THE CAMBRIDGE HISTORY OF
THE ENGLISH NOVEL

The Cambridge History of the English Novel chronicles an ever-changing body of fiction across three centuries. An interwoven narrative of the novel's progress unfolds in more than fifty chapters, charting continuities and innovations of structure, tracing lines of influence in terms of themes and techniques, and showing how greater and lesser authors shape the genre. Pushing beyond the usual period-centered boundaries, the *History*'s emphasis on form reveals the range and depth the novel has achieved in English. This book will be indispensable for research libraries and scholars, but is accessibly written for students. Authoritative, bold, and clear, the *History* raises multiple useful questions for future visions of the invention and reinvention of the novel.

ROBERT L. CASERIO is Professor of English at the Pennsylvania State University.

CLEMENT HAWES is Professor of English and History at the University of Michigan.

THE CAMBRIDGE

HISTORY OF

THE ENGLISH NOVEL

⋆

Edited by
ROBERT L. CASERIO
and
CLEMENT HAWES

CAMBRIDGE
UNIVERSITY PRESS

CAMBRIDGE UNIVERSITY PRESS
Cambridge, New York, Melbourne, Madrid, Cape Town,
Singapore, São Paulo, Delhi, Tokyo, Mexico City

Cambridge University Press
The Edinburgh Building, Cambridge CB2 8RU, UK

Published in the United States of America by Cambridge University Press, New York

www.cambridge.org
Information on this title: www.cambridge.org/9780521194952

© Cambridge University Press 2012

First published 2012

Printed in the United Kingdom at the University Press, Cambridge

A catalogue record for this publication is available from the British Library

Library of Congress Cataloguing in Publication data
The Cambridge history of the English novel / edited by Robert L. Caserio and Clement Hawes.
p.   cm.
Includes bibliographical references and index.
ISBN 978-0-521-19495-2
1. English fiction – History and criticism.   I. Caserio, Robert L., 1944–   II. Hawes, Clement.
PR823.C27   2012
823.009–dc23
2011036933

ISBN 978-0-521-19495-2 Hardback

Contents

Contents

Contents

Contents

VIII

Contents

Illustrations

x

Contributors

AMANDA ANDERSON, Johns Hopkins University
DEREK ATTRIDGE, University of York
LIZ BELLAMY, City College Norwich
BARBARA M. BENEDICT, Trinity College, Hartford
SCOTT BLACK, University of Utah
MARK BLACKWELL, University of Hartford
ROBERT L. CASERIO, Pennsylvania State University, University Park
PETER CHILDS, University of Gloucestershire
J. A. DOWNIE, Goldsmiths College, University of London
JAMES F. ENGLISH, University of Pennsylvania
CHARLES FERRALL, Victoria University of Wellington
CAROL HOULIHAN FLYNN, Tufts University
AARON FOGEL, Boston University
PETER K. GARRETT, University of Illinois, Urbana
JONATHAN GREENBERG, Montclair State University
GEORGE HAGGERTY, University of California, Riverside
ROBERT HAMPSON, Royal Holloway, University of London
CLEMENT HAWES, University of Michigan, Ann Arbor
DOMINIC HEAD, University of Nottingham
ALLAN HEPBURN, McGill University
C. L. INNES, Kent University
DAVID JAMES, University of Nottingham
EDWARD JAMES, University College Dublin
PETER KALLINEY, University of Kentucky
RICHARD A. KAYE, Hunter College and The Graduate Center, City University of New York
SUZANNE KEEN, Washington and Lee University
THOMAS KEYMER, University of Toronto
CHRISTOPHER LANE, Northwestern University
CAROLYN LESJAK, Simon Fraser University
BRIGID LOWE, Trinity College, Cambridge University
MARINA MACKAY, Washington University, St. Louis
PHILLIP MALLETT, University of St. Andrews
ROBERT MARKLEY, University of Illinois at Urbana-Champaign
STEFANIE MARKOVITS, Yale University

List of contributors

ELIZABETH MASLEN, Institute of English Studies, University of London
JESSE MATZ, Kenyon College
ELAINE MCGIRR, Royal Holloway, University of London
FARAH MENDLESOHN, Middlesex University
JULIAN MURPHET, University of New South Wales
DEBORAH EPSTEIN NORD, Princeton University
FRANCIS O'GORMAN, University of Leeds
ALAN PALMER, independent scholar
MURRAY PITTOCK, University of Glasgow
BARRY V. QUALLS, Rutgers University, New Brunswick
JOHN RICHETTI, University of Pennsylvania
ELEANOR SHEVLIN, West Chester University
MORAG SHIACH, Queen Mary, University of London
JANET SORENSEN, University of California, Berkeley
PHILIP TEW, Brunel University
CYNTHIA WALL, University of Virginia
PATRICIA WAUGH, Durham University
BARRY WELLER, University of Utah
MARK WOLLAEGER, Vanderbilt University
GREGORY WOODS, Nottingham Trent University
LISA ZUNSHINE, University of Kentucky

Acknowledgments

The support of Ray Ryan and Maartje Scheltens at Cambridge University Press has made this project possible throughout. We thank them for their leadership and encouragement.

We are deeply indebted to Jodie Hodgson at the Press for guiding us through production. And without Hilary Scannell's rigorous copy editing and Mike Leach's brave construction of the index we could not have come through.

We are grateful to the anonymous readers of our prospectus for the volume; to our contributors for working collaboratively with us over an extended time period; and to Claire Slagis and Christopher Cascio, who helped in the preparation of the manuscript.

An earlier version of chapter 26 appears in Alan Palmer, *Social Minds in the Novel* (Columbus: Ohio State University Press, 2010). The version here is printed with the permission of Ohio State University Press.

Lastly, Robert L. Caserio would like to thank his partner, Kristoffer O. Jacobson, and Clement Hawes would like to thank his partner, Mrinalini Sinha, for patiently sustaining our work on this history.

Introduction

ROBERT L. CASERIO AND CLEMENT HAWES

I

Some important English novels have been popular; some have not; but our volume is not a history of bestsellers. Granted, the novel is not an entirely autonomous literary form, developing in isolation from the influence of market forces. Nor does it develop in isolation from politics, national or international. Far from it: no one could seriously make such an argument. And yet if the novel sees at all – if it offers unique insights – it does so through the ceaseless making, breaking, and remaking of literary forms. Every decision that a novelist makes is formally mediated, and retracing those decisions provides access to the history of the novel. By attending to this history of formal innovations one begins to understand the range and depth of which the English novel has been capable. We hope, even though the *Cambridge History* concludes by affirming the enduring power of romance, that our way of turning the novel's progress into history is less quixotic than the quest of the Knight of the Woeful Countenance.

The challenging side of the genre never fades from view: it does, after all, create something new under the sun. To be sure, the aesthetic and the political avant-garde do not necessarily coincide. And, in any case, as Mikhail Bakhtin points out, any one asserted perspective in the novel is usually rendered relative to others with which it is in conflict. The novel belongs to a virtual, what-if space in which "messages" themselves are put into play, rendered indeterminate, ambiguous, and relative. A direct communication can be "decoded," in the argot of our time, but a novel cannot because a novel is not a glorified bumper sticker. The mere act of the novelist's fleshing out incidents and giving substance to character tends to force a certain complexity on the articulated politics of a given novel.

We do not aim merely to reinforce so-called "canonicity" – a misnomer, given that the lists of texts we study in English departments are neither sacred nor carved in stone. Cultural staying power is an index, nevertheless, of relative richness. Of all genres, moreover, the novel is the most open to appropriation by relative outsiders. Classical learning – the product of a gentleman's education – was unnecessary to work well in the genre: a factor in the vernacular achievements of Daniel Defoe and Samuel Richardson. Thanks to this vernacular vein, by the later eighteenth century there are more women than men writing novels; and the names Burney, Edgeworth, and Austen foreshadow the stunning achievements of George Eliot, the Brontë sisters, and many more. The rise of women writers goes hand in hand with the unfolding of the novel.

The novel is the first literary form to show sympathetically the experience of people who are not merely "common" but actively oppressed. Daniel Defoe's *Moll Flanders* announces in 1722 something very new on the horizon. Moll herself might be the most resilient character in all of literary history. Almost every prevailing social structure seems designed to press her down and yet, like a cork, she always bobs back up – and she eventually prospers. Among the earliest novels, *Moll Flanders* illustrates the articulation in Defoe of economic deprivation with colonizing fantasies. For Defoe, writing at the particular conjuncture of the early eighteenth century, the economic opportunity of settling the New World figures as an escape valve from the bare-bones existence available for many within the confines set by the social order at home. Moll's prosperity is intertwined with colonial settlement and (domestic) slavery. Or, if you prefer to think of *Oroonoko* (1688) as the first novel, one finds there a tragic story revolving around the slave-revolt led by the title character, an enslaved African prince. With politics that are a mirror-image opposite to Defoe's, Aphra Behn weaves together her support for absolute monarchy with a repudiation of the practice of enslaving African royalty. The novel is not anti-slavery as such – after all, the hero, Oroonoko, owns and traffics in slaves – but it does resist slavery that "levels" a captured prince to common servitude. Behn's novel may accurately be said to resist a specifically *racialized* slavery.

Such themes touch on explosive conflicts in national and global history. And so our approaching the English novel specifically through literary form may seem vaguely precious, or even a throwback to some age of ersatz innocence when we turned a blind eye to ideological concerns. And yet even a subtly challenging form can be immensely productive – to invoke a telling pun – of novel thinking. Boring clichés about "breaking all the rules" are crude and unhelpful. One must distinguish between innovations that work, pragmatically, and those that do not. Some innovations are not replicated in subsequent novels – they do not "stick," so to speak – and these do not belong properly to the history of the English novel. They remain sports, one-offs, dead-ends.

There are different degrees of innovation.[1] A change merely in *how the strategy of the genre is instantiated* can be significant indeed. Certainly the metafictional experiments of Fielding – above all, the narrative intrusions in *Tom Jones* (1749) – qualify as one such innovation. One might likewise point to Jane Austen's pivotal use of free indirect discourse: a perspective that is ostensibly third person but dips at will into the coolly self-serving thoughts of a given character. Austen's wittiest ironies stem from her ability to frame occasional flashes of mind-reading with a third-person perspective. A still more innovative text may *change the strategy of the novel itself*. An example of such a work is *Tristram Shandy* (1759–67). Yet despite its radical frustration of narrative progress, *Tristram Shandy* has proven to be an immensely influential text. We hope this volume helps to capture the endless dialectic in the novel between the familiar and the defamiliarized.

What sort of story does the history of the English novel make? Are the novel and capitalism twins – born at the same moments for reasons having to do with, say, individualism, economic and cultural? Or, on the contrary, does the novel maintain conservative loyalties aplenty – say, for starters, to the principle of arranged marriage and so to aristocratic solidarity? Such would be one dimension of the strong case for seeing the novel as perpetually entangled with romance: the older genre that it might mock, as in *Don Quixote*, but never seems finally to displace. And what about all those vast estates that are up for grabs in so many novels? If a major piece of real estate is deeded to hero and heroine, we are more likely to rejoice for the good guys than to agitate against private property. And yet this truth throws into relief the unconventional plot of *Tom Jones* (1749). Though illegitimate – a bastard – Fielding's hero does indeed inherit the Allworthy estate. Fielding's challenge in *Tom Jones* to a tenacious literary convention is of course simultaneously a utopian challenge to the social and legal understanding of legitimacy. That Parliament had in 1688 broken the Stuart succession no doubt licensed his imagination. In *Tom Jones*, indeed, it is Squire Western – the countrified, hard-drinking, fox-hunting patriarch – who still believes, even after the debacle of 1745, in the lost cause of Stuart absolutism. More amusing than dangerous, Squire Western, that blustering font of reactionary attitudes, is scarcely less vivid as a comic creation than Falstaff or the Wife of Bath.

"Marriage-plot" novels of the eighteenth century negotiate with a constrictive ideology, sometimes showing a dazzling sophistication, but they seldom challenge the very choice for women to marry as directly as did Mary Astell in *Some Reflections upon Marriage* (1700). Such novelistic pragmatism offers a fine-grained analysis of the situation of individual women while only occasionally reflecting directly on the condition of women as a group. The dilemmas of such a female protagonist as Frances Burney's *ingénue* Evelina show the sense, as John Richetti argues, in which "the individual" is a problem for rather than a *fait accompli* of the early novel. The eighteenth-century novel had other crucial formal agendas as well, of course, other fish to fry, from satire to fantasy to self-reflexivity. It takes both the individual and the factual not as given but as problematic. The nascent form explores the frictions arising from "novel" conceptions of authority, agency, and knowledge. Samuel Richardson's *Clarissa* (1748) thus produces the darker knowledge stemming from an act of rape, stripping away the insulation from psychological consequences that the aristocratic rapist had banked on.

Our topical account of the novel in this volume is not mainly based on statistical patterns and regularities. Important as those are – literature depends on conventions – we are no less interested in the innovations visible in the unfolding of a remarkably sophisticated literary form. Important innovations figure the possibility of living differently. By the same token, romance – usually regarded as conservative – can give voice to very deep wishes, including the political desire for utopias of all sorts. We read best when we read with an alertness to utopian desires.

Tristram Shandy made clear in the 1760s that the notion of a "true" history cannot be taken too literally. That is to say, no history can live up to the demand for completeness. Like the perfect map mentioned by Borges – perfectly accurate because it is the same size as the territory it represents – perfect history would be useless. Life requires forgetting, and maps must be miniaturized. And so we generally say someone was born on a certain day instead of going back, as Sterne does, to the wildly complicated, and gruesomely interrupted, moment of Tristram's conception. And yet Sterne hits on an insoluble problem. One's "birthday" is a conventional origin that simplifies a multiply determined and frighteningly random beginning. Put that process under a microscope and further modes of randomness emerge. No wonder that *Tristram Shandy* casts a critical light on such collective "grand narratives" as the origins of a given nation. The resonance may be discomfiting, of course, even for a smaller-scale project such as the history of a literary genre. If there is an afterlife, Sterne is no doubt smiling indulgently at the earnest effort of the brave editors to tell the story of the novel.

We take at least this much from Sterne: a good history, to be effective, must sometimes defamiliarize. We are not willing to lose the plot entirely, however – to dispense with the suggestive contours of a larger story. *The Cambridge History* likewise includes plenty of engaged readings of novels. We cannot see afresh unless we sometimes read closely: the alternative is to take everything as "already read." Aside from the rather snide attitude this promotes, the inevitable result is to repeat clichés. And so even as we recognize that repetitions and inertia are crucial, we largely eschew the "distant reading" proposed by rival theorists of the genre. Just as we can recognize various degrees of invention in the novel, we must also make use of reading that is flexibly calibrated in its ability to zoom in and out.

If there is any model that might help to visualize this developmental complexity perhaps we must think not of a neatly branching family tree but a very tangled bush. We recognize fully, in any case, that all books are open at once to those who will read them. Sometimes the impact of a given text will register much later. *Tristram Shandy* begins to get its full due only in the twentieth century. As this example suggests, moreover, literary evolution sometimes proceeds like its biological counterpart: not by gradual degrees, that is, but by unpredictable leaps in one or another aspect of the form. The perception that Sterne is "postmodern" or "our contemporary" seems awkward if juxtaposed with the equally strong claim that he is "modern" in the narrower sense: a key inspiration for Joyce and Virginia Woolf. The tangled bush of novelistic development, however, always turns back on itself, reflectively, renewing itself through unpredictable and sudden transformations. So the novel perpetually transplants its past and renews itself.

II

Only a few of the following chapters concentrate on single authors. Satisfying as exclusive acts of attention can be – one thinks of D. A. Miller's superlative close reading of Austen in *Jane Austen, or The Secret of Style* (2003) – our goal has been to interweave novelists and novels in the light of Henry James's remark that ideally relations stop nowhere.

James admits the necessity of stopping them somewhere, of course. We make an initial arrest of relations in our use of the unreliable term "English," to which we cling under the prevailing limitations of scholarship. However, in repeatedly turning some chapters towards an engagement with four nations – England, Scotland, Wales, Ireland – we underline our unease with confining nomenclature. Had we overleaped limitations entirely, we would have had to reproduce Franco Moretti's brilliantly globalizing project on the novel, as well as his desire to replace close reading with what he calls distant reading in *Graphs, Maps, Trees: Abstract Models for Literary History* (2005). Although our writers read both closely and distantly, for the most part ours is a middle-distance project. The ideal reader of this book will want to cultivate a like distance, by making use of the way its chapters move between close scrutiny of particular writers and particular formal or generic variants of prose fiction to more comprehensive views that push beyond the usual author-centered or period-centered boundaries. In so doing, the reader will be able to compare, against the grain of temporal sequence, the "English" novel's changing or persistent modes of representing phenomena such as the four nations (as well as other places and spaces at home and abroad) in chapters 5, 10, 20, 31, and 44; or representations of eros (8, 27, 49); or the genre's formal consonance with the way we know the world (9, 26). Chapters 37, 38, and 47 comprise a cluster on formal experiment in the twentieth century; but when has the novel not been experimental? Readers who bring the chapters on the eighteenth century (and before) together with the later chapters on experiment will see continuity no less than change.

Those examples are only some of the trans-temporal groupings suggested by the way this history is arranged. It places readers at a middle distance *vis-à-vis* the novel's long career in the hope that new syntheses of awareness will result. The chapters about non-fictional discourses (such as law, science, and new media) provide further occasions for synthesis – and for contemplating continuities and differences between novels and their environments. Even despite such chapters, however, our history might seem insufficiently committed to the temporal or historical "situatedness" (as we say now) that professional discipline favors. The discipline here shows itself in competition, as well as collaboration, with the history of the novel. For both are caught up in a dispute about reality. When the heroine of D. H. Lawrence's *St. Mawr* (1925) wonders "What was real? What under heaven was real?"[2] she voices a question that the novel has been raising since *Don Quixote*. Scholarship, depending on the phase it is passing through, might claim that only social history outside of fiction, or the history of political movements and conflicts, is the touchstone of reality; or it might answer that romance is no less real than history. Whatever the answer, the uncertain, even treacherous relations between history and fiction are the heart of the perplexity. This volume's critical middle distance intends to keep the perplexity vivid. Doing so entails complicity with Ralph W. Rader's claim that "The understanding of genres in history is a very different thing from the history of genres, and the connection between them is . . . tenuous and problematical."[3]

The history of the novel, like fictional narrative (the original time machine), is in time and out of it, retrospective and prospective and immediately present, in a way that complements fiction's confluence with history, and flight from it. Periodizing and sequential literary histories resist what Mieke Bal calls "pre-posterousness": a "shared time" of artists and audiences that transcends sequence, making distinction between "before" and "after" difficult.[4] Postmodernist fiction often is characterized by its addiction to pastiche sequels or prequels of the lives of famous characters from fictions past. How, then, do we characterize what is happening in 1904 when Walter de la Mare's eponymous hero Henry Brocken encounters Jane Eyre, Gulliver, and Bunyan's Pilgrim in their existences before or after their published histories? *Henry Brocken* is preposterously postmodern, just as are Flann O'Brien's fictions from the 1930s. In a similar way, "modernism," at odds with what is Victorian, turns up already in Hardy's *A Laodicean* (1881). Hardy's heroine and her private telegraph represent "modernism";[5] her house, exemplifying "mushroom modernism" (40), is also on the verge of postmodernism, because its ironic owner prefers "an eclectic" architecture. Preposterously, she wants to be "romantic and historical" and simultaneously "of today" (100). When we consider periodization preposterously, we can use it to unsettle the assumptions of a later moment, including our own. Such assumptions might include contentions that in the eighteenth century there was a self, before we learned that the self is illusory; or that there was a non-problematic idea of nationhood, before we learned otherwise.[6] We hope it will not be easy to maintain such assumptions in the face of our chapters on the rise of the novel. Even as their writers respect historical rigor, they justifiably intermingle concerns shared by past and present.

"Situated" literary history must continually seek to solve the mysteries of transhistorical fellow-feeling. Ford Madox Ford's *The March of Literature* (1938) estimates Trollope's *Framley Parsonage* (1860) "higher than any other English novel," and names Trollope, "except perhaps for Jane Austen, the greatest of all specifically English novelists."[7] The collaborator with Conrad, the canonizer of James and Conrad, the *echt*-modernist writer of *The Good Soldier* (1914), makes this judgment! What this incident of literary history is about might be, on the one hand, Ford's penchant for the colloquial directness of Trollope's realism (Ford's impressionism is an outgrowth of realism); and, on the other hand, Ford's interest in the difficulties of controlling impulsiveness (which Trollope's narrative dramatizes). *The Good Soldier* evokes uncontrollable impulse; *Parade's End* (1924–1928) insists that even the most justifiable vehement impulses can be, and ought to be, controllable. If this is the way to understand Ford's evaluation, one might see Trollope's Lord Lufton and Lucy Robarts as prefigurations of the desire, and the difficult historical world, that Valentine Wannop and Christopher Tietjens eventually reduce to happiness and order, in decided contrast to the lovers in Ford's earlier novel.

Ford can always model the difficulty of "situating" novelists in definitive historical or literary-historical frameworks, even though a magisterial recovery of the modernist Ford by Max Saunders and other scholars in recent decades has been accomplished. *The Good Soldier*'s modernist experiments with narrative disjunction seem not only to complement erotic anarchy, but also to suggest that even the best human lives are "broken, tumultuous, agonized and unromantic"[8] because no principle of intelligibility is discoverable for them. Yet at the same time that Ford's novel presents eros as a raging ahistorical darkness, it makes partial historical sense of the agony by referring it to the still unresolved conflict between Catholic and Protestant forms of life. In doing so Ford attaches *The Good Soldier*'s modernism to his trilogy of historical novels *The Fifth Queen* (1906–1908), and thereby – of all things for a modernist – to the content and the form of Walter Scott's fiction. That the influence of Scott remains at work in English modernism (in Conrad too, with Dickens as mediator) means the stubborn influence of romance in unlikely places. Embedded as *Parade's End* is in contemporary history and in Ford's modernist *progression d'effet*, its hero and heroine are from the romance world, and attempt to maintain an elevation of impulse and action that realism and history (and modernism, conventionally understood) do not permit. But the modernist Ford, the historical novelist-realist Ford, and the romance-writing Ford are one and the same; and the unity of such a trinity is another example of Rader's contention that the history of the novel is not reducible to the novel in history.

The novel form has remained a curiously alternative one, resistant to assimilation despite its copy-cat relation to other discourses. At its natal moment the English novel and the law are as close as Fielding and *Tom Jones*. But what Jerome Bruner says about the relation of fictional narrative to law – that, in contrast to legal discourse, the novel "evokes familiar life with the aim of disturbing our expectations about it the better to arouse our sense of what might lie beyond it"; or that the novel, as a component of literature in general, "looks to the possible, the figurative. Law looks to the actual, the literal . . . Literature errs towards the fantastic, law towards the banality of the habitual"[9] – sounds a note of general disjunction between fiction and the real-world protocols that it apes. Joyce's twins, Shem and Shaun, in *Finnegans Wake* (1939) might constitute an allegory of fiction's shamming of the real (Shem stands for novels, not just for Joyce). However assiduously the genre's Shem-like character takes on the appearance of a discursive alter ego or twin, there is always shamming to be reckoned with.

A primary sign of the disjunction and the sham, affecting content and form alike, is romance. The most prominent simultaneous twin and target of romance in novelistic tradition is real history. This volume, in repeatedly striking romance as a keynote – romance in many varieties, but above all in Henry James's senses of "all the things we never can directly know" and of "experience ... uncontrolled by our general sense of 'the way things happen'"[10] – unsettles the certainties we assign to history proper, and to investigations in its light. Fictional character might serve this tendency to contravene history. The way novel readers attach themselves to Clarissa or Clarissa Dalloway as figures who rise clear of their entrammeling stories suggests that readers respond to a timeless effect novelists themselves aim at. Dickens's imagination of Sydney Carton in *A Tale of Two Cities* (1859) moves towards doubling what Carton achieves in history with a ghostly, hermetic intensity that trumps temporal and historical phenomena. Despite the narrative record, Carton's famous closing words are presented by Dickens as probably not spoken aloud, hence never heard.[11] Their unheard sound suggests that even Dickensian narrative cannot encompass its most crucial utterance. Indeed what requires Carton's death is a narrative: the secret history Dr. Manette has left behind in the Bastille, and that the Defarges bring forward to condemn Darnay (and his scapegoat Carton). Here historical narrative betrays character, and character's power depends on being apart from it.

Romance has a similar distancing function, even though its vehicle is storytelling. What Dickens famously cultivates as the romantic side of familiar things weighs in, just as fictional character often does, against the counter-claims of real history. Romance suggests fiction's autonomy (of the kind that modernist fiction makes into an aesthetic principle, perhaps as a new twist on romance), and fiction's consequent flouting of worldly accountability. That this flouting betrays responsibility, especially responsibility to social and political analysis and human progress, worries critics. Yet the treachery of fiction can constitute a point of political and historical repair, a place from which writers and readers can see how reality outside of fiction is the more humanly traitorous thing. Graham Greene's *The Human Factor* (1978) presents a double agent, Castle, who uses volumes of classic fiction in which to encode information for the Soviets. "He put *Clarissa Harlowe* back in the bookcase" is the first clue to his treachery.[12] He subsequently draws on *War and Peace* and *The Way We Live Now* as matrices of secret transmission. The motive for Castle's treachery is no mere double-cross, however. Castle is white, and his wife is a South African black. Their bond developed in the struggle against apartheid, which brought Castle into loving contact with an anti-racist communist ally. Castle becomes a traitor out of loyalty to that comrade – an act of political decency that is continuous with his decent domestic life. In contrast, the powers Castle works for at home are immoral: they murder a friend of Castle's who they think is the source of Castle's leaks. The Russian government is no better. Rescuing him when his treachery is discovered, it provides an asylum that seals him off forever from his beloved wife and child. In search of consolation he turns to *Robinson Crusoe*. If novels are treacherous things, they also provide a secular saving grace. Part of their grace is the toughness of judgment that their distance from ordinary worldly allegiances affords them.

Greene's novel shares with Doris Lessing's work a sobering demonstration of the bankruptcy of extant models of world-historical political order, whether they are reactionary, conservative, or progressive. Iain Sinclair is one of the brilliant contemporary heirs of what Greene and Lessing have woven into the English novel in the way of criticism of historical and political realities. Perhaps no recent English fiction epitomizes the accumulated tradition's wily relation to history more than Sinclair's. Significantly, his writing arrives in the midst of a historiographical turn among novelists that is not unequivocally appealing. Before postmodernism fiction tends to assign an at least equal authority to a novel's historical components and to its autonomous, imaginative, and romance components. In contrast, in historical novels such as J. G. Farrell's *The Singapore Grip* (1978), the novel takes on the air of a history classroom, in which the characters, whoever they are and whatever they do, seem to be students digesting textbook lessons. Farrell's narrative *donnée* is Victorian – a quasi-orphan inherits his father's Empire-derived rubber business in Singapore, and must dispose of the world-historical class and ethnic conflicts he also is heir to. The Victorian aspect in itself is laudably preposterous; yet there is more invention, and more unresolved political, even revolutionary, *élan* in Disraeli's *Sybil* or Charlotte Brontë's *Shirley* than in Farrell's latter-day offshoot. Both history and fiction in Farrell can seem to be inert inheritances.

Sinclair's *Downriver* (1991) faces a new dilemma: a commodification of history that goes hand in hand with marketplace neo-liberalism. International capital now speculates in real estate, especially where it can find dilapidated urban areas that it can "develop" and hawk in terms of "historic" locations and renewals. The resulting "colonizing the past"[13] and the profits from it mark an intensification of buying and selling that Sinclair's writing satirizes, with a fierceness that reminds one of Wyndham Lewis. "The authentic whiff of heritage" (93) goes hand in hand with "vertiginous increase of property values" (135): so much for earnest interest in history, or for disinterested interest in the present. Global capital produces "a past that is narcotic" (176) as well as submitted to lucrative thematizing. Sinclair's fiction registers a savage dissent from turning history into property. What Sinclair's narrator ("Sinclair") says of immigration – "It can always be sentimentalized, but never re-created. It is as persistent and irreversible as the passage of glaciers and cannot – without diminishing its courage – be codified, and trapped in cases of nostalgia" (136) – applies to the past and the present as his fiction attempts to evoke them. Both temporalities have yielded to a greed that is simultaneously callous and sentimental, and that is of a piece with a collective state in which we have been "conned into worshipping nothing better than the synthesis . . . of [our] defects" (379).

In order for Sinclair to keep clear of how history itself has become the object of a new highest stage of capitalism, Sinclair's fiction must find a way to revive the historical novel, in decided counterpoint to the "renewal" and the "development" that is universally a matter of enthusiastic investment, no matter how ultimately swindling (of the poor and the lost if not of the rich). The path of counter-renewal in *Downriver* is formidably rigorous; it must renovate in terms of "a morbid checklist of roadside halts" (396) rather than in terms of an upbeat progress; it must renew in terms of visionary solicitations – the romance element – that oppose gnostic and gothic insanities of the kind dramatized in Peter Ackroyd's *Hawksmoor* (1985) (the novelist Mary Butts's visionary opposition to the occultist Aleister Crowley is Sinclair's model). It also must mourn in the present the future deaths that worldly development and bogus "renewal" bring about.

At the same time as it bites the hand of the world that feeds it, however, *Downriver* is also a collection of "fate tales": a repository of "after-images of unredeemed pain" (335), and "an uncompleted folk song" (392) that history can barely register, indeed cannot encompass in the way that fiction might. The historical record becomes only "the point of embarkation" (342) for the novelist; what he searches, and researches, is the emanations of the record. Temporally the emanations "slip . . . further out, abdicate . . . the strident exhibitionism of the present tense: lurk . . . like a stray dog, somewhere beyond the circle of firelight" (343). Meanwhile, the *places* of history are more searchable as the point of embarkation, so that Sinclair's fiction exhumes what lies beneath the development of real estate, trying to recover from the grasp of indecent use "the last slab[s] of unclaimed territory" (238) in the heart of the new financial empire. But speculation must fight speculation, in another Shem–Shaun (or Jekyll–Hyde) contest; the speculative, theoretical aspect of fiction must fight off its economic double.

The allies in the battle are the fictions of the past. It is the novel downriver, late in its history, that Sinclair exemplifies; but the example is full of evocations and direct enlistments of the tradition. However, in the literary realm also there is a heritage industry: "heritage fakes" called "literature," gaining publication and book prizes, so that, in the literary realm, it appears, as well as in the political and economic realm, "all those greedy pastiches have become the only available reality" (297). Just as Sinclair's novel must fight fire with fire in terms of history-writing, so it must fight fire with fire in terms of novel-writing. Enlisting Stevenson's romance adventure, Lewis Carroll's fantasy, Conrad's dark historical vision, and Butts's white magic to help him, Sinclair suggests that a downriver location is not necessarily an untrustworthy reality – even if it is no longer anchored in realism or trust in "history" – and that a novelist's alliance with prede-cessors is not inertial.

The current popularity of science fiction and fantasy does not mean an end of "the novel," but a resurgence of the perennial novelistic intermixing with romance. It is noteworthy that in Nicholas Mosley's *Inventing God* (2003) Mosley's narrative mode reverts to sheer romance, in order to handle contemporary history's fusion of political, economic, and religious wars. Mosley's international and multi-religious array of characters sets out on adventures to find a sacred object: the remains or the living person of a charismatic thinker about religion who disappeared in the Middle East in the 1990s. Coincidences in the course of the quest interrelate the questers; and one young female protagonist, an Israeli abducted from Jerusalem by terrorists, and rescued from them in northern Iraq by a Sufi Muslim, under-goes a change of identity. At times she appears to have been resurrected, and to have become an angel. The disguises and wonders of ancient romance are come again, even as the novel ends with the attack on the World Trade Center. It does so to suggest that, if the motives of the attack were religious, one has to get at the roots of the "so-called invention of God," and grasp anew what in the invention is at stake (apparently, human autonomy and exercise of choice), in order to see the catastrophe in a way that leads forward.

Mosley's form, despite its backward aspects – what could be more backward than romance quest? – also leads forward, as one might expect from the author of the *Catastrophe Practice* series novel (1979–1990). For the romance matrix of *Inventing God* is combined with Mosley's characteristic formal innovation: a narrative that progresses by means of second-person interrogative address. It is by asking questions that his story moves ahead. We hope that our history of the novel will be seen to have raised multiple useful questions for future visions of the invention and reinvention of the genre.

Notes

1. We have transposed those degrees of innovation from their analytical use in a different medium. See Leonard Meyer, "Innovation, Choice, and the History of Music," *Critical Inquiry* 9 (1983), 517–544.
2. D. H. Lawrence, *The Woman Who Rode Away, St. Mawr, The Princess* (London: Penguin Books, 2006), p. 152.
3. Ralph W. Rader, "The Emergence of the Novel in England: Genre in History vs. History of Genre," *Narrative* 1: 1 (1993), 69–83, 69.
4. Mieke Bal, *Quoting Caravaggio: Contemporary Art, Preposterous History* (University of Chicago Press, 1999), p. 7.
5. Thomas Hardy, *A Laodicean: A Story of Today*, ed. J. H. Stape (London: J. M Dent, 1997), pp. 93, 193.
6. Clement Hawes, *The British Eighteenth Century and Global Critique* (New York: Palgrave Macmillan, 2005), pp. 71–72.
7. Ford Madox Ford, *The March of Literature: From Confucius' Day to Our Own* (New York: The Dial Press, 1938), pp. 788–789.
8. Ford Madox Ford, *The Good Soldier* (Harmondsworth: Penguin Books, 1972), p. 213.
9. Jerome Bruner, *Making Stories: Law, Literature, Life* (New York: Farrar, Straus and Giroux, 2002), pp. 49, 61.
10. Henry James, *The Art of the Novel: Critical Prefaces* (New York: Charles Scribner's Sons, 1934), pp. 32, 34.
11. See Richard Maxwell's Introduction to his edition of Charles Dickens, *A Tale of Two Cities* (London: Penguin Books, 2000), p. xxvii. For multiple relevances to the present volume, see also Richard Maxwell, *The Historical Novel in Europe, 1650–1950* (Cambridge University Press, 2009).
12. Graham Greene, *The Human Factor* (London: Bodley Head, 1978), p. 12.
13. Iain Sinclair, *Downriver* (London: HarperCollins Publishers, 1991), p. 62.

I

The novel before "the novel"

JOHN RICHETTI

All societies possess narrative traditions, myths, and legends about gods and heroes, often in verse. In literate as opposed to oral societies, prose narrative also seems to be an inevitable development, and in Western culture from Greek antiquity onwards there is a rich tradition of prose fictions that are called "novels" by some literary historians. But literary historians have also insisted that long prose narratives beginning in the early to mid-seventeenth century in Europe are radically distinct from their predecessors, and that they inaugurate a type of fiction peculiar to Western modernity that is by custom referred to as "the novel," the form that expresses the special qualities of modern Western experience.

The most influential account of the modern novel is Georg Lukács's *The Theory of the Novel: A Historico-Philosophical Essay on the Forms of Great Epic Literature* (1920). "The Novel," he says, "is the epic of a world that has been abandoned by God." The novel reveals "that meaning can never quite penetrate reality, but that without meaning reality would disintegrate into the nothingness of inessentiality."[1] For Lukács ancient epic and novel are polar opposites, with the novel dramatizing the distinctive nature of modern experience at its most problematic, especially when set against the epic that gave "form to a totality of life that is rounded from within" (60). Whereas the epic assumes that the world has form and significance, the novel is about a frustrated seeking for the meaningful coherence that epic takes for granted. The novel reveals a profound irony in modern life "within which things appear as isolated and yet connected, as full of value and yet totally devoid of it, as abstract fragments and as concrete autonomous life, as flowering and as decaying, as the infliction of suffering and as suffering itself" (74).

The Russian literary critic Mikhail Bakhtin found in the novel more than simply a prose narrative genre that emerged in the European seventeenth century. He defined as novelistic the linguistic energies that, beginning in late antiquity, reached out through narrative to what he called a "zone of maximal contact with the present (with contemporary reality) in all its openendedness."[2] In this emergence of the novelistic spirit, Bakhtin wrote, narrative became "permeated with laughter, irony, humor, elements of self-parody ... an inde-terminacy, a certain semantic openendedness, a living contact with unfinished, still evolving contemporary reality" (7). Comparing classical epic and drama with this novelistic mode, Bakhtin (like Lukács) saw the essence of those genres in their ahistorical perspective. Epic, he asserts, represents in a frozen heroic idiom an archaic, monumental past that in its remote grandeur is completely cut off from contemporary reality and actual, living speech. For Bakhtin the spirit of novelistic discourse lay in comic or parodic resistance to literary language and decorum, with their repressively hierarchical approach to the world. Such resistance, he said, was licensed by ordinary, everyday experience. In the most influential formulation of his thesis, Bakhtin defined the novel as a rendering of the dynamic process of reality not in a unitary and "monologic" literary language but in what he called the "dialogic" process of actual language where competing voices compete and collide, as human beings incessantly shape their reality by means of rival forms of language. The modern novel features "a diversity of social speech types ... and a diversity of individual voices" (262).

For Bakhtin, to trace the emergence of the "modern" novel in its early stages is to mark enduring continuities as well as to define radical differences. Bakhtin and Lukács represent two distinct approaches that may well comple-ment each other, especially when we look at the book that many consider the first modern European novel, *Don Quixote by* Miguel de Cervantes (1547–1616, Part I, 1605, Part II, 1615). Don Quixote is like one of Lukács's novelistic heroes, a seeker for totality in a world where no such unity exists. Lukács says of *Don Quixote*, in fact, that "the first great novel of world literature stands at the beginning of the time when the Christian God began to forsake the world ... when the world, released from its paradoxical anchorage in a beyond that is truly present, was abandoned to its immanent meaninglessness" (103). Quixote has constructed from the romances of chivalry that he has read obsessively the idealized world of his fantasies, and those illusions rub against the grain of the actualities of his specific identity in early seventeenth-century Spain as a modest hidalgo (a noble landowner). Quixote's fantasies, couched in the heightened language of the romances and founded on a world where magic and larger-than-life heroism prevail, run up against the common sense of his squire, Sancho Panza, whose peasant idiom and reliance on the folk wisdom of the proverbs he is always quoting collide with Quixote's exalted language and chivalric ideals. Master and squire – the one gaunt and ethereal, the other stocky and solid (*panza* is Spanish for stomach) – in their physical appearance and in their opposing idioms and perspectives on the world exemplify Bakhtin's heteroglossia.

For one example of this opposition, consider the moment when Don Quixote sees in the dust raised by two flocks of sheep that are approaching

> two armies in full march to attack each other, and engage in the middle of that spacious plain; for every hour and minute of the day, his imagination was engrossed by those battles, inchantments, dreadful accidents, extravagant amours and rhodomontades, which are recorded in books of chivalry.[3]

Sancho warns his master that these armies are only "ewes and lambs you are going to attack! ... What madness possesses you! Consider, here are no giants, nor knights, nor cats, nor arms, nor shields quartered or whole; nor inverted azures, and the devil knows what: was there ever such distraction?" (128). Sancho can only wonder not just about Don Quixote's chivalric terminology but his inexplicable madness. When the armies he sees advancing are revealed as merely sheep (and later when the giants he charges turn out to be windmills), Don Quixote has a ready explanation:

> How strangely can that miscreant inchanter, who is my enemy, transmography things to thwart me? Know, Sancho, that it is a very easy matter for negromancers to make us assume what shapes they please; and the malicious wretch who persecutes me, envying the glory I should have gained in this battle, hath doubtless metamorphosed the squadrons of the foe into flocks of sheep. (129)

Don Quixote's madness is coherent, psychologically true to what he believes but false to the material realities that the narrative renders. However, he is no ordinary madman; he is eloquent and learned, deeply thoughtful, with a clear sense of the moral value of the chivalric calling, which the novel implicitly contrasts with the narrow self-seeking of the ordinary people he encounters. As the mundane opposites of the mad visionary Quixote, however, these ordinary people exemplify the realism of Cervantes' novel. David Quint has made the point that in "the very structure and narrative progress" of *Don Quixote* "Cervantes mimics and charts the arrival" of a modern world "that is beginning to succeed the feudal aristocratic order," which is of course the world that his hero "tries to reenact."[4] So despite what the curate perceives as his excellent intellect, Don Quixote precisely in his mad adherence to chivalry illuminates by comic contrast the secular modernity that Cervantes' novel represents.

Don Quixote is a narrative hybrid. The chivalric career that its hero aspires to follow becomes in practice a variation on the picaresque as he and Sancho in their wandering encounter a variety of folk from a cross-section of social classes. Of course, Don Quixote is not a petty criminal (*pícaro* is Spanish for rogue) like the hero of the anonymous *Lazarillo de Tormes* (1554), a short tale of a resourceful servant boy who turns the tables on his cruel masters, or like the minor criminals who are the protagonists of Francisco de Quevedo's *El Buscón* (1604) and Mateo Alemán's *Guzmán de Alfarache* (1599–1604). In its episodic form, *Don Quixote* is short on plot but strong on the theme; the hero's "Quixotic" personality in all its intense singularity is the driving center of the book. As the philosopher José Ortega y Gasset put it, characters in novels "interest us not because of what they are doing; rather the opposite, what they do interests us because it is they who do it."[5] Novels are not about intrinsically significant or heroic events – for example, the founding of a city, the slaying of a dragon or a tyrant, or the defeat of an enemy – but about characters who are interesting by virtue of that richly particularized individuality that novels can evoke. Novelistic persons are presented as uniquely themselves but also in many ways just like ordinary readers rather than heroes or gods. Don Quixote is both mad and extra-ordinary and yet recognizably familiar, like us.

Don Quixote thus helps us understand how the "modern" novel is distinct from earlier prose narratives. To mark crucial differences we can turn back to those few surviving ancient "novels" (conventionally called the "Greek romances") originating in the period from about the first to the fourth century AD. These narratives are set in the Greek world of an earlier period (the Greek Hellenistic world from the conquests of Alexander the Great until Egypt was conquered by the Romans, from 330 to 30 BC, encompassing Greece, Persia, Egypt, and the lower Mediterranean, including Sicily and southern Italy). Chariton's *Chaereas and Callirhoe*, Heliodorus' *An Ethiopian Story*, Achilles Tatius' *Leucippe and Clitophon*, Xenophon of Ephesus' *An Ephesian Tale*, and Longus' *Daphnis and Chloe* – the best-known and most influential on later fiction, all dating from the first three centuries AD – tend to have similarly formulaic plots: adventures in which the heroes, always extravagantly beautiful young lovers, are separated and endure numerous ordeals and horrendous trials before their final happy reunion. Many episodes, some bizarre and often violent, are unified by the efforts of the protagonists to strive for such a happy reunion. They resemble those old film serials in which the main characters are left in dire straits at the end of each episode and somehow manage to live on and continue the story in the next episode.

Despite their superficial piety – the appeals of the characters to various deities and even occasional appearances of gods, such as in *Daphnis and Chloe* when Pan himself speaks (in a dream) to one of the characters – the determining force in these narratives is Fortune or Fate, blind, amoral, random. For example, in Chariton's *Chaereas and Callirhoe*, the heroine, Callirhoe, resolves to be true to her husband, Chaereas, from whom she has been separated by various disasters, but the narrator tells us that "Fortune outwitted her ... Fortune, against whom alone human calculation has no power. For Fortune relishes victory, and anything may be expected of her."[6] In Achilles Tatius' *Leucippe and Clitophon* the hero observes that "often the celestial powers delight to whisper to us at night about what the future holds – not that we may contrive a defense to forestall it (for no one can rise above fate) but that we may bear it more lightly when it comes" (*CAGN*, 178). Coincidences and arbitrary disasters are the rule in this world rather than divine intervention, with rational and material explanations provided for just about all of the extraordinary events that take place. Yet prophetic dreams as well as magic and at times divine visitors or visions are featured; the world of the romances is thus mysterious, with causality uncertain and fate capricious. For example in Heliodorus' *An Ethiopian Story*, one of the characters tells of a divine visitation or a dream in which he was instructed how to act when "Apollo and Artemis appeared to me, so I imagined – if indeed I did imagine it and not see them for real" (*CAGN*, 418–419). Such spiritual uncertainty marks one key difference from the secular, entirely materialistic perspective of the modern novel.

The Greek romances are, nonetheless, about human interactions in very particularized social and historical settings, and as Tomas Hägg notes, there is a historical accuracy in what looks to modern readers like pure fantasy. For example, piracy was a real problem, reaching as he says "grotesque proportion in the Hellenistic period," and there was, more generally, widespread political instability with deep social divisions in the Hellenistic cities that did not obtain in the classical Greek city states.[7] As Hägg explains, commerce was expanding and sea travel in the Mediterranean and Black Sea was easily managed although risky. The demotic Greek that was understood throughout the region created the cosmopolitan world of the romances. So their complicated plots have a basis in these historical conditions, and they may be said to represent in a realistic manner the resistance that human agents put up against the arbitrary twists of fate or fortune in this unpredictable "modern" Hellenistic world.

Despite that "realism," a character or a narrator will ascribe some wondrous turn of events to "either some divine power or some fortune that arbitrates over human destiny" (*CAGN*, 492). So speaks the narrator of *An Ethiopian Story*, the longest, most sophisticated, and complicated of the ancient novels, full of bewildering sub-plots featuring an enormous cast of characters, a variety of locales, and spectacular events, but centered around a pair of lovers – Theagenes and Charikleia – beset by travails and obstacles to their happiness. A deserted ship surrounded with corpses and the remains of a banquet in marshland at the mouth of the Nile: that is the backdrop for our first view of them, the scene an example of the idealized representation of characters in ancient Greek fiction. The intensely pictorial and to that extent static and self-consciously "literary" nature of this picture illustrates the characteristic style of the romances, designed to provoke admiration and pathos rather than to provide insight into character:

> On a rock sat a girl, a creature of such indescribable beauty that one might have taken her for a goddess. Despite her great distress at her plight, she had an air of courage and nobility. On her head she wore a crown of laurel; from her shoulders hung a quiver; her left arm leant on the bow, the hand hanging relaxed at the wrist ... Her head was bowed, and she gazed steadily at a young man lying at her feet. He was terribly wounded and seemed to be barely conscious, coming round from the verge of death as if from a deep sleep. Even so he had a radiant, manly beauty, and his cheek appeared more gleaming white because of the red streak of blood running down it.
>
> (*CAGN*, 354)

The Egyptian bandits who observe this scene take the couple captive but are succeeded by another group of brigands who chase them away (such bewildering successions of events are a feature of all the romances and these miscellaneous accretions of incidents are significantly different from the measured tempo of most modern novels). Charikleia tells the bandits that she and Theagenes are brother and sister (to protect her lover from the bandit chief, Thyamis, who is struck by her beauty and nobility and plans to make her his wife). This is only the first of several captivities she endures before the story ends. They are, she tells her captor, priest of Apollo and priestess of Artemis, from Ephesus, Ionian Greeks on their way to Delos with many of their fellow citizens on "a sacred embassy" (371). After Thyamis is captured in a battle with rival brigands, the Greek captives escape but their troubles are only beginning, and the narrative looks back as we learn that Charikleia was exposed by her mother, found by an unnamed black man who offers the child to Charikles, a Delphic priest resident in Egypt, who raises her. When Theagenes, a descendant of Achilles, arrives leading a delegation from Thessaly to perform a ritual sacrifice, he and Charikleia fall instantly in love, the standard emotional event in the romances.

Foundlings, abandoned infants, left with tokens that hint at their identity, are a recurrent motif in the romances, and plots turn on the eventual discovery of true identity. Charikleia is actually the daughter of Queen Persinna and King Hydaspes of Ethiopia. As emerges later, Charikleia was exposed by the queen when she was born with white skin; her color was the result of her mother's gazing on a picture of Andromeda at her conception; and Persinna would have been accused of adultery if the girl had survived. But Persinna has commissioned a priest, Kalasiris, to find her child, and he recounts the adventures that led to their capture by pirates, with the results we saw at the beginning of the story (rival groups among the pirates had slaughtered each other at a banquet on shore). The story ends in Egypt and Ethiopia with a war between the Persian rulers of Egypt and Hydaspes, the king of Ethiopia. After the Ethiopian victory in an epic battle, Charikleia and Theagenes are captured and brought before the king. About to be sacrificed to thank the gods for victory, Charikleia produces tokens left with her when she was exposed, and after various complications and near-disasters for the young couple they are finally spared and preparations made for their marriage.

Heliodorus' book offers an enormous variety of scene and action; the plot is in fact too complicated to summarize adequately, and I have omitted many of its twists and turns and important characters. *An Ethiopian Story* is a narrative extravaganza, full of violence and predictable mayhem along with wondrous developments, although some of the other Greek romances come close to it in their multiplicity of characters and events. It is, therefore, no wonder that the conception of character in the Greek romances is quite distinct from the representation of individual psychology in the modern novel. There is a stylized sameness about the characters in the romances that the modern novel consistently avoids as it reaches for such eccentric or even unique figures as Cervantes' knight. Consider for one key feature in the Greek romances the invariability of the heroines' sexual allure. In *Chaereas and Callirhoe*, for example, every man who looks at the heroine instantly falls madly in love with her, and in *An Ephesian Tale* every man who meets the heroine, Anthia, is smitten to the point of obsession. Such automatic reactions move the plot along, but for the modern reader of novels the effect is farcical and mechanical. Under the pressure of the extravagant turns of Fate that bedevil them, characters in the romances respond with human feelings, of course, but the rendition of such feelings is invariably stagy, exteriorized, and schematic.

As the translators into English of the Greek romances note, the best of them are intensely literary, echoing and paraphrasing classic literary texts such as the Homeric epics and the Greek tragedies. They tend toward melodramatic rather than strictly narrative form, and as in drama the emphasis is on action, on staged scenes rather than on introspection or the examination of moral and social ideas. For an example that makes the dramatic quality of the romances overt, *Chaereas and Callirhoe* features a trial at the Persian king's court in which the heroine's first husband, Chaereas, thought to be dead, appears. The heroine has been sold into slavery and married to her purchaser, Dionysius. The trial has been provoked by his accusing Mithridates, one of the Persian king's satraps, of attempting to seduce Callirhoe. Mithridates testifies in his defense and calls on Chaereas to appear:

> When she saw him, Callirhoe cried out, "Chaereas! Are you alive?" and made to run to him. But Dionysius held her back, blocked the way, and would not let them embrace. Who could fitly describe that scene in court? What dramatist ever staged such an astonishing story? It was like a play packed with passionate scenes, with emotions tumbling over each other – weeping and rejoicing, astonishment and pity, disbelief and prayers. How happy all were for Chaereas! How glad for Mithridates! For Dionysius, how sorrowful! As for Callirhoe, they did not know what to think. She was in total confusion and stood there unable to utter a word – she could only gaze wide-eyed at Chaereas.   (*CAGN*, 85)

The romances deliver variety, surprise, and wonder (like that experienced by Callirhoe when she sees Chaereas). The modern novel values such things, but they are not central to its form and purpose, and indeed much of the time novels work to demystify wonder and to invoke a mundane reality that deflates it.

Heliodorus' *An Ethiopian Story* appeared in French in 1547, and Achilles Tatius' *Leucippe and Clitophon* was widely translated, including an English version in 1579. Other Greek novels were translated into the major European languages in the sixteenth century. Neglected during the Middle Ages, the Greek romances began to be read again during the Renaissance, and their influence lingered through the ensuing centuries. That influence encouraged loose, episodic plotting, but the tradition of prose romance also promoted an emphasis on elegant elaboration, on leisurely style over narrative substance and economy. (It is worth noting that Henry Fielding's first two novels, *Joseph Andrews* [1742] and *Tom Jones* [1749] follow the plot pattern of the romances, complete with foundlings and separated lovers.) Richardson named his heroine Pamela after one of the characters in Sir Philip Sidney's *Arcadia* (1590), which resembles Heliodorus' *An Ethiopian Story* but was also influenced by Renaissance pastoral romances such as Jacopo Sannazaro's *Arcadia* (1504) and Jorge Montemayor's *Diana Enamorada* (1552). Sidney's romance is nowadays an almost unreadable curiosity but valuable as an example of what the novel when it emerges will reject but also revise and reprocess.

Arcadia has a simple plot: two shipwrecked princes and cousins, Musidorus and Pyrocles, fall in love with Pamela and Philoclea, daughters of Duke Basilius, ruler of Arcadia. Basilius has gone with his family to live in a rural village after a frightening prediction from the Delphic oracle that his elder daughter will be stolen from him, that his younger will marry badly, and that a foreigner will usurp his throne. This simple plot is complicated by the twists and turns of fate as well as a host of minor or subordinate characters, but chiefly by the elaborately rhetorical style of the narrative. For one example from early in the narrative: Musidorus comes upon Pyrocles, who has disguised himself as an Amazon (Zelmane), and recognizes him by his voice:

> entering into the arbour, he perceived indeed that it was *Pyrocles* thus disguised, wherewith not receiving so much joy to have found him, as grief so to have found him, amazedly looking upon him (as Apollo is painted when he saw Daphne suddenly turned into a Laurel), he was not able to bring forth a word. So that *Pyrocles* (who had as much shame as *Musidorus* had sorrow) rising to him, would have formed a substantial excuse; but his insinuation being of blushing, and his division of sighs, his whole oration stood upon a short narration, what was the causer of this Metamorphosis? But by that time *Musidorus* had gathered his spirits together, and yet casting a gastful countenance upon him (as if he would conjure some strange spirits) he thus spake unto him.
>
> And is it possible, that this is *Pyrocles*, the only young Prince in the world, formed by nature, and framed by education, to the true exercise of virtue? Or is it indeed some *Amazon* that hath counterfeited the face of my friend, in this sort to vex me? For likelier sure I would have thought it, that any outward face might have been disguised, than that the face of so excellent a mind could have been thus blemished.[8]

Sidney's leisurely narrative pace accommodates such mannered speaking, with its careful parallelisms and exhaustive descriptions. Note as well the pictorial mythological image – Musidorus, astonished, is like Apollo looking at Daphne turned into a laurel, and in this pictorialism Sidney is imitating a feature of the Greek romances. Although Don Quixote's speeches have much in common with this courtly language, they express a distinctive personality within a context in which eloquence is subordinated to material circumstances –

as it is not in the *Arcadia*. Pyrocles, Musidorus, and other characters (except for the rustics and shepherds) all speak in the same way; their courtly rhetoric is deliberately artificial and does not aspire like speech in the modern novel to express a particularized individual in a specifically realized temporal world.

Popular fiction writers in late sixteenth-century England use less rarified approaches to language, but the mannered expressiveness remains central. Thomas Nashe's picaresque *The Unfortunate Traveller or The Life of Jack Wilton* (1594) is the demotic contemporary of Sidney's romance, rapid, energetic, and purposeful where Sidney's book is leisurely and convoluted. Nashe's book is also specifically historical, set in the reign of Henry VIII, where the hero-narrator, Jack Wilton, is a "a certain kind of an appendix or page, belonging or appertaining in or unto the confines of the English Court; where what my credit was, a number of my creditors that I cozened can testify." [9] Jack is a rogue, a trickster, a heartless con man, and when he goes from England to France to follow the wars his movements match his mercurial and inventive prose: "Over sea with my implements I got me, where hearing the King of France and the Switzers were together by the ears, I made towards them as fast as I could, thinking to thrust myself into that faction that was strongest" (*ibid.*). *The Unfortunate Traveller* is verbally inventive and violently comic, even revolting for modern readers. The grotesque cruelty that Nashe depicts is the polar opposite of the elegant pastoralism of the *Arcadia*, but despite the actual geographical settings in England, France, and Italy the effect is not realistic but fantastic, focussed on Jack's rhetorical embroiderings. At the very end of the book, for a vivid example, Jack describes the execution of a criminal in Rome:

> The executioner needed no exhortation hereunto, for of his own nature was he hackster good enough. Old excellent he was at a boneache. At the first chop with his wood-knife would he fish for a man's heart and fetch it out as easily as a plum from the bottom of a porridge pot. He would crack necks as fast as a cook cracks eggs; a fiddler cannot turn his pin so soon as he would turn a man off the ladder. Bravely did he drum on this Cutwolfe's bones, not breaking them outright but, like a saddler knocking in of tacks, jarring on them quaveringly with his hammer a great while together. No joint about him but with a hatchet he had for the nonce he disjointed half, and then with boiling lead soldered up the wounds from bleeding. (369)

Although Nashe's similes for the executioner's grisly craft are drawn from ordinary life – a plum at the bottom of a porridge pot, a saddler at his craft – Jack's description is both rhetorical and heartlessly realistic, striking a balance between describing action and rhetorical articulation. That balance is actually rare in English fiction in the late sixteenth and early seventeenth century. One very popular style that is purely rhetorical elaboration is John Lyly's in *Euphues: The Anatomy of Wit* (1578), which by 1636 had run to nineteen editions.[10] In its exaggerated attention to language, Lyly's book is in novelistic terms a blind alley, a choice of fullness of language over action and character development that the novel will in the eighteenth century define itself by drastically modifying. All we really know about the characters in *Euphues* is how they employ language; the narrative action is precisely the manipulation of language in elaborate self-expression (that does not reveal a self). For one example, here is Euphues wooing Lucilla in Naples:

> coming to Naples but to fetch fire, as the byword is, not to make my place of abode, I have found such flames that I can neither quench them with the water of free will, neither cool them with wisdom. For as the hop, the pole being never so high, groweth to the end, or as the dry beech, kindled at the root, never leaveth until it come to the top; or as one drop of poison disperseth itself into every vein, so affection having caught hold of my heart and the sparkles of love kindled my liver, will suddenly, though secretly, flame up into my head and spread itself into every sinew.[11]

Lucilla is the mistress of Euphues' friend, Philautus. But Lucilla betrays Euphues and the two friends are reconciled. Like the balance in the plot – the alienation of two friends and then their reconciliation – the language is all about antithesis and balance, and in its rehearsal of quasi-proverbial wisdom it offers readers a static and universalized human and natural world that has nothing to do with the modern novel's essentially socio-historical contextual-izing of experience.

Over the course of the late sixteenth and through the seventeenth centuries, English fiction moves away from the rhetorical richness (or excess in the case of *Euphues*) and the rarified subject matter of the romance tradition. From the Elizabethan age through the seventeenth century, prose fiction has a number of diverse strands and subject matters, some more important than others, and with the increase in literacy as the century progresses there is a corresponding increase in the production of prose narratives at various levels of sophistica-tion. (Salzman puts the number of new works published in the seventeenth century at 450, with 213 of those translations [*English Prose Fiction*, 114].) In the late 1500s there is a native strain about middle- and even working-class characters such as in Thomas Deloney's *Thomas of Reading* (1598) and *Jacke of Newberry* (1597–1598), whose heroes are prosperous clothiers. Popular Spanish and French picaresque fiction from this period narrates the racy lives of marginal characters, "picaros," rogues, or criminals and renders the lower levels of society. Such books were widely read in English translations through the seventeenth century. Richard Head and Francis Kirkman's popular *The English Rogue* (1665 but appearing in sequels and abridgments until 1759), imitated in titles such as *The French Rogue* (1672) or *The Dutch Rogue* (1683), is closely modeled on Alemán's book. At the end of the seventeenth century many accounts of actual criminals appeared in quasi-fictional form influenced by the picaresque tradition, such as Francis Kirkman's *The Counterfeit Lady Unveiled* (1673), the life of a con-woman named Mary Moders, and Elkanah Settle's *The Complete Memoirs of the Life of that Notorious Impostor Will Morrell* (1694). Defoe's narratives, *Moll Flanders* (1722) and *Colonel Jack* (1722), in the early eighteenth century owe a good deal to this tradition, but there is little in the earlier fictions that is properly novelistic, although their interest in the actualities of life at the lower levels of society looks forward to the later novel's preoccupation with such experience.

Some popular prose narratives did, indeed, possess novelistic qualities mixed with traditional techniques and purposes. The most important example is a religious allegory, John Bunyan's *The Pilgrim's Progress* (1678), the story of a man named Christian as he awakens to his need to set off on a dangerous path to salvation. Written in a plain but powerful style, it features lively dialogue among a cast of recognizable English folk in realistic settings. Christian's story belongs to the medieval genre of a dream vision; it also resembles a romance to the extent that the hero undergoes the perils of his journey like a medieval knight, brandishing sword and shield to defeat monsters and to reach the heavenly city. *The Pilgrim's Progress* is also satiric in its depiction of worldly characters that stand in Christian's way to salvation (Mr. Wordly Wiseman, Pliable, Talkative) and places where temptations abound for the pilgrim like Vanity Fair. Where the picaresque tradition values action and subversive protagonists, *The Pilgrim's Progress* dramatizes the moral struggles, both external and internal, of its hero as he makes his way to salvation. For one revealing incident, Christian and one of his companions, Hopeful, are captured by Giant Despair. The moment is both allegorical and a way of rendering the travelers' psychological state, and literal and external, as the Giant Despair, an implicitly aristocratic oppressor, locks these simple travelers up in his castle, beats them senseless, and advises them to kill themselves:

> he told them, that since they were never like to come out of that place, their only way would be, forthwith to make an end of themselves, either with Knife, Halter, or Poison: For why, said he, should you chuse life, seeing it is

attended with such bitterness. But they desired him to let them go; with that he looked ugly upon them, and rushing to them, had doubtless made an end of them himself, but that he fell into one of his fits; (for he sometimes in sunshine weather fell into fits) and lost (for a time) the use of his hand: wherefore he withdrew, and left them, (as before) to consider what to do.[12]

Particular narrative detail contains and promotes generalized allegorical meaning, since Despair (what on the allegorical level Christian and Faithful are suffering from) is incapable of decisive action like suicide. But the scene makes perfect narrative sense without the allegory, even if it is enriched by it. That double effect is the guiding principle of Bunyan's book, the literal and the allegorical cooperating and inter-animating one another. *Pilgrim's Progress* is thereby an anticipation of what the novel at its most complex can achieve: external actions and events that are rendered fully but point to psychological, moral, and social-historical meaningfulness.

Among the most popular narrative genres during the last decades of the seventeenth century and the first three or four decades of the eighteenth was amatory fiction, a simplified derivative of the romance tradition produced by many women writers, pre-eminently Aphra Behn (1640–1689) and Eliza Haywood (1693–1756). Such works were also influenced by contemporary multi-volume French romances that were widely read in translation, such as Honoré d'Urfé's *L'Astrée* (1607–1633), Madeleine de Scudéry's *Artamène, ou le grand Cyrus* (1649–1653), and *Clélie* (1654–1660), and especially the much shorter and more psychologically acute *The Princesse de Clèves* by Madame de Lafayette (1678; English translation 1679). Shorter, narrower in setting and focus than the romances of antiquity, amatory fictions dealt with erotic relationships, with the intensities of heterosexual love. The English amatory novel, as Rosalind Ballaster has explored it, was also directly influenced by the popularity of the translation of the anonymous *Lettres Portugaises* (1669) translated in 1678 as *Five Love-Letters from a Nun to a Cavalier*, in which a nun writes to the man responsible for her seduction in an emotional style that was "ostentatiously 'natural' and implicitly associated with female desire."[13]

"Romance" in this period acquires the meanings now attached to it, and this is an important step in the emergence of the modern novel. Erotic love, as these romances explore it, is a defining emotion, a means of self-exploration and discovery that is often tragic but also psychologically revealing, exemplifying the specific individuality of the lovers, granting primacy to the intense interiority of particular persons, especially women. *The Princesse de Clèves*, for example, ponders the heroine's ethical and emotional dilemma about whether to marry the man with whom she fell in love (chastely) while her husband was alive.

The narrative examines her state of mind as she recalls her husband's death and her passion for her lover, M. de Nemours:

> she remembered too that this same man who she now thought could marry her was the one she had loved during her husband's lifetime, the one who had caused his death; she remembered that, as he lay dying, he had even expressed the fear that she might marry him; and, in the austerity of her virtue, she was so wounded by this thought that she now felt it to be scarcely less of a crime to marry M. de Nemours than it had seemed to love him while her husband was alive. She gave herself up to these reflections, fatal as they were to her happiness, and reinforced them still further with other reasons . . . Yet this conviction, inspired as it was by her reason and virtue, failed to carry her heart with it.[14]

Ethical and emotional subtlety such as Madame de Lafayette's novel features is invariably missing in the racy romances of Aphra Behn, although most of her novels have a courtly setting and aristocratic characters like *The Princesse de Clèves*. Instead, those novellas and her one book-length narrative, *Love Letters Between a Nobleman and His Sister* (1684–1687) rehearse (with some interesting variations in which women are the sexual aggressors) the seduction of vulnerable and innocent young women by predatory aristocratic libertine males. The exception is her extraordinary *Oroonoko: or, The History of the Royal Slave* (1688), set in Surinam, where Behn, herself the narrator as the title-page announces, claims to have witnessed the events surrounding the history of her hero, an African prince betrayed into South American slavery. Despite the local color the narrator includes about life in Surinam, this is a romance as well in the sense that Oroonoko is a heroically perfect character, like a doomed hero out of Restoration heroic tragedy (Behn's novella was turned into a play by Thomas Southerne in 1696). To some extent all of Behn's romances are escapist thrillers, meant to stimulate erotic fantasy as well as vicarious participation in glamorous worlds of sex and power.

On the other hand, for all the formulaic extravagance of its plots and the conventionality of the characters, amatory fiction marks a shift from the artificiality of the courtly romance tradition toward a simpler, more direct literary manner, and in thematic terms an intense if embattled individuality is granted to its young and inexperienced heroines. Moreover, amatory fiction in this period often includes a double voicing by which the narrator's analytical intelligence establishes the possibility of a critical distance from the values of the characters. Implicitly, the libertine ethos of the seducers is at times exposed by that narrative voice as a matter of gender and class privilege, and a realistic critique, in contrast to the fantastic eroticism of the narrative proper, of patriarchal ideologies is set in motion.

This amatory novel does not seek to render a social-historical totality like the mature mid-eighteenth-century novel, or for that matter to explore the psychology of its characters in depth. Such inclusiveness is ruled out by the entertaining formula of the seduction plot that restricts the action to aristocratic love intrigues, and in the single most popular instance of the genre, Eliza Haywood's *Love in Excess; or, The Fatal Inquiry; a Novel* (1719), by the many variations on amatory business. *Love in Excess* is popular fiction, a "bodice ripper," with many erotic near-consummations and frantic articulations of desire. But on the other hand it is an exploration of the workings of desire, especially in young women, and the narrator's analysis of love and its powerful, indeed irresistible, effects seems to be meant seriously and to provide knowledge of emotional realities:

> When love once becomes in our power, it ceases to be worthy of that name; no man really possest with it, *can* be master of his actions; and whatever effects it may enforce, are no more to be condemned, than poverty, sickness, deformity or any other misfortune incident to humane nature . . . These *insipids*, who know nothing of the matter, tell us very gravely, that we ought to love with moderation and discretion. [15]

Note Haywood's strong insistence on impulses almost beyond the control of the will, an emphasis on an irresistible emotional determinism that is absent from Renaissance romances. Haywood's *Love in Excess* focusses mainly on female erotic self-discovery, so that despite its melodramatic excess it traces a process of individual development and even transformation.

A related if more varied and complex approach to characterization, with a corresponding exploration of ethical and psychological tensions, will for readers and critics of the time emerge in the novels of the 1730s and 1740s, especially in the fictions of Richardson and Fielding. In its moralizing interruption of the romantic drive of the story, a defensive anxiety about the unreality of the characters being evoked, Haywood's novel looks forward to the emergence of the English novel in full flower twenty or so years later in the works of Richardson and Fielding. In William B. Warner's account of the English novel in the mid-eighteenth century, formulaic narrative entertainments like Haywood's are crucial because they provoke in response a reformation of fiction by Defoe, Richardson, and Fielding that offers instead instruction and moral improvement for readers.[16] Romantic entertainment needed defending in 1719, it seems, and one can say that in the same year that

Defoe's *Robinson Crusoe* as well as *Love in Excess* were published, standards of verisimilitude and plausibility were in the air. The modern English novel emerges in this uneasy co-existence and competition between romance and realism.

Notes

1. Georg Lukács, *The Theory of the Novel: A Historico-Philosophical Essay on the Forms of Great Epic Literature*, trans. Anna Bostock (Boston, MA: MIT Press, 1974), p. 88.
2. Mikhail Bakhtin, *The Dialogic Imagination: Four Essays*, trans. Michael Holquist (Austin: University of Texas Press, 1981), p. 11.
3. Miguel de Cervantes, *The Adventures of Don Quixote De La Mancha* trans. Tobias Smollett, with an introduction by Carlos Fuentes (New York: Farrar, Straus and Giroux, 1986), p. 125. Smollett's translation is from 1755.
4. David Quint, *The Novel of Modern Times: A New Reading of Don Quijote* (Princeton University Press, 2003), p. x.
5. José Ortega y Gasset, *The Dehumanization of Art and Other Writings* (New York: Doubleday, 1956), pp. 61–62.
6. *Collected Ancient Greek Novels*, ed. B. P. Reardon (Berkeley: University of California Press, 1989), p. 46. Hereafter referred to as *CAGN*.
7. Tomas Hägg, *The Novel in Antiquity* (Berkeley: University of California Press, 1983), pp. 84–85.
8. Sir Philip Sidney, *The Countesse of Pembrokes Arcadia*, ed. Albert Feuillerat (Cambridge University Press, 1963), pp. 76–77. I have modernized some spelling.
9. Thomas Nashe, *The Unfortunate Traveller and Other Works* (New York: Penguin, 1972), p. 276.
10. Paul Salzman, *English Prose Fiction 1558–1700: A Critical History* (Oxford: Clarendon Press, 1985), p. 35.
11. John Lyly, *Euphues: The Anatomy of Wit, Euphues & His England*, ed. Morris William Croll and Harry Clemons (New York: Russell and Russell, 1964), p. 57.
12. John Bunyan, *The Pilgrim's Progress* (London: Oxford University Press, 1962), p. 142.
13. Rosalind Ballaster, *Seductive Forms: Women's Amatory Fiction from 1684 to 1740* (Oxford: Clarendon Press, 1992), pp. 62–63.
14. Madame de Lafayette, *The Princesse de Clèves*, trans. Terence Cave (Oxford University Press, 1999), p. 142.
15. Eliza Haywood, *Love in Excess; or, The Fatal Enquiry; a Novel*, ed. David Oakleaf (Peterborough, ON: Broadview Press, 2000), pp. 205–206.
16. William Beatty Warner, *Licensing Entertainment: The Elevation of Novel Reading in Britain, 1684–1750* (Berkeley: University of California Press, 2004), pp. xiii, 277.

2

Biographical form in the novel

J. A. DOWNIE

I

More than half a century after the publication in 1957 of Ian Watt's seminal study *The Rise of the Novel*, those who conceive of the origins and development of the English novel largely in evolutionary terms still do not seem fully to appreciate the challenge presented to the expectations of contemporary "novel and romance readers" by the publication towards the end of April 1719 of *The Life and Strange Surprizing Adventures of Robinson Crusoe of York, Mariner . . . Written by Himself.* Daniel Defoe made strenuous efforts not only to distinguish his narratives from mere "Novels and Romances," but also to convince his readers that what they were reading was "not a Story, but a History."[1] In itself, this particular ploy was not new. In the dedication to *The Fair Jilt* (1688), for instance, Aphra Behn maintained that "this little History" was not "Fiction," but "Reality, and Matter of Fact, and acted in this our latter Age,"[2] and most of Behn's immediate female successors, as Rosalind Ballaster has noted,[3] tended to resort to this type of substantiating claim. However, in drawing his readers' attention in the prefaces to his narratives to the relationship between fact and fiction, Defoe emphasized the biographical element in his stories to an extent hitherto unheard of, and the response in the first half of the 1720s to the authenticating devices adopted in his series of spurious autobiographies appears to have been significantly different from that which occurred in the previous century.

   In any consideration of the relationship between the emerging English novel and existing literary forms, it is imperative that the terms used by Defoe's contemporaries to describe prose fiction be investigated. Fifty years before the publication of *Robinson Crusoe*, for instance, the bookseller Francis Kirkman observed that the old chivalric romances "are now grown so scarce that you can hardly purchase them, and yet they are not worth the Printing agen, being now out of use and esteem by an other sort of Historyes, which are called *Romances*, some whereof are written originally in *English*."[4] Kirkman's linking of "Historyes" and romances is of interest because it was largely after the Restoration that the term "romance" began to be used to distinguish fictitious tales from "real" history, as is indicated by this entry in Blount's *Glossographia* (1661): "we now give the name *Romance* most commonly to a feigned History writ in Prose."[5] And it is in this context that Mary Davys's observation that "those Sort of Writings call'd *Novels*" were "out of Use and Fashion" should be read: "the Ladies (for whose Service they were chiefly design'd) have been taken up with Amusements of more Use and Improvement; I mean History and Travels; with which the Relation of Probable Feign'd Stories can by no means stand in competition."[6] Given the date of this remark, 1725, it supplies a link between Blount's implication that the term "history" was applicable both to "real" and to "feigned" stories, and Davys's assertion that ladies were "taken up with . . . History and Travels" in the mid-1720s also suggests that she was referring to the sort of narratives produced by Defoe (and others) during the brief upturn in the publication of prose fiction that followed on from *Robinson Crusoe*.

Defoe's narratives changed what was expected from biographies, not simply by pretending that they were the genuine autobiographies of real-life adventurers, rogues, and criminals, but also by their foregrounding of the relationship between fact and fiction. There can be no doubt that Defoe was perfectly aware of what he was doing. Thus although he dismissed *Letters Writ by a Turkish Spy* as "a Meer Romance,"[7] he maintained that *Roxana* was radically different because "the Foundation of This is laid in Truth of *Fact*; and so the Work is not a Story, but a History" (1). Defoe's insistence that his fictions were based on fact actually predates the publication of *Robinson Crusoe*. "Tho' much of the Story is Historical, and might be made to appear true in Fact," he wrote in the Introduction to the first part of *The Family Instructor* (1715), "yet the Author resolving not to give the least hint that should lead to Persons, has been obliged to leave it Uncertain to the Reader, whether it be a History or a Parable; believing it may be either way adapted to the sincere Design."[8] Interestingly, Defoe wrote in very similar terms in the preface to *Colonel Jack* (1723): "neither is it of the least Moment to enquire whether the Colonel hath told his own Story true or not; If he has made it a *History* or a *Parable*, it will be equally useful, and capable of doing Good."[9]

By comparing *The Family Instructor* and *Colonel Jack* with biblical parables in this way, Defoe opens up the possibility of an allegorical dimension to his writings, much as he does in *Serious Reflections during the Life and Surprising Adventures of Robinson Crusoe* (1720) in what appears to have been a knee-jerk response to Charles Gildon's allegation that the "Story" told in *Robinson Crusoe* "is feign'd, that the Names are borrow'd, and that it is all a Romance." In response, "Robinson Crusoe" affirmed "that the Story, though Allegorical, is also Historical ... there is a Man alive, and well known too, the Actions of whose Life are the just Subject of these Volumes, and to whom most Part of the Story most directly alludes, this may be depended on for Truth, and to this I set my Name."[10] While his insistence that his narratives were allegorically if not historically true seems to be part of the tradition that led Bunyan to justify *The Pilgrim's Progress* on the grounds that it worked through similitudes, potentially of more significance are Defoe's assertions in the relevant prefaces that *Crusoe* was an actual personal account, that *Colonel Jack* is his own narrator, and that *Roxana* was a history, not a mere story.

Patently, not all of Defoe's contemporaries were taken in by his professions. In the preface to *The strange adventures of the Count Vinevil and his family* (1721), Penelope Aubin followed Gildon's lead by maintaining that: "As for the Truth of what this Narrative contains, since *Robinson Cruso* has been so well receiv'd, which is more improbable, I know no reason why this should be thought a Fiction."[11] Two years later the anonymous author of *The Highland Rogue: or, the Memorable Actions of the Celebrated Robert Mac-gregor, commonly called Rob-Roy* went further in actually suggesting that three of what we now know as Defoe's novels were simply spurious. "It is not a romantic Tale that the Reader is here presented with, but a real History," he insisted: "Not the Adventures of a *Robinson Crusoe*, a *Colonel Jack*, or a *Moll Flanders*, but the Actions of the *Highland Rogue*; a Man that has been too notorious to pass for a meer imaginary Person."[12]

The link between Defoe's narratives and biography, particularly criminal biography, has of course not passed unnoticed by critics. As the differences between Defoe's narratives and existing biographical forms are more striking than their similarities, however, the extent to which his contemporary readers would have appreciated the analogy must be debatable. Defoe's narratives differ from "standard criminal biography" in a number of ways, including not only their openings and their endings, but also the sense in which they suggest an implied author "standing behind its narrator and speaking through him or her to an audience which, at some level aware of its complex relation to the text, is encouraged to respond critically; to perform, in other words, a variety of interpretive acts."[13]

Perhaps the best example of Defoe's insinuating that a consciousness other than that of the putative narrator is at work in his fiction is the way in which, from the opening sentence of the preface to *Moll Flanders* onwards, seeds of doubt are sown in the minds of his contemporary readers about the status of the narrative which is ostensibly being introduced. Thus after suggesting that what is on offer is "a private History," he not only observes how "the World" has been "taken up of late with Novels and Romances," he also invites "the Reader to pass his own Opinion upon the ensuing Sheets, and take it just as he pleases."[14] Whether or not mystification is the effect that Defoe is seeking to achieve by this opening gambit, when he goes on to explain that it has been necessary to bowdlerize the text – indeed that the "Pen employ'd in finishing her Story, and making it what you now see it to be, has had no little Difficulty to put it into a Dress fit to be seen, and to make it speak Language fit to be read" (i–ii) – the reader might be forgiven for wondering exactly what moral point the publisher of this allegedly genuine "private History" is trying to make.

As the preface proceeds painstakingly, if not entirely convincingly, to articulate "a few of the serious Inferences which we are led by the Hand to in this Book," it appears that Defoe has anticipated that his readers might be a little uncertain about his narrative purpose. Thus he suggests that "this Work is chiefly recommended to those who know how to read it," and that "it is hoped such Readers will be more pleased with the Moral than the Fable, with the Application than with the Relation, and with the End of the Writer than with the Life of the Person written of" (iii). But who is this "Writer" to whom Defoe is referring? Is it Moll? Is it "the Pen" employed in tidying up her memoranda for publication? Or is it an implied author standing behind – and distanced from – these carefully contrived rhetorical postures? The phrase Defoe uses is not only nicely ambiguous, it also deliberately privileges authorial intention over biographical accuracy, thereby turning on their head the claims to authenticity of Behn and her disciples.

And if we turn to the actual examples of moral instruction offered by Defoe in the preface, it is difficult to avoid the notion that these cautionary tales are oddly materialistic for a book ostensibly concerned with spiritual guidance. Prominent among those offered "as so many warnings to honest People" of how to avoid being "drawn in, plunder'd and robb'd" is Moll's "robbing a little innocent Child, dress'd fine by the vanity of the Mother, to go to the Dancing-School" (iv–v). In this way Defoe draws attention to what is perhaps the finest instance of Moll's attempting to shift the blame for her actions on to others:

> THIS String of Beads was worth about Twelve or Fourteen Pounds, I suppose it might formerly have been the Mother's, for it was too big for the Child's Wear, but that, perhaps, the Vanity of the Mother to have her Child look Fine at the Dancing School, had made her let the Child wear it, and no doubt the Child had a Maid sent to take care of it, but she, like a careless Jade, was taken

up perhaps with some Fellow that had met her by the way, and so the poor
Baby wandred till it fell into my hands.   (202)

By constructing a fiction to justify her conduct, Moll succeeds in distancing
herself by several removes from the consequences of her actions. It was not my
fault, Moll maintains, but "perhaps" the mother's; or if not the mother's, then
the maid "no doubt . . . sent to take care of it," who "was taken up perhaps with
some Fellow." It can be plausibly argued that, in psychological terms, sheer
supposition on this scale is a remarkable indication of the extent to which Moll is
in denial, more especially as she goes on to insist that as she "had a great many
tender Thoughts about [her] yet," she "did the Child no harm" (202).

Even more significant, however, is the way in which this episode demonstrates the extent to which, in Defoe's hands, the first-person narrative is
revealed as not merely partial, but as actually a construct of the narrator's
imagination rather than an objective account of what took place. And if this
is the case, then it seems reasonable to consider what the response of Defoe's
first readers to Moll's equivocations might have been. Given that she has
already explained that "the Devil put me upon killing the Child in the dark
Alley, that it might not cry" (200), perhaps Defoe is inviting "those who know
how to read it" to assess the validity of the narrator's own account of her
actions. Passages such as these, then, suggest that authorial irony is at work in
Moll Flanders in the form of a technique which distances the implied author
from the narrator. Further, in that the version of events readers are being
presented with by Defoe is actually *retrospective* first-person narrative, the wry
observation made at the conclusion of the preface – that at the end of her life
Moll was "not so Extraordinary a Penitent, as she was at first" (vi) – might well
be thought to be peculiarly apposite.

II

While it is possible to describe Defoe's narratives as spurious autobiographies in
which the narrators' claims to tell their own stories truthfully are systematically
undermined by the real author through irony, Fielding insisted that his "true
histories" offered his readers not fact, but fiction. For instance, the truth claims
of those who profess to write history are pointedly brought into prominence in
the important chapter that opens book iii of *Joseph Andrews*. Significantly entitled
"Matter prefatory in Praise of Biography," Fielding painstakingly distinguishes for
rhetorical effect between "the Authority of those Romance-Writers, who intitle
their Books, the History of *England*, the History of *France*, the History of

Spain, &c.," and "the Facts" delivered by "us Biographers," as these, paradoxically, "may be relied on, tho' we often mistake the Age and Country wherein they happened."[15] This distinction leads on to Fielding's famous declaration that although he "describe[s] not Men, but Manners; not an Individual, but a Species," his characters are nevertheless "taken from Life," and that he has written "little more than I have seen" (vol. II, 5).

In drawing attention to the relationship between fact and fiction in this way, Fielding not only implies that all historical accounts are inevitably partial and all historical interpretation subjective, but (like Defoe) he also responds to existing literary forms. Thus the title-pages of *Joseph Andrews* declare that it is "Written in Imitation of The *Manner* of CERVANTES, Author of *Don Quixote*," while the preface warns "the mere *English* Reader" against expecting "a different Idea of Romance with [i.e. from] the Author of these little Volumes," lest he should "expect a kind of Entertainment, not to be found, nor which was even intended, in the following Pages" (vol. I, iii). Critics continue to debate whether Fielding was being entirely serious in suggesting that his prose fiction ought to be compared with Homer's lost comic epic, the *Margites*, but the opening chapter's references to both Colley Cibber's pretentious autobiography, *An Apology for the Life of Mr. Colley Cibber*, and "the Memoirs of Mrs. *Andrews*" – in other words, Richardson's blockbuster, *Pamela* – are exploited to allow him to draw attention to "the exact Rules of Biography" (vol. I, iii).

From the vantage point of the twenty-first century we might be tempted to sneer at the self-consciousness with which these ideas are introduced, but they seem to have been taken seriously by Fielding's contemporaries. Thus Francis Coventry, without any apparent irony, explained why it was appropriate that this "new Species of Writing," which Fielding called "true history," might be described as biography:

> But as Mr. *Fielding* first introduc'd this new kind of Biography, he restrain'd it with Laws which should ever after be deem'd sacred by all that attempted his Manner; which I propose to give a brief Account of . . .
>
> As this Sort of Writing was intended as a Contrast to those in which the Reader was even to suppose all the Characters ideal, and every Circumstance quite imaginary, 'twas thought necessary, to give it a greater Air of Truth, to entitle it *an History*.[16]

Coventry took his cue from a sentence in the opening chapter to the second book of *Tom Jones* (1749) in which Fielding mischievously declared that: "as I am, in reality, the Founder of a new Province of Writing, so I am at liberty to make what Laws I please therein." "'Tho' we have properly enough entitled this our Work, a History, and not a Life; nor an Apology for a Life, as is more in Fashion," Fielding explained, the ostensible purpose of the chapter was to show "what Kind of a History this is; what it is like, and what it is not like."[17] Fielding's narrative self-consciousness serves an important rhetorical purpose. In book III, chapter 7 of *Tom Jones* – in which the narrator begs the reader's pardon for himself appearing "by Way of Chorus, on the Stage" (vol. I, 139) – he refers to his characters as his actors. Fielding is the puppet-master, and he never allows his readers to forget that he is pulling the (always visible) strings.

By inserting a series of alienation devices into his narrative, Fielding deliberately distances his readers from the story they are reading. Thus the series of critical tasks which, from the outset, his readers are set can be interpreted as an array of rhetorical ploys introduced so that they can be manipulated. One of the reasons Fielding does this is to force them to choose between several possible interpretations of a particular character's actions. One of the finest examples of this at work occurs immediately after the battle between Tom and Western and Blifil and Thwackum following on from Tom's retiring into the thicket with Molly Seagrim. "For now a more melancholy and a more lovely Object lay motionless before them," Fielding writes. "This was no other than the charming *Sophia* herself, who, from the Sight of Blood, or from Fear for her Father, or for some other Reason, had fallen down in a Swoon, before any one could get to her Assistance" (vol. I, 298). While the first two reasons given are plausible, it is the "some other Reason" teasingly suggested by Fielding-as-narrator that is telling. The reader has to work out that Sophia has swooned because of the sight of Tom, "almost covered with Blood, part of which was naturally his own, and Part had been lately the Property of the Reverend Mr. *Thwackum*" (vol. I, 298).

In this way the "much celebrated Biographer of *Joseph Andrews*, and *Tom Jones*"[18] complicates his earlier insistence that he will not "pay a Visit into the inmost Recesses of his [Blifil's] Mind, as some scandalous People search into the most secret Affairs of their Friends, and often pry into their Closets and Cupboards, only to discover their Poverty and Meanness to the World" (vol. I, 161). Even though it seems to have been a primary consideration in Watt's distinction between "internal" and "external" approaches to characterization, Fielding's assertion should not be taken at face value. As Robert L. Chibka has recently emphasized, Fielding's narrator "pays a number of such visits,"[19] and of course the reader is subsequently given authoritative information about Blifil's character:

> As there are some Minds whose Affections, like Master *Blifil's*, are solely placed on one single Person, whose Interest and Indulgence alone they consider on every Occasion; regarding the Good and Ill of all others as merely indifferent, any farther than as they contribute to the Pleasure or Advantage of that Person: So there is a different Temper of Mind which borrows a Degree of Virtue even from Self-love. Such can never receive any kind of Satisfaction from another, without loving the Creature to whom that Satisfaction is owing, and without making its Well-being in some sort necessary to their own Ease.
>
> Of this latter Species was our Heroe.   (vol. I, 181)

This can hardly be interpreted as anything other than authoritative, third-person commentary, telling us what to think about Blifil. But to be sure Fielding has been carefully contriving to allow us, as readers, to form our own judgment of Blifil's character from the moment we are first introduced to Tom and Blifil in book III, chapter 2 onwards, and presumably, by this point in the narrative, we have done so.

Fielding, then, alternates between "internal" and "external" approaches to characterization, just as his narratives (to use Roland Barthes's famous formulation) are both "readerly" and "writerly." While he accepts that his readers will read "for the story," and that they will therefore be eager to find out what happens "in the end," he is reluctant to allow us simply to escape into the narrative: hence the alienation devices to make us pause and reflect on what we have just read.

The most obvious examples of this strategy at work are of course the opening chapters to each book. In turn, the best of these to illustrate the point is book VI, chapter 1, "Of Love," which opens by pointing out how: "In our last Book we have been obliged to deal pretty much with the Passion of Love; and, in our succeeding Book, shall be forced to handle this Subject still more largely." After a brief disquisition exposing "certain Philosophers [who], among many other wonderful Discoveries, pretend to have found out, that there is no such Passion in the human Breast" (vol. II, 1), Fielding ends up addressing the reader directly. "Examine your Heart, my good Reader, and resolve whether you do believe these Matters with me," the narrator insists. "If you do, you may now proceed to their Exemplification in the following Pages; if you do not, you have, I assure you, already read more than you have understood." From this point onwards, when Fielding directly questions the reader with such parenthetical asides as "how justly let the Reader determine," or "as the Reader will himself very easily perceive them" (vol. II, 5), he is implicitly assuming that he is one of the "upper Graduates in Criticism" to whom he referred in an early chapter (vol. I, 109).

By setting tests for his readers, Fielding sets out to prevent his narratives from being merely "readerly." This is why, despite making their fictitious nature perfectly plain, he nonetheless refers to them as "true histories." And because he is "an Historian, who professes to draw his Materials from Nature only" (vol. III, 195), Fielding's histories of the adventures of Joseph Andrews, and of his friend Mr. Abraham Adams, and of Tom Jones, a foundling, insinuate that they reveal a higher truth about human nature precisely because they are *fictitious* biographies, even though it is often assumed that, especially in comparison with Richardson's, Fielding's characters lack psychological depth. Notoriously, according to Boswell, Samuel Johnson remarked: "that there was as great a difference between them as between a man who knew how a watch was made, and a man who could tell the hour by looking on the dial-plate."[20] It is for this reason, one assumes, that Mark Kinkead-Weekes memorably asserted that: "Fielding isn't all that interested in what goes on inside his characters, but is very much interested in what goes on inside his readers."[21] The second half of this sentence is not merely unobjectionable, but central to an understanding of Fielding as a "writerly" rather than a "readerly" writer; it is at the heart of his use of an insistent "I" manipulating his characters as if they were his actors. However, I am less convinced that Fielding was uninterested in presenting characters who were psychologically unconvincing, which would, it seems to me, be tantamount to undermining his insistence that "I have writ little more than I have seen." As a biographer, albeit a biographer of fictitious people, Fielding sought to describe characters which, because they were lifelike, were therefore psychologically convincing also.

III

In the *Dictionary* Johnson famously defined the word "novel" as "a small tale, generally of love," and in an equally famous *Rambler* essay he condemned romances but offered qualified approval of "familiar histories" on the grounds that they "may perhaps be made of greater use than the solemnities of professed morality, and convey the knowledge of vice and virtue with more efficacy than axioms and definitions."[22] Therefore despite his criticism of *Tom Jones* as "so vicious a book,"[23] he actually appears to have endorsed the efforts of fiction-writers who could be "approved as just copyers of human manners," and when he turned to writing prose fiction himself to pay for his mother's funeral expenses he described his effort as simply a "little story book." "The title will be The choice of Life or The History of – Prince of Abissinia," he explained to William Strahan on 20 January 1759,[24] although when it actually appeared in print it was entitled *The History of Rasselas, Prince of Abissinia*.

Rasselas has been criticized as formless but, from the opening paragraph's exhortation to "[y]e who listen with credulity to the whispers of fancy, and pursue with eagerness the phantoms of hope" to "attend to the history of Rasselas prince of Abissinia"[25] onwards, it is patently biographical in form. And whether it is regarded as bipartite or tripartite in structure, it is essentially a consideration of "human manners" in line with what Johnson had advocated in his *Rambler* essay on fiction. Set entirely in Abyssinia and Egypt, it is clearly intended to throw English and European manners into sharp relief, and it is for this reason that Imlac explains how Europeans "are less unhappy than we, but they are not happy," because "[h]uman life is every where a state in which much is to be endured, and little to be enjoyed" (355). Gwin J. Kolb has pointed out that Imlac's history, "although modelled on the story-within-a-story device common in oriental tales . . . contrasts sharply with such tales."[26]

Johnson's own fiction, then, is an example of "familiar history" which deliberately departs from the "wild strain of imagination" found in heroic romance in favor of "accidents that daily happen in the world" (*Rambler*, 19). Imlac's account of his life is in effect a pseudo-autobiography within a pseudo-biography which, immediately preceding the chapter in which Rasselas discovers the means of escape from the happy valley, serves as a prelude to the account of the Prince's own investigation into the various ways in which men choose to live their lives. He resolves "to begin his experiments upon life" (364) as soon as he arrives in Cairo, and the following sixteen chapters comprise his (and his sister Nekayah's) survey of human manners. This section of the narrative comes to an abrupt end on the abduction of Nekayah's maid, Pekuah, on a visit to the pyramids. Depressed because she is forced to return to Cairo without her, Nekayah is exhorted by Imlac not to "suffer life to stagnate; it will grow muddy for want of motion; commit yourself again to the current of the world" (392).

This is a crucial element of Johnson's story in which, in conclusion, "nothing is concluded" (418). It has been well observed by Walter Jackson Bate that, among other things, *Rasselas* is a sort of miniature *Bildungsroman*, in which Imlac functions as the Prince's mentor. As life is a state in which much is to be endured, the central theme of Johnson's "familiar history" is that withdrawal from the world is not really an option. In this sense, the happy valley, like Crusoe's island, can be regarded as a state of mind in which, as Rasselas discovers through his conversations with Imlac, "some desire is necessary to keep life in motion, and he, whose real wants are supplied, must admit those of fancy" (348). Sage advice to a young man who had previously "past four months in resolving to lose no more time in idle resolves" (342). As fictitious biography *Rasselas* is scarcely to be accused of contradicting Johnson's dictum that "works of fiction" should "exhibit life in its true state" (*Rambler*, 20). Despite arguing that "many characters ought never to be drawn" in fiction, Johnson nevertheless maintained that, while it had to be shown, vice "should always disgust" (*Rambler*, 22, 24). Accordingly, the four travelers encounter a series of examples of vice and folly and, having recognized them as such, in each case they turn from them in disgust. This allows them "to regulate their own practices" and, in turn, offers a model of behavior for the reader to follow. To this extent, therefore, it can be argued that, despite the famous title of the final chapter, *Rasselas* is not really a tale in which, in conclusion, nothing is concluded.

IV

When corresponding with Robert Dodsley about the publication of *The Life and Opinions of Tristram Shandy, Gentleman*, Sterne proposed "to print a lean Edition in 2 small Vols, of the Size of Rasselas, & on the same paper and Type, – at my own Expence merely to feel the Pulse of the World."[27] The reference to *Rasselas* is of interest if for no other reason than that, although *Tristram Shandy* is shot through with allusions to Sterne's satiric forebears, Lucian, Rabelais, Cervantes, Burton, and Swift, not to mention Shakespeare and Montaigne, Sterne notoriously failed to mention Defoe, Richardson, Fielding, and their contemporaries (although he satirized Smollett as Smelfungus in *A Sentimental Journey*). This has not prevented critics from positioning *Tristram Shandy* firmly within the novel tradition, however. Given that Sterne appears to anticipate many of the preoccupations of twentieth- and twenty-first-century novelists, this is understandable, if potentially misleading. According to Tim Parnell: "*Tristram Shandy*'s deliberately hybrid discourse is a hotch-potch that includes conventional fictional narrative, historiography, travel writing, philosophical and scientific discourses, essayistic digressions and an extraordinary mélange of language and registers." While it is valid to point out that this "suggests at once Tristram's encyclopaedic ambitions and the impossibility of any one book or genre offering a full or adequate rendering of the world,"[28] it also indicates that Sterne was keenly aware of pre-existing narrative forms, and that he ruthlessly exploited them in his best-selling pseudo-autobiography.

One of the best examples of this awareness at work is to be found in the passage in book II, chapter 8, in which Tristram controversially points out that: "It is about an hour and a half's tolerable good reading since my uncle *Toby* rung the bell, when *Obadiah* was order'd to saddle a horse, and go for Dr. *Slop*, the man-midwife." [29] He goes on to introduce the notion of an "intractable hyper-critick" who insists that the reading time which has actually elapsed is "no more than two minutes, thirteen seconds and three-fifths." It is not simply that Sterne is patently playing with narrative time to which I wish to draw attention so much as the conclusion that he equally playfully draws from it: according to Tristram, the discrepancy which the intractable hypercritic insists he has found will "damn me biographically, rendering my book, from this very moment, a profess'd ROMANCE, which, before, was a book apocryphal" (119–120). Here Sterne is quite clearly using the term "romance" to mean a feigned or made-up story, as it had been used by fiction-writers at least since the publication of Blount's *Glossographia*. How seriously we should take his apparent desire to distinguish *Tristram Shandy* from the romance is complicated not only by the fact that the *Oxford English Dictionary* cites this passage as the first instance of the use of the adverb "biographically," but also by Sterne's neologism, "book apocryphal." Sterne plays on the reader's uncertainty about whether *Tristram Shandy* is a genuine autobiography or merely a work of fiction.

Those critics who seek to position *Tristram Shandy* squarely within the emerging novel tradition do not appear sufficiently to have taken into consideration the possible connotations of Sterne's playful distinction between romance and what he is writing. Like Fielding, perhaps, Sterne was deliberately differentiating between the older form of fiction in which (as Congreve put it) "lofty language, miraculous contingencies, and impossible performances elevate and surprise the reader into a giddy delight," and new fiction "of a more familiar nature."[30] When he draws his readers' attention to the possibility that what they are reading is "a book apocryphal," if not "a story of a roasted horse" (vol. 1, 337), however, he appears to be indebted to Sir Thomas Urquhart's 1653 translation of Rabelais's *Gargantua and Pantagruel*, according to which "the story of *Ronypatafam*, or *Lamibaudichon*, interpreted by some to be the tale of a tub, or of a roasted horse, savours of *Apocrypha*, and is not an authentick history."[31] Given what Sterne says in his "short essay upon the character of St. Peter" in sermon XXXI of *The Sermons of Mr. Yorick* (1769), it is difficult to avoid the conclusion that deliberately distinguishing between truth and fiction was high on his agenda. He insisted that his character of Peter was drawn:

> with truth and sobriety, representing it as it was, as consisting of virtues the most worthy of imitation, – and grounded, not upon apocryphal accounts and legendary inventions, the wardrobe from whence popery dresses out her saints upon these days – but upon matters of fact in the ancient Scriptures, in which all christians agree. – [32]

Deliberately identified with Sterne himself in the episode in which Corporal Trim reads a sermon to Walter Shandy, Uncle Toby and Dr. Slop on the text, "For we *trust* we have a good Conscience" (Hebrews 13:18), Yorick is introduced as the vicar of the parish in which Tristram was born, and commemorated by the famous black page. It can scarcely be denied that, particularly in describing Tristram's continental escapades, Sterne drew on his own experiences, while Yorick was of course subsequently resurrected as the first-person narrator of his sentimental autobiography, *A Sentimental Journey*. Sterne, then, not only complicates the relationship between fact and fiction by drawing attention to the doubtful status of his narrative as autobiography, but by "signing correspondence with the names of his characters, Tristram and Yorick, and deliberately blurring the lines between his biological self and his literary creations,"[33] he also contrives to remind his readers (as Fielding had done) of the limitations of both authentic and fictitious "history."

Take, for instance, the passage in book III, chapter 20, in which the narrator, having managed to get all his "heroes" off his hands for a moment, sits down to write "The Author's Preface." Who, in narrative terms, is the "I" who concedes that "in publishing it, – I have appealed to the world," before going on to remark that: "All I know of the matter is, – when I sat down, my intent was to write a good book; and as far as the tenuity of my understanding would hold out, – a wise, aye, and a discreet" (vol. 1, 227)? In this instance the "I" would appear to be Sterne – the "Author" – at least as much as Tristram Shandy, the ostensible autobiographer and narrator. This is an important consideration. If the extent to which Sterne was drawing on the fiction of the 1740s and the 1750s is uncertain, the circumstantial details of the everyday life of the Shandy family which he offers his readers – from the ostensible account of Tristram's conception in the opening chapter to Uncle Toby's courtship of the Widow Wadman in volume IX – strongly suggest that *Tristram Shandy* is nonetheless a story drawn (in Fielding's phrase) "from Nature only." For all his narrative playfulness, Sterne, on one level, is simply another "just copyer of human manners." While Montaigne's *Essays* is an obvious influence on the form of *Tristram Shandy*, in making Tristram undertake "to write not only my life, but my opinions also" (vol. 1, 9) it could be argued that Sterne is following Johnson's theory and Fielding's practice.

Like Fielding, Sterne is interested to the point of preoccupation with what is going on in his readers' minds. As Thackeray observes: "He is always looking in my face, watching his effect."[34] Further, the pseudo-autobiographical form Sterne assumes prevents him from "running [his] history all upon heaps" merely to satisfy the "vicious taste . . . of reading straight forwards, more in quest of the adventures, than of the deep erudition and knowledge which a book of this cast, if read over as it should be, would infallibly impart with them" (vol. I, 75). The humor with which Sterne introduces such ideas should not be allowed to detract from the seriousness with which he suggests that: "The mind should be accustomed to make wise reflections, and draw curious conclusions as it goes along" (vol. I, 65). On this view, even the sensibility for which Sterne was chiefly admired by his contemporaries might be regarded as evidence of a belief that the art of fiction was capable of revealing higher "truths" about the human condition than the mere "factual" historian.

V

In the "small monograph" which he published in 1930 under the title *The English Novel from the Earliest Days to the Death of Joseph Conrad*, Ford Madox Ford lamented what he described as "the present vogue" for the fictitious lives of real-life historical figures, which he called "novelized biography."[35] Ford failed, however, to comment on the novel's relationship, from its earliest days, to history and biography. Defoe, Fielding, Johnson, and Sterne all exploited the relationship between fact and fiction for their various rhetorical ends. While Defoe insinuated that, unlike mere "novels and romances," his narratives were genuine autobiographies – not "stories," but "histories" – Fielding maintained that his accounts of the adventures of patently fictitious characters were actually "true histories" that revealed more about "real life" and human nature than, on the one hand, the old-fashioned romance and, on the other, "those Romance-Writers, who intitle their Books, the History of *England*, the History of *France*, of *Spain*, &c." (*Joseph Andrews*, vol. II, 1). And if Johnson's exemplary *History of Rasselas, Prince of Abissinia* is essentially a "familiar history" which, despite its exotic setting, largely describes "accidents that daily happen in the world," Sterne's *Tristram Shandy* – the first two volumes of which appeared in the same year as *Rasselas* – still seems to be playing games with readers' expectations by suggesting that they suspend judgment about the authenticity of his fictitious autobiography. In this sense, if in no other, Sterne might be regarded as working within the boundaries between truth and fiction that had been deliberately set by Fielding.

Notes

1. For these particular phrases, see *The Fortunes and Misfortunes of The Famous Moll Flanders*, ed. Liz Bellamy (London: Pickering and Chatto, 2009), p. 23; and *Roxana*,

or The Fortunate Mistress, ed. P. N. Furbank (London: Pickering and Chatto, 2009), p. 21.

2. Aphra Behn, *The Fair Jilt* (London: R. Holt for Will. Canning, 1688), "The Epistle Dedicatory."

3. Rosalind Ballaster, *Seductive Forms: Women's Amatory Fiction from 1684 to 1740* (Oxford: Clarendon Press, 1992), p. 155.

4. Francis Kirkman, *The Famous and Delectable History of Don Bellianis of Greece, Or, The Honour of Chivalry* (London: Francis Kirkman, 1673), "To the Reader."

5. T[homas] B[lount], *Glossographia: Or A Dictionary, Interpreting All Such Hard Words of Whatsoever Language, Now Used in Our Refined English Tongue* (2nd edn, London: George Sawbridge, 1661), s.v. "Romance."

6. *The Works of Mrs. Davys: Consisting of, Plays, Novels, Poems, and Familiar Letters* (London: Printed for the Author, 1725), p. iii.

7. *The Letters of Daniel Defoe*, ed. George Harris Healey (Oxford: Clarendon Press, 1958), p. 38.

8. *Religious and Didactic Writings of Daniel Defoe. Vol. 1: The Family Instructor*, ed. P. N. Furbank (London: Pickering and Chatto, 2006), p. 47.

9. Daniel Defoe, *The History and Remarkable Life of the Truly Honourable Col. Jacque*, ed. Maurice Hindle (London: Pickering and Chatto, 2009), p. 32.

10. Daniel Defoe, *Serious Reflections during the Life and Surprising Adventures of Robinson Crusoe*, ed. G. A. Starr (London: Pickering and Chatto, 2008), p. 51.

11. Penelope Aubin, *The strange adventures of the Count Vinevil and his family* (London, 1721), p. 6.

12. Quoted in John J. Richetti, *Popular Fiction Before Richardson: Narrative Patterns 1700–1739* (Oxford: Clarendon Press, 1969), p. 45.

13. Lincoln B. Faller, *Crime and Defoe: A New Kind of Writing* (Cambridge University Press, 1993), pp. 53, 61.

14. [Daniel Defoe], *The Fortunes and Misfortunes Of the Famous Moll Flanders, &c* (London, 1722), p. [1], Eighteenth Century Collections Online, Detroit: Gale Language Learning, 2008.

15. Henry Fielding, *The History of the Adventures of Joseph Andrews, and of his Friend Mr. Abraham Adams*, 2 vols. (London, 1742), vol. II, pp. 1–2, Eighteenth Century Collections Online, Detroit: Gale Language Learning, 2008.

16. Francis Coventry, *An Essay on the New Species of Writing founded by Mr Fielding: with a Word or Two upon the Modern State of Criticism* (London: W. Owen, 1751), pp. 16, 18.

17. Henry Fielding, *The History of Tom Jones, A Foundling*, 4 vols. (London, 1749), vol. I, pp. 59–60, 57, Eighteenth Century Collections Online, Detroit: Gale Language Learning, 2008.

18. Anon., *The History of Charlotte Summers, the Fortunate Parish Girl*, 2 vols. (London: Printed for the Author [1750]), vol. I, p. 3.

19. Robert L. Chibka, "Henry Fielding, Mentalist: Ins and Outs of Narration in *Tom Jones*," *Henry Fielding In Our Time: Papers Presented at the Tercentenary Conference*, ed. J. A. Downie (Newcastle-upon-Tyne: Cambridge Scholars Press, 2008), pp. 81–112, 92.

20. James Boswell, *Life of Johnson*, ed. G. B. Hill and L. F. Powell, 6 vols. (Oxford: Clarendon Press, 1934–1950), vol. II, pp. 48–49.
21. Mark Kinkead-Weekes, "Out of the Thicket in *Tom Jones*," *British Journal for Eighteenth-Century Studies* 3: 1 (1980), 1–19, 7.
22. Samuel Johnson, *The Rambler*, 10th edn. (London, 1784), p. 21 (Saturday, March 31, 1750).
23. Hannah More's *Memoirs*, quoted in *Johnsonian Miscellanies*, ed. G. B. Hill, 2 vols. (Oxford: Clarendon Press, 1897), vol. II, p. 190.
24. Walter Jackson Bate, *Samuel Johnson* (London: Chatto and Windus, 1978), pp. 336–337.
25. Samuel Johnson, *Rasselas, Prince of Abysinnia* in The Oxford Authors, *Samuel Johnson*, ed. Donald Greene (Oxford University Press, 1984), p. 335.
26. Gwin J. Kolb, "The Structure of *Rasselas*," *PMLA* 66: 5, (1951), 698–717, 707.
27. *The Correspondence of Robert Dodsley 1733–1764*, ed. James E. Tierney (Cambridge University Press, 1988), p. 421.
28. Tim Parnell, Introduction, in Laurence Sterne, *The Life and Opinions of Tristram Shandy, Gentleman*, ed. Tim Parnell (London and North Clarendon, VT: J. M. Dent and Charles E. Tuttle, 2000), p. xxii.
29. Laurence Sterne, *The Life and Opinions of Tristram Shandy, Gentleman*, ed. Melvyn New and Joan New, 3 vols. (Gainesville: University Presses of Florida, 1978), vol. I, pp. 119–120.
30. [William Congreve], *Incognita: or, Lover and Duty Reconcil'd. A Novel* (London, 1692), preface.
31. [Sir Thomas Urquhart], *The Second Book Of the Works of Mr. Francis Rabelais* (London: Richard Baddeley, 1653), p. 80.
32. [Laurence Sterne,] *The Sermons of Mr. Yorick*, 2 vols. (London, 1769), vol. II, p. 107.
33. Christopher Fanning, "Sterne and Print Culture," in *The Cambridge Companion to Laurence Sterne*, ed. Thomas Keymer (Cambridge University Press, 2009), p. 126.
34. *The Complete Works of William Makepeace Thackeray*, 22 vols. (Boston: Houghton Mifflin, 1889), vol. XIII, p. 306.
35. Ford Madox Ford, *The English Novel from the Earliest Days to the Death of Joseph Conrad* (London: Constable, 1930), p. 13.

3

Legal discourse and novelistic form

ELEANOR SHEVLIN

. . . the customary law is a fiction from beginning to end: and it is in the way of fiction if at all that we must speak of it.

Jeremy Bentham, Of Laws in General (c. 1782)

The Novel . . . gives a familiar relation of such things, as pass every day before our eyes, such as may happen to our friend, or to ourselves; and the perfection of it, is to represent every scene in so easy and natural a manner, and to them appear so probable, as to deceive us into a persuasion . . . that all is real.

Clara Reeve, The Progress of Romance (1785)

The law, woven inextricably into the fabric of eighteenth-century English life, exercised a pervasive presence across social ranks. For most persons the law served as their main exposure to government and politics,[1] but its associations stretched far beyond governance and state affairs. Literal and figurative reminders of the law passed every day before the eyes of the English populace in the form of public executions, marriage settlements, bankruptcies, gaming restrictions, debtors' prisons, land enclosures, wills, navy press gangs, deeds of ownership, estate disputes, to list only a few. Those and similar reminders also filled the pages of eighteenth-century fictional narratives. Reworked as plot devices, thematic threads, or instruments of verisimilitude, matters of law infused fictional narratives with the stuff of lived experience and contributed to their persuasiveness "that all is real."[2] It is perhaps unremarkable that eighteenth-century novels, given their concern with replicating the real of everyday experience, embraced the law. More noteworthy but less acknowledged is the extent to which the law embraced fiction.

Fictions of law arose "to resolve novel legal questions through arguments of equivalence and creative analogical reasoning"; they signify "the growing pains of the language of the law."[3] As English society shed its feudal past and moved steadily to a capitalist mode of operation, its legal system remained rooted in its medieval origins. When new situations occurred that existing laws either did not cover or could not handle adequately, fictions were devised and treated as fact in order to circumvent the inconveniences or inadequacies occasioned by outmoded jurisprudence. English law, in short, adopted legal fictions as a procedural technique for responding to changing social situations and cultural conditions. In addressing those changes legal fictions, much like early novels, trafficked in fictions of persons, places, and social relations. They constructed the personages of "John Doe" and "Richard Roe" to transform freeholds into leaseholds;[4] to avow that Paris was actually in London, or Calais really in Kent, to secure jurisdiction over disputes outside of England;[5] and to recast a private debt between two civil parties as one owed to the king to gain access to the court of the Exchequer.[6] The imaginative reconstructions operated within the broader framework of the common law and served to perpetuate the larger fiction that English law had been unchanging from time out of mind.

One of the most cogent demonstrations of the law's embrace of fictions is the jurist William Blackstone's *Commentaries on the Laws of England* (1765–1769), a work that dominated eighteenth-century understanding of the law. Although legal fictions had a long tradition in the common law, Blackstone recognizes that their presence may at first "startle" his lay audience.[7] While Blackstone's treatment of legal fictions at times suggests his anxiety over their use,[8] he consistently emphasizes their necessity and equity. These "series of minute contrivances," he explains, are undertaken to achieve "substantial and speedy justice" without causing "any great legislative revolution" in the common law (vol. III, 267–268). Once the fictions are understood, citizens will come to see them as "highly beneficial" and necessary "to prevent a mischief, or remedy an inconvenience, that might result from the general rule of law" (vol. III, 43). Yet it is not just its explications of legal fictions that constitute this work's engagement with fiction. A primary goal of the *Commentaries* is "to render the whole [English law] intelligible to the unformed minds of beginners" by providing "a general map of the law, marking out the shape of the country, its connexions and boundaries, its greater divisions and principal cities" (vol. I, 35). In executing this task Blackstone's work arguably enacts a kind of "novelization" of the common law. Aided by a graceful, coherent narrative and rich use of fictions and metaphoric language, the *Commentaries* refashions the nation's past to suit prevailing views about English rights. Its resulting four-volume "map" of the law depicts a historically revised, ethically motivated, and timelessly harmonious legal system whose illumination is aimed at providing the literate lay population with not only a better understanding of the law but also, by extension, of their own everyday world. Like legal fictions and early novels, the *Commentaries* relies on inventions and suspending disbelief to construct its particular world view as accepted reality. Its transformation of the Norman Conquest from a military defeat into a rhetorical contest in which the English emerge victorious, unconquered with their liberties intact, offers a prominent example (vol. II, 50–52). In the process verbal maneuverings frame the strategy of fiction as a respected, accepted technique of the law that other discourses could adapt to achieve their particular ends.

As this overview intimates, juxtaposing the ways in which fictions operated within early novels and the law reveals a reciprocal, at times constitutive relationship, between the two realms.[9] Characterized not only by shared thematic concerns but also similar discursive practices and ideological preoccupations, this relationship was born of broader social, political, psychological, and cultural alterations that distinguished England from the Continent. As one cultural critic has noted, in Anglo-American law literary and legal "discourses inform each other because they share the same cultural root buried deep in the seventeenth century."[10] In the wake of seventeenth-century socio-political upheavals the English reimagined their past, claiming liberty and property as God-given rights from time immemorial to be foundational tenets. This mythic national patrimony contributed significantly to the idea of England's legal uniqueness among its continental counterparts[11] and generated a cultural consciousness well suited to fostering fictions of individuality and ownership. Such cultural consciousness helped to spur significant changes in the law alongside the growth of prose fiction purporting to be true. The subsequent cross-fertilization between eighteenth-century law and the era's novels was predicated not just on a shared investment in fictions but also on a deep engagement with conceptions of property and its regulation. The *raison d'être* of eighteenth-century English law, property also constituted the thematic substance of the early novels. Changing conceptions of property and the way it structured social relations fueled the need for legal fictions and drove the plots of fictions known today as novels.

Within this context Blackstone's geographic analogy of *Commentaries* as a map is telling, for it figuratively equates the law with land. By 1688 property in land reigned supreme as a determinant of social and political power, a view the *Commentaries* promoted through its vision of the world as governed by and for the propertied.[12] Yet this supremacy was increasingly being challenged by new forms of commercial property such as paper money, promissory notes, speculation in stocks, and other credit-based entities, as well as by new notions of the self and subjectivity. Indeed, that Blackstone refers to the English as "a polite and *commercial* people" subtly evokes the power that new forms of property were wielding throughout the century (vol. III, 326; emphasis added).[13] While the world-making that Blackstone effects in his *Commentaries* produced a particular view about the way in which English law structured society, realistic fictional narratives were ideally positioned not only to replicate this view but to offer contesting visions as well. By constructing imaginary lands of everyday happenings that claim to be real, early novels encapsulate the contests over the changing nature of property, legally defined in terms of "real" (land and immovables) and "personal" (movable goods as well as the property one has in one's self),[14] that permeated eighteenth-century English life and preoccupied English courts.[15]

A shared set of characteristics – ranging from ontological links with changing social conditions and shifting roles of property to a mutual employment of land and fictional persons – distinguishes the novel's functional relationship with the law from other literary forms. More than merely a system of procedures, the common law developed "substantive rules purporting to regulate in some detail how people should behave, to analyze the relationships of life into a comprehensible system of rights and duties" (Milsom, "Blackstone's Achievement," 4). Those functions – providing rules aimed at regulating behavior and analyzing human relationships to clarify the workings of society – mirror the purposes that early novels in their prefaces and narrative commentary profess to fulfill. This functional correspondence between the law and eighteenth-century novels is strengthened by the novel's semantic correlative in the law. Long before "novel" became the accepted term for realistic prose fiction, the word possessed legal currency. Originating in Roman law, the term "novels" – or *novellae*, the Latin form commonly used in legal texts – denotes addenda or supplements to recorded laws. These "new constitutions" addressed "new questions [as they] happened to arise" (Blackstone, *Commentaries*, vol. I, 81). Ontologically akin to legal fictions, novels in a legal context were newly instituted codes. While legal novels altered the body of established law by adding new codes, legal fictions preserved the illusion that English law was timeless and unchanging through a series of maneuvers. In the literary realm, however, the functions associated with legal novels and fictions of law not only co-existed but operated in tandem.

Like *novellae*, early eighteenth-century fictional narratives defined themselves as dealing with new and unusual situations in novel and uncommon ways. As Sarah Fielding rhetorically asked, "In what does the Novelty so much required in these kind of Writings consist? . . . Must it not therefore be said to consist in putting known and remarkable Characters into new Situations?"[16] Similar claims to novelty, strange situations, and remarkable circumstances characterize novelistic discourse, from Daniel Defoe's title pages and Henry Fielding's prefatorial claim that *The History of the Adventures of Joseph Andrews* (1742) presents a "Species of writing . . . hitherto unattempted in our Language,"[17] to countless other examples. Early English literary novels embodied the word's legal meaning by operating as extensions of the established law. The increasing ascendancy of personal property gave rise to "new situations" that literary novels were well positioned to tackle. As cultural supplements to the official law, early novels afforded a forum for positing, championing, complicating, and dismissing competing opinions and solutions about how property should regulate social relations beyond the purview of the Court of Common Pleas, King's Bench, Chancery, and the Inns of Court. Legal fictions' enactments of "a series of minute contrivances," in turn, parallel the intricate, inventive paths that plots of novels devised in detailing particular versions of property relations against the backdrop of ongoing eighteenth-century social changes. And just as fictions of law perform verbal maneuvers that enable action within the guise of unchanging procedures, so, too, do the "minute contrivances" of early literary novels act as narrative devices that advance storylines about property within the guise of dramatic events. Not only do the law's strategies and rationales for employing fictions resurface in realistic narrative, but the early English novel's thematic preoccupation with property is an essential component of its reworking of the law.

In their role as "new constitutions" and their employment of "minute contrivances," early novels also adopted the logic of the English trial. As Martin Kayman has noted, unlike the continental trial that "is structured as an inquest, a search for the truth, the English trial is adversarial in nature: it presupposes the possibility of rival representations of events."[18] At the level of genre, early novels themselves serve as rival representations of institutional law. At the level of individual works, novels explore rival representations of events within their pages, often adopting the habits of legal reasoning to assess their respective merits. The numerous novels born of actual legal cases make explicit the ways that this literary form performed as a public hearing that aired opinions and resolutions about how property relations should regulate English society. In *Memoirs of an Unfortunate Young Nobleman* (1743), for instance, Eliza Haywood refashions the events surrounding *Annesley* v. *Anglesea* (1743), the suit that James Annesley brought against his uncle the

Earl of Anglesea to regain his inherited title and accompanying Irish estates, to champion the nephew's rights. Using legal affidavits, Benjamin Victor's *The Widow of the Wood* (1755) relates the charges and suits ensuing from Sir William Wolseley's private marriage to his widowed but much younger neighbor Anne Whitby; Whitby, already pregnant with another man's child, falsely claimed that she had married this man before her union with Wolseley. In the epistolary novel *The History of a Late Infamous Adventure, Between a Great Man and a Fair Citizen* (1768), the events preceding Lord Baltimore's trial for the abduction and rape of Sarah Woodcock, a milliner, are fictionally rendered. In all those novels property questions occupy center stage: who owns the Annesley property? Was Wolseley defrauded of the property he held in Whitby through his marriage to her? Did Whitby's desire to preserve the property that she had in her good name and that she wished her unborn child to inherit drive her claims? Did Lord Baltimore invade the ultimate form of Sarah Woodcock's personal property, her body?

While such explicit bonds with actual legal cases are absent from most early fictional narratives, the same concerns with acquiring, preserving, and reassigning property surface throughout the works we know today as eighteenth-century novels. Whether we consider Robinson Crusoe's desire to acquire more and more property, Pamela's pleas to preserve her most prized property, Tom Jones's becoming heir to Allworthy's property, or Peregrine Pickle's fallings in and out of property, what we quickly see is how much the right of property governed the imagination of these works. As the plots of early novels embraced property as an overriding concern, they distanced themselves more and more from the intrigues of French romances. In doing so their plots adhered more faithfully to the etymological derivation of the English word "plot" from "plat," whose general meaning ranged from an area of land or a diagram of something, especially that of a piece of ground, to the plan of a fictional work (*Oxford English Dictionary*, n. "plat" 1.1; 2.3–4, 6) and whose legal meaning referred to a "map, or representation on paper, of a piece of land subdivided into lots . . . usually drawn to scale."[19]

Though scheming and intrigue certainly persist in early English novels, these elements emerge domesticated and subordinate to property concerns; and their narratives favor mapping representations of social relations drawn to the scale of the everyday. The stratagems propelling the plots of Daniel Defoe's novels from *Robinson Crusoe* (1719) to *Roxana* (1724), for instance, are undertaken to accumulate property and solidify a protagonist's place in the world. Similarly, the machinations found in Henry Fielding's *Tom Jones* (1749) – be they executed by the Blifils, Sr. or Jr., by Molly Seagrim, or by

Mr. Fitzpatrick – are all motivated by property interests. And in Samuel Richardson's *Clarissa* (1747–1748), the scheming that occupies its plot is essentially driven by desires to acquire or secure property – whether those desires for property are formed by the Harlowes' greediness for enlarging the family's fortune, Lovelace's fixation on making Clarissa his property, or Clarissa's battles to maintain the personal property she has in her self. All these manifestations of property concerns directly treat property as a force ordering eighteenth-century English social relations. Yet while the *Commentaries* envisioned the world as being governed by and for the propertied, early fictional narratives offered a multiplicity of views on how fictions of land, law, and self interacted in structuring and regulating society, and it is to these views that we now turn.[20]

"Property is a way of looking at the world, as well as a means of sharing it out"[21]

Daniel Defoe's Robinson Crusoe, Moll Flanders, and Roxana all exhibit an insatiable desire for accumulating property, both real and personal. For these characters, an obsession with property signifies not only cravings for material goods but also anxieties about survival. In a world governed by property, the unceasing pursuit of possessions and land translates as self-preservation. Within this context the narratives of Crusoe, Moll, and Roxana are as much discourses about *homo juridicus* as they are models of *homo economicus*. At the start of Defoe's *Robinson Crusoe*, Crusoe recounts that his father had "design'd me for the Law; but I would be satisfied with nothing but going to Sea."[22] Crusoe's decision to spurn his father's wishes and pursue a mariner's life propels the novel's plot, but his choice does not mark the end of the work's engagement with the law. Rather, the narrative itself adopts the design of the law through its procedural mode and thematic concerns. Its series of minute contrivances, ranging from Crusoe's first rash departure from home to his shipwreck en route to Guinea, not only lands Crusoe on an uninhabited island, but an ensuing set of contrivances also results in his achieving dominion over this property in land and the property that Friday has in himself. While Crusoe's claims of being the exclusive proprietor of "the whole Country" and its "absolute Lord and Law-giver" allude satirically to absolutism (203), they also gesture to the fictions that underpin the divine rights of kings and those of landed property owners. This gesture becomes explicit pages later when the ruse that Crusoe is the island's English governor proves to be an effective strategy in securing the mutineers' surrender despite its being "all a Fiction" (226).

Defoe's interest in exploring legal issues and reformulating property relations surfaces again and again in his fictions as the rights accorded by real property collide with those derived from the property that one has in one's self and in one's labor. Like *Robinson Crusoe*, debates about real and personal property in *The Fortunes and Misfortunes of The Famous Moll Flanders* (1722) and *Roxana, or The Fortunate Mistress* (1724) traverse wide geographies that extend beyond England's physical borders and work to expose the fluidity of land and its ties to competing forms of commercial and personal property. In the process the two works' multi-layered treatment of property underscores more broadly the lack of protection that the law afforded women and the economic hardship, if not destitution, that could and did result from their legal status. These works' examination of property, law, and self, undertaken through a chain of minute contrivances, juxtaposes legal issues with moral concerns. Moll's diverse wranglings with the law and her conscience and Roxana's "property" speech to the Dutch merchant represent just a few of the numerous examples of this juxtaposition. Property was so central an explanatory concept for Defoe that he envisioned even God's authority over humanity as a property right: God's "Right to rule over us, is founded upon his Property in us."[23] By linking Providence, property, and the whole of humanity, Defoe reconfigures personhood as a viable counterpart to the social and legal authority associated with immovable property. Applied as an interpretive lens, English law, deeply invested in both personal and fixed property, supplies a broader perspective in which critical views of Defoe's novels as spiritual autobiographies, criminal biographies,[24] or treatises hailing economic individualism can not only co-exist but also be shown to interact. Read as cultural hearings on English law, Defoe's novels grapple with the right to possess and preserve one's self in ways that highlight the fissures and fictions of a legal system aimed at protecting the propertied.

Competing visions of the law's formulation of property rights also drive the plot of Samuel Richardson's *Pamela* (1740). Richardson's novel questions the power that landed property wields over the worth of the individual self in ways that unsettle notions of English rights and liberties in terms of status and gender. As a printer Richardson acquired intimate knowledge of the propertied classes and the workings of the law, including its legal fictions. From the 1720s on he printed numerous private bills for both the Commons and the Lords. Most of this printing involved "purely private and personal matters, such as estates, wills, marriage settlements, and the like."[25] This employment familiarized Richardson not only with legal terms and tenets but also with an array of legal maneuverings such as surname substitutions[26] aimed at transforming fictions into desired social "truths." The tensions between personal and landed property as well as those between moral and legal authority that dominate *Pamela* reflect the knowledge Richardson would have gained from printing these Acts. As Janine Barchas has observed about the graphic resemblance between Pamela's reply to Mr. B.'s "naughty Articles" and legal reference texts, Richardson's rhetorical use of the law accentuates Mr. B.'s and Pamela's sharply demarcated realms of moral authority, the gravity of her situation, and the tangible costs of maintaining her principles.[27]

Pamela's determination to preserve the property she has in her self at all costs not only seems incredible and artful to the propertied and privileged Squire B., but her steadfastness also fuels the novel's events as both sides struggle to maintain their vision of property relations. Early on in her captivity, Pamela indignantly asks, "[H]ow came I to be his Property? What Right has he in me, but such as a Thief may plead to stolen Goods?" Her keeper Mrs. Jewkes responds, "This is downright Rebellion" and adds that if she were in Squire B.'s place, "he should not have his Property in [Pamela] long questionable."[28] While Pamela views the right to the property she has in her self as incontrovertible and Mr. B.'s claims on her person as specious, Mrs. Jewkes sees his right as unquestionable and Pamela's analogy as fomenting rebellion against established norms. Mr. B., who is a magistrate, also employs the metaphorical language of stolen property, equating Pamela as property that Parson Williams has attempted "to invade" (305), and "rob . . . me of" (282). Jewkes's and Squire B.'s stance is substantiated by the law's delineation of the master–servant relationship as a property contract in which the master gains ownership rights to the servant's service (Blackstone, *Commentaries*, vol. I, 417). While Mr. B. and Jewkes broadly construe what constitutes "service," their attitude largely conforms to dominant social norms surrounding female servants, especially those held by socially privileged males. The diametrically opposed conceptions of self and rights that Pamela's and Squire B.'s figurative uses of stolen property convey encapsulate the novel's central conflicts over property's regulatory power and the locus of moral authority and virtue.

Operating as the novel's narrative mode, Pamela's letters and journals also function as testimony and documentary evidence. Richardson's printing of potentially dangerous material[29] early in his career might well have heightened his understanding of the legal significance of manuscripts and handwriting as potent signifiers of individuality and "witnesses" of the self.[30] As late as 1683 Algernon Sidney was convicted, albeit not without controversy, of treason based on papers identified as being written by his hand and used in court as the second "witness" required for conviction (Blackstone, *Commentaries*, vol. IV, 80). In *Pamela* Richardson uses handwriting and personal papers akin to the roles such materials play in the legal realm. With pen seemingly perpetually in hand, Pamela inscribes again and again the authority she has in her self as she simultaneously produces written witness after witness to her trials. The discovery of her first writing parcel transforms her trials into a "Trial" with Mr. B. as its self-appointed "Judge" (230). Pamela's writings, initially deemed "treasonable Papers" (228), furnish the evidence of her "true" self that will ultimately convince Squire B. of her virtue.

Ordered to submit her remaining writings by Mr. B., Pamela "must all undress" to retrieve the papers (235). Sewn into her garments, the writings literally and figuratively embody her self. By stripping herself of them and delivering them to Mr. B., Pamela relinquishes much of the property she holds in her self. That she subsequently reverses her attitude toward her former captor leads to further loss. With her marriage to Mr. B., Pamela becomes a feme covert under the law, forfeiting her legal personhood: "the very being or legal existence of the woman is suspended during the marriage" (Blackstone, *Commentaries,* vol. I, 430). The once "treasonable" papers bearing witness of her self have become the property of Mr. B. who controls their circulation (455). Their challenge to a social order that privileges landed birth and treats moral authority as a monopoly of the propertied has been domesticated as virtuous inspiration. Likewise, the fictions surrounding the "[un]Changeableness of human Estates" and "Gentle-folks, that brag of their ancient Blood" (258) that Pamela's writings expose have been subsumed by Mr. B.'s fictions that "a Man ennobles the Woman he takes, be she *who* she will" (422) and that "Equality" not "Obligation" defines his marriage (350). That the married Pamela welcomes the prospect of being "improv'd" by Mr. B. and vows that she has "no Will but [his]" makes a fiction of her former self, confirming her hypocrisy for those already skeptical readers (351). The ties between virtue and the propertied have been loosened, but Pamela, whether servant or wife, remains the property of her landed master.

If we regard Richardson's *Pamela* as a bill of complaint, then Henry Fielding's *Shamela* (1741) offers the defense's answer. After *Shamela* Fielding's novels abandon the adversarial position of respondent and assume the mantle of magistrate. Although *Joseph Andrews, Tom Jones,* and *Amelia* (1751) all explore the shifting relationships among property, social order, and morality, the law informs those works in ways notably different from its role in Richardson's first novel. Among the most significant divergences is Fielding's choice of an omniscient narrator over the first-person narrator favored by Richardson, Defoe, and others. Such a choice reflects Fielding's attitudes about the limitations of personal testimony in both law and fiction.[31] This belief cuts across his novels, and explicit references to such testimony's shortcomings appear in all three. *Joseph Andrews*, for example, registers Fielding's mistrust of such testimony through irony: "Informations from his own Mouth; which, in the Opinion of some Moderns is the best and indeed only Evidence" (62), while *Tom Jones* explains his reasoning: "Not that Jones desired to conceal or disguise the truth ... but, in reality, so it happened, and so it will always happen ... when a man tells his own story."[32] And *Amelia* proposes Fielding's remedy: "had the Magistrate been endued with much Sagacity ... he would have employed some Labour in cross-examining the Watchmen," or at least he would have "sen[t] for the other Persons who were present."[33] For Fielding, relying on a single voice or even on a selective few will only result in a partial, prejudiced report; only by receiving all accounts and sifting through their inconsistencies and contradictions can readers render a fair judgment.

Fielding's preference for the omniscient narrator also speaks to his views of property's role as a regulating force of social relations. Yet it does so in ways more complex than an "all-knowing" narrator or a narrator claiming absolute powers as "the founder of a new province of writing" might suggest (*Tom Jones*, 88). Along with others, Nicholas Hudson has encouraged reconsidering conventional views of Fielding as an inflexible representative of the old social order, and argues that situating *Tom Jones* within "its social, philosophical, and political context" enables a more nuanced, complicated picture to emerge.[34] Examining Fielding's fictions through the frame of law and property yields similar results. While in many ways this lens sharpens the focus of his belief in social order, hierarchical structures, and a commitment to landed property as a touchstone against which other forms of property are adjudged, it also suggests a far more flexible view of status, one fixed not on virtue but instead on one's capacity for judgment and the ability to exercise such judgment to achieve justice. Thus, what Fielding often exposes are fictions of justice ostensibly achieved by the workings of the law and often arising from deficiencies in judgment resulting from incompetence, greed, self-interest, pride, incomplete knowledge of the circumstances, or similar causes. That the servant girl in *Joseph Andrews*, for instance, produces the evidence needed for the thief's conviction when all others around her fail is telling, and operates both as a criticism of her "betters" and as an indication that the possession of judgment is not relegated to a particular rank or ranks.

Within this context Fielding's narrators, steeped in their use of forensic rhetoric,[35] perform a special role as both legal counsel and reader's guide. As Alexander Welsh has said of *Tom Jones*, Fielding's narrators are "manager[s] of the evidence" (58). Not only does an evidentiary manager intimate a different relationship with readers from that an absolute lawgiver would have, but it also implicitly emphasizes ability and judgment over status. Fielding, an experienced lawyer and magistrate, possessed the professional legal expertise to create narrators who could perform this role expertly. His penchant for having his narrators develop relationships with readers, though their extent would certainly depend on a given reader's understanding, positions them as jurors, as Ian Watt suggested so many years ago.[36] The narratives of his works follow the procedures of arguments at trial, and readers, as Welsh reminds us, must suspend judgment until all the accounts and facts are concluded. As Fielding's narrator in *Amelia* proclaims, "[t]here is no Exercise of the Mind of a sensible Reader more pleasant than the tracing the several small and almost imperceptible Links in every Chain of Events by which all the great Actions of the World are produced" (482).

The breadth of legal topics and attention to legal procedures in Fielding's novels render his fictional corpus a sort of compendium of Blackstone's *Commentaries*. Trials abound in it, but his works also either mention or incorporate discussions of diverse types of writs, dueling, highway robbery, laws of evidence, ejectment, illegitimacy, theft, transportation, *habeas corpus*, bankruptcy, capital punishment, the game laws, petit larceny, entailed estates, manslaughter, debt, criminal conversation, settlement laws, impressment, forgery, perjury, the assize courts, specific prisons, penalties for various crimes, and various judicial roles from justices with no legal training to bailiffs, law clerks, solicitors, and many other topics.[37] Often shrouded in comic guise, these frequent occurrences of the law in the narratives carry serious intentions. Fielding's extended treatment of evidence of theft and stolen property in *Joseph Andrews*, for example, illustrates the multiple purposes such sequences serve (55–57). Eschewing Richardson's metaphorical use of stolen property, Fielding instead addresses an actual point of law – *bona waviata* – alongside comic exchanges that end with the flippant remark, "So the Lord of the Manor is the Receiver of stolen Goods" (57). Here and elsewhere in his novels such incidents ultimately criticize both the law's seemingly anachronistic, often tortuous workings and its frequent inability to produce justice. Fielding's continued satirizing of the clergyman Barnabas and the Surgeon as pseudo-practitioners of the law also draws attention to the need for sound professional training – or at the very least sound judgment. More importantly, as he does throughout his novels, Fielding demonstrates that legal terminology alone does not a lawyer make, and, worse, that its use can obstruct the ends of justice. Instead, his novels suggest that it is not legal diction but rather its habits of thinking – its underlying assumptions – that hold the key to its operations. Such a position closely resembles legal theorist James Boyd White's notion of the "invisible discourse of the law" that arises from its "'cultural syntax,' the invisible expectations governing the way the words are ... used."[38] That White developed his theory as a means of advocating legal literacy among lay persons extends some parallels to the type of ethical reasoning and observation that Fielding is promoting in his works.

Not only does the law pervade the imagination of realistic eighteenth-century novels, canonical and the non-canonical alike, but it also exercises a particularly forceful relationship with gothic fictions. That relationship speaks to the rise of new social anxieties, and indicates fresh challenges to conceptions of property as a regulatory force. The gothic novel's appropriations of feudal elements hark back to the roots of common law, and act to dispel fictions of the law's unchangeableness and of its role as guarantor of liberties. Blackstone's description of legal fictions anticipates this appropriation in an architectural metaphor that commingles novelistic discourse with the law:

> We inherit an old Gothic castle, erected in the days of chivalry, but fitted up for a modern inhabitant. The moated ramparts, the embattled towers, and the trophied halls, are magnificent and venerable, but useless. The inferior apartments, now converted into rooms of convenience are chearful and commodious, though their approaches are winding and difficult.
>
> (*Commentaries*, vol. III, 268)

Through their strategic employment of gothic architecture, scenery, and labyrinthine passageways, gothic novels lay bare the decay – what Sue Chaplin terms "the 'fragility'" – of law, and project the legal system's capacity for inducing terror and a sense of overwhelming oppression.[39]

Here is a new turn in the novel's relation to legal discourse. Amid an already troubled arena of foreign and domestic politics, law as an institution was itself changing. Robert Shoemaker has noted that in the latter decades of the eighteenth century, "growing frustration at the cost, delays, and complexities of the legal system," coupled with "the seemingly unending tide of malicious prosecutions," resulted in more and more of the population, especially the urban middle class, feeling increasingly alienated and distanced from law. Shoemaker's link between the social malaise surrounding the courts and law and the development and popularity of gothic novels with their representations of "law as an oppressive system which terrified those caught up in it"[40] – a description that cannot but help to evoke William Godwin's *Things as They Are; or, The Adventures of Caleb Williams* (1794) – is further strengthened when filtered through the lens of property. With the proximity of social upheaval across the Channel causing fear of similar property eruptions in England and, perhaps equally important, with the loss of England's former colonial property in North America (an amputation of England's phantom extension of itself bolstered by such legal fictions as Boston equals London), the nexus of property, land, and self in imaginative narratives of everyday occurrences purporting to be real lost its patina of plausibility.

In keeping with his declaration that the common law "is a fiction from beginning to end,"[41] Jeremy Bentham deemed the *Commentaries* an "excursion into the land of fancy" in which metaphors create "imaginary objects" disguised as laws.[42] Few others at the time shared his view; yet the way was prepared for change.

Notes

1. John Brewer, "The Wilkites and the Law, 1763–74," in *An Ungovernable People: The English and Their Law in the Seventeenth and Eighteenth Centuries*, ed. John Brewer and John A. Styles (New Brunswick: Rutgers University Press, 1980), p. 133.

2. David Punter usefully overviews three key areas of the law's representation in eighteenth-century fiction. See Punter, "Fictional Representation of the Law in the Eighteenth Century," *Eighteenth-Century Studies* 16: 1 (1982), 47–74.

3. Nancy J. Knauer, "Legal Fictions and Juristic Truths," *St. Thomas Law Review* 23: 1 (2010), 1–51, 3; Lon L. Fuller, *Legal Fictions* (Stanford University Press, 1967), p. 22.

4. R. S. White, *Natural Law in English Renaissance Literature* (Cambridge University Press, 1996), pp. 89–90; J. H. Baker, *An Introduction to Legal History* (3rd edn, London: Butterworths, 1990), pp. 341–343.

5. Y. B. Pasch. 20 Hen. VI, fo. 28, pl. 21; Y. B. Mich. 15 Edw. IV, fo. 14, pl. 18.

6. William Blackstone, *Commentaries on the Laws of England: A Facsimile of the First Edition of 1765–1769*, 4 vols. (University of Chicago Press, 1979), vol. III, p. 45.

7. Blackstone wrote for a lay audience. S. F. C. Milsom, "The Nature of Blackstone's Achievement," *Oxford Journal of Legal Studies* 1: 1 (1981), 1–12.

8. John H. Langbein, introduction to Blackstone, *Commentaries*, vol. III, p. v.

9. For an extended discussion, see Eleanor Shevlin, "'Imaginary Productions' and 'Minute Contrivances': Law, Fiction, and Property in Eighteenth-Century England," *Studies in Eighteenth-Century Culture* 28 (1999), 131–154.

10. Jane Gaines refers specifically to the emergence of the bourgeois subject and laws governing intellectual property, but these roots extend beyond copyright

law; Gaines, *Contested Culture: The Image, the Voice, and the Law* (Chapel Hill: University of North Carolina Press, 1991), p. 23.

11. For most in post-1688 England, liberties ceased to be something the king gave to the people but instead became firmly ensconced as God-given rights and never constitutionally part of the king's jurisdiction. Howard Nenner, "Liberty, Law, and Property: The Constitution in Retrospect from 1689," in *Liberty Secured? Britain Before and After 1688*, ed. J. R. Jones (Stanford University Press, 1992), pp. 88–121, esp. pp. 88–89.

12. While Blackstone's introduction notes that the study of law can benefit various ranks, it focusses on the propertied segment of society; his allegiance to this group is, at the very least, implicit throughout the *Commentaries*.

13. This characterization also recalls the social status associated with eighteenth-century realistic fictions, both in terms of the audiences traditionally aligned with those works and the perspectives that their fictional works typically feature.

14. Legally defined, both real and personal property consist entirely of "things": "The objects of dominion or property are *things*, as contradistinguished from *persons*: and things are by the law of England distributed into two kinds; things *real*, and things *personal*. Things real are such as permanent, fixed, and immovoe-able, which cannot be carried out of their place; as lands and tenements: things personal are goods, money, and all other moveables; which may attend the owner's person wherever he thinks proper to go" (Blackstone, *Commentaries*, vol. II, p. 16).

15. Between 1688 and 1820 the number of capital statutes increased about fourfold, from about fifty in number to over two hundred such Acts. On the whole this increase consisted almost entirely of legislation responding to offenses against property; see Sir Leon Radzinowicz, *A History of English Criminal Law and its Administration from 1750*, 4 vols. (London: Stevens, 1948–1968), vol. I, p. 4. For a specific look at the actual effects of this legislation, see Douglas Hay, "Property, Authority, and the Criminal Law," in *Albion's Fatal Tree: Crime and Society in Eighteenth-Century England* (New York: Pantheon, 1975), pp. 17–63.

16. Sarah Fielding, *The Adventures of David Simple. Volume the Last, in Which His History Is Concluded* (London, 1753), Eighteenth-Century Collections Online, p. vi.

17. Henry Fielding, *The History of the Adventures of Joseph Andrews*, ed. Douglas Brooks-Davies; rev. and intro. by Thomas Keymer (Oxford University Press, 1999), p. 8.

18. Martin Kayman, "The Englishness of the English Novel, and 'The Glory of the English Law,'" *British and American Studies/Revista de Studii Britanice și Americane* 10 (2004), 225–236, 230.

19. "plat," *Black's Law Dictionary* (rev. 4th edn. St. Paul, MN: West Publishing, 1968), p. 1309.

20. For a recent examination of the ways early prose fiction participated in a rethinking of law, land, property, and self, see Susan Paterson Glover, *Engendering Legitimacy: Law, Property, and Early Eighteenth-Century Fiction* (Lewisburg, PA: Bucknell University Press, 2006).

21. Paul Langford, *Public Life and the Propertied Englishman 1689–1798* (Oxford: Clarendon Press, 1991), pp. 4–5.

22. Daniel Defoe, *The Life and Strange Surprizing Adventures of Robinson Crusoe*, ed. Thomas Keymer (Oxford University Press, 2009), p. 5.

23. Daniel Defoe, *Review*, publication no. 44 of the Facsimile Text Society, Facsimile Book 7, May 7, 1706, to September 21, 1706 of vol. III (New York: Columbia University Press, 1938), July 13, 1706, p. 334.

24. Hal Gladfelder offers extended examinations of the ties between criminality and Defoe's work in *Criminality and Narrative in Eighteenth-Century England* (Baltimore, MD: Johns Hopkins University Press, 2001), pp. 93–149.

25. Keith Maslen asserts that "in his lifetime Richardson was the major printer" of these Acts. See Maslen, "Samuel Richardson as Printer: Expanding the Canon," in *Order and Connexion: Studies in Bibliography and Book History*, ed. R. C. Alston (Cambridge: D. S. Brewer, 1997), pp. 15–16.

26. Surname substitution established the fiction of an unbroken line of male descendants within a given family. For the relationship between this practice and novels, see Eleanor F. Shevlin, "Titular Claims of Female Surnames in Eighteenth-Century Fiction," in *Women, Property, and the Letters of the Law in Early Modern England*, ed. Nancy E. Wright, Margaret W. Ferguson, and A. R. Buck (University of Toronto Press, 2004), pp. 256–280.

27. Janine Barchas, *Graphic Design, Print Culture, and the Eighteenth-Century Novel* (Cambridge University Press, 2003), pp. 182–184.

28. Samuel Richardson, *Pamela: or, Virtue Rewarded*, ed. Thomas Keymer (Oxford University Press, 2001), p. 126.

29. John A. Dussinger, "Richardson, Samuel (bap. 1689, d. 1761)," *Oxford Dictionary of National Biography* (Oxford University Press, 2004); online edition, accessed January, 2008.

30. In the post-classical Latin period the term *manuscriptum* could denote "documents which derived evidential value from being written by a particular person." See "manuscript, adj. and n.," *Oxford English Dictionary* Online, Oxford University Press, accessed November, 2010.

31. Alexander Welsh, *Strong Representations: Narrative and Circumstantial Evidence in England* (Baltimore, MD and London: Johns Hopkins University Press, 1992), pp. 48–49, 57–62. See Gladfelder, *Criminality and Narrative*, pp. 155–156, 179–180.

32. Henry Fielding, *The History of Tom Jones*, ed. R. P. C. Mutter (London: Penguin Books, 1985), pp. 378–379.

33. Henry Fielding, *Amelia*, ed. Linda Bree (Peterborough, ON: Broadview Press, 2010), p. 63.

34. Nicholas Hudson, "Tom Jones," in *The Cambridge Companion to Henry Fielding*, ed. Claude Julian Rawson (Cambridge University Press, 2007), pp. 80–82.

35. Glen McClish, "Henry Fielding, the Novel, and Classical Legal Rhetoric," *Rhetorica* 14: 4 (1996), 413–440.

36. Ian Watt, *The Rise of the Novel: Studies in Defoe, Richardson, Fielding* (Berkeley: University of California Press, 1957), p. 31.

37. Simon Stern's insightful reading of *Tom Jones* as commentary on copyright debate adds to this list. See Stern, *"Tom Jones* and the Economies of Copyright," *Eighteenth-Century Fiction* 9: 4 (1997), 429–444.
38. James Boyd White, "The Invisible Discourse of the Law," *Heracles' Bow: Essays on the Rhetoric and Poetics of Law* (Madison: University of Wisconsin Press, 1985), p. 72.
39. Chaplin's second chapter situates newly emerging legal models in the eighteenth century against the backdrop of William Blackstone's "'romance' of the English common law in the *Commentaries on the Laws of England.*" Sue Chaplin, *The Gothic and the Rule of Law, 1764–1820* (New York: Palgrave Macmillan, 2007), p. 4.
40. Robert Brink Shoemaker, *London Mob: Violence and Disorder in Eighteenth-Century England* (London: Continuum, 2007), pp. 236–237.
41. Jeremy Bentham, *Of Laws in General*, ed. H. L. A. Hart (London: Athlone Press, 1970), p. 193. Although Bentham had finished most of *Of Laws in General* by 1782, it was not published until the twentieth century.
42. Jeremy Bentham, *A Comment on the Commentaries*, ed. J. H. Burns and H. L. A. Hart (Oxford University Press, 2008), pp. 10–11.

4

Novelistic history

CLEMENT HAWES

... all historians ought to be punctual, candid, and dispassionate, that neither interest, rancour, fear, or affection may mislead them from the road of truth, whose master is history, that rival of time, that depository of past actions, witness of the past, example and pattern of the present, and oracle of future ages.

Miguel de Cervantes, *Don Quixote* (1605), trans. Tobias Smollett (1755)

England's seventeenth-century intellectual revolution is often taken to have launched a revolutionary approach to the truth that led, by the time of the eighteenth century, to the new genre of the novel. So far as it goes, that account cannot be gainsaid: new methods, based either on direct observation or on inference from statistical regularities, introduced a novel language and tonality for approximating the truth. Literary imitations of personally verified truth and of "political arithmetic" followed in due course: Daniel Defoe's *A Journal of the Plague Year* (1722) illustrates both at once. A new "culture of fact"[1] did indeed raise the threshold of credibility in many quarters. Who can doubt that the eighteenth-century emergence of the novel registered the adaptation of older literary genres, especially epic and romance, to a new standard of fact-like plausibility? This accommodation to probable characters and plots, however, by no means exhausts the variety of possible relations in the eighteenth century between narrative history and narrative fiction. Rendering the past in eighteenth-century fiction goes far beyond the novel's mimicry of eye-witness authority or political arithmetic. To take these visible elements as the essence of the early novel's treatment of matters historical serves only to eclipse its striking engagement with the methodology of writing history – in short, with historiography.

Key historiographical *aperçus* abound in the eighteenth-century British novel. Early novelists are acutely responsive to what Paul Ricoeur describes as "the enigmatic notion of a trace *of the past*."[2] No less than historians proper, those writing fictional history approach the question of access to a past that, by definition, exists only by way of its lingering effects: incomplete, cryptic, evanescent, and conflicting traces that require active and principled "reading." The early novel is thus not merely concerned with a mimesis of history – with an accurate imitation of *what* happened – but, and above all, with *how* history is reconstructed from its traces. Along with *Tristram Shandy*, *Gulliver's Travels*, *Tom Jones*, and *Castle Rackrent* exemplify an eighteenth-century mode by which novelistic fictions engaged with the protocols of history-writing. And though an empirical strain can indeed be mapped in the eighteenth-century novel – an effort to mimic fact-like particulars – the specifically historical achievement of the innovative genre lies elsewhere than in a finely granulated verisimilitude. That vibrant achievement lies, rather, in the early novel's broader historiographical turn: its penchant for writing about the writing of history.

The novel and history

Intellectual debate about the nature of history was far more open during the eighteenth century than we may assume now. Seventeenth-century narrative history had itself been conspicuously divided, in the wake of Bacon's empirical revolution, between antiquarians and humanists. While writing their historical accounts, more traditional humanist authors avoided an overzealous grubbing for facts in moldy archives. Their primary criterion remained narrative excellence, a rhetorical issue. The earlier meaning of "fact" had been closer to *feat*: a human action or deed (Shapiro, *A Culture of Fact*, 34). The "Modern" fascination with factuality thus competed with the "Ancient" humanist emphasis on effective storytelling, sometimes within the same historian's work.[3] It is perhaps only with Edward Gibbon's *Decline and Fall of the Roman Empire* (1776) that "erudite" and "eloquent" history were skillfully integrated.[4]

Ian Watt's influential account of the "rise of the novel," a trajectory he ties organically to emerging bourgeois culture, overstresses one side of the new genre's relations with written history. "The modern novel," he writes, "is closely allied ... to the realist epistemology of the modern period."[5] The persistence of aristocratic values such as honor and virtue – and so the enduring allure of humanist historiography – is scanted in Watt's account. Indeed, major novelists of the eighteenth century, as John F. Tinkler contends, "took over and extended the rhetorical history of the humanists."[6] Rhetorical eloquence and narrative strength were, for early British novelists, a valid means of coming to terms with a past of which the function was to supply examples. That recounted past was necessarily virtual, as Everett Zimmerman points out, existing only "in the mediation that connects past and present," and such virtuality was an arena in which "novelistic fiction" could claim "all that history might perhaps claim."[7] Long before the digital age, both memory and imagination, as Pierre Lévy writes, were among the "vectors of virtualiza- tion."[8] The virtual nature of fiction intersected, moreover, with the character- istic concern in humanist history with what was possible, what might have happened: an implicit potency.

In Britain the eighteenth-century novel and eighteenth-century history- writing shared the same intellectual universe. Only in the nineteenth century would Leopold von Ranke's emphasis on primary sources, critically used, and "facts alone" become the basis of professional training for historians.[9] The discipline of (vernacular) Literature would be even slower to emerge in elite universities. Eighteenth-century study of the classics was a matter of gram- mar, rhetoric, and civic awareness. The exposure in 1711 as an impostor of the fake Formosan George Psalmanazar demonstrates that lies stood then in relation to truth exactly as one would expect now. Less immediately trans- parent, however, is the intricate relation of *fiction* to *history*. The concept of a "Historian of private Life" – a self-definition invoked by the narrator of *Tom Jones* (1749) – begins to open up the richness of the early novel's engagement with both history and historiography. Henry Fielding opposes a specifically private history to the inauthenticity of public history, according to Zimmerman, in order to show the way "to a kind of history that can only be fully achieved (or, more precisely, simulated) in the novel" (Zimmerman, *Boundaries of Fiction*, 161). A paradox comes into sharp focus: Fielding's narrator flaunts his own role as the artistic creator of his characters and plot. He nevertheless insistently claims, despite such ostentatiously acknowledged fictionality, to be writing history. Fielding's narrator combines "a theory of literary construction and historical reconstruction" (Zimmerman, *Boundaries of Fiction*, 147). And indeed, the eighteenth-century novel's generic intimacy with history illuminates a familiar oddity. Seventeenth- and eighteenth- century novelistic fictions in English often present themselves as the written lives of their title characters. Delarivier Manley, contrasting long French romances with succinct novels, refers to the latter as "little histories" in her ruminations about genre in the preface to *The Secret History of Queen Zarah and the Zarazanians* (1705).[10]

A corollary, as J. Paul Hunter points out, is that openly acknowledged fiction was by no means the norm, especially in the earlier part of the eight- eenth century. In the half-century following the Glorious Revolution, literary gestures apparently claiming a literal-minded "truth" were common. Hunter enumerates the authenticating tropes:

> In the short run, novels insisted that they were copied from newly discovered manuscripts, collections of letters found by passersby or collected by arbiters who wanted to set family history straight, memoranda left behind to instruct later generations, secret memoirs surreptitiously made public – stories found, pieced together, made public in spite of efforts to suppress them, or specially revealed, but never made up.[11]

Such documentary "traces" are pseudo-survivals from the fictive past that they themselves create. To be sure, this very proximity sometimes serves to undermine the truth claims of history. In book III of *Gulliver's Travels*, Gulliver is able, through sorcery in the land of Glubbdubbdrib, to conjure up and question the spirits of famous people from the past. What Gulliver discovers is that the classic historians produced a pack of endlessly repeated lies. And in *Tom Jones* the narrator scolds the first Earl of Clarendon for recycling an implausible ghost story in his *History of the Rebellion* (1702–1704). Fielding's narrator suggests that in such a "solemn" work the ghost episode might better have been omitted, as he puts it, "in Complaisance to the Scepticism of a Reader."[12] If "fiction" could shade into mere unacknowledged confabulation, it could also serve as the medium for the literary assertion of a specifically historical authority.

By the time of Fielding, it had become possible for novelists to come out of the closet to celebrate "their fiction, their imagination, their conscious art" (Hunter, "Protesting Fiction," 306). The word "history," nevertheless, remains ubiquitous in the titles of novels throughout the rest of the eighteenth century. One meaning of this equivocal word at the time, now archaic, was simply "prose narrative." For many humanist intellectuals, aiming to *apply* the exemplary lessons of history in the hermeneutic sense, the "truth" simply did not depend on literal facts alone. Henry St. John, Viscount Bolingbroke, thus appeals to "any man of candor, whether his doubts concerning the truth of history have hindered him from applying the examples he has met with in it, and from judging of the present, and sometimes of the future, by the past?"[13] The project of mining of history for usable examples delinks historical truth from factuality.

Novelistic history

The eighteenth-century novel's affinity with history – and especially with its humanistic variant – included self-conscious deliberation about historical method. It "exposed," as Zimmerman writes, "the limits of the verifiable" (*Boundaries of Fiction*, 21). Consider the sharply etched musings, in the works of Swift, Fielding, Sterne, and Edgeworth, on the nature of historical sources – the weak or sturdy peg on which the credibility of a narrative must hang. In making an issue of the reliability and proper use of historical sources, these authors build towards a systematically reflective approach to our always mediated access to historical truth.

Gulliver's Travels (1726) comes at the question of sources from an especially challenging angle. Swift marries an extravagantly improbable tale to the authenticating tokens of factual discourse: documentary evidence, eye-witness reportage, and insistent attestations to the narrator's veracity. With its seamless mixture of precise quantitative data and tall tales, Swift's mock-novel is deliberately unthinkable. Our "source" for *Gulliver's Travels* itself is of course a shipboard surgeon and captain whose bland frontispiece portrait testifies to his "real" existence. Lemuel Gulliver tells us that we can verify his story about Brobdingnagian wasps at Gresham College – the early home of the Royal Society – to which he has donated three of their gigantic stingers. Gulliver refers familiarly to a real person, William Dampier, a well-known sailor-narrator, map-maker, and buccaneer, as "Cousin Dampier." Even as he asks us ("gullibly") to swallow talking horses, a flying island, and men twelve times larger and twelve times smaller than the narrator, Swift takes extraordinary care with the persuasive force of such scrupulously documented details in *Gulliver's Travels*.

More than any other eighteenth-century author, Swift suggests the possibility that foregrounded facts could be embedded within – or, indeed, partly constituted by – egregious fantasies lurking in the background. Swift had in mind, among other possible satirical targets, the political fantasia that sustains the *oeuvre* of Sir William Petty, seventeenth-century founder of "political arithmetic." As Surveyor-General of Ireland, Petty had provided the data required – maps and demographic statistics – to enable English Protestants to confiscate "Papist" land. A favorite scheme that Petty entertains is to transport the Irish and Scottish Highland populations to Britain:

> And here I will beg leave (among the several matters which I intend for serious) to interpose a jocular, and perhaps a ridiculous digression, and which I desire Men to look on rather as a Dream or Revery, than a rational Proposition; the which is, that if all the *moveables* and People of *Ireland*, and of the *Highlands of Scotland*, were transported into the rest of *Great Britain*; that then the King and his Subjects would thereby become more *Rich* and *Strong*, both *offensively* and *defensively*, than now they are.[14]

Petty relies throughout his work on the appearance of quantitative precision and impartiality.[15] Swift's most famous response to such statistical fact-mongering is *A*

Modest Proposal (1729). *Gulliver's Travels* develops a closely related critique specifically to satirize both voyage literature and the early novel as vehicles for a seemingly objective discourse in which facts are tendentiously assembled to prop up an imperial project.

The penetrating ability to unpack, evaluate, and reconstruct historical sources is near the narrative heart of *Tom Jones*. For Fielding, the truth is indeed not to be discovered from a single perspective only. As per his profession as a magistrate, Fielding emphasizes the meticulous sifting of evidence in *Tom Jones*, the weakness of second-hand testimony, the unreliability of rumors, and the imperfect credibility of eye-witnesses. He would not have blinked at R. G. Collingwood's definition of history as "a web of imaginative reconstruction."[16] No wonder, then, that the historian and novelist commingle so freely in *Tom Jones*.

The early novel asks how, given the sheer cumulative bulk of related information, one isolates a relevant historical source. This question is pushed to the limit by Laurence Sterne in a defense of *Tristram Shandy's* compulsion, as a narrator, to digress. The passage elaborates on Cervantes' "road-of-truth" *topos* used in the epigraph to this essay:

> when a man sits down to write a history, – tho' it be but the history of *Jack Hickathrift* or *Tom Thumb*, he knows no more than his heels what lets and confounded hinderances he is to meet with in his way, – or what a dance he may be led, by one excursion or another, before all is over. Could a historiographer drive on his history, as a muleteer drives on his mule, – straight forward; – for instance, from Rome all the way to Loretto, without ever once turning his head aside, either to the right hand or to the left, – he might venture to foretell you to an hour when he should get to his journey's end; – but the thing is, morally speaking, impossible: For, if he is a man of the least spirit, he will have fifty deviations from a straight line to make with this or that party as he goes along, which he can no ways avoid. He will have views and prospects to himself perpetually soliciting his eye, which he can no more help standing still to look at than he can fly; he will moreover have various
>
> > Accounts to reconcile;
> > Anecdotes to pick up;
> > Inscriptions to make out;
> > Stories to weave in;
> > Traditions to sift;
> > Personages to call upon . . .[17]

One will never find a more insouciant critique of the historian's desire to be comprehensive and exhaustive, to master the archives. The production of written history is conditioned from the outset by the pressure-cooker of time.

The temporalities in play in the writing of history – the time of a historical event, the time of its writing by mortals, and the time of its reading by mortals – are teased apart in *Tristram Shandy* and shown to be incommensurable. "I am this month one whole year older than I was this time twelvemonth; and having got, as you perceive, almost into the middle of my fourth volume – and no farther than my first day's life – 'tis demonstrative that I have three hundred and sixty-four days more life to write just now, than when I first begun" (341). No wonder that Tristram Shandy as a narrator constitutes history-writing as endless.

Sterne likewise reflects on the worrisome opacity of sources with discrepant and unshared memories. For starters, the grinding conflict between Tristram Shandy's parents makes one wonder how far to trust the story of his conception. Our confidence in the "homunculus" story wanes because of another context as well: Walter Shandy's conspicuous use of historical explanation to produce a reassuring illusion of mastery. Tristram's misfortunes began "nine months before ever he came into the world" (4). So says Walter Shandy, explaining Tristram Shandy's failure to make a figure in the world. But perhaps it is not merely Tristram's shortcomings that are at stake in this anecdote, but his very paternity. If Walter Shandy's documented episodes of sciatica and travel imply that he was out of action during Tristram's conception, then the "homunculus" story serves to screen a perturbing anomaly in family history. Not unlike Clarendon in his *History of the Rebellion* – an account by a participant in the events described – Tristram Shandy writes in order to make sense of ruptures and discontinuities. Although Clarendon presents the commonwealth government of 1649–1660 as an "aberration," he does not pretend that the monarchy experienced a gapless succession. As Leo Braudy writes, "the continuity that survives is the continuity of Clarendon's own perspective."[18] In contrast to even that minimal anchor, Tristram presents a history in which even his perspective is marked by seams and patches (Braudy, *Narrative Form*, 177–178).

The retrospective fabrication of origins is a common abuse in certain kinds of evolutionary writing about "peoples." Nowhere is Sterne's scrutiny of such continuous histories more telling than in the revisionary "history" of Tristram's nose. The genealogical interpolation performed by Walter Shandy illustrates how memory rewrites history. Although Tristram's nose was accidentally mashed by Dr. Slop's forceps, Walter Shandy seeks the explanatory origin of its mangled shape elsewhere, in a snub-nosed ancestor from the time of Henry VIII. The supposed origin of Tristram's nasal short-comings is Walter Shandy's belated fabrication. Sterne provides in such examples of narrative backfilling a critique of invented traditions. Just at the moment that linguistics and folkloric movements were constructing supposed pedigrees for designated "peoples," Sterne diagnosed their invented nature and belated provenance.

That solid sources in themselves by no means guarantee a trustworthy narrative is a crucial theme of Edgeworth's *Castle Rackrent* (1800). *Castle Rackrent* is a fictitious oral history mediated by a literate editor. The voice of Thady Quirk is left in something close to a raw state. The editor "cooks" his Hibernian English by glossing peculiar idioms and providing ethnographic commentary on Irish customs. The editorial voice, in the context of *Castle Rackrent* as a whole, manifests a superiority complex incompatible with an engaged encounter with Thady Quirk's story. Even while introducing a "native informant," then, *Castle Rackrent* revives in a new way the humanist mock-scholia of the Scriblerian authors, once again making visible the potential arrogance of the editor's framing words. The normative editorial discourse is thus positioned not only as Protestant, Anglo-Irish, metropolitan, and literate but as condescending to the Catholic, local, indigenous, and unlettered but intelligent narrator of *Castle Rackrent*. This structuring antagonism is the deepest historical truth that Edgeworth's novel makes palpable.

A second example of the eighteenth-century novel's engagement with historical method lies in its subtle explorations of the relation between social forces and personal experience. Consider the concerted way that Swift, Fielding, Sterne, and Edgeworth explore the intersection between typically conservative public institutions and private motives in the making of history. Human beings make history, and individuals shape their lives, but they do so (to paraphrase Marx) under circumstances not of their own choosing. A lopsided imbalance between the two sides of this equation very often launches the stories taken up by the early novel. The anonymous condition of the "pre-political" common people was almost universal and yet seldom represented with any depth prior to the novel. "Private" persons, it must be noted, were simply "nonentities on the great stage of public affairs" (Tinkler, "Humanist History," 531). More negatively still, the realm of private interests threatens, by way of such smooth hypocrites as Tom Jones's half-brother Blifil, to corrupt the public good. To make public the polarized experiences of deprivation and privilege contributed to the creation of the public as a self-conscious political force. And though "public" might designate the dead weight of the institutional past, it could also name a historically new intersubjective agency that had the potential to challenge the legacies of past oppression. In this sense, the novel, despite its putative immersion in individualistic habits of being, serves above all to *deprivatize* modern life.

Swift's portrayal of Gulliver's ultimate alienation serves precisely as a deprivatizing commentary on the *history* of private life insofar as it has been invaded by the collective violence of colonial history. Gulliver's violent change in book IV – from identifying with the human race to identifying with the Houyhnhnms only – recasts his shipmates, his family, and even himself as odious "Yahoos." He *snaps*, separating himself utterly from the socio-symbolic world and history of his family and his readers. In historiographical terms, Swift achieves a series of aims: first, to draw attention to the terrifying suddenness of historical change; second, to address its retroactive effects on the remembered past; and third, to exploit the satirical resonance of Gulliver's repudiation of Englishness. Gulliver's seemingly private and domestic alienation reads as a form of imperial blowback: he is to England what Friday is to his Caribbean homeland. Gulliver's estrangement is finally another way for Swift to problematize England's imperial history.

Fielding could be said to reverse the public–private equation described above in Swift. In showing historical causality as working through given social circumstances, Fielding makes a point about the gulf between any given individual experience and a more comprehensive understanding. As an illegitimate foundling, the character Tom Jones is from the outset beset by forces beyond his control. Fielding's frame-breaking device aims precisely to get beyond a politics of identification with the limited perspective of the protagonist. Fielding famously violates the reader's illusion of immersion in the protagonist's world. The naïve "private" perspective of Tom Jones is juxtaposed with a panoramic and worldly representation of society at large, civil antagonisms and all.

Fielding stretches the capacity of the eighteenth-century novel to reflect on the "making" of history as belonging simultaneously to private experience and to public institutions and conflicts. His novel is set during the Forty-Five and Tom briefly enlists to fight for Protestantism and King George against the Jacobites. However, such major historical actors as Bonnie Prince Charlie and the Duke of Cumberland remain off stage. The conflict between Jacobites and the House of Hanover is instead registered in the novel through much more ordinary socio-historical types, all of whom are satirized: the reactionary Jacobite, Squire Western; the superstitious Jacobite, Benjamin Partridge; and the pretentious "progressive," Mrs. Western. More broadly, the predatory sexual relationship that Lady Bellaston establishes with humble Tom continues the "class-struggle" theme that begins when Tom is barred, on grounds of low birth, from marrying Sophia Western.

"Private history" could of course involve more typical overtones of personal intimacies and erotic foibles. Among Zimmerman's examples of "private history" is the significance, to Tom and Sophia Western exclusively, of Sophia's muff. The muff is a trace of her presence, at the inn at Upton, on the very night that Tom was sporting himself with Mrs. Waters. "Muff" was slang, then as now, for the feminine pubic triangle, and so a metonymy for the female genitals. Though Braudy compares the imputed meaning of "muff" to the famous "china scene" in *The Country Wife* (Braudy, *Narrative Form*, 177–178), Fielding's tone is not bawdy hilarity. Unlike Horner and Dainty Fidget, Tom and Sophia could never exchange a dazzling series of *double entendres* based on the muff. Fielding's less explicit symbol creates room for a specifically novelistic history in which the erotic vulnerability of individuals is figured by an intimation of unspoken depths.

The prevailing motor of history in *Tom Jones* is ultimately to be found in frequently comic negotiations between private desire and prevailing social institutions. Even as Tom Jones and Sophia Western are joined, the fractures of civil society – the residue of the Forty-Five – are knitted up. Tom is substantially a Hanoverian hero but stylistically parallel to Bonnie Prince Charlie: dashing, sexually magnetic, even willing to risk death, or murder, in a duel over honor. For Peter J. Carlton this can be read as an olive branch extended by Fielding to a defeated adversary: a delicate reweaving of Jacobite flair, as it were, into the national fabric.[19] The life of an individual, Tom Jones, carries the potential – one person at a time, as it were – of patching up the conflicts that had recently unraveled the social fabric. Here is the ultimate public intervention by the "Historian of private Life"!

For Fielding, as a self-proclaimed "Historian of private Life," it was clear that public and private intersected in the concept of legitimacy. By taking up the Forty-Five in connection with the politics of legitimacy – it was England's last dynastic war, and the final chapter of the Glorious Revolution – Fielding thus engages with the public level of historical actions. Britain's socio-symbolic structure is made to register, consolidate, and legitimate a change – Parliament's breaking of the Stuart succession in 1688 – that foregrounds the problem of political innovation. By changing the very rules of political legitimation, the events of 1688–1689, the Glorious Revolution, could be taken to imply that public choice is not bound forever by past arrangements. Humanist historians had thought that political communities confronted crises and either survived or perished according to leadership based on civic virtue:

devotion to the public good. Alongside this traditional sense of "virtue" we encounter novelistic takes on the *virtù* provocatively elaborated by Niccolò Machiavelli: bold action, however ruthless, that succeeds as a matter of *Realpolitik*.[20] This revisionary *virtù*, as J. G. A. Pocock notes, enables Machiavelli to ponder political innovation – rule outside the traditional frames of legitimacy.[21] Both "virtue" and *virtù* enter into the conceptual architecture of the early novel.

In teasing out the resonance between the bastard Tom Jones and the Hanover family, imported from Germany in 1715, Homer Obed Brown is right to link private and public legitimacy. However remote Georges I and II were from proper succession in strict genealogical terms, the threat of the Forty-Five had convinced Fielding that a Protestant "bastard of history"[22] was precisely what Britain needed on the throne. By the logic of this resonance, one pragmatic fiction of retroactive legitimation (Tom's promotion to the heir of Allworthy) validates another. Hence the *virtù* of Squire Allworthy's private act: it echoes the audacious logic that broke the inert pattern by which the *ancien régime* reproduced itself. That Fielding refuses any references to providential causation, unlike Bishop Gilbert Burnet in the latter's *History of My Own Time* (1724, 1734), underlines his focus on human possibilities and choices. For a sovereign community such as the nation, Fielding implies that a collective decision to change the rules is not only a settled *fait accompli* but a self-legitimating feat – an audacious act, on behalf of innovation, of *virtù*. Although Fielding's Shamela is forever prating about her "vartue" in *Shamela* (1741), this is a send-up of Pamela's "virtue" in Samuel Richardson's novel bearing her name (1740). The satire pertains not to the concept as such, but to its puritanical reduction to chastity, itself still further reduced in *Shamela* to a fraudulent bargaining chip. Fielding has little use for the merely private.

In Sterne the genre of the novel is stretched by attention to historiographical issues surrounding private memory in particular. Sterne brings an appropriately hermeneutic emphasis to the hints in *Tristram Shandy* of unbearable wartime experiences: traumas that make a hash of memory. As Uncle Toby's obsession with "fortifications" indicates, Sterne anticipated the psychoanalytic concept of defense mechanisms. We are thus presented with behaviors for which the causes are camouflaged by psychological defensiveness. Uncle Toby, "wounded by Words," simply cannot symbolize – put into words – the nature of the wound to his groin. "History" appears indirectly here as the "trace" of trauma, as a symptom. The historical trace that solicits interpretation is obliquely expressed – it bespeaks a failure of symbolization – and yet it is imperfectly erased or repressed.[23] A more demanding practice of "reading" historical events, attuned to such oblique and yet persisting traces, is required to take their full measure. As Frank Palmeri points out, for Sterne the "novelistic" effect of making public matters so peculiar and intimate has implications for the writing of history. The enigma of Uncle Toby's obsession exposes precisely what has been omitted from the public record of sieges and battles: "the particular individual histories of the thousands who were wounded, captured, defeated, or otherwise scarred during the battle."[24] Through Sterne's discontinuous and pointedly novelistic history, *Tristram Shandy* begins to suggest how to "read" a past so traumatic as to be accessible only through engagement with those mediations of memory that are too idiosyncratic, too enigmatically expressed, to serve as testimony in the ordinary public record. What Tristram says of Locke's *Essay Upon the Human Understanding* – that it is "a history book ... of what passes in a man's mind" (98) – is in this sense true, above all, of *Tristram Shandy* itself.

Tristram Shandy projects a world in which public and private spheres threaten to drift catastrophically apart. Moreover, in telling the story of his own life, Tristram begins to tell the story of Uncle Toby's life: a "digression," of course, but more deeply a deliberate attack on the tidy separation of "individual" lives. The scanty "events" in the novel mostly involve accidental assaults on male members (the pun is intended) of the Shandy family. The result is, in the words of Patrick Parrinder, "a comprehensive defeat for the *jus paternum*, or Law of the Father, and an ironic victory for the idea of the novel as cock-and-bull narrative and scapegrace offspring of the ancient epic."[25] Gravity, having steered a canon ball much too near Uncle Toby, strikes again when Tristram is a very young boy: a window sash, stripped of its counterweight, slams down on his penis. After Walter Shandy accepts that his only living son may have been unsexed, he seems resigned, remarking to Mrs. Shandy that "I'll put him, however, into breeches" (522). Public language does not fully clarify what has happened: breeches will cover up male credentials that are, in Tristram's case, suspect at best. But not only in Tristram's case: the ineffectual Shandy males represent a tragi-comic gap between the penis and the seemingly virile language of public "virtue" and *virtù*.

With the downfall of an old order comes the politicized revision of its public institutions and norms. Another version of the interplay of public meaning and private intentions – this time in a narrative of historical decline – animates Maria Edgeworth's *Castle Rackrent*. Both the brevity of Edgeworth's novella and the breathless pace of its telling render the effect absurdist rather than tragic. There is no ultimate triumph of barbarism and religion (Edward Gibbon's summary of the medieval era), but the novel might be seen as a mock-epic version of Gibbon's themes. The decline and fall of an old order in eighteenth-century Ireland (represented by the Rackrents) and the emergence of a new one from its interstices (as seen in the figure of Jason Quirk) drive the narrative logic. Causality operates on several levels simultaneously. In the *longue durée*, the motor of history, *à la* Fernand Braudel,[26] might be considered geographical, especially as it involves Ireland's proximity to England. The novel also evokes the conditioning weight of *mentalités*. By foregrounding the longstanding master–servant relationship between two families, the Rackrents and the Quirks, Edgeworth captures the inertia of class-bound mentalities. Beyond this interfamilial relationship, however, the class struggle between tenants and landlords forms another level of causality: Braudel's *conjuncture*, a third term, as it were, between structure and event. The sheer scale on which this multi-leveled sense of causality operates seems at first to dwarf human agency, much less that of any private individual. Yet *Castle Rackrent*, which founds the historical novel – it predates Sir Walter Scott's *Waverley* (1814) – finally qualifies the sway of impersonal forces in its account of historical causality.

Among Edgeworth's notable contributions to the historical novel is the use of the generations in a private family to figure discrete historical periods of public history: periodization through "domestic" generations. In *Castle Rackrent* one finds a sort of minor heroic age (the age of Sir Patrick); an age of fruitless legal snarls around land ownership (the age of Sir Murtaugh); an age of absentee landlords (the age of Sir Kit); and the age of the old regime's descent into the abyss (the age of Sir Condy). Generational change, whether through Edgeworth's Rackrents, Faulkner's Compsons, or García Márquez's Buendías, resonates with epochal change. As such, causality in Edgeworth's novel brings together both Braudel's temporal durations and "public" and "private" histories.

In *Castle Rackrent* the personal and the social intermesh in a compelling representation of historical change as a rupture with longstanding *mentalités*. There is a single subtle event in *Castle Rackrent*, one recounted with elaborate nonchalance by Thady Quirk, which in retrospect stands out as the narrative pivot. When Jason Quirk decides to buy some of the Rackrents' mortgaged land, his father Thady lets it be known in the neighborhood "that no one need bid against us."[27] Jason goes on to acquire that piece of land, and then he acquires as well a comprehensive knowledge of the vulnerable financial position of the Rackrent family and sets out to buy up its debts. Thady's quiet but decisive break with feudal loyalty to the Rackrents – the mentality to which he continues to give lipservice – has revolutionary repercussions. In the texture of time represented by *Castle Rackrent*, this is a major rupture indeed, enabling the servant's clever son to inherit the Rackrent estate.

Despite the manifest and cumulative inadequacies of the Rackrent family, we feel considerable ambivalence when Jason Quirk takes over. Nothing truly heroic has been lost, and yet the passage to a recognizably capitalist order is surprisingly painful. Here we encounter another novelistic take on Machiavellian *virtù*. Though Fortuna, "bitch-goddess of unpredictability,"[28] generally determines one's fate, the singular man of *virtù* can reverse the equation by remaking his own circumstances. Edgeworth's coldly competent Jason recalls John Gay's calculating Peachum: a negative intimation of the capitalist future based on private greed. Even so, and for better or worse, Jason Quirk is undoubtedly the man of *virtù*: the one character in the story who acts to seize time's forelock, remakes his circumstances, and so "makes history" by ditching feudal public norms altogether. Here, as so often in the following centuries, it is difficult to distinguish the opportunistic entrepreneur from the sociopath.

The novel and history, again

We need to rethink the relationship between the novel and history at this pre-disciplinary moment. In accumulating and validating historical knowledge, humanist historians had given first priority to exemplary value and narrative excellence. Rhetorically eloquent stories added to the virtual warehouse of basic situations and strategies. As historians, the humanists aimed to be responsible not primarily to the factual details of past events but to their creative potential, as so many narrative unfoldings, of the logic of a reality that encompasses both the actual and the possible. Human actions, moreover, do not speak for themselves: they require both emplotment and hermeneutic midwifery. "Like a text," as Paul Ricoeur writes, "human action is an open work."[29] "Acts embody intersubjective meanings," as Quentin Skinner puts it, "that we can hope to read off."[30]

The early novel, despite its ties to an emerging discourse of facticity, represents less a break from this humanist tradition than a reaffirmation and refinement of it: a mode in which the factual is constitutively interwoven with possibilities. We should not be content to say, with Milan Kundera, that the early novel (by way of Cervantes and his *Don Quixote*, 1605) "tears through the curtain of legend and romance" to reach "the comical nakedness of [the world's] prose."[31] The early novel is concerned with the difficulty, or even the impossibility, of tearing through any such curtain of romance. In 1605 Cervantes pretended in volume 1 of *Don Quixote* to be merely the obsessive reader who had hired a translator, a "Morisco *aljamiado*" in the Jewish quarter of Toledo, to translate his supposed original: an Arabic manuscript written by a fictitious Arab historian. This fiction continues in volume II, which appeared in 1615, just after the expulsion from Spain of the Moriscos. To Cervantes' layered fiction, María Rosa Menocal poses a rhetorical question: "Who is that translator, after all," she asks, "but a crypto-Muslim beneath a Christian veneer, decipherer of a language that is crypto-Castilian underneath an Arabic veneer?"[32] Aside from illustrating the promiscuity of intercultural appropriations, such intricately folded layers of cultural memory militate against any "final" unveiling.

That this metafictive story is all related to us by one Cide Hamet Benengeli, an Arab historian, confirms a founding novelistic trope in *Don Quixote*: a turn precisely *away* from a too easy and overly literal relation to "factual" history as such. A cultural outsider in terms both of social class and religion tells the story. "The Muslim world," as Walter Cohen puts it, "enters *Don Quixote* above all as narration, not representation."[33] Cervantes makes an amusing problem of the original narrator's distance from Christian Spain: "However, if any objection can be stated to the truth of this, it can be no other, but that the author was an Arab, of a nation but too much addicted to falsehood, tho' as they are at present our enemies, it may be supposed that he has rather failed than exceeded in the representation of our hero's exploits" (67). In such a passage Cervantes makes us reflect, historiographically, on the inability of history-writing itself to escape from historical conflict. The early English novel, by the same token, did not merely simulate antiquarian historical writing by way of evidentiary claims about what really happened. Like the humanist historians before them, and like Cervantes, early authors of the British novel attended, above all, to history as a problematic – to *how* history is framed, written, and used ("applied"). These are metahistorical issues that no methodology, however positivistic, can long evade. As an artistic practice of moral, political, and epistemological inquiry into the textual representation of temporal existence, the early novel's *historiographical* turn on the road to truth produced not merely *the novel in history* or even *history in the novel* but something more challenging: *novelistic history*.

Notes

1. Barbara J. Shapiro, *A Culture of Fact: England, 1550–1720* (Ithaca, NY: Cornell University Press, 2000).
2. Paul Ricoeur, *Time and Narrative*, trans. Kathleen Blamey and David Pellauer, 3 vols. (University of Chicago Press, 1985), vol. III, p. 306, n.4.

3. Robert Mayer, *History and the Early English Novel: Matters of Facts from Bacon to Defoe* (Cambridge University Press, 1997).

4. Anthony Grafton, *The Footnote: A Curious History* (London: Faber and Faber, 1997), pp. 97–99.

5. Ian Watt, *The Rise of the Novel: Studies in Defoe, Richardson, and Fielding* (Berkeley: University of California Press, 1957), p. 62.

6. John F. Tinkler, "Humanist History and the English Novel in the Eighteenth Century," *Studies in Philology* 85: 4 (1988), 510–537, 511.

7. Everett Zimmerman, *The Boundaries of Fiction: History and the Eighteenth-Century British Novel* (Ithaca, NY: Cornell University Press, 1996), p. 6.

8. Pierre Lévy, *Becoming Virtual: Reality in a Digital Age* (New York: Plenum Trade, 1998), p. 28.

9. Georg G. Iggers, *Historiography in the Twentieth Century: From Scientific Objectivity to the Postmodern Challenge* (Middletown, PA: Wesleyan University Press, 1997), pp. 24–25.

10. Mary Delarivier Manley, *The Novels of Mary Delarivier Manley*, ed. Patricia Köster, 2 vols. (Gainesville: University of Florida Press, 1971), vol. 1, p. 2.

11. J. Paul Hunter, "Protesting Fiction, Constructing History," in *The Historical Imagination in Early Modern Britain: History, Rhetoric, and Fiction, 1500–1800*, ed. Donald R. Kelley and David Harris Sacks (Cambridge University Press, 1997), p. 311.

12. Henry Fielding, *The History of Tom Jones, a Foundling*, ed. Martin Battestin (Middletown, PA: Wesleyan University Press, 1975), p. 401.

13. Henry St. John, Viscount Bolingbroke, *Letters on the Study and Use of History*, 8, 72, 58, in *Historical Writings*, ed. Isaac Kramnick (University of Chicago Press, 1972), pp. 53, 57.

14. Sir William Petty, *Essays in Political Arithmetick* (London: 1711), p. 225.

15. See Mary Poovey, *A History of the Modern Fact* (University of Chicago Press, 1998).

16. R. G. Collingwood, *The Idea of History*, ed. Jan van der Dussen (rev. edn, Oxford University Press, 1993), p. 242.

17. Laurence Sterne, *The Life and Opinions of Tristram Shandy, Gentleman*, ed. Melvyn New and Joan New, 3 vols. (Gainesville: University Presses of Florida, 1978), vol. 1, pp. 41–42.

18. Leo Braudy, *Narrative Form in History and Fiction* (Princeton University Press, 1970), p. 18.

19. Peter J. Carlton, "The Mitigated Truth: Tom Jones's Double Heroism," *Studies in the Novel* 19: 4 (1987), 397–409; and "*Tom Jones* and the '45 Once Again," *Studies in the Novel* 20: 4 (1988), 361–373.

20. Niccolò Machiavelli, *The Prince*, ed. Quentin Skinner and Russell Price (Cambridge University Press, 1988), pp. 103–104.

21. J. G. A. Pocock, *The Machiavellian Moment: Florentine Political Thought and the Atlantic Republican Tradition* (Princeton University Press, 1975), p. 113.

22. Homer Obed Brown, "Tom Jones: The 'Bastard' of History," in *Institutions of the English Novel: From Defoe to Scott* (Philadelphia: University of Pennsylvania Press, 1997), pp. 82–115.

23. See Gilbert C. Chaitin, *Rhetoric and Culture in Lacan* (Cambridge University Press, 1996), p. 198.

24. Frank Palmeri, *Satire in Narrative: Petronius, Swift, Gibbon, Melville, and Pynchon* (Austin: University of Texas Press, 1990), p. 208.

25. Patrick Parrinder, *Nation and Novel: The English Novel from its Origin to the Present Day* (Oxford University Press, 2006), pp. 91–92.

26. Fernand Braudel, *On History*, trans. Sarah Matthews (University of Chicago Press, 1980). For *longue durée*, *structure*, and *conjuncture* respectively, see pp. 28–32, 122, and 74–75.

27. Maria Edgeworth, *Castle Rackrent*, ed. George Watson, intro. Kathryn J. Kirkpatrick (Oxford University Press), p. 22.

28. Alasdair MacIntyre, *After Virtue* (3rd edn, University of Notre Dame Press, 2007), p. 93.

29. Paul Ricoeur, *From Text to Action: Essays in Hermeneutics, II*, trans. Kathleen Blamey and John B. Thompson (Evanston, IL: Northwestern University Press, 1991), p. 155.

30. Quentin Skinner, *Visions of Politics*. Vol. I: *Regarding Method* (Cambridge University Press, 2002), p. 120.

31. Milan Kundera, *The Curtain: An Essay in Seven Parts*, trans. Linda Asher (London: Faber and Faber, 2007), p. 92.

32. María Rosa Menocal, *The Ornament of the World: How Muslims, Jews, and Christians Created a Culture of Tolerance in Medieval Spain* (New York: Little, Brown and Company, 2002), p. 261.

33. Walter Cohen, "Eurasian Fiction," *The Global South* 1: 2 (2007), 104.

5

Interiorities

ELAINE McGIRR

Pamela (1740) was not the first novel to start a craze – Defoe's *Robinson Crusoe* (1719) inspired sequels, pamphlets, and even a restaurant – and nor was it the first novel to be denounced; but the quality and intensity of attention it received resonated far beyond that particular book and the characters and fashions described therein. *Pamela*, and the controversy it sparked, transformed a loose, inchoate form into the modern novel. *Pamela* shifted attention away from events and questions of truthfulness onto character and questions of believability. Early novels, like *Oroonoko* and *Moll Flanders*, made truth claims, stressing that the events they described really happened.[1] *Pamela* purported to be a true story as well, but because the stakes were so high – social advancement through the power of narrative – Pamela's believability, rather than *Pamela*'s fictiveness, took center stage: responses such as Henry Fielding's *Shamela* (1741) argued that Pamela was a hypocrite; he asserted that her virtue was fictional, not her existence. *Pamela*'s epistolary format, its insistent location in the present tense, instantly raised questions of character, of self-presentation, and of the ability ever really to gain access to the workings of another person's mind, in life or fiction. Pamela did not just spark a craze: it redefined the way both writers and readers approached the novel. Carolyn Steadman argues that Pamela "is all selfhood, all inside, and [her] depth as a point of reference for female interiority has been immense."[2] But it was not only women who viewed both *Pamela* and Pamela as touchstones. Male novelists, readers, and even fictional characters were also quick to respond to the possibilities and potential dangers posed by Pamela's radical, seemingly unmediated self-representation. Master and servant: love and labor in the English industrial age.

After *Pamela* the question of identity was never far from readers' minds, and the difficulty of presenting legible and believable characters plagued authors. Readers wanted characters who were individuals rather than types, who had subjective interiority. However, identity, which is personal and public,

80

internal and external, is itself an unstable category. As we shall see in *Pamela*, identity – wife or whore, Mistress Andrews or Mrs. B. – can be unstable even when character – Pamela – is fixed. Finally, the furor surrounding *Pamela* also reminds us that questions about identity are always also bound up in questions of representation and interpretation. Pamela's protestations of her truthfulness and innocence raised as many suspicions as they assuaged and sparked a debate about identity, self-expression, and interpretation still raging today. Is the self knowable? If so, can that self be reliably communicated? Representing oneself is always an act of translation or metaphor; interpreting another's character is always an act of reading. Bodies and words are made to signify hearts and minds, but that externalizing process also calls attention to the very gap it attempts to overwrite.

Debates about the self quickly become debates about the reliability of the tools available for writing and reading the self. Anxiety about the legibility of character was not, of course, limited to fiction. But novels, unlike real life or even drama, could give readers access to both faces and hearts. Reading character, whether on a page or in the street, is an interpretive act that, as John Locke argued in *An Essay Concerning Human Understanding* (1690), "depends much less on a belief in essence than upon the empirical data of appearances and situation."[3]

Unfortunately, appearances and situation are nearly always misleading. Deceitful intentions are thus not the only cause of misreadings. Character is judged and evaluated by appearances and situations because those are the only gauges available, but experience – and novels – teach us just how inadequate those gauges are.

The novel was the perfect medium in which to present individuality and interiority. It could tackle the question of reading other people and paint characters who were credible, for it could employ means that were not available in other media: it could convincingly narrate thoughts, point out interpretive clues, and describe events from multiple perspectives. Novels created space not just for complex and contradictory emotions, but for their adequate expression. The novel could make use of the poetic and imaginative power of language. Metaphors and similes, comparisons, direct addresses, descriptions, and explications have force in the novel because readers, unlike theater-goers, are not presented with visual distractions. The novel can expose what is invisible and intangible. At the same time, the novel can also imitate reality and encourage readers to trust its narrative. So *Pamela*'s epistolary form not only created an intimate relationship between reader and character, but it also created a plausible reason for both the heroine's volubility and her isolation.

The novel form had other advantages as well. Unlike biography it was not bound by known or knowable fact. It is no accident that most early novels are fictional biographies: they are ultimately more satisfying than actual biographies because they fill in the gaps of what we know by including thoughts, motives, and conversation. Conversation would be key in the novel's creation of characters with lifelike interior depths: characters in novels could speak and think for themselves in their own distinctive voices. Only in novels can individuals be truly legible, can external signs be correctly matched with their interior causes; only in a novel can we know for sure if a woman blushes from confusion or guilt. This surety is comforting, but also alarming, for while readers are reassured that the "real" Evelina or Camilla or Pamela can be known, their travails also remind us of how misleading surfaces can be, and how prone to error are our judgments.

Providing characters with more voice and providing readers with unmediated access to their thoughts may have helped develop legible and recognizable characters, but it did not solve the problem of believability, or necessarily close the gap between seeming and being. For although Syrena Tricksy and Shamela Andrews were obliging enough to tell their mothers – and their readers – what their real thoughts were, thus exposing their true characters, their illegibility to the men in their stories highlighted the danger of relying on a single perspective. Starting with *Joseph Andrews* (1743), his second response to *Pamela*, Fielding moved away from Richardson's intimate first-person narratives. His omniscient narrators tell readers what characters do not know or do not want to tell, and Fielding's tone does not leave the reader in any doubt as to interpretation. The narrator's ironic voice punctures characters' duplicity and self-deception. Fielding's narrator directs readers' responses to characters, both within and without the novel: he teaches us how to read through misleading surfaces to the "true self" hidden beneath.

Richardson continued to refine his first-person narratives, but he too worried about misreadings, not least those of readers attracted to his villain Lovelace. With each novel he added more perspectives. In *Clarissa* (1747–1748) he balanced his heroine's correspondence by including more responses and opposing viewpoints from the Harlowes as well as Lovelace's correspondence with Belford. By his third novel, *Sir Charles Grandison* (1753), his hero and heroine even comment and respond to each other's acts of self-representation. This layering of perspective allowed Richardson to maintain his intimate focus on "his girls" without repeating the *Pamela* problem: in contrast to Pamela's voice, Clarissa and Harriet's voices are complemented by their correspondents, as well as contrasted by others. This matrix of letters works to confirm the heroines' characters and reassure readers that Clarissa's and Harriet's self-representations are accurate portrayals.

Half a century after the *Pamela* controversy, novelists were still torn between articulating character from within and drawing it out from an external perspective. Frances Burney's first novel, *Evelina* (1778), echoes *Pamela* in more than the ingenuous narrative voice of its heroine. But Burney escaped the *Pamela* problem: her exemplar of female virtue is beset by misinterpretation within the novel, preempting and correcting potential bad readers. Despite the success of *Evelina*, Burney turns away from the epistolary form in her later novels, most spectacularly in her last, *The Wanderer* (1818). Like Evelina, Juliet's true identity is obscured – readers do not even learn her "real" name until the third volume – but here the comparison ends. Whereas Evelina speaks for herself, Juliet's inability to name herself – she is known only as "Ellis" in the novel's first part – is central to her inability to tell her own story of paternal abandonment and forced marriage. She is as voiceless as she is nameless. Burney uses third-person narration to distance readers from her beleaguered heroine in order to create pathos and to encourage readers to view Ellis sympathetically. She does not want readers to identify with her heroine or to see and feel the novel's events through her eyes. Interiority is here expressed by obscuring it: instead of offering unmediated access to Juliet's inner life, Burney narrates the difficulty of unburdening oneself.

Problems of believability

Pamela did more than allow a servant to tell her own story of resistance to sexual predation. Its ambiguity, and the excitement and unease it generated, stem in part from its exposure of the fundamental insecurity of personal identity, of the ways in which external signs and associations can impart new values and assign new characterizations. The novel demonstrates how identity shifts according to circumstances, and offers readers an unparalleled glimpse into the heroine's mind to prove its case. Whereas earlier novels, like *Moll Flanders* (1722), were presented as retrospective memoirs – a *Life* told after it had been lived – *Pamela* is written to the moment, in the present tense, before the heroine's status is fixed as wife or whore. This ambiguity highlights the problem of interiority: readers are exposed to characters still in the making, whose choices and adventures shape and change them. In contrast *Moll Flanders* and other, similarly retrospective *Lives*, suggest that character is fixed, static, essential.

Moll Flanders asserts not only its truthfulness – as opposed to fictiveness – but also common fame: "My True Name is [. . .] well known in the Records, or Registers,"[4] Moll tells readers, reassuring them that her narrative can be cross-referenced and certified. But it also reassures readers that her narrative has already happened, that the story is fixed: before the novel even begins, we know that "in her last Scene at *Maryland*, and *Virginia*, many pleasant things happen'd, which makes that part of her Life very agreeable" (5). There is no suspense about Moll's character or her fate: she was born and bred into wickedness and sin, but grew into penitence. Defoe, claiming status as editor rather than author, uses his preface to explain the novel's retrospective present tense:

> Throughout the infinite variety of this Book . . . there is not a wicked Action in any Part of it, but is first or last rendered Unhappy and Unfortunate: There is not a superlative Villain brought upon the Stage but either he is brought to an unhappy End, or brought to be a Penitent: There is not an ill thing mention'd, but it is condemn'd, even in the Relations, nor a virtuous just Thing, but it carries its Praise along with it. (3)

Thus, even though his heroine is "made to tell her own Tale" (1) in the present tense, as if her story were still unfolding, the conclusions that have already been drawn from them ensure that access to Moll's "true" thoughts and feelings are unnecessary, for we already know how to read her. She is an exemplar, not an individual. Her life has literally been rewritten: "her" original thoughts and style were unacceptable. The new-dressed Moll is "made" by Defoe; he explicitly tells readers that he is *not* negotiating access to someone else's real thoughts, feelings, or self-expression. Despite its first-person, present-tense structure, Moll never speaks for herself in the novel that bears her name.

In contrast, *Pamela* tells a story that is as immediate as it is unapologetic. Pamela's voice and the structure of *Pamela* mark its complete divorce both from idealized romance and from rogue's tales. Pamela, as Ian Watt argues, is an individual, with an individuated life story and singular character.[5] Singularity, however, is also a reassurance of exceptionality. Pamela, and the contest over her character, demonstrates not just the dangerous gap between seeming and being, but also the gap between difference (singularity) and identity (similarity). Michael McKeon argues that the new bourgeois form of the novel posed a challenge to the older aristocratic form of the romance: the novel, with its insistence on verisimilitude (as seen in Richardson's "epic of the everyday") and individuality defines itself against the ideals and universals of romance and epic (McKeon, *Origins*, 20–22, 131–175). Deep characterization is revolutionary: by making heroes out of private people, and by making private people knowable, the novel insists that personal merit, rather than birth, makes worth. As is the case with *Pamela*, this can be seen as an attack on class privilege. Pamela tells us as much:

> were my *life* in question, instead of my *virtue*, I would not wish to involve any body in the least difficulty for so worthless a poor creature. But, O sir! my *soul* is of equal importance with the soul of a princess, though in quality I am but upon a foot with the meanest slave.[6]

Pamela admits her social "worthlessness," but asserts the pricelessness of her soul. She frequently asserts both her independence and her intrinsic worth. As Mr. B. is also the local justice of the peace, resisting his will should also be read as resisting the law. Yet Pamela refuses to submit, and claims a status as an individual and a woman that would normally be denied her – in the romance tradition, a lady's maid would not even have a name of her own, but would be assigned a trait name like *Pert* or the category name *Betty*. This individualism is seen in Pamela making herself into a novel. It is Pamela's story we are getting, not that of Mr. B. her social (and sexual) superior. Not only is she our narrator, as she writes to the moment in her letters and diary, but she quite literally fashions herself; for instance, she conflates her "story" and her person by sewing her diary into her petticoats, thus making the tale of her resistance to sexual predation the physical barrier between herself and Mr. B. Pamela makes herself legible, and in so doing lays claim to a new identity, a new status.

Pamela's "virtue" defines both her sex and her status, and the signification of this intangible quality changes slightly over the course of the novel. In Pamela's conflict with Mr. B., her virtue seems to be little more than her virginity – the point Fielding makes with Shamela's "vartue." However, once Pamela's virtuous tale seduces Mr. B. into making her his wife, her "virtue" becomes something a little less sex-specific; virtue becomes her narrative voice and her personal merit, intangible qualities that do not disappear after the marriage night. This virtue is also seductive: Pamela wins over the local gentry and Lady Davers, convincing all of them that she deserves her new place in society. This secondary conflict – over status, not sex – is the stage on which the debate of personal "goodness" rather than inherited "greatness" described by McKeon is fought and won. Not only is Lady Davers forced to acknowledge her brother's misalliance and recognize Pamela as her sister and equal, but she, prompting readers, is forced to admit that Pamela *deserved* to be elevated from servant to lady. Pamela's legibility, her ability to make her heart and her virtue transparent and knowable, inspires both confidence and love. Her ability to narrate her "self" ennobles Pamela and makes her worthy of Mr. B.'s honorable addresses.

The perfections of Pamela seem to turn social hierarchy on its head. The personal qualities of Pamela are measured against the reigning signifiers of wealth and birth, and hers come out trumps. The dialectical relationship between the novel and the romance means, however, that while the novel has progressive impulses that are in conflict with romance ideology, it also necessarily has conservative impulses that align it with romance, which, after all, carried more cultural authority than its rival. This is the case in *Pamela*. Although her virtue is rewarded, her singularity is emphasized throughout. Pamela may merit social elevation, but the novel is far from democratic: nowhere is it suggested that social hierarchy should be abolished, or even that everyone has equal intrinsic merit. Furthermore, despite her frequent "saucy" observations about the inadequacies of the nobility, of their faulty educations, their intemperance, and frequent dullness, Pamela wants nothing more than to be absorbed into that world. Her gender ensures that she will be, because

> the difference is, a man ennobles the woman he takes, be she *who* she will; and adopts her into his own rank, be it *what* it will: but a woman, though never so nobly born, debases herself by a mean marriage, and descends from her own rank, to that of him she stoops to marry . . . when a duke lifts a private person into his own rank, he is still her *head*, by virtue of being her husband: but, when a lady descends to marry a groom, is not that groom her *head*? Does not that difference strike you? and what lady of quality ought to respect another, who has set a groom *above* her? (441–442)

Pamela's virtue is gendered, something Fielding seized upon in *Joseph Andrews*. Her intrinsic worth as a human being can only be valued because by marrying Mr. B. she gives up her individuality and is subsumed into her husband's identity. *Pamela* becomes, then, not so much the story of a servant worth as much as a princess – the radical reading – but a much more conservative plot: the story of status inconsistency, of a "lost" princess returned to her rightful place. Pamela's identity is confirmed through marriage to Mr. B.: it is a place she belonged in all along, not a new character she will assume. When Pamela becomes Mrs. B., she ceases to be the radically individual subject, a problem Richardson tackles in the continuation of *Pamela*. However, her status, her identity, is assured, so narrative focus naturally turns to more external events and concerns.

Ultimately, *Pamela* is an ambiguous novel, and this ambiguity provides ample space for resistant, parodic, and oppositional readings. But *Pamela* is also unambiguously sincere. While the tensions in the plot and form suggest wildly different interpretations of Pamela, both readings agree on her essential goodness and encourage the reader to trust her narrative. However, two of the first responses to *Pamela*, Henry Fielding's *Shamela* (1741) and Eliza Haywood's *Anti-Pamela* (1741) do challenge her goodness. Both articulate a cynical belief in the disjunction between self-representation and self, between seeming and being. Both parodies abandon ambiguity and demand the same negative interpretation of all acts of female self-representation. Shamela and Syrena are both expert whores, practiced in the art of deceiving men by appearing to be what they desire, by appearing virtuous and concealing their sexual appetites. For Fielding and Haywood, first-person narration is the least trustworthy form because personal correspondence, whether written or told, is always a carefully crafted fiction. In this fallen world, Fielding warns, hypocrisy is the norm, not the exception, and anyone who seems too good to be true is in reality no better than she should be. But this cuts through the tricky question of being and seeming as neatly as Richardson's transparent heroines and villains: readers can assume characters are the opposite of what they would seem. Fielding and Haywood are just as didactic as Richardson, but where he wanted to teach the art of self-expression, they warn of the danger of deception. Fielding and Haywood are worried about readers falling prey to fictions. Shamela and Syrena are extreme and cynical responses to Pamela, but they usefully demonstrate both the public concern with reading character and the tools at the novelist's disposal.

Fielding's great fear is that if supposedly intrinsic qualities, like virtue, can be learned, then they can be counterfeited or assumed: someone who does not possess virtue can learn to "act" like someone who does and be rewarded. In *Pamela* – as in conduct books – the underlying assumption is that by following the pattern of virtue (e.g. Pamela) the reader can become truly virtuous. Fielding is less sure. Shamela's performance of virtue does not reform her character, but confirms her in vice. Most troubling is the ease with which she acts her part: the immediacy and claustrophobia of writing to the moment leaves no time for rational reflection or space for critical distance.

Acting is central to any understanding of the construction of identity in the eighteenth century. In *Shamela*, in his opening letter of false praise, Fielding has Parson "Tickletext" extol *Pamela* for the closeness with which "Thought is everywhere cloathed by the Expression"[7] and then reminds us of how tight Pamela's country dress is and how often we see her naked – with "pride of ornament" cast off. It is a nice conceit – that Richardson's words perfectly represent the ideas – but when parsed, we can see the problems inherent in the metaphor. First, there is the obvious problem that Tickletext himself cannot escape – the closeness of expression, the immediacy of description, and detailed descriptions are closer to pornography than moral discourse: "oh! I feel an Emotion even while I am relating this!" (322) ejaculates the Parson. Despite Richardson's claims to the contrary, *Pamela* was a sexy book; Richardson's own affection for his creation turned the scenes of her virtue in distress into an opportunity for voyeurism. But that is not the only problem with the clothing analogy. Pamela's wardrobe is used to chronicle her social position, from her country maid's dress to the fashionable silks Mr. B. insists she wear after their marriage. Throughout the novel, the transformative power of clothing is highlighted: Pamela is assumed to be what she wears. Her country garb "metamorphoses" her and makes her unrecognizable to her friends and master. Her ability to change clothes reminds us that identity is not fixed but rather assumed, and, moreover, that clothes are often false symbols of status. Both Pamela and Mr. B. disguise themselves frequently: Pamela is not a country maid; Mr. B. is not a maid. If clothes, the most external of signifiers, have such power to confer identity, then what need is there for interiority? Indeed, if clothes really do make the man (or woman), then is there any interior self to express?

Pamela raises fundamental questions about the legibility of identity. *Pamela* argues that it is possible to articulate the self through novelization: Pamela makes herself known by transforming her distracting and unclear physical body into a coherent and readable text. Pamela's papers are both her armour and her unveiling; they keep her physically safe long enough for first Mr. B. and then Lady Davers to gain greater intimacy. This tantalizing promise – the transmutation of identity into word – was as frightening as it was intoxicating, for any act of translation leaves room for distortion, deceit, or mistake. The novel seemed to provide an index to humanity, and reassured readers that true character could be divined and adequately rewarded. But at the same time the novel's patent recourse to narrative devices reminded readers that the dream of legibility of character, of self, was fiction after all.

Problems of authority

The impossibility of ever really transcribing the self is humorously described in Charlotte Lennox's *The Female Quixote* (1751), whose heroine, Arabella, wants to be as transparent as a character in a novel. She instructs her maid Lucy as follows:

> Recount all my words and actions, even the smallest and most inconsiderable, but also all my thoughts, however instantaneous; relate exactly every change of my countenance; number all my smiles, half-smiles, blushes, turnings pale, glances, pauses, full-stops, interruptions; the rise and falling of my voice; every motion of my eyes; and every gesture which I have used for these ten years past; nor omit the smallest circumstance that relates to me.[8]

Arabella's imperious command is the logical expectation of a confirmed novel-reader. She is not questing after fame or even feminine agency, but transparency: she longs to be legible, for her self to be clear to her readers. She wants her external signs to be itemized and glossed so that their significance can be known. That this task is impossible is at once the source of the novel's humour and also its pathos.

The novel's increasing focus on interior life goes beyond contemporary anxiety about hypocrisy and acting. The novel was engaged in serious debate about the very nature of human existence, and raised many of the same questions about the nature of the self as did the "serious" genres of moral philosophy and biography. Debate about the nature and meaning of human-kind was not new to the eighteenth century, but John Locke's *Essay Concerning Human Understanding* signaled a paradigm shift by arguing that consciousness begins as a blank slate – without innate ideas – and is formed through experience, through sensation and reflection. Humanity, therefore, is made by its surroundings, education, and relationships. Furthermore, if consciousness is the defining feature of selfhood, then moral responsibility – virtue – is fully attributable to the subject, rather than to fate.

The Life and Opinions of Tristram Shandy, Gentleman (1759–1767) tackles the same existential problems with gusto and provocative humor. Tristram, a first-person narrator displaced from his own "life," makes light of the impossibility of ever expressing, let alone knowing, the self. Laurence Sterne uses *Tristram* to ask what constitutes a character or a life. Sterne argues that the only way to understand a character is to follow his mind through its musings and associations. Therefore his novel does not narrate his hero's coming of age, or even his picaresque misadventures, but rather allows Tristram to express whatever seems relevant to him and to share the stories, experiences, smells, and books that made him. As John Locke explained in his 1693 reflections on education: "the little and almost insensible impressions on our tender infancies have very important and lasting consequences."[9] Tristram is not in fact displaced from his fictional *Life*, which famously digresses from his conception and does not get around to his birth until the end of the third volume: the unwound clock, the pre-nuptial agreement, and the bad weather are at the heart of Tristram's character. Likewise, Uncle Toby's centrality in Tristram's life means that Toby should be the central figure in his *Life*.

Digression, then, is not losing track of the narrative, for it *is* the narrative:

> I have constructed the main work and the adventitious parts of it with such intersections, and have so complicated and involved the digressive and progressive movements, one wheel within another, that the whole machine, in general, has been kept a-going; – and, what's more, it shall be kept a-going these forty years, if it pleases the fountain of health to bless me so long with life and good spirits.[10]

Tristram's digressions, like the cogs in a clock, may appear to be flying off in separate directions, but they combine perfectly to move the narrative – and time – forward. The chapter on digressions, then, is a narrative version of winding Mrs. Shandy's clock. And just as winding the clock was central to Tristram's conception, so, then, are digressions central to his *Life*. But Tristram's digressions are more than narrative foreplay. Digression, Sterne teaches us through *Tristram Shandy*, is the purest expression of character because it exposes the intricate web of allusions and associations that makes up one's frame of reference. By exposing the inner workings of his mind, Tristram hopes to explain himself and make himself legible to others – a project in which he, like the Female Quixote, is doomed to fail.

Tristram, like one of Richardson's heroines, writes in the first person and the present tense. He is doing his best to write to the moment, the difficulty of which is comically epitomized by Tristram's father, Walter. Walter's attempts to complete the *Tristrapaedia* are always doomed to failure because his son grows faster than he can write. While the *Tristrapaedia* is an affectionate jab at the logical absurdity of writing to the moment, Sterne takes the narrative conceit to its logical conclusion. Tristram is writing his own life in the present tense – not retrospectively telling the story of a single episode, but telling the story of his whole life while he is still living it. Therefore Tristram's narrative can have no direction, no clear trajectory, because the end has not yet happened. Tristram's *Life and Opinions* will only end with his life, and no man can foresee his own death.

The opacity of identity celebrated in *Tristram Shandy* reassures readers that the novel need not smooth over epistemological failures, but can revel in them. Life, and indeed *Lives*, may not travel in a straight line, but beauty, poetry, humor, friendship, and love are found in the serpentines and switchbacks. Furthermore, Tristram's inability to narrate his history is ultimately profoundly illuminating: where moral philosophy and biography struggle, *The Life and Opinions of Tristram Shandy* offers a method for describing a life and exposing character that is both effective and entertaining.

Problems of interpretation

The eponymous heroine of *Evelina* (1778) faces a different problem from Tristram Shandy. She appears all too easy to read and to interpret, and those about her constantly judge her character based on appearance and situation, circumstances that are always against her. Evelina unwittingly yet continually finds herself in the wrong company, in the wrong dress, and at the wrong door. Her ignorance of social custom is interpreted variously as levity, insensibility, and rudeness. With so many others all too ready to ascribe bad character and motives to Evelina, and with the rules of decorum conspiring to keep her silent, the epistolary format offers Burney's heroine her only opportunity of self-expression.

Like *Pamela*, the plot of *Evelina* describes the testing and ultimate discovery of a young woman's identity. The novel charts her development from a nobody to a recognized and recognizable somebody. Whereas the status of Tristram Shandy, Gentleman, is confirmed on the title-page, Evelina's status is far murkier. She is made vulnerable to misreadings because she can lay claim to an individual subjectivity only; her mysterious history separates her from the usual markers of class and family identity. Evelina's name – the first clue to her identity – derives from her mother's maiden name, Evelyn. Because her father will not own her, she cannot use her real surname, Belmont. But to use her mother's surname would admit the illegitimacy everyone assumes for her. So her guardian Villars creates a new identity for her: *Anville*. Despite Margaret Doody's attention to *Anville* as an (imperfect) anagram of *Evelina*,[11] it might be more useful to think of the suggestive connections in the surnames found in the novel: *Vill-ars*, *Or-Ville*, and *An-Ville*. This triangular relationship – Evelina, her "more-than father," and her "more-than brother" – represents a natural grouping whose similarity of character is represented by the similarity of name. To be sure, Doody's argument about the importance of maternal inheritance and Burney's (and Evelina's) refusal to abandon autonomous female identity seems absolutely central, not only to *Evelina*, but to any investigation of the translation of interiority into visible and readable signs.

Although Carolyn Evelyn died, she lives on through Evelina: it is the daughter's marked resemblance to the mother – external signifiers, not interiority – that finally wins the day. By inheriting her mother's face as well as name, Evelina can finally prove her identity, and reclaim her rightful place in the world. *Evelina* narrates the complex relationship between interior subjectivity and external signifiers in a Lockean world. Knowing and/or reading character is of vital importance, but as Tristram and Arabella likewise discover, the self is always mediated through external signs, associations, and surroundings. Polly Green was not only recognized as Miss Belmont but believed herself to be Miss Belmont because she was presented as such. Burney's neat resolution argues that external signifiers such as circumstances and associations might cause confusion and mistaken identification, but that external signifiers will also lead careful observers to the truth.

Evelina is clearly troubled about her incomplete identity, signing her first letter to Villars "Evelina --- -----." The blank, as Doody and other critics have noted, links Evelina to the "Blank" in the dedicatory poem, connecting the heroine to the "author of [Frances Burney's] Being." But it also has more troubling connections to eighteenth-century figurations of female sex and the feminine gender. She does not simply sign off "Evelina," as she does elsewhere in the novel: she adds a dash to signify the missing family name. The dash signifies a lack, an absence: it is not too much of a stretch to connect it to that other "lack," female genitalia. In this reading, Evelina, because she lacks a secure place in the patriarchy, is reduced to the sexual.

This is a recurring theme in Burney's novels. In *The Wanderer*, and to some extent in *Cecilia* and *Camilla*, Burney dramatizes the near impossibility of achieving female "self-dependence" and maintaining female respectability. And it is not just the punctuation that makes this point. Because she cannot confidently assign herself a place in the world she has entered, Evelina is consistently classed with more unfortunate and/or less virtuous women – women who live by their "nothings." Lovel and Willoughby assume that because she is "nobody" she is therefore available for insult and sexual predation. Evelina is slighted and neglected at Clifton Hill because its fashionable inhabitants (excepting Lord Orville) think her missing surname makes her a nobody. But this is the least troubling of Evelina's misadventures; it is much worse when anyone actually does take notice of her. She is mistaken for an actress and a prostitute. Willoughby attempts to take advantage of her lack of protection. And less immediately dangerous is the assumption that she would marry her insufferable cousin Branghton or Mr. Smith; that a girl whose only dowry is her beauty must sell and sell quickly. *Evelina* draws attention to Evelina's lifelike, interior depths by narrating the pain caused by ignoring interiority. No one within the novel acknowledges Evelina's right to have her own thoughts, feelings, or soul: she is a blank to be filled in as the interests of others determine. Burney's moral is clear: Evelina's story may be singular, but her plight is all too common.

Evelina is Burney's only epistolary novel, and the only one to be written in the first person. In the preface to *Camilla* (1796) Burney draws a distinction between the historian or biographer and the novelist, between the narration of actions and the painter of interiority: "The historian of life finds less of difficulty and of intricacy to develop, in its accidents and adventures, than the investigator of the human heart in its feelings and its changes." [12]

Mediated self-expression

In later novels Burney exposes the hearts of her heroines by combining the disclosure of first-person narration with the contextualizing gaze of a third-person narrator. Camilla, Cecilia, and Juliet express themselves indirectly through an omniscient narrator. The direct speech and thoughts of the heroines are mediated through, and combined with, narratorial commentary, blurring the boundaries between character and narrator. This meeting of external and internal, this free indirect discourse, combines the intimacy of first-person narration with the objectivity and reliability of third-person narration. It allows the novelist to document his or her character's feelings and clearly and unambiguously to map them to physical expression or utterance, or to mark and explain the disruption between body, word, and emotion. By speaking through the narrator, characters are freed from charges that they are crafting their own fictions – being Shamelas – yet still given an authorial space from which to speak directly to readers and in their own distinctive voices. Free indirect discourse was a popular and largely successful solution to the problems of interpretation, authority, and believability I have detailed above.

Free indirect discourse not only lends narrative authority to subjective utterance, but also creates a channel for unvoiced and unspeakable thoughts; it allows characters like Burney's to be subversively witty, judgmental, and knowing without losing the appearance of, and reputation for, sociability. Free indirect discourse in this vein, which Helen Dry describes as a "narrated monologue" that "might represent a transcript of a character's conscious thoughts," [13] is perhaps best employed in Jane Austen's novels, from demonstrations of Elizabeth Bennet's ready wit to Fanny Price's thoughtful ruminations. Free indirect discourse can also illuminate characters like Emma

Woodhouse, who are used to expressing themselves, but often mean more, or at least better, than they say.[14] Despite asserting that Emma would be a "heroine no-one but myself will much like,"[15] and whose social superiority can be offputting, particularly for modern readers, Austen works hard to contextualize, explain, and offset Emma's faults. Her use of free indirect discourse collapses the potential distance between reader and heroine and creates a space for Emma's self-awareness and interiority:

> With Tuesday came the agreeable prospect of seeing him again, and for a longer time than hitherto; of judging of his general manners, and by inference, of the meaning of his manners towards herself; of guessing how soon it might be necessary for her to throw coldness into her air.[16]

The unreferenced pronoun "herself" immediately introduces Emma's subjectivity. Moving quickly and seamlessly from external description to interiorized thoughts, the novel allows readers to gain both subjective and objective views of its heroine – to undergo the process of self-discovery with Emma.

Emma's isolation and superiority risk alienating her not just from the society of Hartfield, but from her self as well. However, despite opening the novel with a playful admission of her heroine's "disposition to think a little too well of herself" (1), Austen's use of free indirect discourse rather emphasizes the fact that Emma is only too aware of her faults and failings, including her vain disposition. Nowhere is this self-awareness more evident than after the disastrous trip to Box Hill. When Mr. Knightley reprimands her for insulting Miss Bates, "Emma recollected, blushed, was sorry, but tried to laugh it off" (339), but the sting to her conscience went deep:

> A whole evening of back-gammon with her father, was felicity to it. *There*, indeed, lay real pleasure, for there she was giving up the sweetest hours of the twenty-four to his comfort; and feeling that, unmerited as might be the degree of his fond affection and confiding esteem, she could not, in her general conduct, be open to any severe reproach. As a daughter, she hoped she was not without a heart. She hoped no one could have said to her, "How could you be so unfeeling to your father? – I must, I will tell you truths while I can." Miss Bates should never again – no, never! If attention, in future, could do away the past, she might hope to be forgiven. She had been often remiss, her conscience told her so; remiss, perhaps, more in thought than fact; scornful, ungracious. (443–444)

Despite the third-person tags, this passage narrates Emma's thoughts and gives them vent – "Miss Bates should never again –." This passage does not merely describe the state of Emma's heart but narrates the process of her self-examination and self-reproach. Rather than allow Emma to announce her penitence directly to readers, which would trigger problems of believability, it is folded into the narrator's moral compass and voice.

Emma's self-reflection and knowingness offer one index of how much novelistic representation of psychological depth had changed since *Pamela*. But her obsession with explaining herself, and her repeated frustrations at being mistaken and misunderstood, also suggest that nothing had changed. Emma, like Arabella or Evelina, is still frustrated by her inability to make herself known and understood. Evelina suffers in part because the language of self-expression available to her – the swoons and blushes so effective for Pamela – has become hackneyed through repetition and satire and is no longer trusted as an authentic index of "real" feeling. Women blush, we are reminded again and again, through guilt as well as innocence, and innocence can be "put on" like a mask or theatrical role. The problem for Burney's and Austen's heroines is not that they do not have a "stable self" to articulate, but that there is no reliable, shared language with which to express themselves. For self-expression to be "authentic," and believable, it has to be spontaneous, personal, and unperformed. However, anything that is spontaneous, personal, and unperformed is also illegible. Once a language becomes legible, it also resonates as contrived and false and can only articulate a role, rather than an "essential" self. Interiority, then, is always vexed by expression. Access to hearts and minds, thoughts and feelings, is only ever available through fiction, because interiority must be brought to the surface, and psychological depth flattened out into text, in order to be made legible.

Notes

1. For more on truth claims, see Lennard Davis, *Factual Fictions: The Origins of the English Novel* (Philadelphia: University of Pennsylvania Press, 1983) and Michael McKeon, *The Origins of the English Novel 1600–1740* (Baltimore, MD: Johns Hopkins University Press, 2002).
2. Carolyn Steadman, *Master and Servant: Love and Labour in the English Industrial Age* (Cambridge University Press, 2007), p. 164.
3. Peter H. Nidditch, Introduction to John Locke, *An Essay Concerning Human Understanding*, ed. Peter H. Nidditch (Oxford University Press, 1979), p. viii.
4. Daniel Defoe, *The Fortunes and Misfortunes of the Famous Moll Flanders*, ed. G. A. Starr (Oxford University Press, 1995), p. 7.
5. Ian Watt, *The Rise of the Novel: Studies in Defoe, Richardson, Fielding* (Los Angeles: University of California Press, 1957), pp. 135–173.

6. Samuel Richardson, *Pamela*, ed. Peter Sabor and Margaret Ann Doody (Oxford University Press, 2001), p. 197.

7. Henry Fielding, *Joseph Andrews* and *Shamela*, ed. Martin C. Battestin (London: Penguin Books, 1965), p. 321.

8. Charlotte Lennox, *The Female Quixote*, ed. Margaret Dalziel and Margaret Ann Doody (London: Penguin Books, 1997), pp. 121–122.

9. John Locke, *Some Thoughts Concerning Education*, ed. Ruth W. Grant and Nathan Tarcov (Indianapolis: Hackett Publishing, 1996), p. 10.

10. Laurence Sterne, *The Life and Opinions of Tristram Shandy, Gentleman*, ed. Howard Anderson (New York: Norton, 1980), p. 164.

11. Margaret Anne Doody, *Frances Burney: The Life in the Works* (New Brunswick: Rutgers University Press, 1988), pp. 40–41.

12. Fanny Burney, *Camilla*, ed. Edward Allen Bloom and Lillian Bloom (Oxford University Press, 1999), p. 7.

13. Helen Dry, "Syntax and Point of View in Jane Austen's *Emma*," *Studies in Romanticism* 16 (1977), 87–99, 88.

14. See Daniel P. Gunn, "Free Indirect Discourse and Narrative Authority in *Emma*," *Narrative*, 12: 1 (2004), 35–54.

15. James Edward Austen-Leigh, *A Memoir of Jane Austen*, ed. R. W. Chapman (Oxford University Press, 1967), p. 157.

16. Jane Austen, *Emma* (Oxford University Press, 1995), p. 176.

6

Samuel Richardson

CAROL HOULIHAN FLYNN

Writing to Johannes Stinstra in 1753, Samuel Richardson revealed his child-hood fascination for learning the secrets of the heart. He began his writing career as a precocious busybody whose curiosity thrived in his crowded urban world. Neighbors, particularly young women, revealed small sins and desires to serious young Samuel. One victim under his surveillance took offense. Richardson was "not Eleven Years old when [he] wrote, spontaneously, to a Widow of near Fifty ... who was ... continually fomenting Quarrels & Disturbances, by Backbiting & Scandal." Adopting "the Stile and Address of a Person in Years," Richardson "expostulated with her. But my Handwriting was known." The boy was discovered and "chid" for his freedoms, but he continued to be an "early Favourite with all the young Women of Taste & Reading in the Neighbourhood," reading to them while they sewed. When he was "not more than Thirteen," he served as "Secretary" to several young women who needed help in writing their love letters. We have then a "bashful" and grave adolescent writer in the making, given to impersonations, happy to act as amanuensis to encourage or chide, "at the very time that the Heart ... was open before me, overflowing," and the lover was "dreading to be taken at her Word."[1]

Just as happy to expostulate with a backbiting zealot, Richardson finds power in assuming a character while exposing the heart. In both examples the power of the impersonated style, that of the elderly scold or the nervous lover disguising her feelings, is profound. Significantly, Richardson used "the letter" at an early age to steal into his reader's consciousness, disguising his moral as mere entertainment. He also liked to insinuate his fantasies of sexual struggle, fantasies made moralistic to allow them safe passage into the reader's aroused heart.

The term "busybody" comes to mind not just to describe young Samuel's writing other people's love letters and reducing a censorious widow to tears. All his life, Richardson was busy writing, demanding responses from his family, friends, readers, and critics. A most reactive writer, he answered critics of *Pamela* (1740) with second and third editions bristling with defenses of his work, finally producing a sequel to quell distrust in Pamela's behavior in "high-life." When readers like Lady Bradshaigh and Hester Mulso objected to the way he abused Clarissa, as well as his gentle readers, he answered their criticism in chiding, sometimes strident letters. His line of defense culminates in his third edition of *Clarissa* (1751), designed as tightly as a legal case to defend Clarissa's reputation as well as his own. Indeed, his fictional characters labor to defend their reputations. Pamela distributes her letters to her neighbors to illustrate not just her story, but also her moral and epistolary style. Clarissa's distribution is more crucial; she collects all the documents in the text to expose Lovelace's plots and exonerate her actions posthumously.

Richardson's compulsive attention to the received meaning of his work compelled him to "restore" passages, collect "Sentiments," and revise prefaces, conclusions, and footnotes. Luckily, Richardson was a busybody who could employ his own press on his behalf. His first publication, *The Apprentice's Vade Mecum* (1734) demonstrates his commitment to his printing community, where apprentices needed to be protected, indeed perfected, for the good of the profession.

In *The Apprentice's Vade Mecum*, Richardson writes as a Master familiar with the habits of apprentices in his own printing business, one who also fears the "Degeneracy of the Times, and the Prophaneness and Immorality, and even the open Infidelity" corrupting society. This is why the apprentice had to be controlled. The Master Printer, however, has no interest in finding "Faults in the Master," or in reforming society. Instead he wants to "endeavour to prevent or reform [faults] in the Servant, who when he comes to be Master, in his Turn, may contribute to amend the age."[2] It is the pliable state of the apprentice, his potential to grow into a model either moral or profane, that matters. His target, the boy, can be trained to reform society when he comes into his own power. Not that *Vade Mecum* offers a radical reform of present flaws. Although apprentices were often mistreated in the "real world,"[3] Richardson's model must bind himself to the rule of the master, and shun "the Company of all such as would inspire him with a *mean* or *disrespectful* Opinion of the Master or his *Family*." Beware "the *Spy-fault*, the *Back-biter*, the *Detractor*, the *Ingrateful*, the *Betrayer of Secrets*" (45). The Master "is intitled to have a Veil drawn over his Infirmities." However flagrant his faults might be, the Master is "not accountable for them to the Insolence of a Servant" (47). And however severe the superior, the inferior apprentice must still be "curb'd and held in." Obliging behavior always earns the "greater

Merit" (50). For relief, Richardson allows his apprentice to attend one play a year: George Lillo's *London Merchant* (1731). In this choice he reveals his early fascination with two opposing dramatic elements: the inculcation of morality and the representation of seductive and powerful characters who unsettle conventional moral standards. This tantalizing dialectic never disappears from his work.

In 1740, at the age of fifty-one, Richardson began writing *Familiar Letters on Important Occasions*, to offer epistolary models of "Use to . . . Country Readers . . . Will it be any Harm," he asks Stinstra, "in a Piece . . . written so low, if we should instruct them how they should think & act in common Cases, as well as indite for themselves?" (*Selected Letters*, 232). Some directives seem quite simple: the perils of keeping a horse, the dangers of courting a flighty young woman. Filial piety is an unquestioned duty, regardless of paternal behavior. A rebuke to "an irregular Address, when it is not thought proper wholly to discourage" it, creates the possibility for an interesting ambiguity seldom offered in the collection. His epistolary models became even more ambiguous in letters 138 and 139 instructing "handsome Girls, who were obliged to go out to Service . . . how to avoid the Snares that might be laid against their Virtue." When a girl complains about her master's attempts on her virtue, her father tells her to "come directly away."[4] And "hence," Richardson tells Stinstra, "sprung Pamela" (*Selected Letters*, 232).

The lure of the familiar letter, the perfect instrument to carry passionate secrets, seems to have stolen Richardson away from his writing guide and into his first novel. His own handsome girl does not follow her own father's entreaty to come home, but stays on, inciting Mr. B.'s passion as she works on his embroidered vest. Richardson eventually returned to his epistolary project, in 1741, but only after *Pamela* had completely altered his sense of his vocation.

Richardson, a most reactive novelist, received essential energy from the responses of his readers. He unspooled his career responding to the engulfing wave of criticism that met *Pamela*. Written in a heat in two months, the novel was first read by members of his household in manuscript, revised and published in 1740, and revised again in five more editions by 1741. He defended his "girl" in thousands of textual changes, and in prefatory materials full of puffery and praise. He continued preserving Pamela from detractors in a two-volume sequel filled with the dangers and temptations of "high life" that she masters. He was still revising the novel months before he died in 1761.

Richardson spent much longer than two months to write his first edition of *Clarissa*. It took seven years, during which time he shared versions of his manuscript with countless "friends," and made substantial cuts according to their directions to bring the work into some sort of manageable size. He published the novel in seven volumes in 1747 and 1748, responding to the complaints of readers insisting that Clarissa and Lovelace marry. His second (1749) and third (1751) editions contain so many cuts, added material, footnotes, printer's ornaments, and printer's bullets to signify his alterations, that he published *Letters and Passages Restored From the Original Manuscripts of the History of Clarissa* (1751) to contain them. In comparison with his earlier novels, *Sir Charles Grandison* (1753) appears to be more stable, but Richardson still made changes in the second (1753) and third (1754) editions that reflected the questions he kept posing to his circle of readers and critics. In *A Collection Of the Moral and Instructive Sentiments, Maxims, Cautions, and Reflexions* (1755),[5] culled from all three novels, he cemented his "meaning" alphabetically from an "Address to the Rich" (*Pamela*) *to* "Zeal and Zealous" (*Grandison*). The fragmentary nature of its design goes against the desire Richardson cherished to make the meaning of his "moral" inescapable. He also wrote, rewrote, and copied hundreds of personal letters in defense of his fiction. He may have written "to the moment," but he constantly changed that moment to one that he could better control, one less likely to be "misread."

And what were these ignorant misreadings that he kept correcting? From the beginning, he was accused of teasing the reader with "warm scenes" while ostensibly making his moral case. Certainly that was the main problem for readers like Henry Fielding, who famously created *Shamela* to expose the hypocrisy lurking in the pious maid who refuses to "leave" her master, but stays on to reform him. Richardson defended his warm scenes as late as 1755, arguing that "Instruction, Madam, is the Pill; Amusement is the Gilding" (*Selected Letters*, 322). What was being gilded was not so obvious. Mr. B. was to cease and desist, and give in to the morality being packaged in the delightfully gilded form of Pamela. Her delicious subservience as well as her physical beauty makes her ascendancy into moral instructor easy to swallow. This is not so simply worked out in *Clarissa*. There, Richardson refuses to "reform" his rake, but leaves his readers struggling to find meaning in a bleak world that sacrifices its finest woman to flawed patriarchal power. Scenes of rape, rapture, and resistance draw readers in, but they are left without a place to stand, let alone a moral to cherish.

Richardson never stopped imagining fictional situations that would produce female subjects willing to internalize their subordinate place in the patriarchal system. While he labored to control errant female imaginations, he worked just as hard to "steal in" his intentions by refashioning the patriarchal style and the shape of masculinity to make his lessons more acceptable and even attractive. Patriarchy itself, redesigned to attract the female reader, remains his most significant authorial act. What developed, however, when he began writing his novels, went far beyond his initial intentions. For he also developed a style that tended to inflame readers even as he insisted that their desires must be contained. His epistolary style invited his readers to internalize not only his moral instruction but also the passions he was laboring to quell.

Pamela

Richardson informs his reader on the frontispiece of *Pamela* that he has published his novel "In order to cultivate the Principles of VIRTUE and RELIGION in the Minds of the YOUTH of BOTH SEXES." He promises that although his narrative entertains "by a Variety of *curious* and *affecting* INCIDENTS," he has "divested" his piece of "all those Images, which in too many Pieces calculated for Amusement only, tend to *inflame* the Minds they should *instruct*."[6] One definition of "divest" is "to unclothe, undress, disrobe, and strip of clothing." The author seems not only to promise to move his reader with curious and affecting incidents, but to make his reader safe with a sanitizing strip-tease. Before it even begins, the text is filling the youthful mind with notions both curious and affecting. Never recovering from its unsettling divestment, the novel is energized by the ambiguous relationship that its author has to the moral task ahead. A laudatory letter to the "Editor of PAMELA," positioned directly before the first of Pamela's letters, continues to imagine divesting the text and its girl of superfluous garments in a heated commendation of the novel's simple style:

> [N]eedless Decorations . . . like too much Drapery in Sculpture and Statuary, will but incumber it . . . let us have . . . *Pamela* . . . in her own Words . . . Produce her to us in her neat Country Apparel, such as she appear'd in on her intended Departure to her Parents . . . Such a Dress will best edify and entertain. (9)

The writer, possibly one Reverend William Webster, or even Richardson himself, as Fielding insinuates in *Shamela* (see *Pamela*, 526, n.10), admires Pamela's "new Garb" designed to suit her humble condition. Rejecting her late mistress's presents of silk and linen cast-offs, she writes that "I trick'd myself up as well as I could in my new Garb," and "shew'd" off her homespun dress, down "to my Under-petticoat," to Mrs. Jervis. Displaying herself to

Mr. B. in a low "curchee," she reports that her master, "cunning as *Lucifer*," has mistaken her for her "sister." He "took me about the neck," to kiss her "for all [she] could do." While Pamela insists that he recognize her as *"Pamela, her own self,"* he attacks her for her "villainy" in disguising "herself." "Who is it you put your Tricks upon?" he asks (56). This question has been debated by readers ever since. Even Pamela *"her own self"* seems confused, complaining that she has been "in disguise" ever since she left her parents' home.

"In disguise" as a work designed for the cultivation of virtue and religion, *Pamela* aroused readers with more than morality on their minds. While it is not the first novel to make such an impression on the British reading public, it is certainly the first novel to polarize its readers so completely, creating legions of Pamelists and anti-Pamelists debating the novel's meaning. And just what made the novel so incendiary? Primarily its morality, mixed with a plot of brutal seduction and rape attempts that are foiled, but toyed with for hundreds of pages. Pamela makes her case against B.'s attempts in irresistible descriptions of her tousled and disordered self. "I have been, and am, in a strange Fluster, and I suppose . . . [Mrs. Jervis will] say I have been full-pert" (59). "Full-pert" enough to be called saucy slut and to throw her apron over her head, and while undercover, "full-pert" enough to act as a mime in a scene that turns menace into comedy:

> I clasp'd my Hands together thro' my Apron, over-joy'd at this, 'tho I was so soon to go away: For naughty as he has been to me, I wish his Prosperity with all my Heart . . . Well, *Pamela*, said he, you need not now be afraid to speak to me; tell me what you lifted up your Hands at? I said not a Word. Says he, If you like what I have said, give me your Hand upon it. I held my Hand thro' my Apron, for I could not speak to him, and he took hold of it. (66)

When Mr. B. presses Pamela's arm, we are reminded that he has already "made my Arm black and blue; for the Marks are upon it still" (57). This time he "press'd it, tho' less hard than he did my Arm the Day before" (67). Sitting with her apron thrown over head, holding out her hand, presumably the hand that belongs to the black and blue arm, Pamela is both funny and disturbing, just as her own desires to flee are undercut by her tendency to linger, over-joyed as she is "'tho" she will be leaving so soon. Departure could not be soon enough unless a certain degree of passion as well as indignation is being covered up in this scene.

Her appreciation of a lesser form of assault vanishes, however, when Mr. B. attacks Pamela for her "Freedom of Speech of me last Night!" Pamela rebukes him while addressing God, refusing to hold her tongue. At times like this, the saucy servant seems to be a truly revolutionary character, one that asserts her rights as a natural citizen with liberties that she will not relinquish. But the moment, however radical, is subsumed by continued play between the two, for next morning, B. is at it again, displaying a costly new suit even as he insults her. The gap between horrific sexual harassment – the bruises, the sprained ankle, the imposition of raw physical power over the helpless young woman – and the somewhat playful disguises that both characters adopt makes the work itself remarkably unstable.

But most importantly it is also the gap between the revolutionary implications of a text that insists that every girl (or at least Pamela) has the soul of a princess and the true level of domesticated inequality that is demanded once Pamela is truly "Mr. B.'s" that makes Richardson's novel so unsettling. Pamela's insistence on her personal worth struck a nerve in her readers, many no doubt in transition, imagining their own ascendency through their self-improvement, freed perhaps by the very literacy that enfranchised Pamela. Her letters are designed to forge a sympathetic identification between reader and writer. While Mr. B. is learning to love his victim through her letters, so are Richardson's readers. What they end up loving, however, is a refined Pamela, turned into her lover's most revered possession. Her equality becomes restricted through domesticated use.

So long as she is physically fighting back, stripped of clothing, losing her shoes, Pamela is reduced to a body that still remains powerful because of her resistance as well as her distress. But once virtue in distress triumphs and she becomes the future Mrs. B., her body becomes sacred, no longer subject to thrusts and prods. She still suffers, however, the pains of her position. When her father surprises her with a visit, in front of Mr. B.'s neighbors all assembled to admire her virtues, she springs up and overturns the table, throws herself at her father's feet, and down she sinks in a furor of filial piety. She is praised for "painfully delight[ing] the company" (294–295). While her resistance makes her Mr. B.'s equal, demonstrating her ability to match him in wit and energy, once she is no longer fighting him, her energetic insistence upon equality disappears. Instead she voluntarily takes on her servitude. "He shall always be my Master; and I shall think myself more and more his Servant" (303).

Mr. B. demands that his wife watch and study his temper, and "draw a kind Veil over [his] faults" (445–446), sounding much like Richardson's Master laying down the law to his apprentices in *Vade Mecum*. Pamela numbers Mr. B.'s required rules of behavior from one to forty-eight, finding them "all very tolerable" (448–451). While ostensibly reforming a "rake," Richardson is really laying down the law to reform the early modern family. Pamela's servant status makes her the perfect wife, eager to take on household duties, preferring the company of her husband to the rowdy gang of early modern ladies of quality who gad about playing cards and cheating on their spouses. As the editor observes at the end of the novel, *"Ladies of Condition"* should make themselves useful in "their Duty to God, Charity to the Poor and Sick, and the different Branches of Household Management," all of which "ought to take up the most considerable Portions of their Time" (502). No mention here of reading novels or writing letters, for we know how dangerous the epistolary habit can become.

However conservative Pamela's allegiance to the patriarchy that B. embodies, Richardson's early critics seemed to read her triumph as a threat to a society that depended upon fixed sexual and social roles. The very ability that Pamela demonstrates to cross class lines, as well as her talent at displaying a "tricked up" sexuality, provoked attacks on her authenticity that served more than anything else to promote his novel as well as his sequel in 1742. Richardson insisted that he unwillingly wrote his sequel to counter John Kelly's *Pamela's Conduct in High Life* (1741), an act of piracy and robbery that he could not allow. He also used the further adventures of Pamela to keep demonstrating the domestic excellence of his subservient paragon while laying down the law. Thomas Keymer and Peter Sabor make clear in their six-volume collection of anti-*Pamela* documents[7] the power that the Pamela controversy generated. No wonder that the ubiquitous *Pamela* along with Haywood's *Anti-Pamela* showed up on the Roman Catholic index of prohibited books. While he undeniably benefited in money and fame from the extraordinary explosion of Pamelania that filled the literary marketplace in the 1740s, Richardson also seems to have suffered from the incessant critique that such imitations made of the moral fabric of his work. While it is doubtful that his novel was produced merely to demonstrate the reformation of a rake, it is clear that he took away from the publishing experience a very simple dictum: to avoid reforming a rake ever again. The novel that followed, however, was anything but simple.

Clarissa

In *Clarissa* (1748) Richardson's rake Lovelace seems designed for hellfire; from his first letter he lays down his principles of woman-hating love-making. He loves Clarissa, "this proud Beauty," but loves his fantasies of revenge even more. His soul will glow with revenge when she is secured "in spite of her own inflexible heart: Mine, without condition; without reformation-promises." Then, he exults, "shall I have all the rascals, and rascalesses of the family come creeping to me . . . to kneel at the foot-stool of my throne."[8] But in the first two volumes of the novel, Richardson concentrates less on Lovelace's villainy and more on the strains of domestic conduct, the dark structural flaws of the bourgeois family that Richardson labors to both sustain and subvert. He places his heroine in an impossible situation, answering to the unreasonable demands of her inferior brother, sister, uncle, mother, and father. For, as he indicates in his novel, in his own letters to his agitated correspondents, in footnotes and "collected sentiments," filial piety must be upheld regardless of the behavior of the father. "[T]he want of duty on one part justifies not the non-performance of it on the other, where there is a reciprocal duty," he writes to Susanna Highmore in 1749, defensively explaining how his novel works. Performance "on one side, when it is not performed on the other, gives something so like a merit, that I am ready almost to worship the good mind that can do it." Thus the Harlowe parents "are made more cruel, more implacable, more punishable in short, in order to inculcate this very doctrine, that the want of duty on one side enhances the merit on the other, where it is performed" (*Selected Letters*, 131–132). His "Zeal" in supporting "the Parental Authority" is so strong that he tells an American correspondent, Frances Grainger, that he considers his novel "*The Whole Duty of Woman*," a work designed "as something more than a mere Novel or Romance, or Kill-time." It would seem that his novel endorses a patriarchy run wild, because "there was a Necessity for some such Piece to be written" (*Selected Letters*, 141). The culture made him do it.

It is important to realize how much Richardson depended upon his connection to his readers and critics while he wrote his novels. A writer approximating his exploitation of critical disagreement might be Alexander Pope, who made great use of his own attackers and official enemies in his *Dunciad Variorum* (1729). That work sold out in record time to readers addicted to the controversies stirred up in every vitriolic couplet and footnote that Pope offered in attacking his critics. Pope, however, was writing satire, a genre that thrives on attack. Richardson is unusual in the way he privately depends upon the jabs and disagreements of readers he labors to conquer. Richardson does not necessarily expose readers who question his tactics like Hester Mulso, bristling with irritation over his authoritarian treatment, or Susanna Highmore timidly disagreeing with his unfair measures. He writes to his detractors intimately and obsessively, and in his letters we can particularly see the way his "intentions," seemingly misunderstood from the start (or you might say "seen through" his readers), drive him to justify his powerfully unstable novel.

Often he invited readers into the creative process. Richardson sent Aaron Hill an early version of *Clarissa* "in a series of vellum volumes with blank pages interleaved for Hill's comments," comments he mostly disregarded.[9] Sometimes readers barged in, like Lady Bradshaigh and her sister, Lady Echlin. Bradshaigh rewrote his text in its margins, while Echlin offered an alternative ending, both finding places in the text to resist, reform, and rewrite.[10] Their critical engagement creates a paradigm of resistance, what Florian Stuber calls a partnership in creating a text in perpetual state of revision. The text is always "in flux, unfinished, open always to reshaping, refining, rewriting," while "readers are partners in the shaping process of the text" (*Clarissa*, vol. 1, "Introduction," 11). Yes and no, since Richardson in his lifetime had the last word in print. He created, however, a text that still inspires frustrated engagement.

Critics enter the text because they want to change its meaning, and in the interpretive process, they, we, are really taking issue with the limitations not so much of a text as of its culture, and our culture. The contradictions that characterize the author's ideological position as a sympathetic patriarch who loves to support women to keep them in their place radically force disparate and mutually engaged positions of interrogation. This explains how in the 1980s Richardson could be read as feminist or patriarchal, bourgeois or revolutionary, by critics often working out of similar desires to fix the meaning of often contradictory texts. Even if that meaning is one that celebrates diversity and disjunction of meaning, the reader, however sophisticated, finds herself blocked by Richardson's own insistence in sacrificing his "girl" to notions of patriarchal supremacy. She is not any girl, but the cynosure of her world: "Every eye . . . is upon you with the expectation of an example," Anna Howe warns her in her first letter. *"Rather useful than glaring,"* her "deserved motto," Clarissa is "pushed into blaze" (vol. 1, 3–4). To douse the flames of her notoriety, she will dispense advice (much like young Richardson), providing models of behavior to be followed even posthumously. In her last days she demonstrates the correct way to write a will, find an executor, and publish the truth of her story. She even corrects herself in her letters, admitting her mistakes compulsively to Anna Howe as she questions every move she makes toward Lovelace and toward death.

The problem for Richardson was to propel such a saint into the arms of such a heartless seducer. To do so, he explores the violent dysfunction of the bourgeois family, rejecting the comic possibilities of marriage and reformation to turn courtship into tragedy. Through the letters of four very different writers, Clarissa Harlowe, paragon, Anna Howe, egalitarian spitfire, Robert

Lovelace, cynical and imaginative terrorist, and John Belford, rake turning into sentimental gentleman, the novel interrogates the inequalities of the female condition, the necessity for female subordination, the inequities of bourgeois privilege, the necessity of bourgeois solidarity, and the illusion of romantic love. But of all the categories investigated, the most brutal is the domestic. Clarissa may be brought down by her faith in herself, but she is sacrificed by the unfeeling machinations of her nuclear family, determined to torture her into compliance all the while the text insists that the family be held sacred.

Early on, her siblings supported by her uncles, all threatened by Clarissa's heiress status, try to force her into marrying "the odious Solmes sitting asquat between my Mother and Sister, with *so much* assurance." A Grendel figure, awkwardly reptilian, a "bent and broad-shouldered creature," he squats, once more "with his ugly weight" so near to her that he presses upon her sacred hoop (vol. 1, 92–93). Solmes's monstrous "assurance" reinforces the power of a patriarchal system that depends upon the sacrifice of its daughters and wives. Clarissa's mother has long ago given over to the demands of Clarissa's gouty and disabled father who nonetheless rules almost off stage through his big voice. He reinforces the demands of the rest of the family determined to suppress Clarissa's sentimental power of "moving," her ability to penetrate the hearts and minds of her audience.

It is of course the "editor" who moves us in a collection of letters written to, stolen from, copied, and forged by the four correspondents. The epistolary multiplication is essential to the "moving" power of the novel. Readers experience the action of the novel in many different ways, drawn in by the conflicting desires of the correspondents, sometimes even fooled by the extravagant lies that Lovelace makes even to Belford. The extreme length of the novel magnifies this process of revision always ongoing in the text and in the reader herself. Can we trust Anna Howe, or Clarissa herself, so staunchly refusing to recognize the "throbs" Anna detects in her omissions; can we believe anything about Lovelace, a writer endorsed partially by the loyal Belford who cedes a great deal of trust in him by at least refraining from attacking his early activities? The editor labors to control his readers' responses to the perilously tragic unfolding of a seduction plot that drives Clarissa out of her "garden" into a Satanic Lovelace's arms. She is imprisoned by her own internalized rules of conduct, her punctilio, while she becomes unwittingly the prisoner of Lovelace who has hidden her in a brothel disguised as a middle-class lodging. The successful transformation undermines the tenets of the bourgeois world Clarissa depends upon. Armed with her spiritual resources and her letters from an untried Anna Howe who never really delivers the support she promises, Clarissa performs virtue in distress based on commonplace principles of conduct that fail to protect her.

Lovelace's assault stems from his own mechanical position as heir to generations of rakes, constructed out of the aristocratic scrap heap of Restoration models, a little Horner here, a pinch of Dorimant there. He anachronistically wages war against the Harlowes, just risen up from the "dunghill" of upward mobility. When Lovelace castigates the Harlowe family for its upwardly mobile pretensions, is he making a case that Richardson endorses? Or is it part of a larger cultural attack on the bourgeois reader? When Anna Howe meets Lovelace at Colonel Ambrose's ball after the rape she is revolted by the assembly's general indifference to Clarissa's state, and even more outraged at the way Lovelace is embraced by a crowd that will always love a lord. Which is more loathsome: the middle class (home of the Harlowes and their neighbors who refused to protect Clarissa) or the aristocracy (where doddering Lord M. and his nieces love to be shocked by Lovelace's exploits)?

Clarissa dies because she has internalized a lethal bourgeois conduct code fragmented by the conflicting demands that it makes on women. No seducer could have a better opponent. She so diligently checks Lovelace's moves that the protean, witty rake, who thinks of himself as a Caesar, an emperor, the Grand Signor, and even Satan, cannot even begin to rape her without the help of "Mother" Sinclair, who goads him to rape a drugged and helpless victim. The pivotal part that Sinclair plays illustrates Richardson's judgment that *"[t]here is no wickedness like the wickedness of a woman."*[11] Or as Lovelace would put it, "A fallen woman is a worse devil than even a profligate man" (vol. III, 308). Her evil only exaggerates the dilemma that Lovelace sees to be the impossibility facing women in general when they cease being angel in imagination and descend into being a woman in body. Such cultural misogyny forces Clarissa's "end" to be complete precisely because it does not allow a middle ground between imaginary sublimity and the horror of body. Only Clarissa's death allows her to escape the moral categories enforced by the text that would define her raped state to be a damaged and fallen one.

Before her death Clarissa tries to rewrite her damaged self as she experiments with both form and content. Her first writings are fragmented and disjointed, expressed in short bursts that the editor places eccentrically around the page. She composes herself, however, in several ways. With Job as her model, she creates a series of "Meditations." Urged to prosecute Lovelace for rape, she chooses instead to publish her very own story, using Belford as

editor to collect the letters between him and Lovelace, between Clarissa and
Anna Howe, as well as the many other letters sent between family, friends,
and even enemies (Solmes, Joseph Leman, Tomlinson), all assembled to
become the text that we read. Clarissa also inscribes herself on the cover of
her coffin, allegorizing herself in carvings of "the head of a white Lily snapt
short off, and just falling from the stalk," "a crowned serpent, with its tail in its
mouth, forming a ring, the emblem of Eternity," and a winged hour-glass (vol.
VII, 311–312). The serpent ring can also be read as a sign of eternal desire,
offering not closure but another level of ambiguity suggesting a still conflicted
heart. Clarissa's final literary work, her Will and Testament, reclaims her
estate, redistributing her goods to supporters like Mama Norton and Dolly
Hervey. Her Will includes Lovelace: "If . . . as I am Nobody's, he insist upon
viewing *her dead*, whom he ONCE before saw in a manner dead, let his gay
curiosity be gratified" (vol. VIII, 98). This clause, arousing suspicions of
Clarissa's drugged condition during her rape, sends her cousin Morden on a
mission of revenge. He kills Lovelace in a duel as the Will releases vengeful
desires that Clarissa could suppress only while living.

Clarissa's posthumous triumph is minimized by the great loss that her
death creates. If Clarissa must be sacrificed, what early modern reader could
withstand her tests? Exposed to the troubling vision of daughters sacrificed to
maintain a social order, the reader might simply decide to let the social
markers stay in place. This is the cultural bargain that Richardson drives.
Ravishing his readers with dramatic representations of the perverse inequities
of the cultural system that contains them, his text exposes the limitations of
their powers. The reader might "enjoy" her pain, an appropriately sentimental
response. Lady Bradshaigh reports with some degree of pleasure her agony:
"Had you seen me, I surely should have moved your pity. When alone, in
agonies would I lay down the book, take it up again, walk about the room, let
fall a flood of tears, wipe my eyes, read again, perhaps not three lines, throw
away the book, crying out . . . I cannot go on."[12]

Richardson appreciated the agitated distress expressed by his disempow-
ered correspondents. While he teases them with intimations of their limited
powers, he still answered some of them in his revisions, for Richardson was as
interested in correcting his texts as Clarissa was in correcting and revising
herself. The third edition of his novel particularly demonstrates the investment he had in perfecting his text. With an eye on his detractors, he blackened
Lovelace in footnotes and additions to the text, including one of Lovelace's
most imaginative and daunting plots, to rape Anna Howe and her mother off
the Isle of Man. Lovelace is hailed as a heroic villain as he is marched through

London, his life spared, his ascendancy reassured. Richardson signifies his textual additions with bullets and indicates the individual characters with printing ornaments to denote their place on the page. Clarissa is a rose, Anna a fleur-de-lis, Lovelace a manic collection of asterisks, and Belford, surely Richardson's editorial surrogate, an acorn. The revisions were sold independently as *Letters and Passages Restored* (1751) so that readers could become careful editors themselves, correcting their own readings as they made the necessary changes. But the essential change would be to agree with Richardson at last, brought down by his bullets.

Sir Charles Grandison

Sir Charles Grandison can be seen as one last experiment by Richardson to correct his readers. While he attempted in his revisions and footnotes to blacken Lovelace's character, in his third novel Richardson degrades the rake entirely, knocking three front teeth out of an unsuccessful villain's mouth. In the character of Grandison we find the lineaments of Lovelace sanitized and made respectable. The hero is one of the finest swordsmen of his day, but he refuses to duel. He is also one of society's best-dressed young men, not out of vanity, but to honor a father who does not really deserve obedience. Sir Charles exerts great power in social and domestic circles, righting the wrongs where disorder might lurk. As "executor," he turns housekeepers who have been living in sin with their now deceased masters out of doors with great civility, offering miscreants the chance to reform. As a model of civic manliness, he enjoys acting out Lovelace's wildest fantasies of conquest. While Lovelace imagines "dropping the handkerchief" before Anna Howe and Clarissa in his own private harem, Sir Charles approaches in real life a form of polygamy in his triangular sentimental friendship with Harriet Byron and the divine Clementina, who has run mad with love for him. In fact, no fewer than five ladies of quality in the neighborhood would be willing to stand before him and let him choose one of them (vol. II, 43).

His sister, Charlotte Grandison, particularly suffers under his domestic rule. Married to an inferior husband who appears to be slightly simple, although loving and rich, she learns to be "matronized" by his goodness, particularly when she is sunk into being a "Mama." She must sink her reason, and give way to her feelings to become the "whole" wife and mother, for as she realizes, "I think too much . . . and consideration is no friend to wedlock" (vol. II, 320).

Harriet Byron comes to the novel with great cultural capital as a witty and beautiful heiress, scorning the power of men who pretend to exalt the women they intend to ruin. Abducted from a masquerade, she barely escapes rape when Sir Charles comes to her rescue. His rescue mortifies her, but then he will witness other low moments, taming Harriet in these encounters. Humiliated by her physical and mental sufferings, Harriet learns to be proud of her "inferiority" to Sir Charles, and dedicates herself to obliging the man in all things. She learns what it is to be "Nobody," a creature of raised sensibilities but lowered "self-consequence." Her compliance, a voluntary subjugation, is demanded of all truly superior female characters. Richardson confided to Miss Mulso that "after a proper amount of mortification," he intended to "raise" Harriet, humbled by a love grown more pure, for "suspense in love is a mortifier" (*Selected Letters*, 190).

Female mortification could be Richardson's greatest legacy to the novel. Frances Burney developed its pains in all of her novels. She delineates the adventures of "Nobody," Evelina always under the eye of Orville, Cecilia driving herself mad in the attempts to please oppositional guardians blocking her marriage, and Camilla, exposed for her petty crimes, under the surveillance of a careful lover and his watchful tutor. Tracing the line of female voluntary mortification from Richardson through Burney into Jane Austen, moving on to Maria Edgeworth into George Eliot, can only remind us how powerfully the perils of mortification, elevation, and degradation, so strangely mixed, entered into the English novel, never to be entirely removed. We read Richardson's novels to steal into his extraordinary characters, to learn their secrets, their passions, and their struggles. But then we are left with the patriarchal paradigms that have been smuggled in for our edification. It is positively mortifying.

Notes

1. Samuel Richardson, *Selected Letters*, ed. John Preston (Oxford: Clarendon Press, 1964), pp. 230–231.
2. Samuel Richardson, *The Apprentice's Vade Mecum* (New York: Garland Publishing, 1974), p. v.
3. For discussion of apprentice murders see my *Samuel Richardson: A Man of Letters* (Princeton University Press, 1982), pp. 8–12.
4. Samuel Richardson, *Familiar Letters*, ed. Brian W. Downs (London: George Routledge and Sons, 1928), pp. 124–131, p. 166.
5. *Samuel Richardson's Published Commentary on Clarissa, 1747–65*, ed. John A. Dussinger and Ann Jessie Van Sant (London: Pickering and Chatto, 1998). Peter Sabor, "Teaching *Pamela* and *Clarissa* through Richardson's Correspondence," in *Approaches to Teaching the Novels of Samuel Richardson*, ed. Lisa Zunshine and Jocelyn Harris (New York: Modern Languages Association, 2006) discusses the

problems with editions of the correspondence and announces that Cambridge University Press has commissioned a complete edition of Richardson's works and correspondence.

6. Samuel Richardson, *Pamela: or, Virtue Rewarded*, ed. Thomas Keymer and Alice Wakely (Oxford University Press, 2008), p. 1.

7. Thomas Keymer and Peter Sabor, *The Pamela Controversy: Criticism and Adaptations of Samuel Richardson's Pamela, 1740–1750* (London: Pickering and Chatto, 2001).

8. Samuel Richardson, *Clarissa: Or, The History of a Young Lady*, 3rd edn [1751], *The Clarissa Project*, ed. Florian Stuber, 8 vols. (New York: AMS Press, 1990), vol. i, pp. 195, 200–201.

9. As cited in T. C. Duncan Eaves and Ben D. Kimpel, *Samuel Richardson: A Biography* (Oxford: Clarendon Press, 1971), p. 206.

10. Janice Broder, "Lady Bradshaigh Reads and Writes *Clarissa*: The Marginal Notes in Her First Edition," *Clarissa and Her Readers*, ed. Carol Houlihan Flynn and Edward Copeland (New York: AMS Press, 1999), pp. 97–117.

11. Samuel Richardson, *Sir Charles Grandison*, ed. Jocelyn Harris, 3 vols. (London: Oxford University Press, 1972), vol. ii, p. 28.

12. *The Correspondence of Samuel Richardson*, ed. Anna Laetitia Barbauld, 6 vols. (London, 1804), vol. iv, pp. 240–242.

7

Domesticities and novel narratives

CYNTHIA WALL

The house, quite obviously, is a privileged entity for a phenomenological study of the intimate values of inside space . . . For our house is
our corner of the world . . . [A]ll really inhabited space bears the
essence of the notion of home . . .

Gaston Bachelard, *The Poetics of Space* (1957)

[H]aving settled my houshold Stuff and Habitation, made me a Table
and a Chair, and all as handsome about me as I could, I began to keep
my Journal.

Daniel Defoe, *Robinson Crusoe* (1719)

Robinson Crusoe, who left a comfortable middle-class home in England, finds
himself stranded on a deserted island, and promptly creates a comfortable
middle-class home in its midst. He makes his new corner of the world into a
house – two houses, to be precise: his main "fortress" and his "country
retreat," complete with his "family" of dogs, cats, goats, and a parrot, with
handy shelves, misshapen pots, raisins, and an umbrella. And when his household stuff is settled, he can begin to write.

Crusoe's domestic management supplies a vignette for the eighteenth-
century British novel, which in such sweeping ways is all about home: finding
it, losing it, running away from it, replicating it, furnishing it, inhabiting
it, remembering it, haunting it. Even the picaresque novels, "homeless" as
their rogues go ranging round the world, define themselves by the absence
of home, the picaro living by his wits on other people's doorsteps. The house,
which houses the home, the domestic, is site of plot, character, action, setting:
she is pursued through the chamber; he brandishes a sword in the hall;
they meet in the parlor; they avoid each other in the garden; she drops in an
elbow-chair; he eavesdrops from the closet; she points the poignard at her
breast in the dining-room; they take two chapters to descend a staircase.
As Amanda Vickery notes: "Universal but unexamined, homes are implicated

in and backdrop to the history of power, gender, the family, privacy, consumerism, design and the decorative arts."[1] The good fat eighteenth-century novel offered commodious lodgings for the exploration of new family patterns (courtship, marriage, children, servants) and all the radiating (or concentric) concerns of money, estate, status, politics, religion, gender, etiquette, autonomy, and Turkey carpets.

This chapter will offer a set of house-plans for various novelistic domesticities: one for those who set up house, who determine its physical and social parameters, build its walls literally or conceptually, not only within the novel but also for the cultural space outside it; one for the happy families, who offer – in their past, present, or future – a model (or range of models) for domestic tranquility, whether mainstream or alternative; one for those who find "domestic tranquility" an oxymoron, and either run like mad from it, fingers in their ears, or go mad and die from it; and finally, one for those who occupy the home (to use Freud's term) in an *unheimlich* sort of way, haunting or being haunted by the most familiar and intimate of spaces. Novels house households; they carve out the spaces in which to imagine and enact the various cultural dramas of eighteenth-century domestic life. To paraphrase Gaston Bachelard, the novel itself bears the essence of the notion of home.[2]

Setting up house

Daniel Defoe's *The Life and Strange Surprizing Adventures of Robinson Crusoe of York, Mariner* (1719) is often read as a colonialist tract, with the emphasis on Crusoe's staking out ownership of the island, subordinating and evangelizing Friday, killing cannibals, and setting himself up as governor. But as Pat Rogers and more recently Susan Fraiman have shown, Crusoe has a cozy domestic side that is all about home and hearth. For outsiders and castaways, as Fraiman puts it, "domestic spaces and domestic labor mean neither propriety nor status nor captivity and drudgery but rather safety, sanity, and self-expression – survival in the most basic sense."[3] Crusoe, in setting up house on his apparently deserted island, explicitly sets up what is at stake in eighteenth-century domesticity: comfort, security, stability, and identity. Crusoe designs the house-plan and shows us the scaffolding for home and family.

He begins by transporting the ship that wrecked him and turning it into a center of utilitarian self-protection:

> I made me a Table and a Chair . . . out of the short Pieces of Boards that I
> brought on my Raft from the Ship: But when I had wrought out some Boards,

as above, I made large Shelves of the Breadth of a Foot and Half one over another, all along one Side of my Cave, to lay all my Tools, Nails, and Iron-work, and in a Word, to separate every thing at large in their Places, that I might come easily at them; I knock'd Pieces into the Wall of the Rock to hang my Guns and all things that would hang up.

So that had my Cave been to be seen, it look'd like a general Magazine of all Necessary things, and I had every thing so ready at my Hand, that it was a great Pleasure to me to see all my Goods in such Order, and especially to find my Stock of all Necessaries so great.[4]

The pleasure in order soon expands into a pleasure in comfort. Crusoe finds melons, grapes, and limes, and makes raisins and lime-water; he discovers he has sown corn, and makes bread: "as well as in the best Oven in the World, I bak'd my Barley Loaves, and became in little Time a meer Pastry-Cook into the Bargain; for I made my self several Cakes of the Rice, and Puddings" (123). He finds a pastoral paradise on the other side of the island where he builds "a little kind of a Bower" (101) and fancies: "now I had my Country-House, and my Sea-Coast-House" (102). And circling his fireside, or ovenside, is his "family": the parrot, the dog, the tame little goats, and the cats. Crusoe reiterates his pleasure in his domesticity more often than he complains of his desolation:

> I cannot express what a Satisfaction it was to me, to come into my old Hutch, and lye down in my Hamock-Bed: This little wandring Journey, without settled Place of abode, had been so unpleasant to me, that my own House, as I call'd it to my self, was a perfect Settlement to me, compar'd to that; and it rendred every Thing about me so comfortable, that I resolv'd I would never go a great Way from it again, while it should be my Lot to stay on the Island. (111)

Indeed, the iterations of his domestic happiness are also iterations of his domestic security; both comfort and security are wrapped around the act of writing about comfort and security (when his household was settled, he began to keep his journal). Over and over he tells us he will not bother us again with the details of building his camouflaging wall around his fortress/ hutch/ house; over and over he repeats the details of building his wall. The securities and comforts he creates on his island he re-creates in writing of them. The building and the writing give the homeless man a settled place of abode, a center from which to write.

Given that his "home" is more or less a bunch of wooden sticks in a pile of sand, we are tempted to think that his constructions of domesticity are largely metaphorical, except insofar, as Bachelard says, as "all really inhabited space bears the essence of the notion of home." But that is why *Robinson Crusoe* is such a useful place to begin the exploration of novelistic domesticities: it distills the essence of the notion of home. "Family," in early eighteenth-century Britain, was as capacious an idea as "domestic," and had as its first meaning "The servants of a house or establishment; the household. *Obs.*"; its second includes "The body of persons who live in one house or under one head, including parents, children, servants, etc." – or dogs, cats, goats, and parrots (*Oxford English Dictionary*).

Samuel Richardson's Pamela in *Pamela* (1740) and Harriet Byron in his *Sir Charles Grandison* (1753–1754) offered more apparently conventional patterns for constructing domestic security, comfort, and happiness. Pamela, the fifteen-year-old servant girl who defends her virtue from her lusty young master Mr. B., radically insisting on the right to say "no" to *le droit du seigneur* ("How came I to be his Property?"),[5] ends up chastely marrying the squire, encountering the shining barbed boundaries of life among the gentry. Pamela learns to set up house in new ways as she moves from servant-as-family to wife-as-family; what happens (sexually) to a servant girl "hurts no Family," as randy Sir Simon observes (134), but what happens to a wife certainly does. The contrast between Pamela as saucy servant and as meek wife, which so irritates and disappoints many readers, is in part redeemed by the spirited way in which she draws as well as observes the social boundaries during her encounter with her redoubtable sister-in-law, Lady Davers, and Lady Davers's impertinent nephew Jacky. It is a tricky situation: the marriage has been private, but Lady Davers suspects that Pamela is now her brother's mistress – and fears that she is his wife. Because the marriage has been private, and it is not her place to go announcing it, Pamela cannot openly defy Lady Davers. But because she is Mr. B.'s wife, she can no longer act the servant. Plus, Lady Davers *is* Mr. B.'s sister, and the future lies ahead. The bullying in-laws use all the physical furniture in a dining parlor to trap Pamela with the metaphysical furniture of propriety, blocking the door, pushing her into chairs, demanding servitude and answers:

> Dost hear, *Chastity*? said [Lady Davers]. Help me to a Glass of Wine, when I bid thee.–What! not stir! Then I'll come and help thee to one. Still I stirr'd not, and fanning myself, continu'd silent. Said she, When I have ask'd thee, Meek-ones, half a dozen Questions together, I suppose thou wilt answer them all at once! Pretty Creature, is not that it?
> I was so vex'd, I bit a Piece of my Fan out, not knowing what I did; but still I said nothing, and did nothing but flutter it, and fan myself. (388)

Pamela employs silence and immobility effectively, to keep up the walls of self-respecting resistance without transgressing into active disrespect. Eventually she pulls together energy and ingenuity and jumps out the window and runs away; Mr. B. later approves of her entire behavior (401). Pamela has successfully negotiated the most complicated domestic space of all: her social status.

Harriet Byron, in *Sir Charles Grandison*, has things much easier, once she has endured several hundred pages of waiting for Sir Charles to deal with his Italian obligations. When Harriet finally becomes Lady Grandison, she ushers into the eighteenth-century novel one of its most ultimately influential features: detailed interior description. Entering the life – and house – of her choice, she takes visual as well as actual possession: "O my dearest, dearest grandmamma! Here I am! The declared mistress of this spacious house, and the happiest of human creatures!"[6] (In that order? She is as house-proud as any Defovian character could be.) Sir Charles shows her around, affirming: "The whole house, my dear, said he, and every person and thing belonging to it, is yours: But this apartment is more particularly so. Let what is amiss in it, be altered as you would have it." And then she begins what to some critics has seemed a rather blue-collar insertion of an auction catalogue or country-house guide: an itemized survey of the furnishings, colors, fabrics, and ornaments of Grandison Hall. The room of her own is a drawing-room "elegantly furnished. It is hung with a light green velvet, delicately ornamented; the chairs of the same; the frames of them gilt; as is the frame of a noble cabinet in it." Richardson here is actually quite consciously importing into his text the kind of spatial detail that by mid-century was permeating public consciousness with *things* – a welter of new, affordable, mass-produced, or imported goods – in advertisements, shop windows, newspapers, satires, auction catalogues, and country-house guides. Susan Stewart has argued that

> [w]e can see in eighteenth- and nineteenth-century realistic novels echoes of two major themes of bourgeois life: individuation and refinement ... The description of the material world, the world of things, is necessary for a description of the hero's or heroine's progress through that world, and the "finer" the description, the "finer" the writing.[7]

From this perspective Harriet's meticulous cataloguing of the colors and textures and lived geometry of Grandison Hall is not *just* a textual praxis, not *just* a guide to a country house, but a textual reproduction of the spaces of her domestic identity. Bringing the workhorse of description into novelistic space becomes an act of domestication and gentrification; these are fine spaces she has got herself into. Household description absorbs the cataloguing logic into the space and meaning of narrative, reassembling and reuniting the *things* of a house into the *meaning* of a house.[8]

Happy families

Domestic happiness in one sense is not a good topic for a novel; happiness just rather sits there and glows. But in novelistic explorations of domesticity, happy models exist – must exist, in order for the exploration to have direction. Or, as Samuel Johnson argued, as "these books are written chiefly to the young, the ignorant, and the idle, to whom they serve as lectures of conduct and introductions into life,"[9] so novels ought to supply Positive Role Models. But because of their plot-dampening effects, the models usually occupy margins, beyond the borders of the book – the past, the future – or in the corners of secondary characters, so that the center can continue its scurry.

In one early novelistic narrative, however, happiness in the sense of domestic comfort remains foregrounded, the tragedy pushed quietly to the side. In John Bunyan's *The Pilgrim's Progress* (1678), Christian abandons his family to seek salvation, and dies. But in Part II of *The Pilgrim's Progress* (1684), when Christiana, her children, and her friend Mercy follow after Christian, they have a remarkably cheerful, comfortable journey, spending goodly time in nice people's houses and houselike inns, with plenty of tasty food and lots of singing. Even the weather assists to cheer them on: they have a good *"Sun-shine Morning"*;[10] they are contented rather than tormented in the green Valley of Humiliation (188); they go through the Valley of the Shadow of Death in *daylight* (189). The Keeper of the Wicket-Gate ushers them into a "Summer-Parler" (150) where they talk comfortably among themselves, and when they continue on, "the weather [was] very comfortable to them" (152). At the House of the Interpreter, Mercy at first cannot sleep for happiness, but the Narrator of the Margins assures us of "Mercy's *good nights rest*" (163). As they leave, Mr. Interpreter gives Christiana "a piece of Pomgranate ... a piece of an Honey-comb, and a little Bottle of Spirits" (170). There is roast lamb with sauce at the House Beautiful, and at the inn run by Mr. Gaius (Mr. Hospitality – Romans 16:23, 3 John 1–6), the cook, *Taste-that-which-is-good*, whips up heave-shoulder, wave-breast, a dish of milk well-crumbed, butter and honey, apples, nuts, and good red wine (205). Even Christiana's death, compared to Christian's, is gentle and happy (240). The happy family bring their harmonious domesticity out of their house, on the road, and into whatever space they enter. *Pilgrim's Progress*, Part II demonstrates quite firmly that you can take it with you.

Henry Fielding's *Tom Jones* (1749) begins in Squire Allworthy's Paradise Hall. A widower now, Allworthy had had a model marriage, the template for Tom and Sophia at the other end of the text. The negative models abound, of course: book II, chapter 8, titled *A Receipt to regain the lost Affections of a Wife, which hath never been known to fail in the most desperate Cases*, is all about Captain Blifil's death and how nicely it reconciled his wife Bridget to his memory. Squire Western treated his wife, Sophia's mother, as a "faithful upper serv- ant";[11] the schoolteacher Partridge's wife is compared to Socrates', the famous fishwife; Sophia's friend Mrs. Fitzpatrick complains that "the Law hath fool- ishly omitted this Office of Vice-Husband" (399) to accommodate women not happy with their primary husband; and yet, and yet . . . even the Narrator is in love with Sophia because she reminds him of his late wife (98, 102). Mrs. Miller, widow, mother, landlady, and socially insignificant figure, as she

> was one of the most innocent Creatures in the World, so she was one of the most chearful. She never thought, nor spoke, nor wished any ill, and had constantly that Desire of pleasing, which may be called the happiest of all Desires in this, that it scarce ever fails of attaining its Ends, when not disgraced by Affection. In short, though her Power was very small, she was in her Heart one of the warmest Friends . . . (456)

This acme of local domesticity generates the power of a *dea ex machina* at the end: she stands up to her patron Allworthy in Jones's defense, she visits Tom in prison and gives him Sophia's letter, and she rightly sees through Blifil. Fielding, like most of the great satirists of the eighteenth century, believed in the "good heart" – the respect for others, the worth of sympathy and generosity and integrity and honesty, the value of courtesy, the power of forgiveness. Not only domestic happiness, but an even larger possibility of wider social benevolence, is predicated in the novel's orderly structure, beneficently causal trajectory, and the explicitness of the conclusion. For Fielding, domestic happiness is a real possibility, even in this dark world.

Oliver Goldsmith's *The Vicar of Wakefield* (1766) offers up the perfect Happy Family as fortune's sacrificial lambs, but the Primroses pass their various tests and emerge if anything happier than ever on the other side. In their first chapter, in their first prosperity, the prosperity itself is still a close, "snug" domesticity, filled with pickling, preserving, cookery, and housekeeping, with "migrations from the blue bed to the brown," living near the road and welcoming travelers with gooseberry wine.[12] Even when the family fortunes collapse in the second chapter, nothing punctures the vicar's sturdy optimism; the description of the new smaller dwelling is full of happy little details:

> My house consisted of but one story, and was covered in thatch, which gave it an air of great snugness: the walls on the inside were nicely white-washed, and my daughters undertook to adorn them with pictures of their own designing. Though the same room served us for parlour and kitchen, that only made it the warmer. Besides, as it was kept with the utmost neatness, the dishes, plates, and coppers, being well scoured, and all disposed in bright rows on the shelves, the eye was agreeably relieved, and did not want richer furniture.
> (24–25)

A 1792 edition of the novel features an engraving of a comfortable thatched-roof house nestled among leafy trees, behind a low welcoming wall, framed by graceful clusters of trees in the foreground. It is the very image of domestic snugness (Figure 1).

And so, rather unexpectedly, is Clara Reeve's gothic novel, *The Old English Baron* (1778). In its aim to domesticate Horace Walpole's supernaturally infused *The Castle of Otranto* (1764), it is all about eggs and bacon and settling household accounts and having parental, protective ghosts. The novel eschews any suspense: any reader paying any attention immediately links up the identity clues stuffed along the way, from the first moment Sir Philip sees Edmund Twyford in the field and thinks how much the boy looks like his old chum. We have a detailed description of the derelict, reportedly haunted room that Edmund bravely offers to occupy, where the wind blows out the lamp, things rustle, and "the furniture, by long neglect, was decayed and dropping to pieces; the bed was devoured by moths, and occupied by the rats."[13] But the only ghosts to haunt Edmund are those of his parents, appearing in a dream, and that story is told only after we are reassured that Edmund has slept well through the night and awakens to the "orient beams" of sunshine (38). The plot marches predictably and satisfactorily along until All Is Discovered and we simply need to sort out who gets the plate, linen, furniture, farming stock, and utensils. The story really is not gothic, except for a few trappings; it is a happily-ever-after domestic lesson.

Frances Burney's *Evelina* (1778) sends Lord Orville gracefully down the Perfect Husband runway towards young Evelina Anville, who is introduced into London society with a fog around her identity. Eighteenth-century culture packed worlds of significance into the smallest gestures, which Evelina observes and records. As the debauched Lord Merton says to his fiancée Lady Louisa: "'You have been, as you always are,' said he, twisting his

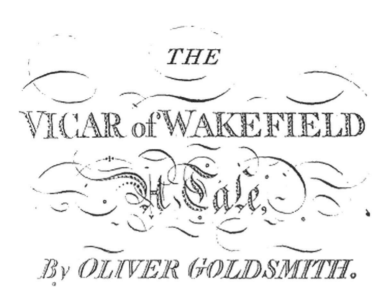

1 Oliver Goldsmith, *The Vicar of Wakefield*, 4th edn. (London: Ogilby & Speare, 1792), title-page; © The British Library Board (012612.f.16)

whip with his fingers, 'all sweetness.'"[14] The Lord and the Lady have been, for different reasons (lust and jealousy), studiously snubbing Evelina in the parlour of Mrs. Beaumont. "But, when Lord Orville appeared, the scene changed: he came up stairs last, and seeing me sit alone, not only spoke to me directly, but drew a chair next mine, and honoured me with his entire attention" (289). The smallest gestures with a whip or a chair may define the larger contours of domestic habitability.

Not all Happy Families are programmed into the same domestic plan, however. Fanny Hill, in John Cleland's sweetly pornographic *Memoirs of a Woman of Pleasure* (1749), finds proper bourgeois happiness in the world with her first and last love, Charles – *almost* like her more respectable sister-heroines. In spite of bulging at the middle with every conceivable act of (and metaphor for) sex, the beginning and end of this novel blazon true love and domestic harmony with Charles, whose "even sweetness of [temper] made him seem born for domestic happiness: tender, naturally polite, and gentle-mannered."[15] In Laurence Sterne's *Tristram Shandy* (1759–1769), although Walter and Elizabeth Shandy may seem lacking in the perfect marriage department, Uncle Toby and Corporal Trim perfectly make up for it: they have a deeply satisfying, compatible partnership in their mutual devotion to their scale-model reproduction of the Siege of Namur (1773) (Figure 2). Uncle Toby's amours may have disappointed him, but not his life with Trim. Sarah Scott's *Millenium Hall* (1762) imagines an institution for healthy living set up for ladies alone: "There are twelve of us that live here. We have every one a house of two rooms, as you may see, beside other conveniencies, and each a little garden, but though we are separate, we agree as well, perhaps better, than if we lived together, and all help one another."[16] Lemuel Gulliver, in book II of Jonathan Swift's *Gulliver's Travels* (1726), lives happily among the giant Brobdingnagians in a portable box. Although the eighteenth-century models for domestic happiness seem from a distance to prescribe strong husbands and docile wives, the best-ordered houses (in the largest sense) accommodate a most interesting variety of configurations, including feminized heroes, independent heroines, and peripatetic domesticity.

"Domestyc enimyes"

The phrase comes from a sixteenth-century example (George Joye, *The exposicion of Daniel the Prophete* [1545]) in the *Oxford English Dictionary* illustrating a definition of "domesticity": "Lo here maye ye see this beast to be no

The Smoking Batteries.

2 George Cruikshank, plate VIII to *Tristram Shandy*, "The Smoking Batteries"

stranger . . . he is therefore a domestyc enimye." For all the happy families on the margins of novelistic domesticity, the enemies within march the plots violently along. Although it has been a critical commonplace to view the eighteenth-century novelistic tragedy as the product of (usually) female transgressions against the patriarchal code, in the largest narratives a different reading is possible: the dominant cultural/moral code is itself the transgression, and enacting it – abiding by the domestic laws of the conduct books – logically ends in self-destruction. The most literal example is Christian, in Bunyan's *The Pilgrim's Progress*, who runs desperately from his wife and children with his fingers in his ears, because staying home means quite literally going to hell. But the families in Richardson's *Clarissa* (1747–1748), Frances Sheridan's *The Memoirs of Miss Sidney Bidulph* (1761), and Sophia Lee's *The Recess* (1785), all expose the devastating fault-lines running just under the surface of some apparently smooth cultural assumptions.

Model daughter, model granddaughter Clarissa Harlowe's first words capture her entire situation: "How you oppress me, my dearest friend."[17] (And all dearest friend Anna is asking for is the inside information on the reported disturbances in the Harlowe household.) All of Clarissa's "friends" oppress her: her father and brother and uncles want her to marry the repulsive Solmes to aggrandize their estate; all the family oppose the arrogant, aristocratic Robert Lovelace as a suitor; her spiteful sister Arabella is jealous of her beauty and belovedness; her mother and aunts behave much too femininely in failing to oppose or even remonstrate with the family gentlemen. All Clarissa asks for is the right to say no to their choice of a husband; she will give up every other right or interest, but that is not enough. To escape a forced marriage Clarissa finds herself in the clutches of Lovelace, who dangles marriage in front of her but really wants to test her virtue to the ultimate limit: he has never failed to seduce before. The family overtly and Lovelace covertly insist that she submit. Strand by strand, they wrap her into paralysis. Lovelace finally drugs and rapes her; she refuses to marry him and goes into a decline; her family refuse to believe she is ill; and no one really realizes what they are doing until she is dead. In the hundreds of pages between rape and death, Clarissa (and the reader) wonder ceaselessly where in that intricate net of actions she went wrong, what she could have done otherwise at any particular moment. In a text as finely textured as this one, the motivations, the causes, the choices, the decisions are finely, precisely ground, and the best answer might be that at no single point would it have made better sense for Clarissa to do other than what she did, given her information, her situation, and her principles. Family and lover combine to shape her to death. From Clarissa's closet nailed shut at home to her coffin returned home, Clarissa is squeezed out of her own life: her family "fill[s] up the doorway" (51), Lovelace wants to rip out her heart and keep it in a jar – even Anna (along with Richardson's readers) wants her to marry Lovelace after the rape. If Clarissa had obeyed her parents and married Solmes, or defied her parents and married

Lovelace in the beginning, or married Lovelace after the rape, she would have annihilated herself. By insisting on remaining to her own self true, she died.

Clarissa had plenty of people around her criticizing her every move (even sometimes Anna); no one could say anything against any single action of Sidney Bidulph. As daughter, lover, wife, mother, widow, she does exactly what eighteenth-century culture demands: submit, self-deny, look the other way, forgive. And every single right and feminine decision she makes ends up in disaster for herself and everyone around her. Frances Sheridan ruthlessly follows the logic of female submission to its terrible conclusion: the implosion of family itself in a sort of moral anorexia. Early on, Sidney murmurs: "I am positive, if I were let alone, I should be as happy as ever."[18] She is forced to break off her match with Orlando Faulkland because her mother believes him to be a rake; Lady Bidulph then insists she marry Mr. Arnold, who actually is unfaithful; Sidney pretends not to notice, and after he ruins the family fortune, she dutifully welcomes him back into her arms; after he dies and she is free to marry Faulkland, she instead pushes him into doing the right thing by marrying the Miss Burchell he was supposed to have seduced; Miss Burchell turns out to be another fiend, crocodile, ape, toad, like the Mrs. Gerrarde who seduced Mr. Arnold; Faulkland goes mad; the memoirs end in mid-sentence, with an added fragment that foreshadows even greater tragedies. Sidney's brother George had told her: "your good intentions [are] productive of nothing but evil" (328). She herself cries, "[M]y best purposes, by some unseen power, are perverted from their ends" (391). Every decision she makes is founded on the principle of female duty; every decision she makes destroys the known world. In this case, the "domestyc enimye" is the proper lady, the submissive daughter, the dutiful wife, the self-sacrificing mother, the self-denying lover.

But it is not just parents and guardians and lovers who can destroy from the inside. Sisters make good enemies, too. Sophia Lee's novel *The Recess* (1785) is the story of twin sisters, Matilda and Ellinor, daughters of Mary Queen of Scots by a secret marriage to the Duke of Norfolk, who grow up in a secret recess, hidden as children from the overworld of politics and recorded facts. As women, they emerge into history's arms, so to speak: Matilda marries and has a daughter by Robert Dudley, Earl of Leicester and favorite of Queen Elizabeth; Ellinor falls into requited love with Robert Devereux, Earl of Essex and favorite of Queen Elizabeth. The sisters say they are devoted to each other. But under closer examination, it is rather disconcerting to observe just how unsisterly *The Recess* appears to be. From early in the narrative, Matilda's self-consciousness seems to translate seamlessly into self-satisfaction: "Shall I confess my vanity?

When I looked in the glass, I did not think I should be neglected, even at court . . . The clearness of my complexion, and the delicacy of my features, left me no equal, but my sister."[19] Ellinor, it turns out, is to blame for their mother's death: "Lovely, ill-fated sister," Matilda apostrophizes a letter, "it was you then who accelerated our hapless mother's death! . . . I plainly perceive my sister indiscreetly wore the duplicate proof of our birth . . . while mine is yet treasured in the secret cabinet at Kenilworth" (134). Matilda also manages to sit passively by as her best friend, Rose Cecil, commits suicide. Matilda's narrative is interrupted by Ellinor's, which rather flatly contradicts much of what Matilda thinks and says. Matilda's aunt kills Leicester; Matilda's daughter deceives her and dies poisoned because of adultery.

Domestic enemies indeed. Happy families may wait as models in the margins of eighteenth-century novels, but in the center of the text, beware the heart of domesticity.

Haunted houses

> Whole Streets seem'd to be desolated, and not to be shut up only, but to be emptied of their Inhabitants; Doors were left open, Windows stood shattering with the Wind in empty Houses, for want of People to shut them.
> Daniel Defoe, *A Journal of the Plague Year* (1722)[20]

So writes "H. F.," a London saddler caught in the 1665 Great Plague, which claimed "An Hundred Thousand Souls" (238), emptying the city, destabilizing its meanings. *A Journal of the Plague Year* is a historical novel that explores what happens when the familiar world becomes unutterably strange and there is no such thing as a reliable sign. A number of eighteenth-century novels might be called novels of haunting, in that they reflect the ordinary world as suddenly unfamiliar, its regular inhabitants "unseen or immaterial visitants" (*Oxford English Dictionary*, "to haunt"):

> Passing thro' *Token-House-Yard* in *Lothbury*, of a sudden a Casement violently opened just over my Head, and a Woman gave three frightful Skreetches, and then cry'd, *Oh! Death, Death, Death!* in a most inimitable Tone, and which struck me with Horror and a Chilness, in my very Blood. There was no Body to be seen in the whole Street, neither did any other Window open; for People had no Curiosity now in any Case; or could any Body help one another; so I went on to pass into *Bell-Alley*. (79)

For H. F. and the world of plague-stricken London, voices have no bodies and too many bodies are silent.

In Ann Radcliffe's gothic classic, *The Mysteries of Udolpho* (1794), as Terry Castle has shown, it is not so much the dark brooding castle that haunts the text, but the "supernaturalization of everyday life,"[21] the uncanny (or *unheimlich*) aspects of the warm everyday world of Emily St. Aubert's home in France, La Vallée. Her beloved Valancourt, never much of a hero in the grand scheme of things, is someone she never manages to recognize: she frequently mistakes him for someone else (the villain Montoni, suggestively enough);[22] she fancies someone in the shadows near the fishing-house and she shrieks – it turns out to be Valancourt: "I have haunted this place," he explains (151–152). As Castle puts it, "to love in the novel is to become ghostly oneself" (124). That ghostliness itself suggests some ambivalence, a "you're not quite real to me." Valancourt rather ungallantly turns Emily into a ghost when they are forced to separate: "I shall look, and cannot see you; shall try to recollect your features – and the impression will be fled from my imagination; – to hear the tones of your voice, and even memory will be silent!" (154). Throughout her time imprisoned in the castle of Udolpho, Emily thinks the mysterious music is a sign of Valancourt's presence; it is not. And even at the end, when they are together and reconciled, Valancourt is difficult to recognize (667).

But it is not just Valancourt. When Emily returns home to La Vallée after her father's death, the novel spends significant space on the transformation of the interior. As an interior, it is occupied – its objects determined, its contours shaped – first by the father:

> Not an object, on which her eye glanced, but awakened some remembrance, that led immediately to the subject of her grief. Her favourite plants, which St. Aubert had taught her to nurse; the little drawings, that adorned the room, which his taste had instructed her to execute; the books, that he had selected for her use, and which they had read together; her musical instruments, whose sounds he loved so well, and which he sometimes awakened himself – every object gave new force to sorrow ... There was an arm chair, in which he used to sit; she shrunk when she observed it, for she had so often seen him seated there, and the idea of him rose so distinctly to her mind, that she almost fancied she saw him before her.   (94–95)

St. Aubert, even in memory, owns and fills up every bit of space, historically and metaphorically. But then: "She walked slowly to the chair, and seated herself in it" (95). Emily seating herself in her father's chair on that first day is just the first small gesture of a larger reappropriation, as she quietly seats herself in his patriarchal position. In time, "she could bear to read the books she had before read with her father; to sit in his chair in the library – to watch the flowers his hand had planted – to awaken the tones of that instrument his fingers had pressed, and sometimes even to play his favourite air" (99). The verbs, and then the objects, become hers. Ownership of this domestic interior and these domestic objects has been reversed; Emily makes herself at home. In some cases, domesticity requires an exorcism.

The eighteenth-century novel was very interested in the eighteenth-century house, and the domestic narratives occurring inside it. Amanda Vickery points out that "women's history has long viewed home as a container of women, especially of middle-class women – a doll's house, a gilded cage, a suffocating prison" (3). But that is a blinkered view. The house is far too complicated a structure, with meanings in windows and corners and stairways and doors, in parlors and dining-rooms and bedchambers and halls, in patterns and textures and *objets d'art*, in the small gestures of social space.

We might set down the image of Emily sitting in her father's chair as a metonym for the gestures and furnishings and behaviors of domesticity in the eighteenth-century novel. Between the sixteenth and the eighteenth centuries, as Daniel Roche argues, the chair "conquers the social space."[23] Robinson Crusoe made a table and a chair, and so could begin his journal. Pamela finds a corner, first in her late lady's dressing-room, and then in her own closet, to write her epistolary story. Sir Charles Grandison pulls up a chair between his late father's mistress and his unforgiving sisters, and so (like Lord Orville and his chair) changes radically for the better the social temperature in the room (364). In Jane Austen's *Pride and Prejudice* (1797, 1813), Mr. Darcy realizes he has pulled his chair too interestedly close to Elizabeth Bennet, and hastily slides back. In the same novel, Elizabeth approves her friend Charlotte's domestic seating arrangements with her husband Mr. Collins, with the women sitting in a backwards-facing room – to avoid Mr. Collins. And in *Tristram Shandy* Sterne compresses the whole of human sensibility in one small domestic gesture, as Uncle Toby, "rising from his chair, and going a-cross the room," lifts up the sash to release a fly: "go poor Devil, get thee gone, why should I hurt thee? – This world surely is wide enough to hold both thee and me."[24] The spaces of home, for better or for worse, are the spaces of narrative; the narratives of home are the preoccupations of male and female characters, male and female novelists, male and female readers. As novels are inhabited spaces, they bear, in Bachelard's words, "the essence of the notion of home"; they open up for us the many corners of inhabited life.

Notes

1. Amanda Vickery, *Behind Closed Doors: At Home in Georgian England* (New Haven, CT: Yale University Press, 2009), p. 3.

2. Gaston Bachelard, *The Poetics of Space*, trans. Maria Jolas (Boston, MA: Beacon, 1969), p. 5.

3. Susan Fraiman, "Shelter Writing: Desperate Housekeeping from *Crusoe* to *Queer Eye*," *New Literary History* 37: 2 (2006), 341–359, 341. See also Pat Rogers, "Crusoe's Home," *Essays in Criticism* 24: 4 (1974), 375–390.

4. Daniel Defoe, *Robinson Crusoe*, ed. J. Donald Crowley (Oxford University Press, 1972, 1998), pp. 68–69.

5. Samuel Richardson, *Pamela*, ed. Thomas Keymer and Alice Wakely (Oxford University Press, 2001), p. 126.

6. Samuel Richardson, *Sir Charles Grandison*, ed. Jocelyn Harris, 3 vols. (London: Oxford University Press, 1972), vol. II, p. 269.

7. Susan Stewart, *On Longing: Narratives of the Miniature, the Gigantic, the Souvenir, the Collection* (Durham, NC and London: Duke University Press, 1993), p. 28.

8. Pages 117–118 have been adapted from Cynthia Wall, *The Prose of Things: Transformations of Description in the Eighteenth Century* (University of Chicago Press, 2006).

9. Samuel Johnson, *The Rambler* (10th edn, London, 1784), p. 21 (Saturday, March 31, 1750).

10. John Bunyan, *The Pilgrim's Progress*, II (1684), ed. Cynthia Wall (New York: W. W. Norton, 2009), p. 144.

11. Henry Fielding, *Tom Jones*, ed. Sheridan Baker (2nd edn, New York: Norton, 1995), pp. 10, 92.

12. Oliver Goldsmith, *The Vicar of Wakefield*, ed. Arthur Friedman (Oxford University Press, 1974, 2006), p. 9.

13. Clara Reeve, *The Old English Baron*, ed. James Trainer (Oxford University Press, 2003), p. 36.

14. Frances Burney, *Evelina*, ed. Edward Bloom (Oxford University Press, 2002), p. 280.

15. John Cleland, *Memoirs of a Woman of Pleasure*, ed. Peter Sabor (Oxford University Press, 1985, 1999), p. 48.

16. Sarah Scott, *A Description of Millenium Hall and the Country Adjacent*, ed. Jane Spencer (New York: Penguin Books, Virago Press, 1986), p. 13.

17. Samuel Richardson, *Clarissa, or, The History of a Young Lady*, ed. Angus Ross (Harmondsworth: Penguin, 1985, 2004), p. 41.

18. Frances Sheridan, *The Memoirs of Miss Sidney Bidulph*, ed. Patricia Köster and Jean Coates Cleary (Oxford University Press, 1995), p. 83.

19. Sophia Lee, *The Recess*, ed. April Allison (Lexington: University of Kentucky Press, 2000), p. 14.

20. Daniel Defoe, *A Journal of the Plague Year*, ed. Cynthia Wall (London and New York: Penguin, 2003), p. 164.

21. Terry Castle, "The Spectralization of the Other in *The Mysteries of Udolpho*," *The Female Thermometer: Eighteenth-Century Culture and the Invention of the Uncanny* (Oxford University Press, 1995), p. 123.

22. Ann Radcliffe, *The Mysteries of Udolpho*, ed. Bonamy Dobrée (Oxford University Press, 1966, 1998), p. 145.

23. Daniel Roche, *A History of Everyday Things: The Birth of Consumption in France, 1600–1800*, trans. Brian Pearce (Cambridge University Press, 2000), p. 173.

24. Laurence Sterne, *The Life and Opinions of Tristram Shandy, Gentleman*, ed. Ian Campbell Ross (Oxford University Press, 1983, 1998), p. 91.

8

Obscenity and the erotics of fiction

THOMAS KEYMER

Thirty years after publishing *Memoirs of a Woman of Pleasure* (1748–1749), the most celebrated erotic novel in the language, John Cleland was still boasting about its periphrastic delicacy of style. His ornate diction originated in a kind of wager, he told James Boswell, undertaken to demonstrate "that one could write so freely about a woman of the town without resorting to the coarseness of [*L'École*] *des filles*, which had quite plain words." This was a telling contrast, for *L'École des filles*, a libertine dialogue of 1655, had long been a byword for brazen obscenity. Seized and burned by the Paris authorities within weeks of its first appearance, it was also suppressed in London when the publisher of an English translation was fined "for printing divers obscene & lascivious bookes, one called *The School of Venus.*"[1] But Cleland's claim was not only to have transcended, in his elaborate circumlocutions, the most scandalous pornographic writing of the previous century. By eschewing the gross literalism of *L'École des filles*, he had also achieved a sensuality unmatched by the most sophisticated literary bawdry of his own day. The language of the body in *Tristram Shandy*, Laurence Sterne's Rabelaisian masterpiece of 1759–1767, was likewise "too plain," and Cleland had told Sterne so to his face. "I reproved him, saying, 'it gives no sensations.' Said he: 'You have furnished me a vindication. It can do no harm.' 'But,' [I said,] 'if you had a pupil who wrote c– on a wall, would not you flog him?' He never forgave me" (Boswell, *Laird of Auchinleck*, 76; Foxon, *Libertine Literature*, 9–11).

The most likely date of Cleland's conversation with Sterne is 1760 or 1761, though there is no knowing for sure that it really took place. If it did, it is hard to imagine Sterne at the height of his fame being quite so easily silenced, or bothering to bear a grudge against – as Cleland inescapably was by then – a disgraced and struggling hack. That said, Cleland's anecdote is significant for the history of the novel on several grounds. First, it indicates just how central sexuality was as a thematic and rhetorical concern for novelists of the period, before the stricter decorum of the nineteenth century banished eroticism to the coy displacements of the mainstream novel – the strawberry-eating in Hardy's *Tess of the d'Urbervilles* (1891), for example – or to the tawdry underworld of Victorian pornography. Second, the story reminds us how self-conscious novelists were about the most effective register in which to articulate the erotic, as though finding in the representation of sexuality – or in Cleland's words "the creation of sensations" – a special version of the larger challenge they faced as pioneers of the novel. This was to make their fictional worlds imaginatively present for readers. Third, Cleland's story implies a large claim for the originality of his scandalous text: a claim to have broken with the norms of early modern pornography and opened up for the novel, in its handling of sexual experience, a fresh and powerful language of representation. This is a questionable but heuristically enabling claim, and scrutiny of it allows us to trace a mutually animating interplay between the discourses of obscenity and fiction across more than a century.

Cleland was right, of course, to stress the crude directness of early pornographic prose. Behind *L'École des filles* lies the Italian tradition of Pietro Aretino, best known in England for the obscene sonnets he wrote as pendants to the mannerist engravings of *I modi* (1524), the notorious album of sexual positions designed by Giulio Romano. Graphic in every sense, these statuesque "postures" had a vigorous underground circulation, and spawned a progeny gleefully observed by a journalist of 1699 in the bookselling district by St. Paul's cathedral, "where as many smutty Prints were staring the Church in the Face, as a Learned Debauchee ever found in *Aretine*'s Postures."[2] More significant as literary models were Aretino's *Ragionamenti* (1534–1536), a series of erotic-didactic dialogues between women that use their form to explore the arts of the courtesan while also parodying formally comparable texts and practices in higher spheres. Well into the next century, the *Ragionamenti* generated a thriving subgenre of "whore dialogues" in which pornographic elements coexist with skeptical or satirical critiques of the philosophical, political, or religious norms of the day.

This is pornography in the strict etymological sense of "whore writing" – writing about whores; writing that is whorish in itself, proceeding in the same manner toward the same effect – though "proto-pornography" is sometimes preferred for works of this kind, not only because they precede the Victorian articulation of pornography as a category but also because they pursue additional purposes.[3] Thus the pseudo-Aretine *La puttana errante* of 1531, which was to inspire the scurrilous English serial *The Wandring Whore* (1660–1663), combines ribald sexual specifications with jeering anti-clerical satire. A century later Ferrante Pallavicino, whose *La retorica della puttana* (1642) was adapted in English as *The Whores Rhetorick* (1683), was executed in the papal enclave of Avignon not for obscenity but for the more alarming crime of impiety. Dialogue is crucial in all these texts, not only as a means of dramatizing initiation or seduction, or as a discursive parallel to the genital "conversation" of intercourse, but also as a mechanism for interrogating or destabilizing official truths, as sometimes seems the primary impulse.

In this context *L'École des filles* marks a point of transition: not only the emergence of France in place of Italy as the epicentre of pornographic output, but also the emergence of a "pure" pornography, uncomplicated by, or at least no longer subordinate to, the freethinking agenda of intellectual libertinism. This in turn marks the emergence of obscenity as a regulatory category, definable by the historical fact of censorial attention. Stripped of philosophical skepticism and theological heterodoxy, the salacious dialogues of *L'École des filles* "g[a]ve censors nowhere else to look but at sexuality," as one literary historian puts it, "thereby forcing them to learn to censor an area in which their mission did not originally lie."[4] Here was obscenity for its own sake, or for the sake of creating sensations. There is no better witness to the efficacy of *L'École des filles* in this regard than that seventeenth-century Boswell, the indefatigable diarist and lecher Samuel Pepys. Several copies of the French text survived the flames of 1655, and in the following decade Pepys found an imported reprint in a London bookshop, pulling it off the shelf, he reports, as an elegant-looking gift for his Huguenot wife. Instead *L'École des filles* turned out to be "the most bawdy, lewd book that ever I saw, rather worse than *putana errante* – so that I was ashamed of reading in it." Nonetheless Pepys was back in the shop within weeks, "and there stayed an hour and bought that idle, roguish book *L'escholle des Filles*" – a book he now thinks, in a rationale that recurs through the period in more or less tongue-in-cheek form, "not amiss for a sober man once to read over to inform himself in the villainy of the world." The next evening Pepys informs himself to the full, narrating the outcome in an argot that nicely reflects the polyglot origins of early pornography. The evening then ends in a guilty private restaging of the censors' bonfire: "I to my chamber, where I did read through *L'escholle des Filles* . . . for information sake (but it did hazer my prick para stand all the while, and una vez to decharger); and after I had done it, I burned it."[5]

As in France, the censorial authorities in seventeenth-century England were primarily concerned with blasphemy and sedition, and the regulation of obscenity was a piecemeal affair, improvised in response to particular provocations through the mechanisms of common law. No clear statute against obscene publication existed in the Restoration period, or indeed until 1857, though it may have been in view of recent efforts such as *The Wandring Whore* and a partial translation of Aretino entitled *The Crafty Whore* (1658) that the Licensing Act of 1662 rather vaguely prohibited books "contrary to good life or good manners." There is little evidence that this formulation generated actual pre-censorship on grounds of obscenity; and the Licenser and Surveyor of the Press, Roger L'Estrange, who once estimated that 200,000 "Seditious Copies" were printed in the first two years of the Restoration,[6] had his hands full as things were. Yet it is also clear that a temporary lapse of the Licensing Act between 1679 and 1685 (the Act lapsed permanently in 1695) was treated in practice as an opportunity to publish English versions of French pornography, as though licensing had been an obstacle before.

The licensing lapse of 1679–1685 saw publication of *The School of Venus . . . Being the Translation of the French L'Escoles des filles* (1680), *Venus in the Cloister, or, the Nun in Her Smock* (1683, from Jean Barrin's exuberant *Vénus dans le cloître*), *The Whores Rhetorick* (1683, from Pallavicino, with supplements from Aretino), and *A Dialogue between a Married Lady, and a Maid Tullia Octavia* (1684, from Nicholas Chorier's *Satyra Sodatica*). Suspension of pre-censorship did not mean immunity from retrospective sanction, however, and these years also brought prosecutions that began to establish a case-law tradition concerning obscene libel. Printers and/or booksellers were prosecuted in 1680 for *The School of Venus*, 1683 for *The Whores Rhetorick*, 1684 for *Tullia Octavia*, and 1688 for *The School of Venus* and *Tullia Octavia* again (perhaps in new editions).[7]

With their *tarses* and *pintles*, their *firkling* and *swiving*, all these translations are couched in a sexually explicit idiom that has partly dropped from the language. "Plain words" are a feature common to them all, even in cases where the French (or, with Chorier, Latin) originals were euphemistic. Chorier especially was seen in the period as a stylist whose prose could give "a Sort of Merit to Lewdness," but it is clear enough from the one sentence we have from the English text (quoted in the bookseller's indictment of 1688) that little of this finesse survived the translation: "He took his pricke out finding it all wet with my spending, and having wiped it and me, he immediately put it in again and began to thrust with great vigour."[8] This was not just incompetence on the translator's part, but resulted instead from an expressive strategy that we might, however incongruously, connect with the plain-style priorities of Royal Society scientists or puritan spiritual autobiographers in the same era. The method is briskly theorized in *The School of Venus*, in which the worldly Frances sees no need "to describe a Monysyllable by new words . . . For the heat of love will neither give us leave or time to run divisions, so that all we can pronounce is, come my dear Soul, take me by the Prick, and put it into thy Cunt, which sure is much better then to say, take me by the Gristle, which grows at the bottom of my Belly, and put it into thy loves Paradice."

To which, efficiently aroused, the *ingénue* Katy replies: "Your very bare Narration is able to make one's Cunt stand a tip toe."[9]

It was not seditious content as such, Annabel Patterson argues, but the explicit transmission of seditious content, in defiance of informally understood codes of ambiguity and indirection, that provoked political censorship in the seventeenth century.[10] The same may well be true of pornographic writing. In the confrontational literalism of their "monysyllables," the translations singled out for prosecution in the 1680s overstepped a lexical mark that *Venus in the Cloister*, though adding transgressive spice (lesbianism, flagellation) to the plain-vanilla content of other works, kept largely within. More patient of euphemism than *The School of Venus*, *Venus in the Cloister* even carries a mock-dedication to the "Most Worthy Abbess of *Loves Paradice*," pointedly retrieving an idiom rejected in the earlier work. In the text itself, the lead interlocutor despairs of the capacity of any language to capture the thrill of "Amourously Lanching the tongue between the Lips of the Object one Adores" – an act she never performs on a fellow devotee "without being Ravisht into an Extasy, and without feeling through all my Body an extraordinary Titilation, and a certain I know not what, that I cannot express to thee, than by telling thee, that it is a secret Pleasure which spreads it self Universally into all the most secret parts of my self."[11]

When *Venus in the Cloister* was eventually prosecuted for obscene libel, as happened following its 1724 republication by the flamboyant pornocrat Edmund Curll, it was clearly a proxy target. It has sometimes been assumed that Curll's edition (a new translation) was selected for retribution because its voluptuous scenes of lesbian sexuality crossed the line that made heteronormative obscenity tolerable in the period. But Curll's recent biographers have established that state, not gender, politics were the real issue. To be sure, Curll gained more notoriety than any previous pornographer for the effrontery of the output that poured from his "Literatory" in forms ranging from lubricious pseudo-medical treatises to gloating reports of rape and sodomy trials. But he was really being punished for publishing politically damaging revelations by a renegade government spy, and he highlighted the arbitrariness of the case against him by protesting that *Venus in the Cloister* had circulated openly in the 1680s without legal retribution.[12] Also central to Curll's defense was a legal precedent of 1708 that placed corruption of manners, and specifically "bawdy stuff, that reflects on no person," beyond the reach of libel law because – the Dworkin–MacKinnon ordinance being centuries away – it defamed no individual or group. As the judge in this earlier case had ruled, "a libel must be against some particular person or persons, or against the government." Dubious official maneuvers were therefore needed to secure Curll's conviction, notably a pedantic redefinition of "libel" as simply "little book" (*libellus*), and the removal of a judge who swallowed Curll's supplementary defense that *Venus in the Cloister* was in fact a public-spirited satire "to expose the *Romish* Priests, ... and Popish Religion."[13] The paradox is that the decisive legal ruling against obscenity, on which all subsequent cases were based until the Obscene Publications Act of 1959 and its aftermath (the *Chatterley* trial in 1960, the prosecution of *Fanny Hill* in 1963–1964), originated in a cynical exercise to punish a publisher for something else.

When Curll returned to pornography in his last years, he did so in a more euphemistic style. Purportedly the work of Roger Pheukuewell, *A New Description of Merryland* (1740) was the first in a series of ribald, innuendo-laden pamphlets that detailed the lush topography of an eroticized island, an alluring world of opulent labial inlets and luxuriant vaginal creeks. The real author was a member of Curll's literary named Thomas Stretser, who numbered among his aliases *Philogynes Clitorides* (author of *The Natural History of the Frutex Vulvaria* [1732]), and *Leonhard Fucksius* (a learned authority cited in *The Natural History of the Arbor Vitae* [1732]), both these works being tittering burlesques of pre-Linnaean botany that Curll then reissued on the back of *Merryland*. Also included in the series – in a promotional tactic known to the period as "Curlism" – was a bogus denunciation of *Merryland* entitled *Merryland Displayed* (1741); and a reprint of another relic from the publishing window of 1679–1685, *Erotopolis: the Present State of Bettyland* (1684), an obscene parody of Restoration voyage-narrative that was probably Stretser's inspiration. As with earlier pornography, it is important to note the self-consciousness about language on show in the *Merryland* series, especially in *Merryland Displayed*. Here Stretser laments the popularity of his own porno-topia with fashionable ladies, "because (as they pretend) there is not a baudy Word in it." With mock outrage, he deplores the social acceptance of *double entendres* evidenced by the work's reception, "there not being a Page ... without some smutty Allusion, which it seems now-a-Days is not looked on as immodest, nor is any Thing so esteemed, tho' ever so lascivious, but what is expressed in the coarsest, plainest Terms."[14] This also seems to have remained the legal assumption, and Curll was never prosecuted for the series. Periphrastic erotica was tolerable; outright obscenity was not – a situation confirmed soon afterwards by the trial and conviction of several small-time printers and booksellers who were pirating Curllian and related pornography. Among their wares were works such as *Merryland* and *Frutex Vulvaria*, but it was an illustrative supplement of their own (an album of engravings entitled "A Compleat Set of Charts of the Coasts of Merryland"), and reprints of old offenders such as *The School of Venus*, that precipitated official action.

Alongside the development of erotic periphrasis as a strategy for avoiding prosecution, the other factor complicating Cleland's account of *Memoirs of a Woman of Pleasure* as an unprecedented break with the obscene norms of the pornographic tradition is that other novelists had been making this break for almost a century. The phenomenon that Ian Watt famously characterized as the "rise" of the novel is now often seen as a more conscious effort at "elevation," a slow and arduous campaign on the part of novelists to lift the genre clear of its abiding reputation as uncomfortably like pornography in itself. John Milton's disparaging use of the term "amatorious novel" in 1644 and Henry Vaughan's excoriation of "lascivious fictions" in 1655[15] are two examples of an anti-novel discourse that had lost none of its virulence a century later, and in the 1740s the preference of both Richardson and Henry Fielding for "History" as a generic label had everything to do with the illicit reputation of the material then normally designated by the term "novel." The spate of pornography of which *Venus in the Cloister* formed part also generated bawdy novelistic texts such as *Aloisia, or the Amours of Octavia Englished* (1681), an opportunist fiction that strategically confused itself with Chorier's work; and *The London Jilt* (1683), a raunchy picaresque novel which in its subtitle, "The Politick Whore," clearly evoked the Aretino–Pallavicino tradition. The pattern repeats itself in the 1720s, when Curll was a prolific publisher of trashy novellas with titles like *The Amorous Priest* and *The Virgin-Seducer*.

For some, obscene libels and amatory novels were hard to tell apart, and the reputation of the latter is nicely caught when voracious Lady Manlove in Colley Cibber's comedy *Woman's Wit* (1697) borrows "a French novel" from Major Rakish. "Being told there was one deadly smutty page in it, she very discreetly begged him to double it down, that she might be sure to avoid it"; she then returns the book with the offending page "more thumbed and blurred, than the beginning of a schoolboy's accidence."[16]

Exactly how many real readers approached novels in this spirit can only be guessed, but the book trade provided plentiful, and increasingly explicit, opportunities (though some of these are now lost, such as *The History of Don B.*, confiscated and destroyed in 1745, evidently a translation of the clandestine French novel *Dom Bougre* [1741]). Then there was the embarrassment of the sexually fixated ancient novel, which until recently has been treated as irrelevant to modern developments, though very much on the radar for writers at the time. Of greatest interest is the case of Petronius, whose fragmentary, transgressive *Satyricon* was first assembled in its modern form in a landmark Amsterdam edition of 1669. Curll was not yet an apprentice when the first English Petronius appeared in 1694, but one of his earliest ventures was a Latin edition of 1707, and he was probably involved in the much-reprinted *Satyrical Works of Titus Petronius Arbiter* in 1708. Even before these publications, the *Satyricon* was a creative resource for English writers, and among the cleverest pre-Restoration experiments in fiction is Walter Charleton's *The Ephesian Matron* (1659), a sensuous, intellectually elaborate re-reading of one of the bawdy Milesian tales interpolated in Petronius' text. In its original form, the tale is a masterpiece of black comedy in which a famously chaste widow starts off grieving by her husband's tomb, and ends up not only copulating with a passing soldier but also crucifying the husband's corpse (a ruse she devises to save her new lover from punishment for losing another corpse). Though resisting the misogynist moral of the Latin text, which he turns instead into a fable of human endurance, Charleton playfully intensifies the widow's transgression, and even has her make love on top of the coffin. His primary interest is in catching the alluring physicality of her reconnection with life, "her *lips*, swelling with a delicious vermillion tincture, and gently trembling." In this endeavour his prose goes far beyond the original in its lingering evocation of sexual ecstasy, even though this, he concedes with a rueful sense of the transient and ineffable, "cannot be described, so as to be understood by any, but such as feel it, nor those, but when they feel it."[17]

Acknowledgments like this notwithstanding, Petronius continued to stimulate efforts to render sexual experience in language, the extreme case being a work apparently prosecuted at the instigation of Cleland himself, when, diverting attention from his own novel, he pointed to a yet more outrageous publication the same year, "a Pamphlet evidently in defence of Sodomy" that had been "perhaps rather overlooked than tolerated."[18] This was Thomas Cannon's *Ancient and Modern Pederasty Investigated and Exemplify'd* (1749), an impassioned exercise in faux-denunciation that now survives only as quoted in legal records. Clearly the widow of Ephesus was no use for Cannon's purpose, but among his sources was a companion tale from Petronius about erotic awakening, this time involving a boy who, bribed, seduced and at one point more or less raped by his wily tutor, then goes on to exhaust the tutor with insatiable sexual demands. It indicates the difficulties posed by this somewhat dubious fantasy that even Curll, in whose 1708 edition the Pergamene boy becomes a "pretty Lady," sensed a need for circumspection, and Cannon was courting disaster in the reckless, salivating embellishments of his own version. Not content with the faithful gendering of the 1694 translation, in which the boy's tutor recalls pressing "his snowy breasts, that swelling seem'd to meet my hands, and, half smothering him with Kisses, hasten'd to that last and greatest joy," Cannon shifts the passage into a torrid historical present and a frenzied Rochesterian idiom of mutual climax, all of which was solemnly transcribed for the court: "So first I fill my Grasp with his milk white Breasts; presently cleave to him in a Kiss of all Parts; then each fond Wish to one fierce Point contract. My Joys launch into Inexpressibleness: expiring and recovering I rush to expire anew upon the dissolving lovely Dissolver." Somewhat optimistically, the printer of *Ancient and Modern Pederasty* claimed under examination to have accepted Cannon's surface explanation that all this expiring and dissolving "was Design'd to explode the Crime and make it hateful to all Mankind." Cannon's own defense is unrecorded, but it is noteworthy that when publishing an abject recantation a few years later, he did so in code recalling the libertine tradition, as though to pass off his real offense as one of atheism, not obscene libel or atrocious prose.[19]

There is nothing quite as extravagant as this in the home-grown novel before Cleland, but the erotic idiom cultivated between 1680 and 1730 by the so-called "fair Triumvirate of Wit" – Aphra Behn, Delarivier Manley, and Eliza Haywood – presupposes a diverse audience with varying tastes.[20] Embracing both male and female perspectives, and representing erotic writing as an aphrodisiac resource – the use of "amorous Books" as "Preparatives for Love" is a recurring plot device (Haywood, *Secret Histories*, vol. I, 84; vol. II, 34) – amatory novels dominated the emerging market for fiction for half a century. The mode powerfully arises in Behn's three-part scandal novel *Love-Letters between a Nobleman and His Sister* (1684–1687), in which a pervasive vocabulary of seduction, betrayal, tyranny, and conquest links the sexual intrigues of Behn's decadent characters with the conspiratorial Whig politics of the day. Dwelling on the aroused bodies of her protagonists Sylvia and Philander, Behn honed a high-octane style that flows in the next generation into Manley's *roman à clef The New Atalantis* (1709). Here too, adapting the mobile perspective of Behn's multi-voiced narrative form, Manley's text objectifies both male and female bodies, and typically both at once, with voyeuristic fervor. In one typically exclamatory passage, "she clos'd her Eyes with languishing Delight! deliver'd up the possession of her Lips and Breath to the amorous Invader . . . and, in a word, gave her whole Person into his Arms, in meltings full of delight!" Almost inevitably, in a fiction committed to a language of the senses more eloquent than words, Manley's formulations culminate in the inexpressibility trope: "The Duke by that lovely Extasie, carry'd beyond himself, sunk over the expiring Fair, in Raptures too powerful for description!"[21]

One could miss the fact that this overwrought passage leaves Charlot and the Duke no further forward than first base. But this is as far as Manley's language goes at any point, and indeed when Charlot is punitively raped a few pages later, the narration is more elliptical. And though *The New Atalantis* drew journalistic fire for revelling in the depravity it claimed to expose, in legal terms it was the political, not erotic, charge of the work that led to Manley's brief arrest in 1709. Only in later fiction such as *The Power of Love: In Seven Novels* (1720), based indirectly on sixteenth-century French and Italian novellas, and published by Curll, could she truthfully claim to be writing only "amorous Trifles" innocent of seditious implication.[22] It was Haywood in the 1720s who refined the erotic idiom of Behn and Manley into an elegant, fashionable literature that Kathryn King has described as a "sexualized sublime," relentlessly focussed on the physical and psychological transports of love and expressing "the ineffable bliss of sexual ecstasy."[23] Among the most interesting follow-ups to *Love in Excess* (1719–1720), in which Haywood developed this mode, is *Fantomina* (1724), in which a shape-shifting heroine continually reinvents her identity to captivate a fickle lover. One disguise involves an overt replay of the Ephesian matron tale, but the most effective is a plain country dress that overwhelms the genteel Beauplaisir with the thrill of class transgression "till he had ravaged all, and glutted each rapacious Sense." Haywood finally punctures this fantasy of erotic masquerade when, just as Fantomina has "another Project in *Embrio*," she instead falls literally pregnant. In a teasing conclusion that may nod among other things toward the tradition of cloistral pornography, the heroine is abruptly packed off to "a Monastery in France" (Haywood, *Secret Histories*, vol. III, 271–272, 280, 292).

Until recently, literary history has represented the major novelists of the mid-eighteenth century as largely indifferent and immune to the amatory tradition. Privately, Richardson excoriated "the Behn's, the Manley's, and the Haywood's," and he publicly presented his first novel, *Pamela* (1740), as the recuperation of an illicit genre, an antidote to "such Novels and Romances, as have a Tendency to inflame and corrupt."[24] Fielding mocked Haywood as the histrionic "Mrs. Novel" of his comedy *The Author's Farce* (1730), and in *Tom Jones* (1749) he drolly characterizes a rakish fortune-hunter by introducing him "in Bed reading one of Mrs. *Behn*'s Novels; for he had been instructed . . . that he would find no more effectual Method of recommending himself to the Ladies than the improving his Understanding, and filling his Mind with good Literature."[25]

Yet in practice both these novelists were closer to the amatory tradition, and indeed the pornographic tradition, than first appears. Even as he composed *Tom Jones*, Fielding was also turning out salacious potboilers like *The Female Husband* (1746), a catchpenny pamphlet about a cross-dressed, dildo-wielding lesbian fraudster, "Mrs. *Mary*, otherwise Mr. *George Hamilton*," a work selflessly produced to warn the public against "monstrous and unnatural desires."[26] (Fielding frequently lampooned Curll; he also learned from him.) Amatory conventions often lurk in the margins of Fielding's novels, and in *Joseph Andrews* (1742) the interpolated "History of Leonora, or The Unfortunate Jilt" is a colorless imitation of intrigue novels such as Haywood's *The City Jilt* (1726). More often, however, Fielding subjects these conventions to irony and implicit critique, and he targets in particular the air-brushed idealizations and casually legitimized rapes of the amatory mode. One thinks of the burlesque moment when, in *Jonathan Wild* (1743), one of Wild's gangsters ravishes Laetitia Snap, "or at least would have ravished her, if she had not, by a timely Compliance, prevented him," or again, in *Tom Jones*, of rustic Molly Seagrim's failure to look like "a *Circassian* Maid . . . attired for the Grand Signior's Seraglio" when she and Tom head off, unaccompanied by the narrator, to mollock in the sukebind. Here and elsewhere, sex typically happens off stage, in the blank space between paragraphs, or "the thickest Part of the Grove."[27] But Fielding also loads his fiction with outrageous *double entendres*, even if modern readers sometimes fail to hear them. Sophia's muff has recently become a prime exhibit in the burgeoning field of thing theory. But as the innuendos accumulate – "Mr. *Jones*, you will stretch my Lady's Muff and spoil it" – early readers knew exactly what they were dealing with.[28] *Tom Jones* was less a forswearing of indecency than a mischievous test of its limits.

The more complicated case is that of Richardson, who when disparaging Haywood neglected to add that some years earlier his own printing-house had produced several novels for the 1732 edition of her collected works. Not only that; a striking feature of the volumes printed by Richardson, not shared by others in the same collection or by earlier Haywood printings, is their strategic use of printers' ornaments – throbbing hearts, simpering Cupids – to highlight the erotic identity of the text. Then there was the odd coincidence that the friend Richardson used as *Pamela*'s promoter in chief, the charismatic poet Aaron Hill, had been Haywood's mentor and patron two decades beforehand, and may even have been a model for the amiable seducer D'Elmont in *Love in Excess*. It is tempting to suppose that Fielding recognized this incongruous connection when in *Shamela*, his instant parody of 1741, he cleverly rewrote Hill's effusive, moralizing commendations of the novel as a voyeuristic, even masturbatory, response: "Oh! I feel an Emotion even while I am relating this: Methinks I see *Pamela* . . . with all the Pride of Ornament cast off" (*Shamela*, 155). Fielding also places *Venus in the Cloister* and part of *The New Atalantis* in Shamela's personal library, deftly inaugurating a series of attacks on *Pamela* as, for all its moral pretensions, a work of covert erotica. The most strident was *Pamela Censured* (1741), denouncing the whole premise of Richardson's novel as a pretext for pornography, and losing no opportunity to allege local instances of obscene innuendo and *Venus in the Cloister*-style perversion. Worse still, at the height of the *Merryland* craze, *Pamela Censured* was rumoured to be "a Piece of *Curlism*" or "a Bookseller's Contrivance, for recommending the Purchase of *Pamela*," with Richardson himself pulling the strings.

Richardson drew on amatory fiction not only for his plot structure and for local scenarios (Pamela's change into plain rustic dress, with its aphrodisiac effect on Mr. B., is an obvious play on *Fantomina*). He also absorbed, redeployed, and sometimes even outdid the heady lexis of Haywoodian eroticism, most clearly in his monumental *Clarissa* of 1747–1748. Yet he always appropriated amatory conventions with a critical edge. His technique of presenting fictional plots in terms of competing generic assumptions begins to emerge in *Pamela*, where Mr. B. sees events as constituting a kind of novel, and in this context Mr. B.'s assurance to Pamela that he understands "in what manner to wind up the Catastrophe of the pretty Novel"[29] is a fairly blatant threat of Haywoodian rape. For her part, Pamela narrates the story in the style of spiritual biography, the inwardness and piety of her writing implying a constant rebuke to the novelistic insouciance of her assailant. But it is in what Richardson called the "double yet separate" narrative structure of the novel, where the antihero Lovelace engineers an amatory plot and narrates it in amatory style alongside the morally rigorous counter-narrative of his victim, that the technique is given free rein, to powerful ironic effect. Thus Clarissa's realist account of her abduction by Lovelace undermines his Haywoodian fantasy of the same event, which draws on the rhetoric of seduction novels – "She was even fainting, when I clasped her in my supporting arms . . . How near, how sweetly near, the throbbing partners!" – to reinvent the scene as a passionate elopement.[30] Not least through effects of juxtaposition, amatory fiction is redefined here as a mode of casual objectification, while *Clarissa* as a whole becomes, in its patient examination of sexual violence in all its aspects, a sustained critique of novelistic trivializations of rape as matter for pornographic entertainment.

It should be clear by now that when *Memoirs of a Woman of Pleasure* reached print shortly after *Clarissa*, Cleland had much more before him by way of available idiom than the "plain words" of *L'École des filles*, and that a rich variety of ingredients was in place to draw on as he revised and expanded his much earlier manuscript drafts of the novel. The published version is marked throughout by Richardson's techniques of representational immediacy and circumstantial particularity, sometimes justifying his heroine's "minute detail of things," sometimes casting her narrative – "I see! I feel! the delicious velvet tip . . . oh! my pen drops from me" – as a lewd parody of Richardsonian "writing to the moment."[31] Also in play was the ancient novel (Harriet's tale of aquasex draws on *The Pastoral Amours of Daphnis and Chloe*, a 1719 translation from Longus); and Fanny's penchant for peephole voyeurism reworks the "keyhole testimony" conventions of trial reports, a thriving pornographic sub-genre of the period. Cleland's most important periphrastic resource is a set of metaphors from botany and topography that flows from the *Frutex Vulvaria* and *Merryland* traditions of pseudo-natural history, to which he adds a new mock-scientific dimension of his own by playing on recent treatises about mechanism and electricity. A further set of metaphors – Fanny and her fellow prostitutes as "noviciates" or "devotees" (Cleland, *Memoirs*, 92–93) – recalls the seventeenth-century world of cloistral pornography, and in its larger structures of both form and plot – Fanny's intimate narration to a female confidante; her initiation and graduation in sexual experience – *Memoirs of a Woman of Pleasure* modernizes the Aretine tradition of the whore dialogue. Throughout all this the novel is distinguished by a high degree of self-consciousness about its language and the limits of its language. Though capable of delicate painterly evocations – Harriet's breasts "had such an effect on the eye as to seem flesh hardening into marble" (Cleland, *Memoirs*, 118) – Fanny repeatedly falls back on the inexpressibility trope, inviting readers to imagine or figure to themselves beauties, and especially sensations, she cannot describe, or to recognize that some experiences lie "beyond the expression of words, or even the paint of thought" (Cleland, *Memoirs*, 115). Midway through the novel comes an elaborate theorization of erotic language, of the need for the "imagination and sensibility" of readers to supplement it, and of the rhetorical difficulty of steering "between the revoltingness of gross, rank, and vulgar expressions, and the ridicule of mincing metaphors and affected circumlocutions" (Cleland, *Memoirs*, 91).

Cleland evidently expected this ostentatious literariness, and his rigorous avoidance in the narrative of literal obscenity, to exempt him from prosecution. The wheels moved slowly, but he was arrested late in 1749, and at that point urged release of his publisher Ralph Griffiths (and of his printer), who "were deceived by my avoiding those rank words in the work, which are all that they Judge of obscenity by, and made them think the Line was drawn between them, and all danger of Law whatever." The line, however, had moved. It is clear that the content represented, not merely the language of representation, was now the issue. One reason is perhaps that Cleland's state-of-the-art novelistic techniques made this content look more dangerous than in earlier works, and it may be significant that the driving force behind his prosecution was Bishop Thomas Sherlock, an informed and enthusiastic admirer of Richardson's novels. Whatever the cause, the outcome is clear. The perversities that *Venus in the Cloister* had gotten away with in the 1680s – flagellation, homosexuality – became central to the case against *Memoirs of a Woman of Pleasure* in 1749, as they were again when an unexpurgated text was republished in 1963. On the first count, Cleland probably did not help by claiming in mitigation that he had made his flagellant a layman, when his real-life model was "a Divine of the Church of England" – to which he added that the clergy in general were statistically over-represented among purchasers of the book (Foxon, *Libertine Literature*, 55, 54). On the second count, his exposure of *Ancient and Modern Pederasty* was not enough to divert attention from the brief but graphic sodomy scene in his own work, and the various revivals, adaptations, and piracies of *Memoirs of a Woman of Pleasure* over the next few years were all careful to omit the offending paragraphs. By the 1780s even the rarified homoeroticism of William Beckford's *Vathek* (1786) and his manuscript "Episodes of Vathek" was beyond the pale, and Beckford judiciously buried his most transgressive material, notably the love story between Alasi and Firouz, two young princes, in the unpublished "Episodes."

For Sterne, however, tolerance thresholds could be a subject for casual play. From the botched conception that opens the work to the "cock and bull" innuendo at its close, *Tristram Shandy* was sexual through and through, and its bawdy *double entendres* may owe more to the *Merryland* tradition than has been recognized. There is a direct line between Stretser's obscene gags about the genital "*Curtains, Hornworks,* and *Ramparts*" of Merryland and Sterne's teasing play on the language of fortification, from Slop's innuendos about the "curtins and horn-works" of Toby's fortifications, or Tristram's simple recipe for avoiding bawdy: "Scratch Backside out, and put *Cover'd-way* in, – 'tis a Metaphor."[32] But the bawdry of *Tristram Shandy* was always a matter of jest, not risk; and in *A Sentimental Journey* (1768) Sterne's writing modulates into a more delicate, even poignant, mode of erotic suggestion. Playing on the inexpressibility trope that haunts prior traditions in both pornography and the novel, Sterne also passes on to his readers responsibility for obscene meaning, and wittily rebukes them when they transgress. When Tristram writes a chapter about noses he means by the word "a Nose, and nothing more, or less." On the most famous page of *Tristram Shandy*, left blank because the lustful, concupiscent Mrs. Wadman defies description, readers must imagine her beauty for themselves, and draw their own widow of Eboracum (258, 565).

Notes

1. James Boswell, *Laird of Auchinleck, 1778–1782*, ed. Joseph W. Reed and Frederick A. Pottle (New York: McGraw-Hill, 1977), pp. 76–77 (April 13, 1779). For the 1688 indictment against the printer of *The School of Venus*, see David Foxon, *Libertine Literature in England, 1660–1745* (New York: University Books, 1965), p. 11.

2. Edward Ward, *The London-Spy Compleat*, 2 vols. (1703), vol. I, p. 96.

3. The earliest recorded instance of "pornography" in *Oxford English Dictionary Online* is from 1842; earlier usages in French include the title of Restif de la Bretonne's prurient treatise on prostitution, *Le Pornographe* (1769).

4. Joan DeJean, *The Reinvention of Obscenity: Sex, Lies, and Tabloids in Early Modern France* (University of Chicago Press, 2002), p. 83.

5. *The Diary of Samuel Pepys*, vol. IX: *1668–9*, ed. Robert Latham and William Matthews (London: Bell and Hyman, 1971), p. 22 (January 13, 1668), pp. 57–58 (February 8); p. 58 (February 9); p. 59 (February 9).

6. Anne Dunan-Page and Beth Lynch, *Roger L'Estrange and the Making of Restoration Culture* (Aldershot: Ashgate, 2008), p. 194.

7. Foxon, *Libertine Literature*, 9–11; Roger Thompson, "Two Early Editions of Restoration Erotica," *The Library* 32 (1977), 45–48.

8. Chorier is praised alongside Petronius and Rochester in a 1707 source quoted by James Grantham Turner, *Schooling Sex: Libertine Literature and Erotic Education in Italy, France, and England, 1534–1685* (Oxford University Press, 2003), p. 357; for the 1684 indictment see Thompson, "Two Early Editions," p. 47.

9. *The School of Venus* (1680), in *When Flesh Becomes Word: an Anthology of Early Eighteenth-Century Libertine Literature*, ed. Bradford K. Mudge (New York: Oxford University Press, 2004), pp. 44–45.

10. Annabel Patterson, *Censorship and Interpretation: The Conditions of Writing and Reading in Early Modern England* (new edn, Madison: University of Wisconsin Press, 1991), pp. 3–31.

11. *Venus in the Cloister* (1683), pp. A2, 151–152.

12. Paul Baines and Pat Rogers, *Edmund Curll, Bookseller* (Oxford: Clarendon Press, 2007), pp. 155 ("Lewd & Infamous Books"), 208 ("Literatory"), 155–169 *passim*; see also Foxon, *Libertine Literature*, pp. 14–15.

13. Donald Thomas, *A Long Time Burning: The History of Literary Censorship in England* (London: Routledge, 1969), pp. 78 (quoting Judge Powell, *Rex* v. *Read*), 82 (quoting Judge Fortescue, *Rex* v. *Curll*).

14. Thomas Stretser, *Merryland Displayed* (1741), pp. 5–6.

15. In, respectively, the expanded *Doctrine and Discipline of Divorce* (1644) and the 1655 preface to *Silex Scintillans*.

16. *The Plays of Colley Cibber*, vol. I, ed. Timothy J. Viator and William J. Burling (Madison: Fairleigh Dickinson University Press, 2001), p. 186 (III.iv.269–274); an accidence is a grammar textbook.

17. Walter Charleton, *The Ephesian Matron* (1659), pp. 47, 51.

18. Foxon, *Libertine Literature*, 54, quoting Cleland's letter to an investigating official of November 13, 1749.

19. *The Satyr of Titus Petronius Arbiter* (2nd edn, 1694), part ii, p. 13; Hal Gladfelder, "In Search of Lost Texts: Thomas Cannon's *Ancient and Modern Pederasty Investigated and Exemplify'd*," *Eighteenth-Century Life* 31 (2007), 46, 26. Gladfelder writes that the recantation referred to in a later legal document is not known (28), but it clearly exists as the preface ("The Author's Retraction") to Cannon's *Treatise of Charity* (1753).

20. The phrase was coined by James Sterling in a commendatory poem to Haywood: see her *Secret Histories, Novels, and Poems*, 4 vols. (3rd edn, 1732), vol. I, [p. 2].

21. *Selected Works of Delarivier Manley*, ed. Rachel Carnell and Ruth Herman, 5 vols. (London: Pickering and Chatto, 2005), vol. II, p. 44.

22. For Richard Steele's critique in the *Tatler*, see no. 74 (September, 29 1709).

23. Kathryn R. King, "New Contexts for Early Novels by Women: The Case of Eliza Haywood, Aaron Hill, and the Hillarians, 1719–1725," in *A Companion to the Eighteenth-Century English Novel*, ed. Paula R. Backscheider and Catherine Ingrassia (Oxford: Blackwell, 2005), p. 265.

24. *Selected Letters of Samuel Richardson*, ed. John Carroll (Oxford: Clarendon Press, 1964), pp. 46–47, n.173.

25. Henry Fielding, *Tom Jones*, ed. Martin C. Battestin and Fredson Bowers (Oxford: Clarendon Press, 1974), p. 530.

26. Henry Fielding, *The Journal of a Voyage to Lisbon, Shamela, and Occasional Writings*, ed. Martin C. Battestin (Oxford: Clarendon Press, 2008), pp. 365, 381.

27. Henry Fielding, *Miscellanies* III, ed. Bertrand A. Goldgar and Hugh Amory (Oxford: Clarendon Press, 1993), p. 109; *Tom Jones*, pp. 256–257.

28. *Tom Jones*, p. 207; see Orbelius, *An Examen of the History of Tom Jones* (1749), p. 46.

29. Samuel Richardson, *Pamela*, ed. Thomas Keymer and Alice Wakely (Oxford University Press, 2001), p. 232.

30. Samuel Richardson, *Clarissa*, ed. Angus Ross (Harmondsworth: Penguin Books, 1985), p. 400.

31. John Cleland, *Memoirs of a Woman of Pleasure*, ed. Peter Sabor (Oxford University Press, 1985), pp. 84, 183.

32. Thomas Stretser, *A New Description of Merryland* (1740), p. 14; Laurence Sterne, *Tristram Shandy*, ed. Melvyn New et al. (Gainesville: University Presses of Florida, 1978–1984), pp. 128, 116.

9

Cognitive alternatives to interiority

LISA ZUNSHINE

What we call the interiority of a fictional character is a cognitive-historical construct. That is, it emerges out of the interaction between our *theory of mind* – our evolved cognitive adaptation for explaining people's behavior in terms of their mental states, such as thoughts, desires, feelings, and intentions – and historically contingent ways of describing and interpreting behavior and mental states. At no point can the cognitive be separated from the historical, although various interpretive systems have considered and continue to consider them in isolation. Thus traditional literary analysis has been mostly unaware of the cognitive aspect of fictional interiority, while some over-zealous evolutionary literary critics pointedly ignore the role of history in literary endeavor. My goal here is to posit an interpretive model that is grounded in the workings of our cognitive adaptation for reading mental states into behavior and that is sensitive to particular cultural preoccupations of a given historical period. Specifically, I show how the eighteenth century's uneasy fascination with hypocrisy and madness informed the writers' intuitive reliance on their readers' cognitive predispositions as they worked to create an illusion of interiority of their socially troubling and personally troubled characters.

The cognitive and the historical

As an introductory illustration of the ongoing interplay between the cognitive and historical, consider a conversation that takes place in Laurence Sterne's *Tristram Shandy* (1759–1767), when Walter Shandy, Uncle Toby, Yorick, and Corporal Trim gather one evening around the fire in Shandy-hall. Yorick has just read out loud a long passage from Rabelais's *Gargantua*, in which Gymnast and Captain Tripet turn somersaults on the croup of a horse, and now Walter prepares to share with the company his own manuscript, *Tristrapaedia*:

I have advanced nothing in *Tristrapaedia*, but what is as clear as any one proposition in *Euclid*. – Reach me, *Trim*, that book from off the scritoir: – it has often been in my mind, continued my father, to have read it over both to you, Yorick, and to my brother Toby, and I think it a little unfriendly in myself, in not having done it long ago: – shall we have a short chapter or two now, and a chapter or two thereafter, as occasions serve; and so on, till we get through the whole? My uncle Toby and Yorick made obeisance which was proper; and the corporal, though he was not included in the compliment, laid his hand upon his breast, and made his bow at the same time. – The company smiled. *Trim*, quoth my father, has paid the full price for staying out the *entertainment*. – He did not seem to relish the play, replied Yorick – 'Twas a Tom-fool-battle, an' please your reverence, of captain *Tripet's* and that other officer, making so many summersets, as they advanced; – the *French* come on capering now and then in that way, – but not quite so much.

My uncle Toby never felt the consciousness of his existence with more complacency than what the corporal's, and his own reflections, made him so at that moment; – he lighted his pipe, – Yorick drew his chair closer to the table, – Trim snuff'd the candle, – my father stir'd up the fire, – took up the book, – cough'd twice, and begun.[1]

Why does Trim snuff the candle? We make sense of his behavior by exercising our theory of mind, that is, by attributing to Trim a certain intention: he *wants* to make the flame brighter so that Walter Shandy can see the pages of *Tristrapaedia* better. In fact, we can read an even more complex mental state into Trim's action: he has just had a chance to voice his disapproval of the "battle" described in *Gargantua*, and he is flattered to be part of the discussion, particularly as it seems to draw on his military expertise, even if Walter has not initially paid him the "compliment" of having wanted to read *Tristrapaedia* to him as well as to Yorick and Toby. So by snuffing the candle Trim is not only making the pages more visible for Walter but also signaling his readiness to be included in this conversation and his satisfaction at having his opinion considered and respected by his "betters."

But wait! Are Trim's actions not in fact incomprehensible? If he wants to make it easier for Walter to see the pages of *Tristrapaedia* and also wants to signal that he belongs to this conversation, why would he snuff – that is, put out – the candle? As it turns out, the meaning of the word "snuff" has changed over the last two centuries. For Sterne's contemporaries, "snuffing the candle" meant "brightening its flame by freeing the candle from its excess wick, either by pinching or cutting off its snuff (the part of the wick partially consumed in burning)."[2] This is to say that, prepared as we are to explain the characters' observable behavior in terms of underlying mental states, our explanations can be woefully wrong, if not downright impossible, unless we also know something about the historically contingent linguistic environment in which a given text was written and first read.

And the problem with words changing their meanings as time goes by is, of course, only the tip of our interpretive iceberg. To get a fuller picture of the feelings animating the behavior of the protagonists in this passage, we have to know, for example, that the reason Yorick quotes a passage from *Gargantua*, in which Gymnast and Captain Tripet do acrobatics in lieu of fighting, is not to comment on the effectiveness or futility of a particular way of waging the battle – which is how Trim takes it – but to satirize the practices of English "polemic divines" (New, *Tristram Shandy* n. 6). Armed with this literary-historical insight, we begin to appreciate the complexity of mental states underlying the nondescript actions of Toby as he lights his pipe, of Yorick as he draws his chair closer to the table, and of Walter Shandy as he stirs up the fire.

Toby is happy about having humored his own comrade (for it was Toby who, knowing that Trim would enjoy "the description of a battle," invited Trim to join them just as Yorick was about to read the passage from *Gargantua*). Yorick and Walter are sharing a joke about the similarities between the arguments of the "polemical divines" and the antics of Gymnast and Captain Tripet – a joke of which Trim is not aware at all (and they know it), and which Toby appreciates only to a point because he is more happily preoccupied with Trim's satisfaction about voicing his opinion of that "Tom-fool-battle" and about being thus included in the conversation. Finally, Yorick must also be pleased about humoring his host as Walter is about to read "a chapter or two" from his *Tristrapaedia*.

You notice that to make sense of this passage, we speak of Trim, Yorick, Walter, and Toby as endowed with interiority, that is, capable of a rich variety of mental states. This practice of treating fictional characters like real people has been long decried by literary critics, who see it as corrupting discussions both in classrooms and in non-academic reading environments, such as book clubs. With the advent of research in theory of mind, I think it is time for us to admit that we have been fighting a "Tom-fool-battle" of our own (and have been cheating at it, too), to reconcile ourselves to the fact that all of us, undergraduates, professors of literature, and book-club devotees, treat fictional characters as real people, and to focus instead on historically specific strategies used by writers intuitively to exploit this "weakness" of their readers.

To clarify the role played by theory of mind (also known as "mind-reading" – clumsy terms both) in our perception of fictional characters, consider this. After a certain age, people "cannot turn off their mind-reading skills even if they want to. All human actions are forevermore perceived to be the products of unobservable mental states, and every behavior, therefore, is subject to intense sociocognitive scrutiny."[3] The results of this "scrutiny" are far from perfect: we misread and misinterpret minds all the time, and we remain subject to people's conscious and subconscious manipulation of our perception of their mental states. Still, flawed as our mind-reading is, it is the default way by which we construct and navigate our social environment. When theory of mind is impaired – as it appears to be with the autism-spectrum condition – we are faced with social challenges of a different order of magnitude.[4]

So important is mind-reading for our species, that, at least on some level, we do not distinguish between attributing states of mind to real people and attributing them to fictional characters. Figuring out what an attractive stranger encountered by a fictional protagonist in a bookshop is thinking feels almost as important as figuring out what a real-life attractive stranger is thinking as she looks us in the eye and holds forth on how she enjoyed reading the book that we currently have in our hands. Thus the pleasure afforded by following various minds in fictional narratives is to a significant degree a *social* pleasure – an illusory but satisfying confirmation that we remain competent players in the social game that is our life. (Not surprisingly, patients with theory-of-mind deficits, such as those with autism-spectrum condition, exhibit a striking lack of interest in stories about people, both fictional and non-fictional.)[5]

Talking about fictional characters as if they were real people is thus not a sign of the lack of readerly sophistication, but simply the reflection of the fact that the same cognitive adaptations that evolved to process information about the mental states of real people also process information about the mental states of fictional characters. Literary scholars are just as guilty of this offense as are lay readers. The main difference between "us" and "them" is that we can consciously adjust certain aspects of our mind-reading when we deal with a work of fiction, indeed may *enjoy* adjusting them, as a function of our personal mind-reading idiosyncrasies translated into the career of literary critic.

That is, on the one hand, we attribute "real" mental states to characters with the same gusto as do our undergraduates. Think: when five minutes ago, you read the sentence, "Reach me, *Trim*, that book from off the scritoir," did you really pause to remind yourself that you were dealing with a fictional construct, "Walter Shandy," who is portrayed so as to create an impression in the reader that he "wants" (well, actually "he" should be in quotation marks, too) another fictional construct, "Corporal Trim," to "do" something for "him"? Probably not. More likely, you simply skimmed over that sentence without even noticing that your theory-of-mind adaptations interpreted it as "Walter wants Trim to get him the book off the scritoir" – which is almost exactly the same kind of work that these adaptations would have performed had I, in your hearing, asked my daughter to reach me a book off the shelf.

On the other hand, more so than lay readers, we are apt at adjusting our mind-reading mode to introduce mental states of other "people" into our discussion of the novel: those of the novel's author, its actual and/or implied narrator, its variously historically situated readers, as well as living and dead literary critics and philosophers. For example, we may ask what was Sterne's own position on polemic divines? Or, what does Tristram, the novel's narrator, *mean* when he says that Yorick "read, or pretended to read" that long passage from Rabelais? What effect does this little interjection – "pretended to read" – have on contemporary readers, and what effect might it have had on Sterne's eighteenth-century readers?

When we ask our students to consider such questions, it may seem that we encourage them to move away from treating fictional characters as real people and train them instead to see the novel as a historically situated artifact that uses a variety of narrative techniques to engage with ideological, aesthetic, and psychological agendas – techniques that may come into sharper focus if we consider them via conceptual frameworks developed by various classical and modern thinkers. And train them we do. Make no mistake, however: the only way by which we can achieve this is by expanding the circle of entities whose minds we read *as if they were real people*.

Not only do we ourselves treat fictional characters as if they were capable of a broad variety of mental states (as real people are) to make sense of the story when we first read it; not only do we casually refer to these characters' and the author's mental states in our subsequent discussions with students; not only do we introduce more "people" into our conversation, such as Freud, Derrida, and Marx, and talk about them as if we know what they would think about the text; but we also cannot produce a single interpretation of the text without constructing ever more elaborate and/or surprising attributions of thoughts, feelings, and intentions. Every single one of our exegeses involves attribution and interpretation of mental states, and none of our classroom conversations or scholarly publications would be practicable if we had to stop every minute and issue a disclaimer to the effect that we *seem* to be talking about real minds but we are really talking about fictional constructs.

What all this adds up to is that the cognitive perspective on fictional interiorities commits us, *more than any other theoretical perspective*, to historicizing. As an evolved cognitive adaptation that has been with us for hundreds of thousands of years, theory of mind does not change across the whole species just because a particular group of readers (say, eighteenth-century European middle-class devotees of sentimental novels, or twenty-first-century North American professors of literature and their students) happen to be in an environment that calls for a particularly elaborate attribution and interpretation of fictional minds. It follows then that a literary text from the tenth century BC (such as parts of the Hebrew Bible), a novel written between the second and third centuries AD (such as Heliodorus' *Aithiopika*), a Norse saga from the fourteenth century AD, Sterne's *Tristram Shandy*, and Zadie Smith's *On Beauty* all feed and stimulate the same enduring socio-cognitive need to attribute and interpret mental states. But if they *all* do it, we have no way of explaining what feels like a very palpable difference in the representation of fictional interiority origi-nating in different time periods and cultures. That is, we have no way of explaining it unless we focus on specific historical circumstances that encour-age – or discourage! – the production and consumption of different modes of mind-reading in fictional representations.

In the rest of this chapter, I discuss one strategy used by eighteenth-century writers to construct fictional interiority, a strategy that both reflected and critiqued the period's obsession with the mutability of the social self. The reason that I had to start with the long introductory discussion on theory of mind is that we can now talk about this particular strategy without making it bear more interpretive weight than it ought to bear. That is, instead of saying that the advance of this strategy heralded a broader cultural shift in the perception of subjectivity (a kind of claim routinely made by scholars of every literary period), I can advance a more modest and defensible argument. I can say that this strategy was just one of many ways in which eighteenth-century writers intuitively built on their readers' evolved cognitive eagerness to read mental states into behavior; that they did it by negotiating some of the period's immediate cultural preoccupations; and that, by developing a new way of representing fictional interiority, they did not change their readers' mind-reading *adaptations* (which, again, had remained constant for hundreds of thousands of years and will remain so for the foreseeable future), but they certainly changed their readers' mind-reading *environment*, as well as that of future readers and writers. The cognitive-historicist frame-work advocated by this chapter presupposes a constant give-and-take among the text, the culture, and the mind, with interiority as a moving target, a shifting overlap of all three.

Multiple mental states

Although as inveterate mind-readers we need only a mere whiff of a cue to see a mental state behind a behavior, it has been argued that one particularly socio-cognitively satisfying pattern of fictional mind-reading involves interaction among three mental states (no matter how many physical bodies these mental states may represent: one, two, or a crowd of a hundred and fifty). Eighteenth-century writers explored a wide variety of social situations that allowed for such mental triangulations. In constructing such situations, however, they had to hierarchize the cognitive complexity of their characters; that is, they had to decide which characters should be able to represent more mental states than others.

For example, when the title protagonist of Eliza Haywood's *Fantomina* (1724), who impersonates different women to keep up the interest of her lover, Beauplaisir (who does not know that all of his mistresses are actually the same person), receives two letters from Beauplaisir – one addressed to "Widow Bloomer," his fresher conquest, whom he is eager to see immediately, another to his by now "stale" passion, "Fantomina," whom he needs to put off for the sake of the Widow and to whom he thus lies about being busy – the mind-reading dynamics of the scene put her at the apex of its mental triangulation:

> Traytor! (cry'd she) as soon as she had read [both of Beauplaisir's letters], 'tis thus our silly, fond, believing Sex are serv'd when they put Faith in Man: So had I been deceiv'd and cheated, had I like the rest believ'd, and sat down mourning in Absence, and vainly waiting recover'd Tendernesses ... But I have outwitted even the most Subtle of the deceiving Kind, and while he thinks to fool me, is himself the only beguiled Person.[6]

Observe that Beauplaisir imagines two mental states – his own and the presumably fooled Fantomina – whereas Fantomina imagines three: her own, Beauplaisir's as he imagines the fooled Fantomina, and the presumably fooled Fantomina's. To put it differently, she is capable of representing the feelings of Fantomina as represented by Beauplaisir, thus engaging in what cognitive scientists call a third-level cognitive *embedment*. If we correlate fictional interiority with the ability to embed multiple mental states we begin to see the workings of the narrative mechanism that endows some characters with "more" interiority than others. At least for now, Fantomina is on top of the cognitive "food chain," and as such she is the most interesting character in the story.

The writer's intuitive decision about which of her characters will carry on complex mind-reading embedments and which will have to settle for simpler ones can be informed by considerations of social class, of gender or race, or of any other parameter reflecting the current ideological investments of the society. The characters not capable of representing anybody's mental states except their own, such as Lady Bertram from Jane Austen's *Mansfield Park* (1814), may come across as stupid or flat, their interiority at the lowest ebb; but the characters capable of representing multiply embedded mental states may come across as peculiarly misguided, betrayed as it were by their cognitive complexity into ethically questionable or socially debilitating behavior. It seems that readers' perception of interiority imposes a cost on a fictional character, though the exact form of this cost is figured on a case-by-case basis, reflecting, among other things, specific cultural preoccupations of the moment. In what follows, I consider two models of eighteenth-century fictional interiority – one constructed specifically via the characters' capacity for embedding multiple mental states, and another constructed via their capacity for considering perspectives differing from their own – and discuss the costs associated with each model.

Hypocrisy

Eighteenth-century anxiety about the mutability and endless performativity of the self, and the resulting uneasy view of hypocrisy as a social glue, are well-established topics in recent scholarship, explored in such studies as Blakey Vermeule's *The Party of Humanity: Writing Moral Psychology in Eighteenth-Century Britain* (2000), Patricia Meyer Spacks's *Privacy: Concealing the Eighteenth-Century Self* (2003), and Jenny Davidson's *Hypocrisy and The Politics of Politeness* (2004). From the cognitive perspective espoused by this chapter, hypocrisy is a quintessential mind-reading phenomenon: an endeavor to subtly convince another person that she knows your thoughts and feelings and that these thoughts and feelings are congenial to her own. It presupposes a third-level mental embedment ("I know that you like X, so I *want* you to *think* that I *like* X, too") and as such presents a particularly inviting subject for fictional and non-fictional explorations.

Looking at how the eighteenth century treated its hypocrites, one gets an impression that non-fictional discourses were more forgiving than fictional ones. Thus *The English Theophrastus* (1702) refuses to pass judgment on hypocrisy, admitting instead with world-weary resignation that not only is sincerity a particularly insidious performance of openness ("Half-witted People can never be sincere ... Sincerity ... is only a more cunning and shrewd sort of Dissimulation, to insinuate our selves into the Confidence of other People"), but also that every social interaction involves mutual manipulation ("All Men [strive to] appear what they have a mind to be taken for: So that we may say, That the World is made up of nothing but formal Countenance and Shews.").[7]

The Earl of Chesterfield's *Letters to His Son* (1774) is a heartfelt glorification of social hypocrisy. Its author frankly delights in his capacity for adapting to the minds of others and fervently wants his son to learn this social grace. Thus describing his younger self: "My passion for pleasing was so strong (and I am very glad it was so), that I own to you fairly, I wished to make every woman I saw in love with me, and every man I met admire me."[8] On strategies of making people like you: be attentive to small things that they value, for "attention to such trifles flatters self-love much more than greater things, as it makes people think themselves almost the only objects of your thoughts and care" (Chesterfield, *Letters to His Son*, vol. I:29). On pleasing people whose opinion you, in fact, despise:

> As women are a considerable, or at least a pretty numerous part of company; and as their suffrages go a great way toward establishing a man's character in the fashionable part of the world (which is of great importance to the fortune and figure he proposes to make in it), it is necessary to please them.

However:

> The man of sense only trifles with them, plays with them, humors and flatters them, as he does with a sprightly forward child; but he neither consults them about, nor trusts them with serious matters; though he often makes them believe that he does both; which is the thing in the world that they are proud of ... [for] being justly distrustful that men in general look upon them in a trifling light, they almost adore that man who talks more seriously to them, and who seems to consult and trust them ...
> (Chesterfield, *Letters to His Son*, vol. II:107)

It is tempting to see the period's fictional narratives as offering a wishful corrective to the successful careers of real-life hypocrites. Think of one assiduous third-level embedder, Blifil, from Fielding's *Tom Jones* (1749), who endeavors to convince every person instrumental to his social advancement that he shares his world view. Already at sixteen, he has "address enough ... to recommend himself at one and the same time" to both his mentors, Thwackum and Square, in spite of their opposing views: "With one he was all religion, with the other he was all virtue." Moreover, by praising Thwackum and Square to Allworthy behind their backs, Blifil not only ensures that they would think that he sincerely values their instructions (for he knows that Allworthy repeats "all such compliments to the persons for whose use they were meant"), but that his uncle, too, would find such panegyrics "extremely grateful," as they so loudly resound "the praise of that singular plan of education" which Allworthy "laid down" for the boys.[9]

A real-life Blifil would have been very likely to succeed in a world in which sincerity was "only a more cunning and shrewd sort of Dissimulation, to insinuate our selves into the Confidence of other People." Fielding, of course, does not let him get away with anything, finally unmasking him in front of Allworthy. True, Blifil does not end up completely destroyed – in fact, when we last see him he is clawing his way back to the top by using his old strategy of pleasing people who matter, such as turning Methodist "in hopes of marrying a very rich widow of that sect, whose estate lies in that part of the kingdom" for which he wants to "purchase a seat in the next Parliament" (869). Still, within the moral economy of the novel he remains an irredeemable villain.

Similarly, Thomas Holcroft's *Hugh Trevor* (1797) contains a panoply of third-level embedders none of whom suffers a complete worldly fiasco, but each of whom is intended to strike the reader as repugnant in his own way: from the reverend Enoch Ellis, whose life is one "necessary endeavor to please"; and the Earl of Idford, who wants to flatter a brilliant thinker and public speaker Mr. *** and thus proclaims – *when that gentleman is present* – that he "would rather be Mr. *** than a prince of blood"; to the Lord Bishop, who, together with his friend, the Dean, sprinkle their dinner conversation with crude obscenities while "hypocritically [avoiding] words which the ear could not endure," so as not to alienate completely the other people present. Hugh himself has to learn not to be "too eager in [his] thirst of approbation," a thirst which leads him, among other things, to such repulsive displays of hypocrisy as complimenting the bishop on his cathedral sermon (which Hugh himself wrote, but "his lordship" shamelessly passed for his own and, worse yet, completely mangled by his "spiritless" delivery, "thick" voice, and "ridiculous" cadences).[10]

It seems, in other words, that eighteenth-century fictional characters who practice third-level cognitive embedment for the purposes of social elevation get condemned as hypocrites and judged harshly, as opposed to characters who demonstrate an acute awareness of other people's mental states – which also frequently calls for a third-level mental attribution – but have no worldly ambitions and thus refuse to manipulate others by pretending that they share their feelings (e.g. Tom Jones himself, as well as Turl and Mr. Evelyn from *Hugh Trevor*). The novels' distaste for the mind-reading pattern (i.e. Theophrastian "sincerity" and Chesterfieldian "graces") that in real life could indeed be rewarded by social advancement is quite striking. Cognitive construction of fictional interiority becomes an ideological endeavor, enabling what John Richetti sees as the "deeply critical" view of "more traditionalist authors such as Fielding" of the "emerging modern self and the new kind of society that encourages it."[11]

Madness

Madness attracted and repelled eighteenth-century readers and writers as strongly as did hypocrisy, and as such it has received sustained attention from modern scholars, from Michel Foucault (*Madness and Civilization*, 1965) and Max Byrd (*Visits to Bedlam: Madness and Literature in the Eighteenth Century*, 1974) to Clement Hawes (*Mania and Literary Style: The Rhetoric of Enthusiasm from the Ranters to Christopher Smart*, 1996) and Allan Ingram and Michelle Faubert (*Cultural Constructions of Madness in Eighteenth Century Writing*, 2005). To consider representations of madness from the cognitive perspective taken by this chapter, we may ask to what extent madness was correlated with particular constructions of fictional interiority. To put this differently, is there a cognitive method to eighteenth-century madness, that is, will we understand better at least some forms of it if we adapt the vocabulary of mind-reading and embedded mental states?

One distinguishing feature of many eighteenth-century mad (or just eccentric in ways that strike observers as mad) fictional characters is their misplaced mind-attribution. That is, they attribute mental states either to entities that do not have any (such as natural phenomena) or to entities whose mental states should matter little or not at all in one's everyday life (such as other fictional characters or imaginary creatures). What is interesting about this "mad" behavior is that it builds on an essential aspect of our mind-reading endowment, which, under normal conditions, is crucial for our social functioning: namely, the capacity for being aware of other people's perspectives, particularly when they differ from our own.

In fact, deficits of this capacity manifest themselves early enough in a child's development to be used as the ground for diagnosing autism. The test administered to four-year-olds (the age of four being an important threshold in the maturation of theory of mind) involves putting a child in a situation in which she has to demonstrate an understanding that other people may entertain false beliefs, that is, that they may believe that something that she *knows* to be the case is not so. Neurotypical children pass this "false belief" test, while children with autism-spectrum condition generally do not.

Hence one strategy for creating the illusion of interiority of fictional characters is to have them be aware of differing perspectives of the same subject. Maria Edgeworth uses this strategy in the opening paragraph of her

Castle Rackrent (1800). The novel's narrator, Thady Quirk, tells us how different people in and out of the "family" view *him*: he is "honest Thady" to some, "old Thady" to others, "poor Thady" to yet others, Thady-to-be-disregarded to his own son, and "true and loyal" Thady in his own eyes:

> Having out of friendship for the family, upon whose estate, praised be Heaven! I and mine have lived rent free time out of mind, voluntarily undertaken to publish the Memoirs of the Rackrent Family, I think it is my duty to say a few words, in the first place, concerning myself. – My real name is Thady Quirk, though in the family I have always been known by no other than *'honest Thady'* – afterwards, in the time of Sir Murtagh, deceased, I remember to hear them calling me *'old Thady;'* and now I'm come to *'poor Thady'* – for I wear a long great coat winter and summer . . . to look at me, you would hardly think *'poor Thady'* was the father of attorney Quirk; he is a high gentleman, and never minds what poor Thady says, and having better than 1500 a-year, landed estate, looks down upon honest Thady, but I wash my hands of his doings, and as I have lived so will I die, true and loyal to the family.[12]

Note that, defined in terms of the character's ability to consider different perspectives, fictional interiority does not necessarily translate into intellectual sophistication or a heightened capacity for empathy. That is, such a character may still come across as naïve (as Thady does; though some critics also read his naïveté as a clever mask adapted by a manipulative and "self-serving man")[13] or as obnoxiously self-centered. Thus Lady Clementina from Elizabeth Inchbald's *Nature and Art* (1796) is acutely aware of other people's perspectives, yet all she can think of is what all these different people think about *her*:

> If she complained she was ill, it was with the certainty that her languor would be admired; if she boasted she was well, it was that the spectators could admire her glowing health; if she laughed, it was because she thought it made her look pretty; if she cried, it was because she thought it made her look prettier still. – If she scolded her servants, it was from vanity, to show her knowledge superior to theirs; and she was kind to them for the same motive, that her benevolence might excite their admiration. – Forward and impertinent in the company of her equals from the vanity of supposing herself above them, she was bashful even to shamefacedness in the presence of her superiors, because her vanity told her she engrossed all their observation.[14]

In other words, a character's relative cognitive complexity (that is, her ability to embed mental states of numerous other people), which strongly contributes to our perception of her interiority, can be disconnected from her intelligence and, in fact, from any true awareness of other people's states of mind. A character can be an assiduous mind-reader, yet a hopeless solipsist; "neurotypical" as far as her theory of mind goes, yet lacking in empathetic imagination.

She can also be mad. The difference between such characters as Lady Clementina, on one hand, and Jonathan Swift's Gulliver (*Gulliver's Travels*, 1726), Charlotte Lennox's Arabella (*The Female Quixote*, 1752), and Samuel Johnson's Astronomer (*Rasselas*, 1759) on another, is that solipsistic as the first group can be, they seek their reflection in the minds of socially acceptable / sanctioned others, whereas the Astronomer looks for it in the minds that are not "really" there. It is as if their theory of mind was working in overdrive, not discriminating between those whose opinion about them should matter and those who simply cannot have any opinion.

Take Gulliver. It is not just that he has what Michael Seidel calls "an image problem," not knowing "whether he looks good small or big"; "whether features of his face look better symmetrically disposed or awry"; "whether his pathetic body would serve him better shaped like a horse's"; "whether his sounds and smells are as offensive to everyone else as they are to him"[15] – after all, Lady Clementina has a kind of an "image problem" too – the trouble is that he turns for answers to these questions to the creatures who (according to one interpretive tradition)[16] might be mere figments of his imagination: tiny Lilliputians, giants from Brobdingnag, inhabitants of a flying island, and talking horses. It is his reflection in their minds that matters to him – to the exclusion of people whose opinion *ought* to matter. As he puts it in the letter to his Cousin Sympson: "The united Praise of the whole [human] Race would be of less Consequence to me, than the neighing of those two degenerate Houyhnhnms I keep in my Stable; because, from these, degenerate as they are, I still improve in some Virtues, without any Mixture of Vice."[17]

Just so, Arabella from *The Female Quixote* cares deeply about the opinion of phantoms but not about that of her actual acquaintances. In stark contrast to her cousin, Mr. Glanville, who writhes in embarrassment when he imagines what the people whom they meet, such as Sir George, must think of Arabella's odd behavior, Arabella is concerned with how she would look in the eyes of the characters from her beloved Romances; in the eyes of the historians who would come to write the "History" of her adventures; and in the eyes of the future readers of that "History." Thus, upon receiving a letter from Sir George, which, she suspects, contains a confession of love, she debates with herself whether she should read it and thus have her suspicion confirmed, which must necessarily result in her banishing Sir George from her presence forever. No Romance heroine that she can think of would read such a letter, hence *"fearful of transgressing the Laws of Romance*, by indulging a Curiosity *not justifiable by Example*, [Arabella resolves] to return this Letter unopened." Further deliberation on the matter even makes her angry, and she speaks to the letter thus:

> Presumptuous Paper! . . . Bold Repository of thy Master's daring Thoughts! *Shall I not be blamed by all, who, hereafter, will hear or read my History*, if, contrary to the Apprehensions I have, that thou containest a Confession that will displease me, I open thy Seal and become accessory to thy Writer's Guilt, by deigning to make myself acquainted with it?[18]

Finally, the Astronomer from *Rasselas*, convinced that the sun listens "to [his] dictates," passing "from tropic to tropic by [his] directions," that the clouds, "at [his] call," pour their waters, and that the Nile overflows "at [his] command," is not merely attributing mental states to natural events (a phenomenon that cognitive psychologist Jesse M. Bering would see as building on our "existential theory of mind"). He also values the opinion of the nebulous entities who bestowed "this distinction" on him more than that of ordinary people, whose ridicule and incredulity he is prepared to disregard. Thus when he discovers in Imlac, who listens to his story, "some tokens of amazement and doubt," he observes that, "not to be easily credited will neither surprise nor offend [him]; for [he is], probably, the first of human beings to whom this trust has been imparted."[19]

These three cases of irrational mind-attribution are relatively clear cut: as long as Gulliver, Arabella, and the Astronomer privilege the good opinion of phantoms over that of the "real" people, they could be considered mad. (Arabella and the Astronomer eventually "get better" by learning to seek their reflections in the "right" minds.) Other fictional characters who construct their self-image by reading the minds of others walk a thinner line. Members of their social circle may pronounce them insane when they choose to be reflected by the people whose thoughts about them should not matter – because of their class, race, gender, or a particular ideological concern of the moment. After all, a Chesterfieldian "man of sense" (as opposed to what: a man who is silly? Irrational? Insane?) must not really care about what women think of his affairs – he must only make them think that he cares.

Portraying a fictional character as aware of her reflection in the minds of others is one strategy for making us perceive her as having interiority – a *cognitive* strategy. Deciding *whose* minds she should or should not be reflected in is an intensely ideological, culture-specific choice, made first by the writer but then – again and anew – by the reader situated in a particular historical moment. Fictional interiority is thus a social phenomenon, but as such it is always a cognitive-historical construct. Hence to Deidre Lynch's argument that "individuated psychological meanings ... do not come naturally" to readers of any historical period, that they are instead "social productions, objects of contest as well as of collaboration" that "become intelligible in historically specific, institutionally mediated ways,"[20] I would add that they are always cognitive productions as well.

Notes

1. Laurence Sterne, *The Life and Opinions of Tristram Shandy, Gentleman*, ed. Melvyn New (Florida Edition: Penguin Classics, 1998), p. 321.
2. Melvyn New, "Notes," in Sterne, *Tristram Shandy*, 622, n. 3.
3. Jesse M. Bering, "The Existential Theory of Mind," *Review of General Psychology* 6: 1 (2002), 12.
4. See Simon Baron-Cohen, *Mindblindness: An Essay on Autism and Theory of Mind* (Cambridge, MA: MIT Press, 1995).
5. See Jennifer Barnes, "Reading Preferences and Social Cognition," manuscript in preparation.
6. Eliza Fowler Haywood, *Fantomina and Other Works* (Orchard Park, NY: Broadview Press, 2004), p. 59.
7. Abel Boyer, *The English Theophrastus: or, the Manners of the Age. Being the Modern Characters of the Court, the Town, and the City* (London: Printed for W. Turner, 1702), p. 205.
8. Philip Dormer Stanhope Chesterfield (Earl of), *Letters to His Son: On the Fine Art of Becoming a Man of the World*, 2 vols. (Washington, DC and London: M. Walter Dunne, 1901), vol. 1: 31.
9. Henry Fielding, *Tom Jones* (New York: Oxford University Press, 1996), p. 116.
10. Thomas Holcroft, *Hugh Trevor* (Oxford University Press, 1978), pp. 102, 133, 148, 118, 138.
11. John Richetti, Introduction, in *The Cambridge Companion to the Eighteenth-Century Novel* (Cambridge University Press, 1996), p. 8.
12. Maria Edgeworth, *Castle Rackrent* (London: Oxford University Press, 1964), pp. 7–8.
13. Erica Bauermeister, Jesse Larsen, and Holly Smith, *500 Great Books by Women: A Reader's Guide* (New York: Penguin, 1994), p. 39.
14. Eizabeth Inchbald, *Nature and Art* (Orchard Park, NY: Broadview Press, 2004), p. 50.
15. Michael Seidel, "*Gulliver's Travels* and the Contracts of Fiction," in *The Cambridge Companion to the Eighteenth-Century Novel*, ed. John Richetti (Cambridge University Press, 1996), p. 75.

16. For a strong view of Gulliver's madness, see Seidel's Introduction in Jonathan Swift, *Gulliver's Travels* (New York: Barnes and Noble, 2004), pp. xiii–xv; for an opposing view, see Claude Julien Rawson, *Swift* (London: Sphere, 1971), p. 191.

17. Jonathan Swift, *Gulliver's Travels* (New York: Oxford University Press, 2005), pp. 9–10.

18. Charlotte Lennox, *The Female Quixote* (London: Penguin Books, 2006), p. 198, emphasis added.

19. Samuel Johnson, "The History of Rasselas, Prince of Abissinia," in *Samuel Johnson: Prose and Poetry* (Cambridge, MA: Harvard University Press, 1967), p. 466.

20. Deidre Lynch, *The Economy of Character: Novels, Market Culture, and the Business of Inner Meaning* (University of Chicago Press, 1998), p. 9.

10

The novel, the British nation, and Britain's four kingdoms

JANET SORENSEN

In eighteenth-century Britain many of the writings we now call novels functioned as a national form on a number of levels. As a technology of national consciousness along lines Benedict Anderson has described, eighteenth-century novels helped British readers imagine the simultaneous, intertwined existence of fellow Britons. While daily newspapers offered the most widespread and immediate version of printed matter consumed con-currently across vast regions, the circulation of novels throughout the nation and their subsequent reviews, imitations, and sequels, sometimes within the pages of periodical publications, would also underwrite a consciousness of shared cultural touch-points across a geographically diverse English reading population within a roughly contemporaneous time frame. Samuel Richardson's *Pamela* (1740) illuminates this phenomenon in particularly high relief, and contemporary criticism of that bestselling book, whether affirma-tive or oppositional, frequently spoke of its impact on the nation. Within novels themselves writers developed narrative strategies for representing the consciousness of simultaneity that is crucial for imagining the nation – so much so that writers could poke fun at the convention. A discomfited Tristram returns "to my mother" several chapters after leaving her eaves-dropping on his father and uncle through a chink in the door.[1] The intrusive narrator of Henry Fielding's *Joseph Andrews*, having broken off the narration of the near-rape of Fanny to relate the dialogue between a Poet and Player, doubles back to "poor *Fanny*, whom we left in so deplorable a Condition."[2]

While novels helped readers imagine national others – both other readers and multiple characters and their actions in any given moment of time – the traversing of space that structures the plot of many eighteenth-century British novels also helped readers map the geographic contours of the British nation. The extent to which Fielding's novels describe a specifically British space has been the subject of debate, but the relationship between domestic travel writing such as Daniel Defoe's *Tour of the Whole Island of*

Great Britain (1724–1726) and the British novels that set their protagonists in motion on the highways and byways of Great Britain is unmistakable. For the traveling narrators of both Defoe's *Tour* and Tobias Smollett's *Expedition of Humphry Clinker* (1771), it is by their natural resources and locally produced commodities that ye shall know the nation and its regions, near and far. It is the circulation of those goods, in turn, that joins the nation's disparate regions together.[3] While *Humphry Clinker*'s Matthew Bramble might be far less enthusiastic about the goods that have made their way from the nation's coasts to its center – he finds revolting, for instance, London's barrels of green oysters brought in from the coast – like Defoe's traveler, his, and his fellow travelers', epistolary descriptions of the movement of both people and things illuminates a circuitry capable, for better or worse, of tying together the variety found in Great Britain.

The mobile heroes and heroines of eighteenth-century novels witness not only a kaleidoscopic assortment of British places and products but also of British peoples, languages, and manners. *Roderick Random*'s reluctant eponymous adventurer becomes acquainted with a range of Britons and their vernaculars, including the Welshman Mr. Morgan and his "strange dialect," both in his trek from Scotland to London and aboard a Cartagena-bound naval ship.[4] Taking leave of their native Wales, the touring Bramble family of *Humphry Clinker* meets up with the wide array of people and their various dialects – from Irish dancing-masters to proud Scots veterans – that forms a composite picture of eighteenth-century Britain. Their epistolary records of their journey, in turn, register in the novel's pages several regionally inflected Englishes, exposing not just characters but readers to the "strange dialects" to be found across Britain. Moreover, characters' and their immediate families' own mobility explain their slippery relations to regional and national origins. Defoe's archetypal English molls and footpads all have transcontinental connections, and even his iconic Robinson Crusoe has a German father and (anglicized) surname. Humphry Clinker is not quite the "Wiltshire lad" he believes himself to be but is of Welsh origins as the natural son of Matthew Bramble; the Scottish Roderick Random discovers that his father has become a Caribbean plantation owner; the "Scotch poet" of Frances Burney's *Evelina* (1778) has English parents, and the heroine's grandmother Madame Duval has resided for so many years in France that she now denounces "the horrible ill-breeding of the English ... so beastly a nation";[5] the O'Shaughlins of Maria Edgeworth's *Castle Rackrent* (1800) take the English name of Rackrent (and the Protestant religion), while Edgeworth's Lady Clonbrony in *The Absentee* (1812), although born in England, can never convince anyone she is not Irish, and, conversely, her Irish-named niece, Grace Nugent, is revealed by the novel's end to be not Irish but English. All suggest a fundamental fluidity within Britain, often moving beyond its shores, that makes impossible any fixed sense of region, nation, and personal identity.

For some theorists, the syncretic mix of goods, landscapes, people, manners, and languages encountered in the movement through the nation finds its fullest generic incarnation in the novel. It is not only novels' temporal grammar of simultaneity or frequent picaresque movement across space that helps enable national consciousness, but its very formal capaciousness, accommodating and promoting a sense of diversity, especially linguistic diversity, so central to the emerging understanding of the nation as horizontal and inclusive.[6] For Mikhail Bakhtin, the "speeches of narrators, inserted genres, the speech of characters" all make possible the novel's "multiplicity of social voices."[7] Less often noted, but equally important to Bakhtin's analysis, however, is how novels participate in "the internal stratification of any single national language" (262). Novels represent not simply a random range of individual languages and styles but also maintain a "higher unity" (263) that sorts and hierarchizes those languages – and their speakers – into a single national language. Frances Burney's *Evelina* reproduces the language of the "vulgar and low-bred" (140) Branghtons, their spoken "crinkum-crankum"s (137) and their "n't"s (115); but their inferior place in the social order and their distinction from the novel's heroine is pronounced at exactly such moments. Similarly, the outlandish language of *Humphry Clinker*'s Tabitha Bramble and her maid, Win, locates them on the fringes of British society.

Significantly, then, such ordering of language within novels is pointedly not the mere recording of a range of oral languages, but the textual creation of difference and value. Tabitha and Win's language, as analysts have shown, was no accurate representation of Welsh dialect but a fabricated concoction.[8] Representations of such languages might do less to widen the sense of what might be meant by the term "British" and do more, in their very idiosyncratic oddness, to make a newly codified standard English seem itself less strange. Edgeworth's *The Absentee* graphically represents Lady Clonbrony's unsuccessful attempts to speak an English uninflected by Irish dialect. As the novel literally makes visible her dialect-inflected language in print, in such phrases as "the PINT nearest my heart" and "prolong the DEES of courtship," for instance, it also, and perhaps more importantly, makes invisible and leaves unmarked the particular dialect that is standard English.[9]

Naturalizing a hypostatized standard English (a standard English increasingly found in the pages of novels, especially in the words of external narrators) was vitally important for consolidating national consciousness. The very idea of such a language promised to unify an otherwise heterogeneous array of people and places in novels and their readers. But what might be the limit points of such containment? After all, writers of the period, such as David Hume and Oliver Goldsmith, believed that it was in "vulgar English" that the true character of the nation was to be found. And the customs of the people, not polished metropolitan practices, were at the heart of a political rhetoric that founded authority on Britain's ancient constitution.[10] David Hume saw the refinements of cosmopolitanism as a threat to national character.[11] Oliver Goldsmith writes, "the polite of every country pretty nearly resemble each other ... in an estimate of the genius of the people, we must look among the sons of unpolished rusticity."[12] Against a newly established polite standard English and refined elite society stood the colorful manners and languages of motley rustics, unpolished and uneducated, where the true "genius of the people" might be said to reside, representations of which made their way into novels – Thomas Keymer, for instance, has noted Pamela's strong Bedfordshire dialect and low language, and links it to her vulgar origins.[13]

Those daughters and "sons of unpolished rusticity," an unmixed "vulgar English," were, however, something of a vanishing point. The vulgar English, as commentators have noted, had always been a very mixed thing – Defoe's poem *The True-Born Englishman* described the English race as "mongrel, half-bred." More recently Patrick Parrinder writes, "the nation was constituted by successive waves of immigrants," and "it goes without saying that many 'English' writers are of Welsh, Scottish, Irish ... origin" (including Hume and Goldsmith).[14]

Novels' textualization of the rough edges and regional differences not yet polished away by London society were also necessarily moves into the embattled political territory of the relations between the "four kingdoms" (England, Wales, Scotland, and Ireland) and the nation of Great Britain, relations which were especially pressing in the eighteenth century. Scotland and England had only recently, and with difficulty, in the 1707 Act of Union, formed the nation of Great Britain by England's incorporation of the kingdom of Scotland – itself a divided land of Scots and Scots Gaelic speakers – imagined as a persistent threat to British sovereignty. Wales, although it had been incorporated centuries earlier, retained its sense of a discrete society. In the late seventeenth and early eighteenth centuries antiquaries were busy unearthing evidence of Wales's (and Scotland's and Ireland's) separate and heroic past and linguistic pre-eminence.[15] Ireland, not part of the British nation at all, more a colony, until the politically and rhetorically unconvincing union of the two that formed the "United Kingdom of Great Britain and Ireland" in 1800, nonetheless exerted a considerable force within Britain in the eighteenth century. A country that the English had brutalized and partially conquered in a long-shared history, Ireland continued to figure as a mysterious presence, a nearby but largely unknown land, with its own Gaelic language. Many Anglo-Irish ferried back and forth across the Irish Sea – Jonathan Swift, Oliver Goldsmith, Thomas Percy, and Edmund Burke, to name a few.

Early-eighteenth-century non-fiction prose representations of the relationships among the four kingdoms often figured them in embroiled domestic or failed erotic unions. A political tract by Swift had allegorized Ireland, for instance, as an "Injured Lady" whose house "was parted" from her inconstant English lover's "by a river."[16] The Injured Lady characterizes her triumphant rival, Scotland, in turn, as "ill shaped; she hath bad features, and a worse complexion; She hath a stinking breath and twenty ill smells about her" (104). For many a novel character, other Celtic spaces represented something of a black hole, into which they projected ludicrous imaginings. *Humphry Clinker*'s Win Jenkins represents Welsh Britons so ignorant of the world of their compatriots to the north as to imagine it separated from England by a body of water. The English Horatio of Lady Morgan's *The Wild Irish Girl* (1806) admits to conjuring the image of "an Irish chieftain and his family ... seated round their domestic fire in a state of perfect nudity ... broil[ing] an enemy ... whenever the Irish were mentioned."[17]

What formal innovations of the eighteenth-century novel could render visible and even affiliate such unknown entities? A good answer to this question might begin with what Catherine Gallagher has called "the rise of fictionality" in eighteenth-century English writing, and that technique's ability to create characters with "peculiar affective force."[18] In her description of eighteenth-century fiction Gallagher emphasizes not its realism but its oft-neglected overt fictionality; and she perceives an incontrovertible link between the openly unreal, if plausible, quality of fictional characters, their explicit non-existence, and the "reader's experience of them as deeply and impossibly familiar" (356). Readers can know characters with a depth and intimacy not possible in real life and, as Gallagher writes, "because we know their accessibility means fictionality, we are inclined to surrender to the other side of their double impact: their seductive familiarity, immediacy and intimacy" (356). In fictional characters "we seem to encounter something with the layers of a person but without the usual epistemological constraints on our knowledge" (357). To whom but the reader of fiction, for instance, would the intimate details of Joseph Andrews' and Fanny's embrace be available – how

Fanny's "violent Love made her more than passive in [Joseph's] Embraces; and she often pulled him to her Breast with a soft Pressure, which, tho' perhaps it would not have squeezed an Insect to death, caused more Emotion in the Heart of Joseph, than the closest Cornish Hug could have done" (42)? Part of the pleasure of novel reading – literally eroticized in this passage – derives from that dual sense of, on the one hand, the seeming personhood of a character, created through the assignation of a proper name and the depiction of probable experiential details of his or her everyday life (such as vernacular phrases like "Cornish hugs") and, on the other hand, the impossibly intimate knowledge of thoughts and feelings to which the fiction reader gains access. The open fictionality posed by the radically public nature of the supposedly private also induces an affective connection to character.

This sense of fictionality's powers of unreal and affect-generating revelation is doubly loaded in the case of fiction and characters hailing from Ireland, Scotland, or Wales, as they bear the representative weight not only of a fictional person but also of Irishness, Scottishness, or Welshness. Novels might provide what Patrick Parrinder describes as an "inside view of a society or nation, just as it gives us access to personal experiences different from our own" (1). In their portrait of the lives and customs specific to the spaces of Ireland, Scotland, or, less often, Wales, novels suggest that it is there that the foreign, with its enhanced inaccessibility, is located – a foreignness which must also be affiliated. Morgan's *The Wild Irish Girl* figures the rather exaggerated "epistemological constraints on our knowledge" of Ireland in a series of scenes in which the protagonist, Horatio, struggles to get a glimpse of usually obscured worlds and their unwitting and unaware subjects. He writes of how "I approached – removed the barrier . . . and I found myself alone in the centre of this miserable asylum of human wretchedness – the residence of an Irish peasant" (20). Hastening from this scene Horatio goes on to peer into a barn filled with weaving, singing, Gaelic-speaking women, and enjoys a moment of unobserved observation. Not long after this he secures his first images of his soon-to-be beloved, Glorvina: "I climbed, with some difficulty, the ruins of a parapet wall, which encircled this wing of the castle, and which rose so immediately under the casement as to give me, when I stood on it, a perfect view of the interior of that apartment to which it belonged" (52). These scenes dramatize a sense of access to the usually impenetrable; Horatio's presence is not unlike the invisible presence of the reader witnessing the intimacy of Joseph Andrews and Fanny. Although the spell will be broken – a tittering crew of women discover Horatio's presence at the barn; he loudly tumbles off the parapet wall – these initial scenes frame subsequent action, in which

Horatio becomes a full participant, with a sense of being privy to something usually withheld from view.

In *The Wild Irish Girl* Horatio, the English lord banished to his father's properties in Ireland for his youthful excesses, becomes something akin to the narrator of contemporary works of fiction because of his ability to describe the private recesses of another's – an Irish woman's – mind. In an epistolary form that provides realism's details – he writes of such things as the bit of seabiscuit in his pocket that he offers a poor peasant, and the old damask drapery of his bed – Horatio also has the improbable ability to reveal the intimate inner cogitations and feelings of the Irish Glorvina, with whom he falls in love. While Glorvina appears as a prototypically and tantalizingly unknown Irish woman, Horatio can also write with assurance that she is

> deep in the metaphysics of love. She is perpetually awakening ardor by restraint, and stealing enjoyment from privation. She still persists in bringing the priest with her to the drawing-desk; but it is evident she does not the less enjoy that casual absence which leaves us sometimes alone . . . – even though they are enjoyed in silent confusion. (162)

Horatio's narration reminds readers of the authority of the English to represent the Irish, but the narrative technique also promotes the conscious fiction and resulting affective response of making readers party to the private thoughts of an enigmatic and glamorous Irish woman.

Such fictional availability is also at work in Smollett's *Roderick Random* (1748). Here a first-person narrator, Roderick, shares with readers the private musings he does not share with fellow characters: "We traveled half a mile without exchanging one word; my thoughts being engrossed by the knavery of the world" (47). When a Londoner taunts him for the long red hair that marks him as a Scot, and Roderick shares with readers the emotional response he could not reveal to his tormentor or those watching – "I was incensed at this usage, but afraid of resenting it, because I happened to be in a strange place, and perceived the person who spoke to me was a brawny fellow" (63) – the fictional easement recruits readers' allegiance, and not simply to a first-person narrator but also to a Scot who can share his feelings of persecution with non-Scots only in the realms of fiction.

Given the profound inaccessibility of shared meaning, of thoughts and emotions that could be known in another, it is little wonder that fictionality's promise and open ruse of utter knowability holds such power. The fantasy of secret access – to another's intimate thoughts, feelings, and even sufferings – saturates, and is perhaps displaced to, the experience of reading about decidedly alternative spaces in late-eighteenth- and early-nineteenth-century novels. Such moments, despite the realist techniques on which they draw, are also openly moments of fiction. Readers know, and are reminded by the improbably intimate details to which they gain access, that these characters are not flesh and blood. For Gallagher the social pay-off of this fictionality is that it places readers "in the lofty position of one who speculates" (346). In demanding readers' "ironic credulity," novels cultivate the sort of "flexible mental states" (346) necessary to participate in the actions and relations characteristic of modernity. A mind trained in speculation, for instance, could effectively intervene in a credit-based market economy that demanded imaginative projections about paper currency or investment risks.

Such speculation could also be crucial for imagining the nation and one's membership in it. A reader might conjecture about a Scots or Irish person or even occupy his position, but always as a function of open fiction. In this sense the concept of the nation itself and of national affiliation is more a function of "imaginative play," of knowing provisionality, than an essential, enduring certitude – an understanding especially useful in an expanding nation in which one increasingly encountered "foreigners" who must also be imagined as fellow countrymen. Indeed, national identity and the acquisition of local knowledge become a function of fluid identifications and performativity. It is by traveling incognito through various parts of his father's Irish estate that Colambre of Edgeworth's *The Absentee* becomes intimate with the once unknown local space of his father's Irish property, such as specific patches of unfixed road, what the postillion calls "THE BAD STEP" (106). In the disguise that allows access to the otherwise inaccessible, Colambre catalogues the details of everyday life that were to become the stock-in-trade of Walter Scott's regional descriptions, such as the "clean trenchers, hot potatoes, milk, eggs, bacon, and 'kindly welcome to all'" (113) that appear in an Irish tenants' cottage. It is only as a concealed, self-effacing presence that Colambre could witness those details as well as "various schemes for outwitting the agents and defrauding the landlord" (120), his own father. Alternatively, it is by this means and through the quotidian but loaded minutiae of their everyday life itemized by Colambre that he and readers develop affective relationships with those very defrauding renters.

The provisionality of fiction that emerges with the formal realism and new narrative techniques developed in eighteenth-century Britain facilitated what Gallagher calls "affective speculation," imagining what it might be to love someone without formal commitment (346). Gallagher limits her discussion of this ability to marriageable young people increasingly free to choose – and thus needing to speculate about – potential spouses, but the term might be widened to include the all-important eighteenth-century concept of sympathy. Writing about the well-known representation of sympathy in the initial confrontation and subsequent snuff-box exchange between Yorick and the monk in Sterne's *Sentimental Journey*, Thomas Jefferson commented on its power to school readers, whether it was fictional or not: "We neither know nor care whether [he] really went to France, whether he was there accosted by the poor Franciscan . . . or whether the whole be not a fiction. In either case we are equally sorrowful at the rebuke, and secretly resolve we will never do so."[19] The point might be, however, that it is precisely the element of fiction, the speculative, overtly imagined quality of such exchanges, that has an impact upon, and reforms, a reader. Moral philosophers in particular, perhaps from an acute sense, as Irish and Scots, of the need for a model of sympathetic interaction that could imaginatively underwrite greater social inclusiveness, foregrounded the fictional in such relations. The Scots-Irish Francis Hutcheson points to readers' investment in virtuous fictional characters as the very evidence of a moral sense. From the fact that readers care about fictional characters, from whom they have no hope of benefit, "It is plain" Hutcheson writes, "we have some secret Sense which determines our Approbation without regard to Self-Interest."[20] One's ability to sympathize with fictional characters demonstrates, and might develop, a moral sense crucially removed from any perception of selfish advantage that might be derived from connections to real people and their actions. Similarly, as Gallagher has shown, David Hume emphasizes the sympathetic availability of fictional characters precisely because they have no property, even in themselves, that might disturb or inhibit the free bestowal of sympathy.[21]

In the Scotsman Adam Smith's account sympathy involves a considerable labor of speculation, the prolonged posing of a fiction, in which one party can enter into the sentiments of the person principally concerned, only if that observed person conjectures correctly, and can "bring down his emotions to what the spectator can go along with."[22] Scottish novelists and novelists writing about Ireland drew from Smith's notions of civic sympathy to stage their own fictional scenes of sympathetic exchange, with direct bearing on the vexed relations between Britain's incorporated kingdoms. In Smollett's *Humphry Clinker*, as Evan Gottlieb notes, successful Smithian speculation allows for the sociable society of Scotsman Captain Lismahago and Welshman Matthew Bramble.[23] Although the two frequently dispute on different subjects from their own national viewpoint, "Mr. Bramble set a guard over his own irascibility . . . and when, in spite of all his efforts, he began to wax warm, the other prudently cooled in the same proportion" (191). That Matthew's nephew narrates this interaction, and in epistolary form, is especially important – he, and the reader, must do their own speculation on this exchange, and are in turn brought into this provisional emotional economy, an affective speculation directed toward fellow Britons in the face of their most dogged differences.

Similarly, in Morgan's *The Wild Irish Girl* readers watch as Horatio, an English man of *"confirmed prejudice"* (13, italics in original) enters a part of Ireland where he most expects "primeval ferocity" (17). He finds instead an Irish peasant who successfully dampens his emotional response to his life's hardships, including famine and a dying wife, thereby eliciting the deepest sympathy from Horatio. Horatio writes of their exchange, again in a letter, that private/public form whose openness invites oddly affective identification, "art thou then (I mentally exclaimed) that intemperate, cruel, idle savage, an Irish peasant? With an heart thus tenderly alive to the finest feelings of humanity . . . sustaining the unsatisfied wants of nature without a murmur?" (25).

In these novels it is not the English but the Celts of Welsh, Scottish, or Irish extraction who are especially predisposed to affective speculation. Horatio discovers the Irish to be a "warm-hearted people, who find in the name of stranger, an irresistible lure to every kind attention" (16). By the time of the publication of *Evelina*, the idea of the sentimental Celt had taken hold enough to provide a stock figure in Burney's "poor Scotch poet" (217), Macartney. But the use of this figure in eighteenth-century English novels is not simple. The Scotch poet Evelina first beholds is a melancholic, suicidal soul. Yet although Macartney suffers intensely from his thwarted love and predictably pens verses over it, it is Evelina who proves the feeling, sentimental character.[24] "[I]lliberally detested for being a Scotchman" (218), Mr. Macartney, while he elicits scorn from the ill-bred Branghtons (who refer to him as the "Scotch mope"), educes feelings of sympathy from Evelina. She, and not Mr. Macartney, is the sentimental soul, for it is she who feels sympathy for him, in preventing his suicide, "really too affecting to be borne" (224), and she faints. Evelina models an affective speculation for readers, seeming to base her treatment of Macartney on hypotheticals of which the Branghtons are incapable – what if this man were family? How would I treat him? For this speculative work she, and readers, receive recompense; Mr. Macartney turns out not only to be English like herself, but her own brother. Evelina's admirable abilities at affective speculation form the basis for a social cohesion in which the strangers of society literally become one's family. And those Scots strangers shed their overly sensitive Scotch poet-persona in the process.

All heart to the head, and hard-heartedness, of the English, the sentimental Celt that Horatio describes and that Burney invokes is a familiar and lingering stereotype. Yet the eighteenth-century texts and characters that develop this figure abound in complexity, in some cases troubling the very "lure" of the stranger behind national or even intimate social unity. Henry Mackenzie's immensely popular sentimental novel *The Man of Feeling* (1771), for instance, did much to promote the idea of the sentimental Scot in the figure of its protagonist, Harley. Extraordinarily sensitive, Harley repeatedly bursts into tears at the stories told by the suffering strangers he meets in his journey from Scotland to London and back. Yet his powers of sympathy are disabling – when his tearful responses become too much, Harley becomes stupefied and wordless. Rather than fostering community in his sympathetic response to these scenes of strong feeling Harley often flees the social scene altogether. Finally, his overwhelming love for the unattainable Miss Walton (and exposure to a contagion when visiting a friend) result in his own death. In these moments, as Maureen Harkin observes, this sentimental novel illustrates the "failure of shared sentiment to effect the production of community."[25] Moreover, the very formal structure of this novel – its series of sentimental tableaux as opposed to anything like a single, unitary plot, its often confusing, fragmented narration of unrelated stories, and even its announced status as a lost manuscript currently being used as wadding in a gun (the ultimate anti-social object!) would all assert what Harkin sees as Mackenzie's estimation of the "powerlessness of texts to reform readers" (319).

A similar case might be made for Sterne's *A Sentimental Journey through France and Italy* (1768). Like *The Man of Feeling*, *A Sentimental Journey* consists of a series of sketches of sentimental scenes without much plot to speak of. The work's structural disjunction stresses not the power of texts to reform readers but the powerlessness of texts to even hold themselves together, foregrounded in the work's inclusion of stray bits and pieces, such as a drummer's letter to a corporal's wife, for some reason on the person of Yorick's servant, La Fleur; and a fragment lifted from Burton's *The Anatomy of Melancholy*, which was itself copied from Lucian. This narrative, filled with dashes of questionable meaning, ends inconclusively, mid-sentence, repeatedly and ultimately withholding knowable, common verbal signification as well as the sense of sociality that such communicative exchange might bring.

Alternatively, the text proffers the possibility of sentimental exchange beyond words and beyond nations. Through the extra-verbal communication of blushes, tears, and softly pressed hands English Yorick experiences powerful sentimental feelings with a number of foreign nationals. Ambiguity haunts those scenes, however. The exact meaning of the handholding between Yorick and a traveling woman remains murky, shading into sexual innuendo. "The pulsations of the arteries along my fingers pressing across hers," Yorick claims, "told her what was passing within me: she looked down" (26). Yet this remains a narcissistic speculation, unconfirmed by anything the woman says, followed as it is by silence. At best, what have been communicated are the mechanical workings of his body and not the unique sentiments of an individual soul. Both Sterne's and Mackenzie's novels reveal the ways in which an understanding of the most sentimental nature, even between two people alone, is always incomplete and unknowable, even to themselves. Such a vision leaves little room for intra- or transnational sentimental unions.

Yorick oscillates between what he imagines to be cosmopolitan sentiment, crossing national divides, and his insistence that sentiment stops at national boundaries. Indulging in characterizations of national types Yorick enters the looming shadow cast by borders when he finds himself without a passport in France during the Seven Years' War. Yorick also avers that chief among the "impediments in communicating our sensations out of our own sphere" is "want of languages" (13). His fumbled French quotations throughout the text serve as constant *aides-mémoire* of how much can be lost in translation. One's national language, then, seems to be the principle of exclusion for sentimental exchange. Yet even as Yorick makes his case for the notion that "the balance of sentimental commerce is always against the expatriated adventurer" (13), he uses an English term (of Latin origin) that obscures his meaning by multiplying it. "Nature has set up by her own unquestionable authority certain boundaries and fences to circumscribe the discontent of man," he writes, "laying him under almost insuperable obligations to work out his ease, and to sustain his sufferings at home" (13). Because of his use of "to circumscribe," it is not clear whether Yorick thinks nature limits or merely sketches man's unhappiness in establishing those boundaries. Even a single term of a national language, instead of establishing and maintaining a sentimental community, threatens to confound and divide language users. The ambiguity of sentiments, verbal and non-verbal, reminds us that if the novel is a national form, sometimes drawing from the language of sentiment, the fissions of national discourse inhere within it.

National tales, as Lady Morgan's and Maria Edgeworth's novels written in the wake of the union between Ireland and Britain have been called, would seem to resolve the continuing tensions between the English and Irish, making the unknown known, and offering plots of successful marriage between English and Irish or Scots as a rejoinder to earlier allegories of failed domestic union. As some of the first novels to declare their status as national novels, the national tales work to accrue authority to the novel as a form capable of entering official public debate. They cull some of their authority from a newly institutionalized historiography of the respective nations' developmental stages, a conjectural history in which all societies might be mapped onto a universal, linear history of development. In such mapping the pronounced edges of salient regional and national differences become not just spatial but temporal differences; and novels more and more narrate particular customs, practices, and even languages as throwbacks to an earlier period. The co-existence of the characters of those places, their manners and languages, with metropolitan narrators and readers, becomes a simultaneity of anachronism.

In this temporal mapping and its attendant formulation (roughly, "they are what we once were"), a sentimental bridging of disparate times becomes the work that novels need to do in order to bind regions and peoples together. The details of domestic life lovingly rendered in fiction are self-consciously weighted with geopolitical meaning – the trencher and silver tankard have the pull of both an individual childhood and a distant social past. But the notion of sentimental connection in these contexts too is itself extremely fraught, not least because of continuing associations of sentiment with residual Celtic spaces and because of the way the association problematizes the chronology of conjectural history. Not unlike Mackenzie's Harley, the Celtic female partners of the Celtic-English unions of national tales are often sentimental figures. In *The Wild Irish Girl* Horatio describes "the varying hue of [Glorvina's] mutable complexion, which seemed to ebb and flow to the impulse of every sentiment" (73). Yet in deploying the figure of the sentimental Celt, these novels, like *The Man of Feeling*, relegate sentimentalism itself to the past, thereby suggesting that the strong capacity for sentiment is anachronistic in the face of an improving modernization.[26] Such a move endangered the very Enlightenment time grid on which the national tale was based, undoing contemporary understandings of sentiment and sympathy as emotions that were characteristic of members of a developed polite society.[27]

A similar unraveling takes place formally, as national tales represent the distinct spaces of Scotland or Ireland through temporally graduated generic filters. In the national tale, the novel, whose deep indebtedness to romance its authors usually disavowed, must deliberately deploy the romance motif of a concluding erotic union. At the same time, these novels consign Ireland and Scotland to romance. Upon first arriving on the shores of Ireland, Horatio views it through the lens of that fantasy-based genre, romance, observing a boat "the oars of which were plied by six men, whose statures, limbs, and features, declared them the lingering progeny of the once formidable race of Irish giants" (14). In a well-worn trope of the period (in William Collins's "Ode on the Popular Superstitions of the Highlands of Scotland," for example), the Celtic space Horatio records is romance itself. He writes to his friend that if he could accurately render what he saw through the Irish castle window "you would think the mimic copy fabulous; the celestial visitant of an over-heated imagination" (53), describing what he sees in remote Ireland as "like some pictured story of romantic fiction" (51). In contrast, the expanding footnotes and authenticating editorial apparatuses of such works turn to the rhetoric of evidence and reason and the rational observation that is the hallmark of the genre of the modern Irish tour. Critics have noted how Maria Edgeworth in particular draws from the language of economic improvement and efficiency in the modern generic protocols she brings to the depictions of the past still extant in Ireland.

If novels increasingly defined regional difference in temporalized generic terms, however, national tales, the works most interested in representing those differences, manipulated those conventions to surprising ends. Edgeworth's interventions were particularly canny. Her footnotes to *Castle Rackrent* at times satirize the form in good Scriblerian style, as in the first footnote, which traces the cultural history of the "long great coat" worn by the story's narrator, Thady, back through Spenser's writings, to the Jews, the Chaldees, the Egyptians, the Greeks, and the Romans.[28] Alongside those send-ups, however, appear footnotes of serious contemporary political commentary, such as the exposé of the "Middle men" who rack exorbitant rents from Irish tenants (73). By offering multiple versions of the footnote, *Castle Rackrent* explodes the sense of shared, singular, and unquestionably authoritative meaning associated with that genre.

In analyzing the national tale, it is important to understand these novels' response to, and deployment of, adjacent temporally situated genres in relation not simply to Celtic regions but to English narrators. National tales, as Ferris argues, "rewrote the metropolitan travel-figure by mobilizing the old romance plot of encounter to subject this figure to a disorientation that altered his (more rarely her) center of both personal and national being."[29] Thus, through the use of the generic formula of romance, a representative modern English touring figure like Horatio becomes himself the object of another's knowledge, as the Irish women wonder at his inability to speak Gaelic and as Glorvina and her family tend to his bruised, incapacitated body after he has fallen from his perch while peeping into their castle's casement. In the repeated scenes of Horatio's discomfort in the foreign space of Ireland, it is he, and not the Irish subjects he describes, who becomes the fictionally knowable terrain of the novel. Readers, trained in the techniques of fictionality, and its invitation to affective speculation, place themselves in Horatio's position. Once there, however, they find themselves not in the "lofty" location of controlled discernment but in a state of bafflement and incomprehension. We have seen that the sympathy the sentimental novel offers with one hand it takes away with another. In the new occasions for sympathy found in the national tale, Ferris argues, sympathy ceases to be a "mediating emotion between separate entities" at all. It is, rather, "the activation of internal disequilibrium," not a Smithian but a Humean model "in which sympathy insinuates itself into and disturbs the regular flow of one's consciousness. It makes pivotal the initial moment of internal estrangement" (13). Changes in the form of the novel, including its techniques of fictionality and the models of sympathy they encourage, might well be "intimately linked to *changes* in national consciousness," as Patrick Parrinder argues (*Nation and Novel*, 6, emphasis added). Those formal innovations might even make possible new ways of understanding the nation and one's relationship to its imagined members. Throughout the period, however, the ability to imagine the nation remained dependent on the provisional and the fictional, on the process of affiliating with strangeness, and on continually re-creating it.

Notes

1. Laurence Sterne, *Tristram Shandy*, ed. Howard Anderson (New York: Norton, 1980), pp. 250, 258.
2. Henry Fielding, *Joseph Andrews*, ed. Douglas Brooks-Davies and Thomas Keymer (Oxford University Press, 1999), p. 232.
3. See Betty Schellenberg, "Imagining the Nation in Defoe's *Tour thro' the Whole Island of Great Britain*," ELH 62 (1995), 295–312.
4. Tobias Smollett, *The Adventures of Roderick Random*, ed. Paul Gabriel Boucé (Oxford University Press, 1988), p. 145.
5. Frances Burney, *Evelina*, ed. Kristina Straub (Boston, MA: Bedford Books, 1997), p. 112.
6. Benedict Anderson, in *Imagined Communities: Reflections on the Origin and Spread of Nationalism* (London: Verso, 1993), refers to the nation as "a deep, horizontal

comradeship" (p. 16), as opposed to the vertical, top-down political organization of monarchic states.

7. M. M. Bakhtin, "Discourse in the Novel," in *The Dialogic Imagination*, ed. Michael Holquist, trans. Caryl Emerson and Michael Holquist (Austin: University of Texas Press, 1981), p. 263.

8. See W. Arthur Boggs, "Dialectical Ingenuity in *Humphry Clinker*," *Papers on English Language and Literature* 1 (1965), 327–337.

9. Maria Edgeworth, *The Absentee* (Middlesex: Echo Press, 2007), p. 56.

10. See John Barrell, *English Literature in History: An Equal Wide Survey 1730–1780* (London: Hutchinson, 1983).

11. David Hume, "Of National Characters," in *Essays, Moral, Political and Literary*, ed. Eugene Miller (Indianapolis: Liberty Press, 1987).

12. Oliver Goldsmith, *The Citizen of the World*, 2 vols. (London: Dent, 1900), vol. II, p. 173.

13. Thomas Keymer, Introduction, in Samuel Richardson, *Pamela*, ed. Thomas Keymer and Alice Wakely (Oxford: World's Classics, 2001), p. xxvii.

14. Patrick Parrinder, *Nation and Novel* (Oxford University Press, 2006), p. 18.

15. See, for example Edward Lhuyd, *Archaeologia Britannica* (Oxford, 1699). Rosemary Sweet provides a comprehensive guide to antiquarianism in *Antiquaries: The Discovery of the Past in Eighteenth-Century Britain* (London and New York: Hambledon, 2004).

16. Jonathan Swift, "The Story of the Injured Lady" in *Miscellanies*, 2 vols. (London: 1746), vol. II, p. 104.

17. Sydney Owenson, Lady Morgan, *The Wild Irish Girl* (Oxford University Press, 2008), p. 13.

18. Catherine Gallagher, "The Rise of Fictionality," in *The Novel*, Vol. 1: *History, Geography, and Culture*, ed. Franco Moretti (Princeton University Press, 2006), pp. 336–363, 356.

19. Cited in note to Laurence Sterne, *A Sentimental Journey*, ed. Melvyn New and W. G. Day (Indianapolis: Hackett, 2006), p. 7.

20. Francis Hutcheson *An Inquiry into the Original of Our Ideas of Beauty and Virtue*, ed. Wolfgang Leidhold (Indianapolis: Liberty Fund, 2008), p. 92.

21. See Catherine Gallagher, *Nobody's Story: The Vanishing Acts of Women Writers in the Marketplace, 1670–1820* (Berkeley: University of California Press, 1995).

22. Adam Smith, *Theory of Moral Sentiments*, ed. D. D. Raphael and A. L. Macfie (Indianapolis: Liberty Fund, 1982), p. 23.

23. Evan Gottlieb, *Feeling British: Sympathy and National Identity in Scottish and English Writing, 1707–1832* (Cranbury, NJ: Associated University Presses, 2007), p. 92.

24. For an extended discussion of the sentimental relationship between Evelina and Macartney see Juliet Shields, *Sentimental Literature and Anglo-Scottish Identity, 1745–1820* (Cambridge University Press, 2010).

25. Maureen Harkin, "Mackenzie's *Man of Feeling*: Embalming Sensibility," *ELH* 61 (1991), 317–340, 319.

26. Harkin, p. 321, makes this observation in relation to Harley.
27. See Ian Duncan, "Scotland and the Novel," in *The Cambridge Companion to Fiction in the Romantic Period*, ed. Richard Maxwell and Katie Trumpener (Cambridge University Press, 2008), pp. 251–264.
28. Maria Edgeworth, *Castle Rackrent* and *Ennui*, ed. Marilyn Butler (London: Penguin, 1992), p. 65.
29. Ina Ferris, *The Romantic National Tale and the Question of Ireland* (Cambridge University Press, 2007), p. 11.

Money's productivity in narrative fiction

LIZ BELLAMY

The prose fictions of the early eighteenth century were preoccupied with wandering protagonists circulating through a disparate society accumulating not only moral experience but also the wealth that would enable them to settle down at the end of novels. Simultaneously the emerging discourse of political economy posed questions about the nature of value, the function of circulation, and the role of the individual that were similar to questions being raised within fiction. And while characters circulated within novels, novels circulated within society. The novel was therefore both a forum for the exploration of the system of exchange, and an object within that developing system.

Several writers on the origins of the novel have noted the recurrence of words with an economic significance in the lexis of creating and disseminating stories. "Account," "circulate," "tale," "tell," "retail," "recount," "credit" and "creditable" all have a commercial as well as a narrative significance, emphasizing the importance of circulation and creditworthiness in establishing the value of both stories and coins. The overlap in terminology is matched by an overlap in personnel. As well as being the acknowledged "father of the novel," Defoe contributed to the developing discourse of economic analysis, while Swift wrote about coinage in his *Drapier's Letters* before penning *Gulliver's Travels*. This chapter will examine the relationship between economics and fiction, through analysis of the significance of money in some of the narratives of the eighteenth and early nineteenth centuries, showing how literature not only explored systems of circulation and exchange, but also revealed anxieties about the dangers of an economy based on paper money, credit, speculation, and consumption. Patrick Brantlinger has argued that, like money, "the novel is simultaneously a form of debt and of wealth, and a commodity in search of buyers,"[1] and Deidre Lynch has argued that eighteenth-century readers used their experience of novels as a means of comprehending the nature and significance of the marketplace. While critical interpretations of the precise significance of fictional representations of finance may differ, there is a general consensus that the histories of money and the novel are closely intertwined.

The discourse of political economy developed in the seventeenth century with the work of commentators and pamphleteers who considered practical issues such as the value of the coinage or the rate of import or export tariffs. The subject began to be treated in a more systematic fashion with Sir William Petty's *Essays on Political Arithmetic* (1682–1687), which provided facts and figures to support theories that had been previously based largely on unsubstantiated assertion. Petty emphasized the importance of trade and circulation and identified consumption as a means of stimulating the economy and promoting wealth. Moreover the "superlucration" or accumulation of "gold, silver, precious stones, &c.," which were "morally speaking perpetuall & universal wealth" was identified as the primary purpose of the state. Wealth was presented as a source of national strength and social harmony, instead of being associated with luxurious consumption that would weaken the nation. Trade was facilitated by the availability of money, and generated a diverse range of specialized occupations, including "Divines, Physicians, Lawyers, Soldiers, Seamen" as well as "Trades of pleasure and ornament as Parks, perfumes, jewells, musicians, comedians &c."[2]

This was a very different image of the state from that propagated within more conservative discourses, in that it replaced an essentially static social model with a fundamentally dynamic one. While the traditional image of society fostered by religious and moral works emphasized the importance of a hierarchical system based on the maintenance of power and wealth within a stable hereditary aristocracy, the mercantilist writers on political economy celebrated the movement of wealth between individuals. The uneasy co-existence of these competing images of society was revealed by the reaction to the publication of Bernard Mandeville's poem *The Grumbling Hive, or Knaves Turned Honest* (1705), reissued with a prose exposition in 1714 as *The Fable of the Bees, or, Private Vices, Public Benefits*. Mandeville's fable uses the metaphor of a hive of bees to explore what happens when a complex commercial society begins to practice the virtues of austerity and frugality advocated within moral discourse. Industry is destroyed once the bees no longer consume goods that they do not need; the increased health that results from virtuous abstinence means that the medical profession is not required; and the army and the legal profession are redundant because there are no longer any pointless foreign wars or unnecessary litigation. The ultimate consequence of the bees' decision to turn honest is the destruction of the prosperity of the hive.

Mandeville gained notoriety for the theory encapsulated in his subtitle that private vices represent public benefits, but none of the moral and religious writers was able to provide an effective critique of the economic basis of his ethical paradox. An instinctive belief that virtue resided in avoidance of excessive consumption was in conflict with a growing recognition within economic works that the maximization of prosperity was the ultimate end of the state, and that consumption, accumulation, and circulation were to be celebrated as signs of that prosperity. The social and moral implications of this conflict reverberated through representations of the state for at least a century after the publication of Mandeville's work.

The economic ideas scattered through the tracts and treatises of the seventeenth and early eighteenth centuries were consolidated and given systematic form with the publication of Adam Smith's *Inquiry into the Nature and Causes of the Wealth of Nations* (1776). Smith identified the importance of money in facilitating the exchange of goods, thus making possible accumulation and unequal distribution. He emphasized the role of the division of labor both in improving productivity and in entrenching inequality, by confining the majority of individuals to repetitively tedious tasks which would restrict their mental capacity. Smith's model therefore develops both Mandeville's insight into the importance of the economic system as a means of maintaining national strength and prosperity and also his awareness that the source of this prosperity was itself a cause of moral debility and potential social problems.

Novels thus developed within a climate in which the structure of society was being scrutinized by multiple discourses. Money, whether as coin or in the form of paper money and bills of exchange, generated debate over the nature of value. James Thompson has argued that political economy and the novel can both be seen as responses to this crisis of value, since "each in its own way describes or represents or figures value and at the same time is charged with explaining it."[3] Circulation could be represented as a means of acquiring and establishing value, or as a threat to the traditional status quo. Acquisition could be presented as a measure of social success and the ultimate end of individual endeavor, or as a sign of a destabilizing self-interest that had the potential to undermine the state. Defoe's heroes and heroines are all preoccupied with how to get and how to keep money. By entitling his 1722 novel *The Fortunes and Misfortunes of Moll Flanders* and his 1724 tale *The Fortunate Mistress* (now more commonly called *Roxana*), Defoe signaled the interdependence of the concept of destiny and the pursuit of financial security. Defoe's protagonists recognize that they have their own fortunes to make; establishing a solid economic position is crucial in securing their social identity. The classical concept of the blind goddess Fortuna deciding the fate of characters through the turning of her wheel is displaced in Defoe with an emphasis on the efforts of the individual to establish his or her own credit in society. Robinson Crusoe's laborious efforts to construct the consumer society ironically reinforce the importance of precisely the mechanisms of exchange and the division of labor that his island lacks. In *Moll Flanders* the energy of the protagonist is directed towards the accumulation of money as a means of achieving social acceptability and moral reformation, even though the money is largely acquired through dishonest means. The celebration of Moll's social fluidity is undermined by the connection of her industry with criminality, which impedes rather than enhances the working of the economic system.

Roxana's accumulation is similarly compromised by being associated with immorality through the sale of her body to a series of generous partners. In both *Moll Flanders* and *Roxana* the association of sex with financial gain is manifested in scenes in which sexual foreplay is enlivened by gifts of coins. Roxana's landlord took a silk purse containing sixty guineas and "threw them into my Lap, and concluded all the rest of his Discourse with Kisses, and Protestations of his Love; of which indeed, I had abundant Proof."[4] For Roxana the proof is in the guineas rather than the kisses, but the sexual significance of the gift is manifested in its location in her lap. When the French Prince places "a fine Necklace of Diamonds" round Roxana's neck, her reaction is described in terms reminiscent of sexual excitement as she recounts that "If I had an Ounce of Blood in me, that did not fly up into my Face, Neck, and Breasts, it must be from some Interruption in the Vessels; I was all on fire with the Sight" (73).

Material reward and sexual pleasure are conflated throughout Roxana's narrative and this emphasis on the thrill of wealth may be connected to the fact that Roxana, like Moll, has experienced the despair that comes from lack of money. On the desertion of her first husband, Roxana is left with "five little Children" without "one Shilling . . . to buy them Victuals." Having "sent *Amy* out with a Silver Spoon, to sell it, and bring something from the Butcher's," she is "sitting on the Ground, with a great Heap of old Rags, Linnen, and other things . . . looking over them, to see if I had any thing . . . that would Sell or Pawn for a little Money" (17). Clothes and silver cutlery, the symbols of consumer society that Moll most frequently steals, are being reduced back to a depreciated cash value, in a reversal of the process of consumption. This is the ultimate symbol of how far Roxana has fallen.

Once restored to society, Roxana, like Moll, uses consumption as a form of self-construction, disguising her identity through different modes of dress, as a gentlewoman, a Quaker, and most famously as the exotic Turkish dancer Roxana. Her value is acquired rather than inherited, and is inscribed through the acquisition of goods that in moral discourse would be eschewed as luxury because inappropriate to her true social position. Roxana, like Moll, becomes obsessed with wealth, but she is afflicted with anxieties about the disposition of her money similar to those that had previously been expressed by Defoe in *Colonel Jack* (1722). As Roxana says, "thinking of it sometimes, almost distracted me, for want of knowing how to dispose of it" (110). Roxana gives the reader a detailed description of how she solves this problem. Although Alexander Pope inveighed in his "Epistle to Bathurst" against "Blest Paper-credit! last and best supply!/ That lends Corruption lighter wings to fly!" Roxana sees paper credit, in the form of notes and bonds, not as a symbol of the insubstantiality and unreliability of the economic system, but rather as a practical solution to the difficulties inherent in the storage and transfer of wealth. Given that the novel was published only four years after the spectacular financial collapse of the South Sea Bubble, this was a contentious stance. Moreover Roxana discovers that by investing her money, she can keep it safe while earning interest of 3 per cent; and so she becomes as expert in the financial system, "as any She-Merchant of them all" (131). Critics have commented on the influence of the conduct or advice book on Defoe's fiction, but here the novel has some of the functions of a work such as *The Complete English Tradesman* in providing advice on the best means of saving and transporting money. It can almost be seen as a guide to the banking system for prospective investors. Money is presented as inherently productive rather than simply a mechanism to facilitate exchange. Moreover, this celebration of paper money and bills shows the transformative power of the process of writing that can convert worthless paper into substantial sums, and critics have drawn parallels between this power and the development of fiction itself.

But while investment is portrayed in affirmative terms, the same is not true of Roxana's mercenary motivation. When faced with a proposal of marriage from the Dutch Merchant, Roxana provides reasons for her refusal, but when the Merchant removes her only real objection to the match, i.e. that it would involve giving up control of her money, she is too embarrassed to accept, for if she had agreed to marry him at this point

> I then did as good as confess, that it was upon the Account of my Money that I refus'd him; and that tho' I cou'd give up my Virtue, and expose myself, yet I wou'd not give up my Money, which, tho' it was true, yet was really too gross for me to acknowledge. (147)

Roxana cannot admit that her motives are purely mercenary, and instead appeals to abstract concepts of liberty and independence. Moreover, despite her cele-bration of the financial system, she is ultimately unable to gain satisfaction from her wealth because of her guilt about the means through which it has been acquired. When she finally marries the Dutch Merchant she is reluctant to combine his *"honest well-gotten Estate "* with her *"ill-got Wealth"* (259).

Defoe's works are preoccupied with economics, but focus on perversions of the economic system: Moll and Colonel Jack get rich through crime; Captain Singleton from piracy; Roxana from prostitution. Robinson Crusoe is stranded on an island where there is no system of exchange because there is nobody to exchange with, and in *A Journal of the Plague Year* (1722) exchange is compromised because circulation is associated with the spread not of prosperity but of disease. The catastrophic effects of the plague are manifested in the seizing up of exchange and movement since "Merchandizing was at a full Stop," "Navigation was at a Stop," and "all Trades being stopt, Employment ceased."[5] Yet while the narrator, H.F., confines his household in accordance with the official instructions, he continues to wander the streets of London and provides detailed descriptions of the measures that people took to maintain commerce while minimizing the dangers of infection. Ultimately H.F. rejects confinement as a solution to the problem of disease, arguing that "it seemed to have no manner of publick Good in it, equal or proportionable to the grievous Burthen that it was to the particular Families, that were so shut up" (166). Sandra Sherman has identified the plague as a figuration of credit, and connected the shutting up of houses with the shutting up of conversations, arguing that both are equally impossible, and constitute fictions of stability within a world of shifting values.[6]

The emphasis in Defoe's works on circulation, investment, and exchange can ultimately be read as an endorsement of the new financial system and the concept of liquidity. In novels that are characterized by the rapidity of the movement of their protagonists through society, Defoe celebrates a dynamic rather than a static social model, and provides a focus on the acquisition of capital which was not to be a feature of the novel for the rest of the century. As Samuel Macey observes, Defoe provided "the first prose epics of the common man and woman motivated by the accumulation of wealth on this earth."[7] Thereafter, novels became more preoccupied with the distribution of money rather than the means by which it was amassed, and in some texts the use of money and the ethics of consumption were still the subject of debate. Brantlinger identifies a reactionary counter-discourse in the work of writers such as Pope and Swift that "attacked public credit as a form of idolatry or fetishism" (6).

Jonathan Swift's *Drapier's Letters* (1724) had the polemical purpose of protesting against the introduction of William Wood's debased copper coinage into Ireland. Metal coin was usually seen as intrinsically valuable, in contrast to bills and paper currency that were dependent on the maintenance of credit. But the coin minted by Wood had a face value that was far in excess of the cost of the metal it contained. By emphasizing this disparity, the *Drapier's Letters* reinforced a belief in intrinsic value, suggesting that the people of Ireland should refuse to use a currency that departed from this principle. The Drapier inveighs against corruption in the award of the contract to Wood, but he also attacks the imperialism of the measure, which is portrayed as a mechanism for leaching wealth from Ireland to England. Yet the new Irish coins only represented in extreme form the state of the currency throughout Britain, which had become severely debased. Intrinsic value was increasingly being displaced in economic thought by the idea that, as Crusoe discovered on his island, the value of coins was as dependent on the maintenance of credit as the value of notes. By invoking the specter of intrinsic value, the Drapier employed a residual economic ideology to reinforce an emergent nationalist discourse.

The function of money is further explored by Swift in *Gulliver's Travels* (1726), where Gulliver uses money as a way of signaling to the farmer in Brobdingnag that he is a civilized and intelligent creature. He empties his purse containing "six *Spanish*-Pieces of four Pistoles each, besides twenty or thirty smaller Coins" into the hand of the farmer who "seemed to be wholly ignorant what they were."[8] The inhabitants of Lilliput and Brobdingnag are initially portrayed as perplexed by money, for the Lilliputian officers despatched to search Gulliver's pockets report that they found "several round flat Pieces of white and red Metal of different Bulk" (29) without apparently identifying the pieces as coins. Yet it soon becomes apparent that both countries have money economies, and in both countries Gulliver is perceived in monetary terms. He is represented as a cause of economic crisis within Lilliput, for the Lord High Treasurer reports to the Emperor that:

> He was forced to take up Money at great Discount; that Exchequer Bills would not circulate under nine *per Cent*. below Par; that I had cost his Majesty above a Million and a half of *Sprugs* . . . and upon the whole, that it would be adviseable in the Emperor to take the first fair Occasion of dismissing me. (58)

The cost of maintaining Gulliver has led to a shortage of credit and an increase in government debt, with a consequent rise in interest rates. Brantlinger argues that Gulliver thus becomes a metaphor for the national debt. In Brobdingnag, on the other hand, Gulliver is sold to the Queen for "a Thousand Pieces of Gold" (91). Yet Gulliver served the Lilliputian state, destroying the fleet of the neighboring island, perhaps reinforcing the connection between the national debt and the pursuit of an aggressive foreign policy. In Brobdingnag, in contrast, he can perform no useful function and is therefore a luxury commodity and his value is increased accordingly.

In his conversations with the King of Brobdingnag and the Houyhnhnm Master, Gulliver has difficulty explaining the nature of the British economy. The King is perplexed by government debt and "at a Loss how a Kingdom could run out of its Estate like a private Person. He asked me, who were our Creditors? And, where we found the Money to pay them?" (119). The King of Brobdingnag emphasizes the importance of public virtue within his own state, but the unspoken answer to his question draws attention to the dominance of private interest within the British polity. The corruption that was identified with the executive in the *Drapier's Letters* is here extended to encompass all those who have lent money to the government and thereby profited from the perpetuation of national debt. Colin Nicholson has drawn attention to the topicality of this critique in the aftermath of the collapse of the South Sea Company, in which 450 members of the two Houses of Parliament had bought stock.[9]

In the land of the horses the Houyhnhnm Master is unable to understand the use of money. Gulliver's account is reminiscent of Petty and Mandeville and anticipates Smith in drawing attention to the importance of money as the cause of luxury and economic inequality. It is due to money that "the rich Man enjoyed the Fruit of the Poor Man's Labour, and . . . the Bulk of our People was forced to live miserably . . . to make a few live plentifully" (234). Gulliver's apparent difficulty in explaining the function of money and government debt draws attention to the irrationality of the economic system, and this impression is reinforced by the remarks of the Houyhnhnm Master. He relates Gulliver's account of the exchange economy to behavior observed in the savage humanoid creatures, the Yahoos. The Master describes how:

> In some Fields in his Country, there are certain *shining Stones* of several Colours, whereof the *Yahoos* are violently fond . . . My master said, he could never discover the Reason of this unnatural Appetite, or how these *Stones* could be of any Use to a *Yahoo* ; but now he believed it might proceed from the same Principle of *Avarice*, which I had ascribed to Mankind. (242)

The economic system is identified with irrational greed and a childish wish for brightly coloured baubles, combined with a selfish desire to possess those objects to the exclusion of others. Gulliver's association of money with civilized society is therefore ironically subverted by the end of the book, so that the novel presents a very different view of the economic system from Roxana's enthusiastic endorsement of the credit economy and the virtues of the financial system.

The importance of the processes of circulation and exchange, and their function in tying together an otherwise disparate society, are manifested in a fictional sub-genre that emerged in the eighteenth century and has been labeled the "it-narrative" or "novel of circulation." These works follow the adventures of an object-narrator, such as a pen, peg top, sofa, or hackney coach, or an animal such as a dog or cat. Many of the narratives trace the adventures of coins or bank notes, the best known being Charles Johnstone's *Chrysal: Or, The Adventures of a Guinea* (1760–1765). The use of the object-narrator makes possible an exploration of society that prioritizes the impersonal relationships of exchange rather than the affective relationships of human protagonists. On his arrival in the Bank of England, Chrysal is alarmed to be thrown onto a large heap of guineas which "seemed to threaten a long state of inactivity, before it might come to my turn to be brought into action." The military lexis appears to endorse the guinea's enthusiasm for entering the economic field of action, and this is reinforced when we are told that he soon found himself "agreeably mistaken, and that the *circulation* there was too quick to admit of such delay." Yet this celebration of circulation is satirically undermined when Chrysal recounts that he was "that very day paid out to a noble lord, in his pension from the ministry."[10] While Chrysal is occasionally used in the exchange of goods, he is more often transferred through gambling, bribery, prostitution, peculation, the misappropriation of charitable funds, the supply of substandard goods to the navy, or, as here, in the payment of a pension to a corrupt official. The guinea's portrayal of circulation as a form of public service is therefore ironic, and can be read as an indictment of the function of money in the economy, resonant of the diatribe of the King of Brobdingnag rather than the commercial enthusiasm of Defoe.

Oliver Goldsmith's *Citizen of the World* (1762) presents a very different view of the economic system from the perspective of a Chinese philosopher, Altangi, writing to a correspondent in China. Altangi defends luxury as a means of increasing demand for goods, and therefore enhancing circulation, prosperity, and the interdependence of society. He argues that "to luxury we owe not only the greatest part of our knowledge, but even our virtues" and "as it increases our wants, encreases our capacity for happiness."[11] The luxurious man

> stands in need of a thousand different artists to furnish out his happiness; it is more likely, therefore, that he should be a good citizen who is connected by motives of self-interest with so many, than the abstemious man who is united to none. (55)

This identification of self-interest as the fundamental bond within a disparate society was developed in Adam Smith's observation in *The Wealth of Nations* that "it is not from the benevolence of the butcher, the brewer, or the baker that we expect our dinner, but from regard to their own self-interest."[12] The philosopher Altangi reorients the Mandevillian paradox to suggest that public benefits must be construed as private virtues, and he even anticipates Smith's paradigmatic illustration of the division of labor by referring to the fact that "Not less than ten different hands are acquired [sic] to make a pin" (Goldsmith, *Citizen of the World*, vol. ii, 55–56).

In Goldsmith's novel *The Vicar of Wakefield* (1766), however, the enthusiasm for the economic system is tempered by an account of the socially disruptive impact of luxury that harks back to the moral critique of consumption. The Vicar is entertained in a gentleman's house, unaware that his host is in fact the butler who "in his master's absence, had a mind to cut a figure, and be for a while the gentleman himself."[13] Mainly as a result of the burgeoning spread of consumption, the Vicar is unable to distinguish the false gentleman from the true. The butler incident generalizes the Vicar's own struggles to restrain the vanity and luxury of his family in order to render their consumption appropriate to their means. Yet the resolution of the novel makes it clear that luxury and pretension are conceived as minor foibles rather than vices, and even the butler is forgiven on the Vicar's intercession.

The eighteenth-century novel therefore encompasses a range of perspectives on the economic system and the use of money, with some writers celebrating the importance of circulation and exchange and others condemning the luxurious consumption of goods as a mechanism for eroding social distinctions. Yet the ideological inclusivity of the novel form ensures that many works incorporate elements of both perspectives, manifesting the uncertainty over the emergent economic ethos that had been evident in the reactions to Mandeville's paradox. In Tobias Smollett's epistolary novel, *The Expedition of Humphry Clinker* (1771), the critique of modern commercial society is put into the mouth of the misanthropic conservative Matthew Bramble in letters to his friend and physician, Dr. Lewis. Bramble expresses his dissatisfaction with the social promiscuity which he perceives to be the consequence of the increased circulation of money, and rails against "the general tide of luxury, which hath overspread the nation."[14] Yet this perspective is balanced by the letters of Bramble's nephew Jery, who takes a much more affirmative view of the increase in affluence and social mobility. He recounts how he:

> Took the liberty to differ in opinion from Mr Bramble, when he observed, that the mixture of people in the entertainments of this place was destructive of all order and urbanity; that it rendered the plebeians insufferably arrogant

and troublesome, and vulgarized the deportment and sentiments of those
who moved in the upper spheres of life.   (51)

Bramble makes an explicit connection between social and economic change,
and shows his adherence to an outdated concept of intrinsic value when he
argues that the mixing of classes "was worse . . . than debasing the gold coin of
the nation." Jery argues that the eagerness of the lower orders "to imitate the
dress and equipage of their superiors" will lead to a general refinement in
manners, to which Bramble's old friend Quin sardonically replies: "Yes . . . as a
plate of marmalade would improve a pan of sirreverence [excrement]" (51).

The potentially destructive impact of the consumer economy is manifested
in the contrast between the estate of Bramble's friend Baynard, which has
been wasted through the extravagance of his wife, and the modest but well-
managed household of Mr. Dennison, who has retired from the world to a life
of simple austerity. Yet Bramble's preoccupation with social promiscuity is
to some extent assuaged in the course of the narrative by his travels through
the country, and especially through the Borders and Scotland, where he finds
what he regards as a more honest and less pretentious way of life. Bramble's
free circulation, meeting people from a range of different backgrounds, is in
contrast with his desire to restrain the social mobility of others, to prevent the
debasing of the coin of the aristocracy. Furthermore, Bramble's conservative
stance is ironically undermined by the revelation of his own youthful social
promiscuity that resulted in the birth of Humphry Clinker to Dorothy
Twyford, bar-keeper at the Angel at Chippenham. The end of the novel
sees the moderation of Bramble's static social model, as he admits the
illegitimate Clinker not into the ranks of the gentry, but into the respectable
position of farm manager, with the possibility of appointment to the post of
vestry clerk. Moreover in the last letter of this epistolary novel, the arguments against the promiscuous mixing of classes are expressed not by
Bramble but by the servant Win Jenkins, wife of the erstwhile Humphry
Clinker, now Humphry Loyd. The novel ends with Win's abjuration to a
fellow servant that:

> Being, by God's blessing, removed to a higher spear, you'll excuse my being
> familiar with the lower sarvents of the family; but, as I trust you'll behave
> respectful, and keep a proper distance, you may always depend upon the
> good will and purtection of
>
> Yours,
> W. Loyd

The opposition to social promiscuity is satirized by being articulated by the barely literate Win. The novel therefore uses the epistolary form to dramatize the tensions between a model of society based on a mercantilist emphasis on the importance of consumption, circulation, and exchange, and a traditional static social model. Bramble outlines the disruption created by increased consumption, but ironically he acquires a more moderate perspective through the very process of circulation which he has sought to restrict.

The traditional resolution of retreat to an organic country estate, to foster the virtues of aristocratic benevolence in isolation from the complex economic nexus, is therefore undermined by the novel's critique of the social ethos on which this system depends. The narrative importance of movement and exchange in the picaresque novels of Defoe, Smollett, and Fielding necessarily subverts the ideological significance of plot resolutions that restore stasis. Circulation is presented as the prelude to a period of stability, when the hero and heroine retreat to the country estate, yet this conclusion is only achieved as a consequence of a sequence of adventures that reinforces the fact that status and value are subject to negotiation through the process of circulation.

In Maria Edgeworth's *Castle Rackrent* (1800) the static social model of the hereditary aristocracy is undermined by association not with images of idyllic retreat but with ideas of decay, dysfunction, and unproductive parasitism. The history of the Rackrent family recounted by the "illiterate old steward,"[15] Thady Quirk, presents a series of Irish stereotypes, from the alcoholic Sir Patrick, the parsimonious and litigious Sir Murtagh, and the gambling Sir Kit to the useless Sir Condy. Each of these landlords contributes to the erosion of the Rackrent estate, and the exploitation of the tenantry that funds their foibles is highlighted by Thady's narrative, despite his reiteration that he will not say anything against "the honour of the family." Thady's ostentatious attempts to exculpate the Rackrents only emphasize the extent of their culpability. When the reckless gambling of the absentee Sir Kit leads to repeated requests for money, Thady reports that his agent:

> Ferreted the tenants out of their lives – not a week without a call for money – drafts upon drafts from Sir Kit – but I laid it all to the fault of the agent; for, says I, what can Sir Kit do with so much cash, and he a single man?   (21)

The Rackrents represent an aristocracy that is ultimately self-consuming and moribund, divorced from the productive economy. Yet the novel does not present an uncomplicated contrast between an ideologically bankrupt, inefficient landed class and a dynamic and meritocratic elite, any more than it presents a simple contrast between a native Irish peasantry and an Anglo-Irish elite.[16] The threat to the Rackrent family comes from within the household, in the form of the scheming and unscrupulous Jason Quirk, son of the supposedly loyal retainer Thady. While Jason is shown to have a legal and commercial knowledge that enables him to profit from the decline in the Rackrent family, his main strength is his ability to exploit the vanity and vices of successive landlords, as he plays on their willingness to exchange future interest for immediate gratification. Jason is in many respects no different from the Rackrents, in that he too is motivated by a predominant passion, but his passion involves the accumulation rather than the dissipation of wealth. He has no sense of benevolence or paternalism, but in this he is just like the Rackrents. Edgeworth's novel therefore represents an indictment of the aristocratic ethos, by indicating the hollowness of its paternalistic claims, but without suggesting any viable alternative system of values.

Edward Copeland has argued that the novel from the 1790s was fundamentally preoccupied with "the amount of spendable income in the heroine's pocket,"[17] and Jane Austen's novels, in particular, contain very precise references to the financial status of the characters. The opening of *Sense and Sensibility* (1811) outlines the economic predicament of Mrs. Dashwood and her daughters, who are forced to retrench their expenditure on their father's death since the estate is inherited by a son from her dead husband's previous marriage. When Austen revised the novel for the second edition many of the changes were designed to clarify this legal and financial position. The introduction of Mrs. Jennings at the opening of chapter 8 contains no description of her appearance, but rather the information that "Mrs Jennings was a widow, with an ample jointure."[18] The focus on female characters within Austen's novels means that there is a great emphasis on settlements, jointures, wills etc., and therefore on the disposition and distribution of wealth rather than its creation. These overt references challenge the tendency in fiction to present marriage as an affective union based on true love, brought about despite acquisitive relations. Austen exposes the continuing importance of mercenary considerations within the novel and within marriage, satirizing the affective ethos in the exaggerated sensibility of Marianne Dashwood, who believes in love at first sight and the impossibility of a second attachment. Yet while Marianne's unrestrained emotions and romantic ideas are exposed as inappropriate for the modern world, symbolized by her eventual marriage to her unromantic second lover Colonel Brandon, purely mercenary behavior is equally censured through the portrayal of her first lover Willoughby, who is characterized by callousness and self-serving hypocrisy. The prudential yet sincere approach to marriage is celebrated in the character of Elinor

Dashwood, and Deidre Lynch has shown how Elinor's prudence is manifested in the economy of her lexis.[19]

In William Makepeace Thackeray's *The Newcomes* (1855), dynastic ambition and mercenary motivation are represented as inimical to the happiness of members of society through a series of disastrous marriages forged by economic interest. Ethel Newcome protests that:

> There never were, since the world began, people so unblushingly sordid! We own it, and are proud of it. We barter rank against money, and money against rank, day after day... We are as much sold as Turkish women; the only difference being that our masters may have but one Circassian at a time.[20]

When the mercenary marriage of Barnes Newcome ends in shameful ignominy, the narrator pairs financial scrutiny with divine judgment in asking "When the whole of the accounts of that wretched bankruptcy are brought up for final Audit, which of the unhappy partners shall be shown to be most guilty?" (595). The metaphor reinforces the connections between the marriage plots of *The Newcomes* and the theme of reckless financial speculation.

The Newcomes, along with a swath of other mid-nineteenth-century novels, such as Dickens's *Martin Chuzzlewit* (1843–1844) and *Little Dorrit* (1855–1857) and Trollope's *The Way We Live Now* (1875), marks a return to interest in the acquisition, rather than simply the distribution, of money. But the mechanisms for the creation of wealth in those novels, whether the Bundelcund Banking Corporation in *The Newcomes*, the Anglo-Bengalee Railway Company in *Martin Chuzzlewit*, Merdle's Bank in *Little Dorrit*, or the Great South Central Pacific and Mexican Railway in *The Way We Live Now*, are all forms of financial bubble. In both *The Newcomes* and *The Way We Live Now* the activities of the financiers are metonymically represented in the activities of a group of feckless young aristocrats, who gamble away their patrimony, their promissory notes providing a metaphor for the shares exchanged by the older generation.

In Defoe's novels wealth is frequently acquired through dishonest means, but this does not reflect on the value and importance of wealth itself. Money is presented as a means of attaining a virtuous life, through retirement from the sphere of dishonest action, and the financial system is a fundamentally virtuous mechanism against which dishonest activities can be measured. In the nineteenth-century novels the systems of peculation and misappropriation are not represented as perversions of the economic system, but rather as the system itself. The mercenary marriage market, the financial bubble, and the card table comprise a series of nesting metaphors, in which all represent one another, and all come to symbolize what is presented as a universal desire to gain a living through cheating, over-reaching, and exploiting other people. In *The Newcomes* the extent and perniciousness of the system is emphasized by the fact that the swindle is perpetrated not by some evil criminal mastermind, but by the amiable and naïve military hero, Tom Newcome. The eighteenth-century distrust of money and finance, manifested by the King of Brobdingnag and Matthew Bramble, has metamorphosed into a nineteenth-century disgust at an economic system which is shown as having displaced or stifled true productivity and true affection, and afflicted everybody within society. When the hero and heroine are finally united at the end of the novel, the happy resolution is undermined by the suggestion in the closing lines of *The Newcomes* that such an ending is only possible in "happy, harmless Fable-land." In real life there is only injustice; and the only resolution is death. Thus the novel, which for a century and a half provided a forum for the exploration and criticism of the economic system, and analyzed the relationship between affective and moral values, is ultimately presented as a world that is illusory, since it has a justice and benevolence that do not exist outside fiction. The "poet of Fable-land . . . deals out bags of sovereigns which won't buy anything" (774).

Notes

1. Patrick Brantlinger, *Fictions of State: Culture and Credit in Britain, 1694–1994* (Ithaca, NY: Cornell University Press, 1996), p. 45.
2. Sir William Petty, *The Petty Papers* (London: Constable, 1927), p. 213.
3. James Thompson, *Models of Value: Eighteenth-Century Political Economy and the Novel* (Durham, NC: Duke University Press, 1996), p. 3.
4. Daniel Defoe, *Roxana: The Fortunate Mistress* (Oxford: World's Classics, 1996), p. 42.
5. Daniel Defoe, *A Journal of the Plague Year* (Oxford: World's Classics, 1998), pp. 94–95.
6. Sandra Sherman, *Finance and Fictionality in the Early Eighteenth Century: Accounting for Defoe* (Cambridge University Press, 1996), pp. 145–149.
7. Samuel Macey, *Money and the Novel* (Victoria, BC: Sono Nis Press, 1983), p. 9.
8. Jonathan Swift, *Gulliver's Travels* (Oxford: World's Classics, 2005), p. 80.
9. Colin Nicholson, *Writing and the Rise of Finance* (Cambridge University Press, 1994), p. 106.
10. Charles Johnstone, *Chrysal: Or, The Adventures of a Guinea*, 2 vols. (London, 1760–1765), vol. I, p. 94.
11. Oliver Goldsmith, *The Citizen of the World*, 2 vols. (London: Dent, 1891), letter XI, vol. I, p. 53.
12. Adam Smith, *The Wealth of Nations*, Books I–III (Harmondsworth: Penguin, 1986), p. 119.
13. Oliver Goldsmith, *The Vicar of Wakefield* (Oxford: World's Classics, 1999), p. 99.

14. Tobias Smollett, *The Expedition of Humphry Clinker* (Oxford: World's Classics, 1984), p. 36.
15. Maria Edgeworth, *Castle Rackrent* (Oxford: World's Classics, 1980), p. 3.
16. Liz Bellamy, "Regionalism and Nationalism: Maria Edgeworth, Walter Scott and the Definition of Britishness," in *The Regional Novel in Britain and Ireland 1800–1990*, ed. K. D. M. Snell (Cambridge University Press, 1998), pp. 58–64.
17. Edward Copeland, *Women Writing About Money* (Cambridge University Press, 1995), p. 10.
18. Jane Austen, *Sense and Sensibility* (Oxford: World's Classics, 2004), p. 28.
19. Deidre Lynch, *The Economy of Character* (University of Chicago Press, 1998), pp. 232–235.
20. William Makepeace Thackeray, *The Newcomes* (London: Everyman, 1994), pp. 324–325.

12

"The southern unknown countries": imagining the Pacific in the eighteenth-century novel

ROBERT MARKLEY

By the time James Cook was killed in 1779 at Kealakekua Bay on the Big Island of Hawai'i, the Pacific Ocean had been mapped and remapped by dozens of fictional and non-fictional texts.[1] Even before the news of his death reached England, popular accounts of Cook's first two voyages had begun to trans-form Polynesia into an idyllic realm of tropical beaches and exotic cultures or, more ominously, into a beleaguered paradise assaulted by merchants and missionaries. For readers before 1770, however, the Pacific was conceived as a mosaic of more-or-less distinct regions and spheres of influence that, in different ways, fulfilled three crucial, if imaginary, roles. First, the islands east of the Indonesian archipelago (and the imaginary continent of Terra Australis Incognita) offered the prospect of an insatiable market for European exports and an inexhaustible storehouse of gold, spices, and exotic goods; second, the civilizations of China and Japan offered the luxury goods (tea and porcelain) in demand across Europe and access to complex trading networks across East Asia that could multiply profits severalfold; and third, the west coast of the Americas stoked dreams of breaking the Spanish monopoly on gold and silver mining, disrupting Spanish trade across the Pacific, and blocking French designs to control the slave trade in the Caribbean and Central America.[2]

Despite their differences, these regions were often joined in grand visions of British expansion across thousands of miles of ocean. Writing in his *Review of the State of the English Nation* in 1711, Defoe cautions against get-rich-quick schemes for colonizing the Pacific, yet nonetheless asserts that "there is Room enough on the Western Coast of America, call'd the South Seas, for us to Fix, Plant, Settle, and Establish a Flourishing Trade, without Injuring, Encroaching on, or perhaps in the least Invading the Property or Commerce of the

Spaniards."[3] This vision of a South Seas of infinite resources and endlessly "Flourishing Trade" derived, in part, from the extravagant claims by seventeenth-century British explorers, notably John Narborough and William Dampier, and helped to fuel the speculative frenzy for South Sea Company stock between 1712 and 1720. Yet British enthusiasm for Pacific exploration persisted after the collapse of the South Sea Bubble in the autumn of 1720, and this stubborn optimism suggests the ways in which the Pacific marked a fundamental dialectic in the national imagination: the hopes that Pacific trade and colonization would cement Britain's status as a global power; and the fears that failure in the South Seas would undermine its naval power, economic ambitions, and political influence. To a significant extent, eighteenth-century fiction set in the Pacific, particularly Defoe's novels, can be read as compensatory efforts to reconcile these hopes and fears; what British expeditions to the Pacific failed to accomplish in reality could be imagined in fiction by projecting onto the South Seas fantastic visions of a "Flourishing Trade."

Taken together, several works of fiction of the 1720s – Jonathan Swift's *Gulliver's Travels* and Daniel Defoe's *Captain Singleton* and *A New Voyage Round the World* – supplement traditional histories of the novel by making problematic the ways in which early eighteenth-century fiction became entangled with visions of the South Seas as a crucial theater for expanding Britain's economic and naval power. These works are not necessarily representative of the huge body of fiction available to readers before the 1770s, but they proved crucial in structuring both the wishful thinking that motivated British voyages to the Pacific and the satiric skepticism that these unrealistic expectations provoked. Defoe and Swift recast a long tradition of voyage literature in order to define the Pacific as a theater for reimagining Britain's national identity. No realistic narrative could comprehend an unbounded ocean whose shorelines faded off the northern and southern edges of maps. Their novels, in this context, present contrasting versions of British ventures in the Pacific: Gulliver adrift on his misadventures versus Defoe's heroes negotiating always incomplete transitions from piracy and opportunism to sustained commercial success. Given its roots in voyage literature, it is not surprising that fiction set in the Pacific often seems tangential to the development of the eighteenth-century novel. Nonetheless, in the century before Britain established colonies in the Far East, novels such as *Captain Singleton* and *Gulliver's Travels* demonstrate the ways in which the Pacific helped to shape the nation's ability to imagine itself, culturally as well as economically, as a global power.

Fiction and non-fiction

Early in 1720 when Defoe sent his pirate-hero, Bob Singleton, into the Pacific, he could draw on a rich tradition of voyage literature that described the hardships, profit-taking, and flag-planting that stirred British dreams of a "Flourishing Trade." Before the advent of steamships, voyages to the Pacific around Cape Horn were expensive, dangerous, and time consuming, beset by the omnipresent threats of storms, scurvy, supply shortages, shipwreck, mutiny, and attacks from Spanish ships off the coasts of Chile and Peru and Dutch ships in the East Indies. Beginning in the sixteenth century, accounts of the often harrowing voyages to the Pacific constituted a popular genre that interlaced tales of adventure, shipwreck, mutiny, and naval raids with commercial reconnaissance, nationalist propaganda, skewed cultural anthropology, and schemes for future commerce and colonization.[4] In the late seventeenth century readers in Britain avidly consumed the eye-witness accounts of the buccaneers, including William Dampier, Basil Ringrose, and Lionel Wafer, who raided the Spanish colonies in South and Central America in the 1680s; and who, in the case of Dampier, parlayed such experiences into the command of three voyages to locate and explore Terra Australis Incognita.[5] Significantly, both tales of buccaneer raids and accounts of sanctioned naval expeditions display what Glyndwr Williams calls "a process of enlargement and literary polishing"[6] – a self-conscious recasting by ghost-writers of oral accounts, ships' logs, and officers' journals into literary artifacts designed to appeal to a readership eager for tales of adventure and investment opportunities. In this regard, the fictionalizing of the Pacific preceded and helped to define the contours of the novels of the 1720s.

Tellingly, Defoe's final novel, *A New Voyage Round the World by a Course Never Sailed Before* (1725), appropriates the title of Dampier's *A New Voyage Round the World* (1697) and its recycling by later writers and publishers eager to cash in on a popular genre. William Funnell, Woodes Rogers, George Shelvocke, William Betagh, and Richard Walter and Benjamin Robins all promised their readers "new voyages around the world."[7] The buccaneering roots of these works reflect the hard realities of ventures into the Pacific: because the British launched no successful commercial ventures in the Pacific before 1800, all of these "new voyages" turned to preying on Spanish ships, raiding Spanish colonies in Chile and Peru, as Sir Francis Drake had done in the 1570s, and then sailing across the Pacific and using their booty to trade for spices, silks, and porcelain in the Far East.[8] Rogers' mission, though, had no successor for thirty years, and the South Sea Company never sent a ship into the Pacific.

To market their narratives of actual voyages, authors, ghostwriters, and booksellers had to compress radically the day-to-day entries of logbooks and journals of three to four years at sea and to censor potentially sensitive navigational information that might prove more useful for Dutch and Spanish rivals than for British readers. With few glorious successes to trumpet, tales of circumnavigation remain episodic and, in some ways, unfulfilling. For Defoe in *A New Voyage Round the World*, "The History of the Voyage" need not recount facts "useful indeed for Seamen going thither again, and *how few are they?*",[9] but must link the various regions of the Pacific – from Terra Australis Incognita to Peru – *imaginatively*; and in his own work, he harnesses tales of Pacific adventure to larger generic and ideological ends. Particularly in *A New Voyage*, his nameless hero embodies the virtues of an ideal commander. For Swift, in contrast, the "History of the Voyage" becomes a satiric tale of the senses of disorientation and eroding selfhood that plague the usually hapless Gulliver in voyages that never reach their ostensible destinations.

Captain Singleton *and* A New Voyage Round the World

Defoe's novels set in the Pacific offer distinct but complementary visions of the South Seas. If *Captain Singleton* reworks a tradition of pirate literature that Defoe himself had helped to shape, *A New Voyage* reasserts the novelist's faith in the prospects of a "Flourishing Trade" in the wake of the South Sea Bubble, which had exposed the Company's schemes for trade, privateering, and exploration in the South Seas as little more than a smoke-screen for financial corruption. Published in June 1720, two months before the collapse of the Company's stock, *Singleton* outlines the novelistic opportunities that the Pacific offers. In *The Farther Adventures of Robinson Crusoe* (1719), Crusoe, now in his late sixties, becomes a merchant in Southeast Asia, and his quest for profits eventually takes him along the coast of China, to Beijing, and then across Siberia in a caravan; Singleton, in contrast, reaches the waters of the far southwestern Pacific and begins his ultimate transition from pirate to merchant. As Hans Turley argues, Singleton, like the older Crusoe, is distinguished less by an interiorized psychology than by his rebellion against hierarchies of command on navy vessels, civilized behavior, legal strictures, and moral consciousness.[10] What distinguishes Singleton is not simply his outlaw status as an "enemy to all mankind" (the legal definition of piracy in the eighteenth century) but the ways in which he displaces the dangers of eighteenth-century voyages to the South Seas onto a vision of profit and ultimately reform.

Singleton's adventures in the second half of the novel highlight the stark differences that Defoe and his contemporaries perceived between potential trading partners in the far western Pacific. Confronted by Dutch ships among "the infinite Number of Islands which lye in [the] Seas" of Southeast Asia, Singleton fights when he has the advantage and shrewdly negotiates when he senses the opportunity: after running a captured ship aground and stealing its merchandise, he gives its sailors the option of joining his crew.[11] Clandestine trade and piracy bring Singleton enough money to convince him that *"we were rich enough"* to leave "Rummaging among the Spice Islands" (198), and he adjusts to temporary setbacks by setting a new mercantile course. Unlike the mutual suspicion that characterizes Singleton's encounters with the Dutch, his negotiations with the Chinese merchants are marked by a civility that is essential as both the basis *for* and the product *of* mutually beneficial commerce. This scene is not Defoe's "realistic" depiction of Anglo-Chinese trading encounters in the eighteenth century, but a fictional rendering of the mutually reinforcing values of mutual self-interest, good-faith bargaining, and profitable trade that he had advocated in his 1711 numbers of the *Review*. In this respect, Singleton's turn to commercial civility provides the moral platform for his eventual renunciation of his life as a pirate, if not the fortune he has accumulated. An episode wherein negotiations with the Chinese leave both the reformed pirates and the Chinese "exceedingly well satisfied" (201) tells us less about a change in Singleton's moral psychology or a dawning recognition of his past crimes than it does about his strategic flexibility and new-found zeal for trade. Because the wealthy regions of the China Sea hold the promise of nutmegs, cloves, silks, teas, and (above all else) gold bullion, trade becomes – for Defoe as it does for Singleton – the logical extension and evolutionary end of piracy. Piracy offers him the means to invest in a complex regional economy that produces "Civility" as well as profit.

In this respect, *Singleton* makes the Pacific a logical stage for the theatrics of his repentance precisely because the novel asks its readers to imagine the mutually constitutive discourses of trade and civility as a means for the hero to secure a stable, if secretive, identity. Wealth produces reformation, even if Singleton and his partner Quaker William's future in London rests on the disguised homoerotic bonds that isolate them from society. Yet the riches that Singleton and William accumulate from "turn[ing] Merchants" are a fantastic projection of what trade in the "great Pacifick" offers, and Defoe yokes their wealth to two of the great dreams – or delusions – of eighteenth-century voyage literature: reopening trade to the closed nation of Japan and finding a sea-route to the Pacific across the arctic wastes of North America.

Immediately after concluding their dealings with the Chinese merchants, William tries to persuade Singleton to sail to Japan in order to rescue thirteen English sailors shipwrecked "upon a great Rock in a stormy Night where they lost their Ship and the rest of their Men were drowned" (201–202). Japan had been closed to all Europeans except for a single Dutch trading outpost since 1638, the year that professing Christianity was made a capital offense, and native converts were massacred.[12] The source of William's tale is "a kind of Religious, or *Japan* Priest, who spoke some Words of *English*" (201), having learned them from sailors who had been pressured to denounce the Christian religion and worship what Defoe calls "their God, an Idol" (202). The "Japan Priest" rescued the sailors, making it possible for them to save their lives by sailing away. The sailors in turn have told the priest, who relays it to William, that they originally voyaged to Japan via the North Pole: in other words, that they have discovered a new route to the East. In this embedded tale, Defoe gives fictional form to the centuries-long dream of finding a sea route across the Canadian Arctic, the fabled Northwest Passage that motivated expeditions from the sixteenth to the late eighteenth centuries.[13] William sees for himself only a scrawled, one-sentence narrative left behind by the sailors, *"We came from Greenland, and from the North Pole"* (203), that marks the limits of geographical knowledge at the border between plausible narrative and pure fantasy.

Defoe's treatment of this twice-removed tale of the crew's "noble Discover[y]" differs, as we shall see, from Swift's handling in *Gulliver's Travels* of Japan, the only actual country that Gulliver visits in his travels across the Pacific. In *Singleton* Japan exists beyond the horizons of first-hand knowledge, trade, and English ambition, linked to the tale of an impossible voyage and the sacrifice of Englishmen who cannot be rescued. The Japanese remain beyond the collective suggested by "Mankind." Although the crew captures and loots a Japanese merchant ship in one of their raids, the Japanese empire lies outside of the "Adventures and Pyracies" that the title promises. It becomes instead a kind of talisman for two centuries of British ambitions to exploit the Northwest Passage as a comparatively fast and inexpensive sea-route to the great empires and trading emporia of the Pacific. The marooned sailors who vanish from the narrative are Defoe's ciphers for the thousands of lost seamen who never completed their global circumnavigations. Their ghosts haunt English dreams of Pacific wealth. It is only in fiction that these dreams can be realized.

In *A New Voyage Round the World*, Defoe relocates the prospect of an infinitely profitable trade from the China Sea to the shores of the imaginary great southern continent. The undiscovered or under-explored lands of the

South Pacific offer endless reserves of gold and valuable commodities. In contrast to *Singleton*'s focus on "Adventures and Pyracies," *A New Voyage* offers fantasies of mercantile opportunism that refurbish the arguments that Defoe had made in 1711 when he devoted twelve numbers of his *Review* to promoting the South Sea Company. Repeatedly in the *Review* Defoe argues that if England were to drive the French from the Pacific, the ensuing trade would be of immense advantage to Britain. *A New Voyage* envisions the immensity by inverting the route of actual circumnavigations: an English ship reaps vast profits by sailing eastward around the Cape of Good Hope and across the Indian Ocean, then discovers a new continent in the Pacific, new trade in Chile, and ideal conditions for colonies in South America. In the post-Bubble disenchantment of the mid 1720s, no cartel of investors awaits the hero at the end; indeed the financing of the improbable voyage comes from a single anonymous investor in London, who conveniently dies so that the narrator can keep the profits.

Defoe distances *A New Voyage* from the traditions of voyage literature, declaring that, instead of a conventional story-less journal, he is providing a "manner of relating" "observations" that is "perfectly new in its form" (3–4). Defoe's claims for the originality of his novel, significantly, are aesthetic, even metafictional; it is the imagination of the author that will make particulars "agreeable" and ensure a narrative and conceptual unity that will turn a "variety of incidents" into a believable first-person account. Yet even as Defoe mocks previous tales of circumnavigation, he appropriates and reworks the assumptions and values that underlie their voyages. His novel is a "history of the voyage" related by an individual who becomes no more than his account of the crew's adventures. What voyage literature can only promise, Defoe asserts his novel will deliver. The "indifferent author" whom Defoe has in mind is Dampier, whose accounts of his three contentious and unprofitable missions to map the coasts of Australia and discover new markets for British trade devolve into long stretches of "directions for [future] sailors coming that way." What distinguishes Defoe's novel from Dampier's narratives is its redefinition of the genre to exclude the descriptions of scurvy, dissension, violence, and death that are the staples of non-fictional accounts of circumnavigation. For Defoe, the narrative coherence of his history reflects the single-mindedness of his visions of wealth to be made in the Pacific. Moll Flanders and Bob Singleton reform after they have become rich, but the narrator of *A New Voyage* has no need to leave a life of rampant acquisitiveness because he already exists in a privileged state: the success of the voyage legitimizes his actions and identity by redefining "character" in the mutually constitutive terms of morality and trade.[14] And the narrative "form" dramatizes new strategies of command aboard ship that recast the frustrations of previous circumnavigations into a dream vision of mercantile aggrandizement.

Although the hero of *A New Voyage* shares the pirate's ability to command by consensus, he is no Bob Singleton. Defoe's treatment of the abortive mutiny in *A New Voyage* rewrites the Madagascar episodes in *Captain Singleton* by emphasizing the superiority of cogently planned trading ventures over piracy or mere opportunism. The hero quickly pardons all but two of the mutineers; he then sends one of them, the second mate and ringleader, to spy on a crew of pirates on Madagascar. After learning that the pirates are merely "a crew of unresolved divided rogues . . . [with] nobody to command, and therefore nobody to obey" (64–65), the now-reformed second mate convinces those tired of their immoral, and not very profitable, ways to join the expedition for the remainder of the voyage. Yet to the extent that the hero's moral and psychological identity is defined by his strategies of command and control, his integrity as a character becomes as imaginary as his vision of the boundless wealth of the Pacific. Defoe's heroes, as they sail the Pacific, rely on the prospect of "infinite Advantage" as a way to justify the coherence of a *retrospectively* constructed self: that is, Singleton can reform himself, and the narrator of *A New Voyage* simultaneously can disclaim the need for self-reformation, because the captain and crew have returned to England wealthy men. The success of their voyages grants hero and narrator the narrative authority – the aesthetic authority – to recount the ways in which they shaped their strategies of self-command into tales of moral reclamation and consensual will. The hero of Defoe's final novel is a different kind of character from Roxana or Moll Flanders because his self-justification lies in already having overcome the dangers and frustrations of trade in the Pacific.

While it may be tempting to write off *A New Voyage* as a failed or eccentric experiment, Defoe seems intent on pressing narrative fiction into the service of something approaching science fiction: a near-future, alternative history of commercial triumph. In his preface to the third volume of his Crusoe trilogy, the *Serious Reflections* (1720), Defoe castigates his critics who claim that his novels elevate make-believe over moral purpose. Speaking in the persona of Crusoe, he declares "that the Story, though Allegorical, is also Historical; and that it is the beautiful Representation of a Life . . . sincerely adapted to, and intended for the common Good of Mankind," while reminding his readers that "the Fable is always made for the Moral, not the Moral for the Fable."[15] Although *A New Voyage* shares more with Crusoe's *Farther Adventures* than with the far better-known first volume of the trilogy, it too privileges a

"Moral" over a "Fable"; now the moral is defined in terms of the "common Good" of British commercialism.

The undiscovered lands of the Pacific that the narrator visits exist in the liminal spaces between allegory and history; the hero claims that

> I lay it down as a Foundation; that whoever, Sailing over the *South-Seas*, keeps a stated Distance from the Tropick to the Latitude of fifty six, to sixty Degrees, and steers *Eastward* towards the *Straights of Magellan*, shall never fail to discover new Worlds, new Nations, and new inexhaustible Funds of Wealth and Commerce, such as never were yet known to the Merchants of *Europe*.   (*A New Voyage*, 131)

The uncharted regions they supposedly inhabit (far to the south of Macquarie Island and its penguin colonies) are the imaginary – and essential – landscape of an ideology of capitalist expansion, the fictions of "inexhaustible Funds of Wealth and Commerce" that justify outlays of men, ships, and money. The promise of these "new Worlds," for Defoe, renders schemes of Pacific trade and exploration rational enterprises, blurring distinctions between fiction and fact, speculation and investment. These "new nations," with "no Manufactures or Materials for Manufactures of their own" (131) must remain imaginary because to "civilize" them would bring them into economies of scarcity, self-interest, and commercial competition. If that were to happen, these lands would offer not "the best Merchandise and Return in the World" (131), but only refractions of the contentious histories and ongoing antagonism that Swift satirizes in the rivalry between Lilliput and Blefuscu.

Gulliver in Japan

Where Defoe sees new horizons of economic expansion in the Pacific, Swift finds only the abjection of the Western self and the shipwreck of mercantile fantasies. While Defoe offers the prospect of British explorers outflanking their European rivals, Gulliver's voyages through an imaginary Pacific in *Travels* are punctuated in book III by two encounters with natives of actual countries: the Japanese and Dutch pirates who capture the hero at the beginning of the book, and the Japanese Emperor who aids him at its end. As several critics have noted, Swift uses these encounters to satirize the Dutch, extending and updating the criticisms that Swift had published in 1711 and 1712; *The Conduct of the Allies*, in particular, skewers the Netherlands, England's erstwhile ally in the War of Spanish Succession, as unreliable, duplicitous, and self-aggrandizing.[16] For much of *Gulliver's Travels*, Swift pushes aside or satirically exaggerates previous accounts of South Seas voyaging, but in writing about Japan he draws on a rich and varied tradition of European commentary that paradoxically both idealizes the country as a bastion of propriety, power, and patriarchal authority and anathematizes the Japanese for their near-total ban on foreign trade and their brutal suppression of Christianity.[17] Like many of his contemporaries, Swift recognized the limitations of British power in the Pacific, and his satire ultimately seems directed less at the exaggerations of travel narratives than the kinds of commercial and colonial adventurism that Defoe promoted.[18] In this respect Gulliver's trip to Japan represents a brief but telling disruption of eurocentric discourses of imperialism, techno-military supremacy, and religious authority. Unlike the Master Houyhnhnm and the King of Brobdingnag, the Japanese Emperor is neither an impossible ideal nor a satiric scourge; instead he embodies the limits of Western authority and offers a corrective to the adventurism and corruption that Swift identifies with England's colonial ambitions. In the background of Swift's depiction of the Japanese lies his recognition that the empire's violent suppression of Christianity in the seventeenth century challenged the fundamental tenets of European commercial expansionism and religious proselytizing.[19] Swift, in short, dramatizes what Defoe avoids: the prospect of a Far Eastern empire that mocks British pretensions to commercial expansion in the Pacific.

Gulliver's adventures in book III begin with an abortive trading venture: sailing from Tonquin, he is captured by Japanese pirates. The villain of this encounter, though, is not the Japanese captain but a Dutchman, in league with the pirates, who, "jabbering to us in his own Language, swore we should be tyed Back to Back, and thrown into the Sea."[20] Swift's vilification of the Dutchman recalls John Dryden's caricatures of the evil merchants of the Dutch East India Company in his tragedy *Amboyna* (1672), a propagandistic indictment of the torture and execution of twelve British merchants in the Moluccas in 1623.[21] Despite the Dutchman's efforts, the Japanese captain manages to save Gulliver's life and then, when the hero is "set a-drift in a small Canoe, with Paddles and a Sail, and four Days Provisions," proves "so kind [as] to double [the food and water] out of his own Stores" (139). This episode dramatizes Swift's satiric point that his hero finds "more Mercy in a Heathen, than in a Brother Christian" (139), yet the Japanese pirate is not presented as a complex psychological creation but as an embodiment of the humane qualities that the Dutchman lacks. In this respect, Swift displaces onto the "jabbering" Dutchman the paranoia about foreigners and Christians that was encoded in the edicts of successive shoguns in Tokugawa Japan.[22]

At the end of book III, the Emperor of Japan exhibits the same kind of sympathy for Gulliver's plight as the pirate captain; he, too, embodies the antithesis of the injustice and cynical self-interest that characterize Dutch apostasy in the Far East. Ironically, the only way that Gulliver can return to England is to pose as a Dutchman in order to secure a passage from the fictional island of Luggnagg to a real, but sketchily drawn, Japan. Gulliver's reception by the Emperor recalls nostalgically accounts of the seventeenth-century English sailor, Will Adams, who prospered at the court in Edo as a translator, advisor, and minor samurai official.[23] Rather than the ritual prostrations and indignities that Gulliver must perform in Luggnagg, his treatment in Edo is improbably decorous and friendly, and shunts aside the ritual humiliation, described in contemporary European sources, required of supplicants prostrating themselves before the Shogun. In fact, Swift's Emperor helps Gulliver avoid the otherwise compulsory ritual of *yefumi* (literally, trampling on the crucifix) that symbolized both the political allegiance of the Emperor's subjects to the throne and the Dutch subservience to Japanese authority.

Shortly before Swift published *Gulliver's Travels*, Engelbert Kaempfer's *History of Japan* appeared. This was an account of his service as a physician on the tiny Dutch outpost of Deshima in Nagasaki harbor. Barred from contact with all Japanese except through official translators and a handful of officials, the Dutch made themselves virtual prisoners in exchange for a carefully monitored trade. In his *History*, the primary European source on Japanese culture published during the eighteenth century, Kaempfer describes at length the ritual abjections that Dutch ambassadors had to undergo at the Shogun's court.[24] Performed during the merchants' annual audiences with the Shogun, desecration of Christian icons represents, for Swift, Dutch complicity in subordinating religion to an unhealthy desire for profits and their perverse willingness to humiliate themselves. Gulliver's petition to avoid *"trampling upon the Crucifix"* meets with the Shogun's initial disbelief: "he seemed a little surprised; and said he believed I was the first of my Countrymen who ever made any Scruple in this Point; and he began to doubt whether I was a real *Hollander* or no; but rather suspected I must be a CHRISTIAN" (200). Swift's opposition of "Hollander" and "CHRISTIAN" turns the Dutch into satiric butts, even as it suggests the sense of disorientation, or disidentification, that plagues Europeans in the far western Pacific. Like Singleton, Gulliver must deny his national identity in order to preserve his life and avoid apostasy. Swift's hero can preserve his sense of himself as an Englishman only by subterfuge, only by avoiding, with the Emperor's connivance, the rituals of abjection that characterize the Dutch. It is the Dutch crew, not the Japanese officials, who pester Gulliver on board the ship that will carry him back to Europe – sardonically named the *Amboyna* – about whether he has complied with the ritual of *yefumi*. The Dutch have internalized the performative conditions of their own abjection, and therefore represent the nightmarish loss of integrity and identity that is treated more comically in Gulliver's professed desire in book IV to transform himself into a Houyhnhnm. For Swift, the pursuit of the Pacific dreams that animate Defoe's writing lead to a loss of a normative sense of selfhood.

The afterlife of new voyages

Charged with raiding Spanish shipping and disrupting New Spain's trade in bullion, Commodore George Anson (later Lord Admiral of the British navy) led a wartime expedition around Cape Horn and into the South Seas in the early 1740s. In 1743, in a desperate effort to stave off disaster, Anson's only remaining warship, the *Centurion*, successfully ambushed and captured the Manila Galleon off the coast of the Philippines. Forced to return to Canton to refit his vessel, Anson behaved more like a buccaneer on shore than a representative of the British nation in the chief trading entrepôt of the wealthy Qing Empire. Edward Page, the chief merchant for the East India Company in the Chinese port, describes the Commodore's behavior as "a Case Extraordinary, and could not but Create some Disgust & aversion in the Chinese Government"; he describes the venerable Hong merchant, Suqua, telling Anson that the Chinese consider him "as a little man, and greatly [the] Inferiour" of the Viceroy in Canton.[25] Page's "Little Secret History" is devoted to describing his efforts to restrain Anson from disrupting the Company's lucrative trade in Canton.

The contrastive official account of this voyage, Walter and Robins's *A Voyage Round the World*, turns the commodore into a heroic embodiment of British decisiveness, power, and courage, and metamorphoses the Chinese into caricatures of cowering and effete natives. In episodes such as this, the Anson of the *Voyage* introjects the violence of the pirate warring against merchant shipping, and then projects it as the embodiment of stalwart British national identity. To the extent that the authors of Anson's *Voyage* rework a tradition of voyage literature given to overt nationalism and narratives of self-justification, they ignore Swift's satire, and reanimate Defoe's heroes. The fable, as Defoe would have it, is shaped to the moral.

More than twenty years later, John Hawkesworth, who had edited Swift's works, was paid the huge sum of £6,000 to turn the journals of the commanders of four British expeditions to the South Pacific between 1764 and 1771 into a single, marketable narrative. Hawkesworth recast observations from logbooks and journals into *An Account of the Voyages Undertaken by the Order of His Present Majesty for Making Discoveries in the Southern Hemisphere* (1773), a book both widely read and disparaged for turning four often desultory accounts into a unified first-person narrative, written from the perspective of a refined English gentleman of sensibility and means.

Like Defoe in writing *A New Voyage* as a "history," Hawkesworth grapples with the problem of converting observations of seas, winds, tides, and coast-lines into a narrative form that re-creates the experiential dimensions of such voyages. He defends his decision to write in the first person by claiming that:

> it was readily acknowledged [by the various commanders], that a narrative in the first person, would, by bringing the Adventurer and the Reader nearer together, without the intervention of a stranger, more strongly excite an interest, and consequently afford more entertainment . . . if it was written in the name of the several Commanders, I could exhibit only a naked narrative, without any opinion or sentiment of my own, however fair the occasion.[26]

His concern that a "naked narrative" will not sell many copies justifies, to his mind, appropriating novelistic strategies to (re)construct a fictional "I" – a subject removed from the experiences that the various commanders describe. Hawkesworth also believes that "opinion" and "sentiment" are essential strategies for allowing his readers to identify with "the Adventurer," a quasi-allegorical figure who embodies minute observation and general judgments about native cultures and natural wonders prompted by "occasion[s]" that demand commentary. By subsuming the wide variety of experiences that the commanders describe in their journals into "the Adventurer," the writer constructs a benevolent version of Defoe's hero in *A New Voyage*.

In rewriting a tradition of new voyages, Hawkesworth redefines both the "Adventurer" and the nature of adventure itself. Cultural "sentiment" – dis-interested reflection and a form of omniscient narration – becomes the mark of the stability of a British identity in the far reaches of the Pacific. Hawkesworth's *Account*, in this respect, redefines Defoe's sense of a "useful and diverting" narrative by downplaying economic motivations for British ventures in the Pacific. It offers instead a strategy of literary exchange-value that foregrounds the ways in which the record of mere experiences can be fictionalized and thereby made *more* useful, *more* diverting. This holds because individual experiences can be sifted and combined to discover the truths contained within history, and cultural encounters can be rewritten as the commerce between native innocence and civilized knowledge. In the process, as Hawkesworth rewrites the strategies that Defoe had employed to negotiate between "History" and a "useful and diverting narrative," the self is recast as a novelistic abstraction.

Coda

Ultimately, the Pacific functions on a number of levels to mark the limits of British power and ambition. By the time of the founding of the Australian penal colony at Botany Bay in 1788, Defoe's faith in the "new Worlds" of the South Pacific had become fantasies of a bygone era. Nonetheless, the imaginative distances between Swift's Lilliput and Botany Bay suggest something of the conceptual work that the novel undertook in the eighteenth-century Pacific. As the native peoples of Australia, Aotearoa, the Canadian Northwest, and Polynesia replaced the Lilliputians, talking horses, and Brobdingnagians of the 1720s, the half-pirate, half-merchant of the early century was being transformed in fiction, non-fiction, and the hybrid exemplified by Hawkesworth into the abstract figure of the authoritative novelistic "I" – as much a product of the imagination as Defoe's heroes. This "I" of "sentiment" and "opinion" allowed the new worlds of Polynesia and Micronesia to be plotted within anglocentric narratives of human progress, invariably to the benefit of an emerging colonial power. Given England's fascination with the Pacific in the wake of Cook's voyages, the *"Southern* unknown Countries" had ceased to be the chimeras that Dampier and Defoe had imagined, and instead were the early locations of its transformation into an arena of colonial conflict.

Notes

1. On Cook's much-debated death see John Gascoigne, *Captain Cook: Voyager Between Worlds* (London: Hambledon, 2007), esp. pp. 214–219; and Anne Salmond, *The Trial of the Cannibal Dog: The Remarkable Story of Captain Cook's Encounters in the South Seas* (New Haven, CT: Yale University Press, 2003).
2. See O. H. K. Spate, *The Pacific Since Magellan*, vol. II, *Monopolists and Freebooters* (Minneapolis: University of Minnesota Press, 1983); J. C. Beaglehole, *The Exploration of the Pacific* (3rd edn, Stanford University Press, 1966); William Eisler, *The Furthest Shore: Images of Terra Australis from the Middle Ages to Captain Cook* (Cambridge University Press, 1995).
3. Daniel Defoe, *Review of the State of the English Nation* 8: 49 (July 17, 1711).

4. C. R. Boxer, ed. and trans., *The Tragic History of the Sea*, rev. edn with additional translation by Josiah Blackmore (Minneapolis: University of Minnesota Press, 2001).
5. For the exploits of the buccaneers, see A. O. Exquemelin, *Bucaniers of America . . . Inlarged with two Additional Relations, viz. The one of Captain Cook, and the Other of Captain Sharp* (London, 1684), and Basil Ringrose, *Bucaniers of America. The Second Volume Containing the Dangerous Voyage and Bold Attempts of Captain Bartholomew Sharp and Others; Performed upon the Coasts of the South Sea* (London, 1685). See Derek Howse and Norman Thrower, eds., *A Buccaneer's Atlas: Basil Ringrose's South Sea* (Berkeley and Los Angeles: University of California Press, 1992); Peter T. Bradley, *The Lure of Peru: Maritime Intrusions into the South Sea* (New York: St. Martins, 1989); and Diana and Michael Preston, *A Pirate of Exquisite Mind: The Life of William Dampier: Explorer, Naturalist and Buccaneer* (Sydney: Doubleday, 2004).
6. Glyndwr Williams, *The Great South Sea: English Voyages and Encounters 1570–1750* (New Haven, CT: Yale University Press, 1997), p. 113.
7. William Funnell, *A Voyage Round the World* (London, 1707); Woodes Rogers, *A Cruising Voyage Round the World* (London, 1712); George Shelvocke, *A Voyage Round the World by Way of the Great South Sea* (London, 1726); William Betagh, *A Voyage Round the World* (London, 1728); and Richard Walter, *A Voyage Round the World, in the Years MDCCXL, I, II, III, IV. By George Anson* (London, 1748); Richard Walter and Benjamin Robins, *A Voyage Round the World 1740–4 Compiled from the Papers of George Lord Anson* (1748).
8. Glyndwr Williams, "'The Inexhaustible Fountain of Gold': English Projects and Ventures in the South Seas, 1670–1750," in *Perspectives of Empire: Essays Presented to Gerald S. Graham*, ed. John E. Flint and Glyndwr Williams (London: Longman, 1973), pp. 27–53.
9. Daniel Defoe, *A New Voyage Round the World by a Course Never Sailed Before*, ed. John McVeagh (London: Pickering and Chatto, 2009), p. 30.
10. Hans Turley, *Rum, Sodomy, and the Lash: Piracy, Sexuality, and Masculine Identity* (New York University Press, 1999).
11. Daniel Defoe, *The Life, Adventures, and Pyracies of the Famous Captain Singleton*, ed. Shiv Kumar, with introduction by Penelope Wilson (New York: Oxford University Press, 1990), p. 191.
12. See Derek Massarella, *A World Elsewhere: Europe's Encounter with Japan in the Sixteenth and Seventeenth Centuries* (New Haven, CT: Yale University Press, 1990), and Jacques Proust, *Europe through the Prism of Japan: Sixteenth to Eighteenth Centuries*, trans. Elizabeth Bell (University of Notre Dame Press, 2002).
13. See Glyn Williams, *Voyages of Delusion: The Search for the Northwest Passage in the Age of Reason* (London: HarperCollins, 2002).
14. See Deidre Lynch, *The Economy of Character: Novels, Market Culture, and the Business of Inner Meaning* (University of Chicago Press, 1998).
15. Daniel Defoe, *Serious Reflections during the Life and Surprising Adventures of Robinson Crusoe* (London: W. Taylor, 1720), A2v, A2r.

16. See Anne Barbeau Gardiner, "Swift on the Dutch East India Merchants: The Context of the 1672–73 War Literature," *Huntington Library Quarterly* 54 (1991), 234–252. See also Neil Rennie, *Far-Fetched Facts: The Literature of Travel and the Idea of the South Seas* (Oxford: Clarendon Press, 1995), pp. 76–82; Maurice Johnson, Kitagawa Muncharu, and Philip Williams, *Gulliver's Travels and Japan* (Doshisha University: Amherst House, 1977); John Dussinger, "Gulliver in Japan: Another Possible Source," *Notes and Queries* 39, n.s. (1992), 464–467; and Hermann Real and Heinz Vienken, "Swift's 'Trampling upon the Crucifix' Once More," *Notes and Queries* 30, n.s. (1983), 513–514.

17. Engelbertus Kaempfer, *The History of Japan*, trans. J. G. Scheuchzer (London, 1727). On the significance of this work and its composition and publishing history, see Beatrice Bodart-Bailey and Derek Massarella, eds., *The Furthest Goal: Engelbert Kaempfer's Encounter with Tokugawa Japan* (Folkestone, Kent: Japan Library, 1995); Annette Keogh, "Oriental Translations: Linguistic Explorations into the Closed Nation of Japan," *The Eighteenth Century: Theory and Interpretation* 45 (2006), 171–191; and Elizabeth Kowaleski Wallace, "The First Samurai: Isolationism in Engelbert Kaempfer's 1727 *History of Japan*," *The Eighteenth Century: Theory and Interpretation* 48 (2007), 111–124.

18. See Clement Hawes, "Three Times Round the Globe: Gulliver and Colonial Discourse," *Cultural Critique* 18 (1991), 187–214; Claude Rawson, *God, Gulliver, and Genocide: Barbarism and the European Imagination, 1492–1945* (New York: Oxford University Press, 2001); and Anna Neill, *British Discovery Literature and the Rise of Global Commerce* (London: Palgrave, 2002), pp. 110–119.

19. In addition to Kaempfer's *History of Japan*, see Arnoldus Montanus, *Atlas Japanensis: Being Remarkable Addresses by Way of Embassy from the East-India Company of the United Provinces to the Emperor of Japan*, trans. John Ogilby (London, 1670); Francis Caron and Joost Schorten, *A Description of the Mighty Kingdoms of Japan and Siam*, trans. Roger Manley (London, 1671); and Jean Crasset, *The History of the Church of Japan*, trans. N. N., 2 vols. (London, 1705).

20. Herbert Davis, ed., *Gulliver's Travels*, in the *Prose Works of Jonathan Swift*, 14 vols. (Oxford: Shakespeare's Head Press, 1941), vol. XI, 138.

21. Robert Markley, *The Far East and the English Imagination, 1600–1740* (Cambridge University Press, 2006), pp. 143–176.

22. The standard account of the limitations and fall of Christianity in Japan is George Elison's *Deus Destroyed: The Image of Christianity in Early Modern Japan* (Cambridge, MA: Harvard University Press, 1973); see also C. R. Boxer, *The Christian Century in Japan: 1549–1650* (Berkeley: University of California Press, 1951); and Hubert Cieslik, "The Case of Christovão Ferreira," *Monumenta Nipponica* 29 (1974), 1–54.

23. See Giles Milton, *Samurai William: The Adventurer Who Unlocked Japan* (London: Hodder and Stoughton, 2002).

24. See Keogh, "Oriental Translations"; Markley, *Far East and the English Imagination*, 259–262; and Kowaleski Wallace, "The First Samurai."

25. Edward Page, "A Little Secret History of Affairs at Canton in the Year 1743 when the Centurion, Commodore Anson was lying in the River," November 18, 1765, MS 2894, Oregon Historical Society, Portland, 1–2, 4.
26. John Hawkesworth, *An Account of the Voyages Undertaken by the Order of His Present Majesty for Making Discoveries in the Southern Hemisphere*, 3 vols. (2nd edn, London, 1773), vol. 1, iv–v.

13

Editorial fictions: paratexts, fragments, and the novel

BARBARA M. BENEDICT

Eighteenth-century novels are full of lies and jokes. They bear false imprints and attributions; authors masquerade as editors; satires are veiled as documents; typographical signals, poems, songs, anecdotes, parables, sermons, philosophical commentary, pictorial vignettes, and unfinished tales interrupt the narrative. These appear not only within the text, but before, after, above, and below it in a riot of frontispieces, epigraphs, prefaces, tables of contents, dedicatory and admiring letters, interpolated tales, documents and reports, footnotes, glosses, chapter headings, songs, poems, inset tales, printers' ornaments and illustrations, and indexes. These paratexts divert readers' attention from the narrative to the text's documentary status: its authenticity and authority. Paratexts challenge the very possibility of representation by making textual transmission and the experience of fragmentation part of the process of reading the novel. Form qualifies content.

Editorial defense: Defoe and narrative authenticity

Daniel Defoe's *Moll Flanders* (1722) establishes authenticity by purporting to be an autobiography. Like memoirs and eyewitness accounts, autobiographies claim to be literal truth, but a narrative's authenticity does not guarantee its morality. *Moll Flanders* meets the conflicting needs of didacticism and credibility with an elaborate preface that negotiates the rival claims of authenticity and morality, accuracy and art. The novel appears to be a transcription of Moll's own account of her life. Its title guarantees entertainment by advertising variety and excitement:

> The Fortunes and Misfortunes of the Famous Moll Flanders, &c. Who was Born in Newgate, And during a Life of continu'd Variety, for Threescore Years, besides her childhood, was Twelve Year a *Whore*, five times a *Wife*

(whereof once to her own Brother), Twelve Year a *Thief*, Eight Year a Transported *Felon in Virginia*, at last grew Rich, lived *Honest*, and died a *Penitent*. Written from her own Memorandums.

The preface advertises the "abundance of delightful incidents," interspersing episodes of crime with "solemn resolutions of virtue."[1] Variety was itself a prime aesthetic value throughout eighteenth-century culture, and Defoe's promise of scandal tale, travelogue, criminal confession, and spiritual auto-biography promises variety in full. This "infinite variety" – a phrase lifted from Enobarbus' famous description of Cleopatra in Shakespeare's *Antony and Cleopatra* – is central to the novel's appeal. Defoe's preface, indeed, stresses the work's artistic principles by twinning morality and structure. It calls on "Advocates for the Stage" to defend the morality of *Moll Flanders* as "in all Ages" they have persuaded "People that their Plays are useful, and that they ought to be allow'd in the most civiliz'd and in the most religious Government" (iv). In identifying the novel with a revered literary genre, Defoe coopts for his chronicle of low life the prestige of high culture.

Despite this artistry, as "editor" Defoe claims the manuscript's literal truth. He observes that the story does not end with Moll's death, "for no Body can write their own Life to the full End of it, unless they can write it after they are dead" (i). He thus makes the narrative's gaps and evasions proof of its authenticity. At the same time, recognizing that nothing proves a narrative's plausibility so much as the invitation to doubt it, he explains that "The Author is here supposed to be writing her own History" (i): the term "supposed" simultaneously invites readers to question Moll's reliability, and to suspend their disbelief in it. This paradox, whereby the narrative is true and untrue, factual and fictional, is intensified by the role of the pseudo-editor. As "editor," Defoe abdicates responsibility for the novel's veracity: he merely transcribes what he has read, consequently introducing the possibility that this is a true story precisely by disavowing authoritative knowledge of whether it is. He begins the preface by declaring that "The World is so taken up of late with Novels and Romances, that it will be hard for a private History to be taken for Genuine . . . and on this Account we must be content to leave the Reader to pass his own Opinion upon the ensuing Sheets, and take it just as he pleases" (i). Yet this editor also confesses that he has meddled with the manuscript, erasing, shortening, and bowdlerizing episodes to shape it "with the utmost care, to virtuous and religious uses." He further admits that:

> It is true, that the original of this Story is put into new Words, and the Stile of the famous Lady. . .is a little alter'd, particularly she is made to tell her own

Tale in modester Words than she told it at first; the Copy which came first to
Hand having been written in a Language more like one still in Newgate than
one grown Penitent and Humble, as she afterwards pretends to be.   (i)

This admission permits several readings of the narrator: Moll might be
penitent; Moll might be lying; Moll might be trying to be honest, but
deceiving herself; Moll might be a fiction. This panoply of possibilities
undermines the stability of the novel's truth, and gives readers the authority
to interpret it.

The dynamic whereby textual instability authorizes readers' interpretations
reflects the contemporary concern with the utility of the new genre. Defoe
stresses the moral and pragmatic uses that *Moll Flanders* offers readers, as
Defoe repeatedly abdicates editorial responsibility:

> this work is chiefly recommended to those who know how to read it, and how
> to make the good uses of it. . .All the Exploits of this Lady of Fame. . .stand as
> so many warnings to honest People to beware of 'em, intimating to 'em by
> what Methods innocent People are drawn in, plunder'd, and robb'd, and by
> Consequence how to avoid them.   (iv–v)

He cites several specific examples as lessons in urban survival: the episode
of the little girl dressed by her vain mother in a golden chain that attracts
Moll's momentarily murderous avarice, for example, and the pickpocket-
ing of "the Gold-Watch from the young Ladies side in the park." Each is a
"good Memento" for the reader, as the depiction of the Virginians should
teach readers that "unwearied Industry will go a great way to deliver us
from" misery (v). The preface thus models the moral way to read
narrative.

The preface of *Moll Flanders* sets out the conflicting principles that shape the
novel: art, artlessness, authenticity, utility, morality, and variety. As a retrospective account, Moll's bipartite perspective both records events episodically,
and imposes a didactic structure of spiritual awakening and repentance that
pits the immediacy of experience against the moralizing function of reflection.
The inconsistencies between those points of view represent realistically the
chaos of experience, *both* the immediate experience of undergoing and reading
about adventures, *and* that of reflecting or reading about them later. This is
Defoe's attempt to justify the novel on the basis of its accuracy in representing
real life, which extends to the reader: the experience of reading reprises Moll's
own experience in writing up her life. Thus the actual engagement of the
reader with print becomes part of the moral effect of a novel.

Authentic transmission: Richardson and epistolary authorship

Moll Flanders introduces another important element to the novel: female experience, understood from inside. Since, however, female desire in itself was transgressive, portraying it in public print presented a problem of credibility and morality. Samuel Richardson approached this problem by making the documentary form of the novel central to the understanding of virtue itself. His three epistolary novels – *Pamela, or Virtue Rewarded* (1740), *Clarissa Harlowe* (1747–1748), and the seven-volume *The History of Sir Charles Grandison: In a series of letters published from the original, by the editor of Pamela and Clarissa* (1753) – present the narrative as heroines' letters being written to their intimates in the midst of exciting experience. This technique makes narrative dramatic or drama narrative because it represents the writer's feelings and thoughts at the moment they are occurring, thus avoiding the problem of retrospective editing by the self-justifying writer. The heroines' confessions, moreover, contain a dramatic irony that enables Richardson's reader to spy out the women's unrealized desires. How the letters are written, who writes them, why and when, and how they are preserved become part of the plot: letters comment upon letters, as writers upon writers, and hence, the mid-eighteenth-century novel becomes longer and longer.

Sir Charles Grandison is a patchwork of forms. It centers on the love affair between Harriet Byron and the eponymous hero, and the effect of this on their circle of acquaintances. The first volume recounts Harriet's abduction by Sir Hargrave Pollexfen, and Sir Charles's Christian refusal to duel with him: it contrasts adventure and philosophy. The remaining six volumes describe Harriet's increasing love for Sir Charles, complicated by his prior romantic entanglement with the Roman Catholic Lady Clementina. The English sub-plot is interrupted by two volumes detailing Lady Clementina's moral dilemma of choosing between her love for Sir Charles and her religion; her ensuing madness; and Sir Charles's visit to Italy to resolve their affair. Sentimental vignettes portraying excessive feeling juxtapose satirical descriptions of social interaction: the novel juggles scenes of comedy, melodrama, and morality. Both memoirist and observer, the primary correspondent, Harriet, juxtaposes reflective letters about her feelings with descriptions of her circle, and other genres, even the legal transcriptions by a functionary named Henry Coates of *"A Conference between* Sir Charles Grandison, Bart. *and* James Bagenhall, *Esq."*[2] Harriet herself employs maxims, proverbs, quotes, and jokes from both popular and high literature; transcribes prayers and songs; and even invents a series of letters written by her new acquaintances that, encapsulating their virtues and flaws in their own idiosyncratic diction, describe Harriet! These devices underscore Harriet's artistry, and thus the fictionality of her own letters. Further: these imagined epistles train readers in how to read by showing the way language reveals character. Elsewhere, Harriet reproduces the conversation between members of her social group in dramatic dialogue, presented as a play script. While this strains credibility, since no one could reproduce such dialogue verbatim, by erasing traces of Harriet, the recorder, it also frees readers to contrast ways of understanding social interaction, and to interpret the conversation themselves. In place of verisimilitude, Richardson presents a medley of modes, designed to elicit from his audience a medley of responses. He thus introduces heteroglossia, the articulation of multiple perspectives in idiomatic language (as M. M. Bakhtin formulated it), into the novel genre.[3]

Letters supposedly enclosed within letters also present contrasting perspectives. The very first letter in the novel, written from Lucy Selby to Harriet, contains an epistle from Harriet's suitor Mr. Greville to his friend, Lady Frampton. Lucy explains that Greville has agreed to permit her to show Harriet the letter once he has "scratched over passages... with so many little flourishes (as you will see) that he thought they could not be read." However, Lucy adds that "the ink I furnished him with happening to be paler than his, you will find he was not cunning enough. I promised to return it" (vol. 1, 7). While the letter enables Richardson to provide his readers with a thorough description of Harriet that reveals the writer quite as well as the character written about, it also interrupts the illusion of reading a manuscript with reminders of print. A footnote marked "(a)" explains that "the passages in this letter thus mark'd [in quotation marks] are those which in the preceding one are said to be scratched out, and yet were legible by holding up the Letter to the light" (vol. 1, 5). The footnote supplies readers with a crib; the editorial apparatus maps how to read print as manuscript. At the same time, this printer's conceit retains the illusion of authenticity. Writers' comments also prompt interpretation: for example, Harriet encloses both the penitent letter by William Wilson, Sir Hargrave's accomplice in the attempted abduction of Harriet, and the generous response forgiving him by Sir Charles (vol. 1, 37). Harriet prompts the interpretation of a reader – both of her own, Lucy, and of Richardson's reader – with the comment that it is a "short Letter, so for the lenity, of mercy, of generous and humane care for the future good of a criminal...enables one to judge of the truly heroic Charles Grandison" (vol. 1, 36, 272). Harriet's commentary serves as the paratext explaining Sir Charles's masculine brevity.

Alternating letters also contrast feelings, while footnotes map the narrative by explaining which parts of the letters were deleted or restored, and intra-textual references explicate the sequence of reception. For example, Richardson as "editor" prints letters recounting Harriet's rescue before those describing the distress of her relatives, still ignorant of her recovery, and includes a postscript clarifying this (vol. I, 203). In other instances, Richardson underscores the intimate connection between the reader, privileged to see all the letters, and the writers. In a footnote following her self-revealing meditation on love, for example, Harriet writes to Lucy: "On reperusal of the latter part of this letter [which I have enclosed in Hooks,] if you can avoid it, read it not before my uncle" (vol. I, 407).

Richardson's typography makes the physical status of the book part of its fictional realism. Each writer has his or her own printer's ornament, separating sections of narrative as the author is forced to break off: these ornaments represent time. In one instance, after three of her characteristic rosettes appear on the page, Harriet writes: "I was obliged to lay down my pen. – See how the paper blistered" (vol. I, 281). The rosettes here symbolize Harriet's tears. Harriet herself employs various techniques to differentiate her responses from her narrative: she writes, for example,

> My cousins will have it, that I am far gone in a certain passion [*They* speak quite out]; and with a man that has given me no encouragement – Encouragement! how meanly sounds that word! I cannot say, but I might prefer, if I were to have my choice – one man to another – but that is a different thing from being run away with by so *vehement* a folly as they are ready to ascribe to me.   (vol. II, I)

Her exclamation points, brackets, italics, and dashes visually dramatize her conflicting rush of emotions – the debate between her conscious and unconscious, admitted and denied feelings. Transgressive feelings even threaten to stifle her ability to write: she records that all his relatives think "That Sir Charles's great struggle, his great grief, is owing – His great struggle … is between his *Compassion* for the unhappy Clementina, and his *Love* – for – Somebody else" (vol. III, 37). Her self-editing, exclamatory rhetoric, and interruptions of narrative become conventions of sentimental literature, but so too does Richardson's self-conscious disruption of the illusion of manuscript authenticity.

Although Richardson edited his own works in a sprawling series of annotations and supplements, he largely abandoned the editorial pretense in *Sir Charles Grandison*. Pleading in the preface, "How such remarkable collections of private Letters fell into [the Editor's] hands, he hopes the Reader will not think it very necessary to enquire," he explains that he intends to "produce into public View the Character and Actions of a Man of True Honor" (vol. 1, 3). His front and end matter openly point to his didactic purpose. An initial two-column play list of the "Names of the Principle Persons," with men on the left and women on the right, followed by a section naming the "Italians," presents the novel as a moral drama, and the preface defends the hero as "the Example of a Man acting uniformly well thro' a Variety of trying Scenes, because all his Actions are regulated by one steady Principle" (vol. 1, 5). Richardson also appended to the last volume "an historical and caracteristical index"; an account of the piracy of Dublin printers; and two letters by Richardson responding to readers' complaints. These extra texts, like his long *Letters and Passages Restored from the Original Manuscripts of the History of 'Clarissa'* (1751), dispel the illusion of authenticity in order to thrust the novel into a moral conversation between author and readers. Indeed, Richardson repackaged his work, including the letters, as *A Collection of the Moral and Instructive Sentiments, Maxims, Cautions, and Reflections, contained in the histories of Pamela, Clarissa, and Sir Charles Grandison* (1755). This volume clips sentences from the novels, and presents them in an anthology of aphorisms, arranged alphabetically and according to each novel. In his concluding letter to the *Collection*, he explains that his method compels such clarification:

> that these observations lie scattered … in different parts of the story, is owing, a good deal, to the manner of writing, (to the moment, as it may be called) as occasions arose in the progress of the story: A manner of writing that has its conveniences and inconveniences. The *latter*, in such cases as that before us [in which the reader misunderstands or fails to grasp the intentions of the author]; the *former*, in giving opportunities to describe the agitations that fill the heart, in the progress of a material and interesting subject, the event of which remains undecided.[4]

Since narrative disrupts moral, Richardson provides authoritative interpretations – yet ones that are supplementary, even marginal, to readers' own experience. This anthology demonstrates the ways in which novels contain and spur multiple genres, escaping formal boundaries and breeding texts that serially substitute or overlay each other – a palimpsest of fiction.

Mocking authenticity: Sterne and the collapse of representation

Richardson's self-conscious attention to textual transmission fractured the novel's form by exposing the artifice in documentary authenticity.

However, earlier writers had already derided the authenticity of printed texts, and the concomitant conceit of the non-interventionist editor. The most prominent writers of the five-member Scriblerus Club, Jonathan Swift and Alexander Pope, issued a series of mock-documents illustrating the obfuscation of false learning and its power to indict the writer himself. In place of the simple reliance on the speaker's reliability that they thought – or pretended that they thought – Defoe had intended, they invented texts, full of trickery, in which the speakers were eminently untrustworthy.

Swift's *The Tale of the Tub* (*c.* 1696, published 1704) achieves this by interrupting the metaphorical narrative with meandering digressions, contradictions, and unfinished episodes. The story itself takes the form of a parable on the history of Christianity in which three sons, Peter (the Roman Catholic Church), Martin (the Anglican Church), and Jack (the Calvinist Church) grow decadent, disobedient to their father, and quarrelsome. However, its preface explains that the title derives from sailors' practice of distracting whales from attacking their ship by tossing them an empty tub; while this anecdote alludes to Thomas Hobbes's political treatise, *The Leviathan, or the Matter, Form, and Power of a Commonwealth, Ecclesiastical and Civil* (1651), it also represents Swift's distracting method. By reversing the central and the marginal narratives, the text destabilizes reading, and challenges the meaning of Hobbes's own subtitle about "Matter" and "Form." False learning, exemplified by the titular allusion itself, became part of the troubling nature of representation. Pope's satire, *The Memoirs of Martinus Scriblerus* (1741), similarly attacks false learning: the mock-autobiography of a Gulliver-like pedant, it reveals the speaker's unwitting stupidity in the course of becoming a critic, a physician, a philosopher, and an explorer. Such satire peaks in Pope's *Dunciad* (1744), a mock-epic, lambasting all Pope's literary rivals, in which the riotous, ironic and labyrinthine footnotes bubble up the page like a surge of sewage: some pages contain as little as two lines of Pope's text while the rest of the page is devoted to vitriolic footnote commentary. Intertextual and intra-textual devices merge so that the differentiation between the main text and the sub-text dissolves.

This deconstruction of genre characterizes the great novel of the later eighteenth century, Laurence Sterne's nine-volume *The Life and Opinions of Tristram Shandy, Gentleman*, published serially between 1759 and 1767, supplemented by *A Sentimental Journey* in 1768. In both length and form, *Tristram Shandy* embodies the impossibility of representing in finite print thoughts and feelings as they occur. The novel purports to be the autobiography of a hero *manqué*, but his stream of consciousness snakes and veers away from linear narrative, outpacing his life; the experience he records becomes the experience of the writing. In fact, although the book apparently starts with Tristram's conception, he is not born until volume IV, and his preface appears as a separate unit within chapter 20 at the end of volume III. Tristram's dilemma skewers contemporary learning, particularly John Locke's theory of causation, and thus satirizes narrative itself: Tristram cannot find his beginning without finding the beginning, in turn, of that beginning – the novel spins in infinite regression. Even the opening, which describes the interrupted, diverted orgasm that generated Tristram, is not a true beginning, since it necessitates an explanation of why the interruption occurred. It does, however, explain the narrative's method – a series of interruptions and digressions. Chapters frequently end with a dash that indicates a digression, as Tristram's racing thoughts branch away. Conscious even of this, Tristram includes a chapter on chapters, and another on digressions themselves.

The novel purports to explain Tristram's mysterious inadequacy, but neither this nor its cause are ever clear. Is it the result of a curtain sash falling on his penis as he was held out of a window as an infant to urinate, or his father's interrupted orgasm, or his natal extraction from his mother by means of forceps, or his accidentally flattened nose? Each of these possibilities pulls Tristram away from his tale into the jumble of associative digressions that annihilate the possibility of logical structure. Interpolations and paratextual and typographical jokes further disrupt the narrative: the lengthy curse of Ernulphus, Bishop of Rochester, interrupts the story early on, and "Slawkenbergius's Tale," a treatise on noses, printed in Latin and translated in English on facing pages, for example, occupies much of volume IV, a circumlocution leading to the mistake of failing to name Tristram Trismegistus. Meretriciously learned footnotes, passages fractured by rows of asterisks or dashes indicating edited text, pointing hands, a black page symbolizing Yorick's death, a blank page inviting readers to insert an imaginative portrait of the ideal woman to represent Widow Wadman, and a host of other devices deconstruct the representative power of either print or narrative. Sterne portrays this representational quandary by Sir Toby's "narrative line," exemplified by a squiggle on the page.[5] The final words of the book address its fundamental existentialism: when Tristram's mother asks, "L–d!. . .what is all this story about? –," Yorick replies, "A COCK and a BULL. . .And one of the best of its kind, I ever heard" (vol. IX, 145).

Thus, instead of Tristram's own life, the novel includes a medley of stories about its minor characters. Many recount his irascible father Walter's obsessions and theories, particularly concerning doctors and Tristram's own education, supplanted by his father's authoring a treatise dedicated to the subject, the *Tristrapaedia*; many others concern Tristram's sentimental Uncle Toby, preoccupied by his experiences in the war, and engaged in replaying the siege of Namur with miniature embattlements on his bowling-green. Toby's frustrated amours with the Widow Wadman become metaphorically reflective of Tristram's own problems with expression and relationships, since Toby himself has suffered a mysterious wound in the groin during the war. So tender are Toby's sympathies, indeed, that he frees a fly, rather than harm it. Toby's devoted Corporal Trim is also wounded, albeit in the knee.

Tristram Shandy not only dismantles causality and narrative, however: it also establishes the conventions of sentimental aesthetics that insistently draw attention to the inadequacy of language, especially print, to represent true feeling. *A Sentimental Journey through France and Italy* (1768) exemplifies this technique: instead of descriptions of countryside, industry, or famous sites, Yorick details in brief chapters the sequential, emotional impulses produced by his encounters with assorted characters, including a mendicant monk, a florist, and a chambermaid, as he moves through "the great SENSORIUM of the world!"[6] As well as Sterne's trademark digressions, omissions, and print jokes, the book contains Yorick's discovery of an ancient manuscript of Euripides' *Andromeda*, used as wrapping paper for a bouquet of flowers that his servant, improbably named La Fleur, gave to his mistress. This device mocks the manuscript status of the book itself. Thus, writing can never represent reality but only itself. Authenticity is hoist on its own petard, the marginal becomes central, and digression becomes the novel.

Found manuscripts: Mackenzie, Radcliffe, and sentimental conventions

Sterne's dismantling of the logical conventions of narrative in favor of expressions of fragmented, momentary impulse becomes fundamental to the sentimental novel. Henry Mackenzie's *The Man of Feeling* (1771) epitomizes the technique of portraying moments of feeling, stimulated by impressions and severed from sequential plot, in both form and content. A pair of mirroring narrative frames structures a story composed of episodes involving the sentimental hero Harley, and concluding with his death from passionate but stifled love. The first frame is established by the preface. This opens as an anecdote by Mackenzie's persona, the "editor," of his chance discovery of the manuscript being used as gun-wadding by his companion, a curate, on a futile hunting excursion, as he similarly uses "an edition of one of the German Illustrissimi,"

i.e. German and Dutch philosophers.[7] When the companions exchange manuscripts, Mackenzie hints that his novel serves the reader in the same way that
philosophy serves conventional religion, as a personal prompt to morality. At
the same time, the mutual disregard that the curate and the editor display for
the other's preferred reading underscores Mackenzie's ambition to replace
conventional morality with sentimentalism. Just as the manuscript has been
discarded by insensitive readers, so it can be discovered by sensitive ones. In the
preface's final paragraph, the editor describes his discovery as:

> a bundle of little episodes, put together without art, and of no importance on
> the whole, with something of nature and little else in them. I was a good deal
> affected with some very trifling passages in it; and had the name of a
> Marmontel, a Rousseau, or a Richardson, been on the title-page –'tis odds
> that I should have wept:
>   But one is ashamed to be pleased with the works of one knows not
> whom.   (viii)

This artful declaration of artlessness pricks readers to dismiss critical judgment
in favor of a willingness to empathize, weep, and laugh. It also echoes the joke
that the editor has indeed found what he was hunting for, not in shedding
animals' blood, but in feeling pity for the novel's hero. By isolating the final
sentiment as its own paragraph, Mackenzie's "editor" prods readers to replace
prejudice with feeling, as Rousseau prescribed.

The second narrative frame unveils the fiction that editing is a transparent
process. According to the curate, the manuscript was left in the rooms of a
mysterious, "grave, oddish kind of man," known as The Ghost (vi). It is so
badly penned, so disjointed that "the author [is never] in one strain for two
chapters together," and lacks even "a single syllogism from beginning to end"
(vii). This ghosted transmission results in fragmented chapters, asterisks, and
haphazard breaks in script and plot that reinforce both the fiction of authenticity and the disconnections of sentimental experience. The novel opens, for
example, with chapter 11, which describes The Ghost's mournful recollection
of a departed friend, Ben Silton, who is entirely peripheral to the plot.
Mackenzie reinforces the disjointedness of this opening instantly with a footnote: "The Reader will remember, that the Editor is accountable only for
scattered chapters, and fragments of chapters; the curate must answer for the
rest" (i). Further chapters sketch out a brief biography of Harley in loosely
chronological episodes: his education; his encounter with Miss Walton, whom
he loves; his journey to London in pursuit of his inheritance; and his experiences with London characters.

Sequence, however, is constantly interrupted: chapter 21, for example, contains a polemic by a misanthrope on *"honour"* and *"politeness,"* which the editor considers to be another writer's. His footnote remarks:

> Though the Curate could not remember having shewn this chapter to any body, yet I strongly suspect that these political observations are the work of a later pen than the rest of this performance. There seems to have been, by some accident, a hiatus in the manuscript, from these words, "Expectation of a jointure," to these, "In short, man is a selfish animal," where the present blank ends; and some other person (for the hand is different, and the ink whiter) has filled part of it with some sentiments of his own. Whoever he was, he seems to have catched some portion of the snarling spirit of the man he personates. (78)

By underscoring both this peculiar rhetoric and the joke that associates greed with bestiality, Mackenzie solicits readers to sew together the themes of the novel – particularly hypocrisy – from its patchwork fabric. This structure ironically projects the fiction that, discovered serendipitously, the manuscript is artless, incomplete, anonymous, unwanted, and should therefore be read as naïve; the reader's sympathetic response indeed enacts moral virtue. The jokes, frames, missing chapters and passages, and footnotes facilitate contrasting, serial moments of emotion, and insist on the text's mediation.

Mackenzie's sentimental story of parted lovers, *Julia de Roubigné, a tale. In a series of letters* (1777), reworking *Romeo and Juliet* and Rousseau's *Julie, ou la Nouvelle Héloïse* (1761), translates this structure into epistolary form. Again using the conceit of a found manuscript, Mackenzie's editorial persona explains his "discovery" of the letters that comprise *Julia de Roubigné* as the result of a gift from the son of a French friend, who discovered them when they were being sold to a grocer for vegetable wrapping paper. As in *The Man of Feeling*, this deliberate play with the materiality and dubious value of the novel intensifies the ambiguity of the manuscript's value and genre. The story is divided between the eponymous heroine's sorrowful, passionate letters mourning her lost love Savillon, who has journeyed to Martinique, and those of her jealous husband, the stern soldier the Marquis Louis de Montauban; but it also includes letters by Savillon, by his traveling companion, Beauvaris, who dies on the voyage, and by Beauvaris's faithful wife. This structure alternates gentle sentiment with tyrannical judgment, travelogue with anecdote. Paratextual commentary highlights the tale's accidental incompleteness. In one instance, the "editor" footnotes a letter concerning the abuses of slavery:

> It is proper to apologize to the reader for introducing a letter for purely episodical reasons. I might tell him, that it is not altogether unnecessary, as it introduces to

his acquaintance a person, whose correspondent Savillon becomes at a future period; but I must once more resort to an egotism for the reason: the picture is exhibited to please myself and I could not resist the desire of communicating it.[8]

Like the alternating letters, these paratexts toss readers back and forth between pathos, irony, outrage, reflection, pedantry, humor, and pity.

This aesthetic of strong contrast becomes a structural element of the novel particularly in gothic and Romantic fiction. It is facilitated by the convention of the found manuscript, since authorless or ancient scripts release author and reader from the constrictions of contemporary realism. Horace Walpole's *The Castle of Otranto, a Gothic Story. Translated by William Marshal, Gent. From the original Italian of Onuphrio Muralto, Canon of the Church of St. Nicholas at Otranto* (1764), the first "gothic" novel, abandons verisimilitude for a series of shocking effects. In it the tyrant Manfred, grandson of a usurper who has murdered the rightful prince Alfonso, is punished for his villainies by supernatural events that fulfill a prophecy: the descent of Alfonso's enormous, black-plumed casque in the center of his castle, crushing Manfred's son; and sighing paintings whose figures walk out from the gallery walls. Manfred's incestuous violence contrasts with the virtue of the beautiful and blameless heroines Hippolita, Isabella, and Matilda, and the hero Theodore. By presenting the script as translation of an Italian account of events from the twelfth and thirteenth centuries, Walpole's narrative method, supposedly rooted in primitive culture, is designed to arouse irrational awe.

Ann Radcliffe's *Mysteries of Udolpho, a romance; interspersed with some pieces of poetry* (1794) achieves this effect differently. The lengthy and complex story is fundamentally sentimental: it portrays the hopes, fears, terrors, sadness, love, and piety of the beautiful, sensitive, and innocent Emily St. Aubert. Upon the death of her mother, Emily and her weakening father travel to the Pyrenees, where they encounter the vacillating but noble Valancourt, with whom Emily falls in love. However, the death of her father compels her to live with a shallow and frivolous aunt, who is married to the tyrannical Marquis Montoni. As Emily's guardian, Montoni forces her to accompany him to his remote castle, where mysterious night-time noises and abandoned, bloodstained weapons arouse her fears of murder, ghosts, and unknown crimes. After a series of false leads and mysterious clues, including distracting sub-plots involving her father's possible infidelity, her courtship by another suitor, Dupont, and the mystery of the mad nun Agnes, Emily discovers that another aunt, the Marchioness de Villeroi, was murdered by Laurentini, Montoni's mistress, and that Montoni leads a band of rebel soldiers. The plot concludes with Emily's recovery of her inheritance, and reconciliation with Valancourt.

Radcliffe sets the story in 1584 and the years following in order to avoid conventional probability while still portraying characters with which readers might identify. It also allows her strong contrasts and simple effects in a range of registers: violent pre-Enlightenment men confronting submissive, powerless women; comically simple servants contrasted with delicate, sophisticated gentry; the shallow gaiety of decadent society in the face of private, spiritual contemplation; the wildness of the forests and mountains of the Continent in comparison with the peaceful calm of the valleys; art versus nature; and ultimately faith, fear, and superstition as opposed to reason. The contrasts of emotion and character appear in the narrative method. Picturesque descriptions of sublime, natural beauties alternate with accounts of Emily's thoughts and social experiences; genre scenes depicting happy peasants or banditti on the hills, borrowed from contemporary painting, break free from the narrative to create a patchwork of moments of still contemplation between the intervallic rush of events. Radcliffe heads her chapters with passages of poetry as epigraphs, particularly by the proto-Romantic Thomson and by Shakespeare: these set the mood for the reader, inviting her to compare poetry, painting, and prose, and to form a parallel between the sentiment expressed by the epigraphs and its narrative illustration. In addition, poems by Radcliffe appear within the text as alternative modes of understanding the feelings stimulated by the scenes.

Most markedly, however, the plot is rendered tantalizingly obscure because it is told from the point of view of the inexperienced and superstitious heroine in the midst of experiencing it. Although the narrative appears to be rendered from an omniscient, third-person point of view, Radcliffe uses the technique of free indirect discourse to present what is actually Emily's perspective in third-person language. For example, when the heroine perceives her father weeping over a miniature painting, she suspects it to be a portrait of his lover, yet the text hints that Emily has mistaken, not what she sees, but how she sees it:

> Emily could scarcely believe what she saw to be real. She never knew till now that he had a picture of any other lady than her mother, much less that he had one which he evidently valued so highly; but having looked repeatedly, to be certain that it was not the resemblance of Madame St. Aubert [her mother], she became entirely confident that it was designed for that of some other person.[9]

The phrase "what she saw to be real" should alert readers to her faulty perception. Again, when Emily, who is deeply suspicious that her guardian has murdered his mistress Laurentini, encounters while wandering the castle a wax *memento mori* of a skeleton behind a curtain, she sees it as a rotting corpse. So, too, does the reader, for the narrative represents Emily's perceptions, colored by her feelings, rather than objective reality. Repeatedly Radcliffe's narrative employs uncertainty: interpretations or predictions are "probable," or might "perhaps" be true. Cumulatively, those devices shuttle readers between different modes of interpretation and levels of certainty. It is not the story, but the feelings evoked by reading it that produce its meaning. Radcliffe employs narrative effects to mystify the reader, a mystification that heuristically parallels the heroine's own experience.

The aesthetic of contrast, however, also structures both didactic and ironic narrative. Elizabeth Inchbald's *A Simple Story* (1791) bluntly concludes as a recommendation for "A PROPER EDUCATION" for women.[10] The narrative depicts in the first two volumes the relationship between the flighty, vain but witty heroine Miss Milner, and her stern and moralistic guardian and suitor, Dorriforth. Almost entirely conducted in dialogue, the story juxtaposes the gay repartee of the rambunctious heroine with the repressive lectures of Dorriforth, who himself wavers between demanding total obedience and respecting Miss Milner's desires. While this might seem a banal plot, Inchbald shatters her reader's expectations by a second pair of volumes, set seventeen years later in which Miss Milner, now Lady Elmwood, has committed adultery, and been exiled to poverty and remorse, while her husband has stiffened into a tyrant who has banished his only daughter, and plans to leave his estate to his nephew Lord Rushbrooke. Such an ending to the "simple story" forces readers to rethink their reading of previous volumes, since what seemed a happy ending now appears a tragic one. Not only does the second half of the story revise the moral of the first, but it criticizes the conventional plot of courtship fiction. By depicting the Elmwoods' daughter, Matilda, as a perfectly obedient and virtuous version of Miss Milner, finally rewarded by inheritance and love, Inchbald implies that the second two volumes are an alternative version of the story in the first. This structure of providing several versions of a plot appears in later fiction, notably Emily Brontë's *Wuthering Heights* (1847).

Maria Edgeworth's mock-gothic *Castle Rackrent; An Hibernian Tale. Taken from the facts, and from the manners of the Irish squires, before the year 1782* (1800) uses textual instability to mock the narrative convention of naïve authenticity. Set in the recent past, it purports to be a verbatim transcription of the reminiscences of an illiterate Irish servant, Thady, who recounts the lives of four generations of the ramshackle Rackrent squires. In the preface, the Scriblerian editor stresses Thady's reliability:

> The prevailing taste of the public anecdote, has been censored and ridiculed by critics, who aspire to the character of superior wisdom: but if we consider it in a proper point of view, this taste is an incontestable proof of the good sense and profoundly philosophic temper of the present times...besides, there is much uncertainty even in the best authenticated ancient or modern history; and that love of truth... leads to a love of secret memoirs, and private anecdotes.[11]

Thady's self-representation as scrupulously honest, foolishly sentimental, and totally loyal explodes the convention that simple folk are good, and anecdotes true and moral: the reader quickly perceives ignorance, prejudice, duplicity, moral sloth, and graft, since Thady's son, like Uriah Heep, ends up with the estate and all the money. This realization occurs despite the editor's notes and glossary, which fussily and unnecessarily translate Thady's dialect, and provide irrelevant, irritatingly detailed antiquarian explanations of Irish customs and manners; for example, *"Childer"* is glossed with "this is the manner in which many of Thady's rank, and others in Ireland, formerly pronounced the word *children*" (25). Edgeworth thus mirrors the unreliability of conversation with the unreliability of commentary.

By jostling readers with texts, digressions, and paratexts that, sprouting like mushrooms, disrupt narrative, and highlight instabilities of source and transmission, eighteenth-century novels revel in a riot of heteroglossia of voice and form. Some novelistic offshoots become genres themselves. Anthologies, miscellanies, and collections of stylistic "Beauties," for example, encouraged readers to compare authors. Like the multiple narratives and varied effects of the early novel, such genres undermine didactic and linear narrative, and redefine – or indeed define – the novel as a collection of fragmented impressions, a welter of varied forms producing an encyclopedic experience. This "baggy monster," as Henry James termed the novel as he inherited it, decentered narrative, and permitted writers to make not only content or characters, but tone, plot, narrative, and the very act of representation the subject of the novel itself.

Notes

1. Daniel Defoe, *The Fortunes and Misfortunes of the famous Moll Flanders* (London: W. Chetwood, 1722), p. iv.
2. Samuel Richardson, *The History of Sir Charles Grandison: In a series of letters published from the original, by the editor of Pamela and Clarissa*, 7 vols. (London: for S. Richardson, 1753): vol. i, letter 45, pp. 310–315.
3. M. M. Bakhtin, *The Dialogic Imagination*, ed. and trans. Michael Holquist (Austin: University of Texas Press, 1981).

4. Samuel Richardson, *A Collection of the Moral and Instructive Sentiments, Maxims, Cautions, and Reflections, contained in the histories of Pamela, Clarissa, and Sir Charles Grandison* (London: for S. Richardson, 1755), p. 408.
5. Laurence Sterne, *The Life and Opinions of Tristram Shandy, Gentleman*, 9 vols. (London: for T. Beckett and P. A. DeHondt, 1760–1767), vol. IX, p. 17.
6. Laurence Sterne, *A Sentimental Journey through France and Italy, By Mr. Yorick*, 2 vols. (London: for T. Becket and P. A. DeHondt, 1768), vol. II, p. 182.
7. Henry Mackenzie, *The Man of Feeling* (London: T. Cadell, 1771), p. viii.
8. Henry Mackenzie, *Julia de Roubigné*, 2 vols. (London: for W. Strahan; and T. Cadell, 1777), vol. II, letter 29, p. 46.
9. Ann Radcliffe's *Mysteries of Udolpho, a romance; interspersed with some pieces of poetry*, 4 vols. (London: for G. G. and J. Robinson, 1794), vol. I, pp. 2, 69–70.
10. Elizabeth Inchbald, *A Simple Story*, 4 vols. (London: G. G. and J. Robinson, 1791), vol. IV, p. 157.
11. Maria Edgeworth, *Castle Rackrent; An Hibernian Tale. Taken from the facts, and from the manners of the Irish squires, before the year 1782*, 4 vols. (London: for J. Johnson, 1800), vol. I, p. iii.

14

Extraordinary narrators: metafiction and it-narratives

MARK BLACKWELL

The *Oxford English Dictionary*'s entry for the term "metafiction" – "Fiction in which the author self-consciously alludes to the artificiality or literariness of a work by parodying or departing from novelistic conventions" – emphasizes the form's dependence on established artistic norms and, through later invocations of naturalism and postmodernism, its short pedigree. Indeed, the best-known studies of metafiction in English have focussed on works published during the last century or so. As a consequence, metafiction is often construed as a relatively recent response to the shopworn conventions of realism. Patricia Waugh, for instance, has described metafiction as deliberately countering the expectations established by traditional fiction through its "opposition ... to the language of the realistic novel."[1] However, the notion that metafictive play is the twentieth century's cheeky challenge to the hegemony of the realist novel is complicated by numerous examples of metafictional experimentation before the advent of "realist imperialism."[2] Waugh admits that postmodernism's "formal techniques seem often to have originated" from eighteenth-century predecessors (23–24), and Linda Hutcheon likewise acknowledges "the novel's early self-consciousness."[3] Nonetheless, both Waugh and Hutcheon concern themselves largely with twentieth-century works that respond to the nineteenth century's "reification of ... a temporally limited concept of 'realism' into a definition of the entire genre" (Hutcheon, *Narcissistic Narrative*, 94).

Unfortunately, our standard definition of metafiction, similarly reified and period bound, risks skewing our understanding of earlier metafictional texts, and is unlikely to help us comprehend the relationship between experimental eighteenth-century narratives and the developing protocols of what Ian Watt called formal realism.[4] Indeed, the old saw that "new developments in fiction have always tended to evolve through the parody of older or outworn conventions" (Waugh, *Metafiction*, 69) would seem to be complicated by the more or less simultaneous eighteenth-century interest in what Hutcheon terms mimesis of product and mimesis of process – that is, by the period's parallel investments in producing the effects of the real and in exploring self-consciously the narrative mechanisms that generate those effects (Hutcheon, *Narcissistic Narrative*, 38–39). Traditional assumptions about the sequential relationship – and the sure distinction – between realist fiction and metafiction demand careful scrutiny. Such scrutiny might challenge received wisdom – about both the emergence of realism and the development of metafiction – by recognizing the distinctive ways in which eighteenth-century writers "explore[d] a *theory* of fiction through the *practice* of writing fiction" (Waugh, *Metafiction*, 2). Metafictional experimentation might then be considered not only the refuge of self-consciously innovative writers seeking freedom from the constraints of settled conventions, but also a common practice of writers working in an environment relatively free of entrenched precedents, an environment in which writers' habits and readers' expectations are emergent rather than settled.

Many writers implicated in the story of the novel's development in England betray considerable interest in the identity and role of the narrator, in the protocols of reliable testimony, and in the rhetoric of fiction. In her epistle dedicatory to *Oroonoko* (1688), for example, Aphra Behn worries about the impossibility of distinguishing fact from fiction: "If there be any thing that seems Romantick, I beseech your Lordship to consider, these Countries do, in all things, so differ from ours, that they produce unconceivable Wonders; at least, they appear so to us, because New and Strange."[5] Intimations of formal realism soon appear in the narrator's eschewal of "Invention," in the work's use of real proper names, and in the descriptive precision with which the natural environment of Surinam and the customs of its natives are represented. Yet, as Behn's dedication intimates, the sometimes jarring juxtaposition of different sets of narrative conventions (the language of travel narrative and natural history for Surinam, the discourse of romance heroism for Oroonoko), like the narrator's self-consciousness about her role in the events described, renders *Oroonoko* a text with implications for the history of metafiction.

For instance, Behn's express thematization of the problem of truth-telling – recall Oroonoko's manipulation by Europeans' lies – raises questions about language's capacity to conjure images that are false or imaginary (to say the thing which is not, as Swift's Houyhnhnms put it) and thus explores the sometimes hazy distinction between fictive referents and real referents, between literary language, which creates its own realm of imaginary objects, and the kinds of language intended to describe things that exist in a world outside the text. The possibility of confusing real and fictive referents forms part of the story of the novel from its very beginning; witness the man from la Mancha's inability to distinguish the landscape through which he travels from the world evoked by chivalric romances in Cervantes' *Don Quixote* (1605, 1615). Oroonoko's struggle with such problems of reference crests at story's end, when his crisis of faith in verbal signs drives him to a rhetoric of the body whose persuasive limit is suicide: "*Look ye, ye faithless Crew*, said he, '*tis not Life I seek, nor am I afraid of Dying*; and, at that Word, cut a piece of Flesh from his own Throat, and threw it at 'em" (62–63). Unsure that mere words will move his interlocutors, Oroonoko borrows the suasive strategy of the native war-captains who mutilate themselves to prove their mettle (50). By slicing flesh from his throat, Oroonoko effectively points the contrast between the voice, which can conjure a "faithless" referent, and the material basis of speech, a little piece of the empirical world of objects which can serve as reliable physical evidence of his resolution. In the event, Oroonoko's enemies take from him a morbid lesson in the art of suasion, as they use the display of his quartered corpse to communicate emphatically the dangers of disobedience, transforming his body into a sign that serves their own purposes. Their gruesomely parodic cooptation of Oroonoko's rhetoric of truth echoes in a different key the narrator's early allusion to the set of Surinamese feathers she presented to the King's Theatre, where they served as the costume of the title character in *The Indian Queen*. The feathers function simultaneously as empirical evidence of the wonders and customs of Surinam, and as a means of materializing an imaginary native heroine. Like the text's other reflections on the problem of faithful representation and forceful persuasion, moments like these suggest that Behn is as interested in meditating on the problematic relationship between fiction and empirical reality as she is in telling Oroonoko's tale. They demonstrate that Behn recognizes the capacity of things to speak, and the importance of invoking – or inventing – the material grounds of truth claims.

The self-consciousness about narrative method evident in *Oroonoko* remains a conspicuous attribute even of such works as *Robinson Crusoe* (1719) and *Pamela* (1740), privileged examples in most accounts of the rise of novelistic realism. Both novels betray a preoccupation with the relationship between narrative form and the "effect of the real" that threatens to exceed the demands of verisimilitude. After a preface addressing the difficulty of distinguishing fact from fiction, Crusoe himself calls attention to the form that his tale takes, interrupting his first-person retrospective narration to include a copy of the journal he kept while shipwrecked. The journal is presumably the factual storehouse upon which Crusoe relies as he reconstructs his early experiences on the island, and thus serves as (pseudo-)material evidence of the authenticity of his account. It also presumably gets readers closer to Crusoe's state of mind during his time as a castaway. Yet its appearance is jarring. First, it recapitulates circumstances already related, offering readers two different versions of the same events.[6] Second, its early entries have been retrospectively reconstructed, by a Crusoe closer to the events described, to be sure, but by a Crusoe nonetheless distant from the man who experienced them, one who at last has the time, materials, and equanimity to record them: "at first I was in too much hurry, and ... discomposure of mind, and my journal would ha' been full of many dull things. For example I must have said thus ...."[7] What follows is a hypothetical journal entry that Crusoe supposes he might have written had he recorded his experiences "at first," an entry that does not differ radically from the actual one a page later. There is not here the type of frame-breaking that the metafiction of John Barth or of postwar experiments in English fiction have made familiar. Neither Crusoe nor an external narrator addresses readers to remind them that this is all make-believe. Yet the intrusion of Crusoe's journal interrupts his tale and focusses attention instead on how the story is being told and what its evidentiary basis might be, thereby reminding readers that his "Life" has been fashioned from words, and might have been arranged otherwise.

Dorrit Cohn's claim that "the real world becomes fiction only by revealing the hidden side of the human beings who inhabit it" implies that fictional representation depends on the development of technologies for disclosing subjective experience, for enabling readers to know characters "precisely in ways we could never know people in real life."[8] Behn's narrator-participant, confidante of the hero, and Defoe's journal are examples of such technologies, even as Oroonoko's self-mutilation and Crusoe's competing accounts of the same events signal potential problems with the convincing revelation of interiority. Richardson's experimentation in the *Familiar Letters* (1741) with epistolary templates for the transmission of stock inquiries and the successful communication of personal information resulted in a fiction, *Pamela* (1740), that registers the ways in which conventions of discourse mediate our access to the subjectivity of others. Richardson's preface by the editor, together with the apparatus of encomiastic letters that accompanied even early editions of the text, fosters the illusion that the work reprints documentary evidence of the real-world adventures of a servant girl, but by explicitly addressing questions of style and encouraging the work's own conflation of text and character, of *Pamela* and Pamela, these paratexts also make the novel's language opaque, calling attention to the ways in which Pamela's simplicity and virtue are not simply facts of the world represented by language, but effects constructed in and through language.

Likewise Mr. B.'s waxing interest in Pamela as a creature of words: Mr. B.'s importunate demand for access to Pamela's person is displaced in volume II by his equally insistent command that she turn over her papers, and then that she "continue your Relation . . . [in order] that this wondrous Story be perfect, and we, your Friends, may read and admire you."[9] The theme is maintained later in the novel with the appearance of Lady Davers, who is disinclined to believe that her brother has married Pamela – "So you want to make out a Story, do you?" – but later asks permission to peruse Pamela's writings, predicting that the "Sight of your Papers" will reconcile her to her new sister-in-law (329, 375). These allusions to the belief-inducing, world-making power of language recall all the prefatory material mingling admiration of Pamela's unadorned "Innocence and beautiful simplicity" with praise for the "beautiful simplicity of the Style, and a happy Propriety and Clearness of Expression" (7, 4). To be sure, this emphasis on the austerity of the prose seems designed to preempt accusations of artifice and fictionality. Yet it adumbrates a more complicated affirmation of language's mediation of truth, and of the power of stories to transform our interpretation of supposed facts about the world. As Mr. B.'s own syntax in the passage above suggests, reading *Pamela* and admiring Pamela are inextricably intertwined.

Thus, even some of the storied ancestors of realism betray concerns with the formal resources of fictional representation, with the distinction between real and fictive referents, and with problems of convincingly communicating the truth of private experience, concerns that give these texts a subtle and perhaps unexpected metafictive cast. Jonathan Swift's worries about the emerging protocols of verisimilitude and his skepticism about the role that print texts play in mediating access to truth, be it political and religious truth, the truth of subjective experience, or truths about unfamiliar places and peoples, motivated his own satirical experiments with narrative reliability, especially with the paratexts that sanctify the contents of printed books. Swift's *Tale of a Tub* (1704) includes dedications by author and bookseller, a letter from the bookseller to the reader, a preface, and an introduction; it is also peppered with footnotes that, together with these other customary appurtenances of printed books, pretend to validate the text as a reliable medium for the communication of truth but in fact call readers' attention to the mechanical artifice by means of which print texts generate the appearance of the real.

Likewise the preliminary matter in *Gulliver's Travels* (1726), including the letter from the imaginary publisher, Sympson, explaining the provenance of the text and vouching for Gulliver's veracity and the letter from Gulliver complaining that Sympson has published a corrupted, error-riddled version of his travels. These paratexts divert readers from the main event, Gulliver's narration of his adventures, yet they help to foster the text's mimetic illusion even as they call attention to the strategies by which print manufactures such illusions. Like *A Tale of a Tub*, whose digressions distract readers from a tale that is itself, as the narrator admits, a diversion, *Gulliver's Travels* plays complex, self-conscious games with the paratextual customs and narrative conventions that govern the relationship between reader and writer.

Frame-breaking narrators who address the reader and explicitly call attention to the artifice of the stories they recount become more common and conspicuous in the middle of the eighteenth century. The narrator of Henry Fielding's *Tom Jones* (1749) makes a spectacle of himself to avoid the deceptive pretenses of fiction with which Defoe and Richardson experimented. By having his narrator address readers directly as each of the novel's eighteen books begins, Fielding distances them from the story and encourages their reflection on both the means by which the story's events are represented and the relationship between the world fabricated in the text and the world they inhabit. Fielding's narrator intrudes upon the reader not only in the opening chapter of each book, but throughout the novel. Even chapter descriptions sometimes have the effect of highlighting the distinction between the matter of the story and the manner in which it is told so as to remind readers that their experience is manufactured by carefully articulated rhetorical mechanisms. Titles such as that for the final chapter of book IV, "The Arrival of a Surgeon. His Operations, and a long Dialogue between Sophia and her Maid," focus exclusively on the story's events. But others, such as that for the fourth chapter of book I, "The Reader's Neck brought into Danger by a Description; his Escape, and the great Condescension of Miss Bridget Allworthy," call attention to the relationship between what is described – Mr. Allworthy and his hilly estate – and how it is described – in an elevated manner that ennobles its subject – and thus play with the gap between the physical dangers that characters in the story-world might face, either at the top of Allworthy's hill or on the "ridge of wild Mountains" visible from his property, and the rhetorical dangers that attend both reader and writer as they make the transition from the high style suitable to Allworthy and his environs to the homelier language accompanying his sister's appearance.[10]

Indeed, Fielding often mixes narrative registers archly, as in the title for the sixth chapter of book I, "Mrs. Deborah is introduced into the Parish, with a Simile," which conflates a character's arrival in a particular location in the story-world with the manner in which that advent is described by the narrator (33). The opening of book IV provides yet another example, as the book is described as "Containing the Time of a Year," while the chapter that immediately follows that heading is entitled "Containing five Pages of Paper" (99). Fielding juxtaposes measurement in an internal frame of reference, the amount of time that passes in the story-world, against a different, external standard, the amount of physical space occupied by the first chapter of the book. By reminding readers of the material basis of the story they hold in their hands – the paper it is printed on – Fielding distances them from the story, encouraging them to see the book itself rather than the events – the imaginary time – it contains.

Moreover, by depicting an author as "Master of an Ordinary" and readers as customers who "pay for what they eat," Fielding portrays novel-reading as a process of commercial negotiation and exchange in which readers commit resources of attention and time in return for nourishing pleasure that "gratif[ies] their palates" (25). This vision of fiction as an article of consumption was taken up by imitators who traded on Fielding's style in order to make their own literary products more appealing to prospective consumers. The narrator of *The History of Charlotte Summers, the Fortunate Parish Girl* (1750), for example, rewrites Fielding's metaphor of comestible fiction, portraying himself not as an "Ordinary-Keeper" but as a publican offering "excellent Biberage."[11] By claiming to be Fielding's illegitimate, poetical offspring, this narrator not only makes a story of literary influence into the kind of tale – unrecognized affiliation, obscured identity – that Fielding likes to tell, but emphasizes the commodity status of fiction, the fact that stories are less imitations of life than copies, with an eye to the market, of other stories. The invocation of Fielding readies readers for a garrulous narrator and a high degree of reflexivity, but *Charlotte Summers* goes *Tom Jones* one better in its self-conscious play with its status as fiction and in its challenge to verisimilitude. The narrator closes the fourth chapter of book I with the suggestion that the reader take a nap; "only let him remember," the narrator recommends, "that he left off at the end of the 4th Chapter" (67). Despite a descriptive heading that focuses on Miss Summers, chapter 5 begins with Miss Arabella Dimple asking her maid Polly to retrieve a book: "Pray step down to the Parlour, and bring me up the first Volume of the *Parish Girl* I was reading in the Afternoon. I think I left it on the Spinnet" (67–68). The maid asks her lady where she left off, and a conversation ensues about the "ugly Custom of thumbing and spoiling the Leaves," a practice rendered unnecessary in books "divided into Chapters" such as *Charlotte Summers* and *Tom Jones*. Miss Dimple asks that Polly begin reading the seventh chapter, but quickly stops her – "you read too fast; and I don't understand one Word of what you are saying" – before commanding that she "Look back to the End of that Chapter where the Blockhead of an Author bids us take a Nap, and remember where he left off" (68). Once they find their previous stopping point, the novel proper at last resumes – the tale of Charlotte Summers, parish girl, rather than a digression about a reader of that very tale.

This inset scene of reading calls attention to the book as an object among other objects, like the spinnet upon which it was left, a material thing that can be dog-eared and mishandled, yet one that, under the right conditions, comes alive for its readers. It also suggests that a carefully designed book can lend itself to the reading practices of its users. Its representation of those practices manifests an awareness of reading as a process in time, and of the idea that narrative resources may be marshaled not only to serve the ends of temporal verisimilitude, but also to cater to the habits of readers who consume these novel commodities piece by piece, at different hours, at varying paces, and in changing locations.

Narrative intrusions and metafictive games reach their eighteenth-century apogee in Laurence Sterne's *Tristram Shandy* (1759–1767). Like its forebears, including *Tom Jones*, *Charlotte Summers*, and *A Tale of a Tub*, *Tristram Shandy* delays the appearance of its putative protagonist, it digresses, it addresses its readers, it acknowledges its status as a material thing, and it comments upon its own progress, even offering schematic diagrams of the trajectory of its plot. Yet Sterne differs from his predecessors in elevating his narrative culs-de-sac and intellectual excursuses and puns so as to render them the main event of *Tristram Shandy*, its very substance. As is intimated by the narrator's scorn for those intent on "reading straight forwards, more in quest of the adventures, than of the deep erudition and knowledge" offered by his book, *Tristram Shandy* concerns itself less with the plot of Tristram's life than with the accidents, digressions, misprisions, and interruptions that, while appearing to be distractions from and deferrals of his autobiography, constitute a type of story and a kind of reading experience uniquely its own.[12]

The narrator's resistance to straightforward narrative is perhaps most clearly evinced in his knowing manipulation of various dimensions of time – that necessary to write the tale, that necessary to read it, and that theoretically taken up by the events described. The most famous example of this temporal play is the narrator's mock-rueful acknowledgement that he is writing his life more slowly than he is living it (225–226). Elsewhere, a mismatch between Walter Shandy's subjective experience of time and an objective measure of the time that has passed inspires a discussion of the succession of ideas (146). Yet Sterne's most sustained exploration of fiction's different temporalities comes in the opening volume of *Tristram Shandy*. First, the narrator registers the particular times at which he is writing, noting in chapter 18 that the date is March 9, 1759, while proclaiming three chapters later that he writes on "March 26, 1759, and betwixt the hours of nine and ten in the morning" (48). Though only minutes have passed for readers who have read these chapters continuously, over a fortnight has passed for the narrator. Nonetheless, he complains in chapter 21, "I write in such a hurry," citing the breathless haste with which he is forced to scribble as justification for his failure to provide a citation (47). Besides the time spent reading or writing, and readers' and writer's subjective apprehension of those durations, Sterne adds another layer of complexity, beginning in this same chapter the famously long suspension of Uncle Toby's response to Walter's question about what is happening above stairs on the day Tristram is born. "I think," Toby begins, only to have the completion of that thought delayed until the sixth chapter of volume II (47, 76). The consecutive narration of the events surrounding Tristram's birth is interrupted, and a reading time that seemed quick by comparison with the weeks that elapsed in the text's writing now seems slow by comparison with the little time that has passed in the world of Walter and Toby – almost no time at all.

Sterne's deliberate temporal sleight of hand in this section of *Tristram Shandy* is of a piece with his manipulation of readers' expectations of sequence when he inserts a dedication after the work has begun (10), includes a preface in volume III (149), and, in the final volume, places the eighteenth and nineteenth chapters after chapter 25. Such games manifest Sterne's metafictive predilections and reveal his interest in the extraordinary, Prospero-like power of the narrator to shape the text as he will. But these temporal irregularities also betray Sterne's awareness of varied and desultory practices of reading, practices that the most intrusive and controlling narrator cannot regulate any more successfully than Walter Shandy can govern Tristram's upbringing. *Tristram Shandy*'s reflections on accident and chance as determinants of life and as motors of narrative dovetail with its acknowledgment that texts are ephemeral, reading practices contingent and arbitrary, and imaginations unmanageable.

The eighteenth-century popularity of the found-manuscript device, in which a frame narrator purports to have discovered or been entrusted with the very text readers hold in their hands, reflects this period interest in textual ephemerality, narrative discontinuity, and the contingency of reading. Typically, the manuscript was treated as mere stuff before being rescued from its unwitting possessor. In Charles Johnstone's *Chrysal: Or, The Adventures of a Guinea* (1760–1765), for example, the publisher reports having discovered the manuscript after spying one of its leaves serving a family "instead of a plate to hold their butter."[13] Having assembled as many pages as he could recover, the publisher offers the manuscript in its "present mutilated condition" and promises that the original "shall be deposited in the public library of one of the universities, as soon as the work is printed," presumably so that skeptics may consult empirical evidence of the story's truth (xxii, xxiii–xxiv). Like the letter in epistolary fictions, the found-manuscript device highlights the material status of the text to generate a sheen of objectivity, yet simultaneously emphasizes its vulnerability to material degradation and misconstruction. The repurposing of the manuscript pages – their use as butter plates, trunk linings, or gun-wadding – underscores the text's mutability, just as the dissemination of the manuscript, often painstakingly reassembled by an editor, draws attention to fragmentation and dispersal as threats to the coherence of an individual life, a text, and a reader's experience of that text. Yet the found-manuscript device also establishes a fresh profile for the eighteenth-century narrator. Unlike the master of ceremonies who narrates *Tom Jones*, or the archly self-conscious figure in *Tristram Shandy*, both the frame narrator who introduces a found manuscript and the narrator of the recovered text are presented as guileless beneficiaries of a happy accident with no particular audience in mind and no overarching plan. Hence, the device positions a text as authentic, as untainted by the forces of the print market exactly because its status as a fugitive object not penned for sale imbues it with a worth distinct from and extraneous to the values of market culture.

In Henry Mackenzie's *The Man of Feeling* (1771), an introduction explains how the editor procured broken shards of the history of Harley, the titular man of feeling, from a curate who used the manuscript as wadding for his gun. The curate received the "bundle of papers" from a farmer who found them in the room of a "grave, oddish kind of man" who presumably sketched episodes from Harley's life before departing the parish.[14] The manuscript is in pieces – it begins with chapter 11, and some later chapters are either missing altogether or incomplete – yet even before the depredations of the hunting curate, it was a "medley," a "bundle of little episodes"; as the curate puts it, "I could never find the author in one strain for two chapters together" (48–49). The reticence of both Harley and his would-be memoirist, the happenstance organization of the narrative, and the fragmentation of the manuscript conspire to generate an aura of authenticity that depends on the notion that the text was not composed with publication in mind and, like Harley himself, intrudes itself upon our attention almost against its will, without the scheming forethought that would betray its designs on unsuspecting readers.

The experiences of discontinuity and contingency so cleverly distilled in the found-manuscript trope, like the effacement of the narrator so artfully effected therein, are explored more systematically in a curious sub-genre of eighteenth-century fiction, the it-narrative. In it-narratives, objects and animals – coaches, coats, donkeys, lice – serve as protagonists and, most often, narrators, typically recounting tales they collect while circulating among different human possessors. One of the most successful, *Chrysal*, details the experiences of a gold coin whose travels from hand to hand and from land to land have provided it with a panoramic view of ranks, professions, and nations as well as an opportunity to collect political arcana. Like most it-fictions, *Chrysal* is an episodic collage that risks devolving into a jumble of character sketches and anecdotes. Reading such works is a bit like viewing a photographic image comprised of pixels which are themselves photographs, so that there is a tension between the constituent images, each of which solicits the viewer's attention, and the larger picture which they collectively form. The challenge of assembling from *Chrysal*'s varied episodes a coherent experience of the entire text became even more difficult after Johnstone added volumes III and IV in 1765, for, rather than functioning as a sequel that recounts Chrysal's further adventures, the final volumes elaborate earlier scenes and add new tales to be intercalated among the previous episodes. Johnstone's use of the found-manuscript trope as a framing device is therefore particularly apt, for it provides a material analogue for the reader's experience of episodic discontinuity and narrative contingency. It also serves as an analogue for the most surprising aspect of it-narratives, namely, their violation of the commonsense assumption that inanimate objects and non-human animals have no point of view and no subjective depth. The marvelous discovery that a taken-for-granted object – the waste paper whereon an overlooked manuscript is scribbled – can give voice to an absent human subject anticipates the governing trope of all it-fictions, the unexpected capacity of things and pets to speak as if human.

Because the protagonists of it-narratives typically have little power to move themselves, choose their companions, or determine a course of action, they are, as Sterne might say, "the sport of contingencies," and they carry picaresque fiction to a logical extreme adumbrated in the early work of Tobias

Smollett, whose characters bounce from adventure to adventure with a zigzagging randomness that Smollett likens to the movement of a tennis ball.[15] The loose episodic structure of most it-narratives would seem to share more in common with the unpredictable haphazardness upon which *Tristram Shandy*'s narrator prides himself than with the carefully orchestrated suspense and the tightly wrought plotting that distinguish *Tom Jones*'s more overtly controlling narrator. Yet it-narratives share with both works – and with Smollett's novels, which range from first-person retrospective narration, to varieties of third-person narration, to multi-party epistolary fiction – an interest in expanding fiction's compass by experimenting with the capacities and the identity of the narrator.

The most evident precursor of eighteenth-century it-fictions is Apuleius' *Metamorphosis* (or *Golden Ass*), which details the adventures of a man transformed into a beast. Indeed, Charles Gildon's *The Golden Spy* (1709), perhaps the first it-narrative in English, appeared shortly after he published a loose translation of Apuleius entitled *The New Metamorphosis . . . Being The Golden Ass . . . Alter'd and Improv'd to the Modern Times and Manners* (1708). Gildon's extended title suggests that, despite its classical provenance, the it-narrative appeals predominantly to a taste for novelty and modernity. *Oroonoko*, *Robinson Crusoe*, and *Gulliver's Travels* all exploited the attraction that exotic places, unfamiliar people, new objects, and novel situations would have for readers. Part of the it-narrative's popularity likely derived from a form of domestic exoticism that consists in imagining animals and objects as persons with secret inner lives, and in thus seeing, Don Quixote-like, fantastic possibilities in the disenchanted world of everyday things.

In his revised version of Apuleius, Gildon substituted a lapdog for an ass because he considered this domestic animal more likely to enjoy privileged access to concealed information: "An Ass . . . cou'd scarce come into any Place where there cou'd be any Secret Transacted . . . But a fine *Bologna* Lap-Dog is admitted to the Closets, Cabinets, and Bedchambers of the Fair, and the Great."[16] Gildon's choice may have inspired Francis Coventry's *The History of Pompey the Little, or The Life and Adventures of a Lap-Dog* (1751), a novel dedicated to Fielding that, like *Tom Jones*, conveys its hero's story through an external narrator. Though Pompey does not recount his own experiences, he has imputed to him a human-like consciousness, and his love affairs and vicissitudes are treated as if experienced by a roguish human – a jolly dog like Tom Jones, perhaps. Much of the novel concerns the "characters" Pompey encounters as he makes the rounds of various owners, humans to whom he has access exactly because a handsome lapdog, unlike an ass, is a fashionable commodity with currency.

The importance of currency in it-narratives – a combination of fluid circulation, contemporariness, and voguish prevalence – may explain why the storytelling objects in Gildon's *Golden Spy* are coins, and why so many eighteenth-century writers chose a form of money or a mode of transportation as their "Machine for the Discovery of secret Vices" (Gildon, *New Metamorphosis*, vol. I, n.p.). The human narrator of *The Golden Spy* muses, "what noble and diverting Discoveries might be made, could any of the *Louis d'Ore's* or *Guineas* reveal by discourse what Affairs they have negotiated, and those secret Intrigues, which have produc'd strange and terrible Effects in Kingdoms, and Families."[17] The ribaldry of Crébillon *fils*'s *Le sopha* (1742) and Diderot's *Les bijoux indiscrets* (1748) exemplifies one diverting purpose to which a privileged knowledge of others' private affairs might be turned. It-narrators also share something in common with the narrators of secret history, who boast behind-the-scenes access to historical actors and therefore witness the hidden springs and private machinations that shape current events. The relative invisibility of "its" permits them proximity to people of all kinds – the louis d'or in Gildon's *Golden Spy* boasts, "I have been in every station of Life, from the Prince to the Peasant" (13) – and to secrets those people would be loath to disclose before other humans.

Thus, it-narratives are the generic cousins of one brand of spy fiction, in which narrators enjoy a profession, a technological advantage, or a supernatural endowment that makes them privy to others' secret doings, or even their hidden thoughts. The subtitle of *The Birmingham Counterfeit* (1779), "Invisible Spectator," discloses the it-narrative's dependence on the figure of the spy or spectator so prevalent during the eighteenth century. In Le Sage's *Le diable boiteux* (1707, 1726), translated by Smollett as *The Devil upon Crutches*, a devil rewards his liberator by lifting the roofs of houses to reveal what passes behind closed doors. The devil offers more than an external perspective on those whose domestic lives are thus revealed, promising his charge that, by "discovering . . . inward and hidden motives" and plumbing "the true and real sources of human actions," he will enjoy "a perfect insight" into their characters.[18] The narrator of Eliza Haywood's *Invisible Spy* (1755) inherits two items from a "Cabinet of Curiosities": a belt of invisibility and a "wonderful tablet," a sort of pocket-book that "receives the impression of every word that is spoken, in as distinct a manner as if engrav'd."[19] The narrator of *The Sentimental Spy* (1773) is a footman whose position as a servant provides him with many opportunities to "peep" at his employers. *The Balloon, or Aerostatic Spy* (1786) exploits period enthusiasm for the latest technological advance; its narrator is carried into space by a hot-air balloon and there meets an "Aerostatic Spirit" with the power to "shew you what is passing in various parts of the globe."[20] In all such spy fictions, narrators are endowed with special capacities for surveying and, in Haywood, reliably recording secret goings on.

The difficulty of ferreting out and communicating hidden truths is addressed differently in another kind of spy fiction popular during the eighteenth century, in which an ostensibly disinterested and therefore unbiased outsider – a Turkish spy in Giovanni Marana's *Eight Volumes of Letters Writ by a Turkish Spy* (1691–1694), a Persian emissary in Montesquieu's *Les Lettres persanes* (1725), a Chinese philosopher in Goldsmith's *Citizen of the World* (1760–1761) – records his impressions of the European people and customs he encounters. The spies enjoy an outsider's perspective which imbues them with an aura of impartiality and defamiliarizes practices that seem natural to readers. As the editor of *Letters from a Persian in England* puts it, "there is a Pleasure in knowing how Things *Here* affect a Foreigner," who "must be suppos'd more impartial than our Countrymen when they speak of their own admir'd Customs, and favourite Opinions."[21] Because objects and animals enjoy a distance from humans that promises a fresh and dispassionate viewpoint unavailable by other means, they participate in the period vogue for this type of spy fiction. Indeed, the unusual combination of an unmatched proximity to human secrets and a presumably cool, objective distance from human affairs generates extraordinary narrative possibilities for sentient things.

In his *History and Adventures of an Atom* (1769) Smollett ingeniously marries an insider's privileged access to others with an unjaundiced outsider's perspective by selecting an atom as his narrator. Smollett's atom speaks to the frame narrator, Nathaniel Peacock, from his own pineal gland – "I heard a shrill, small voice, seemingly proceeding from a chink or crevice in my own pericranium," Peacock reports – about the political intrigue that it witnessed at the Japanese court while stationed first under the toenail of the monarch and then in the hindquarters of an important minister.[22] Though *The Adventures of an Atom* is largely a secret history of ministerial politics during the reign of George II, it also experiments, however wryly, with the best means of providing a narrator with access to the shadowy motivations of a story's main actors. For the narrating atom is in a special position to provide a doubly inside view – of the behind-closed-doors interactions between king and minister, certainly, but also of the deeper material cause of the minister's ambitious itch, a struggle between two of the atoms in his rump. Indeed, Smollett's text is an early send-up of the conventions of the it-narrative. Having traveled around the globe occupying various bodies, animal, vegetable, and mineral, its narrator is unmatched in the social, geographical, and ontological range of its circulation. As an atom lodged in humans' brains or buttocks, it boasts unusual access to others' interiority. And its hasty iteration of the metamorphoses it underwent before lodging in Peacock pokes fun at episodic promiscuity, casting an unsavory light on the implicit claim of most it-narratives – that humans are connected to other humans, even strangers, through the filthy things with which they come in contact, things they share unaware.

Smollett does not write straightforward historical narrative in *The Adventures of an Atom*, nor does he experiment with free indirect discourse. Yet he does compose a *roman-à-clef* that exploits the capacity of an extraordinary narrator – an atom – to spy on others from a uniquely intimate vantage point that oddly mingles internal and external narrative perspectives. *The Adventures of an Atom* struggles with the best means of narrating both public and private truths, recounting contemporary historical events while simultaneously negotiating the relationship between a fictively constituted interiority and the medium through which that inside is made visible. More broadly, Smollett's text, like the others discussed in this chapter, testifies to the extraordinary experimental energy and the unsettling generic ambiguity so characteristic of eighteenth-century narrative, an energy and an ambiguity that complicate any too-simple distinction between subjects and objects, people and things, narrators and characters – or realism and its discontents.

Notes

1. Patricia Waugh, *Metafiction: The Theory and Practice of Self-Conscious Fiction* (London: Methuen, 1984), p. 11.
2. Linda Hutcheon, "Metafictional Implications for Novelistic Reference," in *On Referring in Literature*, ed. Anna Whiteside and Michael Issacharoff (Bloomington: Indiana University Press, 1987), p. 4.
3. Linda Hutcheon, *Narcissistic Narrative: The Metafictional Paradox* (Waterloo, ON: Wilfrid Laurier University Press, 1980), p. 9.
4. Ian Watt, *The Rise of the Novel: Studies in Defoe, Richardson, and Fielding* (Berkeley: University of California Press, 1957).
5. Aphra Behn, *Oroonoko*, ed. Joanna Lipking (New York: Norton, 1997), p. 7.
6. Defoe's contemporary, Charles Gildon, complained, "you have been forc'd to give us the same Reflections over and over again, as well as repeat the same Fact afterwards in a Journal, which before you had told us in plain Narration" (*The Life and Strange Surprising Adventures of Mr. D – – de F –, of London* [London, 1719], p. 31).
7. Daniel Defoe, *Robinson Crusoe*, ed. Angus Ross (New York: Penguin, 1985), p. 82.
8. Dorrit Cohn, *Transparent Minds: Narrative Modes for Presenting Consciousness in Fiction* (Princeton University Press, 1978), p. 5.

9. Samuel Richardson, *Pamela, or Virtue Rewarded*, ed. T. C. Duncan Eaves and B. D. Kimpel (Boston: Houghton Mifflin, 1971), p. 255.

10. Henry Fielding, *Tom Jones*, ed. Sheridan Baker (New York: Norton, 1995), p. 30.

11. *The History of Charlotte Summers, the Fortunate Parish Girl* (London, 1750), pp. 4, 2.

12. Laurence Sterne, *The Life and Opinions of Tristram Shandy, Gentleman*, ed. Robert Folkenflik (New York: Modern Library, 2004), p. 44.

13. Charles Johnstone, *Chrysal: Or, The Adventures of a Guinea*, 4 vols. (5th edn, London, 1766), vol. I, p. x.

14. Henry Mackenzie, *The Man of Feeling*, ed. Maureen Harkin (Peterborough, ON: Broadview, 2005), p. 48.

15. Laurence Sterne, *A Sentimental Journey through France and Italy*, ed. Graham Petrie (New York: Penguin, 1986), p. 29; Tobias Smollett, *The Adventures of Roderick Random*, ed. P.-G. Boucé (Oxford University Press, 1982), p. 1.

16. Charles Gildon, preface, *The New Metamorphosis ... Being The Golden Ass of Lucius Apuleius*, 2 vols. (London, 1708), vol. I, n.p.

17. Charles Gildon, *The Golden Spy* (London, 1709), p. 3.

18. Alain René Le Sage, *The Devil upon Crutches*, trans. Tobias Smollett, ed. O. M. Brack, Jr. and Leslie A. Chilton (Athens: University of Georgia Press, 2005), p. 19.

19. Eliza Haywood, *The Invisible Spy*, 4 vols. (London, 1755), vol. I, pp. 2, 4, 10.

20. *The Balloon, or Aerostatic Spy*, 2 vols. (London, 1786), vol. I, p. 84.

21. *Letters from a Persian in England, to his Friend at Ispahan* (4th edn, London, 1735), p. vi.

22. Tobias Smollett, *The History and Adventures of an Atom*, ed. O. M. Brack, Jr. and Robert Adams Day (Athens: University of Georgia Press, 1989), p. 5.

15

Romance redivivus

SCOTT BLACK

Agnes and the bleeding nun

Sometimes you get the ghost instead of the girl. In the long backstory of Raymond in Matthew Lewis's *The Monk* (1796), Agnes (Raymond's beloved) is imprisoned by her jealous aunt in a German castle. Agnes forms a plan to escape by impersonating the Bleeding Nun, a ghost who appears annually and for whom the castle gates will be opened. It would not be dignified, the skeptical, scoffing Agnes quips, to let the ghost slink out through the keyhole. Raymond waits for Agnes in a carriage and whisks her away. But once they stop to rest, Agnes disappears. It turns out that Raymond has picked up the actual ghost and left the disguised Agnes at the castle gates wondering where her lover is.[1] The old, superstitious story that the modern, skeptical Agnes sought to use for her own purposes turns out to be true.

This scene is both a winking, self-conscious comment on Lewis's own project and a parable of literary history more generally. Old stories live strange afterlives in their retellings and even in their instrumental repurposings. *The Monk* itself is a joyously naughty romp through many residual narrative tropes, or at least tropes that are considered residual in recent accounts of the novel. In the midst of Enlightenment, at the end of the century in which realism rises and novels help to develop the formal technology of modernity, Lewis offers an outrageous fable of blasphemous crime, abused innocence, and demonic stagecraft. When the ghost story that Agnes adopts to outwit her aunt turns out to be true – when she uses the silly superstitions of her jailers to escape, only to have the actual object of those superstitions thwart her plans – Lewis suggests that the self-conscious anachronisms of his own narrative may have force beyond their ironic adaptations. Storytelling, even in its most modern forms, traffics in the extraordinary, the fantastic, even the supernatural, in order to register the real (if not realist) experiences of desire and imagination. In this chapter, I shall explore the eighteenth-century

British novel from the perspective of those alien shadows, which never really go away. Reading is not necessarily a modern activity, and, as Raymond and Agnes learn, the intent to use those old stories for your own purposes does not keep them from taking you places you did not mean to go.

The history of the novel is commonly told as part of the history of modernity: a realistic form helps to dispel the mists of superstition and teaches readers how to understand themselves in modern terms. In such accounts, the novel either supersedes or instrumentalizes romance.[2] But the distinction between romance and novel was unstable throughout the long eighteenth century and easily breaks down when it comes to particulars. In his "Essay on Romance" (1824) Walter Scott starts with Samuel Johnson's definition, "a military fable of the middle ages; a tale of wild adventures in love and chivalry," but says that "wild adventures" are "almost the only absolutely essential ingredient" of romance. In his own definition Scott distinguishes romance, which "turns upon marvellous or uncommon incidents," from novels, which are "accommodated to the ordinary train of human events, and the modern state of society," but immediately notes "there may exist compositions which it is difficult to assign precisely or exclusively to the one class or the other; and which, in fact, partake of the nature of both."[3] Such interlacings of the uncommon and the ordinary can be found at the several origins of romance itself, and have been said to define the invention of the genre in late antiquity and its rise in medieval France. John Winkler argues that romance is "invented" (in the sense of found) when foreign stories are read in new places.[4] The origins of medieval French romance are likewise effects of translating and adapting old works (the "matters" of Rome and Britain) into the vernacular. Simon Gaunt notes that "romance" comes from *mettre en roman* (to translate into the vernacular), and Eugène Vinaver argues that romance "rises" in twelfth-century France when the work of elucidating traditional material is written into the text.[5]

Romance is an echo chamber in which we hear the reverberation of old forms in new works. Northrop Frye discusses romance in terms of the old forms, describing it as formulaic, anti-representational, and more self-consciously situated in literary conventions than in historical contexts.[6] Fredric Jameson discusses romance in terms of its new work, and critiques Frye for eliding historical differences. Jameson explains the persistence of romance's modal continuities as indicating structural absences within particular historical contexts. Frye's echoes thus become a way to examine the chamber.[7] Though each privileges one or the other, both Frye and Jameson see romance as formed at the intersection of two scales of time – a mediating hinge and a relay between long time and local time, and so a resource to explore their critical interaction. Although Jameson's own readings always rest in synchronic histor-ical situations, his account of the novel as "layered or marbled" and organized by generic discontinuities points to the possibilities of a less synchronized resolu-tion of the tensions between the historical use and the mythic force inherent in reading such texts (*Political Unconscious*, 144). Romance can provoke desires that are not allayed or explained away, and a literary history adequate to the strange loops of romance need not be organized by the putative progress of history.

The modernity of the novel is an interpretive choice, not a historical fact. Starting from the defining problem of romance – negotiating the adventures consequent on uncommon provocations – offers another way through a longer and wider history of prose fiction. Recent scholarship on eighteenth-century print culture has stressed the importance of translations, republications, and collections in both literary and book history.[8] The contexts of the book trade suggest the need for an account of the novel geared to the "operation[s] of translation and transformation" that define the form and history of romance.[9] Romance tells the story of extraordinary intrusions from (or as if from) other worlds, and in turn romance is itself a strange intrusion that may provoke in its readers versions of the adventures it narrates. How does the eighteenth-century English novel look from the perspective of romance?

This chapter surveys the resources of romance as an array of possibilities arranged in a "progress" in the older, spatial sense, not the modern sense of temporal advance. In the following section I outline some representative uses of romance, including its use thematically as a tool of social critique and moral exhortation; its formal use as a narrative game for play and pleasure; its historical use as a relay between the adaptation of older conventions and the production, and reproduction, of books. I then turn to several English Quixotes that critique the reading invited by such works, and next consider English gothic romance as a critique of romance writing. We must in the end consider romance – a transplanted alien lodged in eighteenth-century collections of novels – as itself a meditation on the alien provocations that are at the heart of romance, in both its narratives and its history. Literary history is best imagined as a reader facing a bookshelf jumbled with the resources of many times, any one of which can be read, re-read, and perhaps realized. Romance is formed of the puzzles, pleasures, and promises of such readerly encounters.

Stories of virtue: exciting attention

In the preface to *The Old English Baron* (1778), Clara Reeve writes: "The business of Romance is, first, to excite the attention; and second, to direct it to some useful, or at least innocent, end."[10] The second half of this Horatian project is, of course, hard to guarantee. In the castle of Udolpho, Emily sits down with a book "to enliven her attention," demonstrating her susceptibility to the mysteries of Udolpho.[11] Romance excites and enlivens attention by presenting lively and intensified characters, often lovers, undergoing "wild adventures," often to realize their fated love. Pierre-Daniel Huet defines romance as "fictions of love adventures."[12] And while the topic of love is now a critical embarrassment, in the eighteenth century it was widely considered the defining trait of romances and novels (whether these terms were taken as synonyms or antonyms). Love, at least, offers a paradigmatic instance of the sudden intrusion (Smollett calls it a "rude shock") that generates adventures, and Huet's definition suggests a way of thinking about the modal force and generic structure of romance: excitation of desire (love) and interlace of plot (adventures).[13]

Worlds collide in Aphra Behn's *Oroonoko* (1688). The plot is organized by the eponymous hero's forced movement from an Africa presented in the idealized terms of romance to a Surinam presented as the site of a degraded, barbaric modernity. Oroonoko and Imoinda, his beloved, embody the traditional romance values of nobility, honor, and constancy. They are initially tested by a standard conflict as the king, Oroonoko's grandfather (lecherous, old, and in the way), claims Imoinda for himself and Oroonoko struggles with the conflict between love and duty. The story unfolds in the familiar way: after secretly communicating through the language of eyes, Oroonoko sneaks into the seraglio in which Imoinda is imprisoned (it is equipped, naturally, with a gate in an Italianate orange grove), and together they bemoan "the hard Fate of Youth and Beauty."[14] Once she establishes this literary landscape, Behn thrusts her conventional lovers into a harsher, modern world, both to test them and to test that world by the ideals they represent.

Oroonoko's movement from the receding milieu of romance to a more historically specified world figures both the genre's literary and social history, exemplifying its originary dynamic (a stranger in a strange land) and its usefulness for moral and political projects. When Oroonoko is tricked into slavery by a lying ship captain (38), Behn critiques the ideology of racial difference for misrecognizing what the text presents as the proper distinctions of status. The captain sees Oroonoko in terms of his race, not his royal quality. Likewise, modern slavery is condemned because it is commercial. Oroonoko is dishonorably betrayed into slavery instead of being honorably conquered. (Oroonoko himself trades his prisoners of war as slaves [36].) Race-based chattel slavery is condemned, but from the perspective of a residual ideology.

Without the bulwarks of aristocracy, Behn suggests, the modern world has fallen into a state of nature where brutal power and savage violence rule, not honor and grace. The graphic torture to which Oroonoko is subjected at the end is a powerful image of modernity, pitting the power of a usurping upstart, Banister, against the honor of a wrongly enslaved prince. Stoically, heroically (while smoking a pipe), Oroonoko dies to prove his nobility (79–80), and we are left with only his story to remind us of a better world. The sacrifice and apotheosis of Oroonoko into *Oroonoko* offers a compensatory trace of the vanishing aristocracy he personifies, as romance serves as the site where such residual values go to live out their half-lives as nostalgic dreams. The story is necessarily double, itself mediating the crossing of worlds it narrates, and enacting the genre's rhythm of relay – making of exile a promise it hopes, perhaps, to be redeemed in reading.

Jane Barker also uses the genre to advocate for lost causes. She offers her *Exilius; or, the Banish'd Roman* (1715) as a "New Romance" that promotes an anachronistic "Heroick Love" in a world of "Interest and loose Gallantry."[15] Like Behn, Barker uses her romance to recommend an ideal, figured by interlocking stories of constant lovers overcoming a variety of obstacles, against which to measure cultural decline. But while there is no reason to doubt the sincerity of Barker's project of reformation, her claim that love has gone to the dogs is tricky, performing as it does a standard generic gesture, one indeed found at the origin of romance. In *Yvain* Chrétien de Troyes writes: "People today do not fall in love or love as they used to. They do not even have the desire to hear talk of love."[16] The belatedness of romance is itself a generic trope. Does Barker reach for the genre because she wants reform or does she activate the critical gesture when she chooses the genre? Probably both of these, and indeed *Exilius* is organized by a rhythm of moral exhortation and engaging action that is itself part of its generic profile. Virtuous proclamations punctuate the explosively proliferating narrative twists, and it is not clear which serves the other. The action proves the characters' virtue and models it for readers, but equally the characters function as tokens of a conventional plot. (Perhaps Barker's prefatory moral claims function like those of Daniel Defoe, her contemporary, as so many thin fig-leaves of piety to excuse another kind of readerly pleasure?)

But it is surely tendentious to choose between the "mixed modes" of romance.[17] If Barker frames her narrative with a claim for its moral usefulness, she also remarks the extraordinary narrative register proper to the adventures of love. In the third story of the cycle, Exilius says: "There we pass'd our Moments in a serene or rather insipid Tranquillity, each succeeding Day supplanted its Predecessor, without the least Adventure to render any one remarkable" (191). Happily (for us) or unhappily (for him), Exilius' insipid tranquility does not last. *Exilius* is built for speed, and its rapid generation of plots enlivens attention with the pleasures of game-playing and pattern-matching. The overall story is pieced together through interlacing narratives as two groups of bereft lovers tell interlocking stories of five pairs of lovers finding their ways to each other. The interleaving creates patterns of echo and variation on the standard themes of constancy and mutability, while also ratcheting up the narrative stakes and enabling various strategies of delay, misdirection, and misrecognition. The adventures themselves feature a famil-iar array of remarkable devices: a cruel father who kidnaps and attempts to rape his own daughter but is prevented by a mysterious stranger; shipwrecks, pirates, enslavement, palace intrigues; imprisonments and escapes through secret passageways; counterfeit letters, disappearing bodies, slain characters returning to life; prophecies; a traveler's tale of supernatural sea monsters; disguises and hidden identities disclosed by birthmarks and characters who pop up *ex machina* to tell surprising backstories; and of course challenges to the constancy of lovers, who resist the blandishments and threats of royal captors to prove their virtue and justify their marriages. The thematic coordinates (soliloquies on the limits of stoicism, for instance, or aristocratic excoriations of rebellious mobs) feel perfunctory and as much grist for the machinery of intersecting stories as the narrative clichés that eventually knot them together in the expected patterns. The often dizzying complexity of the stories and the sheer speed of their proliferation go along with the elevation of characters, diction, and themes: all are strategies designed to carry readers away on Barker's roller-coaster of story.

With its complex narrative interlace, its elevated characters, and its setting in a vaguely ancient Roman Sardinia, *Exilius* is a Mediterranean romance, and reminds us of the continued presence of even such ancient genres in eighteenth-century Britain. Two years after Barker's adaptation of this late classical genre, a new translation of Heliodorus' foundational *Aithiopika* was published (1717), the second of three in the long eighteenth century (1686, 1789).[18] The overlapping presence of these various strands – and not the displacement of earlier forms – suggests that the formal technology of romance may offer a model of its literary history as well. Romance is formed by the self-conscious adaptation of alien forms (Heliodorus offers a model of this as well).[19] And throughout the eight-eenth century English novels borrowed broadly from foreign and past texts as well as contemporary life to model moral behavior for readers and (or?) to claim their attention with provocative fictions of intensified desire. Despite critical rumors to the contrary, traditional plots do not disappear with the rise of realism, nor do fantastic elements or outlandish loves.[20] (Realist works are structured by them too.) And such fantasy is lodged in the collections that institutionalize the novel.

A djinni and a shape-shifting charm are central to Hawkesworth's *Almoran and Hamet* (1761); prophetic dreams and magical doors to Reeve's *Old English Baron* (1778); flying people and universal emancipation to Robert Paltock's *Peter Wilkins* (1750). Each of these works serves as a relay between older narrative traditions and the new publishing ventures that develop the canons of the novel.[21] Hawkesworth adapts Johnson's *Rasselas* (itself an anti-exotic adaptation of Oriental tales); Reeve adapts Walpole's *Castle of Otranto* (itself an adaptation of popular vernacular traditions); and Paltock adapts Defoe's *Robinson Crusoe* (itself an adaptation of travelers' tales). And each work is republished in later collections of novels: *Peter Wilkins* is reprinted in Harrison's *Novelist's Magazine* (1780–89); *Almoran and Hamet*, in Harrison and Barbauld's British Novelists (1810); and *Old English Baron* both in Barbauld and in Scott's Ballantyne's Novelist's Library (1821–1824). Both internally, in a history of forms, and externally, in a history of books, these works demonstrate that the putatively defining (and differentiating) realism of the modern novel co-exists alongside the vigorous continuation and dissemination of older forms and modern adaptations of them. And if the narrative pleasures of such anachronistic fantasies remain available to excite the attention, so do excited readers who seek to realize their reading adventures.

English Quixotes

The two worlds juxtaposed in *Oroonoko* are hyperbolically polarized. Behn does gesture towards her reader's own world at the margin of the text when she remarks that her work will be competing with other entertainment options in London (7). Likewise Barker's and Reeve's prefatory materials appeal to contemporary readers, whom they hope to entertain and perhaps reform. But romance can be self-critical as well as critical. Explicating the dynamic of reading marginally registered by Behn and Reeve is the work of *Don Quixote* and Cervantes' English followers. If intensified, idealized characters like Oroonoko and Exilius are formed of the modal elevations of romance, Charlotte Lennox's *The Female Quixote* (1752) explores their effects by sending an intensity-seeking reader of such texts into the world.

Arabella, the Female Quixote, is formed by romance and unable to distinguish between the force of her immersive reading and prosaic reality.

Arabella's reading mistakes are tested by a range of responses: her uncle Sir Charles's confusion, her cousin Miss Glanville's jealous maliciousness, her suitor Sir George's cynical abuse, her lover Mr. Glanville's sympathetic despair. Arabella figures the anachronism of romance's persistence into the modern world, and each of her interlocutors figures a modern critical response to romance. Miss Glanville, an unimaginative literalist who does not read and has no imagination, offers an inverted mirror of Arabella. Each is absorbed by a narrow band of experience, and the comedy of their interactions depends on the perspectival clash of literalisms as a tiresome world of fashion and a fantastic world of passion talk past each other. From Miss Glanville's perspective we laugh at Arabella's absurdity and from Arabella's we cringe at Miss Glanville's crassness. In her simplicity Miss Glanville is as ridiculous as Arabella, but Sir George and Mr. Glanville are more witting readers of romance – and of Arabella – and so offer the novel's real critical tests, and indeed the kind of responses needed to enjoy the perspectival play of the young ladies' scenes. Sir George is playing a double game, pretending to laugh at Arabella with Miss Glanville while actually courting Arabella in a language Miss Glanville cannot understand. But though Sir George is not only mocking Arabella as Miss Glanville thinks, he is not really taking her seriously either. Sir George "was perfectly well acquainted with the chief Characters in most of the French Romances; could tell every thing that was borrowed from them, in all the new Novels that came out," and uses this knowledge to court Arabella in the style to which she aspires.[22]

The novel presents Sir George's canny, instrumental use of romance – he tells an elaborate romance about himself and stages one to discredit Mr. Glanville – as manipulative abuse of Arabella's Quixotic obsession, part of his attempt to perpetrate the larger outrage of marrying her for mercenary purposes. In this way, Sir George is a figure of a modernity in which love is just a lie told by interest and loose gallantry. And his instrumental repurposings of romance misfire. In his own story, Sir George paints himself as inconstant, and his staged performance leads to real violence. In contrast, the narrative celebrates Mr. Glanville, who wants to cure Arabella of her folly and undergoes a series of ordeals to prove his devotion. While Sir George takes the position of a modern author of romance, Mr. Glanville is entangled in a strange, modern version of one, and finds himself undergoing amusingly bookish trials – rescuing Arabella's romances from a threatened *auto-da-fé*, enduring an ordeal of reading, and trying to protect Arabella from the consequences of her ridiculous reading.

But if *The Female Quixote* mocks and demystifies the enchantments of reading, it does not in fact demystify love or love stories. The novel starts with the problems caused by reading love stories – Arabella "was taught to believe, that love was the ruling Principle of the World" (7) – but ends with a ringing endorsement of true love (383). Lennox is finally not concerned either to replace romance with an equally limited mundane literalism or to instrumentalize it as an ironic tool of disenchanted modern matrimony. Rather, she adopts as her narrative frame the structure of the love adventures she satirizes. Arabella's cure is rewarded with marriage as the critique of romance's provocative modal excess is resolved within its own generic structure. At the beginning of the novel Arabella is said to have read romances in bad translations (7). *The Female Quixote* is a better translation of romance, self-critically mocking its misleading force, but at the same time depending on its appeal to desire as an antidote to the reductive literalism and materialism of modernity.

Don Quixote's impossible love for the imaginary Dulcinea was part of his madness, and when he wakes from his delusion, he dies alone. But eighteenth-century English Quixotes are structured by double plots of Quixotic obsession and love adventures; they suffer their Cervantic aches and heal them too.[23] Like *The Female Quixote*, both Tobias Smollett's *Launcelot Greaves* (1760–1761) and Richard Graves' *Spiritual Quixote* (1773) are organized by twin plots in which Quixotic adventures are interleaved with, and resolved by, love stories. In both, Quixotic reading is minimized (even erased by Smollett) and the Quixotic figure used to offer a normative model for broader satiric projects, critiquing religion (Graves) and law and politics (Smollett). But if they focus less than Lennox on the mechanisms of readerly transmission, both Graves and Smollett adopt Cervantes' dense intertextuality and literary self-consciousness, and in this context their adoptions of romance narrative arcs suggest a critical perspective on the narrative interlace that structures romance in both its sentimental and Quixotic forms.

Graves naturalizes the trigger of Wildgoose's spiritual Quixotism and nationalizes its object. The roots of Wildgoose's Quixotism are carefully traced through a series of linked causes, starting with a spat with the vicar and leading to enflamed readings of seventeenth-century puritan works, whose "phrenzy" and "enthusiasm" he imbibes and decides to emulate by turning Methodist itinerant. In his "Essay on Quixotism," Graves announces that the project of his novel is to satirize such modern itinerant reformers, who "by the mere force of imagination, have conjured up the powers of darkness in an enlightened age."[24] But at the same time he defends "another species, or rather a slighter degree of Quixotism," the desire to imitate what we read, and the value of fancy and imagination more generally (40). *The Spiritual Quixote* finally moderates but does not do away with Wildgoose's religious enthusiasm, and it recuperates "enthusiasm of another kind" for the love story. The seams of Graves's narrative weave are made visible in the wry chapter (which sounds like Sterne and Fielding) that introduces the heroine, Miss Townsend:

> Should any of my amiable country-women, I say, smit with the love of novelty, carry home this trifling volume from some Circulating-library; and throwing herself negligently upon her settee or sopha – or even on the feet of her truckle-bed – have patience to attend two such odd fellows thus far; she will probably be disgusted that she has not been entertained with a single love-tale, which are generally looked upon as essential to works of this kind; and not only make a principal part of every episode, but are usually interwoven with the body of the fable. (77)

Graves duly offers Miss Townsend's history, one of several interwoven stories that give the narrative the tight snakes-and-ladders feel of traditional romance (and *Quixote* as well). Characters from seemingly digressive stories regularly pop up in the main story. And at one Cervantic moment, Graves's real source crosses into the fiction. Graves structures Wildgoose's spiritual adventures with episodes and language from the actual journals of Whitefield and Wesley, and in a baroquely metafictional twist, Wesley himself makes an appearance in the novel, suggesting a meeting Wesley might write into the journals that form the basis of Wildgoose's fictional adventures. Graves never reverts to the "amiable country-woman" he invokes, but the playful self-reflexivity of his narrative interweave suggests that the reader's pleasure in the modulation of the Quixotic enthusiasm into love is meant to be remarked as well as indulged by the reader.

If *The Spiritual Quixote* attenuates the problem of reading, *Launcelot Greaves* cuts it completely. Arabella's madness was Quixotically generated and Wildgoose's Quixotically amplified by reading, but Launcelot is born with his obsession. His Quixotically extravagant benevolence has no trigger, and though intensified by frustrated love it actually precedes his falling in love (58–59, 64); he is just born good and so ill fitted to a corrupt world. Though framed as a Quixote, and appearing in a narrative studded with incidents borrowed from the novel, Launcelot is presented as a version of the chivalric ideal that Cervantes critiques. The distinction is underlined by the fact that Launcelot refurbishes his family's ancestral armor rather than constructing fake armor as Quixote does. Launcelot's Quixotism is moral and social, not epistemological. He aims "to enforce, not violate laws" (86), and says he is "not mad like Don Quixote – I see objects as they really are and quarrel only with the foes of virtue and decorum" (50). A figure of ideal generosity and justice, Greaves offers a point of moral reference against which to satirize a corrupt world and an example of the active virtue one expects of a knight, rescuing Aurelia, his ideal and fated lover, from a runaway coach, highwaymen, impostor officers, and a madhouse. Indeed, Smollett seems to answer Cervantes' critique by offering a modern-dress chivalric romance. Rather than the love story emerging out of a residual, errant knightliness, as with Quixote, Launcelot's errantry serves as a complication in the love story. And in English fashion, Launcelot's cure is rewarded by a conventional marriage.

Gothic games: stories of vice

In English Quixotes, the effects of impassioned reading are critiqued within the generic structures that excite them. The satisfactions of romance answer its provocations. One mark of this is the unselfconscious use of the convention of dreams and desires forecasting narrative realizations: Jerry, Wildgoose's Sancho, dreams of his long-lost son, who turns up a couple of pages later, and there is a similar moment in *Launcelot Greaves*.[25] This kind of story logic organizes Charlotte Dacre's *Zofloya* (1806). The strange, inexplicable Zofloya first appears in Victoria's dream, after a long series of unbridled passions and crimes prove her susceptible to his evil influence, and then he pops up just when he is wanted, appearing "as if informed by sympathetic influence of her wishes."[26] Your thoughts, he tells her, have power to attract me. Called by "the dreadful, the terrific, the surprising" (242), Zofloya at once embodies Victoria's desire and is the narrative device by which it is realized. The misanthropic Ferret is the variously disguised instigator of all the narrative obstacles of *Launcelot Greaves*, but the secret engines of plot are amplified into supernaturally evil agents in gothic narratives. Like Vathek's Giaour, Victoria's Zofloya turns out to have staged the crimes that make up the narrative in order to claim her back as his, the devil's, own.[27] If English Quixotes manage the desire generated by reading within conventional romance narratives, one strand of gothic romances stages its narratives as themselves effects of intensified desire. (Ann Radcliffe's romances work differently, demystifying the suspicion of supernatural machinery into merely human, though extraordinary, criminality. The subterranean architecture of fear in *A Sicilian Romance* (1790) turns out to hide not the ghost of an ancient crime but the victim of a present one – though the effect is a spooky, if natural, resurrection of Julia's dead mother.)[28]

In *The Monk* Matilda's supernatural plotting also turns out to have underwritten the whole narrative. Matilda first appears in the guise of an especially devoted and attentive novice in the monk Ambrosio's monastery; once she has earned Ambrosio's affection, she reveals that she is a woman, and one who uncannily resembles the icon of the Madonna Ambrosio adores. When they have sex, then (after she has sucked snake poison from his wound) Ambrosio achieves something like a sinning trifecta: sleeping with a boy, a woman, and Mary herself. We find out later that the coincidence of Matilda's resembling the Madonna is less remarkable than it seems at first. Matilda herself modeled for the picture in order to excite Ambrosio's less than spiritual devotion. The novel puts an exclamation point on the Monk's blasphemy when Matilda is finally revealed to be a demon. The holy representation is demonic, and the entire narrative itself turns out to have been staged, like the holy icon, as a satanic snare. It is all an enjoyable narrative game, of course. Or does *The Monk* narrate the demonic inspiration that authored it, figuring Lewis's own pact with the devil in the Monk's, and Lewis's demonically inspired narrative production in Matilda's? In the playfully intensified false bottoms – Matilda's resemblance to the icon is first a sexy accident, then erotic play, and then demonic ploy – the conventional coincidences that structure romance turn out to be supernatural realizations of desire. Gothic romances explore the flipside of the Quixote problem, realizing as narrative the intensified desires that representations provoke. This is the conceptual loop, or progress, of romance. Quixotic reading generates desire and gothic narrates the realization of desire.

The afterlife of forms

If reading romances looks Quixotic, writing romances looks demonic, a Faustian bargain. The changing significance of Matilda's picture suggests that the activities of desire are never really innocent or accidental. (And, precisely to underline the transgressiveness of desire, Ambrosio is a monk.) Reeve's pious claim that the pleasures of romance are, if not useful, at least innocent, is tested by the gothic romance she helped spawn. The narrative games that variously play out the effects of desire, whether naturally or supernaturally, are attempts to deal with the force of the accidents that are integral to romance, modally, narratively, and historically. Though sage advisors at the moment of happy endings often vindicate the straightening out of narrative kinks by invoking providence, such supernatural explanations often sound as rote as the resolutions they help decorate. The efficacy of strange representations is much weirder than that.

One of the most powerful meditations on the force of romance and its originary interplay of form and desire is Lafayette's *Zayde*. I include this in an account of the English novel to make a point about the shape and content (foreign, translated, reprinted) of British print culture and literary history. First published in French (1670), *Zayde* was translated into English in 1678 (two editions), reprinted in 1690 and 1737, and included in Samuel Croxall's *Select Collection of Novels* (1720, 1722, 1729, 1766) and Elizabeth Griffith's *Collection of Novels* (1777). The first English edition of 1678 was called a "novel," while the second edition of 1678 was called a "romance."[29] A naturalized alien intrusion at the fuzzy border of romance and novel, *Zayde* was the original context of Huet's *Traité de l'origine des romans* (which prefaced it in the original French and in Croxall's *Collection*) and itself an exploration of the origins of romance.

A gracefully intertwined network of stories, *Zayde* is organized by the misunderstanding of Consalve and Zayde, each of whom loves the other but mistakes the other's love for love of a rival. In *Zayde*, in a Möbius strip of narrative structure, we return to the first scene from the perspective of the other lover. At the start, Consalve recognizes that he resembles someone Zayde loves, and in one of those puzzling paradoxes that punctuate classical romance he thinks he owes her affection to what keeps that affection from him: "it's not me she sees, and it's not me she's thinking of when she looks at me; I remind her of the only thing I wish I could make her forget" (48). After prolific narrative complications, we learn that Consalve resembles the portrait of the lover for whom, according to the Egyptian astrologer Albumazar, Zayde is destined (171). At first Zayde had not taken Albumazar's prediction seriously, but she starts to wonder when she sees Theodoric (as Consalve is known at this point).

> "Up until now," said Zayde, "I hadn't taken what Albumazar said as a real prediction, but now I admit that since seeing Theodoric, it has begun to make an impression. I thought it quite extraordinary to have both found a man who resembled the portrait and felt an inclination for him. It surprises me when I think that he foresaw my feelings for Theodoric, and I find his person so charming that if indeed I am destined for a man who resembles him, then what should have made for my happiness will end up being my life's greatest misfortune. This resemblance has fooled my inclination, which is now drawn to someone I do not belong with, and perhaps so prepossessed that I will no longer be able to love the man I am supposed to." (174)

Zayde's desire underwrites her belief in the prediction even as the prediction seems to guide her desire; but then her belief in the prediction seems to block her desire.

Zayde's situation mirrors Consalve's, as she too is worried about a paradoxical love for the *Doppelgänger* of a proper lover and jealous of a rival who turns out to be herself. These confusions are cleared up, but the formal obstacles of portrait and prophecy remain. In typical fashion, the narrative knot is unraveled by a *pater ex machina* (Heliodorus uses this device and so does Barker). Zayde's father, Zulema, appears at the end to explain that the portrait is indeed of Consalve, whom the painter, by whim, painted in African clothes. The prediction, it turns out, was a ploy on the part of Zulema and Albumazar to trick Zayde into marrying the Prince of Fez, whom they mistakenly believe the portrait represents. But Consalve is the attenuated reference of the fancy-dress portrait, and the narrative vindicates the recognitions of desire mediated by translation. More strangely, though, this false prophecy turns out to be true. "The same words that Albumazar pronounced because of a mistaken resemblance have become, without his intending it to be so, a real prediction" (193). Forms have a strange agency, which works despite the intentions supposed to guide those forms. While the supernatural explanation turns out to be a bogus human trick, it still brings about what it prophesies. This is Lafayette's comment on the real mystery at the heart of her genre: prophecy is demystified as patriarchal deceit but its efficacy is naturalized as desire. False prophecies guide real affections and fiction can thus be realized. The reality of stories may be found not in their referential function but in their transmission and perhaps realization in a reader.

The mystery of romance – the situation the genre as narrative returns to over and over again and the situation that organizes its generic history – is that fictions have a strangely forceful, productive, seemingly prophetic power. Not because they are mythically forceful but because, despite their strangeness, they can provoke and shape readerly desires. The mechanism of Lewis's fable of the ghostly survival of stories is naturalized by Lafayette when the representation of Consalve dressed as an African Muslim – a figure perhaps for the novel's own Spanish dress – provokes in Zayde an enlivened if mistaken attention. Prompted by a fictional supernatural machinery, Zayde quixotically seeks to realize the desire excited by that attention: "I thought it quite extraordinary to have both found a man who resembled the portrait and felt an inclination for him" (174). The coordination of recognition and inclination is indeed extraordinary but not so surprising. If romance exists to relay, or play with, or critique alien intrusions (and the best romances do all at once), it depends on the strange loops inherent in reading. Narratives of desire seek to provoke readerly versions of the desire they represent. Reading gives you a taste of possibilities that only in the modern confusions of realism – the assumption that signs are bound by referents or stories by reality – look like lies. When we read we know that such lies can redeem their promises in the very pleasures and passions excited in reading.

Notes

1. Matthew Lewis, *The Monk*, ed. Howard Anderson (New York: Oxford University Press, 1980), pp. 139–165.
2. Supersedes: J. Paul Hunter, *Before Novels: The Cultural Contexts of Eighteenth-Century English Fiction* (New York: Norton, 1990), pp. 23, 28. Instrumentalizes: Michael McKeon, *The Origins of the English Novel 1600–1740* (Baltimore, MD: Johns Hopkins University Press, 1987), pp. 268, 392–393.
3. Walter Scott, "Essay on Romance," in *Essays on Chivalry, Romance, and The Drama* (London: Frederick Warne, 1887), p. 65.
4. John Winkler, "The Invention of Romance," in *The Search for the Ancient Novel*, ed. James Tatum (Baltimore, MD: Johns Hopkins University Press, 1994), pp. 35–36.
5. Simon Gaunt, "Romance and other genres," in *The Cambridge Companion to Medieval Romance*, ed. Roberta L. Krueger (New York: Cambridge University Press, 2000), p. 45; Eugène Vinaver, *The Rise of Romance* (New York: Oxford University Press, 1971), pp. 17–18, 21, 68.
6. Northrop Frye, *The Secular Scripture: A Study of the Structure of Romance* (Cambridge, MA: Harvard University Press, 1976), pp. 37–38, 55, 59–60.
7. Fredric Jameson, *The Political Unconscious: Narrative as Socially Symbolic Act* (Ithaca, NY: Cornell University Press, 1981), pp. 135, 138–139.
8. J. A. Downie, "The Making of the English Novel," *Eighteenth-Century Fiction* 9: 3 (1997), 1–22, 21–22; Mary Helen McMurran, "National or Transnational? The Eighteenth-Century Novel," in *The Literary Channel: The Inter-National Invention of the Novel*, ed. Margaret Cohen and Carolyn Dever (Princeton University Press, 2002), pp. 51–53; James Raven, *The Business of Books: Booksellers and the English Book Trade 1450–1850* (New Haven: Yale University Press, 2007), p. 2.
9. Barbara Fuchs, *Romance* (New York: Routledge, 2004), p. 50.
10. Clara Reeve, *The Old English Baron*, ed. James Trainer (New York: Oxford University Press, 2003), p. 3.
11. Ann Radcliffe, *The Mysteries of Udolpho*, ed. Jacqueline Howard (New York: Penguin, 2001), p. 240.
12. Pierre-Daniel Huet, *The History of Romances*, trans. Stephen Lewis (London, 1715), p. 3.
13. Tobias Smollett, *The Life and Adventures of Sir Launcelot Greaves*, ed. Peter Wagner (New York: Penguin, 1988). Robert Bage also calls love a rude shock in *Hermsprong*, ed. Peter Faulkner (New York: Oxford University Press, 1985), p. 89.
14. Aphra Behn, *Oroonoko*, ed. Joanna Lipking (New York: Norton, 2000), pp. 22, 26, 29.
15. Jane Barker, Preface, *Exilius; or, the Banish'd Roman*, ed. Josephine Grieder (New York: Garland, 1973), p. A2. *Exilius* was reprinted as vol. 1 of *The Entertaining Novels of Jane Barker*, 2 vols. (1719, 1736, 1743).
16. Chrétien de Troyes, "The Knight with the Lion," *The Complete Romances of Chrétien de Troyes*, trans. David Staines (Bloomington: Indiana University Press, 1993), p. 321.

17. Corinne Saunders, Introduction, *A Companion to Romance* (Malden, MA: Blackwell, 2004), pp. 3, 5.

18. The year after *Exilius*, Richard Blackmore repeats the familiar claim about Heliodorus as the Homer of prose fiction in "An Essay Upon Epick Poetry," in *Essays upon Several Subjects* (London, 1716), pp. 29–30. For Heliodorus' influence, see Alban K. Forcione, *Cervantes, Aristotle, and the Persiles* (Princeton University Press, 1970), pp. 50–51, where Huet's claim about Heliodorus as prose fiction's Homer is quoted.

19. See my "Reading Mistakes in Heliodorus," in *Eighteenth Century: Theory and Interpretation*, 52: 3/4 (2011).

20. Ian Watt, *The Rise of the Novel: Studies in Defoe, Richardson, and Fielding* (Berkeley: University of California Press, 1957), pp. 15, 33.

21. Richard C. Taylor, "James Harrison, *The Novelist's Magazine*, and the Early Canonizing of the English Novel," *Studies in English Literature* 33 (1993), 629–643; Claudia L. Johnson, "'Let Me Make the Novels of a Country': Barbauld's *The British Novelists* (1810/1820)," *Novel* 34: 2 (2001), 163–179.

22. Charlotte Lennox, *The Female Quixote*, ed. Margaret Dalziel (New York: Oxford University Press, 1989), pp. 129–130.

23. For Fielding's use of this double structure, see my "Anachronism and the Uses of Form in *Joseph Andrews*," *Novel* 38: 2/3 (2005), 147–164.

24. Richard Graves, *The Spiritual Quixote*, ed. Clarence Tracy (New York: Oxford University Press, 1967), pp. 19–20, 27, 29.

25. This device is used in realist novels, too, as when Anna Karenina uncannily dreams her own death scene.

26. Charlotte Dacre, *Zofloya, or The Moor*, ed. Kim Ian Michasiw (New York: Oxford University Press, 2008), pp. 136–137, 166.

27. William Beckford, *Vathek*, ed. Kenneth W. Graham (Peterborough, ON: Broadview, 2001), p. 148. Frances Sheridan's "History of Nourjahad" also turns out to be an elaborately staged illusion (*Oriental Tales*, ed. Robert L. Mack [New York: Oxford University Press, 1992], p. 194).

28. Ann Radcliffe, *A Sicilian Romance*, ed. Alison Milbank (New York: Oxford University Press, 2008), pp. 173–174.

29. Marie-Madeleine Pioche de la Vergne, Comtesse de Lafayette, *Zayde*, trans. Nicholas Paige (University of Chicago Press, 2006), p. 29.

16

Gothic success and gothic failure: formal innovation in a much-maligned genre

GEORGE HAGGERTY

Gothic fiction emerged from a dream and subsided into infamy, but in the years 1764–1810 it included works that were thematically challenging and formally innovative; and much that first took shape in gothic fiction changed the face of novel-writing for generations after its lurid heyday. The rather infamous inception of the gothic novel – Horace Walpole recounts a dream in which antiquarian imaginings led him to scribble far into the night – is repeated and recast in other famous gothic iterations such as Mary Shelley's *Frankenstein* (1818) and Henry James's *The Turn of the Screw* (1898). Most important, however, are the details of Walpole's dream itself and the ways in which it inspired an incipient gothic technique. Walpole's account, addressed to his friend William Cole, describes the dream in full:

> Your partiality to me and Strawberry [Hill] have I hope inclined you to excuse the wildness of the story. You will even have found some traits to put you in mind of this place. When you read of the picture quitting its panel, did not you recollect the portrait of Lord Falkland all in white in my gallery? Shall I even confess to you what was the origin of this romance? I waked one morning in the beginning of last June from a dream, of which all I could recover was, that I had thought myself in an ancient castle (a very natural dream for a head filled like mine with Gothic story) and that on the upper-most banister of a great staircase I saw a gigantic hand in armour. In the evening I sat down and began to write, without knowing in the least what I intended to say or relate. The work grew on my hands, and I grew fond of it – add that I was very glad to think of anything rather than politics – In short I was so engrossed with my tale, which I completed in less than two months, that one evening I wrote from the time I had drunk my tea, about six o'clock, till half an hour after one in the morning, when my hand and fingers were so weary, that I could not hold the pen to finish the sentence, but left Matilda and Isabella talking, in the middle of a paragraph. You will laugh at my earnest-ness, but if I have amused you by retracing with any fidelity the manners of

ancient days, I am content, and give you leave to think me as idle as you please.[1]

This passage tells just about everything we need to know about the genesis of the novel: not only about Walpole's private obsession with antiquarian materials and modes of home décor – Strawberry Hill, his house in Twickenham, was a gothic treasure-trove even in his own lifetime – but also about the ways in which those materials affected his fictional imagination. Walpole projects the features of his dream into this first gothic novel because for him the materials themselves – the oversized helmet, the gigantic sword, and the expanding statue – begin to tell a story. Walpole scribbles into the night because these details speak to him.

The nightmare effects come first in gothic fiction. The effects *create* the narrative, just as Walpole's dreamscape creates the terms of his novelistic experiment. The first gothic novel included other features that return with later examples of the form. It was published anonymously, and the original preface talks as follows about the work's being "found in the library of an ancient catholic family in the north of England. It was printed at Naples, in the black letter, in 1529."[2] The anonymity, the Italian Catholic setting, and the mysterious origin of the manuscript all become familiar gothic tropes by the early years of the nineteenth century. Most important, however, is the year in which the tale is set. Walpole's gothic novel uses historical distance as a key feature of his text. This innovation in setting had the most profound effect on Walpole's imitators. Once gothic fiction had been established in its historically gothic setting, then every lurid story of religious excess, abuse of power, or familial persecution began to have a logic of its own.

Walpole's novel itself is a simple and sometimes almost laughable account of supernatural events that finally shake the resolve of the usurping Prince Manfred, who in the end admits defeat when the true inheritor of the principality is recognized and celebrated. Not laughable, however, is the account of Manfred's pursuit of the innocent Isabella, who had been betrothed to his son Conrad. By pressing his suit for her hand, Manfred causes her to flee, and the flight of Isabella within the gloomy confines of the castle's subterranean regions is one of the signal set pieces of the novel. Not coincidentally, this is the first gothic moment of erotic fear:

> The lower part of the castle was hollowed into several intricate cloisters; and it was not easy for one under so much anxiety to find the door that opened into the cavern. An awful silence reigned throughout those subterraneous regions, except now and then some blasts of wind that shook the doors she

had passed, and which grating on the rusty hinges were re-echoed through
that long labyrinth of darkness.   (26)

Walpole may not have known that he was providing terms for what would
come to be known as "female gothic"; but he understood that female vulnerability was an area of great fictional potential. Here Walpole does what becomes
the hallmark of gothic fiction: in a single image he combines the sexual anxiety
of a victimized female, the incestuous desire of a libidinous male, the use of the
actual physical features of the castle to represent political and sexual entrapment,
and an atmosphere deftly rendered to produce terror and gloom. This scene is
retold hundreds of times in gothic fiction. Because he understands that gothic
fiction can represent abject terror and frenzied aggression in ways that other
fiction only approximates, Walpole's depiction of this moment, and others like
it, takes on a kind of talismanic importance in the history of gothic fiction.[3]

In his preface to the second edition of *The Castle of Otranto*, Walpole explains
his literary endeavor in this way:

> It was an attempt to blend two kinds of romance, the ancient and the modern.
> In the former all was imagination and improbability; in the latter, nature is
> always intended to be, and sometimes has been, copied with success. Invention
> has not been wanting; but the great resources of fancy have been dammed up
> by a strict adherence to common life.   (9)

Walpole does this in part by introducing supernatural elements into his quasi-
realistic narrative, but he also invests psychic life with erotic terror, and that
does as much to "blend two kinds of romance." When Isabella dashes away
from this predatory prince, she recalls persecuted heroines from the past, but
she also hints at a feature that gothic heroines often share: although they do not
submit to aggression, they somehow, in many cases at least, manage to escape.

Ghostliness is secondary to erotic terror in gothic fiction; it combines with it
to make interior torments greater than anything that the supernatural world
could supply. When the supernatural is "explained" in novels by Radcliffe and
her contemporaries, that explanation is often more harrowing – murder, incest,
prolonged incarceration – than anything that supernatural agents were
threatening.

Mention of Ann Radcliffe suggests that "female gothic" might offer a different perspective on pursuit and sexual terror, but that does not seem to be the
case. Radcliffe, to name only the most famous of the female writers of gothic
fiction from the later eighteenth century, develops the trope of erotic pursuit
into the very structure of her novels. Everything that happens in Radcliffe's
novels is motivated by the persecution of the young female heroine by an

autocratic male aggressor. Some critics have been led to claim that Radcliffe's heroines are actually attracted to the villainous figures that pursue them.[4] I have argued against this approach. Even so, it might make sense to discuss Ellena di Rosalba's relation to the evil monk Schedoni in such terms. She for long imagines that he is her father. In this novel and in Radcliffe's other work, however, the malevolent paternal figure is rejected in favor of the ineffectual and indeed emasculated hero of the work. The latter joins with the heroine in the articulation of a bond other than the terrorizing masculine victimization that the novels recount.[5] Rather than extend the victimization that was begun in Walpole's novel, then, Radcliffe places women in threatening situations and then shows them ways to resist the victimization that seems so inevitable.

One of the techniques Radcliffe uses to make this resistance persuasive is the landscape description so often commented on in her works. At times her set descriptions of the Apennines or the Alps seem gratuitous. But this is far from true, for in almost every key landscape description in Radcliffe's novels, a heroine is there to take in the scene and to be moved by its sublime power. This ability to engage with the beauties of nature calms the heroine, but it also teaches her how to draw calm from communicating with her inmost self.

Take the scene in which Ellena, the heroine of *The Italian, or, The Confessional of the Black Penitents* (1797), is incarcerated in the Convent of San Stephano. Alone in her room, she feels brutalized and lonely, but when one of the nuns, the kindly Sister Olivia, gives her the key to the turret, she finds there a source of consolation that can sustain her in her convent ordeal:

> She ascended the winding steps hastily, and found the key led only to a door, opening into a small room, where nothing remarkable appeared, till she approached the windows, and beheld thence an horizon, and a landscape spread below, whose grandeur awakened all her heart. The consciousness of her prison was lost, while her eyes ranged over the wide and freely-sublime scene without ... Ellena, with a dreadful pleasure, looked down them, shagged as they were with larch, and frequently darkened by lines of gigantic pine bending along the rocky ledges, till her eye rested on the thick chestnut woods that extended over their winding base, and which, softening to the plains, seemed to form a gradation between the variegated cultivation there, and the awful wildness of the rocks above ... To Ellena, whose mind was capable of being highly elevated, or, sweetly soothed, by scenes of nature, the discovery of this little turret was an important circumstance.[6]

How important a circumstance can be seen in the passage itself: Radcliffe gives us an almost textbook description of the working of the sublime here. Ellena is elevated and soothed by the visual scene. The "dreadful pleasure" she takes in the scene before her causes her to lose consciousness of her prison. This psychological dynamic enables her to resist the pressure that is put on her there. The landscape description functions in the plot and has significance in the outcome of this incarceration.

Even these few novelists might begin to suggest a range of techniques and *topoi* that typify gothic fiction and provide some of its irresistible power. To be sure, not all critics agree that gothic novels are powerful. One of the most articulate critics of "gothic failure" is Elizabeth Napier, who sees two opposed currents in the gothic novel: "a tendency towards moral and structural stabilizing characteristic of much previous eighteenth-century fiction . . . and a contrary inclination towards fragmentation, instability and moral ambivalence." She goes on to say that the gothic novel "remains essentially a genre of imbalance because its authors finally neither subscribed to either extreme nor found a middle way between them."[7] I have previously made a different case: that "what really takes place is a process of formal insurgency, a rejection of the conventional demands of the novel form, first within the gloomy confines of the gothic novel, causing disruption and inconsistency, and later in a liberated and liberating alternative to the conventional novel. Gothic fiction, in other words, plays out a formal drama which is itself gothic in its implications" (Haggerty, *Gothic Fiction*, 3). The gothic tale, so I have argued, emerged from the novel itself to give gothic writers a coherent rationale and powerful effect. Gothic novels are most successful when effects are gauged precisely to the situations that give them rise and when narrative excesses are placed within a single internal narrative perspective. All these things happen in the gothic novel from time to time; and when they do, even otherwise sensationalist novels take on real complexity and power.

Matthew Lewis's 1796 novel, *The Monk*, demonstrates the uses of sensationalism. One of the most shocking scenes is the one in which the conflicted monk, Ambrosio, murders the mother of his intended sexual victim, Antonia. Antonia's mother was suspicious of the supposedly upstanding monk, and entered her daughter's bedroom to discover Ambrosio's lascivious advances:

> "Attempt not to fly!" said She; "You quit this room not without witnesses of your guilt."
> Ambrosio struggled in vain to disengage himself. Elvira quitted not her hold, but redoubled her cries for succour. The Friar's danger grew more urgent. He expected every moment to hear people assembling at her voice; And worked up to madness by the approach of ruin, He adopted a resolution equally desperate and savage. Turning round suddenly, with one hand He grasped Elvira's throat so as to prevent her continuing her clamour, and with

the other, dashing her violently to the ground, He dragged her towards the Bed. Confused by this unexpected attack, She scarcely had power to strive at forcing herself from his grasp: While the Monk, snatching the pillow from beneath her Daughter's head, covering with it Elvira's face, and pressing his knee upon her stomach with all his strength, endeavoured to put an end to her existence. He succeeded but too well . . . The Monk took off the pillow, and gazed upon her. Her face was covered with a frightful blackness: Her limbs moved no more; The blood was chilled in her veins; Her heart had forgotten to beat, and her hands were stiff and frozen. Ambrosio beheld before him that once noble form, now become a Corse, cold, senseless and disgusting.[8]

The novelist seems to take pleasure in the brutality of the attack, and Ambrosio's moment of violence is depicted in grim detail. Because Ambrosio has been attempting the rape of Antonia, the violence carries a sexual valence. Consider also Lewis's pre-Freudian version of the family romance: the woman Ambrosio is on the bed struggling with to the death is in fact his mother. The devil throws out this detail for Ambrosio to contemplate, just before he casts the sinner into the abyss. Lewis's seemingly gratuitous scene of violence, then, is deeply connected to Ambrosio's own psychology. Such a brutal perversion of Oedipal desire is Lewis's attempt to explain the insatiable sexual monstrosity of his hero.

One of the most striking features of *The Monk* is the internal narrative of Raymond and Agnes, sometimes called the story of the Bleeding Nun. This is yet another story of sexual violence and retribution, neatly contained within the limits of family; but this time the victim seems to be the young man, Raymond, who hopes to run off with Agnes, the young woman whom he loves and who loves him in return. They are thwarted when they attempt to use the local lore about a "Bleeding Nun" who walks the halls of Agnes's castle at one night in the year as the clock strikes one. Agnes and Raymond dismiss the claims of local superstition, and disguise Agnes as the nun to better enable their flight from jealous and overbearing parents. Raymond has a carriage ready, and when Agnes appears, the carriage takes off at a remarkable speed. When the carriage crashes, Raymond is taken to an upper chamber. There he recounts the following eerie encounter that occurs during the first night of recuperation, when he is trying to sleep:

That repose I wooed in vain. The agitation of my bosom chased away sleep. Restless in my mind, in spite of the fatigue of my body I continued to toss about from side to side, till the Clock in a neighbouring Steeple struck 'One'. As I listened to the mournful hollow sound, and heard it die away in the wind, I felt a sudden chilliness spread itself over my body. I shuddered without knowing wherefore; Cold dews poured down my forehead, and my hair stood bristling with alarm. Suddenly I heard slow and heavy steps ascending the stair-case. By an involuntary movement I started up in my bed, and drew back the curtain. A single rush-light, which glimmered upon the hearth shed a faint gleam through the apartment, which was hung with tapestry. The door was thrown open with violence. A figure entered, and drew near my Bed with solemn measured steps. With trembling apprehension I examined this mid-night Visitor. God Almighty! It was the Bleeding Nun! It was my lost Companion! Her face was still veiled, but She no longer held her Lamp and dagger. She lifted up her veil slowly. What a sight presented itself to my startled eyes! I beheld before me an animated Corse.   (159–160)

The virtues of first-person narrative in this instance are obvious. Raymond's fears are delineated so as to maximize their affective power. Lewis was familiar with German tales of terror, and he employed their techniques of immediacy.

The horrors here are as familial as those surrounding Ambrosio's murder of Elvira. The Bleeding Nun's story is one of broken vows, illicit marriage, and betrayal. She was murdered by her supposed lover, the brother of her husband, and left unburied in the place called Lindenberg's hole. In order to gain peace and offer the nun final rest, Raymond needs to travel there and bury her bones. Once he has done so, he is free to pursue Agnes once more.

Both these examples from *The Monk* show how seemingly sensationalist scenes can be made to serve the purposes of gothic narrative. Charlotte Dacre, sometimes known as Rosa Matilda in honor of characters in *The Monk*, used sensationalism in different ways. Her own gothic masterpiece, *Zofloya, or The Moor* (1806), creates one of the most villainous heroines of gothic fiction, the beautiful and willful Victoria; and Dacre avoids first-person narrative to create instead a moral-psychological narrative voice that explains Victoria's excessive behavior by pointing out the illicit love affair of her mother and making connections between maternal neglect and a daughter's villainy. To make certain that her family romance hits home, moreover, Victoria involves her brother in a series of unnatural crimes that are as vivid as they are gruesome. Leonardo suffers from the same maternal transgression; but he becomes the plaything of the vicious and vindictive Megalena Strozzi, who sends him to destroy Victoria's lover, Berenza; but instead he finds himself in an incestuous encounter with Victoria herself.

The narrative also introduces Zofloya, the Moor of the title, who also becomes, as the narrative unfolds, a sort of demonic double for Victoria, who enables her to realize her desires only to punish her with eternal damnation at the end. Victoria's chief object of desire is her husband's brother Henriquez.

Henriquez seems immune to her charms, and instead he dotes on his darling and much more feminine Lilla. With the help of Zofloya, Victoria murders her husband, incarcerates Lilla, and then has a voluptuous sexual encounter with Henriquez while assuming his wife's form. When Henriquez recognizes what he has done, he falls on his own sword, cursing Victoria as he does. In a further chilling scene, Victoria murders Lilla. This scene stands out as one of the most brutal in gothic fiction:

> Nerved anew by this feeble attempt to escape her vengeance, Victoria pursued her flying victim. At the uttermost edge of the mountain she gained upon her, when Lilla perceiving that hope of escape was vain, caught frantic, for safety, at the scathed branches of a blasted oak, that, bowed by repeated storms, hung almost perpendicularly over the yawning depth beneath. – Round these, she twisted her slender arms, while, waving to and fro with her gentle weight over the immeasurable abyss, they seemed to promise but precarious support.[9]

Lilla is objectified as a victim here – a pale reflection of Victoria, she becomes the perfect answer to Victoria's surging rage. Her "slender arms" and wounded hand make her attractive as well as pathetic, in the terms that the novel has established. She is an object of obsessive erotic fascination to Victoria. Lilla represents the devoted femininity that Victoria has sacrificed to her desire to be like her mother. Like her indeed! This is as intense a scene as the novel offers, and in its brutal, physical intensity resides all the frustration of that originary foreclosure. Victoria wanders in a frustrating and horrifyingly normative desire, that is, because she has lost the mother whom she loved (Haggerty, *Queer Gothic*, 36–41).

When Victoria meets that mother again in the robbers' cave where her brother and Megalena have ended up, she simply rejects her; and in doing do she turns to the Moor who has befriended her with an affection that is as erotically charged as her relations with her mother are brutally cold. "[S]he loved, yet trembled at the inscrutable Zofloya" (245), and in the arms of this "presumed lover" (244), she tells him, "Wert thou always with me Zofloya, ... black melancholy and gloomy visions would never agitate my soul" (249). But her mother continues to be a source of pain only. Nature, the novel asks, or nurture? But beneath the thematic clarity of this encounter, another level of personal intensity is at work as well. Dacre sees this relation between mother and daughter as so totally formative that it could be seen as the basis of narrative itself. When Victoria says "that which I have been, my mother made me" (258), she gets at the very heart of gothic interest in the depths of selfhood. Dacre realizes the violence and brutality of subjectivity itself, and she plays out this violence, with the help of the radical alterity that Zofloya represents, to victimize everyone to whom she is close. It is a stunning, breathtaking display of personal aggression and rage. But of course Victoria is the one who is finally cast down into the abyss.

Another route entirely is suggested by Sophia Lee, who combines the gothic with the sentimental. In her historical gothic thriller, *The Recess* (1783), Lee blends sensibility and the gothic so successfully that later writers were able to use the historical approach to considerable effect. Most gothic fiction is historical to some degree. After all, it was Walpole's antiquarian interests that led him to write the first gothic novel. Nevertheless, the history is usually vaguely medieval and Italian so as not to step on the toes of (Protestant) English readers and their knowledge of English history. Lee does almost the opposite: she takes some of the most familiar passages of English history and rewrites them for her own female, if not feminist, purposes.

Lee chooses to retell the story of Queen Elizabeth I and Mary, Queen of Scots. She creates two daughters of Mary, who are hidden away in infancy, in the "recess" of the title, which comprises a cave-like series of chambers underground but on the grounds of an enormous abbey. Formerly a convent, the space is cave-like but consists of various rooms, centered on "a vaulted passage" whose light "proceeded from casements of painted glass, so infinitely above our reach we could never seek a world beyond."[10] This remembered space assumes a suggestive womb-like quality, and the distinctly charged memories of this childhood world are suffused with the idea of the girls' mother, the majestic but threateningly distant (and doomed) Mary, Queen of Scots. Just as Mary is a mother both inaccessible and dangerous – should the girls be acknowledged publicly, their lives would surely be in danger – the maternal space is the scene of horror (the incestuous relation of their foster parents, their own brutal incarceration and near-rape) as well as love (both between the sisters and among them and their historically important male companions, Leicester and Essex). The tale of unhappiness and loss that besets them – each is doomed to misery in love and wretchedness in life – returns repeatedly to this exotic space and the foredoomed happiness that it represents. In the end, however, it can only torment these girls with all they lack. The literally "absent" mother hovers over the work with a similarly threatening presence that always seems to promise happiness while bringing misery and despair. If later gothicists create maternal specters to challenge heroines with the limits of their own subjectivity, Lee tries, as it were, to *maternalize* history itself: to depict it as harrowing in a particularly female way.

The novel's special quality, however, lies in the possibility of female relations it dramatizes. Not just the girls' attraction to the always tantalizingly close mother, Mary Stuart, renders this work uniquely centered on women: the same goes also for their relations with their foster mother, Mrs. Marlow; with the antagonist, Queen Elizabeth; with friends; with servants; and, most especially, with each other. In many ways like Sarah Scott's female-centered novel *Millenium Hall* (1762), *The Recess* celebrates women-centered affection and eroticizes maternal relations with unswerving flair. Lee was determined to defy social conventions by her attention to sexual relations that were unacceptable to late-eighteenth-century society. She also defies the generally lesser position of women in that society. Lee manages to create a historical precedent for the eroticization of female relations, sisterly as well as mother–daughter: a new analytical lens is thus needed. Lee is very strong in characterization, and her work was read with historical interest in her time and beyond. What Lee was able to show with *The Recess* was that history could be retold for the purposes of gothic and sentimental narrative. Other gothicists used history persuasively as well.[11]

One last female gothic writer deserves to be included here, if only because her novels offer such a contrast to the writers considered so far. She is Regina Maria Roche, an Irish writer who settled in London after her marriage. *The Children of the Abbey* (1796) is a novel to be placed among the most renowned gothic novels on account of its religious valence and its attempt to rehabilitate the Catholic clergy. Nuns and priests are good characters in this novel. The heroine is persecuted and threatening scenes abound, but what is always true is that members of the Roman Catholic clergy offer succor and support of kinds rarely imagined in other gothic works. Even the good sister Olivia in Radcliffe's *The Italian* turns out to be first a mother and second a nun; but in Roche's work nuns are motherly without any blood connections to the heroine at all. Restrained in its use of wicked monks and nuns, *The Children of the Abbey* nevertheless tells a tale that deeply intertwines religion and sexuality. The heirs of Dunheath Abbey, Amanda Fitzalan, the heroine of the tale, and her brother Oscar, are nefariously disinherited and forced to struggle separately for survival. Amanda is sent by her widowed father to live with friends, but she very quickly becomes the victim of jealous competitors. She is a beautiful and unassuming girl, and a rumor spreads that she is somehow dishonorable. Out of the welter of suspicion and disappointment, Amanda finds solace in the form of a Catholic nun. The nun does not accuse, threaten, or victimize in any way. But even in this novel, the consoling force of the convent is often suggestive.

In one of the most powerful scenes in the novel, Amanda searches for her lost mother in the chamber in which she imagined that woman had died. The excitement is palpable here, and Amanda moves forward with a temerity that

marks her as a gothic *ingénue*. At the same time, the scene has all the quality of
a dream: the darkness, the sudden moonlight, the room of indeterminate size,
and finally the consoling portrait once again. But she finds that all is not what
it seems:

> Amanda . . . at last came to the door, it was closed, not fastened; she pushed it
> gently open, and could just discern a spacious room; this she supposed had
> been her mother's dressing-room; the moon-beams . . . suddenly darted
> through the casements . . . She advanced into the room; at the upper end of
> it something white attracted her notice: She concluded it to be the portrait of
> Lady Malvina's mother . . . She went up to examine it; but her horror may be
> better conceived than described, when she found herself not by a picture, but
> the real form of a woman, with a death-like countenance! She screamed
> wildly at the terrifying spectre, for such she believed it to be, and quick as
> lightening flew from the room. Again the moon was obscured by a cloud, and
> she involved in utter darkness. She ran with such violence, that, as she
> reached the door at the end of the gallery, she fell against it. Extremely
> hurt, she had not the power to move for a few minutes; but while she
> involuntarily paused, she heard footsteps. Wild with terror, she instantly
> recovered her faculties and attempted opening it . . . at that moment she
> felt an icy hand upon her's![12]

This ghostly presence – maternal and enabling, even if not her actual
mother – shimmers with erotic feeling. After all, the girl who is prowling
through the castle in the middle of the night has suffered emotional stress
and personal disappointment of various kinds. But still she thinks that the
dark, gothic chamber will offer her some kind of satisfaction, some thrill of
discovery. She takes her readers with her into this darkness, and she
challenges them to experience these thrills with the almost physical intensity
that she displays. As the tension builds, the mysteriously threatening cold
white figure follows, chases her, places its hand on hers, gives the scene a
peculiar power that earns it a place among the other gothic novels of its time.
Amanda was drawn to the chapel as a way of discovering something about
her lost mother. Instead, she confronts a ghostly presence that clasps her
with an icy grip. Her own past and the lost mother seem to threaten from
somewhere beyond the grave. Here she must confront her deepest fears.
Amanda is of course up to this challenge, and the novel ends happily. But it
does not do that without presenting many more harrowing scenes to rattle
the sensitive reader.[13]

The novelist William Godwin raises issues that anticipate the concerns of
many writers in the Romantic period; and his novel *Caleb Williams* (1794) is a

stunning achievement that deserves to be placed among the most compelling novels in the English tradition. *Things as They Are; or, A History of Caleb Williams* is told in an engrossing first-person narrative technique that makes the very most of what gothicists before Godwin had achieved. He understood that psychological effects are best rendered in first-person narrative, and he understood that a degree of confusion and uncertainty on the part of the narrator would only heighten those effects. Caleb Williams, the title character, is constantly struggling to understand what is happening to him, and he is confused, at first, because he does not fully comprehend the depravity of human nature. Even later, when he comes to this understanding and tries to turn to the law for help – even there he is confronted with how little his lower-class plea can mean in a system devised to render him powerless.[14]

Some of the most compelling scenes in the novel are those in which Caleb confronts his master and benefactor, Falkland, only gradually recognizing that this man is in fact his nemesis. The scenes in which this transpires are all in some ways like this one in which he is discovered looking through a trunk in Falkland's room, which he attempts when there is a fire on the grounds:

> I was in the act of lifting up the lid, when Mr. Falkland, entered, wild, breathless, distracted in his looks! He had been brought home from a considerable distance by the sight of the flames. At the moment of his appearance, the lid dropped from my hand. He no sooner saw me than his eyes emitted sparks of rage. He ran with eagerness to the brace of loaded pistols which hung in the room, and, seizing one, presented it to my head. I saw his design, and sprang to avoid it; but, with the same rapidity with which he had formed his resolution, he changed it, and instantly went to the window, and flung the pistol to the court below. He bade me begone with his usual irresistible energy; and, overcome as I already was by the horror of the detection, I eagerly complied.[15]

Falkland catches Caleb in an act that threatens his privacy, and his reaction is violent. Caleb feels himself to be in the wrong, even though he suspects Falkland of a capital crime, and he absconds guiltily, which plays into Falkland's ultimate game. Whatever Caleb does, he feels that he is in the wrong; this is in part because of Falkland's position and power and in part because Caleb must always be victim to this social superior.

Godwin's gothic technique takes what was implied in earlier gothic fiction – the wielding of power and the victimization of the powerless – and he makes of it an irresistible trope. Falkland pursues him relentlessly throughout the novel, and renders his life a nightmare of persecution and incarceration. At the end, Caleb may triumph over his enemy – there are two endings, and in the one Godwin finally settled on, he does – but that does not make him any the less a victim. After he has denounced Falkland in a court of law, he tells us that Falkland praised his "elevation of mind":

> I record the praises bestowed on me by Falkland, not because I deserve them, but because they serve to aggravate the baseness of my cruelty. He survived this dreadful scene but three days. I have been his murderer. It was fit that he should praise my patience, who has fallen a victim, life and fame, to my precipitation! It would have been merciful in comparison, if I planted a dagger in his heart. He would have thanked me for my kindness. But, atrocious, execrable wretch that I have been! I wantonly inflicted on him an anguish a thousand times worse than death. (433)

Caleb blames himself in this final scene, and the victory is Pyrrhic at best. Caleb does not feel released from Falkland's victimization, but instead he feels that he has himself been the aggressive murderer. He takes responsibility for the death of this villainous man precisely because he cannot imagine that his own life is worth that of his social superior. This gothic novel has portrayed a harrowing account of social inequity even while Godwin makes it one of the greatest psychological thrillers in English.

Far from failing at its formal challenges, gothic fiction was a laboratory for the exploration of narrative techniques. Psychological fiction, first-person narrative, the uses of history, female violence, and female desire, incest tropes: all these elements animate the pages of gothic fiction and make this genre unavoidably compelling. Jane Austen mocked the gothic in her masterly parody, *Northanger Abbey* (1817). But when Austen mocks the genre, she also pays it compliments that it well deserves. Catherine Morland is talking to Henry Tilney, the man she is losing her heart to, and his sister, when she finds herself celebrating the talents of Mrs. Radcliffe. They are in Bath, and they have arrived at Beechen Cliff:

> "I never look at it," said Catherine, as they walked along the side of the river, "without thinking of the south of France."
> "You have been abroad then?" said Henry, a little surprised.
> "Oh! no, I only mean what I have read about. It always puts me in mind of the country Emily and her father travelled through, in the 'Mysteries of Udolpho'. But you never read novels, I dare say?"
> "Why not?"
> "Because they are not clever enough for you – gentlemen read better books."
> "The person, be it gentleman or lady, who has not pleasure in a good novel, must be intolerably stupid. I have read all Mrs. Radcliffe's works, and most of them with pleasure. The Mysteries of Udolpho, when I had once

begun it, I could not lay down again; – I remember finishing it in two days – my hair standing on end the whole time."

"Yes," added Miss Tilney, "and I remember that you undertook to read it to me, and that when I was called away for only five minutes to answer a note, instead of waiting for me, you took the volume into the Hermitage-walk, and I was obliged to stay until you had finished it."[16]

This passage belies the usual impression that Austen attacks gothic fiction in her novel of gothic parody. In fact, at the same time that she shows how gothicism can lead an impressionable young girl astray, as it does Catherine Morland, Austen begins to explain the popularity of gothic fiction. For all Catherine's gothic exaggeration of the situation at Northanger Abbey – suspecting lurid missives in the drawers of a locked cabinet and instead finding a laundry list – she has some reason to suspect General Tilney of having murdered his wife. Henry is appalled that she could imagine such a thing, but General Tilney is an autocratic and condescendingly paternal figure. He has a demeaning attitude toward Catherine, which produces her imagining of him as a villain. Her gothic reading almost seems to have helped her in this situation – as, indeed, it helped countless readers to gain a sense of themselves and to imagine a world outside the confines of their village or urban setting.

Gothic fiction still has the ability, as Henry Tilney remarks, to take us out of ourselves and to involve us in a compelling fictional world. At its most successful, gothic fiction is challenging and expanding in the ways that Edmund Burke suggests the sublime can be. As Burke said, "The passion caused by the great and sublime in nature ... is Astonishment; and astonishment is that state of the soul, in which all its motions are suspended, with some degree of horror. In this case the mind is so entirely filled with its object, that it cannot entertain any other."[17] Gothic writers are interested in finding ways to effect this process of suspension. At times they do it by suggestion, innuendo, and lofty descriptions; at others by depicting horrifying scenes and brutal encounters; but the intention is the same – to astonish the readers and move them out of themselves. More often than not, the gothic novelists achieved this: therein lies their greatness.

Notes

1. *The Yale Edition of Horace Walpole's Correspondence*, ed. W. S. Lewis, 48 vols. *Horace Walpole's Correspondence with The Rev. William Cole*, vols. I and II, ed. W. S. Lewis and A. Dayle Wallace (New Haven: Yale University Press, 1937), vol. I, p. 88.
2. Horace Walpole, *The Castle of Otranto*, ed. Michael Gamer (London: Penguin, 2001), p. 5.

3. See George E. Haggerty, *Queer Gothic* (Champagne-Urbana: University of Illinois Press, 2006), p. 22.

4. Cynthia Griffin Wolff, "The Radcliffean Gothic Model: A Form for Feminine Sexuality," *Modern Language Studies* 9 (1979), 98–113, 103–104.

5. See, for instance, George E. Haggerty, "The Pleasures of Victimization in *The Romance of the Forest*," in *Unnatural Affections: Women and Fiction in the Later Eighteenth Century* (Bloomington: Indiana University Press, 1998), pp. 158–170.

6. Ann Radcliffe, *The Italian, or The Confessional of the Black Penitents*, ed. Frederick Garber (Oxford University Press, 1984), p. 90.

7. Elizabeth Napier, *The Failure of Gothic: Problems of Disjunction in an Eighteenth-century Literary Form* (Oxford: Clarendon Press, 1987), p. 5; see also George E. Haggerty, *Gothic Fiction/Gothic Form* (University Park, PA: Pennsylvania State University Press, 1989), p. 2.

8. Matthew Lewis, *The Monk*, ed. Howard Anderson (Oxford University Press, 1980), pp. 303–304.

9. Charlotte Dacre, *Zofloya, or the Moor* (1806), ed. Kim Ian Michasiw (Oxford University Press, 1997), p. 225.

10. Sophia Lee, *The Recess; or, A Tale of Other Times*, ed. April Alliston (Lexington: University Press of Kentucky, 2000), p. 8.

11. For the historical importance of the novel, see April Alliston, Introduction, *The Recess*, pp. ix–xliv.

12. Regina Maria Roche, *The Children of the Abbey* (Whitefish, MT: Kissinger Publishing, n.d.), pp. 446–447.

13. For more on this novel, see Haggerty, *Queer Gothic*, pp. 72–75.

14. On surveillance and pursuit in the novel, see James Thompson, "Surveillance in Godwin's *Caleb Williams*," in *Gothic Fictions: Prohibition/Transgression*, ed. Kenneth Graham (New York: AMS Press, 1989), pp. 173–198.

15. William Godwin, *Caleb Williams*, ed. Gary Handwerk and A. A. Markley (Peterborough, ON: Broadview, 2000), p. 211.

16. Jane Austen, *Northanger Abbey*, ed. John Davie (London: Oxford University Press, 1990), p. 82.

17. Edmund Burke, *On the Philosophical Origins of Our Ideas of the Sublime and the Beautiful*, ed. J. T. Bolton (New York: Columbia University Press, 1958), p. 58.

17

Sir Walter Scott: historiography contested by fiction

MURRAY PITTOCK

Sir Walter Scott's perceived "Scottishness" has been a handicap to the understanding of his work in the postwar world. The rise of an aestheticized vision
of the Romantic period, combined with a focus on the Coleridgean imagination and the Lake Poets in general, rerouted Romantic criticism away from
its origins in language, politics, and society and towards the realms of transcendent vision. Scott and Burns suffered more from this shift than other
Romantic writers in the British Isles, and the situation was not relieved by a
turn in the focus of Romantic criticism in the 1980s towards a historicist
approach and enlarged canon.[1] Whereas in the 1930s Scott's novels were
being set at School Certificate for pupils in English schools, in the 1980s it
was not unknown for English academics to believe that he was almost
impenetrable to their undergraduates. Nor was the situation in Scotland
better, despite the launch of the Edinburgh Edition of the Waverley novels
in 1985, a project which initiated a new wave in the textual editing of Scotland's
major authors. Signs of revival in North America have not yet significantly
altered this picture.

Scott is commonly credited with inventing the historical novel. This is the
case made by Georg Lukács in *The Historical Novel* (1936–1937; English translation, 1962). Lukács argues that historical settings in novels that predate Scott
(mostly gothic or quasi-gothic novels) do not acknowledge periodicity, which
Scott achieves by portraying "the struggles and antagonisms of history by
means of characters who always represent social trends and historical forces."[2]
Scott is a kind of Hegelian ignorant of Hegel; and Hegel lays the groundwork
for Marx. Lukács is firmly writing from a Marxist perspective.

Marxism enabled Lukács's beguiling systematizations to be influential, but
his arguments are flawed because of inaccuracy and their reductive quality.[3]
Lukács's grasp of history is inexact: in discussing *Rob Roy* (1817), Lukács is
at odds with its setting by eighty years; Scott confuses Cameronians with

Cromwellians in *The Heart of Midlothian* (1818); and Lukács claims that "Scott very seldom speaks of the present"(32), a strange comment on the author of *The Letters of Malachi Malagrowther* (1826) and the *Life of Napoleon* (1827). Potentially more serious errors, though, are the facts that Lukács is incorrect about the history of the novel, and that he himself is (as a Marxist) an inheritor of the Enlightenment paradigm of stadial development which he recognizes in Scott, but only as evidence of the author's accuracy, his "objectivity" (60) and "*historic faithfulness*" (65), not as an intellectual model which has its own problems, as Scott perhaps recognized more than Lukács does.

Scott's world is one of national, not of class, struggle; and his inheritance comprises not only the Enlightenment model, but the national tale and the apparatus of gothic fiction. Maria Edgeworth had pioneered ideas of periodicity and their political implications in *Castle Rackrent* (1800); Anne Radcliffe had prefigured Scott's worlds of ancestral local and "emergent" national loyalties, and also anticipates him in her use of landscape and depiction of a hero in *Castles of Athlin and Dunbayne* (1789). What Scott does is to forge a more sophisticated representation of history in fiction which – if not for the first time (here Lukács is right in general though wrong in detail) – rests on a developed historiographical infrastructure. The past becomes no longer a realm for the free play of fantasy, as it had hitherto been in much fictional representation (a state of affairs which has returned to haunt us today), but instead a place where things happen for a reason; where character and situation register the pressure of circumstance and changing times.

Scott's historiographical model rests on two main foundations. Scott is indebted to the Scottish Enlightenment historians David Hume and William Robertson, and to the concept of stadial history, the view that history progresses through the same stages in all human societies, but at different rates, and that knowledge of the stages enables the condition of modernity to be discerned. Stadialism is the historiographical theory developed in detail in Scotland amid a highly educated society trying rapidly to catch up with English economic wealth and assimilate to English cultural norms. Hence the differential speeds of "uneven development" that stadialism identifies, as Chandler notes (*England in 1819*, 131).

Adam Smith as well as Robertson endorsed this model, which was to form in the nineteenth century an important component in Whig historiography. Whig historiography sees history as a progressive march to liberty and (often) manifest destiny. Hume's model in his *History of England* (1754–1762) had posited a division within Scotland between "Germanic" Lowlands, characterized as liberty loving, forward looking, commercially minded, and easily integrated into Britain; and "Celtic" Highlands, characterized as backward looking, indolent, rebellious, and violent. For Hume the Highlanders are locked in a Hobbesian state of nature, immune to the refinements of civility. Smith's jurisprudence lectures of 1762 depict four stages of society: "1st, the Age of Hunters; 2ndly, the Age of Shepherds; 3dly, the Age of Agriculture; and 4thly, the Age of Commerce." For Robertson the defeat of the Jacobites and the triumph of the British state have led to an end of history, at least to the end of Scotland's history. Robertson, while promoting Scotland as a place of learning and politesse, also begins the process whereby the importance of the Scottish past is to be dismissed. As he writes at the outset of his *History of Scotland* (1759): "Nations, as well as men, arrive at maturity by degrees, and the events, which happened during their infancy or early youth . . . deserve not to be remembered." This metaphor of the "youth" of nations becomes central for Scott. In him the "old Scotland" of the Jacobites, the Catholics, and Highland society is doomed to be superseded by a superior, more civilized (and more British) state of affairs, and by a mutually comprehensible standard language. Scott takes from Robertson the idea that the Scots past, Gaelic, the Stuarts, and Scottish independence could be a source of pathos and nostalgia (as in Robertson's portrayal of Mary, Queen of Scots), but not of continuing political or linguistic relevance.[4]

These developments in eighteenth-century Scottish thought on which Scott relies run parallel with attempts to eradicate so-called "Scotticisms" from speech. Those were seen to detract from the need to assimilate to a common British culture in order to exchange ideas and commerce freely, without misunderstanding, in a shared public sphere. Scots had been dominant in Scottish poetry, most recently through Burns; but Scott's poetry – which made his name – is in standard English. His novels use Scots more intensively, but even here Scott's heroes, the protagonists who represent the "new" Scotland/ Britain, are English, half-English, or speak standard English, in a kind of stadial socio-linguistics. The more forward looking a character is the more standard is its English. Scott also represents middle- and upper-class Scots as conforming broadly to a standard English in their speech, though that was not true in his day, still less in the period settings of his novels. To most Enlightenment thinkers modernity is a universal aspiration, pursuit of which requires a standard language.

This historical and linguistic stadialism is at the root of Scott's detailed display of the past in order to advocate and confirm the virtues of the future. The future is British and regulated by general principles of applicability, in line with Enlightenment rationality. In *Ivanhoe* (1819) Norman and Saxon must be reconciled to begin the building of a unified England free of ethnic tensions; in *Waverley* (1814) Jacobite violence on behalf of an old independent Scotland and its native kings must be destroyed in order to build British unity. Unity will make England and Scotland stronger, and halt Scotland's tendencies to inter-necine violence. These are symbolized in the mountain torrent of chapter 22 of *Waverley*, where a consciously picturesque landscape forms the backdrop to Flora MacIvor's wooing of Waverley to the Jacobite cause; the violent tendencies are present in her brother's clannishness, in the quarrelsome Lowland lairds, and the thieving and kidnapping Donald Bean Lean. Scott uses the picturesque to herald Scotland's beauty, but also to show incompat-ibility between the inhabitants of its Highlands and the emergent British polity. Like their unimproved landscapes and environments the Jacobites are immature, and belong personally as well as politically to an earlier stage of development. The Baron of Bradwardine and Fergus MacIvor, the two leading Jacobites of *Waverley*, are presented as childish or at best adolescent, following Robertson's dictum about the childhood of nations. In *Old Mortality* (1816) the move to modernity is one away from sectarian strife; in *The Antiquary* (1816) Scotland forgets its old quarrels to unite against revolutionary France; in *The Heart of Midlothian* (1818) an ordinary Scot secures British intervention against the unjust consequences of her own country's laws; while in *Rob Roy* the world of British mercantilist modernity is set against the violent tensions of upland Stirlingshire and Perthshire. The complex theories of the Scottish Enlightenment's project of modernization seem perfectly realized in Scott's prose narratives.

But the project of modernization is only one of the main foundations of Scott's fiction, and is held in tension by the second. If the theories that govern the development of history appear to be of general applicability, the characters and situations through which they arise are ineluctably particular. It is in the particularity of narrative that its charm lies for the reader. Redgauntlet's Solway in *Redgauntlet* (1824), Flora's enchanted glen in *Waverley*, Ravenswood's Wolf's Crag in *The Bride of Lammermoor* (1819) are all intensely realized particular places, where character and situation intersect in a seduc-tive, authentic way. The *locus amoenus*, the special place of enchantment, power, or resistance stands in tension with the universalizing principles of the Scottish Enlightenment, and their presumption of a common goal of commerce, sympathy, politeness and moderation (Lukács's "middle way," *The Historical Novel*, 31).

The Enlightenment thinkers had suggested that climate and landscape altered character: what if they did so irreducibly, so that the individual thus formed must either be destroyed or repressed in order to be incorporated into new political structures? In his depiction of the *locus amoenus*, another set of intellectual underpinnings is at work in Scott: those of the national tale. The Irish national tale, particularly in the hands of Maria Edgeworth, "enjoyed Continental fame." Its origins have been traced back by Joep Leerssen to George Howard's *The Siege of Tamor* (1773) and Frances Dobbs's *The Patriot King* (1774) which, in pursuit of "Grattanite patriotism," "utilize native Ireland on behalf of the Anglican Protestant public sphere" (Pittock, *Romanticism*, 93).[5] Critical opinions differ as to how radical this tradition is. Edgeworth is hard to enlist on the side of radical nationalism, Sydney MacKeon/Owenson less so: but the national tale liberates the imagination and representation of Irish difference, and by conceptualizing the nation as a separate entity in the era of Union helps give it a voice. (By the early nineteenth century, the national tale serves the idea of a national literature in Ireland; by the 1820s novels such as John Banim's *Boyne Water* are presenting Enlightenment notions of progress as themselves agents of cruelty, a view shared by Thomas Moore's *Memoirs of Captain Rock* [1824].)

Edgeworth's *Castle Rackrent* and Owenson's *The Wild Irish Girl* (1806) define the genre. By cultivating the idea of Irish particularity and separateness, and exhibiting the injustices of past (and present) Irish society, these novels challenge universal values on behalf of local conditions. Anglo-Scottish or Scottish writers Jane Porter (1776–1850), Susan Ferrier (1782–1854) and Christian Johnstone (1781–1857) all respond with their national tales, Porter being the earliest: *Thaddeus of Warsaw* (1803) celebrates the struggle for Polish independence, while *The Scottish Chiefs* (1810) describes the fight for Scottish freedom under William Wallace. In response to Jane Porter's novel Scott probably began *Waverley* in 1810 rather than, as traditionally assumed, in 1805, as Peter Garside argues; Edgeworth's *The Absentee* (1812) might have spurred Scott to complete the then unfinished manuscript.[6] *Waverley*'s use of the picturesque alludes to Owenson, and Flora's harping in (and on) the wild Highlands is a knowing tribute to Owenson's heroine. Nor does Scott's debt to Ireland disappear: elements of the plot and landscape of Charles Maturin's *Milesian Chief* (1812) enter *The Bride of Lammermoor*, while the name of Moncada in *The Surgeon's Daughter* (1825) is borrowed from Moncada in Maturin's *Melmoth the Wanderer* (1820).

Although *The Milesian Chief* is set in the present (the "Milesian Chief" goes off to fight in the Rising of 1798), and Scott's chronological distancing softens the politics of the pasts he portrays, the intense realization of locality in his work undermines the architecture of stadial historiographical closure that claims to abolish the politics of such localities. The means by which Scott inscribes the Enlightenment text are thus the means by which he undermines its claims to general applicability. If having one's foot on one's "native heath" changes name, conduct, and even personality, as it does for Rob Roy, where can one locate the universal and universalizable human subject of Adam Smith's *Theory of Moral Sentiments* (6th edition, 1790) (a text ironized in the national tale tradition by Edgeworth in *Ennui* [1809])? The trial of Evan Dhu MacCombich in *Waverley* shows the brutality behind the laughter in the courtroom from those who cannot possibly share the habits, customs, and expectations of the Gaidhealtachd. In "The Two Drovers" (1827) mutual Anglo-Scottish misunderstanding of minute particularities of cultural differ- ence leads to tragedy; in "The Highland Widow" (1827), old Elspat's son, torn between loyalty to his mother (who symbolizes a feminized Scotland, like the Sean Bhean Bhocht of Irish tradition) and the British army, is destroyed. Even Scott's use of standard English as a linguistic agent of British solidarity is held in tension by the role Scots plays in Jeanie Deans's plea to the queen in *The Heart of Midlothian*, or in Edie Ochiltree's use of Scots in *The Antiquary*, which signifies his commonsense grasp of the continuities of local history.

It is not just language, character, and situation that Scott employs to create a locality and particularity at odds with the overarching narrative drive to a reconciling unity. Other forms of cultural specificity challenge the possibility of English or British homogeneity. In *Ivanhoe* the reconciliation of Saxon and Norman is undercut by a deep unattractiveness in Norman society, and by the fact that Isaac and Rebecca, the Jews, are "oppressed and outcast from any possible Christian history ... only finding refuge in a Muslim land" (Pittock, *Romanticism*, 200–201). The Plantagenet expulsion of the Jews from England (in fact by Edward I, not Richard I) haunts the novel, demonstrating – as do in their different ways *The Talisman* (1825) and *The Betrothed* (1825) – the limitations of the Crusades in all the tales that concern them. The Germanic Saxons can join with the Norman aristocracy in forging English liberty and unity: but there is no room for the Jews, and though Rebecca ministers so tenderly to Ivanhoe, his marriage with her is unthinkable. Ivanhoe would never dream of burning the Jewess alive as a witch, as the Templars almost do, but she is definitely removed from what for him constitutes an equal humanity. Scott's realization of repressed, destroyed, exiled, or alienated identities might not at all points be innocent of contemporary caricature or lazy cliché; but it is extraordinarily sensitive, and renders him in this dimension of his work a postcolonial novelist.

The form of Scott's historical fiction retains its resilience not because it is an accurate historical depiction, but because it is not one. For Scott is always aware that "romance and real history have the same common origin," and that the "unifying order" of history is invented by ourselves, as his 1824 *Encyclopaedia Britannica* entry on "Romance" makes clear. The great architecture of Scott's historical novel rests on a paradox: that its ostensibly Enlightenment historiographical principles of organization and evidence-led accuracy, mimicked by Scott's notes and allusions rather than confirmed by them, are ultimately held to ransom by the sympathy they extend to the past, and not reinforced by the past in Robertsonian mode. That past is irreducible because of, not in spite of, its localization. It operates in the Herderian space of particularity, which is defined in opposition, or at least in dialogue, since Herder's teaching exemplified some of the Enlightenment premises whose conclusions he sought to interrogate. Its categories are slippery. Andrew Lincoln points out that in *Rob Roy*, Bailie Nicol Jarvie, the figure of modern commerce to set against the Highland cateran Rob Roy, is implicated in the slave trade; it is also made clear in the novel that, as Rob Roy's relative, his personal identity is contingent on his situation just as much as his international moral responsibility is. In the same novel Di Vernon sees, as Lincoln puts it, Frank Osbaldistone's "politeness as part of a colonising project" that reduces women to the role of passivity. Di and Helen MacGregor resist the reduction. Scott often presents his strong women being quelled; but he presents an unusual number of them suffering this process. Although in comparison with Irish national tales Scott appears to support modernization by weakening and generalizing "the material grounds of political discontent," he repeatedly complicates his categories in doing so. Lincoln notes that the crusading knight with the red cross at the opening of *The Talisman* is a sly reference to the opening of *The Faerie Queene*. Scott's love of chivalric fiction might seem to endorse the Crusaders: but it is they who manifest the high-handedness and bigotry deemed typical of the Orient, while the Duessa-like Saladin, present in different disguises, manifests the virtues of hospitality, chivalry, and disinterested generosity.[7]

This kind of approach can be seen as early as *Guy Mannering* (1815). Although Scott presents the novel as "a tale of private life" rather than historic struggle, it too advances and retreats from the presumptions of Enlightenment stadialism. Guy Mannering is the modern Englishman, charmed by the local peculiarities of the Bertrams/Dingawaies of Kippletringan in Galloway, when in the early 1760s he enjoys their hospitality by chance. Yet while Godfrey Bertram (a ridiculously anglicized name for a Galloway laird, as Scott well knew) speaks broad Scots, he also yearns to be a justice of the peace, an English office introduced into Scotland by James VI. When he eventually succeeds in this goal, he abandons the customary loyalties of old Scotland to become a tyrannizing squirearch like the Falkland or Tyrrel of Godwin's *Caleb Williams*; this ancient Scottish family adopts characteristically English vices. (Scott's dim view of justices of the peace is evident in other texts, such as *Rob Roy* and *Redgauntlet*).

The chief victims of Bertram's tyranny are the Gypsies who once were tolerated on his lands. They are brutally evicted, a process that damages not only them, but the whole community. The Gypsies are repeatedly associated with the East, and with Egypt: Scott is aware that the Gypsies are alleged to have come from Egypt, and also that Egypt is the origin of the Scots according to the traditional national foundation myth. The Gypsies are also categorized as Maroons, the ex-slave group in Jamaica whose defence of their independence had been supported in Parliament by R. B. Sheridan not many years before. They are markedly Orientalized, in other words; and Bertram the Scottish laird is playing out a grim localist version of empire in his own parish.

Meanwhile Mannering, the supposedly rational modern Oxford graduate who has foretold the risky future of the laird's son Harry by his use of astrology, has spent a generation in India as a hero of the British Empire. His role has been a violent one: "it was he relieved Cuddiebum, and defended Chingalore, and defeated the great Mahratta chief, Ram Jolli Bundleman" as his servant comically puts it, with a disregard for the name of the foreigner and foreign place that marks the colonizer.[8] Mannering has acted against the Easterners who are not Scots as Bertram has acted against those who are. Despite Mannering's good qualities, his pride and violence are stressed, and he almost kills Bertram's son in a duel in the rather preposterous main plot of the novel. But it is the sub-plots that count. Bertram the Scottish laird is less traditional than he appears, and more like Mannering, the imperial warlord, who is less rational than he appears. There is an uncomfortable parallel between Mannering's vaguely known and much-approved violence abroad, and Bertram's well-known and little-approved violence against the "eastern" Gypsies at home. Would we approve of Mannering less if we knew more of his conduct in India? The evils of the local world might reflect the violence of the global one, but we are better judges in contexts we know; and this hint on Scott's part surely endorses ancient loyalties, and cautions against their destruction anywhere. Although Meg Merrilies the Gypsy remains true to such loyalties, and despite being evicted by Bertram, gives her life to save his son, at the end she dies almost alone and neglected, while Bertram receives the accolades of the tenantry who do nothing for him. Meg's death is the death of an old world of loyalty and obligation that will not return; the shallower plaudits of the tenantry, which appear so like a happy ending, can be read as signs of the new age of transient affections and shallow novelties.

As Scott aged, and as the high reputation Scottish troops won in the Napoleonic wars gave way to peacetime British centralism, Scott's non-fictional writing, in his *Journal* and in the *Malachi Malagrowther* letters (based on Swift's *Drapier's Letters*), shows closer adherence to the Irish national tale, at the expense of the Enlightenment's optimistic formulae. More of Scott's fiction shows his increasing reservations about historical progress: in *Redgauntlet* the process of modernity is as much an unsavory struggle for power as what it replaces. It was this novel of Scott's which is in some ways the model used by Dickens in *A Tale of Two Cities* (1859). Nonetheless, despite Scott's increasing reservations, on the whole his popularity stems from what was widely seen as an ultimately unproblematic version of the tension between Scottish particularity and British unity. The British reader read Scott in the belief that the challenges to history in his work had been resolved, and that what was retained as difference was an amusing zone of local color, with the faintest frisson of unfamiliarity and threat. Familiar with the proto-Whig approach of Robertson and Hume, readers could see in Scott an ostensibly similar route to closure, to modernity and dismissal of the past, even if Scott's endless realizations of that past might seem prima facie evidence of an unwillingness to discard it.

But for a continental readership, matters were different. To those unfamiliar with the Jacobite threat and the Enlightenment narrative of British reconciliation, Scott's realized localities appeared central, their defeat temporary. Scott could be perceived as a radical, even a dangerous writer. To read Scott within even a "four nations" British context is always to read incompletely: to read him against the Romanticisms of continental Europe is to read this incompleteness back into his work. For Poles, Czechs, or Hungarians, among others, what might be called the taxonomy of glory, the identification of the antiquity of one's society and culture as essential to its individuation, was a more important component of Scott than his reconciliatory closures. He made the particularities of history live. Macpherson had provided mood music for "the literatures of Europe" to "define their independent position on the literary map by tracing themselves back to a foundational epic," in the process converting epic from a universal to a national genre.[9]

Scott was equally and immediately influential in anglophone writing. Among his earliest followers in England are W. Harrison Ainsworth and Edward Bulwer Lytton: Ainsworth's *Boscobel* (1872) is close to a direct imitation of *Woodstock* (1826). In *Rookwood* (1834) Ainsworth, blending Scott's grasp of historical gothic with the subject matter of the Newgate novel, creates a fiction that inserts itself into "history": Dick Turpin's ride from London to York. Ainsworth also attempts to create a regional novel for Lancashire based on Scott's example. Sometimes he links Lancashire to the Scottian theme of the Stuarts and the Jacobites, as in *Preston Fight* (1875), *The Leaguer of Lathom* (1876), and *The Manchester Rebels* (1873). His most successful creation under this head is *The Lancashire Witches* (1849), which mingles recusancy, the Gothic, the Pendle witch trials of 1612, and local dialect in a powerful exposition of Lancashire tradition and culture. If Ainsworth offered a novel based on Scott's settings and accessories (as did R. D. Blackmore in *Lorna Doone* [1850]), Bulwer Lytton crudely follows a version of Scott's politics with a succession of Whig heroes, prophetic of English modernity, a tactic also taken by Charles Kingsley in *Hereward the Wake* (1865), which presents a romanticized Whig image of the Anglo-Saxon patriot, a "lowland" hero in contrast to the Highlanders of Scott.

Among Scott's most important heirs in England is William Thackeray, whose *Henry Esmond* (1853) is indebted to Jacobite subject matter. But Thackeray's reflective opening, although copied from Scott, evinces a clear *parti pris*, which sneers at the Baron of Bradwardine's historic court office in *Waverley* under the guise of the "hereditary Grand Bootjack of the Empire." What in Scott is touching and dignified if faintly ridiculous is in Thackeray a piece of nonsense. The end of the novel is equally direct: "With the sound of King George's trumpets, all the vain hopes of the weak and foolish young Pretender were blown away."[10] Historical tension is absent in Thackeray: character, situation, and historical change are alike steamrollered beneath what E. P. Thompson calls the enormous condescension of posterity.

Dickens's use of Scott's example can be seen in *A Tale of Two Cities*, where Scott's device of setting two worlds against one another is presented in a way which fails to endorse either. From the mutual mistrust and suspicion evident in the episode of the stopping of the Dover coach at the beginning of the novel to Sydney Carton's memorable if sentimental sacrifice at the end, both England and France are seen as societies that do not always act justly or reward merit, whatever the differing nature of their internal political arrangements. Mutual suspicion and dislike is strongly present throughout all the social arrangements depicted, although France in particular is corrupt and oppressive both as a monarchical and as a republican state. Charles Darnay, who is positioned midway between England and France, and in the latter between the *ancien régime* and the new world of liberty, is clearly a version of the mild-mannered Scott hero caught in the midst of political processes from which he remains in some degree detached: a Henry Morton or a Frank Osbaldistone. In *Barnaby Rudge* (1840–1841) Dickens precisely fulfills the "'Tis Sixty Years Since" retrospection of *Waverley*. However, being the intensely Whig writer that he is (for example, in *A Child's History of England* [1852–1854]), Dickens tends to see the past as a tale of conflict, cruelty, and vanity with which contemporary society on the whole compares very favorably, a simplistic view that makes it difficult to accommodate the subtleties of Scott.

In *North and South* (1850) Elizabeth Gaskell uses Scott's "two worlds" technique in a novel of contemporary life. Here too there is a Stuart subtext, for Milton Northern is not only a mill town (Manchester), but also represents a Miltonic tradition of Nonconformity and a sturdy if somewhat coarsely and directly expressed independence and radicalism, opposed to the comfortable and rural crown-and-country Anglican conformity of the south. George Eliot in *Middlemarch* (1871–1872) – wavering, as the title suggests, between the two worlds written of by Gaskell – does not show two worlds in opposition, but represents the conflict between the old and the new about the time of the 1832 Reform Act, forty years "since" rather than Scott's sixty. *Middlemarch* shows that Scott's approach to the novel can be applied on a localized and depoliticized scale, and this is how Thomas Hardy uses it also, as he revisits the way in which a changing environment and changes of consciousness intersect in *Tess of the d'Urbervilles* (1891). *The Mayor of Casterbridge* (1886) continues *Waverley*'s method of commencing its action half a century before the time of its publication. Hardy also employs themes and episodes from Scott's narratives. As W. M. Parker points out in his preface to *Guy Mannering*, Hardy's "well-known opening formula of placing a solitary figure in the landscape" (5) is borrowed from Scott, while Henchard's rescue of Lucetta Templeman from the bull in *Casterbridge* is probably derived from Edgar Ravenswood's deliverance of Lucy Ashton from a similar attack in *The Bride of Lammermoor*.

It was perhaps ultimately from Edgeworth's national tale and not Scott's that Joseph Conrad takes the device of the unreliable narrator for *Heart of Darkness* (1899), although Stevenson's *The Master of Ballantrae* (1889) and H. Rider Haggard's *She* (1885) are probably closer influences. But Conrad and Ford Madox Ford's collaboration in *Romance* (1903), and their use of the device of a passive anti-hero in John Kemp, shows the marked continuing influence of *Waverley*. *Romance* demonstrates that even masters of modernism remain heirs of Scott. In Conrad's *Nostromo* (1904), wherein Giorgio Viola is the exponent of Italian republicanism in a South American context whose ethnic and political tensions are exacerbated by a history of foreign occupation, the nation of Costaguana contains opposing political ideologies reminiscent of those in Scott. And Costaguana's troubles, like Giorgio's, echo those that are damaging to Italy in Alessandro Manzoni's *The Betrothed* (1824), another continental offspring of Scott's.

Scott's influence on Scottish writing was even more profound. He endorses the Jacobite cause and the last struggles for Scottish independence in the eighteenth century as "matter of Scotland," a perpetual subject for fictional treatment. James Grant's *The Scottish Cavalier* (1852) and, more centrally, Robert Louis Stevenson's *Kidnapped* (1886), *Catriona* (1893), and *The Master of Ballantrae* (1889) derive from this inheritance, although Stevenson explores Scotland in primarily psychological rather than historiographical terms. How *The Master* exhibits and revises Scott's impact on the novel form in the latter half of the nineteenth century merits special notice.

Stevenson unites Edgeworth's national tale with the Scottian narrative model and with the intensely divided selfhood of James Hogg's Scott-influenced *Memoirs and Confessions of a Justified Sinner* (1824). Stevenson's primary narrator, the Ballantrae family steward Mackellar (an echo of Edgeworth's Thady in *Castle Rackrent*) presents a tale that is a self-confessedly partisan account of his loyalty to Henry Durie, Lord Durrisdeer. Henry's brother James is, by right of primogeniture, the real heir of Durrisdeer; but he becomes a Jacobite fugitive. Mackellar's perspective blackens the reputation of James. Although Mackellar does not enter the family service until the end of 1748, he confidently traces the origin of the divided family to 1745–1746, purporting to be an objective spectator while confessedly nurturing "an unnatural jealousy" of the fugitive Master. The latter is presented almost as an anti-hero from literature rather than life: he quotes Lovelace, and reads *Clarissa* (in which another Lovelace is the villain); but he is also – in true, inflated Jacobite style – likened to Aeneas. Mackellar displays at times a shockingly brutal directness towards members of the family, which we can – reading between the lines – link to Henry's implacable hatred of the Master, whom both Henry and Mackellar try to kill. Although it is the Master whom Mackellar presents as a figure of Satanic charm and malevolence, the evidence is that it is Henry whose pride is overdeveloped. The Master's closeness to and kindness to his Indian servant and companion, Secundra Dass, is notable (the Master even dresses in Indian clothes); Mackellar does not realize until the end of the novel that Dass speaks English, because – it is evident – his Orientalist stereotypes prevent him from understanding Dass's humanity as the exile and displaced person James Durie understands Dass to be. Henry Durie sees Dass simply as "a black deil," a devil who serves the greater devil he believes his brother is.

While Henry and Mackellar represent Whig modernity and the Master the Jacobite past, it is they who are the more superstitious, brutal, and racist. The Master's physical brutality is there only in the secondhand report of another adventurer's narrative, which while it might be reliable, is distanced twice over, by its teller and by its location. Progress, as a historical phenomenon and an ideology, is vitiated; and a repeated metaphor of tossing a coin in the narrative signifies not only the doubleness of the brothers and the Scottish character, but also the fact that there are two sides to every story, that virtues in the past are lost in journeying to the future. The introduction of Sir William Johnson/MacShane, the Irish eighteenth-century general who was sympathetic to the colonial peoples of North America (as indeed the narrative points out), as a character in the last chapters of the book provides a control of sorts to Mackellar's tale, as it is evident that Sir William thinks that Henry is insane. Stevenson subjects Scott's historiographical model to the psychology of the victor's self-interest, as indeed Scott had begun to do in *Redgauntlet*. In doing so Stevenson marks a major development of the Scottian novel, even though Stevenson's deceptively readable narrative disguises rather than reveals the revolutionary innovation.[11]

In the United States Scott's initial influence on James Fenimore Cooper, including the transference of Scott's historiographical model to *The Last of the Mohicans* (1826) and other Deerslayer novels, has been overshadowed by the critique by Mark Twain of Scott's alleged influence on the mores and ideals of the Confederate South. Although it is precisely Scott's detailed thematic use of linguistic registers that is adopted by Twain in *Huckleberry Finn* (1884) ("painstakingly, and with the trustworthy guidance and support of personal familiarity with these several forms of speech," as Twain puts it in his Explanatory), in *Life on the Mississippi* (1883) Twain attacks Scott and "his mediaeval business" forcefully, as an assault on the principles of "liberty, humanity and progress":

> Then comes Sir Walter Scott with his enchantments . . . sets the world in love with dreams and phantoms . . . with the sillinesses and emptinesses, sham grandeurs, sham gauds, and sham chivalries of a brainless and worthless long-vanished society. He did measureless harm; more real and lasting harm, perhaps, than any other individual that ever wrote . . . Sir Walter had so large a hand in making Southern character, as it existed before the war, that he is in great measure responsible for the war.[12]

Twain's critical attack on Scott is followed by a fictional one directed at *Ivanhoe*, which Twain in *Life on the Mississippi* contrasts with *Don Quixote* as mystifying what the latter had demystified. When in 1889 in *A Connecticut*

Yankee at King Arthur's Court Twain introduces a commercially minded Yankee arms manufacturer into the world of sixth-century Camelot, the world depicted is much closer to that of twelfth-century *Ivanhoe*, the most popular of all Scott's novels over much of the world. Morgan, the Yankee hero, "a Yankee of the Yankees," and thus the enemy of the Southern states, literally "dynamites the old chivalric and autocratic order" at the end of the book, when he wipes out the medieval age with the technology of the Gatling gun. In Twain's version of socio-linguistic stadialism the knights speak the language of Scott mediated through decades of poorer quality Victorian romances; they cannot understand economics; they lie and exaggerate and thus contribute to the romanticization of the sordid social system they represent. Twain's evident if humorous loathing for the ridiculousness of chivalry is only mildly moderated by the gloomy foreshadowing of an age of total war in the slaughter initiated by American technology as the book draws to a close.[13]

Despite Twain's attacks Scott's novels influence American modernism as well as British. As Richard Milum points out, comments on William Faulkner's more sympathetic closeness to Scott have been an intermittent leitmotif of Faulkner criticism. Echoes of *The Heart of Midlothian* and *Quentin Durward* (1823) in Faulkner have been identified by leading critics; and the "cavalier" heritage, with its "feudal and chivalric" aspects and its idealized women, forms a major strand in the Yoknapatawpha chronicles generally. But although the links between Scott and potent Southern mythology are well understood, Faulkner's approach to Scott's form is more complex than is usually thought.[14] Quentin MacLachlan, the aboriginal member of the Compson family in Faulkner's fictional universe of "Yoknapatawpha" ("split land", a reflection of Scott's method of using landscape as a proxy for the human divisions caused by time and belief), is a Jacobite refugee who "fled to Carolina from Culloden Moor."[15] The Compsons are a dynasty for whom dispossession is a recurring trope that is all too real; their lack of mental balance is more than an echo of the juvenile savagery and passions of some of Scott's own clan of irreconcilables, who struggle with the modernity that destroys them.

The decline in history teaching across much of the Western world since the 1930s has served to make Scott's model more difficult to follow for a new generation of readers, and the exponential rise of fantasy in the post-Tolkien world has in many respects changed historiography into fodder for manipulative fictions. In such a world it is not altogether surprising that Scott's complex historical model is in decline: but its long reach across the globe and the contemporaneity of its challenge are evidence not only of its great importance to the novel, but its continuing relevance to a world where those who have not learnt from the past or its mistakes are repeating them.

Notes

1. For fuller discussion see Murray Pittock, *Scottish and Irish Romanticism* (Oxford University Press, 2008), ch. 1.
2. Georg Lukács, *The Historical Novel*, trans. Hannah and Stanley Mitchell (Harmondsworth: Penguin, 1976), p. 33.
3. See James Chandler, *England in 1819* (Chicago University Press, 1998), pp. xv, 41–42.
4. Adam Smith, *Lectures on Jurisprudence*, ed. R. L. Meek, D. D. Raphael, and P. G. Stein (Indianapolis: Liberty Classics, 1982), p. 14; William Robertson, *The History of Scotland*, 2 vols. (London: Jones & Co., 1827), vol. 1, pp. xviii, 1.
5. Alastair Fowler, *Kinds of Literature* (Oxford: Clarendon Press, 1982), p. 228; Joep Leerssen, "'Interesting to all the world': Fiction, Interest and the Public Sphere," in *The Irish Novel in the Nineteenth Century*, ed. Jacqueline Belanger (Dublin: Four Courts, 2005), p. 61.
6. Peter Garside and Anthony Mandal, "Producing Fiction in Britain, 1800–1829," *Cardiff Corvey* 1 (n.d.); Peter Garside, "Popular Fiction and the National Tale: Hidden Origins of Scott's *Waverley*," *Nineteenth-Century Literature* 46: 1 (1991), 30–53.
7. Andrew Lincoln, *Walter Scott and Modernity* (Edinburgh University Press, 2007), pp. 56, 108, 127, 133, 135. I am indebted to my doctoral student Kang-yen Chiu for observations on *The Talisman*.
8. Sir Walter Scott, *Guy Mannering*, ed. P. D. Garside (Edinburgh University Press, 1999), p. 66.
9. Joep Leerssen, "Ossian and the Rise of Literary Historicism," in *The Reception of Ossian in Europe*, ed. Howard Gaskill (London: Continuum, 2003), p. 125.
10. William Thackeray, *Henry Esmond* (London and Glasgow: Collins, n.d.), pp. 14, 454.
11. Robert Louis Stevenson, *The Master of Ballantrae* (London and Glasgow: Collins, n.d.), pp. 22, 298.
12. Mark Twain, *Tom Sawyer* and *Huckleberry Finn* (London: Collins, 1953), p. 202; Mark Twain, *Life on the Mississippi*, ed. Shelley Fisher Fishkin, Willie Morris, and Laurence Howe (New York: Oxford University Press, 1996), pp. 465, 467–469.
13. Mark Twain, *A Connecticut Yankee at King Arthur's Court*, ed. Justin Kaplan (Harmondsworth: Penguin, 1976), pp. 21, 36.
14. Richard A. Milum, "Faulkner and the Cavalier Tradition," *American Literature* 45: 4 (1974), 580–589; Elizabeth M. Kerr, *William Faulkner's Yoknapatawpha* (New York: Fordham University Press, 1985), pp. 95, 97.
15. William Faulkner, "Appendix: Compson 1699–1945," in *The Sound and the Fury*, ed. David Minter (2nd edn, New York: Norton, 1994), p. 204.

18

How and where we live now: Edgeworth, Austen, Dickens, and Trollope

BARRY WELLER

After chapters of broad social comedy centering on Lady Clonbrony's extravagant bid for acceptance by London high society, Maria Edgeworth's *The Absentee* (1812) takes a remarkable turn. Lord Colambre, Lady Clonbrony's son, both a native of Ireland and a stranger to it (hence the novel's title), arrives in Dublin, and immediately each detail of the setting is etched with representative significance as Lord Colambre begins to test his mother's contempt for the country that supplies the family's precarious means of support. Within pages the novel offers a conspectus of the transformations the Irish capital has undergone since the Act of Union – always the decisive historical marker in Edgeworth's fiction. The nobility had retreated to their country houses or gone abroad, and "commerce rose into the vacated seats of rank; wealth rose into the place of birth."[1] Within a few years, however, the "want of manners [and] knowledge, in the *nouveaux riches*" leads to ridicule and bankruptcy (83–84). Worst of all, the Irish peasantry become outrageously exploited by agents of the absentee landlords; and the absentees in turn become victims of their own efforts to match the expenditure and the snobbery of the English. For the Irish the result is an international network of well-nigh insoluble debts. The debts are exacerbated by the geographical and historical distance between England and Ireland.

Edgeworth maps the two nations in a way that demarcates the almost uniform unpleasantness of the English, and the mixed character, for good and for ill, of every class of the Irish. The mixture expresses the imperfectly achieved adjustments of the reconfiguration of Ireland's classes resulting from the Union. The overview of Ireland's recent past is unusually conscious and explicit about its historical vantage point. But what is "historical" here? "Lady Clonbrony . . ., in terms of detestation, described Dublin such as it appeared to her soon after the Union; lord Clonbrony . . . painted it with convivial enthusiasm, such as he saw it long and long before the Union" (82). History, as the Clonbrony couple represents it, is not just something "long and long before" the present; history is a contemporary split consciousness that results from the intermixture of past and present times and social orders, all going on simultaneously, even when the present (like Lady Clonbrony) repudiates its origins, and seeks liberty from the past altogether. If Edgeworth's treatment of the contemporary scene of national and class differences and economic entanglements leads her to emphasize contrastive geographical places rather than contrasting temporalities, her narrative also must illustrate the way the Irish and the English live now by evoking a dialogue between past and present. Lord Colambre, returning to his Irish birthplace and discovering the disastrous contemporary reality that absenteeism has forged, proceeds to attempt to set it right in what appears to be a restoration of a time before the alienating effects of English imperialism and modern finance. Nevertheless, Colambre also must repudiate the past: he must learn that he has mistakenly construed as illegitimate the history of the woman he has loved; he must also discover that her past is English, not Irish. The discovery means that Colambre and the narrative's alliance is with the English present, after all; with contemporary life's freedom from the past as well as determination by it.

Edgeworth's narrative, mobilizing the previously fixed constituents of past historical and social order, perpetuates the class reconfiguration that is both a trouble and an opportunity. *The Absentee* identifies the reconfiguration with fiction's present, and with the presence of history. Jane Austen's use of narrative in *Persuasion* (1818) echoes Edgeworth's interweaving of contemporary life with a new sense of historically motivated economic order and with contrastive places and spaces. Austen's heroine Anne Elliot has been wrongly persuaded to break her engagement to a navy captain, who represents the contemporary upward mobility initiated by the Napoleonic wars. Anne's family and her most trusted advisor have argued that Anne must respect the "importance" derived from "rank and consequence," hence not wed a self-made new man. But eight years after her broken engagement Anne knows that "honesty" such as the captain's outweighs the claims of historical lineage.[2] The renewal of Anne's romance with her former fiancé occurs when her pompous father, thanks to a convergence of his wasteful expenditure (he might as well be an absentee) and the war's reconfiguration of class, is forced to rent his ancestral home to the captain's brother-in-law, an admiral. Anne is unhoused, and relocated to the village of Uppercross, where she learns that even a minor distance between places constitutes each as a separate "little social commonwealth" (69). As part of her mobility among such commonwealths, to which she sensitively adapts without losing her self-possession, Anne encounters the captain. Her movement strengthens her resolve to become free of the decaying aristocratic, landowning past. To be sure, both she and the captain are fixedly faithful to their shared private history; and both repudiate the promiscuous social mobility of Bath, where Anne's father and snobbish elder sister have retreated. Honesty appears to be invalid in that community. But that is partly because in Bath pretentious respect for past "importance" and "rank" blinds the city's inhabitants to the fluidity of the social order that newly marks historical life. Anne and her captain, faithful to that present innovation, find it to be compatible with honesty, even if the compatibility has not become a norm.

Edgeworth and Austen provide an instructive preview of how nineteenth-century narrative coordinates the elaboration of historically conscious realism with a representation of places, each of which amounts to a contemporary "social commonwealth." Walter Scott, in the wake of Edgeworth and Austen, might have sought to differentiate his work from theirs by shifting the contemporary conflicts they dramatize back into the past, in order to make the historical present appear to be the resolution of those conflicts. In the name of Scott Georg Lukács more or less fights off the notion that the contemporary novel is itself historical: "With [Scott's successor] Balzac," Lukacs says, "the historical novel which in Scott grew out of the English social novel, returns to the presentation of contemporary society. The age of the classical historical novel is therewith closed."[3] Nevertheless, Lukács concedes that "Balzac's deepest experience was the necessity of the historical process, the necessity for the present to be as it was" (96). Lukács also admits that the "compression of historically portrayed events into a relatively brief period" (from 1789 to 1848) allows Balzac to breathe "entirely the great historical spirit of [Scott]" and with greater "historical concreteness" (95), even though Balzac addresses the contemporary world primarily.

Edgeworth and Austen also demonstrate that it is not only novelists who treat the past as the necessary prehistory of the present who can envision the present historically. Scott does it too. Lukács neglects to note that in *Chronicles of the Canongate* (1827) Scott gives us a contemporary life (and a Scottish variant of an absentee). His present-day narrator Chrystal Croftangry has been away from his hereditary Lanarkshire estate long enough to register the decay (in which he has played a role) of both the property and his family reputation. "Long enough" means Chrystal's single lifetime, which measures major changes in the relations that constitute a local or national community. Renouncing his ambition to redeem his paternal property, Chrystal retreats to the Canongate district of Edinburgh, once his refuge from creditors, now a "local situation . . . favourable to [his] undertaking,"[4] a publishing venture that will chronicle the past of Scotland (and that resembles the Waverley novels). Indeed, Chrystal sees "two [historical] extremities of the moral world" inscribed and still visible on the very face of Edinburgh: "the huge city, dark with the smoke of ages, and groaning with the various sounds of active industry or idle revel, and the lofty and craggy hill, silent and solitary as the grave . . . a throne to the majestic but terrible Genius of feudal times" (51–52). Despite the contrast, chronicles of the present age can close the gap between temporal and social extremities. Chrystal's published histories emphasize the intermingling of past and present Scotlands. The present can be understood in the same terms as, or as an immediate outgrowth of, the recent history that lives in the conversation and memoirs of Chrystal's acquaintanceship, and that is "spatialized" there as well.

Edgeworth, Austen, and Scott enlarge their representation of the present to encompass the temporal and spatial forces that produce it. Charles Dickens and Anthony Trollope's narratives follow suit. Almost all of Dickens's novels are historical, either as a matter of direct statement ("Thirty years ago, Marseilles lay burning in the sun, one day")[5] or through broadening the reference to the present ("In these times of ours, though concerning the exact year there is no need to be precise").[6] Those references to the past emphasize the historicity of the present. Trollope's Barsetshire and Palliser cycles present an English counterpart to *La Comédie humaine*, tracing historical changes in political and ecclesiastical power not only as they affect the fortunes of individual families but as they affect the institutional character of contemporary society as a whole – the current commonwealth, once again. The full title of Dickens's *Hard Times, for These Times* (1854) and the title of Trollope's *The Way We Live Now* (1875) pose the question of how "we" construe the temporal moment we inhabit; these titles imply a consciousness, whether articulated or not, of how the present differs from the past. Both continuity and change are presumed to be subjects of investigation for the sake of understanding the world in its current totality of relations.

As Elizabeth Ermarth argues, the narrative medium of the mid-century British novel in itself establishes the novel as historical, assuming a homogeneous and neutral temporal space within which events, objects, and actions are meaningful in terms of one another – if the time and patience to trace the infinite ramifications of their relations are available. Such tracing becomes the novelist's vocation. To ask the question "What connexion can there be, between the place in Lincolnshire, the house in town, the Mercury in powder, and the whereabouts of Jo the outlaw with the broom?"[7] is to assume the possibility of an answer, and the reiteration of the increasingly rhetorical question affirms that axiom: "What connexion can there have been between many people in the innumerable histories of this world, who, from opposite sides of great gulfs, have, nevertheless, been very curiously brought together!"

(219). The slide from the present tense into first a conditional and then a present perfect illustrates Ermarth's point that the present is implicitly in constant emergence from a past, which gestates its own future revelations. The gaps in the sequence are visible, even foregrounded, but there is no absolute rupture.

Dickens's emphasis on distances that both separate and join is symptomatic. The form of the English novel of the present, comprehensively conceived, is different from the continental model, because it responds to the historical specificity of English society and its resistance to unifying centers. Lauren Goodlad makes clear that the lateral expansion of explanatory relationships that constitutes Romantic and Victorian versions of historical realism is particularly suited to representing the diffuse character of Victorian regulatory and administrative structures, and the basis of that diffusion in separate places. "Throughout the century Britain's ruling classes strove to govern *indirectly* ... in ways that encouraged self-help, philanthropy, voluntarism, and local government."[8] This preference for the ad hoc and the local remained in tension with all-embracing liberal or radical aspirations toward social amelioration. To impose upon such agglomerative practices the kind of totalizing narrative favored by continental theorists such as Marx (or Lukács) was difficult for English novelists because even Marxian dialectics conform to a swifter and more linear plot than either the economic and political history of nineteenth-century England or its fictional representations would permit.

What the English novel, as practiced by Edgeworth, Austen, Dickens, Trollope, and others, substitutes for linear narrative (and explanatory) trajectories is the experience of moving between one milieu – one set of narrative possibilities – and another, and waiting for the connections to emerge. The suspension of overt analysis or explanation is analogous to the novelist, his characters, and his readers' immersion in the still unfolding plot of history. By the same token the resolution of Victorian novels often seems arbitrary or foreshortened in response to the complications of motive and consequence they explore. However copiously Dickens treats his readers to glimpses of his characters' subsequent stories, their endings are increasingly tentative (Esther Summerson's broken-off "even supposing---" ends *Bleak House*). The two endings of *Great Expectations* (1861) might be taken as an ultimate indecision, and despite the comfort Mortimer Lightwood derives from Twemlow's affirmation of the gentleman's code, it is Lightwood's repeated doubt ("Now I wonder ... whether *you* are the Voice of Society!" [889]) that echoes most strongly through the final chapter of *Our Mutual Friend* (1865). Still, as Ermarth suggests, this open-endedness is fundamentally optimistic: "Historical narratives capture that sense, so broadly evident across a varying cultural range, that whatever things are now, they could always be otherwise."[9]

Telling the present as historical requires that novelists make the descriptive component of narrative more prominent. The thrust of historical meaning is encapsulated in places and spaces. In *The Condition of the Working Class in England in 1844* Friedrich Engels anatomizes the "irrational" and "planless construction" of working-class housing in Manchester and the damage it does to the health and morals of workers.[10] Engels's writing is as passionate and polemical as most rhetorically heightened passages of *Bleak House* ("in such dwellings only a physically degenerate race, robbed of all humanity, reduced physically and morally to bestiality, could feel comfortable and at home" [Engels, *Condition of the Working Class*, 75]); but Engels's survey is as well supplied with facts, even tables, as a Gradgrind of liberal disposition could desire. Dickens shares the discursive indignation of Engels, and is responsive to the same facts. Hence, as a narrative artist he is torn: the Coketown in *Hard Times* is no less motivated by a desire for an accurate portrayal of the historical present – of it as fact – as it is motivated by a desire to keep description within the bounds of narrative, subordinated to the unfolding of a novel. Motivated therefore by a double responsibility to history and to fiction, the narrative is not surprisingly about conflicts among fact, description, and imaginative storytelling; it is itself that conflict.

The first full evocation of Coketown occurs as Gradgrind and Bounderby search the town for Sissy Jupe's circus folk, in order to announce the ineducable Sissy's expulsion from Gradgrind's "fact-ory," his school. For several pages, however, the ambulatory industrialists, and the narrative proper, are left behind for the sake of extensive description. Or, as Dickens says, "Let us strike the keynote, Coketown, before pursuing our tune."[11] The keynote description emphasizes "a town of red brick, or of brick that would have been red if the smoke and ashes had allowed it . . . a river that ran purple with ill-smelling dye . . . a rattling and a trembling all day long" (20). But lest the keynote exhibit an over-reliance on present fact, and therefore show the narrative tune in step with Gradgrind after all, Dickens turns the description back towards storytelling (in pursuit of circus-like fancy) by seeming to locate Coketown in two places at once. One place is factual-historical: Coketown is the necessary outcome of the industrial revolution of sixty years since. But the time and place of Coketown's present are not fixed by the past or even by the present. They can always be otherwise. Hence Dickens's description of present spaces moves into realms of possibility. The red and black of the city are savage war paint, the smoke an interminable serpent, and the up-and-down movement of the steam piston is like the head of a melancholy mad elephant. The intense metaphoricity of these passages is part of Dickens's counterplot against fact and the merely utilitarian uses of language. However ironically, the illuminated factories are "like Fairy palaces" (52); however close to Engels's facts, what is closer to truth, Dickens suggests, is the metaphorical departure from fact whereby Stephen Blackpool's tenement becomes the center of a labyrinth controlled by the monstrous Minotaur of profit and the laws regulating marriage. When Louisa Gradgrind tells her uncomprehending father that, "There seems to be nothing there" – in the world of contemporary fact – "but languid and monotonous smoke. Yet when the night comes, Fire bursts out . . .!" (78), she underlines her author's hope that imaginative fiction can be such fire, liberating the present from the history that imposes its distorting impact on contemporary life. In Edgeworth and Austen mobility – from class to class, from place to place – collaborates in the process of defining present history both in alliance with the past and as a counter to the past; in Dickens metaphor and analogy's heightened place in narrative becomes a new expression of progressive mobilization.

Nevertheless, Dickens's hopeful investment in such mobility weakens as his novelistic career unfolds. The depiction of Coketown is a less optimistic revision of Dickens's already ambivalent portrayal of an industrial town in the "Steel and Iron" chapter of *Bleak House* (1853). Despite the "coalpits and ashes . . . blighted verdure, scorching fires" of "the iron country farther north," the hands from Mr. Rouncewell's factory are "sinewy and strong" (846), his family attractive, well educated, and welcoming, and the iron he makes holds the promise not only of genuine usefulness but of further productivity. Moreover, the novel's early chapters imply that the ironmaster's success results from his own mechanical ingenuity. His activity has a discernible origin. In contrast, Coketown seems monstrously self-born. Bounderby is a self-made man in a different sense than he boasts: the story of his early days is a forgery.

At issue in Dickens's gathering pessimism about the social commonwealths he portrays in *Bleak House* and *Hard Times* is his characteristic equivocation about the claims of the past on the present. To what extent should the past be respected, to what extent put to the torch? Engels brilliantly supplies a genetic historical narrative of how industrial cities or the proletariat came into being (or "was called into existence by the introduction of machinery" [19]). Part of Dickens's critique of British industrial capitalism suggests that it denies its own historicity and therefore presents its current economic arrangements as natural and inevitable. *Hard Times* shows Dickens critical of industrial capitalism's erasure of the past. One of its chapter titles, "The Great Manufacturer," teasingly promises that we are about to read a satirical portrait of Mr. Bounderby, because in chapter 12 we have seen him through the adoring eyes of his mother. "The Great Manufacturer," however, is Time, which "brought its varying seasons even into that wilderness of smoke and brick" (71). Time acts rapidly upon Louisa, Sissy, and Tom, but "Mr. Gradgrind himself seemed stationary in his course, and underwent no alteration" (71). That is because Gradgrindism refuses alteration. The commercial imagination (or lack of imagination) that informs the historical present refuses to acknowledge the power and necessity of temporal process by foreclosing temporal alternatives. Dickens criticizes commercially motivated foreclosure of the future as well as erasure of the past as early as *Dombey and Son* (1848), where Dombey projects his son's future only inasmuch as it fixedly maintains the present of the Firm:

> [The] feeling uppermost in [Mr. Dombey's] mind, now and constantly intensifying, and increasing in it as Paul grew older, was impatience . . . [If] [his heart's] very hard surface could receive the impression of any image, the image of that son was there . . . not . . . as an infant, or as a boy, but as a grown man – the 'Son' of the Firm. Therefore he was impatient to advance into the future, and to hurry over the intervening passages of his history.[12]

The son's "intervening passages" of history turn out to be all too brief; the novel recovers them for itself by its own dilation of the volatile interval, with all its possibilities of development, between past and future; between fact and imagination.

Dickens's and Trollope's attitudes toward the relative claims of past and present differ significantly. Dickens objects to the erasure of the past, and plots toward a revelation of what has been erased. Chesney Wold in *Bleak House* represents the interest and imaginative claims of history, as in Scott. But Dickens portrays Chesney Wold as history's dead hand, a house that stands aloof from economic productivity and, for that matter, the professions. Esther is naïvely overwhelmed by its rose-flushed beauty, but her response is prophetic: "The house with gable and chimney, and tower, and turret . . . seemed scarcely real in its light solidity" (246), as though echoing Marx's and Engels's verdict on inherited certainties: "All that is solid melts into air."[13] If there is a touch of elegy in Dickens's treatment of Chesney Wold, elsewhere his recoil from historical nostalgia is unequivocal. He despises the medievalism of Mrs. Skewton ("Those darling bygone times . . . with their delicious fortresses, and their dear old dungeons, and their delightful places of torture . . .! How dreadfully we have degenerated!" [*Dombey and Son*, 375]), and Chancery law is odious because of its preoccupation with legacies. The spontaneous combustion of Krook, known to his neighbors as the "Lord Chancellor," expresses a wish to eradicate the accumulated rubbish of a world of precedents. In contrast, Trollope, as we shall see, employing a topographical narrative grammar as a mark of historicity, finds residual value in the Church, the squirearchy, and the nobility. When he lampoons Dickens as Mr. Popular Sentiment, the sobriquet expresses Trollope's disdain for the rival novelist's impatience with present-day fact as well as inherited stabilities. "In former times . . . [w]hen evils were to be reformed, reformers set about their heavy task with grave decorum and laborious argument" whereas now "imaginary agonies touch more than true sorrows, and monthly novels convince, when learned quartos fail to do so."[14]

Trollope's critique implies that Dickens is celebratory of the present: "when he has made the working classes comfortable . . . there will be nothing left for him to do" (*The Warden*, 206). But for Dickens the challenge is to *imagine* a better present (or future) – not to materialize it; hence, again, his insistent recourse to metaphor. To remain in communion with the past produces obsessive repetition (like Dr. Manette's shoemaking in *A Tale of Two Cities* [1859]) or paralysis (like that of Mrs. Clennam in *Little Dorrit* [1857]). But to enter the present is also a problem: in the case of William Dorrit the improvisatory life in prison hardens into not only a duration but an identity; freed from the Marshalsea he discovers he has become his own prison and can neither annul the past nor feel at home in contemporary society – in large part because he cannot comprehend or will not acknowledge the very history he must leave behind him. Dorrit perhaps projects dilemmas that structure Dickens's narrative art at its formal as well as thematic level: it increasingly enacts a desperate attempt to be liberated from the constraining past, and to be recalled to present life; but its mimesis of the present, including increased movement among classes and national "commonwealths," is not a satisfying alternative, even when the claims of the past have been liquidated. Moreover, in *Little Dorrit* the ruling coalition between the Circumlocution Office and Mr. Merdle's financial manipulations provides no hope that Louisa's "Fire" will clear the contemporary air. Merdle's economic speculations that have no grounding in fact horribly parody *Hard Times*'s Fancy, suggesting that the imaginative realm has been fatally tainted by the speculative one.

The present becomes weightless and ahistorical thanks to the entrepreneurs and speculators. In *Our Mutual Friend* and Trollope's *The Way We Live Now* the emphasis shifts from industrial production to the production and circulation of modern capital – already, by the mid-nineteenth century, coming unglued from the former. In Trollope, to be sure, modern affluence stands in contrast with the values represented by landed property, but the former must constantly rescue the latter, for worse rather than for better. On the fraud and vanity of contemporary economic and social arrangements, Dickens and Trollope concur. If Coketown, relative to Rouncewell's iron country, represents a movement in the direction of luxury goods, London in *Our Mutual Friend* seems wholly divorced from primary production. Manufacture appears in the form of Mr. Venus's taxidermy or Jenny Wren's repurposing of waste material from Fledgeby's shop, just as bodies are retrieved from the Thames and the detritus of daily life swells the dust mounds that constitute the novel's most conspicuous source of wealth. The paper factory where Lizzie Hexam finds work and refuge is upstream and remote from the metropolis. It is apt that the industrial product here should be paper, not only because of the novel's preoccupation with reading and writing, but because "the mysterious paper currency which circulates in London when the wind blows" (191) evokes dust heaps – it is litter – and the traffic in shares that accord status in the world of Veneerings and Podsnaps:

> Have no antecedents, no established character, no cultivation, no Ideas, no manners, have Shares . . . Where does he come from? Shares. Where is he going? Shares . . . Has he any principles? Shares. What squeezes him into Parliament? Shares. Perhaps he never of himself achieved success in anything, never originated anything, never produced anything? Sufficient answer to all; Shares. (263)

In the medium of shares history becomes irrelevant.

Pace Trollope, Dickens is not sanguine about the efficacy of systematic reform. Like *Hard Times*, *Our Mutual Friend* foregrounds the failure of educational formation as a social project, and if the ideological (utilitarian) motivation of the project is more muted in the later novel, its execution also seems more haphazard. The site of Charley Hexam's introduction to learning is "oppressive and disagreeable . . . crowded, noisy and confusing; half the pupils dropped asleep, or fell into a state of waking stupefaction" (263). The misfit of educational goals and means continues in the better school to which Charley is promoted; for while Bradley Headstone's mechanical inventory of knowledge and "decent formal" attire bespeaks obsessive order, the school is located in a neighborhood whose random assemblage recalls Engels's description of Manchester, as though "taken in blocks out of a box by a child of particularly incoherent mind" (*Our Mutual Friend*, 268). The novel's triumphs of learning occur in spite of, rather than because of, the schools. Charley's acquisition of literacy, moreover, proves merely a self-serving instrument of social mobility, which by this point in Dickens has become a mode of shamming, in utter contrast to the honest mobility applauded in *Persuasion*. Fortunately Lizzie

Hexam exemplifies a still live promise in class reconfiguration. Lizzie scavenges what she needs, emotionally and intellectually as well as physically, from a social landscape that offers little without an exorbitant price. Her hard-won ability to read and write completes important circuits of communication between other characters. At the beginning of the novel she recoils from her father's Thames-side life; but by the end she has put her skills as an oarswoman to good use, fishing her future husband from the river. Unlike William Dorrit, she can both recuperate and incorporate the past in the present.

Dickens's mocking passage about the power of shares seems descriptive of the influence wielded by Melmotte in *The Way We Live Now*. Though antithetical in most respects to his Dickensian counterpart, the self-canceling and nearly invisible Merdle, Melmotte's larger-than-life presence may make him the most Dickensian character in Trollope's novels. It is the contrast of Melmotte and his obfuscated origins with the rest of Trollope's fictional world that makes his uniqueness most apparent. The spatial homogeneity of Trollope's novels is remarkable – not that all the settings of his action are alike but that Trollope's even, understated narration delineates the ensemble of social places and institutions that spread out from London, as though he were filling out a map. Narrative time, and past stories, again give way to, or merge with, spatializing descriptions.

As a historian, therefore – and he surely is the historian of political realignment during the era of Reform – Trollope defines himself in large part by negation. The first chapter of *The Way We Live Now* introduces Lady Carbury's *Criminal Queens*, history as a repository of lurid anecdote, and throughout Trollope's novels journalism is too sordidly instrumental to serve as even a first draft of history. As Ermarth astutely observes concerning Trollope's focus on the nuances of conversation and manners, "as in all good historical novels, the author represents not a particular situation so much as the grammar of a situation, and shows that social life is all about that grammar, and not about simpler causalities" (155). The grammar and the mapping replace the "simpler causalities" of conventional history. Ermarth observes that this approach requires the circumscription of Trollope's material, and thereby suggests that Trollope could be considered an heir to Austen. Certainly *Framley Parsonage* (1861), which Ford Madox Ford "in his private preferences place[d] higher than any other English novel,"[15] has in Lucy Robarts a heroine to compare with Austen's protagonists.

Each of Trollope's novels has its own literal and moral topography. The plot of *Framley Parsonage* in effect begins when Mark Robarts travels from the precincts of Framley Court, which include his vicarage, the mean, ugly church, boys' and girls' school, a grocer's shop (owned by the pew-opener), etc., to Chaldicotes in West Barsetshire, where, by the lights of his patroness Lady Lufton, competing political interests wickedly prevail. Chaldicotes is not only the seat of the Whig member Mr. Sowerby but the center of the "Chaldicotes set," presided over by the licentious Duke of Omnium. That Robarts should try to break free of the enclosure of Framley – Lady Lufton has supplied him not only with a living but with a wife – seems inevitable; it also proves disastrous. Courting political friendships, including connection to the prelates of Barchester, and advancement in the church, Robarts is manipulated into co-signing a loan for Sowerby; in the end he is rescued from bankruptcy and disgrace only by the generosity of his boyhood friend, Lady Lufton's son, and thus reabsorbed into the world of Framley. Only the romantic plot, in which Mark's sister Lucy proves an unwitting obstacle to Lady Lufton's plans for her son's marriage, qualifies, or palliates, the claustrophobic circularity of this movement.

Meanwhile, a contest over the lease of Chaldicotes eventually becomes a struggle for the soul of Barsetshire, that is, whether the integrity of its estates and its attachment to tradition can be defended against the drive toward economic exploitation. (An echo of *The Absentee*'s dilemmas sounds itself here.) Robarts's career enacts the defenselessness. The function in the narrative of the indigent clergyman Mr. Crawley might be to enact a radical defense. But in Mr. Crawley the defense is isolated and joyless poverty, an almost savage austerity.

London, even in the Barsetshire novels, is increasingly the source of political influence and hence preferment. The pulse of Trollope's plots and of the characters' trajectories is defined by alternating movement to and from the metropolis. In *The Way We Live Now* country gentlemen and their families (as exemplified by the Longestaffes) are drawn to London as the locus of capital, prestige, and matrimonial possibility. It is no longer a question simply of going to London for "the season," as in an eighteenth-century novel; the social stakes are far more substantial. Melmotte, the embodiment of London's restless striving, excels in self-advertisement, throwing lavish balls at his house in Grosvenor Square. This house is virtually rebuilt in order to entertain the Emperor of China at an elite dinner to be attended by royalty and two hundred guests, sitting down, as a national affirmation, "in the dining-room of a British merchant."[16] Melmotte's reputation for wealth attracts opportunities for enlarging that wealth, including the American project of the South Central Pacific and Mexican Railway – as phantasmatic in its prospects as the extent of Melmotte's affluence: "The object of Fisker, Montague, and Montague was not to make a railway to Vera Cruz, but to float a company" (77). The Beargarden Club, where young men of title foregather to eat, drink, gossip, and gamble, similarly operates on a principle of constant expenditure and borrowed credit (and like Melmotte's enterprises, will crash by the end of the novel).

The values of landed property and rural stability are honorably, if somewhat dully, upheld by Roger Carbury of Carbury Hall in Suffolk. The family and property date back to the Wars of the Roses. But land no longer suffices to produce a comfortable income. Carbury Hall is surrounded by grander estates, whose owners have made their fortunes elsewhere. Melmotte too seeks to establish himself in this neighborhood, an indication that landowning still signifies social status more firmly than metropolitan display. It is the Longestaffes' precarious and mortgaged standing that creates the opening for Melmotte. (The young men seeking refuge from their creditors also enact centrifugal movement away from the capital.) In fact most of the novel's relationships can be mapped as spreading outward from Carbury Hall, rather than from the gaudier, more conspicuous center of Melmotte and London. Returning to Carbury Hall is always the narrative's default position; it is not surprising that the final chapter is "Down in Suffolk." Nevertheless, in its final appearance Carbury Hall is a place of melancholy self-sacrifice: Roger yields his beloved cousin Hetta, surrenders his hatred of the man who has stolen her heart, and devotes himself to solitude. Roger's askesis, as a response to what "Shares," and Melmotte, and the present social commonwealths have wrought, is another version, albeit softer, of Mr. Crawley's stern withdrawal from worldliness. This is a far cry from the happy results of historical change and mobility in Edgeworth and Austen, whereby a new re-engagement with the present is made possible. It is not a far cry from Dickens. His figures also come to withdraw from the present. When Arthur Clennam, financially ruined by his involvement with Merdle, and Little Dorrit at last go "quietly down into the roaring streets, inseparable and blessed," they separate decidedly from the social commonwealth because the historical present has come to belong to "the uproar" of "the noisy and the eager . . . the arrogant . . . the froward and the vain" (802).

To enumerate the settings of Trollope's novels (and of Dickens's more expansive ones) is to provide a skeleton key of their action – and of their authors' understanding of the shifting balance between competing sectors of the English polity, and between competing histories or breaks with history. It also provides a measure of Dickens's and Trollope's differences. Although both provide the broad coordinates of a contemporary social reality, Trollope rarely fills a space as memorably as Dickens. In terms of *Our Mutual Friend* alone, one thinks of Mr. Venus's shop; the Podsnaps' or Veneerings' dining-rooms; the differentiated zones of Boffin's Bower; the wingless windmill in which Lizzie Hexam is discovered before the fire; or the shared apartment of Eugene Wrayburn and Mortimer Lightwood, furnished with items chosen to inspire domesticity. Dickens's novels offer a more jagged, excited ride – occasionally exalted, occasionally bathetic – than Trollope's, where metaphors never threaten to usurp the description of an empirically accessible reality. The pleasures of reading Trollope derive from his precise observation, and from his characters' plausible motives and interests, despite those breathtaking moments in which they embrace (or abandon) some intransigently idealistic principle. In contrast with such intransigence, much as he admires it, Trollope inhabits his narratives' present England with relative comfort, on the whole without yearning for transformation. But, in contrast, the passionate partiality of Dickens often offers a more immediate conspectus of "the way we live now."

Ermarth rightly contends that Victorian narrative fiction "embodies the collective awareness of a culture" and that this "blend of consciousness, time and language does not belong exclusively to any character, or even to the historical author; the entire range of narrative awareness constitutes it; its narrative expression is precisely Nobody" (89). This constitutive anonymity, encompassing and harmonizing the shifting focalizations of characters and narratorial stances, guarantees the historical space in which the events of the novel can assume meaningful relations to one another. Nevertheless, the stylistic differences of individual authors work against a reader's perception of this underlying uniformity. The controlled, if partially illusory, neutrality of Trollope's narrator could not contrast more strongly with the extravagant, mercurial transformations of Dickens's narrative voice, overtly partisan – even though its allegiances may shift.

One must not overstate the differences, however. Literary history and criticism have always been overeager to keep Dickens and Trollope in separate compartments. Among the remarkable aspects of Trollope's last, unfinished novel, *The Landleaguers* (1882), is his version of a Dickensian child innocent – a ten-year-old convert to Catholicism who unwittingly conspires with murderous Irish rebels against his English landlord father – and the novel's chapter "The State of Ireland," in which Trollope stops his narrative "tune" to deliver a keynote assessment of Anglo-Irish relations and the Land Law of 1881. Although "The State of Ireland" is not the product of any Mr. Popular Sentiment, it is Trollope's version of Dickensian passionate social protest. It is not a radical protest, but it faces the prospect of revolutionary violence in the latest social commonwealth without panic.

The Landleaguers provides an important measure of how much has remained the same in fiction since *The Absentee* – and how much has changed. Dickens and Trollope go beyond the examples of their predecessors in making the quasi-fictional terrains of Coketown and Barsetshire, or the actual terrains of London and Ireland, vehicles for apprehending the historically grounded simultaneity and mutual implication of a social order's constituents. It is arguable that in the succeeding century the precedent of their representational practice in regard to contemporary life and to the places that ground it contributes to novelistic mappings of a non-European and ultimately postcolonial world: the "nation" of Costaguana in Conrad's *Nostromo* (1904), for example, an invented (but nevertheless historically revealing and accurate) outpost of economic imperialism, and synecdoche for an entire continent. In the tradition of the nineteenth-century novel's topographical vision, the harbor town, the mountains, the coastal waters of Conrad's South America renew the convergence of empirical and metaphorical spaces, the perception of place that, as Mieke Bal argues, gives meaning – and, by extension, a historical destiny – to its contours. Fiction in the late twentieth and early twenty-first centuries explosively enlarges the geographical scope of the historical novel – or, rather the novel of the present, understood as historical.

Notes

1. Maria Edgeworth, *The Absentee*, ed. W. J. McCormack and Kim Walker (Oxford University Press), pp. 83–84.
2. Jane Austen, *Persuasion*, ed. D. W. Harding (Harmondsworth: Penguin Books, 1965), pp. 42–43.
3. Georg Lukács, *The Historical Novel*, trans. Hannah and Stanley Mitchell (Harmondsworth: Penguin, 1969), p. 96.
4. Walter Scott, *Chronicles of the Canongate*, ed. Claire Lamont (London: Penguin Books, 2003), p. 51.
5. Charles Dickens, *Little Dorrit*, ed. Harvey Peter Sucksmith (Oxford: Clarendon Press, 1979), p. 1.
6. Charles Dickens, *Our Mutual Friend*, ed. Stephen Gill (London: Penguin, 1985), p. 43.
7. Charles Dickens, *Bleak House* (London: Oxford University Press, 1956), p. 219.
8. Lauren M. E. Goodlad, *Victorian Literature and the Victorian State* (Baltimore, MD and London: Johns Hopkins University Press, 2003), p. 14.
9. Elizabeth Ermarth, *The English Novel in History 1840–1895* (London: Routledge, 1997), p. 114.
10. Friedrich Engels, *The Condition of the Working Class in England*, ed. David McLellan (Oxford University Press, 1999), pp. 60, 67.
11. Charles Dickens, *Hard Times*, ed. George Ford and Sylvere Monod (New York and London: W. W. Norton, 1990), p. 20.
12. Charles Dickens, *Dombey and Son*, ed. Alan Horsman (Oxford: Clarendon Press, 1974), pp. 90–91.

13. Karl Marx and Friedrich Engels, "Manifesto of the Communist Party," in Karl Marx, *The Revolutions of 1848*, ed. David Fernbach (New York: Vintage Books, 1974), p. 70.

14. Anthony Trollope, *The Warden* (New York and London: Oxford University Press, 1989), pp. 205–206.

15. Ford Madox Ford, *The March of Literature* (New York: The Dial Press, 1938), p. 789.

16. Anthony Trollope, *The Way We Live Now* (New York: Modern Library, 1984), p. 327.

19

From Wollstonecraft to Gissing:
the revolutionary emergence of women,
children, and labor in novelistic narrative

CAROLYN LESJAK

The story of how the conditions of women, children, and laborers enter the nineteenth-century English novel is a story, both true and false, about making visible individuals and groups who were previously invisible. False, because these groups' invisibility is a conceit nineteenth-century novels and their critics engage in. After all, it is only because women, children, and laborers are becoming increasingly more visible and felt presences in the social world, subjects who must be reckoned with, that the need for fictive representation arises. And yet true insofar as what is made visible through nineteenth-century novels is less documentary evidence of the real state of women, children, and laborers than imaginative constructions of those subjects produced in their name. The Molls and Roxanas, Pamelas and Clarissas of fiction had already opened the space to be filled by new representations in fiction of the lives of their heirs. The gap between fiction and reality, textuality and experience, is hardly something to bemoan; the gap defines the act of representation broadly, and realism specifically. But narratives that introduce emergent subjects also do something different: because their novelistic representations are demands for social redress, they highlight the distance between the "imaginary or formal 'solutions'" they offer and the problems they set out to "solve."[1] They function as model ideological acts whose success lies paradoxically in their failure: their failure to paper over or mitigate the fact that the social problems they raise and represent are, in the end, "unresolvable social contradictions" (Jameson, *The Political Unconscious* 79).

Evaluation of the novels as "messy," "immature," or "bad" register this so-called failure, as do readings that dismiss them as propaganda: in the former case, they fail in their literariness; in the latter, they are not literary enough. But once the formal problems are seen as symptomatic of all novelistic narratives, topical novels can be recognized for what they are – typical rather than exceptional. Their failure is the failure of all novels: they fail to solve the social contradictions that animate them; but unlike domestic fictions, they leave more marks of their failure precisely because they aim to translate social problems into political action.

All novels of this type desire some kind of revolutionary transformation, often explicitly aiming at electoral and social change through the very act of representing what has gone unrepresented. At the same time, the myriad definitions of revolution that these novels generate unsettle its very meaning. There are as many versions of revolution as there are novels about it, and, indeed, the purpose of such fictions is to narrate and redefine revolution in ways that make it palatable to a primarily middle-class readership. There are clear limitations therefore to how revolutionary these texts can be. They protest injustice and inequality, they demand specific reparations, they make the private public, and they attempt to narrate the most minute and impressionistic of mental processes in order to disrupt and alter the status quo. But they also apologize, capitulate, reconsider, and contain their own revolutionary energy, betray their subjects, and reproduce the status quo. They at once dramatize the impossibility of any individual or group of individuals existing in a discrete relationship to the social whole – and rely on that self-same discrete individual as the ground for their fictions.

It is striking how many novels in the century between 1796 and 1897 have individual names as their titles. The continuity of the titles with earlier eighteenth-century novelistic convention masks a significant underlying difference. Beginning with the publication of Mary Hays's *The Memoirs of Emma Courtney* (1796), there follow Mary Wollstonecraft's *Maria, or the Wrongs of Woman* (1798); William Godwin's *Fleetwood* (1805); Maria Edgeworth's *Helen* (1837); Frances Trollope's *Michael Armstrong, the Factory Boy* (1839); Captain Marryat's *Jacob Faithful* (1834); Charlotte Elizabeth Tonna's *Helen Fleetwood* (1841); Benjamin Disraeli's *Sybil* (1845); Charlotte Brontë's *Jane Eyre* (1847) and *Shirley* (1849); Elizabeth Gaskell's *Mary Barton* (1848); George Eliot's *Felix Holt, the Radical* (1866); and Henry James's *Daisy Miller* (1878) and *The Princess Casamassima* (1886). The names thus invoked perform double duty: they register the utter significance of the individual as the center of narrative interest and, equally, they function as stand-ins for classes or genders or ages that have a potential (and a calling) to transform the social world. While it might be tempting to say that all novelistic characters essentially play this role, something different happens in these narratives precisely because they attempt didactically to further a cause as much as a character.

Mary Wollstonecraft begins *Maria* by saying that the story could have been more dramatic "would I have sacrificed my main object, the desire of exhibiting the misery and oppression, peculiar to women, that arise out of the partial laws and customs of society." This aim, she continues, "restrained my fancy; and the history ought rather to be considered, as of woman, than of an individual."[2] This is an odd apology for a novel hardly lacking in drama, but Wollstonecraft's desire to capture the generic rather than the individual – woman's history rather than Maria's – characterizes the aims of Romantic novelists generally. Written in the wake of the French Revolution and influenced by both Enlightenment thinking and Jacobinism, Romantic novels have at their heart politico-philosophical questions about the proper relationship between reason and passion, which are shown to be integrally connected to the rights and status of women, the validity of women's experience, and the manner in which women's knowledge and experience can be articulated, privately and publicly. The institutional context for those concerns is marriage and its unequal, oppressive structure: in his *Enquiry Concerning Political Justice* (1793) William Godwin likens marriage to a "monopoly, and the worst of monopolies," given men's complete control over their wives.[3]

Fictional texts and political treatises go hand in hand for Romantic novelists: Mary Wollstonecraft imagines *Maria* as the fictional sequel to her earlier essay, *A Vindication of the Rights of Woman* (1792). *Maria* "show[s] the wrongs of different classes of women, equally oppressive, though, from the difference of education, necessarily various" (248). William Godwin's *Fleetwood* (1805) dissects the abusive systemic power of men within marriage. Mary Hays, a friend of both Wollstonecraft and Godwin, offers *Emma Courtney* as a cautionary tale about excessive sentimentality that nonetheless owes its impressive force to the forthrightness with which its heroine expresses her desire and voices, like Maria, strong sexual feelings. Hays and Wollstonecraft do not shirk the equal danger faced by women who want to marry and women who want more than propriety allows. For both kinds of women metaphor becomes terrifying reality: women are "buried alive," becoming slaves to their husbands' wishes and hypocritical notions of virtue; "covered" by the laws of patriarchy, they lose their lives, their children, their ability to refuse sexual relations with their husbands, and their property. In classical nineteenth-century realist novels marriage is more often than not the solution, but in the earlier Jacobin novels marriage is the problem. "Marriage," as Wollstonecraft's Maria pithily notes, "had bastilled me for life" (316–317).

Given few vocational and emotional outlets for women, writing functions for Wollstonecraft and Hays as a political act in and of itself, and goes a long way toward explaining the sensationalist excess of their narratives. They and their heroines are writing for their lives, which appear to depend upon their representation in writing. Moreover, their personal experience and hence autobiography is seen as the appropriate vehicle for the development and expression of abstract Enlightenment principles. Excess in Hays's *Memoirs* takes the form of a series of letters from Emma to the man she loves, Augustus Harley. The more he neglects to respond to her letters, the more letters she writes. While not writing to the moment, as Richardson's Pamela does, Emma's inability to *stop* writing suggests how letters and the epistolary novel serve not merely to reflect but also to actively construct women's emerging identity. These letters attempt to "trace a faithful delineation of the emotions and sentiments of an ingenuous, uncorrupted, mind – a mind formed by solitude, and habits of reflection, to some strength of character."[4] As an individual, who, like all other individuals, has the capacity to reason, Emma has a right, the narrative implies, to write – and to be written to. In fact, the necessarily mediated relations between men and women in the early nineteenth century make letters and writing often the only outlet for the "delineation of the emotions and sentiment" even as they represent a danger- ous breach of propriety. Secrecy, sexual intrigue, and indiscretion circulate in and around women's letters. *Maria* offers a potent example of the seductive power of texts when Maria falls in love with Henry Darnford via his margin- alia in Rousseau's *Héloise* – a text to which Maria has "flown" as "her only refuge from the idea of [Darnford]" (262). But by transposing Darnford onto Rousseau's St. Preux, Maria succumbs to Rousseauian sentiment – and to Darnford.

Even as Romantic novels seek to extend or illuminate the political concerns motivating them, they also demonstrate how complex fictional renderings of newly emerging identities and revolutionary ideas can be. William Godwin's novelistic representation of marriage in *Fleetwood* stops short of advocating what his political treatises do: free love as a possible solution to the hypocrisy and falsehood encouraged by current codes of sexual conduct. In a loose retelling of *Othello*, Godwin narrates Fleetwood's descent into jealousy and misogyny as a series of petty irritations, which, spurred on by the Iago-like Gifford, lead Fleetwood to disown his virtuous wife. While Fleetwood even- tually reunites with Mary, the full force of his power as her husband, as well as the profound misogyny underlying his view of women, defines *Fleetwood's* narrative. It simultaneously critiques Fleetwood's flawed "sentimental educa- tion" and praises the heightened value of women's virtue when tested by the inhumane tribulations of tyrannical men. "There," Fleetwood concludes, admiring Mary, "there is presented to us the most ravishing spectacle that earth can boast. I never till now was sensible of half the merits of my wife."[5] Old ideas of the virtuous woman reassert themselves rather than being over-turned; reform on an individual level – Fleetwood's – supplants Godwin's call in his political tracts for the structural reform of marriage itself.

In contrast Wollstonecraft and Hays refuse Godwin's attempt to recuperate marriage by redefining it. Because Wollstonecraft never finished *Maria*, we cannot know exactly how the novel would have ended; but none of the fragmentary endings in the unfinished manuscript includes marriage. In one version Darnford leaves Maria, who then loses the child of his she is carrying; in another, she commits suicide. The most sanguine of possibilities has Maria, the working-class domestic Jemima, and Maria's first daughter (her husband's child, not Darnford's – whom Jemima miraculously finds) living together in an all-female household, thus anticipating the ending of George Gissing's *The Odd Women* (1893). Hays plays with the idea of a household free of men, concluding her narrative with Emma as the head of an extremely unconven-tional family consisting of her own daughter, her lover's son, and her hus-band's mistress Rachel, who was her former servant. Both her husband and her lover have died, and Emma now fulfills the task of educating the son in the ways of the world. Indeed, the pretense of the novel is that young Augustus is in danger of becoming a libertine like his father. Emma writes her narrative in order to save him from doing to women what Emma's husband and lover have done to her.

In protesting sexual and social inequality and in attempting to write new women into existence, these revolutionary novels say the unspeakable. At one point Emma Courtney offers herself to Augustus Harley, proposing to live conjugally with him outside of marriage. At another, in the midst of narrating the pleasures Maria experiences in her first sexual contact with Henry Darnford, the narrative pauses to consider whether Darnford will turn out to be a cad, the implication being that most if not all men are. And as hard as *Fleetwood* tries to provide closure, the overriding sense is one of failure: the failure to narrate its way out of the sexual and social impasses it renders compellingly.

Clearly, the use of novels to illustrate or affirm the validity of a particular political theory or demand proves to be a difficult business. Hays's narrative moves between declarative statements that read like mini-treatises and impas-sioned prose that argues against the efficacy of reasoned argument. William Godwin speaks through Hays's character Mr. Francis, who consistently advo-cates reason rather than passion; but while Emma values his advice, she rarely follows it. And the trajectory of the narrative indicates that Emma's passionate feelings for Augustus Harley were right insofar as they were reciprocated. Rather than seeing these contradictions as failings, it seems more instructive to read them as the price so-called political novels pay in trying to render contemporary events and politico-philosophical debates in fictional form. Moreover, the turn to autobiography, memoir, or confession as the most appropriate form for this rendering, given the authors' investments in personal experience, can compromise these novels' projects insofar as they have trouble moving from the individual to the social. Reliance on a level of individual heroics can be politically defeating. Nevertheless, these novels can shock readers precisely because for the most part they resist facile solutions to the seemingly intractable problems they represent. They do not shy away from making public the most intimate relations between men and women, and they do not mince matters regarding the degradations suffered and shared by women from the upper classes and from the lowest. They also mark an important moment in literary history before the boundaries between politics and literature are fully solidified.

Later nineteenth-century realist novels temper the excesses of individual biography and attenuate their direct links to political treatises and specific political demands. Nevertheless, the pressing need for social and sexual equality for women and the question of how best both to represent it and to achieve it remains central. Leaving aside what happens to misbehaving or willful nineteenth-century female characters – from Austen's Marianne Dashwood to Eliot's Gwendolen Harleth – conventional women face impossible constraints as a result of the public–private divide. Lady Davenant in Maria Edgeworth's *Helen* (1848) sums up this state when she confesses, "It is hard that my own character – the integrity of a whole life – should avail me nothing! And yet. . .to how few can my character be really known! Women cannot, like men, make their characters known by public actions."[6] Without a public voice, women, like the orphan children activating so many nineteenth-century *Bildungsromane*, continue to be buffeted, suggesting how vulnerable they are to external circumstance and how useful they are therefore to plots that represent their personal and social transformation.

Charlotte Brontë's Jane Eyre, shunted from the Reeds to Lowood to Thornfield Hall, is exemplary in this regard. Completely at the mercy of the Reeds as a child, she asks, "Why was I always suffering, always brow-beaten, always accused, for ever condemned?"[7] Her abusive confinement in the red room confirms her sense of injustice – "'Unjust! – unjust!' said my reason, forced by the agonizing stimulus into precocious though transitory power;

and Resolve, equally wrought up, instigated some strange expedient to achieve escape from insupportable oppression" (15) – and sets the stage for the novel's exploration of Jane's development from a "heterogeneous thing" (15) into Rochester's wife. In its concern with Jane's psyche, as well as the larger social structures limiting women's role in the world, *Jane Eyre* continues the project of Romantic novelists, but now in an altered social and intellectual context. It also looks forward to the New Woman novels at the end of the century in the explicitness with which it explores the erotics of power and the battles for control that take place between Jane and Rochester. The novel sits at the nexus of multiple social conflicts – some stated, others unwittingly present – including gender and class inequalities, the status of women's labor, the nature of revolutionary change, and the role of the British Empire and racial difference in Jane's transformation. Indeed, the novel dramatizes the increasing difficulty of isolating any one social category of identity – be it race, class, gender, age – from the whole complex of social relations being altered in response to the consolidation of a capitalist economy in nineteenth-century Britain.

Is *Jane Eyre* a feminist text, a colonial or imperial text, an "autobiography" as its subtitle claims, an exemplary realist novel, or a gothic tale? And what picture of revolution emerges from Jane's transformation from an orphaned, abused girl to the wife of Rochester? Jane's famous revolutionary credo asserts that women:

> need exercise for their faculties, and a field for their efforts as much as their brothers do; they suffer from too rigid a restraint, too absolute a stagnation, precisely as men would suffer; and it is narrow-minded in their more privileged fellow-creatures to say that they ought to confine themselves to making pudding and knitting stockings, to playing on the piano and embroidering bags. (109)

While the clarity of Jane's feminist demand for "a field" for women's "efforts" is important, and has contributed to the positioning of *Jane Eyre* as a feminist text, the novel offers a less clear-cut view of rebellion and its results. Marriage, once again, constitutes the endpoint of Jane's rebellion even if her marriage to Rochester and the events leading up to it are anything but predictable. Along the way there are forgotten persons, who represent emerging classes with competing claims at odds with Jane's exemplary womanhood: not only the colonial creoles exemplified by Rochester's mad wife, the white Jamaican Bertha Mason, but also beyond her all the invisible imperial subjects who provide the labor and resources to further Britain's development as well as

Jane's. The money Jane receives when her uncle dies not only provides her with the personal independence that allows her to return to Rochester as heiress rather than governess, but also ensures her indebtedness to others whom the novel leaves unseen. Empire subtends Jane's success; it also remains as a literal reminder of the limits of bourgeois individualism and of the bourgeois novelist's representational efforts. Brontë's recourse to a fairy-tale ending – the master will marry the governess! – registers the fantastical nature of this individualistic myth.

Despite the unrealistic nature of so many nineteenth-century marriage plots, marriage ranks consistently as domestic realism's plot of choice for figuring and representing social change. Facilitated by improbable inheritances, fortuitous deaths, maimings, sicknesses, and even the plague (see Harriet Martineau's *Deerbrook* [1840]), realist novels relentlessly bring their unlikely couples together. Realism's paradoxical penchant for the improbable is less a cause for questioning, however, when placed in the broader context of Victorian culture. For much of the nineteenth century, no organized movement existed for furthering women's rights and equality. Women who spoke out spoke without institutional support; women who wrote frequently wrote under male pseudonyms in order to harness the cultural capital needed to be read and received seriously, as something other than a "woman writer." Finally, apart from writing, with its gendered vagaries, few professional opportunities existed for middle-class women; unmarried middle-class Victorian women could be governesses or schoolteachers, roles that all three Brontë sisters filled and that Charlotte and Anne wrote about. Recent work on Victorian psychology shows, moreover, that Brontë's picture of Jane's revolutionary energies is historically specific, inspired by phrenological models of the mind, which conceive of multiple faculties competing with one another and not necessarily leading to harmony. Individuals can regulate those energies as well as abuse them. This view of the psyche precludes domestic ideology's "angel of the house" – a figure that Brontë directly attacks in the novel when she has Jane remonstrate that she "had rather be a *thing* than an angel" (262). Brontë also complicates the Enlightenment contrast between knowledge and feeling that drives Romantic narratives, suggesting a multiplicity of material faculties "warring" in the brain[8] – matched by a multiplicity of generic forms reflecting the intertwined yet conflicting histories of its emerging subjects.

Social problems are simultaneously narrative ones; new subject matter prompts new modes of self-consciousness and a persistent concern with narrative method. The question of method is perhaps most pronounced in nineteenth-century fictional attempts to represent industrial labor and factory workers. Middle-class industrial novelists inherit the problems of typicality that Romantic novelists struggle with in their representations of women and new "men of feeling," and find themselves having to justify their subject matter and vouch for the legitimacy of their characters and the social problems brought to light through them. Dilemmas concerning the agency of revolutionary workers are particularly fraught, given industrial novelists' split allegiances and their need to represent workers without granting them power as a class whose aims are separate from, and opposed to, fiction-writers and readers. These divided interests necessarily put pressure on one another; as Raymond Williams notes about George Eliot, a "unity of idiom" is no longer possible once the English novel introduces new classes into its narratives.[9]

The initial aim of *Michael Armstrong*, Frances Trollope writes, was "to drag into the light of day, and place before the eyes of Englishmen, the hideous mass of injustice and suffering to which thousands of infant laborers are subjected, who toil in our monster spinning-mills."[10] Once readers are aware of this injustice and suffering, the reasoning follows, something will be done about it. Benjamin Disraeli subtitles *Sybil* "The Two Nations" to signify the division between rich and poor, and, characteristically, narrates conversations between his middle- and working-class characters thematizing the divide. The novel's hero, Charles Egremont – and by extension the reader – learns in his conversation with the working-class radical Stephen Morley and Sybil's father, Walter Gerard, that England is split into:

> Two nations: between whom there is no intercourse and no sympathy; who are as ignorant of each other's habits, thoughts and feelings, as if they were dwellers in different zones, or inhabitants of different planets; who . . . are not governed by the same laws.[11]

Characters within the novels can serve as ideal readers, asking naïve, uninformed questions about the working class that the narrative then answers, thereby modeling the interest and engagement desired of readers. Readers are invited to identify with the working class; and, unlike realist fiction generally, such narratives ideally want their readers to *do* something with their new knowledge and identification, or at least to have a different attitude toward the laborers in their midst.

Reaching out in this way confounds the boundaries of fiction. In a dramatic example of this confusion, Frances Trollope revises her plans for *Michael Armstrong* when the real workers, on whom she wants to model the second phase of Michael's life (when he will work for the amelioration of the conditions detailed by his childhood suffering), engage in actions she cannot abide, resorting to violence in the name of their cause. "The cause," she explains, "has been too much sullied, and the sufferers too closely associated in the public eye with those who have been guilty of all she most deprecates, to permit her continuing the work as she intended" (iv). The actions of real working-class operatives impinge on Trollope's willingness to offer to readers her fictional laborers, and Michael Armstrong, in particular, "as objects of public sympathy" (iv). Sympathetic fictional portrayals become signs of political alliance; it is thus more politically expedient, Trollope reasons, to end Michael's story at the end of his childhood, since "no misconstruction of principles, no misconception of motives can exist with regard to an attempt to ameliorate the lot of infant labourers" (iv).

The fear of being misunderstood – or of guilt by association – surfaces frequently in or around industrial novels. Elizabeth Gaskell does not change her tale of Manchester factory life in *Mary Barton*; but her publisher, concerned about her sympathetic portrayal of the working class, asks her to write a preface explaining her motives in order to defuse readers' political ire. Gaskell herself throughout the narrative carefully distinguishes between what her characters feel and what she knows to be the truth, thereby working to keep her own identity and political views separate from those of her characters. George Eliot employs a related strategy when, at the behest of her publisher, she appends to *Felix Holt* an "Address to Working Men" in the voice of her protagonist. Eliot's appendix makes explicit the didactic goals of her novel, which otherwise might go unheeded without such extradiegetic address. The address cautions against precipitous action, and emphasizes workers' patience, duty, responsibility, and, above all, their recognition of the invaluableness of the cultural inheritance that the "endowed classes" possess and the "unendowed multitude" lack.[12]

Eliot's appeal to gradualism (in her case, drawing on the language of organicism) is typical. Visions of revolution in the industrial novel tend toward the ameliorative; they are marked by reconciliations between individuals of different classes or, as in the case of Gaskell's *North and South* (1855), individuals of different segments of the middle class, who in turn represent regions of the country – the industrial north as opposed to the agricultural south – both of which must necessarily play a part in the transformation of England into an industrial, modern economy. Economic and social differences are tempered by representations of cross-class understandings. An ideal scenario in *North and South* involves the novel's southern heroine, Margaret Hale, convincing the northern manufacturer John Thornton of the necessity of listening to his factory hands and of the novel's working-class hero, Nicholas Higgins, partnering with Thornton in a scheme to run a dining-hall inside the factory. Interpersonal relations supplant class distinctions; new modes of social inter-course are shown to be preferable to a new social order; sympathy and fellow feeling arise from individuals meeting face to face and are irrevocably blocked when individuals identify as part of a class. Unions are poor substitutes for Christianity; and working-class violence is never justified – in part because no matter how brutally workers are treated, the novels never translate such brutality into a recognition of the structural violence at the heart of capitalism. Even when Charlotte Elizabeth Tonna's *Helen Fleetwood* leaves its industrialist unconverted by the sorrows of his workers, the means of redress still consists of a Christian stewardship undertaken by masters for their working men, women, and children.

Industrial novels, however, do more than exhibit symptoms of contra-dictions attendant on middle-class representations of the working class. They highlight the impossibility of isolating any one social category, such as class, from any other. Some of their most affecting characters and scenes evoke the social limitations under which women struggle. The extended dialogues between Margaret Hale and John Thornton in *North and South*, rife with political, aesthetic, and personal disagreements as well as sexual frisson and angst, anticipate later New Woman novels in the intensity with which they at once express and chafe against limited possibilities for women. Likewise, *Felix Holt*'s powerful representation of Mrs. Transome's power-lessness threatens to steal the show, and clearly applies in varying degrees to all the female characters. The novel relentlessly ironizes the language of choice for women, be it with respect to Mrs. Transome, the heroine Esther Lyon, or the minor character, Annette Ledru, who is described as "one of your meek little diablesses, who have a will of their own once in their lives – the will to choose their own master" (314).

For the most part, however, these are middle-class ironies; it is a given that workers require masters because of their inchoate or childlike state as newly emerging industrial subjects. Accordingly, workers must choose between individual and class allegiances, a choice that literally kills Stephen Blackpool in Charles Dickens's *Hard Times* (1854) and highlights, more generally, the impossibility of industrial novels sympathetically portraying militant union workers. The vague promise Stephen makes to his beloved Rachel to avoid trouble prevents him, he believes, from joining his fellow workers in support of the union. Stephen can thus act on his individual obligation to Rachel, but that very act renders him incapable of collective action as a power-loom weaver, which in turn leaves him both ostracized from his community and separated from Rachel by dint of his marriage to his unnamed alcoholic wife. He becomes key to other people's stories – he offers a potent counter to Gradgrind's fatuous adherence to facts at the expense of feeling; he figures as the pawn in Tom Gradgrind's plot to rob the bank; he epitomizes the honest, hard-working hand who resists the wiles of opportunistic union men like Slackbridge; and our response to his travails disproves claims that the middle-class does not care about the plight of the working class. But in the process he loses any real agency and any ability to articulate his own condition and that of his fellow workers: "'Tis a muddle, and that's aw," he ineffectually concludes.[13] Individuation in *Hard Times* seems possible only via "fancy" or "wonder," in spaces such as Sleary's circus or Sissy Jupe's imagination, which are already marginal and which intensify the antagonism between individual and group existence.

Another key site of transformative possibility for Dickens, as well as other nineteenth-century novelists, is children. In *Hard Times* Dickens finds in children a certain faith in the world that persists despite their maltreatment. In response to Thomas Gradgrind's injunctions to "never wonder," to never sacrifice fact to fantasy, Louisa Gradgrind finds herself unable to stop wondering. Wonder as a noun merges here with wondering as a mode of thought that counters the cold facts of industrial life in Coketown. Although it does not prevent Louisa from being sold as a pawn to further her father's interests, it does protect her from being irreparably ground down by her suffering. The novel envisions Louisa surrounded ultimately by:

> happy Sissy's happy children loving her; all children loving her; she grown learned in childish lore; thinking no innocent and pretty fancy ever to be despised; trying hard to know her humbler fellow-creatures, and to beautify their lives of machinery and reality with those imaginative graces and delights, without which the heart of infancy will wither up ...   (313)

Henry James also identifies children with wonder. In *What Maisie Knew* (1897) James describes Maisie as the "little feathered shuttlecock" her parents "could fiercely keep flying between them."[14] Rather than bemoan Maisie's state, however, James sees it as the means toward the creation of new sets of relations; he refers to Maisie as "our little wonder-working agent" (5), and throughout the narrative the connections she unwittingly draws among persons circulating around her divorced parents are indeed wondrous – precisely because they are serendipitous. While other nineteenth-century novels about children employ a variety of narrative voices, they share with James a sense that children are more perceptive and sensitive because less biased in their readings of the social world (and James further clarifies that only a girl really has this requisite sensitivity).

Captain Frederick Marryat's sea novel *Jacob Faithful* uses Jacob's adventures on a Thames barge to map the social space of pre-Victorian London, but given its picaresque form, impoverishment and debauchery are rendered lightly and humorously in stark contrast to their treatment in industrial novels or later condition-of-England novels such as Gissing's *Workers in the Dawn* (1880). Jacob moves through his narrative willy-nilly and that is part of his charm. Children in these novels play the role of agentless agents, and as such they epitomize the conundrum of introducing potentially revolutionary subjects into fundamentally bourgeois narratives: they cause change but are not active agents of it; ingenuously awry to the given, they are at once wondrous in their "revolutionary" relationship to the status quo, and ultimately never threatening to that order because their capacity for acting on the world is circumscribed from the outset. Recall, after all, that Frances Trollope refuses to let Michael Armstrong grow up.

To return to James: his reflections on Maisie are important not only for what they say about children but also because they register a marked change in tenor regarding how novelists conceive of emergent social identities. If individual solutions save the day in many mid-century industrial and domestic fictions, by the latter decades of the century material circumstances weigh heavily on individuals. In the wake of Darwin and of materialist theories in the sciences, political economy, and psychology, there is an appreciation for the larger social structures and ideologies within which new subjects are produced. Novelists draw on new social developments regarding women, workers, and children, and self-consciously investigate the status and limits of novelistic narrative and the realist project. Such self-reflexivity is most pronounced in James's prefaces to his novels, where he brings matters of form and content to the fore, and reflects on the challenges he and his fellow nineteenth-century novelists faced in their attempts to capture the experiences of emergent social subjects. In the preface to *The Princess Casamassima*, for example, James muses about the trickiness of finding the place, as a writer, where "one's impelled *bonhomme* may feel enough and 'know' enough – or be in the way of learning enough – for his maximum dramatic value without feeling and knowing too much for his minimum verisimilitude, his proper fusion with the fable."[15] In *What Maisie Knew* as well the challenge is to represent the play of a child's mind without imputing to it impossible knowledge. James thus moves from conveying "what the child might be conceived to have *understood*" to "what my wondering witness materially and inevitably *saw*; a great deal of which quantity she either wouldn't understand at all or would quite misunderstand" (7). For James the new content of his novels constitutes particular forms of knowledge, which in turn require new narrative methods attuned to the material world at its minutest levels.

New forms of fiction also arise directly from new social movements: as the shibboleths of domestic ideology come under direct attack, "sensation" literature of the 1860s disrupts gender norms and the New Woman fiction of the 1890s depicts new, liberated possibilities for women's lives beyond the confines of marriage and the home. Drawing on and spurring a host of social anxieties around the changing status of women, these narratives gain traction from a series of legislative acts gradually increasing women's rights over property and within marriage, as well as the development of a collective social movement for women's rights that include training programs and the creation of other institutional structures to support women, both married and unmarried.

Women in sensation novels and New Woman novels write, work, have love affairs, and lead independent lives outside of marriage. Despite its highly wrought prose, Rhoda Broughton's *Not Wisely But Too Well* (1867) is a sensation novel that follows its New Woman heroine, Kate Chester, from her disastrous affair with a playboy of a lover (with a name to match), Dare Stamer, to the slums of Queenstown where she works as a district visitor and, once the fever hits the slums, as a house-nurse and Sister of Mercy. Kate is *not* saved by romance, either with Dare Stamer – who, Broughton writes, "was not more conceited than men generally are"[16] – or anyone else; instead she remains alone, and isolated from her middle-class family. Mary Cholmondely's *Red Pottage* (1899) also features unconventional women negotiating unconventional lives, and highlights the integral role that writing plays in the construction and the representation of the New Woman – in fact and in fiction. One of its two new women, Hester Gresley, spends most of the novel writing a book, the only copy of which gets destroyed by her brother. Likening her book to a baby, Hester in revenge attempts to kill her brother's son, suggesting just how far New Woman novels have moved outside the conventions of domestic realism.

The fairy-tale endings of mid-nineteenth-century domestic novels have no place in Gissing's *The Odd Women*: material and psychological deprivations are determinant, and the revolutionary energies of its new women necessarily compromised by overlapping and contradictory desires and social pressures. The story of the three Madden sisters undercuts their father's firm Ruskinian belief in the virtues of Victorian domestic ideology and introduces the figure of the modern shopgirl in the youngest sister, Monica Madden, who might be the real new woman of the 1890s. Concurrently, New Woman Rhoda Nunn's feminist beliefs are complicated when she falls in love with Everard Barfoot. Rhoda and Everard engage in intellectual and sexual power struggles with one another, and eventually they separate, both having failed tests of confidence concerning marriage and free love, and Everard's fidelity. Rhoda remains at her business school for young women. Commenting on its success in the final pages of the novel, she concludes, "The world is moving!"[17] Not the novel's final word, however – it ends with Rhoda murmuring "Poor little child!" (386) as she looks down on Monica Madden's parentless baby girl. Significantly, both concluding exclamations make a mockery of the "quiet liberality" (329) and "polished humanism" (367) that Everard opts for in his marriage to Agnes Brissenden.

As the sheer pressure of circumstance increasingly makes itself felt in the pages of fiction and in social fact, liberalism, humanism, and individualism lose much of their luster in the 1890s. How to reconcile the myth of individual, autonomous effort with the increasing knowledge of the material realities determining and delimiting the reach of the individual? How to hold on to a notion of individual redemption in the midst of narratives such as Thomas Hardy's and Gissing's, where individuals, such as Arthur Golding in *Workers in the Dawn*, find themselves "straying amid the billows of life like a wrecked and manless ship upon an ebbing sea."[18] Social systems rather than the individuals within them increasingly come to define the space of the novel. In Hardy's rendering of this space, when individuals do act, they act too late, or in ways that do more harm than good. Knowledge, when it comes, comes after the fact and hence is incapable of guiding action in the present.

At the end of *Mimesis* Erich Auerbach celebrates Virginia Woolf's emphasis on the "random moment" as deeply humanist in its ability to bring diverse individuals together around the "elementary things that men [sic] have in common."[19] But this shared commonness of the quotidian might be read as a recognition that individuals *only* meet on the most basic or mundane of levels. We all eat, need shelter, and are vulnerable to others by dint of our existences as social beings, but these trivial commonalities do not erase the great political and economic realities within which individuals live, acquire, and share their collective social existence. A number of the novels discussed in this chapter have not found their way into the traditional canon, and many are out of print. A number of them are rarely lauded for their literary merit, but are identified instead by reference to their "cause," as social problem novels, industrial fictions, New Woman novels, or (proto-) feminist tracts. Like the label "woman writer," their focus and hence their import is qualified. They are too topical, goes the argument, a charge that even canonical writers open themselves to when they turn to representing events perceived to be contentiously contemporary, as Anthony Trollope does in his last unfinished novel, *The Landleaguers* (1883), which addresses the justifiable character of violence in the Irish Land Wars of the early 1880s.

But this charge already assumes that novels should be something else, a paradoxical assumption, it would seem, when talking about the genre of nineteenth-century realism. Nineteenth-century representations of women, labor, and children succeed by failing. By failing to transcend their own topicality, or escape their typicality – by their assignment of individuals to group categories – they make visible the inevitably partisan nature of what Franco Moretti refers to as the "democratic-universalistic values" to which the English *Bildungsroman* as a form adheres.[20] By failing to solve the problems they raise – but continuing to pose them nonetheless – they act as a thorn in the side of the novel's formal history, and in this way guarantee their continuing importance to the development of English fiction.

Notes

1. Fredric Jameson, *The Political Unconscious: Narrative as a Socially Symbolic Act* (Ithaca, NY: Cornell University Press, 1981), p. 79.
2. Mary Wollstonecraft, *A Vindication of the Rights of Woman* and *The Wrongs of Woman, Or Maria* (New York: Pearson Longman, 2007), p. 247.
3. William Godwin, *Enquiry Concerning Political Justice* (New York: Penguin, 1976), p. 762.
4. Mary Hays, *Memoirs of Emma Courtney* (New York: Oxford University Press, 2000), p. 88.
5. William Godwin, *Fleetwood* (Peterborough, ON: Broadview Press, 2001), p. 423.
6. Maria Edgeworth, *Helen* (London: Macmillan, 1896), pp. 282–284.
7. Charlotte Brontë, *Jane Eyre* (New York: Oxford University Press, 2000), p. 15.
8. Sally Shuttleworth, *Charlotte Brontë and Victorian Psychology* (Cambridge University Press, 1996), p. 154.
9. Raymond Williams, *The Country and the City* (New York: Oxford University Press, 1973), p. 169.
10. Frances Trollope, *The Life and Adventures of Michael Armstrong, Factory Boy* (London: Henry Calhoun, 1840), p. 3.
11. Benjamin Disraeli, *Sybil or the Two Nations* (New York: Penguin, 1980), p. 96.
12. George Eliot, *Felix Holt the Radical* (New York: Penguin, 1984), p. 626.
13. Charles Dickens, *Hard Times* (New York: Penguin, 1985), p. 105.
14. Henry James, *What Maisie Knew* (Oxford University Press, 2008), p. 7.
15. Henry James, *The Princess Casamassima* (New York: Penguin, 1987), p. 41.

16. Rhoda Broughton, *Not Wisely but Too Well* (Dover, NH: Alan Sutton Publishing, 1993), p. 30.
17. George Gissing, *The Odd Women* (New York: Meridian Classic, 1983), p. 386.
18. George Gissing, *Workers in the Dawn* (New York: AMS Press, 1968), pp. 440–441.
19. Erich Auerbach, *Mimesis: The Representation of Reality in Western Literature* (Princeton University Press, 2002), p. 552.
20. Franco Moretti, *The Way of the World: The Bildungsroman in European Culture*, trans. Albert Sbragia (New York: Verso, 1987), pp. 195–196.

20

Spaces and places (I): the four nations

DEBORAH EPSTEIN NORD

In the most often cited passage from Benjamin Disraeli's *Sybil* (1845), the hero, Egremont, encounters two strangers in the ruins of an abbey. The younger of the two describes the lamentable state of England, in which men live in isolation and mere "contiguity" rather than community and cooperation.[1] When Egremont demurs that they inhabit "the greatest nation that ever existed," the stranger inquires which of two different nations he means:

> Two nations: between whom there is no intercourse and no sympathy; who are as ignorant of each other's habits, thoughts and feelings, as if they were dwellers in different zones, or inhabitants of different planets; who are formed by a different breeding, are fed by a different food, are ordered by different manners, and are not governed by the same laws.　　　　(96)

Though the two nations the stranger evokes are "THE RICH AND THE POOR," his description of the tenuous connection between them might apply to numerous social divisions within England or to the relationship between the typical novel-reader – English, middle or upper class, situated in the south of England and especially London – and the many "others" who populate the British Isles.

Disraeli refers to the estranged groups as "nations," a word that captures the cultural, linguistic, and sometimes geographical differences between them. The unknown others are both external and internal to England. They include residents of parts of the United Kingdom that were regarded as separate countries – Ireland, Scotland, and Wales – as well as the urban and rural poor, Jews, Gypsies, Irish immigrants, and inhabitants of the industrial north of England. To represent the lives of those alien others required ethnographic inquiry, an effort of translation, and thick description. In sketches, vignettes, fictional diary entries, annals, and novels, writers might record not just the stories and character types of other "nations" but their holidays, languages, dress, and marriage customs. Though these others might live around the corner or in the next town, their lives and habits were as invisible, or at least as perplexing, to the English reader as if they lived halfway round the globe. A potent mix of xenophobia and "scientific" interest compelled fiction writers to include "strangers" in their narratives, often on the periphery and, in some cases, at the center.

Through the inclusion of strangers and others, novelists raised questions with political, cultural, and personal implications: What is England? What is Englishness? What is an Englishman or woman? How is the British nation to be defined? And how are individual identities to be understood? Linda Colley points out that the eighteenth and early nineteenth centuries recast British national identity, mapping new ideas of region and nation onto older configurations.[2] Wars against a common enemy – France – and adherence to a common religion – Protestantism – forged stronger alliances between England, Scotland, and Wales in the wake of the Act of Union in 1707. A growing interest in antiquarianism produced a new sense of the relationship between ancient and modern Britain and between antiquated ways of life and current practices. Philologists and ethnologists explored genealogies of languages and peoples in an effort to identify common origins and distinct lineages. Novelists like Walter Scott, himself an antiquarian, invented historical narratives to comment on contemporary divisions and estrangements. Matthew Arnold attempted to understand what role older and contiguous cultural traditions, whether Hebraic or Celtic, played in Protestant English society and literature. His estimate of those cultures, despite its condescension, signals that Englishness is a mixed identity, an amalgam of various national and religious strains.

Questions of national, ethnic, and cultural identity find their way into fictional narratives, in part because the novel as it evolves is eminently hospitable to them. Mysteries of origin become regular features of fiction, and a protagonist's quest for the secrets of his or her identity animate narratives from *Moll Flanders* (1722), *Tom Jones* (1749), and *Evelina* (1778) to *Guy Mannering* (1815), *Ivanhoe* (1819), *Oliver Twist* (1837–1838), and *Jane Eyre* (1847). The Freudian family romance, in which a child imagines that it is adopted and that its real parents are of more elevated birth than those who have raised it, structures this period's fictional narratives. A different version, in which the child's true origins are exotic, lowly, or racially tainted, also emerges, especially in Victorian decades. Veiled personal identity could be linked to larger connections and hidden resemblances between peoples. Inheritance is marshaled as a fictional trope in relation to nations as well as individuals. What was the nature of a child's relationship to its father, of a people's connection to its land, and of Ireland or Scotland's tie to England? Could these relationships be represented as parallel phenomena or as metaphors for one another?

The novel's ethnographic impulses, interest in origins, and variegated social panoramas make it fertile ground for representing new and alien groups of people. In turn, curiosity about others and strangers influences the forms of fiction. The sketch flourishes as a way of representing obscure ways of life. Terry Eagleton argues that "anthropological interest can best be filled by the sketch, the cameo, the brief vignette, whose point is to put the characters on consumable display rather than pitch them into dynamic interaction."[3] This observation applies to Dickens's and Mayhew's sketches of the urban underclass, William Cobbett's travelogues of rural life, Mary Russell Mitford's sketches of country villages, John Galt's annals of a Scottish parish, and, at the end of the century, Israel Zangwill's fictional vignettes of East End Jews. Shorter and largely unplotted fictional forms offer not just characters but settings unknown to the general reader: Gypsy camps, Jewish shops, the slums of Manchester, cotton mills in Ayrshire, Irish fields devastated by potato blight, and the stunning landscapes of the Irish countryside. Novels too include such descriptions. Some celebrate the picturesque, some evoke sympathy and indignation, and others offer lessons of history and politics bound up with evocations of place.

Others beyond and within England (1800–1840)

Sydney Owenson's *The Wild Irish Girl* (1806), subtitled "a national tale," plays a formative role in the literature and culture of Irish nationalism, but it also exhibits characteristics common to what we might call the literature of otherness. This epistolary novel ends in the marriage of a formerly wayward English aristocrat, Horatio, to a Gaelic heroine, Glorvina, who embodies the essence of her people. She converts the young Englishman's attitude toward a nation he has suspected of "barbarity" from prejudice to enlightened appreciation.[4] Glorvina, like the protagonist of Madame de Staël's *Corinne; or Italy* (1807), is a Romantic heroine whose identity is inseparable from her national culture. The marriage concluding the narrative joins two cultures and also resolves oedipal and inheritance plots, both common characteristics of period texts that feature national or ethnic otherness.

Owenson's story of romance, inheritance, and cultural reconciliation is virtually eclipsed, however, by the ethnography and travelogue that infuse her narrative and fill it with scholarly footnotes. Glorvina is not only red-headed and "a romp" but "a pedant," and, as the alter ego of her didactic creator, she teaches Horatio Gaelic language and lore (42). The subjects of copious footnotes range from disquisitions on Irish history to discussions of the lyre. The footnotes figure in Owenson's overall aim to elevate Ireland and redeem its reputation among the British reading public. The 1800 Act of Union that constructed the United Kingdom of Great Britain and Ireland discriminated against and oppressed non-Anglicans. Owenson is determined to champion the "real" Ireland – the Celtic or Catholic land of her father's birth. She hopes to elicit from her readers the sentiment Horatio expresses when he declares himself, like the "spirit of Milton," in a "new world, 'vital in every part'" (92). A primary source of Horatio's enlightenment is the picturesque Irish landscape. Conforming to the classic attributes of Romantic sublimity, the mountains of western Ireland inspire a "tranquility tinged with terror, a . . . 'delightful horror'" (19). The land satisfies Horatio's Wertheresque *ennui*; and descriptions of the landscape, like the novel's footnotes, impress the reader with Ireland's natural grandeur and worthiness as a nation.

If Owenson champions the homeland she inherits through her Catholic father, Walter Scott celebrates Scotland in historical novels intended to ensure that his birthplace become familiar to British imaginations. The two countries had been joined by the 1707 Act of Union, and by the beginning of the nineteenth century the bond between them had begun to solidify. Nonetheless, Scott introduces English readers to a history, a landscape, a vernacular, and a set of legendary figures that constitute a distinct and even alien national culture. He revives local literary forms, like the Border tales and ballads he published early in his career, and uncovers the complex, culturally diverse Scottish past. His novels establish a template for fictions about others outside of England but also for fictions that feature indigenous others, such as Gypsies and Jews. Scott's project of Scottish historical recovery is inseparable from his desire to portray marginal and outcast minorities.

Scott's fiction is peppered with mysteries of origin and identity and deeply engaged with dispossession and oedipal strife. In *Guy Mannering* Harry Bertram, the son of a laird, is kidnapped as a child and spends years in India before returning as an adult to his birthplace. Ignorant of his own origins, he turns up as Harry Brown, a propertyless young itinerant. During his exile, an unscrupulous arriviste has taken possession of the laird's castle and attempted to erase Scotland's authentic ancient ways. Scott's hero ultimately discovers his identity, recovers his rightful inheritance, restores custom and tradition, and wins the heart of the woman he loves. Hidden identity and oedipal violence also figure in *The Heart of Midlothian* (1818), in which the illegitimate child of Effie Deans, who was suspected of murdering her son at birth, returns as an outlaw and murders his father, a nobleman. In *Ivanhoe* Scott offers two disguised and temporarily dispossessed sons: Ivanhoe, the "Disinherited Knight," who has been banished by his father Cedric, a Saxon nobleman, and Richard Coeur de Lion, the mysterious "Black Knight," whose younger brother John seeks to usurp the rightful king's throne.

It is not merely the two sons who have been disinherited or exiled in twelfth-century England but the Saxons as a whole and, indeed, their culture and languages. Scott uses the story of Ivanhoe, set well in the past, to promote the acceptance of a mingled culture in the present. As the separate strands of Norman and Saxon are ultimately woven together to make up England, so too will Scotland and England co-exist as distinct but interdependent nations. But *Ivanhoe* includes another "race," one still recognized as alien in the early nineteenth century: the Jews. Isaac of York and his daughter, Rebecca, appear in *Ivanhoe* as both outcasts and objects of desire. Isaac belongs to the lineage of Shakespeare's Shylock, the suspect moneylender, and Rebecca exudes both exotic sensuality and chaste rectitude. She and the purely Saxon Rowena constitute one of Scott's racially inflected female pairs and represent an early example – if not the beginning – of a crucial connection between female sexuality and otherness in narrative fiction.

Scott's fascination with Jews in *Ivanhoe* echoes his preoccupation with Gypsies in *Guy Mannering*. A band of Gypsies occupying the laird's land faces expulsion and exile. Scott takes pains to give us the Gypsies' history, describing their evolution from roaming "banditti" to a "mingled race" of tinkers, fortune-tellers, and musicians.[5] Meg Merrilies, a Gypsy "sibyl" and the novel's most memorable character, acts as the only maternal presence in the life of Harry Bertram. Her people, suspected of participating in his kidnapping, are ultimately vindicated. Like the Jews of *Ivanhoe*, these Gypsies suggest that, as Michael Ragussis says, Scott envisions history as "a lengthy process of racial mixture . . . a record of difference."[6] If the English are a hybrid mixture of Norman, Saxon, and Jew, the Scots possess the mongrel inheritance of Gypsy, Highlander, laird, and vagrant. Ancient, even primitive, ancestors remain importantly alive within contemporary culture and peoples. But Scott's vision of inclusiveness goes only so far. The Gypsies of *Guy Mannering*, forced to leave the laird's property, are dispersed into the wider world. In *Ivanhoe* Isaac and Rebecca are exiled to Spain, and Rebecca commits herself to a celibate life of service. To be sure, Scott's Jews are saved from conversion and Meg Merrilies's influence is celebrated as benign, but the intermingling Scott imagines is cultural and transitory. The hereditary line of alien groups abruptly ends.

Scott's historical digressions and Owenson's lengthy footnotes supply the English reader with information about other nations that finds no easy place within the flow of fictional narrative. John Galt approaches the problem of fiction differently. In *Annals of the Parish* (1821) he appends no notes and eschews plot altogether. Presenting himself as editor, Galt offers the diary-like testament of an Ayrshire minister. Reverend Balwhidder includes an entry for every year between 1760 and 1810, the length of his ministry. This unself-conscious narrator of his own life includes callous comment on his succession of wives and myopic accounts of world-changing historical events. Through him Galt evokes the life and times of a Scottish parish and especially the changes that such a community witnesses in those transitional years. Lint mills burn down and cotton mills are erected; men depart for Jamaica; during the war with America recruiting parties appear in the village. Galt gives us ethnographic detail as well as history and local color, and among the most striking features of the annals is Balwhidder's use of Ayrshire dialect. He employs words like "thole," "outstrapolous," and "galravitchings" without translation or apology. English readers are instructed in a semi-foreign language as they consume a quaint but also fundamentally familiar chronicle of village life.

Novels devoted to the exploration of Ireland and Scotland are kin to forms of travel literature. The exoticism of travel narratives is relocated to nearby counties or replaced by scrutiny of the homely and familiar – the village rather than the harem, the mill rather than the temple or art gallery. In the 1820s and 1830s English writers transfer the emphasis on rural or village life that dominates the literature of Scotland and Ireland to observation of their own country. Mary Russell Mitford, whose *Our Village* (1832) bears the influence of Washington Irving's *Sketch Book* (1819–1820), explicitly compares her object of investigation – the rural village – to that of the continental tourist. "Nothing is so tiresome," she writes, "as to be whirled half over Europe at the chariot-wheels of a hero, to go to sleep in Vienna, and awaken in Madrid."[7] Readers might relish evocations of country villages in Jane Austen's novels or descriptions of Robinson Crusoe's island, but the perusal of a "small neighbourhood" is "as good in sober waking reality as in poetry or prose" (2). Going on foot, Mitford proceeds to vivify the "peculiar charm of English scenery" as well as the familiar but curious figures that populate "our village" (15). She contrasts the rural scene not only with Vienna and Madrid but with the English capital, inviting the "person newly arrived from the heat, the glare, the noise, and the fever of London, to plunge into the labyrinths of the country, and regain the repose of the mind, the calmness of heart, which has been lost in that great

Babel" (100). In Mitford's realistic sketches of ordinary life, the village becomes other, the familiar unfamiliar, and the labyrinth is transposed from urban alleyways to rural lanes.

Writing in the same decades and engaged in an enterprise similar in content and form to Mitford's, William Cobbett chooses horseback rather than tramping on foot to gain access to levels of rural reality that had not previously been represented in print. He begins *Rural Rides* (1830) by telling the reader that he wants to "see the *country*; to see the farmers at *home*, and to see the labourers *in the fields*."[8] No turnpike-roads or country inns for him, but rather the unseen life and labor of rural people, especially agricultural workers. He focuses with great interest on crops and soil, hare-hunting and sheep fairs, enclosure and exploitative landlords. His lengthy subtitle features the phrase "Economical and Political Observations," and perhaps his greatest contribution is to delineate a politics and economics of the land for his urban middle- and upper-class readers. Jane Austen, a reference point for Mitford, regards this world, as Raymond Williams has written, "from inside the houses that Cobbett was passing on the road."[9] Austen's and Cobbett's cast of characters differs radically, a matter not just of inside and out, but of class.

As Cobbett shifts the focus from gentry to laborers, he recasts the idea of the picturesque. Mitford, on foot, favors a relatively tame landscape, while Cobbett, on horseback, has access to a rougher scene. Atop the chalk hills of North Hampshire, he describes the *"hammering"* noise his horse's hoofs make on this iron-like ground, the "stiff loam" that rests on a bottom layer, twenty feet down, of chalk, the wells of water more than *"three hundred feet deep,"* and the chalk dredged up to manure the land (71–72, emphasis in the original). Organizing his sketches by date, he writes that a journey from Hambledon to Thursley on November 24 "was the most interesting day, as far as I know, that I ever passed in my life" (90). "Hawkley hangers [wood on the side of a steep hill], promontories, and stone-roads," he concludes, "will always come into my mind when I see, or hear, of picturesque views" (90). Neither Owenson's sublime Irish mountains nor Mitford's "fairy-land" of hoar-frost (Mitford, *Our Village*, 27), this dramatically elemental English countryside gives Cobbett a new literary other, a new landscape, a new picturesque.

Others within (1840–1870)

Two important Victorian texts exemplify English interest in the "others" amid them: Emily Brontë's *Wuthering Heights* (1847) and Matthew Arnold's *On the Study of Celtic Literature* (1867). Brontë's Heathcliff, a child of unknown origins plucked by Mr. Earnshaw from the streets of Liverpool and variously referred to as a "gipsy brat," a Lascar, a Spanish castaway, and an American, enters the world of the Heights and Thrushcross Grange speaking a foreign tongue – "some gibberish that nobody could understand" – and proceeds to disrupt and rearrange the patterns of two families (91, 77).[10] The quintessential outsider, Heathcliff represents the invasion and uneasy integration of the generic other into English social life. Like many of his literary relations across the Victorian novel, he allows for the examination and partial dismantling of the idea of Englishness.

Brontë's novelistic inquiry via Heathcliff into the meaning of Englishness is mirrored in Arnold's meditation, first delivered as a series of lectures at Oxford, on Celtic literature and its role in English culture. Though Arnold is interested in identifying the essential qualities of Celtic "spirit" and "sensibility," he is equally, if not primarily, concerned with their influence on Englishness. He understands that Celtic culture is constituted by language, land, history, and subject status. The Celtic language in Ireland is "the badge of the beaten race, the property of the vanquished." Nonetheless, like Heathcliff reordering the Earnshaw–Linton lineage, Celtic culture has infiltrated Englishness, infusing it with the lasting and necessary legacy of energy, melancholy, and "natural magic." As a result of the acquisition of these qualities, which verge on caricature (Celtic sensibility is "feminine," "defiant," "extravagant," and has "fairy charm"), English writers can achieve poetic distinction. Celtic literature on the other hand, rather like the barren line of Heathcliff, contributes to the greatness of other cultures but never quite achieves its own. Celtic poetry possesses an "unsurpassable intensity, elevation, and effect" but can neither "master the world" nor "give an adequate interpretation of it." [11]

A host of Victorian writers look at alien others within the culture and economy of the city and, with ethnographic acumen, catalogue the occupations, slang, marital habits, religious practices, and financial dealings of the working- and underclass of London and the industrial towns. Foremost among these is Henry Mayhew, who adapts the ethnographic sketches that Cobbett, Mitford, and Galt use to portray rural life to present the life and labor of the urban *lumpenproletariat*. In his articles for the *Morning Chronicle*, later amplified and published as the four-volume *London Labour and the London Poor* (1851–1852), Mayhew interviews and describes the street workers of the metropolis who remained nearly invisible and largely unknown to a middle-class audience: costermongers, river dredgers, mudlarks, dustmen, prostitutes, and vagrants. As he divides costers into sellers of various items, he also breaks down the urban poor into ethnic communities, most prominently Irish and Jewish. In the first section, titled "Of Wandering Tribes in General," of volume I, Mayhew identifies himself as an "ethnologist" who studies "wanderers and settlers." Redefining otherness in anthropological terms, he asserts that his street-folk are to "citizens" of the city what "nomadic" peoples are to "civilized tribes."[12] The two groups occupy different but interdependent spheres of a shared culture. Just as their versions of the English language differ, so, too, do their customs and beliefs. They constitute a newly observed and recorded urban English world.

In Mayhew's work, as in the works of other mid-nineteenth century writers, Jews and Irish cease to be the exotics and foreigners of Scott and Owenson and appear as fixtures of an urban landscape internal to England. Jews figure prominently in the London sketches and fictions of Charles Dickens, mainly as street people, criminals, shopkeepers, and moneylenders, while Irish take center stage in literary and social scientific evocations as immigrants and workers in the industrial towns of the north of England. In "Meditations in Monmouth Street," one of the *Sketches by Boz* (1836), Dickens introduces his readers to the second-hand clothing trade. Not Mayhew's Jewish hawkers of old clothes bleating out the cry of "'Clo'! 'Clo'!," these Jews have moved into their own shops and become overbearing, "the red-headed and red-whiskered Jews," Boz writes, "who forcibly haul you into a suit of clothes, whether you will or not." [13] Jews populate Dickens's novels, especially the early ones, mainly as minor fixtures of the urban scene. With Fagin, Jewish denizen of the criminal underworld in *Oliver Twist*, however, Dickens creates a memorable Jewish character, disturbing in his predatory and exploitative relationship to small boys and women alike and oddly compelling in his flamboyant, threatening demeanor. "As he glided stealthily along, creeping beneath the shelter of the walls and doorways," Dickens writes of a primordial, atavistic Fagin, "the hideous old man seemed like some loathsome reptile, engendered in the slime and darkness through which he moved: crawling forth, by night, in search of some rich offal for a meal."[14]

Dickens answered concerns about the anti-Semitic aspects of Fagin's characterization by creating another Jew, Riah, friend to Jenny Wren and Lizzie Hexam and apparent usurer in *Our Mutual Friend* (1864–1865).[15] This Jew turns out to be only the front man for a Gentile moneylender, and his exoneration constitutes a form of apology for the offense Dickens had caused with Fagin. Both of Dickens's principal Jewish figures, and most of his incidental ones, are attached to the cash nexus, their suspected or real crimes a form of theft. This association between Jew and illicit money-making is a deeply held tenet of anti-Semitic thinking in the nineteenth century. Anthony Trollope's novels also feature usurious Jews, more likely to be from the high capitalist class than Dickens's street Jews. Melmotte, the swindler-speculator at the heart of *The Way We Live Now* (1875), is never identified as a Jew, though he is taken to be one and offered by Trollope as the quintessential outsider who passes, for a time, as insider.

If the Jew appears in mid-century fiction as *homo economicus*, the typical Irishman takes the role of impoverished worker, often unemployed, alcoholic, and profligate. In *The Condition of the Working Class in England* (1845) Friedrich Engels describes the Irish in Manchester as barely human: "this race," he writes of the inhabitants of Little Ireland, "must really have reached the lowest stage of humanity."[16] Continuing his description of them as a race apart, he remarks on their "Celtic faces," "singing, aspirate brogue," and "Irish-Celtic language," but he extends the defamation by representing the Irish as savages, drunkards, and lovers of pigs (123, 124–125). Most salient for Engels is the "degrading influence" Irish workers have on the English proletariat. "The whole character of the [English] working-class assimilates a great part of the Irish characteristics," he writes, and in time all wages and all workers sink to the lowest common denominator (125). For Engels, Irishness has become the identifying mark of the English proletariat.

The industrial north, with Manchester as its epicenter, spawned a sub-genre of the novel that, as Raymond Williams phrased it, illustrated the "facts of the new society" and, more importantly, its "structure of feeling."[17] Those "facts" include a new set of others: a class of workers, a type of manufacturing and the edifices – factories – where it took place, upwardly mobile manufacturers, industrial towns, and the North of England itself, now an economically and even politically powerful sector of England. The "structure of feeling" that grew up as a response to those facts reflects middle-class fears, sympathy, and revulsion, and, in turn, generates a set of narrative conventions. Elizabeth Gaskell's *North and South* (1855) makes the industrial city and the north of England into virtual protagonists, and the cultural and geographic divisions of the country into a romantic plot. Class strife and reconciliation figure in almost all industrial fictions, as do accounts of starvation, working-class dwellings, strikes, and conditions of labor. In *Mary Barton* (1848) Gaskell introduces her readers to the "new" language of Lancashire dialect and provides definitions of words like "nesh" (tender), "farrantly" (comely), "clem" (to starve), and "mither" (to trouble) in her notes. What might have been exotic in Owenson – a foreign culture, with its separate language and rites – takes on a different status in the industrial novel, with its strong implications that unknown and barely recognizable cultures exist within English borders.

The rural explorations of the 1820s continue into the middle of the century. Although Jews rarely figure in novels of country life, Gypsies are staples of the rural scene. The Irish appear as migrants to English cities but also as citizens of their native country in novels like Trollope's *Castle Richmond* (1860) and *The Landleaguers* (unfinished at Trollope's death in 1883) and William Carleton's *The Black Prophet: A Tale of the Famine* (1847). Both *Castle Richmond* and *The Black Prophet* tell the story of the potato famine, the former through a typical inheritance plot and the latter in the context of a murder and detective story. Carleton extends and deepens the gothic elements in Owenson, and Trollope's *Castle Richmond* includes isolated descriptions of heartbreaking poverty, but in each of these novels the famine, the ravished land, and the brutal facts of Irish history are undigested aspects of narrative, integrated into neither plot nor development of character. Here, narrative fiction seems a form inhospitable to social and political realities.

More conducive to the evocation of otherness in the mid-century is George Borrow's idiosyncratic form of fiction, a hybrid of travelogue, autobiography, *Bildungsroman*, love story, pastoral, and picaresque. In *Lavengro* (1851) and its sequel, *Romany Rye* (1857), Borrow tells the story of his life on the road and among the Romany, the Gypsies of Britain. Like many English writers who take a sympathetic interest in Gypsies, Borrow feels out of place in his family, an ungainly child who survived his more favored brother's death. He leaves home to find his place in the world – a standard feature of *Bildung* – and, after a failed attempt to make his way in London, settles into a vagabond life in the countryside among the people with whom he feels the greatest affinity, the Romany. Among the remarkable features of Borrow's work, perhaps the most salient is his obsession with languages. His alter ego, Lavengro, derives his name from the Romany word for "word master," and, in the course of the fiction-memoir, he learns Irish, Hebrew, Arabic, Danish, and, of course, Romani. For Borrow–Lavengro foreign language takes the place of family, romance, and ambition and comes to define his very identity, origins, and purpose. At the center of all is Romani, the language he comes to believe might "turn out to be the mother of all languages in the world," a "picklock, an open sesame" to all others.[18] Romani reveals the mysteries of linguistic correspondences ("tanner" signifies a sixpence to a Cockney, a little child to an English Gypsy), but it might also open the door to history (196). In Borrow's eyes the primitivism of Gypsy life, reviled by some as degraded, holds the secret of human origins.

The elements of family romance detectable in Borrow's work appear fully elaborated in the fictions of George Eliot, the novelist of the period most profoundly engaged with otherness. Heir to Walter Scott, Eliot devoted entire works to Gypsy and Jewish plots. Descendant of Mary Russell Mitford, she committed herself to the realistic representation of ordinary rural life. Beginning with *Scenes of Clerical Life* (1858) and continuing through *Adam Bede* (1859), *The Mill on the Floss* (1860), *Silas Marner* (1861), and *Middlemarch* (1871–1872), Eliot's narratives focus on unconventional individuals struggling to find their place in provincial societies. She often represents the singularity of these outsiders as a difference of physical type or race. In *Middlemarch* Will Ladislaw's neighbors ridicule him as a Gypsy, Jew, Corsican, or an "Italian with white mice."[19] Maggie Tulliver, the rebellious, dark-haired and dark-skinned heroine of *The Mill on the Floss*, regards herself as a kind of foundling, resembling neither her mother nor her fair cousin Lucy but rather a woman she encounters in a Gypsy camp after she runs away from home. Maggie refers to Scott and de Staël's paradigm of dark and light heroines to evoke her own relationship to Lucy, and her neighbors comment on her bodily difference from other women.[20] A racialized heroine like de Staël's Corinne, Owenson's Glorvina, and Scott's Rebecca, Maggie, unlike these other women, never discovers a country or identity that allows her to survive her difference.

Like Lavengro, Maggie seeks her own true kin. Like him, she imagines herself the child of otherness and of other parents. When Eliot came to write *The Spanish Gypsy* (1868), a narrative poem, and *Daniel Deronda* (1874–1876), she made literal the fantasy of family romance. Fedalma, a Spanish princess, turns out to be the daughter of a Gypsy chieftain, and Deronda, an English gentleman's adopted son, turns out to be a Jew. Both protagonists feel the calling of some vocation associated with their otherness, even before they understand its exact nature. Instead of languishing as outsiders or frustrated anomalies within the communities they occupy, they each set sail for a homeland of their own. Eliot attempts to solve the problem of otherness by making it inborn and hereditary, not just existential, and by giving those who discover their otherness a community and nation elsewhere.

Others and moderns (1870–1900)

In his 1897 essay "The Celtic Element in Literature," W. B. Yeats revises Arnold's *Study of Celtic Literature* by questioning the notion that the "natural magic" Arnold attributes to Celtic forms is a feature confined to Irish culture and poetry. Rather, Yeats emphasizes, this "magic" had a broader genesis and meaning and is "but the ancient religion of the world, the ancient worship of

Nature and that troubled ecstasy before her."²¹ Where Arnold perceives Celtic influences, Yeats sees what is ancient, elemental, and universal; what Arnold regards as "Celtic melancholy," Yeats understands as "primitive melancholy" (183). In Yeats's view the other turns out to be all of us. His general understanding of folk literature, myth, and legend echoes the beliefs of folklorists and philologists in the last decades of the nineteenth century who saw in these forms structures of thought and expression common to all humankind. He defines the English relationship to Nature as "modern," the "way of people who have forgotten the ancient religion" (178). In juxtaposition to this kind of writing Yeats places folklore and folk literature, those revivifying forces that might, in some rare instances, make their way into contemporary literature and art (180). At the end of the essay he suggests that a new literature might derive its symbols from the legends, myths, and tales of old, that folklore might provide the origins of a new modernism.

Thomas Hardy, novelistic chronicler of a slightly fictionalized west country of England, uses the dissonance and interplay between ancient and modern to animate his narratives. From the remains of the old Roman Road that runs through Egdon Heath in *The Return of the Native* (1878) to Stonehenge, where Tess ends her days in *Tess of the d'Urbervilles* (1891), and the ancient walls of Christminster in *Jude the Obscure* (1895), Hardy's Wessex constantly reminds us of the ineluctable presence of the deep past within the modern era. This ancient past constitutes a form of otherness in *fin-de-siècle* England. In the first chapter of *The Return of the Native*, the narrator evokes Egdon Heath by meditating on the relationship between the ancient and the new: "to know that everything around and underneath had been from prehistoric times ... gave ballast to the mind adrift on change, and harassed by the irrepressible New."²² Clym Yeobright, the "native" who returns, is a hybrid, a creature formed by modernity, whose face reveals "the typical countenance of the future" (171). He tries to come to terms with the heath, a place that seems to have "slipped out of its century generations ago," and to cast his lot with enlightenment even while maintaining fealty to the ancient essence of the place (178). Clym's fate is to become a kind of ancient, a blind preacher traveling the land, stuck in the world of the heath. Eustacia Vye, the woman who sees Clym as her means of escape to cosmopolitanism, drowns before she can leave the landscape. Older, primitive forces compete with modern yearnings to claim the souls of Hardy's characters.

Hardy's interest in otherness derives from identification with a particular English geography and its ancient past rather than from an association with a national or ethnic minority. He does not share in what motivates Yeats's response to Arnold: a *fin-de-siècle* trend in which a growing number of out-siders, especially Irish and Jewish writers, author texts about their own people. Writers at the end of the century exhibit a new freedom of perspective and expression that allows for a Yeatsian universalizing of their cultures. At the same time, however, these outsiders also feel free to assume a critical and even a satiric stance toward their own communities.

Amy Levy's *Reuben Sachs* (1889) depicts London Jewish life from the inside and focusses on the striving Jewish middle class. Levy, a poet and novelist educated at Cambridge, does not spare her co-religionists. Underscoring the crassness of the eponymous hero's family, Levy earned the disapprobation of many Jewish readers. One cynical member of the novel's Sachs family remarks of a Gentile friend: "I think that he was shocked at finding us so little like the people in *Daniel Deronda* . . . Ours [is] the religion of materialism. The corn and the wine and the oil; the multiplication of the seed; the conquest of the hostile tribes – these have always had more attraction for us than the harp and crown of a spiritual existence."[23] Not only does Levy indict upper-bourgeois Jewish life, but she also creates a poor, respectable Jewish heroine, Judith Quixano, who attracts a Gentile husband because of the stereotypical exoticism he associates with Jewish women. Levy gestures to the bigotry of conventional representation even as she pillories her own people.

Israel Zangwill was one of the English Jews who initially reacted with dismay to the unflattering image of Jewry in Levy's novel, but he reversed himself after Levy's untimely death by asserting that she had merely told the truth about the foibles of English Jews.[24] Zangwill's approach to such short-comings in *Children of the Ghetto* (1892) proves to be far gentler than Levy's bitter satire, but he imparts with great frankness an extraordinary amount of information about his own people to a largely enthusiastic, wide British audience. His cast of Jewish characters is tremendously varied. It includes penniless East Enders and prosperous entrepreneurs; Zionists and leftists; students of Talmud and students who, like young Solomon Ansell, prefer the adventures of Daredevil Dick; Jews from Poland, Germany, Holland, and Russia; Ashkenazim and Sephardim. Like Levy, Zangwill also debunks stereo-types. Referring back to Mayhew, as Dickens had done in *Our Mutual Friend*, he muses on the old Jewish peddler, the "three-hatted scarecrow of Christian caricature, who shambles along snuffling 'Old clo'," but who, in reality, has "a strenuous inner life."[25] Zangwill's ethnography is remarkable not so much for what it takes in as for what it gives out. The narrative educates its reader in religious practice, internecine debates, favorite foods, and multiple languages. Not only do characters and narrator regularly employ Yiddish, Hebrew,

German, and Russian, but there is also an extensive glossary at the back of the novel for readers to consult. Like Owenson, Scott, Galt, Gaskell, and Borrow, Zangwill translates the "gibberish" of the other for the English reader, at once making comprehensible the speech of the alien and transforming the English language.

Two years after *Children of the Ghetto* appeared, the Irish novelists Edith Somerville and Martin Ross (Violet Martin) published *The Real Charlotte* (1894), an unforgiving send-up of the Protestant Ascendancy in Ireland. In the small town of Lismoyle, the Irish gentry exhibits signs of decline and struggles to hold its own against the English aristocrats who preside over the town's social life and own much of its land. Young and beautiful Francine Fitzpatrick is sent away from Dublin by her failing family to board with her scheming middle-class cousin Charlotte Mullen. Roddy Lambert laments that Irishmen can only make money by selling drink. And Julia Duffy, who remembers the grand and gracious past of her landowning father, now lives in squalor, about to be "processed" for arrears on her rent. Grasping, climbing Charlotte works assiduously to take advantage of others' misfortunes, to exploit Francine's beauty for her own ends, and to gouge the poor washerwomen who live in her slum property. The increasing bleakness of the Irish landscape is matched by the bleak future of the Protestant Ascendancy, symbolized by the loveless marriage and accidental death of the *ingénue* Francine.

Though Somerville and Martin take a satiric view, they also chronicle the daily existence and popular culture of Irish life, introducing English readers to traditions of pantomime and song, much as Zangwill introduces them to *kugel* and the meaning of *chutzpah*. Like Disraeli, who sees the rich and poor of England as separate nations, "inhabitants of different planets," the later novelists, following Owenson, Scott, Mayhew, Eliot, and others, strive to represent and translate otherness. Ethnographers all, they weave the details and plots of alien lives into the fabric of English fiction and of Englishness itself.

Notes

1. Benjamin Disraeli, *Sybil or the Two Nations* (Harmondsworth: Penguin, 1980), p. 95.
2. Linda Colley, *Britons: Forging the Nation, 1707–1837* (New Haven, CT: Yale University Press, 1992).
3. Terry Eagleton, *Heathcliff and the Great Hunger: Studies in Irish Culture* (London: Verso, 1995), p. 208.
4. Sydney Owenson, Lady Morgan, *The Wild Irish Girl* (Oxford University Press, 1999), p. 176.

5. Walter Scott, *Guy Mannering, or, The Astrologer*, 2 vols. (Boston: Estes and Lauriat, 1892), vol. I, p. 157.

6. Michael Ragussis, *Figures of Conversion: "The Jewish Question" and English National Identity* (Durham, NC: Duke University Press, 1995), p. 100.

7. Mary Russell Mitford, *Our Village* (Poole, New York: Woodstock Books, 1996), p. 2.

8. William Cobbett, *Rural Rides* (Baltimore, MD: Penguin, 1967), p. 31.

9. Raymond Williams, *The Country and the City* (London: Chatto and Windus, 1973), p. 112.

10. Emily Brontë, *Wuthering Heights* (Harmondsworth: Penguin, 1965), pp. 91, 77.

11. Matthew Arnold, "On the Study of Celtic Literature," in *Matthew Arnold: Poetry and Prose*, ed. John Bryson (London: Rupert Hart-Davis, 1967), pp. 471, 475, 474, 479.

12. Henry Mayhew, *London Labour and the London Poor*, 4 vols. (New York: Dover, 1968), vol. I, p. 1. Volume I, *The London Street-Folk* (partial), contains an entry on "The Street Irish" (pp. 104–120) and volume II, *The London Street-Folk* (continued), an essay on "The Street Jews" (pp. 115–136).

13. Charles Dickens, *Sketches by Boz* (London: Penguin, 1995), p. 96.

14. Charles Dickens, *Oliver Twist* (Harmondsworth: Penguin, 1985), p. 186.

15. For the story of Dickens, Fagin, and Riah, see Lauriat Lane, "Dickens' Archetypal Jew," *PMLA* 73: 1 (1958), 94–100, and Harry Stone, "Dickens and the Jews," *Victorian Studies* 2 (1959), 223–253.

16. Friedrich Engels, *The Condition of the Working Class in England* (London: Granada, 1969), p. 93.

17. Raymond Williams, *Culture and Society, 1780–1950* (Harmondsworth: Penguin, 1961), p. 99.

18. George Borrow, *Lavengro* (New York: Dover, 1991), pp. 267, 196.

19. George Eliot, *Middlemarch* (London: Penguin, 1994), p. 490.

20. George Eliot, *The Mill on the Floss* (London: Penguin, 1985), pp. 433, 621.

21. W. B. Yeats, "The Celtic Element in Literature," *Essays and Introductions* (London: Macmillan, 1961), p. 176.

22. Thomas Hardy, *The Return of the Native* (New York: Barnes and Noble, 2005), p. 14.

23. Amy Levy, *Reuben Sachs*, ed. Susan David Bernstein (Toronto, ON: Broadview Press, 2006), p. 100.

24. Susan David Bernstein, Introduction to *Reuben Sachs*, p. 39.

25. Israel Zangwill, *Children of the Ghetto: A Study of a Peculiar People* (London: Macmillan, 1932), p. 66.

21

Dickens, Charlotte Brontë, Gaskell: politics and its limits

AMANDA ANDERSON

The nineteenth-century political novel poses a continuing challenge to literary critics and literary historians. Whether identified as "the industrial novel," "the social-problem novel," or, the denomination I favor, "the political novel," this particular genre has proved notoriously difficult to characterize and to classify. Generally, novels are placed into this category because they treat conditions and crises occasioned by the industrial revolution in Britain: the discontent and misery of the working classes; the negative effects of a world increasingly dominated by machinery, alienated labor, and the profit motive; and, not least, the impact of worker uprisings, strikes, and violence (with the example of the French Revolution always in the background). Beyond this constellation of concerns, there is one other key feature of the mid-nineteenth century political novel in England – it tends to position itself as an intervention. In addressing the problems it exposes, that is, the political novel proffers some sort of solution, even if that solution is only the reading of the novel itself (which thereby allows for insight into under-recognized problems, or prompts sympathy for suffering, or otherwise effects a transformation in the reader that might enable a constructive approach to the problems depicted). The nineteenth-century political novel is, in a word, typically sincere, regardless of its ideological orientation.

I propose to examine a number of novels that traditionally fall within this classification, but I will also expand the rubric of the political novel so that it comprehends a broader range of novelistic projects. In doing so, I follow the more capacious definition of the political novel provided by Irving Howe in *Politics and the Novel*. Howe defines the political novel as "a novel in which political ideas play a dominant role or in which the political milieu is the dominant setting."[1] This definition might seem overly elastic, but my aim is to cast a wide net so as to be able to specify more concretely, across a range of literary examples, how politics is understood, and in particular what its limits are imagined to be. There is a well-established body of criticism tracking the conceptual and formal economies of the industrial novel, and one consistent feature of such criticism is the tendency to see competing narrative foci as indicative of a political evasion that is fundamentally conservative in nature. For example, romantic storylines in industrial novels are thought to draw attention away from the political plot, and to enforce a sense of resolution and stability through marriage. Similarly, inconsistencies of mode – among melodrama, tragedy, political argument, documentary realism, and religious homily – are often read as indications of ideologically conditioned impasses. Criticism of this genre remains strongly influenced by Raymond Williams's claim that these novels characteristically give voice to conservative anxieties about unrest or change, and seek to evade politics by redirecting attention to the sphere of moral concern, with its more reassuring scale of aspiration and practice (self-transformation and sympathy).[2]

It is worth pausing, however, before making confident assertions about where a writer or text, let alone a whole genre, falls on the ideological spectrum. Novels are often deemed conservative or liberal (in a pejorative sense) because insufficiently political or radical. Apart from its near tautological form, this judgment reflects a tendency to undervalue, or even dismiss, literary treatments of non-activist forms of politics (politics de-linked from working-class mobilization, grievance, and strike), and to identify non-activist politics with quietist forms of economic liberalism or bourgeois modernity. Lost to view are a range of political forms treated within the novel, including parliamentary and procedural forms, institutional politics, political philosophy, deliberative politics, political argument, and demagogic modes. It is also worth reconsidering the assumption that political novels flee the demands of political life when they accord value to realms outside of politics. In many cases such novels are presenting complex and fluid forms of politics waged in relation to complex and fluid conditions of human existence. In some cases they emphasize an incommensurability between politics and literature. As Howe stresses, any noteworthy aesthetic engagement with politics – whatever the primary political orientations of a text or author might be – will not express political commitment in any simple way; rather, it will be exercised by the complexity of trying to live or enact or promote the political ideals it engages.

This chapter focusses on novels by Charles Dickens, Elizabeth Gaskell, and Charlotte Brontë, with a view to expanding the conception of the relation among politics, form, and ideology. To provide further context, I discuss a number of other novels, including a sample from the early twentieth century. There are several areas of focus. First, I show how many novels use a dynamic formal relation between narratorial and characterological perspectives to work through (or, alternately, act out) key conceptual problems. The tension between the third- and first-person perspectives often reflects a tension between theoretical and existential orientations or, to put it somewhat differently, between a systemic critique largely negative in its assessments, and those moral and practical orientations that might counteract the negative forces under analysis. Second, I will show that the mode of argument, as advanced by the narrator and as engaged in by the characters, is a crucial formal and dramatic feature of the political novel. Argument is often (but by no means necessarily) expressive of a kind of liberal energy that is overlooked in readings that privilege plot closure over other forms. And third, I consider how and when authors conceive of politics as having limits (beyond which one can locate forces that exceed it), and how and when they see politics as linked to, or expressed through, those forces (among those forces I would include art, violence, desire, death, nature, morality, and psychology). I take as axiomatic that different writers conceive the world differently, and that any general theory of the politics of the novel will falter. But there are some useful generalities of form that will allow us to disclose more fully the visions of the authors under discussion.

I begin with Dickens's *Hard Times* (1854), a novel routinely included in the canon of industrial novels. This novel merits attention not only because it is anomalous with respect to Dickens's canon, but also because it departs in important ways from the conventions of the traditional political novel. The critique of utilitarianism mounted by Dickens is ultimately a critique of ideology as fundamentally inadequate to an understanding of human existence. His is therefore an anti-ideological novel, and in a stronger sense than some other industrial novels, such as Gaskell's *North and South* (1855), that stress the complexity of life over the poverty of theory. In its own way, moreover, *Hard Times* is as formally innovative as *Bleak House* (1853); its estranging formal features suggest that established novelistic conventions cannot accommodate self-conscious critique of ideology. *Hard Times* stands out for its taut and compressed quality, its likeness to moral fable rather than realistic narrative, and, perhaps most strikingly, its lack of any typical hero or heroine (we are presented rather with a symbolic configuration of characters, some of whom are morally privileged, and set pieces in which they figure). And, significantly, this novel does not end in marriage, a feature I will discuss presently.[3]

Hard Times represents not only the impossibility of actualizing utilitarian theory, but also the dangers associated with trying to do so – the distorting and maiming effects on personality and moral life that result from attempts to enact or instill a systematic theory. What the novel puts in place of theory is not, as is often asserted, the life of the imagination or the life of feelings, but rather the importance of inspirational moral exemplars. Here Dickens takes a strong stand for persons as over and against either theories or institutions. Through his treatment of Stephen Blackpool's relation to Rachel, and several characters' relation to Sissy Jupe, Dickens implies that one should orient oneself morally not toward principles or theories, but towards an exemplar, a moral hero. (It is no accident that the novel is dedicated to Thomas Carlyle.) Indeed, in the case of Stephen's promising to Rachel that he would not be involved in the labor union, explanation is entirely eschewed, and therefore all position-taking, and ideology itself, becomes moot. He made a promise to her, and he will keep it. We are not told why he made this promise; we are only reminded that he sees Rachel as infallible, as capable of saving his soul. Similarly, Sissy's influence helps to prepare Mr. Gradgrind for conversion, and she serves as an orienting moral beacon after Louisa's crisis.

But the pervading darkness in which these beacons glimmer is intense, and there is more at play than a demonstration of the failure of social engineering. Two aspects of the novel, both expressive of inexorable fate, stand out in this regard: the intense suffering of Louisa Gradgrind, and the trials, and eventual death, of Stephen Blackpool. We might simply read Louisa as the maimed outcome of utilitarian upbringing, but such a reading would fail to capture fully her function in the novel. Louisa represents what exceeds the reach of fact and reason: her tendency to stare into the fire represents inaccessible interiority and an unmet (and possibly combustible) desire. Her non-liberatory self-awareness – negative, dissatisfied, restlessly critical – is diametrically opposed to the protected innocent sincerity of Sissy Jupe. The gap between the two characters is a playing out of the novel's own divided mentality, its unresolved tension between its pervading satirical assessments and its affirmative values. The narrative fascination with Louisa, mirrored by the cynical, dandiacal artist figure Harthouse's fascination with her, isolates tortured consciousness and divided impulse as key objects of aesthetic/erotic interest. The novel is thus pulled away from simple moralizing to a more complex understanding of the gap between social critique and moral aspiration, which it aestheticizes through the figure of Louisa. It is the novel's commitment to this volatilized dynamic that precludes conventional romantic closure, or a standard marriage plot. Separated from Bounderby, Louisa remains an unsettled, live interest, in contrast to Stephen Blackpool, whose death in an abandoned mineshaft evokes not so much industrial negligence as the larger force of universal fate. As Stephen says to Rachel when he lies dying, "When it [the mine] were in work, it killed wi'out need; when 'tis let alone, it kills wi'out need. See how we die an no need, one way an another – in a muddle – every day!"[4] This statement is closer to the vision of Thomas Hardy than to anything else: the naturalism of Blackpool's story, and the irresolvability of Louisa's, show with special power the impersonal forces that thwart the moral and political ambitions of individuals. The critique of political ideology is also centrally about what lies beyond the horizon of any political or sociological framework.

The dual narrative form of *Bleak House* heightens the question of whether any mediation is possible or desirable between the systemic perspective – the totalizing critique of power, society, and institutions – and the perspective of the embedded social actor. It can appear as if the novel aims to champion the David of moral autonomy against the Goliath of social totality, with Esther Summerson asserting her small voice, and her notion of the expanding circles of duty, against the airless, power-laden world of the third-person narrative. But the striking thing about *Bleak House* is that it seems not so much insistent on a moral gap between the first- and third-person narratives, as obsessed with how one might mediate between the two, given the insights that each advances. By and large, Esther's narrative expresses the voice of moral aspiration, and the third-person narrative enacts a particularly searing and bleak form of sociological critique. But their separation is not absolute, and there are a range of mediations between the two, both formal (having to do with character and plot) and rhetorical (having to do with narrative voice). Moreover, tensions between the two narratives, and mediations of them, provide the key aesthetic and interpretive interest of the text. There are figures at home in both narratives, such as Woodcourt, and Bucket, and Esther herself, who essentially gets abducted into the third-person story. Woodcourt can mediate effectively between the forms of knowledge and access associated with the third-person narrative and the values and modes associated with Esther's narrative. This mediation contrasts with the counter-motion represented by Richard, who is slowly destroyed, morally and physically, by his entry into the world of the third-person narrative. Equally interesting are the rhetorical disjunctions. The third-person narrative's strange use of the simple present and its foregrounding of epistemological issues – who knows what? who suspects whom of what? – gives the effect of a world ruled by entrenched power, strategic agency, and corrosive self-interest; and yet it is interrupted by odd moments of moral excoriation that make it seem as though a character has entered the scene to disrupt the impersonal narrative performance.

Conversely, the Esther narrative at times reaches for a larger view, as when Esther wonders why the education system failed to develop Richard's full potential. But perhaps the most interesting and unsettling cross-over moment takes place when the third-person narrator attempts to understand what it is like to be the illiterate Jo:

> It must be a strange state to be like Jo! To shuffle through the streets, unfamiliar with the shapes, and in utter darkness as to the meaning, of those mysterious symbols, so abundant over the shops, and at the corners of streets, and on the doors, and in the windows! To see people read, and to see people write, and to see the postmen deliver letters, and not to have the least idea of all that language – to be, to every scrap of it, stone blind and dumb! It must be very puzzling, to see the good company going to the churches on Sundays, with their books in their hands, and to think (for perhaps Jo does think, at odd times) what does it all mean, and if it means anything to anybody, how comes it that it means nothing to me?[5]

The passage forces the reader to break out of the comfort of being moved by scenes of sympathy between characters, and to contemplate instead the effect of reading about the lives of those who are profoundly socially marginalized. Rather than seeing the third-person narrative as simply capturing the conditions of pervasive power, then, it seems more interesting to think of the novel as a complex formal enactment of the estranging but also enabling consequences of attempting to think the moral and the sociological perspectives in relation to one another. The novel uses the informing tension between first- and third-person perspectives to help promote such thinking; and it indirectly makes the case for enlisting narrative's formal resources as a way to move beyond limiting conceptual approaches to poverty and social injustice. It therefore makes a claim for the aesthetic as a power that can further moral, political, and social understanding, in part through occasional breachings of the structuring gap between sociological and moral perspectives. The implications are more hopeful here than they are in *Hard Times*, where the aesthetic interest in Louisa's tortured consciousness seems to eclipse, rather than channel, the concerns of a morally conscientious social critic. A similar eclipsing effect is created by figures like Rosa Dartle in *David Copperfield* (1849–1850), or Miss Wade in *Little Dorrit* (1857).

Elizabeth Gaskell's novels have often been adduced as exercises in political evasion. Rather than truly confront problems of urban industrialism, the criticism goes, Gaskell appeals to an ethic of sympathy that ultimately upholds the status quo and enforces the power of the middle class. Even though she is credited with interesting formal innovations and a commitment to portraying working-class culture and life, there is often a sense that the novels disappoint, both in their failure to proffer solutions adequate to the problem depicted and in their tendency to allow romantic plots to eclipse the political substance.

Certainly, marks of class-based unease are discernible in Gaskell's novels, especially in *Mary Barton* (1848), where the narrator seems particularly anxious to contextualize and explain the violence of the workers, on the one hand, and the immovability of the masters, on the other. But Gaskell's fiction also represents a powerful working through of the challenges attending emergent democratic modernity. The industrial novel is a key precursor to the novel of ideas, and is pathbreaking in its presentation of ideological and philosophical positions. Much of this work is done through the mode of (embedded) argument. Gaskell is interestingly self-conscious about this, even going so far as to show how inhospitable the traditional novel is to the mode of argumentative dialogue about matters political. The central example here would be the scene, in *Mary Barton*'s eighth chapter, in which the romance plot is ambushed by the political plot. Jem Wilson, an industrious and apolitical young worker, has come to visit his love interest, Mary Barton. The chapter frames the scene through Jem's eyes, and he is anxious and distracted when Mary's father, John Barton, holds forth on economic and political issues, promoting the workers' cause. But the chapter performs an interesting volte-face, forcing the reader, by way of a long narratorial intervention that interrupts the chapter's focalization through Jem, to pay attention to the issues that John has been discussing. This tactic is a self-conscious reframing of formal conventions so as to redirect audiences toward a new form of novelistic, readerly scrutiny of social and political problems.

More interesting still is Gaskell's use, in *North and South* (1855), of a mode of argumentative dialogue to forward romantic and political plots simultaneously. Almost entirely abandoning her use of a moderating, appeasing narrator, Gaskell places the substance of ideological disagreement in dialogues between Margaret Hale and Mr. Thornton, and between the workers and members of the middle class. Margaret and Mr. Thornton argue over the relative merits of Christian responsibility, on the one hand, and economic liberalism on the other (though Mr. Thornton also espouses a strong form of paternalistic authority). And, interestingly, what emerges as the guiding value at the end of the novel is precisely the need for ongoing dialogue. While it is certainly the case that what prevails is a Christianized liberalism that favors the continued power of the current system, refined through modest reforms, it seems important to register Gaskell's privileging of continuing collective deliberation, which is a primary component of democratic practice, and which crucially counters the sense of closure wrought by the romantic plot. It is worth considering more fully the literary history of this formal feature. Beginning with Austen's *Pride and Prejudice* (1813), a romantically charged form of socially and politically critical dialogue has been a key element of the courtship novel, and it is interesting to note where argument stands at the conclusion of Austen's narrative. While *Pride and Prejudice* legitimates a reformed Pemberley, it does so in large part by holding up the relation between Darcy and Elizabeth as exemplary. And what is the form of that relationship? It is one that privileges argumentation and the bringing of the energy of attraction to the service of direct, extensive, and mutually improving debate. Argument is important, because it keeps critique and self-examination vital. There is no question that the sharpness of Elizabeth's critique has been softened, but the active air of challenge and debate is very much alive at the end of the novel, where we read that Elizabeth's habit of challenging Darcy is instructive to Georgiana, effectively schooling the next half-generation in a mode of lively debate. What is innovative about *North and South* is the insistence that the energy of debate will continue within the institutional sphere of the factory, supported by the forms that were put in play through the "antagonistic friendship" of Margaret and Mr. Thornton.[6] To imagine that Gaskell's use of marriage to close the narrative downgrades the important role played by argument in revisioning class relations is to read simplistically in terms of plot. This is an all-too-common tendency in readings of the industrial novel.

In Gaskell politics is generally conceived in two ways – as irruptive and violent, and as reformist and institutional. In either case political commitments tend to take shape in response not only to events in the social or political sphere but also, and more immediately, to experiences of catastrophic personal loss that suspend the forms of domestic, familial everydayness underwriting moral strength and sympathetic engagement with others. The abrupt loss of such grounding, typically through the death of a parent or child, is the catalyst for political awakening, of either the violent or the more piecemeal, reformist kind. Violence is seen as the wrong moral choice, though Gaskell often stresses that it is a result of desperation. Interestingly, an experience of violence can serve to redirect individuals toward the more desirable form of piecemeal, reformist politics. For Gaskell life in the economic sphere – in the factory or the workplace – should ideally foster forms of collaborative exchange similar to those that characterize everyday domestic life. The fact that Thornton's house abuts his factory is not a confusion of spheres but a promising proximity, one that supports his eventual commitment to engage in habitual and familiar forms of interaction with his workers.

Gaskell's interest in loss as a form of experience that exceeds, yet also prompts, the social, action-oriented character of political life speaks to a more general tension in the political novel between the immediately felt social problems of the day, and those ineluctable, and typically harsh, experiences associated with universal conditions of existence – loss, fate, nature, human nature, violence, and isolation. It impoverishes our understanding of these novels if we deem them evasive or conservative when they acknowledge forces that exceed the political. Charlotte Brontë's *Shirley* (1849), for example, is often classed as a conservative novel, despite its formal oddities. On the surface it reprises familiar elements of the industrial novel, especially in its admixture of concern for working-class suffering and fear of working-class violence. As in Gaskell's novels, there is an industrial entrepreneur (Robert Moore), who both strongly defends the values of progressive industrialism (science and progress) and goes through a kind of conversion (aided by the female emotional intelligence of his love interest), learning to be more sympathetic toward the struggles and sufferings of his fellow man. But despite such core elements, this novel defies classification in multiple ways. It has an experimental formal quality, marked by a changeable (even capricious) narrative voice. There is a proliferation of sub-plots and minor characters, and a doubling of the romantic plot (via two couples, and at least three active triangles among the four lovers). The romantic plot is not simply a matter of two couples and temporary misalignments/misunderstandings. Rather, the forms of characterological value in the novel are mobile and varying – manifesting themselves as, among other things, aristocratic valor, entrepreneurial vocation, stoicism, and charisma – and they exert forms of magnetism and allure that do not allow for an easy or stable understanding of either individual virtue or ideal romantic pairing. In addition, there is an internal doubling within the political plot, insofar as power, suffering, and discontent have not only to do with conditions of class, but also of gender.

Even apart from its proliferation of values and sites of interest, Brontë's narrative poses a challenge to any possibility of normative stability by emphasizing the capricious force of individual nature and temperament, and the ineluctability of power as a medium for all relations. From one perspective, the challenge to norms expresses Brontë's Romanticism, her privileging of individuality, emotion, and imagination over social life and social forms. This orientation is clearly difficult to reconcile with, or reduce to, any clear political ideology, though there are critics who will equate it with political conservatism and bourgeois interests, especially given the fact that Robert Moore's individualism accompanies a strong commitment to *laissez-faire* principles and the unregulated economic behavior that accompanies those principles. But viewed more comprehensively, the novel wreaks havoc with any one-to-one correspondence between social position and political ideology. One particularly telling instance is Mr. Yorke, for whom revolt (or commitment to republicanism and equality) is "in his blood."[7] Individual temperament acts almost as a surd, with the bad nature of Caroline's father an unexplained, but life-determining, fact. Also left resolutely open is the question of whether one's suffering can be attributed to social conditions. Does Caroline Helstone's suffering have to do with constraints placed upon women generally, or is it keyed to far-reaching existential emptiness and loss? Keeping such questions in a kind of volatilized flux, this novel makes it very hard to identify clear values within the political register, as the narrator's own parting insistence on the novel's lack of a moral exemplifies.

Perhaps even more interesting is the novel's treatment of power as a primary medium of social life, and therefore necessarily a basic condition of love relations, and of all ethics and politics. We have become used, after Foucault, to speaking of power as positive rather than negative, but it is worth pondering how radical Brontë's approach was during her time, and certainly in the context of the genre of the political novel. While many political novels stress the ways in which the human condition exceeds the limits of politics narrowly conceived, Brontë stands out for her treatment of unavoidable ways in which power is a fact of human relations – in the charisma of individuals, in the expression and enactment of love, and in familial and economic structures. This is a viewpoint that cannot be reduced to either a radical or a conservative perspective, though it certainly has been interpreted often enough as the latter, and especially when the mere insistence on the medium of power is taken as a reconciliation with entrenched hierarchies. But – to take one example – the relation between Shirley Keeldar and Louis Moore is less expressive of Shirley's capitulation to the dominance of her man than her active staging of power and submission. For Brontë power is a fundamental and volatile fact of human relations, one to which individuals ideally have a performative rather than passive relation: this is the more basic way in which her novels are political. Coupled with this is a strong and explicit resistance, moreover, to the reductions of political thought or ideology itself (as shown for example in Shirley's argument with Mr. Yorke in chapter 21).

In its radical refusal to accord explanatory primacy to social convention and established political frameworks, *Shirley* expresses a spirit also at play in Emily Brontë's *Wuthering Heights* (1847). Emily is often regarded as the more anti-social of the two novelists, and there is certainly a stronger sense of negative freedom in *Wuthering Heights*, where violence is attributed to society itself, and a dream of absolute severance from any social constraint is sustained. But because *Shirley* works on and through the conventions of the political novel, it has some powerful anti-ideological effects that are essentially sidestepped in the more stark conceptual schema of *Wuthering Heights* (which, admittedly, does not announce itself as an industrial novel).

In the story of Caroline Helstone and her mother, *Shirley* emphasizes personal loss, and keys it to a gendered scenario. The loss of the mother is primary, and the suffering of women especially acute, in part because women are less able to engage in public forms of self-actualization, and therefore remain more focussed on the experience of loss. This gendered emotional stall or paralysis makes its force felt across any number of political novels, expressing a bleak contrast to the forms of progressive optimism that often characterize their plots. One is tempted to see this feature as a precursor of the naturalism that Hardy represents more comprehensively; but it would be more accurate to see it as a constant that takes shape differently across novels of the realist and modernist period.

In this regard George Eliot's *Felix Holt, the Radical* (1866) is worth considering, because it is the sole political novel in a corpus by an author who has an ambitious philosophical, historical, and sociological outlook, one that includes a conviction of the ineluctability of natural and social laws. Eliot is interested in showing, among other things, how individuals suffer the consequences of actions that they cannot ever fully own, given the mesh of circumstances that constrains what they are capable of doing, or becoming. But she also insists on the moral desirability, and potency, of affirming the larger webs of relations in which one finds oneself, and avoiding harmful actions, given their ramifying negative effects. These practices will contribute both to moral self-development and to the good of the community. *Felix Holt* uses its titular hero both to make the case for moral vigilance as the source of self-development and to register a profound distaste for the hubris of political intentionality. The two aims are somewhat in tension with one another, insofar as the first assumes the possibility of self-actualization, while the second cautions that effects may outrun intentions in the case of individual intervention into collective political arenas. The first is hortatory and progressive, the second has a quietist emphasis (and raises the question of whether, for Eliot, all political interventions overstep the bounds of morally responsible action). The novel is forced into paradox, using Felix Holt as a charismatic figure who enters the public sphere in order to enjoin crowds not to engage in political action, hence to teach a general withdrawal from the public sphere. Indeed there is a larger force of negation in his personality – he makes clear that he is motivated in large part by "what he should hate to be."[8] What this amounts to is a kind of anti-political purism, one whose lesson is more fully enforced by means of the disastrous consequences that ensue when Felix aims to redirect a protesting mob, and ends up committing manslaughter.

Shadowing the political plot is not only the romantic plot between Esther and Felix, but also the tale of deceit surrounding Mrs. Transome and Mr. Jermyn. Emphasized here are the fateful consequences of a moral fall, and the extended anguish it imposes on Mrs. Transome. Ultimately the bleak view animating the Transome plot, its emphasis on the ramifying effects of conscious wrongdoing, is echoed in the political plot's dim view of efficacious moral action. The force of nature and passion (Mrs. Transome has a sexual fall; Felix at one point refers to his rages as "drunkenness without wine") powerfully undermines the aims of reason and culture (147). Interestingly, however, it is precisely the tragic consequences of those forces, and indeed their often hidden elements, that serve to intensify realist narrative for Eliot, to provide it with an expressive force that reaches beyond the normal forms of social and even ethical communication ("Many an inherited sorrow that has marred a life has been breathed into no human ear" [10]).

For Eliot political aspiration (even the kind of anti-political politics espoused by Felix) takes shape in relation to the breadth of human existence, and must contend with all the forces that undermine and derail even the most thoughtful moral actors. If one simply rushes to call Eliot a conservative when assessing *Felix Holt*, one risks missing her more potent assessment of the context of all action, an assessment that transcends ideology, and that across her opus serves as the dynamic and vital ground of all forms of aspiration.

The tension between the existential ground of action and action itself is potently expressed in modernist novels, but it would be misleading, as I hope my readings have shown, to credit modernism with a turn to ontological or existential questions, when the realist novel is already exercised by them. The degree and kind of emphasis might be said to vary, in relation to both individual authors and the broader literary period designations, but the continuity between the political novels of the nineteenth century and the early twentieth is more striking than their differences. One might consider E. M. Forster's *Howards End* (1910) and Conrad's *Nostromo* (1904), which notably foreground the relation between the political and the existential. *Howards End* stages an encounter between the cosmopolitan, argument-oriented world of the Schlegels, and the potent Mrs. Wilcox, who figures the force of place, connection, and nature. The Schlegels are crucially disarmed when Mrs. Wilcox imposes her mute negations on their lively debates. The novel's interest in the displacements occasioned by modern life, and in the loss of an organic relation to others and to the land one inhabits, has a dual focus and dual system of value – on the one hand, there is an impulse to move, as in the case of Margaret Schlegel, beyond words (and the dissension they cause): to simply be with others and to embrace both social heterogeneity and the natural world. But on the other hand, there is a recognition that such a move is utterly dependent on the discursive and reflective forms that allow one to recognize the need for calm acceptance. It is only after Margaret has argued a need to overcome the divisions that issue from social hierarchy and power, and has forced her disquisition upon Henry, that she can come to embrace what is. Forster's novel is therefore still, quite powerfully, a social problem novel, and it exerts its force by keeping in play the intractable energies of the social and the natural, in ways reminiscent of Gaskell, of Eliot, and of the Brontës.

Conrad's *Nostromo* might appear to be the modernist *Aufhebung* of the political novel, in its kaleidoscopic treatment of perspectives, interests, and motivations. Seemingly above ideology and mobile in relation to value, *Nostromo* self-consciously uses the conventions of the political novel, placing under erasure key stabilizing forms of the nineteenth-century novel – moral conversion, sincerity, reform, the marriage plot. In their place we find the values of art, myth, and nature (including national character and natural temperament) operating as elemental powers in relation to which politics are dwarfed and diminished. In addition, a restless irony, a shifting assessment of characters and events, makes assessments of political life, and in particular political idealism, both context bound and secondary. And yet, even as the novel's formal features draw attention from the political to the aesthetic register, there is also a kind of cynical political judgment abiding throughout, an insistence that assertions cannot be taken at face value, but are always traceable to interests and passions, and often parrot well-established ideologies that either secure existing relations of power, or assist in the imposition of newer regimes that continue to retain advantages for the few at the expense of the many.

From this perspective, there is a kind of ideology critique at play, but it is an incidental effect of a broader sweep of skeptical assessment and ironic presentation. Moreover, the cynicism is counterbalanced by a more neutral appraisal of the inevitability of value-making. The text is so even handed about motive, especially what we might call core meaning-giving motives (or existential orientations), that it seems to negate its own work of ideology critique. The novel reflects, ultimately, a kind of incomplete pragmatism, a recognition of the contingent and interested nature of ideals and values, and an uneven acceptance of that fact, one that oscillates between a skeptical and an existential framework. This results in interesting modifications of the notions of character and moral commitment, as well as the use of romance. Mrs. Gould serves not so much to inspire Mr. Gould as to channel an emerging recognition that his idealism is ultimately a pathology (a "fetish" or a "fixed idea").[9] The romance between Decoud and Antonia serves as the occasion for forms of argument not between benighted liberalism and moral reform (as in, say, Gaskell's *North and South*), but rather as a higher level face-off between skepticism and idealism, which, as the core cognitive interest in the novel, is both aestheticized and eroticized. The afterlife of traditional value is housed in the sheer commitment of Antonia and the radiant and embodied morality of Mrs. Gould. But like the Garibaldino's owl-of-Minerva republicanism (which is nostalgic and characterological, rather than self-standing), these values are ultimately grounded in existentially situated characters who choose what matters to them, rather than simply standing for something that transcends them. This both dwarfs the political pretensions at play and allows for the possibility of their utter seriousness. In this way the novel seems to deflate, or at least radically recast, the question, which so exercised Dickens, of the tension between the critical and existential viewpoints.

The ultimate achievement of the political novel broadly construed, realist and modernist, lies precisely in this playing out of the tension between the moral-existential viewpoint, and the systemic or critical one (sociology, ideology critique, irony/skepticism). What has often been deemed the failure of the political novel – its partial insertion of an alien perspective or agenda – is actually its defining problematic, as it brings the novel form's determining interest in lived experience into play with those diverse frameworks of understanding that shape critical thinking about political life.

It is worth considering, by way of conclusion, the one form of the political novel that seems most immune to the question of whether politically it succeeds or fails – the political novel of manners. The political novel of manners combines the features of the novel of manners and the political novel. It is like the novel of manners in that, while it is certainly interested in the milieu it treats (in this case, the political milieu), it departs from the more traditional political novel in that it does not appear to set out a problem that needs solving, but to show how political life sustains itself. Anthony Trollope's Palliser novels, the key representative of this genre from the period under discussion, show how conventions and practices shape the institutions of governing, emphasizing the use of social power as a key component of political power (demonstrated memorably through Glencora Palliser). Moreover, in his more direct treatment of parliamentary politics, Trollope is at once ironic and pragmatic. Empty forms of political life are exposed, yet political purism of the kind that the Duke tends toward is shown to be quixotic and ineffectual.

Trollope's effectiveness as a political novelist has to do with the pressure he puts upon apparent accommodation to the way we live now. He does this in two ways. First, by showing how certain political trends, especially a growing liberalism, are exerting force on the world of taken-for-granted manners, and thereby bringing political forces into the life of society in a disruptive way. In *The Prime Minister* (1876) we see this with the introduction of Lopez and his prejudiced reception by society. Even as Trollope emphasizes ethical character (who is judged to be good and who bad), there is an insistent critique of prejudice that relies in part upon the very disruptions instigated by less than reputable figures. The critique often plays out through argument, and maintains a clear-eyed distinction between liberal principle (people should not be judged on the basis of their social standing) and moral judgment (some people of lesser standing or unknown origin may in fact turn out to be immoral).

Second, apart from the interruptive energy of liberal principle, there is also Trollope's insistence on ways in which psychological dispositions, and temperament more generally, mediate all commitments to principle. This is reminiscent of Charlotte Brontë (and anticipates Conrad), though there is in Trollope a more developed catalogue of types than in Brontë, and a perverse delight in showing how psychology can skew professed beliefs. The Duke's procedural purism leads him to the narrow cause of decimal coinage. Yet Trollope typically maintains a kind of dual position: acknowledging moral courage, and also showing its all-too-human features (stubbornness, recalcitrance, pure habit). Insofar as this is not so much an undermining of questions of value, a trumping of morality by psychology, as it is a complex presentation of contexts for the espousal of political principle, there is a way in which Trollope's novels are different in tone from the traditional industrial novel, but share with it this key feature. In a way, all political novels are political novels of manners, if we understand the latter not as a complacent, ironic presentation of an enclosed world stabilized by conventions, but rather as a novelistic project that shows the tension between political ideas and the manifold forces that condition and shape human existence, both individual and collective.

Notes

1. Irving Howe, *Politics and the Novel* (Chicago: Ivan R. Dee, 1987), p. 17.
2. Raymond Williams, *Culture and Society: 1780–1950* (New York: Columbia University Press, 1958), pp. 87–109. For key examples of the two approaches specified, see Ruth Bernard Yeazell, "Why Political Novels Have Heroines: Sybil, Mary Barton, and Felix Holt," *Novel* 18 (1985), 126–144 and Catherine Gallagher, *The Industrial Reformation of English Fiction: Social Discourse and Narrative Form, 1832–1867* (University of Chicago Press, 1985), ch. 3.
3. These characterizations draw on discussions of the novel by F. R. Leavis, *The Great Tradition* (Garden City, NY: Doubleday, 1954) and David Lodge, *Working with Structuralism* (Boston: Routledge and Kegan Paul, 1981).
4. Charles Dickens, *Hard Times* (Norton: New York, 2001), p. 203.

5. Charles Dickens, *Bleak House* (Harmondsworth: Penguin, 2003), p. 257.
6. Elizabeth Gaskell, *North and South* (New York: Norton, 2005), p. 219.
7. Charlotte Brontë, *Shirley* (Harmondsworth: Penguin, 2006), p. 45.
8. George Eliot, *Felix Holt, The Radical* (Harmondsworth: Penguin, 1995), p. 259.
9. Joseph Conrad, *Nostromo* (Harmondsworth: Penguin, 2007), pp. 175, 298.

22

Populations: pictures of prose in Hardy, Austen, Eliot, and Thackeray

AARON FOGEL

Rules for formatting the publication of prose include: a rectangular block of print; random, moot line breaks, which are accidents of printing; word-density on the page, crowded by comparison with most verse; arbitrary page breaks, numbered independently of the originating manuscript; and nets or lacings of white spaces between words and sentences. There is another condition, due to prose's printed format: any reprinted prose text past or future can reposition words on the page (higher, lower, left, right, centered).

Those elements make a mental picture of prose for us. We would usually recognize a prose page, as well as verse or a statistical table, from across a room. The picture might be at work though not thought about most of the time while we read. The surface shapes and rules of prose might also be an unconscious force acting on the history of thought. The neutral givens of prose could be prompts, though not imperatives, toward certain kinds of thinking. Intermittently, and by secondary gestures, novelists perhaps have represented the regulating conditions of their own prose medium. They have sometimes worked the look of the prose page understatedly into a general figurativeness, so that prose's seemingly neutral shapes ground the themes and interpretations of the novelists' worlds. The everyday prose page – not the illuminated or typographically daring one, but the minimal, recognizable least square of common print – amounts to a paradox of hypertrophied ordinari-ness, of what is "most ordinary," a condition to be reinterpreted by novels. Thoughts about prose's print format – among print options an abstract, extremely evolved historical form – might take place through the medium of the novel.

A tradition of prose-picturing scenes, images, and events would result in fiction. Those scenes would have become famous just because they had semi-consciously faced or mirrored prose as a picture without directly saying so. The tragicomic marionette, Prose-page-ness, subliminally thematized in its horizontal-vertical dance, might even be as widespread as "story," "dialogue," "reliability," "point-of-view," or "irony," but with an obvious qualification: this theme hides away from any recognized rollcall of novelists' crafts. To some extent it goes against our sense of prosaic sanity and of "the" novel to say that at times novelistic prose calligrams itself. A little Borgesian – the claim that there "must be" such a tradition assumes, also, readers who have looked at print other than to read it – from five or twenty feet away, or too closely, as well as from an ordinary middle distance.

According to this hypothesis, prose must have been surprised into meaning regarding its own look at heightened moments in English fiction. There would have to have been wit about the prose page that has kept itself metaphorical. Specific images from the world (rectangular windows, etc.) become events that have to remain unrelated to the page, because they invite too-obvious figuration, like bad puns. The world has many things in everyday life – rectangular mirrors or tables or cards, for instance – that cannot be "prose"-symbols disguised. But at the same time the question of prose format as not really neutral returns. And so there might be unresolved radical questions about rectangularity in the whole tradition. The best-known, even best instance, at once amplifying and shattering "the" prose page, would of course be the black page(s) mourning Yorick in *Tristram Shandy* (1759). Sterne's block plays at being a reminder of the prose page itself by way of a mock-fulfillment of page design. Absolute content, that prose page acts out and finds the limit. When, earlier, Defoe's *A Journal of the Plague Year* (1722) reproduces 1665 Bills of Mortality, in some nowhere land between verse and prose, the other point of interest here, besides Defoe's great superimposition of two or three publics (then and now) reading plague numbers, would be the difference between prose format, statistical format, and poems, all of them in their own typographic relation, among other things, to "populations": to an abstraction that cannot be seen.

Who are "too menny"?

The famous and terrible last note by Little Jude in Part VI, chapter 2 of Hardy's *Jude the Obscure* (1896), *"Done because we are too menny,"* has been read variously for the dark pun of its fading last word. But the jolt also comes first: "Done." That word has ironically a state decree's or pronunciamento's authority, but, not as obviously, it consummates the sound of the (maiden) name of his mother (Arabella Donn) early on linked with still more grim irony to his father's first desire to be a "don." Arabella "Donn" (no virgin) became Jude's in lieu of his desire to be a don. It may also sound like "dun," a debt called in. Hardy makes these echoes and thumps only remotely explicit, unheard by the characters. The puns are for readers to overhear, less part of a psychoanalysis of Little Jude than a subtly objective-obscene music, a chord for readers in a choral state.

A reading that excludes this chord as irrelevant or as over-reading would take Little Jude's note to mean only that there are going to be too many other children in his family. One cannot posit complicated chords of meaning here without doing violence to prose's plainness. Nevertheless, one cannot exclude such chords without doing violence to Hardy's craft. The novel invites but also mocks the most grandiose reading of the suicide when the Doctor comments that there is a coming general wish not to live, and that Little Jude represents it. The Doctor might not register the author's view so much as he might be Hardy's darkly comic example of the modern prosaic will to make doomful and allegorically general demographic statements. A resonant sentence spoken by Little Jude is and is not a back-echo to Malthus's vision (in prose) of increasing densities and numbers of people. One has to choose: but it is probably not wrong to read the scene either as an attack on Malthus's idea or a confirmation of it. And the right way, after all, might be to see the catastrophically scary and contradictory relation between prose and such ambivalent demographic visions. Prose has effects on mind: in Little Jude we get a childishly precocious mind's dramatic negative replay of the idea of "overpopulation." That idea, a sort of prose-ridden fantasy, accords with the prose page's density so neatly that it questions where population-fact ends and the hallucinatory power of print takes over, so that Little Jude becomes a bitter "hypostasis" of prose format. Hardy turned to poetry, perhaps because he found prose's "numbers" too diffuse.

Little Jude's note also startles because there are only a few hints in *Jude the Obscure* of any Malthusian theme of populousness. Hardy's are relatively less-populated novels among the nineteenth century's giants. They may even thumb their agrarian noses at the century's virtuoso mega-peopled census-like works. *Jude the Obscure* does have a batch of ensembles and groups: the bar, the young women's barrack-school, a brawl in Shaston, carnival. Mostly, though, the novel feels suggestively under-peopled, lonely. It is as if Hardy were begging off competition with the earlier nineteenth century novel's prolifics. That a horrendous apprehension by a child of the lurid doctrine of overpopulation has become a single piece of paper on the floor in a note he leaves about his perceived family is all the more an oblique condemnation of Malthusian imagination – the economic truth or falsity of his teachings not even in question – for being expressed in prose.

Each nation arguably has had its own fables of demography. For England the word "population" invokes distinctive shades and struggles, derived from the Domesday Book, from crises about what was called "depopulation" (eviction for enclosure), from the eighteenth century's population controversies and theories, and finally from Malthus and all who hated or defended him. Hardy uses "population" as a mild pejorative in his retrospective preface to *Far From the Madding Crowd* (1874). He attributes lost agrarian lore, customs, and terms, for instance the lost "love of fuddling," to the "supplanting of the class of stationary cottagers by an incoming population of more or less migratory laborers."[1] "Population" here is part of a long migratory sentence about cottagers displaced. William Cobbett's agrarian radicalism had cast "population" as a most demeaning term equating rural working people with beasts. Hardy transposes that equivocally onto Little Jude's naïve summation.

The complex by which the word-and-letter densities of prose somehow belong to the world of historical crowds, indirectly "symbolizing" them by way of feelings about old and new alleged scarcities-and-densities of human life and spill and migration, makes a platen on which fiction is pressed. In Hardy's *The Return of the Native* (1878) the heath is an image of collectivity as density. Elias Canetti's sociological study *Crowds and Power*, exploring "crowd symbols" that emblematize European nationalisms, never mentions prose itself as a crowd symbol. The analogy might explain the uncanny fame of Hardy's heath. One doesn't need London to provoke density. All one needs is prose. The effect is less diagrammatic or sociological than aesthetic, a doubt about prose's pure or mere functionalism. One wishes that Raymond Williams had taken on "population" in his *Keywords*.

Hardy's most scenic enactment of the prose page might be the spilling of the sheep, in chapter 5 of *Far From the Madding Crowd*, over the edge of a precipice, where hundreds of them timidly die, goaded by an overzealous and well-meaning young sheepdog-in-training. The episode is titled "A Pastoral Tragedy." Pastoral falls over prose's edge. One strength of this seriocomic image lies in the resemblance between the way the sheep are driven over the edge and the way lines at the end of prose break, passively, as we think, whitely, "by accident." Insomniac night music, this image turns counting sheep into discounting them. Prose ledges contain, endanger, and transfer population-like groups with no comment and no poetic sense of deliberate break.

The emblematization of prose by the relatively random spilling of innocent herds or large groups over edges, borders, bounded spaces: can it be proven? Certainly not. It is itself "over" some line or edge of interpretation by the rules of permissible allegory. *Eppur si muove.* Hardy wrote many poems metrically exacting for idiosyncratic counts and awkwardly beautiful stanza forms. He must have seen, at times, the prose rectangle as stanza-like and as an anti-stanza too. He might have seen a formal connection to the contradictory qualities, counted and uncounted, of the category "population."

The prose page and the world beyond

Closer to Malthus's time, Austen constructs the prose line break into a visual idiom completely different from Hardy's. One passage from Austen's *Emma* (1816), a page-like landscape with a mix of the finite and the unending, maps the class history of England not only by topography but according to a picture-like logic:

> It was hot; and after walking some time over the gardens in a scattered, dispersed way, scarcely any three together, they insensibly followed one another to the delicious shade of a broad short avenue of limes, which stretching beyond the garden at an equal distance from the river, seemed the finish of the pleasure grounds. – It led to nothing: nothing but a view at the end over a low stone wall with high pillars, which seemed intended, in their erection, to give the appearance of an approach to the house, which never had been there. Disputable, however, as might be the taste of such a termination, it was in itself a charming walk, and the view which enclosed it extremely pretty. The considerable slope, at nearly the foot of which the Abbey stood, gradually acquired a steeper form.[2]

Emma is visiting Mr. Knightley's Donwell Abbey. The fall of Hardy's sheep over the field's edge, the leap overboard by Joseph Conrad's Jim – in the later novelists the prose edge will be more dramatically objectified. The modern danger of the edge is missing from Austen's scene. But perspective about stopping and seeing belongs, as here, in prose format, to the way prose lines terminate at random but peaceable blanks. Geometrical, comforting, sane, Austen's prose pictures itself as a better poem than poetry – it sees past the convention of the line break out to the world. There is (almost) no romantic chasm. The eye goes "down" from one prose line to the next *not* suffering a severe fall.

In what comes next the eye moves down to the Abbey Mill Farm. The narrator breaks in to celebrate the English sun, English culture. Lionel Trilling made the passage just after the one above a keynote to what he saw as an idyllic novel. The quotation about the lime-avenue which ends in no building or resolution – and the framing pillars that look out on nothing and everything – could be read not only as a prelude to the picture of England's austere-pleasurable lines and limits and agrarian base (which can be torn apart easily by us for ideological "critique"), but as a metaphorical hymn to the condition of prose. The hymn might guard our "critical prose" against being too certain that it has the power to critique Austen's "ideology" from a position outside hers. The plain eye, moving past the garden, or safety, comes actively to the end of a driving line of trees to look at no house, "only" the world. Ezra Pound's charge that Austen and her people are "hemmed-in" is answered in advance.[3] Metaphorical identities underwrite one sentence in the quotation: the lime-tree path = the end of the old orders of rhyme = England's containment in the world, which is simultaneously openness to the world. The sentence says in effect that England requires no imperialist travel, only thought about its position in space. Austen is an anti-Malthus, de-populationalizing her text, to make space. If there is something conservative in that, there is something radical too about the refusal to "populate."

Nothing else in the novel addresses the special but non-transcendental case of prose in the world so broadly. What the eye sees summarizes English class structure as non-vertigo. Lines of type are not in reality moving "down" the page (it is the eye that moves). There is less emphasis on "higher" and "lower" lines than there would be in a poem. Class structure and rank are given, then quieted, then called unoppressive – the prose page has a less fixed typography as to high or low. (This is not my view of class, but what I see diagrammed in Austen here.)

The opposite can also be argued, clearly. You can certainly try to add *Emma* up to a "demography" (a later word, from the 1850s) with many ranks. Highbury is "populous." The middle class are on their way in; the absolutely and relatively poor are visited almost invisibly; the "gypsies," all five or six of them, invade like French revolutionaries, and are repelled; and four young people are orphaned (Emma, Harriet, Jane, Frank) by illness, parental default, sexual naughtiness, war, and trade. But still, Austen, though allowing that sort of reading, consciously refuses to "populationalize" prose. This can be read as avoidance of history and crowds, or innocence of them. It can also be read as knowledge of and resistance to one side or aspect of the prose page's format. If prose usually carries the thrill of envisioning "populations," Austen's exclusion of that from her world is a marked act. Her prose resists sociological force, and in a radical, not reactionary way, rejects the oppressively dense sense of massive population that is prose and some poetry's Malthusian muse in her time, the hypnotic-demonic census-like act of amassed counts. However, if the scene at Donwell Abbey began programmatically, with picturing the page as Austen's motive, it would not be so strong. It is the sense of a pedestrian movement of description coming upon a scene that is a witty likeness of its writing, the world's parallel "limes" found out by moving through it, that makes it funny and active.

Again no allegorical certainty here: if the landscape were more clearly an allegory of prose it would not be novelistic prose. If allegory were absent entirely, it would not be a novel but a naïve, false realism. The action further combines a Protestant plainness with a remotely Catholic (Donwell Abbey) impulse. That brings us back, uncertainly, to the question "What is a page?" as both a religious and a secular question. If we read Austen's descriptive passage as the ordinary prose page reflecting on itself by extraordinary analogy, Protestant print severity becomes also a Catholic art of medieval illumination of itself. Reading the "plain" Protestant page as itself like a Catholic illumination of its geometry becomes a secular witticism. On an illuminated page from a Book of Hours one can compare things at different ontological levels. Here the ontological mix asks whether we have permission to combine the Protestant page and the Catholic page into a synthesis that becomes England.

George Eliot's scratched mirror

An attempt now at a clarifying interruption: the "population" of a novel does not have to mean its entire cast of characters. Self-contradictory as this sounds, it can be useful to doubt the major words derived from "people," such as "popular," and their claims to self-evident meaning. "Population," among such words, applied to the world, let alone a text, might be worth considering not as a fact but as a trope, and one that is especially tempting to representation by prose. Is a whole "great" novel's dramatis personae, as we almost see it after finishing a book, or by using some accompanying encyclopedic reference guide, comparable to "population" as used in sociology, let alone to whatever it is we mean by population(s) in the world?

An extreme contrary position, resisting the book review cliché ("x novelist has populated the text brilliantly") would see novelistic accumulations and plenitudes of people as not only *not* real "populations," but as critiques of that word and concept – of a prose-effect that reifies "collectivity." Novels can work, through picturing, irony, and overwriting, to undermine and mock reified "populousness" as a readymade idea of what they offer. By a deliberate flattening, the alternative to credulousness about "populations" in texts, the element that *is* most like "population" in all novels is the prose page's surface, seen as inclined to exalt its own distribution of letters and words. Whole philosophies of population may have grown out of this prose-effect: the population of a text is its words and letters. The page will likely differ, from itself, in time and position, on the next reprint, adding to the mystique of history, migratory power, and nomadic force. But the mystique is perhaps the prose page's own.

Belief in the real abundance of people in novels is at once a glorious mimetic sanity, a great collective humanism, and a superstition or hypnosis of plenitude that novels sometimes help us break. Popular skeptical talk about blockbuster movies makes fun of grand casts of thousands – that skepticism might be as sharp as the serious academic attempt to read novels for knowledge of historical demography.

The most famous passage in George Eliot's *Middlemarch* (1872) about representation and multiplicities is the brief parable in chapter 27 about a pier-glass's countless scratches, the effect of a housemaid's polishing, which make a half-illusory circle when a candle is raised to them. This is the most cited passage of homemade ethics from the novel because it has, secondarily and with absorbing power, a grounding irony about the surfaces of writing.

The glass's many scratches became famous because they conform unconsciously not just to reading in general but to the prose page surface in particular. The great simile absorbs interpreters because of its wit and real profundity, and also because it is a classical, less than conscious, instance of prose mirrored by prose. A "pier"-glass is set between two windows, and is probably rectangular. The pier-glass parable that seems so warmly and mockingly profound likewise makes fun of itself as a piece of prose intellectual furniture.

According to the reading I want to suggest, the "first image" we have in our minds *when reading* is not the world's plentiful variety, but the rectangular prose page's multiplicity of "scratches," and its claim to contain all, including multidirectional freedoms. If we read prose rather than verse, it is likely that we have passively chosen in advance the belief that the world is populations, dialectics, dialogic, multiplicities, etc. This presumed diverse knowledge-of-multiplicity-in-advance is itself an icon-worship, an egoism. Faith in it is uncritical. Few readers, I acknowledge, will accept this claim about the parable's suggested ironic meaning-in-reverse, even though it is only a critical possibility, not a dogma about prose; and few will accept an additional claim: that the small marks in the pier-glass parable are made by a figural "housemaid," rather than a personal one, partly because it is no accident that the lowly word "housemaid" has nine different letters, with all five vowels, each once, and is comically visible as a humble parable of letters, a comic letter-image – Eliot at her best? – of plenitude (rubbed and scratched) in alphabetical practice? This "housemaid" belongs to writing and to printed prose. If we start to "see" the prosaic word "housemaid" as an emblem, we are on our way towards the ironic-aesthetic reading Eliot proposes and cannot directly announce in her own art. Detractors of such a reading might use prejudicial labels like "Kabbalistic" or "crazy." Yet the mirror in this scene is held up not only to the world but to the prose page by the prose page. Fully conscious ironic prose, not a realistic, empirical, or plain philosophy in direct contact with the outside world, but a format-for-itself, with its pre-ordained quantifi-cations, necessarily projects its own format-figure, and even so, a little like the egoist, only celebrates its own omniscratchedness as the alleged real, non-egotistical truth of the world.

Eliot's image, then, like Austen's, works ultimately as anti-Malthusian because it is at its best ironic about the reified multiplicity-effect on thinking that prose has. For this to be seen, Malthus has to be figured as perhaps the most powerful, un-ironic population-rhetoric in history. In Malthus the ulti-mate "it," of prose, its effective and even hallucinated force, is that of a "population" "increase," turned into an eminent philosophy that still rides the nightmare of social imagination and justifies our most selfish economics. The crescendoing medium of prose is mistaken for the reality of population increase. Eliot, by contrast, makes us see the egoism of prose's asserted multiplicities. *Middlemarch* is not only a census but an ironic questioning of the will to census. Dickens's *Bleak House* (1853) is not only a census but a tragic anti-census. Call it dialectic, dialogic, phenomenology, multiplicity, what you will, and you will only have the next cookbook recipe for prose's intellectual infatuation with its own multiplicity. All the great theories of the novel – for example, M. M. Bakhtin's dialogic – cannot entirely foreclose this problematic aspect of the cult of prose.

The speculations of *Daniel Deronda* (1876) might depend upon Eliot's late feeling that her earlier great teachings of expansion and "widening" beyond egoism might have been incomplete. Through the figure of the Jews, she reworks the theme toward persons, or a people, who need to do the reverse, to contract from overexpansion. "The" Jews figure in *Deronda* as the dis-persed, diffused population that, directly contrary to the "eng" (narrow) English, needs to stop "widening the circle" of forced worldliness, and to re-contract.

In one of the novel's key moments, Mordecai speaks to the club of poor intellectuals or "Philosophers" (chapter 42), Jews and Christians and scientists together, who have that night been debating, among other things, statistics, and whether quantity is indistinguishable from quality in the study of social conditions. He insists on Jewish participation in the world through a qualitative distinctiveness that is also quantitative. The passage is too long to quote, but one main point distills itself this way: "Let us . . . not renounce our higher gift and say, 'Let us be as if we were not among the populations.'"[4]

The double negative here, the compound litotes typical of Eliot, amounts to a statement that Jews (and human beings in general) should *not* stay aloof or write themselves a special permit to be *not* "among the populations." So the first emphasis almost certainly falls on "among." "Among" recurs in the chapter. A little drolly like a composite Jewish-Christian minyan, the discussion group's moral is: all are "among." It is made pointedly clear that the dialogue takes place *among* different types of lower-class intellectual people. A second reading, though, could shift stress onto "populations." Mordecai's line would take part in the history of nineteenth-century thought about the horrendous logic-defeating category of "population" and the demand it makes on sentences to say something intelligent and clear at once. The Jews are, certainly, and by a vexed logic of sets, not only "among" Europe's populations, but oxymoronically *the* emblem of "population." Eliot seems intellectually gigantic among novelists, and yet she had no logic better or clearer than anyone else's to address the double-bind riddle of seeing one group as singularly *exemplary* of undifferentiated "population"-ness. How can one group be more a population than another? This is nearby the very problem of prose's claim to exemplify in itself a special realism about multiplicities and collectivity, and to exemplify extraordinary ordinariness. A general quantifier ("population") dissolves, revealing its rhetorical status as the mask of a qualitative judgment. "The" Jews were, arguably, in Europe, the exemplary excluded–included population, not a nation, but the quality assigned to quantity, the lowest common denominator of all bids to think inclusion and exclusion without quandary.

The word "population" belongs to this miserable slipperiness. As a word it sometimes works to include, to reduce, to speak for, or to slaughter and exterminate the group referred to. We do not usually add up all the demographers in the world, and call *them* a population. It would imply satire and aggression. We use the word most for missing women, or orphans, or the total of people in a small place, or the homeless. The word is half-reserved for those we at once demean and pretend not to, even though sometimes it is clarifying, and liberatory in relation to other categories. Yet when Mordecai calls for Jews to accept that they are among the *populations*, then, if we italicize that, his self-evident meaning of universal humane participation shows itself to be faulted internally by the other tonalities of the word. It pretends to neutrality, often amounts to pathos, defense, and identification, but also heavily tends toward contempt. Prose is the chosen medium and site for this set of contested meanings of "population": the default mode, the exalted, the reviled, the quantitatively neutral as the qualitative accent.

Put too simply: the ironic "novel" is not only a genre capturing multiplicity, society, and dialogic but, obversely, a radical critique of modern prose's self-mystifying claims to own just those energies. The great ironists, like Austen, Eliot, Hardy, Conrad, entice us into an absorbing prose promise of a full census, but can almost be relied on to withdraw the trance in favor of a bodily prose surface seen as a texture that likes to find multiplicity in itself. This might be so of other formats and media. But when Samuel Beckett's quasi-policeman Moran in *Molloy* (1955) lies in bed at night picturing "masses" that are first visible as mere blotches in his vision in the dark – "Masses of what?" he asks[5] – one answer should be "prose." If we try to shift away to other media, and lose sight of prose's specific character and effect, we will have lost the hidden metaphor (prose equals populations) that makes the term "population" what it is for us.

Thackeray's torn-out page

The subtitle – or signature – of Thackeray's early mock-census *The Book of Snobs* (1846–1847) was "By One Of Themselves." "Themselves" gives dictionaries a run for their money. In the change Thackeray made from the earlier "by one of them," the added "selves" governs the title retroactively. It drawls. It seems a deliberate rhythmic choice. Secure collective identity ("they were themselves again") seems one of the tones. Thackeray's sense is that, despite all the mutual head-knocking forms taken by his fictional puppets, even the loneliest belong to the double condition of being "themselves," people kept intact and in contact by them-ness. "Themselves" also cuts informally against more solemnly author-itarian and impalpable terms like "society," "community," and "population." To be called a "population" is more ominous than to be called a "themselves": you know what happens to populations. "Themselves" sounds more rough-and-tumble. Marxian critiques of this as a bourgeois complacency-in-conflict would hold, but there is something also Marxian in the lively indifference of "them-selves" to the more abstract terms. Lightness has its place. In Thackeray's famous illustration in *Vanity Fair* (1848) that shows Becky throwing the dic-tionary out of a carriage window, that heavy book, the word-population, seems in some ways to fly or float in the air. Thackeray does not project the prose page as a a dark-inked oy-vey for Yorick, a garden of limes looking outside itself, a tragic heath, or a Conradian dark Congo.

Thackeray's indifference to heavy implication about the page surface might stem from his being a cartoonist. That perhaps tends to cancel, or draw his attention away from, any need to brood over the prose page by itself. Pictures are pictures, and prose prose, and both are ad hoc, even if people are shaped like capital letters heading chapters, and vice versa. His antic indignations about politics and parties are serious enough, and his convincing hatred of atrocious wars and massacres; but he also washes over the slightly ridiculous side of prose's potential to brood over itself too fiercely as a political picture of dark collectivity. The evidence is that the problem of population as often discussed theoretically in his time seems to him to need some casual and "irresponsible" spoofing. His early study *Cruikshank* (1840) displays Cruikshank's "Philoprogenitiveness" first. Nineteen figures of one household crowd a rough oval, mostly big-and-sharp-nosed children wreathing, climbing, hugging, and staring around a sharp-nosed papa, with a genteelly pretty and sharp-nosed mama gazing into a cradle of twins. The visual sharp nose in Cruikshank seems a forecast of the name Becky Sharp and a replacement for the aristocrat's elbow. To this tactile, visual sense of all of us "themselves"-people as fleshy sharpers, there is a relaxed, vulgar, easy-does-it prose music, a feel for English bright vowels. Monosyllables and polysyllables cohabit louchely in Thackeray's sentences with a kind of relaxed availability that makes his prose style almost too companionable. What we would call the groupie and the isolato are in Thackeray hard to tell apart. Thackeray is a sort of English Veronese: large festive-sad groups at the banquet never exactly look each other in the eyes though things might be going on under the table.

It is true that all this is dismissible as liberal ideology in Thackeray. "Over"-crowded and sometimes to him "hideous" but erotic groups, like Jews, Indians, and slaves, whom he often treats with a cavalier revulsion and relish, and that we might or might not be disgusted by, are offered as innocent ridicule. The populousness of Thackeray's fiction might be the most complacent in nineteenth-century English literature. Of course this can be set against recent critical work like Mike Davis's *Late Victorian Holocausts* with horrendous ideological implications. But there is something to be said for Thackeray's Malthus lite in a century framed by Malthus-heavy and extreme population fear. Another Thackeray-like picture of "population" by Cruikshank, a complacent visual comedy called "Overpopulation," was used by D. V. Glass in 1973 for a frontispiece to Glass's *Numbering the People: The 18th Century Population Controversy*. "Overpopulation," perhaps our single most morally and politically culpable cliché, is a word with genocidal implications, enhanced by being embedded in the semi-conscious crowdedness of prose itself. That is one reason for attempting a light touch. In Cruikshank's cartoon we see overcrowded London, still another "themselves" incarnate, not so much as snobbish or warlike or even carnivalesque but as an English, plump, audience-like totality, seated in the open air. Every corner of the page is full. Strangely comfy people, by the hundreds, inhabit every vertical-or-horizontal plane, including bridgework and balloon-apartments. In all four corners as well as the center, where a Union Jack calls attention to their distribution in all directions including diagonals, there are about as many people as there are words to a prose page. The people sit on the edges of outdoor urban precipices like audiences on the edge of their seats or words on the edge of prose; almost everyone is served brew.

The cartoon, radically ambiguous, can mean, negatively, that nowadays London looks like this, badly overpopulated by passive blob-people. But it can also mean that this or any assertion of "overpopulation," in the mind, is a cartoon, a picture grounded in print-densities confused with reality. Density is a print illusion that worships its own format, and is another trope of printed prose. A third suggestion: that if domestic London is as crowded as this the result is not a nightmare mob nor a surplus but a sort of huge popular beer-hall and auditorium.

Thackeray's *The Book of Snobs*, after a chapter called "Snobbium Gatherum," rages against the snobbishness (not identical to our meanings) that inhibits free fertility and marriage. Young men and women are discouraged by snobbism from loving outside caste. A punchy voice shouts down Malthus:

> When Punch is king, I declare there shall be no such thing as old maids and old bachelors. The Reverend Mr. Malthus shall be burned annually, instead of Guy Fawkes. Those who don't marry shall go into the workhouse. It shall be a sin for the poorest not to have a pretty girl to love him.[6]

Jack Spiggot's tale then gets told: he lacked money to marry the once beautiful Letty Lovelace, now shriveled and a pill-taker. Jack drinks.

The call to burn Malthus might be spoof and mimicry of Malthus's enemies and not a protest in their key – or both at the same time. But a footnote, if it is to be taken as Thackeray's, not another mock-voice, guiltily qualifies the attack, and defends the right to be celibate. A little like Cobbett when being funny about Malthus, Thackeray seems to feel that Malthusian anxiety needs festive debunking by light tragic farce, by hoots and not by prophetic rage. *Vanity Fair* describes the secret and public (readily visible, nor really furtive) wedding of Becky and Captain Rawdon. Rawdon is on the lam from his patron Miss Crawley. The wedding takes place not just between themselves but as a popular masque for all. "[A] lady very like her" (Becky) gets married amid a list of other elopements. Becky and the Captain, Everycouple, become invisible by being public – they walk into a church and do it. Thackeray's casual narrator ends the paragraph with a faux bow to population theory: "If people only made prudent marriages, what a stop to population there would be!" The next paragraph defends Rawdon's marriage as one of his "honestest actions."

Microsoft Word programming redlines the word "honestest," warning us it does not exist. A strong word here, it can mean that Rawdon makes an honest woman of Becky, but also that their direct lust is good. As an act of para-graphing, Thackeray's putting the merry line about checks to population in last place spoofs printed prose paragraphs themselves, insofar as they are supposed to come to a line in the sand. When a paragraph over-structures itself to add up and "stop" at some sure mock-mathematical proof or verdict it says something like this: us coherent paragraphs have always been like true honest arithmetic in this rational age. Thackeray's successor John Galsworthy spoofs and trivializes "coherent" demographic paragraphing in the sixth para-graph of *In Chancery* (1920), which announces that Forsyte birth-rates have corresponded to interest-rates – 10 percent on Consols meant ten kids, it's down to three – etc.[7] This easy parodic paragraph is droll because it comes close to the heart of prose. Prose delights in being two-sided about its numberings, both as quantifiers and anti-quantifiers, making raw data avail-able and also repudiating raw data as too static for a medium so anti-metrical.

The eighteenth-century typography Thackeray famously used for a first edition of *Henry Esmond* (1852) is a readymade example of the image of prose enlisted for "historical" witness, because it highlights visual changes in prose format. So we could invoke that edition for the argument of this chapter. "History" *is* right there in the general look of prose pages over time. But this example also runs contrary to the more specific theme I am going after. That theme is a pointed and plain but ironic reflection on *the most typical formatting conditions* of prose in one's own age – taken mostly for granted during that age. Prose always, I am arguing, has inclined one way, whatever changes it undergoes; it has always made us think, too much by default, and too easily, that all human large groups are really "populations." Novelistic prose, by contrast, has some-times seen that, or seen through it. The most standard conventional everyday prose format in any era is always covertly *census-like* in its force and impact.

If we ignore the edition of *Henry Esmond* that was set in old typography, we see that Thackeray's historical novel favors a high-spirited festive theme of common "pages" more than any serious historical-typographical antique "special effects." The opening pages of the novel refer repeatedly to the young hero as "the page" and "the little page." I think that, in this patent and even slightly annoying ornate pun, a lot of work gets done concerning the novel form, class, population, and prose pagination. As a noble, orphaned bastard – or as he seems to be – Esmond, no Edmund, remains loyal to his family. He is at once counted within them and left aside. Lord Castlewood and others first use him as a "page." Among the units of composition, the sentence, the word, and the chapter fall more under authorial control than does the page. The page is what, by contrast, the printer, or the random side of typesetting, takes charge of. It – the page – is in one sense torn out, but in another the most independent variable of the prose book.

The more one calls attention to the way most page breaks on any novel's printing *are* half-random, the more "the page" itself, as a general idea, seems clarified by analogy to special-but-typical characters like the world's Esmonds. Esmond "the page" keeps changing his ideological sides and his instrumentalities. A certain thrill canceling one's sense of the initial stodginess of this novel comes when one senses that Esmond, a sort of walking anagram of *le monde* or the world, of the real world in conflict with the artifice of high society, lives out an arbitrary constant: the predictable turning of pages. Esmond acts out the prose page's low place in the order of critical respect. Who pays attention to the practical prose page as a unit of the novel that cannot be as important as narrators or style? And yet, despite the neglect of due attention, it is the "charter" of printed novels to be made up of this page and that. The class-bound but chance-bound novel page can almost be torn out: that would make it ("the" prose page in England, freed from its book) a broadside. The single page even harks back, at many removes, to Magna Carta or Chartism. In this slow-seeming novel, the act of page-turning as suppressed page-tearing becomes a prosaic action of constitutional emancipation.

That prose and population might be linked iconographically in our culture is meant here to be not a dogma but the opening of a critical exploration. It is a way to ask about prose form in novels. To the extent that the origin or home of the novel is the populational prose page, the novel has the self-contradictory task of looking at its own prose as a picture of populations. That picture, in turn, distantly but inevitably drives the novel to take not only a census, but an anti-census, a critique of the format that is a whole order of meaning inherent in printed prose itself.

Notes

1. Thomas Hardy, Preface, *Far From the Madding Crowd* (New York: Harper & Brothers, 1905), p. vii.
2. Jane Austen, *Emma*, ed. Fiona Stafford (London: Penguin Books, 1996), Part III, ch. 6, p. 337.

3. Ezra Pound, review of Robert Frost's *North of Boston*, cited by Janet Todd, *The Cambridge Introduction to Jane Austen* (Cambridge University Press, 2006), p. 33.
4. George Eliot, *Daniel Deronda*, ed. Terence Cave (New York: Penguin Books, 1995), p. 538.
5. Samuel Beckett, *Molloy* (New York: Grove Press, 1955), p. 151.
6. William Makepeace Thackeray, *The Book of Snobs*, in *The Oxford Thackeray*, ed. George Saintsbury, 17 vols. (Oxford University Press), vol. ix, n.d., p. 430.
7. John Galsworthy, *The Forsyte Saga* (Oxford University Press, 1995), p. 351.

23

The novel amid new sciences

PHILLIP MALLETT

"You mean that she is too scientific? So long as she remains the great literary genius that she is, how can she be too scientific? She is simply permeated with the highest culture of the age." Thus Theodora defends her heroine, George Eliot, in Henry James's wittily ambivalent *"Daniel Deronda*: A Conversation."[1] Whether or not it was the highest form of culture, the idea of science is hardly less evident in the Victorian era than the effects of its application. Periodicals and the daily press carried reports on scientific meetings and disputes; *Nature*, dedicated to science, began publishing in 1869. Scientific societies sprang up or reformed themselves, laid claim to new premises or expanded old ones. Enthusiastic amateurs collected fossils, explored rock pools, and gazed at the stars, or stayed indoors to read such bestsellers as Gideon Mantell's *The Wonders of Geology* (1838), Charles Kingsley's *Glaucus; or, the Wonders of the Shore* (1855), and Richard Proctor's *Essays on Astronomy* (1872). Museums, exhibitions, and demonstrations attracted large audiences, while popular lecture series turned professional men of science like Faraday, Tyndall, and Huxley into public figures.

Meanwhile, the notion of what constitutes science was being revised. Originally a synonym for the state of knowing, by around 1700 "science" had come to denote knowledge acquired by study, and more especially an organized body of knowledge, consisting of defined terms, coherent proofs, and regular laws. It is in this sense that political economy, sociology, anthropology, and psychology would later establish themselves as sciences of human behavior. The use of science as the generic name for the separate studies of chemistry, physics, and so forth belongs to the nineteenth century; it was ready to hand when Charles Babbage, William Whewell, and others, despairing of a moribund Royal Society, met in York in 1831 to found the British Association for the Advancement of Science. Even so, those who attended the Association's early meetings were unsure what to call themselves: "philosopher" seemed too grand, *"savant"* dangerously French, "scientist," formed by analogy with "artist," too evidently a neologism. But by 1840, when Whewell defended it in his *Philosophy of the Inductive Sciences*, "scientist" had become the title for the "cultivator of science in general," "science" the collective term for the study of the material world, and both, for admirers and detractors alike, the keywords of a new age.[2]

Theodora speaks of Eliot's mind as "permeated" by science. The metaphor (itself drawn from physics) suggests that scientific ideas both penetrate and diffuse themselves through other forms of discourse; they are everywhere felt to be present, but their origin and the nature of their influence are difficult to track down. How to do so has been one of the concerns of an emerging interdiscipline of "science and literature." In broad terms, there have been three kinds of approach. Earlier studies followed a powerful strain of cultural criticism, typified by Matthew Arnold's 1882 Rede lecture on "Literature and Science," in proposing an essentially reactive model.[3] On this view scientific investigation is rational, objective, and morally neutral; its aim is to uncover discrete "pieces of knowledge," which can be confirmed by observation and experiment. These might cumulatively enforce new "conceptions of the universe," but they have no immediate relation "to our sense for conduct, to our sense for beauty." Science neither responds to nor seeks to "engage the emotions"; that task is left to the transformative imagination of the poet. Literature is the junior partner in a lopsided relationship; the writer may borrow from and give human resonance to the language and concepts of science, but the scientist has nothing to learn from the writer.

The belief that science and literature operate in a state of mutual incomprehension proved stubbornly long lived, as C. P. Snow's 1959 lecture on "The Two Cultures" attests, but it was never wholly dominant, and by the 1980s it was being dismantled. Tess Cosslett's *The "Scientific Movement" and Victorian Literature* (1982) drew attention to the aesthetic, moral, and emotional meanings called into play in the work of scientists like Tyndall, Huxley, and W. K. Clifford. Far from being antithetical, Victorian science and literature pursue similar concerns: the commitment to "truth," the recognition of "law," belief in the unity of, and interrelatedness within, Nature, the role of the imagination in constructing knowledge, the tolerance of contradiction and the openness to mystery – all these are the values of the "prevailing scientific culture," but they are "implicitly assimilated into a wide range of literature."[4] For novelists like Eliot and Hardy, they provide the standard by which the conduct of a Dorothea or Gabriel Oak is approved, that of a Rosamond Vincy or Farmer Boldwood found wanting.

Gillian Beer's seminal *Darwin's Plots* (1983) argued for a still deeper consonance between scientific writing and imaginative literature. Beer began with two key observations. First, mid-Victorian scientists share a common language with other educated readers. They deploy motifs, analogies, and rhetorical strategies whose meanings, at least in part, are already established within the wider literary tradition, and can never be wholly contained; hence Darwin's anxieties about the metaphorical valency of such phrases as "the struggle for existence," or "natural selection." Second, in their preoccupation with time and change, the theories of Lyell and Darwin in particular have close affinities with narrative history and the writing of fiction. *The Origin of Species* (1859) too has a story to tell, which shares the novelist's interest in cause and effect, transformation, hidden lines of kinship and descent, and the role of chance in a deterministic order. The "traffic" between literature and science is "two-way," each informing the other: "not only *ideas* but metaphors, myths, and narrative patterns could move rapidly to and fro between scientists and non-scientists: though not without frequent creative misprision."[5] George Levine's *Darwin and the Novelists* (1988) nudges this argument a step further, to view science and literature as not merely convergent but similarly constituted practices embedded in a particular social formation. His work is accordingly less concerned with "influence" than with the "cultural matrix" from which both science and literature emerge, and which they help to form, and Levine is as much interested in Austen, Dickens, and Trollope, who by and large did not read scientific books, as in Eliot and Hardy, who did. Where Beer's work tracks the migration of evolutionary concepts back and forth between scientists and novelists, Levine proposes a "one-culture" model that embraces both: "a gestalt of the Darwinian imagination," as detectable in fiction as in science.[6]

Levine argued with some care that to emphasize the social, linguistic, and intellectual contexts within which science is done is not to deny its rationality and internal coherence. Precisely this objection has, however, been made by Joseph Carroll, who in *Literary Darwinism: Evolution, Human Nature, and Literature* (2004) accuses Beer and Levine of preferring to flirt with post-structuralist indeterminacy, rather than concede the epistemological authority of science, and of evolutionary biology in particular. Offering itself as a new critical paradigm, literary Darwinism in Carroll's view holds that fiction can most productively be read in search of patterns of human behavior – child bearing and rearing, the battle for resources, competition and cooperation within families and communities – which are taken to be innate and universal, rather than historically contingent. Fiction supplies the data, science the principles on which analysis is to be based, and literary Darwinism the articulation of the two. Claims such as Carroll's that literary scholars should adopt the methods of the natural sciences have in their turn been rejected as reductive,[7] and the most promising recent work in the field continues to test and refine Beer's "two-way traffic" model, especially in relation to writing about medicine, pathology, and the sciences of the mind.

Darwin deprecated his own taste in imaginative literature;[8] Trollope claimed little knowledge of or interest in science. Yet Trollope's realism – "as real," in Hawthorne's words, "as if some giant had hewn a great lump out of the earth and put it under a glass case"[9] – can be correlated to the world uncovered in *The Origin*. The attention paid in the novels to the formation of systems, classes, and groups (the Church, Parliament, the legal profession) and to what it means for individuals to belong to them, is a counterpart to Darwin's fascination with the processes of "structure and coadaptation" at work in nature.[10] Trollope's chosen subject, the "state of progressive change" in personal and social life (*Autobiography*, 319), is the expression of innumerable struggles, if not out and out for existence then at least for power and place, whether among London politicians or the clergy and their wives in the environs of Barchester. Even Septimus Harding in *The Warden* (1854), who wants nothing more than to play his cello and care for his elderly bedesmen at Hiram's Hospital, finds that merely by virtue of his office he and they are in conflict, just as (in Darwin's example) two seedling mistletoes on one branch may "truly be said to struggle with each other" (*The Origin*, 53).

In Trollope's world, as in Darwin's, events unfold gradually, and along intelligible paths, but in neither do they follow a precedent design; Trollope's indifference to the "perfected plot" (*Autobiography*, 232), with its implicit promise of an organizing power, is a fictional analogue to Darwinian dys-teleology. Whether on the public or the private level, beginnings are obscure, endings only apparent. There is, first, no fixed point of origin. The action of the Barsetshire novels turns on questions of Church remuneration, but there is no "original settlement" written down in "ecclesiastical black-letter" which will resolve them; Mark Robarts in *Framley Parsonage* (1861) never chooses to deceive his wife, or betray his patroness, but as he slides slowly into debt, "by degrees his feelings became less acute," and he does both.[11] And second, there are no conclusions: or rather, those offered, such as the marriages of "four couple of sighing lovers" in the final chapter of *Framley Parsonage*, are provided to fulfill the novelist's contract with the reader, not in fidelity to the real world, and are in any case undermined as characters and situations spill over into subsequent novels. The existing state of affairs in the novels as in *The Origin* is always and only the outcome of numerous small adaptive acts over long periods of time, not evidence of a purpose working in or above history.

Trollope's prose is at one with the narrative structure of his novels. It represents itself as describing what any observer might have seen, much as Darwin draws not only on his own observations but on those of his numerous correspondents, and in its apparent neutrality, its refusal to appear surprised, it suggests that the events it reports can be sufficiently accounted for: "How was it possible," the narrator asks, characteristically, "that such a one [as Mark Robarts] should not relish the intimacy of Mr Sowerby?" (*Framley Parsonage*, 26). This sufficiency is, however, only a partial truth. Trollope's realism is flexible; it can accommodate both Lucy Robarts's courage when she declines Lufton's proposal of marriage, and her wisdom when she finally accepts him; moral constancy is not incompatible with a readiness to adapt. But it falters before Lily Dale, whose continued refusal of Johnny Eames in *The Small House at Allington* (1864) borders on the perverse, or Josiah Crawley, the impoverished and at times half-crazed Perpetual Curate of Hogglestock. A man as awkward as his title, Crawley appears *sui generis*, a maladaptation. In a strictly Darwinian world such intransigence would be fatal, but that does not disqualify his protest against the injustice of his lot: "Gift bread chokes in a man's throat and poisons his blood ... You have never tried it" (*Framley Parsonage*, 435). In *The Origin* Darwin offers the consoling belief "that the war of nature is not incessant, that no fear is felt, that death is generally prompt" (66). Just briefly, *Framley Parsonage* allows Crawley's bitterness to give the lie to that polite fiction, but then reinstates it, by ensuring that since he will not adjust to his environment, the environment will adapt itself to him. It does so by finding a hybrid class, ambiguously both natural and cultural, to which he and his opponents can equally belong: "We are," Archdeacon Grantly tells him, "both gentlemen."[12] If the novelist so chooses, as here he does, the spirit of comedy can always trump scientific rigor.

The direct evidence for Dickens's scientific interests is in articles about science that he published in *Household Words* and *All the Year Round*. In the novels it manifests itself as a problem about knowledge: both what may be known, and the processes of knowing. "Facts alone," maintains Thomas Gradgrind, "are wanted in life," but *Hard Times* (1854) – indeed, Dickens's work as a whole – is one long argument against the kind of enquiry, or "ology," which from Facts alone constructs general laws that too often sustain systems and institutions at the expense of the individual. Oliver Twist acquires his surname as the twentieth foundling, T being the twentieth letter of the alphabet, just as Sissy Jupe in *Hard Times* is Girl number 20. Both are victims of the Gradgrindian knowledge of tables, laws, and averages that is charged with the callousness of the New Poor Law in *Oliver Twist* (1838) and with the broken homes, wrecked marriages, and industrial misery in *Hard Times*. Bitzer, Gradgrind's star pupil, understands that the heart is necessary to the circulation of the blood, and can define a horse ("Quadruped. Graminivorous . . ."), but the novel confronts him with what exceeds knowledge of Facts; a horse that dances the polka, and men and women who obey the dictates of the heart rather than "rational" self-interest. Both novels require the fantastic to achieve a partial resolution. Oliver recovers his bourgeois status, but only because in the rhetorical sequence of the novel he figures as "the principle of Good" rather than a historically realized identity; Dickens's claim in the preface, that seemingly "impossible" events in the mundane world may yet disclose "God's truth," is less compelling than his fascination with meaninglessness, passed on after Oliver's rescue to the jailed Fagin and the fleeing Bill Sikes. Sissy Jupe too comes through, but in order to protect the reasons of the heart from the challenge of Gradgrindism Dickens has to render them inarticulate, lisped out by Sleary the Cackler, and "at leatht ath hard to give a name to, ath the wayth of the dogth ith!"[13] What truly needs to be known is beyond the definitions of science.

The problem of knowledge is still more urgent in *Bleak House* (1853) and *Little Dorrit* (1857). In both, society's refusal to admit the great fact of human relatedness prompts analogies with ideas current in thermodynamics in the 1850s. *Bleak House* opens on a day that evokes at once the beginning and the end of time, while the city's spatial coordinates are obscured by the fog, and its inhabitants reduced to "Chance people," isolated particles adrift in a world remote from the uniform space–time posited by Newtonian physics. Entropy, or energy unavailable for useful work, is perpetually increasing. (Clausius coined the term in 1865, but the principle was known from the early 1850s.) Buildings want to fall down, Chesney Wold in Lincolnshire no less than Tom-all-alone's in London; individuals remain fixed in endless repetition, or change only to become still more what they always were, like Krook, transformed by spontaneous combustion to "a dark greasy coating on the walls and ceiling," or Sir Leicester, reduced by a stroke to "perpetual stoppage."[14]

There is of course a counter-movement. Entering the dispute on the age of the sun, William Thomson (later Lord Kelvin) argued that the light and heat essential to life on earth will fail within a few million years, "unless sources now unknown to us are prepared in the great storehouse of creation."[15] Thomson was confident that these sources are being prepared, but outside the realm of the knowable. It is Esther's role in the first-person narrative to act as the avatar of such sources of renewal. Even when illness leaves her temporarily blind, "confused" by "the divisions of time," and lost in a "great black space," she keeps faith that the world is knowable, and action possible: "Perhaps the less I say of these sick experiences, the less tedious and the more intelligible I shall be" (513–514). But while Esther struggles to return damaged lives to use, creating order out of chaos, for most of the characters all experience is sick, tedious and without meaning. In place of the past-tense narration, which suggests completion, the third-person narrative employs the present tense, implicitly questioning the power of overview to bring events to order. Lists, non-hierarchical and indefinitely extensible, as in the account of Krook's shop, or Miss Flite's birds, become the defining rhetorical mode of the novel. Secrets come to light, but too late; as Hortense taunts Bucket, with an emphasis Clausius and Thomson would have understood, he cannot "restore" the murdered Tulkinghorn to life, or re-create Lady Dedlock as an "honorable lady" (773–774). The novel ends with a new Bleak House, but it stands as an imaginative model of desire, an act of will by the novelist. Meaning is projected beyond the world, drawn from "sources now unknown," rather than found within it.

The sunshine that opens *Little Dorrit* is hardly less oppressive than the London fog. Nature, once God's second book, testimony to a loving Deity, in this novel means only itself. The August sun blazes down on the same disorder at Marseilles and in the Marshalsea prison; later it will shine on the metaphorical fall of the House of Merdle, and the literal collapse of Mrs. Clennam's London property. In a paper "On a Universal Tendency in Nature to the Dissipation of Mechanical Energy" (1852), Thomson argued that since "the Creative Power alone" can call energy into existence, or destroy it, energy which appears lost "cannot be annihilation, but must be some transformation of energy";[16] but in *Little Dorrit* waste is everywhere: in every physical environment – in the dust of London, the decay of Venice and the ruins of Rome, even in the Alps, where the snow is trodden into pools of mud – and in every life. The novel is a virtual typology of the ways human energy can be wasted: turned inwards in self-torment (Miss Wade, Tattycoram), thwarted by institutions (Meagles's battle with the Circumlocution Office), drained away by languor or self-doubt (Gowan, Clennam). Even love expresses itself in self-abnegation rather than desire. The few outbursts of energy late in the novel, such as Affery's rebellion against "the clever ones," or Pancks's exposure of the grasping landlord Casby, even the love between Amy and Arthur, moving as it is, and offering some hope that the powers of growth and recovery are not wholly exhausted, are too frail to set against a "universal tendency." The sun still shines in the last chapter, "through the painted figure of Our Saviour," as if trying to recruit some spiritual meaning, but it shines on those going down into the "usual uproar" of the crowded city streets, conceived in this novel, as in *Bleak House*, as a mere aggregate of matter and force. The scientific metaphors suggest the inevitability of defeat; only the fictive energy of the prose remains to assert the novelist's power to resist the forces of decomposition.

George Eliot's response to science is systematic where Dickens's is opportunistic. Her literary realism is premised on a series of linked ideas: the "invariability of sequence which is acknowledged as the basis of physical science"; the principle of continuity, by which "every past phase of human development is part of that education of the human race in which we are sharing"; and the interrelation of the individual and society – more abstractly, of the organism and its environment.[17] All three are in play in *Silas Marner* (1861). In one aspect the novel is an anthropological study, within the framework of Comtean positivism, of the life and customs of urban Lantern Yard and rural Raveloe, in the opening years of the nineteenth century. The differences between the two communities are scrupulously noted, but in each the fetishistic beliefs and resistance to rational explanation attract the narrator's disapproval; Eliot knew how easily religious certainties erode human sympathy. Equally Comtean, however, is the recognition that the need for belief persists into modern times, and must be treated with tolerance. Society, Eliot writes, is *"incarnate history . . .* What has grown up historically can only die out historically, by the gradual operation of necessary laws."[18] Human society is a natural structure; its evolution is as slow and inexorable as the evolution of species.

Implicit in Eliot's concern with social development is the issue of personal identity. In Marner's case psychological continuity is disrupted by the cataleptic fits that admit chance events into his life: he is framed for theft, robbed of his gold, and stands in a trance as Eppie enters his house. The "chasm in his consciousness,"[19] which leaves him unaccountable for his actions, calls into question the idea of a rational unified self, and in the process threatens Eliot's project as a literary realist. To show that real continuity underlies apparent chance, Eliot turns to associationist psychology, particularly as developed by Alexander Bain (himself the son of a weaver), which explains mental states by the formation of habit, and the consequent strengthening of nerve pathways in the brain.[20] Mental states and habits, rooting psychology in physiology, shape the argument and metaphors of the novel. Denied any "channel" for his "sense of mystery," or "pathway" for the expression of his thoughts, Silas turns inward, his life "hardening" by "repetition" into "a mere pulsation of desire" for gold, but with Eppie's arrival, and his gradual re-entry into the community, old "fibres" are "stirred," and old "habits" revive (Eliot uses "habit" and its cognate forms twenty times in the novel); forgotten feelings begin to "vibrate" (as Eppie's feelings vibrate in response to his), and his mind "grow[s] into memory" (15–16, 19, 109, 123, 166, 124). Marner's recovery is a happy reversal of the Midas story of the daughter turned to gold; but for Eliot it is also the recuperation of her own key to all mythologies: the principle of unvarying law.

Middlemarch (1871–1872) was rightly seen as the most overtly scientific of Victorian novels. In 1863 Eliot wrote: "It is the habit of my imagination to strive after as full a vision of the medium in which a character moves as of the character itself."[21] The thought derives from her zoological studies with Lewes, which taught her that organic life subsists in the relation between the organism and the world it inhabits. Since this relation is constantly changing, the survival of the organism entails continuous functional adaptation, which in turn requires an increasingly complex interaction with the environment. The same principles hold within society: social advance leads simultaneously toward greater individuation and greater dependence. This is the truth adumbrated in *Middlemarch* by the interweaving of plots ("Three Love Problems," "Two Temptations"), echoed in the numerous metaphors drawn from biology, and glimpsed by Dorothea when in chapter 80 she recognizes herself as part of "the largeness of the world" and its "involuntary, palpitating life."[22] In "Notes on Form in Art" (1868) Eliot insists on the importance of "organic form," or "the relation of multiplex independent parts to a whole" (*Essays*, 433). The indivisibility of part and whole, of which *Middlemarch* is the supreme example in English fiction, is for Eliot the grand unifying idea from which can be educed the principles of literary form, the laws of biology, and the sociology of provincial life.

Eliot's richest analysis of scientific thought comes in the description of Lydgate's work in chapter 16 of *Middlemarch*. Unlike the Rev. Farebrother's natural history, which stops at collection and classification, Lydgate's research examines structure and function. The biology of the 1830s, guided by Lydgate's hero François Bichat, is concerned to interpret organisms in their temporal aspect. Like the novelist, the biologist wishes to know "how the mysterious mixture [*sc.* "man"] behaves under the varying experiments of Time." For this, observation alone is insufficient: the "minute processes which prepare human misery and joy" are "inaccessible by any sort of lens." They can, however, be "tracked . . . through long pathways of necessary sequence by the inward light which is the last refinement of Energy" (*Middlemarch*, 162–163). This is close to Thomas Huxley's account, in his 1853 essay on

"The Cell Theory," of the need to combine deductive and inductive methods, and to bring in "the powerful aid of the imagination, kept, of course, in due and rigid subordination, to assist the faculties of observation and reasoning."[23] The "inward light" of the disciplined imagination is as necessary to the creation and testing of hypotheses as it is to the construction of stories. This testing, Lydgate argues later, requires the mind to be "continually expanding and shrinking between the whole human horizon and the horizon of an object-glass" (630). In the same way, Eliot's narrator focusses on, say, Bulstrode's self-examination in chapter 61, and then withdraws to reflect on the nature of human deceit and inconsistency. Lydgate's research fails because he frames his question not quite in the way required by the waiting answer; but his methods are exemplary for the novelist.

The finest aspect of Eliot's genius, writes Henry James, is "the combination of her love of general truth and love of the special case."[24] The special case is both one of the triumphs of *Middlemarch* and the source of Eliot's chief difficulties in the novel. In chapter 42 the narrator stumbles in the attempt to understand both Casaubon and Dorothea, as each is said to struggle with feelings – the fear of failure, the sense of moral superiority – of which at the same time they apparently have no knowledge. Lying behind the uncertainty, as in the account of Bulstrode's self-deceptions, or of Rosamond's vacillations in chapter 81, is a model of the mind as federal, one part operating independently of or even against another. Perhaps influenced by her early interest in phrenology, Eliot is unable to reconcile her account of the repression of mental states, so often a central concern in her fiction, with her belief in the indivisibility of part and whole. Instead, the novel turns to the remedial power of human affection. Brooding over his imminent death, alone in his study, Casaubon cannot be understood, but he can be met with love, as Dorothea waits for him at the end of the chapter. "Yet surely, surely," says the narrator of "Janet's Repentance" (1857), "the only true knowledge of our fellow-man is that which enables us to feel with him."[25] The power and the burden of the kind of knowledge that begins and ends in sympathy (and its possible relation to gender) are as deeply the theme of Eliot's fiction as her commitment to scientific means of observation, imagination, and generalization.

"'The very ground-thought of Science,' Hardy copied into his notebook, 'is to treat man as part of the natural order.'"[26] In Hardy's fiction this means not just that men and women work outdoors, but that they are simultaneously alien presences in nature, as suggested by the abrupt shifts of scale and perspective – the fleeting set against the permanent, the microscopic against the panoramic – and caught up helplessly in its energies, whether the instinctual life of Egdon Heath, the struggle for existence in the woods of Little Hintock, or the appetite for joy that surges through the Vale of the Great Dairies. Like Comte, whose work he read in the mid-1870s, Hardy asserts the physical basis of our affective life. Subjectivity in the novels is registered not through introspection or free indirect discourse – the usual means of the psychological novelist – but somatically, in terms of physical sensation (changes in the rhythm of the blood, or the breath), or altered perception of the outer world. Hardy's characters are in thrall to physiological process; they flush, palpitate, quiver, as much as they think. Gilles Deleuze suggests that they are not so much "people or subjects" as "collections of intensive sensations."[27] Humanity in Hardy's novels is not merely part of the natural order, but subordinated within it.

But Hardy is ambivalent. His reading in contemporary science led him toward what Max Weber calls "the disenchantment of the world": a vision of a morally indifferent universe, subject to determining laws, in which consciousness is the unintended byproduct of chance organizations of matter. Yet this is not his only view of our relation to the natural world. More than a dozen of Hardy's notebook entries taken from Comte relate to "Fetishism," understood as the tendency to view objects in nature as animate. In *The Return of the Native* (1878) this appears partly in the form of what Edward Tylor designates "survivals," vestiges of "primitive" cultures living on in attenuated form into a nominally Christian age.[28] Thus the bonfires at the beginning of the novel commemorate "the instinctive and resistant act of man" to seek heat and light, and the maypole dance at the close "the instincts of merry England": "the impulses of all such outlandish hamlets are pagan still."[29] In a darker shape, pagan traditions inform Susan Nunsuch's witchcraft against Eustacia. The narrator faithfully records those moods and rituals, but he does so as a man of advanced culture, mindful of the distinction between the Egdon mumming, which is "a fossilized survival" carried on without excitement, and "a spurious reproduction," taken up at that moment in history where inherited traditions are consciously reacquired as heritage (122). The inhabitants of Egdon are unaware that their ceremonies have their origins in a prehistoric past; the narrator, who knows, is by that very knowledge cut off from them.

But to recognize the beliefs of the heath-dwellers as atavistic is not to dismiss all sense of a spiritual relation between humanity and the natural world. Typically ironized, as when Henry Knight suspects Nature of feline trickery as he hangs on the Cliff without a Name in *A Pair of Blue Eyes* (1873), the spiritual sense nonetheless refuses to die away. In the passage describing Clym's "curious microscopic" life, cutting furze in the midst of bees, butterflies, grasshoppers, and rabbits, a Darwinian sense of the energy and abundance of the world combines with a Pre-Raphaelite intensity of observation; for a moment all becomes foreground, suggesting the impossible plenitude of a life fully immersed in the particularities of touch, sound, sight, and movement. There is more than the pathetic fallacy in the description of the heath on the night Eustacia dies: "Never was harmony more perfect than that between the chaos of her mind and the chaos of the world without" (253–254, 358). When the anthropologist Edward Clodd referred the superstitions of the Dorset peasantry to "the barbaric idea which confuses persons and things," Hardy addded that this idea is "also common to the highest imaginative genius – that of the poet."[30] The idea is also, cautiously, allowed to edge its way into the fiction. In Hardy, as not in Tylor, a "barbaric" and a "modern" view of life are allowed to co-exist rather than succeed each other.

Hardy's evolutionary and broadly materialist philosophy led him, as it led Darwin, to question the boundary between the cultural and the natural, the learned and the instinctual. Hardy's last three novels, influenced by the work of Henry Maudsley and August Weismann on heredity, explore the idea that we carry our destinies ready formed within us. Weismann in *Essays on Heredity* (1885) proposed the existence of "germ cells" as a mechanism for inheritance; Maudsley spelled out the implications. Our life-stories are scripted in the lives of our forebears; we inherit them as we inherit our features: "the decrees of destiny have gone forth, and [we] cannot withstand nor reverse them."[31] Tess fulfills the legend of the d'Urberville coach, Jude and Sue act out the curse of the House of Fawley, Pierston is doomed every twenty years to court an Avice Caro. Angel wonders what "obscure strain in the d'Urberville blood" led Tess to murder Alec, Jude confesses that he carries in him "the germs of every human infirmity": Tess, Jude, and Sue all, at times, lose the sense of themselves as subjects.[32] But Hardy refuses to concede everything to biological determinism. Culture, not nature, is the site of their disabilities, and the main energy of the novels is directed against the social, economic, and religious forces that weigh down on them. Neither individual temperament, nor class identity, in Hardy's fiction, is finally reducible to biology.

George Gissing is less resistant to the explanatory power of medical and social science. As Marx and Engels had noticed, the theory of natural selection, originally suggested by the Malthusian principle that the human population would inevitably outgrow the resources needed to sustain it, had since been returned from the animal and plant world to history, and used to naturalize competition as the inevitable law of society. From here it was all too easy to conflate class separation and biological difference. In *The Nether World* (1889)

Gissing represents the urban environment as at once the cause and the out-come of racial decline. Both socio-economic and hereditarian explanations are invoked, but with no attempt to reconcile them; chapter 9, titled "Pathological," attributes Clara Hewett's misery equally to "social tyranny" and "the disease inherent in her being."[33] Contemporary discourses of degen-eration brought to the fore the question hidden in the phrase "the survival of the fittest": fitness for what? In *The Nether World* Sidney Kirkwood's delight in art and the natural world unfits him for life in the slums; Clem Peckover, triumphantly at ease there, is an apt example of Ray Lankester's 1880 defi-nition of a degenerate organism as one adapted "to *less* varied and *less* complex conditions of life."[34] Sidney's work, making jewels for the denizens of an unseen upper world, is both the type of alienated labor, in which the worker's activity, as Marx saw in the 1840s, is the loss of himself, and an instance of Darwin's account of parasitism, with the striking difference that in Gissing the parasite is the more rather than the less complex being. Poverty and biology predetermine personality; escape is barely imaginable. The naturalism of *The Nether World* reflects, as Lukács argues, the disillusionment of the passive observer of a reified world; all it can offer is isolated pictures of the morbid variety of slum life.[35] Gissing's personal investment in the value of literary creation proves of no more account than Kirkwood's talent as a draughtsman; both are reduced to baffled spectatorship of a world that seems incapable of change.

H. G. Wells's scientific romances of the 1890s offer still bleaker readings of class struggle and degeneration, within a vision of global entropy. *The Island of Dr. Moreau* (1896) demolishes the assumption of human superiority over the natural world. The plasticity of living forms admits no distinction between men and beasts: Moreau's surgery creates beast-men who speak, think, and institute laws, only to revert to their animal natures; Prendick and his fellows, driven by hunger, regress towards murder and cannibalism. In the *Descent of Man* (1871), Darwin saw morality develop from the social instincts among animals. Wells is closer to the Huxley of "Evolution and Ethics" (1893), for whom the instincts are anti-social, and the ethical life one which depends precisely on *not* following nature. Moreau's impassivity before suffering enacts the "moral indifference" of the cosmos, before which, Huxley argues, "the conscience of man" stands revolted.[36] Humanity belongs to nature, but is not at home in it.

The Traveller in *The Time Machine* (1895) describes mankind in the remote future as divided into two species, fulfilling the logic of contemporary class separation. An etiolated upper class, weakened by leisure and a too perfect security, has devolved into the Eloi, graceful but childlike beings of diminished stature and energy, and without secondary sexual characteristics. They are preyed on by the Morlocks, half-simian and half-human descendants of the proletariat, who instead of dying out, or being bred out of existence, have wholly adapted to their nether world conditions. It is a future that realizes the worst fears of theorists of degeneration, and of eugenicists like Francis Galton in *Inquiries into Human Faculty and its Development* (1883), but so far as it depends on choices made in the present, it allows room for intervention. Not so, however, with the Traveller's further report of the heat-death of the universe and the disappearance of human life, leaving the world to giant crab-like creatures, and finally a "round thing" resembling a medusa. The cosmic process leads only to extinction.

In his "Discourse introductory to a Course of Lectures on Chemistry," delivered at the Royal Institution in 1802, Humphrey Davy urged the scientist to "interrogate nature with power ... as a master." By the close of the century, the interrogation suggested that mankind was not master over nature, but part of it, and like all other parts subject to the laws that science had worked to discover. The next great advances were in physics and psychology – the discovery of electrons, x-rays, radioactivity, the interpretation of dreams – but the science of the twentieth century is to be at once less accessible to the non-specialist, and more troubling to human self-esteem. Reflecting on what the Traveller has to report in *The Time Machine*, the Narrator can only bow his head: "If that is so, it remains for us to live as though it were not so."[37]

Notes

1. Henry James, "*Daniel Deronda*: A Conversation" (1876); repr. in *George Eliot: the Critical Heritage*, ed. David Carroll (London: Routledge and Kegan Paul, 1971), p. 427.
2. Sidney Ross, "Scientist: The Story of a Word," *Annals of Science*, 18 (1962), 65–85.
3. The pioneering accounts are by Lionel Stevenson, *Darwin Among the Poets* (University of Chicago Press, 1932), and Leo Henkin, *Darwinism in the English Novel, 1860–1910* (New York: Corporate Press, 1940).
4. Tess Cosslett, *The "Scientific Movement" and Victorian Literature* (Brighton: Harvester Press, 1982), p. 3.
5. Gillian Beer, *Darwin's Plots: Evolutionary Narrative in Darwin, George Eliot and Nineteenth-Century Fiction* (2nd edn, Cambridge University Press, 2000), p. 5: emphases in original.
6. George Levine, *Darwin and the Novelists: Patterns of Science in Victorian Fiction* (University of Chicago Press, 1988), p. 13.

7. For summary and critique, see Gowan Dowson, "Literature and Science under the Microscope," *Journal of Victorian Culture*, 11: 2 (2006), 301–315.

8. Darwin's reading notebook for 1855 records, without comment: "The Warden (a novel)."

9. Quoted by Trollope, in *An Autobiography*, ed. P. D. Edwards (Oxford University Press, 1980), p. 144.

10. Charles Darwin, *The Origin of Species*, ed. Gillian Beer (Oxford University Press, 1996), p. 4.

11. Anthony Trollope, *Framley Parsonage*, ed. P. D. Edwards (Oxford University Press, 1980), pp. 168, 64.

12. Anthony Trollope, *The Last Chronicle of Barset*, ed. Stephen Gill (Oxford University Press, 1980), p. 885.

13. Charles Dickens, *Hard Times*, ed. Paul Schlicke (Oxford University Press, 1989), p. 390.

14. Charles Dickens, *Bleak House*, ed. Stephen Gill (Oxford University Press, 1996), pp. 476, 173.

15. "On the Age of the Sun's Heat," *Macmillan's Magazine* 5 (March 1862), 388–393.

16. *Proceedings of the Royal Society of Edinburgh* 3 (April 1852), 139.

17. George Eliot, "The Progress of the Intellect," in *Essays of George Eliot*, ed. Thomas Pinney (London: Routledge and Kegan Paul, 1963), p. 31.

18. George Eliot, "The Natural History of German Life" (1856), in *Essays*, p. 287 (emphases in original).

19. George Eliot, *Silas Marner*, ed. Terence Cave (Oxford University Press, 1996), p. 108.

20. As well as with Bain's *The Senses and the Intellect* (1855) and *The Emotions and the Will* (1859), Eliot was familiar with associationism from John Stuart Mill and G. H. Lewes.

21. *The George Eliot Letters*, ed. Gordon S. Haight, 9 vols. (New Haven, CT: Yale University Press, 1954–78), vol. IV, p. 97.

22. George Eliot, *Middlemarch*, ed. David Carroll (Oxford University Press, 1997), p. 776.

23. Thomas Huxley, *Scientific Memoirs*, 5 vols. (London: Macmillan, 1898–1903), vol. I, pp. 248–249.

24. Henry James, "George Eliot's Life" (1885); repr. in *George Eliot: The Critical Heritage*, ed. David Carroll (London: Routledge and Kegan Paul, 1971), p. 498.

25. George Eliot, *Scenes of Clerical Life*, ed. Thomas Noble (Oxford University Press, 2000), p. 229.

26. Thomas Hardy, *The Literary Notebooks of Thomas Hardy*, ed. Lennart A. Björk, 2 vols. (London: Macmillan,1985), vol. I, p. 65: transcribed from John Addington Symonds, *Studies of the Greek Poets* (London: Smith, Elder & Co., 1876), p. 389.

27. Gilles Deleuze and Claire Parnet, *Dialogues*, trans. Hugh Tomlinson and Barbara Habberjam (New York: Columbia University Press, 1987), pp. 39–40.

28. See Edward Tylor, *Primitive Culture: Researches into the Development of Mythology, Philosophy, Religion, Art, and Custom*, 2 vols. (London: John Murray, 1871).

29. Thomas Hardy, *The Return of the Native*, ed. Simon Gatrell (Oxford University Press, 1990), pp. 15, 389–390.
30. *The Life and Work of Thomas Hardy, by Thomas Hardy*, ed. Michael Millgate (London: Macmillan, 1984), p. 241.
31. Henry Maudsley, *The Pathology of Mind* (New York: Appleton and Co., 1880), p. 89.
32. Thomas Hardy, *Tess of the d'Urbervilles*, ed. Juliet Grindle and Simon Gatrell (Oxford University Press, 2005), p. 408; *Jude the Obscure*, ed. Patricia Ingham (Oxford University Press, 1985), p. 279.
33. George Gissing, *The Nether World*, ed. John Goode (Brighton: Harvester Press, 1982), p. 86.
34. E. Ray Lankester, *Degeneration: A Chapter in Darwinism* (London: Macmillan, 1880), p. 32 (emphases in original).
35. Georg Lukács, "Narrate or Describe?" in *Writer and Critic*, ed. and trans. Arthur Kahn (London: Merlin Press, 1970), p. 114.
36. Thomas Huxley, "Evolution and Ethics," in *Collected Essays*, 9 vols. (London: Macmillan, 1893–1894), vol. IX, p. 59.
37. H. G. Wells, *The Time Machine*, ed. Patrick Parrinder (London: Penguin Books, 2005), p. 91.

24

George Eliot's past and present: emblematic histories

BARRY V. QUALLS

> Would'st read thy self, and read thou know'st not what
> And yet know whether thou art blest or not,
> By reading the same lines? O then come hither,
> And lay my Book, thy Hand and Heart together.
>
> *Pilgrim's Progress*

> No radiant angel came across the gloom with a clear message for her.
> In those times, as now ... [s]uch truth as came to them was brought
> confusedly in the voices and deeds of men not at all like the seraphs of
> unfailing wing and piercing vision.
>
> *Romola*[1]

"In those times, as now": with this characteristic phrase George Eliot writes of past and present and of the absence of those spiritual symbols that would confirm belief and lead characters toward the promised land – somewhere. Maggie Tulliver's journey in *The Mill on the Floss* toward the metaphorical "Promised Land" is, the narrator notes, "thirsty, trackless, uncertain" (251). The endings of all of George Eliot's novels leave one, if not dissatisfied, then certain that promised lands are at most imagined ideas about moral sympathy and, sometimes, belief; they are not Dickensian communities grouped around the hearth. Dickens's endings have no part of George Eliot's commitment to realism.

Born in 1819 into a world of vast change – "Since yesterday, a century has passed away," we hear in *Middlemarch* (1872) (378) – George Eliot more than all Victorian novelists encompasses the movements of mind that characterize Queen Victoria's England. Beginning her life as an intensely Evangelical Christian, she became the translator of David Friedrich Strauss's *Leben Jesu* (1846) and Ludwig Feuerbach's *Essence of Christianity* (1854), an editor at the

I thank Deirdre David and Christiane Gannon for their readings of this chapter.

radical *Westminster Review*, and "the first great *godless* writer of fiction that has appeared in England . . . the first legitimate fruit of our modern atheistic pietism," "the emblem of a generation distracted between the intense need of believing and the difficulty of belief."[2] George Eliot brings to the writing of fiction an unparalleled understanding of the philosophical and epistemological issues and challenges of modernity, and a sense of the novel as anything but entertainment. Her novels, with their commitment to a realism grounded in the particularities of human experience and with their rejection of the "heroic artisan and sentimental peasant"[3] and of the melodramatic devices that put these characters in action, are the century's great meditations on the nature of fiction, on representing character amid change, and on depicting English life past and present.

Celebrated in her time for what appeared to be the Wordsworthian pastorals of *Adam Bede* (1859), *The Mill on the Floss* (1860), and *Silas Marner* (1861), George Eliot repeatedly challenges her own work; repeatedly asks questions about the conventions of fiction; and experiments with narrative form. She uses the *Bildung* genre to chart the progresses of her protagonists; but she combines it – she cannot help combining it – with the traditional spiritualized progress narrative that she and her readers inherit from Bunyan and from the Christian Bible. Finally, in her narrators, she creates one of the signal compelling voices in Victorian England for charting the signs of the times, the dislocations caused by industrialism, urbanization, Darwin, and the "march of mind." In her 1856 review of Wilhelm von Riehl's *The Natural History of German Life*, she writes:

> The nature of European men has its roots intertwined with the past, and can only be developed by allowing those roots to remain undisturbed while the process of development is going on, until that perfect ripeness of the seed which carries with it a life independent of the root. This vital connection with the past is much more vividly felt on the Continent than in England, where we have to recal it by an effort of memory and reflection; for though our English life is in its core intensely traditional, Protestantism and commerce have modernized the face of the land and the aspects of society in a far greater degree than in any continental country.
>
> (Pinney, *Essays of George Eliot*, 88–89)

George Eliot's sense of the severance of past and present in England leads her to create narrators as remembrancers; then as historians, anthropologists of past and present; and finally as writers of parable and even myth. She sees her novels as "incarnate history" (her phrase for Riehl's understanding of "people as they are"), realist representations that extend human sympathies towards all people, not just novelized characters.

How George Eliot came to write incarnate histories is the subject of this chapter. First I place her in the context of Thomas Carlyle's analysis of past and present. She saw in Carlyle a "reverence for the great and godlike under every sort of earthly mummery" (Pinney, *Essays of George Eliot*, 214–215). Then I place her in the context of the novel as she confronts it, and examine her construction of narrators and the ways she experiments with the form of the novel in order to find the voice and language that would bring to readers a "strong terrible vision" of the work of awakening human sympathies. If her earlier writing gives pleasure as a picture of life in "Merry England," in *Daniel Deronda* (1876) she turns away not from the "faithful account of men and things as they have mirrored themselves in my mind" (*Adam Bede*, 175), but from representing those accounts in a realist form. Realism could not be the total picture. A strong vision requires parable, requires finally the structures and voice of Scott *and* of Bunyan and the Bible. I conclude with an examination of her two great experiments as a moral "romancist," *Silas Marner* and *Daniel Deronda*. Novels, she discovers in her "experiments in life," need the typical, the parable, the memories sustained in Israel's history if they are to school the reader's heart and thus be more than entertainments.[4] No wonder her readers came to see her books as "second Bibles" (*George Eliot Letters*, vol. VI, 340).

Recasting Pilgrim's progress

> There is no longer any God for us! God's Laws are become a Greatest-Happiness Principle, a Parliamentary Expediency: the Heavens overreach us only as [a]...butt of Herschel-telescopes to shoot science at, to shoot sentimentalities at: – in our and old Jonson's dialect, man has lost the *soul* out of him...This is verily the plague-spot; centre of the universal Social Gangrene, threatening all modern things with frightful death.
>
> Carlyle, *Past and Present* (1843)[5]

Thomas Carlyle's analysis of the condition of England charts the break between past and present that was palpably *the* sign of the times and that produced the "Social Gangrene" that was always his subject. His voice and the images by which he represents the modern world address the reader directly; yet they recall Bunyan and those didactic exhortations that are so much a part of the conduct book and sermonic traditions of the nineteenth century.

Of course Carlyle does not sound like other writers – and certainly not like George Eliot. He declared, when critics asked why the "unmeaning" style of *Sartor Resartus*, that an age of revolutions would not hear prophetic voices if their language still lodged readers in the eighteenth century. His writing seeks to force connections with the reader, and tries to use language as more than "mere *words*" (*Heroes*, vol. v, 8), more than the debased verbal currencies of modernity.[6] In *The French Revolution* he proclaims that the history is "a journeying together" of reader and author, each of whom, "by the nature of him, is definable as 'an incarnated Word'" (vol. IV, 323). To write this history Carlyle repeatedly invokes contemporary England. Even the characters are not all "real"; alongside Mirabeau and "sea-green" Robespierre, he offers "Eatall, Do Nothing, Janus Bifrons, or *Mr. Facing-both-ways*, as vernacular Bunyan has it!'" (vol. III, 289). Astonishingly, he writes history in the present tense, and urges us to meditate on this subversive choice:

> For indeed it is a most lying thing that same Past Tense always: so beautiful, sad, almost Elysian-sacred, "in the moonlight of Memory," it seems; and *seems* only . . . Not *there* does Fear dwell . . . but it dwells *here* haunting us, tracking us . . . making the Tense a mere Present one! (vol. IV, 81)

This meditation on verb tense reminds us that Carlyle is always about *now*. Scott's *'Tis Sixty Years Since*, the subtitle of *Waverley*, does not interest him; there is no fear there, no material for vision. Only the godless present offers realities:

> Isolation is the sum-total of wretchedness to man. To be cut off, to be left solitary: to have a world alien, not your world; all a hostile camp for you . . . Encased each in his transparent 'ice-palace;' our brother visible in his, making signals and gesticulations to us; – visible but forever unattainable: on his bosom we shall never rest, nor he on ours. It was not a God that did this; no! (*Past and Present*, 271)

This great passage is about the breaking down of all signs, all spiritual languages, in nineteenth-century England. To combat this breakage, the Editor in *Sartor Resartus*, which Carlyle calls "a kind of Didactic novel," gives a *Pilgrim's-Progress* shape to the life writings of the German Diogenes Teufelsdröckh; and the Editor, like the voice in all of Carlyle's writing, constantly urges the reader to meditate on what these signs mean *for* the reader.

Carlyle's voice is (with modifications and moderations) the voice of many narrators of the Victorian novel, that interrupting voice that talks with the reader about the way we live now and about the way we write narratives in a godless world. His is the voice that reminds us that the novel is serious, not merely entertainment. For Carlyle it should provide "doctrine," "reproof," "edification," "healing," "guidance," "a divine awakening voice" for the "heroic that is in all men," as he proclaims in his essay on Scott, in whom he did not find those things. There is room for romance, but "Romance exists now, and formerly, and evermore it exists, strictly speaking, in Reality alone" (vol. XVIII, 329). In George Levine's apt comment, Victorian novels, so many seeking Paradise Regained, become anti-romance romances, existing on the boundaries of fiction and non-fiction.[7]

If Carlyle hopes that words create a world of pilgrims "in friendly company" and that romance helps us discover the spiritual in the modern "real," some contemporary novelists believe otherwise. Thackeray refuses the role of sage; he is the puppet-master in *Vanity Fair*, the "brother" in *Pendennis*. He agrees that author and reader should be in "constant communication" – in "a sort of confidential talk" – but that talk is not about spiritual progress. Isolation for him characterizes modern life: "How lonely we are in the world! How selfish and secret, everybody! . . . you and I are but a pair of infinite isolations, with some fellow-islands a little more or less near to us."[8] Thackeray refuses all comforts of moral language. He concludes *Pendennis* (1850) with a comment on the "ordainer of the lottery" under whose dispensation "the false and worthless live and prosper," and adds: "knowing how mean the best of us is, let us give a hand of charity to Arthur Pendennis, with all his faults and shortcomings, who does not claim to be a hero, but only a man and brother" (785). We are not far here, in mid-century, from Thomas Hardy's *Jude the Obscure* (1895), whose protagonist goes on pilgrimage to Christminster but never finds sacred space, nor hears voices whose words are more than empty. Ironically, what Jude hears are celebrations of Remembrance Games. There is no romance in reality, no remembrance of a moral world, simply death.

Yet Dickens and George Eliot agree with Bulwer Lytton that the novel *must* have a "moral signification" combined with "an obvious popular interest in character and incident." Bulwer found this "double plot" "a striking characteristic of the art of our century," necessary to show "life as it is . . . life in its spiritual and mystic as well as its more visible and fleshly characteristics." For him, "without some gleams of the supernatural, Man is not man, nor Nature, nature."[9] Dickens accepts this sense of what Carlyle calls "natural supernaturalism" as a given. His art is at once the most embedded in Victorian popular urban culture and the most determined to keep the old tropes of Bunyan alive. Those innocent orphans that George Eliot finds so impossible Dickens places amid a hellish world, and says why:

> Look around upon the world of odious sights . . . And then calling up some
> ghastly child, with stunted form and wicked face, hold forth on its unnatural

sinfulness, and lament its being, so early, far away from Heaven – but think a little of its having been conceived, and born, and bred, in Hell! . . .

Oh for a good spirit who would take the house-tops off . . . and show a Christian people what dark shapes issue from amidst their homes, to swell the retinue of the Destroying Angel as he moves forth among them!¹⁰

This long meditation on the unnatural world is one of the most striking, and Carlylean, passages in Victorian fiction. For Dickens the novelist's work is to take the house-tops off. The passage reminds us of why Dickens makes as much use of the present tense as Carlyle. He parallels the present-tense narrator in *Bleak House* with the consoling voice of the autobiographer Esther Summerson, who assumes that God's loving hand is at work shaping her life. The former narrator sees only a world of no progresses, just dullness and inanition; the latter finds order. By the time of *Our Mutual Friend*, Dickens's present-tense passages simply chart life lived happily on a dunghill.

George Eliot agrees with Bulwer's sense of the need of a double plot and Dickens's sense of how the demon-empires inside our selves and our homes need representation. But she gives those emphases a very different context. Her realism says no to Dickens's melodramatic coincidences and ready use of good and evil characters (imagine how she would represent Blandois in *Little Dorrit*, or Oliver Twist). She turns to Scott, in whom she finds "the unequalled model of historical romancists" (Pinney, *Essays of George Eliot*, 128). She treasures his strong sense that fiction must be given a context of actual history if the novel is to be "real." She treasures his handling of human beings from the lower classes. She registers his sense that the old and "romantic" are being replaced by modernity. If his male protagonists waver, if they seem unable to act with the decisiveness of their antagonists – and of many of his women (Rebecca in *Ivanhoe*) – George Eliot sees how modernity cripples their power of action; and she registers this in novels that focus on men and women densely embedded in the local and the particular, whose lives are never severed from the wider history outside their communities.

All of this comes from a writer whose insistence on the real makes her scrupulous in her representations of character and in her handling of novelistic conventions. "So I am content to tell my simple story," her narrator says in *Adam Bede*, "without trying to make things seem better than they were; dreading nothing, indeed, but falsity, which, in spite of one's best efforts, there is reason to dread. Falsehood is so easy, truth so difficult" (176). Yet readers see that George Eliot uses narrative conventions; each of the novels has its share of melodramatic goings on of the kind she laments in Dickens. In *Adam Bede* Hetty Sorrell's affair with Arthur Donnithorne, her killing of her baby, and her trial and "rescue" could come from any stage melodrama, as could Maggie Tulliver's flight with, and from, Stephen Guest in *The Mill on the Floss*. George Levine argues tellingly that the "constraints of the realist imagination need to be violated if the narrative is to be 'realistic.'" For him, George Eliot must make use of the methods of storytelling of the sensation novel, certainly the best selling sub-genre of fiction in the 1860s, if her fiction is to succeed in exiling the scandalous and corrupt, in reasserting the "real" and ordinary. "Realist characters find themselves in sensation novels" by necessity.[11] Levine's argument rightly places George Eliot's practices in the context of contemporary novelistic practice – and also articulates the reasons why realism is so difficult a project.

George Eliot's combination of a realist aesthetic with contemporary sensation-novel practices makes it all the more important to find the "romance in the real" that produces the "double plot," the moral signage making her texts dense with meaning and implication. Thus she uses "character typing" through naming (think of Bulstrode, Hetty Sorrell, Raffles, Rosamond, Dorothea) and invests objects with more than mere description, all in a "push towards allegory" (Levine, *Boundaries of Fiction*, 159). Though she finds the stories and tropes of the Bible forever redefined by the German higher critics in their historicizing of sacred texts, she relies on them increasingly in her work. Her realism is at once insistently secular and religious, a natural history and a secular scripture. All of her words have behind them Strauss's understanding of the Bible's truth as mythic and Feuerbach's urging that Love is "our Saviour and Redeemer ... for God has not saved us, but love, which transcends the difference between the divine and human personality."[12] The name of Eliot's Dorothea reminds us again and again of the pathos of Casaubon's situation; he can never see that the "key" to his life is this "gift of God," not his mythologies.

The point can be made from well-nigh every chapter George Eliot writes. But one passage from *Middlemarch* deserves special attention:

> The objects of her rescue were not to be sought out by her fancy: they were chosen for her. She yearned towards the perfect Right, that it might make a throne within her, and rule her errant will. "What should I do – how should I act now, this very day, if I could clutch my own pain, and compel it to silence, and think of those three?"
> It had taken long for her to come to that question, and there was light piercing into the room. She opened her curtains, and looked out towards the bit of road that lay in view, with fields beyond, outside the entrance-gates. On the road there was a man with a bundle on his back and a woman carrying a

baby ... Far off in the bending sky was the pearly light; and she felt the largeness of the world and the manifold wakings of men to labour and endurance. She was a part of that involuntary, palpitating life, and could neither look out on it from her luxurious shelter as a mere spectator, nor hide her eyes in selfish complaining. (776)

In a chapter whose epigraph is from Wordsworth's "Ode to Duty," George Eliot needs Bunyan to inform her realism. The man with the burden on his back recalls Bunyan's pilgrim, going on progress. The sense of the "perfect Right" rewrites the idea of God into Dorothea's nature, as she realizes. The "What should I do?" that comes from this awareness quotes a question that Bunyan's pilgrim asked – "What shall I do to be saved?" – and recasts it. Finally, the sense that Dorothea is a part of this wider human life makes George Eliot's moral point: she is a part of this progress toward self-renunciation and the ready sympathy with others.

The typical in the real

George Eliot is the novelist as anthropologist. Her use of history helps make her so. All her novels are set in the past except *Daniel Deronda*, and hers is a past like Scott's, shadowed by the looming change that her narrators have already experienced. Both *Felix Holt* (1866) and *Middlemarch* are set at the time of the first Reform Bill. The very name "Middlemarch" calls our attention to the allegorical suggestiveness that forms so much of George Eliot's moral sign system: a community, and nation, in the middle of its progress. Even in the earlier "pastoral" novels, there is a sense of change: the narrators speak from the present. The remarkable close of *Silas Marner*, where the weaver returns to Lantern Yard to revisit the past, shows the chapel where he was betrayed replaced by a factory. George Eliot lets us see, through the meditations of her characters *and* narrators, that memory may lie unless there is the reality of history's particularities to give it moral urgency, to suggest that it is more than mere fact.

It is these narrators who constitute the remarkable contribution that George Eliot makes to the form of English fiction: anthropologist as Words-worthian remembrancer at the outset; then anthropologist as historian (*Middlemarch* is a *Survey of Provincial Life*, and its narrator invokes Fielding and Herodotus); finally in *Daniel Deronda* "historical romancist." But she is also always a moralist: a novelist determined to talk with readers about the comforts of story read one way, and the moral pressures of story read another; she is determined to find the typical, the parable, in the particular. The earlier novels recall a world before readers "had been to Exeter Hall, or heard a popular preacher, or read *Tracts for the Times* and *Sartor Resartus*" (*Adam Bede*, 429); the later ones present a harsher world shadowed by Darwin where the natural may only be that: nature red in tooth and claw. Each "story is told as the thing remembered, not as the thing invented," Barbara Hardy notes.[13] In *Adam Bede*, with its epigraph from Wordsworth's *The Excursion*, the narrator is an actual male presence who has talked to Adam in old age. In *The Mill on the Floss* the opening chapter presents a narrator awakened from dreaming of the past by the present-day commercial reality of a bustling riverside town. Throughout there are invocations of memory that indicate George Eliot's alliance with Wordsworth:

> what grove of tropic palms, what strange ferns or splendid broad-petalled blossoms, could ever thrill such deep and delicate fibres within me as this home scene? These familiar flowers, these well-remembered bird notes, this sky ... such things ... are the mother tongue of our imagination, the language that is laden with all the subtle inextricable associations the fleeting hours of our childhood left behind them. Our delight in the sunshine on the deep bladed grass to-day, might be no more than the faint perception of wearied souls, if it were not for the sunshine and the grass in the far-off years which still live in us, and transform our perception into love.   (41–42)

If "the loves and sanctities of our life had no deep immovable roots in memory" (152), the narrator declares, how can life rise above barrenness? The question haunts George Eliot's narrators – and changes the nature of her realism.

The problem comes first in the nature of the work of memory. The story of *Mill* and its moral discussions with readers do not work easily together. The "roots intertwined with the past" that will be a persistent metaphor in George Eliot's work are in the world of Maggie Tulliver replaced by respectability's deadness to memory and to aspirations for a wider spiritual life. The narrator represents the Dodsons and their world in St. Ogg's as "a kind of population out of keeping with the earth on which they live"; theirs is a "variation of Protestantism unknown to Bossuet" (238). Unlike the golden pastoral of Hayslope in *Adam Bede*, St. Ogg's is Bunyan's town of Carnal Policy, where commerce and "respectable" Protestantism have severed any connection between past and present that the narrator cherishes. The narrator may speak of the "golden gates of childhood" but the reader rarely experiences this. Maggie Tulliver may long "for something that would link together the wonderful impressions of this mysterious life, and give her soul a sense of home in it" (205; the word "home" is crucial throughout the novel) and she may believe in a binding past with the narrator's intensity – "If the past is not to bind us, where can duty lie? We should have no law but the inclination of the moment" (417) – but these needs are never answered. That home and the remembered, or imagined, past offer Maggie no guides to a promised land.

Readers respond intensely to George Eliot's representation of Maggie. But throughout there is a sense that Maggie's "past" is a fiction desperately believed in, not lived through rooted experience in a community. Indeed, Maggie never seems organic to this community. We can see George Eliot working to make the phenomena of St. Ogg's *mean* more, to provide more moral signage outside her meditations on memory. The seven book titles insist on a reading of the story that the narrative makes very difficult: I: Boy and Girl, II: School-Time; III: The Downfall; IV: The Valley of Humiliation; V: Wheat and Tares; VI: The Great Temptation; VII: The Final Rescue. This is Wordsworth and Bunyan brought together: the Wordsworthian glow of childhood is made a pilgrim's progress – but to where? And the "final rescue," literal enough in the book, does not fulfill the allegorical suggestiveness of book VII's title. The "final rescue" is a fiction not experienced. The narrator's great comment at the end, "To eyes that have dwelt on the past, [Nature] makes no thorough repair" (459), is a moving acknowledgment of what memory cannot do. Nor this novel.

Daniel Deronda says at one point in his musings that memory is too easy: "There's no disappointment in memory, and one's exaggerations are always on the good side" (362). This insight George Eliot learns as she explores the nature of narration. Memory fictionalizes and gives comfort; but it does not propel us toward "good strong terrible vision [that] will save you" (224). In *Felix Holt* she calls the first storyteller in the introduction a coachman, at once Wordsworth's Wanderer and Dante's Virgil; and there is no Merry England to be recalled:

> The coachman was an excellent traveling companion and commentator on the landscape: he could tell the names of sites and persons, and explain the meanings of groups, as well as the shade of Virgil in a more memorable journey; he had as many stories about parishes, and the men and women in them, as the Wanderer in the "Excursion" . . . [B]ut the recent initiation of Railways had embittered him: he now, as in a perpetual vision, saw the ruined country strewn with shattered limbs . . . Still he would soon relapse from the high prophetic strain to the familiar one of narrative.　　　　(9)

There is no comfort of memory here. A modern narrator, George Eliot comes to learn, must see more: strong vision severed from history's particularities is not the product of comforting recollection; if narrative is to have moral meaning, narrative cannot be divorced from parable and prophecy:

> The poets have told us of a dolorous enchanted forest in the under world. The thorn bushes there, and the thick-barked stems, have human histories hidden in them; the power of unuttered cries dwells in the passionless-seeming branches ... These things are a parable. (11)

"These things are a parable": George Eliot repeats this line in *Middlemarch*, and will write a parable in *Daniel Deronda*. She will also preface each chapter of her last three novels with epigraphs designed to connect the characters of the narrative with characters and ideas from literature, philosophy, poetry; designed also to give a "text" for the readers' meditations as they encounter the "real" world of the novel. The epigraphs constitute George Eliot's investigation into how to make her words more than "mere *words*," how to ensure that the reader registers her narratives morally. Like the book titles of *Mill* and Eliot's endless allusions to other texts, these mottoes proclaim with Bunyan, "I have used similitudes." They work against the realism that threatens to undermine, even obliterate, the typical sign.

George Eliot always seeks the "typical" (86) in the real. She is convinced that words that are only *words* do not reach the reader as does language that evokes the types, symbols, and narratives of memory. She understands that the particularities of her realism carry no double sense unless those particularities are also typical, also emblems recalling sacred texts that connect readers, characters, and novelist in human sympathy. She naturalizes the sacred in order to ensure its presence in her Straussian and Feuerbachian texts. She urges her readers to see the humanly sacred in the material world, to locate the parable in the particular. Hers is an art of natural supernaturalism.

Scriptured realism

Twice in her career George Eliot baldly moves into religious "romance," opting for her version of Walter Scott's "historical romancist." In *Silas Marner* and *Daniel Deronda*, she says "no" to the realist strategies that had given her narrators and their stories form. *Silas Marner* introduces the double plot as one of the necessary elements of her realism, and it uses coincidence with the abandon of Dickens. One plot offers a legendary tale of a miser, uprooted by lies from his religious community, who settles in "Merry England," loses the gold earned by his weaving, and finds it replaced on New Year's Eve by a golden-haired child. The second plot involves Godfrey Cass, whose "promised land" (131) is a place ruled by chance: chance that his past marriage will not somehow become public; chance that the child of this relationship will never be revealed as his; chance that his wife and the community of Raveloe will always think well of him. The plots are connected by the fact that the child is Godfrey's, and the robber of the gold his brother.

Silas Marner is in essential ways the representative text of George Eliot's fiction. Its "typical" emphasis is secured through constructing Silas as a pilgrim with a burden on his back who "looked like the remnants of a disinherited race" (3). He comes to live in a world "aloof from the currents of industrial energy and Puritan earnestness" (21), a place of rootedness that he could never have imagined. Raveloe's inhabitants attend church, but have little knowledge of the scriptures and less of the Bible-based Christianity that has shaped Silas's life. Beginning his life among the most emphatic of religious sects, he finds his faith in God and community shattered by a Bible-ordained drawing of lots. In Raveloe, when the child Eppie mysteriously appears, he never hesitates to see her as "sent" to him by God. The remnants of his past, the structures of belief, still abide in him through memory, and insert him into a new "communion" (129). He names Eppie after the Bible's Hephzibah: "Thou shalt no more be termed Forsaken; neither shall thy land any more be called desolate: but thou shalt be called Hephzibah, and thy land Beulah: for the Lord delighteth in thee" (Isaiah 62:4). Here the Bible's language joins with the Wordsworth motto on the title page (also about the gift of love a child brings) to give Marner "a consciousness of unity between his past and present" (138) and "the presentiment of some Power presiding over his life" (109). Memories of biblical texts, now animated by the experience of new love and rootedness in human community, propel him to transcend the world of chance that had nearly destroyed his soul.

But Eppie's coming performs no work for her actual father. Godfrey Cass – we register how George Eliot "types" his Christian name – is condemned to a childless marriage. A comment from his wife to Eppie when she and Godfrey seek to claim Eppie as their own indicates the allegorical method of George Eliot's tale:

> "What you say is natural, my dear child – it's natural you should cling to those who've brought you up," she said mildly; "but there's a duty you owe to your lawful father." (167)

Law and "duty" give way to Love; the "natural" world of providential order that Marner has found through Eppie triumphs over Godfrey's world of chance. The tale of Silas and his golden child is sacred romance; the history of Godfrey Cass is petty reality. Silas's "romance" pushes into Godfrey's self-enclosed consciousness, and gives him a vision of connectedness, and loss. Raveloe *is* a "better place" (83) for those with vision. Romance allows history also to become parable.

As it does in *Daniel Deronda*. There is no Merry England here; just the present where characters escape to gambling dens on the Continent; where Providence, according to one minister, arranges wealthy marriages; and where religious language has become "religious nomenclature," its deformation complete for the wealthy English who are the subject of half of the novel. About one protagonist, Gwendolen Harleth, the narrator laments that she has grown up rooted to no place:

> A human life, I think, should be well rooted in some spot of a native land, where it may get the love of tender kinship for the face of earth, ... for whatever will give that early home a familiar unmistakable difference amidst the future widening of knowledge: a spot where the definiteness of early memories may be inwrought with affection ...
> (16)

This passage would be at home in *The Mill on the Floss* or *Silas Marner*. Here it carries a sound of resignation, or of revolutionary nostalgia.

The passage indicates how different *Daniel Deronda* is from *Middlemarch*. In this last novel there is no "real" native land for a rooted life. George Eliot consequently takes her plot from the biblical histories of Israel's exile and its determination to return to the Promised Land. The novel's formal construction insists on our recognition of its other protagonist Daniel Deronda as a type (the word is everywhere), a new Moses, and of the epic historical foundation of the text. There are allusions to Tasso's *Gerusalemme Liberata*, to Handel's *Rinaldo* (Daniel's love interest, Mirah, takes her name from its character Almirena), and to Dante's *Commedia*. For George Eliot the necessary strong vision cannot come from pastoral memories. She has finally, baldly, made Israel's history, its "historic memories," the necessary foundation of English moral life – if any is possible. In "The Modern Hep! Hep! Hep!" (in *Impressions of Theophrastus Such* [1879]), she writes of Israel's place in the "deep immovable roots" of English spiritual life: its literature has "furnished all our devotional language," it is "the very hearth of our own religion," "the birthplace of common memories and habits of mind."[14] The "past revelations and discipline" (*George Eliot Letters*, vol. VI, 216–217) that Eliot finds sustaining at the end of her career require a return to Israel and to what the novel's Jewish prophet Mordecai calls its "divine principle of action, choice, resolved memory" (459); "Israel is the heart of mankind," he says, "if we mean by heart the core of affection which binds a race and its families in dutiful love" (453).

Daniel Deronda, who needs roots as strongly as does Gwendolen Harleth, finds his identity and his life's work in discovering that he is Jewish. His preparation and Gwendolen's for seeking a promised land begin at that moment in each of their lives when they are forced to ask the question of Bunyan's pilgrim, "What shall I do?" Meeting in a casino, each needs to find a "pathway" (the word is everywhere) toward a sense of freedom – Daniel "felt himself in no sense free" (138) and Gwendolen views "the life before her as an entrance into a penitentiary" (231) – even if freedom is very different for a man and a woman. By the novel's end Daniel will discover his Jewish heritage and will prepare for a life of action. He also is reunited with the powers of the typological imagination toward which he has always yearned.

Gwendolen's possibility for progress is uncertain, less "resolved." She encounters the demon-empires within that her delighted gazing into mirrors never exposes her to; and she comes to see that there is a world beyond the self. This self-performer who had once said she knew *Gerusalemme Liberata* "by heart" (37) comes through her experience of Deronda to know what "by heart" means; she finds in her education the beginning of a life of "escape from herself," an exit from her "labyrinth" into a life where she knows, in Deronda's words, "more of the way in which your life presses on others, and their life on yours" (388). Yet this experience of vision leaves her solitary, "with the look of one athirst towards the sound of unseen waters" (658). The image from the biblical texts places her – but it promises what? The promised land, spiritual and physical, for a woman in Victoria's England, is uncertain indeed.

Each of these protagonists needs the other to find a sense of vision; neither's "accustomed pattern" (epigraph, 202) of reading the world has prepared them for what encountering the other means. Yet what happens here indicates George Eliot's sense of, or resignation to, the limitations of her typological realism for representing women who would be more than gifts of God to those around them. Deronda's mother rejects her heritage as bondage; she has no desire to patrol the moral territories typical for good women; she has acted to abandon those territories:

> "Had I not a rightful claim to be something more than a mere daughter and mother? . . . you can never imagine what it is to have a man's force of genius in you, and yet to suffer the slavery of being a girl. To have a pattern cut out – 'this is the Jewish woman; this is what you must be; this is what you are wanted for.'" (570, 541)

Here George Eliot allows much that she values to be questioned. She allows her readers to see the dangers – to a woman's life and to the novelist's moral realism – of the myths and typologies that animate her and her Deronda. Yet finally this novelist cannot imagine a world without moral memories. Bunyan's question "Whether we were of the Israelites, or no?" is hers. And it is the scriptured text for *Daniel Deronda*.

For George Eliot the Jewish and Christian literary traditions, with their tropes and metaphors that form an essential part of human memory, constitute the foundations of the moral lives, the shaping dreams, of women and men in nineteenth-century England. What Eliot writes in an 1855 review states the "religious" principle that guided her as novelist: "The idea of a God who not only sympathizes with all we feel and endure for our fellow-men, but who will pour new life into our too languid love, and give firmness to our vacillating purpose, is an extension and multiplication of the effects produced by human sympathy" (Pinney, *Essays of George Eliot*, 188).

George Eliot could never have written D. H. Lawrence's *The Man Who Died* (1929), could never have presented a Christ revived who connects to a vestal virgin in the Fertile Crescent as Lawrence does – even if their reasons for using the tropes of Judaeo-Christianity are remarkably similar. For her, such a bold move would have undermined those memories of the sacred that she considered the foundation of fellow-feeling. Yet she and Lawrence, paradoxically and finally not surprisingly, are united in their sense of the novel as the "one bright book of life."[15]

Notes

1. All quotations in this chapter from George Eliot's novels are from Oxford World's Classics, Oxford University Press editions, except *Felix Holt*: *Adam Bede*, ed. Valentine Cunningham (1998); *The Mill on the Floss*, ed. Gordon S. Haight (1998); *Silas Marner*, ed. Terence Cave (1998); *Romola*, ed. Andrew Brown (1994); *Middlemarch*, ed. David Carroll (1998); *Daniel Deronda*, ed. Graham Handley (1998). *Felix Holt*, ed. Fred C. Thompson (Oxford: Clarendon Press, 1980).
2. W. H. Mallock and Lord Acton, in *George Eliot: The Critical Heritage*, ed. David Carroll (London: Routledge and Kegan Paul, 1971), pp. 453–454, 463.
3. George Eliot, *Westminster Review*, July, 1856; reprinted in *Essays of George Eliot*, ed. Thomas Pinney (New York: Columbia University Press, 1963), pp. 288–289.
4. *The George Eliot Letters*, ed. Gordon S. Haight, 9 vols. (New Haven, CT: Yale University Press, 1954–78), vol. VI, pp. 216–217.
5. Thomas Carlyle, *Past and Present*, ed. Richard D. Altick (Boston, MA: Houghton Mifflin, 1965), p. 139.

6. References to Carlyle's writings, except for *Sartor Resartus* and *Past and Present*, are to *The Works of Thomas Carlyle*, ed. H. D. Traill, 30 vols. (New York: Charles Scribner's Sons, 1896–1901).

7. George Levine, *The Boundaries of Fiction* (Princeton University Press, 1968), p. 15.

8. William Makepeace Thackeray, *Pendennis*, ed. Donald Hewes (Harmondsworth: Penguin, 1972), pp. 785, 177–178.

9. Edward Bulwer-Lytton, *Caxtoniana: A Series of Essays on Life, Literature, and Manners* (New York: Harper and Brothers, 1864), pp. 317–319; preface to *Ernest Maltravers* (London: George Routledge and Sons, nd), p. viii; *A Strange Story* (New York: J. F. Taylor, 1897), p. xiv.

10. Charles Dickens, *Dombey and Son*, ed. Alan Horsman (Oxford: Clarendon, 1974), pp. 619–620.

11. George Levine, *How to Read the Victorian Novel* (Oxford: Wiley-Blackwell, 2008), pp. 142–146.

12. Ludwig Feuerbach, *The Essence of Christianity*, trans. George Eliot (New York: Harper and Brothers, 1957), p. 53. See my "George Eliot and Religion," in *The Cambridge Companion to George Eliot*, ed. George Levine (Cambridge University Press, 2001), pp. 119–137.

13. Barbara Hardy, *The Novels of George Eliot* (New York: Oxford University Press, 1967), p. 137.

14. George Eliot, *Impressions of Theophrastus Such*, ed. Nancy Henry (University of Iowa Press, 1994), pp. 160–161, 151, 144, 156.

15. D. H. Lawrence, "Why the Novel Matters," in *Selected Literary Criticism*, ed. Anthony Beal (New York: Viking, 1966), p. 107.

25

The *Bildungsroman*

BRIGID LOWE

The *Bildungsroman*, or novel of self-development, is often said to have originated in Goethe's *Wilhelm Meister* (1795), and to have crossed the Channel
in Thomas Carlyle's famous 1824 translation. However, it is tempting to
include in a history of the English *Bildungsroman* earlier literary landmarks
such as *Robinson Crusoe* (1719), *Clarissa* (1748), *Tom Jones* (1749), *Tristram Shandy*
(1759–1767), the novels of Fanny Burney and a number of those of Scott and
Austen. Indeed, the fact that most eighteenth- and nineteenth-century English
novels are deeply concerned with self-development suggests that the term
Bildungsroman should be considered as describing a central tendency of the
English novel *sui generis*. Carlyle's translation of *Wilhelm Meister* coincided
with intensified focus on inward psychological development, as opposed to
outward adventures and progress, and the nineteenth-century heyday of the
Bildungsroman in English saw significant formal developments tailored to the
intensification.

   The very unlikeness of *Wilhelm Meister* to any English *Bildungsroman* that
precedes or follows it points toward the particularities of the English species.[1]
Wilhelm's story, like that of the heroes of Scott's *Rob Roy* (1818) or Thackeray's
Pendennis (1848–1850), begins with his struggle to escape a humdrum
bourgeois future in favor of a romantic alternative. But Wilhelm inherits a
large fortune, and thereby comes to inhabit a social dimension in which rules
of conduct are extremely flexible. In contrast English heroes typically find
their desires and choices radically constrained by economic realities and socio-
moral codes. The economic, moral, and social constraints, or the lack of them,
have great formal implications. In English *Bildungsromane* rigid nineteenth-
century rules of sexual conduct also are great plot drivers. *Bildungsromane* with
female protagonists are sometimes treated as marginal to the genre, but the
especially narrow constraints placed on women in Victorian Britain render
them in many ways paradigmatic heroes. Whether male or female, however,

the protagonists of English *Bildungsromane* almost always begin impoverished – unless, like Dorothea Brooke of *Middlemarch* (1872), wealth actually hampers their actions. In many cases too – *Jane Eyre* (1847), *Wuthering Heights* (1847), *David Copperfield* (1850), *Great Expectations* (1861), *Tess of the d'Urbervilles* (1891), *The Way of all Flesh* (1903) – hostile, malevolent, incompetent, or unsympathetic parents or step-parents get in the way of the development of their offspring or wards; and, in doing so, they further funnel narrative energy. Thus the plots of English *Bildungsromane* are driven by the external constraints that attend their protagonists' growing up – a process that is posed as inherently problematical, reflecting, perhaps, the anxieties of a modern age increasingly at the mercy of an ever-accelerated rate of growth and change.

Wilhelm Meister is free to follow the wayward and unpredictable prompt-ings of his own impulses. While they eventually lead him toward a marriage that marks his achievement of maturity, the mental processes and external forces leading him there are hard to grasp. The reader feels no more sense of narrative necessity than Wilhelm feels economic or social exigency. The absence is reinforced by the final revelation that a secret society of intellectuals has been guiding and shaping Wilhelm's self-development. This *Bildungsroman*, it seems, can be concluded only by becoming a "philosophical romance" more like Johnson's *Rasselas* (1759) than a realist novel. We watch Wilhelm's process of development, but the narrative mode does not allow us to trace the interplay between inward impulse and outward influence and constraint that is the essence of the *Bildungsroman* in English. Wilhelm's vacillations are lightly ironized by the narrator, but at other times he acts as a mouthpiece for Goethe's own views. On the occasions when difference does arise between his perspective and that of the narrator, the extent of the distance between them is hard to judge. This uncertainty militates against the sort of immersion in a dynamic, evolving individual perspective that we find in the *Bildungsroman* in English.

The reader's access to, and evaluation of, a character's interiority depend on manipulations of narrative mode. In Jane Austen's novels either a consistent focalization of the narrative through an all-but infallible primary character, such as Eleanor in *Sense and Sensibility* (1811), or a precisely calibrated use of free indirect discourse, keeps readers actively engaged in assessing the exact distance between the passing and conflicting impressions of the character and the decisive judgment of the narrator – as well as the objective social and moral order reflected by that judgment. When in *Emma* (1816) Emma and Mr. Knightley differ in their assessment of Mr. Elton's interest in Harriet Smith, we cannot be long in doubt of the "right" interpretation (i.e. that Elton's interest in money precludes his having any "passion" for Harriet), in spite of the speciousness of Emma's internal reasoning:

> [Mr Knightley] certainly might have heard Mr. Elton speak with more unreserve than she had ever done, and Mr. Elton might not be of an imprudent, inconsiderate disposition as to money-matters; he might naturally be rather attentive than otherwise to them; but then, Mr. Knightley did not make due allowance for the influence of a strong passion at war with all interested motives.[2]

The reiterated "might" flags a mind – Emma's – arguing with itself, attempting to achieve belief in its own reasonableness – as does the attempt at balance and moderation suggested by "rather attentive than otherwise." However, "but then" marks a reversion toward a strongly held preconception, as "might" becomes "did not," and the sentence, freed of the stilted punctuation of reasonableness, careers headlong back toward Emma's blind unqualified faith in "the influence of a strong passion at war with all interested motives." Through Austen's sophisticated modes of narration, we have first-hand access to the learning process of the maturing protagonist, and can even enter into it with her. But the rhetorical finesse in the manipulation of double perspective – the narrator's and the character's – creates a fictional world in which varying perspectives can be intimately understood and sympathized with, but also measured against a scrupulously analyzed and justified code of conduct. The narrative mode itself reveals the distance that Emma needs to travel toward maturity, for Austen's narration embodies the confident adulthood that is the goal of the *Bildungsroman*. Such maturity reaches through the egoism of youth, the temptations of circumstance, and the unquestioning acceptance of vulgar social norms, toward a conscientious yet self-protecting individual judgment unbiased by selfish wishfulness.

Austen's use of a narrative mode that combines intimacy with a sense of the distance to be traveled is formative for the English *Bildungsroman*. For example, Dickens's use of free indirect discourse and dual perspective in *Great Expectations* (1861), where the voice of the mature narrator continually, with more or less explicitness bracketing the perspective of young Pip, contributes to make that novel one of the greatest *Bildungsromane* in English. However, the resounding confidence of Austen's narratorial perspective is seldom equaled in later novelists, in whose narratives the inevitable pain, loss, and risk involved in growing up is brought to the fore, and the very possibility of achieving maturity is placed in question.

While narratives of self-development began to flourish in English fiction, Wordsworth was refining *The Prelude*. Though not published until 1850, when the English *Bildungsroman* was already in full bloom, its central emphasis on the deep sources of the self in childhood had already been expressed by Wordsworth in poems such as "Ode: Intimations of Immortality From Recollections of Early Childhood" (1807). His idea that "The Child is father of the Man" is a guiding principle of *Bildungsromane* as various as *Jane Eyre* (1847), *Wuthering Heights* (1847), *Dombey and Son* (1848), *David Copperfield* (1850), *Great Expectations*, *The Mill on the Floss* (1860), *Jude the Obscure* (1895) and *A Portrait of the Artist as a Young Man* (1916).

This focus on early childhood has crucial formal implications. In the second chapter of *David Copperfield*, "I Observe," Dickens spells out a version of the suggestion in "Intimations of Immortality" that "The things which I have seen I now can see no more":

> The first objects that assume a distinct presence before me, as I look far back, into the blank of my infancy, are my mother with her pretty hair and youthful shape, and Peggotty, with no shape at all, and eyes so dark that they seemed to darken their whole neighbourhood in her face . . .
>
> I believe I can remember these two at a little distance apart, dwarfed to my sight by stooping down or kneeling on the floor, and I going unsteadily from the one to the other . . .
>
> I believe the power of observation in numbers of very young children to be quite wonderful for its closeness and accuracy. Indeed I think that most grown men who are remarkable in this respect, may with greater propriety be said not to have lost the faculty, than to have acquired it.[3]

Echoing Wordsworth, Dickens claims for the *Bildungsroman* the sensuous, imagistic function heretofore the territory of Romantic poetry. He might almost be talking about what, since his time, psychologists have called "eidetic" memory – memory that not only recalls details with extraordinary accuracy, but (and this is what is distinctive about it) does so without subsuming them to abstract or generalized patterns or categories of thought. Some children do have such special eidetic faculty; but in most the abstraction of mature thought-patterns soon seems to eclipse it. Maturation is precisely this process of sub-suming the particular to the general – of finding patterns in our world, and of placing our own individuality within a network of determined roles and choices.

Dickens's sustained, immediate sensuousness – a narrative capture of eidetic memory – is relatively new to the novel, and only partly discoverable in Fielding and Austen. When Fielding sets out to describe the childhood home of *Tom Jones*, he descends from generalized description into a metafictional joke that deflates the reality effect:

> a fine park, composed of very unequal ground, and agreeably varied with all the diversity that hills, lawns, wood, and water, laid out with admirable taste . . .

could give . . . Reader, take care, I have unadvisedly led thee to the top of as high a hill as Mr Allworthy's, and how to get thee down without breaking thy neck, I do not well know. However, let us e'en venture to slide down together.[4]

And when the heroine of *Emma* has a rare and transformative encounter with a landscape, the terms of the description quickly become saturated with some of the narrator's core values:

> The considerable slope . . . gradually acquired a steeper form . . . and at half a mile distant was a bank of considerable abruptness and grandeur, well clothed with wood; – and at the bottom of this bank, favourably placed and sheltered, rose the Abbey-Mill Farm . . .
>
> It was a sweet view – sweet to the eye and the mind. English verdure, English culture, English comfort, seen under a sun bright, without being oppressive. (283)

The contrastingly distinctive, profuse detail of the Victorian *Bildungsroman*, infused with what Austen might have found an almost "oppressive" emotional intensity not subsumed to analysis, is designed to capture the world of childhood. And the formal investment in the visionary significance of the particular indicates an emotional commitment to childhood as perhaps the height, rather than merely the root, of any individual development.

The immediacy of the child's view is conveyed not just through evocative detail, but also through first-person narrative, or an external narrator's first-person presence. Combining first-person with present-tense narration further narrows the space for the imposition of abstract meanings upon experience:

> now I see the outside of our house, with the latticed bedroom-windows standing open to let in the sweet-smelling air . . . Now I am in the garden at the back, beyond the yard where the empty pigeon-house and dog-kennel are – a very preserve of butterflies. (*David Copperfield*, 15)

> Now I can turn my eyes towards the mill again, and watch the unresting wheel sending out its diamond jets of water. That little girl is watching it too. . .It is time [she] went in, I think; and there is a very bright fire to tempt her: the red light shines out under the deepening grey of the sky. It is time too for me to leave off resting my arms on the cold stone of this bridge.[5]

Vivid details of movement, sight, smell, touch, help a reader share a particular moment of experience with the child protagonist. A naïve immediacy of perspective is also suggested by unframed incidental detail. *Jane Eyre* plunges us into the quotidian of the heroine's childhood experience in its very first line: "There was no possibility of taking a walk that day. We had been wandering, indeed, in the leafless shrubbery an hour in the morning."[6] The simplicity of the child's point of view especially licences this indulgence of the incidental, which has since come to be recognized as a hallmark of realist fiction. The *Bildungsroman* narrative is constructed from the gathering impingement of patterns of meaning and practical constraints upon a sensuous and emotional stream.

Developmental progress begins with an existential experience of identity. So, at the start of *Great Expectations*, the narrator records that:

> My first most vivid and broad impression of the identity of things, seems to me to have been gained on a memorable raw afternoon towards evening. At such a time I found out for certain, that this bleak place overgrown with nettles was the churchyard; and that Philip Pirrip, late of this parish, and also Georgiana wife of the above, were dead and buried ... that the dark flat wilderness beyond the churchyard, intersected with dykes and mounds and gates, with scattered cattle feeding on it, was the marshes; and that the low leaden line beyond, was the river; and that the distant savage lair from which the wind was rushing, was the sea; and that the small bundle of shivers growing afraid of it all and beginning to cry, was Pip.[7]

The repetitive syntax emphasizes interpretation, the arduous effort of decoding the flux of sensuous information, as each detail in turn is translated ("was the churchyard ... was the river ... was the sea ... was Pip"). "Vivid," "raw," "overgrown" impressions must be enclosed, broken up by the dykes of meaning. From a child's perspective, the plain of significance is darkened and flattened like the marshes, experience is a wilderness "scattered" with an assemblage of incidentals. Personality is not clear edged, but is a loosely formed "bundle" of sensations, "shivers." The story of Pip's maturation will be a constant effort to call his impressions to order, to give the right names to his experiences, the right name to himself. In *Wuthering Heights* the imagistic conglomeration of the child ghost with many names, lost on the moor where the paths are obscured by the "dark night coming down prematurely, and sky and hills mingled in one bitter whirl of wind and suffocating snow," conveys the same impression of an identity struggling to emerge from amorphous being.[8] So too do young David Copperfield's invocations of blankness, darkness, and shapelessness in his recollection of his earliest memories.

Dickens's seemingly unfiltered blend of incidental sensuous and material detail with unassimilated verbal fragments ("late of this parish," "also Georgiana") looks forward to the opening of Joyce's *Portrait of the Artist*, which closely echoes Pip's self-naming. "Once upon a time ... there was a moocow coming down along the road and this moocow ... met a nicens little boy ... He was baby tuckoo."[9] The radical subjectivism of Victorian fiction's childhood memories, such as David's recollection of figures "dwarfed to my sight by stooping down or kneeling on the floor," looks forward to modernism. Like David, Stephen Dedalus starts his story with the disordered impressions of a toddler: "Dante gave him a cachou every time he brought her a piece of tissue paper" (5). The child Stephen's impressions of warmth and cold when he wets the bed, and of the smell of the oilsheet, have the multi-sensuous vividness of his Victorian forebears. As young Copperfield looks into his past, time, as well as things and space, lack structure, "A great wind rises, and the summer is gone in a moment. We are playing in the winter twilight, dancing about the parlour" (15). In the same way Joyce moves us from Stephen's infancy to his schooldays in the space of a page. The school scene he conjures is sketched in lines similar to Pip's vision of the marshes: "The evening was pale and chilly and after every charge and thud of the footballers the greasy leather orb flew like a heavy bird through the grey light" (6). It is not surprising that Joyce's *Bildungsroman* paves the way toward his later more radical experimentalism, for in rooting narratives of personal development in the distinctively registered impressions of childhood, Victorian *Bildungsromane* give a new dimension to realism, capable even of carrying it beyond itself.

While Dickens describes the child's observation as characterized by "closeness and accuracy," others have seen in his conjuring of childhood worlds Wordsworth's "visonary gleam," the "glory and . . . freshness of a dream." Charlotte Brontë also, in *Shirley* (1849), a novel that reflects explicitly and emotionally on the nature and limits of realism, draws attention to how the perspective of childhood differs from that of adulthood:

> Before that time our world is heroic, its inhabitants half-divine or semi-demon; its scenes are dream-scenes; darker woods and stranger hills, brighter skies, more dangerous waters, sweeter flowers, more tempting fruits, wider plains, drearier deserts, sunnier fields than are found in nature, over-spread our enchanted globe.[10]

Using their protagonists' progress from childhood to adulthood, Brontë, Dickens, Eliot, and Hardy, among others, are able to carry forward strands of the emotional and imaginative intensity of a childhood perspective into their later narrative and, in doing so, to bring a fruitful tension into the forms and perspectives of realist fiction. There is a stylistic oscillation between naturalism and symbolism, fantasy and allegory – as in *Shirley* where the allegorical description of childhood innocence introduces a chapter of dry realism about "The Curates at Tea." By beginning their life-stories in childhood, these authors can introduce the fairy-tale tropes that are in evidence in *Great Expectations* and *Jane Eyre* where, cheek by jowl with the heightened realism of the incidental and the quotidian, wicked step-mothers, fairy godmothers, princes and princesses in disguise, and sleeping-beauty castles abound.

Like "Intimations of Immortality," childhood-rooted *Bildungsromane* seem deeply colored by a sort of neo-Platonism. In Dickens, Charlotte and Emily Brontë, and the early George Eliot, the boundary between myth and reality is challenged by youthful passions yearning for a oneness of world and spirit. The river in *The Mill on the Floss* is at one time the focus for a meticulous material description and sociological analysis, and at another the realm of myth and legend, a symbolic force capable of sweeping away the limits of realism and dissolving the divisions established by maturation. David Copperfield looks back regretfully to a paradisal childhood, "with a high fence, and a gate and padlock; where the fruit clusters on the trees, riper and richer than fruit has ever been since, in any other garden, and where my mother gathers some in a basket while I stand by, bolting furtive gooseberries" (15). Growing up seems a movement away from an original unity, and the narrative style, in which the presence of a mature narrator combines with vivid occupation of the child's perspective, serves to highlight the painfully yawning gap between innocence and experience.

The life-paths available, the social narratives at hand, seem too narrow for the breadth and depth of feeling embodied by the child protagonist. This can produce acute dissonance, something of the feeling of Emily Brontë's Catherine waking from a fevered dream:

> I thought . . . that I was enclosed in the oak-panelled bed at home . . . the whole last seven years of my life grew a blank! . . . I was a child . . . my misery arose from the separation that Hindley had ordered between me, and Heathcliff – I was laid alone, for the first time . . . memory burst in – my late anguish was swallowed in a paroxysm of despair . . . at twelve years old, I had been wrenched from the Heights, and every early association . . . and been converted, at a stroke into Mrs. Linton, the lady of Thrushcross Grange, and the wife of a stranger; an exile, and outcast, thenceforth, from what had been my world.
>
> (110–111)

Deep metaphysical problems in relation to the identity of the self over time are at issue here, dramatized within a novel whose generic unity is dazzlingly divided between a mythical, epic, Romantic portrayal of passion, and a realistic record of alienating social arrangements.

The loss, as well as, or instead of, the achievement involved in maturation is a dominant theme in mid-century, Romantically inflected *Bildungsromane*, as the emotional intensity of childhood is perpetuated in adulthood in the form of passionate longing for return or reunion. The outcast adult narrator seeks to re-enter an Edenic childhood. Especially in the early novels of Dickens and Eliot, flawed social codes – and, in particular, the beguiling appeal that conventional social narratives bear for the needy growing protagonists – are part of the difficulty. But the problem seems to lie much deeper – in the misfit between the wayward, uncontainable strength of human passions and the narrow logic of earthly existence. In novels like *The Mill on the Floss* and *Wuthering Heights*, unity can be restored only through death: the epitaph on the tombstone of Maggie and Tom reads "In death they were not divided" (522); and Heathcliff dreams of "dissolving" with Catherine in the grave (255).

In these examples the yearning for original unity is often figured, as in Byron's or Shelley's poetry, in terms of a love narrative between siblings or pseudo-siblings. Catherine's dream is of her first separation from Heathcliff, who, "more myself than I am" (71), represents the goal of authentic selfhood. This is the case with David Copperfield and his unfallen "sister" Agnes, and with Pip and Estella. Their relationships are authenticated by belonging to both childhood and adulthood – they guarantee an organic wholeness of self, the identity of child and man. In *Villette* (1853) Lucy remarks of Polly Home, on the day she sees Polly reunited with her childhood playmate and future husband, that:

> her eyes were the eyes of one who can remember; one whose childhood does not fade like a dream . . . She would not take life, loosely and incoherently, in parts, and let one season slip as she entered on another: she would retain and add; often review from the commencement, and so grow in harmony and consistency.[11]

Where there is no sibling-like lover to guarantee wholeness and authenticity of self, there is often instead a soul-mate to play a similar or even more transcendent role. The soul-mate proves that the world, beneath the hostile incidentals of social constraint and practical necessity, is a home fit to grow up in. This vision is spelt out by Dinah Craik: "Heaven guides all true lovers that are to be husband and wife – leads them from the farthest corners of the world . . . to their own appointed home in one another's arms."[12] This pervasive popular ideal has perhaps its fullest expression in the Victorian *Bildungsroman*, and it is there something rather new for the novel. Jane Austen's heroines demonstrate their achieved maturity by freely choosing a partner on the basis of a combination of everyday social emotions and reasoned judgment – "gratitude and esteem," "strong esteem and lively friendship."[13] But the heroes of Victorian *Bildungsromane* are guided by fate toward an ideal counterpart who guarantees at once their true identity and their place in a universe that has a depth beyond its contingencies. Catherine and Heathcliff, Jane and Rochester, are perhaps the greatest examples of such transcendentally united couples, defying the very laws of nature in their inter-communing. As such, they place the novels of which they are the heroes at the very limits of fictional realism.

But the Romantic narrative of the achievement of self through soul-mate is also reworked, writ small, in the materialist providentialism of the self-help narratives of Craik. According to this vision each individual must strive, through industry and prudence, to reach the place allotted him by God. The eponymous hero of *John Halifax, Gentleman* (1856), proclaims "I am what God made me, *and* what, with His blessing, I will make myself."[14] The universe is so fashioned as to guarantee his progress – self-made men "have in them the instinct to rise; and as surely as water regains its own level, so do they, from however low a source, ascend to theirs" (361). The ultimate proof of John's gentlemanly self is his marriage with the high-born Ursula, a marriage demonstrating "the truth . . . that we *are* equals" (198). Like Estella in *Great Expectations*, Ursula makes her lover ashamed of his working hands and dress. But Craik treats the melding of social aspiration and love with none of the ambivalence Dickens directed at it – here sexual passion provides a spiritual validation of social and economic competition.

There is ambivalence, however, at the heart of *John Halifax*. If John's history seems a triumphant assertion of the power and centrality of the individual self, the picture is rather different when we consider the life-story of the narrator, Phineas Fletcher. His is hardly a story at all. As a permanent invalid Phineas demonstrates no power of self-assertion or self-determination, and is debarred from marriage. Life without marriage, Craik suggests, is "unnatural," and yet it is a fact: reality and essence come painfully apart. Against, or within, the sublime egoism of the Romantic ideal of destiny, grows up a tragic *Bildungsroman* where the world stubbornly resists the needs of the soul. Patterns of narration are inverted to replace a triumphant keynote with a melancholy one. First-person narration serves not to naturalize a concentration on the tale of one life, but rather to show up the degree to which self-development can be squeezed or crushed by circumstance. The life stories of Phineas Fletcher, Lucy Snow of *Villette*, and Esther Summerson of Dickens's *Bleak House* (1853) are all but effaced by the pressures of the other lives they narrate, as they challenge us to maintain interest in them despite what they insist is their colorless lack of interest. These narrators are negatively defined – Lucy is not imaginative, Esther is not clever. Such narratives make emotional capital out of the violation of our expectation of a hero-centered *Bildungsroman* universe. Lucy Snow's story is made poignant by the fact that it is always at risk of being obscured and obstructed by another, more familiar and more obviously heroic narrative. The first two thirds of *Villette* wind toward the typical consolidation of ego through return to origins, but the selves thus consolidated are those of the childhood friends Graham and Polly, not of the narrator, who is only thrust further from her oldest ties by their union. Lucy at last finds her fragile moment of self-realization with a soul-mate radically different from herself in age, in temper, in religion, and in background. Her self-fulfillment remains fragile to the end, as the narrative concludes with the probable drowning of her prospective husband. Her isolated, embattled sense of herself seems, in the end, in danger of fading, again unrecognized, into the blankness of the final page. Brontë's last novel clings to Romantic ideals of a nurturing universe, but does so almost against all hope.

The metaphysical complacence that seems to shape the narrative of John Halifax's ascent is indeed the exception, rather than the rule, among English *Bildungsromane*. Other novelists exploit the conventions of the form to explore not so much the profound fragility of selfhood, but rather of life itself. Dickens's *Dombey and Son* shocks us by cutting off the life of the would-be hero at the end of the first volume. Having used the techniques of intimate focalization – developed into something very close to modernist stream of consciousness – to put us behind the eyes of young Paul, Dickens's violation of our expectations when he dies has a powerfully jarring effect. Hardy creates a similar feeling in *Tess of the d'Urbervilles*, where focalized narration brings us into a lover-like intimacy with the heroine. In both novels, the death of the central character brings about a formal crisis – how can the narration go on when the point from which it emanated is obliterated? *Dombey*, not without strain, becomes the story of another life, and *Tess* continues just long enough for us to sense an eerie distance and vacuity in the narrator's perspective.

The final chapter of *Tess* contains no human sound, as Angel and Liza-Lu, described to us as though they were strangers, watch for the sign of Tess's execution from the distant hilltop by the white milestone, their faces "shrunk to half their natural size."[15] The contrast between the confident metaphysical implications of the optimistic version of the Romantically inflected *Bildungsroman* and Tess's particular tragedy allows a profound reflection on the nature of consciousness itself, and on the condition of human selves in an increasingly secularized world. Hardy points out that Tess "was not an existence, an experience, a passion, a structure of sensations, to anybody but herself. To all humankind besides Tess was only a passing thought" (103). This observation highlights the artificiality of the *Bildungsroman* – the sort of sustained engagement and attention we bestow upon the hero is not paralleled anywhere in the real world. "Upon her sensations the whole world depended to Tess; through her existence all her fellow-creatures existed, to her" (172). Both the artificiality and the inescapability of the subjective prism through which the narration of any life must pass is part of the emotional dynamic. The narrator's loving understanding of Tess highlights the fact that, without any reliable God or soul-mate to turn to, she, and other human beings like her, are ultimately alone in their apprehensions of themselves.

Jude the Obscure is another rebellion against the providentialism implicit in the patterns of earlier *Bildungsromane*. The forces of competition here are not benign as in *John Halifax*, but cruel and bloody, and sexual passion leads not to individual validation but to disaster. Biological and social forces dominate individuals, and defy the narrative form designed for more human purposes. With Jude and Sue even human passion itself begins to resist narration, as each fails to claim or identify with their own erratic opinions, emotions, and actions. There is overwhelming resistance to self-fulfillment from both without and within.

In the face of such resistance, the Romantic, neo-Platonic heritage of the *Bildungsroman* needs another channel. The *Bildungsroman* hero has always been akin to the artist – Jane Eyre is an accomplished sketcher, David Copperfield writes novels, Shirley Keeldar shows the depth of her soul in her essays. But, as the fortunate Polly Home's personal history of "harmony and consistency" suggests, life fulfilled by love itself becomes art. In novels such as Craik's *Olive* (1850) success as an artist is succeeded and eclipsed by success in love. What Craik says of life is even truer of many Victorian stories of maturation: "there are other things in life besides love: but . . . love is the very heart of life, the pivot upon which its whole machinery turns" (*The Woman's Kingdom*, 15). But, after Hardy, there is a new pivot – if unity and completeness are to be found anywhere, they are to be found only in art. The sensuous passion of the Romantic *Bildungsroman* flows into the *Künstlerroman* – the story of the growth of an artist. Joyce, in *Portrait of an Artist*, breaks up the familiar patterns of realist narrative to create a new myth of fulfillment and unity: though the artist's life might be fractured by the alienation of social, economic and physical existence, his experience can find unity in its expression in art.

There is, however, a counter-strain. If *Bildungsromane* and *Künstlerromane* with their roots in childhood typify a Romantic version of the *Bildungsroman*, Thackeray's *Pendennis* is a formative example of what we might call the realist *Bildungsroman*. The "hero" is only barely such – we get only a sentence-long glimpse of him in his childhood, just enough to ground the muted attachment we feel to the flawed young man. His story, like Wilhelm's, begins with a romance with an actress; but the relationship, rather than ending in operatic discoveries of infidelity and the abject death of the hero's first love, concludes with the marriage of the good-natured but materialistic actress to a wealthier man. The third-person narrator places a firm and ironic distance between us and all the protagonists. Like a true Romantic hero, Arthur Pendennis ultimately harbors himself in the arms of a childhood companion, almost a sibling. But, rather than being his fated soul-mate, Laura Bell becomes Arthur's wife only after discovering that the man she most respects and loves is married already. Our hero's central narrative, like those of Scott's heroes, is thus radically contingent on the life-story of others. This is an anti-Romantic narrative, in which there is no heroic, glory-trailing, expansive-souled hero, no divine plan, nor any society of learned aristocrats in the wings, to guide each to the fate he deserves. Pendennis is a hero only in the context of a world in which authenticity is rare indeed, and in which compromise is inevitable.

In *Pendennis* the ironical tone of the narrator makes the compromises and contingency and littleness of social life and of human nature seem a matter for regret and even bitterness – but in later realist life-stories this sense fades, replaced by a disinterested exploration of the role of chance and uncertainty in maturation. Anthony Trollope's *Phineas Finn* (1867) carefully maintains a parity of importance between the love-plot and the plot of vocation, while creating uncomfortable clashes and congruencies between the two. Like Pendennis the financially vulnerable Phineas finds that success and honor in his career as a Member of Parliament becomes contingent on his choice of a wealthy wife. But what was for Arthur a matter of maintaining integrity in the face of worldly temptation, is for Phineas a much more radical – and, by implication, inevitable – blurring of different orders of personal desire and social ambition. The difficulty of maintaining political integrity in a world of entangled imperatives and interests is mirrored and confusingly overlapped by the difficulty of maintaining integrity in love. Phineas himself is honest but also eminently adaptable – in and out of love like a fiddler's elbow – and eventually finds his best purchase on integrity through an almost gratuitous choice of the woman least likely to further his career. She is the pseudo-sister familiar from the Romantic *Bildungsroman*, but Phineas seems drawn to her by no inevitable fate. The novel is full of marriages that almost happen or almost do not, and there is a constant foregrounding of the fact that things might easily have turned out differently. That *Phineas* is part of the Palliser series of novels further disrupts the sense of determinate possibilities – and indeed, like Elinor in the Barchester series, Phineas returns in a later novel, *Phineas Redux* (1874), as a widower ready for another marriage – to the wealthy Madame

Goesler, whom he had almost married in the earlier novel, and whose wealth opens up for him the possibility of a disinterested political career. Here, as in *Can You Forgive Her?* (1865) and *The Duke's Children* (1880), successful personal development is not a matter of destiny or of inevitable organic process, but of good-humored negotiation with, and openness to, the world's complexities and compromises.

George Eliot, also, became increasingly interested in such complexities. *The Mill on the Floss* is a Romantic *Bildungsroman* in tragic mode. But when in *Middlemarch* Eliot asks "why always Dorothea?" she makes a theme of the formal choices characteristic of *Bildungsromane*, and reflects ambivalently on the moral dimension of such choices.[16] The famous pier-glass analogy, used to suggest the egoism of Rosamund, in which the random scratches on a surface, when a candle shines on them, "seem to arrange themselves in a fine series of concentric circles round that little sun," can also be seen as a reflection of the traditional narrative practice behind the *Bildungsroman*. Rosamund imagines that she has "a Providence of her own who had kindly made her more charming than other girls, and who seemed to have arranged Fred's illness and Mr. Wrench's mistake in order to bring her and Lydgate within effective proximity" (248). The authors of *Bildungsromane* often act as such providence – and by the very devices through which they shape their narratives can suggest a vision whereby individual needs are in some way answered by the structure of the universe. But *Middlemarch*, as a multi-stranded *Bildungsroman*, attempts to move away from such egoism, emphasizing instead how each life is shaped by the lives around it, and by wider social forces beyond it.

It might seem perverse to treat *Middlemarch* as a *Bildungsroman*, but there is hardly a novel in English more self-consciously reflective upon the processes of personal development. Eliot proclaims her intention of "unravelling certain human lots," and her emphasis is explicitly developmental: as Mr. Farebrother says, "'character is not cut in marble – it is not something solid and unalterable. It is something living and changing'" (132, 692). Repeatedly Eliot's narrative lays claim to areas of experience hitherto left outside narrative. It is committed, for example, to tracing moments of personal development in characters who do not possess "young skins that look blooming in spite of trouble" (261). And in relation to Lydgate's career, Eliot observes that the story of men "who once meant to shape their own deeds and alter the world a little . . . coming to be shapen after the average and fit to be packed by the gross, is hardly ever told" (135). Trollope and Craik, it is true, also deal with vocational development, but perhaps only novels of religious experience had hitherto allotted to secular vocation the gravity with which it is treated in *Middlemarch*.

This emphasis on goals aside from marriage raises gender conflicts. As Trollope frequently points out, "a girl unless she marries becomes nothing."[17] But *Middlemarch* does more than just criticize or reflect upon particular social conditions. It questions the very forms of "the history of man, and how the mysterious mixture behaves under the varying experiments of Time" (3); and it questions the ways in which not only the possible trajectories of human development but also the narratives in which such development can be captured depend upon a distinct social "medium." The story of Dorothea's life is framed with reference to different kinds of narrative as well as to different ways of life. The life-story of a historical figure, St. Theresa, to whom Dorothea is compared, is an epic – while the story of the fictional Antigone, with whose life-story Dorothea's is also compared, is inseparable from the conventions of Greek drama. Eliot contrasts her narrative with epic and drama, and contrasts it too with the way Fielding narrates his "comic epic poem in prose." Dorothea's *Bildungsroman* is shaped by effort to find a channel for aspirations of an epic scale in fragmented modern times, without a background of "coherent social faith and order" (3). And Eliot's effort is to tell the tale of such aspirations in a world that seems increasingly resistant to traditional narrative structure. Though *Middlemarch* does not begin with childhood, and while it refuses the Romantic vision of a nurturing universe that is like "an udder to feed our supreme selves" (198), it nevertheless uses forms established by earlier *Bildungsromane*. It emphasizes the incidental and particular, weighs competing forces of imagination and reality, and works to engage us, not through our admiration for the characters' "far-resonant action," but through our sympathy with visionary yearnings and aspirations more or less hampered and constrained by tangled circumstances.

Notes

1. Jeffrey L. Sammons, "The Mystery of the Missing *Bildungsroman*, or: What Happened to Wilhelm Meister's Legacy?" *Genre* 14: 2 (1981), 229–246.
2. Jane Austen, *Emma* (Oxford University Press, 2003), p. 54.
3. Charles Dickens, *David Copperfield* (Oxford University Press, 1999), pp. 12–13.
4. Henry Fielding, *Tom Jones* (Oxford University Press, 1996), p. 37.
5. George Eliot, *The Mill on the Floss* (Oxford University Press, 1996), p. 8.
6. Charlotte Brontë, *Jane Eyre* (Oxford University Press, 2000), p. 7.
7. Charles Dickens, *Great Expectations* (Oxford University Press, 2008), pp. 3–4.
8. Emily Brontë, *Wuthering Heights* (Oxford University Press, 1995), p. 11.
9. James Joyce, *A Portrait of the Artist as a Young Man* (Oxford University Press, 2000), p. 5.

10. Charlotte Brontë, *Shirley* (Oxford University Press, 2007), p. 83.
11. Charlotte Brontë, *Villette* (Oxford University Press, 2000), p. 276.
12. Dinah Mulock Craik, *The Woman's Kingdom: A Love Story* (London: Hurst and Blackett, 1897), p. 38.
13. Jane Austen, *Pride and Prejudice* (Oxford University Press, 2004), p. 211, and *Sense and Sensibility* (Oxford University Press, 2004), p. 288.
14. Dinah Mulock Craik, *John Halifax, Gentleman* (London and Glasgow: Collins, 1930), p. 181, emphasis added.
15. Thomas Hardy, *Tess of the d'Urbervilles* (Oxford University Press, 2005), p. 419.
16. George Eliot, *Middlemarch* (Oxford University Press, 1997), p. 261.
17. Anthony Trollope, *The Duke's Children* (Oxford University Press, 1983), p. 614.

26

The novel and social cognition: internalist and externalist perspectives

ALAN PALMER

It is only shallow people who do not judge by appearances. The true mystery of the world is the visible, not the invisible.

Oscar Wilde

In Jane Austen's *Emma* (1816), near the beginning of the famous outing to Box Hill, we are told that:

> Seven miles were travelled in expectation of enjoyment, and *everybody* had **a burst of admiration** on first arriving; but in the general amount of the day there was deficiency. There was *a languor, a want of spirits, a want of union*, which could not be got over. *They separated too much into parties* . . . Mr and Mrs Elton, indeed, **showed** no unwillingness to mix, and be as **agreeable** as they could . . . Emma . . . had never **seen** Frank Churchill so dull and stupid . . . [but he] **grew talkative and gay**, making her his first object. **Every distinguishing attention** that could be paid, was paid to her. To amuse her, and be agreeable **in her eyes, seemed** all that he cared for – and Emma . . . gave him . . . **friendly encouragement** . . . though in *the judgement of most people looking on* it must have had such an **appearance** as no English word but flirtation could very well describe.[1]

Much, though not all, of the cognitive functioning described in this passage is being shared between characters. These are social minds in action because they are, in general, public, embodied, and so available to each other.[2] The italicized phrases show that thought can be shared between groups of individuals. Everyone feels the need to engage together in admiration-behavior. The feelings of languor and want of spirits, and the resulting want of union, are jointly experienced. The need to separate into small parties is collectively felt. The judgment on Emma's and Frank's flirtatious behavior is a group one that is shared by most of the people present.

421

In addition, the emboldened phrases describe thought that is visible and public. The language used by the narrator emphasizes this point. Emma "sees" that Frank Churchill is dull and stupid. It "seems" that all he wants is to be agreeable "in her eyes." Their behavior has the "appearance" of flirtation. The Eltons "showed" no unwillingness to mix. "A burst of admiration," "agreeable" behavior and "friendly encouragement" all involve actions that are indicative of the desire to show to others that the appropriate sensations of admiration, agreeableness, and friendliness are in fact being felt. I put the point in this way because, of course, there is some manipulation of the visible nature of thought going on in the passage. People might secretly not be as admiring when they first arrive as they want others to think. Frank Churchill is pretending because he wants others to believe that he has stronger feelings for Emma than he actually has, in order to conceal his secret engagement to Jane Fairfax. To a lesser extent Emma is also putting on a show for Frank and the others. So there is a balance here between the public and the private. But these pretenses can only work if thought is generally visible and public. Otherwise, if no one ever knew what anyone else was thinking, what would be the point of pretense?

The dangers that can arise from the easy availability of thought to others are explicitly recognized later in the chapter. In order to rouse the party and provoke some witty repartee, to reduce the separation and increase the union, Frank Churchill exclaims: "I am ordered by Miss Woodhouse . . . to say, that she desires to know what you are all thinking of" (363). Mr. Knightley sees that Emma is playing with fire and cautions her by asking "Is Miss Woodhouse sure that she would like to hear what we are all thinking of?" (363). Emma ignores the warning, plows on with her conceit, humiliates Miss Bates, and later incurs Mr. Knightley's stinging rebuke. She is made to feel painfully aware of the emotional consequences of the pursuit of knowledge of other minds.

It is a cliché of literary studies that, whereas novels can give us direct access to the minds of characters, by contrast, in reality, we can never know what other people are thinking. This is the sort of thing that sounds true while it is being said, but, in other contexts, can sound like nonsense. To believe it requires a considerable degree of cognitive dissonance in order to contradict the weight of evidence in our everyday experience. All of us, every day, know for a lot of the time what other people are thinking. This is especially true of our loved ones, close friends, family, and colleagues at work. It is also true of our encounters with total strangers. How could it be possible for two people to hold a coherent conversation without at least some knowledge of each other's thought processes? I am not saying that we *always* know *all* of what other people are thinking. That would be as silly as the cliché that we *never* know. Sometimes we know what other people are thinking without them having to say anything; at other times we do not know what they are thinking even though they are trying to tell us. Sometimes we have secret thoughts that no one else will ever know about; at other times, other people, especially those close to us, will know better than we do what we are thinking.

The passage just quoted is an example of one that benefits from an *externalist perspective*. For a contrasting illustration of an *internalist perspective* (both terms are explained below), we can consider a scene in Walter Scott's *Waverley* (1814), in which Waverley is interviewed by a local laird, together with a clergyman, about his supposed Jacobite activities:

> When Waverley retired, the laird and clergyman sat down in silence to their evening meal . . . Each mused over the particulars of the examination, and each viewed it through the medium of his own feelings . . . The wide difference of their habit and education often occasioned a great discrepancy in their respective deductions from admitted premises.[3]

As a presentation of mental functioning, this passage strikingly emphasizes the differences between the two minds. It presents characters who have completely different ways of thinking and widely divergent views on another mind: Waverley's. The ensuing discussion makes it clear that the laird is of a dour and suspicious caste, and consequently sees the young man as a violent and dangerous rebel; the clergyman is more trusting and optimistic by nature and consequently regards him (more accurately, as it turns out) as a decent young innocent abroad. In effect, they are constructing utterly different minds for the same character. Significantly, the two men have great difficulty in understanding each other's thought processes. There is no meeting of minds. This is a picture of consciousness as private, solitary, and inaccessible to others. The emphasis is on the gaps between people, the difficulties that we all sometimes experience in understanding the thought processes of others, the barriers that make it difficult for people to think together or in cooperation with each other.

Speaking very broadly, there are two perspectives on the mind: the externalist and the internalist. The two perspectives form more of a continuum than an either/or dichotomy, but the distinction is, in general, a valid one. An externalist perspective on the mind stresses those aspects that are outer, active, public, social, behavioral, evident, embodied, and engaged. An internalist perspective on the mind stresses those aspects that are inner, introspective, private, solitary, individual, psychological, mysterious, and detached.

I use the term "social mind" to describe those aspects of the whole mind that are revealed through the externalist perspective.

Within the real-mind disciplines of psychology and philosophy there is a good deal of interest in *the mind beyond the skin* (as opposed to *the mind inside the skull*): the realization that mental functioning cannot be understood merely by analyzing what goes on within the skull but can only be fully comprehended once it has been seen in its social and physical context. Social psychologists routinely use the terms "mind" and "mental action" not only about individuals, but also about groups of people. They argue that it is appropriate to say of a group that it decides, for example, or that it remembers. One might ask what is achieved by talking in this way, instead of simply referring to individuals who pool their resources and work in cooperation together. The advocates of the concept of distributed cognition – theoretical anthropologists Gregory Bateson and Clifford Geertz, philosophers Andy Clark, David Chalmers, and Daniel Dennett, and psychologists Edwin Hutchins and James Wertsch are examples – all stress that the purpose of the concept is increased explanatory power. In their view, the way to delineate a cognitive system is to draw the limiting line so that one does not leave things inexplicable.

An important part of social mind is our capacity for "inter-mental thought." Such thinking is joint, group, shared, or collective, as opposed to intra-mental, or individual, or private. It is also known as "socially distributed," "situated," or "extended cognition," and also, especially in literary studies, as "intersubjectivity." The concept of inter-mental thought applies to such activities as problem-solving, joint decision-making, and group action. Inter-mental thought is a crucially important component of fictional narrative because, just as in real life, where much of our thinking is done in groups, much of the mental functioning that occurs in novels is done by large organizations, small groups, work colleagues, friends, families, couples, and other inter-mental units. Those units are to be found in profusion in the nineteenth-century novel. It could plausibly be argued that the subject matter of novels of this period is the formation, development, maintenance, modification, and breakdown of those inter-mental systems. Because story-worlds are profoundly social in nature, novels necessarily contain a good deal of inter-mental thinking. However, inter-mental thought in the novel has been invisible to traditional literary-critical approaches. Indeed, many of the samples of inter-mental thought that follow would not even count as examples of thought and consciousness within those approaches. Nevertheless, inter-mental thought becomes clearly visible in the light of the cognitive approach to literature that underpins this chapter.

A good deal of the significance of the thought that is represented in nineteenth-century novels is lost if only the internalist perspective is employed. Those novels are preoccupied with the balance between public and private thought, inter-mental and intra-mental functioning, social and individual minds. Novelists use differing emphases to display the balance. Jane Austen, Maria Edgeworth, Elizabeth Gaskell, George Eliot, Charles Dickens, Wilkie Collins, and Anthony Trollope tend to assume that characters' thought processes are often transparent and public. In their stories, consequently, secrets, the device around which so many of their plots revolve, are difficult to keep. In contrast, other writers, such as Walter Scott and Henry James, are more ambivalent about social minds, and are often more comfortable with the assumption that minds are usually inaccessible and private.

It is common, when reading discussions of the sustained inside views of characters' private minds in the novels of writers such as Henry James, to be told that, by contrast, characters in novels by, say, Charles Dickens, are really only ever seen from the outside. We only see their surface. They are flat when they should be round. The effect is often to sound rather patronizing about Dickens's achievement. "Brilliant novelist in his way, of course, but without the *depth* of James!" This chapter will reverse that perspective. In cognitive terms, nearly all of one's life is spent on the surface, on the outside, in the sense that all of the minds with which one is involved (with the admittedly rather important exception of one's own!) are only ever experienced on the surface, and from the outside. From this point of view, it is not surprising that Oscar Wilde said that it is only shallow people who do not judge by appearances, and that the true mystery of the world is the visible, not the invisible. Dickens is a novelist of appearances, and of what is visible, and his achievement can only be fully appreciated from an externalist perspective.

There is an explicit and self-conscious debate within a wide range of nineteenth-century novels about the balance between social and private minds. In Anthony Trollope's *The Warden* (1855), for example, Trollope explicitly dramatizes characters reading other characters' minds:

> Mr. Harding knew that the attorney-general regarded him as little better than a fool, but that he did not mind; he and the attorney-general had not much in common between them; he knew also that others, whom he did care about, would think so too; but Eleanor, he was sure, would exult in what he had done, and the bishop, he trusted, would sympathize with him.[4]

The passage vividly indicates the necessity of seeing the character of Mr. Harding as situated within a distributed cognitive network. As part of this network, he and the bishop form a small inter-mental unit of long standing. "The bishop and Mr. Harding loved each other warmly" (37), and, for this reason, "Mr. Harding determined to open his mind and confess his doubts" (38). The important point is that he feels able, in this telling phrase, to "open his mind" to the mind of another. There is often no need for words: when the bishop puts his hand on his knee as a gesture of comfort, "Mr. Harding well knew what that pressure meant" (40).

Charlotte Brontë's novel *Shirley* (1849) is another text in which there are frequent mentions of the visibility of our thought: "Men rarely like such of their fellows as read their inward nature too clearly and truly."[5] This novel is extraordinary in combining staginess and clunkiness in the presentation of the internalist perspective (by such means as elaborate spoken soliloquies or highly unlikely diary entries) with sensitivity, fluidity, and insight in the presentation of the externalist perspective. One example of the latter is a beautiful and moving passage in which, following a period of estrangement, Shirley and Louis Moore's minds start to work together again in perfect unison. They renew themselves as an inter-mental unit by slipping into their familiar roles of tutor and pupil (378–389).

The externalist perspective is an opportunity to widen and deepen our conception of such apparently internalist notions as character, interiority, subjectivity, and identity. Individuals do not exist in a vacuum. As the passage above shows, Mr. Harding can only be fully understood in terms of his functioning within inter-mental units. Similarly, characters have to be seen in relation to the units that they are *not* part of (for example, when they are identified as outsiders, scapegoats, and so on). The workings of social minds can also be used to identify patterns in relationships that might not be apparent from the use of more orthodox analysis. In Anne Brontë's *The Tenant of Wildfell Hall* (1848) there are few examples of characters knowing what other characters are thinking. The one exception is the relationship between Helen, the heroine tenant, and Hargrave, the sexual predator who tries unsuccessfully to seduce her. During brief passages of dialogue, there are at least seven explicit references to one of them being able to read the mind of the other. (I have discovered only six other examples in the rest of the novel.) On the face of it, this finding seems surprising. Helen says that she finds Hargrave's attentions abhorrent. However, the evidence of the closeness of their joint mental functioning suggests that her feelings for him might be deeper and more complex than her own narration, as contained in her diary, is willing to admit.

A sense of social entanglement (especially through the medium of gossip) is particularly strong in the nineteenth-century novel. In Jane Austen's *Sense and*

Sensibility (1811) Marianne in particular suffers from the public ways in which what she regards as her innermost feelings are openly discussed by such people as Mrs. Jennings. Emotional suffering is often related to the visibility of emotion. Brandon, on entering the room on one occasion, sees Marianne rush past him because she cannot contain her intense disappointment that he is not Willoughby. This pains him deeply.

Wilkie Collins is very similar to Dickens in his emphasis on external surfaces: the looks, facial expressions, bodily movements, and sign language by which characters read the minds of, and communicate with, other characters. This is unsurprising, given the close working relationship between Collins and Dickens. "Surface" is a word that recurs throughout Collins's *No Name* (1862). There is little direct report of internal thought in the novel, which continuously demonstrates that much of our thinking can be seen by others:

> When [Magdalen] withdrew [her hands from her face], all the four persons in the room noticed a change in her. Something in her expression had altered, subtly and silently; something which made the familiar features suddenly look strange, even to her sister and Miss Garth; something, through all after years, never to be forgotten in connection with that day – and never to be described.[6]

Magdalen's sister, governess, solicitor, and family friend can see the change in her mental functioning. It is so marked that it is unforgettable for them. On the other hand, the balance between the internal and the external must always be stressed. Although others can see the change in Magdalen's face, it is strange to them. They do not know its precise nature. She keeps her decision (her intention to avenge the wrong done to her and her sister) a secret from them.

Shirley, Maria Edgeworth's *Helen* (1837), and Elizabeth Gaskell's *Wives and Daughters* (1865) are similarly preoccupied with secrets: how much can be concealed from others? For how long? And for what purpose? In *Helen* it is believed that a man who has recently died and who was the lover of her friend Cecilia was in fact Helen's lover. Out of loyalty to Cecilia, Helen cannot tell the truth. The plot of *Helen* hinges on this secret. In *Wives and Daughters* Mrs. Gibson has a secretive nature; Osborne is secretly married; Roger and then Molly discover the marriage, and are forced to keep Osborne's secret; Cynthia conceals her relationship with Preston; Molly finds it out and has another secret to keep. There are passages in this novel, often about Cynthia, in which characters either think about or discuss the difficulty of hiding things from others. The difficulty of concealment is precisely the point. On the face of it, the combination of secrets with social minds seems paradoxical. But the juxtaposition of those apparently disparate elements highlights the difficulties that characters experience when trying to keep secrets from other minds within a community in which people tend to be open and cognitively available to each other. Characters who attempt to hide something are forever fearful that their actions, facial expressions, looks, blushes, and silences will give them away, especially to other characters who know them well.

I will now survey types of inter-mental units in nineteenth-century novels, starting with large and medium-sized ones, and then discussing small units comprised by parents and daughters, or sisters or near-sisters.

One of the most important characters in George Eliot's *Middlemarch* (1872) is the town of Middlemarch. I call the inter-mental functioning of the inhabitants of the town "the Middlemarch mind."[7] The town is not just a social context within which individual characters operate; it *literally*, and not just metaphorically, has a mind of its own. The Middlemarch mind is complex, interesting, clearly visible to a close reader of the text, and vitally important to an understanding of the novel because it explains a good deal of the motivation behind the actions of the other main characters. In looking at the construction of Middlemarch in the novel's opening pages, it is clear that the narrator's initial descriptions of the three individual minds of Dorothea, Celia, and Mr. Brooke are saturated with this group mind, and focalized through it. Once the existence of the Middlemarch mind has been established, the fine shades of inter-mental thought and the complexity of the relationships between inter-mental and intra-mental thought in the rest of the novel can be fully appreciated. Over the course of the text, readers are able to identify a number of distinct, separate Middlemarch minds within the single inter-mental unit that is initially constructed. An analysis of the class structure of the town reveals the existence of separate and well-defined upper-class, middle-class, and working-class minds. This collective framework also makes it possible to see the myriad other fluid and fleeting inter-mental units that occur in the text, and to appreciate the socially situated identities of individual characters. Examples of the latter include characters inside large inter-mental units who act as spokespeople or mouthpieces for their views (Mrs. Cadwallader, Mrs. Dollop, etc.), and also those who, like Lydgate, Dorothea, and Ladislaw, find themselves outside those units and become the object of their inter-mental judgments.

The large inter-mental units in Charles Dickens's *Little Dorrit* (1857) include the speculators who invest in Merdle and are subsequently ruined by him, the Marshalsea prison, and "Society." The speculators are always referred to as a unit, even though, like most large units, it is necessarily a fuzzy set that is composed of individuals who bought into Merdle's financial schemes. "All people knew (or thought they knew) that he had made himself immensely rich."[8] "Nobody . . . knew what he had done; but everybody knew him to be the greatest that had appeared" (627). When explanations for Merdle's death are sought, the entirely spurious physical condition of "pressure" is jointly decided upon and, in an interesting echo of the sort of language used in *Middlemarch*, the narrator remarks that this is "entirely satisfactory to the public mind" (775). In a chilling analysis of the working of this type of inter-mental thought, one which lies behind the exploitative cognitive functioning of the medium-sized units of the Barnacle family and the Circumlocution Office, Ferdinand Barnacle remarks to Clennam in the Marshalsea, "Pardon me, but I think you really have no idea how the human bees will swarm to the beating of any old tin kettle; in that fact lies the complete manual of governing them" (807).

Mr. Harding in *The Warden* quotes an old proverb: "Every one knows where his own shoe pinches!" (175). This is an internalist motto which vividly expresses the apparent truth that only we know what we are experiencing and no one else can. (But suppose one notices that one's companion is hobbling. He stops, takes off his shoe and inspects it, rubs his foot in a particular place, puts a plaster on it, and so on. Is this not fairly close to knowing where his shoe is pinching?) But the proverb is at odds with the tenor of the novel, which is profoundly externalist. The role of the local community, in the form of "gossip," "rumour," and "scandal," is as important as that of the town of Middlemarch. Mr. Harding feels that "all the world knew" (35) about his circumstances. "All Barchester was by the ears about it" (89). The sense of oppression that he feels is similar to that felt by Dorothea, Lydgate, and Ladislaw. The role of the town of Hollingford in *Wives and Daughters* is as frequently mentioned. Its collective mind exerts pressure on Mr. Gibson to marry again (he asks "Why did people think" that he had to remarry),[9] and its speculations about Mr. Gibson's past are similar to those about Lydgate's. (There are curious parallels between the characters of Gibson and Lydgate: both are cultivated country-town doctors who are interested in scientific research, but who blunder into unfortunate marriages with shallow women.)

Anne Elliot in Jane Austen's *Persuasion* (1818) is another character who, like Mr. Harding, cannot be seen in isolation. Apart from her secret feelings for Wentworth, her mind is public and social. In Bakhtinian terms, it is dialogic, frequently anticipating the views of others, successfully or not, and often judged by others, favorably or not. This inescapability of the social has a profound effect on the value judgments that are made about her. Anne is generally favorably judged because she has tact and a sweet character "which must have placed her high with any people of real understanding."[10] Austen's emphasis on the social nature of cognitive functioning is relentless. In the discussion between Anne and Mr. Elliot on what constitutes "good company," the phrase is used seven times in ten lines of text (162). An important aspect of the socially situated quality of Anne's identity is her role within a shifting, ever-changing group of people (or, in my terms, within a medium-sized inter-mental unit) that consists, in the main, of Charles and Mary Musgrove, Henrietta and Louisa, Admiral and Mrs. Croft, Captain Wentworth, Captain and Mrs. Harville, Captain Benwick, and Charles Hayter. There are frequent references to Anne's self-conscious feelings about the workings of the unit and her role within it:

> Anne had not wanted this visit to Uppercross, to learn that a removal from one set of people to another, though at a distance of only three miles, will often include a total change of conversation, opinion, and idea . . . With the prospect of spending at least two more months at Uppercross, it was highly incumbent on her to clothe her imagination, her memory, and all her ideas in as much of Uppercross as possible. (69–70)

This passage, in demonstrating beyond doubt the narrator's awareness of the externalist perspective, might surprise one by sounding so much like George Eliot. It makes it easy to see how *Middlemarch* came to be written. Austen's language is not as obviously cognitive as that in *Middlemarch* (in my experience, the language of no other English novel of the nineteenth century is), but the sensibility, the sensitivity to the workings of social minds, is the same.

A very different medium-sized unit operates in Joseph Conrad's *The Nigger of the "Narcissus"* (1897). It is the crew of the ship. At one point, the men that comprise this crew attempt to rescue the black man of the title, James Wait:

> A rage to fling things overboard possessed us. We worked fiercely, cutting our hands and speaking brutally to one another . . . The agony of his fear wrung our hearts so terribly that we longed to abandon him, to get out of that place . . . to get out of his hearing, back on the poop where we could wait passively for death in incomparable repose.[11]

This is extremely complex inter-mental thought. It starts with an emotion (rage) that is presented *causally*, that is, as an intention to perform an action (flinging things overboard) and therefore as a cause of that action. The intention is presumably unfulfilled and so the action remains hypothetical. The passage then presents realized joint action: intense labor, and the unintended consequence of hands being cut; then speech. Both actions are expressed in ways that vividly convey shared states of mind: working fiercely and speaking brutally. Next, a complex of strong emotions (hearts being wrung) is described as a response to an individual's emotion (Wait's agony of fear). This is followed by another causal emotion (longing), presented as an unfulfilled intention that relates to two decisions that are not made (wanting to abandon him and to get out of his hearing). This short passage concludes with a hypothetical desire to wait passively for death. Some emotions are implied, but not explicitly stated: compassion, fear, desperation, and so on. The thought processes are initially focussed on an individual, Wait, but then become almost mystical or metaphysical ("waiting passively for death in incomparable repose").

Any reader's concern regarding what might seem to be "illicit" access to individual mental functioning in Conrad's text (how can the first-person, or homodiegetic, narrator know what is going on in the minds of his shipmates?) is allayed within the externalist perspective, where at least some knowledge of the mental states of others is the expected norm, not a mysterious aberration. *"Narcissus"* is a good example of a narrative that can be illuminated by a discussion of its social minds. Within the tradition of the action novel, this is a novel of social action; within the tradition of the novel of consciousness, this is a novel of collective consciousness.

With regard to small inter-mental units, close cognitive relationships between parents and daughters are a notable feature. In *Shirley*, while Caroline is being nursed by her mother, Mrs. Pryor, the two "coalesced in wondrous union" (331). "Mrs Pryor could not complete her broken sentences . . . but Caroline comprehended" (296). Shirley does not need to be told that Caroline and Mrs. Pryor are mother and daughter – she sees it by watching them together. However, she conceals from them the fact that she knows it: "I may be communicative, yet know where to stop" (354). When the mother and daughter discuss love and marriage, their discussion contributes to the explicit debate about social minds to which I referred earlier. Caroline suggests that "Where affection is reciprocal and sincere, and minds are harmonious, marriage *must* be happy." Her mother disagrees, arguing that "It is never wholly happy. Two people can never literally be as one" (300). I referred above to the balance between public and private thought, inter-mental and intra-mental functioning, social and individual minds; this discussion maintains the balance by remaining unresolved. There is a close relationship between Mr. Gibson and Molly in *Wives and Daughters*, with frequent references to their ability to know what the other is thinking. "We understand each other" (76). Molly feels great pain at her father's decision to suspend the explicit working of the unit following his marriage. He makes the decision because he does not want to appear to be disloyal to his new wife. Molly is sorrowful that there are now things that he knows that she does not know. They enter into an unspoken pact that the inter-mental quality of their relationship should become implicit because there is no meeting of minds in his new marriage.

Mr. Harding also forms a close inter-mental unit with his younger daughter, Eleanor. "He knew that she loved John Bold" (84). She knows that he is upset by the affair of the hospital. Of course, even inter-mental relationships contain misunderstandings and concealments. Mr. Harding wrongly thinks at one point that Eleanor is more worried about herself than about him (85). Initially, he suffers in silence, and for a long time he cannot tell anyone, even Eleanor, what he is thinking and feeling. On the other hand, he cannot "prevent her from seeing that he was disturbed" (127–128). "Eleanor saw well how it was" (128). His isolation hurts her: her desire is "to be allowed to share his sorrows" (130). Tellingly, she exclaims: "Oh! papa, your face tells so much; though you won't speak to me with your voice, I know how it is with you every time I look at you" (135). She knows some of what he is thinking, but not all of it. She knows that he is suffering, but not badly enough to make him want to resign. Finally, he tells her everything "till he laid bare the inmost corners of his heart" (136). It is worth mentioning that mind-reading is an important element in joint action: Mr. Harding gives Eleanor a letter to his son-in-law saying that he is going to London to speak to the attorney general "with the perfect, though not expressed, understanding that its delivery was to be delayed" (210).

An interesting pattern in these novels is the high degree of inter-mentality between sisters or near-sisters. Examples include Elinor and Marianne in *Sense and Sensibility* (real sisters), Molly and Cynthia in *Wives and Daughters* (step-sisters), Shirley and Caroline in *Shirley* (close friends who become sisters-in-law), and Helen and Cecilia in *Helen* (almost-sisters). Shirley and Caroline fascinatingly debate the visibility of thought, and of emotion in particular. Caroline: "I saw you disturbed." Shirley: "You saw nothing, Caroline. I can cover my feelings." But then, Shirley: "You can never tell how your look, mien, carriage, shook me . . . I soon saw you were diffident" (340). Shirley then "took Caroline in her arms, gave her one look, one kiss, then said – 'You are better'" (353). However, the familiar theme of the patchiness and unreliability of inter-mental thought recurs. Caroline remarks to Shirley: "I thought I knew you quite well: I begin to find myself mistaken" (357). In another similarly complex scene, Caroline tells Robert Moore about an intimate conversation between her and Shirley that probes the mechanisms of inter-mentalism (474–475). Caroline explains to Robert that Shirley tells her some things but not others; Caroline can guess and infer some aspects of Shirley's mind but not all of them. What neither finds out about the other is the identity of the person whom they love. In *Wives and Daughters* there are frequent occasions on which Molly and Cynthia know what the other is thinking, and they are able to communicate by means of looks and gestures (for example, their disapproval of Mrs. Gibson's behavior). As always, though, the picture is mixed. Cynthia does not know about the most important aspect of Molly's mind: she does not suspect Molly's feelings for Roger.

Any survey of internalist and externalist perspectives in the nineteenth-century novel would be incomplete without attention to Henry James. I will, therefore, before concluding with some general remarks, comment on a curious feature of one of his unjustly neglected books, *The Tragic Muse* (1890). During conversations in novels, a character will sometimes not quite follow what another character has said and will ask the other to explain what the other meant to say. In the James novel there are, extraordinarily, at least 175 examples of this phenomenon. One might think that, after all, this is Henry James, and his characters will be prone to employ masterly indirection in order to avoid being understood, or to pretend misunderstanding. However, this novel is different from other Henry James novels in having very few Machiavellian schemers and plotters. Characters here are trying to be straightforward with each other and the vast majority of their non-understandings are genuine. It is just that their minds are private, solitary, and mysterious. As a result, characters' conversations are too gnomic for easy communication. The tone is typically cagey – characters circle each other watchfully, never saying precisely what they mean, not through deceit, but through self-absorption. Only rarely does a reader get a clear sense of characters knowing each other's minds, because James's characters do not put themselves in the place of others and ask themselves: what does that person already know, and what do I need to tell in order to make my statements intelligible? In almost every conversation in the novel, statements have to be made more explicit because the original formulation is unclear to the interlocutors. As a result, communication is a laborious effort. The predominant feeling is of apartness. There is never any feeling of a meeting of minds, of two characters being on the same wavelength. Revealingly, the narrator describes two participants in one conversation as "speaking a different language."[12]

One might consider the contrast between the story-world of James's novel and those of the novels of Austen, Edgeworth, Gaskell, and Eliot. In cognitive terms, it is quite a distance to travel back from *The Tragic Muse* – where characters do not know what others are thinking, despite their endlessly trying to explain – to the many earlier novels in which characters often know what others are thinking without the need for speech. Within the externalist paradigm, the emphasis is on *ease* of communication; within the internalist one, the emphasis is on the *difficulty* of communication. However, it is important not to exaggerate the differences between the Scott and James novels and the others under discussion. It is certainly not black and white – we are talking about shades of grey. Miriam Rooth in *The Tragic Muse* baffles others because she is a supreme actress, but James shows her supreme ability to penetrate the mind of Nick Dormer, whom she loves hopelessly. In both *Waverley* and *The Tragic Muse*, characters do occasionally know what others are thinking. Equally, as I have shown, there are many secrets and frequent misunderstandings and mind-misreadings in the other novels. There are more secrets, in fact, in the externalist novels than in *Waverley* and *The Tragic Muse*. Nevertheless, the general tendency of the two sorts of novels is unmistakably different. The few examples of inter-mentality in the James novel have to be set against the 175-odd occasions when it is conspicuously absent.

It is an obvious truth that the sorting of literary tradition into historical periods is necessarily arbitrary. The novel form does not, of necessity, change utterly at the beginning of each century to suit the classificatory needs of future literary historians. Indeed, it is one of the strengths of this volume that it is organized precisely in order to complicate and question such easy and neat categories as "the nineteenth-century novel." On the other hand, though, it is possible to paint a picture of the history of the English novel that does, as it happens, fit into divisions into centuries. There was a change at the beginning of the nineteenth century, due in the main to the genius of Jane Austen, and it is possible to trace a satisfying line of descent from Austen through Edgeworth and the Brontës to Dickens and Collins, Gaskell, and Eliot, and then on to James and Conrad. There is then a very different change at the beginning of the twentieth century with the coming of the modernist movement. Although many features of the English novel will not fit comfortably into a satisfyingly schematic picture, from an externalist perspective on social minds the picture is a genuinely illuminating one. The novel of the nineteenth century explores tensions between the internalist and externalist perspectives, between social and private minds, in ways that are noticeably different from both the eighteenth-century novel and the twentieth- and early twenty-first-century novel. This is not to say that the novels of other periods are not interested in social minds. The differences lie in the degree of interest, and the ways in which this aspect of the novel is presented and examined.

The standard story for the historical development of the representation of consciousness in the English novel follows what might be termed a "speech category trajectory."[13] Very roughly, this begins with the reliance of narratives before Jane Austen on authors' or narrators' externalized reports of characters' thoughts. Then, from Austen onwards until, say, Henry James, novels are marked by a growing preponderance of free indirect discourse. With the modernist novels of the early twentieth century, stream of consciousness and interior monologue become dominant modes of narration. Leaving aside quibbles regarding the accuracy of this history (its possible overestimation, perhaps, of the amount and importance of free indirect discourse at the expense of external reports of thought), it is an indispensible aid to an understanding of the history of the novel. However, if we want a *complete* picture of the historical development of the representation of *whole* fictional minds, the speech-category trajectory has to be supplemented by others such as the history of the representation of social minds. It is possible that this narrative might well intersect at a number of points with the speech category account. It could be, perhaps, that Jane Austen is the first great English novelist of social minds, just as she is the first of free indirect discourse. That sounds quite likely to me.

Given that a history of social minds would consider all of the novelists under discussion as historically embedded figures, several questions arise. Are the workings of social minds more salient in authors I have discussed than in authors of the same period whom limited space prevents me from considering? In what ways are social minds more salient in nineteenth-century novels than in the novels of earlier and later periods? Is the nineteenth century a privileged moment in which great novelists capture the *universal* condition that we all share and that has since been obscured by assumptions limiting the power of narrative to expose the full extent of this condition? Or, alternatively, are social minds a unique characteristic of the nineteenth-century British society that is the subject matter of nineteenth-century novelists?

Notes

1. Jane Austen, *Emma* (Harmondsworth: Penguin, 1996), pp. 303–304, emphases added.
2. See also this volume's ch. 9 by Lisa Zunshine on minds in the eighteenth-century novel.
3. Walter Scott, *Waverley* (Harmondsworth: Penguin, 1972), pp. 250–251.
4. Anthony Trollope, *The Warden* (Harmondsworth: Penguin, 2004), pp. 237–238.
5. Charlotte Brontë, *Shirley* (London: Everyman, 1975), p. 215.

6. Wilkie Collins, *No Name* (Harmondsworth: Penguin, 1994), p. 124.
7. In *Social Minds in the Novel* (Columbus: Ohio State University Press, 2011), ch. 3.
8. Charles Dickens, *Little Dorrit* (Harmondsworth: Penguin, 1967), p. 611.
9. Elizabeth Gaskell, *Wives and Daughters* (Harmondsworth: Penguin, 1969), p. 104.
10. Jane Austen, *Persuasion* (Harmondsworth: Penguin, 1965), p. 37.
11. Joseph Conrad, *The Nigger of the "Narcissus"* (Harmondsworth: Penguin, 2007), p. 54.
12. Henry James, *The Tragic Muse* (Harmondsworth: Penguin, 1995), p. 346.
13. See my *Fictional Minds* (Lincoln: University of Nebraska Press, 2004), ch. 3.

27

Clamors of eros

RICHARD A. KAYE

The two swore that at every other time of their lives till death took
them, they would assuredly believe, feel, and desire precisely as they
had believed, felt, and desired during the few preceding weeks. . . .
[N]obody seemed at all surprised at what they swore.

Thomas Hardy, *Jude the Obscure* (1895)[1]

Hardy's passage detailing the marriage of Jude and Arabella is as saturated
in ironies as it is in harsh social criticism. In wryly paraphrasing the terms of their
marriage contract, Hardy has substituted "feel" and "desire" where "love" and
"honour" appear in the Book of Common Prayer's solemnization of matrimony. It is carnal passion, not love, that has united the couple, an ill-fated
alliance whose numbing monotony is accentuated in the deforming repetition
of the marital vow. Society has consecrated "desire" (misrecognizing it as
"love") as the basis for marriage when it should comprehend desire as short-
lived. In *Jude the Obscure* it is not so much the familiar Hardyesque elements
"nature" and "fate" that ensnare his restless protagonists but the ludicrous laws
that require marriage to solidify momentary escapades into lifelong commitments. With *Jude* the inhabitable microcosm that Jane Austen's fiction made out
of love-consecrated marriage becomes at the century's end a prison-house.

In writing with such acerbity Hardy anticipates a distinction that animates
literary critics attending to Victorian fiction a century later. For of all the
reconceptualizations in the 1980s and 1990s, none has been more influential
than the deployment of "desire" where once "love" or "courtship" had
demarcated intimate relations in fiction. The value of "desire" as an animating
concept arises from its subtlety and allusiveness, encompassing a range of
impulses and fantasies, enacted or not, and whether or not they find institutional substantiation. Social historians might fret over marriage and divorce
rates, historians of sexuality are bound to parse legal obstacles to new
perversities, and biographers might lack evidence of the bedroom dalliances

437

of their subjects, but critics have felt increasingly free to hypothesize the Sapphic dimension in the relation between Jane Eyre and Helen Burns, the spell that the dashing entrepreneur Donald Farfrae casts over Michael Henchard, or the same-sex carnal energies released by fictional vampires. In the case of *Wuthering Heights* (1847), popularly misconstrued as a narrative of "romantic love," "desire" is efficacious, since it better suggests the anarchic relation between Heathcliff and Catherine, ridden with intimations of adolescent lust, sado-masochism, and semi-incestuous feelings – in short, "desires" inassimilable to everything socially acceptable.

What is valuable in such "desire"-driven criticism and what it also obscures is my object in the following pages. I will propose some alternative arguments, with special attention to Hardy, Elizabeth Gaskell, and Oscar Wilde, about those novelists' uses of eros as thematic material. Hardy remains the pioneering Victorian novelist, taking up the thematics of the socially clamorous and untenable forms of desire, from the Sapphic bedroom scene in his first novel, *Desperate Remedies* (1871) to the last works, *Tess of the d'Urbervilles* (1891), *Jude*, and *The Well-Beloved* (1897). But in addition to grappling with eros Victorian novelists thoughtfully consider self-denying celibate life, particularly for "unmarriageable" or professionally ambitious women; and they do so in the context of threats produced by what I will discuss as "animality." In further considering Hardy, and then exploring Gaskell's *Mary Barton* (1856), I hope to demonstrate how the crisis of erotic desire at the heart of a social-problem novel relates to a radical political agenda, one that promotes an understanding of sexuality as an ally of working-class aspirations. *Mary Barton* makes its argument about female sexuality not in the psychological terms familiar from the Brontës or George Eliot, but in terms of class conflict, even as it draws on the fierce moral rationale on which the other writers rely. Hence Gaskell's novel is in keeping with revolutionary sexual theorists of the mid-Victorian period, chief among them Friedrich Engels. Finally, I explore *The Picture of Dorian Gray* (1891). By now a "queer reading" of *Dorian Gray* is an orthodox endeavor. Critics have been far less attentive, however, to the novel's revisionary formal achievement – to how it overturns the *Bildungsroman* tradition.

In engaging recent criticism I do not forget an earlier generation of critics who focus on fiction's erotic imaginary. Steven Marcus's *The Other Victorians* (1966) scrutinized innumerable pornographic texts, and posits a "pornotopia" – the "imagination of the entire universe under the sign of sexuality" – as a defining feature of a Victorian counter-world.[2] Michel Foucault criticized Marcus for confining erotica to a safely annexed underground, but in fact Marcus vigorously de-sequesters pornographic discourse by demonstrating how *The Lustful Turk* (1828) and *The Amatory Experiences of a Surgeon* (1881) borrow the language of sentimentalism, so that "psychological obsession and literary convention" together characterize Victorian pornography. Marcus's notion of pornography as a hybrid sub-genre of "high" and "low" styles speaks to a key feature of the most notorious Victorian homosexual pornographic text, *Teleny, or the Reverse of the Medal* (1893), perhaps co-authored by Wilde, in which classical allusions interlace same-sex intercourse.

The Victorian pornotopia consorted well with emerging sexological conceptions of the desiring subject in the later nineteenth century. Naturalistic fiction, too, is a highly "sexological" fictional mode, since it presents commonalities between characters of like erotic "temperaments" as crucial to indicting the effects of industrialization on ordinary humanity. In contrast, novels such as Charlotte Brontë's *Jane Eyre* (1847) and *Villette* (1853) that are indebted to realist protocols stress the traits dividing characters, even when affinities between characters and their erotic impulses might be obvious. When Jane is finally confronted with Rochester's sequestered mad wife Bertha, she does not recognize a soul-sister or rival but sees an alien, degraded beast. Even when relations between women are intensely intimate (as they are with Jane's physically demonstrative relation with Helen, or Lucy Snowe's frisky rapport with Ginevra Fanshawe), erotic affinity with other women is disavowed in Brontëan narratives that privilege personal, subjective experience above all else.

Critics reading for "desire" have not attended to the disavowal. Even as late-Victorian sexological science conjured new categories for the conceptual containment of homosexual and lesbian impulses, there is no doubt that the granular individualism of fictional character, which dissolves types into figures with characterological quirks and nuances, works in striking opposition to the categorizations that medical science and law affirm. James's portrait of the pro-woman activist Olive Chancellor in *The Bostonians* (1886), the most psychologically intricate depiction of semi-repressed lesbian desire in nineteenth-century Anglo-American fiction, frustrates any impulse to see her as a specimen of the investment of sexological science in measurable categories of desire. Olive's rival for Verena Tarrant, the Southern lawyer Basil Ransom, schemes to separate Verena from the "emancipation of Olive Chancellor's sex ('what sex was it, great heaven?' he used profanely to ask himself?)" – Ransom himself sounding like a querulous sexologist, his query devalued by a parenthetical submergence.[3]

Although *The Bostonians* individuates sexuality, defying sexology, a unifying social typicality adheres to James's protagonists: Basil is a characteristic post-bellum Southerner; the novel's title invokes recognizable New England female "types," satirizing them as the sexually crackpot offspring of transcendentalism. Still, in continually turning to eros for its material and in relying on delay and deferral as a rationale for narrative itself, the Victorian novel becomes the locus for all the nebulously appearing and receding sensations of arousal that deflect or defy measurement. If the realist novel increasingly resists the reductively classifying dynamics of law and medicine, however, it also registers the toll of transgressions and the pressures of punitive social rules, no more so than when it comes to marriage and its violations. Aside from sensation fiction, in which such works as Mary Elizabeth Braddon's *The Doctor's Wife* (1864) – a re-writing of Flaubert's *Madame Bovary* (1856) – had long indulged torrid portrayals of marital betrayal, adultery belatedly appears in the English novel, lagging behind the content of French fiction. When adulterous relations finally arrive as a subject for James and Ford Madox Ford, they do so because law-courts are increasingly confronted with adultery-driven divorce cases, heralded in front-page newspaper coverage. Sean Latham claims that, beginning with the Wilde trials, sex-scandal generating *romans à clef* challenged prevailing notions of fiction as independent of the social and political sphere, inasmuch as works of literary art emerged as truth-telling, legally actionable texts.[4]

For all their facticity, shocking erotic liaisons always serve as a vehicle for formal discovery in the nineteenth-century novel, as well as an inducement to the reading public's appreciation of formal innovation. Even Austen, whose novels subsume the sexual to the elaborate rituals of courtship, makes eros sub-textually vital to her narratives. In *Emma* (1815) the most deferred secret is Frank Churchill's engagement to Jane Fairfax, a betrothal whose protracted illicitness hints at a carnal intensity that is denied to the heroine. In *Mansfield Park* (1814) Maria Bertram's affair with Henry Crawford leads to her downfall when her husband divorces her and Crawford refuses to wed her (a double disgrace because the scandal appears in a newspaper). Had Crawford not had an affair with Maria, the heroine Fanny Price might have accepted his marriage proposal. George Eliot's *Scenes from Clerical Life* (1858) offers an advanced realism thanks to audacious new subject matter (the first serious depiction of alcoholism in English fiction), yet it is not until *Adam Bede* (1859), with its delineation of seduction, that Eliot is swept to fame by a public excited by lover's betrayals and out-of-wedlock amorous yearning, topics that there-after never disappear from Eliot's fiction. All Anthony Trollope's forty-seven novels concern "love problems." Hardy's themes – erotic threesomes, rape, out-of-wedlock romance – become notorious.

James's plots increasingly require not only spousal betrayal but outlandish erotic intrigue in order to sustain his audience's attention to difficult formal experiments in consciousness. The social optics of adultery as they impinge on a too-innocent mind are pivotal in *The Portrait of a Lady* (1881). Isabel Archer learns that Madame Merle has been her husband's mistress only after Isabel recalls entering a room and realizing that Madame Merle stood while Isabel's husband Osmond sat. A transgression of drawing-room decorum belatedly discloses adultery. By the time James revisits adultery in *The Golden Bowl* (1904) super-subtlety is required to gauge the recessed sexual desires and plots beneath the beguiling sociability of his protagonists. The adulterous lovers and the novelist militate against a world of "vulgar" descriptions. For example, when Prince Amerigo spies his mistress Charlotte Stant enter a room:

> He saw again that her thick hair was, vulgarly speaking, brown, but that there was a shade of tawny autumn leaf in it for "appreciation" – a colour indescribable and of which he had known no other case, something that gave her at moments the sylvan head of a huntress.[5]

With such evocations, this sentence marks Charlotte as a riveting predatory adulteress by rendering her an aesthetic object of exquisitely refined determinations. The essence of the exquisite sensibility lies in the depiction of the adulterers not as malevolent, soul-destroying schemers but as morally nuanced actors whose infidelities must be embraced by the heroine Maggie as inextricably part of "life." Perfection in personal and erotic relations is an unattainable ideal.

Desire, nineteenth-century novels, and critical discontent

Critical emphasis in the 1980s and 1990s on a multiplicity of sexualities sought to escape the limitations of Marxist and formalist approaches that had skirted an exploration of eros in fiction and narrative form. That search was prompted by Roland Barthes's *The Pleasure of the Text* (1972), with its deployment of *plaisir* ("pleasure") and *jouissance* (translated as "bliss" but signifying "orgasm"). In *Reading for the Plot: Design and Intention in Narrative* (1984), Peter Brooks's focus on desire "derives from my dissatisfaction with the . . . formalisms that have dominated critical thinking about narrative."[6] Reviving one of the most vulnerable of Freudian legacies ("drive theory") Brooks claims a "drive of desire" that shapes narrative. Wary of the "drive of desire," feminist criticism sought to expose the ways male desires in fiction construct sexual and gender differences. Hélène Cixous, Luce Irigaray, and Teresa de Lauretis discovered woman-oriented textual "pleasure," insisting on the polymorphous nature of non-phallocentric female eros.

Such developments in criticism brought about the investigation of eros in fiction that I referred to at the start of this chapter. Yet the dissident force of newly discovered eroticisms was often undermined by a co-present emphasis on the novel's reflexive functionalism as an instrument of containment, surveillance, and curtailment. In criticism of the Victorian novel, "subversive" desires became pervasive, but what critics often accentuated was the inevitable inhibition of subversion. The erotic imagination was revealed; but it was also said to be hampered, tamed, or gentrified. Leo Bersani's astringent reading of *Wuthering Heights* construes Brontë's novel as diminished in its second half. For Bersani the novel is bifurcated between a radical anarchic erotic text and a "cozy and conventional" Victorian narrative that provides an imprisoning family-centered solution to the problem of identity.[7] Bersani's construal of desire would have it that narrative intrinsically does violence to existing social forms, a claim foreign to Brooks. But whereas Brooks maintained that desire propels narrative, and feminist critics saw only male-authored texts as proffering violent masculine myths, Bersani viewed narrative, despite its violence, as invariably subduing, containing, and dissipating desire whenever desire is most appealingly disruptive.

The most significant text in determining a critical investment in desire was the first volume of Michel Foucault's *The History of Sexuality* (1978). Arguing against the notion of Victorian society as committed to repression, Foucault contended that nineteenth-century culture produced an avalanche of discourses on eros. In terms of the Victorian novel, however, it was Foucault's examination in *Discipline and Punish* (1975) of surveillance and the "panoptic" strategies of modern society that proved most influential, pre-eminently in D. A. Miller's *The Novel and the Police* (1989), a landmark of Foucault-inspired criticism of Victorian fiction, and in Eve Kosofsky Sedgwick's *Epistemology of the Closet* (1990). In those studies anarchic forms of desire in fiction recede and a figurative imprisonment becomes constitutive of Victorian fiction, which emerges as a policing, closeting, coercively judging instrument of an unseen state apparatus, with endless enabling circuits that produce self-disciplining subjects. Bold as the readings produced by those studies are, a hermetic reiteration among the allegiants of Miller and Sedgwick insisted that the Victorian novel evinces the impossibility of freedom because fictional discourse is invisibly linked to seamlessly interconnected regimes of power. "Like a religion that justifies those who are enriched by the profits of the capitalist system," writes Jeff Nunokawa of Anne Brontë:

or one that counsels resignation to those who labor to produce them, the secular scripture of desire promulgated by novels like *The Tenant of Wildfell Hall* promotes a faith that renders more tenable the sacrifices of desire exacted by that system.[8]

Yet before analogizing *The Tenant of Wildfell Hall* (1848) to repressive ideologies, one should recognize that in a Victorian context the novel is doggedly engaged in a radical agenda – namely, to oppose male dominance in the domestic sphere, which in Brontë's novel leads to an abused wife's decision to flee her home (where her alcoholic husband is initiating their son into male drinking rituals) and to raise her son on her own as a single mother. Any attachment of *The Tenant of Wildfell Hall* to prevailing orthodoxies lies in its ardent attempt to adapt the requisites of a Christian puritan "faith" to a proto-feminist cause.

For a number of more recent critics the readings of Victorian fiction I have surveyed take insufficient measure of the role played by sexuality in a nineteenth-century social order that simultaneously polices and also gives shape to same-sex eros. In *Between Women: Friendship, Desire, and Marriage in Victorian England* (2008), Sharon Marcus expands our understanding of lesbianism in nineteenth-century British fiction. While her title nods to Sedgwick's *Between Men* (1985), a study of repressive homosocial substitutes for homosexuality, *Between Women* supplants Sedgwick's insistence on a uniformly homophobic Victorian culture. Marcus sees heterosexual marriage in Victorian fiction as a mediating institution that enables female same-sex erotic rapport. In a more explicit reproach to Sedgwick, *Queer Dickens: Erotics, Families, Masculinities* (2010), Holly Furneaux forcefully criticizes *Between Men* for its repeated proposition that "Dickensian homoeroticism is most, or only, legible in acts of violence."[9] Rather, Furneaux perceives in Dickens bachelor fathers, men resistant to marriage, and male nurses, in novels that reserve a privileged status to varieties of nurturance, not to a longing for heterosexual reproduction. As the most recent studies suggest, the nineteenth-century British novel repeatedly envisions new modes of erotic freedom as it consciously calibrates the costs of systems of control.

Erotic self-management and animality

To be sure, the Victorian novel strenuously meditates on eros's relation to a surveillance-oriented social realm. At the same time, the novel's focus on sexuality is incited far more by the tensile relations between a highly managed individual identity and a "natural" animal self that cannot be tethered to a human or social code, let alone to surveillance and control.

Darwin's bold conception of nature as destructive of individual destinies unsettles conceptions of the natural, chief among them Rousseau's idealizing notions. George Meredith's *The Ordeal of Richard Feverel* (1859), spoofing the regulation of a young man's libidinal urges by his father Sir Austin's "System," skewers the all-policing parental manipulation of youthful sexual energies. Against Rousseau, Meredith implicitly posits Darwin, who refuses, unlike Sir Austin, to sentimentalize nature as an Eden. Every paternal "rule" about erotic life is exploded in the course of the plot, as Meredith satirizes educational systems intent on creating a "natural" child, the philosophical aim of Rousseau's *Émile* (1762). Meredith's narrative itself refuses to submit to a uniform set of stylistic conceits, for despite its assent to tragic realism in its denouement, the novel is an antic hybrid, employing multiple modal strategies – burlesque, satire, pastiche, fantasy, and melodrama. (One admiring contemporary reviewer notes its "strange contrarieties").[10] Like Thackeray's *Vanity Fair* (1848), another work with an antithetical relation to realism, Meredith's novel stages a comedy of surveillance. Nature is the model for the antic hybrid, brooking no regulation but chance.

But nature's anarchic depth requires management at the surface of individuated life. In *Vanity Fair* Thackeray's narrator is one kind of manager, Becky Sharp, another. The self-conscious narrator-puppeteer is an all-seeing macro-monologist whose volubility frustrates the depiction of psychological depth in the course of representing female sexual prowess as an engine of social aspiration. "You men would sacrifice anything for a pleasure," Becky declares,[11] articulating a well-codified Victorian gender divide regarding libidinal matters; but she herself exemplifies a canny female power based on self-serving restraint. Richard Feverel might have learned from her.

Although Aristotle saw complete continence as conceivable but not natural, Victorian novelists depict the constructive potentialities of self-management or self-denial in matters of sex. In Brontë's *Villette* Lucy Snowe, drawn to two men, repeatedly encounters the ghost of a nun who might have been buried alive for breaking her vows of chastity – a warning of a gothic fate awaiting the heroine. Despite the punitive threat here, sexual renunciation might allow women enhanced intellectual aims, awe-inspiring accomplishments, and serious "occupations." In Wilkie Collins's *The Woman in White* (1860), Walter Hartright confronts two half-sisters, the blue-eyed, doll-like Laura and the memorably mannish, moustache-sporting, heroically sleuthing

Marian Halcombe. Manifestly "unmarriageable," Marian has the virginal strength to investigate the novel's central mystery, becoming a model of perspicacity whom Walter comes to emulate.

The pressure to forge a heterosexual union generates an almost intolerable burden on female characters in fiction. But Marian remains single, and Lucy must survive the apparent loss at sea of her ultimate lover. Unions come and go; survival matters. Sometimes it is rewarded with eros reborn or with mastery of eros. "I think it would be well if all single women were strangled by the time they are thirty," announces the unattached Clara Amedroz in Trollope's *The Belton Estate* (1865), although the novel resolves her quandary by having two men fall in love with her and she with them.[12] Alternative plots, in which the female asserts her power to choose a mate, anticipate (perhaps also help form) Darwin's *The Descent of Man* (1871), where the evolutionist establishes species "courtship" as a live-or-die process in which males perform in a beauty contest for a masterful female.

By century's end, however, many observers worried about a surplus of single women. What could the 44 percent of all British women over forty who had not married *do*? Of what use were they? George Gissing's *The Odd Women* (1893) depicts "useless" females, independent-minded but living precariously because of a low supply of eligible spouses and because they believe eros is a trap. Gissing narrates the challenges facing the charismatic feminist leader Rhoda Nunn, who sees romantic love as an impediment to the cause of women. She rails against novelists for fomenting idealizations of romance: "Love – love – love; a sickening sameness of vulgarity. What is more vulgar than the ideal of novelists? They won't represent the real world; it would be too dull for their readers. In real life, how many woman and men *fall in love*?"[13] Rhoda rejects an affluent bachelor to pursue her pro-woman program of stoical abstinence. Gaskell already had imagined a female-centric community of voluntarily unattached women in *Cranford* (1853), but the community of women that coalesces in *The Odd Women* is motivated by a harsh necessity. (At one point Rhoda's followers celebrate a recent success – until they are checked by the jarring laughter of a prostitute down the street.) Outside of reproduction, men are expendable in Gissing's tale. Although a grim naturalist logic determines much of the novel, lending an unequivocal assent to Rhoda's choices, Gissing concludes with a striking visionary arrangement, in which an all-female makeshift family freely takes on the task of raising the baby girl of a comrade who has died in childbirth. Women's creative aspirations continue to collide with the requirements of marriage and the demands of eros. In Rhoda Broughton's *A Beginner* (1894), a

New Woman novelist courts a man of letters. "She loves his writings; she loves his high character; but does she love *him*?" she wonders, dreaming that "Some day she may find his arms stealing tremblingly presumptuous round her."[14] When she discovers he has penned a hostile review of her novel, bringing her public scorn, she dissolves the courtship, saving the life that her ego rather than eros has made for her.

The novelists' use of Darwin has a notorious dark side. They create apocalyptic scenarios out of his schemas wherein "animality" not only explains the human realm but also threatens to invade it. In *The Realistic Imagination: English Fiction from Frankenstein to Lady Chatterley* (1981) George Levine contended that fictional realism begins with the eviction of the non-human (the expulsion of Frankenstein's monster from the community) and culminates with the return of the non-human in D. H. Lawrence's *Lady Chatterley's Lover* (1928), where the lover game-keeper functions as a symbolic beast. For Levine the cognitive claims of realism are undermined by the inadequately repressed specter of the non-human. Eros is the beast, non-human as well as human. The critical era I have been referring to singled out Bram Stoker's *Dracula* (1897) for its suggestion that heterosexual relations are apocalyptically troubled by the bestiality that overshadows human affairs. The animalistic vampire stands for a perverse underworld: same-sex eros uncontrollably sucking the blood of heterosexual egos. *Fin-de-siècle* texts about eros often register the breakdown of conventional love and mores in formal terms – in the case of *Dracula*, in a disjunctive collage of diaries, letters, "statements," logs, and testimonials – as their protagonists vanquish (but also ambivalently beckon towards) terrifying non-human creatures.

The ambivalence has been read as a symptom of cultural repression of eros, as if eros, free of repression, would not be dangerous. Not repressed, however, it constitutes a profound danger for Lucy Snowe, Marian Halcombe, Gissing's Rhoda, and the others. That is why they must manage it. The danger of an uninhibited immediate relation to eros is summed up in Walter Pater's retelling of the story of Cupid (Eros) and Psyche in *Marius the Epicurean* (1885). Psyche fears that the unknown Eros who desires her is an "evil serpent-thing."[15] Her impatience to discover the identity of her unknown lover makes Eros in effect become the evil she fears it to be. Losing her lover, she must undergo distantiation from Eros before she can recover him. She thereby learns to respect "the *hiddenness* of perfect things" (87) – of Eros – by practicing, however unsteadily, the ego-maintaining labor of self-management and self-possession. Only after that labor, and only through it, can blissful union subsequently occur.

Hardy and dissident desire

Early in *The Mayor of Casterbridge* (1886) Hardy describes Elizabeth-Jane's discernment of the "tigerish affection" that the man she imagines is her father feels for the young Scotsman, Farfrae. Henchard has a "constant liking to have Farfrae near him."[16] An unworldly girl, confronted with "tigerish affection" between men, elects to draw an analogy from animal life as a way of explicating the central cause of Henchard's tragedy, beginning with his drunken decision to sell his wife in the novel's first chapter. The two men strike her as "the inseparables,"[17] as much a couple as the shifting pairs that buffet Hardy's narrative. That Elizabeth-Jane will become Farfrae's wife at the novel's conclusion (after he loses Lucette) relates to a defining dynamic in Hardy's fiction, whereby the objects of one's desire are forever duplicable. In *Tess of the d'Urbervilles* (1891), after Tess's execution for the murder of her husband Alec, it is characteristic of eros in Hardy that Tess's lover Angel Clare walks off hand in hand with Tess's sister Liza-Lu.

Hardy's aesthetic innovation lies in his rendering of sex in symbolically and erotically overheated lyrical vignettes, what Virginia Woolf characterizes as Hardy's "moments of vision . . . passages of astonishing beauty and force" involving a "sudden quickening of power which we cannot foretell, nor he, it seems, control. A single scene breaks off from the rest."[18] Such scenes involve image-laden sexual tensions and yearnings. They function as a spontaneous exposure of unconscious wishes, the imagistic surface registering the erotic conflict far more than the characters themselves.

The scenes also achieve an oblique eroticization of relations without risk of censorship. They can function as subdued moments of unwitting courtship, as when Farfrae encounters Elizabeth-Jane, and blows pollen off of her as she stands immobile. More sensationally they are located in images or incidents such as Bathsheba and Gabriel's standing in an electrical storm in *Far from the Madding Crowd* (1874); Troy's swordplay with Bathsheba in that same novel; Angel Clare's sleep-walking burial of Tess after he learns she is not a virgin. By allowing the reader to grasp the erotically charged import of moments when even Hardy's characters seem sexually unaware, Hardy shapes a sexually cognizant reader. Such moments represent, as well, an effusion of significance, a kind of overload of symbolic import that seals narrative meaning. It is as if the social world, resistant to individual freedom and always casting obstacles before Hardy's protagonists, temporarily must be abandoned for a symbolic and simultaneously natural sphere that can fully accommodate idyllic eros. The moments also can function as testaments to the limits and exhaustion of erotic attraction. Sue Bridehead (the authentic intellectual in a story of a young man whose idea of learning is rote memorization) leaps out of the window from her marriage-bed rather than have physical relations with her husband, Phillotson. Sue is the earliest explicit instance in Victorian fiction of a wife registering disgust at sexual relations with her husband. In a testament to the exhaustion of marriage that is one overt theme in *Jude the Obscure*, Phillotson's neurasthenic self-abnegation allows him to grant Sue an annulment. His action is a pale imitation of Arabella's stoical disavowal of Jude as a husband. Arabella's lack of self-abnegation, and her indomitable erotic character, also testifies to the exhaustion – the inadequacy – of marriage.

Mary Barton and the sexual politics of the social-problem novel

A scene in *Mary Barton* stands out as a notably convulsive moment. Mary learns that her former would-be lover Henry Carson, scion of a prosperous family, has been murdered; and that Jem Wilson, her more recent would-be lover, a poor mechanic, has been arrested as the suspect. Mary is then brutally reprimanded by Jem's mother, who admonishes her for seducing him and then goading him into an act of murder. Mary "staggered on like one in a dream," and as she nears home:

> her impetuous course was arrested by a light touch on her arm, and turning hastily, she saw a little Italian boy, with his humble show-box, – a white mouse, or some such thing. The setting sun cast its red glow on his face, otherwise the olive complexion would have been very pale; and the glittering tear drops hung on the long, curled eyelashes. With his soft voice, and pleading looks, he uttered, in his pretty broken English, the word –
> "Hungry! so hungry."
> And as if to aid by gesture the effect of the solitary word, he pointed to his mouth, with its white quivering lips.
> Mary answered him impatiently, "Oh, lad, hunger is nothing – nothing!"
> And she rapidly passed on . . .[19]

The scene is a moment when the relentlessly grim conditions depicted in *Mary Barton* are registered but are also overridden by protocols more familiar in stories of courtship, where finding relational fulfillment rules supremely. For a moment (but only for a moment, since Mary immediately returns to offer the urchin sustenance), Mary would seem to be rashly claiming that the horrors of hunger are nothing as compared to those of an entangling love triangle. This surrender by the heroine to selfish individual interest as well as to social guilt functions as the repressed underside of the industrial novel. Indeed, as a dictum "Hunger is nothing – nothing!" might well serve as a succinct repudiation of the economistic claims of the social-problem novel itself – claims so successfully realized that Marx saluted Gaskell as part of the "present splendid brotherhood of fiction writers in England ... whose graphic and eloquent pages have issued to the world more political and social truths than have been uttered by all the professional politicians, publicists and moralists put together."[20]

The "love problem" that inaugurates the tragedy of *Mary Barton* stems from its heroine's initially receptive response to attentions from the well-born Harry Carson, leading her to indulge fantasies of becoming his well-heeled wife: "Mary hoped to meet him every day in her walks, blushed when she heard his name, and tried to think of him as her future husband, and above all, tried to think of her as his future wife. Alas poor Mary! Bitter woe did thy weakness work thee!" (41). Yet in the explicit triangle at the heart of *Mary Barton*, she also yearns for the earnest embrace of Jem Wilson. Mary's interest in Carson, meanwhile, has released in Jem a savage male beast:

> Mary loved another! That idea would rise uppermost in his mind, and had to be combated in all its forms of pain. It was, perhaps, no great wonder that she should prefer one so much above Jem in the external things of life. But the gentleman, why did he, with his range of choices among the ladies of the land, why did he stoop down to carry off the poor man's darling? With all the glories of the garden at his hand, why did he prefer to cull the wild-rose, – Jem's own fragrant wild rose?
> ...Then uprose the guilty longing for blood! – The frenzy of jealousy! – Some one should die! He would rather Mary were dead, cold in her grave, than that she were another's. A vision of her pale, sweet face, with her bright hair all bedabbed with gore, seemed to float constantly before his aching eyes. (147)

Jem's vicious jealousy is conspicuously cast in the terms of a class struggle, between the working man and the erotically acquisitive upper-class "gentle-man." As his dejection deepens he dreams that he will "slay himself, and the lovers should love on" (147). His imagination cannot dispense with violence, apparently an inevitable reflex of erotic conflict and class conflict, and the only means to cope with both.

Stressing the novel's norm-substantiating ideological premises, Mary Poovey argues that *Mary Barton* "domesticates politics" as it aims to "human-ize political economy... Gaskell treats class prejudice as the problem to be overcome and the 'natural' attraction of one sex to the other, as part of the solution to social strife."[21] In fact, the novel is far more forward looking about the sexual dynamics of the Mary–Carson–Wilson imbroglio. As Deborah Epstein Nord argues in *Walking the Victorian Streets: Women, Representation, and the City* (1995), in having Mary ultimately reject Harry Carson, despite the temptations he offers, Gaskell defuses the cultural power of texts such as Richardson's *Pamela* (1740) and Brontë's *Jane Eyre* that consecrate marriage as the route of upward mobility for women and that treat marriage as more "natural" than class, or as apart from class conflict.

In *Mary Barton* there is no concealment of class motive. Mary spends a considerable portion of the narrative deflecting, denying, and vanquishing charges that she has wanted to propel herself, via a fantasized marriage to Carson, into a venal factory-owning class. Gaskell ultimately does not so much reaffirm the sexual purity of her mill-worker heroine as redirect Mary's erotic allure so that it serves an ardent working-class cause.

Gaskell's sense that the laboring classes must separately cultivate their most intimate attachments accords with the era's most revolutionary attitudes about sexuality. In Part II, chapter 4, of Friedrich Engels's *The Origin of the Family, Private Property and the State* (1884), Engels appraises monogamy in marriage as a result of the bourgeois male's need to control his patrimony. Perceiving the working-class family as relatively unpolluted by market values, Engels argues that the working poor hold the potential for what he calls "individual sex love," a non-monogamous relation unencumbered by the bourgeois cash nexus. Individual sex love will come to replace the middle-class family. Although *Mary Barton* hardly endorses non-monogamy, it dramatizes the perils of cross-class sexual interactions by depicting its proletarian heroine as recognizing that, while her erotic charms can be deployed across class lines, her ultimate loyalties are to a working-class man. In their narratives of working-class relations between the sexes, Gaskell and Engels struggle to protect the working-class woman from the adulterous, property-bound precincts of upper-middle-class domestic life. Mary's "crime" – what an increasingly aggressive Carson sneeringly refers to as her coquetry – places her at the mercy of town gossip well before the novel's final courtroom scene. Significantly, Mary's imagined transgression, for long stretches of the novel, overshadows the "crime" of lower-class violence against mill-owning burghers.

Mary clears her history of eros at Jem's trial for murder when she is questioned about which lover she prefers:

> "He asks me which of them two I liked best. Perhaps I liked Mr. Harry Carson once – I don't know – I've forgotten; but I loved James Wilson, that's now on

trial, above what tongues can tell – above all else on earth put together; and I love him now better than ever, though he has never known a word of it till this minute." (282)

The vindication articulates its concerns in class terms, but it also insists on the value of a wordless realm in which eros dwells. In light of Gaskell's realism, that realm, however wordless and asocial, belongs to true history. But Gaskell and her heroine are also true to the realm of fiction. The trial scene represents a defense of the genre of the novel against a competing legal authority, and against competing social and moral authorities in general. In the realm of the novel, workers and lovers alike are not compromised by what tongues outside of fiction misleadingly tell about them.

Wilde's counter-*Bildungsroman*

Victorian novelists often depict relations between men in sentimental and physical terms. In Trollope's *Castle Richmond* (1860) a fifteen-year-old enjoys a physical rapport with a twenty-three-year old man who is courting a woman ("Owen would be as tender with him as a woman, allowing the young lad's arm round his body, listening to words which the outer world would have called bosh – and have derided it as girlish").[22] Dickens's depictions of boyhood friendships – of Pip and Magwitch, David Copperfield and Steerforth, Nicholas Nickleby and Smike – have an emotional force, more potent than enduring marriage, by being elegiacally consigned to an unresolved past. Wilde, contrastingly, in *The Picture of Dorian Gray* imagines homoerotically marked male friendship first in terms of a novel of manners, then as a power game for possession of a beautiful male youth, and finally as a gothic tragic fable. Notwithstanding *Dorian's* reputation as the most celebrated homosexual novel of the Victorian era, no man in Wilde's narrative touches another.

That is characteristic of Wilde's perverse play, which also leads Wilde to use *Dorian Gray* to experiment upon the narrative structure of the *Bildungsroman*, wherein the individual's development and its society exist in satisfying complementary relation.[23] The complementarity is achieved, however, only through a process of rigorous personal education, through slow and taxing development. But Wilde once quipped that "Only mediocrities develop." Wilde's boredom with the protocols of bourgeois self-improvement harbored attendant formal ambitions. For Wilde the *Bildungsroman* was at once an aesthetic problem and the perfect representational foil or contrast for an eros that refuses to "produce" or to pliantly respond to familial expectations and social forms; in short, for an eros that refuses to "develop."

The "novel of education" finds a complement in realism's way of tracing personal and historical progress. Wilde undermines *Bildung* and realism together, forging a counter-*Bildungsroman* as he invents a new sub-genre, the homosexual novel of manners. His protagonist is split into antagonistic selves, his soul "mirrored" not in society but in a painting that grotesquely ages as Dorian remains beautifully unaltered. The unfolding supernatural dimension in *Dorian Gray* further reverses the *Bildungsroman* tradition by deviating from realism, subsuming into fantasy questions of societal conflict that are crucial to personal maturation – in Dorian's case, his relation to marriage, and to the homosexual secret masked by his bachelor status. What might be deemed an "unnatural" dilemma in terms of realist or naturalist modes of representation is transformed by a self-conscious literary resolution. The literary resolution, which trumps realism and naturalism with an assertion of artifice, is an aesthetic form of face-saving: Dorian destroys *his* picture, which is tethered to history and morality; Wilde advances his *own* untethered history in its place.

The failure of development on Dorian's part is linked to the novel's sub-textual homoerotics, which aligns the protagonist with an abject, destructive morbidity entailing a retreat from society and a penchant for excessive artifice. The inability of Wilde to write a socially affirmative "queer" text might represent a loss to conceptions of the homosexual subject; but it stands as a victory for a new tradition: modernism. Joyce surely draws on Wilde's society-rejecting aesthete hero for *A Portrait of the Artist as a Young Man* (1916). With Wilde's daring opening pages devoted to males who are courting each other, its hero's refusal of a settled sexual identity, and that hero's apotheosis as a seductive work of art, *The Picture of Dorian Gray* assimilates the history of eros in the British novel into a glittering, self-enclosed orbit.

Notes

1. Thomas Hardy, *Jude the Obscure* (New York: Norton, 2001), p. 48.
2. Steven Marcus, *The Other Victorians* (New York: Bantam Books, 1967), p. 247.
3. Henry James, *The Bostonians* (New York: Barnes and Noble, 2005), pp. 307, 414.
4. See Sean Latham, *The Art of Scandal: Modernism, Libel Law, and the Roman à Clef* (New York: Oxford University Press, 2010).
5. Henry James, *The Golden Bowl* (New York: Everyman, 1992), p. 37.
6. Peter Brooks, *Reading for the Plot* (New York: Alfred Knopf, 1984), p. 47.
7. Leo Bersani, *A Future for Astyanax: Character and Desire in Literature* (Boston: Little Brown, 1976), p. 221.

8. Jeff Nunokawa, "Sexuality in the Victorian Novel," in *The Cambridge Companion to the Victorian Novel*, ed. Deirdre David (New York: Cambridge University Press, 2001), p. 131.

9. Holly Furneaux, *Queer Dickens: Erotics, Families, Masculinities* (New York: Oxford University Press, 2010), p. 15.

10. Samuel Lucas, *London Times*, October 14, 1859, in *George Meredith: The Critical Heritage*, ed. Ioan Williams (New York: Barnes and Noble, 1971), p. 78.

11. William Makepeace Thackeray, *Vanity Fair* (New York: Norton, 1989), p. 307.

12. Anthony Trollope, *The Belton Estate* (Oxford University Press, 1986), p. 113.

13. George Gissing, *The Odd Women* (Toronto, ON: Broadview Press, 1998), p. 82.

14. Rhoda Broughton, *A Beginner* (London: Richard Bentley and Son, 1894), pp. 365–366.

15. Walter Pater, *Marius the Epicurean* (London: Penguin Books, 1985), p. 72.

16. Thomas Hardy, *The Mayor of Casterbridge* (New York: Norton, 2001), p. 71.

17. Denoting homosexual lovers, "the inseparables" appear in what Vladimir Nabokov claims is the first instance in European fiction of homosexual characters, the two fellow officers who disgust Vronski in *Anna Karenina* (the novel was translated into English in 1886, the year in which *The Mayor of Casterbridge* was published). See Vladimir Nabokov, *Lectures on Russian Literature* (New York: Harcourt Brace Jovanovich, 1981), p. 235.

18. Virginia Woolf, "The Novels of Thomas Hardy," in *The Second Common Reader* (New York: Harcourt Brace, 1932), p. 251.

19. Elizabeth Gaskell, *Mary Barton* (New York: Norton, 2008), p. 202.

20. Karl Marx, "The English Middle Class," in *Marx and Engels on Literature and Art* (Moscow: Progress Publishers, 1976), p. 105.

21. Mary Poovey, "Disraeli, Gaskell, and the Condition of England," in *The Columbia History of the British Novel*, ed. John Richetti (New York: Columbia University Press, 1994), p. 530.

22. Anthony Trollope, *Castle Richmond* (New York: Harper, 1860), p. 360.

23. See Franco Moretti, *The Way of the World: The Bildungsroman in European Culture* (London: Verso, 1987).

28

The novel as immoral, anti-social force

CHRISTOPHER LANE

The English novel boasts such a long association with moral uplift that it seems counter-intuitive to argue that it pulls readers in immoral and amoral directions too. Yet although the didactic strains of the *Bildungsroman* and epistolary novel are so prominent as to be undeniable, any suggestion that eighteenth- and nineteenth-century novels aim to cultivate only virtue in their readers is simplistic and needs correcting.

From the earliest decades of the eighteenth century, novels were written as much to entertain as to inform and instruct. Many works aimed at some combination of the three, even playing up their didactic potential to counter allegations that the genre overall was "inferior" to poetry. But for many commentators the kind of entertainment novels provide is as much a source of concern as of delight. By 1750, after Daniel Defoe had famously depicted in *Moll Flanders* a heroine who relishes not being a moral paragon, Dr. Samuel Johnson warns about "the power of example" in fiction, which, he claims, can "take possession of the memory by a kind of violence, and produce effects almost without the intervention of the will." Because such so-called violence can sway "the young, the ignorant, and the idle," he writes, "care ought to be taken that, when the choice is unrestrained, the best examples only should be exhibited; and that which is likely to operate so strongly, should not be mischievous or uncertain in its effects."[1]

Johnson was by no means alone in calling novels frivolous, even dangerous, and in charging that they filled the minds of the impressionable with all kinds of nonsense. For many other critics and for Calvinist preachers, novels that aim chiefly to entertain – especially gothic novels that are designed to shock and thrill – were corruptive, almost immoral, influences, because they were seen almost as lies. Many such novels dwell on exotic, sometimes outlandish, themes with no purpose other than to interest and excite; or they absorb readers for hours of time not devoted to study or prayer. Novels also encourage identification with a broad swath of characters, few of them straightforward moral

454

avatars, and spark fantasies that are apt to detract from religious and secular instruction.

Johnson's concern that novels may "take possession of the memory . . . and produce effects almost without the intervention of the will" clearly points to extreme concern about gullible and naïve readers, including literalists denouncing fiction as a brand of deceit. Still, it is worth taking seriously his argument that novels do influence the mind, in part by agitating fantasies that can involve as much terror or fear as pleasure.

Aware of the novel's dark psychological power, some later commentators believe that its impact can be harnessed to more edifying effect. In 1823, for instance, William Hazlitt published a fascinating contrarian essay, "On the Pleasure of Hating," that explicitly ties the pleasure of hating to reading. According to Hazlitt, not only is hatred endemic in everyone, it can also excite fantasies of revenge that the novel – with its careful pacing of schemes, deceits, and varying retributions – is especially well designed to amplify. To Hazlitt the outcome is closer to poetic than to formal justice, and more enlightening in that respect than Johnson is willing to concede. "The spirit of malevolence survives the practical exertion of it," Hazlitt argues, differentiating acts of violence from the fantasies that can accompany and outlast them. "We learn to curb our will and keep our overt actions within the bounds of humanity, long before we can subdue our sentiments and imaginations to the same mild tone. We give up the external demonstration, the *brute* violence, but cannot part with the essence or principle of hostility."[2]

The reason we cannot do so, he argues, goes beyond the hatred deeply embedded in our psychology; the problem is also that hatred is thoroughly supportive of its operations. "Without something to hate," he says, "we should lose the very spring of thought and action" (127). There is, in short, a productive, almost generative, tie among hatred, imagination, and reading that puts Johnson's concerns about the novel in a more provocative light: fiction elaborates, rather than curbs, asocial and anti-social tensions; it educates us about their intensities and in effect teaches us whom to hate, and why they may be deserving of that hatred. Above all, fiction does so by suspending rational judgment, appealing to primal instincts, and allowing a different set of values to surface with regard to malice and retribution.

Hazlitt notes that, as we read

we throw aside the trammels of civilization, the flimsy veil of humanity. "Off, you lendings!" The wild beast resumes its sway within us, we feel like hunting animals, and as the hound starts in his sleep and rushes on the chase in fancy the heart rouses itself in its native lair, and utters a wild cry of joy, at being restored once more to freedom and lawless unrestrained impulses.   (128)

What narrative unleashes in readers, Hazlitt concludes, is a force opposed to rational control, including self-control. Rather than fearing that force, however, we can learn to understand and possibly even welcome it; for its goal is leveling, or exploding, cant; decrying injustice; and, above all, striving for psychological authenticity. As fiction taps grudges, grievances, and antipathies, it also gives rein to them in a virtual realm that can be enjoyed precisely because it is realistic but vicarious. The result might be more edifying than writers initially intend, Hazlitt suggests, in giving form to animosities that are endemic in all of us, and, however regrettably, in the communities that try to bind us.

"Here are no Jeremy Bentham Panopticons, none of Mr. [Robert] Owen's impassable Parallelograms," Hazlitt almost brags, noting two contemporaneous models of rational behavior that, to him, strike a weak chord in our imaginations. (Dickens clearly thinks so too, as we see in *Hard Times* [1854], his own satire of Benthamite rigidity.) For us readers, Hazlitt explains, there are also *"no long calculations of self-interest"* if we really can lose ourselves in the fictional scenes that absorb us (128).

"There is a secret affinity, a *hankering* after, evil in the human mind," Hazlitt argues, "and . . . it takes a perverse, but a fortunate delight in mischief, since it is a never-failing source of satisfaction" (128; emphasis in original). Similar arguments about *Schadenfreude* recur throughout nineteenth-century philosophy and psychology, particularly in Schopenhauer's *The World as Will and Idea* (1818) and Stirner's iconoclastic study *The Ego and Its Own* (1845), a forerunner to the unapologetic anti-communitarianism of Nietzsche, Dostoyevsky, and Freud. To those writers and thinkers, "community" is synonymous with neither "well-being" nor "contentment." Quite the opposite. The insight renders misanthropy if not appealing, then at least understandable.

Despite its unattractiveness to some, Hazlitt's observation on anti-social thoughts and fantasies helps explain why novels have profoundly visceral effects on us. He makes clear as well why it is important – if not always comfortable – to let fiction guide us somewhat in revealing how other minds work, even if that means representing the grubbier fantasies and ambitions that can stoke heartfelt longings of a nastier kind.

The progressive writer and political journalist William Godwin, father to Mary Shelley, takes a similar line in seeking to enlarge, rather than curb, what he calls "the arduous, the enthusiastic, and the sublime license of imagination."[3] Only "the operation of human passions," he argues, including observation of "the empire of motives whether groveling or elevated," can stir our imaginations sufficiently to bring social concerns alive to us.[4] That may in the end introduce moral concerns through a back door, but it only does so after Godwin has given the imagination free rein to experience the whole "empire of motives" in play.

The same "sublime license" could therefore, Godwin believes, startle readers into awareness of social dilemmas and abuses of power. "What is now presented to the public," he explains in his 1794 *Things as They Are; or, The Adventures of Caleb Williams*, "is a study and delineation of things passing in the moral world," including the troubling consequences of "the spirit and character of the government intrud[ing] itself into every rank of society" (3).

To give readers an almost palpable experience of revenge, injustice, and even terrorism, Godwin's fascinating misanthropic thriller describes in almost fanatical detail the cruelty and vulnerability that ensue from tyranny. Appeals to society and the law for justice are more likely than not to harm Caleb Williams. By using Caleb as a first-person narrator, Godwin also wants to intensify "analysis of the private and internal operations of the mind" (351). His narrative and philosophy therefore have to proceed hand in glove. "I said to myself a thousand times," he later recalls, "'I will write a tale that shall constitute an epoch in the mind of the reader, that no one, after he has read it, shall ever be exactly the same man that he was before'" (350). How he could achieve that effect is a question he has at his fingertips: "What I say shall be incorporated into the very fibres of the soul of him who listens to me" (xxvii). The phrase "very fibres" is critical: Godwin, though disagreeing with Edmund Burke on other matters, adopts his physiological argument of the sublime to give the reader an almost physical sensation of fear, tension, and anxiety.

Certain kinds of novels are, Godwin understands, adept at creating those effects by provoking nervous reactions in transfixed readers. In an excellent introduction to his edition of *Caleb Williams* Maurice Hindle explains that Godwin draws on "one of the earliest, if not the first, of the *Schauer-Romantiks* or 'shudder novels': Naubert's *Herman d'Unna* (1788), using "both volumes of this 'shocker' in the original German while he was working on Volume One" of his own novel (xxvii). Godwin also read accounts of the terror that ensued after the French Revolution, and transposed to largely secular ends the Renaissance treatise *God's Revenge against the Crying and Execrable Sins of Murder, in Thirty Tragical Histories* (1621–1622). This exposition imagines "the beam of the eye of Omniscience . . . as perpetually pursuing the guilty, and laying open his most hidden retreats to the light of day" (Hindle, introduction to *Caleb Williams* xxxiii). For Godwin, the suggestion of relentless, visible guilt is meant less to arouse pious contrition than to generate a sense of dismay about miscarriages of justice – as when the innocent are wrongly imprisoned, even hanged, for crimes they have not committed.

The particular crimes that pepper Godwin's novel, including premeditated murder, stem from a bitter feud between two neighboring squires, Barnabas Tyrrel and Ferdinando Falkland. The latter, newly arrived, takes pride in being thought fair, judicious, and dignified. Tyrrel, galled that Falkland highlights his own autocratic ways, quickly nurses grievances about his neighbor's almost smug demeanor. "To Mr Tyrrel's diseased imagination, every distinction bestowed on his neighbour seemed to be expressly intended as an insult to him" (27).

Because of his "malignant distemper" and "ungovernable" rage, and his mortification in being shown up so dramatically (34, 83), Tyrrel's grudge quickly metastasizes into a lasting, malicious feud. The consequences are disastrous for the two squires and several of their victims – among them Caleb Williams, Falkland's secretary, and Emily Melville, Tyrrel's niece. All are swept up in Tyrrel's desperate bid to destroy Falkland who, he concedes to himself, "poisons all my pleasures. I should be glad to see him torn with tenter-hooks, and to grind his heart-strings with my teeth. I shall know no joy till I see him ruined" (33).

Godwin's careful tracking of Tyrrel's obsession has four consequences worth noting. First, interpersonal relations between the squires become a zero-sum game. Without even trying, Falkland weakens Tyrrel's standing in a society where power relies heavily on the awe and authority that rank can induce. Any shift in public favor may be impalpable, but since to both squires reputation is everything, they monitor it zealously and view its loss with fury.

Second, Godwin's focus brings attention to all the psychological contours of revenge. The latter is broken down into component parts: a "diseased imagination" that perceives malice where none is intended; the "vulgar spite" that quietly stokes a "corrosive bitterness" until it ignites; and the perverse pleasure that turns retribution into a kind of "sport," even (or precisely) when it results in harm to others (27, 78, 69, 317). As Godwin makes apparent, the only way to convey the scale and intensity of Tyrrel's "unexampled malignity" is to force the reader to encounter the "internal operations of [a] mind" that confuses demented rage with truth (90, 351).

Pleasure in the novel is not, however, limited to those who scheme to persecute. Because even appalled witnesses, such as Caleb and the reader, are embroiled in the drama, they become parties to the terrifying thrill that accrues from watching obsessive, malevolent passions unfold, without any capacity to intervene. Caleb's self-appointed role as spy on his patron, emanating from his belief that Falkland has gotten away with murder, thickens the plot further. "When one idea has got possession of the soul," he concedes, speaking his own obsessions here rather than Tyrrel's, "it is scarcely possible to keep it from finding its way to the lips" (118).

The result in him is untold euphoria: "I was conscious to a kind of rapture for which I could not account . . . In the very tempest and hurricane of the passions, I seemed to enjoy the most soul-ravishing calm" (135). At other times in the novel, this pleasure is so intense that it literally makes the characters shake with joy (118).

Because both the narrator and the reader become entangled in "soul-ravishing" primal fantasies, they are caught up in the mechanics of revenge. This is a third consequence of Godwin's tracking of obsession. In one sense the very rationale for plot is the vengeance it tries to record as fully as possible. The unfolding of events also iterates the glee of a persecutor who has rehearsed them beforehand. The pace and intensity of a revenge novel is thus inseparable from the fevered mind that breathlessly awaits satisfaction. That intimate confrontation with a relentless, almost demonic, logic makes reading *Caleb Williams* and other "anti-social" novels both thrilling and disturbing. One cannot determine who gets even, and how, without briefly inhabiting the fathomless cruelty of Tyrrel and Falkland, or identifying with the appalling suffering meted out to Falkland's victim, Caleb.

Fourth, and finally, Godwin's emphasis threatens to corrode the social tie, even to sever it entirely. The rage and anger that erupt in both victim and accuser tilt them toward misanthropy, transforming society from a neutral, even benign, entity into one that seems capable of almost inexhaustible cruelty. When Falkland ingeniously offers a large reward for Caleb's discovery, for example, he not only appeals to the universal mercenary instinct, but also awakens and literalizes a paranoid fantasy that everyone is out to get him. Caleb's "very touch" is made to seem "infectious" (279), as if he carries the plague rather than flees from a murderer's relentless bid to conceal his own crimes.

"I saw my whole species as ready, in one mode or another, to be made the instruments of the tyrant," Caleb notes plaintively (287). Even Caleb's pleading with former friends to rethink whether the accusations against him are just, even plausible, makes them recoil because of their confidence in his apparent villainy. Heartsick thereafter at being made the brunt of "all the ill-will of mankind," he "contract[s] a disgust for life and all its appendages" that turns him against the world, an exemplar of the same type of reclusive misanthropy that beset his enemy, Falkland (297, 314).

Because *Caleb Williams* is to a degree representative of the novel as immoral, anti-social force, it becomes a model for later writers wanting to create similar fantasies and scenarios. Godwin's thematic of revenge enjoys an afterlife in Victorian culture thanks especially to Edward Bulwer Lytton – after Dickens, the second most-widely read novelist of the century. Godwin and Bulwer were friends and for the most part mutual admirers, and the former's celebrated treatise *Political Justice* (1793) is often regarded as one of the latter's greatest intellectual debts.

The influence does not end there. Bulwer's first novel, published when he was twenty-four but drafted three years earlier, is titled *Falkland* (1827). Besides alluding directly to Godwin's villain, it transposes other details from his novel. Its protagonist adores an unhappily married woman called Lady Emily Mandeville, a name that conflates Emily *Melville* in *Caleb Williams* with Godwin's later novel *Mandeville* (1817).[5] Bulwer's Falkland, following Godwin's model, also raves in despair after his Emily dies prematurely. (Her husband discovers that she wants to elope with Falkland; she hemorrhages in shock at his rage.)

There is also a Tyrrell (with a second "l") in Bulwer's *Pelham* (1826), one of the nineteenth century's most popular novels. Bulwer's Tyrrell, again echoing Godwin's, is a wealthy, unscrupulous villain, stabbed by an enemy most assume to be his rival. The echo hints at more than admiration or youthful plagiarism; it signals a debt to Godwin's understanding of revenge.

A similar – though less obvious – debt to Godwin's novel runs through Emily Brontë's *Wuthering Heights* (1847), especially when Heathcliff tyrannizes over his wife, Isabella, in a bid to retaliate against her brother, Edgar Linton. In Anne Brontë's *Tenant of Wildfell Hall* (1848), moreover, itself a partial reworking of the Romantic excesses of *Wuthering Heights*, a debauched and alcoholic Arthur Huntingdon – bearing some likeness to Heathcliff as a character – is forced to experience contrition before he dies anxiously awaiting his fate. His wife, Helen, earlier flees from her husband's abuse and adultery, only to suffer more humiliation from the new community that she quietly and reluctantly joins. Maintaining her anonymity is critical for Helen if she is to avoid discovery and the likelihood that her estranged husband will show up to terrify her and leave with their son. To avoid that risk, she tries to "pass" as a widow, this time grieving for her marriage. But the pious community, troubled by her erratic church attendance, takes a fascinated interest in her. Very quickly, it also interprets her self-protective diffidence as haughty disdain and aggressively rejects her. In that respect, the community almost resumes the role of aggressor that Huntingdon had previously adopted. In *The Tenant of Wildfell Hall*, we might say, community – rather than a single character – functions strongly as a force of vengeance.

The Godwinian and Hazlittian thread also recurs, perhaps surprisingly, in works by George Eliot, a novelist whose interest in fellow-feeling has been called something akin to a "religion of humanity."[6] Even the most ardent defenders of communitarianism acknowledge, however, that there are power-ful anti-social undercurrents in her fiction that complicate and challenge it. These recur quite consistently: from *The Lifted Veil* (1859), *The Mill on the Floss* (1860), and *Romola* (1862–1863), to *Middlemarch* (1871–1872), *Daniel Deronda* (1874), and her last complete work, *Impressions of Theophrastus Such* (1879).

In *The Mill on the Floss* the problem that galvanizes the novel, and with it Tom Tulliver's relentless ambition and partial estrangement from his sister Maggie, is the disastrous feud of Tom and Maggie's father with creditor John Wakem. This neighbor represents Mr. Pivart, the landowner immediately above them, whose irrigation scheme siphons off large amounts of water before it can reach their mill. Tulliver, the miller, sparks a competitive feud with Wakem, which intensifies so dramatically that it makes Wakem go out of his way to harm Tulliver and the family, even to the point of buying Dorlcote Mill and thus appropriating an heirloom that has been in Tulliver's family for generations.

Tulliver is almost paralyzed by anger, fear, and regret. His enemy is insa-tiable. Increasingly hamstrung and desperate, in part from his own role in his family's financial ruin, Tulliver urges his son to record in the family Bible a curse against Wakem: "I wish evil may befall him. Write that."[7]

Still, even issuing a solemn curse is not enough. Like Caleb's curiosity, Tulliver's fury finally boils over. Years of "irritation and hostile triumph" erupt in a "paroxysm of rage" (373). When the two men finally meet on a road and neither is willing to give way, Tulliver takes a riding crop to the man who has worked diligently, systematically, to ruin him. The narrator is at pains to explain why common sense, including the strong likelihood of worsening his family's already dire position, does not prevail: "The sight of the long-hated predominant man down and in his power threw him into a frenzy of trium-phant vengeance" (460). Wakem recovers, even thrives; but for Tulliver the combined shame and over-exertion lead to his premature death. It is as if Eliot were intent on making intemperate rage almost self-canceling.

Not, however, before she expounds at length why such impulses are com-pelling, even fleetingly gratifying. The problem Eliot identifies – the cause of Tulliver's unraveling – is a form of "parenthetic vindictiveness" that seems like a sidebar to the main plot and the psychology it advances, but is in fact central to both. Such "vindictiveness," the narrator insists, yields "pleasure of a complex kind," since it is "not made up of crude malice, but [has] mingling with it the relish of self-approbation" (340). The narrator is adept at explaining why the latter is appealing. "To see an enemy humiliated gives a certain contentment, but this is jejune compared with the highly blent satisfaction of seeing him humiliated by your benevolent action or concession on his behalf. That is a sort of revenge which falls into the scale of virtue" (340).

It is notable that this type of pleasure orients a novel by Eliot; clearly, her ethic of fellow-feeling encounters serious roadblocks not easily remedied by "right thinking" or "right action." Darker anti-social impulses present a real challenge, even to the point of opening a gap in her fiction between the imagined goal of the fiction and the narrator's often-visible trouble in concluding on a sounder note. For one thing, when "parenthetic vindictiveness" begins to influence the secular fate of Eliot's protagonists, as it does quite explicitly in *Silas Marner* and *Romola*, invoking "Providence" thereafter is poor justification for who prevails happily and who is punished by death or unhappiness. And while the vast majority of Victorian novels conform to that logic of rewards and punishments, Eliot helpfully insists that it is an ultimately childish notion of fate. Good conduct does not, alas, guarantee anything: bad things happen to good people.

Wakem enjoys a form of satisfaction that Latimer, the long-suffering protagonist of Eliot's bleak novella *The Lifted Veil*, exposes but in the end cannot eradicate. Cursed, rather than blessed, with a "superadded consciousness" that lets him know exactly what other people are thinking, Latimer discovers that his clairvoyance exposes his friends' duplicity, not their generosity.[8] His "microscopic vision" makes him an unwilling witness to "all the intermediate frivolities, all the suppressed egoism, all the struggling chaos of puerilities, meanness, vague capricious memories, and indolent make-shift thoughts" that others hatch, frequently at his expense (14).[9]

Finding no limit to perfidy, *The Lifted Veil* is Eliot's least optimistic work – one she called a "*jeu de mélancolie*."[10] As Latimer sees "repulsion and antipathy harden into cruel hatred, giving pain only for the sake of wreaking itself" (32), the sensitive intellectual eventually disbelieves in affection, viewing most of his friends as covert enemies. The final blow to his joy – a poignant victory for the supernatural world, given the novella's interest in clairvoyance – falls when he learns that his wife, Bertha, is planning to poison him. Not surprisingly, this knowledge corrodes all remaining fellowship in the tale, leaving the protagonist a confirmed misanthrope: "The relation between me and my fellow-men was . . . deadened" (35–36).

In the end Latimer is poisoned by his wife Bertha, and dies. Yet she does not get off scot-free. On her deathbed, her disgruntled maid, Mrs. Archer, incriminates Bertha. Given a blood transfusion, Mrs. Archer even returns briefly to life, meeting Bertha's eyes "in full recognition – the recognition of hate" (41).

Bertha is accused in the presence of the doctor administering the transfusion, but incredibly he agrees to keep the charge a secret. It is hardly Eliot's finest moment, but (unusually for her) the novella does continue the hatred and violence right to the end.

Romola is of a different order of achievement, yet it too draws centrally on a revenge narrative to galvanize the plot. Set in Renaissance Florence, the novel derives assiduously from Victorian histories of the city and era that it took months to research. It also advances a more complex model of sociability than Eliot's earlier work. Between, on the one hand, the devotional piety of Romola and, on the other, the treachery of her seductive husband, Tito Melema, the novel offers complex shades of gray, representing those of the psychology of crowds, and including Savonarola's cunning adoption of political allegory. Savonarola, "the kill-joy of Florence," manages to whip the public into a frenzy of anti-Medician sentiment with his "fervid piety" and "false certitude about . . . divine intentions" (234).

Through all this complexity drives the revenge motif of the novel: namely, the desire of Baldassare, Tito's adopted father, to kill Tito because of Tito's treachery and ingratitude. Indeed, at one point the narrator hints that the two plots – the revenge plot and the historically based one – are intertwined over this issue, with Baldassare's "ecstasy of self-martyring revenge" bearing an uncanny resemblance to that of the canting, hypocritical redeemer Savonarola (234). Baldassare's ruling passion is to make sure he finally can face his ungrateful "son" and say to him: "I saved you – I nurtured you – I loved you. You forsook me – you robbed me – you denied me. . . . [B]ut there is one draught of sweetness left – *that you shall know agony.*"[11]

Especially at its climactic moments, Eliot's revenge narrative resembles Godwin's by matching her plot with her characters' mania. It is as if she too were intent on harnessing our malicious pleasure in watching characters destroy themselves. The narrator's faithful tracking of Baldassarre's bid for revenge highlights this goal; Eliot not only fleshes out all his retributive fantasies but also repeats over and over his fixated desire to murder his adopted son. Eliot cannot unmask Tito, and thus end the novel, without giving us at least some satisfaction at odds with socially minded fellow-feeling.

Baldassarre's yearning for catharsis must therefore be an attribute we partially share if we are to reach the final chapter. We might recoil from his frenzied monomania and hankering "to see a slow revenge" (270); and the narrator thwarts much of the emotion accompanying the murder to come. Still, as Baldassarre seeks the "one draught of sweetness left" him, it is imperative that his adopted son *not* die during any preliminary confrontation – in short, that the novel place obstacles between Baldassarre and this "sweetness" to prolong its intensity (308). This heightened complicity between the narrative's plotting and Baldassarre's, especially when the narrator decides to reproduce Baldassarre's interior monologue, in effect ventriloquizes what he is thinking:

> Curses on him! I wish I may see him lie with those red lips white and dry as ashes, and when he looks for pity *I wish he may see my face rejoicing in his pain.* It is all a lie – this world is a lie – there is no goodness but in hate.
>
> (270; emphasis added)

Then, as if concerned that we will find this too compelling, the narrator interjects, taking steps to dilute his frothing rage:

> Baldassarre's mind rejected the thought of that brief punishment. His whole soul had been thrilled into immediate unreasoning belief in that eternity of vengeance where he, an undying hate [*sic*], might clutch for ever an undying traitor, and hear that fair smiling hardness cry and moan with anguish. But the primary need and hope was to see a slow revenge under the same sky and on the same earth where he himself had been forsaken and had fainted with despair. And as soon as he tried to concentrate his mind on the means of attaining his end, the sense of his weakness pressed upon him like a frosty ache. (270)

Eliot's compromise thereafter is significant. She lets the murder occur – granting the protagonist, the reader, and the novel their long-deferred satisfaction – but dampens any untoward excitement the act might spawn. We never hear, by the free indirect speech for which she is famous, how Baldassarre *feels* after achieving his aim – surprisingly, given how much else in Baldassarre's head is vividly conveyed. Thus does Eliot try to have it both ways in the 1860s, drawing heavily on the narrative excitement of revenge, while trying to quash and discredit any psychic rationale for it by rendering Baldassarre delirious with rage.

Dickens presents a similar perspective in *Our Mutual Friend* (1865), with Bradley Headstone's near-psychotic stalking of Eugene Wrayburn – again due to a perceived slight. Yet unlike in *Romola*, *Our Mutual Friend* does not try to sequester the rage by limiting it to the avenger. Instead, Dickens peoples his last complete novel with so many rogues, scoundrels, cheats, charlatans, and misanthropes that he renders society part of the problem, rather than suggesting that society might somehow be their lasting solution. He reforms his "harmless misanthrope," Mr. Venus, by allowing Pleasant Riderhood to return his affection.[12] But he also makes Wrayburn's marriage to Lizzie Hexam incompatible with their continued participation in society – a conclusion that Wrayburn reaches solemnly after weighing, then rejecting, what membership in society entails. "But it cannot have been Society that disturbed you," Lizzie cautions. Wrayburn gently corrects her: "I rather think it *was* Society though!" (792).

A comprehensive examination of the many shades of anti-social thought in Dickens's vast corpus would leave few of his works untouched, not *Martin Chuzzlewit* (1843–44), or *Bleak House* (1853), or *Little Dorrit* (1857). Each of these includes protagonists who struggle desperately with the battle of life, one of the Victorians' most intense metaphors, which Dickens helped to popularize.[13] Additionally, his protagonists must carry out this "battle" in societies riddled with crime, indifference, and injustice. Lacking space for analysis of those novels,[14] I will end with two later works that help track the path of anti-social impulses in late-Victorian and Edwardian culture: Anthony Trollope's *An Eye for an Eye* (1879) and Joseph Conrad's *The Secret Agent* (1907).

In Trollope's novella the revenge motif that works out the Old Testament logic of his title stems from the reckless behavior of an immature officer in the hussars, who seduces a young Irish woman when his regiment is stationed briefly on Ireland's west coast. The country is under British rule, and Trollope renders the tensions over Fred Neville and Kate O'Hara's putative marriage as a snapshot of broader colonial struggles between Ireland and its paternalistic neighbor. The British soldiers treat their time in rural Ireland as an adventure, toying with the locals with scant regard for the consequences. Meanwhile, the Irish understandably – though doubtless naïvely – view the soldiers as gallant outsiders who will lift them out of poverty.

Neville is heir to an earldom, which he inherits toward the end of the novella, and his snobbish relatives – concerned about his feckless behavior and the family honor – want him to make a good match. They view with disdain the prospect of his marrying a penniless Roman Catholic and try to release him from an engagement they view as "*a most ruinous alliance*" – indeed, as a "stain" on their reputation.[15] Mrs. O'Hara, meanwhile, is worried about honor of a slightly different kind: the word of a gentleman who has seduced her daughter, thereby destroying her daughter's prospects for marrying anyone else. Alert to Neville's philandering, careless promises, and reluctance to alienate his family, the mother appeals to a more primal form of law and retribution: "An eye for an eye," she says, "and a tooth for a tooth. Is not that justice?" (199).

In exposing all manner of prejudices, including those of Protestants towards Irish Catholics and of English aristocrats toward rural villagers, Trollope falls prey to several prejudices of his own. Kate's father is a captain, a former convict, and a "cadaverous, ill-clothed . . . drunkard" (133). The captain, easily assured that Fred will marry his daughter, winks at his conduct because the match will give his daughter (and thus the captain himself) wealth and rank.

Meanwhile, shrewd Mrs. O'Hara, the prototype for every joke and horror story about meddling mothers-in-law, is said to guard her daughter with "the ferocity of a tigress." She believes that "[m]en are wolves to women" (thereby extending several animalistic metaphors that appear elsewhere) "and utterly merciless when feeding high their lust" (47). "By the living God," she swears before Fred, "if you injure my child I will have the very blood from your heart" (65). She even brings a dagger to their would-be engagement scene and later threatens, "Were you to think of breaking [your word], I would follow you through the world" (154).

A cautionary tale, *An Eye for an Eye* can only end unhappily and, given its title, with melodramatic violence. During a final confrontation on the cliffs, Mrs. O'Hara pushes Fred over a precipice. For a moment it seems as if she too will fall headlong into the abyss, but after she finally kicks him away, "the poor wretch tumble[s] forth alone into eternity" (194). The gratification of revenge is such that Mrs. O'Hara prefers admitting to having killed Fred than claiming, as she could, that he strayed too close to the cliffs and fell accidentally. Since she can only repeat, ad nauseam, "An eye for an eye, and a tooth for a tooth!" she is finally declared insane. The elemental revenge that she enacts is recoded by the authorities (and for Trollope's readers) in largely psychiatric terms.

That shift in perspective and assessment is very much in tune with broader cultural shifts, which by the 1870s invariably view misanthropy as a sickness and pathology.[16] Still, several writers mix that portrayal with earlier depictions of the phenomenon. Among them is Joseph Conrad who, in his 1907 version of an 1894 attempt by anarchists to blow up London's Greenwich Observatory, paints the would-be terrorists in more interesting terms – as deluded rationalists, inept hypocrites, and (in the case of the unnamed Professor) as protofascists.

The Professor, clutching at all times a detonator that can kill him and many others, exhibits a readiness for terrorism that serves more than political ends. Conrad conveys the extraordinary intensity of this character, always mindful of death and prepared for self-extinction. Before making what might be his last foray into the crowd, the Professor toasts "the destruction of what is" and echoes Kurtz's directive, in Conrad's earlier *Heart of Darkness* (1899): "Exterminate all the brutes!"

The Professor is contemptuous of "the weak," whom he considers "the source of all evil on this earth!" yet his desire to eliminate them devolves into monomaniacal self-justification.[17] His hatred is obviously pathological, but Conrad imbues him with a psychology and a belief system that, in less extreme form, afflicts many other characters in the novel – not only Michaelis ("the Apostle") and Karl Yundt, fellow anarchists, but also Mr. Vladimir, the Russian diplomat who orchestrates the bombing, and even the cynical Sir Ethelred, the Home Secretary to whom Verloc reports as a double agent.

What distinguishes the Professor, however, is the degree to which his fanatical beliefs ultimately depersonalize him. The narrator declares:

> He was a force. His thoughts caressed the images of ruin and destruction. He walked frail, insignificant, shabby, miserable – and terrible in the simplicity of his idea calling madness and despair to the regeneration of the world. Nobody looked at him. He passed on unsuspected and deadly, like a pest in the street full of men. (269)

Those are the novel's final words. The Professor is not just parasitic; he is also an entity so devoid of doubt – and so hostile to society – that the narrator can label him a force. Releasing misanthropy from both realist understandings of character and Victorian psychiatric categories, Conrad's novel points to a form of affect beyond socialization and political remedy, a significant way into thinking about fanaticism more generally.[18]

The Secret Agent returns us to arguments Hazlitt raised almost a century earlier, in "On the Pleasure of Hating." In aiming to represent all aspects of psychology, including those that are misanthropic and anti-social, fiction instills in us greater understanding of the range of human emotions. Indeed, in this regard novels might perform quite an important cultural service. They animate such hostilities through the relative control of fiction, thereby helping to ensure that aggressions are not enacted in life. And while that sounds like a variation on the old theme that novels improve us by teaching us to treat others better, the more sanguine effect of Hazlitt's argument and its later incarnations is that we accept the attractiveness of such impulses without sanctioning them in life. The importance of novels, we might say, is that they invite us to enjoy – yet maintain – that crucial difference.

Notes

1. Samuel Johnson, "News," *The Rambler* 4 (London: March 31, 1750), pp. 3–4.
2. William Hazlitt, "On the Pleasure of Hating" (1823), in *The Complete Works of William Hazlitt*, ed. P. P. Howe, 21 vols. (London: Dent, 1931–1934), vol. XII, p. 127.
3. William Godwin, *Things as They Are or The Adventures of Caleb Williams*, ed. Maurice Hindle (London: Penguin, 1988), p. 372.
4. Godwin, "Of History and Romance" (1797), rept. as an appendix to *Caleb Williams*, p. 363.
5. Bulwer may also have had in mind the eighteenth-century philosopher Bernard Mandeville, author of the anti-social treatise *The Fable of the Bees* (1714; rev. 1724), a satire of Shaftesbury's *Sensus Communis: An Essay on the Freedom of Wit and*

Humour, in *Characteristics of Men, Manners, Opinions, Times* (1711). In *Caleb Williams* Emily's infatuation with Falkland is more strongly developed than is Falkland's for her.

6. The phrase is Auguste Comte's, from his *System of Positive Polity, or Treatise on Sociology, Instituting the Religion of Humanity* (1851), and is quoted in Bernard J. Paris, "George Eliot's Religion of Humanity," *George Eliot: A Collection of Critical Essays*, ed. George R. Creeger (Englewood Cliffs, NJ: Prentice-Hall, 1970), p. 13.

7. George Eliot, *The Mill on the Floss* (London: Penguin, 1985), p. 356.

8. George Eliot, *The Lifted Veil* and *Brother Jacob*, ed. Sally Shuttleworth (London: Penguin, 2001), p. 14.

9. These paragraphs are adapted from my earlier study *Hatred and Civility: The Antisocial Life in Victorian England* (New York: Columbia University Press, 2004), pp. 128–129.

10. Eliot to John Blackwood (March 31, 1859), quoted in Sally Shuttleworth's introduction to *The Lifted Veil* and *Brother Jacob*, p. xii.

11. Eliot, *Romola* (London: Penguin, 1996), p. 308; emphasis in the original.

12. Charles Dickens, *Our Mutual Friend* (London: Penguin, 1997), p. 297.

13. Dickens, *The Battle of Life: A Love Story* (London: Bradbury and Evans, 1846).

14. See "Dickensian Malefactors," ch. 2 of *Hatred and Civility*.

15. Anthony Trollope, *An Eye for an Eye* (Oxford University Press, 1992), pp. 69, 159; emphasis in original.

16. See for instance James Cowles Prichard's 1835 *Treatise on Insanity and Other Disorders Affecting the Mind* (New York: Arno, 1973) and C. P. Bronson, *Stammering: Its Effects, Causes and Remedies; Involving Other Nervous Diseases; Such as Hysterics, St. Vitus' Dance, Spasmodic Asthma, Croup, Trembling Palsy, Epileptic Fits, Hypochondria, Misanthropy, Depression of Spirits, Peculiar Weaknesses, &c. &c.* (Boston: Bronson and Beers, 1855).

17. Joseph Conrad, *The Secret Agent: A Simple Tale* (London: Penguin, 1990), p. 263.

18. Adapted from Lane, *Hatred and Civility*, pp. 168–169.

29

Sensations: gothic, horror, crime fiction, detective fiction

PETER K. GARRETT

Throughout the nineteenth century novelists rework the devices of eighteenth-century gothic into new forms of sensational extremity: monster stories from *Frankenstein* (1818) to *Dr. Jekyll and Mr. Hyde* (1886) and *Dracula* (1897), stories of crime and detection from Godwin's *Caleb Williams* (1794) to the Newgate novel and Sherlock Holmes. Even historical fiction from Scott and Hogg to Ainsworth and Reade is gothicized. Whether they appear as preternatural fantasy in the demonic bargains made by Melmoth and Dorian Gray or as scandalous disruptions of mid-Victorian domesticity in the sensation novel, sensational disturbances are always woven into the larger fabric of nineteenth-century fiction. Their extremity is in constant dialogue with the programmatic moderation of realism.

That dialogue already shapes the first "Gothic Story," Horace Walpole's *The Castle of Otranto* (1764). Walpole calls it "an attempt to blend the two kinds of romance, the ancient and the modern," offsetting the traditional romance's "imagination and improbability" with the novel's realistic fidelity to "nature," while "leaving the powers of fancy at liberty to expatiate through the boundless realms of invention."[1] This liberating opportunity works in tension, however, with paranoid plotting that enacts an uncanny return of the repressed in its imaginative revival of outmoded superstitions and its supernatural retributions, visiting the sins of the fathers on their children to the third and fourth generation. Both forms of return, intimations of the preternatural and insistent exposure of past transgressions, animate the fiction that emerges from the ruins of Walpole's haunted castle.

As gothic flourishes and proliferates, the question of the preternatural persists and becomes articulated with other cultural values: opposition between rationally intelligible and supernatural causes in Radcliffe and Lewis becomes part of a larger differentiation between "female" and "male" gothic. In Radcliffe the plight of the persecuted, often confined, heroine becomes the basis for a sensationalism that exercises the imagination of both protagonists and readers, who dread unnamed terrors and thrill in response to apparently supernatural events. After achingly protracted suspense and deferral, the threats are always dissipated and the events explained, but the long intervals produce new and subtler effects of subjectivity. In Lewis subtlety is hardly a concern. The graphic sensationalism of *The Monk* (1796) aggressively inverts Radcliffe's devices: its threatened innocent heroine Antonia is not rescued but raped and murdered, and the supernatural is not explained away in the denouement but shown to be demonically actual, the hidden cause of Ambrosio's fall. Instead of thrilling terror we get the visceral shock of horror, especially from representations of the body's vulnerable and corruptible materiality, as in Agnes's dead baby, to which its imprisoned mother still clings; or the body of the prioress, which an enraged mob continues to abuse "till it became no more than a mass of flesh, unsightly, shapeless, and disgusting."[2] The epitome of such inversions is the episode of the Bleeding Nun, a figure of superstitious legend that Raymond and Agnes believe they can use as a disguise to elope. Their enlightened skepticism is undone by the nun's real ghost, who replaces Agnes and haunts Raymond until she is at last exorcised (with the aid of none other than the Wandering Jew!).

Although such contrasts line up in gendered opposition – passive feminine sensibility against active masculine self-assertion – Radcliffe and Lewis, advancing a characteristic gothic exploration of isolated subjectivity under stress, show how passive and active roles can shift. Radcliffe's confined heroines gain a power of endurance and eventually prevail, while Ambrosio's licentious desires lead to his utter loss of control in a story of perdition whose pattern is repeated by later gothic protagonists. There is ultimately no correlation between these modal differences and the gender of either authors or protagonists. The most remarkable successor to *The Monk* is Charlotte Dacre's *Zofloya* (1806), whose protagonist, Victoria, follows and extends Ambrosio's "masculine" downward path of increasingly unrestrained lust, cruelty, and violence. On the other hand, Radcliffe puts Vivaldi, the hero of *The Italian* (1797), in the "feminine" position of a confined prisoner of the Inquisition and likewise makes him the subject of thrilling intimations of the supernatural, which he must learn to resist. "He almost fancied . . . that he beheld something not of this earth . . . But he checked the imperfect thought . . . and dismissed, as absurd, a supposition, which had begun to thrill his every nerve with horror."[3]

Nineteenth-century gothic fictions demonstrate the continuing expressive potential of such patterns. A clear case is Le Fanu's *Uncle Silas* (1865), written in the heyday of the sensation novel, a creepy recasting of Radcliffe's formula that features a vulnerable young orphaned heroine, Maud, an isolated mansion, Bartram-Haugh, and its sinister eponymous owner, who plots to gain his niece's fortune. Part of what makes Le Fanu's version disturbing is the insidious threat posed by the incestuous or murderous father figure (Silas becomes Maud's guardian in a test of her faith ordained by her father's will), amplifying a factor that already appears briefly in *The Italian*. The unsettling energy tapped by reversing gendered roles can be seen as late as *Dracula*, whose opening sequence condenses a Radcliffe scenario (a naïve young protagonist, a gloomy remote castle, and its mysterious, aristocratic master) with Jonathan Harker in the feminine position, imprisoned by Count Dracula and almost succumbing to sexually aggressive female vampires.

Unlike their eighteenth-century prototypes, *Uncle Silas* and *Dracula* are varieties of first-person narrative, a form that intensifies and relativizes subjective states and that is shared by much nineteenth-century gothic. The pivotal text for this transformation is *Caleb Williams*, which, domesticating and naturalizing gothic motifs of hidden crime and persecution, makes them the basis for a political and psychological thriller. Godwin tells how he began writing in the third person but, becoming dissatisfied, changed to "making the hero of my tale his own historian . . . It was infinitely the best adapted [to] the analysis of the private and internal operations of the mind, . . . laying bare the involutions of motive, and recording the gradually accumulating impulses."[4] Dramatizing Caleb's shifting moods and motives, his growing obsession with Falkland, his exultant detection of his master's guilt, and his subsequent desperation under the implacable persecution that follows, Godwin opens up the vast murky realm of narrative unreliability that many later writers explore. At the same time, by exposing the injustice of "things as they are" (Godwin's original title), indicting the abuses of power and privilege that allow Falkland to discredit and silence Caleb, he links "the private and internal operations of the mind" with contemporary political conditions in the repressive aftermath of the French Revolution.

Many varieties of sensational nineteenth-century narrative can be either traced from Godwin's innovations by direct descent or derived by extrapolation. Stories of detection are the most numerous descendants, directly in the "tales of ratiocination" by Poe, who cites *Caleb Williams* in his "Philosophy of Composition," or in Arthur Conan Doyle, whose Sherlock Holmes cites Poe's Dupin (disparagingly) in *A Study in Scarlet* (1887), and indirectly in all the Victorian novels where detection and mystery plotting play an important role. Dickens's *Bleak House* (1852–1853), which mobilizes both amateur and professional detectives (Inspector Bucket is one of the earliest in English fiction) to uncover Lady Dedlock's secret past, not only elaborates mystery and detection into an expansive multi-plot composition but also follows Godwin in using them to advance a probing diagnosis of diseased social conditions. The real scandal in Dickens's novel is not Lady Dedlock's suppressed affair and illegitimate child but the abyss of ignorance and neglect that separates rich and poor, who "from opposite sides of great gulfs" the unfolding mystery plot brings "together very curiously."[5] Sensation novels, in which scandals like adultery, bigamy, or illegitimacy become more central interests, assign a different function to detection. For figures like the humble drawing master Walter Hartright in Wilkie Collins's *The Woman in White* (1859–1860) or the indolent Robert Audley in Mary Elizabeth Braddon's *Lady Audley's Secret* (1862), investigating the novel's mysteries becomes a process of masculine *Bildung*, offering the male protagonist a transforming active role that leads to his social ascent and power.

The most direct descendant of *Caleb Williams* is Mary Shelley's *Frankenstein*, a filial text dedicated to Godwin. The features of its story that have become modern myth, the "pale student of unhallowed arts" animating "the hideous phantasm of a man," might owe their inspiration to her nightmare vision;[6] but the mode of naturalized gothic, the philosophical reflections on individual development and its social conditions, and especially the narrative dynamics of persecution, the reversible positions of master and slave, flight and pursuit, all recall Godwin. Perhaps no other work shows more clearly how nineteenth-century novelists draw on and transform earlier gothic fiction. The effects of first-person narration are multiplied as the explorer Walton's account not only frames but reflects Frankenstein's with alternative versions of its themes, such as the dangerous quest for knowledge, while the tormented scientist's narrative both contains and is contested by his creature's. Incorporating the creature's version is Shelley's most radical move, distinguishing *Frankenstein* from later monster stories (as well as from most stage and film versions of the novel), by creating an unstable, shifting balance of sympathies that leaves us uncertain which of the antagonists is the more monstrous. Frankenstein's loss of control over his creation is doubled in this escape of meaning from either's rhetorical control.

That loss of control is in turn linked with the way Shelley's characters are impelled by unconscious forces. "There is something at work in my soul," Walton writes of his passion for exploration, "which I do not understand" (231), just as Frankenstein describes his obsession with creating life ("I could not tear my thoughts from my employment, loathsome in itself, but which had taken an irresistible hold of my imagination" [50]), and the creature describes the compulsion that drives him to murder ("I was the slave, not the master of an impulse, which I detested, yet could not disobey" [218]). As in her account of her story's inspiration, Shelley draws on a Romantic psychology of the imagination (Walton's reflection follows his allusion to Coleridge's Ancient Mariner) to develop a sense of hidden psychic energies, the tangled roots of creation and destruction, which are knotted together, doubled like Frankenstein and his creature.

Shelley's novel was soon followed by two other major works of Romantic gothic fiction, Maturin's *Melmoth the Wanderer* (1820) and Hogg's *Memoirs and Confessions of a Justified Sinner* (1824), each developing even more complicated narrative forms as well as plots of persecution and perdition. Maturin carries framing to a disorienting extreme, embedding tales within tales that do not form parts of a single plot but are linked by thematic analogies, particularly between horrifying instances of the perversion of religion into systems of cruelty and oppression. Encompassing all of them is the story of a diabolical pact that impels Melmoth's wanderings: having sold his soul for extended life and forbidden knowledge, he traverses time and space, appearing to those trapped in desperate plights – being falsely imprisoned in a madhouse or condemned by the Inquisition – and offering them escape if they will trade places with him and give up their hope of salvation. None agrees, and in the end Melmoth meets his doom in a spectacular conclusion that recalls and surpasses the last moments of Lewis's Ambrosio.

Hogg also presents a story of perverted religion and damnation, but whereas Maturin's many interpolated tales tend to overwhelm his framing narrative, the "Editor's Narrative" in *Confessions* swells to nearly the length of the recovered text it frames, and struggles with it for narrative authority. The century-old story of Calvinist fanaticism that culminates in the murder of George Colwan by his brother Robert Wringham is first recounted by the editor in a version based on "traditionary facts," "the account as . . . publicly handed down to us," before we read the version given in Robert's "private memoirs."[7] The result is a problem of reliability that becomes increasingly vexed. After the editor's account of Robert's mean-spirited malice, we are liable to read his own self-justifying version of events ironically, feeling sure we already know the truth. But that assurance breaks down as we encounter the traditional gothic problem of the preternatural. The dominant figure in Robert's narrative is his mysterious companion Gil-Martin, who appears as his exact double just after he has been assured he is one of the elect. We may try to construe Gil-Martin, who prompts Robert's escalating series of crimes and who displays preternatural powers of mind-reading and shape-shifting, as a figment of Robert's crazed "private" imagination, but the "public" evidence presented by the editor makes sense only if we credit Gil-Martin's independent existence. And though Robert cannot realize it, we must eventually recognize that his companion is actually the devil, leading him to damnation. The editor's enlightened outlook, however, prevents him from accepting this reading ("in this day, and with the present generation, it will not go down, that a man should be daily tempted by the devil, in the semblance of a fellow-creature" [242]), though he cannot offer a satisfactory alternative, and he concludes in frustrated bafflement: "What can this work be? . . . I cannot tell" (230). Hogg's double narrative of demonic doubling confronts us with the failure of both its narrators – and perhaps its author and readers – to control its meaning.

The editor's postscript does more than simply register his incomprehension; in appending an account of the discovery of the sinner's memoirs, it also foregrounds the novel's engagement with history. The story of finding the text during the exhumation of a remarkably well-preserved corpse offers a graphic image of an encounter with a past that is both remote and yet returns, a characteristic effect of Scottish gothic's "association between the *national* and the *uncanny or supernatural*."[8] For Hogg the past is a history of religious extremism that cannot be reconciled with enlightened modernity. But moderated versions of similar conflicts also run through Scott's enormously influential historical fiction, in which a traditional, premodern Scottish culture that refuses to recede quietly into the past is repeatedly linked with gothic motifs. *Redgauntlet* (1824), published in the same month as Hogg's *Confessions*, offers a striking instance as it reprises with heightened self-consciousness the cultural conflicts that first animated *Waverley*'s representation of the 1745 Jacobite Rebellion ten years earlier. Combining epistolary, journal, and third-person narration, as well as an interpolated ghost story, it works up to the discovery of a renewed Jacobite conspiracy in 1765. At the heart of the plot, therefore, is a return of the repressed past that was itself an insurrection of an older form of life against modernity. Led by the dark, forceful Redgauntlet, successor to a series of gothic hero-villains going back to Walpole's Manfred, the rebellion seems to pose a disturbing threat, yet at the climax it quickly dissolves: the plot is already known, and instead of meeting harsh repression Redgauntlet and the Pretender are allowed to fade away into exile. The renewed rebellion is not only their fantasy, it is also Scott's, since no such events actually occurred, and the novel thus becomes, like many gothic narratives before and after it, a reflection on its own fictive status.[9]

A different kind of eighteenth-century tale becomes a staple of early Victorian sensational fiction as novelists mine the *Newgate Calendar* for stories of notorious criminals, producing such popular and controversial works as Bulwer's *Paul Clifford* (1830) and *Eugene Aram* (1832) and Ainsworth's *Rookwood* (1834). Dickens's *Oliver Twist* (1838) has a contemporary setting but displays several features of the Newgate novel, seen most clearly in its resemblances to Ainsworth's *Jack Sheppard* (1839), whose serialization in *Bentley's Miscellany* overlapped with it. Unlike his earlier *Rookwood*, which is based on the pattern of Radcliffean gothic, Ainsworth's novel, like Dickens's "parish boy's progress," is a Newgate *Bildungsroman*, dramatizing the opposition of the criminal underworld and middle-class respectability through the protagonist's movements back and forth between them. Both draw most of their energy from the outlaws, dwelling knowingly on their hidden haunts, whether the Mint and other eighteenth-century criminal havens or contemporary Saffron Hill and Jacob's Island, and anticipating the atmospheric effects of later urban gothic. The narrative interest of criminality for Dickens's readers is mainly in its threat to claim Oliver ("Once let him feel that he is one of us," gloats Fagin, "and he's ours – ours for life!") and in the more general threat of violence, which finally explodes in Sikes's murder of Nancy.[10] Ainsworth, in contrast, invites his readers' sympathetic involvement with Jack's criminal career and especially his spectacular series of escapes from prison, recounted in admiring detail as Jack surmounts increasingly difficult challenges, which make him a popular hero and dramatize resistance to social constraints. The subversive potential that is defused by Oliver's social salvation finds full expression in the riotous closing scene of Jack's procession from Newgate to Tyburn, which the mob's cheers make seem "more as if he were marching to a triumph, than proceeding to a shameful death."[11]

The fascination with violence and sympathy with the "dangerous classes" that earned the Newgate novel both popular success and critical condemnation are replaced in the 1860s with the allure of uncovering scandalous secrets and transgressions of more elevated figures in novels that quickly garnered the "sensation" label. The first, *The Woman in White*, embodies thrilling sensation in its initial event. Walter Hartright is "strolling along the lonely high road" in the dark "when, in one moment, every drop of blood in my body was brought to a stop by the touch of a hand laid lightly and suddenly on my shoulder from behind me."[12] That light touch, whose startling effect the reader also registers, triggers the novel's intricate plot, which turns on what its characters call "the Secret" and their struggles to hide or discover it. Anne Catherick, the woman in white whom Hartright encounters, has been imprisoned in an asylum because the villainous Sir Percival Glyde believes she knows the secret, and Sir Percival will eventually die in his frantic efforts to preserve it. When

Hartright at last discovers it, he describes his shock: "My head turned giddy – I held to the desk to keep from falling," yet the secret itself turns out to be a legal technicality, the fact that Sir Percival's parents were not married, "that he was not Sir Percival Glyde at all" (529). The more elaborate intrigue, in which the heroine Laura Fairlie, who has become Lady Glyde, is abducted, declared dead, switched with Anne, and imprisoned in her place, also involves threatened class identity, which is a more anxious concern here than physical safety. As the formidable mastermind Count Fosco says in his own defense, "I might have taken Lady Glyde's life ... [but] took her identity instead" (632).

The effort to re-establish Laura's identity motivates the novel's narrative method of assembling texts and testimony, which is Collins's most striking and influential formal innovation. Just as the plot and setting transpose older gothic devices into the terms of domestic realism (the heroine persecuted for her fortune, the doubling of Anne and Laura, the oppressive Blackwater Park), so the composite narrative replaces the unreliability of earlier first-person accounts with a documentary effect of forensic coherence in which each piece of evidence finds its place. Collins's narrative still allows for the interplay of distinctive voices, however, which at one point yields its own sensational effect when Laura's half-sister Marian Halcombe, whose diary constitutes nearly a third of the novel, falls ill and can no longer write. Her last entry breaks off and is followed by a "Postscript" inserted by Fosco, an act of textual molestation as startling as the touch on Hartright's shoulder. Anne's opening appeal is part of a woman's attempt to escape confinement; this moment enacts a contrary impulse of containment. Marian's illness results from getting soaked in the rain while eavesdropping on Fosco and Percival's scheming. Credited by the admiring Fosco with "the foresight and resolution of a man" (346), she manages her surveillance by discarding her voluminous feminine clothing so that "no man could have passed through the narrowest spaces more easily than I" (342). Her illness reverses this bid for masculine agency, ending her roles both as narrator and as active opponent to the villains, and forcefully returns her to the passive position prescribed in the novel's opening line: "This is the story of what a Woman's patience can endure, and what a Man's resolution can achieve" (33).

The disturbances produced by transgressive women and the reassertion of masculine control figure more prominently in several later sensation novels, most spectacularly in *Lady Audley's Secret*. The beautiful Helen Maldon, after marrying and being deserted, transforms herself into the governess Lucy Graham and then becomes Lady Audley. Already technically guilty of bigamy, she goes on to attempt two murders in her efforts to protect herself. The sensational effect of her unwomanly crimes is amplified by the contrast between her innocent "china doll" appearance and the ruthlessness with which she acts, the disquieting qualities disclosed by her "pre-Raphaelite" portrait, which gives "a strange sinister light to the deep blue eyes" and depicts her as "a beautiful fiend."[13] Cornered at last, she claims to be a victim of hereditary insanity, but a specialist who examines her is skeptical. "The lady is not mad . . . She has the cunning of madness with the prudence of intelligence. I will tell you what she is . . . She is dangerous!" (379). And it is as a dangerous woman rather than a madwoman that she is sent off to be confined in a private asylum for the rest of her life.

Braddon continues to exploit the interest of girls gone bad in later novels such as *Aurora Floyd* (1863), and Collins also gives a leading role to a fascinating villainous woman, Lydia Gwilt, in *Armadale* (1866), but the most famous of all the stories of female transgression is Mrs. Henry Wood's *East Lynne* (1861). Often considered a sensation novel because of its elements of mystery plotting (a previous murder, an innocent man falsely accused, investigations by ama-teur detectives, and the climactic exposure of the villain), Wood's bestseller exerts a more scandalous appeal as a sentimental domestic novel that offers a covertly sympathetic view of adultery. Everything about Lady Isabel Vane's situation is calculated to make her vulnerable. Orphaned and penniless, she marries a high-minded but dull man she does not yet love and finds herself sidelined by her officious sister-in-law. Stung into jealousy by her husband's unexplained meetings with another woman, she yields to the manipulations of an unscrupulous former admirer and elopes, taking "a blind leap in a moment of wild passion."[14] Once she "falls from her pedestal" at midpoint, the rest of the novel works to make her fate a warning through both its rhetoric ("Lady – wife – mother! Should you ever be tempted to abandon your home . . ." [237]) and its relentlessly punitive action, in which she is immediately consumed by guilt, soon abandoned by her lover, then injured (and thought killed) in a railway accident. The severity of these admonitions and afflictions, however, licenses the reader's sympathy and prepares for the intense pathos and penitential ordeal of her returning in disguise to serve as governess to her own children, one of which dies in her arms without ever knowing her. She thus becomes a victim whose sufferings demand compassion, and her trans-gression becomes a source of masochistic pleasure.

Other versions of sensation fiction appear in the long career of Charles Reade, who, in addition to exposing contemporary social problems (prison conditions in *It Is Never Too Late to Mend* [1856], lunatic asylums in *Hard Cash* [1863]), sensationalized historical fiction in *Griffith Gaunt* (1866), which provoked outrage over its explicit treatment of sexual infidelity, and in *The Cloister and the Hearth* (1861), an epic narrative of the fifteenth century energized by numerous intrigues and intense set pieces. Unlike Reade, Hardy is not usually associated with the genre, though he begins his career with *Desperate Remedies* (1871), which involves a woman with a mysterious past, illegitimacy, disguise, blackmail, murder, and an extended process of detection. Commentators typically note and deplore the influence of Collins and Braddon on the novel, considering it a false start before Hardy found his way in the Wessex novels, but his later work retains and reworks many of the same concerns and features, such as destructive sexual entanglements and class tensions, as well as deliberately forced coincidences, so that well-known novels like *Tess of the d'Urbervilles* (1891) and *Jude the Obscure* (1895) can be recognized as descendants of sensation fiction.

The most consequential work performed by sensation fiction might be its role in transforming gothic mystery plotting and the rationalized supernatural into detective fiction, which gained extraordinary popularity by the end of the century. I have already noted the early stages of this development from Godwin to Poe and Dickens, as well as the role of amateur detectives in uncovering the suppressed past in *The Woman in White* and *Lady Audley's Secret*. In *The Moonstone* (1868) Collins for the first time constructs his whole plot around the problem of a single crime, the theft of a fabled diamond, developing devices for lengthening the interval between enigma and solution that expand the story into a full-length novel and have since become familiar features of the form, such as a large number of suspects and false leads. The sensation novel's nose for scandal hidden behind respectable appearances comes into play when Sergeant Cuff suspects that Rachel Verinder has herself taken the Moonstone; and again when the actual thief turns out to be the philanthropist Godfrey Ablewhite. The frame story of the Moonstone being plundered and finally restored further questions the established order by representing imperialism as theft and the Indians as the jewel's rightful owners.

Three of Doyle's four Sherlock Holmes novels fill out their narratives with comparable exotic foreign motivations, whether drawn from the wilds of America (evil Mormons in *A Study in Scarlet*, corrupt labor unions in *The Valley of Fear* [1915]) or from India (stolen treasure again in *The Sign of Four* [1890]). Only in *The Hound of the Baskervilles* (1902), which also draws most directly on gothic motifs such as preternatural phenomena and a family curse, does Doyle manage a continuous narrative as tightly constructed as Collins's or his own shorter Holmes stories. But of course the enduring interest in these fictions is not their plotting but the figure of Holmes, who soon became one of those rare and remarkable characters that take on an independent life. Holmes's vitality stems from the opposing forces of detective fiction itself, the exciting disturbance of crime and the incisive power of deductive reason; and though always on the side of righteousness, Holmes also exercises the charismatic fascination that was previously reserved to amoral villains like Fosco.[15]

While sensation fiction often produces its disturbing effects by domesticating gothic, several of the most notable novels of the later nineteenth century return more openly and self-consciously to gothic themes like monstrosity and the preternatural. Stevenson's *Dr. Jekyll and Mr. Hyde*, a monster story that recalls *Frankenstein*, is the first of these. Again a scientist produces and loses control over a creature who is both his double and his antagonist, but here the doubling becomes central as theme and as the focus of a mystery plot that probes the relation between the respectable doctor and his sinister friend. Such plotting clearly draws on the precedent of sensation fiction, as does the novel's narrative method, which joins episodes mainly focalized through the investigating lawyer Utterson with the explanatory accounts of "Doctor Lanyon's Narrative" and "Henry Jekyll's Full Statement of the Case." Also recalling sensation fiction is the contemporary setting, here turned to effects of urban gothic in scenes of streets deserted at night or shrouded in morning fog whose "mournful reinvasion of darkness" makes Soho seem "like a district of some city in a nightmare."[16] But Stevenson's novel produces quite a different effect from earlier sensation novels with its concise structure and elegant style; its economy intensifies suspense and shocking impact while inviting aesthetic appreciation such as Henry James's tribute to its "supremely successful form."[17]

Dr. Jekyll and Mr. Hyde also produces a more radical disturbance than the social scandals unearthed in sensation fiction. Jekyll's initial motive for transforming himself might have been the hidden pursuit of merely "undignified" (presumably sexual) pleasures, "but in the hands of Edward Hyde, they soon began to turn towards the monstrous," toward "drinking pleasure with bestial avidity from any degree of torture to another" (60). This uncontrolled sadistic ferocity is first glimpsed in Enfield's story of Hyde trampling the young girl ("It was hellish to see. It wasn't like a man; it was like some damned Juggernaut" [7]) and reaches full intensity in Jekyll's own account of his brutal unprovoked assault on Carew ("With a transport of glee, I mauled the unresisting body, tasting delight from every blow" [64]). As the pronoun here indicates, Jekyll can at times identify himself with Hyde even at his most monstrous, though at others he tries to insist on their disjunction ("He, I say – I cannot say I. That child of hell had nothing human" [67]). But there is no possibility of either separation or integration; "that insurgent horror was knit to him closer than a wife, closer than an eye, lay caged in his flesh, where he heard it mutter and felt it struggle to be born" (69). The only possible end is their shared destruction.

The preternatural doubling between Dorian Gray and his picture offers another *fin de siècle* version of the hidden life. The gothic elements of Wilde's fable – the Faustian bargain, the magical portrait, and the double as conscience – are clearly recognizable, but they are not such potent sources of disturbance as the novel's unstable mixture of modes. Evocative accounts of decadent aesthetic tastes mingle with brilliant epigrams; worldly comedy alternates with melodrama; vague insinuations of Dorian's secret sins are confronted by the graphically naturalistic description of his murder of Basil Hallward. Working within all the instabilities is a tension that makes Wilde's use of doubling markedly different from Stevenson's. Jekyll can conceal the nature of his double life, but the novel makes it clear that Hyde's monstrosity lies in his sadistic cruelty, which like Freud's death drive takes him beyond the pleasure principle. When Dorian feels "keenly the terrible pleasure of a double life," it is while attending a fashionable dinner party with an appearance of calm grace the evening after he has committed and concealed a violent murder.[18] But as many contemporary and later readers have recognized, the most scandalous transgressions that Dorian's beauty hides are not acts of murderous violence but homosexual liaisons, secrets that the novel, like its author, needs both to disclose and deny, to imagine as both beautiful and monstrous. The time soon came when that tension could no longer be sustained in life as it had been in art, and the disgraced Wilde went into exile under the gothic alias of Sebastian Melmoth.

The last and most lurid of the great nineteenth-century monster stories, Stoker's *Dracula* leaves no uncertainty about the source of disturbance. Both the obscene intimacies of vampirism and the efforts to combat it are insistently sexualized, from Jonathan Harker's near-seduction by the female vampires, to Lucy Westenra's succumbing to Dracula and finally becoming "true dead" after a stake is driven through her heart (both a holy rite and a group rape), to Mina Harker's being forced to drink Dracula's blood. There is also no uncertainty about the reality of the preternatural, both in Dracula's formidable powers, whose extent is elaborately specified, and in the mélange of prophylactics, including garlic and crucifixes, used against him. But while its content mobilizes ancient superstitions and a fearful fascination with the archaic force of polymorphous sexuality, the novel's form is "nineteenth century up-to-date with a vengeance," as Jonathan describes his shorthand diary.[19] Stoker extends Collins's technique of composite narration, incorporating diaries (phonographic as well as shorthand), letters, telegrams, newspaper cuttings, and other documents, just as the plot enacts the sensation novel's updating of older gothic devices in Dracula's move from Transylvania to contemporary England. The assembly of the narrative itself becomes a crucial part of the plot, as the "little band" that forms to fight Dracula share their diaries and the other records, so that they can study the same text that the novel's readers have been reading in order to "arrange [their] plan of battle with this terrible and mysterious enemy" (251). The self-consciousness of this extensive narrative reflexivity, far from distracting our attention, contributes to the novel's absorbing power.

Dracula shows how a sensational gothic fantasy can use realistic techniques "so that a history almost at variance with latter-day belief may stand forth as simple fact" (6). But the traffic flows both ways throughout the nineteenth century: realistic mainstream novels often draw on gothic to achieve their effects, as can be seen in the two most prominent mid-Victorian novelists, Dickens and George Eliot. Gothic informs Dickens's fiction from beginning to end, from the interpolated "Madman's Tale" in *The Pickwick Papers* (1837) to the uncompleted *The Mystery of Edwin Drood* (1870), from a tale of terror like those in *Blackwood's Magazine* to a murder mystery whose power challenges Collins. In both narratives, as in many others Dickens wrote between them, gothic serves to dramatize isolated, deviant subjectivity, whether in the madman's first-person confession or in the brilliantly focalized opening pages of *Drood*, where the reader is immediately plunged into John Jasper's disoriented consciousness as he emerges from an opium dream. As a heightened rendering of self-enclosed, aberrant consciousness, gothic works in tension and dialogue with Dickens's broader social representation, sometimes taking quite subtle forms. Miss Wade's bitter "Confessions of a Self-Tormentor" in *Little Dorrit* (1855–1857), for example, derives from the unreliable first-person gothic tale, but her story and her paranoid resentments resonate widely as she becomes a foil for Amy Dorrit's self-effacing goodness and a double for Arthur Clennam's unacknowledged anger.

Bleak House is not just accented but permeated by gothic effects. We have already noted how it uses mystery plotting and detection to dramatize class divisions, but those public concerns also have their private corollaries in subjective disturbance. When the icy Lady Dedlock becomes faint at recognizing the handwriting of a former lover on a legal document, it is as if she has seen a ghost, a gothic figure that becomes explicit when John Jarndyce passionately warns the young Richard Carstone not to count on getting anything from the Chancery suit. "For the love of God, don't found a hope of expectation on the family curse! Whatever you do this side the grave, never give one lingering glance towards the horrible phantom that has haunted us so many years" (389). Jarndyce and Jarndyce does indeed work like an inherited curse that will eventually claim Richard as another victim, so that the Chancery plot, like the mystery plot of Lady Dedlock's secret, is driven by the dynamics of haunting. In both, impersonal forces rooted in the past overtake and destroy life in the present, a pattern as old as *The Castle of Otranto*. The terror of this fatality is felt – but also resisted – most forcefully in the experience of Esther Summerson, who is told in childhood that she is cursed, "set apart" (31), a doom that seems to be confirmed after she learns Lady Dedlock is her mother and is threatened with exposure. The gothic motif of the Ghost's Walk, a Dedlock family legend of impending calamity, crystal-lizes this dread as she is seized by the thought "that there was a dreadful truth in the legend of the Ghost's Walk; that it was I, who was to bring calamity upon the stately house" (587). Though she manages to overcome her "terror of myself," Dickens suggests that Esther remains haunted by her past to the end.

George Eliot's last novel, *Daniel Deronda* (1876), signals its gothic affinities in its opening epigraph: "Let thy chief terror be of thy own soul . . . ."[20] This warning is aimed most directly at the beautiful "spoiled child" Gwendolen Harleth, who marries for security and status and finds her life turning into a nightmare. The early stages of Gwendolen's development have been rightly praised for their finely observed social and psychological realism, sometimes in order to disparage the romance of Deronda's story. But from the beginning a dark gothic thread of fear runs through her experience, notably in the sequence beginning with the discovery in her new home of a macabre "picture of an upturned dead face, from which an obscure figure seemed to be fleeing with outstretched arms" (27) that reappears to disrupt her performance in a tableau: "She looked like a statue into which a soul of Fear had entered" (61). At the climax, when her feared and hated husband Grandcourt has drowned, the image returns to express her guilt: "His face will not be seen above the water again . . . Not by anyone else – only by me – a dead face – I shall never get away from it" (689). Her guilt stems less from any active responsibility for his death than from her having obsessively desired it. "The thought of his dying would not subsist . . . Fantasies moved within her like ghosts . . . dark rays doing their work invisibly in the broad light" (606). When we encounter the same image of "ghosts upon the daylight" only thirty pages later, it is used by Leonora, Deronda's mother, to explain how she has felt forced to summon him and reveal his Jewish identity, a crucial event in the novel's other plot, which also depends on the power of haunting.

Middlemarch (1871–1872) is one of the greatest achievements of nineteenth-century realism, yet vital components of its broad, richly detailed "study of provincial life," working in dialogical tension with its social representation and attention to ordinary experience, are intense moments of hidden, private subjectivity registered in gothic terms. The most fully developed is the account of Bulstrode's guilty fear when his repressed sordid past returns to haunt him: "Night and day, without interruption save of brief sleep which only wove retrospect and fear into a fantastic present, he felt the scenes of his early life coming between him and everything else."[21] In the hidden experience of her heroine, Eliot probes a different and more troubling form of haunting, produced not in guilty retrospect but prospectively as the narrator renders Dorothea's intense "inward confusion" during her honeymoon in Rome.

> In certain states of dull forlornness Dorothea all her life continued to see the vastness of St. Peter's, the huge bronze canopy, the excited intention of the prophets and evangelists in the mosaics above, and the red drapery which was being hung for Christmas spreading itself everywhere like a disease of the retina. (194)

The shocking, surreal impact of that final image haunts the novel's readers as well. In using sensational extremity to represent "ordinary human life" – here a young bride's feelings of depression and their chronic recurrence – Eliot shows how intricately gothic becomes interwoven in the fabric of nineteenth-century fiction.

Notes

1. Horace Walpole, *The Castle of Otranto: A Gothic Story* (New York: Oxford University Press, 1964), p. 7.
2. Matthew G. Lewis, *The Monk* (New York: Grove Press, 1952), p. 344.
3. Ann Radcliffe, *The Italian* (New York: Oxford University Press, 1981), p. 347.
4. William Godwin, preface to *Fleetwood* (1832) in William Godwin, *Caleb Williams* (New York: Norton, 1977), p. 339.
5. Charles Dickens, *Bleak House* (London: Penguin, 1996), p. 256.
6. Mary Shelley, preface to the third edition (1831) in Mary Shelley, *Frankenstein; or, The Modern Prometheus* (University of Chicago Press, 1982), p. 228.

7. James Hogg, *Private Memoirs and Confessions of a Justified Sinner* (Harmondsworth: Penguin, 1982), p. 68.

8. Ian Duncan, "Walter Scott, James Hogg and Scottish Gothic," in *A Companion to the Gothic*, ed. David Punter (Oxford: Blackwell, 2000), p. 70.

9. On gothic as a reflexive mode, see Peter K. Garrett, *Gothic Reflections: Narrative Force in Nineteenth-Century Fiction* (Ithaca, NY: Cornell University Press, 2003).

10. Charles Dickens, *Oliver Twist, or, The Parish Boy's Progress* (London: Penguin, 2002), p. 159.

11. William Harrison Ainsworth, *Jack Sheppard* (Peterborough, ON: Broadview, 2007), p. 472.

12. Wilkie Collins, *The Woman in White* (Harmondsworth: Penguin, 1974), p. 47.

13. Mary Elizabeth Braddon, *Lady Audley's Secret* (New York: Oxford University Press, 1987), pp. 70–71.

14. Mrs. Henry Wood, *East Lynne* (New Brunswick: Rutgers University Press, 1984), p. 237.

15. Another fascinating mastermind of the period (1895–1891) is Guy Boothby's Dr. Nikola, neither criminal nor detective but a naturalized necromancer.

16. Robert Louis Stevenson, *The Strange Case of Dr. Jekyll and Mr. Hyde* (London: Penguin, 2002), p. 23.

17. Henry James, "Robert Louis Stevenson," in *Robert Louis Stevenson: The Critical Heritage*, ed. Paul Maixner (London: Routledge and Kegan Paul, 1981), p. 308.

18. Oscar Wilde, *The Picture of Dorian Gray* (London: Penguin, 2003), p. 167.

19. Bram Stoker, *Dracula* (London: Penguin, 2003), p. 43.

20. George Eliot, *Daniel Deronda* (London: Penguin, 1995), p. 3.

21. George Eliot, *Middlemarch* (London: Penguin, 1994), p. 615.

30

Realism and romance

FRANCIS O'GORMAN

Contrasts between realism and romance appear easy to make. Realism is a mode of writing embedded in history. It attaches itself to empirical and observable life. Its watchword is credibility. In the nineteenth century realism belongs among the agnostics. It is unconvinced that there is more than what can be known on the earth. It is quintessentially the achievement of the mid-Victorian novel, though its roots and its influence stretch far. Realism proposes the reality of tangible experience. It offers language as that which can call up simulacra of existence in which its readers can believe. The empiricist Aristotle is its remote figurehead. Romance is realism's quirky counter, its opposite number. Romance belongs with Plato and belief in forms and meaning beyond visibility. In the nineteenth century romance makes imaginative enthrallment out of implausibility. It assumes a world beyond what can be touched and tested; its laws are not merely those of the earth. The preoccupations of romance are fantasy, imagination, and strangeness: romance is a mode in which literary language presents phenomena that cannot be measured against what readers think they already know. Realism easily turns to politics; romance to religion. Realism can solicit readers for tears; romance, for surprise, curiosity, bafflement. Realism is a discourse of the senses; romance of the sensational. Realism belongs with satire: a mode of writing rooted in experience. Realism persistently feels the drag of tragedy: it is an expression of the painfulness of being alive. Romance belongs with epic, the gothic, and, for all its terrors, with the comic – the unlikely resolution of human problems through non-human agents, in accord with wish fulfillment.

So realism and romance are sharply contrastive. Are they not? But realism, supposedly rooted in the experience of the world, offers its reader, strangely, the more substantial imaginative challenge from the start. It endeavors, at least on the surface, to disguise its own fictiveness, to hide its nature, and in turn to ask readers to make, curiously enough, an even greater leap of faith than explicit fantasy requires. "'And is this your very sober earnest,'" asks Fergus gravely in response to the hero's announcement in Walter Scott's *Waverley* (1814) that his future happiness depends on Flora MacIvor, "'or are we in the land of romance and fiction?'"[1] Fiction is always imaginative, so Fergus is not wholly wrong to think it simply synonymous with romance. But romance as a nineteenth-century mode of writing does not aspire to cloak the fact that it is peopled with the creations of mind, of dream and imagination. It does not propose to the reader that its correspondence with the actual is the same as realism's: it is more candid about its nature. But the two modes, in the long nineteenth century as elsewhere, are not easily kept apart anyway. If romance and realism express contrasting attitudes, there is no assurance that those attitudes are the authors' or that they will insist on them. The modes are not statements of faith – they are different practices of writing that can be chosen and coordinated. After defeat of the 1745 Jacobite rebellion, Scott's Waverley regards himself afresh. He felt "entitled to say firmly, though perhaps with a sigh, that the romance of his life was ended, and that its real history had now commenced" (vol. II, 281). Romance gives way to history; dreams to a more tangible reality. Flora is replaced by Rose. But that division, the clarity of those two emblematic alternatives, is no guide to fiction's practices in the century that follows.

Fictional language's embrace of the real – I use this term as shorthand, not to obscure ideological weightings and competing philosophical definitions of what the "real" involves – reached its most charismatic exponent in English in George Eliot. But Eliot, creator of a European hero in *Daniel Deronda* (1876), was the most European of mid-Victorian writers. Although her realist project was in part developed from Scott, in part it also is an English interpretation of an earlier French achievement – the novels of Honoré de Balzac. And persistently, through the period, English novelists measured themselves as realists or romancers against the French tradition, however schematized and simplified, just as they assessed their realism against the Russian canvases of Dostoevsky and Tolstoy. *Middlemarch* (1871–1872) is subtitled *A Study of Provincial Life*. Balzac, with *Eugénie Grandet* (1834), had envisaged a series of *Scènes de la vie de province* (scenes of provincial life). The great stretch of *La Comédie humaine*, which those *Scènes* became, followed. *Eugénie Grandet* shapes the exceptional discourse of realism, finding significance in a visible world that is not about Romantic selfhood or God's shaping presence but about human histories, material circumstances. Here was the novel-as-world, as memorial, as recuperation of the past. Émile Zola's Rougon-Macquart series inherits Balzac's ambitions to figure the real in fiction, and transforms his interest in the past into absorption with the present. "'Ah!'" says the artist Claude in Zola's *L'Œuvre* (1886, *The [Great] Work*), "'tout voir et tout peindre!'"[2] This is, literally, a rejection of non-realist academic and historical art in favor of a contemporary manifesto of painting *en plein air*. It is also the motto of a powerful literary realism, with all its stirring hope that language might represent in almost touchable form the experience of being alive. English realists in the later part of the century do not forget Zola.

Realism has a habit of creating series. England answers France with Anthony Trollope's Chronicles of Barsetshire (1855–1867) and his Palliser series (1864–1879). But, like any modern attempts at completeness, realism, whether in a series or a single capacious volume, draws attention to what it has missed out. A sense of need, of reaching but not grasping, generates an implicit mourning that is never far from nineteenth-century realism's endeavors to take hold of experience in its fullness. Realism breathes incompleteness. Its confession is always of what is missing from its ambition "tout voir et tout peindre." When George Eliot at the close of *Middlemarch* asks her readers to remember the benefits of "unhistoric acts,"[3] the words remind them quietly, indirectly, of stories that fiction cannot or is unable to tell, of narratives that will always slip away in the face of the extraordinary plurality of the real. The unknown of human lives is valuable; the unsaid of realism, persistent. Balzac, assessing what realism *could* say, had looked to the immediate history of France. Walter Scott's practice of realism reaches further back to define a mode of historical narrative that remains alive throughout the nineteenth century. Scenes, events, and characters of the Scottish and English past provide the substance of his most persuasive histories: *Old Mortality* (1816), *The Heart of Midlothian* (1818), *Ivanhoe* (1819). His ambition as a chronicler of Scotland's past was, certainly, not to be confined within a single novel. National biographies were knowable in portions: forgetfulness, ignorance, and omission were always part of them.

Edward Bulwer Lytton endeavors to match Scott as a historical novelist. *The Last Days of Pompeii* (1834) and *The Last of The Barons* (1843) are among his ventures in popular historical fiction, with his peculiar fondness for things about to end. But *The Caxtons* (1850) draws on Laurence Sterne's *Tristram Shandy* (1759–1767) and Jane Austen's *Pride and Prejudice* (1813) to fashion a family history that offers a quirky new realism rooted in the quotidian, the familiar, the family. *The Caxtons*, as it narrates the curious life of Pisistratus, its hero, is disconcerted by literary realism's own apparent powers. Even in its title, Bulwer Lytton's text is clearly about print (William Caxton was probably the first person to introduce the printing press to England). In preserving the details of lives, voices, feelings, habits, in writing committed to authenticity, the novel opens up the possibilities of the uncanny power of texts, as Robert Browning would say, to start the past alive. "My father spends his mornings in those *lata silentia*," the narrator reports:

as Virgil calls the world beyond the grave. And a world beyond the grave we may well call that land of the ghosts, – a book collection.

"Pisistratus," said my father one evening, as he arranged his notes before him and rubbed his spectacles, "Pisistratus, a great library is an *awful* place! There, are interred all the remains of men since the Flood."

"It is a burial-place!" quoth my Uncle Roland, who had that day found us out.

"It is an Heraclea!" said my father.

"Please, not such hard words," said the Captain, shaking his head.

"Heraclea was the city of necromancers, in which they raised the dead. Do I want to speak to Cicero? – I invoke him. Do I want to chat in the Athenian market-place, and hear news two thousand years old? – I write down my charm on a slip of paper, and a grave magician calls me up Aristophanes. And we owe all this to our ancest – "

"Ancestors who wrote books; thank you."[4]

Writing that seeks to record "real" things – views, principles, the experience of being alive, even of talking in a marketplace – constitutes a unique gateway to the past. Those who practice such writing are, in the terms of Pisistratus' father, gifted with the potential to endure life. But the conversation enables a reader to ruminate not just on historical archives of personal testimony, but indirectly on Bulwer Lytton's own book, on nineteenth-century realism-as-charm. The notion of writing's connection with the real, despite the passage of time, points subtly to the capacity of literary language to create a simulacrum of vitality that feels, truly, like vitality. There has often seemed to be something of enchantment about that.

The offer of a simulacrum of life is part of realism's promise of engagement with the real. That act of making the *dead* seem alive, however, was also among the most distinctive plots of nineteenth-century romance. Romance figures the uncanny aspirations, the best though seemingly most idealistic aspirations of realism. But for George Eliot the purposes of realism were first and foremost a dedication to the empirical fabric of life. She was not averse to the gothic or to mystery, as *The Lifted Veil* (1859) reveals. But Eliot's realism, agnostic and committed to a morality of sympathy, grows primarily from the firm ground of the new science and a faith in reason. Her realism speaks persistently of a conviction that the earth is the only subject that has a chance of being known. Fiction for Eliot is a secular experiment in recording human lives, in witnessing the results of their deeds and thoughts. It is a form of verbal vivisection with a moral purpose, undertaken in order to fortify human connections beyond the page. Eliot tells her audience in *Adam Bede* (1859), her first full-length experiment with an equivalent in writing of Dutch realist painting, that:

These fellow-mortals, every one, must be accepted as they are … I would not, even if I had the choice, be the clever novelist who could create a world so much better than this, in which we get up in the morning to do our daily work, that you would be likely to turn a harder, colder eye on the dusty streets and the common green fields – on the real breathing men and women, who can be chilled by your indifference or injured by your prejudice; who can be cheered and helped onward by your fellow-feeling, your forbearance, your outspoken, brave justice.[5]

Reading such long sentences aloud aptly exceeds the lung's capacity. The reader feels with literal immediacy, in this rebuke to the "clever novelist" of ideals, the dependence of words on breath, the very element Eliot aspired figuratively to re-create through literary language.

The major realist endeavors of the mid-century, including Eliot's, are typically concerned with rural or high-class lives. Anthony Trollope offers both in the Chronicles of Barsetshire and the Palliser novels. Elizabeth Gaskell's *North and South* (1855) tests the rural against the urban, an educated class against the laboring, while Dickens's *Great Expectations* (1860–1861), depriving rural life of newly mown, idealized charm, is the story of unexpected migration from one class to another. Political and social commentary remains the realist's concern. But those at the close of the century – George Moore, George Gissing, Thomas Hardy – propose a form of writing that takes the earlier realists' habits of tragedy (Eliot's *The Mill on the Floss* [1860], Gaskell's *Sylvia's Lovers* [1863]) into darker territory. As a practice of writing, realism addresses the sublunary; it defies supernatural claims or dimensions. The rich meaning of the lived world is realism's substance. But later realists find that meaning to be dismaying. They make the calamitous failures of human purposes and intention the basis of their disturbing narratives. An element of compelling revulsion is added to the reader's experience of a novel. Zola's audacious Rougon-Macquart novels describe a modernity both toxic and alluring, with ruthlessly unappealing individuals who also are captivating. Gissing's novels of suffering life – *The Nether World* (1889), *New Grub Street* (1891) – bring into English fiction a challenge to readers to discern purpose in human suffering, as does George Moore's most celebrated novel of the dismay, poignancy, and pleasurable misery found in unhistoric acts, *Esther Waters* (1894). Here is an influential realism that points back to Eliot's "real breathing men and women," and finds the representation of their lives to be merely idealism under another name.

Hardy's realism delights in exposing to the reader the failure of realist plots to be plausible. Realism had earlier assumed coherence in the material it narrated; it had offered credible and psychologically convincing reasons for behavior and its consequences. It had developed a sophisticated pattern – most of all in Eliot's writing – of cause and effect. But Hardy, revisiting the territory of *Adam Bede* in *Far from the Madding Crowd* (1874), makes realism pointedly indifferent to the plausibility of cause and effect by fashioning a narrative obtrusively dependent on the novelist's manipulating hand. The reader symptomatically regards Farmer Boldwood's reaction to Bathsheba's mischievous valentine as no more psychologically persuasive than Leontes' jealousy in *The Winter's Tale*. That kind of credibility is not Hardy's aim. His primary concern is with consequences, with the outcome of dramatic situations. Offering the author's guiding intent so clearly, Hardy poses a question about the shape of actual life beyond the page: are purpose and intention only to be found in the fabrications of fiction? Was the novel's fashioning of events the only consoling alternative to the unguided, unruly nature of lived experience? *Far from the Madding Crowd* does not probe those questions directly. But the questions had the potential to tip agnosticism into angst, doubtfulness into the darkly comic misery of Hardy's "God-forgotten" in *Poems of the Past and the Present* (1902).

"Everything human in the book strikes us as factitious and insubstantial," Henry James said in a celebrated rebuke to *Far from the Madding Crowd*: "the only things we believe in are the sheep and the dogs."[6] By James's standards – the psychological realism of *Washington Square* (1880) or *The Portrait of a Lady* (1880–1881) – Hardy is but a melodramatist. Yet Hardy's mode is always composite – melodrama, realism, romance are part of his eclectic, composite way of writing. *The Well-Beloved* (1897) is a peculiarly good example. Is this strange narrative of Jocelyn Pierston's obsession with an ideal that flits from lady to lady a pungent observation on a man's fickleness and self-deception? Or an allegory of a sculptor's search for an ideal's insufficiency in materialized form? Is this a tale of the supernatural or, simply, the odd? Hardy's mixed manner, the fusion of romance with realism, points to the impossibility of making easy associations between those modes and authorial attitudes. And Hardy is certainly not alone in producing and probing fusions of the two. The powerful presence of romance in the nineteenth century, from the beginning to the end, gives the realists a challenge and spur. Arguments are played out, territories marked, and sizeable claims at the close of the period are made about the validity and status of one or the other. But across the long nineteenth century, they come together in single texts in the same way that some of the Pre-Raphaelites – William Holman Hunt, John Everett Millais – use exceptional verisimilitude to illustrate scenes of imagination and myth.

Walter Scott's historical realism gestures to romance. *Kenilworth* (1821) is, indeed, subtitled *A Romance* to signify its departures from historical accuracy.

There is a gothic flavor to *The Bride of Lammermoor* (1819), and ghost stories in *Redgauntlet* (1824). Mary Shelley's *Frankenstein; or, The Modern Prometheus* (1818) and *The Last Man* (1826) are among the late Romantic period's most forceful adventures in romance, a turn from historicity as a mode in order to enable, through a prototype of science fiction, provocative considerations of modern knowledge and the Romantic politics of republicanism. Paradoxically, however, vision and imagination are unexpectedly overthrown in *The Last Man*. Political dreams, visions of better societies, founder in the novel; and the plague that takes all but the narrator Lionel's life is the poisonous antagonist of human endeavor, which wipes out humanity's traces with a fatal indifference. Imagination conjures bleakness so that romance seems for a moment a little like a plague itself. At the close the reader senses that the text hails him or her as oddly deceased, as a mere phantom too. Lionel's final lines envisage spectators of his story who are but the "spirits of the dead" beholding "the tiny bark, freighted with Verney – the LAST MAN."[7] But we are spectators of the last man and *The Last Man* as well, reading Verney's story, watching for the fate of the barque. Romance of tragic and apocalyptic gloom can only end by imaginatively denying life to its readers. It is as if there is something deadly in the imagination itself; as if literary language can neither console nor redeem nor offer an alternative world in compensation for lived life. Romance-reading here is perilous, an immersion in words that have a radical refusal to redeem.

Mary Shelley's novel is immersed in mourning for the ambitions of second-generation Romantics. *The Last Man* is, in that respect too, about the achievements of the dead, even as it looks forward to the twenty-first century. *Frankenstein* had ruminated on the exceptional possibilities of electricity as the secular breath of life. But *The Last Man*, set nearly two hundred years ahead, is about the impotence of medical science to save a race. Science does not drop out of Victorian romance. The quasi-materialist understandings of the world urged imaginative responses, startling narratives. Dickens insists that his account of the spontaneous combustion of Krook in *Bleak House* (1852–1853) is empirically defensible. He publicly denies that he has trespassed into romance even in a novel that, as he says in the preface, "purposely dwelt upon the romantic side of familiar things."[8] Spontaneous combustion is, perhaps, intended to be an example of the realistic side of unfamiliar things. Modern empirical investigation in the Victorian period, including what to modern eyes seems to be pseudo-science, offers worlds too strange to be ignored by novelists. Natural Theology taught men of science earlier that the natural world's design revealed a designer, the extraordinary mind of God. But Victorian empirical investigation and theoretical speculation stretch the extraordinary so that science itself seems to be the source of wonder. As natural philosophers working with Newtonian laws of transfer of energy considered what, precisely, energy was, Bulwer Lytton's *The Coming Race* (1871) invents a new force, Vril, as if figuring one of the marvels that science could not yet understand. Vril has a magnetic power to attract readers then and now. One of the most prominent spokesmen of the new agnostic, empirical science in mid-century, the physicist John Tyndall (1820–1893) robustly defended the "scientific use of the imagination." But nineteenth-century writers of romance have no difficulty with the imaginative use of science.

Fiction spills over into science – and science spills into fiction. Charles Kingsley's account of the natural history of marine life, *Glaucus; or, the Wonders of the Shore* (1855), offers the wonders of the natural world in the form of an empirical romance, urging the reader to understand strangeness that is true, visitable, found in rock pools. *The Water-Babies* (1862–1863), about fictional discoveries in water, provides scenes that are simultaneously enticing and repulsive in their transformation of Darwin's conception, announced in 1859, of the struggle for life through natural selection. The novel's metamorphosis of a scientist's microscopic investigation of water into a fictional investigation of fantastic life born from the mind is a dream of hygiene, a vision of cleanliness. As men of science claimed that the firmest basis of the real was that which was empirically demonstrable, so a scientific conception of the real produced daring forms of literary invention. So did mathematics. Geometry guides *Flatland: A Romance of Many Dimensions* (1884), by "A. Square" (actually the academic and headmaster Edwin Abbott). Here is a world of two dimensions where gender and class assumptions are made plainly visible – exposed, ripe for criticism – in physical shapes. Professional men and gentlemen are pentagons or squares. Women, lines. There is a mathematical playfulness with formulae in Lewis Carroll's enduringly popular *Alice* books too. His prose has all the logic of algebra – logical movements through equations to conclusions. But the fabulous creations of Wonderland also have algebra's opacity to ordinary verbal sense or reasoning. The three sisters of the Dormouse's tale in *Alice's Adventures in Wonderland* (1865) are learning to draw. They draw "everything that begins with an M – ," observes the Dormouse. Why, Alice asks sensibly, "with an M?"

> "Why not?" said the March Hare.
> Alice was silent.[9]

The logic is irrefutable but also ridiculous; it is sound and perverse. Carroll's books, with their violence and potentially terrifying vision of a world where reason stumbles against a charmingly mad sense, offer the reader a glimpse of fantasy made from its apparent opposite.

Bulwer Lytton's realist novel *The Caxtons* contemplates the voices of the dead. Romance returns to the returning dead too. Alice falling down the rabbit-hole suggests a dramatization of death. So does her passage into the mirror in *Through the Looking-Glass, and What Alice Found There* (1871). *Water-Babies* is a drowning as much as a washing fantasy. And George MacDonald's touching children's romance, *At the Back of the North Wind* (1871), delicately imagines new, half-mythic forms of writing about the grave as MacDonald's *Lilith* (1895) would, more darkly. In the gently erotic 1871 tale, the North Wind carries Diamond, the child hero, around the world, finding the place at the back of the wind where language fails to work. It is a "very good place" to be sure, when the life of the body has ceased. But MacDonald's narration is made to feel inadequate. Romance has reached a limit. "I do not know enough about it,"[10] he says of the back of the North Wind, marking a boundary between fantasy and theology, where human imagination ceases on the margin of a claim about life after death. Romance here is a form of Christian mysticism or half-myth-making (it is not hard to see why C. S. Lewis admires MacDonald). MacDonald's romance is a form of authorial assertion that earthly things, human reason, and sublunary experience are not all there is. Imagination recovers, in MacDonald's influential fantasies, something of its vatic, Romantic period identity as a way of glimpsing verities beyond the mere operation of the senses. It is reinvested with a myth of knowledge even when, in such an overtly fantastical novel as *At the Back of the North Wind*, imagination is plainly the generator of – the overtly fantastical.

The searching for lands beyond death, in a century that witnessed major shifts in the authority of Christianity, continued. Marie Corelli, in her prolifically verbal celebration of the longevity of genius, *Ardath: The Story of a Dead Self* (1889), finds reincarnation bizarrely reassuring about the integrity of Old Testament historicity. The romance works its way back through time to affirm that Judaeo-Christian scriptures are grounded in reality. But literary romance, by those without such theological purposes, envisages new ways of speaking on serious subjects all the same, about the loss of the past, the failure of life to survive beyond its natural term. Marcel Proust's multi-volume answer in *À la Recherche du temps perdu* (1913–1927, *In Search of Lost Time*) to Balzac and Zola's multi-volume endeavors to depict a whole culture, historical or contemporary, is an effort to fix in words the life of a single individual. *À la Recherche* is also an act of mourning for language's failure to do precisely that – or that, precisely. Walter Pater's *Marius the Epicurean* (1885) had been, before Proust, an intriguing English version of a philosophical biography. George Du Maurier's romance *Peter Ibbetson* (1891), ruminating on a hope that experience is not lost but stored in an ongoing, indestructible memory, suggests the exceptional power of the mind to recall the past that Proust would more plainly recognize. Memory as figured in *Ibbetson* is like a collective phonograph, a mental faculty akin to Svengalian hypnosis in Du Maurier's *Trilby* (1894) that shows human powers to be outside ordinary science's grasp. "Dreaming true," as *Ibbetson* puts it, is the name of this extraordinary memory that is not a recollection of an individual's life alone, but of his or her ancestors too. To "dream true" is to enable a return, in time travel, even as far back as the age of the mammoth. Such dreaming permits communication with the dead: it is not the promise but the achievement of restoration. Du Maurier's romance is as entranced by secular ways of imagining the continuation of the dead as, in the realist mode, *The Caxtons* is, with its sense of a library full of voices. *Ibbetson* imagines the preservation of *temps perdu*, and romance there dreams of what, later, Proust endeavors to obtain in his celebrated realist immersion in the individual consciousness and his obsession with language's opportunity to re-create a sense of personal interiority.

The dead make themselves felt in Margaret Oliphant's supernatural romances. It is the past's capacity to heal in *The Beleaguered City* (1879) that underlies a narrative of the ghosts of ancestors who protest against a French city's abandonment of Christian worship. The supernatural is self-evident here. But, in Henry James's enigmatic tales, the supernatural may not be there at all. Readable perhaps as psychological realism, as investigations of unbalanced minds, romance in James's hands might just be a realist account of the pathological. In "The Art of Fiction" (1884) James advises novelists to "Try and catch the colour of life itself."[11] But what kinds of life, perhaps, flit through *The Turn of the Screw* (1898) or what supernatural energies are exchanged in *The Sacred Fount* (1901)? The narrations, confined to a single individual's viewpoint, decline to answer. Is the theorist-narrator of *The Sacred Fount* really "crazy,"[12] as Mrs. Briss calls him? We cannot be sure. Realism and romance are held together in a simultaneity of opposites. These are tales like the particles revealed by quantum mechanics that are, in effect, in two places at once.

Modes mixed in different ways: realism asks, paradoxically, for a greater leap of imaginative faith than romance; science provides a new definition of the real that, in the nineteenth century, sustains new forms of fantasy; in their aspirations to recover the past and hear the voices of the dead, romance and realism share similar ambitions; and the torsion of James's romances comes from their capacity to be read as realist too. Elsewhere, the two modes overlap in single novels in other, original forms. The realism of *Adam Bede* gives way to the realism-and-gothic of *Daniel Deronda*, with its rehabilitation of the heroic quest. *Deronda* is Eliot's realist-sensation novel as, earlier, *Jane Eyre* (1847) is Charlotte Brontë's realist-gothic novel. Trollope, a committed realist, rarely relinquishes entirely the possibilities of romance. As he is pleased to conjure a delightfully stagey villain in Obadiah Slope in the Barchester series, so his political novels are shaped by other impulses of romance. He maintains an aura of fantasy in his imaginings of Parliament, and Plantagenet Palliser, the government's best knight, is more a product of a dream than of the difficult realities of modern politics. The air of Shakespeare's *The Tempest* lingers over the end of the Palliser series, in the almost fairy-tale reconciliations and renewals of *The Duke's Children* (1879–1880).

Robert Louis Stevenson's romances include *Treasure Island* (1883) and *The Dynamiter* (1885), a terrorist story suggesting Conrad's *The Secret Agent* (1907, but set in 1886). *Kidnapped* (1886) draws on historical sources while turning to the adventure narrative for shape. Adventure is territory that Alexandre Dumas *père* and his co-author Auguste Maquet had made their own in mid-century France with the musketeer novels, though they too draw richly on historical sources. In Great Britain, G. A. Henty (whose novels include *By Sheer Pluck, a Tale of the Ashanti War*, 1884), H. Rider Haggard, Arthur Conan Doyle, Anthony Hope (of *The Prisoner of Zenda*, 1894 and *Rupert of Hentzau*, 1898), and John Buchan (of *The Thirty-Nine Steps*, 1915) are among those who provide both the homelands and empire with unputdownable adventure narratives, tense stories bound by the logic of fast-paced unitary plots to which more or less everything contributes. (The *Oxford English Dictionary* gives the first instance of "unputdownable" as 1947 – but that was a late arrival for a well-established reading experience.) This gathering of authors helped make romance into a marketable commodity in late Victorian culture, and helped define popular publishing in distinction from the perceived high culture of the realist tradition.

The relationship between popular publishing and high culture, as it is channeled into debates about the nature of romance, can, unsurprisingly, be fractious. H. Rider Haggard's "About Fiction" in the *Contemporary Review* (1887) questions the quality of much that is published, and promotes the durability of romance and its role as a bedrock of literary value. A well-honed romance is, he says audaciously, "perhaps the most difficult art practised by the sons of men."[13] He later regrets saying such a thing. But Haggard remains publicly confident that romance will always attract readers, and that is the best testimony of its enduring strength. Even so stern a judge of literary value as F. R. Leavis admits that longevity indicates worth. Henry James, champion of fiction's ability to figure life, had earlier concentrated attention politely on realism. He observes that others thought the future of fiction was with romance too. Stevenson "would prefer," he remarks, "in a word, any day in the week, Alexandre Dumas to

Honoré de Balzac."[14] But the Jamesian novel is, in intention, imbued with Balzacian life. In "A Humble Remonstrance" (1884), Stevenson responds. He proposes affably that the attempt to compete with life is not what fiction is about. Life is "monstrous, infinite, illogical, abrupt and poignant," he says (his own, certainly, was some of those things): "a work of art, in comparison, is neat, finite, self-contained, rational, flowing and emasculate." What is important is simplicity and the coherence obtained by fiction's "one creative and control-ling thought."[15] Life tips beyond patterns. But the best novels are those taut with the drama of a single, unified plot, in which not a word fails to contribute to the drama's progress and denouement. That is, apart from anything else, quite a good description of *Treasure Island*. James and Stevenson's argument, insofar as it is partly concerned with realism and romance, is primarily a discussion between themselves about their own art. But, both at the national level and in the details of their own writing, their friendly disagreement in *Longman's Magazine* is under-cut by the readiness with which novelists, including James and Stevenson, cross between modes, reaching both for the contact of realism with the lived world and the thrill, focus, and imaginative energy of romance.

F. R. Leavis sensibly maintains the distinction between a novel of ideas and a novel that merely discusses ideas.[16] H. G. Wells's effort to bring science and adventure together afresh at the end of the nineteenth century, if it places him in the second category, marks, nevertheless, a further popular stage of the develop-ment of the romance-realist fusion into tough political fantasy. The conception of the ideological work of a romance–realism fusion inspires William Morris in *News from Nowhere* (1890) and, across the Atlantic, Edward Bellamy in the visionary *Looking Backward: 2000–1887* (1888). In *A Modern Utopia* (1904–1905) Wells brings fantasy into contact with feisty political polemic that proposes headline messages more than detailed analysis, and *In the Days of the Comet* (1906) fuses radical political rumination on the nature of utopia and obviously "mod-ern" urban realism with the romance fantasy of earth's contact with the healing vapors of a comet. The result is a socialist vision that is as convinced of under-lying harmony and order in the world as any work of eighteenth- or nineteenth-century Natural Theology. Fashioning the genre of science fiction, a distinctive form of romance for the twentieth century, Wells corrals science, socialism, and dream into influential form.

Yet literary readers at the end of the nineteenth century read more than literature. Victorian print culture underwent startling expansion. And those readers who knew Stevenson's conversation with James, or Haggard's argu-ment with him, might have recognized a version of those same debates in daily reading on the omnibus, the under- or over-ground railway, the breakfast room, the office. Forms of serial publication at the end of the nineteenth century are plural and they include the flourishing dailies, the newspapers that are products of changes in financial regulation, printing technology, and distribution systems. The newspapers fashioned the concept of "news" and they set the pace for the up-to-dateness and modernity of other forms of periodical publications dependent on them. What was realism and what romance is a question that mattered here as it mattered on the bookshelves. If the newspaper and the range of modern periodicals are the embodiments of the late nineteenth century's enthrallment with what is fashionable and current, with ephemeral experiences *de nos jours*, they are also caught up in politicized and moral argument about what might be knowledge.

No wonder novelists were interested. Anthony Trollope's *The Warden* (1855) had, early on, mused on the power of *The Times* – there called *The Jupiter* – to intervene and shape. "Why should we look to Lord John Russell;" the narrator says, "– why should we regard Palmerston and Gladstone, when Tom Towers [of *The Jupiter*] without a struggle can put us right?"[17] It is an (ironic) claim for a paper's omnipotence in politics and reform; its all-seeing knowledge of real things and capacity for right judgment. These are the decades after Jean Auguste Dominique Ingres had given to the nineteenth century, in his portrait of the journalist Louis-François Bertin (1833), what became an iconic image of modern democracy's new heroes. Yet the notion of a new hero belongs, too, in the world of romance. Journalism and romance are tangled up. Some journalists at the end of the century, W. T. Stead among them, publicly develop their profession's link with the quest, the slaying of contemporary dragons; and play the heroes of their own investigative profession. Some are not averse to deploying their imagination to liven up their reporting, to turn it into a form of entertainment. Guy de Maupassant's *Bel-Ami* (1885) is devastating on the role of falsity in the allegedly trustworthy press. Stead stirs serious controversy over the factuality of his 1885 reports on "The Maiden Tribute of Modern Babylon." And Gissing's journalists in *New Grub Street* find the concept of the modern press dependent on partial information. Neither wholly romance nor realism, there is a form of writing for the "quarter educated." These, Gissing's Whelpdale says, are the men and women who care "for no newspapers except the Sunday ones; what they want is the lightest and frothiest of chit-chatty information – bits of stories, bits of description, bits of scandal, bits of jokes, bits of statistics, bits of foolery."[18] Circulating in contemporary culture, such forms of print are in danger of constituting anything but serious knowledge, even as they are partly rooted in the actual. Endeavoring to depict a key moment in the development of human knowledge in a culture of print media, *New Grub Street* advances itself, a work of fiction, as a more adequate, clear-eyed, and comprehensive guide to the condition of the modern moment than those journalists who claim to traffic in the real for the sake of entertainment.

Biffen, in *New Grub Street*, announces he will write a novel with a quintessential realist title: *Mr. Bailey, Grocer.* "'What's the idea?'" he is asked. "'An objectionable word, that,'" he responds: "'Better say: "What's the reality?"'" (243). In such an exchange the romance/realism argument is epitomized. But if *New Grub Street* is dedicated to the depiction of the hard reality of urban life, in the same way that *Mr. Bailey, Grocer* is, it is important to note that Gissing includes the failure of Biffen's novel with reviewers, who cite its lack of a great romance element: a plot. A "novelist's first duty is to tell a story" (522), shout the newspaper critics in Gissing's novel. They are annoyed by the preponderance of the real in Biffen's text over the pleasures of artistic shape, over story, the drive of sequence, and Stevenson's kind of clear narrative purpose. Realism and romance are inseparable but also at odds in this dissection of how human lives in the midst of grim realities are caught up in fantasies.

The Private Papers of Henry Ryecroft (1903) takes Gissing's preoccupation with the aesthetic and moral meanings of the romance/realism contrast and conjunction into new territory. *The Private Papers* might have been the personal journal that *New Grub Street*'s Edwin Reardon, the doomed writer struggling to make his name, could have written had things worked out. The notes of Ryecroft, a once-struggling author who is now able to retire thanks to a private benefaction, describe a life of ease: he has acquired a perfect housekeeper, books, nature, pleasant solitude, and time for literary rumination. But is this romance or realism? Gissing's silent question is unmissable. No reader can avoid the sharp irony in considering Ryecroft's days of pleasure: a life achieved by a writer of limited accomplishment. Here is privilege from unearned income, wealth from patronage not print. The narrator's reflections are, in turn, saturated with obtrusive irony. "More than half a century of existence," Ryecroft says with characteristic airiness and lack of self-knowledge:

> has taught me that most of the wrong and folly which darken earth is due to those who cannot possess their souls in quiet; that most of the good which saves mankind from destruction comes of life that is led in thoughtful stillness. [19]

Caught up in Gissing's apparently realist prose, Ryecroft is living in a world of romance. As a model for human society, his recommendation is merely impertinent. His own life, freed from the deprivations of Grub Street, is only made possible by a gift. His idle dreaming obscures the foundations of his circumstances; his political recommendations are grounded in a privilege he ignores.

Questions about literary mode are transformed into issues about the writer's life, about the moral failure of living in romance and mistaking it for realism.

Deciding between the two modes of romance and realism is a matter of ethical consequence for Gissing. Recognizing the imaginary in the newspapers is, he thinks, part of a necessary alertness in modern culture to what claims language can make to represent an actuality; discerning what is romance in Henry Ryecroft's account of himself is a matter of moral assessment of a man's life. Realism and romance in the nineteenth century remain distinctive – and they merge into compound forms. But both persistently involve questions about what acts of belief the novel invites, evaluations of the knowledge obtained from writing, and consideration of the pleasures and rewards of reading fiction. For the history and understanding of the English novel, such things do not cease to matter.

Notes

1. Sir Walter Scott, *Waverley*, 2 vols. (Edinburgh: Jack, 1901), vol. i, p. 84.
2. Émile Zola, *Oeuvres complètes*, 12 vols. (Paris: Cercle du livre précieux, 1966–1969), vol. viii, p. 68. "Ah! See everything and paint everything" (my translation).
3. George Eliot, *Middlemarch* (Oxford University Press, 1996), p. 785.
4. Edward Bulwer Lytton, *The Caxtons* (New York: Century, 1902), p. 125.
5. George Eliot, *Adam Bede* (Harmondsworth: Penguin, 1980), p. 222.
6. Henry James, *The Nation* 19 (December 24, 1874), 423–424, 424.
7. Mary Shelley, *The Last Man* (Oxford: Oxford University Press, 1994), p. 470.
8. Charles Dickens, *Bleak House* (Harmondsworth: Penguin, 1971), p. 43.
9. Lewis Carroll, *Alice's Adventures in Wonderland* and *Through the Looking-Glass and What Alice Found There* (Oxford University Press, 1971), p. 67.
10. George MacDonald, *At the Back of the North Wind* (Ware: Wordsworth, 1994), p. 119.
11. Henry James, *The Critical Muse: Selected Literary Criticism* (Harmondsworth: Penguin, 1987), p. 206.
12. Henry James, *The Sacred Fount* (Harmondsworth: Penguin, 1994), p. 187.
13. H. Rider Haggard, "About Fiction," *Contemporary Review* 51 (1887), 172–180, 172.
14. Henry James, "Robert Louis Stevenson," *Century Magazine* 35 (1888), 809–879, 877.
15. Robert Louis Stevenson, *Memories and Portraits* (London: Chatto and Windus, 1887), p. 249.
16. F. R. Leavis, *The Great Tradition* (London: Chatto and Windus, 1948), p. 7.
17. Anthony Trollope, *The Warden* (Harmondsworth: Penguin, 1984), p. 119.
18. George Gissing, *New Grub Street* (Harmondsworth: Penguin, 1998), p. 496.
19. George Gissing, *The Private Papers of Henry Ryecroft* (London: Constable, 1912), pp. 13–14.

31

Spaces and places (II): around the globe

DAVID JAMES

Geographies of nineteenth-century narrative

In the Victorian era the English novel unsettles conventions of representation. It does so by favoring stories about unsettled, displaced characters, and by disturbing its readers with uncomfortable depictions of imperialism abroad. The interlinked levels – formal, figurative, interpretive – through which we can approach the novel's engagement with colonial spaces provide myriad ways of surveying Victorian narratives of empire.

A familiar kind of survey operates at a diegetic level, tracing geopolitical events and foreign or domestic environments as they resonate within the plots of Victorian colonial fiction. A less familiar approach would retell the story of the novel's imperial contexts through a more aesthetically oriented account of its formal tendencies. This alternative approach, which I essay here, does not dispense with literary-political connections; but it does compel us to question linear or evolutionary models of the novel's development from a solely thematic point of view. It provides instead a map of narrative strategies organized by discrete phases of stylistic innovation. Rather than rehearse the assumption that writers become symptoms of their age – producing fiction that passively or unconsciously reflects a time of increasing anxiety about the Empire's legitimacy – we would do better to consider this geopolitical climate from a writerly point of view by exploring the extent to which novelists develop new modes, or test existing ones, for responding to colonial governance.

Concerns about how geographies are described, and to what aesthetic and ideological ends, loom as large for Victorian writers as for those in any period of the English novel. Michel de Certeau assures us that "Every story is a travel story," in one of his most quotable yet vague assertions about textual space.[1] But spatial theory might not altogether unpack the distinctiveness of literary landscapes in classic nineteenth-century realism. I am minded to steer clear of the temptation to invoke space as a tropological abstraction, in order to open

500

the way to a formally precise understanding of how geographies shape narrative experiments. I eschew the usual chronological path, stretching from Sydney Owenson's early portrait of the compromised missionary, to mid-century stories of Eastern fellowship (as W. D. Arnold views them in 1853 amid "the Elysian fields of exiled imagination"),[2] to emerging fictions of Empire's decline that bring literary modernism, via Conrad, into contact with nascent decolonization. Likewise, to perceive Victorian fiction from a purely thematic perspective as a series of imperialist parables is to overlook or distort innovations that writers pursue. *How* novelists register the social, prophetic, and experiential consequences of imperial systems will be my key concern as I consider novelists writing about British sovereignty or about populations or places beyond its ostensible rule.

Victorian writers did not need to go abroad to examine empire's ideological self-justifications. Imperial infrastructures implicitly or allusively parallel manifestations of expansionism, as debates on English soil take the thematic place of fully actualized scenes of foreign events. Mid-century novels from Charlotte Brontë's *Jane Eyre* (1847) and *Villette* (1853) to Thackeray's *The Newcomes* (1853–1855) exemplify how narratives with a domestic ambit connect (at the level of character or economic context) with the ramifications of imperialism abroad. As scholars of Victorian industrial fiction have shown, there is more to the localized concerns of such a reportorial novelist as Benjamin Disraeli, writing in the aftermath of the East India Company. Disraeli's *Sybil* (1844) gestures to India's potential as a burgeoning market resource from the perspective of regional struggle, emblematizing the way mid-Victorian novelists could merge two *scales* of socio-political commentary: combining the criticism of those economic and familial effects of industrialism with an ongoing nationwide interest in Britain's strategic operations abroad.

Disraeli has vested interests in debating in fiction how Britain's imperial leadership might benefit or retrench indigenous working conditions. Given the primacy of debate for Disraeli, the "condition of England novel" – however realist – remains one discursive forum among many for his polemic. Public oratory offers him a proactive medium through which to endorse his prospectus for empire's advancement. In the famous 1872 Crystal Palace speech, Disraeli regards the era of ethnic integration as imminent; but he sidesteps this, praising instead the infrastructure of upward mobility. For inheritors of Britain's colonial enterprise, opportunities for international esteem are there for the taking. "England will have to decide between national and cosmopolitan principles," declares Disraeli. The choice is between a future in which "comfortable England" is "modelled and moulded upon Continental principles" or one in which England continues the growth of "a great country, – an Imperial country – a country where your sons, when they rise, rise to paramount positions, and obtain not merely the esteem of their countrymen, but command the respect of the world."[3]

At the end of the 1870s George Eliot rehearses her skepticism toward cosmopolitanism. In "The Modern Hep! Hep! Hep!" (1879) she addresses those "who have feeling and understanding enough to be conscious of the connection between the patriotic affection and every other affection which lifts us above emigrating rats and free-loving baboons."[4] It is easy to misconstrue the tenor of this essay, constructed as it is through typological assertions in which cataloguing innate human traits causes Eliot's rhetoric to sail close to racism. In impulse the essay complements Disraeli's way of enunciating social propositions under the ruse of salient reminders – the imperative being to warn the population not to forget how Britain assumed the global stature that it has. Leaving their political differences aside, there is a common tonal infusion of cautionary prophecy and rearguard nationalism that inflects Disraeli's and Eliot's respective notions of England's "inevitable fate," an infusion revealing how the "terms and visions of monumental history are central to narratives and practices of the modern state and nation."[5]

Eliot, however, implies more than Disraeli does a distinction between the obligations of state policy to foreign members to whom trade has indelibly bonded Britain, and the monumentality of the nation's image as it might appear to its colonies. It is a distinction that suggests a need to address English integrity as something that transcends the contingencies of everyday political or economic decision-making. And Eliot's preservation of the abstraction of Englishness allows her to re-emphasize the changing roles facing individuals in what is fast becoming a new transnational order, where the colonized can no longer be compartmentalized into racial types if they are to be equal citizens of a global web of responsibility (to adapt Eliot's own renowned metaphor for interconnectedness). Insofar as Eliot's treatment of national conduct concedes that England's "historic rapacity" (404) is inevitable rather than wholly reproachable, she wants to correct the damage wrought by empire but without unequivocally condemning the memory of British supremacy – a memory that needs preserving if England's future is to be secure as a standard of cohesion for other nations in a time of ethnic displacement. For her it is "living force of sentiment in common which makes a national consciousness." A sense of "common humanity" detached from nationality "is not yet enough to feed the rich blood of various activity which makes a complete man." Eliot concludes with the caution that the "time is not come for cosmopolitanism to be highly virtuous, any more than of communism to suffice for social energy" (405).

Eliot champions an "attachment to nationality" (406) by elevating "national consciousness" above the measurable outcomes of geopolitical action. This investment in the organicist conception of nationhood as a "living force" anticipates Ernest Renan's insistence that "The nation, like an individual, is the culmination of a long past of endeavours, sacrifice, and devotion." Eliot concurs with Renan's equation of personal belonging and shared heritage. He argues that the nation represents "a large-scale solidarity, constituted by the feeling of the sacrifices that one has made in the past and of those one is prepared to make in the future."[6] So if Eliot confuses ethnic constitution with ideological action – when she unfavorably equates cosmopolitan coexistence with communism's enforced unanimity – this conflation forms part of her world view. Rather than highlight the idea that England faces a model of community based on racial equity (not just imported resources or other spoils of empire), and that in time this might be productive for English life, Eliot finds it easier to obviate the prospect of inter-ethnic cooperation (whether locally or transnationally) so as to retain the ideality of British self-identification, whose "absence is a privation of the greatest good" (406). Whereas Disraeli equates healthy nationhood with material growth, Eliot downplays economic progress in favor of a vision of secular spiritual solidarity: "national consciousness" as collective faith.

Contrasts between Disraeli and Eliot, even where they share common ground, illustrate the ideologically complex, self-conscious, often cautious senti-ments that shape the geography of nineteenth-century narrative. Such senti-ments resist the received image of Victorian fiction as an immediately mimetic replica of imperial economic and cultural relations, and they necessitate a sensitive account of how writers' responses to Britain's imperial future in turn inform novelistic techniques. In his late work Edward Said reaffirms this need to remain alive to colonialism's implications for *aesthetic* practices, urging us to trace how "different kinds of novels derive some of their aesthetic rationale from changes taking place in the geography and landscape as the result of social contest."[7] Said's sentiments resonate with recent dialogues between literary historians and cultural geographers, who have usefully debated the options for coordinating our readings of material place with those of symbolic or textual space. These metacritical concerns compel us to acknowledge how important it is "not only to discuss space and geography thematically, but also to address them as questions with a profound impact upon how literary and cultural texts are formally assembled."[8] Such is the force with which landscapes shape narrative design. The hero of John Buchan's *Prester John* (1910) exclaims, "Since I came to Blaauwildebeestefontein I had forgotten the mystery I had set out to track in excitement of a new life."[9] Here in capsule form we have confirmation of the power of place to revise original intentions or to divert narrative emplotment and expression down unanticipated paths. Such interactions between landforms and novelistic forms will occupy me here, beginning with the most deceptively rudimentary – because entirely necessary – aspect of Victorian fiction's spatial *poiesis*: description. As a way of making sense of the importance of description, I start where things begin: with writers who use prefaces and other paratexts to spotlight their capacity to describe colonial environments.

Framing empire

Henry Moreton Stanley's preface to *My Kalulu: Prince, King, and Slave: A Story of Central Africa* (1873) opens with a disclaimer:

> In a book of travels some readers prefer the adventures, the incidents of the chase; others prefer what relates to the ethnography of the country; others, geography; others dip into it for matters concerning philology. The person who reads the whole book through is one interested in the subject, or is attracted by its style.[10]

Stanley's anticipative approach to the preferences of his audience enters an established habit of prefatory addresses: an idiom of authorial admission and preemption adopted by Victorian novelists who openly scrutinize their attempts at describing other continents, even before their readers reach an opening chapter. We may see this authorial self-consciousness as resulting from the challenges of reconciling description and action, setting and characterization – challenges heightened by the obligation to detail "the ethnography of the country" while also sustaining our interest in "the incidents of the chase." Stanley admits that all this may be executed at the expense of organic form, for some readers will take to a narrative's "subject," others will be engaged purely "by its style." He seems to acknowledge this severance of matter and manner as the challenge of depicting African "adventures." It gives us pause when looking ahead at how intensely Conrad regards stylization as an index of experiencing colonized continents first hand, because for him style is *not* something that readers can take an interest in without confronting the compulsions and anxieties it discloses.

Of Stanley's antecedents, Mrs. General M. Mainwaring's preface to *The Suttee; or, the Hindu Converts* (1830) is among the most uncomfortable. It opens on a cautionary note, offering an apologia for the extent to which the novel might contradict a reader's expectation that it endorse an imperialist distinction of degrees of civility along racial lines:

> It may be considered requisite, by those who condescend to read this work, to offer some apology for adorning the Hindoo family ... with so many virtues, previous to their conversion to the Christian faith; more particularly, as some of the eminent writers of the present day have represented them in a very different way.[11]

Here the perceived threat has not to do (as it does for Stanley) with the reader's freely choosing among textual components, so much as with the novel's danger to itself, in that its descriptions of indigenous life run the risk of picturing a Hindu community that is so civilized as to disqualify any justification for their conversion to Christian virtue. Seeking to anticipate concerns by "those who condescend to read this work" about how appropriately demeaned the colonized appear in the depiction, the preface expresses an authorial anxiety about how a novel's connotative capacities ultimately exceed any control a writer can exert through the framing remarks of a preface.

Rather than give the wrong impression about the balance of power, Mainwaring's preface intervenes – before one gets to the opposite end of the novel, wherein, with the new converts in tow, the British fleet disembarks. When "some of the sailors, in white dresses, quickly manned the yards" (vol. III, 225), Mainwaring offers a sweeping cross-section of Britain's imperial machinery in action. The profusion of crew members swarming to perform duties with military precision allegorizes in miniature the kind of totalizing governance that protects a colony for what it is. This picture of a programmed duty-to-patriotism is all but enhanced by the impersonality of Mainwaring's narrative voice, as she blankly tracks the way sailors "took their respective stations, some at guns, some ranged on deck – all in a moment were standing still as statues, silent as death, the officers in their full uniform, their noble English faces glowing with the conscious pride of naval superiority" (vol. III, 225). While Mainwaring intends this to be a celebratory representation, it appears that empire's proficiency, far from liberating the English members of its workforce, turns them into automatons.

Other writers put English "naval superiority" to the test. Captain (Frederick) Marryat does so in the guise of a coming-of-age adventure yarn. Alongside Marryat's affinity with the genre of daring colonial excursion, he anticipates Conrad's preoccupation with expeditions as existential self-enquiries, where travel for such characters as Willems, Almayer, and Marlow means confronting the terror of their undiscovered selves. In *The Mission, or Scenes in Africa* (1845) Marryat mixes zoological commentary, potted histories of imperial conquest, and conjecture about the alternative conduct of colonial governance – all filtered through the awe with which Alexander surveys each new episode. That awe germinates in England, where Alexander's fascination with the fate of *The*

Grosvenor's crew, wrecked off the South African coast, shuttles him between excited response to rumor and abstracted contemplation of a world map, until he takes matters into his own hands, and his empirical quest begins.

The wonderment of this youthful observer – in response to immediate environments once he reaches Africa, and in introverted moments of trepidation – is reflected in the narrative discourse, which alternates between spatial documentary and introspection. Marryat intermittently shades into an early version of free indirect style, achieving the same "limpidity of expression" that for Ford Madox Ford made Conrad's "prose seem like the sound of some one talking in a rather low voice into the ear of a person that he liked."[12] When Alexander disembarks the narrative lens turns from sea to mind. Speaking in the "low" tones that Ford would praise in Conrad, Marryat notes that Alexander's "thoughts may be easily imagined," before ventriloquizing his consternation: "Shall I ever see that land [England] again? Shall I ever return, or shall my bones remain in Africa, perhaps not even buried, but bleaching in the desert?"[13]

A comparative calculation of those risks becomes Alexander's self-justification, his way of legitimizing an excursion based purely in his romantic thrill of encountering African wilderness. That thrill has had to be quelled in the presence of his English guardian, Sir Charles Wilmot, to whom he justifies the voyage as practical rather than perilous. Thanks to the imperial missionary project, Africa now seems as close to home as Europe:

> The continual emigration since the Cape has fallen under British government, and the zeal of those who have braved all dangers to make known the Word of God to the heathen and idolater, have in forty years made such an alteration, that I see no more danger in the mission which I propose, than I do in a visit to Naples ... (14)

Something of that brash confidence in the path across continents that the British administration has built survives on his outgoing vessel, and as it "rapidly approached the Cape" (49), Alexander is in high spirits. He agrees to set sail again for Algoa Bay, a threshold zone "gathering in a small space" English emigrants "all united in one feeling, instigated by the same desire, that of independence, and if possible, of wealth" (57–58).

However, the eager "debarkation" of those "beginning a new life" (58) is contrasted in Alexander's perspective with the inscrutable and unpredictable image of the land into which they venture. Presenting itself as "a dark opaque mass" (57), this animistic terrain retains autonomy throughout the novel – figuratively and physically. This is later reflected grammatically, as Marryat tracks alterations in setting through sentences that consign characters to subordinate phrases, especially in moments when "the landscape changed its appearance" (229). The setting assumes grammatical agency over its observers, a power reversal played out at the level of the sentence that effectively – though albeit inadvertently for Marryat – undermines the logic of the mid-Victorian heroic quest. The encountered geography has the potential not only to compromise characters' abilities to comprehend what they perceive, but also to set the novelist a new creative challenge of turning that very perceptual compromise into a source of formal and dramatic interest.

"I tried to give a photograph": classic realism abroad

For *The Mission*'s hero "Everything is comparative" (290). His sentiment encapsulates how essential it is for the novelist to maintain familiar yet vital comparisons between self and other, English pastoralism and African wilderness, even if those contrasts are made only to the sovereign benefit of the English denominators. The comparisons are shallow, because nothing is exposed to the dialectal scrutiny that presumed differences entail. Their purpose is that of reassurance – to reinforce the primacy of national consciousness. Idealized as an ontological abstraction, nationhood can be perceived as a time-honored condition, whose vitality is less dependent upon the immediate pressures of world-historical events than upon personal cultivation of civic patriotism. How to depict this tension between that individualized "activity which makes a complete man," in Eliot's phrase, and the collectively felt ramifications of connecting with Britain's colonial others, is a task that falls to later nineteenth-century novelists.

A little over twenty years after the Imperial Assemblage where the appointment of Queen Victoria as "India's Empress" was confirmed, Flora Annie Steel's *On the Face of the Waters* (1896) scrutinizes the climate of rule in India, following Britain's takeover of a feudal country perceived to be incapable of governing itself in light of generations of invasions and Mughal control. By looking ahead to her novel's survey of the effects of colonial institutions on personal beliefs, Steel contributes to the "genre" of the confessional preface that I address above. She admits that hers is a book "which, in attempting to be at once a story and a history, probably fails in either aim."[14] Continuing with the assurance that "I have not allowed fiction to interfere with fact in the slightest degree," Steel signals to the way "the sham court at Delhi . . . did not need a single touch of fancy in its presentment" (Preface, v). She thereby establishes recourse to "fact" as the grounds, through this prefatory demotion of her own capabilities, upon which we are to value the novel. Steel closes by explaining that she has "tried to give a photograph – that is, a picture in which the differentiation caused by the colour is left out – of a time which neither the fair race nor the dark one is ever likely quite to forget or to forgive" (Preface, vi).

A stripped-down version of classic realism – where the less intricately painted scenes will become the most memorable and uncompromising – is what Steel aspires to. Yet the final product behaves more colorfully, because the democratic "photograph" to which she likens her prose offers a misleading correlative for the pictorial adornments of *On the Face of the Waters*. That is to say, if historical events and places are framed in almost documentary terms, for the *experience* of those situations Steel evidently allows herself more stylistic license:

> The sun sent golden gleams over the short turf worn to dustiness by crowding feet, and the long curves of the river, losing themselves on either side among green fields and mango trees, shone like a burnished shield. On the opposite bank, its minarets showing fragile as cut paper against the sky, rose the Chutter Munzil – the deposed King's favourite palace. Behind it, above the belt of trees dividing the high Residency gardens from the maze of houses and hovels still occupied by the hangers-on to the late Court, the English flag drooped lazily in the calm floods of yellow light. (3)

Even though the scene emerges through the dissolving of figure into ground, topography into metaphor, where a river's defining "curves" merge into the more luminously indistinct "shield" of its reflection – despite this dissolution of line and scale, the prospect offers a pointed tableau. Steel's all-seeing, expansive narrative lens pans round from natural surroundings to the architectural center-piece of occupied territory, the limp ensign of imperialism contrasted some-what grotesquely with the sun's regal "gleams."

Striking this balance between denotation and symbolic insinuation becomes the defining trait of Conrad's incipient impressionism, showcased the year before the appearance of *On the Face of the Waters*, in *Almayer's Folly* (1895). Here, as for Steel, the "bright sunshine of the clear mistless morning" forms not only an illuminating backdrop to Almayer's residence but a central coordinate that "flooded the main path of the settlement" and under whose illuminating rays all other scenic features are arrayed:

> The path was deserted this morning; it stretched its dark yellow surface, hard beaten by the tramp of many bare feet, between clusters of palm trees, whose tall trunks barred it with strong black lines at irregular intervals, while the newly risen sun threw the shadows of their leafy heads far away over the roofs of buildings lining the river, even over the river itself as it flowed swiftly and silently past the deserted houses.[15]

Anticipating Steel's slicing shift in scale from sun to land surfaces ("worn to dustiness by crowding feet"), Conrad's accretive syntax also dissolves distinctions between figure and ground by allowing the earth itself to bear the remnants of absent figures, recently "beaten by the tramp of many bare feet." For both writers the natural landscape is an anthropomorphic presence, and they use light in a manner reminiscent of Kipling's sunlight in *Kim* (1901), "driving broad golden spokes through the lower branches of the mango-trees."[16]

Such scenes instantiate the critical function of crepuscular poetics. Twilight interludes establish a correspondence between literary making and social conduct, rhetorical intensification and intersubjectivity, appearing as a contrast, as Christopher R. Miller writes, "between poetic composition and other forms of work, as a slippage between a pastoral idea of beauty and tranquility and the actual conditions of thought and utterance."[17] In the dwindling light we are drawn closer to the reflecting mind of the character who witnesses the evening spectacle; we are also made aware of the distance between sublimity and conduct, between beautiful (tropical) prospects and the savagery of their imperial occupation. For Conrad landscapes are more than just picturesque. Places are never simply backcloths in his fiction, and nature remains for him the most dramatic antithesis to human vacancy. For Steel, likewise, settings are at once metaphorical and functional, at once visually immersive and intercut with circumstantial information. But like her great impressionist contemporary, Steel intensifies the resources of realist narration to delineate the furrows of indigenous countryside – thereby running the risk, in evoking natural features in aestheticized terms, of finessing the scars of colonial possession.

Formal frontiers of pastoralism: prospects, panoramas, and the novelist's virtuosity

Moving among the particulars of flora, landform, and light, and the portentous, if somewhat universalized, insignias of imperialism (generalities typified by "droop[ing]" flag), Steel builds criticisms of imperialism into the sensual evocation of Indian topography. This synthetic strategy also allows her to ironize, as she does in *Voices in the Night* (1900), the exoticization of the panoramas she frames by characters who thrive on the way the "environment of India had a trick of giving an air of distinction to the Anglo-Saxon."[18] But if panoramic description was a crucial narratological feature of imperialist fiction – every reader, after all, requires and indeed expects cartographical context – then the proportioning of potentially broad-brush prospect visions is far from politically neutral. If Romita Ray is right to remind us that "Art-making in the colonial setting coincided with the development of theories of the picturesque in England," then it seems important to explore the aesthetic and ideological ends to which panoramas are deployed.[19]

This emphasis on evoking domains of control in ocular terms indeed verges on the charming and the picturesque. Going against the grain of chronological analysis, we can find an early precedent in Sydney Owenson's *The Missionary* (1811), a narrative that anticipates Victorian experimenters who invoke pastoral modes to open up new avenues for novelistic realism. On a characterological plane, Owenson's intercultural encounters dramatize the emergence of what Jeffrey Cox calls "competing narratives of conquest and anticonquest," which provide contested visions of "the creation of a new Christian synthesis of East and West in a new Alexandria."[20] At a formal level, however, Owenson incorporates the language of sensibility, writing as a precursor to mid-Victorian sensation fiction by employing opulent spatial imagery to convert physical places – as the preliminary episodes of Hilarion's evangelical journey east progresses – into intensified sensory realms.

The journey stretches "from Tatta to Lahore, by the course of the Indus, and from Lahore to the province of Cashmire." And it is this region that forms "the peculiar object of [Hilarion's] mission," shimmering as "an idea," more so than a literal place, and "belonging to that higher order of genius, which grasps, by a single view, what mediocrity contemplates in detail."[21] Owenson's concentration on intense psychophysical reactions to scenes that complement inner emotions can appear extravagant to us. But this sensationalism becomes the vehicle for Owenson's investigation of the relation between foreign spaces and the senses, catalyzing what Julia M. Wright's "Introduction" to *The Missionary* calls "a pre-psychoanalytic examination of emotion in the context of the needs of society and the individual" (31). And so it happens that in Hilarion's frequent meetings with Luxima, whose "mind" to this missionary "seemed rapt in the wondrous imagery by which she was surrounded" (117), he finds that he has begun speaking "a language not usually his own – the *language of sentiment*" (119). This new vernacular not only represents what has been termed a register of "evangelical entanglement";[22] it also catalyzes the missionary's inner reassessment through a "corrected" visual perception of his exterior environment:

> The sun, as it faded from the horizon, withdrew with its hopes scarcely understood by him who indulged them. Hitherto his mind had received every impression, and combined every idea, through a religious influence; and even the Indian, in all the splendour of her beauty, her youth, and her enthusiasm, had stolen on his imagination solely through the medium of

his zeal. Until this moment, woman was to him a thing unguessed at and unthought of. (123)

More than mere pathetic fallacy, Owenson sets up this panoramic view of the sunset to parallel the new emotional horizon of her protagonist's "mind." Through Hilarion's introjection of this seemingly unremarkable, diurnal spectacle, Owenson utilizes the way that "fad[ing]" luminosity synchronizes antithetically with the missionary's swelling prospect of erotic intimacies "unguessed at," as "every impression" of his former self is now cast in a new affective light.

Panoramic openings and revelations are crucial for Philip Meadows Taylor, writing some twenty years after Owenson's pioneering scrutiny of the missionary project. Taylor's tactic, as in *Tippoo Sultan: A Tale of the Mysore War* (1840), is to use arresting scenic description as a stage set for pivotal encounters that resonate for characters later in their narratives. Honor and longing intermingle as Taylor, like Owenson, builds a plot less out of colonial conquest and its aftershocks than out of the more interiorized matter of torn loyalties and personal guilt. But in placing Taylor in the contemporary context of mid-Victorian dramatizations of indigenous custom, my task is to gauge whether he endorses or surpasses what Brian May calls "that insidious imperialist idealism or 'elementalism' approached by way of its naturalization, a mode resulting when the landscape has been rendered so obdurately solid that it becomes identified with a preternatural, aboriginal substantiality."[23] What Taylor in fact achieves is a way of blending that elementalism – running the risk as he often does of evoking a timeless Indian subcontinent, a monolith of feudalism awaiting progressive change from outside its native order – with practical depictions of the possibilities of economic and demographic development. Taylor feels that the civilization of the intellect would be a unifying discourse for Indian and British culture, rather than a motive for simply expanding trade routes or consolidating the institutional superiority of Christianity. His return to England in 1860, following his period as *The Times*'s foreign correspondent in India from 1840, also spelled his return to fiction as the appropriate forum for putting those ideas of intercultural and intellectual civilization to the test.

In *A Noble Queen* (1878) Taylor engages with the Muslim dominions of Beejapoor and Ahmednugger. We cannot ignore the extent to which his sympathetic attitude toward the preservation of Indian traditions verges on essentialism, for it invokes an undeniably exteriorized perspective on the timelessness of native ritual, while reconsolidating the irreconcilability of Christian, Hindu, and Muslim commitments as a point of continued wonderment. This fascination belies an ethos of alliances cultivated from a distance, and sounds a far cry from the sort of proactive, communicative exchange that is cosmopolitanism's precept for sustaining mutual recognition and accountability. With such ambivalently branching priorities, Taylor oscillates between the humanitarian desire for shared cultural participation and the eroticization of foreign customs through the genre of colonial romance. Tensions between material conditions and romanticized essence are played out stylistically, especially, as we might expect, where Taylor introduces us to "new" places. Anthropomorphism reigns supreme as his first-choice device, as in his description of the "river Krishna," which goes beyond geomorphic features when the narrator pans back from immediate events to show how "the hills themselves were continually distorted by the hot wind and mirage, which had effect on everything about them."[24] We might be tempted to connect Taylor's characteristic method of lending grammatical agency to inanimate topography with Hardy's famous insistence, the year before *A Noble Queen* appeared, that "Art is a disproportioning . . . of realities."[25] But if Hardy's contemporaneous refutation of realism as an adequate mode for landscape depiction sounds akin to Taylor's embellished cadences, the affinity becomes tenuous when we ask ourselves what kind of artistic capital these writers acquire from their respective settings. This is where Hardy and Taylor part company, as Hardy's devotion to Wessex offers a more modest avenue for stylistic virtuosity.

Whereas Hardy, mapping rural Dorset, is compelled to seek what he calls moments of "miraculous animation,"[26] Taylor has more opulent prospects than the Purbeck Hills at his disposal. He capitalizes on this in *A Noble Queen*, taking the opportunity to develop new rhetorical effects from the scenery of underdeveloped communities:

> Trees suddenly appeared to start up, which dwindled into bushes as the party approached them; villages, with their walls and roofs of white slaty limestone, rose into seeming palaces, glittering in the sun, and disappeared; lakes of water seemed to gather together, and again vanish under the fierce blasts of the burning wind, which carried with it at times clouds of choking dust. Men and bullocks ploughing were seen for a moment, then rose quivering and misshapen into the air, and vanished under an increased blast. (vol. 1, 2)

In his own commentary on "The Native Literature of India" (1864), Taylor commends the realist principles of Hindu poetics, a commitment to restraint with "one great charm": that of "present[ing] nothing strange or repulsive to us," with "no oriental hyperboles or strained similes whatever."[27] Yet in the opening above Taylor initially appears to have imbibed this "charm," as he pretends to offer a factual catalogue of environmental conditions. Soon enough, however, the scene's images become animated far beyond the point of documentary realism, as his inventory of the wind's effects precipitates its own linguistic innovations. Taylor assumes a bird's eye view that can scan the scene for what it connotes, rather than record purely what it *is*. The repetition of intransitive verbs ("appeared" ... "seeming" ... "seemed"), whose indication of the mere appearance of indefinite movement ("to start up" ... "to gather together") is then made definitive by the verbs' phonetic connection to the past participle "seen." That is to say, events in the land that hitherto *seemed* to be occurring are now verifiably *seen* to have happened. What yearned toward impressionism now solidifies into reportage. Treading that line, then, between realism and "oriental hyperbole," Taylor can have it both ways: exercising his stylistic agility by accentuating the scene's thrilling wildness for an English audience, while also keeping the whole panorama within the bounds of probability.

This is a difficult balance for any writer to maintain. But Taylor strives to display formal virtuosity while still doing justice to topographical idiosyncrasies, all of which may simply be another "indication," in Said's words, "of how geography can be manipulated, invented, characterized quite apart from a site's merely physical reality" (180). To be sympathetic to Taylor, though, we might infer from his scenic sensationalism a genuine effort to create a *participatory* reading experience, involving us in the action of the land rather than presenting beautified spatial portraits. Undeniably, there can be an imperious aspect to the prospect views that punctuate the novel, not least when Taylor recommends that Beejapoor is fully apprehended when seen from on high, as "From the highest points of these downs many a noble view is obtained of the country around" (*A Noble Queen*, vol. i, 201). But he subsequently assures us that "it is only when the traveler draws near that the illusion is dispelled" (vol. i, 202). This becomes his imperative: to replicate for his reader that sensation of nearness – of proximity and involvement, rather than spectatorial distantiation. In this way, nearness becomes a precept for getting intellectually in touch with regions and customs other than one's own.

This tension between a writerly will-to-experiment and the obligation *not* to embellish the otherness of a place or its population persists for later nineteenth-century novelists. It is a tension between cultivating virtuoso craft and interpolating imperial history that complicates the possibility of representational totality: what Conrad famously describes as the potential "before all to make you *see*," a creative process that demands in every "moving moment that full possession of myself."[28] The impulse is precisely the opposite for a novelist like Olive Schreiner. With a renowned fascination for the complexities of local attachment, Schreiner posits more moderate objectives, for "To paint scenes among which [one] has grown" means forgoing ambition to evoke "Those brilliant phases and shapes which the imagination sees in far-off lands."[29]

Yet contrary aims such as Conrad's and Schreiner's represent merely two poles of a broad aesthetic spectrum along which nineteenth-century writers could develop a poetics of place. Their options are not reducible to any clear choice between totality and locality, or between the panoramic and the perspectival, or between narrative realism and interiority. What they demonstrate instead is what I have tried to show: a complex mediation between a fidelity to the material appearance of environments, and the stylistic opportunities that space itself can afford. As Schreiner admits, "Human life may be painted according to two methods": the "stage method" of realist or naturalist rendition; and "another method – the method of the life we all lead. Here nothing can be prophesied" (xxxix). However fiction might anticipate the conditions by which life might otherwise be lived or led, she implies, what cannot be prophesied by novelist or critic are the most effective modes by which that anticipated liberation of life is to be articulated. But the fact that affective experiences of landscapes "may be painted according to either method," and that nineteenth-century writers dexterously modulate between them despite how different those "methods" can be, is a testament to the contribution that landscapes make to the increasing agility of the novel form. In the spirit of continuing to do justice to that agility we should coordinate ideological and aesthetic ways of reading fiction from this unsettling age.

Notes

1. Michel de Certeau, *The Practice of Everyday Life*, trans. Steven Rendall (Berkeley: University of California Press, 1984), p. 116.
2. W. D. Arnold, *Oakfield; or, Fellowship in the East* (New York: Humanities Press, 1973), p. 56.
3. Benjamin Disraeli, *Selected Speeches*, ed. T. E. Kebbel, 2 vols. (London: Longmans, Green & Co., 1882), vol. II, p. 534.
4. George Eliot, "The Modern Hep! Hep! Hep!," *Essays of George Eliot*, ed. Charles Lee Lewis (New York and Boston: H. M. Caldwell, 1884), p. 403.
5. Saurabh Dube, "Introduction: Enchantments of Modernity," *The South Atlantic Quarterly* 101: 4 (2002), 729–755, 735.

6. Ernest Renan, "What is a Nation?" (1882), trans. Martin Thom, in *Nation and Narration*, ed. Homi Bhabha (London: Routledge, 1990), p. 19.
7. Edward W. Said, "Invention, Memory, and Place," *Critical Inquiry* 26: 2 (2000), 175–192, 182.
8. Andrew Thacker, "The Idea of a Critical Literary Geography," *New Formations* 57 (2005/6), 56–73, 63.
9. John Buchan, *Prester John* (London: Penguin, 1956), p. 40.
10. Henry M. Stanley, Preface, *My Kalulu: Prince, King, and Slave: A Story of Central Africa* (London: Simpson Low, Marston, Low, and Searle, 1873), pp. vi–vii.
11. Mrs. General M. Mainwaring, *The Suttee; or, the Hindoo Converts*, 3 vols. (London: A. K. Newman & Co., 1830), vol. i, p. v.
12. Ford Madox Ford, "On Conrad's Vocabulary" (1928), *Ford Madox Ford: Critical Essays*, ed. Max Saunders and Richard Stang (Manchester: Carcanet, 2002), p. 288.
13. Captain Marryat, *The Mission, or Scenes in Africa* (London: Rex Collings, 1970), p. 17.
14. Flora Annie Steel, Preface, *On the Face of the Waters* (London: Heinemann, 1897), p. v.
15. Joseph Conrad, *Almayer's Folly* (London: Eveleigh Nash and Gayson, 1921), p. 120.
16. Rudyard Kipling, *Kim*, ed. Edward W. Said (London: Penguin, 2000), p. 112.
17. Christopher R. Miller, *The Invention of Evening: Perception and Time in Romantic Poetry* (Cambridge University Press, 2006), p. 12.
18. Flora Annie Steel, *Voices in the Night* (London: Heinemann, 1900), p. 5.
19. Romita Ray, "The Memsahib's Brush: Anglo-Indian Women and the Art of the Picturesque, 1830–1880," in *Orientalism Transposed: The Impact of the Colonies on British Culture*, ed. Dianne Sachko Macleod (Aldershot: Ashgate, 1998), p. 89.
20. Jeffrey Cox, *Imperial Fault Lines: Christianity and Colonial Power in India, 1818–1940* (Stanford University Press, 2002), pp. 48, 50.
21. Sydney Owenson (Lady Morgan), *The Missionary*, ed. Julia M. Wright (Ormskirk, Lancashire, and Peterborough, ON: Broadview Press, 2002), p. 83.
22. Saurabh Dube, "Conversion to Translation: Colonial Registers of a Vernacular Christianity," *The South Atlantic Quarterly* 101: 4 (2002), 807–837, 808.
23. Brian May, "Romancing the Stump: Modernism and Colonialism in Forster's *A Passage to India*," in *Modernism and Colonialism: British and Irish Literature, 1899–1939*, ed. Richard Begam and Michael Valdez Moses (Durham, NC: Duke University Press, 2007), p. 137.
24. Philip Meadows Taylor, *A Noble Queen: A Romance of Indian History*, 3 vols. (London: Kegan Paul, 1878), vol. i, p. 2.
25. Thomas Hardy, *The Life and Work of Thomas Hardy*, ed. Michael Millgate (Basingstoke: Macmillan, 1984), p. 239.
26. Thomas Hardy, *The Literary Notebooks of Thomas Hardy*, ed. Lennart A. Björk, 2 vols. (Basingstoke: Macmillan, 1985), vol. i, p. 63.

27. Philip Meadows Taylor, "The Native Literature of India," in *The Afternoon Lectures on Literature and Art* (London: Bell and Daldy, 1864), p. 132.
28. Joseph Conrad, *Conrad's Prefaces to His Works* (London: Dent, 1937), p. 52; Conrad, "A Familiar Preface," *A Personal Record* (London: Dent, 1975), p. xvii.
29. Olive Schreiner, *The Story of an African Farm*, ed. Joseph Bristow (Oxford University Press, 1998), p. xl.

32

Imperial romance

ROBERT L. CASERIO

Versions of "imperial romance": Walter Scott and Edward Said

The idea that the history of the English novel includes a Victorian and Edwardian sub-genre called "imperial romance" has emerged forcibly in literary studies since the 1980s. "In romance," Wendy Katz writes, in contrast to the "realist and naturalist fiction of the period," there is "a logical congeniality with messianic interpretations of Empire[,] ... ruling class stability," and racism.[1] Patrick Brantlinger, designating the temporal span of the sub-genre between Captain Marryat's novels and Conrad's, argues that the "impressionism of Conrad's novels and their romance features are identical ... and ... both threaten to submerge or 'derealize' the critique of empire."[2] Indeed, because "the romance conventions that Conrad reshapes carry with them the polarizations of racial thought" (265) characteristic of imperialism, his fiction "suggests the moral bankruptcy of his own literary project" (275).

But is imperial romance a sub-genre, or the novel itself? Edward Said's *Culture and Imperialism* (1993) diagnoses a "tragic limitation" in Conrad: "though he could see clearly that on one level imperialism was essentially pure dominance and land-grabbing, he could not then conclude that imperialism had to end."[3] Conrad's tragedy inheres in his medium. For, according to Said, the novel, whether realistic or romantic, amounts to a perpetual imperial romance. "Without empire," Said writes, "there is no European novel ... [I]f we study the impulses giving rise to it, we shall see the far from accidental convergence between the patterns of narrative authority constitutive of the novel ... and ... a complex ideological configuration underlying the tendency to imperialism" (69–70).

Walter Scott is mentioned by Said as a consolidator of the novel's imperialist essence. It is surprising, however, that Scott's *The Surgeon's Daughter* (1827), given its relevance to Said's claims, is not part of Said's reading. What are the "patterns of narrative authority" that constitute *The Surgeon's Daughter*? The novel, according to its narrator, is about the "silent . . . laying of the foundations" of the "immense" British Empire.[4] The foundations are exhibited in terms of Scott's characteristic merger of particular lives with world-historical ideologies. If those are "the patterns of narrative authority" Said refers to, in *The Surgeon's Daughter* they do unusual work.

Usually the hero in Scott is a middle-of-the-road male who reconciles progressive bourgeois forms of life with the hierarchies and authoritarianisms that the middle classes revolutionized. *The Surgeon's Daughter* alters the pattern. The middle figure is Richard Middlemas, bastard offspring of a Jewish mother and Catholic father and the ward of a Scottish presbyterian surgeon. Middlemas becomes an imperialist adventurer in India, where his exploitative schemes – partly in service to the Crown, partly in service to the East India Company – lead to his death at the hands of Hyder Ali of Mysore. There are no reconciliations. The eponymous Menie, who blindly loves Middlemas and follows him to India, returns to Scotland to lead an isolated life. Another male protagonist, Hartley, a surgeon who is Middlemas's rival for the hand of Menie, dies in India, "a victim to his professional courage, in withstanding the progress of a contagious distemper" (285). Hyder Ali, having learned English trustworthiness from Middlemas, announces that he will be at war with the Empire.

It is difficult to read *The Surgeon's Daughter* without identifying the romance of empire as the "contagious distemper" that kills Hartley, and is fatal for the other characters. To that extent, Scott is abreast of a post-1970s generation of critics. But he also implies a literary history and a political moral that are alternatives to what critical authority has endorsed in the last thirty years. To suggest those alternatives, I begin by proposing that Scott's narrative patternings insist on the incoherence of modern British imperialism. They locate the incoherence in historical contradictions that are always exemplified in his narratives.

The contradictions in *The Surgeon's Daughter* are patent. The surgeon, Dr. Grey, a presbyterian scientist and hence an exemplar of modernity's rational temper, takes into his household a male child whose illegitimacy represents authoritarian and reactionary creeds and social structures. The doctor resents Menie because her birth "caused" her mother's death, so he gives pride of place to the imperious orphan at the expense of his daughter's precedence. Self-contradictorily, the modern father acts like a patriarch. When Grey accepts Hartley, who is English, as an apprentice surgeon, the rivalry between Middlemas and Hartley becomes the narrative of a historical crossroads. What union, with what representative man, will best shape the future of a daughter of Scotland, indeed of Scotland herself?

In rejecting union with Hartley, Menie rejects a representative of English life who has no dedication to empire. She misguidedly allies herself with English adventurers who replace Enlightenment principles with the lawless caprice of a superseded era. In Middlemas the revolutionary thrust of capitalism is conformed to monarchy's absolutism. The result is Scottish and English historical regression. When one of the English figures in India is made to say "We are all upon the adventure in India" (253), Scott is identifying the English with the supreme political adventurer of his other novels: the Pretender.

The sign of the Pretender's return, and of the revival of his ideology, is self-enclosure in romance. Middlemas imagines himself as a changeling prince, destined for the repossession of a lost kingdom. When at age fourteen he learns the facts of his parentage, he falls from the heights of "the boldest flights of poetry" to "humble prose" (180–181). A reunion with his long-lost parents (a stock episode in romance) results in Middlemas's angry rejection of them: they are too ordinary for him to tolerate. But then India appears on his horizon. "Oh, Delhi! Oh, Golconda! . . . India, where gold is won by steel, where a brave man cannot pitch his desire so high, but that he may realize it" (198). A disreputable Englishman, Hillary, abets the romance, inciting Middlemas with tales of a military tour of India that brings Hillary wealth, affairs with native women, and – with "no scruples of conscience" – dominion over "black rascals" (202).

Hillary trepans Middlemas even before the latter arrives in India: evidence of the "high" character of English enterprise. But in India Middlemas finds another ally, an Englishwoman who has gone native, and who proposes to deliver Mysore to British troops, for an appropriate sum. Middlemas's schemes with the Begum lead him into romance disguise – a blackface intrigue that makes it more possible for him to betray Menie, whom he uses as a pawn in the plot to also betray Mysore. As the English Begum and Middlemas represent the Empire, it is a violent superimposition of romance fantasies upon present life.

To be sure, the present of Scott's novel is fifty years past, which allows Scott's narrator, Chrystal Croftangry, to remark that the British in India have changed for the better by 1827. But Chrystal's narrative also exhibits the slowness of change, the contradiction-laden persistence of the past in the present. And the figure to whom Scott (and Chrystal) most draws sympathy is Hartley. He is unable to rescue Menie from Middlemas's plot: "A lover of romance might have meditated some means of effecting her release by force or address; but Hartley ... had no spirit of adventure" (277). Too consistently modern and realistic for that, he is the better part of England. There is no Scottish union with that part; its capacity to heal worldly ills is incompatible with political and economic exploitation. It is notable that Scott's Hyder Ali, refusing subordination, exercises his "internal sense of right" (285), in contrast to the wrongness of external – i.e. English – coercions that surround him.

Is it possible to read Scott's narrative as fortifying empire? Scott's novel provokes antipathy to modernity's renewal of romance adventure in the guise of imperialism; but it also depends upon romance prototypes – orphans, disguises, quests – as a vehicle for criticizing geopolitical translations of romance into reality. The dependence confirms Said's contention that the realist novel and imperial romance are one and the same. But Scott's dialectical interplay of the contrasting fictional kinds is essential to the novel's anti-imperialist ethos.

Said's introduction to *Culture and Imperialism* suggests that the opposition to empire enacted by the narrative of *The Surgeon's Daughter* would qualify as what Said calls a "nomadic" candidate in a "contrapuntal" literary history. Such a history advocates a perspective that is "fully sensitive to the reality of historical experience [whereby no culture] is single and pure, all are ... extraordinarily differentiated" (xxv). "Nomadic" texts disrupt what otherwise might be construed in terms of "a unitary identity." In the light of that perspective, literary history could allow that Scott's novel escapes convergence with an "ideological configuration underlying the tendency to imperialism." But although Said intends to reject such convergence in favor of nomadic understanding, he does not practice in his text what his introduction advocates. His text is impelled to advance a "consolidated vision" (the title of Said's second chapter) of the past relations of culture and empire.

The consolidation merits further remark because of Said's identification of all English novels with "imperial romance." "It is striking that never, in the novel," Said writes, "is [the] world beyond [England] seen except as subordinate and dominated, the English presence viewed as regulative and normative" (75). A global disparity of power is thus naturalized in fiction. Neither nomadically nor contrapuntally, Said asserts that "there can be no awareness that the novel underscores and accepts the disparity in power ... unless the history of the novel is seen to have the coherence of a continuous enterprise" (75). Imperialism supplies the historian of the novel with the coherence and the continuity. "The aesthetic (hence cultural) grasp of overseas lands amounts to a 'consolidated' vision ... in a whole series of overlapping affirmations, by which a near unanimity of view is sustained" (75).

To support Said's case *Culture and Imperialism* provides multiple reflections on fiction, but few readings of novels. None endows its object with contrapuntal status. The most famous reading – of Austen's *Mansfield Park* (1814) – exemplifies the animus that enlists contrapuntalism on behalf of "consolidation." For Said Austen's narrative shows that Fanny Price is being groomed to inherit Mansfield Park from her uncle, whose estate is funded by his slave-holding property in the West Indies. Fanny's story is thus legible as an imperialist heiress's mind in the making. For Fanny's story to be legible in Said's way, however, a reader must discount Fanny's self-possession in resisting her uncle's domination. For most of the novel Fanny is treated as a slave; the narrative shows that her liberty lies in her refusal to allow exploitation to seduce or conquer her.

The only texts in the critic's "consolidation" that amount to "nomads" are Yeats's poems ("a major international achievement in cultural decolonization" [238]) and Eliot's "The Dry Salvages" (in which there appears "a vision bearing on, if not delivering, true liberation" [281]). Lyric forms can bear on, and Yeats if not Eliot can deliver, true liberation; but fiction by its very form – its patterns of narrative authority – cannot. The present-day political activism behind the criticism is understandable; what is less clear is why the novel and its history do not have parity in the struggle.

Even casual readers might sense that Fanny Price's self-possession exemplifies an overcoming of the world's status quo. Yet the critic must coerce Austen into alignment with imperialism. The coercive pressure recognizes few limits. Brantlinger identifies Philip Meadows Taylor's *Seeta* (1873) – about the Indian Mutiny – as one of no more than three anti-imperialist British novels of the nineteenth century. Accordingly he dismisses libertarian efforts such as Marryat's campaign against the legal impressment of sailors. That deprivation of liberty Brantlinger judges to be marginal. His judgment relies on Marryat's satirical buffoonery concerning the rights of man in *Midshipman Easy* (1836). Yet, *pace* Brantlinger, the buffoonery does not cancel the touching effect of Jack's friendship with the African ex-king and ex-slave Mesty; nor does it prevent Jack, or readers, from applauding Mesty's leadership in a mutiny against impressment. The mutiny enacts the rights of man, after all; and the narrative pattern cannot do without the black man's courageous rebellion. Even in a comic novel that makes fun of rights (partly because it sees rights as emptily abstract without specifically legislated guarantees), a nomadic counter-force counts.

Brantlinger classifies Victorian gothic fictions as imperial romances, and assigns their cause to "anxiety" about the empire. The assignment is tautological, for what constitutes evidence of a cultural anxiety, or of its determination of a literary content or form? Nevertheless, vague evidence can be influential, as in Gauri Viswanathan's argument that literary studies originate as an arm of British rule in India. Because "literature" transmits "attitudes, beliefs, and ideas … entirely unmediated by … political and historical realities,"[5] in Britain's educational policy for India "literature" prevented those it hoodwinked from recognizing the imposition. Yet what Viswanathan means by literary study is unclear: it sometimes means fictions, sometimes means "English studies," sometimes means "history" (141), and almost always means an amalgam that includes Plato, Francis Bacon, Adam Smith, and Schlegel. How the novel functioned in this amalgam that is said by Viswanathan to have declined in influence by the 1850s – after all of thirty years of "conquest" – is not sufficiently obvious to identify "the novel" as a conqueror. The prevailing conqueror, according to Viswanathan's most telling evidence if not to Viswanathan's argument, is religion. The influence of missionary thought upon all culture in the Empire is neglected by the critical ethos that attacks imperial romance, and novels, as prime agents of global adventure. Scott, portraying Middlemas as the bastard of religious authoritarianisms cohabiting with opportunistic seekers of Golconda, is not similarly neglectful.

Revising action and agency in "imperial romance"

An "activist" political impulse, admirably typified in Said's political writing, stamps the work of the critics' address to novels. The activist impulse is also a "realist" one, aligning itself with history against the deceptions that it believes saturate both realism and romance in fiction. It also projects a world in which fiction is as activist as critics want to be. They assign to novels, no less than to capitalists, politicians, clergy, and generals, the ability to enact imperialism; they assign to readers the same agency. A lack of differentiation among agencies of imperialism has become critical "common sense."

Perhaps this is a blinkering over-investment in "action" and "agency." What if there is an ironic critical misprision here? What if the sub-genre is subversive of empire by revising the meanings of action and agency? Imperial romance, I suggest – in its canonical producers – instantiates a criticism of action that is the nineteenth-century English novel's important innovation of romance. Whereas romance tradition emphasizes more than ordinary powers of human action, its latter-day offspring undermine agency even as they represent it, just as they undermine easy distinctions between romance and realism. The subversion, by eroding the power and efficacy of action, makes the activity that is imperialism appear to be a foredoomed surrender to what no agency can control or master. Such an appearance hardly induces novels or readers to fortify empire.

The revisionary perplexing and humbling of agency that develops in this "sub-genre" comprehends a dual nature in all action. The duality is explained in Hannah Arendt's philosophy. According to Arendt, one face of action belongs to *homo faber*, man the maker, who construes his deeds as self-determined realizations of his conscious purposes. *Homo faber* is an unqualified ruler of his actions, and of their meaning. While his kind of action sounds admirable, Arendt thinks it tends to be for worse rather than for better – which is why she seeks to demonstrate that action is not identical only with *homo faber's* version of it.

For Arendt actions are creative precisely because, despite *homo faber's* aims, they escape from intention, producing unpredictable consequences. Becoming autonomous, actions free themselves from their initiators so that they develop anonymity as well as autonomy. Their autonomy and anonymity mean that an initiator of action turns out to be a sufferer, undergoing – rather than mastering – what he enacts. He undergoes others' deeds as well as his own, because a plurality of agents is a condition of doing. An agent suffers a "haphazardness and moral irresponsibility [that are] inherent in a plurality of agents."[6] *Homo faber* responsibly would oppose, and regulate, such pluralities and contingencies. There is nothing wrong with *homo faber* in his place. His place is in the world of making, wherein his work, which ruthlessly hierarchizes ends and means, instrumentalizes all things. But *homo faber's* world should not be thought identical with political possibility. Arendt's provocative contention is that politics inhabits, or should inhabit, a space in which deeds and agents can appear without subordination to *homo faber's* will to mastery. His will is at the back of empire.

Stripped of such will, action takes on a likeness to passion; agency comes to be inextricable from passivity, even from subjection. What do we *do* when agency and passivity become doubles, when doing appears to lose the name of action? That is a question "imperial romance" (even when it is identical with "the novel") propounds, preceding Arendt; and it asks the question by way of pairing dreams of adventure with impairments of deeds of empire. The critical hostility to imperial romance results from the way critics read it as if it were celebrating *homo faber's* instrumentalizing self-determination.

There is one exemplar of "imperial romance" who identifies action exclusively with *homo faber*. It is John Buchan. Buchan's narratives about his South African colonial hero, Richard Hannay, from *The Thirty-Nine Steps* (1915) on, dramatize the hazards of action whereby Hannay and the Empire might lose control of their purposes; but they underwrite the ultimate victory of instrumentalizing design. The pattern for Hannay is established in Buchan's *Prester John* (1910), in which young David Crawfurd defeats John Laputa, a Zulu descendant leading a movement of "Africa for the Africans."[7] Unlike Scott's Hartley, Scottish Crawfurd seeks to dominate adventure, despite his perilous loss of control when he undergoes "a mad desire to be of Laputa's party ... I longed for a leader who should master me and make my soul his own" (86). The adolescent recovers from this infatuation with a charismatic black anti-imperialist. Playing "the chief part" in the death of his opponent, especially because, in a moment of extremity, Crawfurd realizes that "the passive is the next stage to the overwrought" (154), Crawfurd outdistances Laputa as a man of action. He thereupon realizes that "the meaning of the white man's duty ... is the difference between white and black, the gift of responsibility, the power of being in a little way a king; and so long as we know this and practice it, we will rule not in Africa alone but wherever there are dark men" (166).

Buchan exemplifies "imperial romance" as the critics understand it. But they do not read Buchan. They read earlier writers, from Scott to Conrad, as if those others were Buchan. The absence of differentiation obscures the perplexing of action, and a consequent humbling of imperial agencies, in Buchan's predecessors.

Laputa copies H. Rider Haggard's Zulu heroes. Haggard plays the villain in anti-imperialist patterns of critical authority. Laura Chrisman, Haggard's strongest opponent, condemns his Zulu romances. Haggard, by representing his imaginary Zulu Umslopogaas as the lost heir of Shaka, makes himself, a white imperial metropolitan author, "alone ... responsible for preserving the authentic Zulu historical imperial legacy."[8] At the same time, *Nada the Lily* (1892) chronicles the decline of Umslopogaas as a ruling *homo faber* actor. Such picturing of compromised native ability to act, given its racial context, appalls Chrisman, especially when she asserts that Haggard uses the novel to render the "massacre of the Boers" by the Zulu leader Dingane – "the most directly political and rational act of the novel (and the only one, apart from the assassination of Shaka, to have real historical substance)" – "as something meaningless that defies comprehension" (110). It is for Chrisman a rational anti-imperialist offensive, with intelligible historical motives, and a product of agents who represent *homo faber*'s address to the world.

To make today's readers more conscious of their agency as *homo faber* world-builders is Chrisman's aim, just as it is her aim to reveal romancers as the deliberate agents they might have pretended not to be. Assuming that

Haggard "actively" fabricated his fiction in order to fortify imperialism, Chrisman wrestles the romance elements of *Nada the Lily* (it includes wolves who are ghosts of the dead) into line with historical truth, and thereby enforces her assumption. But history seems as elusive of determinate control, and as fragile, as Arendt's version of action. Chrisman depends upon a Zulu-British historian, Jeff Guy, whose work she refers to as "sensitive and meticulously detailed" (75). Within pages, however, the critic finds that Guy "notably ... contradicts himself" (87). She substitutes her reading of Haggard for the historian's research.

When research aims to recover intentions that ruled the past, it might be situating itself contrarily to the way in which human action evades the control of actors, and narrative intelligibility. If actions (no less than historians) contradict themselves, as Arendt suggests; if the power of actions is also their frailty, history becomes hard to tell, a mysterious undergoing. Did Haggard choose romance, with its distance from reality, as a double for history's resistance to *homo faber*'s rule? When *King Solomon's Mines* (1885) ends with Ignosi's decision to seal off – above all from exploitative whites – the native kingdom to which Allan Quatermain has helped restore him, the novel is simultaneously presenting a utopian image of African sovereignty and a sign of its own self-enclosure, its romance distance from historical realism. With a similar metafictional purport, in *Allan Quatermain* (1887) a sealing off of subterranean Zu-Vendis also emphasizes the distance between fiction and history. The distancing is so extreme as to be often laughable: J. M. Barrie's devastating review of *King Solomon's Mines* (1885) shows that, even for Victorians, romance does not automatically inhibit critical powers.

Laugh-provoking or not, the extremes distance a reader from identification with Haggard's extravagances of action. They also direct attention to an aspect of action that concerns character more than deeds. For Arendt the complications of action bring into relief the character of persons caught up in it, in a way that separates who they are from what they do. Haggard's romances open a space for fictive persons who transcend the doings of *homo faber*. The transcendence is underwritten by Haggard's piecemeal achronological narratives. As if independent of entrammeling action, Umslopogaas, Allan, and She reappear across thirty-five years (the trio surfaces last in *She and Allan* [1921], a prequel to *She* [1887]). Allan notes that "each individual personality" is "made up of six or seven [personalities] . . . seldom all together, although one or more of them [is] present continually."[9] The scission of agents marks Arendt's action-compromising plurality of actors. She's ability to act undergoes the plurality, so that she comes to suffer more than she acts. In *Ayesha: The Return of She* (1905) She is all but identical with Isis, yet She also is a mere pawn of deities, required to bear the vengeance of Isis, whom Aphrodite has led her to betray. She's cosmic agency submits to passion in the She stories. In contrast, ordinary or heroic male agency in Haggard – expressed as violent militarism, a symptom of *homo faber*'s controlling willfulness – does not suffer; but, juxtaposed with the women's passions, it looks puny and comical. Umslopogaas is the male exception. Mythological in stature and rhetoric, the Zulu even in defeat, rather than the white men in victory, is offered to readers as the figure to admire. As a test of how Haggard's imperial romance disposes audiences to fortify imperialism, we might remember that *She* inspired Elizabeth Bowen to write – and that her *The Last September* (1929) approves the anti-imperialist destruction of the Anglo-Irish ascendency.

Kipling, in contrast to Haggard, and in line with Scott, does not draw a boundary between realism and romance. *Kim* (1901) is a case in point. But rote identification of Kipling with *Kim* amounts increasingly to prejudicial political response. The prejudice blocks attention to Kipling's aesthetic, which can mitigate the political worries. To focus on Kipling *the novelist*-author of *Kim* is to overlook how little a novelist Kipling is. His major work, the stories, reduces "the novel" to story length, without sacrificing complexity. Kipling is an experimental writer; but his experimental novel, unlike Zola's, is minimalist. If he is unqualifiedly an imperialist, his form strikingly shrinks from expansiveness. The story collections, like the individual tales, must be considered innovative: each volume reconstitutes "the novel" as virtually a mosaic of lyrics rather than narratives, as a constellation of moods, situations, and modes of representation. Realism alternates with romance, and they also are intermingled; naturalism is part of the mix. "At Twenty-Two" (1888) is self-consciously *"Germinal* upside-down."[10] The cumulative effect is a kaleidoscope of attitudes towards action, rather than actions themselves. One of the attitudes expresses the limits of action's wordly efficacy: *homo faber* in Kipling, whether he is a soldier, a colonial administrator, or an artist (Dick Heldar in *The Light That Failed* [1890] is exemplary), must surrender – despite his many inventions – to what is beyond his control.

The stories that emphasize control unquestionably outrage anti-imperialist perspectives. In "The Mutiny of the Mavericks" (1892) an Irish anarchist and anti-Unionist, who wants his fellow-soldiers to mutiny, is misled by his mates. They feign sympathy with his politics until they can punish him by making him die in combat as an alternative to their friendly fire. Such deliberated aggressiveness, invincibly instrumentalizing its objects, is repeated in "On Greenhow Hill" (1892), where Ortheris takes cold-blooded pleasure in killing a rebel deserter from a native military troop. In "Judson and the Empire" (1891) "Bai-Jove-Judson" and a Portuguese colonial official collude to portray Judson as the loser of a territorial squabble with the Portuguese, for the sake of making the Portuguese monarchy look good at a vulnerable moment. The officially opposed imperialists help each other, lest republicanism undo empire.

Yet such stories, for all their affirmation of *homo faber* as an invincible ruler, are juxtaposed by Kipling with narratives that suggest the inevitable undoing of British hegemony. Especially the narratives evoking Afghan and Muslim violence carry no pro-imperialist animus – indeed, when their native narrators speak for themselves, they predict that once England is gone from India, Islam will possess the subcontinent. Even when native subjects do not speak for themselves, their power emerges. "The Lost Legion" (1891) begins with the tale of a native regiment's attempt to join the Indian Mutiny. Blocked by the English, the regiment was forced into Afghanistan, where the Afghans decimated it. Now, thirty years later, "the Indian Government" is attempting to corral an Afghan border thief and murderer without being seen as "a big bullying power" against "a popular leader."[11] During the course of the English operation, the lost legion – a throng of Indian ghosts – harasses it. The ghosts simultaneously frighten the Afghan sentries, so that the English get through and arrest their man. Have the dead mutineers repented their rebellion, seeing that they now aid the government? The story's narrator thinks so; but the narrative's elements exceed his perspective. The lost legion is avenging itself against the Afghan tribe that extinguished it, and is using the English instrumentally, as a subordinate force. The Mutiny continues. The successful action of the English is willy-nilly a surrender. That the mutineers now have become the dominators one can take as their misfortune as well as their victory. For the English it is a surrender to that element of action that cannot be governed. Where there is such surrender, action is difficult to tell apart from passion. In "On Greenhow Hill" Ortheris kills the rebel with "the smile of the artist who looks on the completed work,"[12] i.e. with the control that *homo faber* – who represents the artist's no less than the political ruler's government of means and ends – exalts. But the story is about Learoyd's passion for a lost lover, and in the face of that passion *homo faber*'s control – Ortheris's in this case – appears hideous. Kipling follows this story in the collection *Life's Handicap* with "The Man Who Was," about an English soldier who has gone to pieces at the hands of Russian imperial power. The phenomenon complements Kipling's reduction of "the novel" to mosaic. The Empire, a fabrication of unity, cannot overcome the multiplicity and diversity to which the fabrication inevitably must yield. That is life and action's handicap; when Kipling subtitled the volume "stories of mine own people," he was suggesting that "owning" such a diversity could only be achieved at the cost of control.

The handicapping of action constitutes Kipling's "imperial romance." The imperialist's agency is fissured because he knows that his adventure does not express his superiority, but only his aggressive instrumentalizing rule. A critic does not need to disclose this fissure as an ambiguity underneath Kipling's "really" imperialist commitments. "Naboth" in *Life's Handicap* tells the nasty history of an imperialist who gloatingly strikes back when his good nature is put upon by a native who exploits *him*. But the next story, "The Dream of Duncan Parrenness," suggests Kipling reimagining Middlemas. Parrenness, an eighteenth-century writer, dreams he has become governor-general of the East India Company. The cost of governing, he discovers, will be loss of trust in men and women, loss of "his very heart" – a cost exacted by a double whom he names "Myself" (81). In return for the loss he will receive a temporarily invincible life – and a crust of bread. This story is echoed in "At the End of the Passage," where "a blind face that cries and can't wipe its eyes, a blind face that chases him down corridors" (259) haunts an imperialist administrator. It is his own face. The imperialist character as revealed by his deeds returns in Kipling, intensified by horror, to the historical contradictions that Scott narrates. It is significant that in the 1923 Macmillan Uniform Edition of *Life's Handicap* Kipling moved "Naboth" and "The Dream of Duncan Parrenness" to the end of the volume, thereby underlining the heartlessness of empire.

Is it the case that even if Kipling discerns the ugliness of imperialism, he sees it – fatalistically – as inevitable? Whatever the answer, Kipling's involvement of romance with both realism and naturalism marks his movement away from the worldly status quo as well as his proto-Arendtian grasp of action. Even in *Many Inventions* (1893), whose title emphasizes the products of man the maker, the artist and the ruler serve what the collection's dedicatory lyric names "the true romance," a power mercifully distant from "this our war/Our call and counter-cry" (vii). The distance is merciful because it disengages action from pride and invulnerability. "Judson and the Empire" has a penultimate place in *Many Inventions*; but the concluding story, "Children of the Zodiac," makes the imperialist hi-jinks look gimcrack. And that is because "Children of the Zodiac" is untethered to reality except in its ending, in which the celestial constellations Leo and Virgo (who have become a pair of human lovers, and Leo a narrative artist) undergo subjection to death. The subjection, and the resulting humbling of effort and action, give art and love their value – and constitute their romance. Traditional romance's promoting of human action to the level of divine or near-divine ability is reversed.

I see the reversal as a crucial development of English fiction in the nineteenth century, above all affecting what happens in the imperial romances of Stevenson and Conrad. Stevenson's *The Master of Ballantrae* (1889) pivots on the threefold resurrection of the Master. Human resurrection, as in *The Winter's Tale*, is a traditional romance heightening of mortal abilities. But Stevenson (also resurrecting Scott) subordinates romance to history. The Master is identified, as a Jacobite, with imperial adventure in North America as well as India – in order to remind readers of the resuscitated hierarchies that capitalist egalitarianism was to supersede. The Master's anti-Jacobitical brother and the brother's humble servant turn out to be reactionary Middlemases. Who is the imperialist and who is not one – "so mingled are our dispositions"[13] – becomes impossible to tell. The old imperialism and the new are halves of a split personality (like Kipling's Parrenness), a wonderful but distasteful historical incoherence yet to be resolved.

The resolution cannot be another fortification of empire. In *In the South Seas* (1891–1896) and *A Footnote to History* (1892) Stevenson's explicit challenge to imperialism (scholars, under the influence of Saidian patterns of critical authority, have noted it belatedly) undermines the mode of action, or the way of defining it, that belongs to ruling agents. No imperialist would brook the loss of agentive mastery that Stevenson and Lloyd Osbourne's *The Ebb-Tide* (1894) exemplifies in its errant protagonist, Herrick. The novel, another generic experiment, attaches the wanderings and wonders of romance to a failure of adventure, and of controlling will, in Herrick; and it employs narrative, which depends upon actions and events, to constate the ebb-tide of action itself.

The narrative's revision of *homo faber*'s version of action begins with the opening paragraph's declaration, suggesting synonymy between "activity" and disease, that "European races . . . carry activity and disseminate disease" wherever they go.[14] Herrick, a failure at every job and personal relation in a life journey that beaches him in Tahiti, resolves anew to cure his acedia by arming himself against a sea of troubles, even if it means joining two other losers in an illicit adventure in marine insurance fraud. Is not the tide of human affairs, taken at its flood, the opportunity for fate-mastering direction? Herrick takes Shakespeare, Virgil (the poet of empire), and the romance fantasies of *The Arabian Nights* as inspiration for his renewal of aims. Yet the inspiration leads Herrick into the arms of a prototype of Conrad's Kurtz: Attwater, a self-appointed English possessor of an island empire; a *homo faber* ruling with an amoral iron fist (capriciously killing his native servants in cold blood), all the while that he believes he is appointed by God to govern, to convert the natives, and to profit. Attwater takes the action of epic for his guide, and compounds epic self-dramatization with allegorical justifications of his rule.

Stevenson bundles together in Attwater and Herrick a spectrum of narrative genres to which action is essential. Yet Herrick is a misfit in relation to that essence. So little does he exemplify wicked activity that, in order to demonstrate his innocuousness, Stevenson cannot permit him even the action of suicide. Herrick attempts drowning because he is terrified by both his attraction to Attwater and his compliance with his companions' plan to murder the man. But Herrick botches his suicide, and Stevenson manipulates the telling of it so that the reader cannot ascertain either the agency or the lack of agency in what happens. The description of his newly beached state implies a defeat of action by action:

> With the consequences of his acts he saw himself implacably confronted for the duration of life: stretched upon a cross, and nailed there with . . . his own cowardice . . . [He] told himself no stories . . . even the process of apologetic mythology had ceased . . . [He] did not attempt to rise. (229)

Herrick experiences no resurrection of an active will; only "incredible simplicity of submission to ascertained fact" (228).

The Ebb-Tide's sympathy is with Herrick's withdrawn distance from *vita activa*. After a century of world conquest by economic and spiritual powers (and not by novels), an escape from the tide of active affairs might have seemed to Stevenson a better mode of endurance than any alternative. Might this have seemed so to Conrad also? *In the South Seas, A Footnote to History*, and *The Ebb-Tide* predict *Almayer's Folly* (1895). That novel compassionates Almayer, but also finds utterance in its female figures' hatred for European imperialists. The hatred stuns Almayer, whose romance "dream of wealth and power"[15] derives from the English adventurer Tom Lingard, who in effect colonizes the Dutchman. Lingard makes Almayer feel that he belongs to a romance world of heroes and gods. But romance and realism converge dissonantly at the end of the novel. The Siamese slave-girl Taminah's shout (in frustration that she has not been able to wrest the Hindu ruler Dain Maroola from her Dutch-Malay rival Nina): "'Too late! O senseless white men! He has escaped!'" (146) resonates with the novel's demonstration of European "folly": the white man's illusion of possessing peoples who escape him, despite his profits. Almayer's fellow colonialists dub his new residence their countryman's "folly." The joke is on them. The rebellions of Almayer's wife and daughter testify to the inward demise of any colonial rule that feels at home in the world; and the Europeans are a transient interruption in the standing conflict between Hindus and Muslims. The activity of the Europeans is entrammeled by the uncontrollable plurality of actors and of reversals that is the medium, and the fragility, of deeds.

The focus of scholarship on Conrad's ambiguities has overlooked Conrad's unambiguous humbling of action. In *Nostromo* (1904) the failure of Conrad's Nostromo, as an individual and as a representative of the working class, results from Nostromo's clinging to a belief that willful action secures the achievement of deliberated purposes. Conrad pairs Decoud with Nostromo because Decoud's terror of patience and passion is the obverse of Nostromo's obsessive attachment to the romance of deeds. The obsession is widespread: it engenders the incoherently mingled dispositions in Costaguana that exchange radicalism for reaction, and reaction for radicalism, without making progress. Sustaining suffering and passion, Dr. Monygham is braver than Nostromo and Decoud, and has more insight into Costaguana's conflicts and history than the glamorous pair of males who exemplify *homo faber*.

Hypothesizing an alternative to *homo faber*'s perspective, Arendt suggests that the loss of the name of action can be a gain for political vision. Perhaps Conrad's novella "The Duel" (1907) is a glimpse of the gain. The narrative is set in Napoleonic and Restoration France, so it is both an imperial romance, and a realist fiction. The story is simple: one of Napoleon's officers challenges another to a succession of duels over the course of fifteen years. The motive for the first challenge is trivial; the motive for the subsequent challenges is unfathomable. But the challenged officer repeatedly responds, always feeling the absurdity of the action he and his opponent are engulfed by. The action feels like control to the challenger (who is deluded); it feels like suffering to the one who is challenged. By chance, not by mastery, the challenged officer comes out the superior duelist every time; but he feels each victory as a burden, and when, forgiving his opponent, he saves him from hanging, his reward is yet another duel. While the duelists struggle on, over their heads (so to speak) Napoleon asserts in his own person *homo faber* as emperor; then Louis Bourbon reasserts *homo faber* as king. Less assertive, the duelists beneath the rulers suffer action as a passion without mastery, and experience agency as an undergoing without liberty. If Conrad's dueling pair do not know what they are doing, or do not know what to do with their bafflement, the suggestion of "The Duel's" realistic romance is that rulers should submit to the humbling of action, rather than master or erase it in the wonted imperious style of instrumentalists.

Notes

1. Wendy Katz, *Rider Haggard and the Fiction of Empire* (Cambridge University Press, 1987), p. 33.
2. Patrick Brantlinger, *Rule of Darkness: British Literature and Imperialism, 1830–1914* (Ithaca, NY: Cornell University Press, 1988), p. 265.
3. Edward W. Said, *Culture and Imperialism* (New York: Vintage Books, 1993), p. 30.
4. Walter Scott, *Chronicles of the Canongate*, ed. Claire Lamont (Edinburgh University Press, 2000), p. 201.
5. Gauri Viswanathan, *Masks of Conquest: Literary Study and British Rule in India* (New York: Columbia University Press, 1989), p. 17.
6. Hannah Arendt, *The Human Condition* (University of Chicago Press, 1958), p. 220.
7. John Buchan, *Prester John* (McLean, Virginia: IndyPublish.com, n.d.), p. 56.
8. Laura Chrisman, *Re-reading the Imperial Romance* (Oxford: Clarendon Press, 2000), p. 107.
9. H. Rider Haggard, *She and Allan* (New York: Ballantine Books, 1978), p. 1.
10. Rudyard Kipling, *Soldiers Three* and *In Black and White* (Harmondsworth: Penguin Books, 1993), p. 134.
11. Rudyard Kipling, *Many Inventions* (London: Macmillan, 1893), p. 178.
12. Rudyard Kipling, *Life's Handicap: Being Stories of Mine Own People* (London: Macmillan, 1891), p. 165.
13. Robert Louis Stevenson, *The Master of Ballantrae: A Winter's Tale* (New York: Barnes and Noble, 2006), p. 227.
14. Robert Louis Stevenson, *South Sea Tales*, ed. Roslyn Jolly (Oxford University Press, 1996), p. 123.
15. Joseph Conrad, *Almayer's Folly* (New York: The Modern Library, 2002), p. 3.

33

The art novel: Impressionists
and aesthetes

JESSE MATZ

"That Fiction is an art in every way worthy to be called the sister and the equal of the Arts of Painting, Music, and Poetry" was Walter Besant's argument before the Royal Institution on April 25, 1884.[1] The argument was self-evident to anyone of a continental mentality but not "so generally perceived as to form, so to speak, part of the national mind" (6). England did not generally consider fiction an art. To the English a novelist "is a person who tells stories; just as they used to regard the actor as a man who tumbled on the stage to make the audience laugh, and a musician a man who fiddled to make the people dance" (9). Besant tries to elevate the novel by asserting its ancient primacy, its breadth ("its field is the whole of humanity"), its value ("it creates and develops that sympathy which is a kind of second sight"), and its subtlety in selection, arrangement, and suggestion (31–32). The claim to "subtlety" would have been surprising, even to an audience not inclined to laugh and dance. That fiction is an art distinguished by real aesthetic refinement needed serious proof, and Besant gave it a try – in "The Art of Fiction," and as part of a culture of letters eager to give the English novel the distinction necessary to claim its place among the finest arts.

Henry James became that culture's leading figure, and his response to Besant – his "Art of Fiction," also published in 1884 – sums up the art-novel impulse of the moment. James disagrees with Besant on one crucial point. Besant claims that fiction "is governed by certain laws, methods, and rules," most importantly that "everything in Fiction which is invented, and not the result of personal experience and observation, is worthless" (34). James found this rule decidedly inartistic; its empiricism could only block aesthetic creativity. So James makes a slight but monumental correction: "a novel is in its broadest definition a personal, direct impression of life" – not a personal "experience" or a direct "observation," but something more removed and more fully personal, given to subjectivity and sensibility.[2] Declaring that "impressions *are* experience," James relocates the art of fiction to the realm of personal discretion, staking it upon the shifting ground of subjective perspective. Whereas Besant endorses a realism that leaves no room for art to intervene, James opens up the necessary space for aesthetic insight to flourish, and his "impressions" become widely shared in one trend central to the art novel: literary Impressionism.

James's response to Besant also reflects another trend in the late nineteenth-century art of fiction. He notes that Besant "seems to me to mistake in attempting to say so definitely beforehand what sort of affair the good novel will be" because "the good health of an art which undertakes so immediately to reproduce life must demand that it be fully free" (169–170). Calling for freedom, James speaks the language of aestheticism, the movement that freed art from responsibility to anything but the requirements of art itself. Empirical realism is again the adversary, but for a different reason. Impressionism relocates realism in the operations of subjective perception; aestheticism trades realism for the pleasures of the imagination, giving up the novel's social and moral responsibilities in favor of the delights of artifice.

In Impressionism objective, omniscient narrators give way to limited, fallible ones; narrative coherence becomes flux; stable backdrops dissolve into elusive, portentous atmospheres. Aestheticism produces fiction rarified by the demands of "art for art's sake": neutral narrators give way to flamboyant, sophisticated, knowing *poseurs*; plots become coyly artificial, increasing in drama, adventure, and sensation; the moral of the story gives way to the beauty of the tale. The impressionists include Joseph Conrad, Ford Madox Ford, and Virginia Woolf. The aesthetes include George Meredith, Robert Louis Stevenson, Max Beerbohm, and Oscar Wilde. Impressionists and aesthetes together transform the English novel, changing its motivations and modes, making artfulness its priority. And yet the classifications do not really hold. Even as these writers register their impressions and indulge their imaginations, unforeseen complications lead them to post-Impressionism, to decadence – to the brink of modernism.

"Impressionism" calls to mind striking images – Parliament awash in foggy color, haystacks shading from daylight yellow to dusky purple, pleasure boats on glistering pond-water – but not ideas. Monet and his fellow Impressionists painted pictures without meanings, the better to capture immediate perception and to purify the medium of painting. "Literary Impressionism" sounds like a literary equivalent: a style dedicated to vivid descriptions, without the depth of thought and feeling "literary" ought to signify. Certainly the two Impressionisms share a belief that individual subjective experience is what constitutes reality, and both react against reason and ethics by staking representation on idiosyncratic personal perspectives. Both choose ordinary, personal, momentary subjects over important public or mythic figures or stories of historic interest. Both stress unmediated perception, focussing on the immediacy of the perceiving eye. And indeed some accounts do dismiss literary Impressionism as "merely impressionistic," just a matter of superficial appearances, a category error that mistakes the art of fiction for something appropriate only to painting.

Of course literary Impressionism is not limited to mere appearances or to the flux and fragmentation of merely subjective experience. Its immediate perceptions entail further thinking. Impressions provoke reflections – speculations about the relationship between appearance and reality, recognitions of the bewilderment caused by the flux of modern life, judgments about the ethics of subjectivity.

Joseph Conrad's fiction is full of the vivid landscapes and heady atmospheres that liken Impressionist writing to Impressionist painting. Conrad filters information through the subjective perspectives of idiosyncratic narrators and characters. His non-linear time-schemes jumble present reflections and past events. His locales are less real places than distortions of the perceiving eye and mind, expressing moods derived more from characters' feelings than facts, and intensities of immediate sights and sounds tend to crowd out reasoned judgments and balanced evaluations. But Conrad's atmospherics provoke existential questions. His narrators find their subjective perspectives challenged by stubbornly objective realities. Ethical drama results. His Impressionism begins in "mere appearances," but never ends there.

The Nigger of the "Narcissus" (1897) begins with a famous preface in which Conrad explains his literary art. His goal, he writes, is "to make you *see*," through "an impression conveyed through the senses," and his motivations are those of the literary Impressionist: the intensities of subjective perception are truth-effects, and authentic realism depends upon mimicry of them.[3] But "to make you see" is also to make you understand more keenly; to "do justice to the visible universe" is to "[bring] to light the truth, manifold and one, underlying its every aspect" (vii). Moreover, it is to create human fellowship, since impressions "awaken in the hearts of the beholders that feeling of unavoidable solidarity" that "binds men to each other and all mankind to the visible world" (x). Chaos and emptiness threaten to make human existence meaningless. Solidarity achieved through common feeling redeems it. This argument indicates Impressionism's range: it begins in phenomenological intensity, then becomes an epistemological question, an existential endeavor, and an ethical good.

The Nigger of the "Narcissus" has this range. Its narrator is an ordinary crewman, and his perceptions are vividly personal – for example, his first impression of shipboard life:

> The main deck was dark aft, but halfway from forward, through the open doors of the forecastle, two streaks of brilliant light cut the shadow of the quiet night that lay upon the ship. A hum of voices was heard there, while port and starboard, in the illuminated doorways, silhouettes of moving men appeared for a moment, very black, without relief, like figures cut out of sheet tin. (3)

No full explanation sets this scene; instead, vivid images immerse us in it. But the images begin to connote moods that suggest existential problems. Singleton, "the oldest seaman in the ship," makes an emphatically meaningful impression: "With his spectacles and a venerable white beard, he resembled a learned and savage patriarch, the incarnation of barbarian wisdom serene in the blasphemous turmoil of the world" (6). Likewise, when "the sun [looks] upon [the ship] all day, and every morning rose with a burning round stare of undying curiosity," or when the stars "[surround] the vanquished and tormented ship on all sides: more pitiless than the eyes of a triumphant mob, and as unapproachable as the hearts of men," impressions become symbols, and immediate perceptions are one with wild surmises (29, 77). Impressionism then develops the ethical theme of the novel. In his preface Conrad expresses the hope that prose impressions will "make you see" and encourage human fellowship; but in the novel fellowship is a disaster. Strong feelings do unite the crew just as intense impressions are supposed to unify readers, but the unity in question is demoralizing and destructive: "we were becoming highly humanized, tender, complex, excessively decadent . . . as though we had been overcivilized, and rotten, and without any knowledge of the meaning of life . . . We were inexpressibly vile" (139). Conrad seems to worry that locating human fellowship in "impressions conveyed through the senses" dangerously undermines civilization, knowledge, and meaning, debasing higher goods into "merely impressionistic" feelings after all.

Such ambivalence is essential to Impressionism and to its real significance as a novelistic mode. It derives from the peculiar status of the "impression." Impressions occupy no secure place in the process of perception. Sometimes immediate sensations, sometimes feelings or intuitions, sometimes essential insights, impressions often collapse distinct aspects of human understanding. This peculiar status is good for the way it helps writers like Conrad articulate a new form of realism and promote a new kind of art novel, but it also complicates the effort to tell the kind of stories for which the novel was invented – stories of development from ignorance to wisdom, from innocence and error to maturity and truth.

James's *The Portrait of a Lady* (1881) turns on a momentous impression. Isabel Archer is unaware of the relationship that has secretly shaped her life: Gilbert Osmond and Madame Merle – her malignant husband and her designing friend – once were lovers. At the end of chapter 41 Isabel walks into a room and sees them together, and she gets an impression of surprising intimacy:

> Just beyond the threshold of the drawing-room she stopped short, the reason for her doing so being that she had received an impression. The impression had, in strictness, nothing unprecedented; but she felt it as something new, and the soundlessness of her step gave her time to take in the scene before she interrupted it.[4]

Osmond sits while Madame Merle stands – something "anomalous" because only a close relationship would allow him to keep his seat while a woman is standing. Isabel's impression is just a sighting. But it gives her a dim idea, a shock, a feeling, and a suspicion – all at once. "The thing made an image, lasting only a moment, like a sudden flicker of light. Their relative positions, their absorbed mutual gaze, struck her as something detected. But it was all over before she had seen it": instantaneous, the impression also persists, freezing Isabel in place but also leading her to further thinking. Fleeting but fixating, a hunch and a truth, a visual glimpse and an ethical discovery, Isabel's impression is complex and unstable, a powerful resource for fiction because of its epistemological ambiguity.

Such complexities could only delight Henry James. They are key to the art novel as he and his Impressionist contemporaries conceive it, entailing the narratorial intricacies, figural innovations, temporal diversities, and ethical ambiguities that distinguish the new novelistic art from fictional realism. In *The Portrait of a Lady* Impressionism enables a perspectivalism in which things are not just seen from a fixed point of view but styled by sensibility, colored by the character of the perceiver. Impressionism accounts for the subtlety of James's signature way of rendering "consciousness," and it allows him to mingle present perception and memory in a complex temporal texture. But as it is for Conrad this complexity is also a source of thematic concern. When Isabel's impression ranges from the sight of the scene to the perception of "something detected" and expands to more extensive speculation, it collapses together what fiction might need to keep apart. Consider its effects on Isabel's story. Is Isabel mainly a young woman susceptible to fresh sensations, or is she significantly capable of serious discernment? Impressionism would have it both ways, and indeed the story of *The Portrait of a Lady* is all about the difficulty with which one develops from a fresh, impressionable young person to a seasoned woman capable of firm reasoning and decisive judgment. The possibility of conflict between freshness and fineness pervades James's fiction. Impressionism correlates with his "international theme," for example, which confronts worldly sophisticates with fresh innocents in plot-structures that complicate the perceptual structure through which impressions work.

Behind those enabling complications is the tradition of British empiricism and aesthetic theories that respond to it throughout the nineteenth century. David Hume's Enlightenment philosophy discovered the extent to which impressions were subjective – an extent that became the measure of his radical skepticism. Hume set the standard whereby Impressionism would assert the adequacy of sensuous appearances. And at the same time he established the ambivalence that would inform Impressionism's skeptical themes and plots. This perceptual dynamic characterizes the work of Impressionism's key predecessor, Walter Pater. Declaring his Impressionism in response to Matthew Arnold's famous injunction to "know the object as in itself it really is," Pater notes that one might and should only know one's impression of it: "the first step towards seeing one's object as it really is, is to know one's own impression as it really is."[5] Pater relocates aesthetic judgment in personal sensibility, combining the critical and the creative in essays and fiction prompted by Epicurean sensations. Like Hume, however, Pater sees the tragedy in it. His Epicureanism is shadowed by death; Impressionist intensity must always give way to change and flux, and the pleasure of it devolves into melancholia. Pater's *Marius the Epicurean* (1885) attempts to balance Epicurean and skeptical Impressionisms. And yet the novel is a precursor text in the history of literary Impressionism because it explores Impressionist theory rather than enacting its practice: Marius lives a life inspired and troubled by the principles through which writers like James and Conrad later convert fictional realism to subjective relativism.

The writer most fully to practice Impressionist theory is Ford Madox Ford. His essays on Impressionism argue that fiction must reproduce effects of life as we live it in order to seem real. As he puts it in *Joseph Conrad: A Personal Remembrance*, "we wished to produce on you an effect of life," which meant "[we] must not narrate but render ... impressions."[6] Rendering impressions requires "selection," "surprise," realistic incompleteness in representation of conversations, "*progression d'effet*," and whatever else necessary to give the reader the feeling of immersion in life itself (182–215). Ford's most important novel, *The Good Soldier* (1915), puts principles into practice by radically limiting its narration to the haphazard, partial, often blinded perceptions of a single character. True to life, this narration turns out not to be true in fact. *The Good Soldier* brings the ambivalence begun in Hume to its most extreme expression, because its narrator's Impressionism demonstrates the greatest possible divergences of appearance and reality, between impressions of life and the truth about it.

The narrator of *The Good Soldier*, John Dowell, admits at the outset that he will only be able to relate his impressions. Unsure "how to put this thing down," he opts for Impressionist method: "So I shall just imagine myself for a fortnight or so at one side of the fireplace of a country cottage, with a sympathetic soul opposite me. And I shall go on talking" (19). Rather than try for the authoritative voice of an objective, all-knowing narrator, Dowell falls back on the subjective dynamics of memory, commiseration, bias, and self-indulgence, telling his story "in a very rambling way so that it might be difficult for anyone to find their path through what may be a sort of maze" (167). And he justifies his method of telling his story "as it comes" by noting that "when one discusses an affair – a long, sad affair – one goes back, one goes forward," adding and revising in the process. Dowell "consoles" himself with "thinking that this is a real story and that, after all, real stories are probably told best in the way a person telling a story would tell them. They will then seem most real." Greater "reality" is the effect of Dowell's fragmentary, haphazard narration, which fails at linear organization and tries for effects that might simulate in the reader the feelings of the teller.

But since Dowell's narration also perpetually revises itself – returning to an old impression to correct it with new information – it undermines its own theory of "reality." Dowell concludes an account of an important event by saying, "well, those are my impressions," only to start in again by saying "What had actually happened was this" (104). This alternation is typical. His impressions are most often wrong, so that finally he must confess, "I know nothing – nothing in the world – of the hearts of men. I only know that I am alone – horribly alone" (14). On the one hand, then, Ford and his fiction assert that impressions represent an adequate reality of their own – that of experiential truth or phenomenological plenitude. On the other hand, Ford and his fiction lament a ruinous discrepancy between appearances and reality. Ford ultimately equates Impressionism with a solipsism that is epistemologically and ethically disastrous. This problem sums up the drama of Impressionism, which we have now seen in James and Conrad as well: the conflict between Impressionism's phenomenology and its epistemology is the real story of Impressionism. When this problem becomes a moral dilemma,

Impressionism reverts to an ethical enterprise, despite the hope of its practitioners to free fiction from direct moral responsibility.

The problem of Impressionism, however, does not trouble all its practitioners. Fuller commitment to Impressionist reality enables modernist writers – most notably, Dorothy Richardson and Virginia Woolf – to produce new narrative forms that innovate explorations of subjective consciousness. Richardson's *Pilgrimage* – the thirteen-volume *roman fleuve* published from 1915 to 1967 – most fully exemplifies Impressionism because its subjectivism never comes in for correction or qualification. Miriam Henderson's consciousness encompasses the full range of the novel's world; her consciousness registers all there is to know of it, and her perceptions fully compose it. *Pointed Roofs* (1915), the first volume of *Pilgrimage*, inaugurates Richardson's Impressionist experiment in the representation of "contemplated reality" with one of the first instances of "stream of consciousness" narration.[7] "Late at night," "rushing" in a train toward Germany, Miriam "began to think," and what follows is a welter of fragmentary reflections:

> It was a fool's errand ... To undertake to go to the German school and teach ... to be going there ... with nothing to give ... Her heart beat in her throat. She had never thought of that ... the rules of English grammar? Parsing and analysis ... Anglo Saxon prefixes and suffixes ... gerundial infinitive ... It was too late to look anything up.[8]   (29)

The rushed, inchoate, fragmentary thoughts exemplify Impressionism's tendency toward narrative deformation, a deterioration characteristic of Impressionism's effort to make narrative reflect unstructured dynamics of real human experience. This particular passage tellingly introduces Richardson's approach to consciousness by questioning the "rules of grammar," preferring language impressionistically atomized into pieces of extra-linguistic expressivity. More generally, Richardson presents subjective experience without implying that objective truths ought to correct or even supplement them. At one moment, for example, Miriam is reading a thin volume of German poetry. Her surroundings derealize, and the description of them implies that vague semblances convey reality:

> There was a stirring in the room; beautiful forms rose and stood and spoke and moved about. Someone went to the door. It opened gently with a peaceful sound on to the quiet hall and footsteps ran upstairs. Two figures going out from the *saal* passed in front of the two still sitting quietly grouped in the light of the summer-house. They were challenged as they passed and turned soft profiles and stood talking. Behind the voices – flutings,

single notes, broken phrases – long undisturbed warblings came from the
garden birds.   (142)

Just what the voices might be saying is secondary to their sensory effects; just
what they have to do with the story is secondary to the pattern of their
registration, and plot more generally dissolves into Richardson's impressionist
consciousness.

If Richardson pursues subjectivism to its farthest extremes, Virginia Woolf
pursues radical fulfillment of another key premise: that fiction should dissolve
itself into the flux and fragmentation that actually inform human experience.
Jacob's Room (1922) opens upon a dissolving world, a landscape seen through
tears. As Betty Flanders tries to write a letter, "her eyes fixed, and tears slowly
filled them. The entire bay quivered; the lighthouse wobbled; and she had the
illusion that the mast of Mr. Connor's little yacht was bending like a candle in
the sun."[9] This dissolving landscape indicates the novel's Impressionist intentions, which turn out to be more extensive than the wobbling of lighthouses
and the bending of masts. Woolf's narration quivers beyond Mrs. Flanders's
confusion to a range of perceiving characters whose impressions gradually
piece together an image of the novel's central subject. The result is unique, for
whereas Richardson's Impressionism suggests that personal impressions constitute a strong individual consciousness, and that the greatest reality is the one
made up by the individual mind, Woolf's Impressionism suggests that it is
only the impressions of others that constitute human beings, and never in
complete or lasting ways. One's own impressions are so utterly changeable
that they lay consciousness open to flux and dissolution; life itself is only the
fleeting passage of impressions, barely composing objects and persons into
being, vanishing selfhood away.

Jacob's Room presents its protagonist only through the partial views of his
friends and family. The novel's narrator shifts rapidly but seamlessly from one
point of view to another, proffering images as intense as they are insubstantial.
Ultimately Jacob is less a solid object than a provocation to seek the truth of
life itself – the "unseizable force" that drives us, the "indescribable agitation of
life" that is its essential Impressionist pattern (156, 163). Woolf's goal is less to
represent impressions than to simulate the vitality with which they strike and
pass. What makes her fiction unique is the fact that this penchant for unseiz-
ability and indescribability does not entail skepticism. Whereas other
Impressionists make the inadequacy of impressions a basis for disappointment
and failure, for Woolf it is precisely what makes them true to life, leading her
Impressionist novels to conclusions in which epistemological failures (the kind

familiar from other Impressionists) enable existential affirmations. At the end of *Jacob's Room*, Mrs. Flanders exclaims, "Such confusion everywhere!," and it is clear that Jacob has entirely escaped our understanding. An empty room and Jacob's old shoes reflect his absolute absence. And yet that very absence has generated such "life" that *Jacob's Room* affirms human existence. The novel's Impressionism has shown that life is in the process of guessing at it, rather than in its "real" products. What might read like a darkly skeptical conclusion – the death of a protagonist we have never really come to know – is actually an affirmative one, since "life itself" has abundantly come through even despite the radical failures of real life.

Woolf famously declares her intention to represent "life itself" by recording the "impressions" that strike the mind in the course of ordinary existence.[10] This declaration hearkens back to James's intentions for the art of fiction and intensifies the impulse through which James innovates the form of the art novel. That impulse, however, also takes fiction in a very different direction. Aestheticism focusses art not on the alternative realism of subjective perception but on the unreality of the imagination. As we have seen, Henry James answers Walter Besant's prescriptive realism not only with an Impressionist alternative but also with stress on the necessity of artistic freedom. James is in turn answered by Robert Louis Stevenson. Whereas James writes that fiction ought to be free to represent impressions rather than direct experience, Stevenson urges that art should be more fully free to "[substitute] a certain artificial series of impressions" for reality.[11] In his "Humble Remonstrance" to James and Besant, Stevenson argues that "the novel which is a work of art exists, not by its resemblances to life, which are forced and material, as a shoe must still consist of leather, but by its immeasurable difference from life, which is designed and significant, and is both the method and the meaning of the work" (92). Different from life, art depends not at all on real experience, but wishful thinking; "I believe," Stevenson writes, "that the artist writes with more gusto and effect of those things which he has only wished to do, than of those things which he has done. Desire is a wonderful telescope, and Pisgah is the best discovery" (94). Stevenson's theory is one basis for aestheticism in fiction. Indeed the "art novel" gets its central justification from Stevenson's claim that fiction truly exists at the pleasure of the aesthetic imagination, that it bears no essential relation to life, and that it should be responsible only to the discoveries of desire.

Another basis for aestheticism in fiction is George Meredith's theory of comedy. Just as Stevenson reacts against James's lingering empiricism, in *The Egoist* (1879) Meredith reacts against the "realistic method of a conscientious transcription of all the visible, and a repetition of all the audible," which "is mainly accountable for our present branfulness, and for that prolongation of the vasty and the noisy, out of which, as from an undrained fen, steams the malady of sameness, our modern malady."[12] The age is too scientific; the best remedy for the "modern malady" is art – more specifically, the art of comedy. For Meredith, comedy is fiction's proper mode because it "proposes the correcting of pretentiousness, of inflation, of dullness, and of the vestiges of rawness and grossness to be found among us" (5). Comedy improves upon human reality. "She is the ultimate civilizer," transforming the great mass of human error into a model for human improvement. And pleasure as well, since comedy selects only those elements of the "Book of Earth" that improve us through laughter.

The result for fiction is emphatically different from Impressionism. Impressionism is immediate, without narratorial intrusion, and it stresses subjective verisimilitude. In novels like *The Egoist* aestheticism entails endless narratorial interference, and style is its main substance. It features authorial didacticism to the point of parody and trades mimetic intensity for fine phrasing and elaborate figural flourish. Whereas Impressionism faces the modern moment, Meredith's aestheticism returns to classicism, albeit a classicism light enough to stay *au courant*. Any atmospherics are set-piece sceneries. Wit, rather than skepticism, is the mode of insight; repartee and epigrams are abundant; and stagey dramas appear in place of the subtler realities characteristic of impressionistic moments of being. Artifice utterly resists realism. And aestheticism is therefore very different from Impressionism, even if the two share the impulse to free fiction from direct responsibility to realist representation.

Consider the contrast between impressionist subjectivism and Meredith's figuration of a man watching a beautiful woman: "So, as, for instance, beside a stream, when a flower on the surface extends its petals drowning to subside in the clear still water, we exercise our privilege to be absent in the charmed contemplation of a beautiful natural incident" (278). The elaborate conceit does not try to immerse us in the moment's passion, but rather to encourage disinterested, abstract reflection, a refined recognition of common experience aptly transposed into playfully refined language. Consider the contrast between an Impressionist's immediate way of rendering consciousness and this narratorial account of a woman's sense of herself:

> She sighed and put a tooth on her underlip. The gift of humorous fancy is in
> women fenced round with forbidding placards; they have to choke it; if they

perceive a piece of humour . . . they have to blindfold the mind's eye. They are society's hard-drilled soldiery, Prussians that must march and think in step. It is for the advantage of the civilized world, if you like, since men have decreed it, or matrons have so read the decree; but here and there a younger woman, haply an uncorrected insurgent of the sex matured here and there, feels that her lot was cast with her head in a narrower pit than her limbs.

(67)

The mind's eye does not dominate here. Blinded by decorum, it is suborned by narratorial wit, which only ironically represents this insubordination through comical figuration. Once again, figural finesse mediates emphatically between the reality and the reader. And yet this mediation occurs for the same reason the Impressionists sought immediacy. Meredith's broad metaphor exercises fiction's freedom to depart from factual information, taking that freedom further in order to exploit even more fully the subjective powers of the literary imagination.

Chapter 11 of *The Egoist* includes a disquisition on love. The plot of the novel – Sir Willoughby, the egoist, is to be jilted a second time, by Clara Middleton, who, like her predecessor, finds her fiancé as unbearable as he is eligible – is really a pretext for this sort of performance. Meredith flamboyantly observes love's blindness, exposing the absurdity of egoism through contrast with his own elaborate insight. But the disquisition is itself a pretext for the more purely comical performance that ends it: "And if you ask whether a man, sensitive and a lover, can be so blinded, you are condemned to reperuse the foregoing paragraph" (93). This bit of self-referential narrative play makes literal the artifice that frees aesthetic fiction from responsibility to the real world. *The Egoist*, despite its title, is more about itself than any real human problem, making the question of egoism a chance to display styles of awareness rather than a chance to intervene in social reality. Which is not to say that Meredith's aestheticism departs entirely from social or ethical objectives; rather, it is to say that it puts the pleasures of artifice first, making the other objectives of fiction secondary to the freedom of the imagination.

Artifice is not unique to the fiction of this moment, of course. Novelists had quite often framed their fictions in such a way as to stress their aesthetic provenance, qualifying any mimetic objectives with stress upon the precedence of the literary imagination. George Eliot begins *Adam Bede* equating her earnestly realistic fiction with sorcery: "With a single drop of ink for a mirror, the Egyptian sorcerer undertakes to reveal to any chance comer far-reaching visions of the past. This is what I undertake to do for you, reader."[13] Dickens is of course full of frankly fictive caricatures, stylized set pieces, and neo-gothic revivals, of which the circus figures in *Hard Times*, the melodramas of Chancery, and the habit of Dickensian naming are examples. Even as early as 1819, Sir Walter Scott frames *The Bride of Lammermoor* with an aesthetic dialogue, in which a painter and a writer debate the relative merits of their arts. The painter, Dick Tinto, disdains the paltry drama of literary art, claiming that its "creeping twilight details" render fiction "incapable of receiving that instant and vivid flash of conviction, which darts upon the mind from seeing the happy and expressive combinations of a single scene."[14] The writer – the fictional author of *The Bride of Lammermoor* itself – concedes, and therefore "[endeavors] to render my narrative rather descriptive than dramatic" (20). Scott foregrounds the difference an artist's choices might make, predicting further defections from realism made by later aesthetes.

Realism locates itself in the lives of ordinary people. Aesthetic fiction migrates back up the social scale – in *The Egoist* (which never leaves the grounds of Patterne Hall) and in Stevenson's *Prince Otto* (1885), a fantasy of Bohemian aristocracy and a prime example of the aesthete's "Pisgah" poetics. A tale of court intrigue in fictional Grunewald, *Prince Otto* is the story of an unpopular royal who finally achieves heroism in exile, a fine but misunderstood prince happily overthrown by a fairly comical republican insurrection. A "bibliographical postscript" calls the novel a "historical romance," and indeed Stevenson's novel might seem to be a retrograde reversion to forms of romance that had been outdated by nineteenth-century realism.[15] In the context of the art novel, however, Stevenson's romance is very much of the moment, because it asserts the necessity of subjective invention. The novel may be full of excessively romantic characterizations, formulations, and plot twists – women run about with their black velvet dresses "ruthlessly sweeping in the dirt" (510), and "you betray, I betray, they betray" could be the novel's motto (539) – but its brazen effeteness belies an important aesthetic agenda. As much as *Prince Otto* departs into royalist fantasy, it exemplifies the cultural value of the refined mind: the prince is utterly out of touch, completely disinterested, nothing but a gentleman, but he is therefore capable finally of choosing the fate most desirable from the standpoints both of love and politics, of public and private life. *Prince Otto* implies that the forms of artful imagining enrich the realities of practical existence. The novel ends with the prince having finally won his princess – as if in a dream, lost in the "spring woods" – as "the Republic was declared" (613). This is very clearly the work of an aesthetic novelist writing what "he has only wished," art for its own sake only, but it argues allegorically for the value of aesthetic judgment: free to imagine anything, Stevenson models a world in which a lack of real constraints enables ideal outcomes.

The Egoist and *Prince Otto* have many fellow travelers, in the realms of adventure fiction, neo-romantic fantasy, and comedy of manners. Anthony Hope's *Prisoner of Zenda* (1894) also fantasizes about royalty, giving another good-for-nothing aristocrat (this time, an English one) a chance at true royal valor. Rudolf Rassendyl resembles the future king of Ruritania so much that he is able to impersonate him when a pretender attempts a coup. As the aimless English aristocrat becomes a swashbuckling hero – the rescuer of the prisoner of Zenda, the savior of Ruritania, the real beloved of the princess – the merely aesthetic pleasure of these novels becomes an argument for aesthetic refinement. Even in less knowing novels like Ouida's *Princess Napraxine* (1884), the pleasures of aesthetic royalism make their case, as Nadine Napraxine represents the alternative virtues of perfectly amoral wit, beauty, and passion. Of course, pure pleasure is only a pleasure in novels like Max Beerbohm's *Zuleika Dobson* (1911), in which farce takes over and the aesthetic motive completely disclaims responsibility. Zuleika is a young woman so charming that all of Oxford, including the Duke of Dorset, fall in love with her, and ultimately commit mass suicide in her honor. The comical style of glittery, lacquered, light-classical narration innovated by Meredith here becomes wildly parodic, so dedicated to its own sake that it indulges a fantasy of authorial omnipotence. In the novel's central chapter 11, we learn that fiction has become a factor in Zeus' efforts to woo Clio, the muse of history. He has allowed her to "choose an historian" upon whom to "confer invisibility, inevitability, and psychic penetration, with a flawless memory thrown in."[16] Beerbohm's narrator finds himself "suddenly on Parnassus," and then floating unseen and all-knowing among the characters of his tale. Artifice here becomes the subject of the tale as the art novel subjects even itself to its own essential irresponsibility.

Such irresponsibility could go beyond fun and become decadence. Aestheticism untrammeled could be so self-indulgently artificial as to leave no aesthetic reasons intact. Decadence did not tend to take hold in the English novel, which always held on to some form of representational justification, but it did become the subject of novels intended to test the limits of art in fiction. Oscar Wilde's *The Picture of Dorian Gray* (1891) begins with a preface that articulates the fundamental tenets of aestheticism: "books are well written, or badly written. That is all"; "An ethical sympathy in an artist is an unpardonable mannerism of style"; "All art is quite useless."[17] Similar theories are expressed by the novel's aesthetes, Basil Hallward and Lord Henry Wotton. Basil paints the picture of Dorian Gray, and, by doing so, discovers a new aesthetic vocation – a new way for art to "recreate life" (13). Lord Henry supplies the decadent corollary: upon meeting Dorian Gray, Lord Henry schools him in the aesthetic way to "Live!" by "always searching for new sensations," pursuing "Hedonism" according to the principles that "Beauty is a form of Genius" and that "the true mystery of the world is the visible, not the invisible" (22–23). But Lord Henry's teachings make Dorian such an aesthete that he trades his life for art – becoming his portrait, which not only lives vicariously for him but betrays the costs of aestheticism by portraying Dorian's moral decay. Decadence will out, finally, and Wilde allegorizes the costs of the forms of artifice that give his style its characteristic brilliance. The decadent dandy is also a "dead man," "withered, wrinkled, and loathsome of visage," because the consequence of making an art out of life is poison as well as pleasure (161, 184). Here we reach the art novel's limit case. *The Picture of Dorian Gray* shows what happens when the freedom of the fictional imagination and the reaction against realism goes to its furthest extreme, giving up on responsibility to objectivity, ethics, and practicality. Other writers – Stevenson, Beerbohm, and their successors on into the twentieth century – pursue aestheticism without consequences, but it is Wilde, the writer who most thoroughly theorized aesthetic doctrine, who dramatizes the dangers of artifice.

Just as Stevenson offers his "remonstrance" to what he sees as James's too modest account of the literary imagination, Wilde responds to Walter Pater's theory of Impressionism. As we have seen, Pater had countered Matthew Arnold's claim that aesthetic judgment must "see the object as in itself it really is" with the claim that "the first step towards seeing one's object as it really is, is to know one's own impression as it really is." Wilde takes things further, stressing the need to "see the object as in itself it really is *not*."[18] In this progression from Arnold to Pater to Wilde is the range of theories from realism to Impressionism to aestheticism. Arnold's objectivity had been the goal of the forms of social realism against which the art novel develops its theories of the subjective imagination. Those theories make the imagination either a partner or an exclusive agent in the development of the perspectives by which the art novel asserts its difference from descriptions of the world as it is, its reason for existing apart from other forms of writing that represent but do not transform reality. Transformation through the imagination – partial in Impressionism, complete in the artifice of the aesthetes – or the imagination of worlds unknown not only give the English novel new license but give art a new mode. The art of fiction is the result. Whether or not art can sustain fiction is another question – one often taken up in the plots of art novels, and subsequently a central theoretical question for the novelists of high modernism.

Notes

1. Walter Besant, *The Art of Fiction* (London: Chatto and Windus, 1902), p. 5.
2. Henry James, "The Art of Fiction," in *The Art of Criticism: Henry James on the Theory and Practice of Fiction*, ed. William Veeder and Susan Griffin (University of Chicago Press, 1986), p. 170.
3. Joseph Conrad, *The Nigger of the "Narcissus"* (London: J. M. Dent, 1957), pp. x, ix.
4. James, *The Portrait of a Lady* (Oxford University Press, 1981), p. 442.
5. Matthew Arnold, "On Translating Homer," in *The Complete Prose Works of Matthew Arnold*, ed. Robert H. Super, 11 vols. (Ann Arbor: University of Michigan Press, 1960), vol. i, p. 174; Walter Pater, Introduction, *The Renaissance: Studies in Art and Poetry*, ed. Donald Hill (Berkeley: University of California Press, 1980), p. xix.
6. Ford Madox Ford, *Joseph Conrad: A Personal Remembrance* (London: Duckworth, 1924), p. 182.
7. Dorothy Richardson, "Foreword," *Pilgrimage*, 4 vols. (New York: Alfred A. Knopf, 1967), vol. i, p. 10.
8. Richardson, *Pointed Roofs*, in *Pilgrimage*, vol. i, p. 29.
9. Virginia Woolf, *Jacob's Room* (New York: Harcourt Brace Jovanovich, 1992), p. 7.
10. Woolf, "Modern Novels," *The Essays of Virginia Woolf*, 6 vols. vol. iii: *1919–1924*, ed. Andrew McNeillie (New York: Harcourt Brace Jovanovich, 1991), p. 33.
11. Robert Louis Stevenson, "A Humble Remonstrance," *Henry James and Robert Louis Stevenson: A Record of Friendship and Criticism*, ed. Janet Adam Smith (London: Rupert Hart Davis, 1948), p. 92.
12. George Meredith, "Prelude," *The Egoist* (New York: W. W. Norton, 1979), p. 4.
13. George Eliot, *Adam Bede* (London: Penguin, 1985), p. 49.
14. Sir Walter Scott, *The Bride of Lammermoor* (Boston: Dana Estes, 1893), p. 18.
15. Stevenson, *Prince Otto*, *The Works of Robert Louis Stevenson*, Vallima Edition, 26 vols. (London: William Heinemann, 1922), vol. v, p. 614.
16. Max Beerbohm, *Zuleika Dobson* (London: Penguin, 1967), p. 133.
17. Oscar Wilde, *The Picture of Dorian Gray* (New York: W. W. Norton, 2007), pp. 3–4.
18. Oscar Wilde, "The Critic as Artist," in *The Artist as Critic*, ed. Richard Ellmann (University of Chicago Press, 1969), p. 369.

34

The impact of lyric, drama, and verse narrative on novel form

STEFANIE MARKOVITS

Standing atop the generic food chain of literature, the novel has yet to meet a genre it is unwilling or unable to consume, being equally capable of lyric, epic, and dramatic attitudes. Such is one implication of Bakhtin's recognition of the form's heteroglossic capacity to incorporate a "diversity" of "generic languages" and "inserted genres."[1] This omnivorous approach has served the novel well in a competitive literary marketplace, making it capable of adjusting quickly to changes in the cultural landscape. As Bakhtin writes, compared with other forms, "the novel appears to be a creature from an alien species. It gets on poorly with other genres. It fights for its own hegemony in literature; wherever it triumphs, the other older genres go into decline" (4). The decline, he insists, is based on the novel's integration of other genres and on the transformation that accompanies such integration: "Under conditions of the novel every direct word – epic, lyric, strictly dramatic – is to a greater or lesser degree made into an object . . . that quite often appears ridiculous in this framed condition" (49–50).

But as David Kurnick points out, "we need a more capacious model of generic interaction than one that understands literary forms as engaged in a kind of Darwinian struggle for survival"; we also need to recognize in a new genre traces of what has been left behind, traces that reveal a kind of generic (almost genealogical) nostalgia.[2] Of course, the novel has long been associated with nostalgia: in his *Theory of the Novel*, Georg Lukács describes the genre's "transcendental homelessness," its longing for the lost "totality" of epic, that is (to switch to Friedrich Schiller's terminology, which influences Lukács), its essentially "sentimental" nature.[3] I am reminded of George Eliot's description of Nicholas Bulstrode's phantom limb of memory in *Middlemarch* (1871–1872): any "past" form from which the novel developed "is not simply a dead history, an outworn preparation of the present: it is not a repented error shaken loose from the life: it is a still quivering part" of the genre.[4] And this awareness of loss as well as gain must be felt with special sensitivity, given how many British novelists are also poets (Walter Scott, Emily Brontë, George Eliot, George Meredith, Rudyard Kipling, Thomas Hardy, William Morris, D. H. Lawrence, James Joyce) or aspiring, albeit often frustrated, dramatists (W. M. Thackeray, Charles Dickens, Henry James, Virginia Woolf, Lawrence, Joyce, and – as authors of closet dramas – Eliot and Hardy).

In what follows I argue that we can consider the novel's essentially nostalgic stance through generic cues. The phantom limb of drama – and of narrative verse that is rooted in epic – appears most in relation to ideas of action and agency.[5] Lukács writes of the historical drama that "The decisive dramatic question" is "whether a person can express himself immediately and completely through a deed."[6] One way to approach the realist novel is as a genre in which such expression is no longer feasible. As Angel Clare reflects in Hardy's *Tess of the d'Urbervilles* (1891), "The beauty or ugliness of a character lay not only in its achievements, but in its aims and impulses; its true history lay, not among things done, but among things willed."[7] Novelistic allusions to drama often counter this view, restoring the importance of external deeds. The dramatic/ epic focus on action also correlates with a longing for communal public expression, with faith in an Aristotelian conception of political man, with belief in the human being as a meaningful actor operating in an objective medium that is both socially and historically navigable. In contrast, as Jay Clayton argues forcefully, novelistic gestures toward lyric appear in relation to ideas of individual transcendence of the temporal.[8] The poetic impulse figures as Platonic, in quest of ideals. It seeks access to experience that is extra-narrative, visionary, ahistorical, and fundamentally private, interior, and authentic.

Of course such categorical distinctions iron out complexity. For example, much poetic influence on the British novel during the nineteenth century can be described as either Wordsworthian or Byronic; those trends are poles apart. And as I have already suggested, the idea of "verse" levels distinctions between lyric and epic, an active, narrative mode (also found in ballads) occupying a different discursive territory from the former category, one that in my analysis resembles drama. Similarly, novelistic references to closet drama (an internalized genre) work more by analogy than by contrast. And references to Shakespeare can focus either on his lyric tendencies or his dramatic ones. Moreover, these forms can figure in novels in diverse ways: through inserted quotation and epigraphs, through allusions to authors (by either characters or narrators), and through looser symbolic or structural allusion (as when dependence on dialogue signals a debt to drama). Finally, generic influence operates differently over the period under consideration here: modernist narrative responds not only to Romantic poetry, with its quest for transcendence, but also to the more "novelized" kinds of Victorian poetry (narrative forms like dramatic monologues and verse novels). In the same manner, as the drama becomes novelized under the influence of naturalist playwrights like Ibsen (Lukács, *Historical Novel*, 5; Bakhtin, *Dialogic Imagination* 124), its impact changes from that of Victorian forms such as pantomime and melodrama. Thus the examples that follow can be but gestures towards a method of considering intergeneric relations not only in terms of victor and vanquished but also as indicating the desire to recoup or lament lost energies belonging to displaced genres.

In reviewing the early history of the novel, one observes how self-conscious novelists are in their interactions with other forms. Take, for instance, the moment early in Maria Edgeworth's *Belinda* (1801), in which the author stages a contest between Lady Delacour – symbol of the aristocratic Popean past – and her own heroine – representative of the *arriviste* didactic sentimental novel – through the attempted "rape" of a "lock" of Belinda's hair. Walter Scott offers a striking example of the generic contest. If for most of the nineteenth century poets competed in a marketplace dominated by the novel, at the beginning of this period, Scott enters upon prose in the wake of Byron's sensational rise (of course, Byron himself responds to the novel's post-Scott popularity in the increasingly "novelistic" English cantos of *Don Juan*). Yet Scott's first foray into fiction shows considerable unease about the shift in formal loyalties. Edward Waverley's crisis of conscience concerning his wavering political allegiances can stand in for Scott's feeling toward the new genre he has ambivalently taken up; *Waverley* (1814) thus represents a nostalgic look back at the moment when Scottish song finally gives way to English prose in the Jacobite Rebellion of 1745. And the Borderland setting, merely "Sixty Years Since" (especially when contrasted with the archaic sixteenth-century setting of *The Lady of the Lake* [1810], a verse romance with similar themes and locale), balances the action on the knife's edge between poetry and prose; as Scott warns his readers: "they will meet in the following pages neither a romance of chivalry, nor a tale of modern manners . . . my hero will neither have iron on his shoulders, as of yore, nor on the heels of his boots, as is the present fashion of Bond Street."[9] Still, such a precarious position is hard to maintain, and if *Waverley* suggests the presence of rebellious verse forces that may yet re-emerge to trouble the progress of prose, this battle goes to the novel.

Initially Waverley composes poems that serve both as signs of "the idle dreams of youth" in a "fond ideal world" (lyric vision) and as a "trumpet-call of Truth" that "Bids each fair vision pass away" (epic action) (23). But while

Waverley wishes to forsake lyric for epic, this task proves difficult. Even in its "natural" Highland homeland, for which Scott's hero departs, poetry has become the stuff of sentiment (recall the controversy about Ossian), as the oddly artificial set-up surrounding Flora MacIvor's poetic "Highland Minstrelry" (the title of chapter 22) reveals. As she stands beneath a waterfall – on a bank "decorated with trees and shrubs . . . under the direction of Flora, but so cautiously, that they added to the grace, without diminishing the romantic wildness of the scene" – she sings of the need to resuscitate lost glory. Yet as Fergus McIvor puts it, among the things useless to the "modern Highlander" is "a bard to sing of deeds he dare not imitate" (103). Poetry thus becomes equated with the past. Appropriately, the greatest source of verse in the novel ("his speech was song," Scott writes, quoting Southey's *Thalaba* [38]) is the "natural fool" Davie Gellatly (or Davie Do-nothing), Baron Bradwardine's old retainer, whose versifying idleness offers an oddly distorted mirror-image of our passive hero (40).

Davie's fate is tied to the Bradwardine home, Tully-Veolan. If Wordsworth likened *The Recluse* to a cathedral, Scott uses a Borderland estate to register the progress of his form. We first encounter it through the lens of Spenser, whom Waverley quotes upon seeing the "solitary and seeming enchanted mansion" (37). But after the Jacobite uprising the Hanoverian troops destroy this realm of romance with a brute insensitivity symbolized in the two ancient horse-chestnut trees they "mutilated and defaced." Waverley rescues from "ravage" "a small copy of Ariosto," which he "gather[s] to him as a treasure," a fragment of poetry to shore against the ruins. And this is also how Davie's "old Scottish song" strikes us, as it pierces the "scene of desolation" (297). Yet by the end of the novel, "the felled trees have been removed . . . their stumps grubbed up," and the grass reseeded. The ruined structures have been "replaced by buildings of a lighter and more picturesque appearance" (334), in accordance with the novelistic domesticity in which Waverley and his bride, Rose Bradwardine, will reside. While Davie is still there, his song is no longer recorded; the vestige of romance has now been relegated to a painting of Waverley and Fergus in Highland dress, which hangs in the refurbished (albeit in the old style) dining parlor (338). Nevertheless, as Marshall Brown notes, in Scott "the eventual subordination of poetry is to be understood as sacrifice, not enrichment."[10]

When she discovered *Waverley*'s authorship, Jane Austen complained, "Walter Scott has no business to write novels, especially good ones . . . He has Fame & Profit enough as a Poet, and should not be taking the bread out of other people's mouths."[11] But Austen's own engagement with poetry – Romantic poetry in particular – was significant and increasing throughout her career, culminating in the poetic musings of the heroine of *Persuasion* (1818) who, being "forced into prudence [or prose] in her youth, learned romance as she grew older."[12] *Mansfield Park* (published, like *Waverley*, in 1814) can be read as a contest between lyric and drama that takes full advantage of the capaciousness of novelistic form to tell its story. And, like Scott, Austen uses the fate of a great country estate to consider questions of genre. In such a reading, Fanny Price becomes the defender of poetry, as her nostalgic love of Cowper hints, and her decoration of her little white attic room (a place of vision and private retreat – a place of lyric) with "transparencies" (a visual equivalent to lyric) of Tintern Abbey (Wordsworth), "a cave in Italy" (Byron and Shelley), and "a moonlight lake in Cumberland" (more Wordsworth) confirms.[13] But if Fanny's East room opens a space for the Romantic visionary in Mansfield Park, the house finds itself menaced by drama, and, specifically, by the intrusion of the dramatic, Shakespeare-reading Crawfords, who lead the charge to convert the absent Sir Thomas's billiard-room into a stage for home theatricals that threaten to level the barriers between private and public space. Both house and novel become platforms for the battle between Fanny's lyric consciousness and the Crawfords' dramatic action, and what makes the book exciting – and matter for critical contention – is that Austen's allegiances to the genres appear divided. While the Crawfords might be unmasked as villains by the plot, their energy and verve, their great sociability, and their freedom offer genuine attractions that events cannot fully undermine. Meanwhile Fanny's passivity ("No, indeed, I cannot act" [115]) renders her troublingly unappealing for readers, even as Austen works hard to identify her acute consciousness with moral conscience.

While Austen might have written the occasional poem (including her final composition), her natural style is prose, with a dash of the dramatic thrown in (as her wonderful dialogues suggest). One recalls Mr. Elliot's description of Anne's translation at the concert of "the inverted, transposed, curtailed" lines of an Italian love-song "into clear, comprehensible, elegant English" (*Persuasion*, 151). But Emily Brontë's approach is that of a poet, as her only novel indicates. *Wuthering Heights* (1847) seems to record in its two generations a shift from a Romance (the term elides distinctions between verse and prose) sensibility to a Victorian ethos – a shift that is again figured through the "improvement" of the estate.[14] The novel's conclusion translates the alien, anti-social realm that Lockwood encounters on first entering the Heights into a scene of quiet, novelistic domesticity, in which the now-"cultivated" Hareton (the second generation's Heathcliff) takes reading lessons from a Catherine Heathcliff who is a tamer, more prosaic version of her mother. Yet *Wuthering Heights* is haunted by the specter of lyric, as we discover in the nightmarish dream sequence during Lockwood's stay at the Heights, when Cathy's ghost endeavors violently to gain ingress to the house: "I'm come home, I'd lost my way on the moor!" (20), she exclaims, as though declaring the intent of lyric to re-enter the novel's domestic realm after having wandered with the Romantics in the wilds of nature. And while the work, with its rings of narrative, may appear to contain the subversive energies of poetry, its very dependence upon thresholds (locations of transcendence, of "going beyond" [Clayton, *Romantic Vision*, 1]) and upon crucial narrative gaps indicates an essentially lyric sensibility: verse depends formally on empty space, not only in the "reversals" from line to line but in the blanks between stanzas.

The greatest of gaps is the story of Cathy and Heathcliff's love, a tale we keep circling but never truly reach. Nelly "hasp[s] the window" to the room in which Heathcliff dies (298), as though to keep out what is there on the moors, as though to protect the home from its strangeness (that which has been rendered uncanny, *unheimlich*). But with its beautiful final passage, in which an uncharacteristically lyrical Lockwood "lingers round" the graves of Cathy, Heathcliff, and Edgar "and wonder[s] how any one could ever imagine unquiet slumbers for the sleepers in that quiet earth" (300), the novel hardly achieves closure. Yet the conclusion is Lockwoodian in that we know him to be misreading one last time, assuming an imprisonment – a literal contain-ment in the grave – that could never be. While the lines recall Wordsworth's great lyric, "A slumber did my Spirit seal," we know Cathy and Heathcliff walk still: lyric will out. As Brontë declares in her poem, "To Imagination": "thou art ever there to bring / The hovering vision back."[15]

Surprisingly, Brontë's novel contains no overt references to poetry. But it is dominated by an example of one of Romantic poetry's greatest gifts to the nineteenth-century novel: a Byronic hero, a dark, angry outcast from society, "link'd with one virtue, and a thousand crimes," as Byron put it in *The Corsair* (1814).[16] Lukács calls the Byronic hero "a lyrical protest against the dominion of . . . prose" (*Historical Novel*, 33); if this is true, his presence in many novels strongly indicates generic nostalgia. He is everywhere in the fiction of the first half of the century: consider the eponymous anti-heroes of Edward Bulwer-Lytton's *Pelham* (1828) and *Eugene Aram* (1832), or that of Benjamin Disraeli's *Vivian Grey* (1826), or his Sidonia of *Coningsby* (1844) (Byron himself appears in Disraeli's *Venetia* [1837]). Yet Disraeli exposes Vivian Grey to satire, and in Charlotte Brontë's *Jane Eyre* (1847) the Byronic hero (Rochester) is first blinded and then domesticated by the novel's conclusion. By the time George Meredith (an inveterate experimenter with generic concoctions) writes *The Egoist* (1879), he has become not only a subject of novelistic satire, but his model of poetry has been subjected to a comedic – that is, dramatic – treatment, as the novel's subtitle ("A Comedy in Narrative") and its active heroine's name (Clara Middleton) indicate.

According to Marshall Brown, while the Romantic novel merges romance and reality in its happy integration of verse into prose, "On its rare appearances in Realist novels, poetry usually strikes a sour note" (110). The trend regarding Byronism that I have laid out fits with such a trajectory (although the fusion of forms is always anxious, as we have seen). Yet the great age of Victorian realism is also the era that sees the most concerted efforts to blend poetry and the novel into a new form: the verse novel. Elizabeth Barrett Browning's *Aurora Leigh* (1856), Robert Browning's *The Ring and the Book* (1869), and Alfred Tennyson's *Idylls of the King* (1859–1885) explicitly link their generic hybridity to efforts at melding both ideal and real and past and present. Consider Barrett Browning's description of her "novel-poem" as "An autobiography of a poetess – (not me) . . opposing the practical & the ideal lifes, & showing how the practical & real (so called) is but the external evolution of the ideal & spiritual – that it is from inner to outer";[17] or Robert Browning's central metaphor of a goldsmith combining "Fancy with fact" in order to "resuscitate" history in the dramatic monologues that comprise the "novel country" of his long poem;[18] or Tennyson's King Arthur, "Ideal manhood closed in real man," who stands at the center of a "New-old" poem that reconfigures epic as lyric idylls that express the story of an adulterous marriage.[19]

Similarly, although critics have read the realist novel's anti-theatricality as an effort to cordon off the domestic sphere from the public, masculine, and political stage of the eighteenth-century republic of letters,[20] novelists also turn to dramatic elements in order to reconsider the loss of such space. The ambiguities of the reconsideration surround Thackeray's self-presentation as "Manager of the Performance," as he steps "Before the Curtain" (as he titles his preface) of *Vanity Fair* (1848) to introduce his "puppets." The most agile of theatrical managers is Becky Sharpe, daughter of an opera singer and foil to the dull but dutifully domestic (read: novelistic) Amelia. Becky is not only active but also skilled at dissimulation, as she demonstrates during a game of charades, where she plays Clytemnestra. Thackeray hints that her performance becomes reality when he illustrates a chapter just prior to Jos Sedley's demise with a plate titled "Becky's Second Appearance in the Character of Clytemnestra," in which Becky stands behind a curtain in her husband's room, holding what one assumes to be a phial of poison. All that separates the scene from the sensation fiction of the 1860s is the text's reticence regarding the "murder." "The novelistic genre most allied with theatricality – not only in its clear ties to stage melodrama ["sensation" was a theatrical term], but also in its evocation of the embodied reader response that critics feared would turn reading into enactment" (Allen, *Theater Figures*, 153), sensation fiction also reveals how a novel's stance regarding drama had consequences for gender as well as genre. The Victorian critic E. S. Dallas notes that novelistic "sensation" occurs when women become plotting agents: "The life of women cannot well be described as a life of action. When women are thus put forward to lead the action of a plot, they must be urged into a false position . . . This is what is called sensation."[21] The cultural debate surrounding sensation fiction thus centers on its dangerous effects on female readers: as Becky Sharpe hints, for all that most novelists punish the transgressiveness of their sensational heroines – and support and reward their Amelia Sedleys – the somatic agency of female dramatic energy could lure readers into other allegiances.

Novel-poems and sensation fiction are special cases of sub-genres that develop through strategic alignment with generic "others" (note the simultaneous heydays of these forms, indicating a particular generic disturbance in the 1850s and 1860s). Equally remarkable is the extent to which high realist novels incorporate poetic and dramatic elements – and not merely to expel them. If George Eliot marginalizes verse in her novels by restricting its concrete presence to her epigraphs, the longing expressed by the epigraphs for poetry and drama (from which they quote frequently) is emphasized by the fact that she composes many of them herself. The impulse to create original fragments of poems and plays as necessary appendages to her chapters again suggests how the forms exist as phantom limbs of the novel.

As I argue elsewhere (*Crisis of Action*, chapter 3), while Eliot's early novels look back sentimentally towards a Wordsworthian lyrical past, in her late masterpieces Eliot turns to Romantic poetry's visionary capability in quest of a purified form of political action that avoids the revolutionary inspirations and dangers of drama. Will Ladislaw and (more successfully) Daniel Deronda are repeatedly associated with Shelley, the apostle of the poetic imagination's transformational politics. Meanwhile, drama's attractions and hazards – especially for constricted female agents – are recorded in figures like the Princess (Deronda's mother, who abandons him for her career), Gwendolen Harleth (who fantasizes about a dramatic career as escape from the marriage plot), and Lydgate's first love, the French actress Laure (whose on-stage "slip" of a foot results in her husband's death, thus releasing her from marriage). While such ambivalently presented characters collectively hint at the novelistic orientation we find in Dorothea Brooke's status as heroine of a "home epic," Eliot's feelings are famously divided between admiration of the benefits accruing from "unhistoric acts" and lament at the loss of more overtly epic opportunities (*Middlemarch*, 779, 785). Similarly, I find it indicative that Eliot's least appealing character, Rosamond Vincy, represents novelistic forces, as her tendency to view the world through the lens of "social romance" (109) implies. Like the genre, she appears as a paragon of Darwinian fitness (she is the ultimate survivor); Lydgate ponders "the terrible tenacity of this mild creature" who seems to belong to a "different species" with "opposing interests" to his (549, 560, 657). Interestingly, Rosamond's passive-aggressive novelistic agency is described in terms that align her also with a closeted dramatic impulse: "She was by nature an actress of parts that entered into her physique: she even acted her own character, and so well, that she did not know it to be precisely her own" (109). Like the novel, she has thoroughly internalized drama.

But it is with Dickens that we most frequently associate the dramatic impulse of Victorian fiction, whether through his biography (the youthful audition, the early plays, the friendships with actors, the love of an actress, the rapid transfer of his novels to the stage, the second career of staged readings) or his works: from the play-within-the-novel episodes of *Nicholas Nickleby* (1839) (*Romeo and Juliet*) and *Great Expectations* (1861) (*Hamlet*), to the world of circuses, panto-mimes, public fairs, and melodramas on display in *The Old Curiosity Shop* (1841) and *Hard Times* (1854), his novels are replete with signs of the spectacular Victorian scene.[22] Dickens's use of doubles (often including a performative element, as one figure acts out the repressed desires of another) suggests an essentially theatrical conception of character, and his carefully "directed" plots, with their great reliance on coincidence, demonstrate faith in – or at least desire for – coherent dramatic action. Yet as John Glavin recognizes, in the novels "theaters invariably represent sites and rituals of degradation ... especially for men" – just think of poor Wopsle's fate as Hamlet.[23] *Hamlet* is an interesting play for Dickens to have fixed on in *Great Expectations*, because if Dickens "turned, reluctantly, from stage to page, because the action-prone stage demands from its protagonists a degree of agency Dickens found literally unimaginable" (Glavin, "Dickens and Theatre," 190), *Hamlet*'s notoriously indecisive protagonist and Romantic status as quasi-closet-drama offer an impeded agency that parallels Pip's frustrated and passive containment within the novel's plot. *A Tale of Two Cities* (1859) demonstrates the tensions between Dickens's pro- and anti-theatrical tendencies by pitting the melodrama and spectacle of revolutionary France – communal and exciting, if dangerous – against the bourgeois novelism of London – individualist yet domestic, safe yet dull. The novel culminates in a scene that blends drama with lyric to preserve the novelistic space of the Manette–Darnay family in England: Sydney Carton's self-sacrifice on the scaffold, an act of lyrical transcendence performed before a crowd.

For all Dickens's drama, such moments of lyricism pervade the novels. Louisa Gradgrind stares into the fire, her gesture drawn from Romantic poems like Coleridge's "Frost at Midnight" (her staring also doubles her peering into the circus tent with which *Hard Times* begins). Jenny Wren undergoes visionary musings on Riah's rooftop (in *Our Mutual Friend* [1865]), before she re-enters her ragbag world of the (novelistic) production of marketable dolls made from old scraps. Frequently, as in Carton's death (or indeed Jenny's dream, which looks forward to an escape into heaven), Dickens's lyric impulse emerges in his famous death-scenes (Little Nell's, Paul Dombey's), where it can be cloaked in a religious aura. In death the relentless momentum of Dickens's plotting can pause, and the experience of release, for both writer and reader, is almost physical.

The flight into lyric from the relentlessness of plot emerges most powerfully in the novels of Hardy, in whose later works narrative always functions as a negative force, leading to tragedy. One is reminded of the visionary bleakness of Robert Browning's "Childe Roland to the Dark Tower Came" (1855), in which the quest is to "be fit" "to fail."[24] Browning's bizarre revision of epic romance perhaps recognizes its generic instability in prophetically evolutionary language ("fit"), even as his monologues function (survive) by holding all three modes (epic, lyric, and drama) in tension. Similarly, Hardy pits his lyric style against his tragic narrative drive; indeed as Gillian Beer describes it, Hardy's conception of happiness "is almost always at odds with narrative."[25] Instead, he offers moments of happiness in what might be called "spots of timelessness." These can be stylistic and diffuse, as when the colors red and white punctuate *Tess of the d'Urbervilles*, accruing an almost imagistic (as much as symbolic) agency that helps constitute the pleasure of reading. Or they can be located in passages where plot seems suspended, as in the idyll Tess experiences at Talbothay's dairy (before her tragic attempt to re-enter the plot with the "I do" of her marriage vow), or the sad respite that Angel and Tess enjoy in the deserted mansion, where they resolve "not to think outside of now" (412). These idylls inevitably recall not only the bucolic realm of Tennyson's "English Idyls" but also the fragile landscape of his take on epic, where King Arthur manages to "make the kingdom one," but only (we are reminded) "for a space" (*Idylls*, 21, 35). Yet while Hardy's lyricism offers temporary escape from the carceral effects of the novel (as D. A. Miller describes them), when the police arrive at Stonehenge, Tess and Angel discover the inevitable press of time – both in narrative and in life.

But Hardy's deaths are not moments of lyric. As Beer remarks, "Whereas George Eliot's novels, and Dickens' novels, tend to include death, rather than end with death, Hardy's text pays homage to human scale by ceasing as the hero or heroine dies" (239). So scenes of death confirm novelistic values, offering a closure that gives significance to the idea of individual life stories. Nevertheless, Tess's need "to snatch ripe pleasure before the iron teeth of pain could have time to shut upon her" (195) is one her readers experience almost palpably. As perhaps did Hardy, who escapes fiction for lyric and closet drama after completing *Tess*. When he returns to the landscape of the novels in his later poetry, it is not only to embrace *Moments of Vision* (title of his 1917 collection), but moments that can become eternal by virtue of their collective applicability. Thus in the brief lyric "In Time of 'the Breaking of Nations'" Tess and Angel are transformed into "a maid and her wight," whose generic status (in both senses) ensures that "War's annals will cloud into night / Ere their story die."[26]

As Hardy's poetic prose indicates, the formal experiments of modernist fiction grow out of novelists' conscious interactions with generic "others" and with Victorian generic experiments. Lawrence's rhythmic repetitions in narrative prose and lyrical consideration of the sexual act as a moment of transcendence owe an enormous debt to Hardy, as his simultaneous work on *The Rainbow* (1914) and a critical study of Hardy suggest; Kipling's foreshortened forms of fiction evolve from the Pre-Raphaelite lyric tradition in which he had been raised (his aunt married Edward Burne-Jones). Then there is the case of Henry James. An interest in the theater that overlaps (not incidentally) with concern for the political realm marks James's "middle phase." In *The Princess Casamassima* (1886), James's most overtly political novel, the primal encounter between Hyacinth Robinson and the Princess happens at a theater in which a melodrama is being staged. And in 1890 James begins a frustrating stint as playwright. This failed effort is registered in the move from James's theatrical and political subject matter in *The Tragic Muse* (1890), with its politician-turned-painter hero and its actress heroine, to the internalization of theater and politics in *The Awkward Age* (1899), where theater is relegated to the novel's stylistic mantra of "'Dialogue,' always 'dialogue'!"[27] even as politics gets subsumed into the social scene of Mrs. Brookenham's salon. The extraordinary formal innovations of James's opaque late style emerge from his engagements with the action-centered realms of politics and the theater, realms he admires and yet ultimately rejects for his internal dramas of consciousness.[28] Thus if *The Golden Bowl*'s two-part structure, in which perspective shifts across the interval from "The Prince" to "The Princess," carries a hint of drama, it is more the drama of *The Ring and the Book* than of Shakespeare.

David Kurnick argues that part of James's problem in *The Awkward Age* lay in the novelization of the theater ("Horrible," 122), exemplified by Ibsen, whose works James discusses in his preface. Ibsen's impact also registers in Violet Hunt's *The Maiden's Progress: A Novel in Dialogue* (1894). Like James's novel (and *Belinda* and *Mansfield Park*), this work implicitly links a young girl's "coming out" to a dramatic debut – through its dialogue format, an early scene set at a *bal masqué*, and its heroine's crush on an actor. "Moderna" Maskelyne's dramatic force, though, is decidedly of the day (she reads Ibsen). Thus for all her New Womanly (both *masque*-like and *masculine*) activity, it turns out that the "evolution" she is said to contain includes the novelization of the transgressive form with which Hunt began.[29] While early scenes offer relatively pure stage dialogue and take sparing advantage of the diegetic (i.e. novelistic) opportunities of stage directions (which might have been used to describe both external setting and internal states), as Moderna becomes bored by her liberation from conventions (including, predominantly, the convention of the marriage plot), Hunt turns more and more to forms of closet drama and of novels, offering soliloquies (chapters 8, 21, 29), dialogues marked by quotation marks rather than character cues (chapter 10), extracts from letters (chapter 18), and scenes of unstageable action, including a Trollopean hunt (chapter 26). And if the novel ends with a proposal scene and a kiss that is equally at home on stage and page, this closure occurs only after the hero has chastised Moderna's "bad form" (240).

An article on "Ibsen's New Drama" (1900) was James Joyce's first published work, and while he completed only one play (*Exiles* [1918]), his novels show continuing interest in theater. *A Portrait of the Artist as a Young Man* (1916) contains extended discussions of aesthetics analyzing the distinctions among the dramatic, epic, and lyric modes, but its five-part structure might also be considered theatrical, alluding as it does to the Shakespearean model. *Ulysses* (1922) offers the reader Stephen Dedalus's discourse on Shakespeare (in "Scylla and Charybdis") and suggests throughout that *Hamlet* is almost as important to Stephen's self-fashioning as Homer's *Odyssey* is to Joyce's novel. And Martin Puchner has shown how we can read "Circe" as "an entirely new genre: the narrative closet drama," in which the stage directions must be attributed to a "narrator" in a manner revealing the novel's actual "resistance to the theater" in the very episode that most seems a tribute to it.[30] In *Ulysses* (compare Goethe's *Faust*'s "Walpurgisnacht"), closet drama provides a way to reveal the subconscious and express deviant desires (both longed-for and feared). It also suits Bloom's rather closeted brand of heroism, in which Odysseus' deeds – including the slaughter of the suitors – are dismissed in favor of acts of sympathy.

Bloom's sympathetic imagination is at heart a Romantic construct; Stephen is a poet. If Joyce makes use of drama to internalize it, his novels not only incorporate a range of poetic quotation and original poetry but also depend upon a symbolic structure that is simultaneously rooted in specific lyric poems (most prominently, Yeats's) and the lyric mode itself. Joyce's narrative epiphanies – from Stephen's sight of the girl-bird in *A Portrait*, announcing his vocation as poet, to Bloom and Stephen's fragile union in the shared view of "The heaventree of stars hung with humid nightblue fruit" in *Ulysses*[31] – are essentially moments of lyric transcendence, and (as the quotation suggests) his "prose" always registers this fact in its particular density. Moreover, Joyce's "stream of consciousness" method uses many stylistic adjuncts of verse, with its tendency to skip over words and its fundamentally associative logic.

One might compare it to Virginia Woolf's style in *The Waves* (1931), her novel following the lives of a circle of six friends through rapidly transitioning monologues interspersed by "objective" lyrical descriptions of the sun's annual and diurnal course over the globe. A contemporary article by Woolf indicates her desire to use generic experiment to unsettle authority by quoting Barrett Browning's effort at writing a "novel-poem . . . running into the midst of our conventions."[32] Woolf actually calls *The Waves* a "playpoem," but it owes more to the latter than the former genre, as her description of writing it "to a rhythm not to a plot" hints.[33] Unlike Robert Browning's dramatic monologues, which depend on the assumption that they are spoken in the presence of a (usually identified) listener, the soliloquies of Woolf's novel are "abstract poetic" (*Diary*, vol. III: 185): while speakers are always identified ("said Neville"), they seem always to be speaking to themselves. Yet the book's essentially collective approach shows Woolf's desire – even as she embraces a soliloquizing form that is traditionally associated with the egotistical sublime – to escape the patriarchal implications of the Wordsworthian model for the sake of a more social sense of self.

The Waves describes "moments of being" (Woolf's version of Wordsworthian "spots of time") strung together by words rather than deeds; the title of *Between the Acts* (1941) promises a like avoidance of overt action. The avoidance stems partly from a wartime context; in 1941 the terrible costs of large-scale action were all too apparent (hence also Miss La Trobe's decision to leave the army out of her village-pageant History of England). In fact the only real act to occur "between the acts" takes place when Giles crushes the toad-consuming snake under his heel – a horrifying moment of symbolic masculine energy ("Action relieved him") as well as, perhaps, an attempt to squash the subversive forces of generic hybridity represented by such "monstrous inversion" (as Giles sees it).[34] But the novel simultaneously reveals Woolf's longing for drama in its theatrical subject and writer-director artist-figure and its genuine playpoem status, in which the dialogue of the pageant is faithfully transcribed. For all Isa's poetic murmurs throughout the book, she takes up drama at the end, as the novel concludes with the promise of Giles and Isa's conversation in bed: "Then the curtain rose. They spoke" (136). While the gesture implies that the "real" action of history is novelistic in scope, it also argues that we need to consider this action politically and not allow ourselves to retreat into lyric.

Thus if Romantic novels stake out territory in relation to drama and poetry, and if Victorian fiction turns thematically to other genres to contest its own conventions, modernist novels formally embrace generic hybridity. From Stephen's "cracked lookingglass of a servant" (*Ulysses*, 6) to Miss La Trobe's concluding theatrical gesture, in which her players parade an assortment of mirrors before the audience, the implication is that there is something salutary (albeit also sad) in the lost wholeness of form – that out of generic fissures new hope can spring. And from *Waverley* to *The Waves*, British novelists have taken advantage of a fluidity of generic interaction that reminds us of the flexibility of the novel's vast form, even as it demonstrates how writers struggle both against and with that form's "bright girdle furled."

Notes

1. Mikhail Bakhtin, *The Dialogic Imagination*, trans. Caryl Emerson and Michael Holquist (Austin: University of Texas Press, 1981), pp. 262–263.
2. David Kurnick, "Empty Houses: Thackeray's Theater of Interiority," *Victorian Studies* 48: 2 (2005), 259.
3. Georg Lukács, *The Theory of the Novel*, trans. Anna Bostock (London: Merlin, 1971), pp. 41, 56.
4. George Eliot, *Middlemarch*, ed. David Carroll (Oxford University Press, 1998), pp. 577–578.
5. Kurnik discusses the fate of action in the novel through its relationship to drama. For a broad generic treatment of the failure of action in the period, see Stefanie Markovits, *The Crisis of Action in Nineteenth-Century English Literature* (Columbus: Ohio State University Press, 2006).
6. Georg Lukács, *The Historical Novel*, trans. Hannah and Stanley Mitchell (Lincoln: University of Nebraska Press, 1983), p. 123.
7. Thomas Hardy, *Tess of the d'Urbervilles*, ed. Juliet Grindel and Simon Gatrell (Oxford University Press, 2005), p. 360.
8. Jay Clayton, *Romantic Vision and the Novel* (Cambridge University Press, 1987).
9. Walter Scott, *Waverley*, ed. Claire Lamont (Oxford University Press, 1986), p. 4.

10. Marshall Brown, "Poetry and the Novel," in *The Cambridge Companion to Fiction in the Romantic Period*, ed. Richard Maxwell and Katie Trumpener (Cambridge University Press, 2007), p. 117.

11. *Jane Austen's Letters*, ed. Deirdre Le Faye (Oxford University Press, 1995), p. 277.

12. Jane Austen, *Persuasion*, ed. James Kinsley (Oxford University Press, 2004), p. 30.

13. Jane Austen, *Mansfield Park*, ed. James Kinsley (Oxford University Press, 2003), pp. 44, 120.

14. Emily Brontë, *Wuthering Heights*, ed. Ian Jack (Oxford University Press, 2008), p. 273.

15. *The Poems of Emily Brontë*, ed. Derek Roper (Oxford: Clarendon Press, 1995), p. 154.

16. *Poetical Works of George Gordon, Lord Byron*, ed. Frederick Page, rev. John Jump (Oxford University Press, 1970), p. 303.

17. Elizabeth Barrett Browning, unpublished letter of March 1855, quoted in *Aurora Leigh*, ed. Margaret Reynolds (Athens: Ohio University Press, 1992), pp. 85–86.

18. Robert Browning, *The Ring and the Book*, ed. Thomas Collins and Richard Altick (Peterborough, ON: Broadview, 2001), pp. 22, 31, 56.

19. Alfred Lord Tennyson, *Idylls of the King*, ed. J. M. Gray (London: Penguin, 1996), p. 302. Dino Felluga describes the market's role in the novelization of poetry in "Tennyson's *Idylls*, Pure Poetry and the Market," *SEL* 37 (1997), 783–803; see also his "Verse Novel," in *A Companion to Victorian Poetry*, ed. Richard Cronin, Alison Chapman, and Antony Harrison (New York: Blackwell, 2002), pp. 171–186.

20. See Emily Allen, *Theater Figures: The Production of the Nineteenth-Century British Novel* (Columbus: Ohio State University Press, 2003), pp. 15–17.

21. E. S. Dallas, *The Gay Science*, 2 vols. (London: Chapman and Hall, 1866), vol. II, pp. 296–297.

22. For Dickens and theater see (among others) Carol Hanbery Mackay, ed., *Dramatic Dickens* (London: Macmillan, 1989); Deborah Vlock, *Dickens, Novel Reading, and the Victorian Popular Theatre* (Cambridge University Press, 1998); and Allen, *Theater Figures*, ch. 3.

23. John Glavin, "Dickens and Theatre," in the *Cambridge Companion to Dickens*, ed. John Jordan (Cambridge University Press, 2001), p. 190.

24. *Robert Browning: The Poems*, ed. John Pettigrew, 2 vols. (London: Penguin, 1993), vol. I: 585.

25. Gillian Beer, *Darwin's Plots: Evolutionary Narrative in Darwin, George Eliot and Nineteenth-Century Fiction* (London: Ark, 1985), p. 246.

26. *Thomas Hardy: Selected Poetry*, ed. Samuel Hynes (Oxford University Press, 1996), p. 133.

27. Henry James, preface to *The Awkward Age*, in *The Art of the Novel*, intro. R. P. Blackmur (New York: Charles Scribner's Sons, 1962), p. 107.

28. See Stefanie Markovits, *Crisis of Action*, ch. 4, and Kurnick's account of *The Awkward Age* as closet drama in "'Horrible Impossible': Henry James's Awkward Stage," *The Henry James Review* 26: 2 (2005), 109–129.

29. Violet Hunt, *The Maiden's Progress: A Novel in Dialogue* (New York: Harper and Brothers, 1894), p. 19.

30. Martin Puchner, *Stage Fright: Modernism, Anti-Theatricality, and Drama* (Baltimore, MD: Johns Hopkins University Press, 2002), pp. 100, 90.

31. James Joyce, *Ulysses*, ed. Hans Walter Gabler (New York: Vintage, 1986), p. 573.

32. *Virginia Woolf on Women and Writing*, ed. Michele Barrett (London: Women's Press, 1979), p. 135.

33. *Diary of Virginia Woolf*, ed. Anne Olivier Bell, 5 vols. (London: Hogarth Press, 1977–1984), vol. III, p. 203; *Letters of Virginia Woolf*, ed. Nigel Nicolson and Joanne Trautman, 6 vols. (New York: Harcourt Brace Jovanovich, 1975–80), vol. III, p. 204.

34. Virginia Woolf, *Between the Acts* (London: Vintage, 1992), p. 62.

35

Henry James and Joseph Conrad: the pursuit of autonomy

ROBERT HAMPSON

In the final chapter of *The English Novel* (1930), Ford Madox Ford suggests that "when the dust of *The Yellow Book* period died away" after the trial of Oscar Wilde, there nevertheless remained in the public mind "some conception that novel writing was an art" and that "the novel was a vehicle by means of which every kind of psychological or scientific truth connected with human life and affairs could be very fittingly conveyed."[1] The three names Ford invokes for this moment are Henry James, Stephen Crane, and Joseph Conrad – two Americans and a Pole, who at that moment were neighbours in Kent.[2] For James and for Conrad (as for Ford), the conception of the novel as art comes from Flaubert: this means not only attention to verbal precision (*le mot juste*) and freedom regarding subject matter, but also "the doctrine of the novelist as Creator who should have a Creator's aloofness, rendering the world as he sees it, uttering no comments, falsifying no issues and carrying the subject – the Affair – he has selected for rendering, remorselessly out to its logical conclusion" (123). Moreover, as Pierre Bourdieu argues, the Flaubertian commitment to style and form (and the logic of "the Affair") also has an impact upon the professional milieu in which it operates: it is a pursuit of artistic autonomy that cannot overcome the forces of the marketplace, but that nevertheless establishes a separate realm of literary production and aesthetic value.

Flaubert is committed to the novel's aesthetic freedom from extra-aesthetic aims. According to Bourdieu, Flaubert and the poet Charles Baudelaire are responsible for "the constitution of the literary field as a world apart, subject to its own laws."[3] Thus, "in opposition to 'useful art,' the official and conservative variant of 'social art' . . . and in opposition to bourgeois art, the consenting or unconscious vehicle of an ethical and political *doxa*," literary artists assert "an obedience freely chosen, but unconditional, to the new laws they invent" (77). Bourdieu contextualizes the "heroic times" of this struggle for literary independence by reference to "the reign of money" that follows the rise to power of industrialists and businessmen during the French Second Empire: "uncultured *parvenus* ready to make both the power of money and a vision of the world profoundly hostile to intellectual things triumph within the whole society" (48). Bourdieu outlines the strategies by which Napoleon III produced the structural subordination of the artist to non-artistic purposes, and shows how writers progressively affirmed their autonomy as a form of resistance to the forces of political power and the market.

As part of the resistance at the level of aesthetics, according to Bourdieu, Flaubert "defines and constructs himself in and through a whole series of double negations with which he counters contrasting pairs of styles and authors" (71). In an aesthetic version of "double negations," truth is arrived at by opposing alternative positions – opposing didacticism to formalism, for example; or realism to idealism. In *Madame Bovary* (1857) Flaubert confronts realism and pure art with each other by opposing an apparent commitment to realism to a paramount concern for style; while *Sentimental Education* (1869) is "inscribed at the intersection of the romantic and realist traditions" (100). Bourdieu contends that Flaubert, "in situating himself, as it were, at the geometric intersection of all perspectives, which is also the point of greatest tension . . . forces himself . . . to raise to their highest intensity the set of questions posed in the field" (100). James follows a similar process when he begins to develop his theory of the novel in *French Poets and Novelists* (1878), wherein he negotiates the claims and counter-claims of romance, realism, and naturalism.

Flaubert's commitment to form and style, Bourdieu maintains, both inscribes his work in the history of French literature and affirms the autonomy of the literary field. At the same time Flaubert's "intensified vision of the real" imposes an obligation on the reader, which James and Conrad also require, "to linger over the perceptible form of the text, with its visible and sonorous material, full of correspondences with a real that is situated simultaneously in the order of meaning and in the order of the perceptible, instead of traversing [the text] as if it were a transparent sign, read and yet unseen, in order to proceed directly to the meaning" (109). For James and Conrad the novel's pursuit and "conquest of autonomy" requires, in addition, a foregrounding of the novel's generic and formal negotiations and the novelist's creation of an objectified "Affair" that solicits the reader's engagement with a potential multiplicity of meanings.

Henry James

James's first assertion of the novel's freedom comes in his essay, "The Art of Fiction" (1884), an opportunistic response to Walter Besant's lecture "Fiction as a Fine Art."[4] James at first allies himself with Besant against a public who undervalue the novel and are unsympathetic toward claims for its seriousness as an art form. However, when James goes on to assert that the novel is "at once as free and as serious a branch of literature as any other," the alliance begins to fracture.[5] James rejects Besant's prescriptive approach to fiction: he thinks it is a mistake to attempt "to say so definitely beforehand what sort of an affair the good novel will be" (83). For James "the good health of an art which undertakes so immediately to reproduce life must demand that it be perfectly free" (83). Above all, he contests Besant's view that the novel should have a "conscious moral purpose" (84).

It is also in 1884 that James visits Millbank prison to research the opening of *The Princess Casamassima*. As he recalls in his "Author's Preface," the origin of this novel lies also in "the habit and the interest" of his walking the streets of London. [6] James's perambulations provide the topographic knowledge that underlies the novel, and also give him the glimpse of his subject: "some individual sensitive nature or fine mind, some small obscure intelligent creature ... capable of profiting by all the [aspects of] civilisation ... yet condemned to see these things only from outside" (7–8). As a result of the experience of social exclusion, James's protagonist, Hyacinth Robinson, is attracted to what James describes in his preface as "an aggressive, vindictive, destructive social faith" (16). Here James drew on personal memories: M. Bonnefans, his French teacher at the Fourierist school James attended in Paris in 1856, "a candid 'subversive' opposed to monarchy," is the source for the character of Poupin, "a Republican of the old-fashioned sort, of the note of 1848," a refugee from the Paris Commune, who initiates Hyacinth into the art of book-binding and also teaches him "French and socialism" (84).[7] From these different origins James produces a novel that thematizes the relation between art and politics – or rather (and more problematically), presents them as opposites, a choice between "civilisation" and subversion. Hyacinth is the illegitimate son of a French seamstress, who is in Millbank prison for killing her aristocratic lover, Hyacinth's father. It is through Hyacinth's personal sense of disinheritance, rather than a sense of class solidarity and social injustice, that he turns toward radical politics. Subsequently, after he has widened his social and aesthetic experience through meeting the Princess Casamassima, Hyacinth turns away from his radical political beliefs just when he has vowed to carry out a political assassination, should he be called upon to do so. It is the resulting dilemma that provides the novel's culminating crisis.

Although earlier twentieth-century critics praise the novel for its depiction of "the entire structure of civil society" and for "a brilliantly precise representation of social actuality," these descriptions of the novel hardly hold water.[8] James deliberately restricts the view of upper-class society (with which he was familiar) to Hyacinth's limited experience of it, while the depiction of working-class life and radical politics is restricted by James's lack of experience of both. There is a fine evocation of the working-class London Saturday night (71), of the kind that urban *flâneur* poets of the 1890s would later produce, and there are a few references late in the novel to "the deep perpetual groan of London misery" (234) – "in the east of London that night there were forty thousand men out of work" (235) – but there is very little sense of "social actuality."[9] Hyacinth's childhood home in Lomax Place, Lady Aurora's house in Belgrave Square, Poupin's lodgings in Lisson Grove, the Muniments' tenement rooms in Audley Court, are representative sites in the novel's social mapping, but they have no more depth than the names on a Monopoly board. Captain Sholto's questions, when he visits the Muniments, resemble those of Victorian social visitors: "Now how many families would there be in such a house as this, and what should you say about the sanitary arrangements?" And he goes on to ask about "the position in life, the avocations and habits of the other lodgers, the rent they paid, their relations with each other, both in and out of the family" (181). But these are not the kind of questions that James's novel is concerned with.

A comparison of James with George Gissing makes this clear. Gissing's first novel, *Workers in the Dawn* (1880), initiates a decade of novels committed to alerting the middle-class reading public to the conditions of the urban poor. The novels grow out of Gissing's own experience of poverty in London combined with an aesthetic commitment to realism. *The Nether World* (1889), the last and most impressive of the series, represents the day-to-day struggle for existence of an intersecting group of characters. It is rooted in detailed knowledge of the topography of the area around Clerkenwell and of the kind (and conditions) of work available to the people in this part of London. The novel emphasizes the long hours of labor and the hard conditions that make working-class life little better than slavery. The central character, Sidney Kirkwood, is a working-class man with the instincts of an artist (as James imagines Hyacinth to be), and the novel demonstrates, through Sidney's career and the accumulated pressure of socio-economic detail, the pervasive oppression of poverty: how "Lives may be wasted – worse, far worse than wasted – just because there is no money."[10] As Ruth Livesey notes, the *Charity Organisation Review* (in an article on Gissing's novels in 1891) recommends that "readers of the *Review* who wish to know about the working classes more particularly will find few better instructors than Mr George Gissing."[11]

James's work is not of this documentary type. Admittedly, James's research at Millbank invites a reading of the novel in terms of naturalist fiction. This is reinforced by the way in which Lady Aurora is presented as "the representative of Belgrave Square" (166) and, in consciously socio-scientific terms, Sholto is described as a "specimen" of "the man of fashion" (183). Hyacinth's inheritance from his parents – his mother's French republicanism, his father's British aristocratic background – is repeatedly referred to: Hyacinth, like Arthur Golding in *Workers in the Dawn*, is presented as divided between genetic inheritances. The division between politics and art, between working-class radicalism and upper-class "civilisation," is played out in Hyacinth's hybrid heritage. But this is not a Zolaesque novel of character and environment, of inheritance and environment determining a character's fate. Hyacinth and the Princess Casamassima are exceptions rather than "types," and at the center of the novel is Hyacinth's consciousness, and the choices that Hyacinth must make. The Princess's expressed hostility to social conventions, combined with Hyacinth's transgressive narrative, articulates the novel's own resistance to moral, social, and novelistic conventions. As Martha Nussbaum argues, James's presentation of Hyacinth makes claims for the ethical value of the imagination that are "inseparable from a demand for the artist's freedom of expression."[12]

James's account of young Hyacinth's prison visit to meet his dying mother recalls scenes in Victorian fictions (Oliver Twist's prison visit to Fagin comes to mind) that reflect the idea that exposing children to the punishment of vice and crime is a morally enhancing experience. However, rather than deriving a moral from the experience, James only has Mr. Vetch observe that "'there are people who would tell you it would do him good'" (39). What this means is that *The Princess Casamassima* alludes to various kinds of novel but does not finally conform to the conventions of the kinds it refers to.[13] That Hyacinth is the son of an aristocrat brought up by a dressmaker, who has great expectations for him, prompts the reader to anticipate a novel like *Tom Jones* and *Oliver Twist*, where the narrative works toward the re-establishment of the hero in his rightful class and the regaining of gentlemanly status. Miss Pynsent brings Hyacinth up "like a real little gentleman" (26), and dies believing that this conventional plot will be fulfilled, once Hyacinth has been taken up by Princess Casamassima. However, this narrative archetype exists only in "the dressmaker's romantic mind" (27). In this context, it is important that Hyacinth is himself a reader. When he visits Lady Aurora he is critical of the "puerility" of her taste in French literature and disappointed not to find works by "certain members of an intensely modern school, advanced and consistent realists" (216). Hyacinth is not a character in a naturalist or even a realist novel, but he desires to read such fiction. Later in Paris he is conscious of "echoes and reminiscences" of Balzac and de Musset "in the air" (319). Millicent Bell describes Hyacinth's observations as "inescapably intertextual" (169), and, as Bourdieu argues, this "reflexivity" constitutes "one of the foremost manifestations of the autonomy of a field: the allusion to the internal history of a genre" (101).

The novel's title also sits uneasily with a naturalistic novel of working-class life. In terms of contemporary readers' expectations, it points instead to the "silver fork" genre, "novels portraying the aristocracy" (217), which Hyacinth *has* read. However, James's readers would recognize that James is reviving in the Princess a character from his first novel, *Roderick Hudson* (1875). A transtextual character by James works to affirm for James the autonomy of the literary field.[14] By citing his own work, James creates his own separate fictional sphere. The novel's overall mode of operation also asserts its autonomy. What the novel offers instead of didacticism is explorative patterns – in particular, suggestive parallels and contrasts among characters. This is most obvious in relation to the two visitors to the social world of the novel, Princess Casamassima and Lady Aurora: the former, a "lady amateur" who seeks to commit herself to revolutionary politics out of boredom with her aristocratic life and her rage at being treated as a female commodity; the latter, a social worker, "ashamed of being rich" (100), who has "dedicated her life and her pocket money to the poor and the sick" (105). Another set of explorative relations is set up by the exchange of love interests that takes place early on, whereby the Princess takes over Hyacinth from a working-class girlfriend, and she in turn takes over the gentleman, Captain Sholto, from the Princess.

In James's earlier novel about the Princess we learn that she is the illegitimate daughter of an American mother and an Italian father. Her mother, to fulfill her desire for recovered social status by capitalizing on her daughter's beauty, has more or less sold her daughter into marriage with an Italian prince. James returns to the topic of the American woman married to an Italian prince in his late novel, *The Golden Bowl* (1904). Maggie, the daughter of Adam Verver, an American millionaire and art collector, is married to the Italian. The marriage is a straightforward exchange of American wealth for European culture and history, Adam's millions for the Prince's cultural capital. However, as we would expect from James, this is not part of an exploration of the historical phenomenon of American collectors buying European art, although it obviously refers to it. Instead, James focusses on the emotional and ethical situation, which he complicates by having Adam marry his daughter's friend, Charlotte. When father and daughter continue to spend time together, they leave their spouses to entertain each other. The further complication is that Prince Amerigo and Charlotte (unknown to Adam and his daughter) had earlier fallen in love, but had to give up the relationship "neither of them having the means to marry."[15] The narrative accordingly negotiates the unspeakable topics of incest, sexual failure, and adultery. In doing so it asserts the autonomy of fiction from conventional morality and its freedom to find its subject.

At the same time the novel's complex interplay between the unspeakable and the unspoken requires an intensity of engagement with the fictional world that precludes that privileging of the referential function of fiction advocated by Walter Besant. The novel is divided into two books (and five parts). The first book concentrates on the Prince and explores his position. As Maggie tells him, he is "a rarity, an object of beauty, an object of price," and he has now become part of her father's collection (10). The narrative follows the Prince's attempt to "see" his way through his self-divided relationship with Maggie and Charlotte. The second part centers on Adam and his discovery that Maggie's marriage has "made vacant . . . his immediate foreground" (114). His marriage to Charlotte provides the solution. The third part begins with the new relationship established between the Prince and Charlotte while father and daughter engage in "make-believe renewals of their old life" (184). The first Book emphasizes Maggie's innocence. The second Book follows Maggie's awakening and her need to produce a reconfiguration of the couples without admitting to her father her suspicions about the Prince and Charlotte. Maggie's "assumption of agency" involves an overdue separation from her father, and "an assertion of the sexual bond between her and her husband and a banishing of Charlotte."[16] However, Maggie's negotiations with her husband, her father, and Charlotte must work through the unspoken, through "the prescribed reach of her hypocrisy" (403), and against a background of silent understanding between father and daughter, the Prince and Charlotte. The outcomes, too, are marked by the unspoken. Thus the Prince "replied to nothing, denied nothing, explained nothing, apologised for nothing," yet conveys to Maggie a new "working arrangement" (459), while, in Maggie's climactic discussion with her father, "their acceptance of the unsaid" means that they can "practically" give up "pretending" (492). As a result of the pretences, the lies, and the unspoken, the reader is engaged in intense interpretive activity of the fictional world. This fictional world is maintained, like a Buckminster Fuller geodesic dome, through the autonomous interplay of its own internal tensions.

An obvious focus for interpretive activity is provided by the novel's title. The golden bowl appears when the Prince agrees to accompany Charlotte as she shops for a wedding present for him. From the outset there are ambiguities about this object: it is described as "a drinking vessel larger than a common cup, yet not of exorbitant size" (84), and it is made of crystal, not gold. References to bowls, cups, gold, and crystal subsequently pervade the novel, proliferating meanings. First the bowl suggests the Prince's character, because it is flawed. The shopkeeper's question about the flaw – "if it's something you can't find out, isn't it as good as if it were nothing?" (86) – is countered by Charlotte's ethical response: "Does one make a present . . . of an object that contains, to one's knowledge, a flaw?" (86). The bowl returns metaphorically in the next chapter when Adam describes the Prince in terms of a perfect crystal; and the bowl returns as a memory on a day that Charlotte and the Prince spend together: the Prince describes the day as "like a great gold cup that we must somehow drain together," and Charlotte reminds him of "the gilded crystal bowl in the little Bloomsbury shop" (263) that he refused to accept. The "great gold cup" links the perfection of their day to the perfection of their understanding of each other ("the degree in which people were, in the common phrase, meant for each other" [261]). When, later in the novel, the golden bowl is by chance bought by Maggie, James self-consciously flaunts the artificiality of this narrative device: "the coincidence is extraordinary – the sort of thing that happens mainly in novels and plays" (442). The bowl now represents Maggie's knowledge of the Prince's prior relationship with Charlotte, but is also used to represent the happiness she had looked for in her marriage (456). The bowl is thus presented as an object, a memory, a metaphor, and a central symbol. It is presented for our interpretation, but it is also used by the characters to interpret events to themselves and to others. In fact, the bowl ceases to be an object and becomes both part of the novel's autonomous figurative play and, ultimately, a symbol for the novel itself.

As part of an intense engagement with the autonomous fictional world of the novel, a reader of *The Golden Bowl* becomes caught up in the characters' attempts to understand their experiences. The attempts generate chains of self-consciously presented metaphors and intertextual allusions. The Prince, as he embarks on his marriage, sees himself as Poe's Arthur Gordon Pym setting out on a "great voyage" into an area of mystery (20), while Adam's successful financial career is explained by reference to his reading of "Keats's sonnet about 'stout Cortez': 'To rifle the Golden Isles' had, on the spot, become the business of his future" (104). This unexpected response to Keats's poem raises the possibility that readings can be misreadings. The place of misreadings is explored further through Fanny Assingham's role in the novel.[17] Fanny operates as commentator on the action: she has an "irrepressible interest in other lives" (185), which is also manifested in the novel by her readiness to meddle in them. The degree to which her meddling makes her responsible for the marital problems of the novel, however, is a knowledge she is keen to conceal. At other times her commentary on the action turns her into a comic version of the novelist. Indeed, in an echo of James's voice and plotting, she is forced to consider whether she had not "fallen in love with the beautiful symmetry" of her plan when she thought of Charlotte as a possible wife for Adam (285). Through her the novel's narrative structure and emphasis on interpretation are foregrounded. At the same time, it also becomes apparent that her interpretations have limits. This is exemplified by her turning away from certain knowledge in her relations with the Prince and Charlotte, and by her readiness to lie in order to protect her own position.

Fanny reminds us of the extent to which characters (and autonomy-centered authors?) can deceive, be deceived, and be self-deceiving. This is significant for understanding Maggie's role later in the novel, when author-like she takes over the responsibility for shaping events. Maggie's efforts to create the "harmony" she desires are open to question in the same way as Fanny's. Maggie ruthlessly manipulates the Assinghams and the Prince to bring about the result she requires. Fanny's refusal to confirm Maggie's suspicions is met by Maggie's lie: a pretence that she believes Fanny. She displays similar duplicity in relation to Charlotte, to whom she never reveals what she knows. As Nussbaum shows, attempts to read the novel in terms of Maggie's personal development and her desire for "moral perfection" cannot ignore the explicit sacrifice of Charlotte and the Prince (and the perfection of their relationship) required to bring this about (*Love's Knowledge*, 125, 131). As Maggie realizes, the significance of the "picture of quiet harmonies . . . could be no more, after all, than a matter of interpretation, differing always for a different interpreter" (476). The concern for quiet harmonies can be a project of personal safety at the expense of others. In *The Princess Casamassima* and *The Golden Bowl*, James makes claims for the political and personal value of the autonomous imagination, but also alerts readers to the limits of interpretation by making them self-conscious about their own interpretative activities.

Joseph Conrad

In his Preface to *The Nigger of the "Narcissus,"* Conrad famously asserts his vision of his task as a novelist: "by the power of the written word to make you hear, to make you feel – it is, before all, to make you *see.*" There is an ambiguity in the word *see*: it suggests both an impressionistic fidelity to the visible world and an attempt to penetrate appearances to a deeper truth. However, not enough attention has been paid to the context in which this task is asserted, the position that it opposes: namely what Conrad calls that "wisdom" oriented towards "immediate profit," which seeks edification, consolation, or amusement. None of these, Conrad asserts, is the aim of art. This is another claim on behalf of autonomy. At the same time the preface is careful not to follow aesthetic doctrines of the separation of art from life: like James and Ford, Conrad is concerned with "every kind" of truth of experience and with finding ways – including autonomous ones – of rendering truth for his readers. This means that *The Nigger of the "Narcissus"* is not a straightforward, realistic representation of a sea-voyage. Instead, there is an ethical concern in the work that is embedded in its organization and method of narration. *The Nigger of the "Narcissus"* is constructed "as a series of ethically and politically charged moments, the relations between which are often neither causal nor explicit."[18] Conrad's tale of the voyage also invites analogical historically oriented interpretations: the ship can be read metonymically as a fragment of late-Victorian English society with its challenges to established authority, or it can be read metaphorically as an investigation of "the moral problem of conduct" – how to exist "within sight of eternity."[19] As with James's novels the reader is forced into an interpretive role and into an engagement with the narration and the construction of the narrative as important parts of the work's method of producing meaning and asserting its artistic freedom.

Conrad's novel *The Secret Agent* (1907), like *The Princess Casamassima*, responds to late-nineteenth-century anarchist bombing campaigns. Whereas *The Princess Casamassima* grows out of fears about men ready "to throw bombs into innocent crowds and shoot pistols at their rulers" (196) and out of anxious memories of the European anarchist attacks of the 1860s, *The Secret Agent* is based on the alleged anarchist attempt to bomb the Greenwich Observatory in February, 1894. Interestingly, Conrad follows the anarchist interpretation of the incident as the deed of an *agent provocateur* rather than the official version, which links the attempt to anarchists. In the novel's opening chapters Verloc is assigned by a foreign embassy to carry out a bombing that will pressurize the British government into clamping down on political exiles.

The novel is subsequently constructed in terms of an opposition between anarchists and police, but this is not James's loaded opposition of politics to "civilisation." Instead, the narrator's trenchant and sustained irony undermines both sides through a succession of "ethically and politically charged moments." In a letter to his friend R. B. Cunninghame Graham, Conrad claims that he is not "satirizing the revolutionary world," because all the revolutionaries in the novel (with the exception of "the Professor") are "shams."[20] Conrad's revolutionaries, sitting round the fire in Verloc's parlor or in the basement of the Silenus Restaurant, are as ineffective as James's anarchist group at the "Sun and Moon" pub. Nevertheless, since the shams are the only "revolutionaries" in the novel, the effect is to satirize the entire revolutionary world. At the same time, however, *The Secret Agent* also satirizes the police and politicians. The police investigation uncovers the truth about the explosion, but that truth is not made public, and the motives of the principal policemen are far from disinterested. Inspector Heat is keen to deflect the investigation away from his informant Verloc, while the Assistant Commissioner is equally keen to protect the anarchist celebrity Michaelis (for the sake of his own domestic peace). If the "anarchist" bombing was designed to undermine faith in law and government, Conrad's novel itself effectively – and with exemplary aesthetic autonomy – carries out this work by means of its radically skeptical subversion of all ideological certainties.

The Secret Agent is a novel about anarchists, *agents provocateurs*, police spies, and secret agents for foreign powers, but at its center is a domestic tragedy. It charts the destruction of the Verloc family: the death of Stevie as the outcome of the self-sacrificing plans of his mother and sister designed to protect him; the misalignment at the heart of the Verloc marriage, whereby Verloc has mistakenly believed that he is loved for himself; and the madness and suicide of Winnie Verloc. The remorseless destruction of this family group is part of a deeply pessimistic vision of the atomization of society, with each individual pursuing his separate schemes; and it suggests a larger chaos, in which human plans go awry, and nothing can be relied upon. As with *The Nigger of the "Narcissus,"* the novel's political, ethical, and psychological concerns invite metonymic and metaphorical interpretations. However, *The Secret Agent* is a long way from being what Bourdieu calls a "vehicle of an ethical and political *doxa*," and very far from having what Besant would regard as a "conscious moral purpose." Undeniably it is the product of a strong personal vision, conveying "a direct impression of life." And that direct impression of life is imbued with such a deep skepticism that it seriously challenges a reader's political and ethical values.

The Secret Agent foregrounds Conrad's ethical and political interests even while affirming every novel's generic freedom from subordination to ideological services of any kind. Conrad's later fiction, like James's, flaunts the novel's aesthetic freedom through a succession of formal experiments. In the case of *Victory* (1915) this involves a combination of what James in his prefaces calls his "scenic" method with a high degree of literary intertextuality. In prefaces that James writes for the New York edition of his works the scenic method is said to be derived from James's interest in writing for the stage. The method means a novelist's thinking of "the Affair" of a narrative action in terms of dramatic scenes, and planning the construction of a novel in terms of the successive scenes of a play. James emphasizes the importance of "really constructive dialogue, dialogue organic and dramatic, speaking for itself, representing, and embodying substance and form."[21] In this way the novel is made to stand on its own, just as drama appears to unfold independently of a narrator or arranger.

Whereas the scenic method explicitly intensifies the objectified, apparently autonomous presentation of character and events (thereby demanding the reader's conscious interpretive involvement), intertextuality implicitly asserts the autonomy of the literary sphere. In *Victory* Conrad combines the Jamesian scenic method with intertextuality. The latter is visible in the way Conrad transposes characters and situations from Shakespeare's play *The Tempest* to create his own "island tale": Conrad's Heyst, like Shakespeare's Prospero, lives on an island, where he can spend more time with his books; Jones and Ricardo (like Antonio and Ferdinand) are brought to the island by boat; Jones's likeness to Antonio, who is Prospero's brother, underlines similarities between Heyst and Jones; Ferdinand's chaste love for Miranda is ironically paralleled by Ricardo's feelings for Lena; Pedro corresponds to Caliban; and Wang's likeness to Ariel explains his puzzling ability to appear and disappear at will. *Hamlet* also is subliminally present in *Victory*: in Heyst's relationship with his father; in Heyst's indecisiveness and inability to act; and in similarities between Davidson's role in the final chapter and Horatio's part in *Hamlet*'s finale. These (and other) intertextual patterns in the novel have contradictory implications by means of which Conrad creates an open-ended, multivalent narrative. Together these patterns constitute another method: the mythical method, whereby an apparently realistic text is patterned after a mythical or literary archetype. Joyce's *Ulysses*, referring modern life in Dublin to Homer's *Odyssey*, is a prime example. Conrad's mythical method, like Joyce's, operates through the superimposition of pre-existing plots (such as Shakespeare's). The connections and contradictions among these various plots build intensive interpretive play into the novel. Situating the novel in relation to a constellation of previous texts becomes another way of asserting the autonomy of literature: its references are more to itself than to the world outside it.

Perhaps the most interesting intertextual presence in *Victory* is an earlier work that notoriously asserts the autonomy of the aesthetic. By giving Heyst the forename "Axel," Conrad suggests a link between his narrative and the French poet Villiers de l'Isle Adam's play *Axel*. Both Axels deliberately lead a solitary existence. Both are persuaded by mentors to renounce life. Both are thought to possess hidden treasure – and both are visited by someone from the outside world searching for that treasure. Each is involved with a woman who intrudes into his solitary existence and tries to persuade the man she loves to re-enter life. In *Axel* Axel's relationship with Sara is contrasted with his servant's relationship to a fiancée, just as Axel Heyst's relationship with Lena is contrasted with Wang's relationship with his Alfuro wife. Axel's assertion that "living" should be left to servants is enacted in *Victory* by Wang's protection of his wife and his taking possession of the abandoned settlement at the novel's end. *Axel* concludes with the *Liebestod* of Sara and Axel acted out against "distant murmurs of the wind in the forest vastness, vibrations of the awakening of space, the surge of the plain, the hum of life."[22] The account of Lena's death in *Victory* concludes with similar ambivalence: "The flush of rapture flooding her whole being broke out in a smile of innocent, girlish happiness; and with that divine radiance on her lips she breathed her last, triumphant, seeking for his glance in the shades of death."[23] Here the celebration of romantic love is balanced against the illusion of victory and the suicide from despair. A reader is left with the explorations and evaluations enacted through Conrad's scenic, intertextual, and mythic methods and by the interaction of the characters' conflicting perspectives. Not least, through the intertextual relationship with *Axel*, Conrad makes reference to the aesthetics of art for art's sake in a novel that ambiguously asserts the importance of trusting in life.

For Conrad and Ford, Flaubert's example meant that the novel should be treated as an art form but also that "the novel was a vehicle by means of which every kind of psychological or scientific truth connected with human life and affairs could be very fittingly conveyed." One aspect of the asserted autonomy of the novel is its ability to treat any area of human life without being restricted, as Victorian fiction could be, by what was thought appropriate for the young female reader. Above all, for Conrad and Ford, this means that the novel should be able to address sexuality. James's scenic method bears directly on *Victory*'s serious engagement with sexuality. During February 1914, when Conrad was working on *Victory*, he also was reading Ford's recent book, *Henry James: A Critical Study*.[24] Ford's study demonstrates a detailed engagement with James's prefaces, and might have brought to Conrad's mind the involvement of scenic method with frank treatments of sex. In *The Awkward Age*, for example, James uses "really constructive dialogue" to address the problem of female adolescents and their relations to the sophisticated adult conversation – and the sexual promiscuity – of circles in which their parents move. The novel's concern with what its adolescent heroine Nanda knows about eros maps readily onto the contemporary censorship of fiction in the name of the adolescent female. Indeed, one of the final crises of *The Awkward Age* hinges on the circulation of a scandalous French novel among the central characters, and on the fact that Nanda has read it.

Conrad's familiarity with James's scenic method is also suggested by his correspondence with Basil Macdonald Hastings, with whom he worked on a dramatization of *Victory*. The dramatization was no doubt made easier by the dramatic nature of *Victory*: James's method is evident in the novel's dramatic handling of its materials. After the prologue, the first two parts of the narrative proceed through a series of staged encounters. In each case, there is a precise spatial location and dramatic interaction carried by dialogue. In the latter part of the novel Conrad uses this scenic method to explore the developing relationship between Heyst and Lena, the enforced relationship between Lena and Ricardo, and Mr. Jones's probing of Heyst. As in drama, the dress, body language, and spatial positioning of the characters are often as eloquent as the words they exchange.[25] Even more prominently than James, Conrad uses all these resources, including what "really constructive dialogue" leaves unsaid, in order to explore what cannot be spoken. In *Victory* this includes the emotional and psychological fluctuations of the sexual relationship between Heyst and Lena, the polymorphous perversity and sexual violence of Ricardo, and the homosexuality of Mr. Jones.

For James and Conrad the pursuit – and the conquest – of autonomy means the novelist's freedom to choose his subject without regard to moral or political conventionalities, even though those might need to be negotiated in the presentation of the subject. It means also a conception of the novel as a verbal construct, which should stand as free as possible from its author and his opinions, through the use of the scenic method, the interplay of internal elements of structure and language, and the use of reflexive devices (such as conflicting or hybrid generic signals, mythic method, or intertextuality), all of which point towards the separate sphere of the literary. The novel as James and Conrad produce it "trusts" life, while simultaneously distrusting art's subjection to any demands on it dictated from outside the realm of fiction.

Notes

1. Ford Madox Ford, *The English Novel* (Manchester: Carcanet, 1983), p. 135. The Wilde trial was in 1895. The *Yellow Book* did not publish Wilde, but its association with "decadence" meant that it was caught up in the aftermath of the trial. It ceased publication in 1897.

2. However, when Ford speaks of writers "beginning to pay some attention to manner rather than to matter or morals" (*ibid.*, 133), the writers he refers to are Wilde, Stevenson, Pater, and Meredith.

3. Pierre Bourdieu, *The Rules of Art: Genesis and Structure of the Literary Field*, trans. Susan Emanuel (Cambridge: Polity Press, 1996), p. 48.

4. Walter Besant was a leading figure in the recently founded (1883) Society of Authors, dedicated to gaining professional status for writers and greater legal protection for literary property. This emphasis on writing as the creation of property plays into the structural subordination of the artist to the market. See John Goode, "The Decadent Writer as Producer" in *Decadence and the 1890s*, ed. Ian Fletcher (London: Edward Arnold, 1979), pp. 109–129.

5. Henry James, *Selected Literary Criticism*, ed. Morris Shapiro (London: Peregrine Books, 1968), pp. 78–97, 82.

6. Henry James, *The Princess Casamassima* (New York: Harper and Row, 1968), p. 5.

7. Leon Edel, *The Life of Henry James*, 5 vols. (Harmondsworth: Penguin, 1977), vol. I, p. 110.

8. See Lionel Trilling, *The Liberal Imagination* (New York: Viking Press, 1950), pp. 58–92.

9. One might compare William C. Preston's *The Bitter Cry of Outcast London* (1883).

10. George Gissing, *The Nether World* (London: J. M. Dent, 1973), p. 377. Gissing assumes that art is the domain of that section of a class-structured society which is liberated by wealth from the labor that dehumanizes the masses. See John Goode, *George Gissing: Ideology and Fiction* (London: Vision Press, 1978), p. 54.

11. Cited by Ruth Livesey, "Reading for Character: Women Social Reformers and Narratives of the Urban Poor in Late Victorian and Edwardian London," *Journal of Victorian Culture*, 9: 1 (2004), 43–67, 43–44.

12. Martha Nussbaum, *Love's Knowledge: Essays on Philosophy and Literature* (Oxford University Press, 1990), p. 205.

13. See Millicent Bell, *Meaning in Henry James* (Cambridge, MA: Harvard University Press, 1991), pp. 180–183.

14. I am indebted to Cedric Watts, *The Deceptive Text: An Introduction to Covert Plots* (Sussex: Harvester Press, 1984), pp. 133–149, for the term "transtextual character."

15. Henry James, *The Golden Bowl* (Oxford University Press, 1983), p. 53.

16. Hugh Stevens, *Henry James and Sexuality* (Cambridge University Press, 1998), p. 55.

17. See Nussbaum, *Love's Knowledge*, pp. 157–161.

18. Peter MacDonald, "Men of Letters and Children of the Sea: Conrad and the Henley Circle," *The Conradian*, 21: 1 (1996), 15–56, 37.

19. Joseph Conrad, "Stephen Crane," *Last Essays* (London: J. M.Dent, 1926), p. 138; *The Nigger of the "Narcissus"* (London: J. M. Dent, 1923), p. 25.

20. Letter (October 7, 1907), *The Collected Letters of Joseph Conrad*, ed. Frederick R. Karl and Laurence Davies, 8 vols. (Cambridge University Press, 1988), vol. III, p. 491.

21. See R. P. Blackmur, *The Art of the Novel: Critical Prefaces by Henry James* (New York: Charles Scribner's Sons, 1934), p. 106.

22. Villiers de l'Isle Adam, *Axel*, trans. Marilyn Gaddis Rose (Dublin: Dolmen Press, 1970), p. 175.

23. Joseph Conrad, *Victory* (London: J. M. Dent, 1923), p. 407.

24. Secker published Ford's *Henry James* on January 14, 1914. In a letter (February 23, 1914) to Ford's partner, Violet Hunt, Conrad reports that he has been "tasting it at odd times ever since it arrived." *The Collected Letters of Joseph Conrad*, vol. v, p. 360.

25. For a fuller account of the dramatic nature of *Victory*, see Robert Hampson, "From Stage to Screen," in *Joseph Conrad and the Performing Arts*, ed. Katherine Isobel Baxter and Richard J. Hand (Farnham: Ashgate, 2009), pp. 59–76. For a text of Macdonald Hastings's adaptation, see *The Conradian* 25: 2 (2000), 87–176.

The first novel James Joyce embarked on could hardly be called modernist. *Stephen Hero*, probably started in Dublin in 1903 when Joyce was twenty-one,[1] was to be a thinly disguised autobiography, stylistically undistinguished and immensely long. When he abandoned it, in Trieste in 1905, he referred to the 914 pages he had written as "about half the book."[2] Its planned sixty-three chapters would have told the story of a Dublin boy growing up in an increasingly impoverished middle-class family, throwing off the shackles of Catholicism and bourgeois convention, and embarking upon the lonely path of the writer determined to expose his society's failings. The title, combining a formula from ancient Greek tragedy with the name of the young protagonist, suggests the kind of ironic distancing Joyce was to exploit later in his career. It is hard to discern irony in the eleven chapters that survive: the accounts of the inner world of Joyce's alter ego Stephen Daedalus, and of his interactions with his fellow university students, are not mediated by any sense of stylistic shaping and verbal economy, and as a result feel too close to their subject matter to allow for the play of distancing.

When Joyce recommenced his semi-autobiographical project in 1907, it was with a very different approach to the task. He had in the meantime completed *Dubliners*, and in writing those stories had developed an art of economy and compression that makes *Stephen Hero* seem positively elephantine (curiously, Joyce pursued the two projects side by side, without any apparent stylistic interference between them). The new, much shorter novel, which he called *A Portrait of the Artist as a Young Man*, was probably completed early in 1914; the title alone indicates the complexity Joyce had introduced into his version of the *Künstlerroman*. Is the "artist" to be understood as the creator of the artwork so entitled, as would be the case in the world of painting from which the phrase is borrowed? Or does it have a more generic (and thus more ironic) reference? How deprecating (or self-deprecating) is the emphasis on youthfulness? We can already see, merely responding to the title-page, that Joyce was exploring ways of loading words with shades of meaning that exceed their ordinary communicative function, and that in doing so he was willing to make greater demands on the novel-reader than had hitherto been the norm.

When Joyce began to rewrite *Stephen Hero* as *A Portrait*, among the novels recently published were Conrad's *Lord Jim* (1900), Kipling's *Kim* (1901), Mann's *Buddenbrooks* (1901), and James's *The Ambassadors* (1903). While they all reflect important innovations in matter or manner, none could be thought of as revolutionary. By the time Joyce had finished his novel, evidence for changes in the world of fiction included the appearance of Gertrude Stein's *Three Lives* (1908), D. H. Lawrence's *Sons and Lovers* (1913), and Marcel Proust's *Swann's Way* (1913). (The same years had witnessed Pound's *Personae* poems [1909], Picasso's *Les Demoiselles d'Avignon* canvas [1907], and Stravinsky and Nijinsky's *The Rite of Spring* ballet [1913].) We do not know the order in which Joyce wrote and revised the five chapters of *A Portrait*, and so we cannot say when his most innovative pages were composed, but we can say that the first installment that appeared in *The Egoist* on Joyce's thirty-second birthday, February 2, 1914, marks a turning point in English fiction.

The opening of the novel, in contrast to the shock of unfamiliarity engendered by the first sight of Picasso's *Demoiselles* or the initial bars of Stravinsky's *Rite* (or, three years later, the beginning of Eliot's "The Love Song of J. Alfred Prufrock"), invites the reader into an entirely familiar world, the world of childhood impressions and, as the vehicle for those impressions, the language of childhood:

> Once upon a time and a very good time it was there was a moocow coming down along the road and this moocow that was coming down along the road met a nicens little boy named baby tuckoo . . . . .
>
> His father told him that story: his father looked at him through a glass: he had a hairy face.
>
> He was baby tuckoo. The moocow came down the road where Betty Byrne lived: she sold lemon platt. (25)

Compare this with a representative passage from the last chapter of the novel, when Stephen is about twenty and reflecting on the woman he is perhaps in love with:

> A sense of her innocence moved him almost to pity her, an innocence he had never understood till he had come to the knowledge of it through sin, an innocence which she too had not understood while she was innocent or before the strange humiliation of her nature had first come upon her. Then

first her soul had begun to live as his soul had when he had first sinned: and a
tender compassion filled his heart as he remembered her frail pallor and her
eyes, humbled and saddened by the dark shame of womanhood.   (250)

The style now manifests the sophistication, or pseudo-sophistication, of the
young man, presenting the onset of menstruation as an event to be imagined
and described in elegant Paterian periods – and it is the slightly mannered
articulation of the sentences that keeps alive the possibility of irony at
Stephen's expense.

The adjustment required of a reader to understand and enjoy Joyce's radically new technique is subtle but far-reaching, and it would be required by most
of Joyce's experiments with fiction from then on. Put simply, a reader cannot
establish with any security the position of Joyce's narrator or implied author
vis-à-vis characters and events, because Joyce's language, though carefully
crafted, is unmoored from an intentional source. Just as we cannot be sure
whether Joyce in giving us a title is inviting us to take it literally or ironically, so
we cannot come to rest firmly on a judgment of the character and actions of the
protagonist as his story unfolds. It is not just a question of a complex combination of the admirable and the reprehensible: since Cervantes, the tradition of the
novel had shown itself to be a superb tool for such complication of moral
judgments. Nor is it a matter of the absence of a narrator: the epistolary novel is
only the most obvious narratorless genre in which an implied author can still be
sensed adopting a particular stance (no one would say that *Pamela* lacks an
ethical perspective). Gustave Flaubert in France had shown fifty years earlier
how powerful and unsettling a narrator who refuses to make judgments can be,
and Joyce takes Flaubert's technique even further. *A Portrait*, although some of it
can be read as a relatively traditional, if unusually fastidious, novel of childhood
and adolescent development, is at its most radical when its reader's pleasure is
derived from the exploitation of linguistic resources unanchored in any narrating consciousness. No one is *telling* us that little Stephen is riveted by his father's
storytelling, that he has not yet divorced the world of fiction from the world in
which he lives, and that his perception is of discrete fragments rather than
unified wholes. In the later passage we are not being pushed into making an
assessment of Stephen's mental world as either sensitive or crass, sympathetic or
detached, verbally subtle or vapidly imitative; the responsibility of judgment is
on us as readers.

After the extraordinarily economical initial pages evoke significant and
lasting influences on Stephen's early childhood – among them storytelling,
parental affection, music, political affiliations, religious intolerance, and sexual

prohibition – the novel depicts Stephen's schooldays by means of an increasingly mature style. Joyce's willingness to thrust his reader into unaccustomed territory is particularly evident in the sermon Stephen hears during a religious retreat. Where another novelist would have provided a taste of the sermon's style and a summary of its content, Joyce gives us page after page of Father Arnall's words, most of them devoted to an agonizingly drawn-out depiction of hell. Stephen's newfound religious conviction is not overtly ironized, though in the following chapter his rejection of a priestly vocation and embrace of an artistic one is given equal intensity – and is equally capable of being read ironically. Also a challenge for the novel-reader are Stephen's long conversations with fellow university students in chapter 5, and the sudden, unexplained shift to a series of diary entries with which the book ends. In the latter, the absence of a narrator is obvious, and, unlike Samuel Richardson, Joyce gives us no pointers (or too many pointers) for a final assessment of Stephen.

A Portrait had a mixed reception when it was published, not without difficulties, in the United States in 1916 and in Britain in the following year. Many reviewers were disgusted by the explicitness of the sexual detail and dismayed by the unusual demands the novel made on the reader. But others found that Joyce's reinvention of novelistic style produced a remarkably direct experience of the agonies and joys of growing up and a mordantly powerful evocation of the moral and political tensions of Dublin life around the turn of the century. By then, Joyce had made substantial progress with the work that would eclipse *A Portrait* as a new departure in the tradition of the novel and be held up in due course as the central exhibit in what became known as "modernism." *Ulysses* was published in 1922 not by a recognized publisher – Joyce was unable to find anyone to take the risk – but by a Paris bookshop, Shakespeare and Company.

Again the title signals a new challenge. It issues an invitation to read the novel as a response to Homeric epic and a warning not to expect straightforward realistic narrative. Moreover, when we realize that the book contains no character of this name, but that it does follow the actions, speech, and – especially – thoughts of a Jewish ad-canvasser in Dublin during a single day in 1904, we have to decide whether it is the values of ancient Greek epic or those of the modern urban bourgeoisie that are being made fun of, or whether the effect is to make heroic the quotidian struggles of the early twentieth-century *homme moyen sensuel*. The narrator, as the book begins, is certainly serious about the business of storytelling, and Joyce exploits his astonishing capacity to create sentences at once vivid in their descriptive power and deeply satisfying in their shape and sound. There had been glimpses of this gift in *Dubliners* and *A Portrait*, but in *Ulysses* Joyce is able to give it a free rein. In the first three chapters the meticulous and often poetic style of narration could be understood as a continuation of the method of *A Portrait*: Stephen, now back from his abortive escape to Paris, is more than ever the artist of language, and the narrative style reflects his virtuoso way with words. Here he is standing on the parapet of the Martello tower that houses him in the first episode ("Telemachus"): "Woodshadows floated silently by through the morning peace from the stairhead seaward where he gazed. Inshore and farther out the mirror of water whitened, spurned by lightshod hurrying feet."[3] If the style teeters on the edge of the excessive, and perhaps falls over into it in the final phrase, it is possible to ascribe this to Stephen's overactive verbal imagination.

Chapters 2 and 3 ("Nestor" and "Proteus") give further evidence of Stephen's inventive mental world as he attempts to teach a history class and later goes walking on Sandymount Strand. In the fourth chapter we encounter a contrasting character in Leopold Bloom, who is by no means an artist with words. Yet the narrative style achieves a degree of heightened expressiveness just as effective as any moments in the opening three chapters. Bloom enjoys the sight and smell of sausages in the pork butcher's window, but would never have articulated his pleasure in words such as these: "The shiny links, packed with forcemeat, fed his gaze and he breathed in tranquilly the lukewarm breath of cooked spicy pigs' blood" (4.142). We might posit a highly poetic narrator, but it would be more accurate to say that Joyce encourages us to enjoy the heightened sensory language for its own sake.

We need to return to the first chapter, however, to note the emergence of the most significant technical breakthrough of the first part of the novel. Here is an early example: "Stephen bent forward and peered at the mirror held out to him, cleft by a crooked crack. Hair on end. As he and others see me" (1.136). After the first full sentence, we shift into what is clearly recognizable as a different stylistic mode: full sentences give way to fragments, the past tense to the present, and the third person to the first. Stephen's thoughts are represented as a kind of shorthand, a development of the telegraphic style Joyce had used for the diary entries at the end of *A Portrait*. Once again Joyce has hit upon a technical device, interior monologue, that is startlingly new in the tradition of the English novel (though there are foreshadowings in, for instance, Austen and Dickens) and yet can be rapidly assimilated by the reader as a window into intimate mental recesses. It proves to be an extraordinarily versatile technique in Joyce's hands, conveying erudite associations that occur to Stephen as easily as it conveys a down-to-earth curiosity that motivates Bloom. In giving apparently fuller access to the motley kaleidoscope of a fictional character's inner world than any previous novel had managed, it is engrossing and often highly comic.

The use of an impressionist style to reflect a character's mental world, as announced on the first page of *A Portrait*, and the representation of thought by means of interior monologue, are techniques that continue a tradition of mimetic narrative that had dominated the novel since Defoe (Sterne being the chief exception). Because interior monologue presents the reader with a character's inner world of memories, allusions, and desires that, to the character, are in no need of explanation, the chapters relying on it contain enigmas (though not as many as an accurate transcription of thought would produce). But the enigmas do not create a barrier to empathetic engagement of a traditional sort. The first six chapters rely on interior monologue to introduce us to the two main characters, and there can be no doubt that, had Joyce continued for the remainder of his novel to trace their day's mental and physical adventures using the methods in the opening chapters, the result would have been hailed as a triumph of realism.

One feature of those six chapters, however, is less conventional: the first three, devoted to the younger man, take place concurrently with the next three, devoted to the older man. The only connections between the two sets of chapters seem incidental. For example, Stephen and Bloom – who barely know one another – witness, and are dismayed by, the temporary covering of the sun by the same cloud; both are in mourning; and both feel obliged to leave their places of residence. There is nothing strictly "unrealistic" about such parallels, but they suggest another aspect of *Ulysses* that is equally new and that moves the novel away from the conventions of realism: the novel is significantly more highly structured, and its structure is more foregrounded, than any of its predecessors. Most readers of the book are probably aware that Joyce produced a "schema" allotting each of the eighteen chapters a Homeric title, a location, and an hour of the day as well as emphasis on a specific organ, art, color, symbol, and technique. One has to take the schema – which exists in two rather different versions – with a pinch of salt; it is not, after all, part of the novel, and some elements of it are clearly fanciful. However, the locations and times of day can for the most part be confirmed from the text itself, and the Homeric titles have stuck, making reference to the chapters easier and reminding the reader of the parallel signaled by the title of the book. Thus the title of chapter 4, "Calypso," which introduces Bloom, alludes to book v of the *Odyssey*, which introduces Odysseus, held in thrall by the nymph of that name. Bloom's servitude to his wife Molly is thus colored by an allusion to a very different kind of sexual enslavement, but the characters themselves have no inkling of the connection.

The manifold structural motifs, verbal patterns, and cross-references create an entire layer of meaning that lies outside the characters' ken. The presence of such structural and other elements outside the fictional world has always been a feature of the novel, from titles, chapter headings, and epigraphs, to parallel plots and devices of closure. But as in so many other areas, Joyce takes to new extremes a property which had become habitual for novel readers, and finds fresh resources in it. For instance, even the most apparently realistic chapters are strewn with verbal clues to the Homeric theme. Thus we find in the "Lotus-Eaters" episode (chapter 5) – in which Bloom pursues his secret erotic correspondence under the pen-name "Henry Flower" and reads a letter to which a flower is pinned – thoughts like "His life isn't such a bed of roses," "No roses without thorns," and "Has her roses probably" (5.08, 5.277, 5.285). There is no reason why Bloom should fasten on this word, other than that the playful will of the author is reminding us of the botanical diet, and subsequent misfortune, suffered by some of Odysseus' companions.

One critical ploy in the face of the absence of any narrating consciousness is to appeal to an "Arranger" as the source of extra-narrative patterns. This is to multiply entities unnecessarily, however; it is simpler to think of an implied author who chooses words as well as arranges them. Some readers find this interference with naturalistic illusion irritating; others find it a constant source of delight. It separates Joyce not only from the tradition of the novel that he inherits but also from most of the novelists who were writing at the same time. Perhaps Joyce's closest stylistic confederate is Eliot – who admired what he called Joyce's "mythical method" – in a poem published in the same year as *Ulysses*: *The Waste Land*. To be sure, Joyce's achievement is emphatically that of a novelist; however, he demonstrates that it is possible for readers to enjoy metafictional devices without any lessening of their absorption in the characters' fictional lives.

Six chapters, then, in which Joyce both pushes the novel to new intensities and complexities of realism and at the same time poses a challenge to the implicit claims of realism. This challenge becomes more overt in the seventh chapter, which is named "Aeolus" after Homer's controller of the winds. It is set in a newspaper office where there is much windy rhetoric. The continuity of the narrative, which includes interior monologue by both Stephen and Bloom, is interrupted here by newspaper-style headlines that cannot be ascribed to a narrator. In the next four chapters Joyce uses other ways of exploding any lingering sense of a single narrative voice. In the "Scylla and

Charybdis" episode (chapter 9) we find that the narrative indulges in its own lexical games, including a Homeric pastiche and a miniature play. "Wandering Rocks" (chapter 10) not only presents short fragments of events taking place across Dublin at the same hour of the day (we have now reached 3–4 pm) but interpolates fragments within fragments, constantly halting the reader's progress. The musical theme of "Sirens" (chapter 11) dominates the events and the language of the episode, foregrounding the sound of the words as it leaves realism even further behind.

Another shock awaits the reader at the start of the twelfth chapter, "Cyclops." Having lost faith in a recognizable narrator, we are now given one with a vengeance. He is never named, but his character emerges clearly from his lengthy anecdote about events in Barney Kiernan's pub that involve Bloom and a group of Dublin drinkers at some unstated time in the past (which we know to have been after 5 pm on June 16). The new narrator's racy story is punctured, however, by parodic versions of bits of his tale that erupt without warning, again rendering any narrative continuity precarious. From now on in *Ulysses* stylistic variation is the rule. Although there is a brief return to Bloomian interior monologue in the second part of "Nausicaa" (chapter 13) (the first part adopts the lush manner of popular women's magazines of the time), the remainder of the novel explores at great length – the last five chapters take up about half the book – possibilities offered by a series of invented styles. Thus "Oxen of the Sun" (chapter 14) presents a parade of stylistic pastiches of English prose, "Circe" (chapter 15) is in the form of a theatrical fantasy, "Eumaeus" (chapter 16) comically wanders through the clichés of journalism and public speaking, and "Ithaca" (chapter 17) takes the form of a bizarre catechism in which questioner and respondent remain unidentified. Finally, as if to end with the reassurance of a single consciousness, the "Penelope" episode conveys the thoughts of a single character in the small hours of June 17. Like Homer's Penelope, Molly is a faithful wife; but unlike Penelope she is also a sexual predator.

And the plot? Joyce's departure from the tradition of the novel depends on a downgrading of the importance of the story, though this is not to say that the reader loses interest in the events of the day. The early chapters of *Ulysses* show Stephen thwarted and rudderless. He can neither return to the tower, which Mulligan and Haines have rendered unbearable, nor go home, where his mother's death, his father's irresponsibility, and his siblings' poverty create in him a sense of desperation. His ambitions as a writer receive no encouragement from the Dublin newspaper world or its literary intelligentsia; he is sexually unfulfilled, fretting with guilt about his mother; and he works at a teaching job he hates. Bloom also has his problems: he has not had sexual intercourse with his wife for over ten years; he is still grieving for a son whose death at eleven days was the apparent cause of his sexual rupture with Molly, and for his father, who committed suicide eight years previously. Bloom too cannot go home, because he prefers to let Molly's assignation with her lover Blazes Boylan take its course. Both Stephen and Bloom are isolated in Dublin, Stephen through his own precious sense of superiority, Bloom through his Jewishness and his failure to participate in the camaraderie of the city's male caucus. All these troubles are given full expression, and provide as much human detail as any nineteenth-century novel. The paths of the two characters cross or almost cross several times during the day, but it is not until the "Circe" episode that they interact in a meaningful way: Bloom saves the inebriated Stephen from an awkward encounter with a brothel madam, finds some late-night refreshment for him, and takes him back to Bloom's house in Eccles Street for cocoa and conversation. The fluent novel-reader is quick to pick up the hints of an ending that will resolve much of this unfinished business: Stephen will move into Eccles Street, establish a companionship with Leopold that will compensate for their respective parental and filial absences, instruct Molly in the proper pronunciation of Italian, and provide her with more satisfactory male company than that of Boylan. Should theirs prove to be a sexual relationship, Bloom might be more than ready to acquiesce in it.

But nothing of the sort happens; in the penultimate chapter, Stephen declines Bloom's invitation to stay the night and walks off into the city, destination unknown. There is, nevertheless, a hopeful tinge to the ending: Bloom finds he can accept his wife's infidelity; and Molly's final monologue, after traversing memories and fantasies involving a long series of men, comes to rest in a recall of the day when she and Leopold sealed their union. This is far from the direction in which the plot seemed to be going, though it leaves open the possibility that an anticipated resolution might still occur. Much more important than the teleological thrust of this narrative journey, how-ever, are the pleasures to be lingered over on the way: incidental detail, vivid phrasing, comic exorbitance, subtle patterning, musical language, and a rich exploration of the mind's engagement with both its cultural milieu and its bodily embeddedness. There is also much pleasure to be gained from the portrait of Bloom as the text provides increasing details about his psycholog-ical and moral characteristics, and his past and present life. With Homer's hero in mind, we can enjoy the virtues that Bloom embodies: his open-minded curiosity, his empathetic relation to other beings (including a variety of animals), his lack of self-righteousness or self-assurance, his generosity (in, for instance, assisting Dignam's widow in her financial straits), and his almost unlimited tolerance. When "the Citizen" in Barney Kiernan's pub pushes Bloom beyond his limits, a reader's sympathies are likely to remain with him, even if the text, cheerfully parodying Bloom's ardent championship of love, undermines the temporary illusion of a kind-hearted author lurking behind the unfriendly narrator.

Ulysses quickly became known not just as a very long and difficult book but as an exceptionally dirty book, a reputation heightened by its unavailability (at least legally) in most of the English-speaking world before Judge Woolsey's landmark decision in 1933 declaring it not to be obscene. Joyce's use of taboo words and unsparing depiction of excretory and sexual activities was not merely the result of a desire to *épater les bourgeois* but part of his project of representing with an unprecedented fullness the human animal in all its facets, a project which the technique of interior monologue is also designed to support. The project can also be understood as part of the work's ethical undertaking: whereas Homer celebrates the extraordinary deeds of the mythic hero Odysseus and his companions in their long journey back to Ithaca, Joyce celebrates the ordinary delights and terrors, trials and achievements, of the not-particularly-special urban lower-middle-class individual at the beginning of the twentieth century as he looks for ways to go home. To omit bodily functions and sexual desires would be to shear off a good part of the experience Joyce wants to redeem.

Sex, in particular, had never been treated in this way. Bloom is aroused at several moments during his day; in the "Calypso" and "Lotus-Eaters" episodes his sexual interest is stirred by the "moving hams" of the next-door servant girl, by the stockinged legs of a woman across the street, by the letter from his clandestine correspondent, and by the thought of masturbating in a Turkish bath. When he does masturbate in the "Nausicaa" episode, stimulated by the exhibitionism of a young woman on the beach (and pleased that he had not, after all, done it in the bath), there is no implied moral judgment. Although any sense of fulfillment is shadowed by the element of sadness in the participants' lives, what happens is a strange kind of consensual sex. The "Circe" episode flaunts a different kind of sexual freedom: the world of fantasy, in which sexual identities and sexual practices are not bound by the moral norms of actual behavior. Whether these fantasies should be ascribed to Bloom, or are another manifestation of the text's autonomy as it pursues possibilities unyoked to any notion of fictional character, is left to the reader to decide. Once more Joyce validates an aspect of the human psyche largely unacknowledged by his predecessors except in studies of deviance and criminality. The Dublin setting in which these fantasies occur is its notorious red-light district, but although there is a touch of infernal intensity about the description of the place, the prostitutes who inhabit it are neither falsely glamorized nor treated with moral disapproval. Finally, the unpunctuated sentences of "Penelope" traverse the gamut of sexual memories, yearnings, schemes, and speculations in a mode that is at once comic and convincing – and all the more scandalous to early readers because the gamut occupies the mind of a woman. In inviting acceptance of sexual and bodily needs not talked of in polite company, and often inviting the relishing of such needs, Joyce was joining the postwar attack on prudery and prejudice in a highly effective way.

Another set of oppressive forces feature in *Ulysses*, as they do in all Joyce's previous work. The Catholic Church, and the political establishment in Ireland which supported and was supported by the Church, had been a target of Joyce's criticism since his university days, and he was equally aware of the exploitation of his country by its imperial masters, both in naked political ways and in the more subtle processes of cultural colonization. One of the most memorable passages of *A Portrait* is the account of the Christmas dinner party at which Stephen, still a young boy, hears his father condemn priests for their abandonment of the Irish Home Rule hero John Stewart Parnell over Parnell's adulterous liaison with Katherine O'Shea; all three of Stephen's and Joyce's subsequent targets are involved in the fierce argument – sexual puritanism and hypocrisy, British rule, and Catholic treachery. Yet Joyce's relationship to the Church and the Empire is more complex than his attitude to sexual dishonesty. In *Ulysses* Catholic ritual is rendered comic by having a Jewish outsider witness it, but Bloom's admiration for the Church's skill in promoting itself, though critical, is also funny, and a long way from Stephen's passionate *non serviam*. Stephen himself is fascinated by the richness of the Church's intellectual traditions, and the Jesuits who have taught him throughout his educational career are not treated with unmixed hostility.

Similarly, in spite of Joyce's strong awareness of Ireland's subservient position to its neighbor (exemplified, for instance, in the British soldiers who accost Stephen in "Circe"), the richness of English cultural heritage is not something Joyce is willing to abandon. The serried pastiches of the "Oxen of the Sun" episode make fun of a variety of canonized English styles, but they are not without affection too (the same could be said of the exorbitant versions of Irish sagas in "Cyclops"). Attempts by the Irish Revival to substitute a home-grown alternative never convinced Joyce. While he strongly identified with the Irish campaign for independence, and Parnell remained one of his most admired political heroes, his depiction of an outspoken nationalist in "the citizen" of "Cyclops" is largely unsympathetic, and he allows Bloom, at the end of "Sirens," to punctuate with a fart his reading of the nationalist Robert Emmet's famous speech from the dock. *Ulysses* was undoubtedly effective in promulgating more open attitudes to sexual matters, and perhaps played a part in freeing some readers from the shackles of a narrow religion, but its undermining of British authority, although an important part of the novel's continuing interest today, is unlikely to have been instrumental in the gaining of Irish independence.

Within a few years of its publication, *Ulysses* was widely regarded as a work of extraordinary originality, a work that transgressed the limits of decency and difficulty, but that any cultured individual had to read – and any up-to-date novelist had to take account of, whether by rejection or emulation. Its author, who had moved to Paris from Trieste in 1920 and completed the book there under conditions that would have daunted most writers, became a celebrity in a city alive with artistic creativity.

Instead of resting on his laurels, however, Joyce began immediately on a new work, known until its 1939 publication only as "Work in Progress," several sections of which appeared in journals and small publications. While *Ulysses* constituted for other writers a challenge to rise to, and a hoard of techniques to raid – as it still does – *Finnegans Wake* occupies a more vexed position in the history of the novel. If the earlier book could be said to be both a culmination and a demolition of the realist novel, Joyce's last work can be called a novel only by default, as it lacks most of the features that characterize the genre. A number of critics have attempted valiantly to extract from it rounded characters and a continuous plot, but this can be done only at the expense of what makes the work unlike any other: 628 pages of verbal inventiveness, in which new lexical items – portmanteaus – are formed by jamming words together. The English language is invaded by other languages, proper names are maltreated as much as common nouns, and the world's treasury of writings, historical events, myths, songs, and personages are plundered to enrich the textual fabric. Nothing like this had confronted the reading public before:

> – He shook be ashaped of hempshelves, hiding that shepe in his goat. And for rassembling so bearfellsed the magreedy prince of Roger. Thuthud. Heigh hohse, heigh hohse, our kindom from an orse! Bruni Lanno's woollies on Brani Lonni's hairyparts. And the hunk in his trunk it would be an insalt foul the matter of that cellaring to a pigstrough. (373.13)[4]

As a student Joyce had baffled readers by referring in an article to Giordano Bruno as "the Nolan"; here he combines a reference to Bruno ("Nolan" appears in anagrammatic form) with Leonardo Bruni, historian of Florence, and Brian O'Linn, hero of a song which tells of his wearing of sheepskin breeches, woolly side in. Richard III, who was famously played by Macready, is transformed into "Roger. Thuthud," and it is possible to detect in what follows that king's most famous Shakespearean utterance (as so often, meanings become clearer when the passage is read aloud).

With this density of multiple meaning, esoteric allusion, and linguistic diversity on every page, observing none of the normal constraints on coherence or progression, it is no wonder that Joyce's endeavor met with a great deal of skepticism. The lexical playfulness evident from the opening page of *A Portrait* and the willingness to challenge the norms of narrative progression manifested in its sermons, both tendencies which Joyce exploited more fully in *Ulysses*, now reach outrageous proportions. No one talks of an "Arranger" for this work, let alone a narrator. The portmanteau style, in particular, enables Joyce to take to its furthest limit his relinquishment of authority. Whereas the pun, in its clever combination of two or more meanings, conveys the sense of an author wholly in control of the linguistic material, the multilingual portmanteau, which always offers the possibility of as yet undiscovered associations, leaves the determination of meaning to the reader. Later in his life Joyce gave critics a way of holding the whole diverse work together by suggesting that it could be thought of as a dream, but this hardly enables us to identify a narrative consciousness running from the opening to the end – which, famously, leads back to the opening.

Our understanding of Joyce's ambitious enterprise has been enhanced by recent studies of the many notebooks and drafts that lie behind the published text, a set of manuscript materials which Joyce carefully preserved, perhaps envisaging them as a vast extension to the book. He collected an enormous number of phrases from a wide variety of printed sources and from spoken utterances, and wove those into what began as a series of rather bare anecdotes, fusing words together freely and allowing indications of actions and traits to coagulate into a small number of figures. The most important of these form a family: a father, a mother, twin sons, and a younger girl. Others include a set of four commentators, twelve citizens, and twenty-eight "rainbow girls." To all these he allotted not names but sigla, such as a triangle for the mother and an upside-down V for one of the sons. Once transferred into the work itself, these clusters of traits could be identified as personages, though their names are far from stable. The father figure is most frequently identified by a series of initials, HCE, which can refer to a host of different names or phrases, though by common consent the most reliable is Humphrey Chimpden Earwicker. The mother is ALP or Anna Livia Plurabelle, the sons Shem and Shaun, the daughter

Isobel or Issy. The parents are also associated with Dublin landmarks: the father with the Hill of Howth and Howth Castle and the mother with the River Liffey. But this is only the beginning of the associations.

A central preoccupation of the work is the fall and possible revival of the hero – in the ballad referred to in the title, the corpse of Finnegan is resurrected when splashed with whiskey – and so among the many avatars of HCE are Adam, Jesus, Parnell, Wilde, Ibsen's Master Builder, and Humpty Dumpty. ALP is the defender of her husband in the face of the scandal caused by reports of an impropriety with two girls in Phoenix Park (which doubles for the Garden of Eden), Shem is a bohemian artist, reviled by the representatives of propriety and commerce, Shaun is a smooth-talking public figure who looks down on his brother, and Issy is a figure both of childish innocence and precocious sexuality. All undergo repeated transformations, as they are made to resonate with related figures and events from history, myth, and literature. They feature in multiple retellings of the central story: the male as fallen hero, the woman as defender, the daughter as temptress (Issy translated into the two girls in the park), and the sons as the new generation knocking at the door (Shem and Shaun conjoined spawn a third male figure, and they become the three soldiers who witness and report on HCE's indiscretion). There are many other versions of sexual impropriety, generational challenge, defenses and self-defenses, conflicts between artistic and commercial interests, sunderings and reconciliations (the passage above is part of an attack on the humpbacked HCE for his sexual transgression). As a result of the unexpected combinations and juxtapositions, comedy erupts on every page, whatever the content. The heroic and the mundane, the elite and the popular, are no longer merely juxtaposed; they are fused. Even more than is the case in *Ulysses*, there is no implicit moralizing about sex: it takes a myriad forms, all treated with the same extravagant and forgiving humor. There is, however, an implicit critique running throughout the work: of puritanism, dogmatism, belief in simple origins and predetermined ends, and discourses of racial and cultural purity.

Finnegans Wake has seventeen chapters arranged in four books (there are no headings, as with *Ulysses*), and while some chapters have distinctive stylistic properties (book II, chapter 2 for instance, is in the form of a textbook, with marginal glosses and footnotes), there is nothing like the series of stylistic shifts in *Ulysses*: Joyce's "night language" prevails throughout. After eight chapters introducing the main figures (and much else), the central books expand at length on various aspects of the family's interactions, following a rough progression from evening to night, and the final single-chapter book announces a new dawn. The challenge to the reader is manifold: to make sense, word by word, sentence by sentence, of a distorted version of the English language salted with many other languages, to identify allusions to an encyclopedic array of people, places, and events, and to advance from this level of detail to an appreciation of the larger structures of the book, without the stepping-stones of traditional characters or plot.

Appearing at an inauspicious moment in European history, the book made less of an impact than it might have done, but probably at any time it would have been greeted more by bemusement than endorsement. Unlike *Ulysses*, its influence on other writers has been more a matter of stimulating fresh experimentalism than of providing technical resources that could be further exploited. Among instances of such experimentalism in English are the more extravagant prose fictions of Samuel Beckett, the textual inventions of Christine Brooke-Rose, and the verbal fireworks of Anthony Burgess. The importance of *Finnegans Wake* outside the novel has perhaps been more significant: in music, John Cage draws repeatedly on *Finnegans Wake*, in the theater, Caryl Churchill's *The Skriker* builds on Joyce's linguistic exorbitance, in philosophy, Jacques Derrida acknowledges an important debt to the work, and numerous later poets have been emboldened by its playfulness to sport freely with language.

Thanks to the work of archival researchers, patient explicators, and, compilers of reference works, it is much easier to enjoy the *Wake* than was once the case. Group reading has proved a particularly successful means of approaching it, making possible the pooling of knowledge and insights. Many puzzles remain on every page. We have reached a moment when, after seven decades of scholarly and critical endeavor, we can derive pleasures from Joyce's achievement; but it would be a bold commentator who would claim that we have fully taken its measure.

Notes

1. See Hans Walter Gabler, Introduction, in James Joyce, *A Portrait of the Artist as a Young Man*, ed. Hans Walter Gabler with Walter Hettche (New York: Garland, 1993), pp. 1–18. Gabler contests the more usual dating of 1904.
2. Letter to Grant Richards, March 13, 1906, in James Joyce, *Letters*, 3 vols, Vol. ii, ed. Richard Ellmann (New York: Viking, 1966), p. 132.
3. James Joyce, *Ulysses*, ed. Hans Walter Gabler (London: The Bodley Head, 1986), 1.242. References are to chapter number, first line number.
4. James Joyce, *Finnegans Wake* (London: Faber, 1939). All editions of *Finnegans Wake* have the same pagination. The reference is to page number, first line number.

37

Richardson, Woolf, Lawrence: the modernist novel's experiments with narrative (1)

MARK WOLLAEGER

Dorothy Richardson, Virginia Woolf, and D. H. Lawrence are connoisseurs of consciousness who experiment with new fictional forms in order to redress older fiction's putative falsification of elusive inner realities. Woolf's "Modern Fiction" (1925) strikes a characteristically modernist note of rebellion in the name of inner freedom: "if a writer . . . could base his work upon his own feeling and not upon convention, there would be no plot, no comedy, no tragedy, no love interest or catastrophe in the accepted style."[1] Woolf's choice of pronoun masks and dramatizes her struggle to find new ways to express not only life in its immediacy but *female* experiences of modernity. In 1923 she credits Richardson with inventing a "woman's sentence": "It is of a more elastic fibre than the old, capable of stretching to the extreme, of suspending the frailest particles, of enveloping the vaguest shapes."[2] Richardson too sees her writing as an attempt "to produce a feminine equivalent of the current masculine realism."[3] Although Lawrence has been characterized as the exemplary patriarch targeted by Woolf, Richardson, and feminism generally, Lawrence believes he is enlisting formal innovations to liberate the female voice from long-standing misrepresentation, and to subvert received notions of masculinity and normative sexuality. All three writers are sexual dissidents. Their shared effort to represent more faithfully the fullness of existence – being rather than "mere" doing – underscores the fact that what we call modernism is for many of its practitioners a newly heightened realism.

But if rebellion against the perceived shortcomings of Victorian fiction unites all three in a recognizably modernist structure of feeling, their standing in the modernist canon differs greatly. Woolf's major status – as iconic champion of female modernism, high-brow aesthete, public intellectual, devotee of new media – is now unchallenged. Lawrence and Richardson enjoy less secure positions. Lawrence's working-class origins set him apart from Woolf's Bloomsbury, described by Raymond Williams as a "class fraction" of England's ruling elite.[4] His ambivalence toward literary experimentation militated against his work's inclusion among the formal innovations of Joyce, Woolf, Pound, and T. S. Eliot. Initially Richardson was given precedence over Woolf and Katherine Mansfield: "stream of consciousness," now a standard term in modernist aesthetics, was applied to Richardson's fiction by May Sinclair in a 1918 review of the first three volumes of Richardson's *Pilgrimage*, which Sinclair compares with Joyce's *A Portrait of the Artist as a Young Man*.[5] Yet Richardson sank into oblivion, and the four-volume edition of *Pilgrimage* (and nearly all the individual titles in the series) is out of print in the United States. Although the relative standing of these writers might yet shift, it seems clear that Richardson enjoys a far smaller readership than does Woolf or Lawrence because she goes further than either in pursuing their shared desire to free themselves from inherited constraints of novelistic form. Relative to the broad reading public, Richardson is modernist to a fault.

Some reflections on each writer's relationship to formal innovation will be helpful. Arnold Bennett had the temerity to suggest in a review that Woolf and her contemporaries lacked the ability to create character. Woolf was keen to show that Bennett had it backwards. Attentive to the "spirit," the Georgians, who include Joyce and herself (as well as an honorary oldster, Conrad), are for Woolf better able to capture the essences of characters, in particular the life of ordinary female ones. The distinctive inwardness of such characters, she argues, is lost in the profuse social detail offered by Bennett and his ilk. Woolf mischaracterizes Bennett's progressive naturalism. Nevertheless, she lives up to her aspiration to devise new forms of characterization and new narrative structures adequate to what she understands as the fragmentary quality of modern life, particularly of urban life. Woolf, moving beyond plottedness itself, seeks an entirely new form, which she once considered calling "elegy,"[6] and readers of *To the Lighthouse* (1927) – especially the radically disruptive "Time Passes" section – or the lyrical monologues of *The Waves* (1931) likely agree that Woolf becomes the "free" writer she imagines in "Modern Fiction."

And yet, like Conrad's Marlow, Woolf sometimes feels a need to withdraw her hesitating foot. Faced with *The Waste Land*, for instance, Woolf in "Mr. Bennett and Mrs. Brown" cannot conceal her fear that Eliot's experimentalism has broken an implied contract with the reader. Richardson brings out Woolf's ambivalence even more. Reviewing Richardson's *The Tunnel* (1919), Woolf expresses admiration for Richardson's effort to write beyond "the form provided by tradition," yet she protests the lack of sufficient "unity, significance, or design" within the novel's "helter-skelter of flying fragments." Even when Woolf acknowledges the originality of the "woman's sentence" that Richardson uses to explore "the crannies of Miriam Henderson's consciousness," she notes that the invention is not so much one of form but of content: "it is used to describe a woman's mind by a writer who is neither proud nor afraid of anything that she may discover in the psychology of her sex." Woolf associates Richardson with pretty good company –"Chaucer, Donne, Dickens," all of whom, like Richardson, investigate the perpetual fluidity of emotions – and then notes that Richardson's project unfolds "on an infinitely smaller scale," that the emotions experienced by Miriam are comparatively superficial (*Contemporary Writers*, 125–126). Richardson's fiction, in its radical departure from norms of narration, like *The Waste Land*, goes too far.

Lawrence also evinces a divided attitude toward radical innovation. In the mid-1920s he argues that high-brow and popular fiction, if they are really to matter, require at the very least major surgery – or an exploding bomb. High-brow novelists suffer from a kind of "arrested development" characterized by infantile self-absorption: "'Did I feel a twinge in my little toe, or didn't I?' asks every character of Mr. Joyce or of Miss Richardson or M. Proust." [7] Only some "convulsion or cataclysm" will cure fiction of its excessive self-consciousness, banish abstraction, and let in "a whole line of new emotion" (*Phoenix*, 520). What is wanted is neither full immersion in a flood of facts or impressions, nor the much ballyhooed God-like objectivity theorized by Flaubert and promulgated by Henry James and Ford Madox Ford. And rather than the moralizing of Victorian fiction, Lawrence urges a "finer morality" that comprehends interrelations not just between human beings but between "man and his circumambient universe" (*Phoenix*, 525, 527). For the web of fiction to capture "life" as opposed to mere existence it must attend to the immediacy of embodied feelings and elicit an answering vibration in the body of the reader.

Lawrence is typically better at critique than realization. Excelling in the art of negation, his fiction often falters when it comes to providing a new model. His greatest novel, *Women in Love* (1917), succeeds by dramatizing the dilemma repeatedly. The Brangwen sisters delight in the temptation not to marry, but the prospect of not marrying secretly makes them afraid. Likewise, the novel aspires to transcend the marriage plot that structures traditional English novels but is not quite sure what to put in its place. Not only does *Women in Love* trace the relationship between two couples, but it also betrays a neoclassical investment in symmetry by locating the two key chapters about the couples –"Rabbit" and "Moony" – dead center in the book. Lawrence's Woolf-like ambivalence toward the radically new also plays out in the novel's complex engagement with

Futurism, which carries for Lawrence, as I will show, what Conrad calls the fascination of abomination.

For now let me suggest that while both Lawrence and Woolf are attracted to the notion of aesthetic revolution, they often cling to the role of reformer. Lawrence inveighs against the novelist who puts his thumb on the scale and thereby falsifies life, but his narrators often take up a hectoring posture, and instead of coaxing an answering vibration in readers try to ring them like a bell. And however much Woolf aspires to go beyond plot, comedy, tragedy, love interest, or catastrophe, she writes almost as much in established genres – the *Bildungsroman* (*The Voyage Out* [1915]), the comedy of manners (*Night and Day* [1919]), the family saga (*The Years* [1937]) – as she does in newer forms – the "day-in-the-life-of" novel (*Mrs. Dalloway* [1925]), the lyrical novel (*Jacob's Room* [1922] and *The Waves* [1931]) – or in *sui generis* forms (*To the Lighthouse* [1927], *Orlando* [1928], and *Between the Acts* [1941]).

The twelve volumes of *Pilgrimage* (1915–1938), in contrast, make few concessions to convention or categorization. To be sure, given Richardson's tendency to slip, from time to time, out of external narration into I-narration, *Pilgrimage* sometimes reads like a diary. And because we now know how closely Miriam's life is modeled on Richardson's, *Pilgrimage* can also be read as a *roman à clef*. H. G. Wells, who had an affair with Richardson, acknowledges in 1934 that *Pilgrimage* is "a very curious essay in autobiography."[8] Curious indeed, Richardson's experiment in autobiography is much more experimental than Wells's own. Again, it exceeds characterization. As Woolf observes, *Pilgrimage*'s "chief characteristic ... is one for which we still seek a name" (*Contemporary Writers*, 124). Although early reviewers recognized Richardson's bold innovations by applying such "names" as "Impressionism," "Futurism," "Imagism," and "cubism" to her fiction, the first review of *Pointed Roofs* anticipates later complaints by observing what might be most disorienting: that Richardson writes "as if the reader did not exist."[9] Limiting the virtually plotless separate volumes to Miriam's point of view, Richardson does not bother to explain things that Miriam herself would not need to explain to herself. Thus unless one begins with the first volume and reads in sequence, later additions become increasingly difficult to follow. If there is a central event in *Pilgrimage*, it is an infinitely prolonged one, the continuous unfolding of Miriam Henderson's process of becoming and visions of being. More so than any other modernists who claim to focus intently on ordinary daily life, Richardson really does, and she does so in long, looping, complex sentences that are best described not as "feminine" (*pace* Woolf) but as eccentric. If Lawrence's originality on the level of the sentence lies in his idiosyncratic idioms ("suave loins of darkness") and incantatory rhythms, and Woolf's in her complex figurative language bound within elongated hypotaxis, Richardson's lies in her convoluted, sometimes fractured syntax.

Richardson, Woolf, and Lawrence all turn their attention to consciousness in order to get closer to life, but their shared aim plays out very differently. In Richardson structure dissolves in the vagaries of consciousness. Woolf, for all her attention to the "incessant shower of innumerable atoms," is more openly interested than Richardson in representing the counter-pressure of social institutions that contribute to "myriad impressions" as they impinge on the mind (*The Common Reader: First Series*, 150). This is not to say that Richardson's representation of Miriam's struggle to preserve the integrity of her self against all that would determine it does not carry the force of social critique. Rather, where Richardson's critique tends to be immanent, Woolf's tends toward the polemical. Lawrence sees consciousness as the source of modern society's ills and wants his fiction to explore the generative power of the unconscious and the liberatory potential of desire. But, always secretly in love with whatever he most claims to despise, Lawrence devotes a great deal of attention to the very forms of consciousness (and often the literary forms) he wishes to negate.

The underworld for Lawrence is a non-human "it" at the deepest levels of being. *Women in Love* meditates on the problem of character at an historical moment when the coherence of human identity, Lawrence thinks, is challenged from the inside by the unconscious and from the outside by the instrumental logic of modern technology.

Dismissing the "old stable ego" of character in favor of a labile model, Lawrence asserts: "There is another ego, according to whose action the individual is unrecognizable, and passes through, as it were, allotropic states which it needs a deeper sense than any we've been used to exercise, to discover are states of the same single radically-unchanged element."[10] Lawrence's two books on Freud betray an investment in the logic of deep truths versus superficial epiphenomena, but psychoanalysis ultimately provides a less illuminating context for Lawrence's theory of character than do his meditations on the status of the human in an age of technology. For under the pressure of Lawrence's fascination with the non-human dimension of the human, *Women in Love* begins to articulate an inhuman underplot that complicates the creation of character within the otherwise straightforward structure of the novel.[11]

The underplot transforms human beings into scrims through which one glimpses the contours of their non-human doubles. In "Rabbit" Gerald strikes at the frenzied rabbit "like a hawk"; the rabbit is "like a dragon" or "furry meteorite"; Gudrun looks like a macaw and cries out like a seagull; the governess is like "some elegant beetle."[12] Elsewhere Gerald is like "a piece of radium," a "fatal living metal" (396); and Loerke, a rabbit, troll, or rat. Rather than dehumanization or reification, which imply a transformation imposed by an external agent, what happens in *Women in Love* seems to come from within, and is better described as a form of allotropic non-humanization in which categories located along the continuum of human–animal–thing begin to drift and overlap. When Gudrun first lays eyes on Gerald she sees him both as "an arctic thing" and a "smiling wolf" (14–15). A locus of transgressed boundaries, Gerald is ice, metal, wolf, man, and, as we later see in the "Industrial Magnate" chapter, both God of and cog in the industrial machine. The effect of non-humanization is more subtle with Ursula, the character least likely to morph into an animal or thing. Birkin wants to enter into an "equilibrium" with Ursula, "a pure balance of two single beings:– as the stars balance each other" (148). In Latin "Ursula" means "little bear," which retranslates into Ursa Minor, a constellation; and the notion of Ursula as a minor constellation resonates with her suspicion that what Birkin really wants is a subordinate "satellite" (150). The star motif operates as a metonym for that which is non-human, or beyond the human, but also alive with a radiant energy suggestive of human aspiration.

Lawrence's defense of allotropic characters accompanies his attempt to define his relation to Italian Futurism, the artistic movement enamored of technological modernity. Lawrence welcomes the Futurist critique of dead tradition, which he associates with the stifling "moral scheme" of more traditional fiction, but rejects the elevation of what Marinetti calls "the physiology of matter"; Lawrence champions not matter itself but the exploration of the "non-human" in humanity (*Letters*, vol. II, 182). The slipperiness of this distinction is evident when Lawrence in the same long epistolary paragraph declares his *fascination* with the physiology of matter, and derides the Futurists for looking only for "the phenomena of the science of physics to be found in human being" instead of "looking for the new human phenomenon" (*Letters*, vol. II, 183). Lawrence's hesitation between the human and the non-human expresses his profound ambivalence toward the very categories of the human and the organic that he is usually understood to exalt.

Lawrence's ensuing theory of character reproduces his divided attitude. Elaborating what he means by allotropic states, he writes: "Like as diamond and coal are the same pure single element of carbon. The ordinary novel would trace the history of the diamond – but I say 'diamond, what! This is carbon.' And my diamond might be coal or soot, and my theme is carbon" (*Letters*, vol. II, 183). Lawrence's preference for unchanging carbon over the superficial glitter of diamonds, each of which might have its own distinctive cut or color, shifts the real action of the novel to what Ursula describes as an "under-space . . . where she did not care for people and their idiosyncrasies" (305). This is the realm of the underplot, the space of de-differentiation or allotropic transformation in which the idiosyncrasies that define conscious individuality dissolve into immediacies of primal desire and being. Lawrence's effort to evoke the surge of unconscious energies thus produces a counter-point between the human and non-human in which the vertical axis that plunges down into the non-human interferes with the lucidity of the tradi-tionally "human" story on the plane of the horizontal by undermining the stability of the symbolic oppositions that structure his narrative.

The horizontal lines of the narrative unfold with relative clarity. *Women in Love* traces the fortunes of an "angelic couple" – Birkin and Ursula – and a "demonic couple" – Gerald and Gudrun. They represent numerous contrasts. The most fundamental is between the human / organic and the non-human / mechanical, but the oppositions can be extended almost indefinitely: nature versus technology; authenticity versus irony; sensuality as a path to enlighten-ment versus sensual experience as an end in itself; the invisible versus the visible. As the characters and the pairings are defined against one another, the narrative traces their movements through social scenes, from the humble Brangwen household, the colliery district, and the decadence of London bohemia, to the prosperous Crich household and the aristocratic country estate of Hermione Roddice. In its first half the story advances less through plot than through juxtaposed symbolic tableaux. In the opening paragraphs of chapter 10, for instance, a body–soul contrast underlies Gudrun's staring at the "turgid fleshy structure" of water plants "thrusting up out of mud" while "Ursula was watch-ing the butterflies" (119).

But given the waywardness of allotropic transformation, the contrastive struc-tures are unstable, and the distinctions between characters blur. Sometimes the permeability of boundaries registers in a single word. When "a dark flood of electric passion" (313) flows between Ursula and Birkin, it evokes the spiritualized flows of bodily energy associated with yoga. But when Gerald becomes "sur-charged with [Gudrun's] electric life" (331), electricity names the material flow of energy. We are meant to remember that before hooking up with Gerald, who electrifies the mining operations he inherits from his father, Gudrun dates an electrician. (We are also invited to hear a pun on the magnetism of the industrial magnate.) With key terms threatening to flip into their opposites, much of Lawrence's effort is devoted to preserving distinctions between his characters even as he evokes a subterranean energy that overrides distinctions. It is not surprising, then, that despite Lawrence's efforts to differentiate between Gudrun and Ursula, many readers still cannot do so.

All this makes the writing of something recognizable as a novel difficult. For to recover the elementally non-human from within the human is to imperil identity. But if the shattering of conscious identity appeals to Lawrence, the radical dismantling of novelistic character, pursued for instance by Joyce in the phantasmagoria of Nighttown, does not. Stopping short of such experiments, Lawrence's interest in problems of representation nevertheless becomes increasingly urgent over the course of *Women in Love*. The introduction of the quasi-Futurist artist Loerke, a major figure, late in the novel violates traditional novelistic proprieties; but it gives Lawrence an opportunity to be more explicit about the matters of representation that concern him. The autonomy of the aesthetic object, authorial willfulness, and abstraction become matters of explicit debate between Loerke and Gudrun in the final chapter, but the grounds for the debate are laid long before, in the crucial "Rabbit" and "Moony" chapters.

It is worth sketching how those chapters explore problems of representation that face Richardson and Woolf as well as Lawrence. Each chapter poses questions about the possibility of articulating new modes of being without simply reproducing and accelerating processes of abstraction that Lawrence associates with a lamentable dominance of consciousness over the body.

In "Rabbit," when Gerald gives a drawing lesson to Gudrun's younger sister Winifred, Lawrence worries over the inhumanness of representational abstraction –Winifred's "grotesque diagram" of her dog Looloo stands in for Futurism and cubism – and the loss of respect for the autonomy of the object of representation that might be inherent in abstraction. Lawrence suspects that the activity of representing has been irreversibly compromised by modern media, from abstract painting to radio broadcasts. The implication that Winifred's drawing may injure Looloo through a kind of sympathetic magic – the dog suffers "a subtle injury" under her gaze – also raises the possibility that all representation, not just modes of misrepresentation, entails violence.

The arrival of Gudrun, herself an artist, extends the meditation in the form of an attempt to capture Winifred's pet rabbit, the next creature to sit for her drawing. The ferociously resistant rabbit gouges Gudrun's arm and elicits Gerald's violent efforts to subdue it. In the ensuing struggle for mastery Gerald and Gudrun bond in a sado-masochist thrill that sets the tone for their subsequent relationship: "The long, shallow red rip seemed torn across [Gerald's] brain, tearing the surface of his ultimate consciousness, letting through the forever unconscious, unthinkable red ether of the beyond, the obscene beyond" (242). The "red ether" phrase is crucial. The notion of ether, the substance of nineteenth-century physical theories through which electro-magnetic and light waves were thought to be propagated, was in the news owing to Einstein's special theory of relativity, which dispenses with the need to posit ether. Lawrence's peculiar recovery of ether in "Rabbit" suggests a radiant field of erotic energy that physically connects Gudrun and Gerald before they ever touch. The red ether operates as a connective medium by suffusing space with a kind of distillate of the body. On the other hand, "ether" at this time also evokes "ether-wave telegraphy," or radio, a form of trans-mission that Lawrence groups with jazz and film as evil abstractions from life.

Gudrun and Gerald are thus bonded by an inhuman underplot that fuses wireless circuitry with a seemingly organic "unthinkable" medium of propaga-tion. It becomes clear that their relationship is tainted by technological media – at one moment an image is "photographed upon [Gudrun's] soul" (281) – and that violence inheres in the modes of abstract representation associated with them. The rabbit seems wise to resist their efforts to draw him, for to be drawn is to be drawn into a force field suffused by the disembodying effects of technological mediation.

Lawrence positions "Moony" as the antithesis of "Rabbit"; but if Birkin and Ursula's interaction implies an alternative to Gudrun and Gerald's abstract techno-organic connection, that alternative is never clearly articulated. What Birkin does in "Moony" dramatizes Lawrence's desire for difference even as it acknowledges the difficulty of working out a sustainable alternative. Birkin repeatedly casts stones at the reflection of the moon on the water of a lake. He wants to shatter the reflection, whose re-forming frenzies him. Birkin's compulsive action amounts to an effort to shatter the history of representation in order to recover the immediacy of the moment via the synaesthetic turbulence of the water. The violence of "Rabbit" is here displaced onto a symbolic equivalent of the modernist desire to make it new. Birkin's violence dramatizes Lawrence's ambivalent desire to dispense with representation and mediation altogether. By striking out at the moon's reflection, Birkin attacks doubly reflected light, and his vehemence mirrors Lawrence's hunger for "sheer naked contact, *without an intermediary or mediator*" (*Phoenix*, 147).

Ultimately, however, the shattering of the moon's image reads as a cautionary response to "Rabbit." Whereas Lawrence suggests in "Rabbit" that representa-tion entails a sympathetic magic whereby misrepresentation, figured as diagram-matic abstraction, threatens to wound the autonomous object, in "Moony" he pictures the integrity of the object, figured by the inviolability of the moon, even as he experiments with the willful and continual disfigurement of the moon's image. "Moony" also responds to danger posed by the rising underplot in

"Rabbit." For Birkin's assault on the moon's image suggests the violent threat to coherent identity posed by the identification of the human with the non-human: the repeated destruction and re-formation of the image betrays Lawrence's anxiety that the grounding of the human in the non-human that is fundamental to his allotropic theory of character amounts not to a revelation of the truth of being but to a sparagmos, or ritual tearing asunder, of the human form.

Woolf began her novelistic career the same year Richardson did. Too often overlooked, *The Voyage Out* (1915) registers Woolf's initial effort to break free of the marriage plot and the imperial adventure story. The patterns of figuration that mark Woolf's later novels are already emerging, but on the level of plot the effort to find a new form fails: Rachel the heroine dies after a river journey in South America, seemingly of a combination of fever and symbolic marriage jitters. If Jane Austen's marriage plot, alluded to throughout the novel, claims Rachel, it claims Woolf in *Day and Night* (1919), a relatively conventional novel. Woolf breaks free for good in *Jacob's Room* (1922), an elegiac, impressionist reconstruction of the life of a young man who dies in World War I and whose absence at the center of the novel is wreathed by the impressions of those who knew him.

It is this novel, an experiment in impressionist characterization, that triggers Woolf's exchange with Bennett about the paradigm shift taking place in novel-istic narrative. We have seen how Lawrence breaks new ground in his effort to represent the unconscious; Woolf aims more at the texture of consciousness. Woolf thought her capture of that texture came in the writing of *Mrs. Dalloway*: "It took me a year's groping to discover what I call my tunneling process, by which I tell the past by installments, as I have need of it" (*Writer's Diary*, 60). We see the tunneling process at work on the first page of *Mrs. Dalloway* when Clarissa, stepping out into a London morning, her mind on the doors that will have to be taken off their hinges by Rumpelmayer's men before her party that night, is reminded of her youth, the shift in time and place marked only by a shift into the pluperfect, by the fresh air and her memory of squeaking hinges on windows that opened onto the garden at Bourton some thirty years before. Often narrated monologue of this kind, which traces the movement of charac-ters' minds, shades into more elaborate figurative representations of con-sciousness in which the language is understood not as the character's but as a heightened account offered by an external narrator. Thus we read later that Clarissa, no longer as confident as she once was,

> felt often as she stood hesitating one moment on the threshold of her drawing-room, an exquisite suspense, such as might stay a diver before plunging while

the sea darkens and brightens beneath him, and the waves which threaten to break, but only gently split their surface, roll and conceal and encrust as they just turn over the weeds with pearl.[13]

Woolf's syntax here is typical of her studied attention to norms of grammatical subordination even in her most lyrical sentences.

In *The Waves* Woolf largely dispenses with the narrator. The novel (Woolf's least plotted) is composed almost entirely through the dramatic monologues of her six main characters. The monologues differ from interior monologue insofar as they do not purport to provide transcriptions of thoughts passing through characters' heads but are permeated by patterns of metaphor that stylize their expression. Instead of the distinctive idioms of, say, Joyce's Bloom or Molly, Woolf creates a shared, communal voice in which boundaries between individual identities blur and re-form. Unlike in Lawrence, however, Woolf evidently welcomes the loss of individuation. She fuses dramatic and novelistic modes in this her most experimental novel, in which a shared vocabulary of keywords functions as a narratorial perspective on the divergent idioms of the characters. Woolf returns to the interpenetration of novelistic and dramatic modes in the posthumously published *Between the Acts*, in which dramatic form operates as a communal point of repair for fragmented individual subjectivities. In *The Waves*, however, the external world registers only as data within consciousness: "'How strange,' said Susan, 'the little heaps of sugar look by the side of our plates. Also the mottled peelings of pears, and the plush rims of the looking-glasses.'"[14] In such moments Woolf's project converges with Richardson's investment in the everyday, with the difference that Susan here asserts a defamiliarizing perspective on the ordinary without actually evoking it.

Woolf's experiment upon narrative in *To the Lighthouse* (1927) might be her most successful. The opening section, "The Window," exemplifying Woolf's tunneling, provides an anatomy of the Ramsays' Victorian marriage and family that comes into crisp focus through the eyes of a young painter, Lily Briscoe, whose attraction to the family is ambivalent. The middle section, "Time Passes," narrates the passage of ten years (including, significantly, World War I) as if through a stop-motion animation of the gradual decay of the Ramsays' abandoned summer-house. Aiming to describe what a scene looks like with no human being there to see it, Woolf clearly writes under the influence of film: the inhuman eye of the camera takes the place of Lily and the other characters. The closing section, "The Lighthouse," witnesses the return of Lily and the family, minus those who have died in the intervening years, and culminates in Lily's effort to finish a painting of Mrs. Ramsay and her son that she was unable to complete ten years before. Lily's struggle stands in for Woolf's own efforts to metamorphose her patriarchal Victorian inheritance into a modern, usable form. Lily succeeds in her struggle by abstracting the figures of Mrs. Ramsay and her son into the form of a triangle that can accommodate new content without losing the stability of a recognizable structure. Woolf thus embraces precisely the kind of abstraction that Lawrence distrusts in *Women in Love*.

The most plotted volume of *Pilgrimage*, *Dawn's Left Hand* (1931), also reflects explicitly on life's relation to novelistic form. Though still loosely episodic, *Dawn's Left Hand* is shaped in part by the twin appeals of Hypo Wilson, to whom Miriam loses her virginity, and Amabel, a young woman with whom she falls in love. Miriam drifts between diametric values and forms of sexual intimacy figured in Hypo and Amabel, though it is more accurate to say that her affair with Hypo is less a form of intimacy than a distraction from a deeper bond with Amabel. In Woolf sexual dissidence tends to register obliquely in, say, Clarissa's sexless marriage and the memory of "the most exquisite moment of her whole life" (35), her kiss with Sally Seton in youth. Lawrence in *Women in Love* struggles to find a way to describe the homoerotic relation between Gerald and Birkin, in order to make it seem less sexual and more utopian, a non-competitive blood brotherhood. Richardson shies away from eroticized descriptions of the body, but she nevertheless evokes the intense intimacy of Miriam's attraction to Amabel, who returns her affection, in ways that recall Lawrence's euphemistic descriptions of Birkin's desire for Gerald and of love-making between Birkin and Ursula.

The first sexual contact between Hypo and Miriam is barely recognizable as such; only a passing reference to their "mutual nakedness" assures one that Miriam is giving in to Hypo's long-standing seduction. More important, though, is how Miriam experiences her nakedness. Rather than imagine herself through Hypo's eyes, she sees "the rose-tinted velvety gleaming of her flesh" "with the eyes of Amabel, and with her own eyes opened by Amabel."[15] From here, after a perhaps failed attempt to make love, Miriam and Hypo begin to discuss novel-writing.

Hypo has long urged Miriam to write, and suggests that she become "a feminine George Eliot," a novelist of ideas who Miriam believes writes like a man. (Richardson thought the same about Woolf.) [16] The conversation ranges over James, Conrad, Wells (Hypo's prototype!), and Bennett, prompting Miriam, who finds them all as wanting as Eliot, to think that "a lifetime might be well spent in annotating the male novelists, filling out the vast oblivion in them" (246). Miriam then links what masculine fiction misses to Hypo's perspective as she prepares to describe Amabel to him: "She looked at Amabel though his eyes. And saw almost everything in her escape them" (240). Miriam's effort to instill in Hypo her own vision of Amabel seems hopeless (and resonates with Lawrence's anxieties over representation as distortion); nevertheless, Miriam speaks aloud about Amabel at length. But it is in Miriam's unspoken thoughts preceding and following the dialogue with Hypo that we read about her and Amabel's longing "to get away and lie side by side in the darkness," about "their wordless communion" (243, 245), and about things that Miriam knows would have "fired" Hypo's imagination – Amabel's engagement with socialism and the suffrage movement – but which Miriam considers "secondary" to "mysterious sudden intimacies" (247). Later Hypo and Miriam will make love, but the moment carries nothing of the erotic charge in an earlier moment when Amabel drops to her knees before Miriam and rests her head in Miriam's lap. Underscoring the relevance of such scenes to novelistic tradition, Miriam feels, as Hypo looms over her bed, that he is "trying to edit her mind" (257).

Miriam's ambivalence toward "the art of the novel" also emerges in her thoughts about Henry James. Although Woolf, in her diary entry on tunneling, balks at the formal strictures that Percy Lubbock derives from James in *The Craft of Fiction* (1921), she nevertheless is, like James and Flaubert, a technician. Richardson, in contrast, is less likely to agonize over *le mot juste* than suddenly to toss up from within her tangled syntax an arresting clause or phrase: for instance, "taking leave not so much of them personally as of the condensation of their common life in London" (208). Richardson once offered a devastating critique of late James: "His style, fascinating at first meeting for me can only be, very vulgarly, described as a non-stop waggling of the backside as he hands out, on a salver, sentence after sentence, that yes, if the words had no meaning, would weave its own spell. So what?" (*Windows*, 588). With similar thoughts Miriam, having exulted over *The Ambassadors* in *The Trap* (1925), decries James's ignorance about human nature in *Dawn's Left Hand*, where well-wrought novels are said to feel like "a dreadful enclosure" (239).

The mixed admiration and disdain that Richardson and Miriam show for James's stylistic mastery might explain both the waywardness of Richardson's pronouns – it is not that she cannot discipline her grammatical subjects, she just does not care – and her syntax, which seem Jamesian and anti-Jamesian at once. In the following one-sentence paragraph from *Dawn's Left Hand*, Miriam, in the company of strangers, awaits a train to Paris on her way back to London:

> Contemplating without looking at them and yet unable to escape the spectacle without either closing her eyes or gazing at the ceiling, it seemed to be in the very person of Mr. Orly, seated at the lunch-table in the bare-walled

basement room at Wimpole Street where the confronted lunchers were, beyond the dishes on the table and the unvarying lights and shadows made by the electric light, the only external refuge for unpreoccupied eyes, that she gazed upwards and mentally emitted his humorously despairing sigh, glancing at the same time sideways-down at herself seated at his right hand and just growing aware of the meaning, for him and from his point of view, of one of his kindly sarcasms, and yet obstinately set against admitting any justification for it, desperately refusing to show any sign of awareness and choosing rather to appear idiotic, and justify his sigh, than to give him the satisfaction of seeing her look "rather sick".   (132)

By the fourth clause – "the only external refuge for unpreoccupied eyes" – the sentence will derail even highly attentive readers; but it rewards re-reading.

The difficulty derives from an erosion of temporal subordination within Richardson's unfolding syntax: clauses that describe a remembered moment – "Mr. Orly, seated at the lunch-table" – begin to turn into a new narrative present as they re-create with increasing vividness a spatially and temporally remote scene at Miriam's employers on Wimpole Street. The relevance of this scene to Miriam's current experience in the waiting-room begins to fade as the remembered scene assumes full presence. Jamesian syntax would firmly locate Wimpole Street in the past; but Richardson's syntax loosens, allowing one to wonder what to do with what seems (but is not) an appositional phrase: "the only external refuge for unpreoccupied eyes." With the unexpected completion of the sentence's main clause – "it seemed to be in the very person of Mr. Orly . . . that she gazed upward" – we return to the waiting-room, and we return as well, assuming one has recognized the suspended syntax clicking into place, to relative clarity. But the next clause –"glancing at the same time sideways-down at herself" – slides back into a past that again begins to morph into a new present as Miriam, who *imagined* herself seeing through Orly's eyes, begins to *remember* herself. Miriam recalls having once become aware, from what then was Orly's point of view, of the intent behind one of Orly's sighs or remarks, and remembers as well that she refused at the time to give Orly the satisfaction of letting him know that she had gotten it – all the while, it would seem, remaining aligned with the subject position attributed to Orly in the past as she gazes upwards in the narrative present. The temporal confusion that opens in the middle of the sentence is augmented in part by the false parallelism between "glancing at the same time sideways-down" and "growing aware," which might seem to unfold on the same temporal plane, even though "glancing" indicates the mental gesture in the present of seeing herself in the past, and "growing aware" indicates a past realization.

This only partial explication of Richardson's sentence (is the Jamesian deferral parodically conditioned by Miriam's assumption of a male "point of view"?) begins to get at the complexity of Miriam's response to a man in the waiting-room whose brusque stolidity reminds her of Orly. Orly is the senior partner to Mr. Hancock, the dentist for whom Miriam works; hence the memory anticipates Miriam's return to the office after her holiday abroad. What matters most here is the complex temporality of Richardson's writing. Richardson later explicitly describes Miriam's multivalent grasp of time –"she felt more than the usual familiar sense of everlastingness ... Here it was, blissfully beating its wings ... and coming this time not only from the past but from past and future alike" (221). Richardson's syntax in the sentence quoted above *enacts* the everlastingness.

Though not the devotee of technique that Woolf is in *The Waves*, Richardson never forswears self-conscious literary making, as Lawrence does: "You can't *invent* a design," Lawrence claims, "You recognize it" (*Phoenix*, 525). Indeed, Richardson puts her finger on one of the major challenges posed by fiction's embrace of contingency and immediacy:

> Information there must be, but the moment it's given directly as information, the sense of immediate experience is gone. Yet [to present] nothing but immediate experience spells the titanic failure of Joyce. It is the great & abiding problem of all those who take the inward way, this business of getting something tremendously there as it were unawares. (*Windows*, 68)

Woolf sees a different yet related failure in Richardson and Joyce. Wondering in 1920 how to find "unity" within "the immense possibilities" of form, Woolf tells her diary: "I suppose the danger is the damned egotistical self; which ruins Joyce & Richardson to my mind: is one pliant & rich enough to provide a wall for the book from oneself without its becoming, as in Joyce & Richardson, narrowing & restricting?"[17] Readers of Richardson will recognize the point: how long does one want to be confined to Miriam's consciousness? Perhaps the confinement, together with Richardson's rejection of the life line of plot, accounts for the current low profile of *Pilgrimage*.

Miriam *can* be very hard to take. She remembers exclaiming to her quondam fiancé about Mr. Orly: "One *moment* of my consciousness is wider and deeper than his has been in the whole of his life" (132). Much rests on the degree to which Richardson persuades her readers that this is so. Too often, it seems, Miriam is depth; everyone else, surface. Honesty, authenticity, or damned egotism? All three, perhaps. Ultimately, it is worth emphasizing that Richardson's twelve-volume plunge into Miriam's consciousness does not make her or Richardson solipsists. Through Miriam Richardson is marvelously attentive to the music of everyday life, whether the music be the varying pronunciation of words across England or the "door-sounds" that Miriam remembers from her various lodgings. There is as well in *Pilgrimage* great joy not only in a paradoxical sociability in solitude – a sentiment understood by Lawrence and Woolf – but also in encountering new people and new ideas. Moreover, Miriam, despite the inevitable suffering of existence, makes out just fine. Unlike many women in modernist fiction, she finds more than a measure of happiness in who she is.

Notes

1. Virginia Woolf, "Modern Fiction," in *The Common Reader: First Series*, ed. Andrew McNeillie (New York: Harcourt Brace Jovanovich, 1984), p. 150.
2. Virginia Woolf, *Contemporary Writers* (New York: Harcourt Brace Jovanovich, 1965), p. 124.
3. Dorothy M. Richardson, "Foreword to *Pilgrimage* 1938," in *Modernism: An Anthology of Sources and Documents*, ed. Vassiliki Kolocotroni, Jane Goldman and Olga Taxidou (Edinburgh University Press, 1998), p. 486.
4. Raymond Williams, *Problems in Materialism and Culture* (London: New Left Books, 1980), pp. 148–169.
5. May Sinclair, "From a Review of *Pilgrimage* 1918," in *Modernism*, ed. Kolocotroni, pp. 351–353.
6. Virginia Woolf, *A Writer's Diary*, ed. Leonard Woolf (New York: Harcourt Brace Jovanovich, 1954), p. 78.
7. D. H. Lawrence, *Phoenix: The Posthumous Papers of D. H. Lawrence*, ed. Edward D. McDonald (New York: Viking Press, 1936), pp. 517–518.
8. H. G. Wells, *Experiment in Autobiography* (Boston and Toronto: Little, Brown, 1962), p. 471.
9. Quoted in Gloria G. Fromm, *Dorothy Richardson: A Biography* (Urbana, Chicago, London: University of Illinois Press, 1977), p. 79.
10. D. H. Lawrence, *The Letters of D. H. Lawrence*, ed. James T. Boulton, 8 vols. (Cambridge University Press, 1979), vol. II, p. 183.
11. I thank Cesar Salgado for suggesting "underplot" and *sparagmos* as relevant terms for my discussion of Lawrence.
12. D. H. Lawrence, *Women in Love* (New York: Penguin, 1995), pp. 241, 243, 239.
13. Virginia Woolf, *Mrs. Dalloway* (New York: Harcourt Brace, 2005), pp. 29–30.
14. Virginia Woolf, *The Waves* (New York: Harcourt Brace, 1959), p. 142.
15. Dorothy Richardson, *Dawn's Left Hand*, in *Pilgrimage*, 4 vols. (London: J. M. Dent/Cresset Press, 1938), vol. IV, p. 231.
16. Dorothy Richardson, *Windows on Modernism*, ed. Gloria G. Fromm (Athens and London: University of Georgia Press), p. 400.
17. Virginia Woolf, *The Diary of Virginia Woolf*, ed. Anne Olivier Bell, 5 vols. (San Diego: Harcourt Brace Jovanovich, 1978), vol. II, p. 14.

38

Wells, Forster, Firbank, Lewis, Huxley, Compton-Burnett, Green: the modernist novel's experiments with narrative (II)

JONATHAN GREENBERG

"So much life with (so to speak) so little living"[1] – thus Henry James disparages the fiction of H. G. Wells during a debate about the nature of the novel that helps to establish the canon of modern fiction. Whereas the canonical modernists – Conrad, Ford, Joyce, Woolf, Lawrence – follow James in developing narrative and linguistic innovations to accommodate a newly scrupulous attention to epistemology and psychology, the seven writers surveyed here generally spurn stream of consciousness, often appear indifferent to the exploration of the psyche, and sometimes follow Wells in renouncing Jamesian formal unity. Thus E. M. Forster breaks with modernist practice in relying on a prominent, moralizing narrator, Wyndham Lewis attacks his contemporaries' obsession with interiority, and Wells and Aldous Huxley embrace a didacticism at odds with reigning protocols. Ronald Firbank, Ivy Compton-Burnett, and Henry Green follow James in their attention to style, but they depart from modernist orthodoxy in representing surfaces rather than depths. In voice, structure, style, and characterization, however, a rebellious spirit in all these novelists challenges both inherited and emergent ideas of what a novel is and how a novel's prose can read.

H. G. Wells

The author of science fiction adventures, speculative utopias, and social satires, H. G. Wells has come – due in part to James's criticism – to represent precisely those values (materialism) and methods (didacticism) that modernism rejects. Resisting James's demand for a unifying consciousness, Wells argues that such a focus leads to highly wrought but sterile "tales of nothingness"; the novel, he insists, is not a unified whole but rather "a discursive thing," and the discursiveness that he champions offers an important alternative to Jamesian closure (Edel and Ray, *Henry James*, 249, 136). Wells begins his career writing "scientific romances," which initiate the modern science fiction tradition and spawn numerous adaptations in literature, film, and (famously) radio. Developing the Victorian adventure genre of Haggard, Stevenson, and Kipling, Wells's tales exploit popular scientific notions (vivisection, time travel, alien life) to give a veneer of realist credibility and a frisson of futurist excitement to ancient motifs such as invisibility or the island kingdom. Characterization is sketchy, un-Jamesian, and subordinated to plot; the plots, equally un-Jamesian, reduce the protagonist to the brute conditions of survival. Chapters end with melodramatic discoveries, as in *The Island of Dr. Moreau* (1896): "Could it be ... I thought, that such a thing as the vivisection of men was possible? The question shot like lightning across a tumultuous sky."[2] Frequently a first-person (always male) narrator travels to a new environment, confronts its mysteries, gathers information, and puzzles out conclusions. Yet initial conclusions can prove faulty, allowing for reversals and recognitions, and implicitly championing a steady English empiricism.

For all their stock formulae, however, Wellsian adventures reveal surprising resemblances to the modernist texts against which they are often contrasted, suggesting that the James/Wells debate poses a false choice. The techniques of the impressionism attributed to James, Conrad, and Ford are there in the early Wells's use of narration:

> I heard something breathing, saw something crouched together close beside me. I held my breath, trying to see what it was. It began to move slowly, interminably. Then something soft and warm and moist passed across my hand.
>   All my muscles contracted. I snatched my hand away. A cry of alarm began, and was stifled in my throat. (*IDM*, 191)

Only later is this sensation identified as an animal's "licking kiss." This impressionist technique, which Ian Watt has named delayed decoding, provides subjective and objective perspectives at once, rendering an event's impact on the senses before the focalizing character can cognitively overcome its strangeness. Wells's impressionism even comes complete with modernist invocations of the limits of representation: "I am afraid I cannot convey the peculiar sensations of time travelling. They are excessively unpleasant."[3]

Darwinism is the greatest intellectual provocation for Wells's fantasies. In *Dr. Moreau*, Darwin's discovery of human–animal kinship makes possible the transformation of beasts into men; in *The War of the Worlds* (1898), environmental pressure has rendered the Martians smarter, stronger, and crueler than humans, who "must be to them at least as alien and as lowly as are the monkeys and lemurs to us."[4] Indeed, the net cast by Darwinism in the *fin de siècle* snares multiple social problems – about race, gender, class, sexuality – and Wells fuses questions about the origin of the species with the social concerns of nineteenth-century utopianists. The evolution of the species in *The Time Machine* therefore reflects class struggle, as the subterranean, laboring Morlocks ascend at night to prey on their leisured, effete Eloi "masters." Similarly implicit is the presence of empire, saturated with racial anxieties: in *The War of the Worlds*, the Martian invasion is compared to the British conquest of Tasmania. Wells's visionary fantasies are thus disrupted by gothic nightmares, and his Victorian progressive ideals jostle against *fin de siècle* fears of degeneration.

For the rest of his career Wells exploits the discursive possibilities of fiction to advance his socio-political views. Those views are laid out comprehensively in *A Modern Utopia* (1905), a fiction–philosophy hybrid in which a beneficent world state has established female suffrage, near-universal education, racial equality, minimum wages, vegetarianism, and electric train travel. Despite this utopia's liberalism, however, to maintain its health Wells envisions a government of oligarchs who recognize, from their (mis)reading of Darwin, that "life is a conflict between superior and inferior types";[5] and although Wells scorns the use of Darwin to justify nationalism, patriotism, and racism, he proposes state-enforced eugenicist limits on the reproductive rights of the drunk, the irresponsible, and the insane.

While Wells's *Utopia* aims to solve social problems, his realist fiction of the Edwardian years is content to explore them. *Ann Veronica* (1909), for example, champions new roles for women through a young heroine who defies her father in her pursuit of a scientific education, her suffragist activism, and a scandalous affair with a married teacher. Darwinism is adduced to support the naturalness of sexuality, and to promote a feminism at odds with the teetotaling, vegetarian, and sexually phobic spiritualism preached by Ann Veronica's friend Miss Miniver. In *Ann Veronica*, as in dozens of his other novels, fiction becomes Wells's vehicle for dramatizing an ambitious social reform grounded in scientific materialism.

E. M. Forster

In her canon-making essay "Mr. Bennett and Mrs. Brown" (1924) Virginia Woolf denigrates Wells and other Edwardian "materialists" in favor of more "spiritual" Georgians of her own generation. One Georgian she praises is

E. M. Forster, who shares Woolf's psychological interests and charts delicate fluctuations in the mental lives of his characters; his first novel, *Where Angels Fear to Tread* (1905), is a Jamesian tale of an ambassador sent to retrieve a love-struck Englishwoman from morally dangerous Italy. Yet Forster is hardly Woolf's model modernist. He inserts his own voice loudly into his narrative, refusing to withdraw in god-like Joycean detachment behind the artwork. Like Wells in *Tono-Bungay* (1909) Forster revives the "condition-of-England" sub-genre, and he openly sides with Wells in the debate with James, arguing that "a rigid pattern" too often "shuts the doors on life."[6]

In his most famous novels, *Howards End* (1910) and *A Passage to India* (1924), Forster intertwines the lives of characters around resonant symbols (such as the Marabar Caves in *A Passage*) while upending the Austenian marriage plot. In *Howards End* an engagement promised in the first pages dissolves, and the child born at the novel's end is illegitimate; in *A Passage* another engagement crumbles, and the bachelor Fielding pronounces marriage to be "absurd"[7] – though in a typical Forsterian irony, he himself later marries. Forster himself scorns the "idiotic use of marriage as a finale" (*AN* 38), rejecting its heteronor-mativity along with its wooden conventionality. And although readers complain about conventions in Forster's own plotting, his use of coincidence can highlight parallels or disparities between classes, races, or genders. Forster's focus is thus the search for human connection, forged across boundaries – of class and gender in *Howards End*, of nation and religion in *A Passage*. Yet while his novels advocate liberal humanist values, Forster modifies his liberalism with a quasi-Romantic recognition of what he calls "the unseen" or "Infinity," embodied in both novels by a wise, aging, ultimately beatified mother: Mrs. Wilcox in *Howards End*, Mrs. Moore in *A Passage*. Even as he critiques Christianity, Forster remains unreconciled to Wellsian materialism.

In *Howards End* materialism is represented by ceaseless construction in London, by motorcars spewing smoke across the countryside, and by a pervasive flux "even in the hearts of men."[8] The novel juxtaposes such materialism, associated with the capitalist and patriarchal Wilcox family, with a spiritualism based in culture, expressed by the socialist, feminist Schlegel sisters, Margaret and Helen. Forster's sympathies are with the Schlegels, but he concedes that their bohemian life requires capital accrued by empire, and he recognizes the condescension with which they confront the upward striving of the clerk Leonard Bast. And although the book's conclu-sion might seem like escapism – Margaret, now married to Henry Wilcox, and Helen, now single mother to Leonard's child, inherit the country house of the title – Forster's idyll cannot accommodate Leonard himself, who has been killed for his sexual transgression. Thus, although the novel's epigraph, "only connect," is Forster's most famous expression of his ideals, connection remains more an injunction than an accomplishment.

A Passage to India, which centers on an Englishwoman's false charge of attempted rape against an Indian doctor, similarly stresses the complexities of human relations, and is even more wary than its predecessor of "spurious unity" (94). Whenever Forster's characters triumph over national or religious differences, the novelist tacks the other way, revealing new conflicts and new points of view; as the doctor says, "Nothing embraces the whole of India, nothing, nothing" (160). As Forster indicts the Wilcoxes' conservatism while remaining skeptical of the Schlegels' socialism in *Howards End*, so in *A Passage* he condemns the arrogance of the English without idealizing the Indians. Indeed, the ever-widening perspectives in the novel include those of monkeys, insects, and even stones, as Forster situates his ethnography of Anglo-India within a deep time fathomed by nineteenth-century geology:

> In the days of the prehistoric ocean the southern part of the peninsula already existed, and the high parts of Dravidia have been land since land began, and have seen on the one side the sinking of a continent that joined them to Africa, and on the other the upheaval of the Himalayas from a sea. They are older than anything in the world. (135)

Neither the star-gazing Bloom of *Ulysses*' "Ithaca" nor the eon-leaping hero of Wells's *Time Machine* takes a more cosmic view.

Forster's idiosyncratic narrative voice enables him to mix ironic skepticism with moral conviction. The narrator of *Howards End* is by turns pedantic, ironic, and lyrical, and indulges in present-tense generalizations: "It is thus, if there is any rule, that we ought to die – neither as victim nor as fanatic, but as the seafarer who can greet with an equal eye the deep that he is entering, and the shore that he must leave" (107). The narrator assumes the first person, describes himself as male, and even rehearses an argument with his grocer about raisins. The narrator of *A Passage* is less earnest and intrusive, but he too makes explicit signals to the reader and makes sweeping claims about English and Indians as social groups. This later voice, however, prefers to drop bits of wisdom in passing, or to promote its views through deadpan ironies. ("Aziz was led off weeping. Mr. McBryde was shocked at his downfall, but no Indian ever surprised him, because he had a theory about climatic zones" [184].) In both novels eccentricities of voice illustrate the continuing dialectic in Forster between earnestness and irony, between defending liberal values and recognizing the incompleteness of those values.

Wyndham Lewis

Forster might then connect the passion of Woolf and the prose of Wells, finding middle ground between Woolf's spiritualists and materialists. Yet Woolf's very schema rests upon dichotomies – between essay and novel, content and form, matter and spirit – that circumscribe the way the modernist novel is theorized. So argues Wyndham Lewis, who dismisses "the old battle of the Woolfs and Bennetts" as "a rather childish, that is to say an over-simple, encounter."[9] Lewis denies that the Paterian-Jamesian tradition has any monopoly on access to the soul, and asserts that Bloomsbury aesthetics have reduced the novel to a "salon scale" favored because it can "accommodate [the] not very robust talents" of the writer-critics who deploy it (*MWA* 166, 167). Yet neither does Lewis endorse the methods of Wells and Bennett. In fact, Lewis's booster Ezra Pound lauds Lewis's *Tarr* (1918) for dispensing with "the particular oleosities of the Wellsian genre,"[10] and Lewis himself mocks Wells's utopian imaginings.[11] For Lewis the very terms of the James–Wells or Woolf–Bennett debate ignore the "vigor" of works such as *Ulysses*, and, implicitly, of his own fiction.

Consequently, Lewis relishes combat with both bourgeois culture and the bohemian modernism that claims to oppose it. As a novelist, he works in what Northrop Frye called the "low mimetic" and "ironic" modes, in which the characters are held in lower esteem than their narrators. *Tarr* mocks the would-be artists of the Parisian Left Bank; *The Apes of God* (1930) sends up the pretensions of Bloomsbury and the Sitwell salon; *The Revenge for Love* (1937) derides the radical chic of Oxford-educated communists. As an editor, he attempts to set the terms for a British avant-garde by using his magazine *Blast* (1914–1915) to denounce all rival cultural-artistic movements including naturalism, Impressionism, aestheticism, and Futurism. As a cultural critic, he lambasts the emergent modernist canon: James, Eliot, Stein, Proust, Joyce, Woolf, Hemingway, Faulkner – even Pound, his old partner in crime. Linking these figures to a Bergsonian "time-cult" that overvalues subjective experience, Lewis advocates instead an aesthetic of the eye, external rather than internal, classical rather than romantic, spatial rather than temporal, derived from his own experience as a painter, and allied to the genre of satire.

The title character of *Tarr* lays out his author's anti-modernist modernism, claiming that one condition of art "is absence of *soul*, in the sentimental human sense."[12] He continues, rebuking Pater: "The lines and masses of the statue are its soul. No restless, quick flame-like ego is imagined for the *inside* of it. It has no inside" (300). Lewis by no means expunges the representation of thought;

Firbank, Compton-Burnett, and (sometimes) Green do that more thoroughly. His target is rather a narcissistic *obsession* with consciousness at the expense of the reality principle. Hence *Tarr* repeatedly subjects its characters to contingencies, debunking their artistic ambitions and frustrating their efforts at asserting personal will. In *The Revenge for Love* champagne socialists can never sort out party line from authentic commitment, "bluff" from "belief," and characters appear less as "human persons" than "as big portentous wax-dolls, mysteriously doped with some impenetrable nonsense, out of a Caligari's drug-cabinet."[13] At the novel's end, the heroine's own personality fractures, as she is torn between private, sentimental fantasy, and the brutal reality she confronts in war-torn Spain. For Lewis, the internal life does not transcend the dead externality of the real; instead, reality exposes interiority as a mere hiding place.

Lewis's thinking and his aggression are entangled with his distinctive prose style, which Pound praises as "volcanic" and "brimming with energy" (*Literary Essays*, 424, 425). In Hugh Kenner's words, Lewis creates a "Vorticist prose" that is "composed of phrases, not actions," one that emphasizes nouns and adjectives over verbs, like the block-print salvoes of *Blast*'s Vorticist manifesto. (Kenner cites from "Enemy of the Stars" [1914]: "The stars shone madly in the archaic blank wilderness of the universe, machines of prey.")[14] The vitality of this style persists throughout Lewis's work:

> "Speak, *mujer*."
>   He thundered the "moo-hhhair!" in a shortwinded pant, as if the African aspirate was too much for his sedentary flesh and there was a shortage of wind in his paunch, exhausted by the calls made upon it by the hurtling *jota*.
>
>   (*RL* 23)

If the clash of languages here intimates a political conflict between England and Spain, it also foregrounds the materiality of the signifier, and fractures words into letters and phonemes. Alliterative repetitions and steady accretions of phrases give the sentence a baroque artificiality that offers no lyrical prettiness, nothing in the manner of the middle-brow "beauty-doctor-class" Lewis scorns (*RL* 143). In other places Lewis deploys a grotesque metaphoricity, informed by his painter's eye: "His spine was not as straight as the spine of an honest man should be. A tell-tale crook made an arc at the top of it, on which his head hung – instead of standing up stoutly upon his shoulders, like a rooster upon a dunghill in the act of crowing" (*RL* 118). The energy of Lewis's Vorticist prose derives from a combination of diction, syntax, metaphor, and, not least, underlying dramatic conflict, creating an electric tension; this tension exists equally on the macro-level of the novels, whether in the unceasing verbal sparring between or within characters, or its frequent eruption into actual violence.

Ronald Firbank

Ronald Firbank is as un-Jamesian as Wells or Lewis, though his writing shows little kinship with either Wells's sociological discourses or Lewis's linguistic violence. In Firbank's case, as E. M. Forster notes,[15] it is the lightness of his comic tone that pushes him to the margins of the canon, to the specialized tradition of the camp novel. Not that such a categorization lacks merit; Firbank's short novels brim with queer sexuality, self-mocking play with melodrama, and general delight in opulence and ritual (Catholicism and clothing are equally grist for his mill). Like Max Beerbohm, Firbank makes cameos in his own fiction, and he revels in scatological and sexual innuendo. The language can be as baroque as Lewis's, though with a decidedly less ornery tone: "[She] regard[ed] dreamily the sun's sinking disk, that was illuminating all the Western sky with incarnadine and flamingo-rose. Ominous in the falling dusk, the savannah rolled away, its radiant hues effaced beneath a rapid tide of deepening shadow."[16]

Yet neither Firbank's camp indulgences nor his queer thematics mitigates his technical radicalism. Robert Kiernan calls his books "milestones in the effort of the twentieth-century novel to free itself from nineteenth-century realism," and they open possibilities in both composition and characterization.[17] Firbank's achievement in composition is, in the words of his disciple Evelyn Waugh, to break "the chain of cause and effect" by splintering realist narrative into a collage of fragments which garner interest primarily as local bursts of humor, lyricism, or mood.[18] (*The Waste Land*, with its juxtaposed fragments, its overheard voices, its parataxes and excisions, shares this achievement.) As for characterization, Firbank's lack of interest in plumbing interior depths produces an "objective" method that proves useful not only to Waugh but also to Huxley, Green, Compton-Burnett, and Anthony Powell. Like Lewis, Firbank employs a poetics of surface – even if his affectionate caricatures differ tonally from Lewis's satiric assaults. The result is a thorough suspension of the moral; in Forster's words, Firbank's books "do not introduce the soul nor its attendant scenery of Right and Wrong" (140). Firbank goes where Forster's didacticism never allows, brushing away duty and wisdom to surround the reader with the pleasure of the text.

Two techniques are notable in Firbank's achievement of this freedom. The first is a deconstruction of the conventions of the printed text that derives from

Tristram Shandy. Footnotes, scraps of songs, foreign phrases, onomatopoeic spelling, exclamation points, and capital letters decorate Firbank's page. (In *The Flower Beneath the Foot* (1923), a nun's imprecation is rendered in symbols appropriate to her office: "Maladetta ✠✛✠✛✠!" [89].) Dashes and ellipses compel the reader to collaborate in the author's naughtiness. When a valet opens a bottle of champagne:

> "What he calls a *demi-brune*, sir. In Naples we say *spumanti!*"
> "To – with it."
> "Non é tanto amaro, sir; it's more sharp, as you'd say, than bitter . . ."
> ". . . . . .!!!!!!"
> And language *unmonastic* far into the night reigned supreme.   (107)

Firbank also masters the arrangement of patches of comic dialogue, unattributed or logically disconnected, so that they sound, in Alan Hollinghurst's phrase, "picked up as if by a roving microphone."[19] As Waugh writes: "from the fashionable chatter of his period, vapid and interminable . . . [he] plucked, like tiny brilliant feathers from the breast of a bird, the particles of his design" (58). The writer becomes a stenographer, displaying the verbal found objects of modernity for the reader's delectation.

Firbank's engagement with modernity is thus marked by both immersion and escape. He works with modern forms of discourse like gossip columns and modern milieux like nightclubs, and his characters pursue social advancement, sometimes desperately, in tightly knit enclaves. Yet the absurdities of modern manners also represent an escape: the greater tides of history with their wars and revolutions never wash the sea-coasts of his Bohemias. Firbank enjoys his characters' sensuous pleasures and recognizes their pain, but these feelings are tempered by the detachment of the collector looking for the brilliant fragment. Firbank therefore serves as a pioneer for homosexual writers not by a psychological treatment of the struggles of gay love (as Forster attempts in *Maurice* [1971]), but through his use of irony, indifference, and parody, which suspend morality to reveal desire in both confining and liberating forms. As Christopher Lane argues, "Firbank brings heterosexuality into relief as an elaborate construction" by "casting heterosexuality as an arduous social ritual that veers away from the 'natural' Firbankian affection of each gender for its own."[20]

Firbank's management of feeling and form extends the erotic into all manner of sublimated pleasures. For Hollinghurst, Firbank recognizes "that human behaviour is governed and given meaning by caprice, impulse and yearning, whether erotic, aesthetic or mystical," while Brigid Brophy links her "defence" of his work to a defense of the novel itself, which has been vilified since Cervantes' day for its affinities with daydreaming and the masturbatory.[21] Indeed, Firbank's books are full of reveries and daydreams (as well as the occasional masturbation joke); the pleasures of idle fantasies are the long-repressed pleasures of reading, released from Victorian notions of moral uplift or functional utility. The political force in Firbank lies in his very frivolity.

Aldous Huxley

Improbably blending the influences of Firbank and Wells is Aldous Huxley. Huxley's first novels, written in the 1920s and described as conversation novels or parlor satires, feature Firbankian exchanges of dialogue among the idle and overeducated, arranged in counterpoint; in the 1930s, he undertakes Wellsian speculations that incorporate science fiction and utopian themes, while displaying Wells's rejection of Jamesian unities. Ignoring Proust's dictum that an artwork with ideas in it is like an object with its price tag on, Huxley gains a reputation as a public intellectual, and later as a counter-culture guru. (His book advocating LSD, *The Doors of Perception* [1954], takes its title from Blake and gave Jim Morrison the name for his rock band.)

Although Lewis openly ridicules Huxley's *Point Counter Point* (1928) for its "tone of vulgar complicity with the drearies of suburban library-readers" (*MWA* 302), Huxley follows Lewis in satirizing modernism itself, and he fills his works with mediocre artists who search for aesthetic principles in a modernity where the greatness of Shakespeare and Michelangelo is no longer attainable. A painter, Lypiatt, voices Huxley's rejection of Bloomsbury's (modernist) ideal of significant form:

> Life only comes out of life, out of passion and feeling; it can't come out of theories. That's the stupidity of all this chatter about art for art's sake and the esthetic emotions and purely formal values.[22]

Instead Lypiatt advocates a reintegration of art and life, an art not for art's sake but for god's sake. Yet Huxley, refusing to spare his own mouthpiece, renders Lypiatt a talentless *poseur* whose own formulaic style is best suited for Cinzano advertisements.

The failure of Huxley's artists to find governing values is symptomatic of a culture where the belief-systems of religion and tradition are no longer tenable, but where modern substitutes (promiscuity, parties, intellectual talk) offer only moral and sexual confusion. *Antic Hay* (1923) offers a steady buzz of chatter and rapid movement from scene to scene that formally replicates the mindless activity of 1920s' London. A familiar catalogue of entertainments and technological developments – "Cinemas, newspapers, magazines, gramophones, football matches, wireless telephones" (31) – saturates the public sphere, and even Gumbril's tailor recognizes these amusements not as the liberating gifts of a new capitalist utopia, but as further restraints on the imprisoned modern subject: "take them or leave them if you want to amuse yourself. The ordinary man can't leave them. He takes; and what's that but slavery?" (31). This rejection of capitalist modernity takes center stage in the later science fiction and openly didactic writings.

Huxley's most famous novel, *Brave New World* (1932), retains Huxley's earlier novels of ideas in its critique of modernity, its incorporation of intellectual conversation, and its narrative scaffolding of an ill-fated romance. Yet it also inaugurates a new exploration of genres that continues in *After Many a Summer* (1939), which weds the Hollywood novel to sci-fi speculation about evolution; and in *Ape and Essence* (1948), a post-nuclear dystopia written largely in the form of a screenplay. Like Forster's science fiction effort, "The Machine Stops" (1909), *Brave New World* is a rejoinder to Wells's utopian progressivism; as Jerome Meckier puts it, Huxley takes Wells's proposals about free love, social engineering, and world government "to an alarmingly successful and essentially insane conclusion."[23] (*Crome Yellow* [1921] already spoofs Wells as Mr. Scogan, a pompous elder intellectual who predicts the demise of the family and forecasts a centrally planned society [Meckier, *Aldous Huxley*, 176].) Because *Brave New World*'s critique extends to Soviet totalitarianism, the novel has gained outsize prominence in American secondary school curricula; still, it remains, alongside Wells's *oeuvre*, a foundational text for the dystopian sub-genre.

Brave New World gestures at modernist style – an early chapter moves several sub-plots along through a Firbankian collage of dialogue snippets – but it is unabashedly a novel of ideas. It presents a future in which humans are mass-produced in labs by an all-controlling world state; manipulated through eugenics and behaviorism to accede to the needs of society; raised communally rather than in families; kept in line through happiness drugs and mass entertainments; and prevented from falling in love through the normalization of promiscuity. Yet this future feels like the 1930s: luggage is carried by negro porters, numbers are looked up in telephone books, and men invariably initiate sex and drive the hovercraft on dates. The story pits a Lawrentian primitive, raised on an Indian reservation in New Mexico, against the modern dystopia he calls the brave new world. As Huxley's fellow California *émigré* Theodor Adorno notes, the novel's prediction of the mass production of humans works as a metaphor for the deadening sameness of modernity, a uniformity of thought that includes "the standardized consciousness of millions which revolves in the grooves cut by the communications industry."[24] Yet Adorno also discerns that Huxley's vision of rampant promiscuity "fails to distinguish between the liberation of sexuality and its debasement" (103), aligns the author with reactionary moralists, and condemns capitalism for satisfying human needs rather than for failing to do so.

Fearing that the gains made by science and material progress will outstrip the human capacity to manage their implications, Huxley seizes on the flexibility of the novelistic form, its protean ability to absorb all manner of prose genres, to address his social concerns. Like Wells before him, he fuses novel and essay to further a counter-strain of modernism that implicitly criticizes the claims of autonomous form.

Ivy Compton-Burnett

Ivy Compton-Burnett extends Firbank's innovations with dialogue in a different direction, retaining from the Jamesian tradition a structural severity and a cool observation of the oddities and ironies of human behavior. Her twenty novels display a striking consistency of content, tone, and style. Even the titles – which balance alliterative or parallel terms on either side of an "and" (*Parents and Children, Elders and Betters, A Family and a Fortune, A God and His Gifts*) – are so similar as to suggest a compulsive returning to the scene of some primal literary crime. Her focus is the landed gentry who interested Austen and George Eliot; her stories, usually set in the late Victorian years of the author's childhood, concern the passions, hatreds, jealousies, cruelties, deceptions, and occasional kindnesses of domestic life. The central source of cruelty is typically a tyrannical, miserly parent whose brutality breeds alliances, conspiracies, and affairs among the weaker members of the household – children, wives, tutors, governesses, and omnipresent financially dependent adult relations. While the symmetry and patterning of Compton-Burnett's plots owe a debt to James, they also show a kinship to the middlebrow whodunits of her contemporary Agatha Christie, who similarly withholds crucial plot events until the necessary dramatic moment. Hence Compton-Burnett's stories hinge on revelations of dark secrets: incestuous affairs, illegitimate children, forged wills, secret elopements, murder, infanticide. Yet because the prevailing affect of the novels is blank and detached, these novels seem to skirt the melodramatic rather than to indulge it.

While her focus on rural, isolated families from the past suggests a reluctance to face modernity, Compton-Burnett is a socially engaged satirist who eviscerates sentimental fictions about domesticity. Marriage often seems a refuge for the desperate and a source of the perpetuation of suffering. Even more than Forster she debunks the marriage plot; in *A House and Its Head* (1935) two female cousins (probably lovers) speculate on "a feeling of escape in the spinster population," and burst into "fits of laughter" at the thought of marrying the local rector.[25] The frequency with which inheritance becomes a cause for hatred suggests a further critique of a patrilineal economy. Religion is shown to be a tool of oppression and a shelter for hypocrites.

As astonishing and unique as the narrative content of the novels is their technique. As in parts of Firbank, narration is reduced to a minimum; scenes consist of long exchanges of dialogue. Even the plot is advanced through talk, and the reader may learn of events only when one character relates them to another. The characters are physically described only when first introduced, and then in a manner that can seem deliberately perfunctory or parodic of realism. Meanwhile, the metonymic impulse of realism is virtually non-existent; characters can enter or exit, walk from home to church, or even die without narratorial acknowledgment. This almost exclusive reliance on dialogue banishes both Forsterian narratorial comment and Woolfian exposition of the contents of the mind.

Compton-Burnett's dialogue itself appears stylized and aphoristic because of the formal manners of the class she treats, the intelligence she grants her characters, and the disdain she displays for the conventions of realism. She is not given to Firbank's illusion-shredding jokes, but her manner itself signals the inescapability of artifice, and her obedience to self-imposed rules implies the belief that mastery is revealed through limitation. Still, the author's enigmatic wit emerges in the way that she bends these rules; when she dips beneath the surface of dialogue to reveal characters' thoughts, she keeps to the dialogue form:

> "Is that what you are supposed to be doing, George?" said a voice that George took at first to be of divine origin, but recognized in a moment as of a more alarming source.
> "No. No, sir."
> "Then why are you doing it?"
> "Because I am so plainly fed, that the dining-room pudding was irresistible," said George, but only in his heart.[26]

Because of this dialogic method, often the characters' speech is talk about talk itself. Characters question and parse each other's language, comment on each other's words and silences, probe sub-texts, dismantle figures of speech – and force the same kind of scrutiny on the reader. Indeed, they come to resemble ordinary language philosophers as they analyze speech acts in their complex social contexts. Meanings ramify, and language becomes a weapon and a shield in domestic battle. Consequently, insides and depths can only be provisionally surmised from the painstaking analysis of surfaces:

> "Is that fire smoking?" said Horace Lamb.
> "Yes, it appears to be, my dear boy."
> "I am not asking what it appears to be doing. I asked if it was smoking."
> "Appearances are not held to be a clue to the truth," said his cousin.
> "But we seem to have no other."   (*MM* 3)

This opening encapsulates the problem of Compton-Burnett's fiction, in which appearances may not indicate truth, yet they remain the only guide available.

The meticulous pursuit of meanings and truths behind words and surfaces ultimately suggests a cruelty underlying human relations, and, like Freud, Compton-Burnett suggests that the modernist may be seen as a temporal refugee from a traumatic Victorian past. Fredrick Karl even compares Marcus Lamb's rebuke of his father in *Manservant and Maidservant* (1947) to Kafka's letter to his father:[27] "We are afraid of you. You know we are ... You did not let us have anything; you would not let us be ourselves. If it had not been for Mother, we would rather have been dead" (*MM* 233). Harsh words like these are spoken in novel after novel, since Compton-Burnett's unhappy families are all unhappy in exactly the same way.

Henry Green

In his rigorous self-effacement, his reliance on evocative symbols, and his foregrounding of style, Henry Green continues the high modernist, Jamesian tradition. Yet he also generally presents characters from the outside rather than the inside, deploying free indirect discourse or interior monologue only sporadically; late in his career he takes up novels in dialogue – *Nothing* (1950), *Doting* (1952) – in the manner of Compton-Burnett. Although his literary manner is quite different from that found in Wells's or Huxley's novels of ideas, his works show a persistent interest in social questions, especially those of class, and he even offers an unorthodox dystopia in *Concluding* (1948). In an idiosyncratic way Green thus reconciles the two sides of the James–Wells debate.

Green's work is notable both for its consistency and its variety. Like Compton-Burnett, his titles follow a pattern: all are single words (if the reader supplies a hyphen in *Party Going*); six of the nine are gerunds (if one includes the false gerund, *Nothing*). The consistency in naming reflects a consistent practice – a steady attention to the nuances and peculiarities of human behavior. Yet Green also treats characters from across the social spectrum. *Living* (1929) focuses on workers in a Birmingham iron foundry, *Party Going* (1939) on wealthy young socialites, *Caught* (1943) on firemen during wartime, *Loving* (1945) on English servants in Ireland. This attention registers the social and economic realities of his time – whether through ironic contrasts in *Party Going* between bright young things and their servants, or through ironic parallels in *Living* between upper- and lower-class stories of erotic rejection. Although both sympathy and satire creep into Green's fiction, for the most part he closely observes his characters' behavior with minimal moral judgment and an implicit valuing of the ordinary.

The language of Green's novels demonstrates a distinctive style, or cluster of styles. In his earliest novels he omits articles and certain deictics ("He looked into grate which had pink paper fan in it");[28] his sentences use punctuation sparingly, presenting, as his admirer John Updike says, "bold phrases roped together by a slack and flexible grammar."[29] This language sometimes fosters lyricism, but it also creates awkward disturbances that command the reader's attention. Like Gertrude Stein, he repeats words and phrases with minor variations in order to capture the rhythm of thought rather than its exact language: "So in his thinking he thought now Mr Dupret is dying. He thought how he'd worked fifteen years for Mr Dupret. 'And never a cross word between us.' He began now in his thinking" (*LI* 281). In Green's own apt description, his prose is "not quick as poetry but rather a gathering web of insinuations."[30] To this narratorial language, Green adds the spoken idioms of his characters, and he follows Dickens and the Joyce of *Ulysses*' "Cyclops" in achieving a richness of image and implication through attention to local idiolects: "They're like a pair of squirrels before the winter layin' in a store with your property mum against their marriage if they ever find a parson to be joined in matrimony which I take leave to doubt" (*LO* 162).

Green professes that "the author must keep completely out of the picture,"[31] and his technique tends toward the dramatic. Scene and character take precedence over authorial or narratorial interpretation of events, and he even thematizes his skepticism about knowing other minds, as if to justify his narrative practice: "no one can be sure they know what others are thinking any more than anyone can say where someone is when they are asleep" (*PG*

463). From time to time his narrator will point a moral, or acknowledge the created nature of his tales, yet these interventions are so rare that they appear as deliberate idiosyncrasies or blank jokes, coy acknowledgments of the relaxation of technique.

Green's use of symbols similarly teases rather than satisfies the reader's desire for meaning. On the first page of *Party Going* a woman finds a dead pigeon in a train station, washes it in the lavatory, and wraps it in brown paper; why, we never learn. *Loving*, set in an Irish castle, begins with, "Once upon a day," ends with "happily ever after," and features a lost ring – but the reader must strain to read this work as a fairy tale. As Green comments, "Life, after all, is one discrepancy after another" (*AF* 13). Hence unlike other exponents of surface or scenic methods – Lewis, Firbank, Waugh, and (to a lesser extent) Compton-Burnett – Green does not make his characters into types. His omission of explicit motive works to deepen his characters' psychological complexity, illustrating what Yeats says of *Hamlet* – that nothing has life except the incomplete. Green's characters are in addition often notable for a vital sensuousness, like that of Amabel of *Party Going* drying herself after a bath: "As she went over herself with her towel it was plain that she loved her own shape and skin. When she dried her breasts she wiped them with as much care as she would puppies after she had given them their bath, smiling all the time" (*PG* 480). In short, Green's self-effacement allows his cast of characters to emerge, vibrant in the colors of their varied settings. Thus while Forster rebukes Jamesian formalism for "shutting the doors on life," Green's own attention to technique does just the opposite. Like many other not-quite-canonical modernists, his narrative experiments open doors to what James himself calls not life but living.

Notes

1. Leon Edel and Gordon N. Ray, eds., *Henry James and H. G. Wells: A Record of their Friendship, their Debate on the Art of Fiction, and their Quarrel* (Urbana: University of Illinois Press, 1958), p. 27.
2. H. G. Wells, *The Island of Dr. Moreau: A Critical Text* (Jefferson, NC: McFarland, 1996), p. 108 (hereafter *IDM*).
3. H. G. Wells, *The Time Machine* (New York: Penguin, 2005), p. 19.
4. H. G. Wells, *The Complete Science Fiction Treasury of H. G. Wells* (New York: Knopf, 1978), p. 266.
5. H. G. Wells, *A Modern Utopia* (New York: Penguin, 2005), p. 218.
6. E. M. Forster, *Aspects of the Novel* (New York: Harcourt, 1927), p. 162 (hereafter *AN*).
7. E. M. Forster, *A Passage to India* (New York: Harcourt, 1924), p. 292.
8. E. M. Forster, *Howards End* (New York: Random, 1989), p. 143.

9. Wyndham Lewis, *Men Without Art* (New York: Russell and Russell, 1964), p. 159 (hereafter *MWA*).

10. Ezra Pound, *Literary Essays of Ezra Pound* (New York: New Directions, 1968), p. 429.

11. Wyndham Lewis, *Time and Western Man* (Boston: Beacon, 1957), pp. 257–258.

12. Wyndham Lewis, *Tarr* (Santa Rosa: Black Sparrow, 1990), pp. 299–300.

13. Wyndham Lewis, *The Revenge for Love* (South Bend: Gateway, 1978), p. 147 (hereafter *RL*).

14. Hugh Kenner, *Wyndham Lewis* (Norfolk, CT: New Directions, 1954), p. 14.

15. E. M. Forster, *Abinger Harvest* (London: Edward Arnold, 1953), pp. 135–136.

16. Ronald Firbank, *The Flower Beneath the Foot* and *Prancing Nigger* (Norfolk, CT: New Directions, 1962), pp. 262–263.

17. Robert F. Kiernan, *Frivolity Unbound: Six Masters of the Camp Novel* (New York: Continuum, 1990), p. 49.

18. Evelyn Waugh, *The Essays, Articles and Reviews of Evelyn Waugh*, ed. Donat Gallagher (Boston: Little Brown, 1984), p. 57.

19. Alan Hollinghurst, "The Shy, Steely Ronald Firbank," *The Times Literary Supplement*, November 15, 2006 (http://tls.timesonline.co.uk/article/0,25338–2454703,00.html).

20. Christopher Lane, *The Ruling Passion: British Colonial Allegory and the Paradox of Homosexual Desire* (Durham, NC: Duke, 1995), p. 181.

21. Brigid Brophy, *Prancing Novelist: A Defence of Fiction in the Form of a Critical Biography of Ronald Firbank* (New York: Harper, 1973).

22. Aldous Huxley, *Antic Hay* (Urbana, IL: Dalkey Archive, 1997), p. 67.

23. Jerome Meckier, *Aldous Huxley: Satire and Structure* (New York: Barnes and Noble, 1971), p. 187.

24. Theodor W. Adorno, *Prisms* (Cambridge: MIT Press, 1982), pp. 100, 98.

25. Ivy Compton-Burnett, *A House and Its Head* (New York: New York Review Books, 2001), p. 267.

26. Ivy Compton-Burnett, *Manservant and Maidservant* (New York: New York Review Books, 2001), p. 56 (hereafter *MM*).

27. Fredrick R. Karl, "The Intimate World of Ivy Compton-Burnett," in *British Modernist Fiction, 1920–1945*, ed. Harold Bloom (New York: Chelsea House, 1986), p. 185.

28. Henry Green, *Living, Loving, Party Going* (New York: Penguin, 1978), p. 351 (abbreviations *LI, LO, PG* refer to this edition).

29. John Updike, Introduction, *Living, Loving, Party Going*, p. 12.

30. Henry Green, *Pack My Bag: A Self-Portrait* (New York: New Directions, 1993), p. 84.

31. Henry Green, Interview, "Henry Green: The Art of Fiction #22," *The Paris Review* 19 (1958) (http://www.theparisreview.org/viewinterview.php/prmMID/4800), p. 13 (hereafter *AF*).

39

Beyond autonomy: political dimensions of modernist novels

MORAG SHIACH

The meaning of "autonomy"

"Autonomy" is a powerfully resonant concept in a variety of contexts. In aesthetic theory it refers to a quality specific to art: its capacity to create meanings through its formal properties, and to generate ways of encountering the world that are distinct from other forms of social experience. Artistic autonomy implies that the creation and the judgment of artistic texts require a sensibility and an imagination separate from other sorts of knowledge or practice. In modernism, and in critical responses to modernism, to see artistic experience as separate from, and potentially superior to, other ways of experiencing the world involves focussing on the material and formal properties of the art object. It is the formal autonomy of the artwork that is emphasized for example in A. C. Bradley's *Oxford Lectures on Poetry* (1909) and Clive Bell's *Art* (1914). Critical discussion of modernist literary texts has been powerfully shaped by this idea of aesthetic autonomy, which continues to be important for many critics of modernism.[1]

However, fascination with "autonomy" as the defining nature of artistic objects and aesthetic experience has been contested by critics who see it as denying to art its relation to historical and social experience. Perhaps the most polemical criticism is Peter Bürger's theoretical and critical study, *Theory of the Avant-Garde* (1974). Bürger argues that modern understanding of artistic "autonomy" is historically limited and historically limiting. He proposes thinking about artistic practice in relation to art understood as an ever-changing social institution, and he also insists on the necessity of reintegrating art and life in criticism and artistic practice.

The novels in this chapter do not take a consistent approach to the status of the formal autonomy of the artwork in modernism. Virginia Woolf and May Sinclair reflect on the nature of modernist fiction. They seek in their novels to generate moments of subjective complexity and intensity as well as structures of coherence and integrity that might well be the basis of an argument on behalf of aesthetic autonomy. Other novelists discussed below are no less focussed on the capacity of the novel to generate subjective identifications and sympathies, or to locate individual experience; but they are more inclined to do so within a coherent historical narrative framework. The autonomy of the aesthetic is thus a much less compelling dimension of their texts.

For none of the novelists discussed, however, does any degree of commitment to the autonomy of the aesthetic suggest that their work cannot capture the complexities of social change or cannot question the nature of modern subjectivity. Indeed subjectivity, in particular female subjectivity, is key to all the novels I discuss, and it is seen as a profoundly social and historical question. Shared interest in changing modes of subjectivity in these novels generates a focus on a different understanding of the nature of "autonomy," one that relates more to the freedom of the individual than to the freedom of the artistic text.

As a political or philosophical term, "autonomy" refers to the idea of self-government, and relies on the idea of the individual as a rational being who is able to make free and unforced choices. This powerfully influential political meaning of "autonomy" troubles modernist literary texts, which so frequently stage a battle between the power and integrity of the individual and the consolations (or perhaps the risks) of what is collective or social. One might think of the prominent figure of the *flâneur* within modernist literature: the individual who walks through the urban environment aggressively separate from the urban masses and yet fascinatedly implicated in their existence. For the early twentieth-century critic Walter Benjamin the *flâneur* embodies a new mode of modern subjectivity that oscillates between the heroic assertion of individual autonomy and the seductive, but threatening, immersion in the crowd. "Autonomy" for this modernist protagonist of the city streets can never be an achieved state, but is an ambiguous, sometimes desirable but never fully attainable condition. It is particularly unachieved for women, whose relations to political identity and to public space are different from those of men in the period. In the period before the First World War women did not have the same legal status as men in regard either to ownership of property or to participation in the political process. "Autonomy" might thus have been, and indeed was, an aspiration for many women; but, along with integrity and individuality, autonomy remains in constant tension with more communal or collective forms of subjectivity in the modernist era. For women especially, the forceful claims of egotism that underpin modernism's most distinctive aspirations to innovate[2] are entangled in the languages of sacrifice and of duty, or of social and family life, with which modernist novels are haunted.

Marriage and the possibility of autonomy

Throughout the nineteenth and early twentieth centuries in all Western nations, the institution of marriage saw significant reform, mostly focussed on men and women's respective rights to property and on the possibility of divorce. Historians argue that whereas in the early eighteenth century middle-class women were vital players in social and economic activity that was organized around the family, by the nineteenth century the "separation of spheres" between work and home left women less prominent in terms of economic activity and more closely aligned to domesticity, so that "by the 1830s and 1840s . . . gainful employment for ladies was widely denounced."[3] This implies that women's rights within marriage became increasingly important as a way of mitigating the marginal economic situation they occupied.

Legislative changes in the second half of the nineteenth century enhanced the economic rights of married women. In Great Britain the Married Women's Property Act of 1882 is "arguably the single most important change in the legal status of women . . . [giving] them the legal capacity to act as autonomous economic agents." However, as the *Encyclopaedia Britannica* asserts in 1911, the rights of men and women are still far from equal: "a husband could obtain a divorce for the adultery of his wife, while a wife could only obtain it if her husband's adultery were coupled with cruelty or desertion"; and the *Encyclopaedia* entry notes that in the event of divorce custody of children was inevitably given to the father. [4]

Subsequent legislation brought greater equality of rights. Marriage reformers in the period did not, however, focus simply on legal rights. Marie Stopes's bestselling *Married Love* (1918) controversially expounded techniques of birth control and the importance of a fulfilling sexual relationship between husband and wife. The aim of sex, Stopes write in her preface, "is to increase the joys of marriage, and to show how much sorrow may be avoided." [5]

Stopes's pragmatic approach to fulfillment within marriage could not, however, overcome the profound antipathy toward the institution in some texts of the early twentieth century. The "Feminist Manifesto" by poet and artist Mina Loy in 1914 argues that the institution of marriage is central to women's oppression because it limits their economic as well as their sexual freedom. Loy insists that women must understand that "as conditions are at present constituted – you have the choice between **Parasitism** & **Prostitution** – or **Negation**." [6] Each of these terms resonates with contemporary philosophical and political debates concerning identity and political agency. The logic of Loy's argument would certainly deny the possibility of women's achieving autonomous selfhood within the institution of marriage. Yet Loy also argues passionately for the importance of maternity to the realization of women's individuality, and indeed to the realization of "her race" (93). Loy writes that "each child of a superior woman should be the result of a definite period of psychic development in her life – & not necessarily of a possible irksome & outworn continuance of an alliance" (93). The antithesis Loy constructs between the desire to bear children and the adequacy of marriage to fulfill the desire will emerge as an essential component in novels of the period.

Marriage, autonomy, and the novel

The ability of the novel as a genre to explore the complex constitution of selfhood as well as the experience of historical change and development has long been noted. The subtleties of the novel's handling of narrative point of view, and the structured experience of temporality within the novel, mean that it has an unusual capacity to construct distinct and opposing subjectivities and to situate them within a defined historical and social framework. The interaction of self and circumstance is material that is integral to the development of the form. Given the significant changes and tensions in the institution of marriage, and the increasing desire for women's independent subjectivity in the early years of the twentieth century, it is unsurprising that we find so many novels of the period representing the dilemmas of married women. In representing those dilemmas, however, the novel form could not easily sustain its tradition of representing characters in terms of an achieved individuality. Consequently, for many novelists the psychological, social, and economic constraints of marriage in the early years of the twentieth century seemed incompatible with fictional tradition. The modernist novel thus becomes a privileged site for the exploration of the tensions between marriage as a social institution and autonomy as a desired state of separate and independently secured individuality.

May Sinclair's novel *The Helpmate* (1907) refers in its title ironically to the idea of marriage as a mutually beneficial state of support and friendship. The marriage that is closely scrutinized in the novel is between Walter Majendie, a businessman, and Anne, to whom we are first introduced pointedly as "Mrs Walter Majendie."[7] The marriage is not happy. Anne discovers soon after marrying that her husband has previously had an affair. Her reaction is to surrender to the accomplished fact of marriage, but simultaneously to withdraw into an intense separateness from her husband. She feels revulsion and hatred for her own body, which has become indissociable from the shame she attributes to her husband; but she also determines that "the surrender [to marriage] would be a martyrdom. She was called upon to lay down her will" (18), and to consent to martyrdom. Despite the passivity, however, Anne insists that it is not for her to "subdue the deep repugnance of her soul" (18) towards her husband.

The novel becomes increasingly melodramatic as it heightens the tensions generated by guilt, passivity, and aggression within the marriage. Walter asks rhetorically at one point, "was that being a good wife to him? To divorce her soul, her best self, from him?" (45), and the choice of the verb "divorce" makes it clear that the institution of marriage is what is at stake for Walter, as well as for Sinclair. Walter blames his wife and his marriage for his own subjective dissolution and fragmentation: "And it was she, the helpmate, she who should have kept him whole, who had caused him to be thus sundered from himself and her" (319).

This doomed marriage, only very fleetingly touched by desire, leaves Walter and Anne diminished, ill, and unable to achieve any sense of worth or meaning in their lives. Anne affirmatively experiences intense desire only at one moment. When she holds an infant to her breast "the deep feeling and enchantment of the woods was upon her" (111). The moment leads to a sexual coupling with her husband, and to pregnancy. That the sexual relationship between the couple should be thus strangely mediated by an infant, and that the offspring of the Majendies' union should die when Walter is away from home with his new mistress, is typical of a certain ultimate perversity in *The Helpmate*. It draws to an end, consciously echoing uncomfortable aspects of the finale of Charlotte Bronte's *Jane Eyre* (1847), with Anne assuming all the guilt for the marriage's failure and pledging to care for her husband, now "paralysed down the right side" (413). In the last few pages, a reconciliation is imagined, with Walter recovering his faculties and Anne insisting that she had "sinned against my husband more than he had ever sinned against me" (437). The concluding paragraph, in which "Her drenched eyelids felt his lips upon them. They opened; and in her eyes he saw love risen to immortality through mortal tears" (438), renders Anne's subjectivity chillingly absent. The metonymy that figures Anne through her drenched eyelids offers no viable sense of autonomous selfhood, but rather leaves a bitter taste that the reader is left to ponder.

Elizabeth von Arnim's *The Pastor's Wife* (1914) focuses on the experiences of a young English woman Ingeborg Bullivant and on her marriage to a lugubrious German pastor, Robert Dremmel. The novel begins with Ingeborg in ecstatic mood, experiencing both liberty and autonomy:

> She was in this exalted mood . . . feeling the relish of life, the tang of it . . . And the beauty of it, the *beauty* of it, she thought. She would not have been

surprised if sparks had come crackling out of the tips of her sober gloves . . . for the first time in her life of twenty-two years she was alone.[8]

The ecstasy is partly due to the fact that she has just been cured of an intense toothache, but it is overwhelmingly generated by the sensation of leaving her oppressive family (which exploits her) and traveling through London alone. On an impulse she sets off on a journey to Lucerne, during which she meets Dremmel. Dremmel is a man more interested in agriculture, in fact in the productive properties of manure, than in romance. After only thirty pages, Ingeborg has agreed to marry him, largely because he scares her with images of a likely future wherein she would "remain with your father and solidify into yet one more frostbitten virgin" (38).

Ingeborg's enclosure within powerful patriarchal structures is rendered clearly; and her move from the judgmental and unloving care of her English clerical father to the judgmental and unloving household of her German clerical husband exhibits the paramount power of this structure. The moment of bliss with which the novel opens is cruelly brief, and Ingeborg's capacity for autonomous judgment and actions is undermined at every narrative turn. As soon as she becomes engaged, "she felt engulfed" (56) and also "felt she must be disappearing altogether" (62).

Ingeborg's own mother had surrendered autonomy on marriage and slipped into the status of a perpetual semi-invalid: "Ingeborg's mother had found the sofa as other people find salvation. She was not ill. She had simply discovered in it a refuge" (71). The narrator does not tell us why Ingeborg's mother needed to be saved, and from whom she sought refuge, but it is her husband and the comprehensive requirements of bourgeois marriage that disable her. Ingeborg's own husband offers her no erotic or romantic excitement. And we are told that Ingeborg "had not yet acquired, in spite of his assurances that she undoubtedly would, any real enthusiasm for embracings" (125). Robert's extraordinary self-absorption and his fascination with his work are reminiscent of Casaubon in George Eliot's *Middlemarch*; but Ingeborg has little of Dorothea's quiet heroism.

Ingeborg's one rebellion is to be found in her friendship with an English artist, Edward Ingram. She tells Ingram that she is happy in her marriage because it produces "a very placid and restful state" (372). Ingram dismisses her marriage as destructive, representing "Negation. Death" (372). Yet Ingram, like Dremmel, is simply another figure seeking to control Ingeborg for his own satisfaction. He insists she come to Italy with him so that he can paint her, and the narrative voice remarks that Ingram believes not only that he must make sacrifices for his art "but other people were bound to give up everything too" (376). He persuades Ingeborg that he is dependent on her, thus locking her into another self-negation. Ingram's later inevitable attempt to seduce her echoes her husband's earlier marriage proposal, and produces in Ingeborg a similar state of detachment from her self: "she watched him kissing her hand as though it did not belong to her" (457). She returns to her husband, but he has barely noticed her absence. The novel concludes with the devastating observation that "Herr Dremmel went on writing. He had forgotten Ingeborg" (484).

The narrative arc of *The Pastor's Wife* intensifies the repetition, frustration, and negation that characterize the protagonist's marriage and, the novel implies, the institution of marriage more broadly. Ingeborg's momentary glimpses of excitement and autonomy give way almost farcically quickly to routine and to repetition, thematically and linguistically. Von Arnim employs free indirect discourse to render the texture of Ingeborg's subjectivity without giving to her the benefit of self-knowledge. Ingeborg is controlled, deluded, frustrated; autonomous subjectivity in her is never fully realized.

Virginia Woolf's *Mrs. Dalloway* (1925) explores the internal and external lives of its characters. The structure of the novel is episodic, as its focus moves among individual actions, thoughts, and memories. Mrs. Clarissa Dalloway's daughter and her husband as well as an ex-lover are important, but so too are the people she passes in the street or buys flowers from. Connections among characters range from the intimate and familial, to the casual, and even to the metaphorical. Woolf's free indirect discourse captures the integrity and individuality of each character's mode of speech and thought while also generating the unifying possibility of a narrative discourse that can contain all their voices and perspectives. The novel encompasses only the time and space of one day; and in part the narrative's formal integrity is created by the regular rhythm of daily life.

The integrity is decidedly formal, however. The most important relationship the narrative creates for Mrs. Dalloway is with a character she never even meets: Septimus Warren Smith, a shell-shocked survivor of the First World War. The novel relates Smith and Clarissa through association of images, accidents of co-location, and moral and narrative comparisons, despite the fact that the two characters inhabit worlds that are radically distinct in terms of class, gender, and experience. This relation is achieved so compellingly that by the end of the novel Septimus Warren Smith's suicide can be read as a sacrifice for Mrs. Dalloway: his fragility brings about his destruction and the reader comes to understand that this may be the condition of Mrs. Dalloway's survival:

This life, to be lived to the end, to be walked with serenely; there was in the depths of her heart an awful fear. Even now, quite often if Richard had not been there reading *The Times*, so that she could crouch like a bird and gradually revive, send roaring up that immeasurable delight, rubbing stick to stick, one thing with another, she must have perished. She had escaped. But that young man had killed himself.[9]

Mrs. Dalloway's overcoming of fear, and thus her evading of death, are bound up with the everyday behaviors of her husband Richard. But they also derive from the "immeasurable delight" that is generated by the fact of friction or tension between two beings: stick rubbed against stick or one thing rubbed against another. She survives partly because Septimus does not, because life consists of more than one object and more than one subject, and also because the routines of the domestic and the familial offer her a space in which she can crouch and "gradually revive."

This sense of Mrs. Dalloway's subjective fragility – the fragility of her autonomy – recurs throughout the novel, and is closely connected to her mapping of her affective life. At the start of the novel, Mrs. Dalloway is reflecting on her relationship with Peter, whose offer of marriage she declined in her youth, and on the condition of her marriage to Richard:

> For in marriage a little licence, a little independence there must be between people living together day in day out in the same house; which Richard gave her and she him ... But with Peter everything had to be shared; everything gone into. And it was intolerable, and when it came to that scene in the little garden by the fountain, she had to break with him or they would have been destroyed, both of them ruined, she was convinced. (9)

Married life is apparently tolerable for her because it leaves "a little independence" while her relationship with Peter was a kind of subjective obliteration.

Mrs. Dalloway's view seems definite and certain, but the power of the image of the garden and the fountain suggests something else: desire comes bubbling up to disturb her certainties. The independence that marriage to Richard apparently offers her does not, after all, amount to autonomy. She reflects on "this being Mrs Richard Dalloway" (13), noting that "she had the oddest sense of being invisible; unseen; unknown" (13). In this moment she feels that she is no longer herself, no longer "Clarissa," but rather a cipher in her husband's social being. Peter endorses this sense that Clarissa has lost something of herself to marriage, when he angrily watches her mending a dress: "growing more and more irritated, more and more agitated, for there's nothing in the world so bad for some women as marriage, he thought" (53).

The suggestion that the "independence" Clarissa values in her marriage has been bought at a high price emerges repeatedly. Clarissa sleeps alone in a narrow bed: "the sheets were clean, tight, stretched in a broad white band from side to side. Narrower and narrower would her bed be" (40). Richard had decided that she should sleep alone following a period of illness, and now she regularly sits up alone reading in her bed and waiting to hear his return to the house. She sees this separation and isolation as a failure: "She could see what she lacked ... It was something central which permeated; something warm which broke up surfaces and rippled the cold contact of man and woman, or of women together" (40). The desire she has suppressed in achieving her state of marital separation and independence is expressed repeatedly in powerfully sensuous memories and moments of profound intensity: "Then, for that moment, she had seen an illumination; a match burning in a crocus; an inner meaning almost expressed" (41).

But full expression of inner meaning is never in fact possible. Clarissa moves among blankness, banality, loss, intensity, desire, and stark perplexity, and never arrives at a moment of achieved selfhood. Looking at Peter she is overwhelmed by the belief that "If I had married him, this gaiety would have been mine all day" (60); but this is not an insight in which the reader can trust. We have observed Peter endlessly playing with his penknife in a ritual of suppressed violence; we know that he will follow a young woman secretly through the streets, and we cannot really believe that perpetual gaiety would have been Clarissa's lot.

The novel culminates in a party given by Mrs. Dalloway, at which some of the characters who have populated the novel through memory or anecdote come together. The party is Mrs. Dalloway's creative legacy, the thing she has worked on to give shape and meaning to the day. But the novel leaves the reader less than confident that this creative impulse amounts to the forging of an autonomous selfhood. The last paragraph of the novel contains the succinct and memorable phrase, "For there she was" (255), and we might wish to read this as the triumphant assertion of Mrs. Dalloway's free subjectivity. But the deployment of free indirect discourse leaves the reader unable to determine whose judgment this in fact is. It could be the voice of a narrator establishing an achieved vision and a fulfilled characterization. But it could also be the voice of Peter, who in the preceding paragraphs experiences his own moment of ecstasy and of terror, asking "what is it that fills me with extraordinary excitement?" and concluding, "It is Clarissa" (255). Thus the moment of finality is not what it might seem: it is someone else's epiphany, which Mrs. Dalloway might have provoked but in which she cannot, surely, be said to be fully realized. She remains at the end of the novel incomplete, not fully present, a reminder perhaps of the limitations of being her married self.

Representation and the suffrage movement

"Representation" of social structures and subjective realities is not simply an artistic concept; it also brings with it political questions about power, agency, and legitimacy. As representative structures of democracy became increasingly widespread from the mid-nineteenth century on, women's political representation also became a more pressing cause, which incited campaigns for women's suffrage internationally. In Great Britain the campaigns took the form of a mixture of parliamentary and extra-parliamentary activism until women were finally granted the vote on the same basis as men in 1928. In the early twentieth century in order to advance the cause of votes for women British "suffragettes" deployed violent and confrontational forms of political campaigning that included street demonstrations, vandalism of property, and hunger strikes.

The campaign for women's suffrage provided a frequent and fascinating impulse for the novel's representational aims. The involvement of a character in political activism within the suffrage movement can be a way for a novelist to mark the character as "modern," typically understood as someone who challenges family structures and inherited social roles. Suffrage activism is also frequently figured as a rite of passage, a moment in the development of one or more characters where choices become acute and consequences stark. In relation to the question of autonomy, however, the suffrage activist poses particularly interesting questions for modernist fiction. She (the emphasis is normally on women activists) is someone who aspires to freedom, to self-determination, to economic self-sufficiency, and to political agency, but who also seeks immersion in, and identification with, the collective social and political movement of suffrage activism. This desire for autonomy and simultaneous fascination with collectivism constitutes an organizing thematic and narrative tension. The remainder of this chapter considers the handling of this tension within three novels, and examines the extent to which a narrative or psychological space "beyond autonomy" is realized within them.

The Convert (1907) by Elizabeth Robins opens with its heroine, Vida Levering, expressing contempt for the narrow and shallow social world in which she finds herself: "All the women . . . are trying with might and main to amuse the men, and all the men are more or less permitting the women to succeed."[10] These men and women are represented as discussing the suffrage movement in hostile terms, condemning, for example, "an ignorant little factory girl presuming to stand up in public and interrupt a speech by a minister of the Crown" (67). Despite being exposed to such hostile images of the suffrage movement, Vida decides to attend a suffrage meeting. This decision triggers encounters that lead Vida far from the social milieu of the novel's opening and toward new, partial, and competing identities. At one point Vida meets a suffrage activist, and questions her closely about the mechanism by which she has managed to align herself with the collective impulse: "One of the things I wanted to know, if you don't mind – how you came to be identified with the movement" (184). The question of identification remains important: as part of Vida's own identification with suffrage activism she decides to dress as a poor woman and deliberately expose herself to the social and sexual vulnerabilities that this implies.

The novel then reveals that Vida has not always inhabited the shallow comfortable world in which the reader first encounters her. She had been forced to leave her parental home following a scandal. Without any training or appropriate education she had struggled to earn her living alone: "Some girls think it hardship to have to earn their living. The horror is not to be allowed to" (265). Vida's status as "modern" woman here undergoes an additional twist, as her aspiration to economic freedom is added to her involvement in the suffrage struggle. The vulnerabilities to which her modern aspirations expose her are further revealed when we learn that she had in the past been seduced and then abandoned by an apparently reliable friend.

The complex interrelations among economic freedom, political freedom, and sexual freedom are mapped in *The Convert* onto ideas of danger, loss, and loneliness. The novel ends with Vida sacrificing one form of personal happiness and arguing instead for a fuller sense of self-realization through participation in collective aims:

> She stood staring out into the void. "One woman's mishap – what is that? A thing as trivial to the great world as it's sordid in most eyes. But the time has come when a woman may look about her and say, What general significance has my secret pain? Does it 'join on' to anything? And I find it *does*. I'm no longer simply a woman who has stumbled on the way." With difficulty she controlled the shake in her voice. "I'm one who has got up bruised and bleeding, wiped the dust from her hands and the tears from her face – and said to herself not merely: Here's one luckless woman! but – here is a stone of stumbling to many. Let's see if it can't be moved out of other women's way. And she calls people to come and help. No mortal man, let alone a woman, *by herself*, can move that rock of offence. But," she ended with a sudden sombre flare of enthusiasm, "if *many* help, Geoffrey, the thing can be done." (348)

The triumphal tone of this ending is palpable, and indeed constitutes an interesting challenge to the adequacy of the novel it concludes. If "one woman's mishap" has no fundamental significance, then this must cast retrospective doubt over the aspiration of *The Convert* to use Vida's personal experience in order to represent the struggles and the experiences of the modern woman. The triumphalism is also undercut by other aspects of this concluding paragraph. We note that Vida is staring into the void, that her voice is shaking, that her pain is palpable, and also that the victory of the collective is only at the end a possibility: "if *many* help ... the thing can be done." It is, at best, a partial victory.

Whether "the thing can be done" is also central to H. G. Wells's novel *Ann Veronica* (1909), which is about the aspirations of Ann Veronica Stanley to achieve economic, social, and sexual freedom. The novel is organized as a journey toward self-realization, beginning with Ann Veronica's total immersion in the stifling embrace of her family, moving through chapters with such titles as "The Crisis," in which she leaves home to live alone in London; "Ideals and Reality" and "Biology," in which abstract ideas and pressing desires are reflected on; through "Discords," "The Suffragettes," and "Thoughts in Prison," during which her activist principles are sorely tested; then on to "The Mountains" where she experiences sexual passion and pleasure; and concluding with "In Perspective," wherein she is both happily married and pregnant.

Discussing Wells as a "modernist" novelist is perhaps surprising, because his interest in the novel as a genre is much more connected to the socially or economically oriented ideas that the genre can set in play than to the innovations of aesthetic means whereby it can do so. Wells's own scientific background leads him to see in the novel the potential for staging experiments in human and social development; and his perspective is more related to Zola's naturalism, with its aspiration to deploy "the application of the experimental method to the study of nature and of men,"[11] than to the formal experimentalism associated with modernist novelists such as Woolf, Dorothy Richardson, or James Joyce.

In looking at the interaction of modern social and psychological experiences and modernist fiction, however, Wells's writing raises interesting questions. Wells's life connects him to some of the most important modern writers of the period. His many love affairs include relationships with Elizabeth von Arnim, Rebecca West, and Dorothy Richardson (who introduces Hypo Wilson, a character based on Wells, into her thirteen-volume novel series *Pilgrimage* [1915–1967]); and his friends include Elizabeth Robins. But the conversation between Wells and the developing modernist novel is not simply biographical. In *Ann Veronica* he uses the temporal and thematic resources of the novel to explore the subjective and social strands that come together to construct a particular kind of modern subjectivity.

In this experimental exploration Ann Veronica's participation in the suffrage movement, and her imprisonment for it, play a crucial role. Ann Veronica's decision to become a political activist follows directly from her financial and ultimately sexual entanglement with an older man, and her discovery that the man with whom she is in love is actually married, though separated from his wife:

> "There is only one way out of all this," said Ann Veronica, sitting up in her little bed in the darkness and biting at her nails.
>
> "I thought I was just up against Morningside Park and father, but it is the whole order of things – the whole blessed order of things . . ."[12]

She comes to the view that the present generation of women must sacrifice their individual interests in order to create the conditions of freedom in the future: "there must be a generation of martyrs" (182). The sacrifice she imagines includes the possibility of sexual fulfillment, which is for Ann Veronica at this stage simply another form of "slavery" (182). She thus presents herself at the headquarters of the suffrage movement, declaring "I would like to go to prison" (184).

The representation of the other suffrage activists that follows is far from approving, a fact for which Wells has been widely criticized. They are represented as fanatical, irrational, and potentially dangerous. One of the leaders of the movement is "aggressive and disagreeable" as well as "a person of amazing persuasive power" who is "about as capable of argument as a runaway steamroller" (186). Nevertheless, Ann Veronica is enthused by the suffrage movement, aspires to mingle with "the stream of history" (190) and joins an attempt by the suffragettes to storm the Houses of Parliament. She experiences "the wildest exhilaration" (191), which quickly gives way to disgust and terror as she is manhandled and arrested by the police. She finds herself in prison where "she meditated profoundly through several enormous cold hours on all that had happened and all that she had done since the swirl of the suffrage movement had submerged her personal affairs" (196).

Ann Veronica's period in prison sees her question her identity and her future aspirations, "What am I? What have I got to do with myself?" (201). This reflection leads almost immediately to "a phase of violent reaction against the suffrage movement" (203). She concludes that she cannot feel any strong sense of belonging to the movement because it is based on an antipathy to men that she does not share. But she also repudiates the stronger forms of egotism that she feels she has been guilty of, moving instead toward the "idea of self-sacrifice" (105), understood not as a loss or negation of selfhood, but rather as an acceptance of her self as a social being. This conclusion leads her to reconcile with her family, and to an engagement to a well-meaning "civil servant of some standing" (40).

But this persona of self-sacrificing "compromise and kindness" (206) proves unsustainable. Ann Veronica breaks her engagement and resumes a passionate affair with the married man with whom she has long been in love. She articulates her desire strongly and confidently, facing up to the potential consequences of the scandal that will follow. The sacrifice for passion's sake is one that she accepts – "I want to give myself to you" (250), yet she also aspires to maintain her intellectual integrity and autonomy, and "not to be drowned in the sea of emotions that threatened to submerge her intellectual being" (255).

Is such a yoking of intellectual freedom and passionate renunciation of the self possible? The novel's ending makes this far from clear. In the final chapter Ann Veronica is married to her lover and pregnant with his child, and expecting a social visit from her father and her uncle. It does not appear that she is employed, there is no reference to any life she might have beyond the domestic sphere, and during the dinner she does not participate in intellectual conversations between her husband and her father. Her own conclusion is distinctly melancholy: "the great time is over, and I have to go carefully and bear children" (291). The novel's conclusion sees Ann Veronica in tears, and describing herself rather chillingly as a "silly woman" (292). This ending could be read simply as a product of Wells's own widely documented antipathy toward marriage as an institution; but the problem it poses for the novel is more profound than this: it represents a failure to find any novelistic space for the reconciliation of subjective freedom and sexual or political passion.

May Sinclair also uses the suffrage movement to stage problems and possibilities of autonomous selfhood in a novel published ten years after *The Helpmate*, during the First World War. *The Tree of Heaven* (1917) is divided into three sections: "Peace," "The Vortex," and "Victory." "Peace" is expressed through and in the domestic life of the Harrison family, who live by Hampstead Heath in London, before the outbreak of the First World War: "the house belonged to the Heath and the open country . . . It was lifted high above the town; shut in; utterly secluded."[13]

"The Vortex" begins in 1910. Dorothy Harrison has just graduated from Cambridge University with a first-class degree in economics, and is hosting a suffrage meeting in the family home. Dorothy's response to the meeting is one of intellectual frustration, as she repeatedly asks for clarifications of arguments and of positions held by suffrage activists: "you *must* get it straight" (93); "you really *are* getting a bit mixed" (95). She watches with horror as a friend is drawn into the emotional turmoil of the arguments and the occasion:

> It was Rosalind, not Dorothy, who had been caught and sucked down into the swirl. She whirled in it now, and would go on whirling, under the impression that her movements made it move.
>
> The Vortex fascinated Dorothy even while she resisted it . . . For Dorothy was afraid of the Feminist Vortex . . . she was afraid of the herded women. She disliked the excited faces, and the high voices skirling their battle-cries, and the silly business of committees, and the platform slang. She was sick and shy before the tremor and the surge of collective feeling.   (99–100)

Despite this visceral repudiation of collective feeling, however, Dorothy finds herself caught up in a suffrage action, and arrested. She insists that her behavior rationally responded to circumstances: "I wasn't excited or carried away in the least" (166). In prison, like Ann Veronica, she finds a curious repose and contemplation, "her white-washed prison-cell, its hardness, its nakedness, its quiet, its visionary peace" (171), sharply contrasting with the terrifying energies and demands of the crowd that turns out to celebrate her release: "the soul of the crowd in the hall below her swelled and heaved itself towards her, drawn by the Vortex" (171).

Dorothy asserts the power of her own will against the crowd. "She saved her soul, it stood firm again; she was clear and hard and sane" (172). But the forces unleashed with the Vortex merely prefigure those deadly collective energies that will be unleashed in the final section of the novel, about the First World War. Against Dorothy's confident claiming of the integrity of her soul in the face of the furious currents of collective identity that for her characterize the suffrage agitation we must set the concluding observation made to Dorothy by her mother: "It's you I'm sorriest for. You've had nothing. From beginning to end you had nothing" (303).

If this is what lies "beyond autonomy" within the modernist novel, it carries more than a hint of negation. Autonomy implies an ability to act freely: what Dorothy might designate as action that is "clear and hard and sane." But in all of the novels discussed in this chapter such aspiration toward individual freedom reaches some kind of limit, either in marriage or in political activism. The "vortex" of sexual or political passion troubles the modern aspiration to freedom, and drives the novelistic representation of autonomy toward a "beyond" that, in the words of Ann Veronica, risks producing "a generation of martyrs" (182).

Notes

1. See Charles Altieri, "Why Modernist Claims for Autonomy Matter," *Journal of Modern Literature* 32: 3 (2009), 1–21.
2. See Bruce Clark, *Dora Marsden and Early Modernism: Gender, Individualism, Science* (Ann Arbor: University of Michigan Press, 1996) as well as early-twentieth-century journals *The New Freewoman* or *The Egoist.*
3. Leonore Davidoff and Catherine Hall, *Family Fortunes: Men and Women of the English Middle Class 1780–1850* (London: Routledge, 2002), p. xxi.
4. Mary Lyndon Shanley, *Feminism, Marriage and the Law in Victorian England* (Princeton University Press, 1993), p. 103.
5. Marie Carmichael Stopes, *Married Love*, ed. R. McKibbin (Oxford University Press, 2004), p. 9.
6. Mina Loy, "Feminist Manifesto," in Bonnie Kime Scott, ed., *Gender in Modernism: New Geographies, Complex Intersections* (Urbana: University of Illinois Press, 2007), p. 92. Emphasis in original.
7. May Sinclair, *The Helpmate* (New York: Henry Holt, 1907), p. 1.
8. Elizabeth von Arnim, *The Pastor's Wife* (London: Virago, 1987), p. 2.
9. Virginia Woolf, *Mrs Dalloway*, ed. Claire Tomalin (Oxford University Press, 1992), p. 242.
10. Elizabeth Robins, *The Convert* (London: Macmillan, 1907), p. 28.
11. Émile Zola, "The Experimental Novel," in *The Nineteenth-Century Novel: A Critical Reader*, ed. Stephen Regan (London: Routledge, 2001), pp. 104–117.
12. H. G. Wells, *Ann Veronica* (London: Penguin Classics, 2005), p. 181.
13. May Sinclair, *The Tree of Heaven* (London: Macmillan, 1917), p. 15.

40

Fiction by women: continuities and changes, 1930–1990

ELIZABETH MASLEN

Representative instances: Woolf, Storm Jameson, Lessing, Attia Hosain

While women writers have long been established as contributors to the history of the novel, the sixty-year period covered by this chapter traces developments in experimentation with the novel as a form, and as a vehicle for new and challenging content. Women, now having greater access to education, respond both to the aesthetic debates of the day, and to rapid changes in their cultural, social, and political context. Virginia Woolf, Storm Jameson, Doris Lessing, and Attia Hosain demonstrate the range of women novelists' achievements over a greater part of the century.

Virginia Woolf develops during the 1920s a major tool of modernist writers pioneered by Dorothy Richardson and May Sinclair: the stream of consciousness that reflects the mind's interior monologue. In *A Room of One's Own* (1929) Woolf asks whether the novel is as yet "rightly shaped" for the woman writer's use, given that the form has been dominated by male authors. She is in no doubt that the woman writer will soon adapt novelistic form to her own purposes, "providing some new vehicle, not necessarily in verse, for the poetry in her. For it is the poetry that is still denied outlet."[1] Accordingly, in *The Waves* (1931) Woolf develops poetic devices (such as repeated rhythms and phrases, together with image clusters) that explore the minds of six friends growing from childhood into adulthood. Each phase of their lives is interspersed with lyrical descriptions of sea and seasons, mirroring their maturation – and the simultaneous aging of the British Empire. The characters' closeness is reflected in their similar speech rhythms, as when, still very young, they respond to the early sun's *"blue finger-print of shadow under the leaf by the bedroom window"*; yet even at this early stage they each exhibit a distinctive perspective on life, conveyed through image clusters peculiar to themselves:

> "I see a ring," said Bernard, "hanging above me. It quivers and hangs in a loop of light."
>
> "I see a slab of pale yellow," said Susan, "spreading away until it meets a purple stripe."
>
> "I hear a sound," said Rhoda, "cheep, chirp; cheep, chirp; going up and down."[2]

As the children mature, Woolf introduces an older character, Percival, whose colonialist career in India, where he dies in a riding accident, affects them all. Percival represents the lure and demise of the imperial quest. As the six friends grow apart, their interior monologues trace the growing sense of loss which each experiences; as the novel ends Woolf has Bernard, the storyteller of the group, draw together images of the sea, the end of empire, and the end of life:

> And in me too the wave rises. It swells; it arches its back. I am aware once more of a new desire, something rising beneath me like the proud horse whose rider first spurs and then pulls him back. What enemy do we now perceive advancing against us, you whom I ride now, as we stand pawing this stretch of pavement? It is death. Death is the enemy. It is death against whom I ride with my spear couched and my hair flying back like a young man's, like Percival's, when he galloped in India. I strike spurs into my horse. Against you I will fling myself, unvanquished and unyielding, O Death! (256)

Continuing her quest for innovative form and language, Woolf's next novel, *The Years* (1937), is intimately related to her essay *Three Guineas* (1938). In *Three Guineas* she argues that, despite women's new freedom in the workplace, the masculine urge to dominate in the Victorian home now extends into society at large, thwarting, by exclusions and censorship, women's attempts to avoid masculine aggression. Women should therefore assert themselves by forming a society of Outsiders, with their own agenda for non-aggressive improvements in society and culture. However, in *The Years* Woolf shows both women and men as victims of the masculine ethos dominating society. Men are in some cases thrust into careers that do not suit them; women find themselves either submitting to continuing stereotypes, or to being seen as savage rebels. Woolf shows by unfinished sentences, fractured lines of thought, misreadings of each others' meanings, that communication is disastrously inhibited, and that loneliness pervades. Toward the end of the novel, North longs both to keep his individuality and "at the same time spread out, make a new ripple in human consciousness, be the bubble and the stream, the stream and the bubble – myself and the world together."[3] Yet the language for such thoughts is still inadequate; he feels trapped in a heart of darkness akin to

Joseph Conrad's, where he is "provided only with broken sentences, single words, with which to break through the briar-bush of human bodies, human wills and voices, that bent over him, binding him, blinding him" (391).

Both in *Three Guineas* and *The Years* Woolf explores the constraining effects modern society has on individuals, and she identifies the inadequacy of language as part of the constraint. Storm Jameson, in contrast, distrusts the role of what she terms "desperate stylists" such as Woolf who, she maintains, "devote themselves to the disintegration of language."[4] As political conflicts in the 1930s grew more critical, Jameson expressed in her essay "Documents" (1937) her idea of the writer's role:

> We need documents . . . as timber for the fire some writer will light tomor-
> row morning . . . As the photographer does, so must the writer keep himself
> out of the picture while working ceaselessly to present *fact* from a striking
> (poignant, ironic, penetrating, significant) angle.[5]

Anticipating George Orwell's assertion in 1946 that "good prose is like a window pane,"[6] Jameson insists that the language for her enterprise should be "decent, straight English" (558). Accordingly, her novel *Europe to Let* (1940) is largely based on the reportorial notes she took of conversations and experiences on her own visits to Prague, Budapest, and Vienna in 1938 during the tense European prelude to World War II. Jameson keeps herself out of the narrative by having a male protagonist, Esk, a veteran of World War I, insist for much of the novel on his non-involvement, simply listening and observing. However, "facts" in this narrative are shown as not always easy to establish in the chaotic climate of 1938; as Esk says, "I understand at these moments how provisional and insecure is the shape, the timing of reality that we have agreed upon."[7]

For Jameson, after all, what is stated so confidently in a non-fictional work reveals itself, as for Woolf, to be open to question when explored in a novel. Esk's own stance as "photographer" fluctuates, as Jameson's choice of images shows. At one point Esk insists "What is happening to the men and women clinging to Europe as to a raft does not move me. There have been too many disasters" (237). Yet at another moment he has a surreal vision that forces him to admit his personal sense of guilt, mirroring the unwillingness of the British government to act when fascism is relentlessly advancing:

> A round white Easter egg, rolling across Europe, left on the roads traces of
> blood: Warsaw, Berlin, Vienna, Budapest. Rome, Prague, tomorrow. To be
> devoured with the mind's salt. Shall I say, "Your chatter disgusts me"? No,
> I am not that man. I listen. I am consenting to the business of jackals. When it

is finished, from a safe place I shall condemn what has been done. Do I hear a
cock crow?   (258)

Jameson captures, through familiar images defamiliarized by context, the
nightmare quality of what Esk experiences, despite his wish to remain
detached. Furthermore, when Jameson draws on actual conversations she
has had, she is offering photographic renderings of fact, but she uses rhetorical
devices to ensure their "striking angle" – their emotional impact on her
readers. The employment of rhetorical repetition, in the following passage,
showing how fact is negated by official attitudes, produces a tragic crescendo
when a Viennese Jewish surgeon, his fingers broken by torturers so that he can
never operate again, mimics Nazi denials of the truth:

> It is not true that thousands of people in Austria have been robbed of every-
> thing. That thousands are slowly dying of hunger. That the prisons are
> crowded with people charged with having been born. That others have
> been existing for weeks on a rotten boat in mid-Danube. It is not true that
> the postman is authorised to demand a hundred marks for a package con-
> taining the ashes of your son, he who was taken away last week by enemies
> who were amused by your tears. It is not true that when they have forbidden
> a Jew to work, and knowing that no country will admit him have ordered him
> to leave at once, officials answer the impudent question, "What am I to do?"
> by the retort, "There is always the Danube."   (280)

Here language is shown as horrifically capable of masking and distorting fact.
    Jameson experiments with formal ways of engaging current events through
fiction throughout her long career. In *Black Laurel* (1947) she reworks her
documentary mode for postwar Germany. A young English pilot sees the
European scene in the image of a torture victim, merging public and personal
suffering:

> The hangmen had done their work thoroughly, the body of Europe, flayed
> while still living, was stretched below him in the sunlight, the nerves exposed
> and torn, the fractured bones, the nails rotted, decomposing flesh, a death
> terrible, sordid, poisoned.[8]

In describing the ruins of Berlin, Jameson develops equally graphic images of
the conquered young with their standards warped, while all too many of the
victors, whether military rulers or big business interests, are revealed as
undermining all principles of right or wrong. As one observer says: "In any
society where some men are of no importance, the only justice these get is the
cheap legal sort" (329).

The "cheap legal" justice that separates justice from freedom, and that divorces language from reality, is a major theme in Jameson's work. It is central also to Doris Lessing's career. In Lessing's first novel, *The Grass is Singing* (1950), based in the southern Africa Lessing had just left for life in England, the protagonist Mary is driven to marry as much by the women's magazines she reads as by pressure from her friends. Her husband is similarly seduced by the romantic films of the day. But for husband and wife the reality of marriage on their lonely farm is unhappy. Breaking down under the strain, Mary turns to her black servant Moses for comfort, only to tragically reject him when her white-settler training rebels against their intimacy. After Mary meets a new young white settler, Tony, she fires Moses, and he kills her. Lessing then exposes the ways in which the settler community suppresses evidence about white Mary's murder by black Moses, forcing Tony into unwilling but complicit silence. The narrator gives a lesson in how to interpret settlers' words:

> When old settlers say "One has to understand the country," what they mean is, "You have to get used to our ideas about the native." They are saying, in effect, "Learn our ideas, or otherwise get out: we don't want you."[9]

The gap between word and meaning is as crucial for Lessing as for Woolf and Jameson.

Lessing's setting remains African for the first three volumes of her *Children of Violence* series. *The Golden Notebook* (1962) is set wholly in Britain. Immediately heralded as a classic feminist text for its explorations of female identity, the novel's division into a series of "notebooks" underlines the fragmentation that the protagonist, a woman novelist suffering from writer's block, experiences. Yet structurally the work suggests something else as well, because in its final section Anna, the protagonist, writes the first sentence of her male lover's new novel and he offers the first sentence of hers (in fact the first sentence of Lessing's overarching text). So each of the lovers, as it were, inscribes the other's body in the writing, but creatively, without the urge for dominance. What Anna dreams of is the role of what are termed "boulder pushers,"[10] who strive to arrive at truths about a range of problems, of which gender is only one. She says:

> There's a great black mountain. It's human stupidity. There are a group of people who push a boulder up a mountain. When they've got a few feet up, there's a war, or the wrong sort of revolution, and the boulder rolls down – not to the bottom, it always manages to end a few inches higher than when it

started. So the group of people put their shoulders to the boulder and start pushing again. (544)

"Boulder pushers" are Lessing's prime concern in all her work. She explores the social constraints on both men and women rather than focussing solely on women in terms of gender difference.

Lessing's Anna exhibits many links with preoccupations in Woolf and Jameson's work. For instance, in a passage recalling Jameson's "Documents," Anna notes that:

> The function of the novel seems to be changing; it has become an outpost of journalism; we read novels for information about areas of life we don't know ... Most novels, if they are successful at all, are original in the sense that they report the existence of an area of society, a type of person, not yet admitted to the general literate consciousness. (75)

Anna next echoes those of Woolf's characters who mourn their apartness, their sense of fragmentation:

> Human beings are so divided, are becoming more and more divided *and more subdivided in themselves*, reflecting the world, that they reach out desperately, not knowing they do it, for information about other groups inside their own country, let alone about groups in other countries. It is a blind grasping out for their own wholeness. (75)

Anna also shares with Woolf's North a sense of the inadequacy of language to express her vision; she despairs of ever writing "the only kind of novel which interests me: a book powered with an intellectual or moral passion strong enough to create order, to create a new way of looking at life" (76). Later, again reminiscent of Woolf's North, she comments, "I don't know why I still find it so hard to accept that words are faulty and by their very nature inaccurate. If I thought they were capable of expressing the truth, I wouldn't keep journals which I refuse to let anyone see" (565).

Lessing brought her experience of Africa to England in a way that has been followed by other foreign-born novelists who have enriched native English perspectives and who challenge them. Attia Hosain brings not only the experience of an India before the end of the Raj but also her own literary tradition to bear on the English language in which she writes. Her short stories in *Phoenix Fled* (1953) and her novel *Sunlight on a Broken Column* (1961) are based on her own experiences in India before independence and at the time of Partition. Hosain draws on the poetic traditions of Urdu literature when in the novel a servant responds to the young orphan protagonist's questions about her parents:

> "Your mother? How can I describe her? In yourself you can see her as the moon is seen in a clear pool, like enough, but still a reflection."
> "And my father?"
> "A prince among men. If he had worn rags they would have seemed the robes of a king, and he had a heart that could have folded the world into it."[11]

Richness of style is for Hosain a subordinate vehicle, however, rather than her prime concern; she is, like Jameson and Lessing, a shrewd observer and critic of her society. In both her short stories and her novel, she shows the inequities of the north Indian feudal system in which she grew up (in an extended upper-class Muslim family), offering graphic insights into the lives of the poor. In the short story "Phoenix Fled," she evokes the tragic end of a long-established way of life by describing an old village woman, her skin "loose around the impatient skeleton,"[12] who finds that "her changeless, circumscribed world" is worryingly "quickening its step in noisy haste" as the cars and trains of Western civilization invade the life she knew (11). Hosain does not refer directly to the partition of India and the violence between Hindu and Muslim it brought in its wake. We only hear that the old woman now "feared the departure of the [British] soldiers as once she had feared their arrival"; yet when her neighbors flee the village, she "who had survived the threats of too many years refused to believe in its finality" (14). So she stays in her string bed until "the creaking of the door woke her. She could not see who came, how many. She smelt the flaming thatch, and as shadows came across the courtyard she tried to sit up" (15), and the tale ends.

Hosain's succinct, astringent sketch of the breakdown of a society recalls Jameson's plea for the novelist to be a creator of documents, and shares Woolf, Jameson, and Lessing's sense of personal and social fragmentation. Hosain impartially shows how distrust evolves between Muslim and Muslim, and Muslim and Hindu, at the end of the British empire, constructing a racism in communities where none had previously existed, even though there had been awareness of difference. But Hosain also shows the warmth between friends: the mixture of races and cultures at the deathbed of an old patriarch; the friendships, despite arguments, among Christian Anglo-Indian, passionate Hindu, and devout Muslim girls at college. Hosain's fiction reveals the descent into open enmity and violence as a gradual process within both community and family, opposition to British imperialism giving way to conflict between old friends and neighbors, between brothers, between parents and children. Whereas the death of Woolf's Percival affects his group of friends deeply, both as personal loss and as a symbol for the death of empire, Hosain gives Woolf's versions of personal and social disintegration a much larger-scale Indian perspective. And strikingly in tune with Lessing, Hosain's protagonist, Laila (who, impatient for greater freedom, frequently transgresses the rules of *purdah*, yet loves her restrictive, tradition-bound family) has a yearning awareness of her divided self, in a divided world, that suggests a mirror-image of Anna Wulf's "blind grasping out for . . . wholeness." English fiction increasingly, throughout the latter half of the twentieth century, comes to embrace voices and perspectives from women of other cultures and creeds, all enlisting fiction as a way to come to terms with their changing worlds.

Continuities and change

Woolf, Jameson, Lessing, and Hosain exemplify how fictions by women can both mirror each other and nevertheless draw on unique backgrounds and priorities to reveal continuities and change in novelistic form and in social and cultural conditions.

Woolf is not the only woman to develop a female form of stream of consciousness in the 1930s. Olive Moore and Mary Butts evolve "the poetry that is still denied outlet" in *A Room of One's Own*. Moore's *Spleen* (1930) anticipates Woolf's argument in *Three Guineas* that women should remain outsiders to the competitive aggressions of society. *Spleen's* protagonist meditates on what has brought her, with her severely disabled son, to a peasant community in Italy, away from what she perceives as her repressive and frigid middle-class English life. The core of this novel is woman's role as outsider, even as she delights in the vitality of the community around her. Butts's *Death of Felicity Taverner* (1932) develops the outsider theme differently. Dead Felicity's cousins and friends remember her as a sort of holy fool, abused by her husband, promiscuous in her search for love, an outsider to the conventions of her society. She is linked with a White Russian *émigré*, whose expulsion from his society has destroyed his loyalty to its values, implying the tie between political and personal abuse that Woolf also suggests in *Three Guineas*.

Jean Rhys, Rosamond Lehmann, Elizabeth Bowen, and Stevie Smith also anticipate Woolf's argument for woman as outsider. Rhys's *Voyage in the Dark* (1934) centers on the experience of a young white Creole immigrant in Britain. The demeaning treatment she receives and the effect on her mind foreshadow the revelations of later immigrant novelists. In the 1930s, however, love's continuing involvement with patriarchy reduces to alien status even women born into citizenship "at home." Rosamond Lehmann plots a patriarchy-doomed love affair in two novels, *Invitation to the Waltz* (1932) and *The Weather in the Streets* (1936). In the first she sketches, through incident and through interior monologue, the awakening of love, as her young girl pro-tagonist hurries toward marriage. In the second, this same girl, ten years later, lives in poverty on the fringes of bohemian London, her marriage broken. Abandoned again, she faces a lonely abortion. Both novels combine the inward life of the mind with a portrayal of the young girl as a victim of male domination.

Elizabeth Bowen in *The Death of the Heart* (1938) explores the consciousness of an orphan girl, living with relatives who treat her punctiliously but without love, and the destructive consequences for her and for them as her loneliness finds release in amorous fantasies and prurient spying. Stevie Smith offers yet another way of presenting the workings of the female mind through protag-onists outside the frame of contemporary society. In *Novel on Yellow Paper* (1936) and *Over the Frontier* (1938), Smith's girl protagonist Pompey babbles about men, fashion, race, friends. This babbling involves both girl narrator and reader in current prejudices, as here, in *Over the Frontier*:

> I am in despair for the racial hatred that is running in me in a sudden swift current, in a swift tide of hatred, and Out out damned tooth, damned aching tooth, rotten to the root.
>   Do we not always hate the persecuted?
>   . . . But I have had some very dear Jewish friends.
>   Oh final treachery of the smug goy. Do not all our persecutions of Israel follow upon this smiling sentence?[13]

In *Over the Frontier* Pompey's quirky meditations on men, Germans, and war become darker, drift into a surreal landscape wherein Pompey has donned the uniform and with it the aggression so often assigned solely to the male. "Fact" proves impossible to locate.

Jameson's engagement with the tense European world of the 1930s is matched by a number of women writers who experiment with fictional genres to lure readers into confronting disturbing contemporary conflicts. Naomi Mitchison in *The Corn King and the Spring Queen* (1931) invents an ancient land regulated by fertility rites, and positioned within the conflicting political worlds of Athens, Sparta, and Egypt, in order to explore war and aggression alongside contemporary attitudes to sex, rape, and woman's role in society.

The novel was successful because it was set in the past. When Mitchison provided a modern English setting for similar themes in *We Have Been Warned* (1935), publishers fought shy of the work, and when it was published it was not well received. So Mitchison returned to the past in *The Blood of the Martyrs* (1939), using a Roman setting to debate state persecution and brutality. When one compares Mitchison's social targets with those of Jameson in this decade, it is noticeable that, while Jameson avoids explicitly sexual scenes when setting novels like *Love in Winter* (1935) in her own time and place, Mitchison offends when she emphasizes rape and free love in contemporary Britain. Writers, both men and women, had at this date to be wary not only of official censorship but of their audience's limited capacity for liberal thinking. Unlike Jameson's *Europe to Let*, set abroad, Betty Miller's *Farewell Leicester Square*, an exposure of anti-semitism in contemporary England, initially met the same fate as Mitchison's *We Have Been Warned*. Miller was refused publication in 1935, only getting into print in 1941, when the treatment of Jews by the Nazis could no longer be denied. The obstacles such matters encountered when represented in a contemporary native English setting suggest reasons for Woolf's decision to be forthrightly combative in *Three Guineas*.

Women in the 1930s not only respond to fascism, but also, anticipating the revelations of writers from old Empire and Commonwealth like Hosain, raise questions about imperialism. Winifred Holtby in *Mandoa! Mandoa!* (1933) satirizes a complacent British sense of superiority to African ways that condemns slavery while turning a blind eye to British colonists' own harsh treatment of their workforce in Kenya. A local African slave-owner is wittily aware of the double standards of the imperialist intruders:

> When Bill urged the mercy of unemployment allowance, Talal remarked that in Mandoa, if a noble allowed his slaves to starve, he lost the worth of them. When Bill conceded that Socialists spoke of the British system of wage-slavery, Talal shrugged his shoulders and observed that the attitude of the League of Nations towards his [fellow slave-traders] in Abyssinia was all the more incomprehensible.[14]

Rumer Godden's *The Lady and the Unicorn* (1937), a novel set in Calcutta and narrated from an Anglo-Indian (Eurasian) point of view, centers on the perils of rootlessness for a mixed race girl. A feckless Englishman, whose attraction for the girl is linked to her sightings of ghosts of her European forebears (with whom she identifies), disastrously damages her bond with her loyal Eurasian lover. The girl's painful confusion of identity is echoed in Hosain's depictions of her Eurasian contemporaries in the years leading to Partition.

As World War II broke out, Jameson, true to her aim in *Europe to Let* of opening her readers' eyes to the effects of invasion and occupation on ordinary people, sets her novels in Europe. In *Cousin Honoré* (1940) and *Cloudless May* (1943), she dramatizes the tensions and strains within a small, personalized community, where public and private spheres lose their dividing lines, and come to mirror the historical attitudes and conflicts leading to war. Unlike Jameson, however, most women writing about war concentrate on the home front. Clemence Dane produced a satirical fantasy as war broke out: *The Arrogant History of White Ben* (1939) shows an animated English scarecrow developing into a grim parody of Hitler, backed by elements in the press and the political establishment, and all but destroying England in Nazi style. Phyllis Bottome innovatively steps outside the middle class to portray the effects of war: *London Pride* (1941) centers on children from the East End slums experiencing the Blitz, and being evacuated; and *Within the Cup* (1943) explores the life of a refugee, an Austrian Jewish doctor, haunted by memories of his Aryan wife's betrayal and now caught up in the savage bombing of Plymouth. All these novels offer "striking angles" on the war years.

By the end of the 1940s many women writers reflect on the legacies of war, often with a skepticism that extends modernist doubts about the impossibility of arriving at anything as slippery as "truth." As in *The Waves* loneliness and fragmentation are their continuing themes, often linked with an experience war had brought to the fore: personal betrayal and political treachery. Elizabeth Bowen's *The Heat of the Day* (1948) explores relationships, both public and private, in which the isolation of each person's experience ultimately evades definitive analysis, and the impossibility of speaking or hearing "the truth" inevitably feeds suspicions of betrayal. Stevie Smith's *The Holiday* (1949) is set, not in peacetime, but in what she shrewdly terms the "post-war," as her tearful protagonist mirrors the spirit of existential crisis that preoccupies many writers after the betrayal of humanist aspirations by war's inhumanities. The bleak vision of Orwell's *Nineteen Eighty-Four* (1949) is shared by many. Marghanita Laski's *Little Boy Lost* (1949) explores a man's mind as he searches for his lost son, his emotions numbed by his wife's death under the Nazi occupation of France. The discovery of a child who might or might not be his own, and the father's confused resistance to the child's appeal, echo in personal terms the loss of certainties and safe havens in Jameson's *Black Laurel*. Rose Macaulay's *The World My Wilderness* (1950) also concentrates on the fate of children affected by war, revealing a child's interpretation of postwar England, her perceptions conditioned by her experiences of the Resistance in France. Through her we see Britain as potentially hostile and treacherous territory.

The child draws on Resistance skills to counter the middle-class expectations of her family, and in the process, raises questions about the nature of reality. The bleak postwar world, the world of Jameson's *Black Laurel*, robbed of all certainties and precedents, is the legacy Rebecca West meditates on in her non-fictional accounts of the Nuremburg trial and of the motivation of traitors in *A Train of Powder* (1955) and *The Meaning of Treason* (1949).

In the attempt to find some precedent for the confusions of war, women writers turn again, like Mitchison, to history. Sylvia Townsend Warner in *The Corner That Held Them* (1948) constructs a community of nuns in medieval England, struggling to survive in a world fraught with danger. In conversations that are never archaized, so as to foreground the turbulent fourteenth century's links with the present, Warner makes clear that prejudices and hypocrisies have scarcely changed; calumnies used by the Nazis to whip up anti-semitism are firmly rooted in her late medieval Christian community, while the poor of the Peasants' Uprising reflect the condition of refugees, the displaced and the disenfranchised of the Europe Jameson captures in *Black Laurel*. "The wretchedness of the poor lies below hunger and nakedness," Warner writes.

> It consists in their incessant incertitude and fear, the drudging succession of shift and scheme and subterfuge, the labouring in the quicksand where every step that takes hold of the firm ground is also a step into the danger of condemnation. Not cold and hunger but Law and Justice are the bitterest affliction of the poor.[15]

During the 1950s women writers continue to reassess the past from a postwar perspective. Rosamond Lehmann's *The Echoing Grove* (1953) captures what one character calls a generation of men and women "all in flux."[16] This is the story of two sisters who love and are loved by the same man; their tale is told from several points of view, as friends' perspectives interweave with the protagonists'. The structure is intricate: the reader holds the clues to the emotional lives of the characters, while none of them has the whole picture. This tale anticipates, in its meditations on the ambivalences of gender roles, *The Golden Notebook*.

New voices emerge in the 1950s. Iris Murdoch's *Under the Net* (1954) mixes high comedy, raffish characters, and deep purpose, for Murdoch's novels challenge at their core the bleaker pronouncements of existentialist philosophy. Murdoch, like Jameson, characteristically has central characters in pursuit of "the good," rather than resigned to purposelessness. Another new talent is Muriel Spark, with her puncturing of middle-class coziness, and her manipulation of spare, precise language; in works like *Memento Mori* (1959), her dark, disturbing wit echoes Stevie Smith. But Spark's protagonists are always more cynical, more dangerously manipulative than Smith's. A particularly striking feature of the 1950s is the emergence of a number of works by women like Hosain from the former Empire. Ruth Prawer Jhabvala, by birth European, married to an Indian, provides a perspective that is both from inside the India she portrays, and on the fringe. Her novel *Esmond in India* (1958) exposes how her English protagonist, living in independent India, maintains an imperial sense of superiority, collecting Indian experiences alongside Indian artifacts. He attracts a young Indian girl, brought up to admire English culture, away from her own community; the effect of the theme is fabular, suggesting potential tragedy when West and East confuse rather than enrich each other.

Women's novels of the 1950s herald an increase in innovative writing, a development predicted by Lessing's career. Christine Brooke-Rose in *Out* (1964) experiments with the French *nouveau roman*, revealing how language shapes experience and perceptions, either deliberately or unconsciously. Ann Quin's experimental work responds to the paintings of Francis Bacon and to *nouvelle vague* film, exploring blurred boundaries between fantasy and reality. In Quin's *Three* (1966) scenes are presented in terms of stage or film directions, while a series of notes, some linked, others apparently random, rework interior monologue as unpatterned thought, prone to deceive the thinker even as the thinker aims to deceive others. Fragmentation again lies at the core of these novels. Other women writers develop more accessible experiments with form. Angela Carter creates disturbing dream worlds, fairy tale tipping into nightmare. *The Magic Toyshop* (1967) centers on a young girl exposed to a dysfunctional family dominated by a male tyrant. The style borrows much from surrealism; and the fantasies that characters dream up to sustain their lives affect those around them, with disastrous results. Both fantasy and realism inspire women writers of the 1960s to revitalize explorations of female experience. Margaret Drabble's *A Summer Bird-Cage* (1963), in realist mode and largely based on her own experience, offers glimpses of marriage as entrapment, and of the friendship and tensions between women; Maureen Duffy's *That's How It Was* (1962) concentrates on poverty, single motherhood, illegitimacy. Their effects on a young girl desperately trying to establish who she is are vividly recreated. But in *The Microcosm* (1966), Duffy portrays a dark, lesbian ghetto, blending realism with fantasy, her style a fragmented, staccato collage of historical and contemporary lesbian voices and experiences.

Writers from overseas continue to develop novels that challenge native British traditions. Pre-eminent among these is *Wide Sargasso Sea* (1966), Jean Rhys's postmodern challenge to Charlotte Brontë's depiction of *Jane Eyre*'s madwoman in the attic. Rhys sets Bertha Mason's own tragic story center stage. Yet Rhys is even-handed in her treatment of her Rochester figure, showing him, in sections dedicated to his stream of consciousness, as equally a victim of his era's social prejudices. Even as he tyrannizes over his wife, his role is shaped by prejudices and priorities that portray him as victim as much as villain. Jhabvala in *Get Ready for Battle* (1962) centers on the heartache within a traditional society as it slowly adapts to a changing world: like Hosain, Jhabvala reveals strengths and weaknesses within traditional societies during their struggle to come to terms with the world the British left behind.

Voices from other cultures are increasingly heard during the 1970s. Jhabvala's *Heat and Dust* (1975) brings two eras into conversation, through the diary of a young English girl who goes to India to recover the story of her grandfather's first wife. The different worlds the two protagonists inhabit, the different solutions they find to similar adventures, are evoked with a wealth of period detail (Ashdaf Soueif's *The Map of Love* [1999], about the development of the Palestinian conflict, has a structure similar to *Heat and Dust*). Kamala Markandaya sets most of her novels of the 1950s and 1960s in India. However, in 1972, her *The Nowhere Man* (1972) transports an Indian family to England between the wars. The family seeks to escape the increasing brutality of imperial rule at the end of empire. This novel is unsparing in its exposure of the growing intolerance that her Indian protagonist, a widower by the end of the war, has to confront in his old age. Markandaya reinvents English "realism," drawing on Eastern philosophy and expressing an Indian perspective on the corner of England that the protagonist inhabits. Markandaya, like Hosain, is even-handed in her portrayals: the Indian son's callous neglect of his father, as the young man turns to Western material culture, is set alongside the brutality of the thuggish son of a well-meaning English neighbor. This is a tale of cultures trying to come to terms with each other, but it is also a cutting indictment of the growth of mindless racism in the postwar years. Markandaya's wit and irony are used for both comic and tragic effect: when, for example, the thug and his friends have whipped up a crowd to hound the old man, someone new to the neighborhood shouts "'Bloody Jew'. . . but was quickly squashed as a racist. Since no one wanted those ovens to be lit again."[17]

Buchi Emecheta's *Second-Class Citizen* (1976) also exposes the hardships faced by new arrivals in England; but Emecheta's work is targeted and written differently. There is a hint of oral tradition in the way Emecheta, originally from Nigeria, writes; autobiographically based, the novel reveals the problems confronting a Nigerian wife and mother in England, as she realizes how her husband clings to the African way of treating women, instead of adjusting to the new, more egalitarian society he has entered. Racist attitudes are there, but as a background to the struggle between old African tradition and the potential for a new life in another country. While Markandaya's novel centers on the passionate patience of her old Indian, Emecheta shows a feisty young woman, refusing to identify herself as victim, ready to battle against the old ways and to find her feet in her new home. Finally she breaks free.

During the next decade women writers continue to experiment with new forms and to reinvent established ones; a younger generation builds on what has become nearly a century-long tradition of modern women's writing. Angela Carter's *Nights at the Circus* (1984) develops her magic realism. The language in this novel is earthy, scenes set within scenes kaleidoscopically. But woman is no longer presented as victim; the heroine Fevvers is supremely triumphant in the circus that represents her world in all its absurdities. Fay Weldon, already established as a feminist writer, produces a postmodernist novel, *Puffball* (1980), that employs playfulness and fantasy to explore misunderstandings and treachery in the context of menstrual cycles, pregnancy, and childbirth. Fact and fiction, the stories we are told and those we tell ourselves, are disturbingly set in tandem; again the exploration is about social and personal fragmentation. Jeanette Winterson's first novel, *Oranges Are Not the Only Fruit* (1985), shows lesbian identity sparring wittily with traditional absolutes of good and evil. Anita Brookner's *Hôtel du Lac* (1984) follows the experiences of a women's romance writer. She is locked into a life of observing and listening, helplessly in thrall to her married lover, always denied the kind of domestic life she craves and invents for her own characters. In this novel, which recalls *The Golden Notebook*, Brookner targets the ultra-feminine, what her protagonist terms "the complacent consumers of men with their complicated but unwritten rules of what is due to them."[18]

Notes

1. Virginia Woolf, *A Room of One's Own, Three Guineas*, ed. Morag Shiach (Oxford University Press, 1992), pp. 100–101.
2. Virginia Woolf, *The Waves* (London: Penguin, 1992), p. 6.
3. Virginia Woolf, *The Years*, ed. Hermione Lee (Oxford University Press, 1992), p. 390.
4. Storm Jameson, "The Form of the Novel," in *The Writer's Situation* (London: Macmillan, 1950), pp. 37–61, 54, 55.
5. Storm Jameson, "Documents," in *Modernism: an Anthology of Sources and Documents*, ed. Vassiliki Kolocotroni, Jane Goldman and Olga Taxidou (Edinburgh University Press, 1998), pp. 556–560, 558.

6. George Orwell, "Why I Write," *The Collected Essays, Journalism and Letters of George Orwell, Vol. 1: An Age Like This 1920–1940* (Harmondsworth: Penguin, 1970), pp. 23–30, 30.

7. Storm Jameson, *Europe to Let: the Memoirs of an Obscure Man* (London and New York: Macmillan, 1940), p. 237.

8. Storm Jameson, *The Black Laurel* (London: Macmillan, 1947), p. 35.

9. Doris Lessing, *The Grass is Singing* (Harmondsworth: Penguin, 1969), p. 18.

10. Doris Lessing, *The Golden Notebook* (London: Collins, 1989), p. 544.

11. Attia Hosain, *Sunlight on a Broken Column* (London: Penguin, 1992), pp. 39–40.

12. Attia Hosain, *Phoenix Fled* (London: Virago, 1988), p. 9.

13. Stevie Smith, *Over the Frontier* (London: Virago, 1980), p. 158.

14. Winifred Holtby, *Mandoa, Mandoa!* (London: Virago, 1982), p. 140.

15. Sylvia Townsend Warner, *The Corner That Held Them* (London: Virago, 1988), p. 122.

16. Rosamond Lehmann, *The Echoing Grove* (London: Collins, 1953), p. 311.

17. Kamala Markandaya, *The Nowhere Man* (London: Allen Lane, 1972), p. 391.

18. Anita Brookner, *Hôtel du Lac* (London: Jonathan Cape, 1984), p. 146.

41

The novel amid other discourses

PATRICIA WAUGH

Philosophy, religion, science, they are all of them busy nailing things down, to get a stable equilibrium. Religion, with its nailed-down God . . . philosophy with its fixed ideas; science with its laws . . . But the novel no. The novel is the highest example of subtle interrelatedness that man has discovered . . . If you try to nail anything down, in the novel, either it kills the novel, or the novel gets up and walks away with the nail.[1]

The novel and other disciplines

Lawrence's description of the novel genre as "the highest example of subtle interrelatedness that man has discovered" encapsulates the dialogisms, hybridities, intertextualities, double voicings, and focalization that are celebrated by recent academic criticism. Scholarship thereby constructs the novel as a capacious house, not only full of many windows, but also built ergonomically, with a range of recycled materials. Of course, the novel has never respected disciplinary boundaries, national frontiers, or well-tilled fields and plots; but in the twentieth century its tendencies have seemed ever more promiscuous, democratic, and miscegenated. Novelists, like public intellectuals, have roamed free of academic practices (even when those practices appear not to be restrictive), borrowing and stealing at will, mixing and meshing, parodying and inverting official discourses of knowledge.

Popular science and philosophy, earlier in the century and again from the late 1970s on, after the publication of Richard Dawkins's *The Selfish Gene* (1976), have been similarly free ranging, making new ideas easily available to readers. In the earlier part of the century, new scientific ideas were liberated from academically circumscribed contexts, and made accessible in Arthur Eddington's *The Nature of the Physical World* (1928) and James Jeans's *The Mysterious Universe* (1930). Popular series like the Home University Library of Modern Knowledge (from 1911) conveyed Einstein, Russell, Jeans, Eddington, Freud, Bergson, and Nietzsche to a new and educationally aspirational middle class. Even Russell abandoned his technical academic logic in 1910 to concentrate on his popular book *The Problems of Philosophy* (1913), which Gilbert Murray, its editor, would refer to wryly as "a message to the shop-assistants about philosophy."[2] The later part of the century sees a similar intermingling in the rise of a new sub-genre, a post "two-cultures" novel, initiating explicit dialogues between science and the arts and humanities, with a vaunted overlap between the uncertainties of the New Physics and those of the postmodern condition, or with an affinity between the new biological sciences and the current revival of evolutionism in the psychological sciences. Examples here include almost all of the novels of Ian McEwan and A. S. Byatt, and a range of novels from Iris Murdoch's *A Fairly Honourable Defeat* (1970) and Doris Lessing's *Memoirs of a Survivor* (1974) to Martin Amis's *Time's Arrow* (1991) and Kazuo Ishiguro's *Never Let Me Go* (2005).

But the greater the novelistic inclination to roam indiscriminately, and the greater the intermingling of discourses, the more intense is the novel form's pressure to distill encyclopedic assemblages into the integrity and mastery of an aesthetic design. The argument of this section – and indeed of this chapter – will be that in rising to the challenge of a vigorous and revolutionary contest of specialized faculties and discourses in the university, beginning *circa* 1900, novelists feel the pressure to formally discipline their own procedures and, in this process, they come to reflect on the capacities for knowledge of their own medium. The novel is thereby able more effectively to establish its own disciplinary authority. Through engagement with discourses outside of art's own, the novel discovers and affirms its unique ways of knowing, and establishes its formal seriousness as a high as well as popular art form. This knowledge of a capacity for knowledge that is unavailable within the academy enables it to negotiate the labyrinthine discursive and disciplinary scene, and to establish the significance of its specific kind of narrative knowledge, offering a space between the rock of analytical and positivist epistemologies and the (soft) hard place of Nietzschean (and later postmodern) skepticism. The novel moves from regarding itself at the beginning of the twentieth century as merely an instrument of skepticism to asserting at the beginning of the twenty-first century a more substantial cognitive value that is its own, as well as a morally committed enquiry impossible within academic disciplinary regimes of pure and disinterested research.

Woolf's contrast between life's "luminous halo" – its "semi-transparent envelope" – and art's artificial "gig lamps, symmetrically arranged"; Murdoch's contrast between fiction's "crystalline" discourse and journalism; the novelist as *bricoleur* and as architect – the tension between formal design and contingent detail lies at the heart of debates around the form and function of the novel in the modern period.[3] "Beautiful and bright it should be on the surface," writes Woolf, "but beneath the fabric must be clamped together with bolts of iron."[4] Woolf, recognizing that scholars are more likely than practitioners of the art to ignore this necessary fulcrum, warns the positivist critic who prefers source-hunting to aesthetic appreciation not to forget the formal integrity of the whole, that "a writer's country is a territory within his own brain; and we run the risk of disenchantment if we try to turn such phantom cities into tangible brick and mortar."[5] Meanwhile, Joyce's now famous remark that "I've put in so many enigmas and puzzles that it will keep the professors busy for centuries arguing over what I meant" suggests, in its mildly defensive *hauteur*, his need to dwell on the unique terms of his art.[6]

The novel, the new sciences, and philosophy

But the preoccupation with matter and form, vision and design, virtuality and solidity, also reflects a more pervasive cultural preoccupation with, on the one hand, an often reductionist and medicalized materialism emerging from the new biological sciences (microbiology, bio-medicine, evolutionary theory, neurology, physiology and psychiatry, and the as yet not entirely internally discriminated disciplines of the physiological psychological sciences, psycho-analysis, and anthropology), and on the other, a new, spiritualized virtuality associated with the turn to logic (after Frege's criticism of nineteenth-century empiricism as a species of psychology) and the revolutionary discoveries in mathematical physics (the new sciences of the quantum, the wave theory of light, the rediscovery of the atom, and Einstein's two theories of relativity). A new world is born, where matter is nothing more than space and empty points of light, and where mind might either exist as an alternative patterning of the same elemental forces and / or as an extension of the animal body. In William James's theory of neutral monism, taken up briefly by Russell, "matter is not so material and mind not so mental as is greatly supposed"; even the hardest physical sciences are "making matter less material ... Their world consists of events from which matter is derived by logical construction."[7] Joseph Conrad writes to Edward Garnett on September 29, 1898 in remarkably similar terms of how we "are all composed of the same matter, all matter being that thing of inconceivable tenuity through which the various waves ... are propagated, thus giving birth to our sensations – then emotions – then thought."[8]

But the new sciences raised questions about the fundamental nature of matter and mind that cannot be contained within the frame of science. Complex philosophical world views arose in response to the new discoveries: from the post-Darwinist genealogy of Nietzsche and the psychologies of Ribot, Freud, Janet, and James, and the biologized dualism of Bergson's alternative evolutionism, to the austere "views from nowhere" of the logico-linguistic and analytic revolutions in philosophy out of Cambridge and Vienna. It began to be inappropriate to talk about reality "existing" at macro- or micro-levels, for the smallest particles of matter seemed to be "actual," to act, in that they express mathematical and natural laws, yet can not be described as *res*, as things, "real" in any normal substantive sense. This produced the need for a radical revision of epistemology that could address how to relate the symbols of mathematical abstraction to the material data of empirical observation. Science could no longer be theorized in terms of the old empiricism's inductions from direct observation and controlled testing. Novelists were as eager as philosophers to take up the epistemological challenge or to explore its human effects.

Many of the new sciences – quantum and atomic physics, cosmology, Darwinian evolution, neurology, the new experimental psychologies of Wundt, William James, Ribot, and Janet – are incomplete *as* science according to the ever more stringent criteria for scientific knowledge advanced by analytic philosophy and logical positivist methodology. The novel (and popular scientists such as Eddington and Jeans) therefore seized the opportunity to keep open crucial metaphysical and imaginative questions that philosophy was debarred from addressing within the terms of its new disciplinary procedures. Russell, Moore, Carnap, Wittgenstein, and Popper increasingly saw their role as that of establishing a new unity of the sciences through the construction of a strict method, restricting the definition of knowledge to what can be said with methodological certainty. Whitehead in 1926 argued that "if science is not to degenerate into a medley of ad hoc hypotheses, it must become philosophical and must enter upon a thorough criticism of its foundations."[9] Logical positivists built on Wittgenstein's *Tractatus* (1922), sternly repudiating even Russell's logical empiricism as unsubstantiated metaphysics. In this austere systematization of knowledge, meaning pertains only to those propositions which can be empirically verified or falsified: metaphysics, art, and values are not even candidates for knowledge; according to Carnap, they are simply the expression of those infantile parts of ourselves which still need to believe in "stories."[10]

This philosophical clampdown responded both to the pluralization of disciplines and the specter of pseudoscience that might kindle in the glow of ontological challenges stoking the fires of post-Nietzschean relativism and nihilism. After 1873, the date of publication of the ninth edition of the *Encyclopaedia Britannica*, the Enlightenment project of unifying all knowledge under the umbrella of a scientific rationalism committed to the material and moral improvement of human life seems to reach a crisis point, not simply a disciplinary crisis but one concerning what and how human beings can know and the relation of values to that knowledge (or lack of it). This became therefore a time of *Principias*: of disciplinary returns to fundamentals in the staking out, by each field, of a more robust or substantial turf. James's *Principles of Psychology* (1890), Moore's *Principia Ethica* (1903), Russell and Whitehead's *Principia Mathematica* (1910), Wittgenstein's *Tractatus*, and Moore's pupil I. A. Richards's *Principles of Literary Criticism* (1924) are cases in point. Thomas Kuhn in *The Structure of Scientific Revolutions* (1962) explains how, during periods of disciplinary transition and turmoil, when older systems are breaking down, and newer ones not yet sufficiently validated, an intervening transitional phase ensues. This phase is marked by the agonistic play of different language games and a sense of the growing incommensurability of knowledge systems, to be resolved finally through passionate belief in, rather than scientific proof of, a newly emerged paradigm and its *Weltanschauung*. Whereas an Aristotelian philosopher staring at a stone swinging on a rope will see natural motion constrained by a final cause, a modern scientist will see a pendulum. Each sees a different object, and experiences a different world. But once the philosopher sees the pendulum there is no simple return to the teleological view of the stone.

The proliferation of disciplines, theories, and methodologies *circa* 1900 produced an intense preoccupation with the question of knowledge and reality: what and how do we know and what is it that we know? It also produced a deepening skepticism about the authority and capacity of the academy, with its specialized rationality, to imagine the full implications of living in a world built upon new epistemological assumptions, or to know how to recover the experience of an entirely different kind of world.

But novels have the capacity to build worlds that enable their readers to experience the reality of a scholastic or an enchanted or a forgotten sphere of life, or one whose premises may be very different from their own. Or novels can subject the premises of their own world to a *reductio ad absurdum* that opens them to view for the first time: this is what the exaggeratedly mechanistic parodies of scientific materialism achieve in the novels of Wyndham Lewis, Huxley's *Brave New World* (1931), Beckett's *Watt* (1953), Golding's *The Inheritors* (1955), Spark's *The Driver's Seat* (1970).

If we return to Woolf, it is evident just how much her conception of what might be specifically *modern* in the twentieth-century novel was attached to this new scientific and philosophical outlook. Her famous "Modern Fiction" essay, which rejects the materialism of the Edwardians, rehearses the question of the relationships among life's "luminous halo" (8), and innumerable atoms that constitute the sense data of ordinary experience, and some impersonal and abstract structure that might provide for life's formal coherence (8). In Woolf's fiction the object world is always poised between virtuality and materiality, between "this vastness and this tininess" (*Lighthouse*, 119): in "The Narrow Bridge of Art" she writes of the necessity for the writer to bring the "power of a strict and logical imagination . . . to bear on the data of experience," to raise the novel to an art form that is far more than simply telling a story or providing a consolatory plot.[11] In "Life and the Novelist," influenced by Roger Fry's understanding of post-Impressionism as the reconciliation of vision with design, she condemns "talk-writing," the kind of Impressionism associated with the solipsism of Walter Pater and the sensationalist philosophy of Ernst Mach: "soft and shapeless with words . . . upon real lips" and giving no relief from the "swarm and confusion of life."[12] She insists that the novel must move beyond Impressionism, find a form "like a Chinese coat able to stand by itself" (44).

So if twentieth-century novelists seem often to be Beckettian scavengers in the storehouses and dustbins of academic disciplines and other discourses, they have also felt acutely, as T. S. Eliot suggests, the need for a new "language . . . which is struggling to digest and express new objects, new groups of objects, new feelings, new aspects": a discipline of form that would make the novel itself into a new formal discipline.[13] And if the term *discipline* ordinarily conjures both a more neutral reference to the transparent regulation of knowledge that confers professional legitimation, as well as a more loaded association of a darker undertow of defensive policing, that is also true with respect to the novel and its relations with other discourses.

The Platonic dialogues were the first to advance an argument for the defense of philosophy as the rational foundational discipline of the Academy; because the sciences now occupy that foundational position, modern aesthetic discourses have often found themselves, under both rationalistic and modern scientific regimes of knowledge, relegated to the academic margins or forced to seek ratification in the terms of some other discourse (sociology, history, psychoanalysis). The modern novelist's preoccupation with form, as well as constituting a response to the intellectual revolutions of the modern world, is also prompted by a concern to establish the novel as a serious literary mode at a moment when cognate disciplines such as literary criticism, psychology, anthropology, and linguistics were making new claims for enhanced professional status in an academy dominated by positivist and rationalist models of knowledge. The literary critic Q. D. Leavis in *Fiction and the Reading Public* (1939) invented the term and defined the condition of "middle brow" in such a fashion that it might be applied to almost all non-experimental or realist fiction (especially the so-called "women's novel" by writers such as Elizabeth Taylor, Rosamond Lehmann, Sylvia Townsend Warner), hence as a way of distancing "the women's novel" from academic critical discourse. Although desirous not to be shut in to the academy, Woolf's serious and high-minded novelist narrator in *A Room of One's Own* (1928) is certainly not comfortable in being shut out altogether: in a world of rapid disciplinary change, where the authority to pronounce on knowledge claims seems up for grabs, only the novelistic practice of a newly self-conscious disciplined indisciplinarity might be the means to resolve this dilemma, and to remain both in and out.

"What can be known?," Marlow's final words in *Lord Jim*, and "What does it all mean, then, what can it all mean?," Lily Briscoe's opening question in the final section of Woolf's *To the Lighthouse*, are emblematic *leitmotifs* of modern fiction. Walter Benjamin suggests that the novel form, unlike the story, can never answer those questions for itself, for the novel can do no more than passively reflect, without offering cure or solace, the loss of customary wisdom and the disciplinary pluralization and fragmentation of knowledge in the modern world: "To write a novel means to carry the incommensurable to extremes in the representation of human life."[14] But Woolf's very modern preoccupation with form and with transcending the mere passivity of reflection (a central preoccupation for novelists from Conrad to Doris Lessing to Salman Rushdie), like Lawrence's somewhat grandiose claims for the unique specificity of the novel, seem not so much statements of a passive reflectionism, as the pretensions of a nascent or burgeoning *discipline*, one that might answer to Arnold's late nineteenth-century call for a renewed humanistic "totality," an aesthetic defense against the fragmented and contested methodologies and epistemologies of modern cultures of expertise. Indeed, I. A. Richards's *Principles of Literary Criticism*, appearing in the same year as Lawrence's essay, claimed that poetry might save a sick civilization and do for the modern mind what medicine does for the body; T. S. Eliot's *The Sacred Wood* (1920) promised a new poetic that would heal the dissociated sensibilities of the post-Cartesian era through the inclusivity of the kind of "wit" that is present when the poet can "feel his thought as immediately as the odour of a rose."[15]

The sense that the novel too might not only find a form to accommodate the mess, but might also, in establishing its own capacity to offer a different kind of knowledge, present possible ways out of it, produced a disciplinary "inward turn" that shapes fiction and engages writers as diverse as James, Conrad, Woolf, and Beckett, as well as the later formal and linguistic experimentation of "postmodernists" such as John Fowles, Christine Brooke-Rose, B. S. Johnson, Peter Ackroyd, and Martin Amis. This disciplinary "inward turn" stimulates some of the most brilliant and definitive criticism to be written on the genre: James's prefaces, Forster's *Aspects of the Novel* (1927), Woolf's essays, Rebecca West's "The Strange Necessity" (1926), and the criticism of Ford Madox Ford, Percy Lubbock, Katherine Mansfield, and others.

The novel as an instrument of modern skepticism

What kind of knowledge is given in or learned through a novel? Conrad set out to discover this in *Heart of Darkness* (1902), by way of contrast, embedding an oral tale, a story, the customary mode of knowledge in a pre-scientific era, within its frame. Marlow's story is set up as a kind of talking cure, both a story to be shared for the purposes of camaraderie and solidarity, and a problem to be solved Enlightenment-style: an investigation, requiring an official report, to establish the facts of an affair that lie deep under the surface. In the end both kinds of narrative – the old and the new – are brought into a mutually subversive play of uncertainty. The only salvageable interpretation seems to be that stories are useful as they cover up the things that might be too threatening to know, and that novels, though instruments of modern skeptical knowledge, seem to uncover nothing certain, and do not even offer the solace of the shared tale. What is left (echoing in reverse Woolf's "talk-fiction" observation) is only a "faint uneasiness inspired by this narrative that seemed to shape itself without human lips in the heavy night-air of the river."[16] The total collapse exemplified by Kurtz's report – with its directive to "'exterminate all the brutes'" – is, curiously, a sentiment disturbingly expressed from time to time in the diaries of Bronislaw Malinowski. Malinowski aspired to be the Conrad of anthropology and seems to have developed his fieldwork theory of the participant-observer after reading Conrad's novella and the radical empiricism of William James. Both provided him new epistemological models for the idea of anthropological knowledge as an experiential immersion in a field or culture. Revolutionizing the practices of the discipline when it was published in 1922, Malinowski's *The Argonauts of the Western Pacific* also provided for the development of modern ethnomethodologies that would inform Mass-Observation in the 1930s, and influence the fiction of George Orwell, Aldous Huxley, and William Golding, as well as stimulate the idea of the regional novel from the 1940s on as a kind of auto-ethno-methodology.

What Conrad discovers in his novel, though, are the limitations (as well as strengths) of the observational methods of the participant observer. What is highlighted by the text is the difficulty of getting under and inside the affair, even on an experiential level, largely because of the defenses put up by the human mind in its propensity for self-deception. This defensive model of the mind already at the heart of Nietzsche's writing becomes Nietzsche's major legacy to Freud, who noted, deftly reserving a scientific status for psychoanalysis that he denies to philosophy, that "Nietzsche is a philosopher whose guesses and intuitions agree in the most astonishing way with the findings of psychoanalysis."[17] In exposing the end of the dream of the Enlightenment model of a unified knowledge guiding moral and spiritual progress, and in beginning to explore the possibilities of immersive consciousness, *Heart of Darkness* stands as the entry point into the possibility of the self-knowingness of modern fiction.

When Freud observed in *Civilisation and Its Discontents* (1930) that "it is precisely those communities that occupy contiguous territories and are otherwise closely related to each other that indulge in feuding and mutual mockery,"[18] he alighted astutely on the anxieties of influence running through the disciplines of modern fiction, anthropology, Nietzschean genealogy, and psychoanalysis. For each had discovered for itself that the mind screens the world and the self from itself, and that the human mind is not so much an efficient and transparent scientific instrument for uncovering facts, but a complex organ of an embodied creature that has evolved over eons for survival in a world of dangers, threats, and territorialism. In *Beyond the Pleasure Principle* (1920), Freud elaborates the essentially defensive and inhibitory nature of the mind. The mind, he explains:

> this little fragment of living substance [,] is suspended in the middle of the external world charged with the most powerful energies; and it would be killed by the stimulation emanating from these if it were not provided with a protective shield against stimuli ... in consequence, the energies of the external world are able to pass into the next underlying layers, which have remained living, with only a fragment of their original intensity.[19]

In *Heart of Darkness* Conrad confronts Nietzsche's belief that art is the lie – the conscious deception – that allows us to face the abyss, by encapsulating Marlow's untruthful "redemption" of Kurtz in a framed "story" that allows the novel as a whole to stand outside of the self-deception of the narrator. But it is a cold and bleak place to stand: another promontory over the abyss, the endless regress of modern skepticism.

The anarchist plot in *The Secret Agent* (1907) pivots on the presentation of scientific knowledge as "the sacrosanct fetish" of the bourgeoisie: in this enervated and dissolving culture, where "things don't stand too much looking into,"[20] scientific materialism is hegemonically substituted as a quick fix, a means of evading the care of the soul, entirely unable to provide life with purpose, value, or meaning. Stevie's endless circles are the emblem of a world neurasthenically and entropically winding down into a stultifying lassitude: the rusting sun, the "fat pig" Verloc, the cheap and crumbling façades, the humans indistinguishable from animals or automata, the primal ooze that seeps into the city whose inhabitants, homeless tenants, scuttle from one cheap and grimy location to another. Conrad's novel, with consummate economy, spins a compelling web of interdiscursive and interdisciplinary resonances, threading together chemistry, the second law of thermodynamics, humanity considered as a faltering Helmholzian combustion engine, the bio-medicalization of degeneracy, political economy, and dialectical materialism. For Conrad, as for Nietzsche, the academic disciplining of knowledge produces only a fetishization of scientific rationality. Conrad's "Professor," a sinister pest, remains, elusively haunting the streets, nursing his almost perfected detonator: a direct allusion perhaps to Nietzsche who had also abandoned his professorship in order to write philosophy as dynamite, convinced that "no genuinely radical living for truth is possible in a university."[21]

Lawrence read Nietzsche in 1908 and also renounced philosophy after a disastrous relationship with Russell (whose analytic knowledge is savaged in the short story "The Blind Man"). *The Rainbow* (1915) describes Ursula's acute feelings of estrangement as she looks down at a living creature under the microscope, wondrously observing it move under the slide and thinking, "if it was a conjunction of forces, physical and chemical, what held these forces unified, and for what purpose were they unified?"[22] The terms closely echo Russell's scientific outlook, his insistence that "there is no reason to suppose that living matter is subject to any other law than those to which inanimate matter is subject . . . theoretically explicable in terms of physics and chemistry."[23] But Ursula's subsequent "consummation" conveys Lawrence's conviction of life as an intuited vitality destroyed through the mechanistic world view of modern science and his sympathy with Nietzsche's sense that "an essentially mechanical world would be an essentially 'meaningless' world."[24]

Conrad and Lawrence are novelists who use the novel as a skeptical instrument against life-denying skeptical rationality. Both express the possibility that the novel might somehow provide its own revaluation of values and arrive at a fully modern equivalent of the kind of shared and customary knowledge identified by Benjamin with the heroic age of storytelling. But how can the novel provide an antidote or alternative to, as well as an anatomy of, the analytic and scientific logics of modernity? This has always been one of its preoccupations. Eighteenth-century fiction hones itself against the quasi-disciplinary knowledge "systems" that are the diverse offspring of the brilliant marriage of Cartesian rationalism and Baconian empiricism that gives rise to modern science. Fielding famously declares in *Tom Jones* (1749) that he is writing a history and not a system, though one "system," Adam Smith's *Theory of the Moral Sentiments* (1759), is closely associated with the novel genre: the Sentimentalist systematization of affect as a political tool of resistance to the competitive ethos of the liberal state. The novel's capacity to discipline unruly affect and encourage "sympathy" might contribute to the provision of an adequate substitute for the moral practices of the religious life in a secularized society. Lawrence gives it a primitivist spin in "The Novel and Feelings" (1923), where the novel becomes the prime channel for reconnecting with the "aboriginal jungle of us" without which "we shall degenerate."[25]

More than modern: rethinking the novel's knowledge

But there are other resources for conceiving, in more radical terms, the role of affect in human life and the importance of the novel in relation to it. In *The Expression of the Emotions in Humans and Animals* (1872), Darwin explored the idea that the emotions are fundamentally adaptive and basically evaluative in orienting the organism toward knowledge of its environment. The full implications of this understanding have not gained disciplinary recognition until recently, in the development of the cognitive neurosciences. Though William James's philosophy draws on Darwin's insights into the emotions, his thinking was resisted by British philosophers who, from Moore's *Principia* onward, were anxious to distance themselves from biology, believing it to be an immature science contaminated with evolutionism. James first explored how emotion, the continuous flow of visceral, sensorimotor, and affective response, anchors us, attunes and minutely adjusts our relation to the world, making us aware, more than anything, of the way in which mental life and flourishing are "knit up with the body."[26] Present-day neuroscientists such as Antonio Damasio have now provided clinical evidence of how the affective responses of the body are "integral to the processes of reasoning and decision-making," and how consciousness emerges as a "feeling of a feeling."[27] Phenomenological psychiatry is developing this work to show how our tacit sense of being in the world is dependent upon a continuous flow of existential feeling through which our ontological sense of world and self is constituted. The role of feelings is shown to be even more fundamental than in the *Bildung* of the eighteenth century.

The novel's thinking has always been anti-Cartesian and anti-positivist: its hypotheses are tested not through methodologically regulated arguments or scientific proofs, but through the mimetic construction and perceptual negotiation of imaginative worlds. Its thinking is anti-Cartesian too in its resistance to the scientifically and philosophically triumphalist conceptualization of cognition as the representation, through internal symbols, by a pre-wired brain, of an external world that is also pre-given and inertly available for internal manipulation. The inward turn of modern fiction might be understood as not simply an exploration of the dark places of Freudian psychoanalysis, but as an attempt to understand and represent mind in a fully enactive, embodied, extended way, where rationality is emotional and evaluative as well as logical and calculative. Here, as Woolf knows in "Modern Fiction," mind is not just an instrument for representing the world, but is in the world, constituted by and constitutive of it. Though William James's model of the mind does not admit an unconscious and is optimistically open to experience, especially compared with the essentially defensive model of the Freudian psyche, both James and Freud offer a dynamic, enactive, transformative model that reveals the complex way in which feelings shape both knowledge of the world and the reality of the world (though for Freud, the scientist, there is a reality independent of our grasp of it; for James, the pragmatist, we have far more opportunity, cognitively, to build the world we inhabit).

Not surprisingly, modern novelists have drawn freely on both these enactive and defensive models of mind, often in the same text, as in Woolf's *Mrs. Dalloway* (1925) or Joyce's *Ulysses* (1922), where characters negotiate their way through busy city streets by exemplifying a variety of mental styles. Bloom, for example, is a brilliant study of a mind coping with the frantic mental bombardment of the metropolis by defensively withdrawing from attentive focus and affective evaluation, simply allowing the sights and smells and sounds of the city to wash over him in a steady and endless stream of receptivity and distraction whose syntactical mode, largely paratactic, enacts his refusal or inability to choose or prioritize or admit what is emotionally important to him. Additive, associative, and neutral in effect, his mental style mingles almost indistinguishably with the banalities of popular commercialized culture.

But brilliant as it is, *Ulysses'* virtuosity sometimes overshadows the quieter achievements of Joyce's earlier work. Another masterful representation of consciousness negotiating its environment, constantly readjusting itself, engaging feeling and sensation, memory and desire, "The Dead" in Joyce's *Dubliners* (1914) is also, like *Ulysses*, a meditation on hospitality, exclusion, *heimlichkeit*, and alienation that draws the reader into the complex flow of existential feelings that anchor human beings to their worlds. Joyce presents his protagonist Gabriel, a reluctant bystander at the Misses Morkan's annual feast, through a technique of continuous kinaesthetic foregrounding, positioning him bodily in space, as he constantly looks down or up or away from the gathering. Projecting a posture of cool indifference, Gabriel nevertheless is inflamed with narcissistic investment. As his turbulent and contradictory feelings mount, so the grammar of his figural narration shifts increasingly into the subjunctive mode. He reaches out to the coolness of a window as if he might magically recover his own coolness through its touch. He looks through its dark pane at the snowy spaces of elsewhere until a proleptic mode of consciousness takes over, and an internal drama of his affective life is raised to heroic proportions. To the very end of the story, he is complexly positioned both inside and outside of the gathering, belonging and not belonging.

Modern fiction demonstrates compellingly what happens if the mind withdraws from emotional engagement with the world, as in the method of Cartesian doubt, where everything that is ordinarily taken for granted is put in question and subjected to relentless distrust. Far from producing an ideal rationality, such hyper-awareness leads to a radical alienation that is not far from madness. The body comes to be experienced as an alien thing; the world appears dead, flat, screened off, offering no hierarchy of salience, no pressures toward selective evaluation. Fredric Jameson's "Postmodernism and the Cultural Logic of Late Capitalism" (1984) famously argues that the postmodern condition is characterized by just such a waning of affect, a disruption of temporality marked by the feeling of living in a hyper-real and perpetual present.

Although hyper-reality emerges as the dominant mark of postmodernism, it might be more satisfactorily understood as the failure of the enactive mind, a hyper-reflexivity and inward turning that is an effect of the alienated experience of modernity, and one of the major concerns of novelists from Woolf, Wyndham Lewis, and Rex Warner to William Sansom, Spark, Golding, and J. G. Ballard. Beckett's Cartesian parodies, which draw on the Bergsonian theory of the comic, of the human reduced to automaton, also reveal the disabling *akrasia* that follows from the fundamental disconnection encapsulated in "postmodernism and the logic of late capitalism." Muriel Spark's

The Driver's Seat (1970) represents persons as canisters of exploding laughing gas, combustion engines in a radically dehumanized world dominated by a frame of Cartesian knowledge and scientific materialism that has disastrously divorced body from mind. It is arguable that the divorce continues in postmodernism's hyper-reflexivity, in flight from propositional truth and caught up in the endless language games of linguistic self-referentiality, as in B. S. Johnson's *House Mother Normal* (1971), Ballard's *Crash* (1973), or Beckett's *The Unnamable* (1959): "that's what I feel, an outside and an inside and me in the middle, perhaps that's what I am the thing that divides the world in two . . . I'm neither one side nor the other . . . I'm the tympanum, on one hand the mind, on the other the world, I don't belong to either."[28]

The contrasting model of the enactive mind is explicitly engaged in Ian McEwan's recent novels. Yet there is something oddly redundant about the self-conscious encounter with neuroscience in McEwan's rewriting of Joyce, James, and especially Woolf, whose *Mrs. Dalloway* is an overt intertext for *Saturday* (2005). Woolf had already, eighty years previously, represented mind in ways uncannily close to the new scientific accounts, but without feeling the need for footnotes. McEwan's novel sometimes reads like popular science and reflects the more markedly pedagogic tone of the post-1970s' "two cultures novel." This is never Woolf's way: "When philosophy is not consumed in a novel," Woolf writes in an essay about George Meredith, "it is safe to say that there is something wrong with the philosophy or with the novel or both" (*Collected Essays*, vol. II, 280). But a global humanity now thinks itself and thinks about its thinking through the form of the novel. Why? Woolf writes in another context: "Philosophic words, if one has not been educated at a university, are apt to play one false. What is meant by 'reality'? It would seem to be something very erratic, very undependable – now to be found in a dusty road, now in a scrap of newspaper in the street, now a daffodil in the sun."[29] For the novel practices philosophy as an extension of the ordinary mind engaging the world: the fear of death is a pair of shoes left on a shoreline; an intimation of betrayal, a schoolgirl hat tilted at an irregular angle; a compassionate struggle for self-overcoming, the praise of a pair of boots.

Woolf's *oeuvre* has been important to the development of the present-day novel, for, situated at the heart of the most gifted and academically unattached intellectual culture of the twentieth century, she embarks on a quest, which begins with her first novel – *The Voyage Out* (1918), with its echo of Moore's repudiation of Darwinian ethical naturalism – and reaches its highest achievement in the metaphysical, emotional, aesthetic, and formal quest of *To the Lighthouse* (1927), a novel that engages almost every major philosophical and scientific idea of Woolf's day. What Woolf seeks and finds is an equivalent in the aesthetic realm, in the form of the novel, of the logico-linguistic "backbone" of analytical philosophy: an aesthetically rigorous *affective* cognition, an artistic equivalent of science's logical empiricist robustness. If Conrad is the first modern novelist consciously to use the novel as a skeptical and epistemological instrument to question the limits of its own self-conception, Woolf is the writer who first recognizes the novel's full disciplinary uniqueness: its capacity to capture the "real" in an evolving dialogue with the thought of its age. In this sense it is still the one bright book of life, for, as William James suggests, "the whole feeling of reality, the whole sting and excitement of our ordinary life, depends on our sense that in it things are really being decided from one moment to another, and that it is not the dull rattling of a chain that was found innumerable ages ago" (453).

Notes

1. D. H. Lawrence, "Morality and the Novel" (1924), in D. H. Lawrence, *Selected Criticism*, ed. M. Herbert (Oxford University Press, 1998), p. 174.
2. Quoted in Victor Lowe, *Alfred North Whitehead: The Man and his Work.* vol. I, *1861–1910* (Baltimore, MD: Johns Hopkins University Press, 1985), p. 19.
3. Virginia Woolf, "Modern Fiction," in *The Crowded Dance of Modern Life: Selected Essays of Virginia Woolf*, ed. Rachel Bowlby, 2 vols. (Harmondsworth: Penguin, 1993), vol. II, p. 8; Iris Murdoch, "Against Dryness," in *Iris Murdoch: Existentialists and Mystics: Writings*, ed. Peter Conradi (Harmondsworth: Penguin, 1997), p. 291.
4. Virginia Woolf, *To the Lighthouse* (London: Hogarth Press, 1960), p. 264.
5. Virginia Woolf, *The Essays of Virginia Woolf*, 6 vols. Vol. I, ed. Andrew McNeillie (London: Hogarth Press, 1986), p. 35.
6. Richard Ellmann, *James Joyce* (Oxford University Press, 1982), p. 521.
7. Bertrand Russell, *My Philosophical Development* (London: Allen and Unwin, 1959), p. 151; Bertrand Russell, *The Analysis of Mind* (London: Routledge, 1989), p. 36.
8. Joseph Conrad, *Collected Letters*, 8 vols. Vol. II: *1898–1902*, ed. Frederick R. Karl (Cambridge University Press, 1986), pp. 94–95.
9. A. N. Whitehead, *Science and the Modern World* (Cambridge University Press, 1933), p. 21.
10. Rudolf Carnap, *Philosophy and Logical Syntax* (London: Kegan Paul, 1935), pp. 69–72.
11. Virginia Woolf, "The Narrow Bridge of Art," in Virginia Woolf, *Granite and Rainbow* (London: Hogarth Press, 1958), p. 23.
12. Woolf, *Essays*, vol. II, ed. Andrew McNeillie, p. 42.
13. T. S. Eliot, *The Sacred Wood* (London: Methuen, 1960), p. 150.
14. Walter Benjamin, *Illuminations* (New York: Schocken, 1969), p. 87.

15. T. S. Eliot, *Selected Essays* (London: Faber, 1951), p. 187.
16. Joseph Conrad, *Heart of Darkness* (Harmondsworth: Penguin, 1973), p. 39.
17. Henri Ellenberger, *The Discovery of the Unconscious* (New York: Basic Books, 1970), p. 277.
18. Sigmund Freud, *Civilisation and Its Discontents* (Harmondsworth: Penguin, 2002), p. 50.
19. Sigmund Freud, *On Metapsychology* (Harmondsworth: Penguin, 1999), p. 298.
20. Joseph Conrad, *The Secret Agent* (Oxford University Press, 1983), p. 177.
21. Quoted in Alistair MacIntyre, *Three Rival Versions of Moral Enquiry* (London: Duckworth, 1990), p. 35.
22. D. H. Lawrence, *The Rainbow* (Cambridge University Press, 1989), p. 491.
23. Bertrand Russell, *Human Knowledge: Its Scope and Limits* (New York: Simon and Schuster, 1948), p. 36.
24. Friedrich Nietzsche, *The Gay Science* (New York: Random House, 1991), p. 292.
25. D. H. Lawrence, *Phoenix: The Posthumous Papers of D. H. Lawrence*, ed. Edward D. McDonald (London: Heinemann, 1936), p. 756.
26. William James, The *Principles of Psychology*, 2 vols. (New York: Holt, 1950), vol. II, p. 467.
27. Antonio Damasio, *Descartes' Error: Emotion, Reason and the Human Brain* (New York: HarperCollins, 2000), p. xiii.
28. Samuel Beckett, *Molloy, Malone Dies, The Unnamable* (London: Calder, 1959), p. 386.
29. Virginia Woolf, *A Room of One's Own* (Harmondsworth: Penguin, 2002), p. 109.

42

The novel and thirty years of war

MARINA MACKAY

"It's rather sad," she said one day, "to belong, as we do, to a lost generation. I'm sure in history the two wars will count as one war and that we shall be squashed out of it altogether."

Nancy Mitford, *The Pursuit of Love* (1945)[1]

Anthony Powell's twelve-novel sequence *A Dance to the Music of Time* (1951–1975) opens at an elite public school in 1921, and goes on to recount fifty years in the lives of the narrator Nick Jenkins's postwar generation. Having reached 1937 at the end of the fifth novel, *Casanova's Chinese Restaurant* (1960), the reader opens *The Kindly Ones* (1962), expecting to follow Nick, now in his thirties, into the Second World War. Yet the leisurely opening of this sixth installment is not what Powell's hitherto chronological narration has led us to anticipate. It is a beautiful but unsettled summer's morning in Nick's childhood: the housemaid is having a breakdown, the cook is in mortal fear of suffragettes burning the place down, and the Jenkinses have just learned that shiftless Uncle Giles is about to gatecrash their luncheon party. But when Uncle Giles eventually arrives he brings news that helps to explain why Powell has interrupted his sequential narrative with this extended flashback to events of decades earlier: "They've just assassinated an Austrian archduke down in Bosnia."[2] And then Powell recalls us to the late 1930s: whereas in 1914 "war had come for most people utterly without warning – like being pushed suddenly on a winter's day into a swirling whirlpool of ice-cold water by an acquaintance, unpredictable per-haps but not actively homicidal – war was now materializing in slow motion" (86–87). What motivates Powell's long flashback is an insight central to many retrospective treatments of the Second World War: that knowing this war means knowing it in relation to the last.

Powell was in distinguished company when he suggested that the world wars, with their striking proximity to one another, were better understood together than apart. Early in *The Gathering Storm* (1948), the first volume of his history of the Second World War, Winston Churchill wrote that his histories of 1914–1918 and 1939–1945 would collectively offer "an account of another Thirty Years War," and, indeed, Churchill might have been speaking for Powell and many other twentieth-century commentators on the world wars in fiction when he described his narrative mode as that of "Defoe's *Memoirs of a Cavalier* . . . in which the author hangs the chronicle and discussion of great military and political events upon the thread of the personal experiences of an individual."[3] Churchill's debt to Defoe rightly assumes the interconnectedness of historiography and the novel form, and the interplay of landmark public events and their subjectively experienced realities is seldom more visible than in the fiction of political crisis.

Miniatures: stories of adventure and loss

Before turning to the canonical monuments of modern war fiction – war-haunted modernisms of the early twentieth century; panoramic mid-century novel sequences such as Powell's, with their meditations on the origins and outcomes of world war; the revisionist fictions produced by the millennial culture of commemoration – it may be worth looking briefly at those earlier war fictions that wear their historical ambitions more lightly, miniaturizing world war into a self-contained fantasy of heroic achievement or a poignant snapshot of civilian mourning.

John Buchan's Great War novels, for example, refine global conflict into a winnable fight between the swashbuckling Richard Hannay and a Hunnish mastermind or two. Set in the summer of 1914, *The Thirty-Nine Steps* (1915) turns on a German plot to steal Britain's war plans: "[I]t was no question of preventing a war," Hannay explains, "That was coming, as sure as Christmas," and when war is declared at the end of the novel the hero receives a captain's commission ("But I had done my best service, I think, before I put on khaki").[4] In *Greenmantle* (1916) Hannay thwarts a German plan to rally the Muslim world against the British by fomenting jihad through a fake prophet, while *Mr. Standfast* (1919) sees Hannay, now Brigadier-General, reassigned from the front line to hunt down a German master-spy. The last of the three war novels, *Mr. Standfast* is the most tellingly ambivalent because what begins as a denunciation of British pacifists ("the half-baked, the people whom this war hasn't touched or has touched in the wrong way, the people who split hairs all day and are engrossed in what you and I would call selfish little fads") becomes an altogether different novel once Hannay comes face to face with the villain Graf von Schwabing, "the most dangerous man in all the world."[5] At once a militarist and a coward, von Schwabing is now made representative of the vested aristocratic and financial interests responsible for the very outbreak of the war itself, and when captured he is brought to the front lines of a war Britain is still losing in order to be killed unwittingly by his own side. In these closing scenes of the novel the war is no longer the honorably manly adventure of Buchan's early chapters, the measure by which those hair-splitting pacifists were judged wanting, but something closer to the hateful bloodbath of trench poetry.

And no doubt because of the image of the Great War lastingly promulgated by the soldier poets of the First World War, Buchan's generally unreflective patriotism can make his engaging novels seem a little quaint; virtuous characters in the mid-war *Greenmantle* are much given to declarations along the dashing lines of Sandy Arbuthnot's "I am the servant of my country, and her enemies are mine."[6] Later writers would use the espionage form to foreground in more politically conflicted ways the uncertainties of wartime knowledge as when, for example, Somerset Maugham translated his Great War experiences into the psychologically penetrating stories collected as *Ashenden, Or the British Agent* (1928). In the next war the novel of intrigue would focus on domestic anxiety rather than foreign adventure: in Elizabeth Bowen's *The Heat of the Day* (1949), an Englishwoman comes to learn that her lover, a wounded Dunkirk hero, is using his work with British intelligence to pass national secrets to the Nazis, and in Graham Greene's *The Ministry of Fear* (1943) the melancholy anti-hero Arthur Rowe inadvertently becomes embroiled in a fantastical spy plot at what appears to be a homely charity fete. Given their shared concerns with national belonging and the murkiness and contingency of knowledge, the war novel and the spy novel are, so to speak, natural allies in (as Buchan put it in the dedication to *The Thirty-Nine Steps*) "days when the wildest fictions are so much less improbable than the facts."

Among the Great War stories by the older generation, more in keeping with the dominant cultural memory of the Great War as tragic failure may be those of Rudyard Kipling. Although perhaps no less patriotic in life than Buchan, Kipling's finest fictional treatments of the Great War are concerned not with its manly excitements but with its human costs. In the chilling "Mary Postgate" (1915) a war-bereaved lady companion takes rejuvenating revenge on a downed German airman who may or may not have killed a local child with his last bomb. In "The Gardener" (1925) a woman loses her nephew – perhaps her unacknowledged illegitimate son – to the war, blown up and buried "so neatly that none but an expert would have guessed that anything unpleasant had happened."[7]

Addressing as they do the depredations of war on civilian consciousness, Kipling's subtlest sketches recall not Buchan but modernist-affiliated writers like the much younger Katherine Mansfield, whose brother was killed by a hand grenade in France in 1915, the same year as Kipling lost his son at Loos. Mansfield's war stories, too, explore the moral ambiguities of mourning and the relationships between private grief and public commemoration. Witness, for example, how she and Kipling deploy the beautifully manicured war cemeteries in their stories of the after-war. In "The Gardener" we learn "how easy it was and how little it interfered with life's affairs to go and see one's grave," a powerfully restrained way of implying that although they cannot truly see it ("how little it interfered with life's affairs") survivors of the war have in an important sense *not* survived the war (315). Mansfield's "The Fly" (1923) opens with a comfortable account of such a visit to Flanders ("Couldn't be better if they were at home . . . all as neat as a garden"), but proceeds to describe a war-bereaved father drowning a fly in an inkwell.[8] "He's a plucky little devil," the patriarch thinks in the war-discredited language of the armchair general, all the while dousing the fly with ink: "Never say die" (347). Inevitably he splashes the fly once too often, unconsciously reprising his son's death in the Flanders mud, as if the very manner of his mourning were complicit with the forces that killed the soldier.

Transformations: modernist war fiction

Such apprehensions about the coercive force of civilian expectation are every-where in the modernist fiction of the Great War. The three women in the life of the shell-shocked officer Chris Baldry in Rebecca West's novella *The Return of the Soldier* (1918) are all very different – Chris's wife is a society beauty, his former girlfriend a shabby working-class housewife, and the novel's question-ably reliable narrator his tweedy spinster cousin – but they all collude to have the soldier "cured" and returned to virtually certain death at the Front because a safely amnesiac Chris "would not be quite a man."[9] Virginia Woolf's *Jacob's Room* (1922) also examines the soldier's role in relation to a whole range of patriarchal advantages and responsibilities. Doomed from the instant of his naming, Jacob Flanders is seen first as an indulged infant son; later snapshots of his homosocial adolescence at Cambridge and in London show him wonder-ing whether or not women actually have brains; in the novel's final vignette we watch his mother and best friend clear out his room after he is killed at war. In life and death Jacob is precisely what his culture has made him, a wholly representative figure of what a pacifist suffragette in the Great War veteran Henry Williamson's *How Dear is Life* (1954) calls the "confused rushing of the unprepared to meet the unimagined."[10]

The irreconcilability of prewar ideals with wartime and postwar realities likewise dominates Ford Madox Ford's *Parade's End* tetralogy (1924–1928), in which the consummate English country gentleman Christopher Tietjens goes to war and outlives everything he has known and valued. *"There will be no more parades,"* Tietjens realizes in the passage that gives the sequence its title: "For there won't. There won't, there damn well won't . . . No more Hope, no more Glory, no more parades for you and me any more. Nor for the country . . . nor for the world."[11] D. H. Lawrence's *Lady Chatterley's Lover* (1929) turns to the same traditional country-house milieu in the war's aftermath: the Chatterley estate has lost its men and its trees to the trenches and the heir is impotent in his wheelchair, and all because the unthinkingly patriotic wartime squire had "stood for England and Lloyd George as his forebears had stood for England and St. George: and he never knew there was a difference."[12] Another great working-class modernist, Lewis Grassic Gibbon addressed the Great War's obliteration of traditional ways of life from the point of view of those who worked rural estates rather than owned them in his masterpiece *Sunset Song* (1932). After the destruction of the village by a war that was never really its war, the novel reaches its haunting conclusion with a sermon from a radical minister who takes as his text not the scripture discredited by its jingoistic wartime abuses but Tacitus' famous speech on the annihilation of local cultures by imperialist wars: *They have made a desert and they call it peace.*[13]

In *Rites of Spring* the cultural historian Modris Eksteins argues that modernism's predilection for extremity and outrage both anticipated and abetted the approach of the Great War. His title alludes not only to the scandalous 1913 collaboration of Stravinsky, Nijinski, and Diaghilev, *Le Sacre du Printemps*, but also to the war that came soon after, a war that shared the ballet's shocking modernist dissonance, its death-driven embrace of the sacrificial.[14] It is instructive, however, that Eksteins's focus is on continental modernism: the major British modernists are typically against the war from the outset, and, as novels such as Ford's indicate, even those who voluntarily enlisted would produce devastating critiques of the war in later years. Postwar disillusionments only intensify the modernists' bitter alienation from the national culture. Woolf's *Mrs. Dalloway* (1925) describes the speedy recovery of English culture after the war, endorsing the refusal to recover of the shell-shocked soldier Septimus Smith, one of "these bothering War heroes" a society hostess dismisses in Ford's *Parade's End* (521). Septimus will kill himself rather than cultivate the "sense of proportion" that would allow him to consign the war to the past as his social masters have done ("The War was over," thinks Clarissa Dalloway, "thank Heaven – over").[15] Woolf's *To the Lighthouse* (1927) is primarily set on either side of the war, with the Ramsays' oldest son killed off in parenthesis mid-novel: "[A shell exploded. Twenty or thirty young men were blown up in France, among them Andrew Ramsay, whose death, mercifully, was instantaneous]."[16] The callousness of the gossipy commentary – the hazy "twenty or thirty," the casually brutal "blown up," and that trite "mercifully" – tells us that this is the voice of a community personally unaffected by the loss that Woolf records through its hopelessly inadequate words.

By the time Woolf wrote *The Years* (1937), the aftermath of the Great War and the approach of the next war were collapsing into one another. Accompanied by her niece Peggy, the elderly Eleanor Pargiter walks through London in the novel's "Present Day" section, passing the statue of "a woman in nurse's uniform holding out her hand":

> "The only fine thing that was said in the war," she said aloud, reading the words cut on the pedestal.
> "It didn't come to much," said Peggy sharply.[17]

Readers are expected to recognize the nurse as Edith Cavell, executed by the Germans during the Great War, and to know that the words on the pedestal constitute her celebrated declaration that "patriotism is not enough." That "it didn't come to much" is evidenced in the fatigued omission of the details, as if Cavell's credo were too wearily, meaninglessly familiar to be worth rehearsing in the blighted mid-1930s now that "[o]n every placard at every street corner was Death; or worse – tyranny; brutality; torture; the fall of civilization; the end of freedom" (368).

Woolf famously argues in her pacifist treatise *Three Guineas* (1938) for the formation of the "Outsiders' Society," whose members would resist war by striving "to maintain an attitude of complete indifference" toward it.[18] Such self-conscious detachment was already under massive pressure from current events in Europe. "For it is impossible any longer to take no side," the compilers of *Authors Take Sides on the Spanish War* had declared the previous year.[19] The editors of this pamphlet were largely left-wing poets such as W. H. Auden, Nancy Cunard, and Pablo Neruda, but fiction also took sides: the professional *provocateur* Wyndham Lewis produced *The Revenge for Love* (1937), a satirical treatment of those English fellow travelers drawn to Spain as a fashionable cause, while the communist Sylvia Townsend Warner's historical-political novel *After the Death of Don Juan* (1938) connects Don Juan's legendary feats of sexual exploitation to the economic exploitation of an increasingly resistant Spanish peasantry. Warner returns in her characteristically indirect way to similar questions of subordination and rebellion in *The Corner that Held Them*

(1948), which likewise uses material history to interrogate the material of legend, this time in an East Anglian convent between the emergence of the Black Death and the outbreak of the Peasants' Revolt.

The prose of the 1930s may most generally be characterized by its documentary aesthetic – and certainly the immaculate transparency attained by writers like George Orwell and Christopher Isherwood is an important stylistic accomplishment in its own right – but the novels of such writers as Lewis and Townsend Warner are important reminders of the persistence of alternatively modernist inspirations through the era of the Spanish Civil War and beyond. The Second World War also would see the publication of a number of important late modernist novels, of which the most widely read is likely Woolf's final work, *Between the Acts* (1941). The novel is set three months before the outbreak of war, in the grounds of a country house where a pageant of English literary history is being staged, and, in marked contrast to the sense of alienation marking Woolf's earlier treatments of the national culture, here is an England newly dear because newly endangered by the planes overhead ("And what's the channel ... if they mean to invade us?").[20] The unnamed village in which the novel takes place stands for England itself – characters' names go back to the Domesday Book, to the last invasion of "England" a millennium earlier – though the novel's universalizing impulses are unmistakable. A shower of rain arrives in the final "present day" scene of the pageant, and is no longer simply rain but "all the people in the world weeping ... all people's tears, weeping for all people" (122).

National allegory such as Woolf deploys is one of the dominant modes of anti-realism in Second World War writing, but, rather surprisingly, it produces some of the war's most politically ambiguous fiction. Rex Warner's stunning *The Aerodrome* (1941) describes the steady takeover and occupation of an English village by the airbase on its outskirts, and the encroaching evil of the airbase seems to stand at once for continental-style fascism and, seditiously enough, for the British government in this time of total war, after the Emergency Powers (Defence) Act of 1940 put citizens and their property at the disposal of the state. Storm Jameson's *The Fort* (1941) is set in the spring of 1940, as France fell to the Germans, in a cellar in northern France, and its characters are a mixed group of English, French, and German soldiers, some of them young men and others veterans of the last war. Only in the novel's final line when the Englishman Major Ward addresses a younger compatriot as "Jamie," naming a friend killed in the last war, do we realize that all these characters are ghosts of one or other of the two wars fought on the very same ground within the same quarter-century. Elizabeth Bowen would use the ghost story to similar ends in

"The Demon Lover" (1945), in which a dead soldier from the First World War turns up in blitzed London to reclaim his fiancée of twenty-five years earlier, as if the glorious dead of one war were now the undead of another.

That sense in which the last war remained unfinished business when the next one came around drives Somerset Maugham's *The Razor's Edge* (1944). Though published during the Second World War, which breaks out in the novel's final chapter, the novel seems primarily concerned with the after-effects of the Great War. *The Razor's Edge* tells of the journey through Eastern and Western mystical traditions of a traumatized Great War veteran trying to make sense of the problem of evil, and this particular spiritual inquiry is the most characteristically *Second* World War aspect of Maugham's novel: C. S. Lewis had published *The Problem of Pain*, his classic book on the subject, in 1940. A similar compression of the wars is evident in Henry Green's extraordinary late modernist *Back* (1946), in which a shell-shocked English veteran is repatriated after five years in a German prisoner-of-war camp struggling to forget an unspecified "something in France which he knew, as he valued his reason, that he must always shut out."[21] Underscoring the painful familiarity of the shell-shock narrative, another character driven insane by loss believes that this is still the Great War, and that Charley is her own brother John, killed in 1917. "'They're coming back nervous cases, like they did out of the last war,'" a character haltingly realizes, "and thought that, in that case, then everything was hopeless" (106). "Coming back" in this novel refers not only to the soldier's traumatized return from the Second World War, but also to the traumatic return to British consciousness of a war that ought by now to be dead and buried.

Green wrote two other novels during the war. Based on his experience with London's auxiliary fire service, the opaque *Caught* (1943) is, along with the hallucinatory espionage novels of Greene and Bowen, among the most striking treatments of the psychic dissolutions of the Blitz. His next novel, the peerlessly charming *Loving* (1945), addressed the war from the offbeat perspective of the servants of an aristocratic mansion in the neutral Republic of Ireland ("the most celebrated eighteenth-century folly in Eire that had still to be burned down").[22] With its cheerfully democratic, unworriedly post-imperial mood, *Loving* is sometimes contrasted with Evelyn Waugh's exactly contemporary and differently seductive country-house novel *Brideshead Revisited* (1945), in which memory, snobbery, and Roman Catholicism famously offer their consolations for the privations of military life. Waugh's own best work from the years of the Second World War is the more characteristically savage *Put Out More Flags* (1942), which tells its satirical story of the war's first year through the misadventures of the gentle aesthete Ambrose Silk, clear sighted and high minded, and the feral opportunist Basil Seal. An individualist of an altogether more ruthless stripe than the cultured Ambrose, Basil maintains a wartime ambition that unabashedly appropriates Stanley Baldwin's old denunciation of the 1918 parliament: "'I know what I want,' said Basil. 'I want to be one of those people one heard about in 1919: the hard-faced men who did well out of the war.'"[23]

Continuities: the postwar novel sequence

Waugh returned to the Second World War in his major late work, the *Sword of Honour* trilogy (1952–1961). Perhaps the most neglected of the century's major fictional forms, the novel sequence enjoyed a golden age in the middle of the twentieth century, and one or both of the wars would play a major part in sequences completed or projected by, among others, Patrick Hamilton, Richard Hughes, Olivia Manning, Mervyn Peake, Rebecca West, and Henry Williamson, as well as Powell and Waugh. That the guiding light is Ford's *Parade's End*, which traces the startling transformation of the national culture from the Edwardian era through the sequence's 1920s present, is most clearly visible in Waugh's project. Just as Ford's Tietjens believes that "One could have fought with a clean heart . . . for the eighteenth century against the twentieth" (236), Waugh's Tory traditionalist Guy Crouchback hastens to prepare for war after the Nazi-Soviet pact of August 1939: "The enemy at last was plain in view, huge and hateful, all disguise cast off. It was the Modern Age in arms."[24] After such a beginning, *Sword of Honour* can only be a story of disillusionment, and like Powell's Second World War volumes – *The Valley of Bones* (1964), *The Soldier's Art* (1966), and *The Military Philosophers* (1968) – Waugh's trilogy presents the war as a fundamentally anti-heroic, even bathetic enterprise, an effect heightened by the emphasis, again like Powell's, on his protagonist's age: too young for the last war, would-be knights like Guy Crouchback are too old for this one.

The reaction against "the Modern Age in arms" described in his own contemporary sequence notoriously takes Henry Williamson to further political extremes than the conservatives Waugh and Powell. Participating in the well-documented spate of war (or anti-war) books of the late 1920s, Williamson had written of the First World War in the memoir *The Wet Flanders Plain* (1929) and the illustrated allegory *A Patriot's Progress* (1930), but places his war experience in a broader context in his fifteen-novel sequence *A Chronicle of Ancient Sunlight* (1951–1969), which follows the story of sensitive, nature-loving Phillip

Maddison from the secret marriage of his parents in 1893 through his childhood and adolescence, his First World War service, his uneasy reassimilation into civilian life, and his life as a farmer in the Second World War and beyond. The first of the war novels, *How Dear is Life*, is set in the autumn of 1914, when Phillip is thrilled as well as appalled to participate in the horror show of First Ypres ("fascinated fear" is the phrase used), but in the course of the *Chronicle* Phillip recoils forcefully from an industrial modernity ("the rootless urban industrial mind," "the factory civilisation of the times") of which he comes to see the First World War as symptomatic.[25] This revulsion takes Phillip, as it does his author, to the far right, and in *The Phoenix Generation* (1965) he embraces fascism as a regenerative force, while the following novel, *A Solitary War* (1966), is dedicated to Britain's best-known fascists, Oswald and Diana Mosley, incarcerated as wartime risks to national security. And, speaking of fascism's sometime fellow travelers, it was "a solitary war" also for Wyndham Lewis, who rewrote his wartime Canadian exile as *Self-Condemned* (1954), a bitter parable about the futility and fragility of private principle during what the novel terms "World Ruin, Act II."[26]

At the other end of the political spectrum, the committed Marxist Patrick Hamilton writes of the Second World War in his *Hangover Square* (1941) and *The Slaves of Solitude* (1947), narratives of persecuted virtue that link domestic cruelties to their international counterparts through the covert Nazi sympathies of shabby villains like the narcissistic actress Netta and the boarding-house bully Mr. Thwaites. Hamilton's final work, *The Gorse Trilogy* (1951–1955), looks back to the First World War and its aftermath, and private malevolence is again linked to brutality on the grand scale. When the seedy Ralph Gorse is first introduced in *The West Pier* (1951), a schoolboy in the last winter of peace before the outbreak of the Great War, he is returning from the mandatory military exercises he ominously adores; and, too young to serve in the war, he will masquerade as a decorated gentleman veteran in *Mr. Stimpson and Mr. Gorse* (1953), a devastatingly funny attack on the instrumentalizing of war by people wholly incapable of being touched by the suffering of others. Major Parry, for example, has spent the war at home in a comfortable staff job, but since he has once had an Armistice Day poem published in the local newspaper his misdirected military pride dictates that he repeat this success. Now "having another go at the glorious dead," he is buoyed up by the realization that Passchendaele rhymes with such heavyweight war-poem words as "fail," "bewail," "dale," "grail," and "nightingale:" "Next to Passchendaele, the Major was tremendously anxious to use Ypres. But here, when it came to rhyming, he was totally stumped." [27]

A connoisseur of the crass and the socially awful, Hamilton is most important for his darkly funny presentations of civilian conditions in England, but other mid-century sequences reimagine the world wars from broader, transnational perspectives. Although Richard Hughes never completed his planned sequence "The Human Predicament" the two published volumes, *The Fox in the Attic* (1961) and *The Wooden Shepherdess* (1973), convey the unusual ambition of his project. The opening volume tracks the postwar progress of a young Englishman Augustine Penty-Herbert and his sister Mary, who is married to a Liberal politician as the party implodes in the aftermath of the First World War. Mary's confident belief that "Liberalism and democracy after all isn't just a fashion, it's the permanent trend, it's human nature ... progress" becomes all the more ironic as the sequence goes on, when familial and national upheavals are given a wider context of renascent European crisis.[28] Augustine and Mary's aristocratic Bavarian cousins, the von Kessens, are divided among themselves about Hitler, national savior or vulgar upstart, and *The Wooden Shepherdess* ends shortly after the Röhm Putsch ("Night of the Long Knives") of 1934, with Baron von Kessen and his family still locked in their tragic misunderstandings and underestimations of the nation's new leader.

Olivia Manning provides a different kind of international perspective in *The Balkan Trilogy* (1960–1965) and *The Levant Trilogy* (1977–1980), which, based on her own wartime experience, follow a young English couple, Harriet and Guy Pringle, around Eastern Europe and the Middle East during the war. The first two novels, *The Great Fortune* (1960) and *The Spoilt City* (1962), are set in Romania as it disintegrates under the dual pressures of German economic exploitation and Soviet territorial ambition and place Manning among the handful of British novelists who address the terrible wartime fate of weaker, poorer nations – such "far-away ... people of whom we know nothing" as those Neville Chamberlain had sacrificed to his policy of appeasement.[29] In 1941 Rebecca West had published *Black Lamb and Grey Falcon*, her monumental mythic history-cum-travelogue of the post-1918 state of Yugoslavia, while Storm Jameson had tackled the parallel but perhaps still more lamentable case of Czechoslovakia, the model democracy destroyed at Munich, in her 1940 novel *Europe to Let*. When read alongside the work of more apparently gregarious but in some ways politically narrower male contemporaries such as Powell and Waugh, what also distinguishes Manning's war novels is their deeply believable double focus on the mundane domestic details of the Pringles' daily life and the extraordinary world-historical events in which the Pringles are caught up – Guy Pringle is both a good leftist and a dismally selfish spouse.

Reckonings: contemporary fiction
and the world wars

In both trilogies Manning places the war in the context of a declining empire, exploring in an impressively unchauvinistic way the international consequences both of Britain's authority and of its waning as a world power. Among writers too young to have experienced the Second World War at first hand, its late imperial context is most important to J. G. Farrell, whose *The Singapore Grip* (1978) recounts the fortunes of the colonial rubber magnate Walter Blackett and his family as Singapore is surrendered to the Japanese and the Anglos are forced to confront the prospect of defeat by what they consider a self-evidently inferior race. *The Singapore Grip* is unusual among the retrospective treatments of the wars in its comic irreverence – from the title forward, in fact, which alludes to the collapse of Singapore only via a sexual practice that runs as a dirty joke through the novel. There is the marvelously puncturing sub-plot centered on Walter's jubilee pageant of imperial enterprise ("Walter had allocated Monty the role of Crushing Overheads"); there is the vignette in which the Englishman Matthew is cooked a romantic dinner consisting of baked beans, raw chicken blood, and poached white mice ("it did not taste too bad, but [Matthew] would have liked to have known which end of the mouse he was eating"); a mangy old spaniel awaiting euthanasia but reprieved at the last minute earns the splendid nickname The Human Condition ("'I think that dog must be rotting internally,' remarked Dupigny objectively").[30]

Also among the finest British novels about the war in the Far East is J. G. Ballard's *Empire of the Sun* (1984), based on Ballard's experience as a young teenager interned by the Japanese at the Lunghua camp in Shanghai. The novel follows Jamie/Jim's story from the disintegration of the city's semi-autonomous international settlement through the end of a war he survives thanks only to hard-headed entrepreneurial ingenuity (strategic alliances with the strongest prisoners, stealing rations from the dying, learning to exploit without being too much exploited), and the grimmest of good fortune (the atomic bomb ends the war just as the prisoners are about to be secretly slaughtered). Ballard had spent the years in Lunghua with his parents and sister and the decision to separate his surrogate self from his family is significant because it gives the novel an almost *Robinson Crusoe* flavor. Perhaps Defoe's most critically influential interpreter, Ian Watt writes in his classic *The Rise of the Novel* that Defoe matters because he alone, "among all the great writers of the past, has presented the struggle for survival in the bleak perspectives which recent history has brought back to a commanding position on the human stage."[31] And Watt, another former Japanese prisoner-of-war, knew more than most about how grim that "struggle for survival" could be. Ballard's sequel, *The Kindness of Women* (1991), follows Jim into his life in postwar Britain, ending, in a neat reflection on Ballard's own hybrid autobiographical-fictional method, with the narrator attending the premiere of Steven Spielberg's acclaimed 1987 film version of *Empire of the Sun*.

Although not strictly speaking a novel sequence, read together the Japanese-British Kazuo Ishiguro's *An Artist of the Floating World* (1986) and *The Remains of the Day* (1989) are strikingly similar in their concerns with the relationships between individual choices and pervasive cultures of honor, between high motives and evil outcomes, despite the fact that each novel looks at the Second World War from a completely different geographical situation. Set in Japan shortly after the Second World War, *An Artist of the Floating World* is narrated by a gifted painter tarnished by his former embrace of the imperialist ambitions that took Japan into the war, while collusion with appeasement is the theme of *The Remains of the Day*, also set shortly after the war but this time narrated by the former butler to a Nazi-sympathizing English aristocrat. "I realize there are now those who would condemn the likes of you and me for the very things we were once proud to have achieved," another disgraced survivor of the 1930s tells Ishiguro's artist, in words that would serve equally well for the protagonist of the later novel.[32] The world has changed around Ishiguro's narrators and only belatedly do they come to see how and why, their narratives oscillating between exaggerating and downplaying the narrator's importance to the discredited regime he served.

Through the 1990s and beyond the retrospective war novel would be testing the boundaries between historical and fictional representation by focussing on what gets left out of traditional British records of wars won. Pat Barker, for instance, follows an earlier generation of novelists when she tackles the Great War through the medium of the novel sequence with her much admired *Regeneration* trilogy – *Regeneration* (1991), *The Eye in the Door* (1993), and *The Ghost Road* (1995) – but her project is entirely of its own time in recovering the lost histories of the war. Through the relationship between the shell-shocked protagonist Billy Prior and the munitions worker Sarah Lumb the roles of women in wartime as victims and profiteers are discussed; through the story of the Roper family Barker explores the stigmatization of pacifists and conscientious objectors. Drawing extensively on the work of the pioneering army psychiatrist W. H. R. Rivers, who treated Siegfried Sassoon and Wilfred Owen at the famous Craiglockhart hospital in Edinburgh (Rivers, Sassoon, and Owen are all major characters), the trilogy is concerned above all with the wartime policing of gender ("emotional repression as the essence of manliness") and sexual identity: "After all," Barker's fictional Rivers explains, "in war, you've got this *enormous* emphasis on love between men – comradeship – and everybody approves. But at the same time there's always this little niggle of anxiety. Is it the right *kind* of love?" [33]

Then there are the novels that bring back into view what was once known but long forgotten. In *Atonement* (2001) Ian McEwan takes this approach to the evacuation of the utterly routed British Expeditionary Force at Dunkirk in the late May and early June of 1940. Working-class Robbie has been victimized at the hands of a spoiled middle-class child, and in this central Dunkirk section of the novel his victimization is fatally completed by the same ruling elite that closed ranks to protect the perpetrator of the crime for which Robbie has wrongly been punished. That even Churchill himself, in perhaps the most famous of all his wartime speeches, had described the retreat from the continent as "a colossal military disaster" – "We must be very careful not to assign to this deliverance the attributes of a victory" – did not prevent the speedy rewriting and enduring remembrance of Dunkirk as a signal instance of national pluck.[34] Here McEwan reinstates its chaotic terror, suggesting that such rewriting of wartime events is the national-historical counterpart to the narrator Briony's wholly self-serving reinterpretations of a past in which she has played only a guilty part.

And the novelistic reinterpretations and reconstructions keep coming, to the extent that it would be hard to overstate the continuing importance of the Second World War to British popular and literary culture. For traditionalists this war represents the last moment when the nation came together to play a heroic role on the world stage; for others, the war was the end of the bad old days, the event that transformed class-bound imperial Britain into a post-imperial welfare democracy. The turning point of the century, the war is endlessly revisitable in British novels, films, and television series, its 1940s' austerity chic providing an instantly recognizable and powerfully evocative setting. Ever alert to the pleasures of revisiting the past, Powell writes in his 1973 installment of *A Dance to the Music of Time* about the difficulty of leaving the war behind, and of the "temptation, after all is over, to return to what remains of the machine, examine such paraphernalia as came one's way, pick about among the bent and rusting composite parts."[35] But if such returns feel inevitable they might also be pathological, Powell suggests, and in this final movement of the sequence characters have begun to joke self-referentially about the possibility of death by retrospection: "Am I to be suffocated by nostalgia? Will that be my end?" one character asks, improvising his own obituary: "Mr. Hugh Morland . . .

succumbed to an acute attack of nostalgia, a malady to which he had been a martyr for years" (230). The war-obsessed English novel – and we no less war-obsessed readers – might take note.

Notes

1. Nancy Mitford, *The Pursuit of Love*, *The Nancy Mitford Omnibus* (Harmondsworth: Penguin, 1986), p. 147.
2. Anthony Powell, *The Kindly Ones*, *A Dance to the Music of Time: 2nd Movement* (University of Chicago Press, 1995), p. 69.
3. Winston Churchill, *The Second World War*. Vol. 1: *The Gathering Storm* (Boston: Mariner Books, 1986), p. xiii.
4. John Buchan, *The Thirty-Nine Steps* (London: Penguin, 2004), pp. 39, 113.
5. John Buchan, *Mr. Standfast* (London: Hodder & Stoughton, 1919), pp. 35, 36.
6. John Buchan, *Greenmantle* (Oxford University Press, 2008), p. 257.
7. Rudyard Kipling, "The Gardener," in *War Stories and Poems*, ed. Andrew Rutherford (Oxford University Press, 1999), p. 314.
8. Katherine Mansfield, "The Fly," *Stories* (New York: Vintage, 1991), p. 345.
9. Rebecca West, *The Return of the Soldier* (London: Penguin, 1998), p. 88.
10. Henry Williamson, *How Dear is Life* (London: Macdonald, 1954), p. 164.
11. Ford Madox Ford, *No More Parades*, *Parade's End* (New York: Vintage, 1979), pp. 306–307.
12. D. H. Lawrence, *Lady Chatterley's Lover* (New York: Modern Library, 2001), p. 10.
13. Lewis Grassic Gibbon, *Sunset Song* (London: Penguin, 2007), p. 255.
14. Modris Eksteins, *Rites of Spring: The Great War and the Birth of the Modern Age* (Boston: Houghton Mifflin, 1989).
15. Virginia Woolf, *Mrs. Dalloway* (Orlando, FL: Harcourt, 2005), pp. 94, 4–5.
16. Virginia Woolf, *To the Lighthouse* (Orlando, FL: Harcourt, 2005), p. 137.
17. Virginia Woolf, *The Years* (Orlando, FL: Harcourt, 2008), p. 319.
18. Virginia Woolf, *Three Guineas* (Orlando, FL: Harcourt, 1966), pp. 106, 107.
19. *Authors Take Sides on the Spanish War* (London: Left Review, 1937), n.p.
20. Virginia Woolf, *Between the Acts* (Orlando, FL: Harcourt, 2008), p. 135.
21. Henry Green, *Back* (Champaign, IL: Dalkey Archive Press, 2009), p. 183.
22. Henry Green, *Loving, Living, Party Going* (Harmondsworth: Penguin, 1993), p. 182.
23. Evelyn Waugh, *Put Out More Flags* (Boston: Back Bay, 2002), pp. 52–3.
24. Evelyn Waugh, *Men at Arms*, *Sword of Honour* (New York: Knopf, 1994), p. 10.
25. Henry Williamson, *How Dear is Life* (London: Macdonald, 1954), p. 302; Henry Williamson, *The Dark Lantern* (London: Macdonald, 1951), p. 300; Henry Williamson, *Donkey Boy* (London: Macdonald, 1952), p. 315.
26. Wyndham Lewis, *Self-Condemned* (London: Methuen, 1954), p. 277.
27. Patrick Hamilton, *Mr. Stimpson and Mr. Gorse*, *The Gorse Trilogy* (London: Black Spring, 2007), pp. 356, 287.

28. Richard Hughes, *The Fox in the Attic* (New York: New York Review Books, 2000), p. 59 (ellipsis in original).
29. Neville Chamberlain, *In Search of Peace* (New York: Putnam, 1939), p. 174.
30. J. G. Farrell, *The Singapore Grip* (New York: New York Review Books, 1999), pp. 356, 410, 482.
31. Ian Watt, *The Rise of the Novel* (Berkeley: University of California Press, 2001), pp. 133–134.
32. Kazuo Ishiguro, *An Artist of the Floating World* (New York: Vintage, 1989), p. 94.
33. Pat Barker, *Regeneration* (New York: Plume, 1993), pp. 48, 204.
34. Winston Churchill, *Blood, Toil, Tears, and Sweat: The Speeches of Winston Churchill*, ed. David Cannadine (Boston: Houghton Mifflin, 1989), pp. 162, 160.
35. Anthony Powell, *Temporary Kings, A Dance to the Music of Time: 4th Movement* (University of Chicago Press, 1995), p. 201.

43

Thrillers

ALLAN HEPBURN

Spy and detective novels have a common goal: to thrill. In murder mysteries or shilling shockers, the thrill depends on criminal culpability and the investigation of wrongdoing. Once the thriller raises suspicion, evidence establishes guilt or innocence. Having proven guilt, the thriller arbitrates the punishment of crimes. The classic British detective novel, as written by Dorothy Sayers and Agatha Christie, begins with a murder and ends with the explanation of motive and method of the crime. The classic British spy story, as written by John Buchan and John le Carré, begins with the recruitment of an ordinary fellow into a conspiracy that endangers the life of the protagonist. Both spy and detective novels are compelled by human curiosity, a will to know, even if knowledge entails physical jeopardy. The detective assembles clues until a coherent story emerges; the secret agent construes codes to verify that a conspiracy exists. In all instances, the thriller adopts a stance toward citizenship, social responsibility, and justice.

Both detective and spy novels originate in nineteenth-century fiction. Charles Dickens shadowed the London police and wrote about his experiences in *Household Words*. In *Bleak House* (1853) Dickens documents constabulary techniques in the figure of Inspector Bucket. In Wilkie Collins's *The Moonstone* (1868) Sergeant Cuff investigates the theft of a diamond stolen from a shrine in India. These characters institutionalize curiosity and its thrills within police procedure. Sensation novels published in the 1860s, such as Mary Elizabeth Braddon's *Lady Audley's Secret* (1862) and Sheridan Le Fanu's *Uncle Silas* (1864), dwell on secrets, hidden pasts, and attempts to obtain money by illegal means. Curiosity and its pleasures assume other forms in imperial romances such as Robert Louis Stevenson's *Treasure Island* (1883) and Rudyard Kipling's *Kim* (1901). In Victorian precursors to the detective and spy novel, the protagonist is often an orphan. In *Uncle Silas* Maud becomes the ward of her wicked uncle. In *Treasure Island* Jim Hawkins's father dies and his mother sends him into the world to fend for himself alongside pirates and conspirators. "My curiosity, in a sense, was stronger than my fear," claims Jim.[1] In *Kim* the protagonist's mother dies in obscurity, and his father drinks himself to an early grave. The orphan faces his fears without the benefit of family counsel. A ward of the state, the orphan bears the secrets of individual responsibility, his need for survival set over against the common good.

The orphan is antithetical to the law insofar as the law protects social interests first. In P. D. James's *A Certain Justice* (1997) orphan Garry Ashe lives with "eight foster parents."[2] Having exhausted their patience, he moves in with his dissolute aunt in a housing estate slated for demolition. Unable to bear affection or physical contact, Ashe murders his aunt, then photographs her corpse splayed on a sofa. Venetia Aldridge successfully defends Ashe in court against murder charges. In recompense Ashe seduces Venetia's daughter, Octavia. An only child, Octavia looks "like a Victorian orphan newly released from a children's home" (87). It turns out that Venetia is also an only child, as were both of her parents. So is Harold Naughton, a clerk at the law courts. The lawyer Drysdale Laud is "the indulged only child of prosperous parents" (154). Indeed, almost every character in *A Certain Justice* is an only child. Through no fault of their own, only children – whether they grow up to become law clerks, lawyers, or defendants – maladjusted and self-involved, bear an uncertain relation to the law.

A Certain Justice speculates on the meaning of evidence within jurisprudence. "You can't bring people to law without evidence," says one police officer (365). Ashe creates an alibi that no evidence can disprove. The narrator remarks that, "however odd the circumstances, suspicion wasn't legal proof" (483). Justice is predicated on facts, not hunches: "Isn't the law all about proof?" (139). This principle bears on the murder of Venetia, a crime for which no "plausible solution" is ever found (670). The chief investigator, Adam Dalgliesh, sketches a theory about Venetia's death, but he cannot prove it. In this novel the legal system sustains the illusion of protection and punishment, but the lawyers and the policemen share the opinion that "all human justice is necessarily imperfect" (671). Although Ashe ultimately admits to murdering his aunt, he cannot be tried for the same crime twice. A recidivist without remorse, Ashe forfeits human sympathy along with the legal presumption of innocence.

Spy novels raise a different set of questions about the law, namely that citizenship involves legal obligations to the state. These obligations are clarified in times of duress, especially when the nation is under attack. Thus the earliest espionage narratives represent possible invasion rather than murder of an individual. Sir George Chesney's *Battle of Dorking of 1871* (1871) and

William le Queux's *The Great War in England in 1897* (1894), both forecasting invasions, articulate British fears about national security. In *Spies of the Kaiser* (1909) William Le Queux elaborates a "dastardly scheme by which, immediately before a dash is made upon our shore, a great railway strike is to be organized, ostensibly by socialists, in order to further paralyse our trade and render us in various ways unable to resist the triumphal entry of the foe."[3] Historically, a Directorate of Military Intelligence was established in 1883; its counterpart, a Naval Intelligence Board, was established in 1887. In 1889 Parliament passed the Official Secrets Act, which remained in effect until a more stringent Official Secrets Act was passed in 1911. Those agencies and laws aimed to control the flow of intelligence, especially military secrets, across international borders. They were also designed to regulate foreign nationals within the UK. (In Edgar Wallace's *The Four Just Men* [1905], four self-appointed law-makers threaten a member of parliament who supports the "unjust" Aliens Extradition [Political Offences] Bill.)[4] The Secret Service Bureau, founded in 1909 to safeguard military intelligence and to monitor breaches of secrecy, evolved into specialized sections: the Security Service, or MI5, protects British interests and provides intelligence and counter-intelligence concerning domestic politics, including counter-terrorism; the Secret Intelligence Service, or MI6, is devoted to foreign intelligence. The Security Service Act of 1989 and the Intelligence Services Act of 1994 updated the jurisdiction and powers of British intelligence agencies.

The espionage thriller concerns the flow of secret information. In John le Carré's *The Mission Song* (2006), a half-French, half-Congolese orphan named Bruno Salvador, who resembles bicultural Kim in Kipling's novel, becomes a professional translator specializing in African languages. Living among several cultures, Salvador calls himself a "mid-brown Briton."[5] His nickname in Swahili, *mtoto wa siri*, means "secret child" (8). He becomes an undercover agent privy to a "secret world" (249) of classified information when he translates at a clandestine meeting of African leaders who plan insurrection against the Congolese government with the assistance of corrupt British politicians and businessmen. Despite his efforts to alert the secret service and the media to the impending insurrection, intended as a cover operation for capitalist exploitation, Salvador meets with indifference. He saves his notebooks from the meetings and steals some tapes that would incriminate the leaders, but two crucial tapes go missing. A British mogul – who stands to gain financially from the insurrection – tells Salvador that, without notes or documentation, he has nothing that can be called "either *proof* or *evidence*" (264). Proof is all: without proof, there is no corroboration, and without corroboration, there is no conspiracy.

The concerned parties consider Salvador a "rogue element" (298) bent on compromising a well-laid plan. After ransacking his apartment, British agents extradite Salvador on the grounds that he never legally held a proper passport: "the man who calls himself Bruno Salvador is not now and never has been a British subject, loyal or otherwise" (326). Whatever his good intentions, Salvador, because he is not a citizen, has no right to British protection. Whereas the spy who takes the law into his own hands is usually believed by military intelligence in the end, Salvador's truth-telling is quashed by English secret service agents. His sense of political obligation leads to nothing. *The Mission Song* is not about a military invasion of Britain, along the lines of earlier espionage tales, but about the interdependence of global markets and the greed of European capitalists. Already possessed by transnational interests, the nation is merely a fiction. Extraditing Salvador preserves the notion, however spurious, of a homogeneous British citizenry, in which half-French, half-Congolese interpreters have no place.

Despite the thrills they elicit, detective fiction and spy fiction have profound generic differences. Detective fiction centers on murder, alongside related crimes such as blackmail and bigamy. Spy fiction centers on assassinations and conspiracies, usually sparked by territorial and ideological disputes. Detective fiction is set within the geographic boundaries of Britain, whereas the spaces of spy fiction are international. To pursue their missions, spies cross borders; they perpetrate versions of British democracy abroad. Both spies and detectives make reasonable inferences from available evidence. Evidence in detective fiction is a set of clues, but in spy fiction evidence is a set of languages or codes. Detectives make deductions from tangible evidence, but spies make guesses based on shifting information. Both spies and detectives have suspicions, but detectives suspect people, whereas spies suspect plots and conspiracies. In almost all thrillers careful reasoning prevails. In Agatha Christie's *The Mysterious Affair at Styles* (1921), Hercule Poirot maintains that "all good detective work [is] a mere matter of method."[6] The detective creates an order, whether causal or chronological, out of available evidence. Albert Campion, the detective in Margery Allingham's *The Case of the Late Pig* (1937), gathers information before looking for a pattern: "I collect all the odds and ends I can see and turn out the bag at the lunch hour."[7] Detective fiction ends by naming culprits; spy fiction, by contrast, rarely ends with a cathartic delivery of justice. Law prevails in detective fiction. Ideology prevails in spy thrillers.

Spy and detective fiction also diverge in their representations of violence. In pursuit of criminals, detectives seldom experience physical peril. Spies, once they are recruited into a conspiracy by being in the wrong place at the wrong time, are chased, shot at, tortured, or otherwise endangered. In John Buchan's *The Thirty-Nine Steps* (1915), inquisitive Richard Hannay is pursued across Scotland and England – "I felt the terror of the hunted on me," he reports[8] – before being locked in a storeroom by his arch-enemy. Hannay, an engineer by training, improvises a detonator to blow out the storeroom wall. The blast knocks him unconscious. He hides in a dovecote to catch his breath and plan his next move. In Ian Fleming's novels James Bond routinely suffers immobilization and torture. In *Casino Royale* (1953) Le Chiffre ties Bond to a chair without a seat, then beats his genitals with a paddle. In *Live and Let Die* (1954) a henchman pulls back Bond's little finger until it snaps. Violence is directly represented in such scenes. By comparison, in detective fiction violence often takes place outside the parameters of representation. Murder is committed, but the details of the murder have to be reconstructed when the crime scene is revisited. Horror is explained in most detective fiction with a concluding summary, a chronological account of events. The detective imagines, but does not witness, let alone participate in, violence. There are few exceptions to this rule. In Margery Allingham's *Traitor's Purse* (1941) detective Albert Campion is accused of "slugging a policeman,"[9] but amnesia prevents him from recalling any such incident. When Campion recovers, he cracks a conspiracy to flood the British economy with counterfeit money, a scheme masterminded by a "full-blown enemy agent" (200). Slugging a policeman in the line of duty is justifiable when Britain is to be saved.

Violence in thrillers marks points of dissent or deviation from the status quo. Murder, terrorism, and reprisals also call attention to contradictions in the social and legal aspects of British subjectivity. At the beginning of Joseph Conrad's *Under Western Eyes* (1911), a bomb thrown at a sleigh in the streets of St. Petersburg kills a Russian official and unsuspecting bystanders. The assassin, while acknowledging that he is a terrorist, asserts that "the true destroyers are they who destroy the spirit of progress and truth, not the avengers who merely kill the bodies of the persecutors of human dignity."[10] Violence can be directed at ideas as well as bodies. As in *Under Western Eyes* violence creates the perception of a state of siege in order to test the legal foundations of the government, in this case Russian despotism. Razumov, a student who cares mostly about academic prizes, is recruited by the Russian police to spy on a revolutionary cell in Switzerland. Unable to bear the pressure of living a secret life, he ultimately confesses his double agency to the terrorists. The revolutionaries beat and deafen Razumov. As in most thrillers, bombings and bodily injuries in *Under Western Eyes* redefine individuals as legal and political entities. The thrill, as a sensation that spreads to readers from imperilled characters within a spy or detective novel, stands for the dissonance between individuals and the juridical and political spheres in which they exist.

Spy and detective novels thus register citizenship and conflict through thrilling sensations. Chantal Mouffe argues that democracy requires internal conflict as a guarantor of civil liberties: "far from jeopardizing democracy, agonistic confrontation is in fact its very condition of possibility."[11] Dissent and partisan politics prove that a democracy functions as it ought. Yet thrillers constantly demonstrate the deleterious effects of dissent and terrorism. In detective novels, murder signals a break with the social compact. In spy novels, assassination throws into doubt the authority of the law. Moreover, governments can break the law – as they do repeatedly in spy fiction – on the grounds that necessity dictates such breaches. The German political theorist Carl Schmitt calls war, insurrection, and martial law "states of exception" when governments suspend the law for the putative good of the polity. "Sovereign is he who decides on the exception," claims Schmitt.[12] The authority to break laws implies a power that supersedes juridical authority. Following Schmitt's formulation, Giorgio Agamben argues that states of exception challenge legal definitions of identity: "in both the right of resistance and the state of exception, what is ultimately at issue is the question of the juridical significance of a sphere of action that is in itself extrajuridical."[13] In thrillers, criminals and secret agents work outside the law by murdering people or by tracking down conspirators without the help of government agencies. Disbelieved by the powers that be, spies work against the authority of governments. Thrillers therefore imagine alternative political orders in which individuals assume the responsibilities of citizenship extra-judicially and solve crimes by circumventing law.

Joseph Conrad represents government-directed dissent and conformism in *The Secret Agent* (1907). Adolf Verloc, an *agent provocateur* working in London for a foreign government, is instructed to provoke a public outrage, so he devises a plan to blow up the Greenwich Observatory. His feeble-minded brother-in-law, Stevie, innocent of the plot, trips over a tree root while carrying a bucket of explosive and blows himself up. Meanwhile, a renegade Professor with a bomb attached to his body roams the London streets. The Professor explains his theory of social equivalences: "The terrorist and the policeman both come from the same basket. Revolution, legality – counter moves in the same game; forms of idleness at bottom identical."[14] For the Professor all political maneuvers are a "game," both childish and illusory. Whereas the revolutionaries in *The Secret Agent* believe that human lives are dispensable, the middle classes, confident in their entitlements, believe that everyone, including Members of Parliament and bureaucrats, contributes to national security. Middle-class citizens expect the police to protect their property and civil rights. By contrast, Mr. Vladimir, who comes from abroad, fears authority: "Descended from generations victimized by the instruments of an arbitrary power, he was racially, nationally, and individually afraid of the police" (224). In *The Secret Agent* neither the revolutionaries nor the police achieve their goals. Revolutionary acts cannot dislodge British smugness or the belief in a definable national identity. Stevie's gruesome death passes without notice among the British populace. Only his sister Winnie reacts to it. Winnie murders her husband because she feels that he has betrayed his family obligation to Stevie, not because Verloc is a secret agent. Although Mr. Vladimir considers British laws too permissive – he thinks citizens should have no democratic entitlements – Conrad, combining the spy thriller with a sensational murder, suggests that no actions, however revolutionary, will ever alter British conservatism. Citizens have rights and responsibilities, but they tend to pursue selfish, personal motives, rather than the common good.

The spy and, to a lesser extent, the detective are experts at discerning authentic "Britishness." If the secret agent is a foreigner, he can never penetrate the British upper classes completely. His accent rings false, no matter how perfectly he speaks English. In *The Thirty-Nine Steps*, Richard Hannay, adept at disguises, claims that "A fool tries to look different: a clever man looks the same and *is* different" (103). When Hannay confronts a group of German spies who dress and speak like Englishmen, he is confounded by the perfection of their disguise: "It couldn't be acting, it was too confoundedly genuine" (107). He recognizes one of the men as an interloper by the way that he taps his fingers on his leg. The tiny physical gesture breaks the completeness of the disguise. In Erskine Childers's *The Riddle of the Sands* (1903) Davies and Carruthers also define Englishness by imperceptible signs. Dollmann, a British traitor, pretends to speak only German. His disguise does not come off. His British character reveals itself in minute details. As Carruthers says, "It was something in his looks and manner; you know how different we are from foreigners."[15] Dollmann, frustrated that Carruthers does not understand German, inadvertently shouts "follow me" in perfect English. Carruthers says, "I was quite aware that [Dollmann] knew a few English words, though he had always mispronounced them; an easy trick when your hearer suspects nothing. But I needn't say that just then I was observant of trifles" (72). Hallmarks of British identity, whatever they be, cannot be effaced.

Suaveness – even cosmopolitanism – defines the British spy. Most spies speak several languages. In William Le Queux's *Secrets of the Foreign Office* (1903),

Duckworth Drew, a confidential agent for the British Secret Service, is both gentlemanly and authoritative. By mingling *savoir-faire* with protocol, Drew establishes a tradition of elegance for espionage literature. In Somerset Maugham's *Ashenden, or the British Agent* (1928), Ashenden is recruited to be a spy because he speaks several European languages and because his profession as a writer makes a perfect cover for espionage: a writer can easily justify writing dispatches. Spying, in and of itself, has few rewards. Ashenden's handler tells him, "If you do well you'll get no thanks and if you get into trouble you'll get no help."[16] Having been brought up in Europe, Ashenden shuttles across borders – Britain, France, Switzerland, Italy – with indifference. He approaches every situation with detachment, even when it involves treachery and murder: "People sometimes thought him heartless because he was more often interested in others than attached to them, and even in the few to whom he was attached his eyes saw with equal clearness the merits and the defects" (146).

Like Ashenden, Charles Latimer, the protagonist of Eric Ambler's *A Coffin for Dimitrios* (1939), is a writer who speaks several languages. Meeting a polyglot man in a train, Latimer notes that his "accurate English would give out in the middle of a difficult sentence, which would be completed in very fluent French or German."[17] Latimer teaches political economy in a minor British university before he turns to writing detective novels full-time. Having written about Proudhon and Nazism, he observes European politics keenly. He takes particular interest in theft and drug-smuggling. His integrity places him above the temptations of theft, but he reflects that "as for the motive [of detective novels], money was always, of course, the soundest basis" (304). As an intellectual with leftist tendencies, however, Latimer exempts himself from the money motive; at novel's end, he resists stealing a million francs strewn on the floor of a seedy Paris apartment. Ambler's novel reflects on the legal and social responsibilities owed to "the dangerous class, the political hangers-on, the grafters and mass thrown off by the lowest layers of an old society" (92). Those who take advantage of capitalism through graft and smuggling, those who have shown no sense of duty to any particular country or to a larger sense of human decency, deserve nothing in return. While investigating the nefarious activities of Dimitrios across Europe, acting as a freelance investigator while pretending to gather information for his next detective plot, Latimer distances himself from "the dangerous class," and confirms his allegiance to civic duty.

Duckworth Drew, Ashenden, and Latimer establish a lineage for Ian Fleming's James Bond. Although Bond loves good food and drives fancy cars, he has no inner life. Preparing to kill some enemies of Britain in *For Your Eyes Only* (1962), Bond expresses distaste for assassination. He is only doing his duty: "He had no personal motives against them. This was merely his job – as it was the job of a pest control officer to kill rats."[18] The descriptive terms usually attached to Bond are "cruel" and "cold." In *Live and Let Die* (1954) he wills detachment: "Bond knew he must remain cold and absolutely resolved to fight for their lives to the end."[19] In *Casino Royale* Bond's face is "ironical, brutal, and cold."[20] In the same novel, as if in compensation for his aloofness, Bond exhibits emotion only when a woman is involved: "Like all harsh, cold men, he was easily tipped over into sentiment. She was very beautiful and he felt warm towards her" (169). Whenever he showers, Bond turns the taps to ice cold and keeps his eyes open. His suaveness is built around a resilience to physical pain.

Unlike Bond, George Smiley in John le Carré's *The Spy Who Came in from the Cold* (1963), *Tinker Tailor Soldier Spy* (1974), *The Honourable Schoolboy* (1977), *Smiley's People* (1980), and other novels, carefully plots espionage and counter-espionage activities. Le Carré denounces the image of the macho spy. He criticizes Bond as an example of "the Superman figure who is 'ennobled' by some sort of misty, patriotic ideas and who can commit any crime and break any law in the name of his own society. He's a sort of licensed criminal who, in the name of false patriotism, approves of nasty crimes."[21] Le Carré's protagonists, such as Leamas in *The Spy Who Came in from the Cold*, owe more to existential misfits of the postwar period than to mythic superheroes. They are emotionally unfinished. In *The Looking Glass War* (1965) weakness binds Avery to Leclerc: "at one moment Avery could hate [Leclerc] for his transparent manipulation, detest his prinking gestures as a child detests the affectations of a parent, at the next he ran to protect him, responsible and deeply caring."[22] Although le Carré's agents are often infantile and grim, their operator Smiley possesses a "natural shyness"[23] that his authority as the head of the Secret Service cannot belie. Erudite and worldly wise, Smiley incarnates the sophistication of never being one-upped.

Detectives, too, can be suave or accomplished. Sherlock Holmes plays the violin and likes opera. Adam Dalgliesh, the detective in P. D. James's novels, publishes poetry. Lord Peter Wimsey, the detective of Dorothy Sayers's novels, epitomizes elegance. An aristocrat with an interest in rare books, Lord Peter speaks with an affected accent, dropping terminal "g's" on present participles and adopting American slang when it suits his mood. In *Whose Body?* (1923) Lord Peter clears up the mystery surrounding the sudden appearance of a naked corpse in the bathtub of a mansion flat, which coincides with the sudden disappearance of a respected Jewish financier named Reuben Levy. As part of his investigation, Wimsey visits Dr. Freke, a physician who studies the physiological basis of moral feeling. In Freke's view "horror, fear, sense of responsibility" are merely cerebral sensations.[24] To prove his theory, he spends long days and nights dissecting dead bodies. He longs for the day when he can leave his practice and settle down "to cut up my subjects and write my books in peace" (109).

Like many detective novels in the interwar decades, *Whose Body?* is unabashedly sensational. In the 1920s and 1930s British newspapers headlined the gruesome details of various homicides. In 1922 Edith Thompson and her lover Frederick Bywaters stood trial for slaying Thompson's husband, Percy, in a premeditated street scuffle; Edith claimed to have had no prior knowledge of the murder, but she was tried for the crime nonetheless. In 1924 Patrick Mahon killed his mistress Emily Kaye in a seaside bungalow at Eastbourne. Mahon dismembered Kaye's body, boiled and burned it, and tossed bits of the abused corpse from a train window. In the "Brighton Trunk Murder" in 1934, the torso of an unidentified woman was found in a suitcase in the left-luggage office of the Brighton; the murderer was never identified. In 1935 Dr. Buck Ruxton was found guilty of murdering and dismembering his wife and his maid.

In addition to the media coverage of sensational murders, the flowering of detective fiction in the 1920s can be attributed to another cause: the Great War. The title of *Whose Body?* evokes the missing and unidentified soldiers of the war, some of whom were interred in the mud of the battlefields. The detective novels of Dorothy Sayers, Margery Allingham, Agatha Christie, and Josephine Tey express a culture of national grief and mourning. As Stacy Gillis claims, "The Golden Age detective novel is both a place in which the dismembered and bloody body of the battlefield can be neatly reassembled and a space in which such motifs of the war as shell shock are negotiated."[25] In *Whose Body?* and other novels by Sayers, such as *The Unpleasantness at the Bellona Club* (1928) and *The Nine Tailors* (1934), memories of the war haunt Wimsey. He suffers from symptoms of shell-shock, including recurrent nightmares about trench warfare. In *Whose Body?* he wakes his valet Bunter in the middle of the night with an abject appeal for help: "Tap, tap, tap – they're mining us – but I don't know where – I can't hear – I can't. Listen, you! There it is again – we must find it – we must stop it . . . Listen! Oh, my God! I can't hear – I can't hear anything for the noise of the guns. Can't they stop the guns?" (137). Disjointedness and interruption are stylistic features of *Whose Body?* The novel begins with a telephone call in which Peter cannot hear his mother's voice clearly. During the investigation, police inspectors have "no words for the interferingness of Lord Peter" (88). The novel is crowded with footnotes, letters, an uncle's short biography of Peter – various voices that impede the work of detection but that also register, in a manner reminiscent of *The Waste Land*, the traumatized voices of war survivors.

Detective novels, by virtue of their dwelling on the extent to which classes assert their legal hold on property and rank, constitute a conservative, law-abiding genre. In Arthur Conan Doyle's *The Hound of the Baskervilles* (1902) crotchety Mr. Frankland, who pursues litigation concerning public rights-of-way, proclaims that "law is law."[26] All social interactions take place inside the law; the law, even when it can be expanded or refined because of new court cases, arbitrates human interactions. Many Sherlock Holmes mysteries focus on inheritance as a legal entitlement. In *The Sign of Four* (1890) Holmes solves a mystery about a missing treasure and the rightful inheritance of Miss Marston. Should Miss Marston's rights be upheld in court, she would instantly "change from a needy governess to the richest heiress in England."[27] Although Holmes works alongside the law as a private detective, he views the law as the foundation of a just society. The law punishes; the law rewards. In *The Valley of Fear* (1915) Holmes warns that "the English law is, in the main, a just law. You will get no worse than your deserts from it."[28]

Agatha Christie's eighty-odd detective novels uphold the primacy of property and the right to inherit as guaranteed by British law. When blackmailers try to extort money from Miss Katherine Grey in *The Mystery of the Blue Train* (1928), a lawyer informs her, "'these people have no claim of any kind upon the estate, and if they endeavour to contest the will no court will uphold them.'"[29] In *Sad Cypress* (1940) Mrs. Welman dies intestate: "There are no settlements or trust. Mrs. Welman's money was hers absolutely to do with as she chose," explains her attorney.[30] In *The Body in the Library* (1941) a pair of bounders try to wriggle their way into the good graces of a wealthy, handi-capped man to pilfer his money. According to Franco Moretti, the detective novel as a genre "dispels from the consciousness of the masses the individu-alistic ethos of 'classic' bourgeois culture."[31] Everyone falls under suspicion, including detectives and professionals. Moretti's opinion notwithstanding, the detective novel asserts the legal entitlements of bourgeois culture to money, property, and inheritance. Criminals aspire to become bourgeois through the acquisition of property or money, however illegally got.

Detective fiction reinforces its conservative ethos through an insistence on the uniqueness of every human body. No corpse can substitute for any other. Scotland Yard first used fingerprints in 1901 to establish criminal identity according to uniqueness and individuality. Accordingly, a murder has an exact set of possible suspects and circumstances. Evidence ensures that the victim and the murderer are properly identified. Sometimes identification depends on legal and national definitions of character. In Agatha Christie's *Evil Under the Sun* (1941) actress Arlena Marshall is murdered at a seaside resort. Hercule Poirot happens to be on holiday at the same resort. A Belgian by birth, Poirot scrutinizes British character as it conforms to or differs from the law. Captain Marshall is "very British and unassuming."[32] However, by making observations about British character, Poirot embodies the ambiguities of the law when it comes to proof and national belonging. Mr. Blatt, a loudmouth involved in smuggling, decries Poirot's detective skills as insufficiently British: "'What's wrong with Scotland Yard? Buy British every time for me'" (32). Ultimately Poirot assesses possible perpetrators of crime according to the character of the victim. "There is no such thing as a plain fact of murder," claims Poirot. "Murder springs, nine times out of ten, out of the character and circumstances of the murdered person" (66).

Evil Under the Sun intimates that British subjects, as a body politic, are all more or less alike, but the novel also maintains the legal certainty that no individual can be confused with any other. Looking at sunbathers lying row upon row on the beach, Poirot remarks, "They are just – bodies!" (5). Law, through its capacity to command, forbid, allow, and punish, converts "just – bodies" into individual subjects, as perpetrators or victims. If character plays a part in murder, as Poirot asserts, the demeanour and past of the victim, Arlena Marshall, come into question. She is variously decried as a "gold-digger" and "man eater" (20). An outspoken clergyman calls Arlena "a focus of evil. She *was* Evil! Evil personified!" (128). The clergyman raises the specter of predestination. Some people are born to a life of crime; others are destined to be the victims of crime. Unredeemed by social or moral virtue, Arlena, in the clergyman's opinion, deserves to die. Poirot contradicts this judgment by calling Arlena a *"victim"* (185). Because he understands that bodies can resemble each other without being identical, Poirot solves the mystery of the homicide: when Arlena's "corpse" is first discovered, it is actually one of her killers sprawled on the beach like a cadaver. One body is not another. Nevertheless, all subjects are equal before the law. Murderers isolate themselves from the protection of the law; they are antithetical to social norms and deserve punishment for their isolation.

Graham Greene's thrillers in the 1930s directly engage the question of evil raised in *Evil Under the Sun*. In many respects Greene revises Agatha Christie and Dorothy Sayers. Ida Arnold, the amateur sleuth in *Brighton Rock* (1938), is Greene's response to quizzical Miss Marple and Harriet Vane. The murder in *Stamboul Train* (1932) owes its locale to Christie's *The Mystery of the Blue Train*, while anticipating *Murder on the Orient Express* (1934). Train travel, commonplace in 1930s literature, accentuates problems of citizenship and belonging because travelers cross borders. In *Stamboul Train* Dr. Czinner wonders whether someone who refuses citizenship in any country can justly be called a traitor: "You say that I am a traitor to my country, but I do not recognize my country."[33] While addressing the topic of refugees in the 1930s, the motif of dislocation draws upon the trope of pursuit in spy fiction. In *A Gun for Sale* (1936) Raven thinks, "He wasn't used to being hunted; this was better: to hunt."[34] Greene's thrillers, or "entertainments" as he called them, combine elements of both espionage and detection. In *A Gun for Sale* the detective Mather pursues criminals "with an odd sense of shame, as if he were a spy" (103). In their representation of gangsters, Greene's novels shift the emphasis in detective fiction toward the possibilities of rehabilitation and redemption. Justice is meted out case by case.

Because it offers itself as a "case," the thriller finds its most common analogue in the file or dossier. Many thrillers trace the movement of information through bureaucracies, into archives, then back into the hands of agents. In *A Coffin for Dimitrios* a secret police agent piques Latimer's interest by toying with "the pages inside the folder" containing information on Dimitrios (21). Latimer subsequently visits refugee archives in search of further evidence about the life of this hardened criminal. In *Live and Let Die* Bond peruses information in a "thick brown folder" giving details about a smuggling ring; the file contains "gaps" that need to be filled in (21). In Greene's *The Third Man* (1949) Calloway, a police detective in postwar Vienna, hands Rollo Martins a file containing evidence that Harry Lime adulterated penicillin with sand, causing unspeakable suffering and death for hospitalized children. A file gives facts, but facts are not the same as a story: a story demonstrates motive, causality, reaction, and emotion. As Calloway says, "One's file, you know, is never quite complete; a case is never really closed, even after a century, when all the participants are dead."[35] The file authenticates, although files may contain false and planted information.

In *The Human Factor* (1978), Greene's novel based on the Cambridge spy ring, the so-called "facts" in files are compounded by deliberate lies and misleading information. A Russian agent explains the double-cross to his British counterpart:

> Your people imagined they had an agent in place, here in Moscow. But it was we who had planted him on them. What you gave us he passed back to them. Your reports authenticated him in the eyes of your service, they could check them, and all the time he was passing them other information which we wanted them to believe.[36]

Disinformation mingles with real information. Reports authenticate other reports, but authentication does not increase the truth value of any document.

The dossier provides historical proof. Combined with other dossiers, the case file creates an archive. Contemporary thrillers frequently mask historical investigations. Detection of crime reaches into the past, sometimes the remote past. In Josephine Tey's *The Daughter of Time* (1951) Alan Grant, laid up in hospital, investigates Henry VII's usurpation of the English throne; Grant deduces that Henry defames Richard III to legitimate a tenuous claim to kingship, despite Henry's having no "right by blood" to that high office.[37] In Peter Ackroyd's *Hawksmoor* (1985) a twentieth-century detective investigates a series of murders that occur on the sites of churches built in the eighteenth century. Hawksmoor thinks of murder historically: "stabbings and strangulations were popular in the late eighteenth century ... slashed throats and clubbings in the early nineteenth, poison and mutilation in the latter part of the last century."[38]

Innumerable thrillers represent espionage during the Second World War and the Cold War. Len Deighton draws upon wartime events in *Bomber* (1978), *XPD* (1981), and *Goodbye, Mickey Mouse* (1982). Robert Harris's *Fatherland* (1992), set in 1964, adopts the unhistorical, counter-factual conceit that the Nazis won the war. Searching archives and bank vaults, an investigator named March looks for "documentary proof of what happened to the Jews."[39] March reasons that "investigators turned suspicion [about crimes] into evidence" (337). In Harris's *Enigma* (1995) a mathematician works on cracking the Enigma Code at Bletchley Park during the war. In Sebastian Faulks's *Charlotte Gray* (1998) a Scottish woman parachutes behind enemy lines during the Second World War to help the Resistance. Faulks's subsequent novel, *Devil May Care* (2008), a pastiche of the James Bond novels, is set in the 1960s with references to the Rolling Stones, the Vietnam War, and nuclear destruction. The arch-villain Dr. Gorner despises the unfairness of British foreign policy and consequently wages "a crusade against Britain."[40] Bond comes out of semi-retirement to battle Gorner. However much he wishes to ignore the duties that patriotism exacts – "I don't believe in destiny," Bond claims (45) – he knows that his destiny as a secret agent allows no alternatives.

The thriller posits an alternative world. In a discussion of the pleasures of escaping reality by reading novels, Elizabeth Bowen comments that "The detective story writer isn't trying to trick you into any false emotional participation in the characters or scenes of his story."[41] The detective novel remains at a distance from the reality of the reader. Such distance allows speculation on the juridical and political dimensions of identity. The thriller

represents individuals' interactions with the law, not only as a confirmation
that institutions like the police and bureaucracy are antithetical to individuals,
but also as an assertion that individuals embody duty and undertake detective
work and espionage with very little prompting.

Notes

1. Robert Louis Stevenson, *Treasure Island* (Oxford University Press, 1985), p. 25.
2. P. D. James, *A Certain Justice* (Toronto: Seal Books, 2006), p. 7.
3. William Le Queux, *Spies of the Kaiser* (London: Hurst & Blackett, 1909), p. 312.
4. Edgar Wallace, *The Four Just Men* (London: Tallis, 1905), p. 23.
5. John le Carré, *The Mission Song* (Toronto: Viking, 2006), p. 23.
6. Agatha Christie, *The Mysterious Affair at Styles* (New York: Berkley, 1984), p. 8.
7. Margery Allingham, *The Case of the Late Pig* (London: Vintage, 2005), p. 36.
8. John Buchan, *The Thirty-Nine Steps* (Oxford University Press, 1993), p. 30.
9. Margery Allingham, *Traitor's Purse* (London: Vintage, 2006), p. 9.
10. Joseph Conrad, *Under Western Eyes* (Oxford University Press, 1983), p. 19.
11. Chantal Mouffe, "What Ethics for Democracy?," in *The Turn to Ethics*, ed. Marjorie Garber, Beatrice Hannssen, and Rebecca L. Walkowitz (New York: Routledge, 2000), p. 92.
12. Carl Schmitt, *Political Theology*, trans. George Schwab (Cambridge, MA: MIT Press, 1985), p. 5.
13. Giorgio Agamben, *State of Exception*, trans. Kevin Attell (University of Chicago Press, 2005), p. 11.
14. Joseph Conrad, *The Secret Agent* (Oxford University Press, 1983), p. 69.
15. Erskine Childers, *The Riddle of the Sands* (Oxford University Press, 1998), p. 71.
16. Somerset Maugham, *Ashenden, or the British Agent* (London: Heinemann, 1928), p. 3.
17. Eric Ambler, *A Coffin for Dimitrios* (New York: Vintage, 2001), p. 68.
18. Ian Fleming, *For Your Eyes Only* (London: Penguin, 2002), p. 88.
19. Ian Fleming, *Live and Let Die* (London: Penguin, 2002), p. 263.
20. Ian Fleming, *Casino Royale* (London: Penguin, 2002), p. 9.
21. Quoted in Andrew Lycett, *Ian Fleming: The Man Behind the Mask* (London: Weidenfeld and Nicolson, 1995), p. 449.
22. John le Carré, *The Looking Glass War* (Toronto: Penguin, 1992), p. 47.
23. John le Carré, *The Honourable Schoolboy* (Toronto: Penguin, 2001), p. 57.
24. Dorothy Sayers, *Whose Body?* (London: Hodder and Stoughton, 1968), p. 177.
25. Stacy Gillis, "Consoling Fictions: Mourning, World War One, and Dorothy L. Sayers," in *Modernism and Mourning*, ed. Patricia Rae (Lewisburg: Bucknell University Press, 2007), p. 185.
26. Arthur Conan Doyle, *The Hound of the Baskervilles* (London: Penguin, 2001), p. 115.
27. Arthur Conan Doyle, *The Sign of Four* (Peterborough, ON: Broadview, 2001), pp. 46–47.

28. Arthur Conan Doyle, *The Valley of Fear and Selected Cases* (London: Penguin, 2001), p. 76.
29. Agatha Christie, *The Mystery of the Blue Train* (London: HarperCollins, 2001), p. 85.
30. Agatha Christie, *Sad Cypress* (New York: Berkley, 1984), p. 51.
31. Franco Moretti, *Signs Taken for Wonders: Essays in the Sociology of Literary Forms* (London: Verso, 1983), p. 134.
32. Agatha Christie, *Evil Under the Sun* (New York: Berkley, 1991), pp. 48–49.
33. Graham Greene, *Stamboul Train* (London: Penguin, 1975), p. 102.
34. Graham Greene, *A Gun for Sale* (London: Penguin, 1973), p. 36.
35. Graham Greene, *The Third Man* (London: Penguin, 1971), p. 25.
36. Graham Greene, *The Human Factor* (New York: Simon and Schuster, 1978), p. 339.
37. Josephine Tey, *The Daughter of Time* (London: Penguin, 1954), p. 102.
38. Peter Ackroyd, *Hawksmoor* (New York: Harper, 1985), p. 117.
39. Robert Harris, *Fatherland* (London: Arrow Books, 1992), p. 271.
40. Sebastian Faulks, *Devil May Care* (Toronto: Anchor, 2008) , p. 164.
41. Elizabeth Bowen, *Listening In: Broadcasts, Speeches, and Interviews*, ed. Allan Hepburn (Edinburgh University Press, 2010), p. 251.

44

Novelistic complications of spaces and places: the four nations and regionalism

DOMINIC HEAD

Novelists grapple throughout the twentieth century with concerns related to identity and belonging. After the *"Windrush* generation" and the winding down of the British Empire, the headline treatments of identity had chiefly to do with multiculturalism in an era of postcolonialism. This chapter addresses a different matter: the tension between local allegiances and broader allegiances. How is regional belonging in the twentieth century understood, and how does it fit with national affiliation? How have novelists continued the tradition of regional fiction, and how has "English" identity in relation to place been complicated by the intersecting concerns of the "four nations," especially where Irish, Welsh, and Scottish nationalisms have greater popular impetus than any pursuit of Englishness?

Regional fiction has conventionally been associated with rural experience or with experience focussed on provincial towns in rural settings. (There is an additional complication here, in that regionalism and provincialism are over-lapping terms.) In the context of the twentieth-century English novel, region-alism has its heyday in the 1930s, and is usually deemed to have tailed off after the Second World War. A commonsense explanation for the apparent decline of the regional novel in England might be that the idea of regionalism inevitably changes with the improvement of modes and routes of travel, which have meant that regions are less self-contained than they were.

However, given the nature of novelistic discourse, and its ability to observe the minutiae of local conditions, there are reasons for thinking the opposite: that the novel is a preserve in which regional experience continues to be recorded. Keith Snell argues that the regional novel in Britain and Ireland – and especially England – has been on the increase since the 1980s. His definition identifies "fiction that is set in a recognizable region, and which describes features distinguishing the life, social relations, customs, dialect, or other aspects of the culture of that area and its people." Snell sensibly includes in his definition "fiction with a strong sense of local geography, topography or landscape." In the spirit of Hardy's "novels of character and environment," regional fiction can show "the effects of a particular environment upon the people living in it," even though, notwithstanding its use of detail in its sociological depictions, regional fiction also is expected to use "a particular place or regional culture . . . to illustrate an aspect of life in general."[1]

Snell does not exclude urban fiction from his purview; but he means a kind of urban fiction that treats convincingly an identifiable community with a strong sense of determining local factors. This interaction or tension between the rural and the urban raises larger historical and political questions whereby the treatment of the local is overshadowed by national issues. It is true that novelists of life in the English provinces have been centrally concerned with the nature of social change, and with how social change affects individual lives and communities; and it is quite possible for such writing to have a regional dimension if specific aspects of local experience are held in tension with the broader (national or international) dynamic of social change. But it is also quite possible for the cultivation of the provincial to be non-specific, devoid of local color, and to be a way of focussing marginalized and peripheral experience that is actually determined by the metropolitan center.

In the least inventive manifestations of provincial fiction, it can become chiefly a *hommage* to earlier authors. Angela Thirkell's Barsetshire novels, beginning with *High Rising* (1933), though renowned for their gently satirical treatment of English eccentricity, are inspired by Trollope's "Barsetshire Chronicles," and rely on a settled format. (Thirkell produced more-or-less a book a year for thirty years.) In later expressions – as in William Cooper's *Scenes From Provincial Life* (1950) – it is the posited social dullness of provincial existence that characterizes the portrayal. Cooper's novel is set in an anonymous provincial town (based on Leicester), and it is the dissatisfaction with the ordinary that drives much of the plot, and most especially the ambitions of the narrator, Joe Lunn. Yet at the same time Cooper's novel offers a quiet celebration of ordinary English culture.

From the end of the 1950s, especially in the novels of David Storey and Alan Sillitoe, the depiction of northern working-class experience opened up a new dimension of the urban provincial novel. Storey's *This Sporting Life* (1960) allows us to glimpse the possibility of social mobility, and the break-up of a class model held in place by an ordered provincial existence. To be sure, working-class provincial experience is often portrayed as claustrophobic, as in Sillitoe's *Saturday Night and Sunday Morning* (1958) or Sid Chaplin's *The Day of the Sardine* (1961). Yet, despite the sense of class entrapment, there is also something socially challenging about provincial fiction of this kind.

It is possible to argue that provincialism embodies a specific form of regionalism: a locally determined working environment with its characteristic color and social relations. Yet it is more common to think of the regional as evoking particular rural spaces. In Phyllis Bentley's pioneering account of the English regional novel, the four novelists "who created, developed, and possibly perfected" it are Charlotte Brontë, George Eliot, Thomas Hardy, and Arnold Bennett. For Bentley the notable twentieth-century successors include Mary Webb and Constance Holme, prior to a renaissance in this form of writing in the late 1920s and 1930s, led by Storm Jameson and Winifred Holtby.[2]

Webb's *Precious Bane* (1924) sustains that element of Hardy's vision in which human happiness is predicated on sympathy with the rural environment: it is Prue Sarn's integration with nature that characterizes her inner beauty and steadfast quality (outwardly she is blighted by a hare lip). Prue's union with nature wins her the love of the handsome, noble weaver, Kester Woodseaves. This love plot is pointedly contrasted with the tragic fate of Prue Sarn's brother Gideon, whose ambition leads to tragedy. Webb's morality, guaranteed by the "right" kind of engagement with the rural, epitomizes an earnest form of regionalism that is very much of the period. A passage in a chapter entitled "Dragon-Flies" encapsulates the philosophy of the novel. Here Prue reflects on the beauty of Sarn mere, which is to be a focus of her brother's tragedy, fully conscious that it is "a very mournful place" for much of the year.[3] In this regionalism it is endurance and sanguinity in the face of hardship that is rewarded.

Constance Holme's work celebrates life in the area of Cumbria formerly known as Westmorland, and does so to illustrate a simple philosophy of rural life similar to Webb's: "'Be honest with the land,' say the farmers, 'and it will be honest with you.'"[4] When that contract is broken, Holme's fiction generates great poignancy, as in the conclusion of *Beautiful End* (1918), where elderly Kit Sill's dream of returning to his marsh farm, now occupied by his son and daughter-in-law, dissolves when he actually does return and finds he can no longer retain his fond memories: "there was nothing here for him but the shell of lovely things grown strange."[5] He decides he has no choice but to return to live with his other daughter-in-law, the repressive and unsympathetic Marget.

This sad conclusion is also revealing about the limits of regional writing. Holme's best work, as Glen Cavaliero observes, offers "a comment on human experience and a definition of tragedy." She centers her best novels "round a dream and the nature of its fulfillment and [thereby] comments obliquely on the rural novelist's confrontation of change."[6] The tension in Holme's work, as so often in regional fiction, is between the celebration of an older way of life and the recognition that change is inevitable. Kit Sill's tragedy – the human tragedy of old man who chases after his sustaining memories only to see them crushed – is overlaid by tacit recognition of the inevitability of social change. It is this that makes the poignancy partly unjustified, and limited because slightly cloying.

In establishing the literary history of modern regional fiction it is worth bearing in mind that the aesthetic sensibility it fosters was sometimes deemed to be of questionable taste, even during its heyday. The earnest kind of region-alism in *Precious Bane* and *Beautiful End* is parodied definitively by Stella Gibbons in *Cold Comfort Farm* (1932), although this is not quite the thorough put-down it is sometimes assumed to be. The narrative of the good offices of city girl Flora Poste in undermining the brutish ways of the Starkadders depends upon generic targets that are not fully focussed by Gibbons; moreover, the felicitous love plot, which dilutes the comedy, is itself squarely in the tradition of comic pastoral: the parody is finally absorbed in the less barbed expression of pastiche.

Even within the work of the best-known regional novelists, at the apogee of the genre, the effects are often produced by complex and contradictory impulses. H. E. Bates's *The Poacher* (1935), with its action spanning the period between the 1880s and the 1920s, typifies the Hardyesque nostalgia that is common in the regional-rural English novel in the first half of the twentieth century. The lore of the poacher, inherited by Luke Bishop from his father Buck, becomes a figure for an anachronistic mode of life, its "illegality" a signal of how it is unsuited to the development of social progress. Even when Luke becomes a farmer, the lure of poaching is his undoing: he becomes a social outcast after serving a prison sentence for trespass and assault. This echoes the literal destruction of Buck, fatally wounded by a keeper's gun in a night chase. Yet, despite this demonstration of the destructive effects of poaching, the most vividly imagined episodes in *The Poacher* are, in fact, the night-time hunting scenes, when Buck and Luke are shown to be at one with the Northamptonshire and Bedfordshire fields and woods, and to have a sensuous and lethal understanding of their quarry. It is the loss of this empathic inhabitation of the landscape that is mourned, implicitly, in the retrospective dynamic of the novel. This is clear in the final scene when the outcast Luke finds houses where there had been fields, and cannot find the footpaths he had known. Luke's mystified encounter with two young surveyors in a field, taking measurements for a new housing estate, epitomizes the transition.

The pervasive presence of nostalgia in regional and rural novels requires some explication. It is easy to be misled into assigning specific historical reasons for the presence of nostalgia in the novel form's treatment of rural themes, especially those that lament a lost way of life. But there might be no era in which such nostalgia is not in evidence. It is also easy to assume that nostalgia is a retrograde phenomenon, redolent of a social conservatism that refuses to embrace change. However, the persistence of nostalgia in regional fiction requires a deeper explanation of its function. John Su implies that the nostalgic impulse might be an inherent mark of civilization, since "the longing to return to a lost homeland," as "a central feature of the Western literary tradition," is easily traced back to Homer. Su's immediate purpose is to rehabilitate nostalgia, to explain its recurrence in later twentieth-century fiction. It might be, however, that Su's analysis has a wider application where nostalgic fantasies "provide a means of establishing ethical ideals that can be shared by diverse groups who have in common only a longing for a past that never was."[7] Nostalgia can be consciously self-critical, as is Bates's nostalgia in *The Poacher*, which tacitly acknowledges an inevitable social contradiction. On the one hand, Bates's nostalgia is made questionable by the ambivalent business of poaching, which emerges as self-destructive; on the other hand, the fantasy of rural life is also cultivated. A form of double-consciousness is at work; and, as we shall see, nostalgic double-consciousness is a seminal feature of later novels in this mode.

Winifred Holtby's *South Riding* (1936) is another important regional novel, from within the primary period of the genre. This work anticipates the ways in which, as the century progresses, regional concerns became increasingly enmeshed with larger social questions. *South Riding* represents a significant new departure for the regional novel through its attempt to render the consequences of local government decisions "as part of the unseen pattern of the English landscape."[8] The novel draws on the author's knowledge of the operations of the county council in Yorkshire's East Riding (Holtby's mother was a county alderman); indeed, the separate areas of county council responsibility – "Education," "Agriculture and Small-Holdings," "Housing and Town Planning," etc. – supply the headings for the eight individual books in the novel. If this is a schematic conception, the execution ensures that the regional treatment is pervaded with a political consciousness. This consciousness circumscribes the human drama, but it also colors Holtby's celebratory descriptions of the Yorkshire landscape. If it is a truism to say that the novel is the primary form of discourse for depicting the interaction of the private and the public, *South Riding* is a very special investigation of this capacity, where public decisions in a particular locality are depicted in their ramifications for individual lives. The conception has to be bold to work – the novel has more than 150 characters – and it is this social panorama that helps *South Riding* achieve its status as perhaps the most accomplished instance of what we might think of as "political regionalism."

In its capacious treatment of a region, and its rigorous focus on local government, *South Riding* gives a nod toward the condition-of-England novel. There is a point where regionalism tips over into a consideration of national identity, and it is this alternative emphasis – which can produce quite different novelistic effects – that I trace in the remainder of this chapter. This is not to imply a simple historical dynamic in which the regional merely dissolves into the national. There is a gradual broad trend, in which the purely regional treatment becomes harder to sustain; but it is greatly complicated by counter-examples that blur the contrast. An earlier regional fiction that opens onto larger questions of affiliation is D. H. Lawrence's *The Rainbow* (1915), a complex novel with many strands, one of which is to question the nature of English identity. This concern grows out of a Nottinghamshire family saga: three generations of the Brangwens. A focus of the novel is the quest of Ursula Brangwen for personal realization in typically Lawrentian terms; yet the novel's celebrated conclusion reveals a broader significance to this quest. As Ursula contemplates a rainbow rising above the colliers' houses, the novel's social dynamic is underscored: her quest is intrinsically related to the circumscribed possibilities for life in her native industrial region, and, beyond that circumscription, to the social possibilities of life in an industrialized nation.

Much later in the century, John Fowles's *Daniel Martin* (1977) evinces a comparable complexity and historical self-consciousness. It begins with a traditional Devon harvest scene during the Second World War. For young Daniel Martin this defining image of "his Devon and England" is shattered by the rude intrusion of modernity in the form of a German bomber, an enormous Heinkel, flying just 200 feet above the field, filling Martin with foreboding, and the sense that "he is about to die."[9] This symbolic death is Fowles's way of marking a way of life that is brought to an end after the war. *Daniel Martin* identifies the loss of a collective principle of social organization, after which "we then broke up into tribes and classes, finally into private selves" (179). The novel is not straightforwardly nostalgic for the rural idyll that witnesses the cooperation of different social classes in the harvest ritual; yet the trope of an Edenic moment remains one aspect of Martin's quest for authenticity in the postwar world. The "rural," conceived as geographically bounded, and socially stable, is here made to stand for a world that no longer exists (however strong its nostalgic attractions), and which cannot supply a meaningful model for progress.

The assessment of regionality as a barometer for epochal change is equally apparent in Bruce Chatwin's *On the Black Hill* (1982), which conveys a reverence for place combined with an anti-pastoral awareness of the hardships, psychological as well as economic, that a rural existence can entail. The novel is set in the Black Mountains on the border of England and Wales, used here to explore the notion that everyone needs a place to identify with. The situation of Lewis and Benjamin Jones, hill farmers and identical twins, is simultaneously productive and destructive on account of their self-containment as a unit: they are effective farmers, in control of an expanding holding, yet are increasingly out of touch with a century with which they are only superficially in tandem. (They are born in the year of the Relief of Mafeking [1900].) Chatwin's novel of successive generations experiencing the impact of social change continues a long tradition. England, to the east, is the immediate source of the destructive world beyond, the world which is unsettling the twins' domain. Chatwin registers the tension between an enclosed regionalism and the dissolution of it, and achieves this through the novel's design, especially through the pointed contrast between the South African migrant Theo, a transnational presence, and the Jones twins.

There is a small but select group of twentieth-century novels in which place is given special prominence, to the point where place overshadows the development of character. In *A Glastonbury Romance* (1932) John Cowper Powys chooses a particular English spot – Glastonbury in Somerset – to be the heroic focus of a novel conceived on an epic scale, overlaying the legend of the Holy Grail with a modern morality tale in which the conflict between faith and greed is tied to the treatment of industrial exploitation. Raymond Williams's *People of the Black Mountains* (1990), using the same setting as Chatwin's *On the Black Hill*, places still greater emphasis on place, and embodies a still more radical treatment of the idea of belonging. The work was conceived as a trilogy, spanning the period from 23,000 BC to the twentieth century (and the present day, in its frame of linking passages), although it was left unfinished when Williams died. His grand gesture in this work is to refuse narrative fiction's usual reliance on human continuity: with a few exceptions, each story is set at a much later time than its predecessor, and involves a fresh set of characters. Narrative continuity is thus supplied by place rather than by character. This refusal of the usual narrative contract with the reader makes *People of the Black Mountains* only partially successful; but it is particularly noteworthy because it seems to locate the limits of regional fiction. Williams sidelines social events, so that he can attempt a long social history of place: regionalism on the grandest scale.

A comparable attempt to supply surface narrative continuity through place rather than character is Adam Thorpe's *Ulverton* (1992), which spans over three hundred years (1650–1988), in twelve separate sections comprising a chronological sequence of episodes in the life of a village in southwest England, each written in a different style. Thorpe's real achievement is to make moments of private drama, which are powerful stories in themselves, build into a poetic social history of place. The heroic resistance of under-gardener Percy Cullurne in the face of the enlistment drive of 1914, despite dubious incitements and public humiliation, is the novel's most powerful scene: "I'd rather bide at home," he tells the squire, scandalizing the assembled village.[10]

The elaborate technique of both *People of the Black Mountains* and *Ulverton* emphasizes the necessary connection between place and human history, where that history is conceived as a dialogue between present frames of understanding and an imperfect reconstruction of the past. If an agreed and verifiable history of place is unavailable, there can be no single understanding of regional belonging; but there can be an imaginative attempt to construct a version of regional inhabitation. This involves historical sensitivity toward region, and ancestry, but with an awareness that the effort of reconstruction is piecemeal. Implicit in this is a warning about the risk of seeking particular, exclusive social origins, an idea treated explicitly in Thorpe's later *Pieces of Light* (1998), a return to Ulverton in which a pointed ambivalence about the celebration of place emerges.

If the pursuit of origins implies a dubious, and reactionary motivation, does this not make the celebration of a particular place as a source of human continuity reactionary by definition? And, if so, does this make a stance of postmodern relativity a felicitous feature in the treatment of place and identity, a necessary check on more insidious desires? A brilliant novel that centers on this very tension between the construction of identity and identification with one particular landscape is Graham Swift's *Waterland* (1983). Swift's novel generates its effects by cultivating a sense of crisis about contrasting kinds of narrative. One effect is to produce a grim version of English history, rooted in imperialism and industrial exploitation. In reaction, narrator Tom Crick has recourse to an unorthodox "humble model for progress" in which "the reclamation of land," a process of "repeatedly, never-endingly retrieving what is lost," is analogous to the subjective and selective shoring-up process of telling stories about oneself.[11] Swift gets beyond the play of textuality, however, when the real and the metaphorical are yoked together in the image of siltation. Crick's storytelling is the cultural equivalent of the struggle for land reclamation, and is similarly incomplete. Yet this metaphorical parallel is not transferable: it works specifically, in the British context, for the fens. In this there is an express emphasis on environment as a limit to consciousness, with the repeated references to the flat fenland landscape as an adverse influence on the psyche.

In the work of Chatwin, Williams, Thorpe, and Swift the continuing resonance of regionalism is tested, and is linked to questions of personal identity and belonging, if only obliquely. There are other novels where problems of national identity are more prominent. It is helpful to remember some of the difficulties that surround the conception of national identity. While nationalism has often been considered inherently reactionary, especially by critics of English literature in the twentieth century, in the postcolonial context nationalism has been the focus of a re-evaluation where the nationalism of emergent states is seen as a more congenial force, tending toward new forms of social organization. Such opposing views of nationalism, perceived either as the vehicle for chauvinism, or as the means to a more equitable, negotiated future, are the poles between which the treatment of British national identities in postwar fiction has tended to work. Novelists have been wary of an uncompromising tradition on the one hand, while tentatively contemplating the reinvention of nationality on the other. As a consequence, a third position has emerged: a kind of post-nationalism built on reappraised symbols and traditions that implicitly acknowledges the mongrelized nature of most British identities.

The uncertainty about national identity is, inevitably, most pronounced in refigurations of Englishness, where the legacy of imperialism remains a dominant presence. Indeed, it has been highly unfashionable to contemplate the more stable elements that might comprise an English national character, especially in the second half of the twentieth century, when Englishness was deemed to be tainted with imperialism. As we have seen, John Fowles is one writer who has bucked this trend of silence about English identity. In *Daniel Martin* the English trait of reticence or withdrawal is treated ambivalently, as an indication of both moral failure and potential. Fowles links this moral conundrum to the "archetypal national myth" of Robin Hood, the myth, that is, of moral rectitude facilitated through withdrawal to the "sacred combe" (303, 306). In the figure of the "Just Outlaw" the personification of justice is held in tension with self-righteousness and asocial aloofness. Fowles' intriguing association of genre, myth, and nationality is pursued through Martin's quest for authenticity, but is tempered by an appreciation of the historically contingent relationship between person and place.

The contingent relationship between person and place in relation to Englishness is emphatically tested in Julian Barnes's *England, England* (1998), in which the essential features of England are reduced to a theme park on the Isle of Wight, with all the major tourist attractions reproduced in convenient proximity. This "England, England" comes to supplant "old" England, but the confusion of the authentic and the bogus unleashes a national identity crisis. Barnes's serious purpose, in a book of conflicting moods, is to offer a more philosophical (yet accessible) deliberation on how the culture of the replica has an impact on national identity, where the replica supplants the original. There is, however, a dynamic in the book that is at variance with this insistence on the false or artificial elements of history and identity. In the final section we see an elderly Martha Cochrane (the central character) back in old England, now known as "Anglia," which, in the economic shadow of The Island, has degenerated into a parody of its pre-industrial self. Yet this regression to village quaintness is not without its attractions. The final scene of the village fête, with its May Queen, its four-piece band and village bobby, its seed cake and preserves, pickles, and chutneys, approaches a pastoral idyll. What is significant is how Barnes pushes the cliché – and in this sense the conclusion is a self-conscious fabrication like the rest of the book – until it seems to promise something of value after all.

Barnes's novel is very much in tune with recent theories of nationalism in which the constructed nature of national feeling is emphasized. The more encouraging formulations call for a conscious, responsible approach, in the spirit of what Barnes calls "complex trust."[12] Without doubt the most influential theorist of national identity for critics of the novel is Benedict Anderson, who has persuasively linked the rise of the novel as a form with the emergence of the modern nation state. In Anderson's reading, the nation is defined as "an imagined political community," imagined as limited in geographical scope, and as sovereign in nature. The modern nation is thus an eighteenth-century concept, a product of "an age in which Enlightenment and Revolution were destroying the legitimacy of the divinely-ordained dynastic realm."[13]

For Anderson the emergence of both the newspaper and the novel are historically co-terminous with the modern concept of the nation. This has partly to do with the sense of shared contemporary experience, or simultaneity, that is necessary to the consolidation of a national community. Anderson shows how this experience of simultaneity is emulated in the narrative technique of the novel, where the "meanwhile" of narration connects characters by embedding them in representations of particular societies, and assigns to the reader, in whose mind the connections are realized, a privileged and omniscient vantage point. What the novel produces thereby in the reader, Anderson argues, is the idea of "a sociological organism" moving through time, "a precise analogue of the idea of the nation," also "conceived as a solid community moving steadily down (or up) history." The argument is not simply that the novel emulates the imagined community among strangers, upon which the modern nation depends, but that it might have played a significant role in establishing the terms of the nation, and the confidence the nation breeds in "steady, anonymous, simultaneous activity" (*Imagined Communities*, 24–26). In Anderson's view the imaginary nature of the national community can be a constructive phenomenon to be interpreted, rather than merely a false entity to be condemned; and it is this which gives his theory its productive (and portable) applicability. It is possible to overstate the role of the novel in the construction of national identity; however, those novels that have an enduring cultural resonance have a contribution to make to the collective idea of a national identity that is gradual and incremental.

Because of the close, and often difficult, relationship between England and Ireland, the interaction between the two nations has been registered by novelists throughout the century. Elizabeth Bowen's *The Last September* (1929) is an important work in this connection, a classic Irish "big house" novel which examines the predicament of the Ascendancy at the time of the troubles. Later in the century, J. G. Farrell in *Troubles* (1970) also set a consideration of 1919–1921 against the backdrop of the big house (a hotel in this case), as part of an examination of British nationalism as a form of madness, where such nationalism is a union of Anglo-Irish and British interests. Even when a novel's focus is on Ireland, some element of interaction with England is often felt. Edna O'Brien, for example, like many other Irish writers, had to move to England before she could begin to write about Ireland. In O'Brien's work the impression of Irish identity is determined by the contrary attractions of the country and the city. Her novels of the 1960s, such as *The Lonely Girl* (1962), reveal the historical tension between a Catholic upbringing in rural Ireland and the (ultimately disillusioning) excitement and sexual promise of life in Dublin.

"Irish Culture," writes Declan Kiberd, "exists in a kind of parabolic relation to England's." Consequently, "the Irish, in renovating their own consciousness, may also be helping, wittingly or unwittingly, to reanimate England's."[14] Irish migrants to England would seem to form a primary group for the development of this kind of cross-fertilization. However, much writing about the Irish experience in England, or Britain generally, concerns itself with the shedding of predetermined roles, and the relinquishment of shibboleths, in what amounts to a cultural ground-clearing exercise. A key factor in distinguishing Irish from other migrant groups in Britain is the dream of returning home. While this is a common aim for all migrant groups, the closeness of Ireland gives the dream greater plausibility. In practice this is often a delusion, but its persuasiveness can make the sense of temporary exile a defining conviction of the "Irish-British," a sparsely represented ethnicity in the British novel, perhaps on account of the stigma of failure that has traditionally been attached, in the Irish consciousness, to those emigrating to England. *Home From England* (1995) by James Ryan confronts and explodes the illusions that surround Irish emigration, which is not presented as necessarily temporary or as a source of great sadness. The (unnamed) narrator is entering his teens when his family moves from rural

Ireland to England in the early 1960s. The myth of return pervades the parents' attitudes to life in England, preventing them from a meaningful life in the present. The children, however, soon become acculturated to life in England, so that a generation gap qualifies the dream of return, and articulates it as a regressive myth of nostalgia, rooted in a debilitating nationalism. The final paragraph articulates the narrator's now complete disentanglement from his father's nationalism. He has arrived at a metaphorical "vantage point from which I could see my fields becoming his fields," and from which "his war for independence" comes to resemble the war games of boyhood.[15] Divesting himself of the trappings of an anachronistic, falsifying nationalism, Ryan's anonymous modern Irishman reclaims and redefines the ground on which his identity might be based.

This provisional and ambivalent treatment of nationalism is thoroughly representative of twentieth-century fiction in Britain. Similar sentiments can be detected in the Welsh or the Scottish novel, where the problem of distinguishing the treatment of the regional from the treatment of the national – to return to that conundrum – is especially fraught. Partly, this is a problem of perception. Regionalism can be, as Cairns Craig observes, "an almost all-embracing category in relation to the Scottish novel" because of the critical tendency to identify all Scottish novels "as regional within the traditions of the *English* novel," rather than to distinguish between, say, the Glasgow of James Kelman or the Orkney of George Mackay Brown.[16]

An important writer in relation both to Scottish regionalism and to Scottish national identity is Lewis Grassic Gibbon, a writer we should associate with the Howe of the Mearns, or, less specifically, with the northeast Lowlands if we are to follow Cairns Craig's scrupulous distinctions. Gibbon's trilogy *A Scots Quair* (1932–1934) is partly a retrospective lament for a distinct regional tradition, and a peasant existence, that is lost as a consequence of industrialization. The novel is notable for its rendering of regional dialect; yet this also means that it incorporates a broader plea for Scottish nationalism, since the social changes it registers – especially the way in which standard English stifles local forms of expression – have an urgency that is common to different Scottish regions. The plight of the novel's heroine Chris Guthrie, caught between ancestral tradition and cultural change, is emblematic of a national dilemma. *A Scots Quair* has come to encapsulate a mythical "Scottishness" that has been hugely influential for the national literary imagination.

In Scottish fiction it is often the dominant presence of English culture that represents the force to react against, but that remains present as a negative pole in the equation of nationality. There is also the perennial (and sometimes related) problem of treating tradition and making it malleable, a source of reconstruction. A novelist who treats this problem, obliquely, and as a formal matter, is Alasdair Gray, whose novel *Lanark* (1981) has been highly influential in the development of Scottish fiction from the 1980s onwards. The novel's twin settings, Glasgow and the dystopian fantasy City of Unthank, suggest the two poles – realism and fantasy – between which Gray locates the impetus of his writing. The median position thus established represents a simultaneous challenge to the two fictional codes. The received history of the realist code is disputed in a famous passage in which Glasgow is said to be neglected in artistic representations, and so unavailable for imaginative inhabitation.[17] At the other extreme, the novel's fantastic elements suggest the dangers of the unfettered imagination, where escapism is in the ascendancy.

What can be observed repeatedly in the Scottish novel toward the end of the century is a metanarrative of national identity, often finely poised between imaginative reconstruction, and uncertain angst. Alan Warner's *Morvern Callar* (1995) deliberates in complex manner on the relationship between nation and narration. The eponymous heroine and narrator is a twenty-one-year-old exploited supermarket worker in a remote Highland seaport. The novel opens with her discovery of her boyfriend's corpse, and the suicide note that bequeaths to her his unpublished novel on computer disc. In metafictional terms the silenced Scottish underclass, for which Morvern Callar stands, is released from the neglect of the novelistic imagination. Morvern's spirit of independence is significant. She is particularly responsive to the natural beauty of her surroundings, though this sensitivity is pointedly distinguished from a conventional literary sensibility. Her camping trip to the Mountains demonstrates her affinity with place, her enjoyment of being "in Nature," amid the "loveliness" which is "just silence"; but such trips have also been the occasion for her to dispose of her boyfriend's corpse, previously dismembered to facilitate a staggered burial "all across the land."[18] The pastoral scene symbolically is the site for the disposal of the untrustworthy Scottish novelist with his more conventional mannerisms.

Treatments of place and space in twentieth-century Welsh fiction are often linked to questions of national identity rather than to more narrowly focussed investigations of regionalism. In such treatments a sense of Welsh national identity is commonly predicated on a reaction against Britishness, and the political and cultural dominance it is perceived to represent. The resistance to effacement at the hands of a colonizing Englishness brings problems with it, however. It often involves the attempt to define stable boundaries in the construction of national identity, boundaries that have been surpassed by historical, cultural, and geographical change. In fiction a retreat into a mythology of Welshness has been a frequent response to this challenge. In Alexander Cordell's

Rape of the Fair Country (1959), for example, the family-saga form of historical romance employs, in a predetermined manner, a received history of English oppression in its cultivation of national pride and the love of place. The dynamic is retrogressive, in its dependence on a "finished" and "remembered past," which fails to address "the openness of the present," or "the will to a wider perspective."[19] The inhibiting effect of the backward look is glaringly apparent in Richard Llewellyn's *How Green Was My Valley*, a hugely popular Welsh novel of the postwar period, even though it was published in 1939. Llewellyn's novel is "widely and properly seen as the export version of the Welsh industrial experience" (Williams, "The Welsh Industrial Novel," 227); and it has latterly become infamous on account of its insular and sentimental appeal to place, and the revelation that Llewellyn was born in Hendon (as Vivian Lloyd), and was not the son of a Pembrokeshire miner.

The case of Llewellyn encapsulates the central problem for Welsh writers, where a turning inwards or (historically) backwards might stave off the process of assimilation to Britain, but only by cultivating a false, and so vulnerable, nationalism. What has become increasingly pertinent is a form of cultural explanation that embraces the fact of migration, and heterogeneity, and that acknowledges a counterproductive insistence on origins: a mode, that is, that begins to relinquish the traditional components of the regional novel.

Emyr Humphreys's *Outside the House of Baal* (1965), considered to be possibly "the most canonical of modern Welsh novels," might be the definitive novel of Welsh national decline (Bianchi, "Aztecs in Troedrhiwgwair," 65). The novel employs a complex time frame to juxtapose a postwar present with an unfolding narrative that traces its characters' pasts back to the early years of the twentieth century. Humphreys is acutely conscious of the assimilation of Wales to England, and the encroachment of commercial interests that negate Welsh culture (such as the modern neighborhood pub in the novel, dubbed "The House of Baal"). The careers of the next generation are presented as part of that process of assimilation. But the new generation are moving through and beyond the phase of incorporation. *Outside the House of Baal* suggests – rather against the author's published view – that the adherence to a sickly tradition imposes a straitjacket on the present, cutting it off from its possible futures.

The novels that speak most eloquently to the problems of national identity for the four nations that comprise the British Isles are those that make the question of belonging a *process*, a matter of undoing past affiliations as well as forging new ones. Just as the perception of the bounded region in Britain has come to seem increasingly anachronistic – as has the idea of a circumscribed regional culture – so has the sense of geographical containment in defining the nation-state become less convincing.

Notes

1. K. D. M. Snell, "The Regional Novel: Themes for Interdisciplinary Research," in *The Regional Novel in Britain and Ireland, 1800 – 1990*, ed. K. D. M. Snell (Cambridge University Press, 1998), pp. 1–2.
2. Phyllis Bentley, *The English Regional Novel* (London: Allen and Unwin, 1941), pp. 13, 33–40.
3. Mary Webb, *Precious Bane* (London: Virago, 1980), p. 189.
4. Constance Holme, Preface to *The Lonely Plough* (London: Oxford University Press, 1931), p. viii.
5. Constance Holme, *Beautiful End* (London: Oxford University Press, 1949), p. 219.
6. Glen Cavaliero, *The Rural Tradition in the English Novel, 1900–1939* (Basingstoke: Macmillan, 1978), p. 162.
7. John Su, *Ethics and Nostalgia in the Contemporary Novel* (Cambridge University Press, 2005), pp. 1, 3.
8. Winifred Holtby, "Prefatory Letter to Alderman Mrs. Holtby," *South Riding* (London: Virago, 2007), p. xi.
9. John Fowles, *Daniel Martin* (London: Picador, 1989), p. 11.
10. Adam Thorpe, *Ulverton* (London: Minerva, 1993), p. 233.
11. Graham Swift, *Waterland* (London: Picador, 1984), p. 291.
12. Julian Barnes, *England, England* (London: Jonathan Cape, 1998), p. 264.
13. Benedict Anderson, *Imagined Communities* (London: Verso, 1991), pp. 6–7.
14. Declan Kiberd, "Reinventing England," *Key Words: A Journal of Cultural Materialism* 2 (1999), 56.
15. James Ryan, *Home from England* (London: Phoenix, 1996), p. 184.
16. Cairns Craig, "Scotland and the Regional Novel," in *The Regional Novel in Britain and Ireland, 1880–1990*, ed. K. D. M. Snell (Cambridge University Press, 1998), p. 221.
17. Alasdair Gray, *Lanark: A Life in 4 Books* (London: Picador, 1994), p. 243.
18. Alan Warner, *Morvern Callar* (London: Vintage, 1996), pp. 104, 91.
19. Tony Bianchi, "Aztecs in Troedrhiwgwair: Recent Fictions in Wales," in *Peripheral Visions: Images of Nationhood in Contemporary British Fiction*, ed. Ian A. Bell (Cardiff: University of Wales Press, 1995), p. 48; and Raymond Williams, "The Welsh Industrial Novel," in *Problems in Materialism and Culture* (London: Verso, 1980), p. 227.

45

The series novel: a dominant form

SUZANNE KEEN

If this chapter were charged with the task of describing twentieth-century English children's fiction, until recently a neglected category in literary histories, novels in trilogies and series would loom large. Imagine a literary history of the children's story without Joan Aiken, the Reverend W. Awdry, Enid Blyton, Susan Cooper, Brian Jacques, Michael de Larrabeiti, C. S. Lewis, Hugh Lofting, A. A. Milne, E. Nesbit, K. M. Peyton, Beatrix Potter, Philip Pullman, Arthur Ransome, J. K. Rowling, Rosemary Sutcliffe, or Barbara Willard. Imagine never again visiting those countries of the mind where swallows and amazons rove Lakeland; where Harry, Ron, and Hermione attend Hogwarts; where descendants of British Romans witness in the dark ages the coming of a Celtic Arthur; where Mantlemass stands at the heart of Ashdown forest, persisting from the Wars of the Roses through the English Civil War. Most readers would feel the absence of these dream countries of childhood reading, if they paused to recall the anticipation ignited by the long row of matching covers in a library or bookshop (is this the right summer to begin Noel Streatfeild's *Ballet Shoes* books?), or the melancholy provoked by the end of a series (still disappointed at Narnia's rolling up like a carpet?), or the bittersweet recognition that they have gotten too grown up to enjoy a series anymore (at least until reading aloud to their own children begins).

Why these formative reading experiences, reinforced during most of the twentieth century by radio, television, and film fiction in series, should account for so little in histories of the novel requires explanation: understanding the omission helps to explain a parallel neglect of sequences written for adults. The very plenitude of works in series written for children forges an association between these most expansive, elastic forms of the novel and juvenile appetites for extension and elaboration, for escapist fantasy facilitated by immersion in and re-entry into sustained fictional worlds, for naïve identification with and investment in characters who come to seem like old friends, even when they live in impossible worlds where trains have temper tantrums or schools teach the art of transfiguration. In their most debased forms, children's sequences can come to appear mere franchises (not even written by a real author, or the same author), baldly commercial gambits to hook young readers on the addictive pleasures of the serial dosage of fiction. A pervasive pedagogical narrative maps maturation as a reader onto the young person's ability to enjoy a freestanding classic, to slow down and analyze rather than gulp down the next installment, to dissect instead of consuming. Series fiction may be pleasurable to read, but it is inconvenient to teach, especially when national or state standards emphasize familiarity with a specific list of texts and authors and mastery of literary terminology over the formation of reading habits. Finally, the strong association of series fiction with the less admired sub-genres (fantasy, science fiction, historical romances, mysteries, Westerns, thrillers) has until quite recently supported a developmental narrative in which better, more highly educated readers suppress their appetite for novels in series in favor of critically admired individual works.

Against these discrediting traits, most importantly the association of sequences with works for children, we may set a number of more positive observations available to the distant reader (a reader, in Franco Moretti's mode,[1] who quantifies texts by kind, and notes trends by collecting publication dates) of the twentieth-century English novel. These observations include the dominance of trilogies and sequences as a novelistic form, their evolution to accommodate the *topoi* and shapes of modernity and postmodernity, their continuing popularity with authors, publishers, and readers, and their prominence in (sub-)genres of the novel, such as fantasy and historical fiction, that still boast robust audiences in a period of declining reading. The end of the long exile of the genres from the arena of critical approbation enables re-expansion of the realm of literary fiction officially to include what was there all along, narrative sequences in a variety of kinds. This chapter tells the complicated story of the serial form itself, as inherited from the nineteenth-century English and French novel. Though consigned for many decades to the less-respected sub-genres of the novel (detective fiction, fantasy, historical romances), sequences are so pervasive across the major and minor types of the English novel as to constitute a dominant form, to apply a phrase coined by Raymond Williams.

The extreme variety of representational tasks that trilogies and sequences undertake and the diversity of forms in which they appear, even during the same decades, might explain why these ubiquitous twentieth-century works could be overlooked and remain untaught. The claustrophobic Anglo-Catholic world of Antonia White's Clara Batchelor trilogy (1950–1954) hardly seems related to the scenes of its contemporaries, Anthony Burgess's Malay trilogy, *The Long Day*

Wanes (1956–1959), Anthony Powell's *A Dance to the Music of Time* (1951–1975), or Henry Williamson's *A Chronicle of Ancient Sunlight* (1951–1969). Joyce Cary's first trilogy (1941–1944) could be regarded as the anti-matter to the matter of C. P. Snow's *Strangers and Brothers* (1940–1970) in style and subject: even to bring the Blakean visionary Gully Jimson into the same sentence with the Masters and academicians of Snow stages a social and ideological contrary. Trilogies and sequences exhibit such diversity that they repel efforts at generalization. Thus one goal of this chapter is to establish the varieties of formal and compositional logic observable in twentieth-century trilogies and series, enquiring into the consequences, for form and reception, when novelists sustain narratives beyond the boundaries of the single book. To proceed in the mode of Moretti's distant reading means attending to dates and clusters of texts, counting and graphing rather than pausing to examine any one text closely.

Applying this strategy reveals the high-water mark of sequences and demonstrates that they never entirely disappear, especially if works in popular genres are included. The twentieth century opens with an influential fictional sequence in limbo, as Sir Arthur Conan Doyle has not yet brought Sherlock Holmes back from his evident death at the Reichenbach Falls. Relenting in 1903 with the first of the stories that would be republished in book form as *The Return of Sherlock Holmes* (1905), Doyle consolidates the serial as a fundamental format for detective fiction; by the time he ceases publishing Holmes stories, Agatha Christie and Dorothy Sayers have already launched Hercule Poirot and Lord Peter Wimsey. Popular fiction in the twentieth century is thus never without detective fiction in series, nor is it now, with Robert Barnard, Peter Dickinson, P. D. James, Ruth Rendell, and Alexander McCall Smith still writing them. Though the Holmes stories and novels provide the bridge between the nineteenth and twentieth centuries' fictional sequences, the serial installment in a magazine was only one of the models already in use by Victorian novelists. Magazine serialization could be episodic, featuring freestanding complete stories such as those published by *Strand* magazine, or they could present full novels in weekly or biweekly installments. The association of original serial publication of novels with suspenseful, cliff-hanging episode breaks derives from the prac-tice of Wilkie Collins, Charles Dickens, Elizabeth Gaskell, and Thomas Hardy. Prominent nineteenth-century novelists, notably Dickens, William Thackeray, and George Eliot, sold their long novels in twelve to eighteen softcover monthly numbers over a year or eighteen months. Victorian readers also enjoyed lengthy sequences, from Walter Scott's *Waverley* novels, to the political and ecclesiastical series of Trollope, to Margaret Oliphant's popular *Chronicles of Carlingford*, a novel sequence that began with a serialized story. With all three varieties of serial distribution of fiction in use, readers were habituated to reading novels in accumulating batches: the midstream periodical reviews of individual installments of long novels reveal lively engagement with unfinished stories.

No surprise, then, to find that middle-brow and high-brow literary fiction employs the serial form writ large in novel sequences in the early decades of the twentieth century. By 1920 John Galsworthy, with *The Man of Property* (1906) and *In Chancery* (1920), and Dorothy Richardson, with *Pointed Roofs* (1915), had both begun their very long sequences. Ford Madox Ford publishes his tetralogy *Parade's End* (1924–1928). Comic sequences fit the bill in the 1920s and 1930s, when E. F. Benson's Mapp and Lucia novels, E. M. Delafield's *Provincial Lady* novels are begun, and installments of P. G. Wodehouse's Jeeves and Psmith lines reach large audiences. Paper shortages during the Second World War and the postwar period reduced both the numbers of titles and the print runs of books published until after 1950, but Snow, Cary, and L. P. Hartley all publish trilogies or novels in sequence during this period. Famously, Anthony Trollope's fiction enjoyed a revival during the 1930s and 1940s, which may partly explain the efflorescence of lengthy sequences in the 1950s, when paper supplies were replenished. Powell, Williamson, and Doris Lessing all begin long sequences in the early 1950s, and this period also sees many trilogies (by Burgess, Cary, the Canadian novelist Robertson Davies, Mervyn Peake, J. R. R. Tolkien, Evelyn Waugh, and White). T. S. Eliot's *Four Quartets* (1943, 1944) might have lent high modernist cachet to a near relative of the popular trilogy format: Lawrence Durrell's *Alexandria Quartet* (1957–1962) and Paul Scott's *Raj Quartet* (1966–1975) both aspire to complicate readers' work by elaborating alternative but partial perspectives in a mode reminiscent of modernist fiction by Woolf and Faulkner.

The 1960s and 1970s see a continuance of trilogies and sequences, many of them historical, representing events of a generation earlier, such as the Second World War and the height of the British Empire. Important trilogies by Olivia Manning and Isabel Colegate represent the experience of non-combatants in the East (Manning's Balkan trilogy [1960–1965]) and an appeasement politician's moral failures (Colegate's Orlando trilogy [1968–1973]). Waugh brings his satirical *Sword of Honour* trilogy, which follows the farcical wartime adventures of Guy Crouchback, to a close in 1968. Major sequences begun earlier are still running, so in the 1960s Powell turns out his most mordantly comic depictions of the Second World War as an opportunity for social climbers and amoral chameleons, while Williamson bitterly documents the isolation and persecution of English fascists and sympathizers (*A Solitary War* [1967] is dedicated to Oswald and Diana Mosley). In the late 1970s Oswald Mosley's son Nicholas Mosley begins his important sequence *Catastrophe Practice* (1979–1990), premised on the notion that there is a match between "falsity in the imposition of patterns on writing" and "danger in the impositions of patterns upon life,"[2] a view that certainly discourages literary history that wants to discover such patterns. However, Mosley represents the old patterns in order to explode them, and concludes his sequence with *Hopeful Monsters* (1990), a novel that alludes to the possibility of a leap in evolution through mutation to create "a form of life on the brink either of something new – or of extinction" (*Catastrophe Practice*, 340).

Before novel sequences can be recognized as undergoing the mutations that mark a new and emergent form, however, novels in series – the ultimate loose baggy monsters – must first be understood as an omnipresent, dominant form of the twentieth-century English novel, long appreciated by regular readers if not by academics. In Williams's terms an emergent form can be discovered by scrutinizing the social present, where the "effective formations of most actual art relate to already manifest social formations, dominant or residual, and it is primarily to emergent formations (though often in the form of modification or disturbance in older forms) that the structure of feeling, as solution, relates."[3] While Williams's model tilts toward discovery of the emergent form and its revelations of changing structures of feeling, Moretti's methodology more dispassionately documents how many texts of a particular kind actually occur in a period. By this measure sheer quantity matters.

A dominant form may not be the first choice distinctively to characterize a period in literary history: that honor often falls to scholars of emergent forms to bestow. A dominant form will be ubiquitous, taken-for-granted, sometimes so ordinary as to go unnoticed. (Of course detective fiction comes in series: didn't it always?) It will occur throughout a lived period of history, persisting long enough for members of an earlier generation to still recognize it when they are old, for it will not be dying out like a residual form. Younger people will know it as always around in the background, certainly not the next new thing that the grandparents can't figure out how to operate. Practitioners of work composed in a dominant form will be aware of working in a tradition. This tradition might not be the most respected or celebrated form around (indeed, if it sells well enough to persist, it probably is not) and the tradition might tacitly acknowledge a narrative of decline from the lofty achievement of an admired precursor, or it might frankly avow a wish to keep the old thing going, since it is obviously still working. A dominant form will be capacious enough to contain rivalries of taste and readerly allegiance, developments that excite or dismay, forgotten and unread examples as well as unashamed retreads and open satires of its purposes and parodies of its most noticeable characteristics (Jasper Fforde does this handily in his Thursday Next series).

These variables confirm its dominance. A sure sign of a dominant form rests in its commercial power to capture an author inside a franchise he cannot sell off: Conan Doyle tried that and failed; we shall see if J. K. Rowling can make the break.

Truly a dominant form of twentieth-century fiction, then, sequences occur not only in the genres, where they are ubiquitous (Michael Moorcock's chronicles and trilogies are building blocks of a science fiction multiverse), but also in middle-brow novels documenting the changing mores of society. For instance, Margaret Drabble's *Gates of Ivory* trilogy (1987–1991) can be placed in the condition of England tradition. Sequences also occur in more ambitiously literary fiction (Durrell's *Alexandria Quartet*, Lessing's *Children of Violence* sequence, Powell's *A Dance to the Music of Time*); in self-consciously innovative, experimental works such as Richardson's *Pilgrimage* and Mosley's *Catastrophe Practice*; and in explicitly historical sequences that tackle experiences of empire and war (by Burgess, Manning, Scott, and Waugh). So often preoccupied with the passing of time or the documentation of evanescent period styles (Galsworthy is particularly good at catching the linguistic texture of a moment), some sequences demand consideration against the historical context that undergirds their weighty and lengthy structure. But which history and which context? As Cary writes in the voice of his character Thomas Wilcher in *To Be a Pilgrim* (1942), "History does not move in one current, like the wind across bare seas, but in a thousand streams and eddies, like the wind over a broken landscape . . . We write of an age. But there is no complete age."[4] Sequences seem an especially appropriate form for following more of the eddies of historical change than could be accommodated in a single novel. Nonetheless, two major historical narratives vie for the title of the most persuasive story of the British twentieth century: victory in two successive world wars, with the defense of the island nations and defeat of fascism as its central accomplishments; and the disappearance of the British Empire, with a complementary shrinking of the nation to its islanded confines. Major historical sequences and trilogies can be placed within each of these rival historiographical camps, while several of the longest sequences tell parts of both stories, in ironic or nostalgic modes.

The different emphases of these rival metanarratives support a resurgence of the historical, historiographical, and otherwise temporally demanding fiction that enlarges the novel into sequences, even as they accommodate a range of heritage sentiments (R. M. Delderfield's *God Is An Englishman* series [1970–1973]), imperial apologetics (Simon Raven's *Alms for Oblivion* [1964–1973]), and revisionist history accommodating previously suppressed perspectives (Pat Barker's *Regeneration* trilogy [1991–1995], for instance, gives voice to homosexual and bisexual experience). While several of the lengthiest series, by Richardson and Williamson, follow inward turns that can be read as a narrowing of perspective on the part of literary fiction, others dramatize generational ambitions through time (Galsworthy's Forsytes) and imperial agendas of the past (Patrick O'Brian's Aubrey/Maturin novels [1969–2004]).

Early examples of the very long sequence, Richardson's *Pilgrimage* and Galsworthy's *The Forsyte Chronicles*, share an undoing of imperialist ambitions and values, with story time beginning in the late Victorian period and extending into the period of decolonization; both, despite their length, emphasize the value of limited horizons. In the post-World War II period, Powell describes time as a series of inevitable repetitions, while Lessing breaks the claustrophobic container of the *Bildungsroman* with her fractured, visionary conclusion to *Children of Violence*, *The Four-Gated City* (1969). In the later twentieth century, the historical impulse is no longer sequestered in historical romances, generational sagas, and sequences like those of Powell and Williamson. In the decades of the vaunted "historical turn" of contemporary British fiction (the 1970s and 1980s), sequence writers such as A. S. Byatt, Mosley, and Ferdinand Mount match freestanding historical fiction with reconsiderations of postwar and post-imperial Britain. The search for an adequate form to convey disparate experiences without oversimplifying shows in Byatt and Mosley's flirtations with hybrid genres and in Drabble and Manning's extended geography, running all the way to Cambodia and the Levant. A twenty-first century sequence, Gwyneth Jones's *Bold as Love* novels (2001–2006), is the apotheosis of the devolution series, beginning with dissolution of national government in a near future scenario where England is cut off from the rest of the world by a real and virtual (internet) quarantine and ravaged by Green terrorism.

Though we may often recognize in sequences the formal logic and representational strategies of imperial decline, we should also acknowledge the novel sequence as a form with generous affordances to resist singular trajectories, to complicate homogenizing politics, to utilize both the energies of inwardness and the carnivalesque, and to swerve in unexpected generic and representational directions.

As a token of that variety, consider settings, which sequences employ as devices of continuity. Twentieth-century sequences represent not just the shrinking island of Little England. Many are set in the walks of power: Whitehall, the army and navy, public schools, and universities. London exerts its magnetic pull: the characters of so many sequences by different writers could cross paths at the Café Royal! Yet comic series often centrifuge away from London, to be contained by the boundaries of Britain, as in significant parts of Cary's Gully

Jimson trilogy and Benson's Lucia and Mapp novels. Novel sequences also accommodate a tourist's impulse to trot the globe, as in Delafield's *Diaries of a Provincial Lady* and the Flashman novels by George MacDonald Fraser. This is not simply a postwar, contemporary phenomenon. Galsworthy locates two interludes of his *Forsyte Chronicles* (*A Silent Wooing* and *Passers By* [1927]) in the United States. Even Richardson's introspective character Miriam Henderson goes abroad, for apprentice teaching in *Pointed Roofs* (1915) and Alpine sledding in *Oberland* (1927). In the 1950s it was hard for British people to travel abroad, but their novelists were not so confined, as Burgess, Durrell, and John le Carré show in their sequences. If it is the case that many of the long sequences of the twentieth century dramatize the undoing of imperialist ambitions and values, what happens to novel sequences in the post-imperial contemporary? Have they lost their job? Sequences are certainly still strong presences today in spy thrillers, children's fiction, detective fiction, fantasy, science fiction, and in film and television, where they migrate in the 1960s with *The Forsyte Saga*. Le Carré's novels demonstrate the endurance of the form and its global representational reach. On his website a visitor can move the mouse over a map of the world "to discover the location of le Carré's stories": only Australia and Antarctica are left out.[5] Writers of sequence fiction labor under no obligation to realistic geography, as Terry Pratchett's Discworld, a flat world balanced on four elephants who stand on the back of a turtle, amply demonstrates in three dozen linked novels.

Temporal variety in construction, not just in the time period of their settings, characterizes trilogies and sequences. Both have earlier origins and important precursors in the nineteenth-century novel, which give trilogies a predilection for the chronology of *Bildung*, and release sequences from the obligations of orderly temporality or even generic homogeneity. Vast sequences by Zola and Balzac suggest their capacity to contain works in a surprising variety of genres, even plays, a hint taken up by Mosley in his *Catastrophe Practice*, which begins with "three plays for not acting" and contains film scripts for movies that cannot be made, or Pratchett's Discworld, with its internal miniseries and accommodation of different audiences, including children. The sequence inherited from nineteenth-century precursors consists of distinct, self-contained but interrelated works, not bound by the chronology of the story world, such as Thomas Hardy's Wessex novels. In the twentieth century Snow's eleven-volume *Strangers and Brothers*, which treats story time anachronously until the last four volumes, exemplifies the continuing influence on form of the loose, capacious nineteenth-century French sequence. The descendants of the spatially demarcated French mode, frequently used for satire and pointed social commentary include Faulkner's works set in Yoknapatawpha County (1929–1962), derived in part from Hardy's Wessex. A rival model emerges in the English nineteenth-century novel: Trollope's two major series, the *Chronicles of Barsetshire* and the Pallisers, both obey a stricter set of principles linking locality, proceding mostly chronologically, and conserving central characters. Though it cannot compare to the still robust afterlife of Sherlock Holmes, Trollope's fictional county Barsetshire is extended and reinvented by Angela Thirkell in twenty-nine novels. The formal irony of Thirkell's homage to Trollope's county shows in the inexhaustible extension of sequence-writing as a three-decade project, ended only by her death, in sharp contrast to Trollope's final title: *The* Last *Chronicle of Barset* (1867), he called it, and it was.

Lengthy sequences sometimes happen by accident: Galsworthy's *Forsyte Chronicles* begins as *The Man of Property* in 1906, and not until twelve years later, in story form, does he pick up the thread (in "Indian Summer of a Forsyte") that carries him through twelve more works and three generations of Forsytes, comprising what we now know of as *The Forsyte Saga*, *A Modern Comedy*, and *End of the Chapter*. A similar story is told about the genesis of the *Alexandria Quartet* (1957–1960), though by the time Durrell finished revising it for republication in 1962, he had unified the four parts in a revision that he presents as a book that should be read as a single story. The same can be said of Scott's *The Jewel in the Crown* (1966–1975): one must read all four of the novels to get all the ripples of consequence that radiate out from the first traumatizing action. By way of contrast to Galsworthy's experience, sequence writers sometimes know perfectly well that they are writing works of a specific number: numerological consider-ations in the Christian allegory of Rowling's Harry Potter books (1997–2007) govern their presentation in seven volumes, as planned from the outset. Mosley envisioned a sequence of seven self-contained books, each to focus on figures introduced in the original eclectic first volume, *Catastrophe Practice*.[6] This plan was truncated with the publication of *Hopeful Monsters* (1990), fifth and final installment of the series, a magnificent novel of ideas that fully acknowledges the atrocities, traumas, and ethical failures of the twentieth century while engaging with the philosophy of language and science, technological advances, ideologies, and psychology of the period. Opportunistic extension often turns a planned trilogy into a lengthier sequence.

Both Jones and Rowling write fantasy fiction, a sub-genre where sequences and trilogies have flourished, so much so that it is tempting to locate the original twentieth-century cultivar there. However, trilogies bear a strong family resem-blance to the Victorian triple-decker novel, a form underwritten by publishers' collaboration with the major circulating libraries. An outfit such as Mudie's Library could triple the rental value of an individual novel by doling it out to subscribers in parts. A yearly annual subscription (costing a guinea) got a subscriber one volume at a time. To take home all three parts of *Jane Eyre* (1847), for instance, a subscriber would need three subscriptions. (The analogy with Netflix is exact.) Since circulating libraries accounted for the great bulk of sales of novels' print runs, publishers cooperated. Eventually the availability of cheap reprints and the growth of free circulating libraries weakened Mudie's hold on the publishers. Not until 1894 did Mudie's drop the three-volume expectation, with the immediate result that novellas and shorter novels found publishers beyond periodicals more readily. The three-volume form of the novel does not disappear after 1895. It persists in the internal divisions of novels now published in a single volume: so, for example, in the modern period, Woolf's *To The Lighthouse* (1927) has three segments, as do Elizabeth Bowen's *The House in Paris* (1935) and *The Death of the Heart* (1938), among many other tripartite modern novels.

Kept alive through the modern period by the ghost form of the triple-decker, the three-volume form then finds new life in the mid-twentieth century in trilogies, intentionally so divided or not. This story plays out vividly in genre fiction. Famously, Tolkien's *The Lord of the Rings* was written as a serial – sent in letters to his son during the Second World War – published in a three-volume form because of postwar paper shortages, but intended to be a single novel with divisions into a prologue, six books, and five appendices. Its reputation as a book broken into three can be explained in part by the resonating trilogies of fantasy and science fiction: Peake's Gormenghast books (1946–1959), and Isaac Asimov's *Foundation* trilogy (1951–1953), predating Tolkien's publication. The science-fiction and fantasy trilogy is an enduring form, as in Pullman's *His Dark Materials* (1995–2000). Tolkien's addition of *The Lord of the Rings* (1954–1955) to *The Hobbit* (1937) suggests that the trilogy form, though sturdily embedded in the array of common formats, also invites additive procedures: preludes, interludes, prequels, doubling, and even, in Galsworthy's case, tripling. Once Galsworthy reanimates the scene and personages of *The Man of Property*, he carries on with trilogy-writing, caulking the seams between those thick bricks with short-story-length interludes. The sequence that results does not quite digest the trilogies that comprise it, and they remain the intelligible units. One doesn't just read "a" Galsworthy novel; one reads a trilogy, usually just *The Forsyte Saga*, which remains in print.

Staying in print remains a challenge for writers of lengthy sequences. Sometimes a publisher colludes with a novelist deliberately to mark his progress in a lengthy sequence, catching up the late-joiners among the readership. Powell and his publisher do this, by collecting his novels in threes: *A Dance to the Music of Time* (1962), containing the first three novels; and *Second Movement* (1964), containing three more, are already in print when the seventh novel, *The Valley of Bones*, is published in 1964. This practice points to the challenge of renewing a sequence novelist's readership while the years of composition pass, for beyond the disciplined trilogists (Burgess, Cary, Hartley, Manning), relatively rare are the Durrells who publish four volumes in as many years: Richardson's original readers had to hang in there from 1915 until 1967; O'Brian's from 1969 until 2004; Snow's from 1940 until 1970. This means, in practical terms, that a cross-generational recruitment has to happen for the sequence to maintain an audience, and of the three I just named, Richardson, Snow, and O'Brian, only O'Brian has succeeded in staying in print through 2009, but he only recently died (2000).

The affordances of trilogies and sequences suggest relative advantages and disadvantages when it comes to opportunity to publish, critical reception, and reader loyalty. Early in the century, sequences were appreciated by readers and taste-makers. Galsworthy's 1932 Nobel Prize for literature was awarded late in the author's life, just before the posthumously published conclusion of the *Chronicles* in 1934. Distant reading reveals that the middle decades of the century, from the 1950s through the 1970s, are most hospitable to the initiation of lengthy sequences, but by the time they come to their conclusions, they perhaps activate critical fatigue more readily than admiration. Most often the histories of critical reception spin narratives of decline when evaluating the later installments of longer series. Very few final volumes of lengthier sequences have won major literary prizes, though Mosley's Whitbread Prize for *Hopeful Monsters* bucks the trend. In contrast, trilogies and quartets maintain rather more dignified pedigrees than lengthy sequences and more often achieve honors at their termination. Barker wins the Booker Prize in 1995 for *The Ghost Road*, the third volume of her *Regeneration* trilogy (1991–1995). This award was widely regarded as registering the importance of the whole trilogy. In an unprecedented accomplishment, Pullman wins the 2001 Whitbread Book of the Year for *The Amber Spyglass* (2000), the conclusion to his children's trilogy *His Dark Materials* (1995–2000). These novels are crossover successes from children's fiction to adult readerships and from the fantasy genre to fiction bestsellers. Each installment of prominent genre fiction in sequence form reaches a huge audience, as systematic perusal of the *Sunday* (London) *Times* bestseller list reveals. The most reliable bestsellers in the 1990s and 2000s, reaching gigantic readerships, are fantastic sequences by Pratchett and Rowling. There is even preliminary evidence that the reading habits of the Harry Potter generation, raised on an engrossing fiction that came out in installments as they grew up, have reversed the declining trend in fiction reading documented in a series of studies of adult American readers by the National Endowment of the Humanities and the United States Census Bureau.[7]

A more difficult test of a dominant form than its impact on huge numbers of readers seeks to discover whether writers of lengthy sequences indicate their awareness of working in a tradition. Here the methodology of distant reading cannot help, for the relationships among texts can best be discovered by tracing internal allusions and stylistic influences. Strong evidence of generic and formal consciousness emerges from close reading of twentieth-century novel sequences. Powell's *A Dance to the Music of Time* has a Galsworthy character, St. John Clarke, and tips a hat to Proust. Appropriately to the character of Powell's narrator Nick Jenkins, a passive aggressive quality can be observed in his traverse of Proust's geographical turf: in *The Military Philosophers*, Jenkins only belatedly realizes where he has been. Jenkins's reason for passing through Cabourg, accompanying allied military officers just behind the final advance into Germany at the conclusion of the Second World War, could be regarded as a reproach to weakness, but "a faint sense of disappointment superimposed on an otherwise absorbing inner experience was in its way suitably Proustian too: a reminder of the eternal failure of human life to respond a hundred per cent."[8] Powell makes no claim to outdo his poetic father, but his artistic modesty perhaps is belied by the sheer length of *Dance*. Powell himself is less a strong poet to be slain in oedipal rivalry than a world-weary tolerant uncle to Raven's ribaldry in *Alms for Oblivion*. Without question, both Raven and Frederick Mount self-consciously extend the project of documenting the flow of experience – for white men of a certain recognizable caste – out towards the twenty-first century. Powell is literal uncle by marriage to Mount, author of *The Chronicle of Modern Twilight* (1975–2004). Though Mount's fictional world and its denizens owe more to Powell, his title refers allusively to Williamson's fifteen-volume *Chronicle of Ancient Sunlight*. We should note the dying fall: from remembrance to oblivion, from sunlight to twilight.

To turn back to Henry Williamson, author of the Hawthornden Prize-winning *Tarka the Otter* (1927), of other works in the animal saga vein, and of the great chronological contemporary sequence, *A Chronicle of Ancient Sunlight*, we find not only self-conscious reference to literary precursors, but also a thematic emphasis on environmental decline that typifies twentieth-century English series fiction. In Williamson's partly autobiographical sequence, we find Galsworthy and Richardson in light disguise as patrons and objects of envious contemplation. Williamson embeds Galsworthy's novels within the reading life of Phillip Maddison, though changing the names of both author and Galsworthy's characters. Like Galsworthy and Richardson, Williamson depicts the choking killer smogs of the late nineteenth- and early twentieth-century metropolis and the escape to suburban locations with sweeter air. Like Richardson's Miriam Henderson, Williamson's character Richard Maddison is liberated from London by possession of a bicycle, on which he reaches the countryside, ever further out from London's sprawl. Williamson's elegiac account of the degradation of waterways and despoiling of woods parallels Phillip Maddison's attempt to reverse the family's urbanization by becoming a farmer. At the same time, he becomes a writer, celebrated for his sympathetic portraits of animals, but haunted by traumatic World War I experiences.

Like his contemporary Tolkien, whose Mordor is a polluted as well as an occupied land, Williamson's visionary environmentalism stems from the experiences of trench warfare. In volumes IV–VIII of his *Chronicle*, Williamson describes the Great War in harrowing detail from the perspective of a combatant. *How Dear is Life* (1954), *A Fox Under My Cloak* (1955), *The Golden Virgin* (1957), *Love and the Loveless* (1958), and *A Test to Destruction* (1960) are among the very finest fictional treatments of the war, including the Christmas truce of 1914 and most of the major battles in Belgium and France. Williamson's later fascism, especially his loyalty to Oswald Mosley, whose support for English farming he appreciated, damaged his reputation and led to critical neglect after his death in 1977. He deserves a place in literary history both for his documentary novels of the Great War and for his animal stories, the wild creature counterpart to James Herriot's veterinary sequence about farm animals.

Women writers of lengthy series show a similar consciousness of their precursors: Richardson pays homage to Henry James and defensively acknowledges that Proust got started a few years before she began publishing *Pilgrimage* (1915–1967). A reader of Richardson's *Pilgrimage* will hear strong echoes of her style in Lessing's *Children of Violence* (1952–1969), while Byatt goes so far as to incorporate a character from Iris Murdoch's *The Philosopher's Pupil* (1983) into *Babel Tower* (1996), the third volume of Byatt's Frederica Potter quartet. It may be objected that Murdoch does not write sequences (indeed her novels are freestanding), but her mode of allowing characters from earlier novels to wander into later novels, in minor roles, or simply to reside at addresses nearby characters from other Murdoch novels, suggests the tangential connections of a richly imagined fictional world and an alternative form of narrative extension, different from the generational continuities of Galsworthy, or the diary-like recapturing of daily life of Richardson and Williamson. This form of oblique relation – the tag-you're-it switching of central characters inside the same game – is adopted by Amanda Craig in her five-volume cycle, the *Foreign*

Bodies sequence (1990–2003). The roster of sequences by women writers is lengthy and spans the century possibly because of their prominence in detective fiction, historical romances, and children's literature.

In the twenty-first century the dominant forms, trilogies and sequences, show good health, especially if narrative fiction in film and game formats can be recognized as emergent repackaging of traditional serial materials. Film and prose fiction already interpenetrate in sequences, as in the later volumes of Rowling's Harry Potter novels, where Rowling seems to be writing for the actors committed to playing her characters on screen. Recent literary sequences conceive the present and future of the form in relation to the parallel realms of video games, hypertext fiction, fan fiction, and multiplayer online worlds. Branching path storylines, nested tales within tales, and opportunities for interactivity through imaginative extension or rewriting of an author's fictional world proliferate on the internet. To recognize the emergent forms of sequences requires attention to a wide range of fiction even within the bounds of the traditional print novel. Literate, highly allusive, and character driven, Jones's *Bold as Love* sequence rearranges the political boundaries of literary science fiction, starting with Crisis and Dissolution, the familiar dystopic circumstances. Jones rephrases the question "what's next?" positively: what would it take to build a better realm? And who would you put in the seats of that round table? Jones nominates independent rockstars as her new royalty. Three major musician characters, Ax (half-Sudanese President of the Rock n Roll Reich), Fiorinda (protector of the displaced masses), and Sage (the Zen Self shaman who comes back alive from neuroscience questing) enact an Arthurian saga of power politics and love.

Fantasy sequences tend to allude to earlier traditions, infusing their inventions with high-culture precedents, as in Neil Gaiman's *Sandman* comic series (1989–1996) with its references to Shakespeare and classical mythology. *Bold as Love* (2001), winner of the Arthur C. Clarke Award, Jones's *Castles Made of Sand* (2002), and *Midnight Lamp* (2003) riff on Arthurian themes; *Band of Gypsys* (2005) takes a considerably more Shakespearean turn; and *Rainbow Bridge* (2006), the final installment, tips its hat at Chinese opera, with its tragedies of betrayal and exile. Jones folds those traditions into a freshly conceived fictional world that has accreted playlists, a blog, a website, and a Facebook group. Digital paratexts and the artifacts of social networking now extend out around successful sequences in a newly concentric version of the form.

The narrative structure of David Mitchell's Booker-prize-shortlisted novel, *The Cloud Atlas* (2004), also bears a relationship to the advancing narrative levels of gaming quest narratives as well as to more celebrated literary precursors such as John Barth and Jorge Luis Borges. In *The Cloud Atlas* Mitchell presents a nested set of six novellas, cracked in half and moving toward the future, until the central novella of the distant future ("Sloosha's Crossin' an' Ev'rythin' After"). This is presented in its entirety and marks the midpoint of a narrative that subsequently proceeds backwards in time, completing the narrative with the second halves of the five preceding tales. Linked by hinted reincarnations of a character identified in each novella with a comet birthmark, as well as by the existence of each prior story in its physical form (a holographic recording, a video, a novel manuscript, a set of letters, a diary), Mitchell's novellas resist interpretation as a collection of separate works. Like twentieth-century sequences, Mitchell's miniature sequence demands openness to interruption, toleration of loose ends, and enthusiasm for hybridized generic conventions. That he employs devices of the sequence to spin a warning parable about the destructive consequences of dominion over oppressed races and exploitation of the environment for the entire human species suggests that the form's affiliation with the unraveling of imperialist grand narratives will persist. As Mosley anticipates in *Catastrophe Practice* (1979), from political, economic, and artistic mutations new hybrids may emerge.

Raymond Williams theorizes the co-presence of emergent, dominant, and residual forms: twentieth-century English sequences exist in all three kinds. The emergent versions do not blot out the popular dominant sequences; and the most venerable residual sequences, the descendants of the Holmes stories, hold their own. In his BookWorld comic novelist Jasper Fforde creates a realm where all fictional characters ever invented are alive and on the job, causing trouble for SpecOps literary detective Thursday Next (introduced in *The Eyre Affair* [2001]). In his alternative history science fiction sequence, Fforde invents a Prose Portal that allows human beings to enter that BookWorld (*Lost in a Good Book* [2002]). Who might readers of the twentieth-century English novel meet there? It is a realm populated by denizens of novel sequences: Frodo, Soames, Mma Precious Ramotswe, Bertie Wooster and Jeeves, Inspector Dalgliesh, Lucia and Georgie, the artist Clea painting with her prosthetic hand, poor old Yaki in his distinguished overcoat, Widmerpool.

Notes

1. See Franco Moretti, *Graphs, Maps, Trees: Abstract Models for a Literary History* (London: Verso, 2005).
2. Nicholas Mosley, *Catastrophe Practice* (Elmwood Park, IL: Dalkey Archive Press, 1989), p. 339.

3. Raymond Williams, *Marxism and Literature* (Oxford University Press, 1977), pp. 132–134.

4. Joyce Cary, *To Be a Pilgrim* (London: M. Joseph, 1942), p. 133.

5. *The World of John LeCarré*, www.johnlecarre.com/world.html (accessed 22 June 2009).

6. Peter Lewis, "Nicholas Mosley Biography," http://biography.jrank.org/pages/4611/Mosley-Nicholas.html (accessed 16 June 2009).

7. Compare *Reading on the Rise: A New Chapter in American Literacy*. Office of Research and Analysis (Washington, DC: National Endowment for the Arts, January 2009) with the earlier report, *Reading at Risk: A Survey of Literary Reading in America*, Research Division Report no. 46 (Washington, DC: The National Endowment for the Arts, June 2004).

8. Anthony Powell, *The Military Philosophers* (1968) in *A Dance to the Music of Time, 3rd Movement* (University of Chicago Press, 1995), p. 168.

46

The novel's West Indian revolution

PETER KALLINEY

In the 1940s West Indian fiction was virtually unknown to English and Caribbean readers alike. Writing in 1960, George Lamming could describe the West Indian novelist as someone "who had no existence twenty years ago."[1] A few isolated expatriates – Claude McKay, Jean Rhys, and Eric Walrond – had published important texts in the 1920s and 1930s, but their work had been absorbed into Anglo-American traditions, suggesting little vibrant, continuous literary culture in the region. In the 1950s, however, West Indian literature suddenly seemed ubiquitous, and exuberantly self-conscious. Between 1949 (with Vic Reid's *New Day*) and 1960, over sixty novels by West Indian writers were released, nearly all of them in London. This led observers to predict a fundamental shift toward Commonwealth literature, as it was then known. As early as 1952 the *Times Literary Supplement* expresses hope that "the new generation of West Indian writers" might infuse parochial and inbred English literary culture with much needed fresh blood: "Perhaps in 10, certainly in 20 years from now, West Indian and African literature in the English language should be an accepted part of our, Commonwealth cultural scene."[2] By the end of the decade, West Indian writers were earning strong endorsements from London's most influential literary people.

In retrospect, given the tendency to read the West Indian boom of the 1950s through the lens of postcolonial studies, the metropolitan reaction to those new writers might seem surprisingly congenial. Contextual factors contributed to this trend: the prevailing mood in postwar England was one of deep pessimism about the future of European culture, making English audiences unusually receptive to ideas from non-metropolitan sources; the widely anticipated dissolution of the British Empire fueled a belated interest in the colonial world; and anti-Americanism was rampant in the decade after the war, so writers from the Commonwealth served as a handy bulwark against the prospect of US cultural hegemony. The strained emphasis on "our, Commonwealth scene" in the passage above emphasizes this projection of cultural affinity across the empire.

There are also narrowly aesthetic explanations for the sudden interest in literature from the colonial world. Whereas the young generation of white, metropolitan writers seemed eager to disavow experimental modernism, the new crop of West Indian writers were hailed as the candidates best equipped to develop avant-garde fiction. Lamming, Sam Selvon, and Wilson Harris were more likely to be compared to Eliot, James Joyce, Ezra Pound, and Virginia Woolf than they were to their white, metropolitan contemporaries. Just as important, West Indian novelists were more welcoming of comparisons with modernist writers than were Kingsley Amis, John Braine, or William Golding. As another *Times Literary Supplement* correspondent states the case, readers who have been "brought up on Joyce and Pound" place a high priority on "some kind of verbal excitement which springs from the abrogation of grammatical rules and syntactic laws." The review article contends that readers with a taste for experimentation are more apt to turn to Amos Tutuola or the emerging school of West Indian writers than to their white, metropolitan counterparts.[3]

This chapter offers an overview of West Indian fiction that emphasizes the complexity of interactions between metropolitan and Caribbean writing. West Indian fiction of the 1950s appears anomalous partly because the Caribbean literary tradition has been variously misread, misplaced, and misunderstood. McKay and Rhys are important for this discussion because they are Caribbean writers who are also deeply involved in interwar modernist circles. I also argue that West Indian writers become some of the most compelling readers of Anglo-American modernism after World War II. While many critics of West Indian fiction are inclined either to celebrate it for its independence from metropolitan modernism, or to criticize it for its excessive reliance on European culture, I want to position Caribbean novelists at the forefront of efforts to recuperate and extend the project of experimental fiction inaugurated by their predecessors, both metropolitan and Caribbean.[4] To state the matter more emphatically, I suggest that the way scholars now read experimental modernism – the styles and themes taken to be most expressive and characteristic of the movement – has been influenced greatly by the way postwar West Indian novelists rework modernist techniques. Not only do West Indian writers of the 1950s learn a great deal from their predecessors, Caribbean writing from the postwar period distills and clarifies some of the most important tropes of interwar modernism.

Aside from McKay and Rhys, Joyce is the writer whom West Indian novelists of the 1950s most emulate. *Ulysses* (1922) remains a key text, but *A Portrait of the Artist as a Young Man* (1916), alongside McKay's *Banjo* (1929), provide the salient fictional models for the *Windrush* generation, as they were later dubbed in reference to the *Empire Windrush*, a ship that brought the first postwar West Indian immigrants to England in 1948. Following the lead of *Portrait*'s Stephen Dedalus and *Banjo*'s Ray, the dominant trope of the West Indian revolution is the young, promising, but as yet unaccomplished writer-in-exile. Dedalus's plan to forge in his soul the "uncreated conscience of [his] race," and Ray's desire to transcribe the "instinctive gifts" of unlettered black men, become repeated and transformed in postwar Caribbean fiction.[5] Enduring problems of racial conflict and discrimination, the struggle against imperialism, the tensions between the deracinated intellectual and the mythical folk, and the dubious attractions of exile appear as themes again and again. It is the aspiring writer, the texts suggest, who is best positioned to understand, represent, and manage those competing claims. Both *Banjo* and *Portrait* utilize the basic framework of the *Kunstlerroman* – with its emphasis on the protagonist's emerging aesthetic sensitivity and temperament – but also align the maturation of the artist with a struggle for racial and national emancipation in the context of colonialism.

In a curious development, however, portraits of failed, frustrated, or thwarted artists begin to overrun representations of even moderately successful writers. Hints of miseries in store for the artist *manqué* are undoubtedly prevalent in earlier texts – neither Ray nor Dedalus has much work to his credit by the time their stories come to an end – but postwar West Indian writers, even the most accomplished among them, brood over the problem of artistic futility with remarkable determination. V. S. Naipaul blames the failures of West Indian fiction on its cultural dependency: "Living in a borrowed culture, the West Indian, more than most, needs writers to tell him who he is and where he stands. Here the West Indian writers have failed. Most have so far only reflected and flattered the prejudices of their race or colour groups."[6] Without a secure indigenous literary tradition, West Indian writers fall back on the two things they know instinctively: the mores of their particular social group and the tradition of metropolitan writing, neither of which is perfectly suited to explain Caribbean culture in its entirety. Naipaul's comments allude to historical and sociological difficulties, but his speculations also have a direct bearing on the formal preoccupations of West Indian fiction, where portrayals of writers and failed writers show a heightened awareness of fiction writing as both a craft and a profession.

West Indian background

Before discussing the fiction of the 1950s in more detail, it might be instructive to say a few words about the tradition of Caribbean writing during the interwar years. Lamming's claim that the West Indian novelist develops *sui generis* in the 1950s is misleading. Recent scholarship has rediscovered a West Indian literary tradition that dates to the turn of the twentieth century.[7] The main difference is that the best writers of earlier generations are working in relative isolation from one another – and from their audiences in the Caribbean – making them ripe for incorporation into other literary traditions. The work of Walrond and the early McKay is absorbed into the Harlem Renaissance; McKay of the 1930s becomes more closely associated with francophone literary circles.[8] Rhys, meanwhile, is white and living in Paris during the 1920s; moreover, most of her early work has no identifiably Caribbean characters or settings, making it easy to ignore her place of origin. Even after her reclamation as a West Indian writer in the 1960s – particularly after *Wide Sargasso Sea* (1966) – she is still known in many quarters as an English or British writer.[9]

Other West Indian writers of the 1920s and 1930s stay put, but their wider significance is difficult to establish. The group of writers in Trinidad associated with the literary journal *Beacon* represents the most important indigenous literary movement of the period. It is notable for the introduction of the "yard story" – literature inspired by the black working class, many of whom lived in crowded slums known as barrack yards. Roger Mais's *The Hills Were Joyful Together* (1953) and *Brother Man* (1954), Lamming's *In the Castle of My Skin*, and Naipaul's *Miguel Street* (1959) are some of the 1950s' texts most clearly indebted to *The Beacon* project. Alfred Mendes and C. L. R. James are the group's pioneers – James's only novel, *Minty Alley* (1936), provides the prototype for yard fiction – but both stop writing creatively early in their careers. Their fiction also experiments in limited ways with dialect, which subsequently becomes an increasingly important resource.

Two fledgling cultural institutions of the 1940s laid much of the ground-work for postwar Caribbean literature, nurturing all the postwar writers: the little magazine *Bim* and the radio program *Caribbean Voices*. *Bim* (the name derives from slang for a Barbadian) was spearheaded by Frank Collymore, but it soon outgrew Barbados, becoming the Caribbean's literary journal of record. *Caribbean Voices*, based in London but broadcast to the West Indies, was launched by Una Marson, a Jamaican poet living in England; she got the idea for the program after working closely with George Orwell on a BBC literary show designed for an Indian audience. Henry Swanzy, who succeeded Marson, served as a vital link between metropolitan and Caribbean literary worlds, both of which benefited. On one side, Swanzy had direct contact with the many West Indian writers still living in the Caribbean, as well as with

Collymore, with whom he became fast friends. *Caribbean Voices* broadcast pieces that first appeared in *Bim*, and *Bim* excerpted or reacted to recent broadcasts. On the other side, Swanzy was well connected to London's inner literary circles. He arranged for influential figures such as Stephen Spender and Roy Fuller to become regular guests on the show, and he generously put West Indian writers who came to London in touch with his vast contacts in the publishing world.

As this overview suggests, West Indian writing 1920–1950 exists in forms of collaboration and interchange with metropolitan literary culture. This pattern continues and even intensifies in the 1950s, when most West Indian novelists had decamped to London. It is therefore unsurprising that exile, both physical and spiritual, becomes a recurring motif in the novels. Kamau Brathwaite suggests that "the desire (even the need) to migrate is at the heart of West Indian sensibility: whether that migration is in fact or by metaphor."[10] There is ample precedent in the work of Joyce, McKay, and Rhys, each of whom connects aesthetic freedom with the experience of living abroad. Following the lead of Édouard Glissant, Simon Gikandi develops the concept of *maroonage* and writing "in limbo," suggesting that mobility allows Caribbean writers to borrow from and creatively distort European modernism.[11] Likewise, Paul Gilroy's description of the Black Atlantic as a "counterculture of modernity" also identifies the experience of new world slavery – and resistance – as the foundation of twentieth-century black literature.[12]

George Lamming

Lamming is the most fiercely anti-colonial intellectual of his cohort. Supriya Nair argues that we should read his flirtation with exile as an attempt to destroy the myth of imperial beneficence.[13] Yet Lamming is not immune to, or embarrassed by, the attractions of metropolitan modernism. His first four novels make extensive use of experimental narrative techniques: disorienting temporal and narrative shifts, stream of consciousness, detached irony, and blends of classical allusions and vernacular speech. According to Lamming's introduction, *In the Castle of My Skin* (1953) attempts to capture the texture of life in the rural Barbados of his childhood by discarding the conventions of realism: "There is often no discernable plot, no coherent line of events with a clear, causal connection. Nor is there a central individual consciousness where we focus attention, and through which we can be guided reliably by a logical succession of events."[14] There is no stable narrator, either: although the story loosely follows the adolescence of G., it tacks between first- and third-person narration, in varying styles, making reading the novel a difficult but rewarding undertaking.

Despite Lamming's claim that no central consciousness organizes the narrative, one cannot underestimate the significance of the suggestively named G. The novel opens on his ninth birthday, a day washed out by a historic flood, and concludes with G., much like the author himself, leaving for a teaching post in Trinidad. More significantly, in a self-consciously Joycean flourish, the final chapter of the novel consists of G.'s diary. As he makes his final preparations for departure, the young man reflects on the meaning of his life in the village:

> When I review these relationships they seem so odd. I have always been here on this side and the other person there on that side, and we have both tried to make the sides appear similar in the needs, desires, and ambitions. But it wasn't true. It was never true . . . I am always feeling terrified of being known; not because they really know you, but simply because their claim to this knowledge is a concealed attempt to destroy you . . . They won't know the you that's hidden somewhere in the castle of your skin. (261)

The debt to *Portrait* is unmistakable. G. feels suffocated by the communal life of the village. The novel emphasizes the oppressiveness of living in a place where there is no allowance for privacy and no space for individual ambition. Although G. savors the "sprawling dereliction of that life," he prefers to do so as an expatriate (224). Unlike many of his fellow emigrants, his desire to leave is not purely a matter of material gain – he feels as if his intellectual development will be thwarted unless he moves away.

Lamming's second novel, *The Emigrants* (1954), uses similar formal techniques to chart the growing self-consciousness, and neuroses, of the artist in exile. It begins with another symbolic departure – this time, from the Caribbean to England. Rhys's *Voyage in the Dark* (1934) is the key intertext here, especially in Lamming's descriptions of metropolitan life. The first half of Lamming's novel describes the expectations and fears of a large group of emigrants, culminating in the formation of a provisional community out of representatives of the islands; the second half charts the dissolution of that community in London. Much like *Castle*, *Emigrants* introduces an array of characters, situations, and narrative voices in order to evoke the complexity and diversity of the travelers. Out of this cacophony, a lonely, sullen young poet, Collis, comes to the fore. On the boat, he hovers at the edges of conversations, preferring to eavesdrop rather than venture an opinion of his own. After arrival in London, the story gravitates toward him, and he even seems to narrate at times, although the reader can never be sure. In the novel's tense climax, when the immigrant community faces a serious crisis, they turn to Collis for help: "'Don't ask me anything'," Collis growls. "'Tis about some of your own people'," begs one of his fellow West Indians, to which Collis curtly replies, "'I have no people'."[15] The novel concludes with a contemplative Collis staring out the window.

Together Lamming's first novels suggest that the aspiring West Indian artist occupies an equivocal position, balancing competing allegiances to art and black Atlantic politics. The younger, more idealistic of Lamming's characters begins his travels by affirming his connection to the transatlantic community of black people; in the closing scenes of *Castle*, G. resolves to confirm the revolutionary significance of his blackness by going abroad, where he can compare his experiences with those of others. *Emigrants*, by contrast, shows how the hopeful intellectual has evolved into a more world-weary expatriate, asserting his professional autonomy against the claims of racial and national identity.

McKay's *Banjo* is clearly one of Lamming's models. *Banjo*'s subtitle, *A Story without a Plot*, initiates experiments Lamming would learn from, and extend. Calling attention to its unconventional narrative, *Banjo* also surveys a wide cast of black emigrants, refugees, and castaways making their way through Europe. The protagonist Ray, a Haitian writer, spends most of the novel enjoying the communal life of the Marseilles docks. Yet Ray also insists that his calling as an artist is not always compatible with the ongoing struggle for racial justice:

> "I'll fight . . . if there's a fight on, but if I'm writing a story – well, it's like all of us in this place here, black and brown and white, and I telling a story for the love of it . . . If I am a real story-teller, I won't worry about the differences in complexion of those who listen and those who don't, I'll just identify myself with those who are really listening and tell my story." (115)

If Lamming's first novel partly tells the story of a burgeoning intellectual who is nurtured, but not ultimately sustained, by the rural life of the islands, his second novel clings more ambivalently to principles of aesthetic independence. Significantly, the greatest threat to artistic integrity is not excessive reliance on modernist formal strategies, but instead the immanent political claims of the transnational black community.

Sam Selvon

In 1950 Lamming and Sam Selvon leave Trinidad for England on the same boat. It is Lamming who first labels Selvon as the greatest "folk poet" from the region – no faint praise, considering the source – and the tag sticks fast (*Pleasures*, 224). In one sense, Selvon's early fiction supports this reading. *A Brighter Sun* (1952) and its sequel *Turn Again Tiger* (1958) follow an uneducated young man from a cane-cutting family as he moves from rural Trinidad to Port of Spain. Many of the short stories in *Ways of Sunlight* (1957) also work with the raw material of Trinidad's Indian communities. *The Lonely Londoners* (1956), Selvon's best-known work, is decidedly urban in scope, yet its portrayals of London's expanding, largely uneducated West Indian population, and its experimentations with vernacular speech and calypso make it close in spirit to regional folk literature, as Lamming recognizes.

A different reading might position Selvon as one of the most urbane, avant-garde, and least conventional writers of his generation. Recent commentary on Selvon, such as Susheila Nasta's, emphasizes this perspective. *Lonely Londoners* alludes directly to both *Ulysses* and *Mrs. Dalloway* (1925), especially in the novel's two most famous vignettes: one breathless, unpunctuated scene takes place in London's parks, in summer, while the other describes a rowdy party near the conclusion of the novel. With a wide range of characters drifting in and out of it, the plot does not proceed along temporal lines, nor does it single out any character for special consideration. More importantly, perhaps, the novel's incorporation of stream-of-consciousness narration and its disorienting, episodic structure are embellished by the use of a modified West Indian dialect. Kenneth Ramchand points out in an introduction to the novel that Selvon's dialect is not faithful to the idiom of a particular island – it is an artificial construction, mutually intelligible to West Indians, and with some allowances, to English readers. Unlike earlier Caribbean novels, which reserve vernacular speech primarily for the dialogue of uneducated people, *Lonely Londoners* makes dialect the main vehicle of narration.

This early work of Selvon's contains the most direct allusions to metropolitan modernism, but each of his first four novels goes out of its way to explore the formal possibilities of West Indian fiction. In one of the best commentaries on Selvon, Bruce MacDonald argues that Selvon's innovations in dialect should not be read as an invocation of the folk, but instead as a technically ambitious experiment that allows him to document the frustrations of the artist as well as the simple strengths of peasant culture.[16] Improbably, all his early novels have central characters who are, or aspire to be, writers, autodidacts longing to share their ideas with a reading public. In *Lonely Londoners* the longest-serving Londoner concludes by wondering if he could ever work up his experiences into a novel. Tiger's interest in books is less fleeting and even more unlikely. He deprives himself and his family of material goods in order to buy volumes by Plato, Aristotle, and Shakespeare, imported luxury goods. Like Dedalus, he is both intrigued and disgusted by the filth of his surroundings, often losing himself in imaginative flights. Despite the conflicts caused by his voracious reading, the narrative pivot of *Turn Again* – when Tiger burns all his books – develops entirely from internal psychological pressures, especially the futility of writing stories while living in an impoverished, largely illiterate society. The self-absorption necessary for writing makes the mature Tiger feel guilty, but he also feels shackled by the paucity of intellectual life in Trinidad.

Foster of Selvon's *An Island Is a World* (1955) is no less tortured by internal demons. Friends and relations hector him for brooding too much and working too little: "'You like to think too much, sitting on your tail all day and puzzling about why this and why that,'" his brother upbraids him on more than one occasion.[17] The text is full of Foster's abstract philosophizing, leading critics to dismiss the novel as Selvon's weakest effort, cluttered with long passages of intellectual posturing and relatively light on Selvon's signature flourish, the gently satiric short story. Unlike Tiger, Foster's desire to become a writer leads him to abandon Trinidad for England, where he consorts with a bohemian crowd he comes to despise. Exile turns out to be less liberating and inspiring than he had hoped:

> I used to think that we belonged to the world, that a Trinidadian could go [anywhere] and fit in . . . I used to think of this philosophy as being the broadest, the most universal, that if it ever came to making a decision on an issue involving humanity itself, we'd have an advantage with this disadvantage . . . unbounded by any ties to a country or even a race or creed. But when you leave the country of your birth, it isn't like that at all. (106)

But Selvon's portraits of frustrated, exiled artists do not demonstrate the failures of West Indian literature described by Naipaul, whom I quoted earlier in this essay. Selvon does not fall back clumsily on his particular racial group or caste. Compared to his contemporaries', his writing more insistently ponders the uneasy mix of races and cultures in the Caribbean (Naipaul's *A House for Mr. Biswas* [1961], by contrast, is a far more insular examination of Trinidad's Indian community). Nor, for that matter, does Selvon's work correspond exactly with the prototypical artists of Lamming, McKay, or Joyce, who hem and haw but ultimately accept the necessity of exile. For the early Selvon, the burning desire to write is snuffed out before it really ignites. There is a wistful glance over his shoulder at Percy Bysshe Shelley's identification of poets as the unacknowledged legislators of the world. In Selvon's fantasy, at least, the Caribbean writer is uniquely prepared to rise above and adjudicate the petty jealousies of racial and cultural conflict because he is innately cosmopolitan in outlook. Yet the realities of exile strip the patina from this dream. Selvon anticipates the work of Zadie Smith, yet he is nowhere near as sanguine as she about the possibilities of blissful co-existence. For a brilliantly comic writer, Selvon's ruminations about the function of the artist have a somber edge. The protagonists in his early fiction accept neither the familiar comforts of home nor the anonymity and license of the expatriate. Yet this restlessness and dissatisfaction feed Selvon's experimental appetite, fueling the search for new means of capturing the West Indian story.

V. S. Naipaul

The perpetual quest for a secure home finds its fullest expression in *Biswas*, Naipaul's epic *Bildungsroman*. Relatively little in Naipaul's early fiction prepares readers for the scope and ambition of his fourth novel. Although he was widely regarded as a promising stylist, his early fiction relies heavily on satiric vignettes, many of which are based on eccentric characters well-known throughout Trinidad, much like Selvon. In other words, it is possible to read the early Naipaul as a writer specializing in local color (much to his chagrin – Naipaul famously reacted to being labeled a "West Indian" novelist on promotional materials by canceling his contract with the publisher). *The Mystic Masseur* (1957) and *Miguel Street* certainly fit that mold. Much of this early work is perfectly balanced, demonstrating close attention to detail, but it operates with the cool detachment of a disinterested, haughty observer. *Biswas* also has its cast of eccentrics, but it allows Naipaul for the first time to expand the emotional range of his work, giving his readers an opportunity to consider the deepest ambitions and frustrations of his subjects from a more empathetic perspective.

Naipaul is the most controversial novelist of his generation. Recent publication of an authorized biography makes it clear that he revels in the role of *enfant terrible*.[18] Most of his fellow West Indians disliked both his person and his work, especially his travel writing, and did not hide their feelings from the reading public. Naipaul himself encouraged their enmity and took pains to distance himself from Caribbean culture and politics. As Rob Nixon argues, Naipaul has consistently styled himself as the homeless intellectual, and therefore impersonal and totally impartial, owing allegiance to neither metropolitan nor colonial worlds.[19] This calculated self-portrait has helped Naipaul position himself as an objective yet expert interpreter of the "Third World." His disdainful attitude may rankle fellow Caribbean artists, but his basic contention that exile facilitates intellectual independence is utterly typical of his cohort.

Of Naipaul's early fiction, *The Mystic Masseur* is closest in content and form to *Biswas*. It follows the improbable career of Ganesh Ramsumair, who goes from unlicensed doctor to quasi-religious pundit to spiritual self-help author to populist politician. The narrator embellishes the tale by periodically quoting from Ganesh's memoirs, which he publishes toward the end of his career; Ganesh is credited with writing "the first best-seller" and other "classic" titles of Trinidadian literature.[20] Knowledgeable readers will detect comically deformed echoes of Selvon's *Brighter Sun*: the young protagonist spends nearly all his money on books, tallying his treasures in inches, feet, and yards. As he acquires a reputation for healing and spiritual wisdom, he travels the island with a fleet of taxis to transport his huge collection of books, serving as both fetishes and credentials: he opens them occasionally, but more often uses them as props to impress audiences. In a parody of British Romanticism, Ganesh styles himself an author whose primary task is the healing of souls. He becomes one of the most admired men on the island. Ganesh is a hack and a fraud of quintessentially Caribbean materials, at least in Naipaul's fictional world.

It is easy to forget that *Biswas* too is a *Künstlerroman* of sorts. Naipaul's father, Seepersad, on whose life the novel is based, had ambitions to be a writer, and even gained modest success in his final years. V. S.'s foreword to Seepersad's posthumously collected stories and the foreword to *Biswas* both describe his father's struggles to become a writer in colonial Trinidad. In *Biswas* V.S. channels the "locked up and unused" material of his father's life: Seepersad never "reached that point of rest from which he could look back at his past. His last years, when he found his voice as a writer, were years of especial distress and anxiety; he was part of the dereliction he wrote about."[21] *Biswas* admits a pathos largely absent from V. S.'s other work; after hearing one of his stories read on *Caribbean Voices*, Seepersad writes to his son: "I am beginning to feel I *could* have been a writer" (foreword to *Gurudeva*, 18). Shortly after his father's death, as V. S. tries to summon the energy and inspiration to write about his father's life, the son faces similar challenges: "to have found no talent, to have written no book, to be null and unprotected in the busy world. It is that anxiety – the fear of destitution in all its forms, the vision of the abyss – that lies below the comedy of the present book [*Biswas*]."[22] In V. S.'s hands the portrait of the artist has become the portrait of the miserable, failed artist, paralyzed by a mixture of fear, isolation, and ambition in the face of mass indifference. As later works such as *The Mimic*

Men (1967) and *The Enigma of Arrival* (1987) suggest, the image of the unappreciated or marginalized writer haunts his *oeuvre*.

The authorial ambitions of Mr. Biswas are peripheral to the narrative's main plotlines, yet central to its overall arc of development – or better yet, its chronic underdevelopment, for Biswas retains the aura of stunted youth. The novel follows Biswas from inauspicious birth through his awkward adolescence, indifferent marriage, itinerant career, and undistinguished death. Following the critic Selwyn Cudjoe, one can read *Biswas* as a national or communal allegory, emphasizing the protagonist's humble beginnings in a quasi-feudal Hindu community, followed by a period of acculturation or "creolization," culminating in the more individualistic and urbanized scenes of the concluding chapters.[23] The novel's most memorable set pieces, however, will strike most readers as painstakingly idiosyncratic rather than readily metaphorical: the hilarious rivalries of Hanuman House, the asset-stripping machinations at the Shorthills estate, or the examination rituals that turn the island's young students into fighting cocks. The protagonist's many humiliations – bullied into marriage, nervous breakdown, disastrous attempts to build a home, and forlorn dreams of writing – do not lend themselves to seeing the protagonist as a stand-in for a larger national or racial group. Rather, the pathos of the novel is driven by the fact that Biswas is both a typical Trinidadian and an outlier whose desires are systematically crushed by his environment.

Pericles Lewis's reading of the modernist artist might be productively adapted to this context. Lewis reads Dedalus and other similar characters as Christ-like figures prone to representing themselves as persecuted by, and as unacknowledged saviors of, the emerging nation state.[24] Fawzia Mustafa sees Naipaul's evocation of the persecuted genius as a function of his antipathy toward the West Indies and his determination to fashion himself as a Writer, with all the perquisites and responsibilities entailed therein.[25] But as my comments on Lamming and Selvon indicate, the fascination with the writer as both peripheral and integral to Caribbean culture has a wider currency in the fiction of this period. This reliance on the misunderstood artist-protagonist extends even beyond the major figures I have discussed. In *Black Lightning* (1955), for instance, Roger Mais tells the story of a reclusive blacksmith-sculptor working mysteriously on a likeness of Moses. Gradually, the sculpture of the prophet assumes a life of its own, defeating its increasingly deranged maker, who ultimately kills himself. Edgar Mittelholzer's *A Morning at the Office* (1950; published in the United States as *A Morning in Trinidad*) treats the figure of the artist with a little less gravitas. In this underrated satire of office politics, virtually half of the characters are aspiring artists of one sort or another, including a sketch of Mittelholzer himself, who tries to finance the publication of his work by selling advertising space. Neville Dawes's *The Last Enchantment* (1960), another coming-of-age story, tracks the protagonist's disillusionment with communism and his hidden ambition to be a writer. Paule Marshall's *Brown Girl, Brownstones* (1959) pushes the gender and geographical boundaries of this narrative trope by relocating this familiar narrative to Brooklyn's Barbadian community.

Wilson Harris

Harris is the major figure from this period whose work does not fit the somewhat restrictive model I have described. *The Guyana Quartet*, comprising his first four novels, does not feature any writers, failed or otherwise, unless one is inclined to interpret a land surveyor (Harris's former occupation) as a surrogate artist. In other respects, however, Harris's groundbreaking work again exemplifies the extension of modernist techniques in West Indian fiction. Nearly every critic who writes about *Palace of the Peacock* (1960) begins with comparisons to Joyce and Woolf, also noting the novel's allusions to W. B. Yeats, Samuel Beckett, and Eliot. And Harris is one of the few anglophone writers at the forefront of marvelous (or magic) realism, which many scholars consider a variant of modernism adapted to non-metropolitan contexts. Similarly, no one writing about Harris's work as a literary critic neglects to mention "Tradition, the Writer and Society" and its debt to Eliot's "Tradition and the Individual Talent." Anita Patterson has written about the strong aesthetic connection between Harris and Eliot, reading them both as distinctively new world poets (Harris was known for his poetry, not his prose, before leaving Guyana).[26]

Briefly describing Harris's fiction is a challenge. The closest literary analogy is lyric poetry. Harris's early novels capture moods and imaginative, sometimes mythical, geographies; they do not narrate much in the way of events, nor do his characters become anything definite, with distinct and well-developed personalities. *Palace*, for example, loosely tells the story of nine men and one woman on a river expedition deep into Guyana's hinterland. The expedition takes seven days – Harris clearly evokes creation myths and the legend of El Dorado – culminating in discovery of the Palace, which has an uncanny similarity to *The Waste Land*'s Chapel Perilous. The mythological overtones are supplemented by the novel's evocation of dreaming and fantasy. Early in the narrative we learn that members of the crew are probably ghosts: they all perished on a similar journey some time ago. The men even joke with one another about their invisibility to the living world. To compound matters, one by one the members of the crew succumb to a second death.

As these descriptions imply, the styles of Harris and Naipaul could not be more dissimilar. While Naipaul's sharp satire extracts the absurd essence of his characters and situations for comic effect, Harris's novels offer up characters and environments that are strange and disorienting. This general observation is also true at the level of the sentence. The texture of Naipaul's writing is subtle but definite and incremental; each sentence nudges the reader gently, but distinctly, in one direction. Harris, by contrast, typically refuses to let even his sentences reach definite conclusions, as in this passage from the opening of *Palace*:

> I dreamt I awoke with one dead seeing eye and one living closed eye. I put my dreaming feet on the ground in a room that oppressed me as though I stood in an operating theatre, or a maternity ward, or I felt suddenly, the glaring cell of a prisoner who had been sentenced to die. I arose with a violent giddiness and leaned on a huge rocking-chair. I remembered the first time I had entered this bare curious room; the house stood high and alone in the flat brooding countryside. I had felt the wind rocking me with the oldest uncertainty and desire in the world, the desire to govern or be governed, rule or be ruled for ever. [27]

Skeptical readers have written off such passages as elaborate trickery, fanciful play without any objective beyond demonstrating authorial dexterity. Harris's frank admiration of Anancy stories, in which clever, shape-shifting protagonists defeat stronger but mentally inferior foes, might help explain his fondness for sentences that seem to mutate midstream. Harris has obliquely defended himself against charges of obscurity by explaining that "dream and paradox" are the basis of his "cross-cultural imagination."[28] To understand Guyana, with its unique blend of European, West African, Indian, and indigenous cultures, one needs to accept the paradoxical and the fantastical. Harris replaces exploration of the knowable self – the central motif of the conventional *Bildungsroman* – with the quest for entirely new models of selfhood.

This convenient contrast between Harris and Naipaul suggests that West Indian writers have very different notions about what varieties of modernism can survive transplantation. For Naipaul the detached, ruthlessly unsentimental streak in modernist fiction becomes a valuable tool for describing the absurdities of colonial culture. For Harris development of the linguistic virtuosity of Joyce (or Gertrude Stein) allows him to pursue an entirely different path. Of the group, Lamming employs the techniques most widely associated with interwar modernism, while Selvon is the most successful in pushing dialect beyond its stereotypical applications.

In linking the major West Indian novelists of the 1950s with modernist writing, my goal is not to depoliticize these texts, but rather to insert the Caribbean novel back into the longer history of the novel in English. As this chapter suggests, the implied tension between overtly political novels and more narrowly aesthetic writing is at this stage incipient rather than fully realized. The highly specialized *Künstlerroman* sub-genre permits a surprising degree of flexibility, allowing these novelists to deftly interlink passionate political messages with less instrumental formal tinkering. In his brilliant reading of the *Bildungsroman* in the history of the European novel, Franco Moretti concludes that the genre did nothing to help, and everything to inhibit, the development of modernist formal experimentation (*Portrait* had to be forsaken before *Ulysses* could materialize).[29] But this history works only if we restrict modernism in both historical and geographical terms. After World War II the novel of personal development becomes one of the most compelling narrative patterns in a more recognizably international modernism.

Reading these texts in dialogue with metropolitan modernism allows us to see West Indian fiction as a crucial bridge between earlier and later formal developments in the century. It is not an instance of colonials simply parroting Anglo-American modernism, or provincial writers stumbling across new narrative techniques a generation or two late. With the examples of Joyce, McKay, and Rhys before them, writers from the Caribbean become some of the most admired and committed defenders of formal experimentation in the postwar era. Comparing postwar West Indian novelists with both their metropolitan contemporaries and modernist predecessors shows that the middle of the twentieth century is not a moment when the avant-garde goes into hiding, but instead a period during which the legacy of modernism becomes a global property.

Notes

1. George Lamming, *The Pleasures of Exile* (London: Allison and Busby, 1984), p. 38.
2. Anon [Arthur Calder-Marshall], "West Indian Writers," *Times Literary Supplement* (May 23, 1952), 348.
3. Anon. [James Burns Singer], "The Caribbean Mixture: Variations and Fusions in Race and Style," *Times Literary Supplement* (August 10, 1962), 578.
4. For example, Silvio Torres-Saillant, a leading intellectual historian of the Caribbean, is extremely critical of Caribbean intellectuals who have been eager to seek approval from metropolitan readers. He sees Naipaul, Walcott, Paul

Gilroy, and even Stuart Hall as complicit in the continued cultural subordination of the Caribbean. See *An Intellectual History of the Caribbean* (New York: Palgrave Macmillan, 2006).

5. James Joyce, *A Portrait of the Artist as a Young Man*, ed. Seamus Deane (New York: Penguin, 2003), p. 276; Claude McKay, *Banjo: A Story without a Plot* (New York: Harcourt, 1929), p. 323.

6. V. S. Naipaul, *The Middle Passage: The Caribbean Revisited* (New York: Vintage, 2002), p. 64.

7. See Leah Reade Rosenberg, *Nationalism and the Formation of Caribbean Literature* (New York: Palgrave Macmillan, 2007) and Kenneth Ramchand, *The West Indian Novel and its Background* (New York: Barnes and Noble, 1970).

8. See Brent Hayes Edwards, *The Practice of Diaspora: Literature, Translation, and the Rise of Black Internationalism* (Cambridge, MA: Harvard University Press, 2003).

9. A. Alvarez, "The Best Living English Novelist," *New York Times Book Review* (March 17, 1974), 6–7.

10. L. E. [Kamau] Brathwaite, "Sir Galahad and the Islands," *Bim* 7: 25 (1957), 8.

11. Simon Gikandi, *Writing in Limbo: Modernism and Caribbean Literature* (Ithaca, NY: Cornell University Press, 1992); Édouard Glissant, *Caribbean Discourse*, trans. J. Michael Dash (Charlottesville: University of Virginia Press, 1989).

12. Paul Gilroy, *The Black Atlantic: Modernity and Double-Consciousness* (Cambridge, MA: Harvard University Press, 1993), p. 1.

13. Supriya Nair, *Caliban's Curse: George Lamming and the Revisioning of History* (Ann Arbor: University of Michigan Press, 1996).

14. George Lamming, *In the Castle of My Skin* (Ann Arbor: University of Michigan Press, 1991), p. xxxvi.

15. George Lamming, *The Emigrants* (Ann Arbor: University of Michigan Press, 1994), p. 280.

16. Bruce MacDonald, "Language and Consciousness in Sam Selvon's *A Brighter Sun*," *English Studies in Canada* 2 (1979), 202–215, reprinted in Susheila Nasta, ed. *Critical Perspectives on Sam Selvon* (Washington, DC: Three Continents, 1988), pp. 173–186.

17. Sam Selvon, *An Island Is a World* (Toronto: TSAR Publications, 1993), p. 42.

18. Patrick French, *The World Is What it Is: The Authorized Biography of V. S. Naipaul* (New York: Knopf, 2008).

19. Rob Nixon, *London Calling: V. S. Naipaul, Postcolonial Mandarin* (New York: Oxford University Press, 1992).

20. V. S. Naipaul, *The Mystic Masseur: A Novel* (New York: Vintage, 1985), pp. 132, 152.

21. V. S. Naipaul, foreword to Seepersad Naipaul, *The Adventures of Gurudeva and Other Stories* (London: André Deutsch, 1976), p. 18.

22. V. S. Naipaul, *Literary Occasions: Essays*, ed. Pankaj Mishra (New York: Vintage, 2003), p. 130.

23. Selwyn Cudjoe, *V. S. Naipaul: A Materialist Reading* (Amherst: University of Massachusetts Press, 1988).

24. Pericles Lewis, *Modernism, Nationalism, and the Novel* (New York: Cambridge University Press, 2000).

25. Fawzia Mustafa, *V. S. Naipaul* (New York: Cambridge University Press, 1995).

26. Anita Patterson, *Race, American Literature and Transnational Modernisms* (New York: Cambridge University Press, 2008).

27. Wilson Harris, *Guyana Quartet* (London: Faber and Faber, 1985), p. 19.

28. Wilson Harris, *The Womb of Space: The Cross-Cultural Imagination* (Westport, CT: Greenwood, 1983), p. xvii.

29. Franco Moretti, *The Way of the World: The Bildungsroman in European Culture*, trans. Albert Sbragia (London: Verso, 2000).

47

Postwar renewals of experiment
1945–1979

PHILIP TEW

Both literary experimentation and periodization are complex, contestable acts. All chronological groupings are potentially arbitrary. Yet a logical starting point for the parameters of postwar fiction is the cessation of major hostilities in 1945. Subsequently the nation punctuates a historical *and* ideological shift to the left with the Labour government's landslide election, defeating Winston Churchill. Much postwar fiction is imbued by politicization in response to the prevailing leftist ideological consciousness, which validated the consensus welfarism inspired by the Beveridge Report and the Labour victory.

As to when the postwar literary phase ends, generational and aesthetic changes occur in the mid to late 1970s, alongside seismic cultural and historical transformations. The 1973 oil crisis, the miners' strike, and the three-day week erode the long-standing *Zeitgeist* defined by a consensus familiar to baby-boomers. Any residual ideological common ground collapses with the 1979 election of Margaret Thatcher, confirming another juncture in culture, ideology, and aesthetics. Following the lead of such historical landmarks, I focus on innovative novelists from 1945 to 1979, particularly on experimental texts that Bernard Bergonzi in *The Situation of the Novel* (1970) characterizes as "at a considerable distance from the well-made realistic novel as conventionally understood."[1]

Which elements of form and content justify characterizing particular acts of textualization or authorship as "experimental?" As Émile Zola explains in *The Experimental Novel and Other Essays* (1893), naturalistic novels with their pan-optic vision were originally considered experimental.[2] For Zola such writing responds to the logic of matter and science (16). It aspires to produce precise and true copies of objective Newtonian externalities. However, implicitly Zola admits the inability of such texts to render an entirely faithful mimesis: "I maintain even at this point that we must modify nature, without departing from nature, when we employ the experimental method in our novels" (11).

Later experimental authors doubt the apparent solidity of nature, factuality, and time, and reject mimetic narrative transparency. They foreground the text as device, in the process actively countering, extending, or revealing generic boundaries and possibilities. As for underlying reality: as Iris Murdoch asks in *Existentialists and Mystics: Writings on Philosophy and Literature* (1997) "Does not a stream-of-consciousness novel, like an impressionist picture, imitate something absolutely fundamental?"[3]

Modernism is situated between naturalism and postwar experiment. Modernism's cultural and artistic revolution addresses a Western crisis concerning the loss of traditional meanings. Many critics regard the postwar period as overshadowed by and antagonistic toward modernism, even although modernism at that time enjoyed an academic apotheosis. David Lodge in 1981, looking back on the Movement writers, sees them as "suspicious of, if not actually hostile to, efforts at experimentation in writing."[4] Although in *Lucky Jim* (1953) Movement writer Kingsley Amis does parody provincial followers of Bloomsbury, deriding the elitist Welches, are Lodge's assumptions about postwar anti-modernism entirely accurate? Even the postwar neo-realists subtly appropriate modernist techniques, albeit incorporating them admittedly into more modest modes of experimentation. Amis's novel appears superficially realist, but radically resists that sub-genre in important ways, especially by emphasizing, as modernism does, the unreliability of the narrator, in this case Jim Dixon. Also at times modernist impressionism displaces Amis's comic rationalism. The effects of excessive drunkenness destabilize textual certainties:

> Dixon was alive again. Consciousness was upon him before he could get out of the way; not for him the slow, gracious wandering from the halls of sleep, but a summary, forcible ejection. He lay sprawled too wicked to move, spewed up like a broken spider-crab on the tarry shingle of the morning.[5]

This passage's incongruous symbolism conveys a certain irony, and is in effect a surreal stream of consciousness. The intensity of Dixon's mimicry, his self-interrogations and fear transcend simple amusement, finally undermining his perspective. Amis evokes a domesticated, subtle series of underlying absurdities. Defying conventional realism, Amis first mixes the burlesque, even vaudevillian moments indicated by Dixon's mimicry with a modernist unreliability lurking sub-textually, and then adopts an intense Pooteresque satirical mode, its ironic meanings always multiple.

What legacies from modernism do experimental postwar novelists explicitly draw upon? They follow their predecessors by undermining verisimilitude and correspondence with reality, by negating stock meanings, by implying the unknowable and unsayable. Authors deploy formal means that include linguistic or stylistic emphases, and shifting or layered perspectives. Others utilize ideological perspectives – such as existentialism, Marxism, feminism – that radicalize texts thematically or ideologically. Both aspects can interact simultaneously, as when Woolf combines formal innovation and feminism, and as Joyce does with radically technical innovation and an anti-colonial perspective. Woolf and Joyce variously inspire many postwar writers.

Central to avant-garde fiction are complex modes of reflexivity, radicalizing aspects of narration, style, structure, characterization, and themes. Samuel Beckett, an Irishman writing mostly in French, merits inclusion here because his influence becomes increasingly profound in Britain, his stark, bleak existential postwar writing inspiring several generations. His trilogy of novels *Molloy*, *Malone Dies*, and *The Unnamable* (original versions in French, 1951–1953) explores abjection and existential anguish, challenges traditional narrative and meaning, accentuates modernist inwardness *in extremis* until everything becomes defamilarized, exuding an alienation so absolute that Beckett appears to pose innumerable unanswerable questions. In *The Unnamable* he undermines fiction itself, revealing reflexively the artificiality of his own process. Fiction in Beckett represents not life, but a realm of ideas and paradoxes. His ironic repetitions are suggestive, and yet simultaneously reductive. His playfulness achieves a sense of non-location that renders his landscapes suggestive, haunting, and deathly. They defy mimesis by both embracing and negating the summative obsession that can permeate naturalistic detail. Logical interconnections of elements also are perpetually confounded. In the story "The Expelled" (French version, 1954) the unnamed first-person narrator recalls: "In what had just happened to me there was nothing in the least memorable. It was neither the cradle nor the grave of anything whatever. Or rather it resembled so many other cradles, so many other graves, that I'm lost."[6] The narrator, paranoid, believing himself spied on, remembers only his lawyer's name, Mr. Nidder. His discourse concerns the search for a furnished room aided by a cabman. Eventually he sleeps in a stable (shorn of biblical reference). The tale concludes inconsequentially at dawn, undermining fictional authority and purpose. "I don't know why I told this story. I could just as well have told another. Living souls, you will see how alike they are" (48).

Beckett's postwar plots baffle summary, offering few identifiable coordinates or points of progression. "The End" evokes another anonymous protagonist, in an unnamed environment, living modestly, lodging in locations ranging from a rented basement, to a cave, a shed-like cabin in the mountains, and another shed. The isolation becomes both comforting and alienating: "You become unsociable, it's inevitable. It's enough to make you wonder sometimes if you are on the right planet. Even the words desert you, it's as bad as that ... To contrive a little kingdom, in the midst of the universal muck, then shit on it, ah that was me all over" (*Four Novellas*, 93). Beckett's formal radicalizations threaten not only the meaning of existence, but existence and meaning themselves. Meaning, inscribing an apparent nothingness defined by a paradoxical and banal absurdity, is confounded. *All Strange Away* (1979) stretches prose to its limits by undoing purposive or relatable, sustainable articulation: "Imagination dead imagine. A place, that again. Never another question. A place, then someone in it, that again. Crawl out of the frowsy deathbed and drag it to a place to die in."[7]

In compacted contractions Beckett alludes to narrative expectations, then defies and undermines them. Despite Beckett's example of abject bleakness, however, by borrowing and heightening his ludic elements many novelists in the postwar literary scene adopt explicit comic perspectives as an experimental mode, situating light playfulness alongside dark irony and intense observation of evil and perversity. The overall effect is mordant, undermining joy with pessimism.

The mordant moral ambiguity of the prewar and postwar worlds permeates Muriel Spark's experiments in fiction. Fascism is featured in *The Prime of Miss Jean Brodie* (1961), which retrospectively narrates the fascinations of the eponymous schoolteacher. The past is reconstructed out of conversations about Brodie by student school-friends grown older and looking back. Brodie first admires Mussolini, later Hitler. Is she perverse, culpable, merely silly? "What energy [Brodie] had to spare she now put into political ideas."[8] "'Hitler *was* rather naughty,' [we are told that Brodie says] but at this time she was full of her travels and quite sure the new régime would save the world" (122). Sandy, the novel's protagonist, later a nun, Judas-like betrays her mentor. Sandy's motivations are not morally clearcut, but are as ambiguous as her teacher's. Spark's relation to her characters also is ambiguous. A literary ethos rendering moral judgment only implicit affects the author–character relationship, reintroducing and deepening the possibilities of narrative unreliability. Spark's ironies domesticate and situate nearer to home the moral decline represented by Nazism.

A postwar novelist who fled the Nazis, Polish exile Stefan Themerson, relocated in Britain, produces postwar fiction influential among avant-garde younger writers. Themerson's *Bayamus* (1949), in which violence and anti-semitism in prewar Europe are undercurrents, is a novella introducing readers to the Theatre of Anatomy, and the Theatre of Semantic Poetry, parts of a surreal version of London, explored jointly in ludic, self-reflexive ways by the first-person author-narrator and Bayamus. The narrator tells about the 1920s when an uncle from Warsaw lost a leg falling from a tram after an anti-semitic attack. "I've just looked back through the pages of my manuscript to see if I have already mentioned that he had three legs. I find no mention of it. But since my handwriting is hardly legible I cannot be sure about it. In any case Bayamus had three legs."[9] Themerson's story offers curious twists and turns of plot and retrospection. Born a girl in France Bayamus is saved by Dr. Roux, who hides the child, intending to preserve her for marriage that will produce more tripeds. But at age fourteen Bayamus becomes a male. To intensify the absurdities, the narrative reveals that Bayamus has evolved a rudimentary roller skate on his middle foot, which is discussed in both aesthetic and Darwinian terms. In a brothel episode a girl sings "the Quartier Latin song" (45), a rambling concatenation of ideas tangentially about procreation. Meaning and logic are threatened, or perplexed by concrete poetry and other obscure forms. Philosophical dialogues recur throughout. Themerson's later work *Tom Harris* (1967) explores moral ambiguity via odd characters in London and Italy, where coincidence and synchronicity prevail, the atmosphere odd, surreal, and uncanny. Themerson in the 1960s interacts with an informal group of young writers – led by the controversial and highly influential B. S. Johnson – who also are inspired by the *nouveau roman* and New Wave continental films.

Modernism's inversion of literary convention and tradition survives in such novels as William Golding's *Lord of the Flies* (1954), which overturns the upbeat excitement of boys' adventure stories inherited from their Victorian heyday. Another intertext for Golding is Joseph Conrad's *Heart of Darkness* (1899). Violence permeates Golding's narrative, displacing notions of human innocence. The rational is threatened throughout, and illusions of childhood challenged. In the final episode, moments before an unexpected rescue, Ralph hides, fearing for his life from fire and the boys who are hunting him, his fear rendered in staccato stream of consciousness. "Hide, break the line, climb a tree – which was the best after all? The trouble was you had only one chance."[10] Ralph is forced to counter-attack. In the impressions of his subsequent flight, one senses impulsivity, an intuitive, unmediated consciousness, exuding a visceral and violent connection to the unconscious. This draws on modernists like Woolf and Joyce; but it exhibits mixed feelings about modernism. On the one hand Golding's narrative allies itself with modernism's disenchantment of the world, of adventure stories; on the other hand

Golding's picture of the boys also challenges the epic grandiosity of Woolf and Joyce, expressing moral commentary though the mythopoeic and allegorical structures of precisely children's fiction. Both on a meta-level and thematically, the allegorical mode mimics or parodies modernists' attempts to stand outside of history, and suggests their hubris in adopting externalized, detached perspectives.

If modernist fiction highlights essentially inner subjective struggles, much postwar writing is concerned with discordant, intensely alienated intersubjective social interactions; with commodification of moral values; and public moral and ideological conflicts. Even when postwar writing draws upon the aesthetics of oblique narrative focus, truncated dialogue and quotidian symbolism that one finds, for example, in Woolf's *Jacob's Room* (1922) and *Mrs. Dalloway* (1925), it does so especially to represent persons challenged by alienating and changing social conditions. Anthony Burgess's *A Clockwork Orange* (1962) foregrounds the decline of public morality, a social breakdown epitomized by violent gangs of youths called "droogs." Burgess's protagonist Alex leads a gang that is further distanced from conventional morality by their hostile argot (an artificial dialect created by Burgess): for example, Alex's droogs prepare "to do the ultra-violent on some shivering starry grey-haired ptitsa in a shop and go smecking off with the till's guts."[11] John Fowles revisits the basis of personal morality in *The French Lieutenant's Woman* (1969) by contrasting the apparently *laissez-faire* sexuality of the 1960s with the sexual intensity and restrictions of Victorian Britain. Stressing both personal and historical contingencies, Fowles's novel offers a reader three endings, only one expressing conventional romance and the traditional motherly role of women.

Modernist fiction represents the alienated fate of individuals in urban environments; postwar innovation centers more on ideological dilemmas and social paradoxes, seeking to extend comprehension of alienation in part by exploring existential authenticity. Murdoch reflects the ambivalent postwar intellectual tenor, fascinated by existentialism but critical too. "The existentialist may become so obsessed with the powerful self-assertive figure of his hero (or anti-hero) that he presents a mediocre person as being important and valuable simply because he is contemptuous of society and gets his own way" (226). Both alienation and the assertive rebel are parodied by Spark in Brodie and in the malevolent hunchback Dougal Douglas, protagonist of *The Ballad of Peckham Rye* (1960). Like many postwar novels *The Ballad* adopts overlapping chronological synchronies, short episodes drawing upon Woolfian moments of time, permeated by whimsical banalities. Suggestive, concise, almost epigrammatic dialogue drives forward Spark's plot, conveying complex scenarios implicitly rather than explicitly. Two local factories employ Dougal as an "Arts" man to undertake research into their locality in early mass-observation style. Dougal self-dramatizingly calls attention to two horns he claims to have had removed surgically. His actions exude mischievousness, if not malevolence, his disruptions are radically carnivalesque. Spark creates a fissure between the surface of Dougal's interventions in the Peckham community and the intuitive responses of the factory workers. The novel's ballad-like repetitions express a laconic distance from the plot's eventfulness, and from the realism that inheres in the novel's mundane details. Part of Spark's intention is to parody the contemporary sentimental realism typified by Wolf Mankowitz's *A Kid for Two Farthings* (1953) and the moralistic social realism and interventionism of E. R. Braithwaite's *To Sir, With Love* (1959).The latter also is mocked by B. S. Johnson's protagonist in *Albert Angelo* (1964).

If reflexivity or an exaggerated concern for writing as a process is a common postwar experimental strategy, Lawrence Durrell's novels constituting *The Alexandria Quartet, Justine* (1957), *Balthazar* (1958), *Mountolive* (1958), and *Clea* (1960) qualify for inclusion, being about authorship and its origins in experience and events. These narratives of the late colonial period, describing the intimate lives of a group of friends during intrigues leading up to the Second World War and its aftermath, undermine any view of personality or identity as stable or fixed. Each offers a fragmented narrative about the characters' intersecting passions, secrets, and love lives. Each celebrates cosmopolitanism, their settings evoked as sites of exotic otherness. The effect is both disparate and cumulative, scenes repeated and revisited, the same ground encountered from different perspectives, additional knowledge or contexts demanding that the reader reassess prior understandings. Reality remains visceral (Durrell is indebted to Henry Miller's libertarian influence), detailed, and yet peculiarly insubstantial, for as the schoolteacher narrator, Darley, says in *Justine*, the first novel:

> I am thinking back to the time when for the four of us the known world hardly existed; days became simply... [a] tide of meaningless affairs nosing along the dead level of things, entering no climate, leading us nowhere, demanding of us nothing save the impossible – that we should be.[12]

Narrative self-consciously permeates the novels: the narrator recollects his struggle to account for events; Pursewarden, the Durrell-like novelist, kills himself; a novel by a character named Arnauti is frequently quoted or alluded to by the narrator, and is incorporated by Durrell-Darley in passages describing Justine, who was originally Arnauti's lover. The schoolmaster narrator literally obsesses about this work, serving as a *mise-en-abime*. He relates to his lover by reference to Arnauti's novel, repeatedly quoting his predecessor's descriptions. All four novels are temporally complex, retrospective, impressionistic, the prose and plot determinedly opaque and fragmented for large sections. Modernism is at work again: Durrell's abstract concept of time explicitly cites Proust's work as "the great academy of time-consciousness" (764).

Doris Lessing's *The Golden Notebook* (1962) is multiply self-reflexive, both structurally (the novel *is* the notebooks that are the narrative) and thematically: the narrator is attempting to write a novel. This act of putative authorship ties together women's oppression and an emergent feminism. Annotations in the text also equate author with editor, implying a relationship between Lessing's final text and the four notebooks in which the protagonist Anna Wulf records her life, and from which she hopes to extract the fifth, golden one. The notebooks are schematic and intertwined: the black one features Anna's life in Africa before and during the Second World war; the red notebook records her time as a member of the Communist Party; a yellow notebook is an attempted novel about the painful ending of a love affair; and the blue one represents the journal in which Anna records both everyday facts and her dreams, emotions, and memories. Lessing's autobiographical presence is implicit. Anna Wulf's life largely mirrors her creator's, and its coordinates are ostensibly realistic, describing a bourgeois existence, framed by offspring, ex-spouses, and lovers.

Critical of war and Stalinism, Lessing's novel assesses communism and its contradictions. It foregrounds the growing awareness by politically committed women of patriarchal structures of oppression. However, for all its ideological self-consciousness, the mores of a privileged intellectual class, the political infighting of the left, and their growing disillusionment are the book's essence. A bourgeois intellectual self-concern lies at the heart of this account. Anna might reflect on a lack of mutuality between the classes. "Britain, the middle-class has no knowledge of the lives of the working-people, and vice-versa; and reports and articles and novels are sold across the frontiers, are read as if savage tribes were being investigated."[13] But Lessing's world is largely an introspective, closed one. Lack of knowledge of the working class is hardly transcended, apart from a glimpse of left-wing scholarship boys. Although Lessing criticizes patriarchal control well, the working class remains finally peripheral in such intellectualizations. Anna reaches out for a feminist understanding, but her resolution is banal when toward the novel's end she tells her friend Molly: "And I'm going to join the Labour Party and teach a night-class twice a week for delinquent kids. So we're both going to be integrated with British life at its roots" (649). This simply articulates what Bergonzi calls "the baffled impotence of the English far left" (61).

Although Lessing employs self-referential structures, ironically using a materialist rationality to chronicle the closed, self-regarding world of radical leftist cliques, she proposes that feminism may breach such constraints. Other ideologically committed writers inflect their fiction differently, using an existentialist view (sometimes more credulously than Murdoch) to engage with concrete facts less systematically, far more impressionistically. One conduit is novelist Rayner Heppenstall, who draws consciously on the existentialism of Jean-Paul Sartre and other French intellectuals (many of them, above all Alain Robbe-Grillet, also writers of fiction). Such fiction explores alienation, seismic shifts in moral perspectives, extreme angst, and ideas about authentic commitments. This perspective explains the immense attention to concrete detail and the shifting attitudes in John Fowles's *The Magus* (1966). Fowles's protagonist, Oxford graduate Nicholas Urfe, confesses of his university crowd that

> we argued about essences and existences and called a certain kind of inconsequential behaviour "existential." Less enlightened people would have called it capricious or just plain selfish; but we didn't realize that the heroes, or antiheroes of the French existentialist novels we read were not supposed to be realistic.[14]

Fowles's narrative initially appears realistic, but is increasingly aligned with mythopoeic archetypes, an emphasis whose illusory aspects are reinforced by the central Greek island setting, Phraxos, reverberant with a sense of the past. This environment appears to communicate with Nicholas. Maurice Conchis, the magus figure, manipulates lives and people's apprehension of the real in his "godgame," which he uses to justify the moral ambiguity of his own wartime fascist collaboration, and with which he reveals Nicholas's hidden inner self. The revelation subverts Nicholas's existential certainties. In effect Fowles presents an anti-heroic challenge to figures who fuse patriarchal authority with radicalism (perhaps those figures represent modernist artistic forebears). *The French Lieutenant's Woman* advances more explicitly experimental devices than *The Magus*, although the former's undoing of Nicholas's selfhood is echoed in the latter's multiple endings, which stress the performative, merely contingent nature of identity.

A differently inflected dreamlike mythopoeic and archetypal quality permeates the fiction of Wilson Harris, a Guyanese writer resident and active in Britain from 1959. His prose reflects on the nature of memory and recollection, on how this influences acts of narrative, celebrating their contradictions and failings. In *The Eye of the Scarecrow* (1965) the narrator-protagonist "IDIOT NAMELESS" writes in a journal about his distant past:

> It is this frail visionary organization of memory – one thing against another, and everything apparently laying siege to nothing (while nothing seems to extend into the immaterial capacity and absorption of everything), which highlights the transient figures of the insensible past into ideal erections against chaos, standing, within a measureless ground plan of spiritual recognitions, intimacies and identities.[15]

Resisting "the dead tide of self-indulgent realism" (15, 105), reality and spatiality in Harris are challenged as ways of knowing. Lurking beneath Harris's sense of history is what he calls "the irony and nihilism of spirit I suddenly saw which bore such a close, almost virtuous, resemblance to the unprejudiced reality of freedom" (18–19).

B. S. Johnson's work especially exemplifies the strand of postwar fictional experimentation that reverses modernism's inwardness, extending experimentalism in the direction of social consciousness. Johnson fuses social perspectives with reflexive and innovative structural formalism. The fusion is informed by a class consciousness that explores Johnson's proletarian origins and identity. Not simply echoing modernist precursors, he transcends them. In his second novel, *Albert Angelo* (1964), Johnson uses a plethora of forms and devices. The novel at one level is a precise study of delinquency and the effects of migration in the postcolonial era. Johnson incorporates essays by pupils that describe their teacher, publishing ones – with only marginal revision of names – that Johnson collected while a supply (substitute) teacher in an unruly secondary school. This adapts the notion of the *objet trouvé* of the literary sphere, as does the inclusion of a fortune-teller's flyer (with its oblique parody of T. S. Eliot's *The Waste Land*). Johnson's documentary action epitomizes the experimental writer's desire to convey a fuller sense of exactly those experiential coordinates that realist conventions distort: a hyper-realism in effect.

Johnson extends modernist technique in order to subvert its potential elitism. Nevertheless he partly shares the modernist obsession with the self, only mediating this compulsion with a class perspective that is combative, and that captures an innate ontological truth. He exemplifies the postwar period's radical intellectual and ideological agenda, flouting class positions that maintain capitalist hierarchies. Sifting his memories in *Trawl* (1966), he asserts unequivocally concerning both his childhood *and* the present:

> I became aware of class distinction . . . aware in fact of the class war, which is not an outdated concept, as those of the upper classes who are not completely

dim would con everyone else into believing it is. The class war is being fought
as viciously and destructively of human spirit as it has ever been in England; I
was born on my side, and I cannot and will not desert.[16]

He says of the novelist in his polemical introduction to *Aren't You Rather Young
to be Writing Your Memoirs?* (1973), "If he [a novelist] is serious, he will be
making a statement which attempts to change society towards a condition he
conceives to be better, and he will be making at least implicitly a statement of
faith in the evolution of the form in which he is working."[17]

Johnson's politics are less idealistic than another experimentalist, Christine
Brooke-Rose, whose schematic reworking of the overall context of racial
prejudice in *Out* (1964) is formally innovative, its themes of migration, prejudice, and ecological disaster cleverly worked through, its characters Ukayans,
Uessayans, and ex-Uessessarians. Her dystopian world is intriguing, with the
whites – the "Colourless"[18] – a migrant population in a black-dominated
world. The protagonist endures a recursive, repetitive nightmarish existence,
where any sense of reality is undermined both by the circumstances and the
narration itself. Formally the novel is intricate, with its reversal of prejudicial
conditions of the early 1960s. Yet perhaps finally the text fails to adequately
penetrate the underlying quotidian realities and impact of Britain's economic
and cultural shifts. Beyond a narrative virtuosity, Brooke-Rose tends to
emphasize prejudice itself as the primary underlying problem. In contrast
both Johnson's *Albert Angelo* and the posthumously published *See the Old Lady
Decently* (1975) subtly analyze aspects of Britain's postcolonial realities and the
marginality of lower-class subjects, whose implicit sense of the past shares the
same dynamic element – that of various oppressions – with the present.

Johnson's politicization of values both pervades and mediates his work's
formal devices, locating them, broadening the ongoing relevance of the texts.
Brooke-Rose's engagement is in part moralistic and also didactic; although
Johnson in *Albert Angelo* also offers a "didactic" intention, "social comment on
teaching, to draw attention, too, to improve,"[19] Johnson proselytizes with a
socialistic aim, that of radicalizing, if not revolutionizing the reader, a commitment that will become more complex and developed. Expressing his desire to
want more from the novel genre in the "Disintegration" section toward the
end of *Albert Angelo*, after the "almighty aposiopesis" (167), one senses
Johnson's vexations, – "It's all about frustration" (169); and when he berates
his reader – "Tell me a story, tell me a story. The infants" (169) – the energy
and resentment are still palpable. His structure, his analysis, and the symbolic
and thematic economy work together persuasively. The failings of ideology

and of aesthetic form match his own. Brooke-Rose offers a repeated observation: "It is impossible ever to see the beginning of anything because at the beginning the thing is not recognisable as anything distinct and by the time it has become something distinct the beginning is lost" (196). This perspective, the rhetoric stuttering in its self-belief, like the fictional dissolving of reality in *Out*, might be more consistent and comprehensive than Johnson's vision, but overall Brooke-Rose's novel seems etiolated or abstract.

Brooke-Rose remains the keystone of the intellectual structures upon which her work rests; Johnson challenges his own self, his own working, in an act of humility and immolation often overlooked. In *Albert Angelo*'s disintegration he enumerates his "lies" (172), his omissions (which thus curiously become part of the text), and the changes both willful on his part and those brought about by subsequent physical interventions in the world of objects:

> – So that's another shifting of reality, in the course of the book I've come to see differently events I believed to be fixed, changed my mind about Muriel, I have this other girl, Virginia, now, at the time of writing, very happy too, but who knows what else will have shifted by galleyproof stage, or pageproof stage, or by publication day, or by the time you are reading this? Between writing and galleys, they've cut down some of the trees in Percy Circus, for instance, taken down the railings, you'll just have to take my word for the description, now, now all I can say is That's how it was, then, that's the truth. (172)

Such attempts are controversial. Throughout his career his novels foreground explicitly their status as artifacts, so much so that he risks constantly being accused of gimmickry and innovation for its own sake, critics ignoring his obsession with capturing ontological truth. Johnson objects to the term "experimental" precisely because of its pejorative connotations, not because of the innovative, radical literary praxis it signifies. As Jonathan Coe insists in *Like a Fiery Elephant: The Story of B. S. Johnson* (2004), "if Johnson's work stands up better today than most of the writing of his 'experimental' peers, this has everything to do with the fact that he refused – or was unable – to sacrifice intensity of feeling on the altar of formal ingenuity."[20]

Ann Quin was part of B. S. Johnson's informal avant-garde group. Quin attempts her own revisions of tradition, not just formally. Challenging ideas of psychological normality permeating the postwar period, her work might be regarded as a phenomenological and existential journey into pathological relationships that nevertheless appear enlightening, however painful the epiphanies. Her first novel *Berg* (1964) begins with the vengeful intentions of

Alistair Berg, whose mother was deserted after his birth: "A man called Berg, who changed his name to Greb, came to a seaside town intending to kill his father ..."[21] This opening foregrounds both inversion and oedipal desire, describing a world where sanity and insanity are indistinguishable. The novel offers a highly impressionistic account of the actions of Berg, unrecognized by his father (an aging vaudevillian living with his lover). The narrative blends naturalistic elements with stream of consciousness, current reflections, and events interspersed with acts of memory. Both introspective and reflective, *Berg*'s perspective fluctuates, denying any certainty about external reality or ethical positioning. Quin's supplement to such a neo-modernist stance is the sleazy, threadbare, and violent authenticities of her world, enumerated and celebrated as ontological fact rather than despised, an aesthetic of an ethical void. Based on Brighton Quin's text minimizes the actual environment, creating an archetypal context, which continues in the Mediterranean setting of her *Three* (1966). *Three* is about the relationship of a young woman, referred to as "S," adopted as a companion by a married couple, Ruth and Leonard. S appears to have killed herself as their summer together ends. The couple attempt retrospectively to chart events leading to S's death from memory, diaries, and S's journals and tape-recordings. Quin's novels incorporate popular elements of the thriller, mystery, and crime sub-genres, but flattened to negate the suspense inherent in each.

Another experimenter of great thematic and stylistic intensity who emerges in the 1960s is J. G. Ballard, who initially wrote science fiction while exploring trauma, sexuality, and violence in shorter pieces. His two most extreme texts are *The Atrocity Exhibition* (1970) and *Crash* (1973). The former's fragmentary nature and style evokes the writing of William Burroughs, an American experimentalist much admired by Ballard and who became greatly influential in Britain after 1980. Ballard's novel has a range of characters, with the protagonist mutating identities, evidently versions of the same template. Both text and the putative protagonist return obsessively to the assassination of J. F. Kennedy. As the obsession unfolds, world political events and culture devolve into the iconography of the theme park. A later edition of *The Atrocity Exhibition* features marginalia by Ballard that explicitly explore the process of the text's creation. "The many lists in *The Atrocity Exhibition* were in effect free-association tests. What I find surprising after so many years is how they anticipate the future themes of my fiction."[22] *Crash* intensifies the apparent transgressiveness of human desires. Those of its central characters are unleashed by automobile collisions, its author rendering Sadeian images of car wrecks as a mode of remorseless violence objectifying eros.

In far less intense and fractious mode Iris Murdoch attempts reflexive fiction (by this time almost a populist sub-genre in itself) although in a fairly traditional manner, with *The Black Prince* (1973). It has an "Editor's Foreword" by P. Loxias followed by "Bradley Pearson's Foreword" which appears to refer to Murdoch's book that follows. On a (second) title-page the reader (who is addressed periodically throughout the text) finds:

NOW FOLLOWS BRADLEY PEARSON'S STORY, WHICH IS ENTITLED:
THE BLACK PRINCE: A CELEBRATION OF LOVE.[23]

Murdoch warns the reader through Bradley against any security of self-knowledge, stating that "no philosopher and hardly any novelist has ever managed to explain what that weird stuff, human consciousness, is really made of" (157). Clearly this authorizes Murdoch to construct a bricolage of experimental modes: ironic gestures that supplement the sub-genres of detective fiction and the comic novel of manners. Bradley tells his story from prison, followed by his postscript and "Four Postscripts by Dramatis Personae" (343). Apart from numerous reflections on love, the process of writing and the meaning of art, it is a stretch to see the novel as primarily innovative apart from its synthesis of genres. Its metafictional dimensions, its use of allusion to Hamlet, are highly literary, and cohere with Murdoch's self-reflexive notion of fictionality. Her work offers clear evidence of experimental modes being adapted, albeit with a lower profile, in less radical forms of the novel, another example of the kind of putative incorporation of avant-garde techniques that I considered in regard to *Lucky Jim*.

Alasdair Gray's complex novel, *Lanark* (1981), although published after the end of the periodization I have identified as constituting the postwar, was commenced in 1954 (when most of book 1 was finished) and finally completed in 1976. Before that point sections had appeared in small journals (and most of chapter 12 had featured as the runner-up prize-winner in *The Observer* short story competition in 1958). Hence it qualifies as a characteristic innovative fiction of this literary era, a Byzantine book, full of gothic elements and enigmatic episodes. An epic in its ambitions, it includes autobiographical and dystopic elements, literary allusions and quotations, illustrations, aphorisms, and lengthy footnotes that offer no really pertinent information. Its prologue appears halfway through, and the text features a dialogue between author and character.

Books III and IV appear first and last, telling of Lanark, a stranger suffering from amnesia arriving in Unthank, a city alien to him, lacking daylight. He tries to write an account of himself, beginning *"The first thing I remember I,"*[24] but can construct no real meaning, the manuscript which follows in chapter 3 recollecting his awakening on a train, suffering from amnesia with a rucksack containing a few items. He seems to adopt his name from a tourist-photograph in his train compartment. His pockets are filled with tiny seashells, the latter anticipating the drowning of another character, Duncan Thaw, an eczema sufferer. Thaw's life in Glasgow is described in books I and II, both topographically naturalistic in rendering, detailing Thaw's conflicted youth and school education and his subsequent scholarship at the Glasgow School of Art, where isolated from women despite his desires, his obsessive aesthetic vision drives him to madness, murder (apparently), and drowning.

Gray celebrates oddities and incongruities. Unthank is surreal and contra-dictory, an exaggeration of the entropy Gray senses in Glasgow and Scotland. If Thaw's life is thwarted and oppressed, it is distorted and yet mirrored in the world of Unthank. None of the latter's inhabitants appears to work, many having developed symbolically suggestive and grotesque ailments. Soon Lanark manifests "dragonhide," his arm scaly, physically representing his emotional repression and isolation. He learns that one woman he knows has suffered from mouths on her body, all speaking independently, an uncontrolled cacophony. Meanwhile, Lanark, after a journey reminiscent of a *regressus ad uterum*, finds himself in "The Institute," which tries to cure people of their metaphorically suggestive diseases. Tangentially he is con-fronted through a female voice, that of Rima, with his past life and name. Soon afterwards it is revealed that the Institute's food is the reconstituted remains of those left uncured. Lanark is revolted and hankers for light and freedom. Finally the oracular voice begins an account of Thaw's life, the narrative that follows. In book IV Lanark and Rima attempt to reach the city of Provan by returning to Unthank via emergency Exit 3124 (an allusion to the novel's unusual progression) along the "intercalendrical zone" (373).

Gray's structures and characterization are deliberately arcane, and symbolic unspoken links permeate all levels of the fantastic realm in ways that tie to the more naturalistic sections. Thaw dissolves into madness; and the relation between sane and insane spheres is always unresolved, reminiscent of the complex interchanges of the conscious and unconscious. Gray, projecting himself as Nastler the conjurer, who appears in the Epilogue (a word on the door through which Lanark passes), has Nastler discuss with Lanark the nature of his work in relation to other writers (Blake, Melville, Mervyn Peake, Tolkien, and Tolstoy), and indicates other sources in marginalia ("'dragon-hide'" derives from the "muscular constriction [Wilhelm] Reich calls 'armour-ing'" [496] that defends against repressed emotions, particularly anxiety and rage). Gray's experimentation is largely symbolic and self-reflexive, but ideo-logically Gray also prioritizes regionalism through vocabulary, syntax, and settings. In a radical and highly influential manner, Gray initiates a Scottish fictional renaissance that begins in the 1980s and continues.

The postwar novel revisits experimentation variously and intriguingly. The period sustains a far more complex and continued relation to modernist and avant-garde aesthetics than is generally recognized. It is the prologue to another vibrant and innovative period of new generations of experimental authors who emerge in the 1970s. These include Angela Carter, Martin Amis, and Ian McEwan. Their fiction synthesizes modernist and postwar innova-tions in order to respond to the ultra-commodification of late-capitalist culture. Amis's *Money: A Suicide Note* (1984) intensifies the later period's demotic register, its comedic devices inflected knowingly by cinematic and televisual culture. Fast, aggressive urban lowlife and its tonality is inter-mixed with philosophizing asides, ranting critiques, and slick gags redolent of stand-up comedy. Here the seriousness and reflexivity of what now amounts to a novelistic tradition of experiment finds remarkably popularized expression.

Notes

1. Bernard Bergonzi, *The Situation of the Novel* (London: Macmillan, 1970), p. 75.
2. Émile Zola, *The Experimental Novel and Other Essays*, trans. B. M. Sherman (New York: Cassell, 1893), p. 310.
3. Iris Murdoch, *Existentialists and Mystics: Writings on Philosophy and Literature* (London: Penguin, 1997), p. 244.
4. David Lodge, *Working with Structuralism: Essays and Reviews on Nineteenth- and Twentieth-century Literature* (Boston and London: Routledge and Kegan Paul, 1981), p. 9.
5. Kingsley Amis, *Lucky Jim* (London: Penguin, 1992), p. 61.
6. Samuel Beckett, "The Expelled," *Four Novellas* (London: John Calder, 1977), p. 35.
7. Samuel Beckett, *All Strange Away* (London: John Calder, 1979), p. 7.
8. Muriel Spark, *The Prime of Miss Jean Brodie* (London: Macmillan, 1961), p. 114.
9. Stefan Themerson, *Bayamus* (London: Editions Poetry, 1949), p. 22.
10. William Golding, *Lord of the Flies* (Harmondsworth: Penguin, 1960), p. 188.
11. Anthony Burgess, *A Clockwork Orange* (London: Heinemann, 1962), p. 5.
12. Lawrence Durrell, *The Alexandria Quartet: Justine, Balthazar, Mountolive, Clea* (London: Faber and Faber, 1968), pp. 20–21.
13. Doris Lessing, *The Golden Notebook* (Harmondsworth: Penguin, 1964), p. 68.
14. John Fowles, *The Magus* (London: Jonathan Cape, 1966), p. 5.
15. Wilson Harris, *The Eye of the Scarecrow* (London: Faber and Faber, 1965), p. 16.

16. B. S. Johnson, *Trawl* (London: Secker and Warburg, 1966), p. 53.
17. B. S Johnson, "Introduction," *Aren't You Rather Young to be Writing Your Memoirs?* (London: Hutchinson, 1973), p. 16.
18. Christine Brooke-Rose, *The Christine Brooke-Rose Omnibus, Four Novels: Out, Such, Between, Thru* (Manchester: Carcanet, 1986), p. 68.
19. B. S. Johnson, *Albert Angelo* (London: Constable, 1964), p. 176.
20. Jonathan Coe, *Like a Fiery Elephant: The Story of B. S. Johnson* (London: Picador, 2004), p. 29.
21. Ann Quin, *Berg* (London: John Calder, 1964), p. 1.
22. J. G. Ballard, *The Atrocity Exhibition* (London: Flamingo, 1993), p. 57.
23. Iris Murdoch, *The Black Prince* (New York: Viking Press, 1973), p. 1.
24. Alasdair Gray, *Lanark* (Edinburgh: Canongate, 2002), p. 15.

The English novel since Defoe has oriented itself toward new technologies and media. It has thrived on the social relations sustained by shifting communications networks, whether they have been the epistolary habits and private couriers of the eighteenth century, the nascent print capitalism and circulating libraries of the imperial nation state, or the solidifying technological matrix of Victorian Britain's Penny Post, telegraphs, and railroads. The conventions of literary realism perhaps had to do more with the novel's formal accommodation to adjacent systems of communication (the postage stamp, the telegraph) and transportation than with any progressive attainment of truth.[1] Beyond realism, the "sensation" novels of the later nineteenth century are, according to Nicholas Daly, "the first subgenre in which a Bradshaw's railway schedule and a watch become necessary to the principal characters . . . The pleasures of fictional suspense and the anxieties of clock-watching appear as part of the same historical moment."[2] And from the telegraphic era to the computer era, the "effort to describe . . . in a far more 'life-like', complex, and detailed way than literature had ever done before becomes an attempt to incorporate, mimic, or co-opt the achievements of competing electric media."[3] The novel has absorbed these technologies into its substance through aesthetic trial and error, a process that argues the primacy of "refraction" over "reflection" in the novel's relationship to its rivals.[4]

In the early twentieth century this process rapidly accelerates. Radical technical adjustments and formal or generic modifications that we assign to "modernism" are inseparable from the rise of new communications technology. As never before, "writing and written narrative in general were . . . forced to compete with gramophones, kinetoscopes, and their technologically more advanced successors in the marketplace of inscription."[5] First the rotary press and its mass-circulation dailies, then the narrative art of cinema, followed by the hegemony of radio as a domestic narrative medium: the novel must struggle for its erstwhile position at the center of national storytelling. When James Joyce's Leopold Bloom starts his day by sitting at stool, reading, and then wiping himself with a "tit-bit" of journalistic prose, Joyce satirically puts journalism in its place; but the challenge goes deeper than satire, and requires the form of the novel to absorb the competing alternatives. Joyce expands his stylistic repertoire in order to ward off the threat: *Ulysses* attempts "to exhaust the languages, styles, and idioms to be found in newspapers, letters, telephone conversations, telegrams, protocols, budgets, interrogations . . . post-cards, and so on."[6] *Ulysses* frequently borrows the conventions of the press; Bloom is an advertising canvasser; at a funeral he contemplates installing telephones in coffins to safeguard against live burials, and surmises that gramophone recordings of the voices of the dead in every grave might gratify the bereaved; "Nausicaa" depends upon the titillations of Mutoscope parlors; and the phantasmagoria of "Circe" is derivative of cinematographic animation.[7] Joyce offers a way of seeing the novel not as some archaic cultural form cast down by the onslaught of new media, but as an active "incorporator" and mediator of its technological environment (Danius, *Senses of Modernism*, 185).

Storytelling is not the only front on which new media test the novel's status at the helm of Britain's narrative economy. With unprecedented powers of recording the real, photography, the gramophone, and the cinema end the monopoly the novel long enjoyed over the storage of social information. Realism had occupied itself with an exhaustive cataloguing of cultural data, but once what Stephen Dedalus calls the "ineluctable modality of the visible" is transposed onto strips of celluloid, and the noises of waves are recorded on wax cylinders, we find the novel declaring with redoubled force its will to "make you *see*," and flirting with onomatopoeic horrors such as "a fourworded wavespeech: seesoo, hrss, rsseeiss, ooos."[8] Conrad's impressionism and Joyce's pedantic verbal notations of urban soundscape are legible as desperate tussles with media better able to archive this material than prose is. No writer feels a deeper affinity with the camera's impressionistic eye than Virginia Woolf, whose "Kew Gardens" is an unofficial manifesto for a suitably subjectless prose:

> The light fell either upon the smooth grey back of a pebble, or the shell of a snail with its brown circular veins, or, falling into a raindrop, it expanded with such intensity of red, blue and yellow the thin walls of water that one expected them to burst and disappear.[9]

We might expect it of the narrator too, so firmly wedded is she to the microscopic ecstasies of the garden floor; and yet this kind of prose appears in each of the major novels to follow.

More consequential for the tradition of the novel is the crystallization of a new if unstated aesthetic law: "Ever since December 28, 1895, when the Lumières presented their cinema projector, non-filmability has been an unmistakable criterion for literature."[10] The movement into the subjective interior characteristic of the modern novel should be understood not as a deepening of novelists' sympathy with human beings, but as a reactive relocation of the form's concerns away from recordable surfaces, into the sole remaining non-visual and non-aural substance of modernity: consciousness. "Somewhere or other," quotes Ford's Christopher Tietjens approvingly, "there must surely be / The face not seen: the voice not heard."[11] Joyce's sixty-page ventriloquism of Molly Bloom's pre-dawn musings stands as the *sine qua non* of a novelistic investment in the not-seen, not-heard "streams" of consciousness. Of course, as with any novelistic convention, the codes adapted for transcribing human thought are not the thing itself; but they assert the rights of literature to a front-rank position among the new recording technologies. The dream of a new, heightened realism, beyond the surfaces of sight and sound, drives deep into unmapped recesses of Being. "Real," as Dorothy Richardson puts it. "Reality vibrating behind this effort to drive feeling through words."[12]

On another front, the rise of faster and more efficient communications systems, via intercontinental cable, telephone, automobile, broadcast radio, and airplane, put paid to long-established chronotopic conventions dear to fiction. No longer will provincial heroines of a novel remain trapped in their milieux, dependent on whims of weather and masculine impulse for their diversions: the flick of a switch or a bus ticket can alter everything. The technical principles of the newer media also promise invalidation of stockpiled transitional devices. As threatening as the cinema was – Orwell hated the movies because "Why encourage the art that is destined to replace literature?"[13] – Virginia Woolf nevertheless foresees that film will superannuate awkward ways of getting one's reader from A to B in novels. One senses both anxiety and exhilaration in her published thoughts on this:

> The past could be unrolled, distances could be annihilated. And those terrible dislocations which are inevitable when Tolstoy has to pass from the story of Anna to the story of Levin could be bridged by some device of scenery. We should have the continuity of human life kept before us by the repetition of some object common to both lives.[14]

Cinema at a stroke obviates the need for any rhetorical justification of scenic transitions, the beauty of cinematic montage being its abrupt and utterly compelling fiat.

Winifred Holtby, one of Woolf's earliest commentators, identifies the cinematic principle at work in *Jacob's Room* (1922). Noting the book's dependency on sudden unexplained shifts of scale and perspective, Holtby writes: "these are devices common enough to another form of art. They are the tricks of the cinema. Mrs Woolf has discovered the cinema. There is no reason why it should monopolise powers of expansion and contraction."[15] Holtby herself in her novel *South Riding* (1936) accepts the extraordinary adaptability of the new citizens of modernity in a way that her novel can only strive to emulate. Not film but radio, Keith Williams argues, "furnishes a literal bromide for terminally-ill Lily Sawdon" (66). Indeed *South Riding*, with its intention of tracing the "complex tangle of motives prompting public decisions, the unforeseen consequences of their enactment on private lives,"[16] mirrors the famous aesthetic protocol of the greatest realist, George Eliot. Holtby's conjuring of a multitude of voices from the literary silence of Yorkshire is something like a radiophonic channeling of Eliot. As Ned Schantz remarks, "*Middlemarch* seems to conjure the very media that began to emerge so near its publication. It is a would-be radio novel, a novel that would gather, redirect, and amplify the lost voices of isolated women."[17] Whereas Woolf harnesses cinematic montage, Holtby surfs the airwaves for realist residua.

Elizabeth Bowen's novels are similarly underwritten by the new mechanical speeds and facilities of modernity. For Bowen the old chronotopes of fiction have been made redundant by electronic media and motorcars. *To the North* (1932) and *The House in Paris* (1935) "show how 'transport', in all the senses of the word, deprives the characters of agency, reducing them to puppets of their own technology."[18] The "vast relay systems of modern travel and communication" hoop around the characters to such an extent that they become mere byproducts. These characters are often "motionless in motion, relinquishing their will to the machines that drive them" (103). The telephone wire in *To the North* is the only thing that keeps jittery Cecilia from vanishing altogether. Her condition expresses a growing sense that the human nervous system is no longer contained within an individual body. "In Bowen's fiction, nervousness reveals the interconnectedness of minds, enmeshed in transport networks that traverse the boundary between the human and the technological" (Ellmann, *Elizabeth Bowen*, 111).

Perhaps the new media's greatest challenge to the novel is a sense of "simultaneousness," thanks to the unparalleled speed of transfers. Raised on a pastoral diet of horse-drawn wagons, hand-written letters and walks down village lanes, the English novel is suddenly force-fed the indigestible facts of telephone, radio, and films, which link social atoms in the swiftest possible manner. Yoked to this unmatchable sense of immediacy is the impossible scale of the metropolis: now too sprawling an object for even the capacious form of Dickens and Gissing to represent. Fiction is stranded while the newer technologies effortlessly hook up the "alienated" bodies of London along an electronic axis. Conrad's *The Secret Agent* (1907) is prescient for its allegorical insights into the representational dilemmas at stake. The Professor, a "perfect anarchist," has his body wired to a terrible explosive device, and is himself a new, vibrating medium of death. He lurks in the grimy seams of the city, contemptuous of the populace, which "swarmed numerous like locusts, industrious like ants, thoughtless like a natural force, pushing on blind and orderly and absorbed, impervious to sentiment, to logic, to terror, too."[19] Against this insuperable force he pits his nihilistic individualism in a bid to emulate the instantaneities of the new media – to "move" the masses, whatever the cost: "What if nothing could move them? Such moments came to all men whose ambition aims at a direct grasp upon humanity – to artists, politicians, thinkers, reformers, or saints" (82). So the relation between the destructive medium of his body, and the avant-garde modern artist who will do anything to arouse a response, is declared; and the ratio hinges on the corresponding scale of the urban mass to be aroused. What *will* "move" them? As Tabbi and Wutz put it, "the ponderously slow dissemination of knowledge and desire by the object that we call the book" seems decidedly unequal to the task (*Reading Matters*, 1). The attempt to secure a "direct grasp upon humanity" that artists, like terrorists, must make, will, in the new century, shift away from the novel's turgid representational conventions and toward hard modes of contact like the telegram and the motor-car accident.

Liberal British fiction's most poignant lament, E. M. Forster's *Howards End* (1910), acknowledges its tardiness as a form for connecting the corpuscles of an atomized and stratified modern society. Allegorizing the confrontation of an older, slower discourse network and the emerging fast-paced one through the *mésalliance* between the Schlegel and Wilcox families, Forster beds his novel in the Schlegelian world of intellectual discussion, symphonies, and poetry; from which preserve it looks out at the blistering speed of Wilcoxian "telegrams and anger." Helen Schlegel's early vision of the Wilcoxes is that of the novel regarding its new media environment: "I felt for a moment that the whole Wilcox family was a fraud, just a wall of newspapers and motor-cars and golf-clubs, and that if it fell I should find nothing behind it but panic and emptiness."[20] Given the sense of the Schlegels' historically untenable position in this state of things ("Logically, they had no right to be alive," 290), the novel upholds one meaning of pastoral against the combustion of "telegrams and anger." Meanwhile, the logic of the novel's syrupy mantra, "only connect," is being tapped by new technologies of mediation like the telephone. According to David Trotter, "The challenge telephony set literature was that of grasping the values implicated in a remote exchange of shudders. Telephony threatens literature's existence."[21] Rising to the repeated threat, the novel grasps at whatever powers it finds to remediate the newer currents.

In Dorothy Richardson's *Pilgrimage*, Miriam Henderson, working as a dental receptionist, handles the telephone routinely. In one sequence a wrong number is dialed; a full paragraph of frustrating "Hallo, hallos" later, as Miriam attempts to converse with "a far-off faint angry voice in incoherent reiteration," we realize that it is not the crackling voice of the Other, but the "angry din of the telephone" that holds her, and our, attention – to no narrative purpose.[22] The phone call is a kind of *anti-incident*; the episode engenders a new reading experience in which the otherwise obscured background noise of everyday life rises to the surface, and we encounter it with renovated awareness. With her ears electrically engaged, Miriam's eyes are free to register the world in a state of distracted inattention. The passage stands as a telling allegory of Richardson's fictional technique – extended passages of sheer "noise" that enable a restitution of phenomenological authenticity.

Woolf attempts the same trick, more pointedly, in *Between the Acts* (1941). With "its trains, automobiles, airplanes, paperback books, newspapers, megaphone, and of course its gramophone, *Between the Acts*, more than any of Woolf's previous novels, is beset with machines and commodities."[23] Most important is the gramophone with which Miss La Trobe imposes "unity" upon the messy formlessness of her country pageant – the unfathomed unity of noise. "Chuff, chuff, chuff sounded from the bushes. It was the noise a machine makes when something has gone wrong."[24] Such noise opens a void that envelops listeners not as "subjects" of a state ideology, but as impersonal nerve ends in a network of electronic and mechanical signals:

> Chuff, chuff, chuff went the machine. Could they talk? Could they move? No, for the play was going on. Yet the stage was empty; only the cows moved in the meadows; only the tick of the gramophone needle was heard. The tick, tick, tick seemed to hold them together, tranced. Nothing whatsoever appeared on the stage. (63)

As with Richardson's "distractionism" (so to speak) Woolf suspends representation in order that the empty stage be occupied by the white noise of modernity. Her aesthetic interests lay here – in finding technical means for the

novel to interrupt its compulsive narrativity, to forestall its generic automatisms, and discover a "post-human" domain of empty durations.

Trotter makes the point that, thanks to the telephone, the novel learns
"radically to privatize experience," especially the experience of conversing
with another. Foregrounding dialogue as never before, the English novel
discovers that the "telephone's capacity to by-pass the public sphere – to
collapse time and space into direct contact. . . – has been reconfigured as the
occasion for (relative) social and sexual promiscuity" ("e-Modernism," 19).
The novels of Bowen and Woolf instance this privatization of affect through a
technology lauded for its interconnectivity and its virtual public sphere. In
telephonic scenes notable for their combined placelessness, abstraction, and
intimacy, the novel withdraws into a new regard for "close-miked" conversation; novels become more like screenplays than Dickensian triple-deckers.
The second chapter of John Galsworthy's *Swan Song* (1928), sixth volume of
the *Forsyte Chronicles*, consists of five telephone conversations between
Winifred Dartie, cooped up in her house thanks to the General Strike of
1926, and family members, strangers, and friends. Using the conceit to
highlight his own tendency towards monoclausal sentence construction,
Galsworthy harnesses the telephone as a great shearer-away of flabby rhetoric,
and a generator of convivial bonhomie for isolated women. Winifred begins
by being distressed by the strike, but ends up thinking it "was really something
to talk about; there had been nothing so exciting since the war."[25] Clearly the
medium is the message. Winifred's telephonic switching between five distant
locations in under fifteen minutes suggests a cinematic montage principle also
at work; a significant transitional economy for a writer struggling to keep as
many balls in the air as Galsworthy is in his comedic saga.

The more the novel simulates these new simultaneities, the more it tests
the parameters of form. In its compendious unfinishedness Richardson's
Pilgrimage epitomizes Italo Calvino's description of a kind of modern novel
that, "in the attempt to contain everything possible, does not manage to take
on a form, to create outlines for itself, and so remains incomplete by its very
nature."[26] This consequence of the novel's rivalry with non-symbolic media of
inscription marks mid-century English literature. Building on the prototypes
provided by Richardson, Ford, and Galsworthy the novel cycles explored in
Suzanne Keen's chapter in this *Cambridge History* extend the scope of the form
toward infinity. Emblematic in this regard is Henry Williamson's First World
War soldier-hero Phillip Maddison who, in *The Golden Virgin* (1957), recovers
from his exposure to gas in the trenches at Loos by grafting his brain (which
"never stops") to the prostheses of motorcycle and gramophone.[27] Mechanical

cycles and novel cycles propel the form outward to a mimetic copiousness, overlooking the lesson in economy that Woolf divined at the cinema.

In regard to the modern media's challenge to literary transitions, once it becomes feasible to substitute a mechanically achieved "device of scenery" for the old clunky explanations of a change of location, then by that very measure the "scenery" may grow to eclipse any human dimension in a novel. In an indicative sequence near the outset of *Parade's End*, Ford alternates between two locales: Britain and the Austro-Hungarian empire, the two imperial powers about to be impelled into war. Motivating this potentially disorienting alternation is not only the fact that each location is inhabited by one half of the Tietjens couple, but the fact that their estrangement is about to be overcome by an intercontinental telegraphic exchange. As we alternate scenes in the first three chapters, we tend to focus on the telegrams. These become higher-order linking artifacts, to be close-read and deciphered at length – since they are the "scenery" enabling the narrative switches. Media content rises into formal self-consciousness; something inhuman and inherently "noisy" (spelling errors and a lack of punctuation promote interference) is dictating narrative movement. By chapter 6 of *Some Do Not . . .* (1924), this telegraphic exchange is remediated again by the "ingenious clever stupidities of the telephone" (120) when Tietjens receives a telegram via telephone concerning his wife's demand that he bring with him her maid "Hullo Central" – so named "because she has a tinny voice like a telephone . . . you'd swear it was the Exchange speaking" (35).

As an analogy for the "inhuman" forces giving rise to war, this protracted business exploits the new conventions being foisted on the novel in order to reflect on them critically. By the end of the novel, the telephone has managed a new metaphorical feat, implicating itself with the narrative technique of a novelist whose most typical procedure is to commence slightly after the "event," circle back on it once, and then circle back on it from much greater depth again, in a kind of progressive excavation of what never takes place before us: "His voice – his own voice – came to him as if from the other end of a long-distance telephone. A damn long-distance one! Ten years . . ." (281).

One familiar version of literary history suggests that it is the heroic task of modernism to take flight from the new media ecology, while the emergent phenomenon of bestseller fiction adapts itself to the commercial benefits of slavish accommodation. If Richardson's colossal sequence typifies the former tendency with its adamant refusal of all prepackaged readerly pleasures (no plot, no "big scenes"), the fictions of Agatha Christie and Dorothy L. Sayers typify the latter: a generic subservience whose logic is clearly that of the mass market for new media products – hit songs, melodramatic films, and sensational "yellow" journalism. And yet any responsible cultural history of the period, specifically of its novels, cannot hope to separate these tendencies into irreconcilable blocks. Instead, the mechanical automatisms of detective fiction or newfangled romance infiltrate the innermost cores of the most serious fiction of the times, while some of the newer experimental anti-generic techniques of modernism (such as the interior monologue) can be found lapping against the shores of bestsellerdom. The pure instrumentalism of technological society against which modernism is supposed to have inveighed turns out on closer inspection to be a shibboleth.

If the bestsellers are associated with any one media institution, it is the press. In both phenomena what is sacrificed to mere utility is the English language. "Language suffers from exhaustion and from the feverish delirium of the yellow Press," Cecil Day Lewis writes in 1935.[28] Between Beaverbrook and the pro-fascist Rothermere, the British press joined hands with a stupefy-ing propaganda machine pumping out what Ford calls "mental anodynes with which the English reader of to-day so persistently drugs himself."[29] This machine fed an appetite for stories driven by sensation, incident, melodrama, and patriotism, drawing predominantly on nineteenth-century literary sour-ces. What the "serious" novelist was to do in response to this unprecedented spreading and simultaneous degradation of the substance of writing was far from clear. One option was to join the "romance revival" in the marketplace of fiction, and strive to achieve distinction there.[30]

Another was to pull fiercely away; but never too far. Isa Giles, the frustrated poet in *Between the Acts*, reflects that, although the library is "the nicest room in the house," with its shelves of literary classics forming a humanistic "mirror of the soul," nevertheless "For her generation the newspaper was a book" (26). A 1939 poll shows that "69 per cent of the population over 16 read a national daily paper and 82 per cent a national Sunday" (Williams, *British Writers*, 23). So irresistible were the dailies that Ezra Pound, scourge of the popular press's corruption of language, must define his own "medium" in its very terms: "literature," he wrote in 1934, "is news that stays news."[31] What should be retained from the news is its *newness*, salvaged from the repetitive cliché that vitiates it.

An early attempt to out-sensation the yellow press, H. G. Wells's "scientific romance" *The War of the Worlds* (1897) is delivered in the professional prose of a London journalist, whose rationalistic framework is challenged by the arrival on earth of canisters of Martian death machines. As the full horror of the invasion becomes apparent, the journalist notes caustically the indifference of the established press, and its subsequent immobilization by the interplanetary barrage. All that remains are the narrator's no-nonsense first-person accounts, written in retrospect – an affinity with the immediacy of the broadcast media that Orson Welles seizes upon thirty years later. The press, it turns out, is simply too "slow" as a medium to grapple with the scale and swiftness of the attack; far better this telegraphic notation, drained of all stylistic distinction, in which data can be stored on the hoof for dissemination later. Thus trumping the news, the irony is that Wells's text would help spawn one of the richest sub-genres in twentieth century literary history – science fiction, variably as operatic or utopian as you like.

Perhaps the most brilliant early meditation on what the mass-circulation press portends for serious fiction is again *The Secret Agent*. It is not simply "the press," but the very world that goes with it – modern policing, geopolitical power relations, and that new technology of fear, terrorism – whose consequences Conrad wishes to draw into the novel, which turns upon the execution of an outlandish Wellsian "event" that will be grist for the mills of the newspaper barons. The idea, hatched by the embassy official Vladimir, is to manufacture an incident out of thin air, which will figure so sensationally as an item in the press that the British government will be forced to respond to it as though it were "real." Vladimir's sketch is of particular relevance to Conrad's own concerns: "The attack must have all the shocking senselessness of gratuitous blasphemy. Since bombs are your means of expression, it would be really telling if one could throw a bomb into pure mathematics" (33). What Vladimir means is some explosive outrage directed at Greenwich standard time, that cardinal point around which the "culture of space and time" of the British Empire is synchronized: all its village clocks, railway stations, naval vessels, and colonial outposts. "Conrad could not have picked a more appropriate anarchist objective, a more graphic symbol of centralized political authority"; or of authorial authority, for that matter.[32] The "pure mathematics" of Greenwich held in place the cognitive map of turn-of-the-century England, not only the "machine" which ensured that police and criminals obey the same routines and conventions (92), but also the chronotopic fixtures, of train schedules, matinée sessions, and ferry timetables, by which the Victorian sensation novel is governed. In devising an incident to shatter this matrix of space–time, Vladimir declares war against an entire representational system – ironically, in the very terms of that system.

For nothing is more germane to the architecture of the Victorian novel than "incident." One of the modern novel's principal aesthetic reactions against the mass media's new mechanized sensations is to recoil from anything like "incident" at the level of narration: the anti-incidents of Dorothy

Richardson, the *longueurs* of Joyce and Woolf, all stem from a new reluctance either to say "what happened," or to have anything happen at all. If the yellow press dishes up nothing but events at the expense of language, then the modern novel restitutes language by eschewing "happenings" altogether. Conrad is the prime mover in this delicate aversion from event-laden narration; but what he takes away with one hand, he dishes up with the other. In *The Secret Agent* neither the bomb blast nor Winnie Verloc's murder of her husband, the two most important plotted events, are narrated. Rather, we depart at the point, and arrive in the aftermath, of those gutter-press moments.

The press itself is omnipresent in the metropolis, propagating the incident; and the final irony is that the character who ends up being haunted by the incident, Comrade Ossipon, is so in the terms of the yellow press – its inane phrases repeat themselves maddeningly in his head: *"An impenetrable mystery seems destined to hang forever over this act of madness or despair . . .* Comrade Ossipon was familiar with the beauties of its journalistic style . . . the mystery of a human brain pulsating wrongfully to the rhythm of journalistic phrases" (307, 310–311). What the mass media kept alive was the substance of romance, the ideological homeland of "mystery" and melodramatic coincidences. Wells had contributed the final effort of the novel form to outdo the press in its own terms. Conrad's solution is not exactly to exile such materials from the modern novel, but to internalize them as "quoted" objective evidence, snatched from press cuttings, trade copy, advertisements. The "serious" modern novel places a strict taboo on the incidents that drive narrative in the mass media; but it readmits incidents through the backdoor via an etiquette of citation and collage. In the new media ecology the novel also resists the pull of melodrama and romance, insofar as those have migrated to the world of journalism, hit songs, movies, and radio dramas; but it cannot resist incorporating melodrama and romance ekphrastically – as samples described *in situ* and patched into the novelistic substance with a documentary regard.

Evelyn Waugh is perhaps the writer most affronted by modern media techniques. If *Scoop* (1938) is the eminent example of press satire in the period, it seems a retreat from the audacious formal achievement of *Vile Bodies* (1930). The success of *Vile Bodies* is not its contemporary tale of Bright Young Things whipped into a frenzy by aeroplanes, zeppelins, gossip columns, racing cars, film sets, and telephonic exchanges, but that Waugh has contrived the aptest form for such a chronicle. The impersonal narrative voice flattens outward against the technological domain it charts, and its mode of articulation is fractured to an extent never seen before in British fiction. As the hapless protagonist reels from situation to situation, dialogue is broken up, and telephonically rerouted; and scene shifts happen without any comment, "intercutting rapidly between events and dialogues to produce a modernist 'montage' effect of constant flickering motion."[33] In this case satire facilitates a method sharper than ekphrasis, admitting the new speeds, techniques, and prostheses of the modern media into the formal logic of the text itself – but to what end? For whereas Joyce, eight years earlier, wantonly absorbs every new medium into the complex formal matrix of *Ulysses* in order to extend the life and legitimacy of the book, Waugh's satire is bleak, and the opposite of optimistic for literature. *Vile Bodies* reads more as a death sentence than a declaration of regeneration.

This terminal tendency has strong affinities with another satirist, Wyndham Lewis. Having absorbed the iconoclastic lessons of Marinetti's Futurism, Lewis launches his Vorticist revolt against Bloomsbury and Edwardian England in the name of a kind of technological deadening of the literary text. Lewis's satire rests on a persistent chiasmic inversion, in which human attributes are predicated of machines, and machinic features are ascribed to human characters. For Lewis, "human beings actually are mechanical objects."[34] Throughout his earliest long fiction, *Tarr* (1918), both the eponymous character and his German counterpart Kreisler are repeatedly attended by variations on the adjective "mechanical." In a typical moment, eating a bowl of strawberries is rendered as follows: "To cover reflection, he set himself to finish lunch. The strawberries were devoured mechanically, with unhungry itch to clear the plate. He had become just a devouring-machine, restless if any of the little red balls remained in front of it."[35] This evacuation of will and its supplanting by mechanical motor force lies at the heart of Lewis's method, in which what remains of the "human" is a layer of vulnerable tissue at the mercy of new techniques. Art must side with the new exoskeletons: "*deadness* is the first condition of art. A hippopotamus' armoured hide, a turtle's shell, feathers or machinery . . . The second is absence of *soul*, in the sentimental human sense . . . This is another condition of art; *to have no inside*, nothing you cannot *see*" (299–300).

This startling reversal of literature's concomitant turn "inwards" implies a satiric identification with the technological forces of dehumanization. Rather than evincing the humanistic rhythms of narrative, a novel ought to revel in "sheets of surface decoration and verbal friezes that withhold or interrupt narrative flow in favor of spatialized exposition" (Tabbi and Wutz, *Reading Matters*, 13). A "good" novel will be one proceeding from the second paragraph of Christopher Isherwood's *Goodbye to Berlin* (1939):

> I am a camera with its shutter open, quite passive, recording, not thinking. Recording the man shaving at the window opposite and the woman in the kimono washing her hair. Some day, all this will have to be developed, carefully printed, fixed.[36]

In the monumental English satires of the twentieth century, by Aldous Huxley and George Orwell, this intuition that the media and technologies of modernity will progressively pauperize the human "soul" is elevated to the level of cosmic tragedy, very much against the spirit of Lewis's pitiless laughter. *Brave New World* (1932) and *1984* (1949) depend on readers' agreement that the mass media "dehumanize" the human being.

If any technology epitomizes this trend toward unqualified distrust, it is the hydrogen bomb that presides over the Cold War. Nicholas Mosley's sweeping historical fiction *Hopeful Monsters* (1990) is a "novel of ideas" orchestrated around the paradoxical notion – perhaps in resistance to Huxley and Orwell – that the threat of total nuclear annihilation might be the necessary if not sufficient cause of an imaginative antidote, a messianic apocalypse:

> "But has this not to do with my other illumination about a potentially universally destructive bomb? It may be something like knowledge of this that may make it possible, necessary even, for the other sort of illumination about the self-creativeness of consciousness to be held: no not even to be held – to take off, like some new species of monstrous but life-giving bird – "[37]

This self-conscious interpolation of an "idea" into the unfolding conventionality of an historical fiction cannot avoid the fact that the last time a "novel of ideas" worked was Mann's *Der Zauberberg* (1924); Mosley's late attempt to reprise its mission in high postmodernity speaks of a disregard for the objective history of novelistic form. What the bomb actually portends for the novel's form is a question the English novel never rose to with the urgency of its American counterpart in the hands of Thomas Pynchon, for obvious reasons – Britain never dropped one.

No English novelist seizes the implications of the ongoing technological apocalypse more energetically than J. G. Ballard. Above all in his novel *Crash* (1973) Ballard pushes to the limit the implicit "dehumanization" of a species hard-wired to machines of speed, technologies of spectacle, and (increasingly) data chains and computations. Rather than tilt this apprehension in the direction of dystopia, or give way to a hysterical laughter, Ballard pursues with quiet resolve the consequences of a cybernetic environment on the substance of the novel: its language and its formal architecture. In *Crash*, although characters are named, they share little affinity with the great characters of British fiction. Instead, obeying entirely new codes of interaction and motivation, these named *actants* are better thought of as modal variations of the discourse that predominates throughout: a hypothesis in prose, blending clinical reportage, instruction-manual-ese, and the permutational play of pornography. Only the unmapped territory where violence meets eros can make any imprint on the reading psyche. Ballard's latent Romanticism, which we can detect against the neutralized grain of his prose style, inheres in his last-ditch effort to retain some inalienable "natural" stratum in the midst of a technologically routinized indifference. Making strange love in his car with the now-disabled widow whose husband he has killed in a crash, the narrator is moved to pen this hymn:

> This small space was crowded with angular control surfaces and rounded sections of human bodies interacting in unfamiliar junctions, like the first act of homosexual intercourse inside an Apollo capsule. The volumes of Helen's thighs pressing against my hips, her left fist buried in my shoulder, her mouth grasping at my own, the shape and moisture of her anus as I stroked it with my ring finger, were each overlaid by the inventories of a benevolent technology – the moulded binnacle of the instrument dials, the jutting carapace of the steering column shroud, the extravagant pistol grip of the handbrake.[38]

This is at once bleak, estranging, arousing, and funny. The manner in which the language of auto manuals morphs into crude porn, and is then leavened by incautious experiments in simile and metaphor, gives the prose an impish exuberance, as it looks for new tactics for wrong-footing its reader. Nor would this strange symbiosis of incompatible discursive elements work in quite the same way if it were not dimly sensed that a computer might have generated these streams of text. Rather than dismissing the automata of modernity as mindless machines of habit and propulsion, Ballard finds ways of libidinizing the "posthuman" course of contemporary life from within its most recalcitrant recesses. It remains perhaps the only legitimate path the English novel can take from this point forward.

Less durably successful have been the attempts to incorporate the invisible, coded, computational processes of the new digital information economy into novelistic form. Christine Brooke-Rose's formal reconfiguration of the technical realities of computer technology and digital processing for her "computer trilogy" – *Amalgamemnon* (1984), *Xorandor* (1986), and *Verbivore* (1990) – extends the hypothesis of "language" writing (that all fiction and poetry is before all else linguistic) into the digital domain: interminable text-generation, flamboyant structural determinations, and an excess of "code." *Xorandor* concerns a pair of computer-geek twins who discover a stone that communicates only in DOS, and their various unlikely travails. But what interests is the form in which the narrative is supposedly mediated: the twins' direct notes typed into a pocket computer, radio broadcasts, and electromagnetic tape recordings of previous dialogue. Devolved to these automated and (in one case) processing instruments, the responsibilities of narrative control are caught in an endless loop of authority and reflexivity, resulting in a "wholly ambiguous or wholly indeterminate text."[39] As digital and analogue machines vie with the novel's raw material of "information," at a higher level the novel, as a resilient but one feels superfluous form, strives for a supervenient mastery; but nothing can conjure away the profuse silliness of the plot as such, a problem that the English novel has yet to surmount. Indeed, in perhaps the greatest incorporation of hypertextual and RAM elements into literature, Tom Phillips's *A Humument*, the aggressive yet cannibalistic remediation of a disposable Victorian melodrama (W. H. Mallock's *A Human Document*) results in something that scarcely deserves the name of novel. Part art-work, part poetic textual experiment, Phillips's masterpiece discovers imperceptible codes and contra-narratives embedded within the grain of the published work: a series of spatial dislocations and ruptures within the machinery of the novel, unthinkable without the digital technology that in no way is responsible for Phillips's loving work of handicraft, explodes that superannuated technology and finds among the shards useful elements refunctioned for another media ecology entirely.

Notes

1. Richard Menke, *Telegraphic Realism: Victorian Fiction and Other Information Systems* (Stanford University Press, 2008), p. 3.
2. Nicholas Daly, *Literature, Technology, and Modernity* (Cambridge University Press, 2004), pp. 47, 49.
3. Geoffrey Winthrop-Young, "Undead Networks: Information Processing and Media Boundary Conflicts in Stoker's *Dracula*," in *Literature and Science*, ed. Donald Bruce and Anthony Purdy (Amsterdam: Rodopi, 1994), p. 124.
4. Keith Williams, *British Writers and the Media, 1930–45* (Houndmills: Macmillan, 1996).
5. Joseph Tabbi and Michael Wutz, eds., *Reading Matters: Narrative in the New Media Ecology* (Ithaca: Cornell University Press, 1997), p. 4.
6. Sara Danius, *The Senses of Modernism: Technology, Perception, and Aesthetics* (Ithaca and London: Cornell University Press, 2002), p. 184.
7. Katherine Mullin, *James Joyce, Sexuality and Social Purity* (Cambridge University Press, 2003), pp. 140–170; Keith Williams, "*Ulysses* in Toontown," in *Literature and*

Visual Technologies, ed. Julian Murphet and Lydia Rainford (Houndmills: Palgrave Macmillan, 2003), pp. 96–121.

8. Joseph Conrad, "Preface," in *The Nigger of the "Narcissus," Typhoon and Other Stories* (London: Dent, 1950), p. x; James Joyce, *Ulysses* (London: Penguin, 2000), p. 62.

9. Virginia Woolf, *The Mark on the Wall and Other Short Fiction* (Oxford University Press, 2001), p. 11.

10. Friedrich Kittler, *Gramophone, Film, Typewriter* (Stanford University Press, 1999), p. 173.

11. Ford Madox Ford, *Parade's End* (London: Penguin, 2002), p. 201. He quotes Christina Rossetti.

12. Dorothy Richardson, *Pilgrimage* iv (London: J. M. Dent and Sons, 1967), p. 217.

13. George Orwell, *Keep the Aspidistra Flying* (London: Gollancz, 1936), p. 80.

14. Woolf, *Essays: 1925–1928*, 6 vols. Vol. iv, ed. Andrew McNeillie (London: Hogarth, 1994), p. 352.

15. Quoted in Laura Marcus, *The Tenth Muse* (Oxford University Press, 2007), p. 129.

16. Winifred Holtby, *South Riding* (London: Virago, 1996), p. ix.

17. Ned Schantz, *Gossip, Letters, Phones: The Scandal of Female Networks in Film and Literature* (Oxford University Press, 2008), p. 9.

18. Maud Ellmann, *Elizabeth Bowen: The Shadow Across the Page* (Edinburgh University Press, 2003), p. 98.

19. Joseph Conrad, *The Secret Agent* (London: J. M. Dent and Sons, 1961), p. 81.

20. E. M. Forster, *Howards End* (London: Penguin, 2000), p. 22.

21. David Trotter, "e-Modernism: Telephony in British Fiction 1925–1940," *Critical Quarterly* 51: 1 (2009), 1–32, 3.

22. Richardson, *Pilgrimage* ii (London: J. M. Dent and Sons, 1967), p. 45.

23. Bonnie Kime Scott, "The Subversive Mechanics of Woolf's Gramophone in *Between the Acts*," in *Virginia Woolf in the Age of Mechanical Reproduction*, ed. Pamela L. Caughie (New York: Garland Publishing, 2000), p. 104.

24. Virginia Woolf, *Between the Acts* (London: Hogarth Press, 1941), p. 59.

25. John Galsworthy, *The Forsyte Saga*, 3 vols. (London: Penguin, 2001), vol. ii, p. 570.

26. Italo Calvino, *Six Memos for the Next Millennium* (Cambridge, MA: Harvard University Press, 1988), p. 118.

27. Henry Williamson, *The Golden Virgin* (London: Macdonald, 1957), p. 347.

28. Cecil Day Lewis, *Revolution in Writing* (London: Hogarth, 1935), p. 40.

29. Ford Madox Ford, *The Critical Attitude* (London: Duckworth, 1911), p. 63.

30. See Nicholas Daly, *Modernism, Romance, and the fin de siècle* (Cambridge University Press, 1999).

31. Pound, *ABC of Reading* (London: Routledge, 1934), p. 43.

32. Stephen Kern, *The Culture of Time and Space: 1880–1918* (Cambridge, MA: Harvard University Press, 2003), p. 16.

33. Chris Baldick, *The Modern Movement* (Oxford University Press, 2004), p. 243.

34. Michael North, *Machine-Age Comedy* (Oxford University Press, 2009), p. 117.

35. Wyndham Lewis, *Tarr: The 1918 Version* (Santa Rosa, CA: Black Sparrow Press, 1990), p. 70.

36. Christopher Isherwood, *Goodbye to Berlin* (London: Hogarth Press, 1939), p. 13.
37. Nicholas Mosley, *Hopeful Monsters* (London: Secker and Warburg, 1990), p. 429.
38. J. G. Ballard, *Crash* (London: Jonathan Cape, 1973), pp. 80–81.
39. Robert L. Caserio, "Mobility and Masochism: Christine Brooke-Rose and J. G. Ballard," *Novel* 21: 2/3 (1988), 292–310, 292.

49
Novels of same-sex desire

GREGORY WOODS

After Jonathan Cape was issued with a summons to appear at Bow Street court in November 1928 for having published *The Well of Loneliness*, the novel's author, Radclyffe Hall, spent part of the tense wait for trial listening to her lover, Una Troubridge, reading aloud from Virginia Woolf's new book, *Orlando*. Hall's novel would be banned; Woolf's would not. The two works represent contrasting tendencies in queer fiction: in Hall, an engagement – albeit a pessimistic one – with the social given; in Woolf, an optimistic speculation on alternative possibilities.

The central character of Hall's book, Stephen Gordon, is lonely because she is an "invert" – that is her fate. Congenitally third-sexed, slim-hipped from the cradle, she and another woman of her own masculine kind could never love each other. Yet when she does fall in love with a suitably opposite, feminine woman, conscience forces her to give her up, because such a paragon of real womanhood as Mary Llewellyn can only be fulfilled by getting married to a man and bearing children. Although Stephen is presented as a case study, she is hardly typical. She is anomalous even within her own category of anomalies. Upper class and rich, expressing her author's deeply conservative attitudes to the ownership and husbandry of land, the hierarchy of social order, and the superiority of Englishness, she is disabled by the thought that her lesbianism excludes her from the enjoyment of her natural class privileges. When she meets a community of fellow inverts, both female and male – in a gay bar in Paris that Hall describes as if it were a Purgatorio of queer melancholia – she is unable to identify with them, finding their sense of a collective, defensive identity perverse in itself. The miracle of this book is the affectionate place it still holds in the memories of successive generations of lesbian readers.

Whereas the plodding realism of *The Well of Loneliness* enacts Stephen Gordon's stuffy conventionalism, the sprightly experimentalism of *Orlando* enacts its central character's unwillingness to conform. Orlando lives for several centuries, first as a man and then as a woman. Throughout her career

Woolf insists on the fragmentation of consciousness, a theme that drives her technical experiments with interior monologue in her more modernistic books. But identity, even if it consists of flux, is not necessarily itself in flux. It remains constant. The same is true of Orlando's identity, which withstands the social changes of centuries as well as the physical change of sex. Woolf seems to be demonstrating the matter of sexual definition as a trivial side issue. "Let biologists and psychologists determine," she says, as if indulging children in their games.[1] So much for sexological speculation. In writing her lesbian love letter to Vita Sackville-West, she has more important topics to deal with than lesbianism itself.

Both before and after the change of sex, Orlando is attractive, and indulges his/her attraction to both sexes. But at the turn of the nineteenth century in Woolf's novel all but a few of Orlando's previous freedoms are circumscribed by Victorianism. Before the nineteenth century Orlando might put on a pair of breeches and get out into the city for whatever adventure transpires. She now finds that life's possibilities have been closed off, not only to her but to all other women. *Orlando* unambiguously outlines the view that, far from having progressed, under the Victorians attitudes to gender and sexuality had become increasingly irrational.

In the crucible of Bloomsbury another major voice influences the subsequent telling of queer lives. Lytton Strachey applies the techniques of fiction to the ossified conventions of historical biography, breathing fresh life into a genre that seemed content with churning out formulaic hagiographies of national heroes. In *Eminent Victorians* (1918) Strachey debunks Cardinal Manning, Florence Nightingale, Thomas Arnold, and General Gordon. More daringly, in *Elizabeth and Essex* (1928) he gives not only the public facts of Queen Elizabeth I's career but also a post-Freudian analysis of her neurotic interior life, in particular of her hysterically blocked sexual life. Strachey's Elizabeth is elaborated as a virtually fictional character at the centre of a network of men, some of them her lovers, others each other's. The influence of both of Strachey's books can be seen in a strong biographical tradition that develops in Britain in the second half of the century. This tradition then feeds back into novels in which the lives of historical figures are fully fictionalized. Major novelizations of the lives of gay cultural figures have included Anthony Burgess's *Earthly Powers* (1980) and John Banville's *The Untouchable* (1997), respectively modeled on the lives of Somerset Maugham and Anthony Blunt.

It might be that to a gay reader E. M. Forster's *Maurice* (begun 1913, published 1971) is all the more endearing for its obvious faults, since those were forced on the author by the intractability of the social situation he was attempting, if only in an act of fiction, to resolve. Forster had set himself an impossible task. He seems not to have realized this when he began to write a book with a homosexual central character whose homosexuality would be the point, but he grew reconciled to the impossibility in the end. *Maurice* would exist only in samizdat typescripts until its posthumous publication. The embarrassment Forster was so obviously ducking was not homosexuality itself but the impossibility – in his lifetime – of writing a good book about it.

What had proved so difficult? In brief, the granting of a happy ending to an unexceptional homosexual man, a man without distinguishing qualities. To counter myths of abnormality, Forster's central character, Maurice, had to be normal. Nothing about him should stand out. Average looks, average intelligence, average (middle-class) background. Only one thing about him would make him, if not particularly unusual as a human being, exceptional as the protagonist in a sympathetic narrative by a well-known author: his sexuality. That alone would have to maintain the reader's interest, for it has to be granted that, in all other respects, he is something of a bore.

Once this solid, unassuming, Christian capitalist is in place, Forster seems to feel that no happy ending can convincingly be offered to such a man in English society at the time. Nothing else can explain his construction of the fantasy of Maurice's affair with the gamekeeper Alec Scudder and their escape to the greenwood. Maurice's affair with Alec is far less persuasive than Connie's affair with Mellors in D. H. Lawrence's *Lady Chatterley's Lover* (1928), which was influenced by Lawrence's reading of the typescript of *Maurice*. An American novelist, with a whole continent to dream in, might have gotten away with Forster's ending; but as a solution to the problem of anti-homosexual prejudice in modern England it is implausible. Yet Forster knew that many homosexual Englishmen did live together and, as much by luck as by design, managed to survive. Part of the problem is that Forster did not seem able, or perhaps willing, to imagine two men of the same age and class living together discreetly in the suburbs. The sameness in those two respects would be the main basis of their discretion. Men could live together, but it helped if they spoke with similar accents.

Both *The Well of Loneliness* and *Maurice* follow the conventional structure of the realist *Bildungsroman*, a life history running from early childhood to that point at which, in a novel about a heterosexual central character, a successful courtship would mold emotional immaturity into the balance and stasis of matrimony. *The Well* ends bleakly, with no such resolution. Indeed it promises a continuation of loneliness and exclusion. *Maurice*, by contrast, ends, however implausibly, in happy coupledom. Stephen and Maurice are similar in that they do not know what they are. They do not have words to describe themselves. Maurice is given a copy of Plato; Stephen finds her father's copy of Krafft-Ebing's *Psychopathia Sexualis*. A doctor gives Maurice the word "homosexual." Such basic information is thereby transferred to the isolated gay reader, as is the message: you are not the only one. This then becomes the model, the "case study" model, for the homosexual novel of the mid-twentieth century. A central character is taken as representative of the type of the homosexual individual. Parentage is examined for signs of Freudian causality, education is examined for signs of abuse, early crushes on school friends or teachers are dissected for signs of permanence, and early tastes in the arts and sports, as well as, after school, in potential employment, are set against what might be expected of normality.

Largely because of the legal action against its publication, *The Well of Loneliness* became the best-known novel about lesbianism from that era – perhaps from any era. But other novelists were working on the theme. Rosamond Lehmann's first novel, *Dusty Answer* (1927), is more modern in its impressionistic technique and more progressive in outlook than Hall's book (which was published a year later). *Dusty Answer* was enthusiastically received for having captured the mood of the interwar generation. Its central character Judith Earle becomes involved with her neighbors, a clutch of young cousins of both sexes. While trying to decide which of the boys to fall in love with – one of them evidently, to us if not to Judith, is having a long-term affair with a male fellow student at Cambridge – she herself goes up to university, where she has an intense affair with Jennifer, another student. The dance of relationships eventually petering out – in one way or another, Judith works her way through all of her neighbors – Judith emerges a little older and a lot wiser, finding that she is stronger on her own than she was in combination with any, or even all, of them.

In this same period the fiction of Sylvia Townsend Warner is concerned to show how individuals can liberate themselves from repressive influences and circumstances, whether social or familial or psychological. *Lolly Willowes* (1926) is about a woman who, having lived for many years in the subordinate familial role of spinster aunt, decides to escape to the countryside and live by herself. Even so, she begins to be plagued by an irritating nephew. Only by becoming a witch does she manage to drive him away, and, although in doing so she has had to make a pact with the devil, she comes to a civilized accommodation with him and settles into a calm equilibrium, strengthened by vastly increased self-knowledge. In *Mr. Fortune's Maggot* (1927) Fortune travels as a missionary to a South Sea island, where he falls in love with a boy called Lueli. Distant from the moral restraints of his own country, Fortune fails to subject the islanders to his weakening missionary zeal, managing to convert only the boy to Christianity. But in the end Lueli goes back to his tribal beliefs, and it is Fortune who relinquishes his God. Converted by the islanders' humane paganism, Fortune feels spiritually liberated and enriched by casting off his responsibilities to his Church. The last thing he does for Lueli before leaving the island for good is carve the boy a new idol to worship. In Warner's *Summer Will Show* (1936), set during the 1848 revolutions in Paris, the heroine Minna declares that her beloved Sophia has run away – "From Sunday Schools, and cold-hearted respectability, and hypocrisy, and prison." She adds, crucially, "And domesticity."[2]

The Oscar Wilde scandal of 1895 had taken its toll on homosexual writers. So stridently pervasive had hostile responses been to Wilde and those associated with him – aesthetes as well as sodomites, women as well as men – that it took no great stretch of the imagination, and little by way of paranoid victimhood, for Radclyffe Hall to think of herself, as well as her book, as being marked for conviction, and even for damnation. While *The Well of Loneliness* was in press, Troubridge had read Wilde's "The Ballad of Reading Gaol" and *De Profundis* to Hall, along with the Frank Harris biography of Wilde. Hall was preparing for literary martyrdom. She wanted to be treated as an artist, but expected to be treated as an outcast.

Others developed a more celebratory engagement with Wilde's legacy. Ronald Firbank took Wilde's levity and made light of it. Eschewing attempts to persuade the reader that anything in his books is plausible, meaningful, or true – for Firbank is as skeptical about realism as about other redundant institutions like matrimony – he undercuts every moment in which the lives, loves, and deaths of his characters threaten to become serious. Valuing surface above depth, ornamentation above harmony, and the swoon and the giggle above psychological nuance, his fictions disarm moral judgment, a trick that Wilde himself never quite manages. One of the most influential of gay writers, Firbank helps shape a major strand of serious British comic fiction that includes Evelyn Waugh, Graham Greene, and Muriel Spark.

Firbank revives the Wildean aesthete as the model (some would say the stereotype) for the portrayal of the typical homosexual man – that is, a man untypical among men – for most of the twentieth century. This fictional tradition begins with Basil Hallward and Lord Henry Wotton in Wilde's *The Picture of Dorian Gray* (1890), and is soon continued in the protagonist of the stories in Hector Munro's first collection, *Reginald* (1904), published under the pseudonym "Saki." Reginald has all of Wilde's frivolity, posed shallowness, aesthetic snobbery, paradoxical wit, and contempt for the mundane. His tendency to form inappropriate associations with working-class boys underlines the point. Saki uses strong collective memories of the Wilde scandal to give his stories a whiff of sulphur that no other cultural reference could have provided.

In Evelyn Waugh's fiction the homosexual aesthete is, for better or worse, the paragon of modernity. Although Waugh's novels are comic, and his characters are subject to a degree of satire, Waugh is never contemptuous of their sexuality; indeed, as individuals and as a type, they attract his sympathy and even admiration. They include some of his most memorable characters. In *Put Out More Flags* (1943) Ambrose Silk is Jewish as well as homosexual, a fact that connects him, at one remove, with the greatest catastrophe of the era. His erstwhile lover, Hans, who used to be in the Hitler Youth and then joined the brown-shirts even though also half-Jewish, is now languishing in a concentration camp. Silk's own youth was spent at Eton and Oxford, and later in the Paris of Diaghilev, Cocteau, and Gertrude Stein. Yet for all that he is presented as a privileged and frivolous aesthete, not far from the lisping and limp-wristed cliché that prevails until the years of gay liberation, Waugh does not allow him to become a mere stereotype. Silk (and, at one remove, Hans) has something far more important to stand for than the mere comicality of being queer. Late in the novel Silk writes a memoir in which he constructs Hans as representing "something personal and private in a world where only the mob and the hunting pack had the right to live."[3]

Other examples of the aesthete type include Anthony Blanche in Waugh's *Brideshead Revisited* (1945), Cedric Hampton in Nancy Mitford's *Love in a Cold Climate* (1949), Hew Dallas, a minor character in Jocelyn Brooke's *A Mine of Serpents* (1949), and Donald Butterboy, a hostile caricature of Brian Howard in Wyndham Lewis's *The Roaring Queen* (completed 1936, published 1973). It is worth noting that E. M. Forster, in his anxiety to demonstrate the normality of his main homosexual characters in *Maurice*, gives his aristocratic queen, Risley, the somewhat negative role of being the "that" that more normative men like Maurice are "not like." For Forster, unlike Waugh, Risley is the less modern figure. When placed beside Maurice, who earns his own living and lives in a suburb, Risley seems anachronistically self-indulgent, a far less useful character than Maurice for attracting the common reader's sympathy for the oppressed homosexual.

The Auden generation in the 1930s takes a further step away from the Wildean model, in part by evincing a more explicitly political interest in the well-being of working-class men. As an exemplar of "gay literature" from the period between the Wilde trials and the decriminalization of male homosexual acts in 1967, Christopher Isherwood's *Goodbye to Berlin* (1939) is a model of enforced discretion: an autobiographical account of part of a gay man's life, with the gay bits edited out. Nothing it reveals of the author's life in Germany, or of the identity he has carried back home to England, could lead to scandal or arrest. In that regard, it is safe and circumspect. On the other hand, it can also be read as an ingeniously complex sequence, not of concealments, but of coded revelations. Its most famous sentence – "I am a camera with its shutter open, quite passive, recording, not thinking" – appears at the start of its second paragraph, laying out the rules by which the narrative will proceed. The "I" of Isherwood ("Herr Issyvoo") will reveal nothing of himself, but will studiously focus on anything and anyone but. Narrated by one of its characters, yet avoiding him as a topic, the book pioneers a form of subjective objectivity which, once one considers the vulnerable homosexuality of Christopher Isherwood, must be seen as a strategy of evasion: a way of averting attention from himself even while recording his own experiences of Weimar Berlin. Isherwood could not countenance proceeding as Proust had in *À la Recherche du temps perdu*, where Marcel, the narrator based on himself, is rendered heterosexual. Instead, Isherwood makes Christopher a "passive" observer of a sexual scene in which he himself takes no active part. This leaves him looking, at times, aloof and condescending – for instance, when reflecting humorously on the chaotic personal life of Sally Bowles – and also somewhat sexless.

Isherwood later explained how he had censored himself in *Goodbye to Berlin* and other early books. Not until 1977 could he write a sentence that might have given body to his earlier fictional self: "To Christopher, Berlin meant Boys."[4] His post-gay-liberationist memoir *Christopher and His Kind* adds many of the details that such books as *Lions and Shadows* (1938) and even *Down There on a Visit* (1962) had covered up – such as the fact that he had de-eroticized his description of Otto, in *Goodbye to Berlin*, by giving him "spindly" legs (38). Such subterfuges may have served their purpose of concealing homosexuality from homophobic readers, but *Goodbye to Berlin* also contains revelations of homosexuality for its other readers. Even on a reasonably obtuse reading, the enigmatically detached narrator clearly spends a lot of time in bars frequented by rent-boys; he seems more adept at spotting homosexual men than Sally Bowles, who has been working in Berlin as a call-girl; he blushes and clams up when Landauer asks him about Oscar Wilde; he goes on holiday with an apparently intimate male couple, Peter and Otto; and, perhaps most revealingly, he enjoys with Sally Bowles that relatively rare phenomenon in its day, a male–female friendship with an unexplained lack of romantic or erotic interest. It could be argued that this amounts to evidence of Isherwood's discreet representation of Christopher's discretion: the gay writer represents himself as a gay character, both of them using behavioral and linguistic strategies that will save them from scandal, even while still managing to say what it is they mean.

A nondescript narrator or central character needs vibrant people to talk about. One thinks of Proust's Marcel, ever eager for his next encounter with the Baron de Charlus, or Isherwood's Bradshaw, observing Norris in *Mr. Norris Changes Trains* (1935), or Charles observing Christo Eugenides in Robert Liddell's *Unreal City* (1952). The older, queer individuals these bland younger characters befriend and observe are self-centered and perverse, offering a sensationalist version of the homosexual as a type. So when Isherwood does come to write a "case study" novel about a representative gay individual, he sets him adrift in a heterosexual suburb, mourning the death of his male lover in isolation from other gay individuals. George, the protagonist of *A Single Man* (1964), is just as featureless as Forster's Maurice or Isherwood's own Christopher, but what makes this novel interesting is the manner of its telling – and in particular, the economy of its structure. Its virtuosic, present-tense narrative combines social satire with psychological case study, framed in its opening and closing pages by a surprisingly touching creation and uncreation of the fictive elements that go together to make "George." Isherwood is at his most succinct and (literally) least self-regarding here, and one of the outcomes is an impressively persuasive argument against the prejudging of individuals (even if George is doing precisely that all the time).

Gay literature is as often about the broad spectrum of label-less relationships between friendship and romantic love as it is about characters firmly identified as "homosexual." Some of the best mid-century writing follows on from D. H. Lawrence's passionate explorations of homosocial desire – most vivid in *Women in Love* (completed 1916, published 1920) and *The Plumed Serpent* (1926) – where masculinity is expressed as a desire for the masculine, as much as for its feminine "opposite." In Denton Welch's autobiographical books, the English landscape is beautified by working-class men and boys who are, at most, to be admired and engaged in conversation. Agricultural workers and national servicemen are likewise in constant maneuvers across the landscapes of Jocelyn Brooke's novels, at once menacing and enviably desirable. Orvil Pym in Welch's *In Youth Is Pleasure* (1945) is turned on by the prospect of doing latrine fatigues in a military camp and chastises himself with a leather strap. Duncan in Brooke's *The Scapegoat* (1948) feels unworthy of anything but the (handcuffed) caning his uncle Gerald gives him. Sodomy finds its sublimation in masochism. There is a lot of the boarding-school adolescent in this world view.

T. H. White's *The Once and Future King* (1937–1958) is a sequence of novels with a similar ethos, about boys-becoming-men, and apparently aimed at a readership of boys-becoming-men. The education of a future medieval monarch, conducted by Merlin in the first volume, is tailored to the needs of a modern commoner, and the etiquette of the Round Table, in later volumes, is rendered into dilemmas raised by twentieth-century politics. The Englishness created by Arthur as an ethic of difference from Frenchmen and Celts is recommended as a governing identity to the modern public-schoolboys to whom the books were originally addressed. In this respect, the books develop a tone that sounds like Sir Thomas Mallory restyled by Lord Baden-Powell. As is to be expected, the tetralogy's emotional focus is on the triangle between Arthur, Guenever, and Lancelot, and on its dynamic within the homosocial networks of the Round Table. Lancelot's affection for Arthur is unflinchingly described as "love" throughout. At first a puerile infatuation, these emotions develop into a mature and mutual passion that survives the two men's rivalry for the heart of Guenever. In achieving this quality, such emotion endorses the value of its puerile origins: for White is, although often amused by it, deeply respectful of the convulsive romanticism of boys.

Given the increasing visibility of homosexuality in the 1950s, and the tendency to treat it as a "problem," it is not surprising that even some of the most thoughtful writers become bogged down in popular received wisdom, instead of representing the reality of ordinary lives. Lawrence Durrell's *The Alexandria Quartet* is disappointingly obtuse on homosexuality, despite its epigraphs from the Marquis de Sade and Sigmund Freud, and its nuanced representations of heterosexual love. The main attention to homosexuality is in the second novel, *Balthazar* (1958). The deaths of two homosexual men are this relatively eventless novel's main, and most lurid, events. The death of Scobie, who is beaten up by sailors while dressed as a woman, is hastily whitewashed, to prevent a political scandal. The death of Toto de Brunel, who is pierced in the head with a hat-pin at a carnival party, is similarly covered up. His lover Amar is subsequently acquitted of his murder for lack of evidence. Durrell pays little attention to same-sex love as a matter of everyday life. He takes it for granted, to be sure – and this is itself an advance on the approach of homophobic novelists of the period – but as a peculiarity. Such as it is, the lesbianism in Durrell's fiction is generally framed and voiced by heterosexual men with a vested interest. In *Livia* (1978) – the second volume of *The Avignon Quintet* – Pia and Livia are given shape – and it is a pretty grotesque shape – in the opening chapter's long conversation between their respective husbands, and throughout the novel it is these two voices that continue to attack lesbian women for the injuries they supposedly do their menfolk.

By contrast, throughout her career, Iris Murdoch seems completely comfortable with the fact that same-sex relationships occur at all ages and in all classes. Indeed, that fact is useful to her in mapping the complex plots of her novels, where the unpredictability of sexual object-choice underpins her arguments about contingency. Her own imaginative habits of myth-making do not allow her lazily to rely on the use of standard myths about homosexual personalities and behavior. From *The Bell* (1958) onwards, she represents homosexuality as an unexceptional fact of life, neither more exotic nor stranger than other characteristics of human lives.

The idea of homosexuality as a tragic flaw is so widely and complacently accepted in the social myths of the postwar period that one finds any number of mediocre novelists leading two-dimensional characters, with little originality or ingenuity behind them, through predictable stages of anguish to an apparently inevitable, premature death (by accident, suicide or murder). Only the occasional novelist makes truly resonant use of the association between homosexuality and the fatedness of tragedy. In *Radcliffe* (1963) David Storey builds a modern gothic novel out of two men's violent co-dependency. Neither identifies as homosexual, nor could we define them as lovers. Their sexual collisions are freighted with the symbolism of violation, much as the violence they wreak on each other's bodies is heavy with desire. Not until Radcliffe is put on trial for the murder of the other man, Tolson (Radcliffe the slighter, less physical, more passive of the two), does he speak of himself as a lover of men in general, rather than the mate of one man in particular; and not until he is imprisoned for the murder does he begin to show signs of desire for other men and act on it by propositioning them. So this is not a novel about the social conditions pertaining to male homosexuality in early 1960s' England; only for a few moments at Radcliffe's trial does it raise these matters. Instead, in a manner influenced by the Romanticism of the Brontës and the sexual modernism of Lawrence (most resonantly echoing the latter's 1913 story "The Prussian Officer," plus elements of *Women in Love*), it explores the danger zone between homosocial and homosexual desire, where opposed but compatible masculinities subvert and reinforce each other with explosive strategies of aggressive self-defense. To each the manhood of the other is as much feared and envied as desired, and the manhood of the self is vulnerable to the consequences of acted-on desire.

At the end of the 1950s Angus Wilson made his mark with two collections of short stories, some of them starting a career-long habit of integrating homosexual characters into broader themes of social involvement. *The Wrong Set* (1949) and *Such Darling Dodos* (1950) set a new standard for pinpoint social observation enlivened by an exhilarating grotesquerie that often doled out punishment to unlikeable characters even as the author's liberal humanism sympathizes with their sufferings and humiliations. Each of these collections contains a story on a homosexual theme: in the first, "Et Dona Ferentes," the heart of a paterfamilias is briefly set racing by a visiting teenage youth, but nothing physical can happen between them and the boy goes home early; in "Such Darling Dodos," a middle-aged man visits his cousins and finds himself contrasting his Catholicism with their atheism, his conservatism with their outdated radicalism, his aestheticism with their down-to-earthness, and his homosexuality with their conventionality. In both stories Wilson is feeling his way into what would become a career-long preoccupation, whereby he seeks to locate his own status as a sexual outsider within the central current of postwar social and political developments. His first novel, *Hemlock and After* (1952), includes a spectrum of straight, gay, and bisexual male characters, and the gay ones are on a spectrum from "respectability" to *"loucherie."* As a camp gay man himself, Wilson was strongly aware of the shortcomings of the supposedly "positive," normatively masculine, gay character. And as an astute observer of the British class system, he was well aware that camp was not the sole preserve of the upper-class aesthete.

In none of his novels does Wilson show much interest in that staple of gay fiction, the isolated individual looking for love, nor does he ever bother with the gay version of *Bildungsroman*, the coming-out story. Instead, he portrays homosexual men, whether single or in couples, in a context of varied familial and social relationships. In *The Middle Age of Mrs Eliot* (1958) David and Gordon are normative, quietly masculine, law-abiding, non-predatory, cultured – and celibate. This makes them, in terms of the liberal tolerance envisaged by the authors of the Wolfenden Report (1957), the perfect couple, quietist and sexless. One might imagine that Wilson is presenting them as a positive representation of how civilized a homosexual couple can be. In fact, though, he thinks of their relationship as a travesty. When Gordon dies, David finally realizes that, by eliminating sex from their equation, the guilt-ridden Gordon deprived them of what could have been the crucially transformative element in their love. Without it, they were left as little better than a caricature of a shallow set of moral maxims. In a paradoxical sense Gordon's death is the outcome David deserves. Coupling is not the only available happy ending.

After the partial decriminalization of male homosexual acts in 1967, the 1970s see more explicit narratives from authors who made their reputations during the period of enforced circumspection. Of these novels the one with the highest profile was *Maurice*. After that came shorter pieces in Forster's *The Life to Come*. From L. P. Hartley came his last novel, *The Harness Room* (1971), a meager concoction about the relationship between a teenager and his father's chauffeur, with little of the sensitivity to cross-class relations that had been such a strong aspect of *The Go-Between* (1953). Angus Wilson's *As If By Magic* (1973) is a tonally unpredictable picaresque about a middle-aged English pederast with a penchant for Asian boys, intercut with the amorous experiments of three students, a girl and two boys, who have been reading too much D. H. Lawrence. And Christopher Isherwood published his memoir *Christopher and His Kind*, which lifted the veil on the Berlin stories of the 1930s. Important autobiographies following decriminalization include T. C. Worsley's *Flannelled Fool* (1967), J. R. Ackerley's *My Father and Myself* (1968), and Tom Driberg's *Ruling Passions* (1977).

Francis King's career followed a similar pattern of increasing openness. His first novel *To the Dark Tower* (1946) begins in a mood of suppressed, militaristic homoeroticism comparable with that of Jocelyn Brooke, but develops an awareness that love affairs may flourish, unpredictably and intensely, between pairs of men or women, and that the love lives of homosexuals and heterosexuals overlap in significant respects. King would return to the theme repeatedly in the next sixty years. The most successful of his gay-themed work is *A Domestic Animal* (1970), which portrays a middle-aged Englishman's unrequited love for a younger Italian. King is less interested in the sameness of the two men's sex than in the difference of their sexualities – for Antonio is a married heterosexual with young children – and of their nationalities.

The publication of increasingly forthright narratives had a strangely negative effect on the critical standing of "gay literature" – a newly emergent category – insofar as they confirmed a common view that the literature of homosexuality depended for its quality on the discretion of the closet. The clearest statement of this position came from Jeffrey Meyers in 1977: "The emancipation of the homosexual has led, paradoxically, to the decline of his art."[5] Meyers is referring principally to such novelists as Jean Genet and William Burroughs, whom he judges inferior to their less sexually explicit predecessors. Their explicitness supposedly undermines the quality of work which, in previous decades, would have had to express its themes obliquely, using coded strategies of indirection and metaphor. Reviewers often applied a similar argument to the post-"emancipation" novels of aging authors who had begun their careers more discreetly. The supposed aesthetic weakness of *Maurice* in comparison with *Howards End* (1908), or *The Harness Room* with *The Go-Between*, or *Christopher and His Kind* with *Goodbye to Berlin*, was preemptive proof that young gay novelists would have nothing to gain by following their inclinations down the route – the slippery slope – of sexual explicitness (which usually meant openness about homosexuality).

Explicitness and openness prevailed, however – despite the resistance of critical conservatives – as did feminism and gay liberation. Caeia March's *Three Ply Yarn* (1986) is a good example of a novel with a doctrinaire approach to its sexual politics. Published by the Women's Press, and wearing its author's socialist feminism on its sleeve, it winds together the individual plies of three women's viewpoints into a single yarn, covering half a century of British working-class history. It places its characters' same-sex desires and experiences in a broader social context of familial, homosocial, heterosexual, and homophobic relations. Lesbians here are never a race apart in the manner of Radclyffe Hall, but neither do they belong to a sub-category of male homosexuality. All of the women in the book take part in a collective "herstory" in which their true allegiances are to each other in their struggle to survive the ubiquitous fall-out from male privilege and misogyny.

Unlike so many lesbian writers, even those less politicized than March, gay men can seem to have too much investment in the rewards of masculinity to want to collapse the system that values it. Even avid followers of Firbank like Alan Hollinghurst are careful to establish the masculinity of their main gay characters. It may be that this is the chief difference between the female and male traditions: lesbian novelists are more interested in gender; gay novelists are more interested in sexuality. Certainly, throughout the century lesbian novelists are far more interested than their male counterparts in challenging the sex-gender system. This they do by systematically demonstrating the sheer contingency not only of gender role and sexual object choice, but even of sex itself.

Above all, questioning gender involves questioning accepted patterns of language use. The narrator of Brigid Brophy's obsessively playful novel *In Transit* (1969), a Joycean comedy, realizes s/he has forgotten to which sex s/he belongs. This explains why her/his narrative has to be cast in the first person singular. Clothing offers no clue; nor does name: s/he is baptized Evelyn Hilary, and is known as Pat. Memory comes up with nothing but a succession of co-educational schools. When a meeting with a stranger convinces Pat that he is a man, he descends the stairs to the gents' lavatories, but when he opens his trousers he finds she must be a woman after all. That said, the narrator's continued existence has both masculine and feminine voices (as both Patrick and Patricia), each of which provides the book with a separate ending, one suicidal and the other accidental. One of the main effects of a book so extensively constructed around gendered puns is the impression that not only gender but even sex is a matter of language, its unpredictable idiosyncrasies determined (if that is the word) by contingency.

Applying a more socially realistic mode to similar questions of gender ambiguity, Maureen Duffy's *The Microcosm* (1966), centered on a lesbian bar in London, includes among multiple parallel strands a pastiche eighteenth-century picaresque tale of a woman living as a married man and travelling with a troupe of actors. The central character of Duffy's *Love Child* (1971) is given a gender-neutral name, Kit, and her/his mother's lover, although nicknamed an apparently masculine Ajax, is also left with gender unspecified. Throughout the novel, Kit, a hyper-intelligent youngster, spies on the progress of her mother's affair, but it is when s/he actively intervenes by forging love letters to create the impression that the mother is transferring her affections elsewhere, that Kit's masturbatory voyeurism becomes perversely malevolent and sets in train tragic consequences that nevertheless have the desired aim of reconstructing her/his intimacy with the hitherto distracted mother. In *Alchemy* (2004) Duffy intercuts two narratives: that of Jade Green, a lesbian solicitor in contemporary London, who thinks of herself as a gumshoe of the Philip Marlowe sort, and that of a young woman in Elizabethan England, who cross-dresses as her dead male twin in order to make her way as an autonomous individual. The two threads are barely connected with each other, but their gendered symbolism merges nicely throughout, emphasizing the potentialities of against-the-grain gender performances.

Jeanette Winterson's autobiographical *Oranges Are Not the Only Fruit* (1985) is less about lesbianism – since lesbian characters and relationships are only sketchily delineated – than about homophobia, and perhaps less about that than the familiar *Bildungsroman* theme of the young individual breaking away from family and stultifying tradition. In its mundane details of a girl's life in a family of religious fundamentalists in the north of England, it follows realist conventions. As her career develops, however, Winterson's fiction is all the more technically adventurous the more adventurous her thoughts on gender become. In a genuine unity of content and form, the flexibility of the novel as a genre allows Winterson a corresponding intellectual flexibility that might not have been achievable in polemical non-fiction. *Written on the Body* (1992) has a narrator of unspecified gender, who gives an account of her love for Louise, a woman with a terminal illness. *The Power Book* (2000) goes further in its exploration of the implications of virtual reality for the gendered body, and its parallel narratives of a woman, Ali, living as a man in seventeenth-century Holland, and a present-day love affair narrated by another person of unspecified gender. It is with unforced logic that the novel's last narrator – again, either female or male – has the name Orlando. This homage to Woolf's 1928 fantasy is only one sign among many of Winterson's continuing reverence for the earlier writer's radical experimentalism in the shaping of fictional form to suit the multiple realities of physical and psychological existence.

In Jackie Kay's *Trumpet* (1998) a jazz trumpeter lives her life as a man, even to the extent of getting married to another woman and bringing up an adopted child. Sarah Waters's *Tipping the Velvet* (1998) marks a return to the readerly pleasures of pre-modernist realism and, perhaps, to the solid (if not stolid) fictional values to which Radclyffe Hall had subscribed, yet the convulsions of its plot – with lashings of cross-dressing in a theatrical setting – are no less concerned with gender transformations than the most experimental of Winterson's books.

Soon after the start of the AIDS epidemic in the 1980s, gay men were so insistently and hostilely associated with the epidemic, and with nothing else, that, even for writers with a close personal involvement in the epidemic, it became necessary deliberately to write about other things. Adam Mars-Jones was the first British writer to start producing fiction about AIDS – his stories on that theme appear with Edmund White's in their jointly authored collection *The Darker Proof* (1987) – but his first novel *The Waters of Thirst* (1993) is about a gay man dying of a condition that is not AIDS. Alan Hollinghurst's first novel, *The Swimming-Pool Library* (1988), is set in the summer immediately before news of the epidemic, and in his second, *The Folding Star* (1994), a gay man with AIDS does die – but in a car crash. Not until his fourth, *The Line of Beauty* (2004), does Hollinghurst pay substantive attention to AIDS, in a book set in the worst days of the 1980s but written long after combination therapies had reduced mortality rates and a change of government had reduced hostility rates. In Neil Bartlett's poetic novel about a London gay bar, *Ready to Catch Him Should He Fall* (1990), the customers seem less at risk from HIV – they dutifully help themselves to free condoms at the bar – than from a wave of homophobic attacks across the city. Patrick Gale's *The Facts of Life* (1995) spans a history from the Holocaust to AIDS. It is worth noting that, in resistance to right-wing commentators' argument that AIDS should call an end to gay pleasures, these authors all continue to celebrate the prolific enjoyment of sex.

Notes

1. Virginia Woolf, *Orlando* (London and New York: Penguin, 1993), p. 98.
2. Sylvia Townsend Warner, *Summer Will Show* (London: Virago, 1987), p. 217.
3. Evelyn Waugh, *Put Out More Flags* (London: Penguin, 1943), p. 187.
4. Christopher Isherwood, *Christopher and His Kind* (London: Eyre Methuen, 1977), p. 10.
5. Jeffrey Meyers, *Homosexuality and Literature, 1890–1930* (London: Athlone, 1977), p. 3.

Following an overwhelming victory in the general election of 1906, the Liberal
Party with the support of the newly founded Labour Party passed legislation
that paved the way for the construction of the welfare state in the middle of
the century. The legislation laid the groundwork for health and unemploy-
ment insurance, old age pensions, and minimum wage standards. When the
House of Lords attempted to block the initial reforms, the Commons passed
the Parliament Act of 1911, curbing the upper chamber's powers. Liberalism
according to George Dangerfield in *The Strange Death of Liberal England* meant
tolerance and progressivism. Its death was "strange" because, of the three
outbreaks of illiberalism in the prewar era – that of the suffragists, the striking
unionists, and the Ulster Unionists – only the last was not progressive or
radical. Thus the prewar years can be described as the beginning of what
Ralph Dahrendorf calls the "social democratic century" in Britain, one which
he argues does not end until the 1970s and 1980s.[1]

Social democracy, according to Dahrendorf, emphasizes benevolent
democracy guided by collective obligations; a market-oriented economy that
nevertheless is planned and managed by the state; liberal conditions counterbalanced by social and economic entitlements (rather than merely voting rights)
for all. In 1942 Sir William Beveridge's *Social Insurance and Allied Services* (The
Beveridge Report) provided a blueprint for welfare in England, and became a
bestseller. It announced "in some ways a revolution," "a comprehensive policy
of social progress," beginning with universal "abolition of want," "without
means test," and following up with attacks on "Disease, Ignorance, Squalor
and Idleness."[2]

Beveridge's ideology is rooted in the early part of the century. The year in
which the Great War broke out has been called an *"annus mirabilis"* for the
"proletarian and revolutionary-democratic novel."[3] It saw the publication
of Robert Tressell's *The Ragged Trousered Philanthropists*, Patrick MacGill's

Children of the Dead End, and John MacDougall Hay's *Gillespie* (D. H. Lawrence's *Sons and Lovers* had been published the previous year). The three most prominent writers in the preceding years, George Bernard Shaw, H. G. Wells, and Arnold Bennett, were all "socialists" of one kind or another. Hence the prewar years are also the beginning of what can be called the social democratic era of the novel. Both the realism of Shaw, Wells, and Bennett and the "progressive" and "collectivist" aspects of the New Liberalism with which they were associated were attacked in the pages of the *New Age*, which also published emerging modernists such as Ezra Pound, Wyndham Lewis, T. E. Hulme, and Katherine Mansfield. Yet while this inchoate division between realism and modernism might suggest that the realist novels of the social democratic tradition were often didactic, at least in contrast to the ideology of modernist autonomy, many of the best novels avoid didacticism and expand the range of twentieth-century fiction, while remaining committed to progressive, collective values.

The year 1914 was also the year of Wells's essay "The Contemporary Novel," a re-statement of his opposition to Henry James (and Joseph Conrad), who had criticized him for sacrificing the art of fiction to sociological preoccupations. The novel is, he contends, "the only medium through which we can discuss the great majority of the problems which are being raised in such bristly multitude by our contemporary social development." Yet far from being "a new sort of pulpit," it is or should be characterized by its spacious, multitudinous form and "rambling discursiveness."[4] *A Modern Utopia* (1905) is an example. It advocates a world state administered by a meritocracy of "samurai" (what Hilaire Belloc in the *New Age* would have considered an anticipation of the kind of "Servile State" he condemned); and yet Wells insists that his utopia is "not static but kinetic," its population migratory and utilizing "energy [rather than money] as the standard of value"; and he distinguishes his utopia from all previous utopias for its insistence on multiplicity, difference, and above all individuality – its lack, *pace* Belloc, of servility.[5]

The eponymous heroine of Wells's *Ann Veronica* (1909) goes to jail for her suffragist campaigning but this is only one stage in her progress and one stage in a series of novels (in accordance with Wells's prescription in "The Contemporary Novel" that novels should "flow into one another" [137]) that he began with *A Modern Utopia* (1905) (where he first proposes that mothers should receive wages from the state) and continues in his later anti-marriage novels, *Marriage* (1912), *The Passionate Friends* (1913), and *The Wife of Sir Isaac Harman* (1914). In *The New Machiavelli* (1911) the hero, Richard Remington, moves through every major Edwardian political party as he searches for ways to clear up the "muddle" of contemporary society; but he is eventually brought down by his affair with a young colleague. Conservative mores in regard to sex and gender retard political and social progress. Muddled, one of Wells's favorite words, could also describe the lower-middle-class heroes of *Kipps* (1905) and *The History of Mr Polly* (1910); but both novels present the lives, aspirations, and common decency of a class whose other representatives might include Forster's Leonard Bast and Woolf's Charles Tansley. Outside of Wells's fiction, such figures provoke attitudes ranging from ambivalence to disgust among writers from higher classes.

Despite Wells's inclination for lower-middle-class figures, he opposes fixations on "class," and is largely disengaged from working-class concerns. In contrast *The Ragged Trousered Philanthropists* comprehensively describes working-class labor, in particular that of the painters and decorators of a house renovation company in an English southern coastal town around 1906. The book contains long and frequent passages that derive from radical and socialist pamphlets, even though Tressell insists in his preface that the text "is not a treatise or essay, but a novel" and that "the subject of Socialism ... [is] treated incidentally" (14).[6] Indeed, the workers or "philanthropists" – Tressell names them so because they devotedly donate their lives to the well-being of their bosses – deflate the sermons of Owen, the main character, a house painter and socialist activist. Responding to the skeptical ribbing of his workmates, Owen himself delivers his lectures in a self-mocking fashion, a habit shared by the author who announces at the start of one chapter that Owen's current lecture will be "even more dull and uninteresting" than its predecessors (194). The narrative is entirely in sympathy with its philanthropists, however. The ironic (and angry) demurrers are Tressell's attempts to refuse sentimentalization of the workers and Owen's cause.

The novel unfolds more by spatial juxtapositions than by narrative drive. There is little narrative progression except for a middle-class socialist's *deus ex machina* rescue of Owen and others from "the undefined terror of the future" (585). We see the philanthropists' worksite, a house called "The Cave" that they are renovating, its relatively small scale enabling a complete account of an industry, as well as a class; the worker's home, whose female-dominated economy amounts to a kind of proto-feminism; the pub; the park where political demonstrations take place; the streets haunted by the shuffling unemployed; the countryside where the workers go for a "beano": outings to the countryside become standard pastoral interludes in fiction that represent a characteristic working-class escape from toil and poverty. The novel is a compendium of working-class documents: newspaper articles; business invoices; extracts from books; drawings and diagrams; popular songs; hymns; company, council and benevolent society minutes; circulars; posters; signs; time sheets; dietary rules, etc. Also included is a game, "The Great Money Trick," which is played with the workers' lunch-bread, knives, and coins to demonstrate the Marxist theory of surplus value. Reader-activists can play it for themselves. The novel is a vitriolic polemic on behalf of workers, but also an example of the inventive "rambling discursiveness" prescribed by Wells. Reprinted dozens of times, the novel is said to have inspired readers to help win the 1945 election for Labour.

Work is the main topic of MacGill's *Children of the Dead End*. The narrator Dermod Flynn "progresses" from a ten-year-old hired by a farmer at a Donegal "slave market" to a navvy working in Scotland. Of the two plot lines, one concerns Dermod's quest for his beloved Norah, an impoverished fallen woman discovered on her deathbed. There is more than a touch of melodramatic sentimentality to this ending, but Dermod's desire to rescue Norah comes not from any religious imperative but from his recognition that prostitution is a part of a larger economy. The second and main narrative is Dermod's adventures as a tramp with his roguish mate Moleskin Joe. Whereas Polly's tramping in Wells represents a pastoral escape from the grind of shopkeeping, Dermod and Moleskin Joe are tramps because they are looking for work. The picaresque plot, for all its comedy, cleaves to the realities of lives reduced to the "primeval, animalised and brutish."[7] Dermod's irrepressible mockery is laced with a bitter, laconic irony. A description of how four men hammer into rock a drill held by a man who can be killed by the "smallest error" concludes with the terse observation, "This work is classed as unskilled labour" (183). The lower-class hero or villain of the picaresque novel had always enabled conventional social values to be satirized, but *Children of the Dead End* is possibly the first to place work or its horrendous absence at its center.

The social solidarity of the war years is evoked by both sides of the conflict during the railway strike of 1919, the miners' strike of 1921, and the 1926 General Strike. In Ellen Wilkinson's novel about the General Strike, *Clash* (1929), the war hero Gerry tells the wavering strikers, "[Y]ou stood together in the trenches, don't let your pals down"; while on the eve of the strike the union organizer heroine Joan predicts that for their adversaries it "will be the War atmosphere back again" with "[y]oung men in plus-fours looking important, and silly Society girls patting their heads and sitting up all night to give them cocoa."[8] Joan's social democratic radicalism reflects Wilkinson's : in the postwar Labour victory Wilkinson became the first female Minister of Education.

On all sides of the ideological spectrum the General Strike, despite its duration of only ten days, was seen as inaugurating a new political era. Leonard Woolf maintained that "[w]hen it comes to the practice of politics, anyone writing about his life in the years 1924–1939 must answer the crucial question: 'What did you do in the General Strike?'"[9] Wyndham Lewis remembered that 1926 was "when politics began for me in earnest."[10] In a study of radical writing during the 1920s, John Lucas confirms that "the definitive moment for the 1920s is not the Wall Street Crash but the General Strike."[11] Wells was not in England during the strike but wrote a novel, *Meanwhile* (1927), about men and women in an Italian villa who receive news of the strike by letter, the more prescient of them connecting political events in England with those in Italy under Mussolini.

Despite the Strike's divisiveness the best novels about it not only avoid narrow partisanship but transmute the conventional realist novel into new forms. Storm Jameson's *None Turn Back* (1936) occasionally flares into moments of angrily intrusive partisan comment, yet what is powerful about it is the way in which a complex network of personal relationships between middle- and upper-class characters, who represent a cross-section of professional, industrial, and social elites, transcend political divisions; the novel also portrays individuals forging political allegiances that cross the class divide. In 1937 Jameson called for a socialist literature that would resemble the documentary film, one in which "the writer keep[s] himself out of the picture while working ceaselessly to present the fact from a striking (poignant, ironic, penetrating, significant) angle,"[12] something she had already achieved by treating the political articulations of a range of characters as themselves "facts." From this mosaic of competing voices and opinion the reader infers that the strikers and their supporters were not so much defeated as betrayed by their compliant union and parliamentary leaders. The novel finishes with its female protagonist in hospital recovering from a difficult hysterectomy; but "[s]omething rejoiced in her that she was still alive, able to feel pain" (319). For all the bitterness of defeat there remains the progressive imperative that none should turn back after 1926.

A lack of historical specificity in James Hanley's *The Furys* (1935) allows readers to assume it is about the General Strike, as Hanley probably intends. The novel tells the story of a working-class Irish family in England. The mother, Fanny, resembles Mrs. Morel in *Sons and Lovers* in her ambitions for her children, in particular her youngest son, Peter, whom she compels to train for the priesthood. Violence, both verbal and physical, pervades the novel. Fanny calls members of her husband's family "dirty," strikes Peter, spits in his face, and threatens to kill him. Despite such open bluntness the family, like the neighborhood, is characterized by its members' secrecy and their proclivity to spy on each other. The streams of their consciousness, at times almost paranoid, are at odds. With the exception of dialogue, the novel is composed of interior monologue and free indirect discourse and, as Simon Dentith points out, there is no overarching narrator to control the story, only a parody of such a narrator in the mad "Professor of Anthropology," R. H. Titmouse, who sneeringly observes at a distance from or above the strikers.[13] The only explicit glimpse of history comes through Grandfather Fury's memories of the Great Famine. Struck dumb by a stroke and strapped into his chair, perhaps the grandfather represents a class agony that has yet to be resolved by social democracy.

The novels of Lewis Grassic Gibbon's trilogy *A Scots Quair*, the second of which, *Cloud Howe* (1933), focusses on the General Strike, are the first to dispense with the division between a narrator who uses standard English and characters who speak in dialect. The narration fuses English and Scots vocabulary, syntax, rhythms, and cadences. As the trilogy progresses and its female protagonist Chris Guthrie moves from farmhouse to Manse to a boarding house in an industrial town, this voice becomes more modern, more the voice of the newspapers and political pamphlets than a rural community. Ideological discourses become more intense and insistent. Toward the end of the final novel, *Grey Granite* (1934), Chris's communist son, Ewan, feels the elation of "LIVING HISTORY ONESELF" but he knows that the party which is supposedly making history tells lies and will dispense with him if necessary. He has found "a creed as clear and sharp as a knife" and yet for his mother "religion and God, socialism, nationalism [are] Clouds that sailed darkling into the night."[14] Ewan and Chris are suspended between political belief and an almost mystical disbelief, just as Gibbon's "Contribution to The Writers International Controversy" of 1935 is suspended between his declaration that "all my books are explicit or implicit propaganda" and his dismissal of talk about "decadence" in recent "bourgeois" writing as "Bolshevik blah."[15]

A Scots Quair is narrated mostly in the second person, what Cairns Craig describes as "the voice of the community speaking to itself."[16] The "you" represents multiplicities: the two selves of the heroine, Chris (the one educated, the other the daughter of a crofter); the generic "one" who is subject and object; the characters who speak and listen; the community that gossips maliciously about individuals; and the individuals who resist the malice; the narrator and the reader. But the "you" of the narration also provides a new democratic relationship between individual and community, the voices of those previously unheard now invested with the collective authority of the second person; while the societal voices that would usually speak with the impersonal authority of the third person are now individualized as "you."

At the end of Lewis Jones's novel about the General Strike and its after-math, *We Live* (1939), the communist hero, Len, goes to Spain to fight for the Republicans. As his Welsh village Cwmardy awaits his return, his wife Mary reads one of his letters declaring that "Fascism may kill us, Mary, but it can never kill what we die for."[17] She then reads a letter from one of Len's comrades telling her that Len has been killed. Initially shocked into a trance, Mary soon runs to join a gathering demonstration of those who have also heard the news of Len's death. She is placed in a car at the head of the march while the people sing "The Red Flag," the final lines of which are the novel's last words. The Spanish Civil War had what Cyril Connolly calls its senti-mental "Rupert Brooke period";[18] and as George Orwell argues in "My Country Right or Left" (1940) the public-school cheer-leading and flag-waving "emotions" of Sir Henry Newbolt's "There's a breathless hush in the Close to-night" are "almost exactly the same" as those of John Cornford's Spanish war poem, "Before the Storming of Huesca." But Orwell refuses to sneer at such emotions, asserting instead that "It is exactly the people whose hearts have *never* leapt at the sight of a Union Jack who will flinch from revolution when the moment comes."[19]

Sylvia Townsend Warner's historical novel, *Summer Will Show* (1936), pub-lished just after she and her lover Valentine Ackland joined the Communist Party and traveled to Spain, coolly affirms the revolutionary emotions that Orwell defends. The heroine Sophia Willoughby begins as a Tory landowner and ends in Paris during the Revolution of 1848 reading a tract called *The Communist Manifesto* that she has been distributing for the revolutionaries. But the romantic revolutionary who seduces Sophia, Minna, a Jewish exile from the Russian pogroms and the ex-mistress of her gallivanting husband is depicted as both charismatic and unscrupulous. The novel is about the awakening of Sophia's political conscience but also of her distrust of political idealism. Free of her class at the end she is also destitute and bereft of Minna. *Summer Will Show*, Claire Harman writes, "is an unillusioned book" in which both "idealists and exploiters of ideals are viewed in the same clear light."[20]

Summer Will Show ends with revolution; Orwell's memoir, *Homage to Catalonia* (1938) begins with one. This is one of two major non-fictions by

Orwell that exemplify the literary culture of social democracy. *Homage to Catalonia* starts with Orwell arriving in Barcelona in December 1936 to discover for the first time in his life a town "where the working class was in the saddle."[21] There is no political discourse in these opening pages, but simply details that evoke a total, almost miraculous transformation in the fabric of ordinary life: "[w]aiters and shop-walkers looked you in the face and treated you as an equal"; there is no tipping; there are no "well-dressed" people and private motor cars. Later amid the "boredom, heat, cold, dirt, lice, privation, and occasional danger" at the front Orwell realizes that the militias "were a sort of microcosm of a classless society," something to which he is "deeply attracted" (84). Such informal socialism is not motivated by any heroic sentiment or political ideology, but is "common," "essential," "human," "innate," "decent." "Decency" is a keynote of the text.

In two of his book's chapters, unfortunately relegated to appendices in some later editions, Orwell interrupts the account of his immediate experience to explain the larger political context, and to sift through the lies of the belligerent parties and of journalism about the war. Especially prone to lying are the communists, whom Orwell regards as anti-revolutionary opportunists, especially because they vilified the anarchists and the dissident anarchist group in one of whose militias Orwell fought. The chapters of explanation make sense of how political sectarianism and media bias caused this extraordinary revolution to fail; and they explain the naïveté and misconceptions under which Orwell labored during his politically isolated time at the front.

Homage to Catalonia movingly describes an actual albeit brief moment of socialism, perhaps the only such moment ever described in English literature. For all its novelty and power, however, it perhaps is a less innovative text than Orwell's previous documentary memoir, *The Road to Wigan Pier* (1937). In the autobiographical second section of *Wigan Pier* Orwell describes sharing the lives of the poor in Wigan out of his impulse to "expiate" an "immense weight of guilt" by "submerg[ing]" himself "right down among the oppressed."[22] In *Homage to Catalonia* Orwell is a participant-observer, but in *Road to Wigan Pier* Orwell the participant-observer is himself observed. He is a Malinowskian anthropologist who becomes the object of his or her analysis. In this he shares the project of the contemporary Mass-Observation group, which in its attempt to collect a democratic record – free of ideological and media distortion – of George VI's coronation, May 12, 1937, invited participant volunteers to record *everything* they observed, including their own responses. As the somewhat alarming invitation put it: "Watch yourself. And watch your neighbour."[23] At the time the project was criticized for its triviality and its unreliable demographics. But it was a genuinely democratic attempt to provide a popular anthropology of the everyday life of ordinary people at the margins of an official ceremony of social and political significance.

The democratization of knowledge in the Mass-Observation project, published as *May the Twelfth*, enabled the at times aleatory assemblage of observers' reports and press cuttings to resemble modernist or surrealist montage (one of the three originators, Humphrey Jennings, was a surrealist painter). Without any extraneous information the opening pages, no less than the opening chapters of *Homage to Catalonia*, cannot be distinguished from a novel. Alternatively, many social democratic novels insist on their "documentary" aspects. Tressell informs us that he "invented nothing": there are "no scenes or incidents in the story that [he had] not either witnessed . . . or had conclusive evidence of" (14). MacGill extends facts into form, claiming that "[i]n this true story, as in real life, men and women crop up for a moment, do something or say something, then go away and probably never reappear again" (111). Since its origins in the early eighteenth century, the novel has always presented individual experience within historical time and in particularized places, but novels in the social democratic tradition are if anything even more insistent that they not only document the lives of the silent masses but that they can, as Charles Lamb says of Defoe, be read like "evidence in a court of Justice."[24]

Walter Brierley's *Means-Test Man* (1935) and Walter Greenwood's *Love on the Dole* (1933) are powerful evidence of the conditions of working people on the dole as they negotiate the threat of the means test. Orwell points out that "[t]he most cruel and evil effect of the Means Test is the way in which it breaks up families" (*Wigan Pier*, 73), citing the case of an old age pensioner forced to leave home because his pension would cause his children's dole to be docked. In *Love on the Dole* young Harry is refused relief because his father's dole and his sister Sally's wages are considered sufficient to keep him. The loss of Harry's dole places even stronger tensions on his relationship with his lover Helen. She is pregnant and Harry's father throws him out of the house when this is discovered. The Cook family in *Means-Test Man* – the unemployed miner Jack, his wife Jane and their young son – have only one source of income. The novel focusses on the tensions between Jack and Jane, as the former coal miner, attempting to fill his days with domestic work and child care, becomes emasculated in his own eyes and those of his socially ambitious and at times unsympathetic wife.

The endings of each novel are contrastive and complementary. Every chapter title of *Means-Test Man* names a day of the week, each day indistinguishable from the next except for the arrival on Wednesday of the means-test man, a degrading humiliation for the couple, who must submit to the surveillance of all aspects of their domestic economy to remain eligible for payments. In *Love on the Dole*, in contrast, there is a comic resolution to the two romance plots, the one concerning Harry and Helen and the other Harry's sister Sally and socialist activist Larry. After Larry dies from an assault by a policeman during a peaceful protest against the means test, Sally agrees to be the mistress of the wealthy but repugnant bookie Sam. As a consequence of her new position she is able to find jobs for her brother and unemployed father. Love is impossible on the dole but at least Sally's defiance of social conventions allows the continuation of some kind of life. If the *Means-Test Man* takes naturalism to its limits by refusing to see any alternative to the cycle of soul-destroying weeks, *Love on the Dole* parodies, as Ian Haywood writes, the "conventional property plot of English fiction."[25] Perhaps because of its "happy ending," as well as its less spare prose, *Love on the Dole* proved the more successful novel. The stage version drew huge audiences; the film version was proscribed until 1941, but when it appeared it received reviews whose basic tenor, in the words of the First Lord of the Admiralty, was that "never again must the unemployed become the forgotten men of the Peace."[26]

Although the renaissance of realism oriented toward social democracy during the 1930s saw the publication of nearly 150 novels with "socialist concerns," it was accompanied by a wave of some thirty dystopian fantasies.[27] The culmination of those dystopias is Orwell's *Nineteen Eighty-Four* (1949), but it and many of its predecessors draw upon *A Modern Utopia*, if only by inversion. The prophetic "Voice" in Wells's novel is transmuted into Orwell's O'Brien and Aldous Huxley's Mustapha Mond; the four main classes of mind in *A Modern Utopia* resemble the five castes of Huxley's *Brave New World* (1932); Wells exiles his anti-social characters to islands as does Huxley; and a special book explaining the history of society exists in Wells's utopia, in Katherine Burdekin's *Swastika Night* (1937), and in *Nineteen Eighty-Four*. But one must remember that Wells establishes his career as a writer of dystopian "scientific romances."

Just as the defeats with which *Clash*, *None Turn Back*, *The Furys*, *A Scots Quair* and *Summer Will Show* conclude are in effect incitements to political action, so the nightmarish worlds of *The Time Machine* (1895), in which the rich and the poor have evolved into separate species, the one feeding on the other, and *The War of the Worlds* (1898), where the technological advancement of the Martians has withered their bodies, are to be remedied by the socialism and vitalism expressed in Wells's succeeding novels. Similarly, Rex Warner's *Aerodrome* (1941) presents no alternative to the intertwined worlds of the small English village and the nearby fascist aerodrome, but in Warner's earlier novel, *The Wild Goose Chase* (1937), liberal values of liberty and equality are affirmed, albeit as ones provisionally attained, and under permanent threat. And just as the language of the inhabitants in Patrick Hamilton's *Impromptu in Moribundia* (1939) consists of English words spelled backwards – the most vilified being "tsinummoc" – so the world that Hamilton describes (in which advertising dominates, persons communicate through comic book speech bubbles, and Newboltish play-up-and-play-the-game public-school values prevail) can be easily read backwards to mean the author's communist sympathies. Burdekin sees the basis for fascism as a desire to dominate and degrade women, her clear implication being that the Popular Front needs to include feminism in its anti-fascist arsenal. *Nineteen Eighty-Four* is usually regarded as the bleakest of the dystopias; and yet the liquidation of objective truth by Winston's acceptance that two plus two can equal three or five is belied by its author's realism, and by the transparent prose that Orwell's "Why I Write" tells us he wrote in the service of. The appendix to *Nineteen Eighty-Four*, "The Principles of Newspeak," is written in the past tense. It suggests, as many have noted, that Big Brother's totalitarian society might already have ceased to exist.

If utopias come as much from dystopic despair as from hope, then it is not surprising that the Beveridge Report in the dark year of 1942 should have met with wide, even rapturous support for proclaiming that "[a] revolutionary moment in the world's history is time for revolutions."[28] The victory of Labour two months after VE day made many optimistic that a government pursuing welfare state policies could rebuild the nation and compensate for wartime sacrifices. In J. B. Priestley's *Three Men in New Suits* (1945) three demobbed soldiers from the same battalion, representing a cross-section of society – one is a worker, another a farmer, and the third from the Manor – find themselves alienated from their families and community. The solidarity of their wartime experience amounts to a great, disillusioning contrast with the grasping values of the civilian population. At the end of the novel the upper-class Alan proclaims that "Either the earth must soon be the miserable grave of our species or it must be at last our home, where men can live at peace and can work for other men's happiness." This is immediately deflated in Tressellian fashion by one of the trio crying "Whoa, steady on . . . Yer'll be either preachin' or in Parlyment next."[29] Nevertheless, *Three Men in New Suits* aligns itself not only with the principles of the Beveridge Report that Priestley also championed in his wartime broadcasts but with a modernized version of the historical "organic" societies whose destruction by *laissez-faire* individualism Raymond Williams traces in *Culture and Society*.

One of Alan's antagonists in *Three Men in New Suits* is a newspaper magnate who claims that all the returning soldiers want are "Dog tracks, cheap racing, plenty of football, better movies, good places to eat and drink where they can take their wives, nice holidays" (89). The third great wave of social democratic and realist writing, that of the 1950s and 1960s, registers a significant change – in the direction of the magnate's prophecy – in the lives of the working class. The protagonist of Alan Sillitoe's *Saturday Night and Sunday Morning* (1958), Arthur, observing his father watching television, thinks "The difference before the war and after the war didn't bear thinking about";[30] we first meet John Braine's working-class hero, Joe Lampton, in *Room at the Top* (1959) in expensive clothes and on the make; David Storey's Arthur Machin in *This Sporting Life* (1960) earns more money playing rugby league than most middle-class people; and Nell Dunn's Joy in *Poor Cow* (1967) can move to a "luxury flat" in the suburb of Ruislip because her boyfriend has just pulled off a robbery.[31] Gone are the community values of the prewar novel: Sillitoe's Arthur admires the communists for their non-conformity but will not stomach a government that says "everybody's got to share and share alike" (33); Joe Lampton moves from his working-class community to the top end of a middle-class town; the rugby club is not an alternative to the social hierarchies of a mining town but a microcosm of them; and politics of anything other than the sexual kind do not exist in Joy's world.

With less desperate conditions and greater possibility of class mobility (thanks to the welfare state!) comes *ressentiment*, at least in *Room at the Top*. Joe Lampton's "whole life" is "changed" when he sees a rich young man in an Aston Martin with "a girl with a Riviera suntan" and he decides that he will get what this man has, a decision that means that he will marry his rival's girlfriend and indirectly cause the death of the woman he loves.[32] In *Saturday Night* and *Poor Cow* the main characters have an amoral vitality (albeit crude and even violent and sexually exploitative) that triumphs over the social conventions and bureaucracies attempting to regulate their lives. In *Saturday Night* the narrative shifts from third to second person to register this conflict, the "you" both an automaton working on an industrial lathe and a young man with money in his pocket fantasizing about sex on Saturday nights. Joy, like the Wife of Bath, will exuberantly survive the various men she sexually enjoys; but like Molly Bloom she remains the lover of one in particular. While some critics see authorial condescension in the reproduction of her atrocious spelling ("I'm so raped up in Your love" [39]), the irony is never at her expense but only augments her unquenchable vulgarity. Even *This Sporting Life* ends with laughter: its exploration of Arthur's inarticulate but painfully delicate and complex relationship with the widow Mrs. Hammond finishes with the rugby players in a crowded bath after a game, shrieking with merriment.

In contrast to the latter-day working-class heroes, the problem for the middle-class protagonist of liberal or social democratic values is one of action, of the kinds of duties and responsibilities he must actively assume. In Angus Wilson's *Hemlock and After* (1952), set before the defeat of Labour in 1951, the writer Bernard Sands at the summit of his novel-writing career (and a married man only recently open about his homosexuality) secures welfare state funding to establish a house for young writers, Vardon Hall. This social democratic project and Sands's life appear to disintegrate when a police officer asks if Sands would like to give evidence against a young man for "importuning" and Sands realizes that "he had been ready to join the hounds in the kill"[33] of his own queer kind. As Dominic Head points out, Bernard's "'hemlock' is the self-knowledge that destroys him, his realization of his moral wavering."[34] As the working-class hero's revolt against welfare-state surveillance and control is merely individualist at best and violent and destructive at worst, so the middle-class hero's dissatisfaction with the kind of liberalism that guarantees merely individual freedoms stares at the abyss of human evil. If the working-class hero has an amoral vitality, the middle-class hero is scrupulously anaemic. But there is life after the taking of hemlock. When Bernard dies his wife Ella emerges from her depression and achieves partial success in completing the socialized commitment to writers that her husband had been unable to fulfill. The principles of the Beveridge Report as epitomized by the Vardon Hall project have been severely eroded but not defeated.

Raymond Williams's *Border Country* (1960) and John Berger's *G.* (1972) represent the changing fortunes of social democratic realism when Conservative reaction and neo-liberalism were on the horizon and when the political and philosophical underpinnings of welfare-state ideology were coming under increasing oppositional scrutiny from the New Left. At the start of *Border Country* Matthew Price, a lecturer in economic history at a London university, returns to his Welsh border village after his working-class father suffers a stroke. The border of the title has multiple significations, indicating multiple "countries." Matthew, or Will as he is known in his village, is a former scholarship boy who has crossed the borders of class; he is researching population movements in Wales during the Industrial Revolution but wants to cross the border that divides the abstract and general from the "emotional pattern" or "tissue of . . . common life"; his father is content to remain working as a railway signalman rather than go into business with his politically disillusioned friend Morgan, though their friendship can still cross the divisions that bound their friendship; most importantly, the narrative periodically crosses the border of the present in the 1950s back to Matthew's father's past – in particular to the General Strike of 1926.[35] Like perhaps all novels about working-class life, *Border Country* is a regional novel; but region here only has meaning in opposition to the metropolis. A whole way of life can only be fully understood in its relationship to another.

While Williams's novel utilizes a realism that is closer to Bennett or John Galsworthy's, *G.* marks a full-blown return to the experiments with realism and narrative that characterize modernism. *G.*'s linear narrative is interrupted by the discursive, the diachronic cut through by the synchronic, the two always *à deux*. Gaps between paragraphs and lines draw attention to the text's montage-like construction, and the novel has been compared to cubist painting. Berger's assessment of cubism as a paradigmatically revolutionary form, predicting the values and aims of the Bolshevik revolution, appears in his *Moments of Cubism* (1967); indicative of his political leanings, one of Berger's collections of essays is called *Permanently Red* (1960). The eponymous character of *G.* is a Don Juan figure, who seduces his way across much of Europe in the heyday of modernism and Futurism that precedes the First World War. G. is sometimes little more than a figure for the libido, his psychology given far less attention than the women he seduces; and for most of the novel he is not interested in or he is removed from the political turmoil that surrounds him. But the hero's death – he is killed in Trieste when he is caught up in a riot protesting the declaration of war against Italy – implies that personal sexuality is intertwined with the impersonal forces of history. Indeed Berger's aim for the novel appears to be a recovery of modernism that coordinates its interest in apparently ahistorical forces – eros, for example – with social democratic struggle. *G.*'s dedication to feminist concerns, as a counter-balance to the Don Juan myth, is part of its recovery project. This is the conflict between desire and collective aims that was sounded in *The New Machiavelli*. And *G.*'s narrator, often keeping G. at a distance while the former meditates essayistically on history, language, and sex, renews Wells's "rambling discursiveness" as a necessary adjunct to novelistic form.

After *G.*'s publication Berger relocated himself to Switzerland, where he commenced writing about the experience and fate of contemporary migrant workers. In this he harks back to the tramping era of MacGill: to its progressive political bearings as well as to its modernism and to the compatability of both. In his relocation, the start of an informal exile not long before the election of Margaret Thatcher in 1979, Berger perhaps enacts the beginning of the end of the social democratic era and of fiction's relation to cherished collective concerns.

Notes

1. Ralf Dahrendorf, *Life Chances: Approaches to Social and Political Theory* (London: Weidenfeld and Nicolson, 1980).
2. Sir William Beveridge, *Social Insurance and Allied Services* (New York: Macmillan, 1942), pp. 17, 6, 7.
3. Jack Mitchell, "Early Harvest: Three Anti-Capitalist Novels Published in 1914," in *The Socialist Novel in Britain*, ed. H. Gustav Klaus (Brighton: Harvester Press, 1982), p. 67.
4. *Henry James and H. G. Wells: A Record of their Friendship, their Debate on the Art of Fiction, and their Quarrel*, ed. Leon Edel and Gordon N. Ray (London: Rupert Hart-Davis, 1958), pp. 148, 138.
5. H. G. Wells, *A Modern Utopia* (London: Fisher Unwin, 1905), pp. 5, 78.
6. Robert Tressell, *The Ragged Trousered Philanthropists* (London: Harper Perennial, 2005), p. 14.
7. Patrick MacGill, *Children of the Dead End* (London: Caliban, 1983), p. 120.
8. Ellen Wilkinson, *Clash* (London: Virago, 1989), pp. 143, 41.
9. Leonard Woolf, *Downhill All The Way* (London: Hogarth, 1967), p. 217.
10. Wyndham Lewis, *Blasting and Bombardiering* (Berkeley: University of California Press, 1967), p. 303.
11. John Lucas, *The Radical Twenties: Aspects of Writing, Politics and Culture* (Nottingham: Five Leaves Publishers, 1997), p. 3.
12. Storm Jameson, "New Documents," *Civil Journey* (London: Cassell, 1939), p. 270.
13. Simon Dentith, "James Hanley's *The Furys*: The Modernist Subject Goes on Strike," *Literature and History* 12: 1 (2003), 41–56.
14. Lewis Grassic Gibbon, *A Scots Quair* (London: Hutchinson, 1946), pp. 459, 495, 332.
15. Quoted in *A Twentieth Century Literature Reader: Texts and Debates*, ed. Suman Gupta and David Johnson (London: Routledge, 2005), pp. 49, 48.
16. Cairns Craig, *The Modern Scottish Novel: Narrative and the National Imagination* (Edinburgh University Press, 1999), p. 94.
17. Lewis Jones, *We Live* (London: Lawrence and Wishart, 1939), p. 332.
18. Quoted in Samuel Hynes, *The Auden Generation* (London: Bodley Head, 1976), p. 242.
19. George Orwell, *The Collected Essays, Journalism and Letters*, ed. Sonia Orwell and Ian Angus, 4 vols. (London: Secker and Warburg, 1968), vol. II, p. 540.
20. Claire Harman, Introduction to Sylvia Townsend Warner, *Summer Will Show* (London: Virago, 1987), p. viii.

21. George Orwell, *Homage to Catalonia* (London: Secker and Warburg, 1986), p. 2.

22. George Orwell, *The Road to Wigan Pier* (London: Penguin, 1989), p. 138.

23. Quoted in James Buzard, "Mass-Observation, Modernism and Auto-ethnography," *Modernism/Modernity* 4: 3 (1997), 93–122, 105.

24. Quoted in Ian Watt, *The Rise of the Novel* (Berkeley and Los Angeles: University of California Press, 2001), p. 34.

25. Ian Haywood, *Working-Class Fiction from Chartism to* Trainspotting (Plymouth: Northcote House, 1997), p. 56.

26. Quoted in Constantine Stephen, *"Love on the Dole* and its Reception in the 1930s," *Literature and History* 8: 2 (1982), 245.

27. Andy Croft, "Worlds Without End Foisted Upon the Future – Some Antecedents of *Nineteen Eighty-Four,"* in *Inside the Myth. Orwell: Views From the Left,* ed. Christopher Norris (London: Lawrence and Wishart, 1984), p. 188.

28. Brian Abel-Smith, "The Beveridge Report: Its Origins and Outcomes," *International Social Security Review* 45 (1992), 5–16.

29. J. B. Priestley, *Three Men in New Suits* (London: Heinemann, 1945), p. 170.

30. Alan Sillitoe, *Saturday Night and Sunday Morning* (London: Allen, 1958), p. 25.

31. Nell Dunn, *Poor Cow* (London: Bloomsbury, 1996), p. 4.

32. John Braine, *Room at the Top* (Harmondsworth: Penguin, 1959), pp. 28, 29.

33. Angus Wilson, *Hemlock and After* (Harmondsworth: Penguin, 1956), p. 109.

34. Dominic Head, *The Cambridge Introduction to Modern British Fiction, 1950–2000* (Cambridge University Press, 2002), p. 20.

35. Raymond Williams, *Border Country* (London: Chatto and Windus, 1978), pp. 284, 323.

51

The postcolonial novel: history and memory

C. L. INNES

Implicit in the category "postcolonial" is a concern with the event of colonialism, its consequences, and the representation of both. Consequently, for many postcolonial writers history is the crucible out of which their fiction is fashioned. They respond not only to written histories in terms of content and narrative form, but also to concepts of history. Their novels counterpose memory and history, and myth and history. The opposition between memory and history also involves an attempt to create – or re-create – a collective memory that will be the source of a collective national identity – an imagined community.

In counterposing history and memory, I draw on distinctions that the French historian Pierre Nora delineates in his *Realms of Memory*:

> The acceleration of history: let us try to gauge the significance, beyond metaphor, of this phrase . . . Our interest in *lieux de mémoire* where memory crystallizes and secretes itself has occurred at a particular historical moment, – but torn in such a way as to pose the problem of the embodiment of memory in certain sites where a sense of historical continuity persists. There are *lieux de mémoire*, sites of memory, because there are no longer *milieux de mémoire*, real environments of memory.[1]

Writing about changes in contemporary European society, especially France, caused by rapid advances in technology, the disappearance of agrarian culture, and the impact of globalization, Nora discerns:

> an increasingly rapid slippage of the present into a historical past that is gone for good, a general perception that anything and everything may disappear – these indicate a rupture of equilibrium . . . *a turning point where consciousness of a break with the past is bound up with the sense* that memory has been torn.
>
> (285, Nora's italics)

The rupture he speaks of, that turning point where "consciousness of a break with the past is bound up with the sense that memory has been torn," is most starkly experienced by colonized peoples under the impact of European invasion and occupation, and also, in different ways, by colonial and post-colonial settlers under the impact of exile and resettlement in an alien land. This chapter considers ways in which history and memory enter into dialogue with one another in novels by postcolonial writers.

Almost all anti-colonial literature begins by challenging histories by the colonizers, who all too often consign the colonized to a pre-historical and subhuman state. Hegel famously wrote that Africa existed outside of history:

> The negro as already observed exhibits the natural man in his completely wild and untamed state. We must lay aside all thought of reverence and morality – all that we call feeling – if we would rightly comprehend him; there is nothing harmonious with humanity to be found in this type of character . . . What we properly understand by Africa is the Unhistorical, Undeveloped Spirit . . .[2]

As Edward Said argues, such pronouncements about the colonized worlds and peoples were part of a network of discourses – historical, anthropological, linguistic, and literary – that established Africa, Asia, and the Middle East as candidates for Western intervention and government. Thus the novels of Joseph Conrad and Joyce Cary portray Africa and Asia as static and atavistic worlds. Indeed Cary writes in a 1952 preface to his novel *The African Witch* (1936) that he sought to show:

> certain men and their problems in the tragic background of a continent still little advanced from the Stone Age, and therefore exposed, like no other, to the impact of modern turmoil. An overcrowded raft manned by children who had never seen the sun would have a better chance in a typhoon.[3]

Similarly, Europeans viewed the indigenous peoples of Australia as an unchanging doomed race, so negligible that Captain Cook and future colonial administrators declared Australia *terra nullius* – land owned by nobody – and therefore land that could be occupied and settled by Europeans without regard to previous inhabitants. The Irish too were described by the British as an atavistic race, close kin to Africans, caught up, according to Benjamin Disraeli, in an "unbroken circle of bigotry and blood."[4]

Insofar as the British and French acknowledged that India or Egypt or Turkey had a history, it was seen as a history of decline – each country a land of picturesque ruins and ancient monuments belonging to the past, and now inhabited by a passive, feeble, perhaps decadent and feminine people.

Thus one important task for anti-colonial writers was to challenge the colonialist historical narrative, to assert, in Chinua Achebe's words, "that African peoples did not hear of culture for the first time from Europeans,"[5] and to write themselves into a historical narrative of their own construction. The opening and closing paragraphs of Achebe's first novel, *Things Fall Apart* (1958), illustrate the contrast between a history constructed by an indigenous people, and one constructed by the colonizer:

> Okonkwo was well known throughout the nine villages and even beyond. His fame rested on solid personal achievements. As a young man of eighteen he had brought honor to his village by throwing Amalinze the Cat. Amalinze was the great wrestler who for seven years was unbeaten . . . He was called the Cat because his back would never touch the earth. It was this man that Okonkwo threw in a fight which the old men agreed was one of the fiercest since the founder of their town engaged a spirit of the wild for seven days and seven nights.[6]

Thus Achebe begins his novel by re-creating the illusion of oral history, and the articulation of collective memory, within what Nora terms the environment in which collective memory, nurtured unselfconsciously, is crucial to group identity. (Although Achebe might disagree with the notion that precolonial Igbo society was not consciously promoting social cohesion through storytelling.) Here memory, history, legend, and myth merge into one narrative in which all elements are considered equally true. The narrative voice suggests a village elder addressing an immediate audience, and adding details as they become necessary in order to explain who Amalinze was, and why Okonkwo was esteemed. "The nine villages" make up the extent of his world and his audience; areas outside these boundaries have little significance, and belong to the vague realm "beyond." The narrator represents a collective voice through which the artist speaks *for* his society, not as an individual apart from it.

Achebe's novel tells the story of Okonkwo's resistance to Christian missionaries and British colonial powers, and of his defeat, ending in suicide. The concluding paragraph moves from the points of view of Igbos to the perspective and thoughts of the British District Commissioner:

> The Commissioner went away, taking three or four of the soldiers with him. In the many years in which he had toiled to bring civilization to . . . Africa he had learned a number of things. One of them was that a District Commissioner must never attend to such undignified details as cutting down a hanged man from a tree. Such attention would give the natives a

poor opinion of him. In the book he planned to write he would stress that point. As he walked back to the court he thought about that book ... The story of this man who had killed a messenger and hanged himself would make interesting reading. One could almost write a whole chapter on him. Perhaps not a whole chapter but a reasonable paragraph, at any rate ... [O]ne must be firm in cutting out details. He had already chosen the title of the book, after much thought: *The Pacification of the Primitive Tribes of the Lower Niger.*

(147–148)

This paragraph marks not only the end of the pre-colonial era in Eastern Nigeria, and the defeat of the values and society Okonkwo represents, but also the replacement of an oral culture by a written one. It specifically marks the change from an oral history based on communal memory to a written history based on the gathering of material and the structuring of it in paragraphs and chapters by one individual for a distant and future audience, not an audience that is present to a narrator and responding to him. And rather than reflecting on the community and one of its heroes, it is a history which will bring honor to the writer, for it will be about the District Commissioner's deeds and actions. It is also a history designed to serve the interests and values of European colonizers rather than the colonized.

Of course, there is a paradox in the fact that Achebe draws on European literary culture and English to represent and validate an oral culture and an African language. The paradox is acknowledged in the novel, not least in the title *Things Fall Apart*, drawn from Yeats's poem "The Second Coming." But the title also points up the divergence between European and African histories. For Yeats "things fall apart" with the end of a Christian era, whereas for Achebe's community the advent of Christianity entails disintegration. What I want to emphasize is how the structure of the novel dramatizes a tension between "memory" and "history." We might consider history as a record of change, whereas memory functions as a means of "crystallizing" the past, for, according to Nora, "the purpose of *lieux de mémoire* is to stop time, to block the work of forgetting, to establish a state of things, to immortalize death, to materialize the immaterial" (295–296).

Achebe's novel consists of three parts, the first of which portrays in detail the pre-colonial world of Umuofia, its people, its religious beliefs, and rituals, its stories and proverbs, its daily life, its interactions among men, women, and children. The first part covers almost two-thirds of the novel's pages, while the second and third parts briefly narrate the changes brought by the Christian missionaries and by the District Commissioner who becomes the historian of those changes. The function of the long first section is not only to re-create pre-colonial society, but also to commemorate it; or rather, to create a collective memory that will become the basis for the new nation of Nigeria (the novel was published two years prior to Nigerian independence). And that particular culture becomes memorable, becomes part of the reader's experience, through reiteration and repetition, because proverbs and rituals, such as the passing around of the kola nut, occur again and again. In this way the knowledge of pre-colonial Igbo culture is absorbed not as anthropology, but as an increasingly familiar, immediate part of the reader's world. As a result the memory of the pre-colonial society outweighs the history of the changes brought about by the British. *Things Fall Apart*, more than fifty years after its publication, has itself become a site of memory, a reference point for readers and writers of African literature, who regard it as a foundational African and postcolonial novel.

The creation or re-creation of a collective memory as a base for a national consciousness, or, to use Benedict Anderson's phrase, "an imagined community," is central to other postcolonial fiction. One could think of James Joyce's *Ulysses* (1922), which brings to life its citizens, its voices, its music, its newspapers, its communal and individual memories. At the end of Joyce's *A Portrait of the Artist as a Young Man* (1916), Stephen Dedalus declares that he will now try to forge "the uncreated conscience of [his] race" (using "conscience" in the sense of "consciousness"), and Joyce seeks to fulfill Stephen's ambitious aim with *Ulysses* and *Finnegans Wake* (1939). *Ulysses* restores Dublin and its citizens to us at a moment in time, a period of just one day, June 16, 1904. *Ulysses* thus is "the shout in the street" that for Stephen substitutes everyday human life as a replacement for any grand Hegelian definition of God. But the very act of historical commemoration in *Ulysses* also sets up a tension with history, which Stephen refers to as "the nightmare ... from which he is trying to awake." Joyce's dating of the novel's composition, "1914 to 1921, Trieste–Zurich–Paris," reminds us not only that it is a historical novel, capturing a time that precedes the Easter Rising of 1916, World War I, and the establishment of the Irish Free State, but also that it is a series of memories of another time and other places. And as with Achebe's novel, the title of *Ulysses*, by alluding to Homer's *Odyssey*, reminds us of the tension between an oral rendering of events and places as remembered by Homer, and a written record (in this case the bookish self-consciously literary work by Joyce that we read). Within *Ulysses* there are also conflicting attitudes to history: for Haines, the Englishman, "It seems History is to blame" for Ireland's subjection to English colonialism; he thinks of History as an abstract concept implying an inevitable chain of events for which the English certainly should not be held responsible. Many of the Irish characters in the novel have an entirely opposing point of view, blaming England for everything.

Salman Rushdie's *Midnight's Children* (1981) takes as its central metaphor the abstract notion of a collective history and memory shared by the fictional thousand children born at the moment India became independent at midnight, August 14, 1947. But Rushdie's novel also portrays tensions between different memories, the difficulty of remembering, and the ways in which memory is altered through time. He refers to the "chutnification" of history, but that metaphor, like the trope of preserving and pickling that becomes increasingly important in the novel, more readily applies to the storing of memories than to the recording and writing of history. Rushdie's essay "Imaginary Homelands" examines the gap between a remembered past, the childhood world of an exile, frozen in time, and the reality of a changing world and place. In Anita Desai's *The Clear Light of Day* (1980), that childhood world is imaged for the novel's two sisters not only in the disrepair of the family house they grew up in and the ghostly presences that haunt it, but also by the unremitting repetition of the old recordings played by their autistic brother.

The tension between memory and history will function differently for different readers of these novels. Perhaps one characteristic of postcolonial writing is its acknowledgment of a dual readership, indeed a multiple readership. Readers from Africa, Ireland, and India can experience the novels I have discussed as "insiders"; their response to the worlds those novels commemorate will be one of recognition, and they will participate in the collective memories re-created there as belonging to them, as shared. But readers outside those communities experience the novels as discovery of a new world; their approach might be more like that of anthropologists, and the societies portrayed will seem to belong to an external, objective, or distant "history." (Indeed *Things Fall Apart* is taught in anthropology and history courses in the United States and Britain.) Thus experiences of reading postcolonial texts will vary, depending on the contexts in which readers situate themselves.

The consciousness and inscription of a *double* or multiple audience marks one of the most significant and interesting differences between English, North American, and European modernist or postmodernist writers and anti-colonialist or postcolonial writers. Postcolonial authors foreground and complicate in their texts the issue of divergent and even contrary reader responses. The District Commissioner's response to Okonkwo's story, like Haines's response to the old woman who brings milk to the young men in the Martello tower or his patronizing view of Stephen's theories, are extreme examples of "outsider" readings. Both responses seize upon individual examples to generalize about the society they are observing. Their function is partly to act as a warning: readers are encouraged to disassociate themselves from such distanced responses. In *Midnight's Children*, on the other hand, Padma, the narrator's consort, acts as an interlocutor from the inside, bringing to bear an indigenous oral and folk tradition from which to view the narrator-outsider's literary strategies with skepticism.

But it is not so easy to draw a clear line between "insiders" and "outsiders." One might remember how over a century ago the African American scholar W. E. B. Dubois invoked the notion of a "double consciousness" that is simultaneously inside and outside the black community. Achebe, Rushdie, Said, and Homi Bhabha celebrate their double status as insiders and outsiders in a particular community or culture. In an 1982 interview Achebe makes a comparable point about his double or multiple consciousness as a Nigerian writer:

> I'm an Igbo writer because this is my basic culture; Nigerian, African and a writer . . . no, black first, then a writer. Each of these identities does call for a certain kind of commitment on my part. I must see what it is to be black – and this means being sufficiently intelligent to know how the world is moving and how the black people fare in this world. This is what it means to be black. Or an African – what does Africa mean to the world? When you see an African, what does it mean to a white man?[7]

Achebe's sense of his layered positions, what the black British critic Stuart Hall terms "positionality," also produces a specifically ironic mode of writing. Linda Hutcheon remarks on a shared rhetorical strategy in postmodern and postcolonial writing: "the use of the trope of irony as a doubled or split discourse which has the potential to subvert from within." In both cases irony becomes "a double-talking, forked-tongue mode of address" enabling the writer to "work within existing discourses and contest them at the same time."[8] Ironic doubling manifests itself in many ways: in a disruption of historical time and linear narrative for the sake of frequent movement between past and present; in a revisiting and rewriting by postcolonial writers of canonical literary texts such as *Robinson Crusoe, Heart of Darkness, Jane Eyre, Great Expectations*, and *A Handful of Dust*; in a mixture of genres and modes so that biography, anthropology, newspaper reports, and oral narratives interrupt one another and enter into fictions that alternate between modes of realism and surrealism or magic realism; in a playful interrogation of the colonial language and literary traditions through which the novel is told.

These strategies can be found in novels such as Ama Ata Aidoo's *Our Sister Killjoy: or Reflections from a Black-eyed Squint* (1977), Margaret Atwood's *Alias Grace* (1996), J. M. Coetzee's *Foe* (1986), Pauline Melville's *The Ventriloquist's Tale* (1997), V. S. Naipaul's *Guerillas* (1975) and *A Bend in the River* (1979); Jean Rhys's *Wide Sargasso Sea* (1966), David Dabydeen's *Intended* (1991), Abdulrazak Gurnah's *Paradise* (1994), and Peter Carey's *Jack Maggs* (1997). Aidoo's *Our Sister Killjoy* replaces Conrad's tale of his male narrator's journey into the African interior with a young Ghanaian woman's discovery of a "heart of whiteness" in Bavaria. Instead of the unnamable and inscrutable "horrors" adumbrated by Conrad's Marlow in the Congo, Aidoo's narrator, Sissie, speaks of the horror she encounters in Bavaria – the memories of Hitler, the war widows, the tragic loneliness of the young white woman, Maria, who befriends her. Maria might be seen not only as a Madonna with her child but also as a contemporary version of Kurtz's "Intended" – that blonde white woman who has no identity other than would-be wife and mother – haunting Aidoo's novel, with her dazzling white bedroom, her desperate loneliness, and her ignorance of any worlds outside her home, which is a soulless shrine to the sensual and the material.

Aidoo also replaces Marlow's hypnotic single-voiced narration with a fragmented, multivocal mixture of prose and free verse. The recollection of Sissie the narrator's experiences is interspersed with dialogues and debates with other characters, and also with questioning by the narrator herself of "knowledge gained then" through "knowledge gained since." Typesetting and page lay-out, sometimes with just two or three words on a page, are also used to disrupt or slow the narrative pace. Moreover, the narrator frequently voices distrust of the language and "culture" brought to Africa by European colonizers:

> A common heritage. A
> Dubious bargain that left us
> Plundered of
> Our gold
> Our tongue
> Our life – while our
> Dead fingers clutch
> English – a doubtful weapon fashioned
> Elsewhere to give might to a
> Soul that is already fled.[9]

Conrad's subject matter and geographical settings present a particular challenge to postcolonial writers seeking to rewrite the story of the colonial encounter and its consequences. And because the indeterminacy of perspective and narrative authority is central to readers' experience of Conrad, his influence is far more significant than that of other colonial writers such as Joyce Cary and E. M. Forster who write from within and toward a fixed European perspective, and often employ an omniscient narrative point of view. (Though, to be sure, Forster in *A Passage to India* [1924] acknowledges the difficulty of ascertaining the truth.)

Aidoo's African modernist novel challenges Conrad and other colonialist writers through a series of reversals and oppositions with regard to gender, race, point-of-view, and modes of discourse. The Guyanese-British author David Dabydeen also subverts Conrad through a more postmodern witty playfulness in *The Intended*, in which *Heart of Darkness* (1902) is relocated and "filmed" in the heart of London by a group of schoolboys of Caribbean, African, and Asian descent. In contrast, Naipaul revisits *Heart of Darkness* via East Africa in *A Bend in the River*, revealing through the perspective of an African of Indian descent the shabby pretension, disorder, and defeat typical, as Naipaul sees it, of contemporary Congo (Zaire) and other post-colonies. In contrast to African novelists like Achebe and Aidoo who repudiate Conrad's representation of Africa and other non-European societies, Naipaul expresses a kinship with Conrad, a writer who was

> not a man with a cause, but a man offering, as in *Nostromo* [1904], a vision of the world's half-made societies as places which continually made and unmade themselves and where always "something inherent in the necessities of successful action . . . carried with it the moral degradation of the idea."[10]

Naipaul shares with Conrad not only disenchantment with the consequences of colonialism and an interest in the fault-lines between cultures imposed on one another, but also shares narrative technique. Like Conrad, Naipaul chooses as his central commentator in novels such as *The Mimic Men* (1967) and *A Bend in the River* an unreliable first-person narrator, often detached from, or wearied by, the events and peoples he describes. In the latter novel and in the novella "In a Free State" (1971) Naipaul traces a journey into the interior of the continent as a metaphor for self-discovery and for a susceptibility to irrational and dark forces in the psyche of the "civilized" human being. In this regard Conrad's influence on postcolonial novelists also can be discerned in the Australian Patrick White's *Voss* (1957) and *A Fringe of Leaves* (1976), as well as in the Guyanan-British author Wilson Harris's *Palace of the Peacock* (1960). Patrick White's Australia, like Conrad's Africa, is presented as a land without history or cultural significance, a country of the mind, and the journey of Voss through an increasingly harsh and hostile landscape becomes a metaphor for an existential journey of self-discovery. But whereas Conrad, White, and Harris foreground the disintegration of a European mind in the context of an alien land's isolation from reminders of European culture, Naipaul's *A Bend in the River* portrays an atavistic regression by Ferdinand, a European-educated African youth, and his society. Ferdinand's reversion to "superstition" and ritual is reminiscent of the inexorable degeneration of Joyce Cary's Oxford-educated Louis Aladai in *The African Witch* (1936).

Naipaul's novels assume a complex but nevertheless definable set of boundaries between racial and cultural identities. Although they bring together and blur travel writing, autobiography, and fiction, they nevertheless adhere to the expectations of realist prose writing. In contrast, Wilson Harris, though another admirer of Conrad (and of *Heart of Darkness*, which he describes as a "threshold text" exhibiting the limits and contradictions of colonialist paradigms), argues that realist conventions adopted by writers like Naipaul, at least in early novels like *A House for Mr. Biswas* (1961), are inappropriate for postcolonial novelists. Describing the nineteenth-century realist European novel as the product of European societies concerned with consolidating "their class and other vested interests," Harris declares that:

> "[C]haracter" in the novel rests ... on the self-sufficient individual – on elements of "persuasion" ... rather than "dialogue" or "dialectic." ... The novel of persuasion rests on grounds of apparent common sense: a certain "selection" is made by the writer, the selection of items, manners, uniform conversation, historical situations, etc. all lending themselves to ... present an individual span of life which yields self-conscious and fashionable moralities. The tension which emerges is the tension of individuals – great or small – on an accepted plane of society we are persuaded has an inevitable existence.[11]

Harris goes on to argue that the Caribbean novel should respond to societies in formation, to the fragmented histories of those who inhabit the Caribbean and Latin America (or other postcolonial societies), encouraging "plural forms of profound identity" rather than "a persuasion of singular and pathetic enlightenment" (39–40). In his novel *Palace of the Peacock* Harris transforms the central metaphor and image of Conrad's crew voyaging into the interior of the continent. For Harris an ethnically diverse crew, representing the Portuguese, Amerindian, African, Indian, English, and German strands that have contributed to Guyanese society, merge and flow into past and present characters, and into a dreamlike landscape and journey. The main protagonist, Donne, sometimes imaged on horseback and reminiscent of one of the conquistadors as well as the English metaphysical poet, sometimes referring to Conrad's Kurtz (as when Donne recalls "that horror and that hell he had himself elaborately constructed from which to rule his earth"),[12] merges with members of the crew and with the landscape, so dissolving binary distinctions between native and settler, or civilized person and savage. Although written in prose, in terms of narrative *Palace of the Peacock* seems closer to T. S. Eliot's *The Waste Land*, with its surreal transformations of past and present characters, its symbolically charged landscape, and its metaphysical quest.

Conrad's influence, sometimes mediated through writers like Harris, Naipaul, and Ngugi wa Thiong'o, continues in the works of a later generation of postcolonial novelists, including Abdulrazak Gurnah and Amitav Ghosh. Gurnah's *Paradise* reclaims territory that provides the setting for *Heart of Darkness* and *A Bend in the River*. It also revisits the historical period central to Achebe's and Ngugi wa Thiong'o's early novels, the colonial encounter, in Gurnah's case the German occupation of East Africa. Whereas early postcolonial novels re-create a homogeneous local community as an image of an indigenous national community undermined and oppressed by historical change, later novelists place greater emphasis on diversity and tension within the national community. Spatial difference becomes as significant as changes over time. In *Paradise* Gurnah depicts a complex society shaped by centuries of immigration and trade. The novel begins with the boyhood of Yusuf, whose Muslim Swahili family draw boundaries between themselves and other ethnic and religious groups – the Washenzi, who, according to his father, "have no faith in God and who worship spirits and demons which live in trees and rocks";[13] the Indian storekeeper; the laborers from the interior. But as Yusuf travels from the restricted, restrictive world of his father to encounters with different peoples and cultures, the novel combines adventure fiction with the *Bildungsroman* and romance. The combination is given a deeper cultural context and resonance through its continuing allusion to the Koranic and biblical story of Yusuf/Joseph, the handsome boy and interpreter of dreams, who was sold into bondage. According to some commentators, the Koran's "sura Yusuf" "was recited by the Prophet Mohammed as 'the best story'; it constitutes one of the most narrated popular tales of the oral tradition, [and] continues to the present day to be a centrally important narrative in Islamic cultures."[14]

Yusuf's journey into the interior and his encounter with the greed and cruelty of Europeans, Arabs, and Africans alike, parallels the expedition narrated by another Joseph. Abdulrazak Gurnah states that he understands that "history, far from being a rational discourse, is successively rewritten and fought over to support a particular argument,"[15] and that although his novel does not attempt to rewrite *Heart of Darkness*, he finds Conrad's "ironical view of the whole enterprise of imperialism. . .useful to resonate against. This activity that Conrad saw as destructive to the European mind also destroyed the African mind and landscape."[16] *Paradise* brings to life competing constructions of history as Yusuf, his friend Khalil, his master Aziz, the Sikh mechanic Kalasinga, and the African chief Chatu all create, and seek to impose, their own versions of past and present realities. But the novel discards the maps and charts, the named territories and borders, whereby travelers and readers interpret East Africa. We learn only of "the lakes to the west of the highlands" rather than "Lake Tanganyika" and "Lake Victoria," so that we experience the wonder and awe of discovering the interior for the first time from the perspective of Yusuf's consciousness, which is grounded in a specific cultural mix of anecdotes, stories, and beliefs. The historical markers, the sites of an imposed set of settler memories, are erased, although for the contemporary reader their ghostly presence remains. Gurnah's novel shows how Nora's description of "a turning point where consciousness of a break with the past is bound up with a sense that memory has been torn" is indeed pertinent to the project of postcolonial writers. And *Paradise* implicitly contrasts a series of oral histories, based on memory and attuned to specific landscapes, with the written histories through which contemporary readers have encountered the colonial and postcolonial pasts of Kenya, Tanzania, and Zaire.

Yusuf tells the story of his journey at night-time as Marlow does, but the difference between Marlow's description of the terrain – disorienting fog, confusion, and shadowy figures – and Yusuf's experience of the sublimity and clarity of the mountain heights is striking. Gurnah's narrator passes through experiences of profound disorientation, but emerges into a new and grounded consciousness. In contrast to Marlow's blurred and bemused account of the river banks he passes, Yusuf's report of the mountains and lakes is detailed and precise:

> "The light on the mountain is green," [Yusuf] said. "Like no light I've ever imagined. And the air is as if it has been washed clean. In the morning when the sun strikes the peak of snow, it feels like eternity. Like a moment that will never change ... One afternoon near a lake I saw two fish eagles calmly roosting on a branch of a gum tree. Then suddenly both of them whooped with great energy, two or three fierce yells with neck bent and the open beak pointing at the sky, wings pumping and body stretched taut. After a moment, a faint reply came back across the lake. A few minutes later, a white feather detached itself from the male bird, and in that great silence it drifted slowly to the ground." (180)

This passage marks Yusuf's movement toward a new acuteness of perception, and toward a new eloquence and authority of speech. Prior to the expedition he had been teasingly called a *"feeble kifa urongo"* (meaning living death – a kind of zombie); he asked questions but made no pronouncements, and it was his older friend Khalil and his "Uncle" Aziz who seemed to possess authoritative knowledge. Now it is Khalil who listens enthralled by Yusuf's account of a world beyond, and Khalil whom Yusuf rebukes when his friend rejoices over a savage beating suffered by the Arab foreman of the expedition and delivered on Chatu's orders.

One of Achebe's fiercest criticisms regarding Conrad's portrayal of Africans in *Heart of Darkness* alleges Conrad's refusal "to confer language on the 'rudimentary souls' of Africa. They only 'exchanged short grunting phrases' even among themselves but mostly they were too busy with their frenzy."[17] The emphasis on orality, storytelling, and the power of speech-making in Achebe's novels provides a forceful counter to Conrad's linguistically disadvantaged Africans. Achebe's stress on the full humanity of the Igbo people through the richness and the particularity of their speech is characteristic of other postcolonial fiction, including *Ulysses* and *Midnight's Children*. Gurnah makes articulate not only Yusuf, but also many of his other characters who throughout the novel tell stories and myths from disparate backgrounds. Gurnah shares with other postcolonial novelists a concern to reveal the presence and humanity of marginalized people – women, ethnic minorities, bonded servants – within the larger nation. His use of the Koranic story of Yusuf, rather like Achebe's use of the story of Abraham and Isaac in *Things Fall Apart* with regard to the fate of Ikemefuna, calls attention to the difference between the ending of the ancient and the more modern tale. Whereas the Koran relates Yusuf's rise to power and honor, Gurnah's Yusuf realizes his own powerlessness in comparison with the wealthy Arab merchant certain of his superiority or the European with his flag and soldiers. "But Yusuf had neither a flag nor righteous knowledge with which to claim superior honor, and he thought he understood that the small world he knew was the only one available to him" (236–237).

The novel ends with a defeat in some ways more tragic than Okonkwo's resistance, for Yusuf cannot aspire to heroism, and sees joining the German regiment led by an officer with "the face of a cadaver" (reminiscent of Kurtz) as his only option. Through their responses to the often restricted world around them, and through their speech, the humanity of Khalil, Yusuf, and his beloved Amina is fully realized, so that we understand not only how much they have been damaged, how much has been taken away from them, but also how much is lost through their powerlessness to fulfill their potential.

Amitav Ghosh is a novelist of the same generation as Gurnah whose work responds to Conrad and Naipaul. He has written of his delight on discovering Naipaul's early novels and Naipaul's essay on the ways in which "the flowers of the Caribbean were rendered invisible by the unseen daffodils of text-book English poets."[18] Ghosh goes on to declare that

> it was Naipaul who first made it possible for me to think of myself as a writer in English . . . I read him with that intimate, appalled attention which one reserves for one's most skilful interlocutors. . . . The word "influence" seems inadequate for a circumstance like this: it is as though Naipaul's work were a whetstone against which to sharpen my own awareness of the world. (1)

The Shadow Lines (1988), Ghosh's second novel, develops and reworks the Naipaulian portrayal in *The Mimic Men* (1967) of "a world defined," as Ghosh says, "by what it lacked" (2), and the consequent inability of "Third World" citizens and their leaders to perceive and grasp the reality that surrounds them. Ghosh's title alludes to Conrad's semi-autobiographical *The Shadow-Line* (1916) and like Conrad's novella is a first-person narrative exploring the shadow line that marks the transit from youth to maturity, a moment of realization when the narrator's understanding of the past is transformed. Conrad dedicates his novella to his son Borys "and all others who like himself have crossed in early youth the shadow-line of their generation" through the experience of fighting in World War I. For Ghosh's narrator it is World War II and the partition of India that changes forever the relationships and perceived realities of the older members of his family and their English friends. For the narrator himself it is the communal riots in Calcutta and Dhaka that are later understood as a shadowy moment of change, obscure also because the memory of them has been repressed by the narrator personally and excised from written histories and living memories. The link between the individual memory or absence of it, and a context of written and spoken narratives, is made when the narrator acknowledges that:

> Every word I write about those events of 1964 is the product of a struggle with silence . . . The enemy of silence is speech, but there can be no speech without words, and there can be no words without meanings – so it follows, inexorably, in the manner of syllogisms, that when we try to speak of events of which we do not know the meaning, we must lose ourselves in the silence that lies in the gap between the words and the world.[19]

The struggle with silence, as we learn, the questioning of other people's memories and narratives, is a function not only of time but geography. The shadow lines, in the plural, refer also to the lines drawn on maps, defining national borders and relationships. Such lines create political divisions, and nationalist histories, which in the case of the subdivision of Bengal and of the Indian subcontinent both create and erase individual identities. The earlier partition of India in 1947 is mirrored in the division of the grandmother's family house, with walls built through rooms, and the resulting bitterness between members of a once close family. But such divisions also cut across memories and lived experiences, so that the narrator's grandmother cannot understand how though born in Dhaka, which she thinks of as her home, and from where she once traveled freely back and forth to Calcutta, she now possesses a different national identity.

Although one can see *The Shadow Lines* as a *Bildungsroman* in which the narrator progresses from innocent childhood to enlightened maturity, its structure fluidly evokes the past in the present, and dramatizes the shadow cast by the past on the present in the memories of characters who move between London and Calcutta. Moreover, the memories that impinge on the characters are frequently the memories of others, indeed are invented memories. Influenced by his uncle and mentor Tridib, the narrator tries to explain to his cosmopolitan cousin Ila that "a place does not merely exist, that it has to be invented in one's imagination; that her practical, bustling London was no less invented than mine, neither more nor less true, only very far apart" (21). For Ghosh, even more than for Gurnah, locations function as sites of alternative memories and histories, although for Ghosh it is urban, man-made sites that are particularly evocative. There is irony in the intensity with which Indian visitors like the narrator preserve the histories of buildings in London, histories now forgotten by the Londoners themselves.

Ila's cosmopolitanism differs from that of the narrator's or her uncle Tridib's, in that it engages space rather than time, geographical differences rather than historical ones. It is the airport of any city that defines that city for her. Whereas the narrator's identity and history is grounded in Calcutta, as is his grandmother's in Dhaka, Ila can orient herself as well in one city as another. One might see hers as a postmodern cosmopolitanism rather than a postcolonial one. Ghosh's narrator is at first entranced by Ila's glamor. But as he matures he embraces a different kind of cosmopolitanism, one that acknowledges a multitude of shadow lines, real and imagined, geographical and historical, where spaces are imbued with memories and stories. *The Shadow Lines* articulates an understanding that informs a great many post-colonial novels in that, as Dipesh Chakrabarty puts it, they hold "history, the discipline, and other forms of memory together so that they can help in the interrogation of each other, to work out the ways these immiscible forms of recalling the past are juxtaposed."[20]

Notes

1. Pierre Nora, "Between Memory and History: *Les Lieux de Mémoire*," trans. Marc Roudebush, in *History and Memory in African-American Culture*, ed. Geneviève Fabre and Robert O'Meally (New York: Oxford University Press, 1994), p. 284.

2. G. W. F. Hegel, *The Philosophy of History*, trans. J. Sibree (New York: The Colonial Press, 1900), pp. 91, 99.

3. Joyce Cary, Preface to *The African Witch* (London: Michael Joseph, 1952), p. 12.

4. Benjamin Disraeli, letter to *The Times*, April 18, 1836 (published under the pseudonym "Runnymede" in the series "Letters to Statesmen") http://www.archive.org/stream/whigswhiggismpoloodisruoft/whigswhiggismpoloodisruoft_djvu.txt (accessed December 16, 2010).

5. Chinua Achebe, "The Role of the Writer in a New Nation," *Nigeria Magazine* 81 (1964), 157–160, 157.

6. Chinua Achebe, *Things Fall Apart* (London: Heinemann Educational Books, 1976), p. 3.

7. Quoted by Kwame Anthony Appiah, *In My Father's House* (New York: Oxford University Press, 1992), p. 73.

8. Linda Hutcheon, "'Circling the Downspout of Empire': Post-Colonialism and Postmodernism," *Ariel* 20: 4 (1989), 149–175, 154.

9. Amata Ata Aidoo, *Our Sister Killjoy: Reflections from a Black-Eyed Squint* (Harlow: Longman, 1977), pp. 28–29.

10. V. S. Naipaul, *The Return of Eva Peron* with *The Killings in Trinidad* (London: André Deutsch, 1977), p. 216.

11. Wilson Harris, *Tradition, the Writer, and Society: Critical Essays* (London: New Beacon Press, 1967), pp. 28–29.

12. Wilson Harris, *Palace of the Peacock* (London: Faber, 1960), p. 130.

13. Abdulrazak Gurnah, *Paradise* (London: Hamish Hamilton, 1994), p. 6.

14. Gayane Karen Merguerian and Afsenah Najmabadi, "Zulaykha and Yusuf: Whose 'Best Story'?," *Journal of Middle Eastern Studies* 29: 4 (1997), 485–508, 485.

15. Abdulrazak Gurnah, "An Idea of the Past," *Moving Worlds: A Journal of Transcultural Writings*, Special Issue: *Reflections*, 2: 2 (2002), 16.

16. Quoted in M. Brace, "Question Marks over the Empire's Decision," *The Independent*, 10 September 1994, p. 24.

17. Chinua Achebe, "An Image of Africa," *The Chancellor's Lecture Series, 1974–75* (Amherst: University of Massachusetts Press, 1975), p. 35.

18. Amitav Ghosh, "Naipaul and the Nobel" (2001) http://www.amitavghosh.com/essays/essayfull.php?essayNo=55 (accessed December 16, 2010).
19. Amitav Ghosh, *The Shadow Lines* (New York: Houghton Mifflin, 2005), pp. 213–214.
20. Dipesh Chakrabarty, *Provincializing Europe: Postcolonial Thought and Historical Difference* (Princeton University Press, 2000), pp. 93–94.

52

History and heritage: the English novel's persistent historiographical turn

PETER CHILDS

Historical fiction, "heritage" fiction: a survey

A renewal of the genre of historical fiction has been a defining aspect of literary production since the appearance of John Fowles's *The French Lieutenant's Woman* in 1969. Fowles's reimagining of nineteenth-century history and the Victorian novel heralded a range of new fictions covering multiple historical eras. This flourishing of the historical genre, besides complementing critical theory and self-conscious historiography, contributed to the reorientation of imperial history by postcolonial writers, particularly after the success of Salman Rushdie's *Midnight's Children* in 1981.

In light of a strong probability that the past attracts British novelists because it is grander than the post-imperial present, historical fiction appears to A. S. Byatt to be a way of turning away from the complexities of the contemporary world.[1] This is a viewpoint that has been brought to bear upon Byatt's own writing and on that of others who use contemporary license to lay bare and exploit the past. Richard Bradford writes:

> The notion of the past as an exciting, edifying point of contrast with the present is a mainstay of recent historical fiction but there is a factor that goes beyond this and which is evident in the work of [William] Boyd, [Adam] Thorpe, [Peter] Ackroyd, [Rose] Tremain et al., and it is this. Irrespective of gestures toward lost periods as independent worlds there is a prevailing . . . inclination among practitioners of the new historical novel toward lofty omniscience. The past is offered up in its fascinating . . . peculiarity yet such gestures are underpinned by an implicit claim on the part of the author. The unpredictable mechanisms and trajectories of history seem now to have given way to a state of irreversible stasis and torpidity, and from this secure perspective novelists assume to know the past better than it knew itself.[2]

If Bradford is right, the past becomes the silent subaltern that cannot speak back to the present-day novelist, who treats it as narrative canvas for contemporary ideas.

This is no doubt a distortion, at the very least a perspective to be debated. The debate is further unfolded in this chapter's last section. To be sure, the core of British and Irish historical fiction remains an interplay between present invention and an already documented past. Invention supersedes historical verisimilitude in recent writings because of novelists' awareness of the textual nature of representation and of the possibilities of intertextual richness. While still tracing connections between past and present, the last half-century's historical novelists often do not attempt to depict the past transparently or authentically. But they also do not succumb to an undermining of historical meaning altogether. Instead they question official or accepted understandings of historical narratives (especially nation-centered ones) partly by moving away from conventions in the rendition of character, speech, and place – eschewing reconstruction of the past for reframing of it. Reframing enlists pastiche, irony, self-conscious reflexivity, and overt intertextual reference, as is evident at the start of J. G. Farrell's *The Siege of Krishnapur* (1973), which rewrites the opening of Forster's *A Passage to India* (1924), and toys with the tropes of imperial travel-writing and adventure fiction.

The surge in retrospective fiction has led to an interest in the past as a heritage. "Heritage" is associated – if we follow Robert Hewison's cultural study *The Heritage Industry* (1987) – with an emotionally charged but historically static reconstruction of the past for leisure consumption. Nevertheless, at the same time, according to the historian Raphael Samuel, "Heritage is also proving quite crucial in the construction of postcolonial identities . . . heritage helps to support both a multi-ethnic vision of the future and a more pluralist one of the past."[3] For Farrell the benefit of the historical novel is to recontextualize accepted understanding of the past and defamiliarize the present. For a novelist interested in ideas, the past gives the opportunity to examine people "undergoing history," as Farrell says of *Troubles* (1970), his novel about Ireland's road to independence:

> I wanted . . . to use this period of the past as a metaphor for today, because I believe that however much the superficial detail and customs of life may change over the years . . . life itself does not change very much, indeed all literature that survives must depend on this assumption. Another reason . . . I preferred to use the past is that, as a rule, people have already made up their minds about the present.[4]

In terms of racial politics there is a noticeable shift in the 1990s to a concern with reclaimed histories, the "black Atlantic," and ethnic and religious differences, powerfully explored in novels by S. I. Martin (*Incomparable World* [1996]) and

Caryl Phillips (*Cambridge* [1991]). Similar exploration is evident in novels by white writers, such as Barry Unsworth in *Sacred Hunger* (1992), a condemnation of the eighteenth-century slave trade that exemplifies the shift from novels with an element of "Raj" nostalgia to a more overt concern with the legacy of colonialism. Hari Kunzru's *The Impressionist* (2002) uses myriad literary intertexts to chart colonial mimicry across the first half of the twentieth century. Kunzru's elevation of intertextual over historical reference is a characteristic formal shift. Andrea Levy's *Small Island* (2004) retells postwar British history through the voices of four interlinked multicultural first-person narrators, each supplying a perspective on the legacy of war and empire for race relations. These examples of revisioned heritage can be considered to differ from previous historical fiction in their aim less to describe the prehistory of the present than to write the past in ways that its contemporary novelists did not – or could not.

The legacy of John Fowles

The template for historical and heritage narratives, exhibiting a pronounced temporal double-consciousness, is *The French Lieutenant's Woman*. Fowles offers a contemporary commentary on the (ideas of the) past in theoretical as well as historical hindsight, incorporating specimens of Victorian literature in his text as part of its re-creation of the past, yet simultaneously introducing a sense of alternative narrative possibilities in history as well as art.

The novel is set a hundred years before its writing. Startlingly, Fowles says of *The French Lieutenant's Woman* that "I don't think of it as a historical novel, a genre in which I have very little interest." He notes that a novel is something new and not an attempt to record the past: "You are not trying to write something one of the Victorian novelists forgot to write; but perhaps something one of them failed to write."[5] Aiming to forge an existentialist Victorian novel – a necessarily anachronistic aim – Fowles pictures his male protagonist Charles as someone who has absorbed the facts of evolution in an indifferent, godless universe. Which is to say that Fowles wants to make sure the reader never forgets that his novel is written in 1967, in a post-existentialist and post-Darwinian world. Moreover, Fowles the novelist has absorbed the lessons of his own time, in the avant-garde theories of Alain Robbe-Grillet and Roland Barthes. Accordingly, Fowles wants to unmask the authority of the omniscient author and so places himself in a railway carriage with Charles, where the two of them encounter each other on the same ontological plane. Fowles also contests the boundaries between reality and fiction. This has an especial relevance to writing about the past. He declares in the novel: "You do not even think of your own past as quite real; you dress it up, you gild it or blacken it, censor it, tinker with it . . . fictionalize it, in a word, and put it away on a shelf – your book, your romanticised autobiography."[6] As part of the "romanticised" aspect, Fowles thinks that his characters must speak a distant-sounding language rather than an historically authentic one. For what matters is not authenticity but what will fit with "our psychological picture of the Victorians" ("Notes," 15). Literary dialogue is rarely very close to transcribed language; and this distance foregrounds its artifice, which undermines other impulses toward verisimilitude, including historical accuracy. Furthermore, Fowles believes that writing a novel set in the past from the perspective of the present will involve descriptions that the Victorians would not have under-taken, such as accounts of characters in bed together.

Fowles was not trying to rewrite Victorian fiction, but to comment explic-itly from his era on "An age where woman was sacred; and where you could buy a thirteen-year-old girl for a few pounds" (French Lieutenant's Woman, 231). With a similar recognition of present sensibilities, Fowles makes explicit the future implications of what is happening at the time of his story in ways that would have gone unrecognized in 1867. That Darwinism will "reduce morality to a hypocrisy and duty to a straw hut in a hurricane" (French Lieutenant's Woman, 106) is not a sentiment from the period, even though the metaphor of "the straw hut" might be.

The point to emphasize is that Fowles inaugurates approaches that will be used and modified by future writers of fiction set in the past. A. S. Byatt's Possession (1990) mines the crisis of faith and the rise of Darwinism alongside Fowles-inspired pastiche versions of Tennyson, the Rossettis, and the Brownings. In the 1980s and 1990s Angela Carter, Pat Barker, and Sarah Waters set their characters' lives in the Victorian and Edwardian past, but express the characters' carnal exploits in ways that fiction of the past could not. Barker starts The Eye in the Door (1993), the middle volume of The Regeneration trilogy, by describing two of Billy Prior's sexual encounters, the second of which is with a man, in terms that would have appeared only in Edwardian pornography. Angela Carter explores the sexuality of her Victorian characters in Nights at the Circus (1984) and Sarah Waters's repu-tation is built on post-realist Sapphic takes on Victorian and Edwardian Britain in Tipping the Velvet (1998), Affinity (1999), and Fingersmith (2002). Other formal characteristics that Fowles initiates for later historical or heritage fiction include header quotations from contemporary writings; multiple endings; modern references (e.g. "the Sartrean experience,"

French Lieutenant's Woman, 278); self-conscious clichés ("He knew if he looked into those eyes he was lost," 302); footnotes commenting on the text; and unacknowledged borrowings from the period, such as the closing lines of Fowles's novel, from Matthew Arnold's "To Marguerite" (echoing the poem's use earlier in the text). The writing is neither realist nor "postmodern," but a blend in which self-consciousness is evident throughout, displaying an awareness and use of the conventions of the past as well as engaging and criticizing them from the author's own historical moment, which itself – the claim appears to be – cannot be transcended.

Byatt's indebtedness to Fowles shows itself in a dialogue between experimentalism and realism in her work. The experimental aspect interweaves realist historical fiction with "distance from it by ironizing its conventions."[7] She scrutinizes the past from a modern perspective in *Angels and Insects* (1992), *The Biographer's Tale* (1999), and *The Children's Book* (2009), and most tellingly in *Possession*. With its title signaling "the question of what it means to take hold of the past,"[8] the novel grapples with philosophical questions of historical appropriation that Fowles ignores. Accordingly, the novel mocks its own attempt to give the past its voice through painstaking fidelity to the styles of Victorian poets: the ventriloquisms cannot escape the appropriative impulse that assimilates the past by distorting it. Recognition of the distortion accounts for Byatt's decision to frame the book not as a novel but, according to its subtitle, a (historical) "romance." At the same time, Byatt notes that in the 1950s the historical novel was frowned on as "escapist" or pigeon-holed as "pastoral," but that it has proved more durable than the majority of "urgent fictive confrontations of immediate contemporary reality" despite its being tagged as "nostalgic" and "costume drama" (Byatt, *On Histories and Stories*, 9). (One is reminded of L. H. Meyers's preface to his 1929 novel *The Near and the Far*, which says that the book is not about its ostensible subject, sixteenth-century India, but is an attempt to view the problems of interwar Europe "from the distant vantage point of an imaginary world."[9]) What Byatt suggests is that the present can confront itself by becoming more conscious of its appropriations of the past and of the way those appropriations construct a cultural identity. The logic here is shared by Farrell. Beryl Bainbridge explores another version of Byatt's suggestion in novels about British self-fashioning of its national consciousness. The sinking of the *Titanic* in *Every Man for Himself* (1996), the Crimean War in *Master Georgie* (1998), and Scott's South Pole expedition in *The Birthday Boys* (1991) stimulate readers to reflect self-consciously on what the celebrity of certain historical events means for self-affirming and self-congratulatory constructions of the present.

"Self," and writing about it, is adjudged by Byatt as an exhausted modernist tradition. The historical turn is partly predicated on escape from subjectivity and its inherited authority in fiction. An ally of the escape might be the de-authorizing of classical novelists that occurs when Byatt and others attempt to rewrite the literary "heritage" – i.e. the fiction of the past. This kind of rewriting might well illustrate Hewison's charge that a heritage industry results from the emptiness of the present. But such revision seeks to give readers new ways to read and evaluate the "classics," and to dramatize the way great authors are less original and unique than fantasies about them suggest. Jean Rhys's *Wide Sargasso Sea* (1966), a rewriting of *Jane Eyre*, set the precedent. Toby Litt's *Finding Myself* (2003) situates Woolf's *To the Lighthouse* as a constant intertext. Gilbert Adair's *The Act of Roger Murgatroyd* (2006) and Peter Ackroyd's *The Casebook of Victor Frankenstein* (2008) build on Agatha Christie and Mary Shelley to create response-novels to earlier texts. This is a phenomenon allied to a more conservative trend that produces sequels or prequels to canonical work. Jeffrey Caine's *Heathcliff* (1992) and Lin Haire-Sargeant's *Heathcliff: The Return to Wuthering Heights* (1992) follow Brontë; Sally Beauman's *Rebecca's Tale* (2001) and Susan Hill's *Mrs. De Winter* (1998) rewrite Daphne du Maurier's *Rebecca* (1938). Inevitably there has been a sequel to Waugh, Michael Johnston's *Brideshead Regained: Continuing the Memoirs of Charles Ryder* (2003). These latter ventures seem especially complicit with the commercial packaging of "heritage."

After *The French Lieutenant's Woman* the nineteenth century and the Edwardian period appeared to be as commonplace settings for fiction as the later twentieth century, although the settings exhibit a double historical consciousness, contrasting past and present. Graham Swift's *Ever After* (1992) interleaves a modern story with a Victorian back-history; Giles Foden's *Ladysmith* (1999) is a Boer War novel. These are experimental works that explicitly doubt the power of storytelling but nevertheless remain within the traditions of verisimilitude, as does Julian Barnes's re-examination of Arthur Conan Doyle's real-life investigation of the Edalji horse-maiming case in *Arthur and George* (2005). By contrast, a staunch anti-realism is evident in Carter's *Nights at the Circus*, a fantastical exploration of ideas about first-wave feminism, gender, and sexuality at the end of the nineteenth century. Carter's novel finds gothic kin in Alasdair Gray's Stevensonian *Poor Things* (1992).

Despite the vogue for neo-Victorian fiction, the earlier centuries have steadily asserted their claims to interest. Barry Unsworth's *Morality Play* (1995) is set in the years following the Black Death; John Banville's *Kepler*

(1981), Jeanette Winterson's *Sexing the Cherry* (1989), Ackroyd's *The House of Doctor Dee* (1993), and Lawrence Norfolk's *The Pope's Rhinoceros* (1996) turn to the early modern era. Hilary Mantel's *Wolf Hall*, winner of the Mann Booker Prize in 2009, is described by one of the judges as a "contemporary novel, a modern novel, which happens to be set in the 16th Century."[10] Ronan Bennett's *Havoc in Its Third Year* (2004) is an allegorical scrutiny of religious conflicts in pre-Civil War England, and Rose Tremain's picaresque *Restoration* (1989) is about a medical student who has to survive his own personal revolution when sent away from the court of Charles II.

With regard to fiction set pre-1800, Amy Elias argues that an increasing number of contemporary novels set in the eighteenth century show that fiction is revisiting the inaugural era of modernity, which saw the rise of modern democratic politics, science, medicine, law, industry, and the state.[11] Norfolk's *Lemprière's Dictionary* (1991) values the gifts of modernity, but the number of anti-Enlightenment fictions is impressive. The "heritage" here appears decidedly untrustworthy. Fowles's *A Maggot* (1985) and Ackroyd's *Chatterton* (1987), Ackroyd's study of deadly geometry in the positioning of six London churches in *Hawksmoor* (1985), Unsworth's *Sugar and Rum* (1988) about the Liverpool slave trade, and Malcolm Bradbury's *To the Hermitage* (2000) treating Diderot's encyclopedia, are all darker takes on the legacy of Enlightenment. Philippa Gregory's *Wildacre* trilogy (1987–1990) juxtaposes the eighteenth century with the Thatcherite 1980s, to the credit of neither. Significantly, however, Alex Murray's critical study *Recalling London* (2007) sees writing like Ackroyd's precisely in terms of 1980s' Thatcherite "blue plaque" London redevelopment (focussing on areas like Clerkenwell, Spitalfields, Limehouse, and Holborn), contrasting this with Iain Sinclair's more politically engaged – and, despite its inventiveness, more historically grounded – representation of London as contested psycho-geography in *Downriver* (1991).

The shared relation of historical and heritage novels with postcolonial texts is not to be underestimated. By virtue of the novel form's current intervention in history writing – an intervention that is by now another inheritance – writers rarely considered in the postcolonial camp, such as Philip Hensher, who re-presents Kipling's vision of the Great Game in Afghanistan by writing with knowledge of contemporary Kabul in *The Mulberry Empire* (2002), come into alignment with the postcolonial tradition. The common desire is to counter accepted historical narratives, and to redirect them, by writing against the grain, using the forms of realism to render verisimilitude and causation, but also employing myth or analogy to proceed by parallel and parallax.

The redirection, beginning with Chinua Achebe's subversion of adventure fiction's Africa in *Things Fall Apart* (1958), continues in David Dabydeen, Amitav Ghosh, and Salman Rushdie, whose experiments with narrative form recover other sites of empire from the way official history represents them. And to judge by Mohsin Hamid's *The Reluctant Fundamentalist* (2007), it is narrative not facts or details that matter most: "I am, after all, telling you a history, and in history . . . it is the thrust of one's narrative that counts, not the accuracy of one's details."[12]

For one present generation of novelists the First World War and its aftermath has become a major genealogical touchstone, uncannily repeating the backward look at the war that in the fiction of the 1920s produces Ford Madox Ford's magisterial tetralogy *Parade's End* (1924–1928). In Ford it is the protagonists whose immediate impressions constitute history and yet also misrecognize it, so that they often stand in need of correction. In the historical novels that now revisit the Great War, the novelists themselves continue the revisionary, corrective process. The latest representations range from Sebastian Faulks's *Birdsong* (1993), the story of a family tree leading back to the Western Front, to Adam Thorpe's German-set *Nineteen Twenty-One* (2001), Sebastian Barry's *A Long Long Way* (2005) and Barry Unsworth's *Land of Marvels* (2008). Following on from examples such as Isabel Colegate's *The Shooting Party* (1980), which centers on a country house in 1913 to depict the decay of a class soon to be responsible for the slaughter of millions, Pat Barker's *Regeneration* trilogy revisits the Great War from the perspective of the 1990s, when sexual explicitness is already a long-established inheritance from modernism, and when new doubts about the distorting effects on history of twentieth-century psychology and anthropology undergird doubts about historical truth itself. Environed by such doubts, the trilogy nevertheless presents an attempt at surmounting them.

Set in 1917–1918, *Regeneration* (1991), *The Eye in the Door*, and *The Ghost Road* (1995) trace the effects of war on individual responsibility and identity. Avoiding matter-of-fact realism, Barker peppers the trilogy with ghostly presences and visions of the dead, drawing a parallel between those hauntings and the twentieth century's fascination with memory and recovered pasts. Perhaps unsatisfied that reviews of the trilogy had failed to realize that she was not writing traditionally realistic "historical fiction," Barker in her next novel *Another World* (1998) insists more explicitly on connections between the early and the late twentieth century. She sets the novel in the present but makes it about the past and writes in the continuous present, imitating how the past is still real for traumatized Geordie Lucas, a one-hundred-and-one-year old First

World War veteran who believes his cancer is a consequence of a 1916 bayonet wound – an eighty-year-old injury – that has come back to kill him. For Barker the key fact of the First World War is that it remains in the collective memory as a persistent traumatic experience that has been insufficiently addressed or acknowledged. Barker is not interested in suggesting that the past will be enacted again, but that its presence endures, like defamiliarized public statuary. Barker's war memorial is Geordie, haunted by his part in the death of his brother in the war: a ghost-presence that suggests the proximity of different temporalities, the presence of history – as if behind a layer of wallpaper or a shut door – informing and shaping interpretations of persons and their identities. While the ineffable specter of the past remains, so does the guilt, grief, and mental or physical scars that remain largely unconfronted by a wider society, and even by politicians or historians who speak against the repression of the past but who do not feel the need for confrontation and closure of those for whom the past is a "central silence, a dark star."[13]

A treatment of the past in an earlier novelist, L. P. Hartley (who stands midway between modernism and the end of the twentieth century) can help to focus Barker's interest in the past as a *public* concern. For Hartley in *The Go-Between* (1953) returning to the past is like a venture into a foreign country, and a way of recalling a pre-Great War world, before "the alienation, the destruction, and the disillusionment"[14] of the present. Hartley's Leo Colston, in order to confront his present world-shy condition, must understand the trauma of his part in an illicit love affair and a suicide when he was twelve and on a visit to an upper-class family in rural Norfolk in 1900. Hartley wants to explore the psychology of Leo's longing for a past world he remembers but did not understand; Barker aims to dramatize the lives of individuals to make a connection in public memory. Both novels are interested in story and characterization rather than fictional self-reflexiveness, and both operate through a double-consciousness of two eras; but whereas Leo Colston needs to untangle a prelapsarian Edwardianism that meshes innocence and guilt within a purely private sphere, Barker's book is concerned with representing the War as a collective public legacy.

The interwar years and the Second World War have formed the historical-intertextual backdrop to Penelope Lively's *Moontiger* (1987) and *City of the Mind* (1991), Kazuo Ishiguro's *When We Were Orphans* (2000), Rachel Seiffert's *The Dark Room* (2001), Sarah Waters's *The Night Watch* (2006), and Ian McEwan's *Atonement* (2001). As an example of the dilemma faced by fiction with a pronounced consciousness of different historical eras, *Atonement* places itself in a tradition of novels from Austen to Henry Green in its use of the country house, and so runs the risk of supplementing the staple "heritage" diet of novels about aristocratic big houses. McEwan attempts to subvert this association by intruding a victimized working-class hero in Robbie Turner (and a rapacious upper-class war profiteer who acts with impunity) into the life of a *nouveau riche* family, the Tallises. Their house, Tilney's, is deemed a gauche and tasteless gothic revival pile dating from the 1890s, but it has become a heritage site by the end of the novel when the narrator returns in 1999 to find it has become Tilney's Hotel. McEwan writes of Tilney's: "Morning sunlight, or any light, could not conceal the ugliness of the Tallis home ... bright orange brick, squat, lead-paned baronial Gothic, to be condemned one day in an article by Pevsner."[15] This is no *Brideshead Revisited* recidivism, but a narrative suffused with literary nostalgia for the country-house novel nonetheless, even if one that places an ethical rather than purely aesthetic emphasis on ways of representing the past.

Theoretical perspectives on history and "heritage" in fiction

The historical novel has been the object of considerable critical scrutiny. This has resulted from developments across twentieth-century theories of literature, cultural studies, and postcolonial studies. New historicist and post-modernist approaches to "historiographical metafiction" have complicated modernist and postmodernist relations with the (texts of the) past still further. A convergence between past fiction and historical fiction has also been remarked: a novel from the past, Fredric Jameson writes in *Postmodernism*, "has necessarily become for us a historical one."[16] Like the word-for-word rewriting centuries later of Cervantes' ur-novel *Don Quixote* in Jorge Luis Borges's "Pierre Menard, Author of the Quixote," historical fiction might be distinguishable from the writing of the past only by its later publication date.

The first widely influential theorist of historical fiction is the Hungarian Marxist Georg Lukács who in *The Historical Novel* (1937) understands it to be a genre that emerges in the early nineteenth century, with Walter Scott, as a formal innovation whose purpose is to help depict the social perspective of the middle classes. Lukács argues that accurate depiction of the historical process provides the basis for evaluating (historical) fiction: the historical novel gives, or should give, a trustworthy picture of how the past leads to the present. Other critics have suggested in contrast to Lukács that it is historical particularity that is most significant for the genre.

In 1971 Avrom Fleishman in *The English Historical Novel* claims that "synthetic imagination" has created the best historical fiction. He concludes that since Woolf's *Between the Acts* (1941), which he designates as the first novel to assimilate historicist relativism, it has been impossible "to write convincingly about the past without building the interpretive process into the structure of the work": only methodological self-consciousness can rescue the historical novelist from costume drama.[17] Fleishman, who claims that his book is the first full-length study in English of the English historical novel, was writing at a time when critical interest in the historical novel was markedly low, in part because it had fallen out of fashion with novelists. Fleishman points toward Mary Renault and William Golding as the most interesting contemporary practitioners, and just misses the emergence in *The French Lieutenant's Woman* of a new variety of methodological self-consciousness in historical fiction.

British fiction did not see in itself, or did not sufficiently recognize, the notable postmodernist metahistorical turn in the 1970s that newly characterized fiction in the USA. Bernard Bergonzi, for example, argues in *The Contemporary British Novel*, a collection of essays edited by Malcolm Bradbury in 1979, that only John Berger's *G.* (1972) is comparable to the fabulations of Pynchon, Barth, and Vonnegut. By 1987, however, with the additional notable examples of Fowles, J. G. Farrell's Empire trilogy, and Anthony Burgess's nineteenth-century historical-biographical novels *Napoleon Symphony: A Novel in Four Movements* (1974) and *ABBA ABBA* (on Keats [1977]), it was possible for Neil McEwan to reconsider UK historical fiction in terms of relativistic perspectives, characterizing it as "yesterday reflected in today's consciousness," and emphasizing that "doubts, detected in the periods in which [Farrell's] novels are set, are adjusted to contemporary consciousness."[18]

In *The Character of Truth* Naomi Jacobs understands the increasingly common appearance of real-life figures in 1980s fiction as a result of the reduction of hegemonic realism in historical writing.[19] Though Jacobs chiefly examines US fiction, the shift becomes apparent in British fiction with Burgess (as in *Nothing Like the Sun: A Story of Shakespeare's Love-Life* [1964] and in his novels mentioned above), and unfolds in the mixtures of historical fiction, historical persons, and reworkings of characters from literary history that follow. Examples would be Robert Nye's *Falstaff* (1976) or Peter Ackroyd's reworking of *Little Dorrit* in *The Great Fire of London* (1982) and Ackroyd's imaginative biography of Dickens (1990). Some of the impulse for mixing biography-centered history with fiction might derive from Lytton Strachey's modernist experiments in biography, as in *Elizabeth and Essex: A Tragic History* (1928), while the mythopoeic anti-realist approach to fiction in Carter and Winterson derives from a key modernist genre-bending blend of "biography" and fiction in Woolf's *Orlando* (1928). Jacobs describes such texts as anti-mimetic "recombinant fiction," "a metafictional game confusing the boundaries between all epistemological categories and forcing readers to recognize their own complicity in the reading process and in the preservation of the myths of power that accumulate around public people" (xx) – and around the myths that accumulate about fictional characters and their authors.

All these experiments with history in fiction-writing set in motion a debate that continues among critics of literature and culture and among historians as well. Although historian Samuel Raphael's affirmative assessment appears earlier in this chapter, his description of the impact of metafictional gaming is wary:

> The idea that the past is a plaything of the present, or . . . a 'metafiction', is only beginning to . . . disturb the tranquillity of professional historians . . . These fictions come to us peppered with epigraph and quotation. They criss-cross . . . historical research and invention: they will sometimes incorporate chunks of what scholars would recognize as original documents, duly footnoted or acknowledged . . . But the purpose is not to establish the real but to make it phantasmagoric, and to suggest that history, like reality, is a chimera.   (429)

Jameson in *Postmodernism* (1991) is also wary, lamenting an "insensible colonization of the present by the nostalgia mode" (20) in which wistful reminiscence, intertextuality, and pastiche replace historical writing. For Jameson "aesthetic style" displaces "'real' history" (20), and the coherent experience depicted in Lukácsian historical fiction dissolves into heterogeneity and aleatory fragments. Jameson seeks to remind us that historicity is neither a representation of the past nor the future but "a perception of the present as history" (284). Hewison's views on "heritage" complement Jameson. There is no perception of the present as history if Hewison is correct to claim that:

> the British have shown themselves uncomfortable with the idea of Culture, whereas they have become entirely comfortable with the word "heritage." "Culture" still suggests at best the preoccupation of a snobbish intellectual elite . . ."Heritage" sounds patriotic, even nationalistic, and summons up the splendours of the past – Shakespeare and Windsor Castle, Elgar and Chatsworth – a world of secure values and an unthreatening social order where the arts supply colourful illustrations to the national narrative.[20]

On the opposite side of the debate are equally strong contentions. Elisabeth Wesseling maintains that "contemporary writers. . .critically comment upon historiography by investigating the nature and function of historical knowledge."[21] Postmodernist self-reflexivity, Wesseling and others maintain, unveils through alterity the orthodoxies of historical writing in an established tradition, and stresses a plurality of not only histories but of historiographies, foregrounding their fictiveness as well as their narrative potency. "Heritage" fiction can do the same, despite pejorative use of the term by critics who want to express historical fiction's complicity with exploitative impulses toward commercially successful entertainment or temporally exotic spectacle. Suzanne Keen observes that in this discussion the terms "history" and "heritage" are freighted with academic and popular baggage that carry an unexamined hierarchy of values.[22] It can in any case be forcefully argued that much contemporary historical fiction recognizes itself as a product of a consumer society but can nevertheless respectably engage with the past even though its ways of doing so are distinct from the renunciation of the burden of history in literary modernism, or from the intended objectivity of the realist historical novel.

An obvious example of the nineteenth-century realist historical novel is Tolstoy's *War and Peace* (1865–1869). Founded on meticulous historical reading and ethnographic investigation, Tolstoy's fictionalizing of the Napoleonic era aims at the close examination of real lives and social and political events through the reconstruction of authentic experience. Tolstoy believes that his novel can thus objectively see the myriad causes of the Napoleonic wars; yet in his novel's "Second Epilogue," a long theoretical essay exploring the nature of history, he advances his idea that individual human actions are not free but instead "bound up with the whole course of history and preordained from all eternity."[23] Such confident assertions of the workings of either history or human experience would be rare in modern historical writing; and indeed Tolstoy's "Second Epilogue" becomes an attack on history writing itself. As such, even Tolstoy's monumental historical realism turns out to predict, and to share, the self-reflexive concern with historiographical method characteristic of historical and heritage fiction more than a century later.

Suzanne Keen names and analyzes a strain of historiographical fiction, "the archival," that explicitly discusses models of history, interpretations of history, and the present's treatment of the past in relation to political aims. The phrase "heritage narratives" is a more capacious classification than Keen's specific "romances of the archive" and suggests fiction that in general represents history in terms of contested understandings of the past. To this extent it might be used without pejorative intent to refer to any texts that foreground a self-awareness of their mediation of the past. One recent book on the role of "heritage" sees its formation already in modernism, and employs the term to denote "the creation of a past that is patently ideological and (thus) nostalgic, defining of collective and individual subjects and rationalizing of unsettling social change."[24] In other words, "heritage narratives," by making their ideological biases clear and by explaining radical collective transformations, can have a progressive impact on readers.

Whether we call the fictions at issue "new historical novels" or "heritage narratives," they are works that acknowledge the irretrievable nature of the past outside of its textual materialization, and they make clear that it is present ideology that regulates the depiction of the past. In doing so, they are especially equipped to disclose the unacknowledged fantasies that achieve official, popular, or influential standing in debates about the nature of identity, community, and nationality. Such novels, as I have suggested above about Barker's work, have emerged from historiographic metafiction in order to address public history along with the imaginary pasts and identities that inform it.

In writing about "the present cult of the English country house," Robert Hewison quotes a passage from Nigel Dennis's *Cards of Identity* (1955):

> This sort of house was once a heart and centre of national identity. A whole world lived in relation to it. Millions knew who they were by reference to it. Hundreds of thousands look back at it, and not only grieve for its passing but still depend on it, non-existent though it is, to tell them who they are. Thousands who never knew it are taught every day to cherish its memory and to believe that without it no man will be able to tell his whereabouts again. (63–64)

In response to such "historical" anchors of personal and collective self-recognition, the historiographical novels that originate with Fowles (and perhaps with roots in modernism) are deliberately unsettling. Julian Barnes's *England, England* (1998) parodies a commercial repackaging of the history of England when a powerful business magnate develops the Isle of Wight into a colossal theme park, importing all the main cultural-commercial aspects of the mainland, which is transformed into "Anglia," a backward island that regresses into its bucolic past. Here Barnes satirizes not just the contemporary world, but the constant reinvention of tradition. At the same time, Barnes pursues the criticism of all modes of historiography that entrap readers in fixed narratives and certainties about the world. "History isn't what happened. History is just what historians tell us," he concludes in *A History of the World in 10½ Chapters* (1989).[25] History is thus for Barnes always-already absent, and events are not recorded so much as textualized. It is this process that enables connections between past and present, and that also makes it necessary to acknowledge a gap in knowledge or certainty about different temporalities. Imaginative fabulation can be inserted into the ephemeral historical stories that for the present make sense of the past; but all the ways of making sense are provisional. National stories are especially so and Barnes notes that a quotation from Ernest Renan would have made a perfect epigraph for his book: "Getting its history wrong is part of being a nation."[26]

The proliferation of historical fiction is a literary turn that has accompanied a renewed emphasis on the relationship between (national) history and (national) citizenship in government education policy. This emphasis is distinct from a previous mode of history-teaching that was informed by the legacy of empire. That mode, having moved from a celebratory to a guilt-ridden condition, sits uncomfortably, if at all, alongside a curriculum and culture inclined toward affirmations of identity. But both modes matter less than exploratory pursuits of understanding past and present fictions, whether they appear in the form of history-writing or of novel-writing. The historical turn in the contemporary novel re-examines not only scenes of past national self-fashioning but also the politics of attempts to use history uncritically as a means to shape present or past identities in entertainment, education, and other aspects of public life. The manifestations of this literary re-examination have been apparent everywhere, from the regional novel, which has undergone a renaissance, to the globalized novel that renders the present and the past from the perspective of an interconnected, complex post-9/11 world.

Notes

1. A. S. Byatt, *On Histories and Stories: Selected Essays* (London: Vintage, 2001), *passim*.
2. Richard Bradford, *The Novel Now* (Oxford: Blackwell, 2007), pp. 90–91.
3. Raphael Samuel, *Theatres of Memory*. Vol. 1: *Past and Present in Contemporary Culture* (London: Verso, 1996), p. 308. This more pluralistic view was brought to prominence in the 1970s and 1980s, and continues into the present, for example with Booker-prize winning fiction set in India.
4. Quoted in Neil McEwan, *Perspective in British Historical Fiction Today* (Basingstoke: Macmillan, 1987), p. 125.
5. John Fowles, "Notes on an Unfinished Novel," *Wormholes* (London: Jonathan Cape, 1998), pp. 13–26, 13.
6. John Fowles, *The French Lieutenant's Woman* (London: Granada, 1977), p. 87.
7. Marguerite Alexander, *Flights from Realism* (London: Edward Arnold, 1990), p. 127.

8. Steven Connor, *The English Novel in History 1950–1995* (London: Routledge, 1996), p. 147.

9. L. H. Myers, *The Near and the Far* (London: Jonathan Cape, 1943), p. 8.

10. See http://news.bbc.co.uk/1/hi/entertainment/8292488.stm (accessed October 7, 2009).

11. Amy J. Elias, *Sublime Desire: History and Post-1960s Fiction* (London: Johns Hopkins University Press, 2001), p. 4.

12. Mohsin Hamid, *The Reluctant Fundamentalist* (New York: Harcourt, 2007), p. 118.

13. Pat Barker, *Another World* (Harmondsworth: Penguin, 1999), p. 158.

14. David Leon Higdon, *Shadows of the Past in Contemporary British Fiction* (London: Macmillan, 1984), p. 24.

15. Ian McEwan, *Atonement* (London: Jonathan Cape, 2001), p. 18.

16. Fredric Jameson, *Postmodernism* (London: Verso, 1991), p. 225.

17. Avrom Fleishman, *The English Historical Novel: Walter Scott to Virginia Woolf* (London: Johns Hopkins University Press, 1971), p. 255.

18. Neil McEwan, *Perspective in British Historical Fiction Today* (Basingstoke: Macmillan, 1987), p. 131. McEwan in the phrase about "reflection" is quoting Elizabeth Bowen.

19. Naomi Jacobs, *The Character of Truth: Historical Figures in Contemporary Fiction* (Carbondale: Southern Illinois University Press, 1990), p. xiv.

20. Robert Hewison, *Culture and Consensus: England, Art and Politics Since 1940* (London: Methuen, 1995), p. 306.

21. Elisabeth Wesseling, *Writing History as a Prophet: Postmodernist Innovations of the Historical Novel* (Amsterdam: John Benjamins, 1991), p. 193.

22. Suzanne Keen, *Romances of the Archive in Contemporary British Fiction* (University of Toronto Press, 2001), p. 98. See also Suzanne Keen, "The Historical Turn in British Fiction," in *A Concise Companion to Contemporary British Fiction*, ed. James F. English (Oxford: Blackwell, 2006), pp. 167–187.

23. Leo Tolstoy, *War and Peace*, trans. Rosemary Edmonds (Harmondsworth: Penguin, 1982), p. 719.

24. Andrea Zemgulys, *Modernism and the Locations of Literary Heritage* (Cambridge University Press, 2007), p. 1.

25. Julian Barnes, *A History of the World in 10½ Chapters* (London: Jonathan Cape, 1989), p. 240.

26. Barnes in interview with Vanessa Guignery, "History in Question(s)," in *Conversations with Julian Barnes*, ed. Ryan Roberts and Vanessa Guignery (Jackson: University of Mississippi Press, 2009), p. 59.

53

Twentieth-century satire: the poetics and politics of negativity

JAMES F. ENGLISH

When considering the fate of satire in the twentieth century, it is easy to find ourselves retailing dubious clichés of literary periodization. We are tempted to say that in the passage from Victorian to modernist fiction there comes a fundamental shift in the hierarchy of genres. Satire, which played a crucial role in the emergence of the English novel in the 1700s, only to be largely abandoned by the mid-nineteenth century, suddenly reappears at the *fin de siècle* and within a few decades reclaims its original prominence and stature.[1] Drawing on Northrop Frye's scheme of generic mythos and archetypes, which associates satire with winter, we could then describe the genre's resurgence in the modernist period as part of a major change in the literary climate, the warm sentiment of Victorian fiction giving way to modernism's famed coldness, impersonality, and detachment.

Though reductive and misleading (and not just with regard to the Victorians), this narrative of satire's near-fatal collapse and dramatic recovery is not altogether false. But we should recall that even in its abstract lineaments Frye's scheme allows no pure instances; in each of its six "phases," satire is blended with elements either of tragedy or of comedy. We are dealing with matters of degree rather than kind, and indeed with modalities of affect rather than with genre in the strictly formal sense. What happened toward the turn of the last century is not that a certain kind of text, *the satiric form of the novel*, having been effectively banished in the mid-nineteenth century, suddenly enjoys a revival. It is that a certain persistent modality in English fiction, *the satiric disposition within the novel*, finds considerably more space in which to operate. This occurred in part as novelists sought under the banner of art to decouple their literary labor from the apparatus of commercial publishing, especially from the magazines and lending libraries, which had served as the self-appointed guardians of middle-class standards of literary decency.[2] With the rise of the art novel, writers claimed an ever wider license not only with respect to content, but with respect as well to extreme or unsavory hybridities of form. The novel continued to define an affective range extending from the warm generosity of sentiment through cool and calculated neutrality to the cold ferocity of censure. But novelists began to avail themselves more freely of the least commonly approved, most discomfitingly negative affects – fear, loathing, contempt, repulsion, shame, disgust, dyspepsia – mixing them audaciously and with little regard for generic proprieties into historical novels, comedies of manners, *Bildungsromane*, political allegories, works of naturalism, romances, and so on.

To be sure, the twentieth century offers examples of relatively monoglot or monomodal "satires" – Huxley's *Brave New World* (1932), Orwell's *Animal Farm* (1945), Golding's *Lord of the Flies* (1954) – as well as novelists who are routinely classified as "satirists": Evelyn Waugh, Kingsley and Martin Amis, Iain Sinclair, Geoff Nicholson, Jonathan Coe. But the novels thus situated enjoy rather ambiguous consecration as set texts for the secondary school curriculum, and the novelists thus labeled seem thereby to be marked out more for their limitations than for their achievements. The real story of satire in this period is not to be found in its most obvious or generically perfect instances but in its trans-generic, practically viral itinerary through the very bloodstream of the canon, including the work of the usual suspects just mentioned but also that of less easily classified writers, from Conrad, Lawrence, Joyce, and Woolf through Powell and Rhys, to Lessing, Naipaul, Carter, Winterson, Ishiguro, Rushdie, and many of the most compelling novelists of the new millennium.

An unavoidable (if also for many readers an irksome) point of reference along that route is Wyndham Lewis, self-fashioned "Enemy" of English society between the world wars and the century's most vigorous promoter and practitioner of the satiric mode in fiction and non-fiction. For Lewis satire is the only art suitable to the modern period. Like Juvenal, who said that any poet of second-century Rome would find it difficult *not* to write satire, Lewis regards satire as the default setting for any serious writer of twentieth-century Britain.[3] His notion of the satirist is in one sense very broad, including Shakespeare as well as Swift, and ultimately encompassing "all artists not specifically beauty-doctors" (*MWA*, 85). But in another sense the category is exceedingly narrow, inasmuch as the whole literary and artistic milieu of interwar London seems to Lewis to consist in precisely the kind of literary prettifiers and flatterers who must be excluded. The true satirist, Lewis stresses, aims neither for beauty nor, as Huxley and Orwell would have it, for morality; "the greatest satire," he declares, "is non-moral" (*MWA*, 85). The satirist's goal is not to correct society or to show it a better path forward but to represent its contemporary contours as closely and unflinchingly as possible. Satire is a kind of intensified realism, a divested observation of human behavior, partaking more of the qualities of a natural science than of a moral or conventionally aesthetic practice. Humans, closely observed, are to Lewis, as they are to Swift, ugly and unpleasant animals: they are "Apes," exuding "offensive smells [and] disagreeable moistures," but rendered more hideous and risible than other primates by their carrying on as though they belonged to a loftier order.

At the start of the century, Bergson influentially defined the comic in terms of "something mechanical encrusted on the living"; he saw laughter as our way of collectively punishing those who allow their essential human spirit, their *élan vital*, to be buried beneath the dehumanizing customs and artifices of social routine.[4] Lewis's writings on satire constitute a grim, unwelcome inversion of this formula; what makes people laughable is the fact that beneath all their pretentions to vitality and spontaneity, their claims to be more than mere creatures of animal instinct and social habit, they really are just "machines, governed by routine": tedious, predictable, unreflective, and dull (*MWA*, 93). But while this negation of our habitual self-regard may provoke a kind of laughter, it is not, says Lewis, "a genial guffaw"; "it is tragic, if a thing can be 'tragic' without pity or terror" (*MWA*, 92).

A literature without beauty, without morality, without geniality, without pity or terror sounds like pretty hard going, and it often is with Lewis's fiction. Even some of his best critics confess to having struggled to get through *The Apes of God* (1930),[5] the monstrous satire of Bloomsbury that culminates but also seems to have exhausted Lewis's *Man of the World* project, a multivolume, trans-generic dissection of interwar art and culture. The London art world represented in these works is in fact a world of "men without art," a world in which pampered, overgrown children, devoted followers of the fashion system, and mindless enthusiasts of one or another trendy "cult" (the Youth cult, the Health cult, the Negro cult, the Cinema cult, the Suffrage cult, the Homosexual cult) squabble and sulk and pontificate and fanny about while imagining themselves "noble geniuses." We are invited to survey this appalling wasteland of cultural self-flattery, this infantilized and above all for Lewis *effeminized* sham-society, as a kind of tragedy: an unmanning of the once virile culture of England, which in its prime had been capable of producing the greatest works of literary art. But it is a tragedy more cringe-making than pitiable, more likely to provoke our shame and embarrassment than our terror, certainly offering no catharsis, and no clear prospect of a better society.

In its way, and notwithstanding its programmatic misogyny and homophobia, *The Apes of God* is an impressive achievement. As Lewis himself concedes, there is a problem with the *"poor quality* of his enemies,"[6] consisting as they do of over-moneyed and under-talented arty acquaintances in and around Bloomsbury, people whose failings seem not to warrant such an extreme application of satiric method. And yet it is the affective extremity of Lewis's practice, his incapacity to back things off or tone things down, his refusal of ordinary concessions to the reader, that gives the work its peculiar distinction. With *Apes* Lewis shows just how radically the satiric mode might be extended within the formal contours of a seemingly minor or trivial novelistic genre – the *roman-à-clef*. This is a genre from which modernism, for all its high ambitions, could never quite manage to detach itself, and which threatens to reduce even the monuments of the emerging canon – from Lawrence's *Women in Love* to Woolf's *Orlando* – to the gossipy self-amusements of a coterie. Lewis's solution to this nagging problem of the art novel's trivial twin or shadow genre (the novel of art-world bickering) is to subject it to remorseless satiric practice, pursuing his uncongenial, unbeautiful, non-moral method so far as to transform the execution of a minor-genre work into something new and altogether strange, an experimental novel that has yet to be fully assimilated and that still has the power to disturb and bewilder.

The interwar period was one of perceived social, political, and economic crisis, bordering almost on panic, among the intellectual classes; and it is not surprising that the novels written in that quarter of the century involve some of the bleakest humor, some of the darkest and, in Lewis's sense, most truly satiric laughter in the canon. We can include here Waugh's *Decline and Fall* (1928) and *Vile Bodies* (1930), Huxley's *Brave New World* and *After Many a Summer Dies the Swan* (1939), key episodes of Joyce's *Ulysses* (1922), Woolf's *Between the Acts* (1941), and all of Lewis's most important work. But the tendency of satire, once unleashed, to take things to extremes, to assume a formally and emotionally disruptive power in a novel, is visible already in the earliest works of British modernism, such as Conrad's *The Secret Agent* (1907).

Dedicated to H. G. Wells and billed as a "simple tale of the XIX century," Conrad's novel is in fact a complex and distinctively twentieth-century hybrid. Along with Kipling's *Kim* (1901) it is one of the first true spy novels, a touchstone for later masters of that bestselling form such as Graham Greene and John le Carré as well as the literary original for the virtuosic spy film, *Sabotage* (1936), that earned Alfred Hitchcock a contract in Hollywood. The plot is that of a political thriller, revolving around international espionage and terrorism, featuring an Assistant Commissioner for Scotland Yard who traces a fatal bombing accident in Greenwich Park first to a group of London anarchists and double agents, and then to a reactionary plot hatched by a sinister Russian ambassador. The story is based on an actual incident, the so-called Greenwich Bombing Outrage of 1894, and written at a time when both anarchist violence ("propaganda by deed") and extreme counter-terrorism measures ("states of exception") were topics of wide and sensational news coverage. Yet both the bestseller/thriller ethos and the timely political source material are dominated by an unsettling black humor that many early readers found alienating and cruel, a humor that Conrad effected by pursuing a rigorous "ironic method . . . right through to the end"[7] and by subjecting the whole scene and system of international politics to coruscating satiric disdain.

The Secret Agent has been called a "powerful counterrevolutionary tract"[8] in which bourgeois quietism is tacitly endorsed while radical theorists and practitioners of anarchism are "condemned . . . by a caricatural presentation."[9] But one of the reasons for the novel's enduring influence is that it represents a kind of political satire that does not readily reduce to any such simple vector of political intention. Like Lewis's patently unartistic artists Conrad's anarchists are decidedly unanarchistic, figures of "inert fanaticism, or perhaps rather . . . fanatical inertness" (24), "lazy" "frauds," devoted only to their personal "repose . . . and security" (54). They are indeed so "thoroughly domesticated" that the entire novel threatens continually to slip the genre constraints of spy fiction and adopt those of domestic melodrama (19). The violent climax of the book is not a bombing or a political assassination but a "domestic tiff" (212), ended when the secret agent's wife stabs her husband with the "domestic carving knife" (217), leaving him dead, but looking for all the world like a man "in the fullness of his domestic ease reposing on the sofa" (233). "From a certain point of view," laughs the Assistant Commissioner, after summarizing the bombing plot, "we are here in the presence of a domestic drama" (184).

These bathetic bourgeoisifications of the supposed revolutionaries raise the question of what it is, exactly, that we are meant to be laughing at. As in G. K. Chesterton's more buoyantly frivolous satire of anarchism, *The Man Who Was Thursday* (1908), Conrad's novel seems not to provide a single genuine anarchist for our readerly derision. Its anarchist figures are risible only inasmuch as they resemble the "idle and selfish class . . . the well-fed bourgeoisie": precisely, we would think, anarchism's abhorrent other.[10] But if this establishes the complacent landowning class, the exploiters of labor, as one face or facet of the novel's overdetermined satiric object, it does not thereby position the genuinely committed and effectual anarchist, were one to appear, outside the compass of its mockery. As Freud theorizes in *Jokes and Their*

Relation to the Unconscious, published just two years before Conrad's novel, joke-work involves condensation rather than simple inversion; laughter at Conrad's lazy "fat-pig" anarchists continues to draw on our hostility toward the anarchist even as it recruits our hostility toward the idle and selfish owners of capital.

Indeed, Conrad's satire depends on a virtually unbroken sequence of negations; its dominant trope is *litotes*, or assertion by denial of the opposite. This rhetorical device extends well beyond the ironies of the lazy anarchist, the revolutionary who "is no man of action," and so forth. Politically non-aligned characters are described in much the same language. The victim of the bombing plot, Verloc's half-witted, stammering brother-in-law Stevie, for example, is said to be "no master of phrases," and we are told that "his thoughts lacked clearness and precision," as well (146). Such language would appear to mock the characters by gratuitous comparison with ideals of which they can only fall short. Yet Conrad is scarcely interested in scoring points against stutterers or the mentally handicapped, nor does he encourage us to admire masterful phrase-turning or keenness of intellect. The most articulate and canny figure in the novel – as well as the character most appreciative of ironic humor and most given to biting sarcastic remarks, the book's supreme satirist – is its arch-villain M. Vladimir, the reactionary Russian ambassador who dreams up the bomb plot in the first place, and whose politics of counter-terrorism represent a greater threat to Britain's social harmony and peace than does anarchism itself. And so it goes with all the novel's scornful negations; the positive values on which their satiric force would seem to depend are themselves immediately and no less scornfully negated. "Like to like," observes the misanthropic bomb-maker known as the Professor (though he holds neither degree nor teaching post). "Revolution, legality – counter moves in the same game; forms of idleness at bottom identical" (68).

Ultimately *The Secret Agent* is a novel of what Terry Eagleton calls "ceaseless ... self-detonation," a political novel that leaves itself no political stance or position capable of surviving the ironies of its plot and language.[11] Its disparagements are harnessed to a Nietzschean ambition to move beyond a politics of antithetical choices, effecting a vertiginous, indeed an anarchic unraveling of the whole logic of revolution and reaction that defines its political horizon.

Another way to say this is that satire such as Conrad and Lewis write is reactionary even to the point of disparaging reaction itself, finding risible and pretentious the very impulses that it continues nonetheless to mobilize. I have dwelled on the work of these authors because the extreme yet conflict-laden negativity of such writing, its reflexive disparagement, is fundamental to much of the century's most important fiction. Satire is the most effective conduit for the diffuse but aggressive current of anti-modern reaction that runs through the "long modernism," the fear and loathing of new media, new foods, new buildings and machines, new forms of political organization, new arrangements for daily living. Such reaction does not stop short of the new literary styles and techniques of the modernists themselves, which are reflexively satirized by Lawrence, Woolf, Lewis, and Joyce among others as products of a cultural fashion system increasingly dependent on novelty and gimmick. The early twentieth century saw not only the vast expansion of the advertising industry, but the rise of the public relations business and the apparatus of public-opinion formation. It was a century of ceaselessly escalating hype and ever more elaborately contrived promises of a better, happier future. From a satiric perspective, revolutionary promises, whether of socialism, fascism, or anti-colonial nationalism, are no different from all the other forms of mass-produced and mass-distributed over-optimism; they are just one more variety of propaganda about "modernization" and "progress." The novel's satiric disposition does not rule out, and in fact depends on, a shared desire for social change. Jameson argues that the satirist's "rage at a fallen society" must always involve a secretly "utopian frame of reference."[12] But modernist satire holds only scorn for the cheerleaders of modernity, and recasts their affirmative narratives of progress as narratives, in Orwell's phrase, of "progress toward more pain."[13]

This might suggest a convergence of the satiric mode with the genre of dystopia, which is likewise of course predicated on unarticulated utopian desires. It would be a mistake simply to reduce the one to the other, as the century's generically normative dystopias – including Orwell's – are far from its most searching instances of satire. But to the extent that the century's satiric narratives project a future, it is an unreservedly bleak one, unfolding not toward the bright horizon of social solidarity, economic equality, and robust human health depicted in futurist fiction like H. G. Wells's *Men Like Gods* (1923), but toward apocalypse: the scorched battlefield of total war at the end of Waugh's *Vile Bodies* (1930); the drugged masses in their collective masochistic frenzy at the end of Huxley's *Brave New World* (1931); the absolute triumph of state power over individual will in the closing pages of Orwell's *Nineteen Eighty-Four* (1949); the barren earth of post-nuclear devastation in Angela Carter's *Heroes and Villains* or in the last section of Doris Lessing's *Four-Gated City* (both 1969); the economic and political meltdown of a literally cannibalistic society in the final book of Alasdair Gray's *Lanark* (1980); the

mushroom cloud that signals cataclysmic retribution for postcolonial corruption and patriarchal hubris at the end of Salman Rushdie's *Shame* (1984).

In the shadow of this grim telos, any prophecy of a happier world looks
absurd. Believers and optimists of every sort become objects of derision: not
only ardent socialists or fascists but all political prophets and dreamers; religious
fanatics, mystics, and occultists; vegetarians, teetotalers, and other food faddists;
space-travel enthusiasts, inventors of gadgets, techno-futurists. A recurring
target is the industrialist dream of perfecting society through more efficient
production and wider consumption of faster, more convenient machines. Ford
brought out the Model T in 1908, and this serves as year one of the modern era
("the year of Our Ford") in *Brave New World*. In Huxley's novel the assembly-
line method of production has been extended even to human reproduction,
with babies rigorously standardized and quality controlled through genetic
modification, and "decanted" from their test tubes in several distinct models
or "castes," each dressed in its designated color and fitted for a particular
segment of a society arranged for optimum efficiency of production and
consumption. The worker-caste babies – Delta models – wear khaki and are
trained with electric shocks to retain a strong aversion to higher pleasures
afforded by books and flowers, whose enjoyment would be "gratuitous" and
hence inefficient given the social function for which Deltas have been designed.
Further training by "hypnopaedia," or sleep-learning, ensures that they assume
their appointed social role without friction, taking pride in their superiority over
the Epsilons but never resenting the Alphas or Betas. In political terms this
apotheosis of Fordist capitalism in the achievement of perfect standardization
and quality control over worker habitus is the very opposite and enemy of
anarchism. But the satiric object here remains the fanatical believer in a new
society, the prophet of a modern factory-based paradise. The characters in *Brave
New World* have raised Fordism to the level of a religion and taken the Model T
as their fetish and icon. When referring to the great father ("our Ford") they
make the sign of the T over their stomachs; when annoyed, they take his name
in vain: "Oh Ford! I've gone and woken the children!"[14]

This vitriolic treatment of auto-worshippers and automobilized society
extends in other novels to grimly satiric car crashes and even fatalities, such
as those of Agatha Runcible in *Vile Bodies* and the American academic Glober
in Anthony Powell's *A Dance to the Music of Time* (1951–1975). It reaches an
apotheosis in the novels of J. G. Ballard, where death by automobile has
become a social obsession and a sexual fetish. In *The Atrocity Exhibition* (1971)
clinical response studies are conducted to identify the most stimulating car
crashes:

In 82% of cases massive rear-end collisions were selected with a preference for expressed fecal matter and rectal hemorrhages. Further tests were conducted to define the optimum model-year. These indicate that a three year model lapse with child victims provide the maximum audience excitation (confirmed by manufacturers' studies of the optimum auto disaster).[15]

In *Crash* (1973) the fetishistic fascination with cars and their destructive power erupts in a subculture that derives erotic gratification from the reenactment of violent collisions, crash victims' wounds – "the chests of young women impaled on steering-columns; the cheeks of handsome youths torn on the chromium latches of quarter-lights" – forming "the key to a new sexuality, born from a perverse technology."[16]

Given such scorn for the paradise of Fordist industrialization, one might expect the luddites and greens and neo-primitives to show well, but this is not how things play out under the lights of satire. Alongside the amateur motor-car racers, antique-car collectors, and other enthusiasts of the automobile who provide one satiric line through the twelve novels of Powell's *A Dance to the Music of Time*, runs a no less derisory sequence of mystics, clairvoyants, and devoted followers (descending from the cult of Dr. Trelawney), who represent the very opposite of industrial dreams and modernity-worship. This line culminates in a bizarre cult of robed wanderers led by Leslie "Scorpio" Murtlock, whose limitless egotism, financial parasitism, and creepy sexual practices seem to stand in for everything that is going wrong with England's youth in the 1960s. The final turn of the satiric screw comes when Kenneth Widmerpool, Powell's most brilliantly monstrous creation, who for most of the *Dance* has been a smarmy champion of modern industry and social progress, submits himself to the charismatic power of Murtlock, divests himself of modern trappings, and abandons the "acceptance world" to go back to nature with the hippies. Through this appalling convergence of its counterposed grotesques, Powell's satire declares a plague on both houses; those who embrace the claims and prophecies of some ardent spiritualism or alternative subculture are finally identical with those who thrill to the promises of industrial modernity and bourgeois fulfillment. They are equally dupes of a false future and harbingers of a true calamity.

As these latter examples suggest, the compounded and duplicitous negativity of satire continues beyond the modernist period through the postwar and contemporary novel. The Reverend R. A. Knox remarks in his *Essays in Satire* (1928) that during the interwar years the satiric mode became so habitual in Britain that its very normativity threatened to blunt its disruptive effects, inoculating readers against its "beneficent poison" and hastening its obsolescence.[17] But satire's complicity in its own undoing, its headlong tendency toward excess and exhaustion, proves in fact to be less a threat than an inducement to further satiric production. Its seeming vector of self-negation through the modernist period has been the very path of its subsequent propulsion.

A pivotal text in this regard is Virginia Woolf's final novel, *Between the Acts* (1941). Written at the endpoint of the interwar period, and the last gasp of late modernism (or the first pangs of postmodernism), the book is at once darker and more reflexively satiric than any of Woolf's works. In this novel Woolf accepts that the satirist must operate *within* the compass of mockery and abuse, scorning the very basis of her social critique, the terms and conditions of possibility of her own (modernist) literary production. It is truly a novel without a safety net, leaving intact no vantage of special insight or authority for its author. Miss La Trobe, the novel's artist character, is a modernist not unlike Woolf herself: a social outsider, a sexual suspect, a "difficult" personality swinging between abject insecurity and bullying egotism, and a bold aesthetic experimenter who wants to believe in the power of a new art to transcend and reconcile. The presentation of La Trobe and her work (a village pageant play that constitutes nearly half the novel) is complex but scathing. For all the pageant's heterodox national history and broadly satiric treatment of empire, and despite its many Brechtian self-disruptions, the production only succeeds, to the degree that it succeeds at all, in avowing the imagined national community of the English, a community which, as both La Trobe and Woolf are aware, is in the process of sidelining its artists and heretics so as to cement and unify itself for the work of renewed warfare. La Trobe's distinctly Woolfian experiment – satiric history as epic theater – serves in the novel as a staging of modernism's failed politics.

Doris Lessing enacts something similar in her brilliant, bitter novel about the political predicaments of the postwar period, *The Golden Notebook* (1962). As in *Between the Acts* long stretches of Lessing's novel consist of the work of one of its characters, a woman who shares many of her author's personal traits and frustrated left-wing political convictions, yet who herself often appears less as the subject than as the object of the book's satiric intentions. Indeed, Lessing enfolds a whole series of found or interior texts inside one another – clippings within diaries within novels-in-progress; stories by characters in novels written by other characters; parodies of "serious" works that turn out to be parodies themselves – to create an enigmatic abyssal structure from which there can be no escape into some safe house of narrative sincerity.

The central character, Anna Wulf, is fierce in her denigration of mainstream literature and media – especially of the way they sentimentalize the politics of race, and exploit as exotic backdrop the struggles for independence in the African colonies where she grew up. Yet her own efforts to rise above the anodyne resolutions and liberal clichés of the movies and magazines constantly stumble into self-parody or peter out in culs-de-sac of shame, bewilderment, and exhaustion. As far as the TV and film producers are concerned, Anna's deliberate parodies of bad writing about racial and sexual politics are in fact "perfectly good" pieces of work.[18] Intended to provoke satiric laughter at the entertainment industry, they serve instead as jokes on Anna, exposing her ineffectual ironies, her nugatory cultural politics.

The novel's feminist humor suffers a similar derailment or neutralization. Its vigorous satire of patriarchal prerogatives – in Communist circles no less than in bourgeois society – earned *The Golden Notebook* an important place in the women's movement in the 1960s. Lessing gave freer reign than any previous writer had done to the refractory laughter of women, as for example when Richard, the novel's most successful industrialist, attempts to "talk frankly to women" about his "problem . . . with how to get an erection," and the women simply erupt into "peals of laughter" (30–31). But those who have seen the novel as anticipating the feminism of Hélène Cixous's "Laugh of the Medusa" (1975), advancing feminine mirth as the key to a decisive subversion of the phallic order, fail to contend with the novel's further satiric turns. The laughter of middle-class white women is not by any means the last laugh of *The Golden Notebook*; this very scene of transgression in fact occurs within a putative framing narrative, ironically titled *Free Women*, which turns out to be a parody of Lessing's own earlier realist fiction and a satire of an emergent feminism rendered, from an African anti-colonial standpoint, all but bootless by its failure to come to terms with race and empire. Formally as well as thematically, Lessing treats the whole problem of comic subversion as a kind of Chinese box, each eruption of transgressive laughter achieving only a limited margin of freedom, a faux-emancipatory breaking-out that remains still multiply contained, its limitations and blindnesses becoming themselves a kind of second-order joke that both heightens and sours the original mirth.

Lessing's satire is finally less anticipatory of Cixous's critique of patriarchy than of Peter Sloterdijk's "critique of cynical reason."[19] Lessing perceives a kind of hysterical cynicism and "bad laughter" among the intellectuals of the New Left, a compulsive self-satirizing laughter that she attempts in the *Notebook* to anatomize from within, that is, even while compulsively deploying it herself. The basis of this intervention lies in her Rhodesian background; she saw the intractable reflexive mockery of the New Left as conditioned in part by the awkward and shaming incommensurability between its notion of the revolutionary political subject and the actually existing revolutionary movements in the colonies. In this respect she can be seen as helping to inaugurate the major line of postcolonial *émigré* satirists that extends from V. S. Naipaul, who arrived in England the same year she did (1949), to Salman Rushdie, whose *Satanic Verses* became, forty years later, the century's most controversial novel.

There are of course great differences among these writers. Naipaul is certainly never identified with the left (old or new), and in his early novels, which are considered his most satiric –*The Mystic Masseur* (1957), *The Suffrage of Elvira* (1958), *Miguel Street* (1959), and *A House for Mr. Biswas* (1961) – he advances a more conventional and univocal satire than Lessing's, a satire whose most explicit objects are the colonized rather than the colonizers and whose comedy of political corruption and ineptitude, tending to outright farce, is more reminiscent of Waugh's *Black Mischief* (1932) than of *The Golden Notebook*. What Rob Nixon calls Naipaul's "programmatically negative representation of formerly colonized societies" has drawn much fire from his fellow Caribbean and postcolonial writers, beginning with George Lamming and notably including Edward Said, for whom Naipaul's work is "ignorant, illiterate," and "immoral."[20] But even Naipaul's satire is complex and, in its own way, abyssal, disrupting liberal Western norms and commitments to capitalist "development" and nation-building on the European model that his many detractors have seen as the firm ground of his satiric perspective. The failure of the postcolonial Caribbean definitively to refuse those metropolitan norms is as shameful and embarrassing to Naipaul as its failure competently to emulate them. His satire erupts out of "negative energies" that are partly self-directed and in a sense self-diagnostic. As Homi Bhabha has argued, even Naipaul's most dogmatic denunciations can be seen to illuminate the "psychic and affective structures . . . that inform the politics of everyday life" for the postcolonial subject.[21]

For the detractors of Naipaul's satire, however, any potential insights of postcolonial self-diagnosis are inadequate to offset their lack of political encouragements. "We dare not accept Naipaul's negation," writes the Trinidad and Tobagan poet Eric Roach. "We cannot accept satire and disdain and speak sneeringly as Naipaul does of our generations of failure and incompetence. We must talk of hope."[22] This disavowal of satiric negation, of a literature that lacks *positive images*, has characterized the reception of nearly all postcolonial British satire, from Naipaul and Selvon to Hanif Kureishi and, most recently, Monica Ali (whose *Brick Lane* has been denounced for negative, stereotypical depictions of East London's immigrant

Sylheti community). But it is Rushdie who brought the project of postcolonial satire to its apotheosis of collective outrage and injured feeling.

Having developed a fluidly satiric style of *Bildungsroman*-as-national-allegory in his novel of India, *Midnight's Children* (1981), and injected it with more rage and vitriol in his novel of Pakistan, *Shame* (which was banned in that country), Rushdie undertook a more comprehensive, transnational satiric agenda in *The Satanic Verses* (1989), his novel of postcolonial London, its South Asian-inflected minority communities, and the various national homelands and cultures to which those communities remain consequentially linked. As is well known, this novel was widely banned, burned, and denounced, and a *fatwa*, or religious edict, calling for the death of its author and publishers was pronounced by Iran's Ayatollah Ruholla Khomeini, resulting in a number of deaths and injuries and forcing Rushdie into hiding for much of the next decade.

Without denying the singularity of the *fatwa*, it is important to recognize that many other cultural, political, and religious leaders besides Muslim clerics denounced the novel as offensive to *their* groups or communities – leaving Rushdie with relatively few real defenders outside the metropolitan literati. (And even there, such figures as John Berger and Germaine Greer on the left and Roald Dahl on the right joined the chorus of denuciation against the book and its author.) Christian leaders were incensed by the novel's representative "foot soldier" of Christ, the caricatural Baptist evangelizer Eugene Dumsday, a creationist bore from the American heartland who suffers a partly severed tongue while traveling to India to spread the good news of anti-Darwinism, and ends up, after a surgical repair involving flesh taken from his glutes, "discussing the relics of fossils with his new, buttocky tongue."[23] Secular leaders working in black British neighborhoods recoiled from the novel's stereotyping: its satiric portrayal, for example, of Dr. Uhuru Simba, an obese and misogynistic community activist who is neither a doctor nor from Africa; or of Hanif Johnson, an opportunistic young black civil rights lawyer who affects a Trinidadian accent, keeps a radical-chic address in the slums, and ventriloquizes all the most advantageous languages of community politics ("socialistic, black-radical, anti-anti-anti-racist" [281]). At the other end of the political spectrum, Margaret Thatcher herself ("Mrs. Torture" in the novel) called the *Verses* "deeply offensive" in the way it depicted her government; her Home Secretary objected in particular to the novel's implied comparison of Thatcher's Britain to Hitler's Germany.[24] Though the government was obliged to ensure Rushdie's safety after Khomeini issued the *fatwa*, it was far from pleased at having to extend police protection to a writer whose novel includes extended and scorching satiric treatment of British policemen, depicting them as crazed occultists and racist thugs whose agenda of "community policing" includes strangling one community activist and burning two others to death. Though the *Verses* had been condemned by Khomeini and some left-wing critics as a work essentially "colonialist" in its perspective, it presented to British conservatives a radical indictment of Thatcher's attempted domestic recolonization of Britain's non-white populations.

The novel's programmatic refusal of positive images, its non-stop satirizing and stereotyping of the police and the policed, the English and the Asians, the whites and blacks and everyone in between, its wholesale commitment to the negativities of satire, has been seen as inducing a dubious universalism, a false sense of political and moral equivalence, a typically metropolitan blindness to the real differentials of power that both justify and impede postcolonial struggles for recognition and equality. In its "failure to take seriously" any affirmative political project, Timothy Brennan argues, the novel finally provides us with no more than a "negative and formal parody" of the postcolonial situation.[25] Rushdie's reply to this might be that it is precisely the postcolonial situation, the discursive system or regime within which the various parties to postcolonial struggle are (together with their antagonists) produced, which renders individual subjects as monsters, grotesques, cartoons: already recognizable and potentially laughable *types*. In taking this whole system as the object of a "negative and formal parody," the satirist offers his disguised utopian gesture toward some different and better discourse in which a new politics, a new subjectivity, and a new notion of freedom might be constituted. But in the same stroke he dooms himself to the common fate of failure and ridicule, for in this system the "famous satirist," too, is a laughable type (391). Appearing in the novel as the brilliantly sharp-tongued poet Baal, the satirist is denounced as a blasphemer and a whore of the enemy, and sentenced to death. When he attempts to plead his case before the public, he finds that his ingrained habits of jocularity and invective have cost him any chance for a thoughtful or sympathetic hearing even among his fans.

It is possible, of course, to write satirically without becoming a pariah among the politically engaged. Traditionally, satire ("militant irony," as Frye famously called it) has been seen as a useful weapon for political parties and movements, and the satirist as an effective shock trooper. But over the last century at least, satire has tended to unmoor itself from partisan polemic in order to perform more troubling and ambiguous political work. Few of the century's satirists have embraced as firmly as Lewis the label of "Enemy"; they have not been driven like Rushdie into reclusion. But many have risked a negativity so unconstrained in its extension, so systematic in its application, so unwelcome and improper in its effects, as to confound all normal relations of affinity and alliance. Since the advent of modernism, it has been satire's chosen task to derange the received forms of political praxis no less than the received forms of the novel.

Notes

1. Defoe's first novel *Robinson Crusoe* (1719) was quickly replayed in satiric mode by Swift's *Gulliver's Travels* (1726), and both writers came to the emerging form of the novel as accomplished satirists in other genres, Defoe having written "The True-born Englishman" (1700) and *The Shortest Way with the Dissenters* (1702) and Swift *A Tale of a Tub* (1704) and *The Battle of the Books* (1704).

2. Frank Palmeri, "Narrative Satire in the Nineteenth Century," in *A Companion to Satire*, ed. Ruben Quintero (2nd edn, Oxford: Blackwell, 2007), pp. 361–376.

3. Juvenal's famous dictum was *Difficile est saturam non scribere* ("It is difficult not to write satire"): Juvenal, *Satire 1*, line 30. Lewis remarked that "there is nothing written or painted today which could not be brought under the head of *satire*": Lewis, *Men Without Art*, ed. Seamus Cooney (Santa Barbara, CA: Black Sparrow, 1987), p. 12 (cited hereafter as *MWA*).

4. Henri Bergson, *Laughter* (1900), trans. Wylie Sypher, in *Comedy*, ed. Wylie Sypher (Garden City, NY: Doubleday, 1956), p. 84.

5. Fredric Jameson calls the novel "virtually unreadable for any sustained period of time": Jameson, *Fables of Aggression: Wyndham Lewis, the Modernist as Fascist* (Berkeley: University of California Press, 1979), p. 5.

6. *Wyndham Lewis on Art: Collected Writings, 1913–1956*, ed. C. J. Fox and Walter Michael (New York: Funk and Wagnalls, 1969), p. 267.

7. Conrad, "Author's Note," *The Secret Agent* (Garden City, NY: Doubleday Anchor, 1953), p. 12.

8. Fredric Jameson, *The Political Unconscious: Narrative as a Socially Symbolic Act* (Ithaca, NY: Cornell University Press, 1981), p. 268.

9. Norman Sherry, quoted by Paul Theroux, Introduction, Joseph Conrad, *The Secret Agent* (Penguin Classics, 1990), p. 17.

10. Thus speaks the anarchist leader Mr. X in Conrad's story "The Informer," written just before *The Secret Agent*, and published in 1908 in *A Set of Six* (Garden City, NY: Doubleday, 1922), pp. 78–86.

11. Terry Eagleton, *Criticism and Ideology* (London: Verso, 1978), p. 140.

12. Fredric Jameson, "Third World Literature in the Era of Multinational Capitalism," *Social Text* 15 (1986), 65–88, 80.

13. George Orwell, *Nineteen Eighty-Four* (London: Plume, 2003), p. 276.

14. Aldous Huxley, *Brave New World* (New York: HarperPerennial, 1998), p. 29.

15. J. G. Ball\ard, "Why I Want to Fuck Ronald Reagan," *The Atrocity Exhibition* (San Francisco: Re-Search, 1990), p. 105.

16. J. G. Ballard, *Crash* (New York: Picador, 2001), p. 13.
17. Ronald A. Knox, "On Humour and Satire," *Essays in Satire* (London: Sheed and Ward, 1928), p. 42.
18. Doris Lessing, *The Golden Notebook* (New York: Bantam, 1973), p. 59.
19. Peter Sloterdijk, *Critique of Cynical Reason* (Minneapolis: University of Minnesota Press, 1988).
20. Rob Nixon, *London Calling: V. S. Naipaul, Postcolonial Mandarin* (Oxford University Press, 1992), pp. 6–7; Edward Said, "Intellectuals in the Postcolonial World," *Salmagundi* 70–71 (1986), 44–64, 53.
21. Homi Bhabha, "Adagio," *Critical Inquiry* 31: 2 (2005), 371–380, 373.
22. Quoted in John Clement Ball, *Satire and the Postcolonial Novel* (New York: Routledge, 2003), p. 46.
23. Salman Rushdie, *The Satanic Verses* (New York: 1998), p. 432.
24. Thatcher quoted in Lisa Appignanesi and Sara Maitland, *The Rushdie File* (Syracuse University Press, 1990), p. 114. Sir Geoffrey Howe quoted in W. J. Weatherby, *Salman Rushdie: Sentenced to Death* (New York: Carroll and Graf, 1990), p. 173.
25. Timothy Brennan, *Salman Rushdie and the Third World* (London: Macmillan, 1989), p. 166.

54

Unending romance: science fiction and fantasy in the twentieth century

EDWARD JAMES AND FARAH MENDLESOHN

Writers from Britain and Ireland – English, Scottish, Welsh and Irish – have contributed in large measure to the development of science fiction and fantasy in the world. Horace Walpole, Mary Shelley, H. G. Wells, Bram Stoker, J. R. R. Tolkien and Sir Arthur C. Clarke can all be recognized as major creators of ideas and images that have had a lasting effect on twenty-first century culture. This chapter sketches the history of developments in these genres in the long twentieth century, from H. G. Wells to the present.

In 1824 Sir Walter Scott defined the novel as "a fictitious narrative . . . accommodated to the ordinary train of human events."[1] "Romance," in contrast to romantic fiction, is the word that has often been used for the novel's opposite: a fiction that imaginatively creates a world existing *outside* ordinary human experience. H. G. Wells calls his stories of time travel, space flight, and wondrous invention "scientific romances," which he firmly distinguishes from his "novels," such as *The History of Mr Polly*, and there is still a feeling among some literary critics that works of science fiction and fantasy, the two modern genres that most obviously treat "romance" themes, are not actually "novels." If the novel is concerned above all with relationships between human beings, the modern "romance" is concerned rather more with the relationship between humans and the universe in which they live. The culmination of a "novel" may be saving someone's marriage; the culmination of a "romance" may be saving someone's world. One of the distinctive narratological aspects of the genres is that while they are not inevitably concerned with politics and ethics, authors have worked to develop rhetorical strategies to enable the form to carry exposition that in other modes would be detrimental to the story.

The progenitors of the modern "romance" are many and varied, reflecting the multifarious nature of science fiction and fantasy. Science fiction grew from the extraordinary voyage, from the space travel in Lucian of Samosata's

True History (later second century AD) through to the medieval travel tales of Sir John Mandeville. Often, early discussions of ideal societies, from Sir Thomas More's *Utopia* (1516) onwards, are set in the framework of an imaginary voyage. Eventually we reach the works of Jules Verne (1828–1905), which collectively are known as his *Voyages Extraordinaires*. What all of these have in common is that they were presupposed to take place within the same "when" as the reader. Stories of the future have a much later origin: they date only from the late eighteenth century, and do not become common until the late nineteenth, in a world that has fully accepted the concept of historical progress and the mutability of humanity in the face of changed conditions and opportunities.

Another progenitor of science fiction is the narrative of scientific discovery itself: Mary Shelley's ground-breaking *Frankenstein* (1818) stems directly from the discoveries of Luigi Galvani, a generation earlier, on the effects of electricity on the animal body, and from the discussions of eighteenth- and nineteenth-century philosophers on the nature of "man" and the role of nurture over nature. Yet the lesson nineteenth- and twentieth-century emulators take from *Frankenstein* is often the anti-scientific fear of new inventions and discoveries. Dr. Frankenstein mutates from a figure of a man who fails to marry ethics and science into obsessive anti-social scientists like Dr. Jekyll (Robert Louis Stevenson) or Dr. Moreau (Wells). In the twentieth century a more optimistic and activist model of the scientist and engineer emerges, but for a long time he shares the stage with the mad scientist.

Prophesying disaster had been a popular form of narrative for centuries but as superstition fell in the face of science, such prophesies found for themselves a new home in tales of mad science, and in the new form of the future war story.[2] The success of George Chesney's *The Battle of Dorking* (1871) spawned many emulators, but the aspect of the fiction of dire warning that achieves respectability in the twentieth century is the future dystopia, as in Aldous Huxley's *Brave New World* (1932), Katherine Burdekin's *Swastika Night* (1937), and George Orwell's *Nineteen Eighty-Four* (1949).

The sources of inspiration for modern fantasy are less specific and far broader. This form of "romance" was, before the development of the novel, dominant in European fiction. A modern scholar of both fantasy and medieval literature, Tom Shippey, argues mischievously that the dominant mode of twentieth-century literature is still the fantastic.[3] The word "romance" (*roman* in French) comes from those medieval stories about the heroes of the past (mostly knights associated with Arthur or Charlemagne) which were written in French (*romanice*), and were populated with giants, dragons, and sorcerers as well as knights and maidens requiring rescue. Those stories were immensely popular, supplying early printers with their most commercially successful products, inspiring post-medieval poets such as Ariosto and Spenser, and filling the library of poor obsessed Don Quixote. Well into the nineteenth century those tales were sold as cheap chapbooks by peddlers to people who had little access to printed matter, with the result that the tales remained common currency. Medieval folklore – with its stories about ghosts, vampires, and fairies – fed into the early modern fairy tale, which lies behind much of modern fantasy, and enters directly into modern fantasy, for which it provides stories and tropes. From Horace Walpole's *The Castle of Otranto* (1764), the founding text of the gothic, to the imitations of J. R. R. Tolkien's *The Lord of the Rings* (1954–1955), the founding text of the modern fantasy genre, the Middle Ages and its tales serve as an inspiration and a locale for fantasy.

The modern labels "science fiction" and "fantasy" establish themselves relatively recently and with different levels of success. Wells and those who followed in his steps tend to use "scientific romance" until after the Second World War, when the American term "science fiction" is generally adopted. It had been first used by Hugo Gernsback, an American editor of science fiction, in 1929 and was understood to cover "the Jules Verne, H. G. Wells, and Edgar Allan Poe type of story – a charming romance intermingled with scientific fact and prophetic vision."[4] "Science fiction" was abbreviated to "SF," although the term "sci-fi" (to rhyme with "hi-fi") has come to dominate in recent years, in the media and among younger SF readers. Critics and writers generally prefer to retain "SF," because it yields to expansions such as "speculative fiction," "speculative fabulation," which seem more respectable to those concerned with the status of the genre, and also because it retains the flexibility of a term that must cover material containing very little science. The *idea* of science fiction is fairly clear cut; and although some authors from outside the genre are eager to disassociate their works from the label, to science fiction readers P. D. James's *The Children of Men* (1992) or Stephen Fry's *Making History* (1996) are very clearly part of it.

Fantasy is a much broader and less well-defined genre. The problems created by the absence of a category of "fantasy" can be seen in the way that critics quoted on the dust jacket of early editions of Tolkien's *The Lord of the Rings* responded: they made comparisons with Malory, Spenser, and Ariosto; they claimed that Tolkien distilled "Norse, Teutonic and Celtic" myth; while Naomi Mitchison, herself a well-known SF writer, declared "it's really super science fiction." As is not infrequently the case, it is publishers who define what a genre is. At the end of the 1960s Ballantine Books in New York (the first official paperback publisher of Tolkien in 1965) began to reprint some of the classics of "Adult Fantasy," which lay behind what was to become in the 1970s a commercial boom. Many of the writers, recruited posthumously to legitimate a new publishing category, were English (William Beckford, Ernest Bramah, G. K. Chesterton, E. R. Eddison, H. Rider Haggard, William Hope Hodgson, C. J. Cutliffe Hyne, William Morris, Mervyn Peake), Irish (Lord Dunsany), Scottish (George MacDonald), or Welsh (Arthur Machen), all writers from the early part of the twentieth century, a period that in Britain and Ireland had seen a small but earnest effusion of literary fantasy, horror, ghost stories, and the supernatural. Ballantine's grouping of authors constructed what Brian Attebery later called the "fuzzy set" of fantasy,[5] a group of tap root texts[6] that has remained current under the Gollancz Fantasy Masterworks imprint, which has extended the creation of a body of "classics" central to the field.

The two main manifestations of "romance," science fiction and fantasy, superficially differ in trajectories and styles in the twentieth century. Neither is interested in setting its narrative in the world that we know and experience, and both are interested in speculating "what if?" But science fiction is normally set in the universe as we understand it, following scientific laws and, very often, describing futures which, if not always plausible, are at least possible within current scientific and historical thought. What if there is a nuclear war? What if we run out of fossil fuels? What if we try to colonize Mars? What if we meet aliens? Fantasy, on the other hand, often consciously flouts scientific understandings, and imagines what is thought to be impossible. What if magic existed? What if someone met an angel, or a unicorn? Science fiction treats the possible, fantasy the impossible. There are problems with this loose definition, of course, in that boundaries between possible and impossible depend on individual perception. Many people (far more in America than in Europe) believe in angels: so a novel about angels would not necessarily be perceived as "fantasy" by an author who was a believer. Many scientists do not believe that time travel or faster-than-light space vehicles are possible: are novels that employ those motifs not science fiction, but fantasy? Useful caveats are offered by Paul Kincaid and Farah Mendlesohn, who suggest that science fiction regards the universe as ultimately indifferent to human ideals, but susceptible to human machinations, while fantasy is intimately concerned with human ideals, but is often impervious to attempts to resist fate.

The distinctions between the genres are sometimes deliberately and creatively obscured by the author: some writers explain the fantastic in scientific terms or place science within a fantastical realm. China Miéville's *Perdido Street Station* (2000), the touchstone of the New Weird (see below), has been claimed as both science fiction and as fantasy: the strange cityscape of New Crobuzon and its grotesque inhabitants have the feel of fantasy, and yet the main protagonist is a scientist and all the phenomena can be rationally and scientifically explained. There is also the tradition of alternate history (embraced by both genres) that seems to span the rational and the irrational, both in its construction of alternate histories (frequently justified with reference to scientific parallel world theories) and the possible presence of magic in that alternate. Keith Roberts's *Pavane* (1966) is a good example. Set in England in the late twentieth century, science and technology are developing slowly after the victory of the Spanish Armada and the reimposition of Catholicism has rendered the Scientific Revolution impossible. We discover that the fairies, in which so many believed in the sixteenth century, are still around. *Pavane* is science fiction that suddenly becomes fantasy.

In recent decades fantasy has outsold science fiction, so writing science fiction with a fantasy feel might be considered commercial common sense. But this blurring of the boundaries has been endemic to the form and has prevented the two genres from ever separating completely. Some critics avoid such problems by following the critic John Clute, and using a word drawn from several European languages that encompasses both fantasy and science fiction, as well as other modes or genres that some people would see as separate categories, such as ghost stories: the word is not the ambiguous "romance," but *fantastika*.

In thinking about the history of science fiction in the British Isles in the twentieth century, one inevitably starts with H. G. Wells. Wells published his first successful SF story, "The Time Machine," in 1895, and he died in 1946. For that span of years Wells defines what science fiction is about (the pulp magazines in the USA began with reprints of his work and Verne's). Indeed, what he wrote (and all his significant science fiction had been published by 1914) covers themes that science fiction continues to explore. His novels about time travel, alien invasion (*The War of the Worlds*, 1898), space travel (*The First Men in the Moon*, 1901), artificial creation of new life-forms (*The Island of Dr Moreau*, 1896), invisibility (*The Invisible Man*, 1897), cosmic catastrophe (*In the Days of the Comet*, 1906), future warfare (*The War in the Air*, 1908) became the gold standard for his immediate followers, who consisted of anyone who wrote novels of the future during Wells's lifetime, even those who were attacking what he stood for (such as Aldous Huxley, who was skeptical that the future would be utopian, as Wells in his optimistic moments believed).

The gigantic presence of Wells must not be allowed to obscure his contemporaries: George Griffith, in particular, was a very real rival. *The Angel of the Revolution* (1893), in which a revolutionary fleet of airplanes forces humanity into a world state, was very popular, and Griffith followed it with novels exploring immortality, space flight, telepathy, and other themes. It is worth noting that the short story, usually published in fiction magazines that were proliferating in the decades before the First World War, was just as important for the development of science fiction and fantasy as the novel. As science fiction and fantasy were not yet marginalized, writers such as Rudyard Kipling and Conan Doyle cheerfully wrote stories about scientific advances, and unlike Wells were not averse either to writing ghost stories or stories that likewise belong to the category of "the weird."

The decades before the First World War are the heyday of the uncanny, a category which includes early vampire fiction, domestic ghost stories, and the weird tales of tentacled or divine horror:[7] the Irish writer Bram Stoker publishes *Dracula* in 1897; M. R. James produces *Ghost Stories of an Antiquary* in 1904; in 1906 and 1907 Algernon Blackwood publishes his first two collections of ghost and horror stories. Blackwood was a member of the Hermetic Order of the Golden Dawn (the occultist society of which W. B. Yeats was Imperator between 1900 and 1902); other writers of the weird were members, among whom probably the most interesting was Arthur Machen. He made his name with *The Great God Pan* (1890), in which a young woman is forced into seeing Pan, the Devil, himself. *The Three Impostors* (1895) tells of the eruption of malevolent "Little People" into Victorian London; *The Hill of Dreams* (1907) refers to a Welsh hill where the protagonist has visions of life in Roman Britain. Machen's short story "The Bowmen" probably had the greatest impact: its idea of a supernatural troop of medieval archers arriving to help British soldiers in the trenches at Mons seems to have been directly responsible for the emergence of the legend of the Angels of Mons a few months later.

Early weird fiction carefully bestrides the borderland between science fiction and fantasy. William Hope Hodgson's impressive *oeuvre* is of this kind. *The Boats of the "Glen Carrig"* (1907) imagines strange beings in a sea clogged by seaweed; *The House on the Borderland* (1908) is a house on the threshold of time and space; its occupant experiences terrifying visions, including one of the inhuman far future. Hodgson's most original work is his *The Night Land* (1912), a love story set in the perpetual darkness of a dying Earth, inhabited by enigmatic monsters. Hodgson's fertile imaginings were cut short by a shell at Ypres, in the last months of the First World War.

Weird fiction continues to develop in the postwar period. One example, which barely sold at the time, but which is now regarded as a minor classic, is *A Voyage to Arcturus* (1920) by the Scottish writer David Lindsay. The hero,

Maskull, travels (in mystic fashion) to Tormance, a planet orbiting Arcturus, where his body undergoes transformations and he encounters esoteric philosophic systems. Equally enigmatic and misunderstood are the almost contemporary novels by E. R. Eddison. In *The Worm Ourobouros* (1922) Lessingham travels mystically to what is allegedly the planet Mercury, where he observes a vast and apparently pointless war. Lessingham appears again in Eddison's Zimiamvia sequence, which begins with *Mistress of Mistresses* (1935), whose world of Zimiamvia appears to be the afterlife of the Mercury of the earlier novel. Unlike most fantasy, there is little or no morality in Eddison's work, only a general ennui and despair. He has little influence on later fantasy (partly because of his impenetrable archaising style).

Alongside weird fiction, another form of fantasy, pioneered by Edith Nesbit, can be described as the urban domestic fantasy. Nesbit's narratives for children, including *The Phoenix and the Carpet* (1904) and *The Story of the Amulet* (1906), bring fantasy in to our own cozy world, without any of the sinister edge of horror. Nesbit began a tradition whose best modern exponents are Joan Aiken (the Armitage family stories), Diana Wynne Jones (*Archer's Goon* [1984]), and Neil Gaiman (*Anansi Boys* [2005]). In a similar vein is the singular but outstanding novel *Lud-in-the-Mist* by Hope Mirrlees (1926) which although an "other world" novel – a pastoral story in a pseudo-medieval town – uses the same mode and story form as Nesbit's fantasies. The inhabitants of Lud-in-the-Mist deny the existence of nearby fairyland and the fairy fruit that is smuggled in from it. It is denial, not the fairy fruit itself, that causes ensuing disaster. A much more prolific fantasist is the Irish peer, Lord Dunsany: his evocative short stories of gods, demons, and monstrous beings are published from 1905 onwards, but his most memorable work is probably *The King of Elfland's Daughter* (1924). It is like *Lud-in-the-Mist* a story of the borderland between the "real" world and Faërie, a theme that fascinates British writers, perhaps because the borders of the kingdoms within the Island of Britain (Scotland, England and Wales) have traditionally been so permeable. Of contemporary works, the best in this vein are Robert Holdstock's *Mythago Wood* (1984), which explores the relationship between a family and a "haunted" wood, and Steve Cockayne's *Wanderers and Islanders* (2002), which leaves the reader wondering which of a number of worlds are "real." Perhaps the most successful interwar fantasy was Virginia Woolf's *Orlando* (1928), which has gained readership because its elision of the borderlines of gender has become part of current gender debate.

British writers of the scientific romance at first benefitted from the reputation gained for the form by Wells. Their works were published as hard-back volumes, and were reviewed in the serious press, unlike their American counterparts, whose careers ran mainly in slick and pulp magazines. Yet few are remembered or still in print. One survivor is S. Fowler Wright, whose works reveal considerable imagination. *The Amphibians* (1925) is a vision of the far future, in which humans have already become extinct; its sequel is *The World Below* (1929). His most successful novel is *Deluge* (1927), in which much of the inhabited world disappears below the oceans and the Cotswolds remain as a little archipelago. As Brian Stableford's excellent account of scientific romance points out, while most stories of this kind talk about how difficult it is for survivors to keep up the institutions of civilization, for Wright it is precisely civilization that is to blame for the disasters afflicting humanity.[8] Of those that have not survived in the popular memory, but remain interesting, are the works of suffragist Cicely Hamilton (*Theodore Savage: A Story of the Past or the Future*, 1922) and of the conscientious objector and later Deputy Speaker Barbara Wootton (*London's Burning: A Novel for the Decline and Fall of the Liberal Age*, 1936). Both found the polemical forms of science fiction, then as now, could carry political weight without destroying narrative interest.

Of the interwar writers of scientific romance, Olaf Stapledon is assuredly the most important. His first novel, *Last and First Men* (1930), is a future history of *homo sapiens* and of species that evolve from *homo sapiens*, extending over two billion years. In 1938 it became one of the first Pelican books, the paperback imprint which Penguin used for non-fiction. Stapledon was a teaching philosopher, and Penguin packaged the volume as philosophy or prediction rather than fiction. It is a difficult book to assess, but it contains more ideas than a shelf-full of science fiction by other authors, and its immense sweep in time and space remains awe inspiring and thought provoking. Stapledon followed this with three other impressive works. *Odd John* (1935) and *Sirius* (1944) concern the development of super-intelligence, the first in a man and the second in a dog, and explore questions of morality and psychology which were challenging in their time. Stapledon's masterpiece is *Star Maker* (1937), a vision of the imperfect cosmos and the sufferings of its various intelligent species; his explanation ultimately is that the Star Maker Himself is still evolving, and our universe is just an infant's experiment.

When British and Irish writers were mostly in hardback, British readers also had access to imported American magazines and the new "pulps." Some magazines had their own British reprints, which were usually abridged. The two highly influential magazines edited by John W. Campbell Jr. – *Astounding Science Fiction* and *Unknown* (a fantasy magazine) – both appeared in British reprints throughout the Second World War and beyond, while the even more influential American fantasy magazine *Weird Tales* appeared in British editions and reprints intermittently from 1942 to 1954. American science fiction magazines soon defined the way science fiction readers saw the field, while British writers began to imitate the new, fast-paced fiction, and specifically the narrative innovations, of the so-called "Golden Age" of American science fiction, whose two greatest names are Robert A. Heinlein and Isaac Asimov. Apart from a few serials, most of which were republished in book form after the war, most new science fiction in the USA was in the form of short stories, and most of it was published in the specialist magazines.

It is no accident that the two most widely read SF writers in the UK in the 1950s were both Englishmen who had cut their teeth on short stories for the American magazines: John Wyndham and Arthur C. Clarke. John Wyndham Parkes Lucas Beynon Harris was publishing in American magazines since 1931 as John Beynon Harris and John Beynon, though it is only when he reinvents himself as John Wyndham with *The Day of the Triffids* in 1951 that he becomes a household name in the UK. However, and counter to the impression that can be given of American SF taking over the British market, Wyndham's reinvention involved not just a change of name; it consisted of repackaging himself as a very English writer and the heir to the recently deceased Wells. The formula which Wyndham repeats successfully is known now as the "cosy catastrophe" (a name conferred by Brian Aldiss) and involves British survivors of a disaster who display the Blitz spirit.

Arthur C. Clarke's first professional sale was to *Astounding* in 1946, and for ten years he published a number of much-anthologized stories in the magazines, of which the most famous is "The Sentinel" (adapted by Stanley Kubrick for the film *2001: A Space Odyssey* [1968]]). Most of his novels until the early 1960s are matter-of-fact (and rather wooden) accounts of stages of "the exploration of space" (the title of a non-fiction book he published in 1951): there are novels about the first moon shot, the settlement of both the moon and Mars, and the development of political systems within the solar system. He is best remembered for *Childhood's End* (1953) and *The City and the Stars* (1956), which owe more to the tradition of Wells and Stapledon than they do to American SF. In *Childhood's End* human consciousness is subsumed into the god-like Overmind; in *The City and the Stars* humanity only reaches its full potential when it accepts its lowly place in the galactic system. In contrast to this awareness of the transience and fragility of humanity, by the 1950s American SF, particularly under the influence of editor John W. Campbell, stresses the ability of humanity to accomplish anything in the universe.

The creation of a new British tradition of fantasy is largely the work of one man: Tolkien. This is not to diminish the work of his friend C. S. Lewis, whose seven Narnia books, starting with *The Lion, the Witch and the Wardrobe* in 1950, revitalized British fantasy for children, or the original and disturbing work of Mervyn Peake, who begins exploring the gothic world of Gormenghast Castle with *Titus Groan* in 1946. But a large part of fantasy in the English-speaking world in the last decades of the twentieth century is a reaction to Tolkien's work, either in imitation or rejection. In England, indeed, part of his influence is very direct: a number of British writers of fantasy, including Diana Wynne Jones and Susan Cooper, were taught Old English at Oxford by Professor Tolkien.

Tolkien's fantasy world, Middle-Earth (a designation taken directly from the Old English designation for our own world), was evolving in his head and on paper from his time in the trenches of the First World War. His children's book *The Hobbit* (1937) had been successful, and not long after its publication Tolkien began a continuation. The three volumes of *The Lord of the Rings* are a *tour de force* of world-creation and of form.

For his world-creation Tolkien creates not just a map and a history, but several languages; he explained to W. H. Auden that he wrote his stories to provide a world in which his languages could function.[9] He drew on his knowledge of medieval Europe to create several societies within his world, and to provide them each with a past going back several thousand years, giving his characters a sense of history and tradition. The long-term success of *The Lord of the Rings* (and in several large polls it was voted the favorite British novel of the twentieth century in any genre) can also be ascribed to the powerful integration of Tolkien's own experience of war, and to the degree to which the book captures the political shift in Britain, from the Lords to the Commons, via the shift from Aragorn, the elves, and the wizards to the hobbits of the Shire.

It is not until the late 1970s that the imitations begin. After that, *Lord of the Rings* set the pattern for a publishing phenomenon. Fantasy books had to be in a trilogy; they had to contain a map of the fantasy world; the heroes or heroines had to travel through this world (visiting each place on the map at least once), in the course of their struggle against the evil Dark Lord; and, of course, the Dark Lord had to be defeated at the end and the world restored. A critical change, however, was that now the protagonists frequently went in search of power (Tolkien's hobbits had been determined to *destroy* the object of power). Diana Wynne Jones offers a pitiless and extremely funny critique of this whole phenomenon in *The Tough Guide to Fantasyland* (1996). However, a detailed study of the imitations does not have to appear in a volume about the novel in Britain and Ireland: the bulk of them have been by Americans and, more recently, Australians. On the whole, emulation is not the reaction of British writers of fantasy; indeed some, like the highly prolific Michael Moorcock, write novels that are deliberate attacks on what he considers Tolkien's cozy bourgeois complacency, and current writers such as Juliet McKenna offer further subversions.

Because most writers in SF and fantasy received their start in the magazines, the emergence of an indigenous magazine culture was vitally important, with editors as important as authors: E. J. ("Ted") Carnell, for example. Carnell was a London-based SF fan, who, after several false starts, established Nova Publications in 1949, which eventually produced three regular monthly magazines: *New Worlds* (under his editorship from 1949–1964), *Science Fantasy* (edited by Carnell 1950–1964) and *Science Fiction Adventures* (1958–1963). It was in these magazines that British writers who were to flourish from the 1960s onwards often saw their first publications, and in which they were able to develop their craft. Brian W. Aldiss began publishing science fiction in 1954 in *Science Fantasy*; J. G. Ballard's first stories were in *New Worlds* and *Science Fantasy* in 1956; Michael Moorcock's first SF novel was published in *Science Fiction Adventures* in 1962, and he subsequently published in both *Science Fantasy* and *New Worlds*; Terry Pratchett's first professional sale was in *Science Fantasy* in 1963. One of Carnell's finds was James White, a highly entertaining writer from Northern Ireland (until the twenty-first century there are no significant SF writers from the Irish Republic). Without Ted Carnell science fiction and fantasy would have developed quite differently.

By the early 1960s a number of writers were convinced that the field had become too formulaic, predictable, and self-referential; they wanted it to be less conservative, to reflect the experimental fiction of the "mainstream," and to reincorporate speculative fiction into the mainstream of literature. The chance came when Michael Moorcock took over the editorship of *New Worlds* in mid-1964. Older *New Worlds* writers like Aldiss and Ballard joined the project, and it attracted newer British writers such as Barrington J. Bayley and M. John Harrison, as well as American writers, notably Thomas M. Disch, Pamela Zoline, Samuel R. Delany and John T. Sladek, each of whom came over to London for extended periods. This self-conscious movement became known as the New Wave. It energized writers, pushed science fiction and fantasy in new directions, bringing "taboo" elements (such as sex and politics) into open discussion, discarding clichéd SF themes such as space travel (ironically just as America's space program was reaching its culmination), welcoming experimental new writers such as Josephine Saxton (*The Hieros Gamos of Sam and An Smith*, 1969) and Angela Carter (*Heroes and Villains*, 1969) and alienating many devoted readers of SF and fantasy while recruiting new audiences. Regular production of *New Worlds* ceased in April 1970 but its influence continued. Aldiss's most experimental and surrealist work, *Report on Probability A*, written in 1962, took until 1968, after the New Wave had changed the climate, before he found a publisher for it.

Aldiss and Ballard, the two most important writers associated with *New Worlds*, had already established themselves before the New Wave, and continue on similar trajectories. Ballard adopted science fictional themes in order to subvert them: he had never believed in a future that involved space-flight, his space-ships tend to be rusting away in some disused American backlot, and it is unsurprising that later in his career Ballard turns his back on science fiction altogether. Aldiss, on the other hand, while continually experimenting with realistic fiction, with poetry, and with fantasy, retained a deep affection for classic science fiction, which he expresses in his history of the field, *Billion Year Spree* (1973). He has written on a wide range of themes and has rarely repeated himself. Some critics feel that *Greybeard* (1964) is his greatest work: a story, set in and around Oxford, exploring a world that male sterility has deprived of children. The most impressive novels of the late 1960s and early 1970s come from John Brunner, an English writer whose major works were published first in the USA, and who was not associated with the New Wave at all. *Stand on Zanzibar* (1968) is a complex novel about the social and cultural effects of uncontrolled population expansion; it became the first British book to win the coveted Hugo Award for Best [SF] Novel. He followed this up with novels exploring the western industrial complex and the dangers of pollution; his *The Shockwave Rider* (1975) postulates a communications explosion in the future, and is still remembered among computer scientists for his invention of the concept of the "worm," a computing program that can propagate itself through a network.

Science fiction writers of the 1960s and 1970s are also writers of fantasy, or turn to it in the course of their career. *The Embedding* (1973) is Ian Watson's first example of his intellectual and complex SF, but he also wrote a series of fantasies in the 1980s. Christopher Priest, on the fringes of the New Wave in the 1960s, was writing science fiction in the 1970s, but established his reputation with *The Affirmation* (1981) and subsequent novels, which explore the interface between science fiction and fantasy. Tanith Lee, who writes fantasies for children at the beginning of the 1970s, turns to science fiction for adults in the middle of the decade, before returning almost exclusively to fantasy for the rest of her prolific career. Gwyneth Jones's adult science fiction begins in 1984 with *Divine Endurance*, which presents a richly described far future matriarchy, with a southeast Asian setting. Her Aleutian Trilogy (*White Queen*, *Phoenix Café* and *North Wind*), an exploration of the effect of a small group of aliens on the gender politics of earth, has been followed by *Bold as Love* (2001), a futuristic Arthurian fantasy set in a balkanized Britain. Mary Gentle first comes to prominence as a writer of complex science fiction, with *Golden Witchbreed* (1983) (the story of a female ambassador coming to terms with an alien culture), but by the end of the 1980s she turns to highly sophisticated rewritings of history in fantasy mode, such as *Rats and Gargoyles* (1990) or *Ash: A Secret History* (2000). Even Brian Stableford, who exploits his own scientific training to great effect in the 1970s, turns to fantasy in the 1980s, bringing new twists to stories about vampires and werewolves. In part the shift from SF to fantasy is a response to the market: by the 1990s UK readers are buying more fantasy than science fiction.

One of Britain's best known fantasy writers, Terry Pratchett, also begins with science fiction, but *The Colour of Magic* (1983) is the first of a series of almost forty novels set on the Discworld, a flat world carried on the back of a turtle. *The Colour of Magic* itself is not so much a fantasy as a parody of various popular American fantasies (in the same way that the *Hitch Hiker's Guide to the Galaxy* books (1979–1984) by Douglas Adams are parodies of SF). But the Discworld fills with memorable characters, and the novels become vehicles for comic but often profound satirical comment on the foibles of this world. Satire indeed becomes one of the distinguishing features of British fantasy, with Tom Holt and Robert Rankin the leading exponents.

In the late 1990s two other English fantasy writers, whose works aim at children and young adults, achieve bestseller status: Philip Pullman, whose *His Dark Materials* trilogy, beginning with *Northern Lights* (1995; US title *The Golden Compass*), follows the story of Lyra and Will and their fight to preserve the link between each human and his or her *dæmon*, a companion spirit in the form of an animal. Neither Pullman's focus on sexuality nor his atheism endears him to readers in the USA, but he has achieved critical acclaim in the UK: the third volume of the series won the Whitbread Prize in 2000, the first children's book to do so. J. K. Rowling, whose first Harry Potter book appeared in 1997 (and the last in 2007), had to weather a storm of American complaints that she was encouraging witchcraft. Her seven novels are mostly set in Hogwarts, a school for wizards and witches; long-time readers of fantasy and of British school stories find much that is familiar in them. Rowling has become Britain's wealthiest author in any genre.

Adults as well as children read the books by Pullman and Rowling, and both fantasy and young adult literature have become more respectable. Rowling's

London publisher Bloomsbury has found a bestselling successor to Rowling in Susanna Clarke's *Jonathan Strange and Mr Norrell* (2004), an intricate rewriting of England during the Napoleonic Wars as a period of the revival of traditional English magic. *Jonathan Strange* breaks out of the genre market completely, and confirms that one can write a "novel" in the classical sense with a fantastical framework. Comic books, once they were relabelled "graphic novels," also are something that adults in the UK have become more comfortable with (as adults on the Continent have been for decades). Two of the most respected writers for comics internationally are both English: Alan Moore (author of *Watchmen* [1987]) and Neil Gaiman (author of *The Sandman* series [1989–1996]).

There have always been mainstream writers who have dabbled in science fiction and fantasy, but in the late twentieth century, many writers who consider themselves part of the mainstream demonstrate the degree to which it is no longer possible to stand apart from the speculative tradition: they include Peter Ackroyd, Martin Amis, Stephen Fry, and P. D. James. Of those who have made a deliberate shift, the mainstream author most popular with genre readers is Doris Lessing for her Canopus in Argos series (*The Sirian Experiments* was short-listed for the Booker Prize). More recently, David Mitchell's *Cloud Atlas* (2004) and Kazuo Ishiguro's *Never Let Me Go* (2005) were shortlisted for the juried award for SF published in the UK, the Arthur C. Clarke Award.

The last decade of the twentieth century is a boom time in the UK for SF and fantasy. British writers Colin Greenland, M. John Harrison, Stephen Baxter, Iain M. Banks, Paul McAuley, and Alistair Reynolds subvert and revive the space opera. The alien contact novel is given a shot in the arm by Gwyneth Jones, Karen Traviss, and Liz Williams. Ken MacLeod, Charles Stross, and Jon Courtenay Grimwood turn an eye on economics and international politics. Justina Robson and Stross have become absorbed with the idea of the Singularity: a runaway and unpredictable technological change. Perhaps the distinctive commonality of all of these authors is the way in which they aim for a cynical and politicized optimism, very different both from the American mood and from the "miserabilism" which had characterized British SF in the 1970s. This has been continued and extended by new writers such as Jaine Fenn, Tony Ballantyne, Colin Harvey, and Jon George; but the merging of US and UK publishers and the loss of some imprints is a cause for concern.

The British boom in SF takes place prior to the end of the twentieth century, that in fantasy as the new century opens. Gentle's *Ash* and Miéville's *Perdido Street Station* were the hotly tipped favorites for the Arthur C. Clarke Award in 2001, an award that is technically for science fiction. British fantasy of the new century is edgy and technological, as likely to feature steam engines as tentacles; and frequently both. Sometimes labelled the "New Weird," a category most of whose members deny belonging to, or sometimes "interstitial," modern British fantasy becomes unpredictable and interested in unpredictability. Graham Joyce, Robert Holdstock, Liz Williams, Steve Cockayne, Chris Wooding, Hal Duncan, Alan Campbell, Joe Abercrombie, Jeff Noon, Steph Swainston, K. J. Parker, Kari Sperring, Helen Oyeymi, Mark Charon Newton, and M. D. Lachlan, all seeking to mix the ingredients differently, produce phantasmagoric urban fantasies, absurdist other worlds, and rich historical tapestries, relentlessly interrogative and political. Of the most recent contributions to fantasy some of the best work has been in children's books: Frances Hardinge and Jonathan Stroud both demonstrate that even for the young the form can support complex political discussions of race, class, and cultural conflict.

Notes

1. Quoted in Margaret Drabble, ed., *The Oxford Companion to English Literature* (6th edn, Oxford University Press, 2000), p. 213.
2. I. F. Clarke, *Voices Prophesying War, 1763–1984* (2nd edn, London and New York: Oxford University Press, 1992).
3. Tom Shippey, *J. R. R. Tolkien, Author of the Century* (Boston and New York: Houghton Mifflin, 2000), p. 1.
4. Gary Westfahl, *Hugo Gernsback and the Century of Science Fiction* (Jefferson, NC: McFarland, 2007), p. 20.
5. Brian Attebery, *Strategies of Fantasy* (Bloomington: Indiana University Press, 1992), pp. 12–13.
6. John Clute and John Grant, eds., *The Encyclopedia of Fantasy* (London: Orbit, 1997), pp. 921–922.
7. China Miéville, "Weird Fiction," in *The Routledge Companion to Science Fiction*, ed. Mark Bould, Andrew M. Butler, Adam Roberts, and Sherryl Vint (Abingdon and New York: Routledge, 2009), pp. 510–515.
8. Brian Stableford, *Scientific Romance in Britain, 1890–1950* (London: Fourth Estate, 1985), p. 186.
9. Humphrey Carpenter, ed., *The Letters of J. R. R. Tolkien* (George Allen and Unwin, 1981), p. 214.

Select bibliography

The following suggested readings do not include texts already cited in the chapters and endnotes.

1 The novel before "the novel"

Archibald, Elizabeth. *Incest and the Medieval Imagination*. Oxford University Press, 2001.
Heiserman, Arthur Ray. *The Novel Before the Novel*. University of Chicago Press, 1977.
Reardon, B. P. *The Forms of Greek Romance*. Princeton University Press, 1991.

2 Biographical form

Benstock, Shari. *The Private Self: Theory and Practice of Women's Autobiographical Writings*. Chapel Hill, NC: University of North Carolina Press, 1988.
Faller, Lincoln. *Turned to Account: The Form and Function of Criminal Biography in Late Seventeenth and Early Eighteenth-Century England*. Cambridge University Press, 1988.
Olney, James. *Memory and Narrative: The Weave of Life-Writing*. University of Chicago Press, 1999.

3 Legal discourse and novelistic form

Schmidgen, Wolfram. *Eighteenth-Century Fiction and the Law of Property*. Cambridge University Press, 2002.
Swan, Beth. *Fictions of Law: An Investigation of the Law in Eighteenth-Century English Fiction*. New York and Frankfurt: Peter Lang, 1997.
Zomchik, John P. *Family and the Law in Eighteenth-Century Fiction: The Public Conscience in the Private Sphere*. Cambridge University Press, 1993.

4 Novelistic history

Clingham, Greg. *Johnson, Writing, and Memory*. Cambridge University Press, 2002.
Griffin, Robert J. *Wordsworth's Pope: A Study in Literary Historiography*. Cambridge University Press, 1995.

5 Interiorities

Freeman, Lisa. *Character's Theatre: Genre and Identity on the Eighteenth-Century Stage.* Philadelphia: University of Pennsylvania Press, 2001.

Van Sant, Ann Jesse. *Eighteenth-Century Sensibility and the Novel: The Senses in Social Context.* Cambridge University Press, 2004.

Wahrman, Dror. *The Making of the Modern Self: Identity and Culture in Eighteenth-Century England.* New Haven, CT: Yale University Press, 2004.

6 Samuel Richardson

Barchas, Janine. *Graphic Design, Print Culture, and the Eighteenth-Century Novel.* Cambridge University Press, 2003.

Bueler, Lois E., ed. *Clarissa: The Eighteenth-Century Response, 1747–1804,* 2 vols. New York: AMS Press, 2010.

Keymer, Tom. *Richardson's "Clarissa" and the Eighteenth-Century Reader.* Cambridge University Press, 1992.

McKeon, Michael. *The Secret History of Domesticity: Public, Private, and the Division of Knowledge.* Baltimore, MD: Johns Hopkins University Press, 2005.

Siskin, Clifford. *The Work of Writing.* Baltimore, MD: Johns Hopkins University Press, 1998.

Varey, Simon. *Space and the Eighteenth-Century British Novel.* Cambridge University Press, 1990.

Yount, Janet Aikins, ed. *Clarissa: The Twentieth-Century Response, 1900–1950.* New York: AMS Press, 2011.

7 Domesticity and novel narratives

Armstrong, Nancy. *Desire and Domestic Fiction: A Political History of the Novel.* Oxford University Press, 1990.

Spencer, Jane. *The Rise of the Woman Novelist.* Oxford University Press, 1986.

Thompson, Helen. *Ingenuous Subjection: Compliance and Power in the Eighteenth-Century Domestic Novel.* Philadelphia: University of Pennsylvania Press, 2005.

Tristram, Philippa. *Living Space in Fact and Fiction.* London: Routledge, 1989.

8 Obscenity and erotics of fiction

Darnton, Robert. *The Forbidden Best-Sellers of Revolutionary France.* New York: Norton, 1995.

Ferguson, Frances. *Pornography, The Theory: What Utilitarianism Did to Action.* University of Chicago Press, 2004.

Mudge, Bradford. *The Whore's Story: Women, Pornography, and the British Novel, 1684–1830.* New York: Oxford University Press, 2000.

Peakman, Julie. *Mighty Lewd Books: The Development of Pornography in Eighteenth-Century England.* Basingstoke: Palgrave Macmillan, 2003.

Relihan, Constance Caroline, and Goran V. Stanivukovic, eds. *Prose Fiction and Early Modern Sexualities in England 1570–1640*. New York: Palgrave Macmillan, 2004.

9 Cognitive alternatives to interiority

Richardson, Alan. *The Neural Sublime: Cognitive Theories and Romantic Texts*. Baltimore, MD: Johns Hopkins University Press, 2010.

Vermeule, Blakey. *Why Do We Care About Literary Characters?* Baltimore, MD: Johns Hopkins University Press, 2010.

Zunshine, Lisa, ed. *Introduction to Cognitive Cultural Studies*. Baltimore, MD: Johns Hopkins University Press, 2010.

10 The novel and four kingdoms

Hechter, Michael. *Internal Colonialism: The Celtic Fringe in British National Development*. Berkeley: University of California Press, 1975.

Mullan, John. *Sentiment and Sociability: The Language of Feeling in the Eighteenth Century*. Oxford: Clarendon Press, 1988.

Pittock, Murray G. H. *Inventing and Resisting Britain: Cultural Identities in Britain and Ireland, 1685–1789*. New York: St. Martin's Press, 1997.

11 Money's productivity

Courtemanche, Eleanor. *The "Invisible Hand" and British Fiction, 1818–1860: Adam Smith, Political Economy, and the Genre of Realism*. Basingstoke: Palgrave Macmillan, 2011.

Goux, Jean-Joseph. *The Coiners of Language*, trans. Jennifer Curtis Gage. Norman: University of Oklahoma Press, 1994.

Poovey, Mary. *Genres of the Credit Economy: Mediating Value in Eighteenth- and Nineteenth-Century Britain*. University of Chicago Press, 2008.

Trotter, David. *Circulation: Defoe, Dickens, and the Economies of the Novel*. New York: St. Martin's Press, 1988.

Vernon, John. *Money and Fiction: Literary Realism in the Nineteenth and Early Twentieth Centuries*. Ithaca: Cornell University Press, 1984.

12 Imagining the Pacific

Aravamudan, Srinivas. *Tropicopolitans: Colonialism and Agency, 1688–1804*. Durham, NC: Duke University Press, 1999.

Edwards, Philip. *The Story of the Voyage: Sea Narratives in Eighteenth-Century England*. Cambridge University Press, 1994.

Lamb, Jonathan. *Preserving the Self in the South Seas, 1680–1840*. University of Chicago Press, 2001.

13 Editorial fictions

Benedict, Barbara M. *Framing Feeling: Sentiment and Style in English Prose Fiction, 1745-1800.* New York: AMS Press, 1994.

Keymer, Thomas and Peter Sabor. Pamela *in the Marketplace.* Cambridge University Press, 2005.

Sher, Richard. *The Enlightenment and the Book.* University of Chicago Press, 2007.

St. Clair, William. *The Reading Nation in the Romantic Period.* Cambridge University Press, 2007.

14 Extraordinary narrators

Blackwell, Mark, ed. *The Secret Life of Things: Animals, Objects, and It-Narratives in Eighteenth-Century England.* Lewisburg, PA: Bucknell University Press, 2007.

Keymer, Thomas. *Sterne, the Moderns, and the Novel.* Oxford University Press, 2002.

Lupton, Christina. "The Knowing Book: Authors, It-Narratives and Objectification in the Eighteenth Century." *Novel* 39: 3 (2006), 402–420.

Park, Julie. *The Self and It: Novel Objects in Eighteenth-Century England.* Stanford University Press, 2010.

Spacks, Patricia Meyer. *Novel Beginnings: Experiments in Eighteenth-Century Fiction.* New Haven, CT: Yale University Press, 2006.

15 Romance redivivus

Black, Scott. "The Adventures of Love in *Tom Jones,*" *Henry Fielding in Our Time,* ed. J. A. Downie. Newcastle-upon-Tyne: Cambridge Scholars Press, 2008, 27–50.

Moore, Steven. *The Novel: An Alternative History, Beginnings to 1600.* New York: Continuum, 2010.

Moretti, Franco. "The Novel: History and Theory." *New Left Review* 52 (2008), 111–124.

Radway, Janice A. *Reading the Romance: Women, Patriarchy, and Popular Literature,* 2nd edn. Chapel Hill: University of North Carolina Press, 1991.

Regis, Pamela. *A Natural History of the Romance Novel.* Philadelphia: University of Pennsylvania Press, 2007.

16 Gothic

Kilgour, Maggie. *The Rise of the Gothic Novel.* London: Routledge, 1995.

McFarlane, Cameron. *The Sodomite in Satire and Fiction, 1660–1750.* New York: Columbia University Press, 1997.

Turley, Hans. *Rum, Sodomy, and the Lash: Piracy, Sexuality, and Masculine Identity.* New York University Press, 2001.

17 Walter Scott

Broadie, Alexander, ed. *The Cambridge Companion to the Scottish Enlightenment*. Cambridge University Press, 2003.

Duncan, Ian. *Scott's Shadow*. Princeton University Press, 2007.

O'Brien, Karen. *Narratives of Enlightenment*. Cambridge University Press, 1997.

18 Edgeworth, Austen, Dickens, and Trollope

Bal, Mieke. *Narratology: Introduction to the Theory of Narrative*. 3rd edn. Toronto: University of Toronto Press, 2009.

"Over-Writing as Un-writing: Descriptions, World-Making, and Novelistic Time." *The Novel* Vol. II: *Forms and Themes*, ed. Franco Moretti. Princeton and Oxford: Princeton University Press, 2006, 571–610.

Caserio, Robert L. "The Name of the Horse: *Hard Times*, Semiotics, and the Supernatural," *Novel* 20: 1 (1986), 5–23.

Ermarth, Elizabeth. *Realism and Consensus in the English Novel*. Princeton University Press, 1983.

Moretti, Franco. "Serious Century." *The Novel* Vol. I: *History, Geography, and Culture*, ed. Franco Moretti. Princeton and Oxford: Princeton University Press, 2006, 364–400.

19 Women, children, and labor

Kelly, Gary. *The English Jacobin Novel, 1780–1805*. New York: Oxford University Press, 1976.

Lesjak, Carolyn. *Working Fictions: A Genealogy of the Victorian Novel*. Durham, NC: Duke University Press, 2006.

Plotz, John. *The Crowd: British Literature and Public Politics*. Berkeley: University of California Press, 2000.

Richardson, Angelique and Chris Willis, eds. *The New Woman in Fiction and Fact: Fin de Siècle Feminisms*. New York: Palgrave, 2001.

20 Spaces and places (I)

Bivona, Daniel. *Desire and Contradiction: Imperial Vision and Domestic Debates in Victorian Literature*. Manchester University Press, 1990.

Bodenheimer, Rosemarie. *The Politics of Story in Victorian Fiction*. Ithaca, NY and London: Cornell University Press, 1988.

Duthie, Enid. *The Foreign Vision of Charlotte Brontë*. London: Macmillan, 1975.

Meyer, Susan. *Imperialism at Home: Race and Victorian Women's Fiction*. Ithaca, NY: Cornell University Press, 1996.

Semmel, Bernard. *George Eliot and the Politics of National Inheritance*. New York: Oxford University Press, 1994.

21 Dickens, Charlotte Brontë, Gaskell

Anderson, Amanda. *The Powers of Distance: Cosmopolitanism and the Cultivation of Detachment*. Princeton University Press, 2001.

Cottom, Daniel. *Social Figures: George Eliot, Social History, and Literary Representation*. Minneapolis: University of Minnesota Press, 1987.

Newsom, Robert. *A Likely Story: Probability and Play in Fiction*. New Brunswick: Rutgers University Press, 1988.

Peckham, Morse. *Victorian Revolutionaries: Speculations on Some Heroes of a Culture Crisis*. New York: George Braziller, 1970.

22 Pictures of prose

Bornstein, George, and Theresa Tinkle, eds. *The Iconic Page in Manuscript, Print, and Digital Culture*. Ann Arbor: University of Michigan Press, 1998.

Dworkin, Craig. *Reading the Illegible*. Evanston, IL: Northwestern University Press, 2003.

Hodge, Robert. *Literature as Discourse: Textual Strategies in English and History*. Baltimore, MD: Johns Hopkins University Press, 1990.

Stewart, Garrett. *The Look of Reading: Book, Painting, Text*. University of Chicago Press, 2006.

23 The novel amid new sciences

Beer, Gillian. *Open Fields: Science in Cultural Encounter*. Oxford: Clarendon Press, 1996.

Dale, Peter Allan. *In Pursuit of a Scientific Culture: Science, Art, and Society in the Victorian Age*. Madison: University of Wisconsin Press, 1989.

Levine, George, ed. *One Culture: Essays in Science and Literature*. Madison: University of Wisconsin Press, 1987.

Morton, Peter. *The Vital Science: Biology and the Literary Imagination, 1860–1900*. London: George Allen and Unwin, 1984.

Small, Helen, and Trudi Tate, eds. *Literature, Science, Psychoanalysis, 1830–1970*. Oxford University Press, 2003.

24 George Eliot

Bodenheimer, Rosemarie. *The Real Life of Mary Ann Evans: George Eliot, Her Letters and Fiction*. Ithaca, NY: Cornell University Press, 1994.

Carroll, David. *George Eliot and the Conflict of Interpretations: A Reading of the Novels.* Cambridge University Press, 1992.

Caserio, Robert L. *Plot, Story, and the Novel: From Dickens and Poe to the Modern Period.* Princeton University Press, 1979.

Qualls, Barry V. *The Secular Pilgrims of Victorian Fiction: The Novel as Book of Life.* Cambridge University Press, 1982.

25 The *Bildungsroman*

Abel, Elizabeth, Marianne Hirsch, and Elizabeth Langland, eds. *The Voyage In: Fictions of Female Development.* Hanover, NH: University Press of New England, 1983.

Bakhtin, Mikhail. "The *Bildungsroman* and its Significance in the History of Realism," *Speech Genres and Other Essays,* trans. Vernon W. McGee, ed. Caryl Emerson and Michael Holquist. Austin: University of Texas Press, 1986, 10–59.

Buckley, Jerome Hamilton. *Season of Youth: The Bildungsroman from Dickens to Golding.* Cambridge, MA: Harvard University Press, 1974.

26 The novel and social cognition

Abbott, H. Porter. *The Cambridge Introduction to Narrative,* 2nd edn. Cambridge University Press, 2008.

Case, Alison and Harry E. Shaw, eds. *Reading the Nineteenth-Century Novel: Austen to Eliot.* Oxford: Blackwell, 2008.

Herman, David. *Story Logic: Problems and Possibilities of Narrative.* Lincoln: University of Nebraska Press, 2002.

Lanser, Susan Sniader. *Fictions of Authority: Women Writers and Narrative Voice.* Ithaca, NY: Cornell University Press, 1992.

27 Clamors of eros

Cohen, William. *Sex Scandal: The Private Parts of Victorian Fiction.* Durham, NC: Duke University Press, 1996.

Girard, Rene. *Deceit, Desire, and the Novel: Self and Other in Literary Structure,* trans. Yvonne Freccero. Baltimore, MD: Johns Hopkins University Press, 1976.

Kaye, Richard. *The Flirt's Tragedy: Desire without End in Victorian and Edwardian Fiction.* Charlottesville: University of Virginia Press, 2002.

Leckie, Barbara. *Culture and Adultery: The Novel, the Newspaper, and the Law.* Philadelphia: University of Pennsylvania Press, 1999.

Showalter, Elaine. *Sexual Anarchy: Gender and Culture at the Fin de Siècle.* London: Bloomsbury, 1991.

28 The novel as immoral, anti-social force

Brombert, Victor. *In Praise of Antiheroes: Figures and Themes in Modern European Literature, 1830–1980*. University of Chicago Press, 1999.
Gay, Peter. *The Cultivation of Hatred: The Bourgeois Experience: Victoria to Freud*, vol. III. New York: Norton, 1993.
  Savage Reprisals: Bleak House, Madame Bovary, Buddenbrooks. New York: Norton, 2002.
Karlin, Daniel. *Browning's Hatreds*. Oxford: Clarendon Press, 1993.

29 Sensations

Hogle, Jerrold E., ed. *The Cambridge Companion to Gothic Fiction*. Cambridge University Press, 2002.
Punter, David. *The Literature of Terror: A History of Gothic Fictions from 1765 to the Present*. London: Longman, 1980.
Radford, Andrew. *Victorian Sensation Fiction*. New York: Palgrave Macmillan, 2009.
Robertson, Fiona. *Legitimate Histories: Scott, Gothic, and the Authorities of Fiction*. Oxford University Press, 1994.

30 Realism and romance

Armstrong, Nancy. *Fiction in the Age of Photography: The Legacy of British Realism*. Cambridge, MA: Harvard University Press, 1994.
McGowan, John P. *Representation and Revelation: Victorian Realism from Carlyle to Yeats*. Columbia: University of Missouri Press, 1986.
Rothfield, Lawrence. *Vital Signs: Medical Realism in Nineteenth-Century Fiction*. Princeton University Press, 1994.

31 Spaces and places (II)

Cannadine, David. *Ornamentalism: How the British Saw Their Empire*. London: Allen Lane, 2001.
Daly, Suzanne. "Spinning Cotton: Domestic and Industrial Novels," *Victorian Studies* 50: 2 (2008), 272–278.
Hall, Catherine. *Civilizing Subjects: Metropole and Colony in the English Imagination, 1830–1867*. Cambridge: Polity, 2002.
Koenigsberger, Kurt. *The Novel and the Menagerie: Totality, Englishness, and Empire*. Columbus: Ohio State University Press, 2007.
Kucich, John. *Imperial Masochism: British Fiction, Fantasy, and Social Class*. Princeton University Press, 2007.
Melas, Natalie. *All the Difference in the World: Postcoloniality and the Ends of Comparison*. Stanford University Press, 2007.

32 Imperial romance

Buckton, Oliver S. *Cruising with Robert Louis Stevenson*. Athens: Ohio University Press, 2007.

GoGwilt, Christopher. *The Invention of the West: Joseph Conrad and the Double-Mapping of Europe and Empire*. Stanford University Press, 1995.

Green, Martin. *Dreams of Adventure, Deeds of Empire*. New York: Basic Books, 1979.

Kemp, Sandra. *Kipling's Hidden Narratives*. Oxford: Basil Blackwell, 1988.

White, Andrea. *Joseph Conrad and the Adventure Tradition*. Cambridge University Press, 1993.

Wilson, Angus. *The Strange Ride of Rudyard Kipling: His Life and Works*. New York: The Viking Press, 1977.

33 The art novel

Katz, Tamar. *Impressionist Subjects: Gender, Interiority, and Modernist Fiction in England*. University of Illinois Press, 2000.

Mao, Douglas. *Fateful Beauty: Aesthetic Environments, Juvenile Development, and Literature, 1860–1960*. Princeton University Press, 2008.

Matz, Jesse. *Literary Impressionism and Modernist Aesthetics*. Cambridge University Press, 2001.

34 The impact of lyric, drama, and verse narrative

Brooks, Peter. *The Melodramatic Imagination*. New Haven, CT: Yale University Press, 1976.

Hadley, Elaine. *Melodramatic Tactics: Theatricalized Dissent in the English Marketplace, 1800–1885*. Stanford University Press, 1995.

Litvak, Joseph. *Caught in the Act: Theatricality in the Nineteenth-Century English Novel*. Berkeley: University of California Press, 1992.

Starr, Gabrielle. *Lyric Generations: Poetry and the Novel in the Long Eighteenth Century*. Baltimore, MD: Johns Hopkins University Press, 2004.

Stone, Donald. *The Romantic Impulse in Victorian Fiction*. Cambridge, MA: Harvard University Press, 1980.

35 James and Conrad

Freedman, Jonathan. *Professions of Taste: Henry James, British Aestheticism and Commodity Culture*. Stanford University Press, 1990.

Hampson, Robert, *Conrad's Secrets*. Basingstoke: Palgrave Macmillan, 2011.

Watt, Ian. *Conrad in the Nineteenth Century*. London: Chatto and Windus, 1980.

Winner, Viola Hopkins. *Henry James and the Visual Arts*. Charlottesville: University Press of Virginia, 1970.

36 Joyce

Attridge, Derek, ed. *The Cambridge Companion to James Joyce*, 2nd edn. Cambridge University Press, 2004.
Kenner, Hugh. *Joyce's Voices*. London: Faber, 1978.
Lawrence, Karen. *The Odyssey of Style in "Ulysses."* Princeton University Press, 1981.
Crispi, Luca and Sam Slote, eds. *How Joyce Wrote "Finnegans Wake."* Madison: University of Wisconsin Press, 2007.

37 Richardson, Woolf, Lawrence

Bluemel, Kristin. *Experimenting on the Borders of Modernism: Dorothy Richardson's "Pilgrimage."* Athens and London: University of Georgia Press, 1997.
DiBattista, Maria. *Imagining Virginia Woolf: An Experiment in Critical Biography*. Princeton University Press, 2009.
Wollaeger, Mark. *Modernism, Media, and Propaganda: British Narrative from 1900 to 1945.* Princeton University Press, 2007.

38 Wells, Forster, Firbank, Lewis, Huxley, Compton-Burnett, Green

Caserio, Robert L. *The Novel in England, 1900–1950: History and Theory.* New York: Twayne, 1999.
Greenberg, Jonathan. *Modernism, Satire, and the Novel.* Cambridge University Press, 2011.
Kenner, Hugh. *A Sinking Island: The Modern British Writers.* New York: Knopf, 1998.
Levenson, Michael. *Modernism and the Fate of Individuality: Character and Novelistic Form from Conrad to Woolf.* New York: Cambridge University Press, 1991.
Wilde, Alan. *Horizons of Assent: Modernism, Postmodernism, and the Ironic Imagination.* Baltimore, MD: Johns Hopkins University Press, 1981.

39 Beyond autonomy

Ardis, Ann L. and Leslie W. Lewis, eds. *Women's Experience of Modernity 1875–1945.* Baltimore, MD: Johns Hopkins University Press, 2003.
Liddington, J. and J. Norris. *One Hand Tied Behind Us: Rise of the Women's Suffrage Movement.* London: Virago, 1978.
Pines, Davida. *The Marriage Paradox: Modernist Novels and the Cultural Imperative to Marry.* Gainesville: University of Florida Press, 2005.

40 Fiction by women

Hammill, Faye, Esme Miskimmin, and Ashlie Sponenberg, eds. *Encyclopedia of British Women's Writing, 1900–1950.* London: Palgrave Macmillan, 2006.

Hartley, Jenny. *Millions Like Us: British Women's Fiction of the Second World War*. London: Virago, 1997.

Joannou, Maroula. *Contemporary Women's Writing: from* The Golden Notebook *to* The Colour Purple. Manchester University Press, 2000.

Lassner, Phyllis. *Colonial Strangers: Women Writing the End of the British Empire*. Rutgers University Press, 2004.

Maslen, Elizabeth. *Political and Social Issues in British Women's Fiction, 1928–1968*. London: Palgrave Macmillan, 2001.

41 The novel amid other discourses

Banfield, Ann. *The Phantom Table: Woolf, Fry, Russell and the Epistemology of Modernism*. Cambridge University Press, 2000.

Malinowski, Bronislaw. *A Diary in the Strict Sense of the Term*. New York: Harcourt Brace, 1967.

Pippin, Robert B. *Modernism as a Philosophical Problem*. Oxford: Blackwell, 1991.

Ratcliffe, Matthew. *Phenomenology, Psychiatry and the Sense of Reality*. Oxford University Press, 2008.

Ryan, Judith. *The Vanishing Subject: Early Psychology and Literary Modernism*. University of Chicago Press, 1991.

42 Thirty years of war

Knowles, Sebastian D. G. *A Purgatorial Flame: Seven British Writers in the Second World War*. Philadelphia: University of Pennsylvania Press, 1990.

Munton, Alan. *English Fiction of the Second World War*. London: Faber and Faber, 1989.

Norris, Margot. *Writing War in the Twentieth-Century*. Charlottesville: University Press of Virginia, 1998.

Piette, Adam. *Imagination at War: British Fiction and Poetry, 1939–1945*. London: Macmillan, 1995.

Rawlinson, Mark. *British Writing of the Second World War*. Oxford: Clarendon Press, 2000.

Tate, Trudi. *Modernism, History and the First World War*. Manchester University Press, 1998.

43 Thrillers

Cawelti, John, and Bruce Rosenberg. *The Spy Story*. University of Chicago Press, 1987.

Hepburn, Allan. *Intrigue: Espionage and Culture*. New Haven, CT: Yale University Press, 2005.

James, P. D. *Talking about Detective Fiction*. Toronto: Knopf, 2009.

Kestner, Joseph A. *The Edwardian Detective, 1901–1915*. Brookfield, VT: Ashgate, 2000.

Rowland, Susan. *From Agatha Christie to Ruth Rendell: British Women Writers in Detective and Crime Fiction*. New York: Palgrave, 2001.

Symons, Julian. *The Detective Story in Britain*. London: Longmans, 1962.

44 The four nations and regionalism

Draper, R. P., ed. *The Literature of Region and Nation*. Basingstoke: Macmillan, 1989.

Esty, Jed. *A Shrinking Island: Modernism and National Culture in England*. Princeton University Press, 2004.

James, David. *Contemporary British Fiction and the Artistry of Space: Style, Landscape, Perception*. London: Continuum, 2008.

Keith, W. J. *Regions of the Imagination: The Devᵉ ʳment of British Rural Fiction*. University of Toronto Press, 1988.

45 The series novel

Adams, Hazard. *Joyce Cary's Trilogies: Pursuit of the Particular Real*. Tallahassee: University Press of Florida, 1983.

Budra, Paul and Betty A. Schellenberg, eds. *Part Two: Reflections on the Sequel*. University of Toronto Press, 1998.

Hayward, Jennifer Poole. *Consuming Pleasures: Active Audiences and Serial Fictions from Dickens to Soap Opera*. Lexington: University Press of Kentucky, 1997.

Payne, David. *The Reenchantment of Nineteenth-century Fiction: Dickens, Thackeray, George Eliot, and Serialization*. Houndmills and New York: Palgrave Macmillan, 2005.

46 The novel's West Indian revolution

Donnell, Alison. *Twentieth-Century Caribbean Literature: Critical Moments in Anglophone Literary History*. New York: Routledge, 2006.

Breiner, Laurence. *Introduction to West Indian Poetry*. Cambridge University Press, 1998.

Edmondson, Belinda. *Making Men: Gender, Literary Authority, and Women's Writing in Caribbean Narrative*. Durham, NC: Duke University Press, 1999.

Emery, Mary Lou. *Caribbean Literature and the Visual*. Cambridge University Press, 2004.

Schwarz, Bill, ed. *West Indian Intellectuals in Britain*. Manchester University Press, 2003.

47 Postwar experiment

Giles, Gordon, ed. *Beyond the Words: Eleven Writers in Search of a New Fiction*. London: Hutchinson, 1975.

Josipovici, Gabriel. *The World and the Book: A Study of Modern Fiction*. London: Macmillan, 1971.

The Lessons of Modernism and Other Essays. London: Macmillan, 1987.

Murphy, Richard. *Theorizing the Avant-Garde: Modernism, Expressionism, and the Problem of Postmodernity*. Cambridge University Press, 1998.

Tew, Philip. *B. S. Johnson: A Critical Reading*. Manchester University Press, 2001.

48 The novel amid new technology and media

Avery, Todd. *Radio Modernism: Literature, Ethics, and the BBC, 1922–1938.* Aldershot: Ashgate, 2006.

Cohen, Debra Rae, Michael Coyle and Jane Lewty, eds. *Broadcasting Modernism.* Gainesville: University Press of Florida, 2009.

Gevirtz, Susan. *Narrative's Journey: The Fiction and Film Writing of Dorothy Richardson.* New York: Peter Lang, 1996.

Murphet, Julian. *Multimedia Modernism.* Cambridge University Press, 2009.

49 Same-sex desire

Bristow, Joseph. *Effeminate England: Homoerotic Writing after 1885.* Buckingham: Open University Press, 1995.

Hammond, Paul. *Love Between Men in English Literature.* London: Macmillan, 1996.

Hobby, Elaine, and Chris White. *What Lesbians Do in Books.* London: Women's Press, 1991.

Sinfield, Alan. *The Wilde Century: Effeminacy, Oscar Wilde and the Queer Moment.* London and New York: Cassell, 1994.

Summers, Claude J., ed. *The Gay and Lesbian Literary Heritage: A Reader's Companion to the Writers and Their Works, from Antiquity to the Present.* New York: Henry Holt, 1995.

Woods, Gregory. *A History of Gay Literature: The Male Tradition.* New Haven, CT and London: Yale University Press, 1998.

50 From Wells to John Berger

Dahrendorf, Ralf. *The Modern Social Conflict.* Berkeley: University of California Press, 1988.

Ferrall, Charles. *Modernist Writing and Reactionary Politics.* Cambridge University Press, 2001.

Rose, Jonathan. *The Intellectual Life of the British Working Classes.* New Haven, CT: Yale University Press, 2001.

Wells, H. G. *The New World Order.* New York: Alfred A. Knopf, 1940.

51 Postcolonial novel

Ashcroft, Bill, Gareth Griffiths, and Helen Tiffin. *The Empire Writes Back: Theory and Practice in Postcolonial Literatures.* London: Routledge, 1989.

Boehmer, Elleke. *Colonial and Postcolonial Literature.* Oxford University Press, 1995.

Innes, C. L. *The Cambridge Introduction to Postcolonial Literatures in English.* Cambridge University Press, 2007.

Stein, Mark. *Black British Literature: Novels of Transformation.* Columbus: Ohio State University Press, 2004.

Thieme, John. *Postcolonial Con-texts.* London/New York: Continuum, 2001.

52 History and heritage

Boccardi, Mariadele. *The Contemporary British Historical Novel: Representation, Nation, Empire.* London: Palgrave, 2009.

Childs, Peter. "The English Heritage Industry and Other Trends in the Novel at the Millennium." *A Companion to the British and Irish Novel: 1945–2000*, ed. Brian W. Shaffer. Oxford: Blackwell, 2005, 210–224.

Gutleben, Christian. *Nostalgic Postmodernism: The Victorian Tradition and the Contemporary British Novel.* Amsterdam: Rodopi, 2002.

Head, Dominic. *The State of the Novel.* Oxford: Blackwell, 2008.

Holmes, Frederick M. *The Historical Imagination: Postmodernism and the Treatment of the Past in Contemporary British Fiction.* University of Victoria Press, 1997.

53 Twentieth-century satire

Elliott, Robert C. *The Power of Satire.* Princeton University Press, 1960.

   The Shape of Utopia. University of Chicago Press, 1970.

Frye, Northrop. *The Anatomy of Criticism: Four Essays.* Princeton University Press, 1957.

Overy, Richard. *The Morbid Age: Britain Between the Wars.* London: Allen Lane, 2009.

54 Unending romance

Csicsery-Ronay, Jr., Istvan. *The Seven Beauties of Science Fiction.* Middletown, CT: Wesleyan University Press, 2008.

Hume, Kathryn D. *Fantasy and Mimesis. Responses to Reality in Western Literature.* London: Methuen, 1984.

James, Edward. *Science Fiction in the Twentieth Century.* Oxford University Press, 1994.

Jones, Gwyneth. *Deconstructing the Starships: Science, Fiction and Reality.* Liverpool University Press, 1999.

Kincaid, Paul. *What It Is We Do When We Read Science Fiction.* Harold Wood, Essex: Beccon, 2008.

Mendlesohn, Farah. "Introduction: Reading Science Fiction." *The Cambridge Companion to Science Fiction*, ed. Edward James and Farah Mendlesohn. Cambridge University Press, 2003, 1–15.

   Rhetorics of Fantasy. Middletown, CT: Wesleyan University Press, 2008.

Mendlesohn, Farah and Edward James. *A Short History of Fantasy.* London: Middlesex University Press, 2009.

Index

Novels subject to detailed analysis or frequent reference are indexed by title; those receiving only passing or brief mention appear as subheadings under the author's name. Titles are given in their most familiar (usually shortened) form, e.g. *Tom Jones* not *The History of Tom Jones, a Foundling*.

Deloney, Thomas
Jacke of Newberry 24
Thomas of Reading 24
Dennett, Daniel 424
Dennis, Nigel, *Cards of Identity* 853
Dentith, Simon 812
Derrida, Jacques 151, 595
Desai, Anita, *The Clear Light of Day* 828
desire, preference for term over "love" 437–438
see also sexuality
detective fiction 478–479, 693–707
accomplishments of lead characters 701–702
compared/contrasted with spy fiction 696–698
engagement with new technologies 781–782
forerunners/early examples 471–472, 693–694
historical settings 706
serials 726
treatment of citizenship/conflict 698
treatment of evidence/uniqueness of human body 703–704
treatment of law 703
treatment of violence 696–697
treatments of war 702–703
Diaghilev, Sergei 681
dialect, representations of 164, 165
in West Indian literature 747
A Dialogue between a Married Lady, and a Maid Tullia Octavia (anon.) 134
Dickens, Charles 8, 393–394, 399, 425, 460, 585, 598, 726, 778
anti-social elements 464–465
contrasts with Trollope 299–300, 304–305
criticisms of 300
death scenes 558
depictions of children/childhood 319, 393–394, 408, 409–412; boyhood friendships 451
endings of novels 296–297, 389
engagement with drama 550, 557–558
engagement with poetry 558–559
externalist perspective 425, 427, 434
as forerunner of aestheticism 544–545
gothic elements 481–482
influence of Scott on 286–287
influence on later writers 626
pessimism regarding systematic reform 301–302
as political novelist 342, 354
scientific interests/themes 377–380
treatment of ethnic minorities 333
treatment of history 295
treatment of masculinity 443
treatment of space/distance 296, 304–305
All the Year Round 377
Barnaby Rudge 287
A Child's History of England 287
Dombey and Son 299, 408, 415, 558
Household Words 377, 693
Martin Chuzzlewit 193, 465
The Mystery of Edwin Drood 481
Nicholas Nickleby 557
The Old Curiosity Shop 557, 558
The Pickwick Papers 481
Sketches by Boz 327, 333
see also Bleak House; David Copperfield; Great Expectations; Hard Times; Little Dorrit; Oliver Twist; Our Mutual Friend; A Tale of Two Cities
Dickinson, Peter 726
Diderot, Denis 846
Les Bijoux indiscrets 242
Disch, Thomas M. 882
Disraeli, Benjamin 501–502, 503, 824
Crystal Palace speech 501–502
Coningsby 554
Venetia 554
Vivian Grey 554
see also Sybil
Dobbs, Frances, *The Patriot King* 281
Dodsley, Robert 40
Domesday Book 360
domesticity, defined 122–123
see also families; home
Don Quixote (Cervantes) 1, 3, 6, 15–17, 20, 35, 63, 76–77, 232, 241, 289, 849, 874
English responses/alternatives 248, 252–256
narrative framework 76–77
narrative hybridity 17
Donne, John 598
Doody, Margaret 91, 92
Dostoevsky, Fyodor 456, 486
"double consciousness," in black community 829
Doyle, Arthur Conan 469, 478–479, 495, 726, 729, 845, 877
character of protagonist 701
The Hound of the Baskervilles 478, 703
The Return of Sherlock Holmes 726
The Sign of Four 478, 703
A Study in Scarlet 471, 478
The Valley of Fear 478, 703
Dr Jekyll and Mr Hyde (Stevenson) 469, 479–480, 873
narrative method 479
treatment of sadism 479–480

Eliot, George (Mary Ann Evans) (cont.)
   treatment of history 396
   treatment of identity 380–381
   treatment of plot 394
   zoological studies 381
   Impressions of Theophrastus Such 461
   "Janet's Repentance" 382
   "Notes on Form in Art" *(Essays)* 381
   Scenes of Clerical Life 336, 440
   The Spanish Gypsy 336
   see also *Adam Bede*; *Daniel Deronda*; *Felix Holt
      the Radical*; *The Lifted Veil*; *Middlemarch*;
      The Mill on the Floss; "The Modern Hep!
      Hep! Hep!"; *Romola*; *Silas Marner*
Eliot, T.S. 507, 597, 666, 741
   criticisms of 617
   influence of 752
   "The Dry Salvages" 521
   Four Quartets 727
   "The Love Song of J. Alfred Prufrock" 582
   The Sacred Wood 667
   The Waste Land 587, 597–598, 619, 703, 752,
      766, 833
Elizabeth I 270–271, 792
Emecheta, Buchi, *Second-Class Citizen* 658–659
Emma (Austen) 93–95
   characterization 94–95
   demography 362–363
   landscape description/page layout
      361–363, 409
   narrative techniques 406–407
   psychological depth 95
   role of outward appearance 421–422
   treatment of love 440
Emma Courtney see *The Memoirs of Emma
   Courtney*
emotion, scientific analysis 671–672
   fictional explorations 672–675
Empire 500–514
   conversion (religious), issues relating to
      504–505
   dissolution of 709, 729–730, 740
   domestic structures/settings evoking
      501–502
   fictional critiques of 518–520, 521, 654
   landscape description: anthropomorphism
      512; documentary approach 507–508;
      picturesque treatments 510–513;
      tension between accuracy and
      picturesqueness 513–514; underdeveloped
      communities 512
   literary responses to governance of 500–501
   means of acquisition 502

role in fiction 314–315, 504–507; centrality
   of 517
science-fiction explorations of 614
see also colonies; imperial romance;
   postcolonial literature
Empire of the Sun (1987) 689
empiricist philosophy 538
Engels, Friedrich 299, 384, 438
   The Condition of the Working Class in England
      297, 298, 301, 334
   The Origins of the Family 450
"English" identity/literature, (problems of)
   definition 5, 326, 502–503, 717–718
The English Theophrastus (anon.) 154, 156
Enlightenment ideology, rejection of
   664–665, 846
entropy 378
epic (genre), relationship with novel 63, 419
   see also Homer; *Ulysses*
epistolary novel, narrative techniques/
   problems 82–83, 107–108, 169, 216–219
   letters within letters 217
   and moral viewpoint 454, 583
   and women's identity/rights 311
Ermarth, Elizabeth 295–297, 302, 305
eros/eroticism see sexuality
Erotopolis: The Present State of Bettyland
   (anon.) 136
espionage, legislation aimed at 695
   see also spy fiction
ethnography 327–328, 332–333, 339
eugenics 386
Europe to Let (Jameson) 647–648, 654,
   655, 687
Evelina (Burney) 4, 83, 91–93, 95, 111, 164, 326
   character names, significance of 91–92
   presentation of Scottish character
      172–173, 178
   treatment of domesticity 120–122
   treatment of social inferiority 165
   treatments of gender 92–93
Exilius, or the Banish'd Roman (Barker) 250–251,
   252, 259
   speed of plot development 251
existentialism 762–763, 765
exoticism
   appeal of 241
   transfer to British minorities 330–331, 334
"experimental" fiction
   characteristic features 759
   (problems of) definition 757–758
   social democratic reworkings 820
   see also postwar period